THE COMPLETE ENCYCLOPEDIA OF GOLF

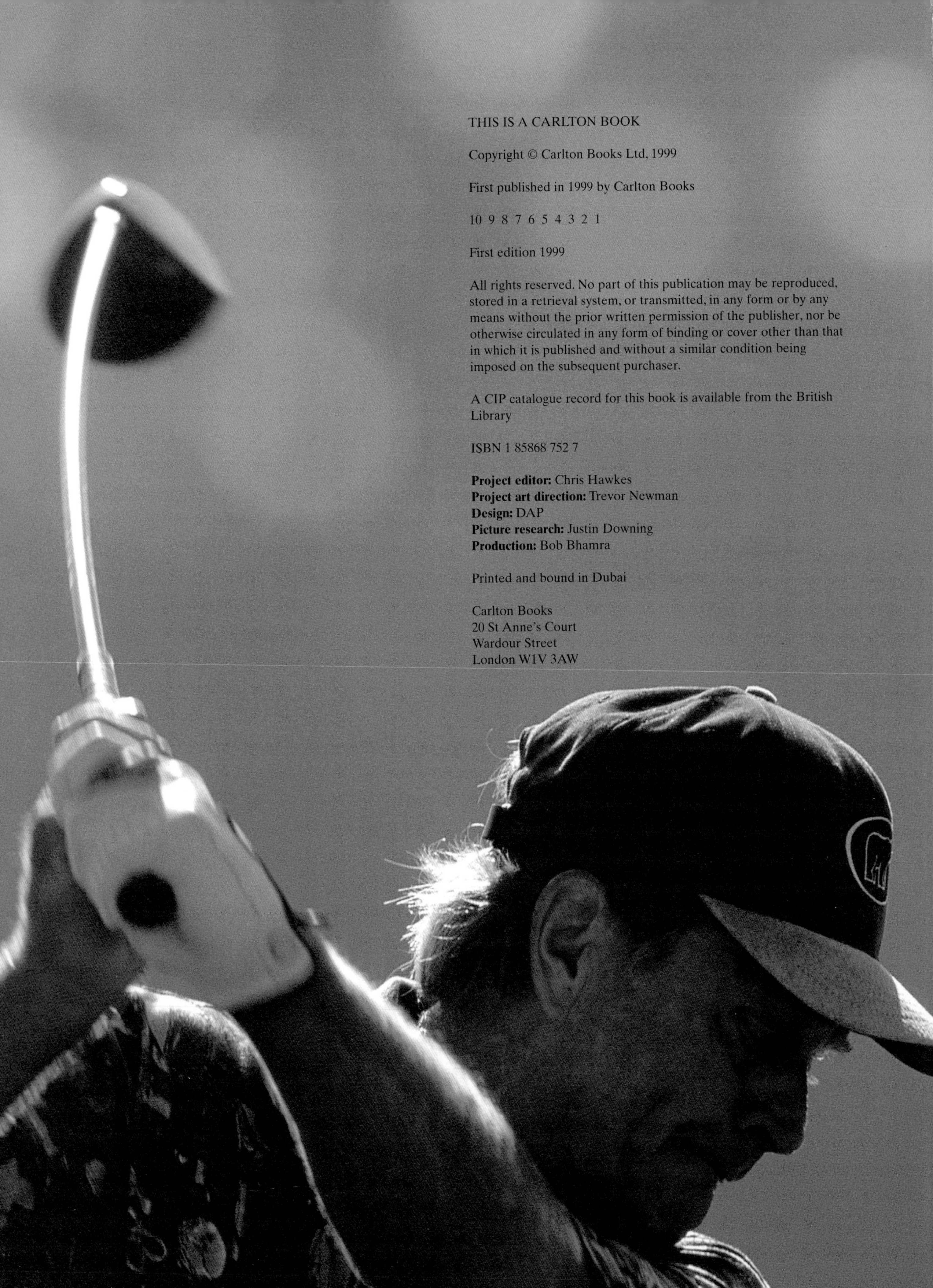

THIS IS A CARLTON BOOK

First published in 1999 by Carlton Books

10 9 8 7 6 5 4 3 2 1

First edition 1999

A CIP catalogue record for this book is available from the British Library

ISBN 1 85868 752 7

Project editor: Chris Hawkes
Project art direction: Trevor Newman
Design: DAP
Picture research: Justin Downing
Production: Bob Bhamra

Printed and bound in Dubai

Carlton Books
20 St Anne's Court
Wardour Street
London W1V 3AW

THE COMPLETE

ENCYCLOPEDIA OF GOLF

DEFINITIVE WORLD GOLF REFERENCE

DEREK LAWRENSON

SPORTS JOURNALIST OF THE YEAR 1999

CONTENTS

Callaway
GOLF

FOREWORD
BY COLIN MONTGOMERIE

The Complete Encyclopedia of Golf is one of the most comprehensive books ever produced on the Royal and Ancient game. Its appeal to me is in its unique combination of quality writing and a wealth of statistics.

All those who know me are well aware of my great love for who did what and when and this book certainly satisfies such curiosity. For example, every player who ever finished in the top 30 in a major championship is mentioned within these pages.

The exploits of the great players throughout this century are explored in considerable detail, while the photography is a real treat for any golf enthusiast.

I have known the author, Derek Lawrenson, for a number of years now and have great respect for his writing in the *Sunday Telegraph*. His love of the game and his knowledge of it is obvious throughout these pages.

This book, however, is more than just another encyclopedia. The decision to rank the 200 best golfers of this century, the top 100 courses and the 50 leading women, is bound to cause debate among readers, but I am delighted to say that any disagreements should be directed to the author, Derek, and not myself!

Happy reading.

Colin Montgomerie
June 1999

Chapter 1

THE EARLY HISTORY OF GOLF

The journalist and broadcaster Michael Parkinson once wrote: "If all the golfers in all the world could be laid end to end, I for one would leave them there." Yet a decade on and he had become a keen convert to the game, to the extent that he regularly regales his readers with stories of his exploits.

The sport's simple virtues have a knack of doing this. What can at first appear a game for old buffers allures most sports-minded people because it is both democratic and cerebral. Heck, in the 1990s, it even became chic and trendy.

Anyone can play golf: fat, thin, tall, short, man, woman, boy, girl. Only those who employ a few of the little grey cells, however, will be successful. One of the biggest thrills the sport can offer is a long drive, yet stand on the tee with the one aim every time of belting the ball as hard as you can and you will not get very far.

The game's earliest beginnings suggest a sport that suffered at the hands of people with a Parkinsonish bent; continual bans were imposed by the Scottish parliament. Yet look at the Scots now? They could hardly be more proud of the fact that they gave the game to the world. And vast numbers on the planet have come to be very thankful that they did.

EARLY HISTORY OF GOLF

Like many sports whose history lies in the dim and distant past, the origins of golf are shrouded in enough mystery to fascinate any budding Holmes. Did the game evolve out of the French pastime *jeu de maille*, or *chole* in Belgium? What about the Dutch game *spel metten colve* (game played with a club), which was well established in the thirteenth century? The truth of the matter is that we honestly do not know; what we do know is that if we accept that the fundamental principle of the game is to hit the ball into a hole, then it began in Scotland.

Early Flemish paintings show the striking of a ball in Kolf, as *spel metten colve* had now become known, but often the target would be a church door; often the game would be indoors and the round object that was struck was the size of a cricket ball. "Clearly Kolf is no more golf than cricket is poker," the Scots poet Andrew Lang sniffily pronounced.

Although the earliest recorded evidence of the game dates back to the middle years of the fifteenth century, it is almost certain that a form of the sport was being played in Scotland many years before that. After all, the first time the sport is ever mentioned is in the bans imposed by the Scottish parliament on "fute-ball, golfe, and uther sik unproffitable sportis". In 1457, King James II declared that "golfe by utterly cryed downe". But for a sport to be utterly cried down it follows that it had to be a widespread pastime carried out by many citizens to provoke such a reaction.

The reasoning behind the ban was to allow Scotland's finest to practise their archery skills so they were better prepared to take on the nasty English. So destructive was the game during these turbulent times that it was blamed for a number of decisive Scottish defeats, most notably at the Battle of Flodden Field in 1513.

By then royal attitudes had completely changed, which may have played its part in the catastrophic loss. The last ban on golf, for example, had come in 1491. In 1502 King James IV had clubs made by a Perth artisan whose usual stock-in-trade was bows and arrows. More clubs and balls were bought the following year for a match with the Earl of Bothwell. The relatively sudden change of heart in the Stuart camp followed close upon James's marriage to the daughter of Henry VII of England. The royal alliance did not, as Flodden and the Jacobite uprisings of the eighteenth century attest, mean the immediate end of war between the two nations, but

Golfers in 1860, the year of the first Open Championship

longer spells of peace and prosperity did take place.

Furthermore, for more than 180 years – until William of Orange replaced James II of England – there was an unbroken line of royal Stuart golfers, including Mary Queen of Scots, who may or may not have been insensitive enough to have played golf shortly after the murder of her husband, Lord Darnley, but whose reputation has suffered ever since from the suspicion that she did.

The worldwide spread of golf received a good start when Queen Elizabeth died and the Stuarts assumed the English throne in 1603, in the shape of King James I. He was the son of Mary Queen of Scots and the unfortunate Lord Darnley, and great-grandson of Margaret Tudor. Margaret was the English wife of James IV of Scotland, none other than our first (known) golfer.

James I proved a powerful influence on golf. Though a century had passed since the Scottish ban on golf had been lifted, James I was moved to make his view known that the common people's right to enjoy sport on Sunday was to be respected, as long as religious observances had been completed first. Charles I repeated this sentiment a few years later. James I, Charles I and II and James II all golfed, and so did Bonny Prince Charlie, who succeeded James II as pretender to the throne of England.

Many a 40-shilling fine was imposed on those who persisted in "tyme of sermonis", but despite this golf flourished, like cricket, in all classes of the community. Early in James I's reign, bishops, noblemen and folk of every rank were busy on Scottish links, while James's two sons were making golf fashionable south of the border by taking it up at their father's behest. The eldest son Henry died at 18, the second son Charles surviving to succeed to the crown, only to lose his head after the Civil War. Charles was golfing on Leith Links, near Edinburgh, on the day he received news of a rebellion in Ireland.

The Restoration of the Monarchy in 1660 brought royal golfers into play again, the most notable being James, Duke of York. James is credited with setting up and playing in the first international match, partnered by a Scottish shoemaker named Patersone, who was no novice at the tee. This Scottish team of Stuart and shoemaker beat two English noblemen, and Patersone was rewarded with enough cash to build a house in Cannongate, Edinburgh (which stood until 1961).

Not until the middle years of the following century did golf take the next step forward. The engine of golf's further development was the social device of the club, until then a strictly political entity. No matter how powerful the ruling bodies of the game, no matter how rich the professional tours become, it is the club that remains the beating heart of the game.

A golf course was just that, a place where people could play golf. They did not pay for the privilege: there was no one to pay, no committee and no greenkeeping costs, since the land over which the game took place was common land, untended apart from grazing animals and rabbits and the more damaging attentions of wind and tide. The links at St Andrews in Fife had, since 1552, been given under licence by Archbishop Hamilton for free and unfettered use of citizens at football, golf and other games. That was the only formal convention.

The rules under which people played were a matter of local custom, on-the-spot agreements and wagers. Score cards had not been invented, and all golf was of the matchplay variety, with handicaps a rudimentary give-and-take between individuals – be they dukes or cobblers. Leading players were, however, already sufficiently celebrated to be the subject of poetry. The next step was to see who was the best player of all.

The defining moment came in 1744 when a group of players – "gentlemen of honour", it goes without saying – well known on Leith Links, presented a petition to the City of Edinburgh to provide a prize for the winning player in an open competition. This was granted by the magistrates in the shape of a Silver Club. The new trophy was carried on the appointed day through the streets of the capital. A code of rules was established. Ten local people entered and the man who came out on top was a local surgeon called John Rattray, who successfully defended his prize the following year.

This man of medicine was quite a cool hand. He went at Bonny Prince Charlie's behest to the aid of the wounded in the Young Pretender's army during the second Jacobite rebellion in 1745. Owing perhaps to the leading Edinburgh golfers having a heavy presence in the law – they still do – he was not arraigned for treason as he might well have been. His escape has been attributed mainly to the efforts of Duncan Forbes of Culloden. Given that he, too, was a "Gentleman Golfer", it just goes to show that useful contacts could be made down at the golf club even then.

A decade after the Edinburgh initiative, 22 "Noblemen and Gentlemen" of St Andrews subscribed for a Silver Club of their own. As at Edinburgh, competition for the silver trophy was the only cement binding together the group of local players. The winner each year was captain of the group, and entrusted with the resolution of any disputes between players.

A second key date in the slow, piecemeal development of the idea of a club came in 1764 when, with no sign yet of the hoped-for challenge for the Silver Club from other parts of Britain, the Edinburgh men moved to restrict entry to competition to "admit such Noblemen and Gentlemen as they approve to be members of the Company of Golfers".

Edinburgh also scored a first in the matter of setting up a code of rules. This they did in 1744, to govern play for their Silver Club, although it is possible that the players at Leith had already put together a rudimentary list of dos and don'ts. The St Andrews men, following suit in 1754, were to abide by a similar codification, employing the principles of simplicity and brevity.

Today's mighty tomes detailing definitions and settling

abstruse queries are a world away from the 13 rules issued in 1754. The first makes strange reading to the modern golfer, since it directs that the player must tee off within a club's length of the hole, which gives an immediate and daunting idea of what the putting surfaces must have been like at the time.

The main principle governing the other 12 is "play the ball as it lies", except when it comes to rest against an opponent's ball or is unplayable in "water, or watery filth", in which case the player may lift his ball, but must allow his opponent a stroke.

All these early rules were, naturally, for matchplay. Once strokeplay became widespread – and strokeplay has always been the most popular form of the game in America – the need arose for exact definitions as to what constitued, to give an obvious example, an unplayable ball. A competitor needed a precise wording, otherwise how would he be able to mark his card accurately?

So the problems began, the beginning of the reputation of the book of rules as manna for insomniacs. A century after the first codification, the game's governing body at St Andrews attempted to define "unplayable". Their explanation required almost as many words as the whole of the original 13 rules.

Rapid growth

And so the word spread. From these small beginnings in the east of Scotland, the irresistible attractions of golf moved south of the border. As with the two pioneering Scottish clubs, the presentation of a trophy in 1766 set Blackheath golfing activities in motion in Kent. Not surprisingly, Blackheath's foundation owed much to the presence of expatriate Scots. Such men were often prime movers in helping the game spread further afield.

It did so with great rapidity and in 1810 came the first mention of a women's competition, at Musselburgh. There had been reports of Scottish officers playing in New York, and of the formation in 1786 of a club in South Carolina. It was another hundred years, however, before the game took root in the United States, and it was pre-dated by the founding of Royal Montreal in 1873.

Golf had already followed the Union Flag to Calcutta in 1829, and Bombay in 1842. Conversely, although the British began business in Hong Kong in the 1840s, golf did not flower there until 1889. Nor did it make the short journey to the Continent until 1856, when Pau, in the shadow of the Pyrenees, was founded for holiday visitors. Scottish soldiers of the Duke of Wellington's peninsula army are said to have played at Pau in 1814, some of them returning 20 years later on holiday – which places them among the very first of the great army of golf tourists, although many English players belonged to the leading Scottish clubs, and journeyed north for their regular silver club and gold medal meetings.

Australia joined the throng in 1870 with the formation of Royal Adelaide, and South Africa in 1885 with Royal Cape.

In the summer of 1887 a New York linen merchant called Robert Lockhard visited St Andrews and purchased six golf clubs and two dozen gutta percha balls for a friend of his, an ex-pat Scot now resident in Yonkers.

It took a while for the clubs to arrive in America, but when he received them John Reid, from Dunfermline, Fife, was thrilled. On February 22, 1888 he went out with five of his friends to play the first "round". All summer they played on what land they could find and then, on November 14, 1888, they met to form the first golf club in America. They called it St Andrew's, using the apostrophe to distinguish it from the original. Their hope was that the name would inspire the same love and affection for the game in America as it had in

Scotland. You could say it was an inspired choice.

The rate of golf course construction in the British Isles was prodigious in Victorian times, mostly with horse, cart and shovel. The railways helped, from St Andrews to Blackheath, and from Sheringham, where the line ran within a few feet of the 17th green, to Aberdovey in west Wales, from Ganton in Yorkshire to Lytham in Lancashire.

Course building reached a feverish pitch in the 1890s as proved by the number of clubs celebrating their centenaries in the last decade of the present century. Curiously, there had been little golf in Ireland before the last years of the nineteenth century, although Belfast set up their club in 1881. Naturally it was a Scot – Sir David Kinloch – who brought the game to Dublin.

The popularity of the game had increased partly through the focus provided by two competitions. In 1860 the Open had been staged for the first time, while 25 years later the first Amateur Championship was held. Here were two summits for players to strive towards.

Among the catalysts leading to the foundation of golf's first major championship was Blackheath's victory, gained by George Glennie and Lt J.C. Stewart, in the International Club Foursomes of 1857 – a competition suggested by Prestwick. This constituted the first Championship Meeting to be played at St Andrews, and the host club were the beaten finalists. The St Andrews club had assumed authority as the game's lawgivers, and their decision to cut the number of holes on their course from 22 to 18 made the latter figure the magic number worldwide.

Golfers had started to assemble in greater numbers by the 1850s

An afternoon stroll – the parklands in St Andrews provided a perfect area for golf (c. 1888)

The following year a singles event was held, attracting a field of 28 from which the publisher, Robert Chambers, emerged victorious. In 1859 another publisher, Robert Clark, who wrote about golf, was much fancied to win, but a big hitter called George Condie strolled to the title by a 6&5 margin.

These three competitions were amateur, but the leading players were celebrated in newspaper reports and verse, and attained the status of national sporting heroes.

The links were the haunt of a great variety of folk, quite apart from the gentlemen amateurs (some of whom played in tall hats – a powerful inducement to keep the head still) and their caddies, whose name, it seems clear, derives from the word *cadet*. This was the term used to describe the young French noblemen who came to Edinburgh with Mary Queen of Scots when she returned after her years at the French court.

Scottish humour, ever sardonic, extended the usage to mean something less complimentary, and so *cadet* journeyed by way of "hanger-on" to "odd jobber" to "porter". In more recent times the word has gone slightly upmarket again, and certainly in the world of the major tours, where the caddies – some of whom earn six-figure salaries – would not thank you for thinking of them as mere porters.

Among the wanderers who would pass by the golfers at the time were people simply enjoying the exercise of a walk;

others kicked a ball about or flew kites. Soldiers drilled, horses were raced, cricket matches were played. On the big days of challenge matches, however, everything changed. With hundreds of pounds sometimes at stake, crowds surrounded the growing band of professionals. They got much closer to the action than would be countenanced today.

After the success of the events they had set in motion in 1857–59, the innovative members of Prestwick turned their attention to the professionals, many of whom started their golfing life as caddies.

It hardly needs saying that the professionals around the middle of the nineteenth century could not make a living from tournament winnings alone; there was no programme of events, and what money they won with their clubs – which they usually fashioned themselves – came from challenge matches for cash.

Club making, which in the early days seemed to become the natural fiefdom of bow makers, was (along with the manufacture of feathery golf balls and teaching) the staple source of income of the early Victorian professional. This state of affairs continued long after the establishment of the first regular Open events.

Allan Robertson, the first golfer to beat 80 at St Andrews, was accepted as the leading player of the day. With his assistant Tom Morris, Robertson ran a thriving feathery ball business out of the window of their workshop, which was the kitchen of Robertson's house. Stuffing a top hat full of feathers into a leather casing was a job for an expert, although even the best could manage no more than three balls a day.

The era of the feathery – preceded almost certainly by lathe-turned wooden balls as used in such games as chole – ended, to Robertson's dismay, with the development of the solid gutta percha ball during the last years of his life; he died in 1859, aged only 44. The popularity of the cheaper "gutty" must have been a severe shock to Robertson, because the family feathery trade had been in existence for so long, run by his grandfather Peter and father Davie before him. The gutty was a solid ball made from the juice of the Malayan percha tree and, unlike the feathery, could be remoulded when damaged – the feathery simply burst open when mistreated, especially in wet weather.

Furthermore, the Robertson and Co. output was reckoned to have been well in excess of 2,000 featheries a year. At half-a-crown each, that came to an annual revenue of about £300, a fair sum in the nineteenth century. The high cost of the feathery in the last days of its dominance no doubt kept many would-be golfers off the course.

Robertson, meanwhile, proved himself the complete professional, for after first declaring of the new projectile "it's nae gowff" he reacted positively to the playing problems set by the fact that it was less responsive and more difficult to get into the air.

He made much greater use of the mid and short irons to fly the ball to the target. Pitching had previously been performed with wooden clubs. Never a long hitter, Robertson obeyed the first rule of golf; he kept the ball in play, and used his new iron technique to get close to the hole with his approach shots.

His death posed the question: who is champion now? Prestwick provided a way of finding out in October, 1860, with the game's first formal competitive tournament at strokeplay – what we now know as the Open. For the last 140 years the golfing calendar has been dominated by this and three other majors: two of them, both amateur events, were replaced as social changes reshaped golf. How appropriate that the youngest of the majors, the Masters, remains the first great international event of the year.

MODERNCROSS

Chapter 2

THE MAJOR TOURNAMENTS

When Bobby Jones won the Grand Slam in 1930, the four tournaments that comprised this feat were the Open and Amateur Championships of Great Britain and America. Clearly, as the golden age of amateur golf receded into the distance following the Second World War, an updated Grand Slam was required.

It was the early 1960s before it came to fruition, with the Masters and the USPGA Championships assimilated in place of the two amateur events. In truth, the line-up is imbalanced: with three of the four major championships in America, it is hardly surprising that United States golfers have dominated. Yet the four events all require different qualities to become champion, which fully explains why only four golfers have ever won all of them at any one time, let alone in the same year.

In recent seasons, attempts have been made to create a fifth major championship, with a number of candidates put up for recognition. The first one was the World Matchplay Championship at Wentworth, the most recent the Players Championship in Florida. All have been rightly rebuffed.
And as the golfing calendar has become ever more cluttered, so spectators and most players have clung even more firmly to these four cherished events as the sport's benchmark.

THE OPEN CHAMPIONSHIP

Which one?

It's funny how Americans get so upset at the British when they start talking about The Open Championship. "You would think the world consisted of only one Open," is the gist of the argument. Yet ask the same people about the tournament that goes on down in Georgia every April, and they will happily waffle on about The Masters, as if that is the only Masters tournament that takes place every year. Ask them about the 1999 venue for the Ryder Cup, and they will proudly tell you that it is taking place at The Country Club, as if that were the only country club in America.

The point is, in all of these instances, that they were the first of their kind, and no further description ought to be necessary to distinguish them. The Open is called the Open because that is what it says on the trophy; the United States Open goes by that name because that is its full title.

Over the years the status of the Open has switched back and forth. Clearly, when it began, it was the most important tournament in the world; then the Americans stopped coming in the 1950s and it lost some of its significance. The arrival of Arnold Palmer and the best Americans of his generation assured the tournament's position once more. Then, about 10 years ago, it was the US Open that again became the most significant tournament for the Americans. Now that position has changed in another evolutionary spin. "The Open is just that, the most important tournament in world golf," says Mark O'Meara. As 1998 Open Champion, he has learned all about the power of the title, and the unrivalled esteem in which it is held around the globe.

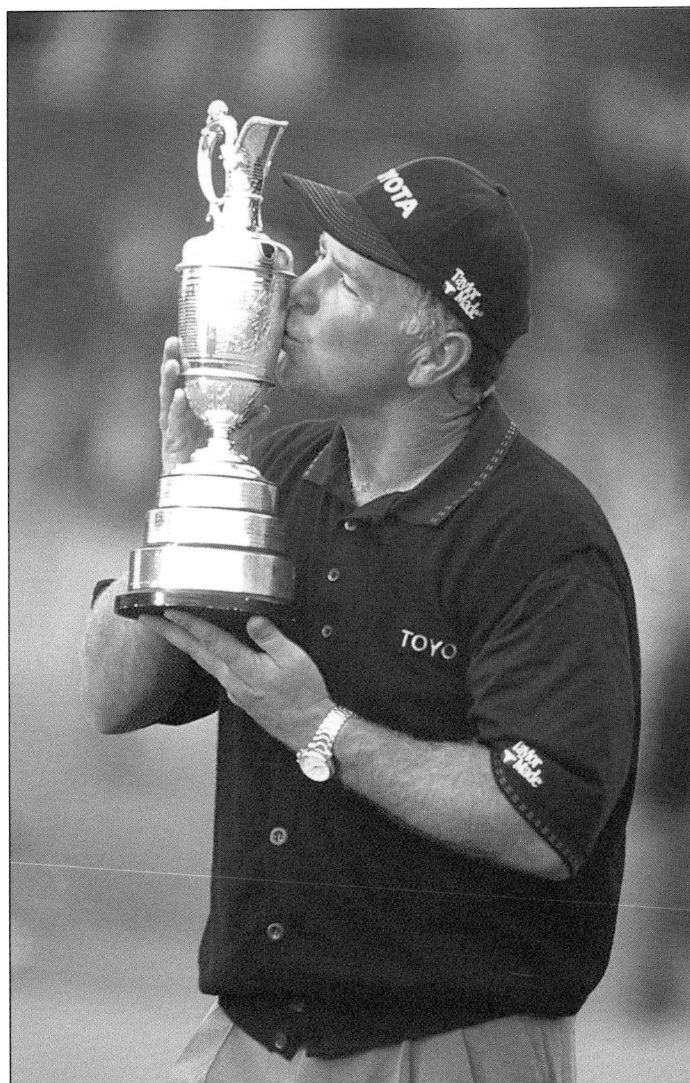

Mark O'Meara – won the "most important of them all"

The early years

Ironically, the Open was not open at all when it began in 1860, at the instigation of Prestwick Golf Club. Just eight players were permitted to enter, and all of them were professionals. The prize was a red morocco Championship Belt put up for competition by the host club, over three rounds at Prestwick's then 12-hole layout.

The idea was to find a successor to the late, great Allan Robertson, who had died the previous year. The golfing community mourned like never before at Robertson's passing. In 1858 he had gone round the Old Course in 79 strokes, a feat as outrageously brilliant as someone shooting 59 today. When he passed away, one Royal and Ancient member said: "They may shut up their shops and toll their bells, for the greatest among them is gone."

In truth, no successor emerged during that tournament at Prestwick. The winning score was recorded by Willie Park from Musselburgh, but few players were impressed with his total of 174; it was not a particularly good effort, even allowing for the then tools of the trade. A number of amateurs were also aggrieved at not being allowed to enter. They took their grievances to Major J.O. Fairlie, the Prestwick member who proposed the competition in the first place. At first he was inclined to permit eight "gentlemen" of distinguished clubs, but changed his mind on the eve of the 1861 competition. "The Belt to be played for tomorrow and on all other occasions until it be otherwise resolved shall be open to all the world," he proclaimed. Almost 140 years on, those words ring more true now than they ever did.

Young Tom Morris

With Robertson gone, his erstwhile rival Old Tom Morris dominated the early years of the Open, alongside Park. Each would win it four times, with Park runner-up on four occasions as well. Hardly anyone else was allowed a look-in until Morris's son, Young Tom, neatly came along at just the right time. In 1867 Old Tom collected his fourth title at the age of 46 years and 99 days, and remains the tournament's oldest winner. The following year his son won and, at 17 years and 161 days, there will surely never be a younger victor.

Young Tom Morris was a prodigy in every sense, a true champion who played golf to a standard never seen before. Here was the first of the long hitters who would come along from time to time over the next 130 years and change the game for ever. At the time the 'bogey' score for Prestwick's 12 holes was 48, but no one had ever got within three shots of it. Until Morris came along, that is. In 1870, Young Tom shot 47 in the first round, signalling his intentions from the first hole, when he became the first man to reach this 500-yarder in three shots.

Playing a new form of golf where the accent was on bold, attacking strokes, he eventually claimed the title by 12 shots, a feat that went unequalled in major championship golf until Tiger Woods won the Masters by the same margin in 1997. Young Tom, the Tiger of his day, had won the Open for the third year in a row, and was accordingly awarded the belt outright. He would achieve one further footnote: in 1868 he scored the tournament's first hole-in-one.

In 1871 there was no championship, as Prestwick was now joined by the Royal and Ancient Golf Club of St Andrews and the Honourable Company of Edinburgh Golfers in the organization of the event. Accordingly, matters were held in abeyance while new ground rules were established. It was agreed that a new trophy, a silver claret jug, be purchased for £30 and played for on a rotation basis on the courses belonging to the three clubs. Furthermore, it was resolved that the tournament be truly open to all-comers, just as Major Fairlie had envisaged a decade earlier.

Prestwick remained the venue for the first tournament for the auld claret jug, and Young Tom Morris carried on from where he had left off to become the first name inscribed on the trophy. The following year, St Andrews golfers predictably dominated the tournament as the Open travelled east to the Old Course for the first time. One of them, Tom Kidd, won by a stroke from Jamie Anderson to collect the first prize of £11.

Young Tom finished third and would go close the following year as well. In 1875 he did not compete. Heartbroken at the death of his young bride in childbirth, he began drinking heavily. On Christmas Day he was found dead by his father. The grief felt by the game was even more profound than when Robertson died. Young Tom was just 24 and possessed skills that would have made him a champion in any era. Such was his fame and popularity, 60 golfing societies put together a fund to erect a moving monument to his genius in the graveyard of St Andrews Cathedral. His father accorded him this posthumous tribute: "I could cope wi' Allan [Robertson] myself, but never wi' Tommy."

The following year the Open should have witnessed its first-ever play-off as Bob Martin and David Strath tied at St Andrews on 36-hole scores of 176. It never took place because Strath was so incensed about a claim against him for disqualification. The charge was that he had played to the 17th hole before the green was clear, so preventing any chance of his ball going on to the road. Strath was cleared of the charge, but chose the route of martyrdom, and refused to participate in the play-off.

The rule on winners keeping the trophy outright disappeared with the award of the claret jug – hardly surprising, given how much it had cost – which was perhaps just as well, as first Jamie Anderson and then Bob Ferguson completed a hat-trick of triumphs. Ferguson, indeed, was denied an unprecedented fourth Open victory in the first play-off that actually went ahead, when Willie Fernie won by a stroke. In 1887 and 1889, Willie Park Jnr won the title, thus becoming the second father-and-son combination to triumph.

Old Tom Morris – dominated the early years of the Open

English arrival

In 1885 the amateur Horace Hutchinson entered the Open for the first time. This was significant in that he was English in an event that up to this point had mostly been contested only by Scots. Over the next few years, Hutchinson would do much to increase the profile of the tournament south of the border and encourage more Englishmen to follow in his path.

One of these was John Ball, a wonderfully talented stroke-maker from Royal Liverpool who became both the first Englishman and the first amateur to win. It did not herald any golden age for amateur golf; only three amateurs have ever won the Open, the others being Bobby Jones (on three occasions) and, before him, Harold Hilton (twice). Incidentally, Hilton – like Ball – came from Royal Liverpool.

Great Triumverate – won 16 Open titles between them

The Great Triumvirate

The reason no golden age occurred was that after Ball came the first shots from the Great Triumvirate. John Henry Taylor took the title on its first trip south of the border, to Royal St George's in 1894, and thereafter that was it for the semi-professionals – the bakers, candlestick makers and plasterers who had dominated the Open to that point.

For the golfing revolution was now in its stride. In 1892, prize money at the Open took a quantum leap upwards, rising from £28 10s to £110. New courses were being added to the rota. After Royal St George's came Hoylake, in 1897. The game, therefore, was ready for professionals in the true sense of the word, men who could take it on to the next stage. Their names were Taylor, James Braid and, above all, Harry Vardon.

Taylor was the first to arrive. He completed a successful defence of the Open in 1895 and at the time was thought invincible. Taylor's style was not elegant, but he garnered a deal of consistency from his flat-footed technique and could hit the ball splendid distances – especially in windy conditions, where his low-ball trajectory came into its own.

Taylor, however, was not as long as Braid, who gave the ball an almighty lash. Like many players, Braid had a few years where he mastered the art of putting, and during that time in the early 1900s he achieved most of his successes.

The greatest of the Great Triumvirate, however, was Vardon, whose easy grace and style made him the choice of the galleries wherever he played. For a while he was close to being unbeatable. Research by the British Golf Museum has shown that in his golden period Vardon entered 52 events and finished either first or second in over half of them. During one dazzling sequence he won 17 out of 22 tournaments he entered. Only Byron Nelson would ever top that sort of dominance when he won 11 tournaments in a row on the US Tour in 1945.

It was chiefly for their performances at the Open, of course, that the Great Triumvirate achieved a fame that would last long beyond their lifetimes. In the 21 Open Championships to take place between 1894 and the outbreak of war in 1914, the three would win no fewer than 16 and the rest of the field five. Vardon would lead the way with six triumphs, with five each for Taylor and Braid.

Naturally it was the friendly rivalry that inspired each of them in turn to still greater heights. After two wins, Taylor was denied in 1896 at a toughened-up Muirfield by the emergence of Vardon, the latter winning a 36-hole play-off between the two by four shots. Hilton won over his home track in 1897, but in 1898 Vardon won again, this time at Prestwick. Here he became the first man to win the Open with four rounds in the 70s, and in 1899 he went ahead of Taylor in terms of Championship victories, three to two, with a win at Sandwich. Back came Taylor at the dawn of the new century, beating Vardon at the Old Course with Braid back in third.

By this stage Braid was wondering if he would ever break the stranglehold of Taylor and Vardon, but he got his chance in 1901 at Muirfield, despite taking 80 for the final round. He was still three ahead of Vardon. Now it was Braid's turn to take charge, while the other two faded. Although Vardon won again in 1903, it would be his last victory for 11 years. During that time, Braid would win on four occasions, while Taylor won once.

And so to the last Open before the war. Over a rivalry lasting 20 years, each man had successfully managed to win the Open on five occasions. Who would prevail one last time, before the war came to rob them of what remained of their vintage years? As it turned out, Braid was far from his best, and would finish in a tie for tenth. Taylor and Vardon, meanwhile, dominated the field once more. After round one, Vardon led following a 73; a second-round 75 saw him maintain his advantage. The following day, however, it looked as if the occasion would belong to Taylor as he strode round Prestwick in 74 shots in the morning, four better than Vardon. Now he was two strokes ahead, with the afternoon round to play. Taylor, though, failed to reproduce his morning form and needed 83 shots to finish. Vardon had won a sixth Open, a record that stands to this day.

After the Great War

When the Open resumed, it was now under the sole auspices of the Royal and Ancient. The six hosting clubs had decided that it was good for the game if there was one controlling body, and 80 years on we can say with complete certainty that it was one of the finest decisions ever taken on behalf of the game. Under the R&A, the sport and the Open have both gone from strength to strength.

Several changes were instantly apparent, with a considerable widening of the course rota. In 1923 Troon hosted its first Open, to be followed by Royal Lytham in 1926, Carnoustie in 1931 and Prince's in 1932. There was one very notable casualty. In 1925 chaos ensued at Prestwick as vast crowds turned up to watch the final day. It was perhaps more by good luck than judgement that no one was seriously injured, as shots came flying over the heads of spectators. Macdonald Smith, one of the challengers for the title, complained that he had to wait too long to play his shots. At times, it is said, he just fired blind over the galleries. What was perfectly clear was that Prestwick had become a delightful anachronism, and would have to be retired from the circuit. In all it had hosted the Open on 24 occasions; in 2000 St Andrews will become the first venue to pass that total when it plays host for the 25th time.

Americans in the ascendant

By the 1920s American golfers were in the ascendancy, and nowhere would they prove the point more than in the Open Championship. From 1924 to 1933 the Open went west every year with wins for Gene Sarazen, James Barnes, Denny Shute and Tommy Armour. But two men in particular would dominate to such an extent that in the nine Opens held from 1922 to 1930 they would win seven between them. Representing all that was good in the professional game was Walter Hagen; for the amateurs there was Bobby Jones.

Rather like Arnold Palmer would in the 1960s, Hagen, with his patronage, was responsible for the American invasion and restoring prestige to the championship after the war. The prevailing mood among his American peers was that if the tournament was good enough for the Haig, then they had better catch the next ocean liner heading east. The British were thrilled to see them, even if their play did overshadow the golf of the home players.

Hagen's victory in 1922 meant that he had won each of the three major championships that existed at the time. Although his style was unorthodox, Hagen made it work for him and he combined it with an unswerving self-belief. Hagen was the first man to douse golf with a splash of colour. "His temperament is more that of a holiday-maker than a prospective champion," the golf correspondent of *The Guardian* sniffily pronounced. Yet that seemingly casual approach enabled him to forget any disappointment. In 1923 he finished second in two of the three majors but simply bounced back the following year to win both of them. His second Open win came at Hoylake in 1924, where he holed from eight feet at the last to defeat Ernest Whitcombe. "Did you know you needed that putt to win?" a reporter asked him afterwards. "Sure, but then no one ever beat me in a play-off," he replied. In *The Times*, Bernard Darwin wrote of Hagen and Whitcombe: "There is this difference between the two, as so often between Hagen and the other man. Hagen just won and the other man just didn't."

Hagen did not defend the trophy in 1925, but returned to Lytham in 1926. It was the first time the championship had been played on the Lancashire coastline, and 10,000 spectators turned up in appreciation. They witnessed perhaps the most dramatic Open to date. Hagen, needing a two at the last to tie, duly asked for the flag to be removed while he played his approach from 150 yards away. For once his impertinence told against him, and he took six. And so the final outcome depended on the wonderful duel taking place out on the course between Al Watrous and Bobby Jones.

At 25 years old, Jones was trying to become the first amateur to win since Harold Hilton in 1897. Watrous, at the age of 26, was labelled as one of the rising stars of American golf. He had certainly showed his potential during the course of a

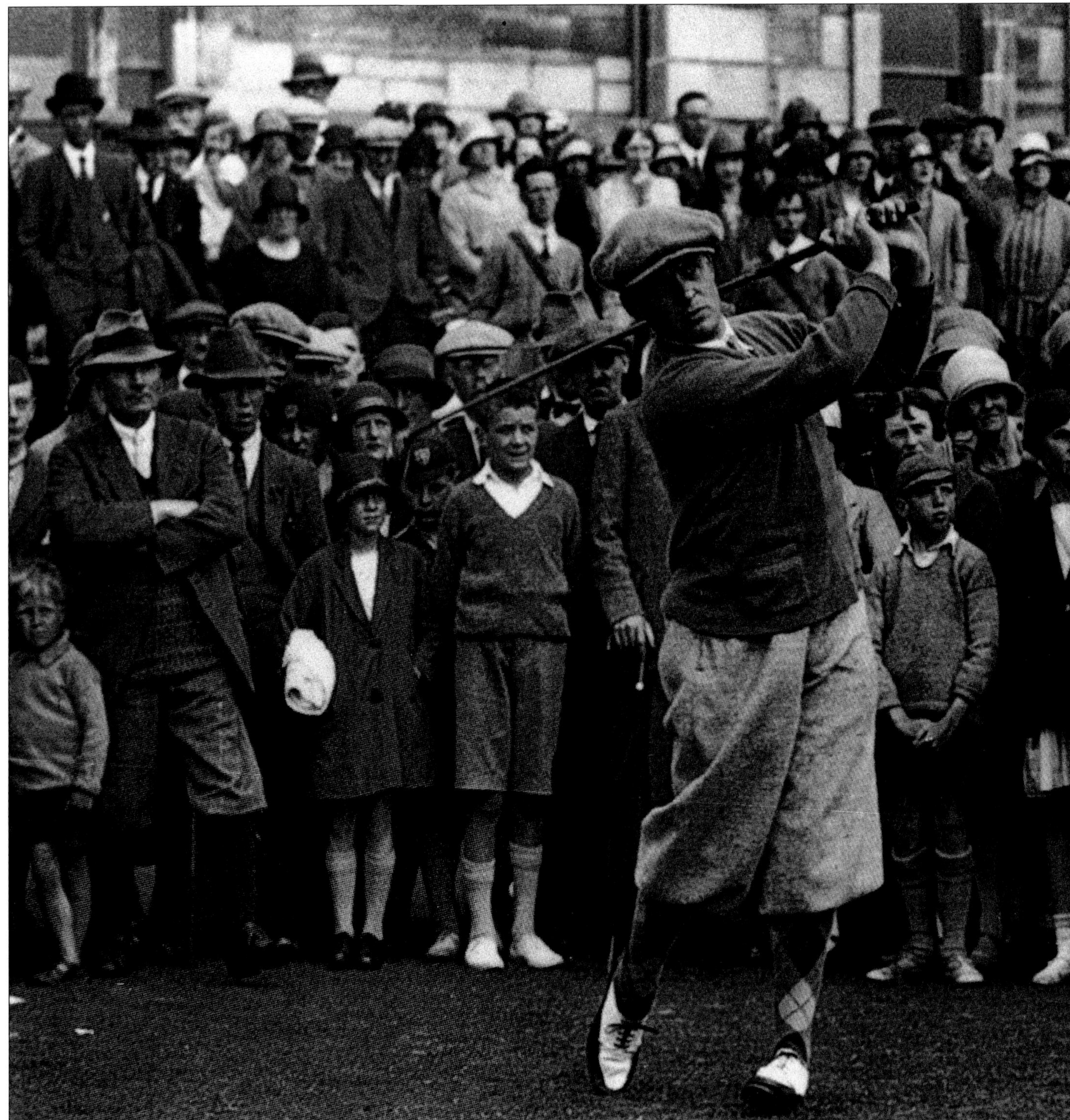

Bobby Jones – the greatest American amateur won the Open Championship on three occasions

magnificent third-round 69. He was two shots ahead of Jones. Back and forth the lead flowed. After six holes the pair were level, but mistakes by Jones at the seventh and the ninth gave Watrous his two-shot lead again going into the final nine. At the 11th Watrous drove poorly and took six, and now Jones was within a stroke. So it remained until the 17th, where the strokes from the tee appeared decisive: Jones had found a bunker, and now would struggle to make the green in two; Watrous had driven perfectly into the middle of the fairway. Watrous played first, a fine shot on to the green. What hope for Jones now? He took an age over the shot, its importance reflected in every deliberation. Eventually he decided to gamble. What was the point of playing short and hoping for a chip and putt? He took on the challenge. With 180 yards to go to the green, most of it carry over bracken and hummock, there was no margin for error. Neither did Jones need any. The ball

finished 12 feet from the pin. Watrous was so rattled he three putted, and then took six down the last.

In his second visit to Britain, Jones had won his first Open. Later, a plaque was erected by the Lytham club to commemorate his decisive blow on the 17th. Jones himself would describe it in his retirement as the best shot he ever struck under pressure.

Jones returned the following year and completed a successful defence at St Andrews. On his first visit to Britain he had played in the Open at the Old Course and tore up his card in the third round in frustration. Now he returned a hero. The impetuous youth was a wise and thoughtful man, and what had once been a den of iniquity was now his favourite course. His winning score of 285 lowered the old record total by no fewer than six shots.

Great Triumvirate bows out

The 1928 Open saw the last appearance by members of the Great Triumvirate. James Braid and Harry Vardon were wizened old fellows by now, approaching 60, and at Sandwich the former shot 316 to finish tied for 41st while Vardon was one shot worse to finish tied for 47th. Intriguingly, Vardon's total was only one stroke worse than the score with which he had managed his first win in the Open in 1896.

Naturally their appearance created some excitement, but the days of British domination were long gone by now. The American invasion was once more considerable, although Jones had stayed at home. But Hagen and Sarazen had both arrived at Sandwich, and in the end it was the former who prevailed over the latter by two strokes. Hagen's prize was £75, which he gave immediately to his caddie.

Hagen's holiday-making

By now he was in his prime, and apparently unstoppable. At Muirfield the following year he trailed Lou Diegel, then USPGA Champion, by two shots going into the final day's last two rounds. How did he prepare for the momentous day? Well, by adopting the temperament of a holiday-maker of course, and partying all night. When reminded in the early hours that Diegel had already been in bed for some time Hagen asked the band to play a little louder and, looking up towards the bedrooms above, quipped: "Yeah, but he ain't sleepin'." The result the next day? Hagen shot two rounds of 75 and won by six strokes. Diegel was third. In six Open appearances Hagen had won the title four times, finished second once and equal third once.

If not Hagen, then surely Jones: that had become the theme of the Open, and so it was at Hoylake in 1930, the year of the latter's "Impregnable Quadrilateral". The Open was part two, the Amateur having already been won at St Andrews. In truth Jones was not at his best at Hoylake, and his scores got worse with every round. By this stage, even moderate golf from him was too much for anyone else to handle. After two rounds Jones had been well clear of the field, but on the morning of the final day Archie Compston raised hopes of a rare British success by breaking the course record with a 68. He had made up no fewer than six shots on Jones to be one in front of him. After lunch his play was as pitiful as it had been majestic before. He limped home with an 82, and once more it was Diegel who finished runner-up, two shots behind the winner.

This would be the last victory recorded by either Hagen or Jones. Their records were superlative, and even better in their way than that compiled by the Great Triumvirate, since there was both the long journey to consider and the fact they were seeing golf courses under conditions they would encounter only once or twice a year at best. It was a measure of both men that they made every visit count.

While Jones went into retirement, Hagen still occasionally showed up. By 1933 he was into his 40s, but he was still good enough to lead after the second round. Perhaps the partying caught up with him on the final day, for he had rounds of 79 and 83, the latter the first time that he had ever shot in the 80s in an Open. At the sharp end of the leaderboard the action could hardly have been more exciting had he been in contention; no fewer than six players finished within a shot of the lead and, heck, one of them was even British.

His name was Syd Easterbrook, and after three rounds he was tied for the lead with the perennial challenger, Leo Diegel. The venue was the Old Course and for the fourth round a fierce wind emerged from the depths of St Andrews Bay. It blew straight into the faces of the players on the homeward half and made life exceptionally difficult over the closing holes.

After the third round Easterbrook was not the only British player in with a chance. Henry Cotton and Abe Mitchell were both tied for the lead as well; alas, Cotton would fade quickly while Mitchell would battle manfully until falling foul of the Road Hole, taking six. It was Diegel and the defending champion, Gene Sarazen, who set the target. Both played well in the last round, overcoming their share of problems like the redoubtable competitors they had become to post a 72-hole total of 293. That was the target, one that Cotton and Mitchell had missed by two strokes.

Craig Wood was the next home. Yes, the Craig Wood who became famous for always finishing second. He shot 75. Now the target was 292. Would he gain his first major? Still out on the course were Denny Shute and Easterbrook. Shute was next to finish, fully an hour after Wood. He came to the last needing a par for a wonderful round of 73 and a tie. His first putt, however, came up short. He took an age over the next one and for an agonizing second it looked as if it would be short as well, until it dropped with its last breath. Now all thoughts turned to Easterbrook, and whether he could make it a three-man play-off. It is estimated that 15,000 people watched him play his closing holes, and British hopes surged and fell with each passing stroke. He had five successive threes from the eighth which gave him a chance of posting the winning score. But the winds began to buffet him and as they did so the strokes disappeared one by one. By the time he came to the 18th he had followed five straight threes with five straight fives. Now he needed a birdie, and when he pulled his second shot to near the clubhouse, the crowd let out a huge groan of disappointment. The game was up. Manfully, Easterbrook rescued par, but he was still a stroke adrift. And so the play-off took place between two Americans the following day where Wood, of course, did what came naturally in such situations and lost. The crowd was left with one lingering thought: after 10 years of American dominance, would a British player ever win the Open again?

British revival

The answer would come swiftly enough the following year when Henry Cotton won the first of six successive British victories. Why the sudden turnaround? Had the home players suddenly become worldbeaters? The truth was rather different. The Depression had choked America and travel across the Atlantic had become prohibitively expensive. Only once did the Americans return in force, and that was in 1937, when they came over anyway for the Ryder Cup. Then came the Second World War and its aftermath, when a ravaged Britain made for a terrible contrast to the dollars that could be earned like confetti at home. Sam Snead came over for the Open in 1946 and was so appalled by what St Andrews had to offer, both in terms of the course and accommodation, that he never returned until 1962 when he was long past his best. And that was after he won!

And so all the Opens between 1934 and 1960, when Arnold Palmer led the next invasion, ought really to carry an asterisk next to them. The auld claret jug was still awarded, but to earn it did not require quite the same acts of derring-do. But there was one great exception, and that was in 1937.

Henry Cotton had shrugged off the massive disappointment of St Andrews in 1933 by pulling off a stylish triumph at Sandwich the following year. Maybe all of the Americans had not been present, but they would have had to have played to the limit of their capabilities to have lived with him, never mind parted him from the trophy; as it was, there was still Gene Sarazen and the defending champion, Denny Shute, to contend with.

Cotton opened with a 67 and then played one of the finest rounds that the Open has ever seen – a 65 that set a new standard for golf in Britain (it would be 1977 before anyone would shoot lower in an Open). His total of 132 smashed the old 36-hole record, too, and when he recorded a 72 in the third round he had the 54-hole record as well. Cotton was now so far ahead that he could afford virtually any score in the final round and still win. In the event, he almost tested the argument, taking 40 strokes to the turn and starting home with three fives. In the end it needed a good finish to break 80; as it was, a 79 still saw him home by five shots.

The 1937 Open fell one week after Great Britain and Ireland had succumbed to customary defeat in the Ryder Cup. The venue was Carnoustie, and Cotton spoke in the days beforehand that he thought a British player could repel the invasion. He did it himself on a course stretched to over 7,000 yards and in conditions that became a trial of strength in themselves.

The tournament was led after the opening day by the American, Ed Dudley, but thereafter the home players bore out the wisdom of Cotton's words. In particular it was a triumph for the Whitcombe brothers, as Reg led after both the second and third rounds and Charles would eventually finish fourth, two strokes ahead of the great Byron Nelson.

Reg Whitcombe's lead going into the final round was three over Cotton, but it did not survive the latter's imperious beginning. In driving rain that would last the whole round, Cotton began: 4, 3, 4, 4, 4, 4. He reached the turn in just 35 shots and from being three behind he was now one ahead. Only Charles Lacey of the Americans maintained the ghost of a chance. Dudley had fallen away with a third-round 78, while Nelson could not maintain the imperious standard of his third-round 71 and shot 74 in the rain after lunch. Then Lacey lost heart as well, impaled by Cotton's superlative golf.

By the time Cotton came to the 18th the crowd lining the hole was 10 deep. It was like a coronation, and in a way it was. Cotton's hero was Walter Hagen, and his approach to the game was almost as flamboyant. He was certainly colourful, and an enormous favourite with the crowds. Now he was fully justifying his natural swagger and confidence. He may have dropped a stroke at the last but a 71 was, in the conditions, as good in its own way as the 65 he had shot at Sandwich. It gave him the trophy by two shots. He had become the first British player to win the Open when all the American Ryder Cup team had been present, and the first since the days of the Great Triumvirate to win the trophy twice.

The following year Reg Whitcombe finally put the famous family name on the auld claret jug, and then in 1939 Dick Burton won the last Open to be played for seven long years. It would be far longer than that before the game's most cherished trophy would regain the lustre it had during the halcyon days of the 1920s and early 1930s.

St Andrews austerity

For Sam Snead, one visit to the east of Scotland was more than enough. That was for the 1937 Open at Carnoustie, when he finished 11th, and he had no desire to return. But sponsors could be persuasive beasts in those days, and when the man from Wilson Sporting Goods pointed out that they were paying him quite a deal of money, and how a victory could hardly do both his own profile and that of the company any harm, Snead reluctantly made the trip. When he got there he described it as "an old, abandoned sort of place", which was somewhat unfair on the German prisoners of war who had worked manfully to get it into some sort of shape.

Sentiment dictated that the Open should begin life again at St Andrews, but the truth of why it was held there may well have been more prosaic; it was probably the only course on the rota that at the time was in any sort of condition to host the event.

Snead was inevitably the favourite to win, but not overwhelmingly so. The war may have robbed Cotton of some of his prime years, but he was still a formidable force; then there was the South African, Bobby Locke, for whom the austere years had done nothing to prevent his waistband expanding by about six inches.

It was roly-poly Locke who led after the first round before Cotton took over the baton with a second successive 70. Cotton was to have a terrible last day, however, ballooning to scores of 76 and 79 as the weather at St Andrews got steadily worse. With a round to play, Snead had pulled level with Locke and Johnny Bulla, one of 11 Americans in total to make the trip.

In the afternoon the wind became a gale, and when Locke came in with a 76 for a total of 294 it appeared that might be good enough to win. The first challenger was the tall, handsome Bulla, who needed only to finish 5, 4 to beat Locke by two strokes. The story of the Open was to be one of continual disappointment for Bulla, the one American who would faithfully support the championship through the troubled period of the next decade. Not that the event ever rewarded his loyalty; on this occasion he three putted both holes to finish 6 and 5, and so tie with the South African.

And so to Snead. He had needed 40 strokes and one temper tantrum to play the more difficult front nine, but he played textbook golf from there on in to claim the trophy by four shots. It was sad that the win never meant anything more to him than "just another tournament victory", but maybe in his dotage he now sees things differently. Certainly he did nothing to endear himself to St Andreans at the time. When asked by a reporter whether he had enjoyed the town he replied: "Whenever you leave the USA boy, you're just camping out."

Naturally Snead was not present to take his place as defending champion at Hoylake in 1947. Indeed the only Americans of note to arrive were Vic Ghezzi, who had lost a play-off for the US Open the previous year, and the promising amateur, Frank Stranahan, who caused quite a stir at the Adelphi Hotel in Liverpool when he arrived with his full weightlifting gear.

Quality at Hoylake

If the course at St Andrews had still to recover fully from the wartime years, the same could not be said of Hoylake, which had long had a tradition of producing the finest greens in the country. No one found them more to his liking than Fred Daly, who caused jubilation in the Emerald Isle by becoming the first player – and, to date, the last – from Ireland to collect the trophy.

At the time it was a triumph celebrated largely only in Ireland, for there was some talk that he was a lucky champion. Daly had completed his fourth round of 72 in the calm of early afternoon, and was safely ensconced in the clubhouse by the time the wind picked up to blow most of the other challengers away. This account fails to take into consideration the capricious nature of links golf. A stroke of luck here and there has decided countless championships: Daly's good fortune was nothing more than in-keeping with this tradition. Even sitting in the clubhouse with the wind raging, Daly had an anxious time of it. At the last Stranahan needed to hole his second shot to force a play-off – and almost did just that, the ball finishing inches from the cup. But Daly was the champion fair and square, over a links that Bernard Darwin would call "the toughest course that I have ever seen".

By 1948 Henry Cotton was aware that time was running out if he was to win the Open for a cherished third time. Already he had done much to restore lustre to British golf, but a third Open title, he felt, would elevate his career to another level. Accordingly, he practised hard leading up to the tournament at Muirfield and in pre-qualifying looked in good shape, shooting a pair of 69s, the best scores on view.

After a first-round 71 Cotton went out on the second day and, under the watching gaze of King George VI, played one of those rounds that leaves his supporters believing that, until Nick Faldo came along and demolished all argument, he was the best British golfer this century.

Walter Hagen's course record of 67 – equalled by Alf Perry eight years later – had stood since 1929, but now Cotton trimmed a stroke from it with a card that contained barely a blemish. He went out in 33, came home in 33, and the only five he marked down was at the third, perhaps the easiest hole on the course, where he had three putts. On the last Cotton had a holeable putt for a 65, but the ball lipped out.

Such was the quality of the round that Cotton had now opened up a four-stroke lead on the field. After the third round Alf Padgham had halved that advantage, but that was the closest anyone would get. Padgham faded after lunch and it was Fred Daly who finished runner-up, though fully five strokes adrift of the imperious Cotton.

The great man had his third Open title, and now there was no question that he was the most worthy successor to the Great Triumvirate. It was as if the player himself felt he had reached the mountain top as well. Thereafter Cotton never played with quite the same intensity as he had before; indeed four years passed before he again filed an entry to the Open. It was another blow to the event, which would struggle to retain its credibility over much of the next decade.

South African challenge

Few players in the history of the Open began as such an overwhelming favourite as Bobby Locke in 1949. This was partly a reflection of the fact that, Ben Hogan apart, the outstanding South African had few peers in world golf. Mostly, however, it was due to the fact that the overseas challenge was skimpy, to say the least.

The feeling in the locker room, then, was that if anyone could beat Locke they would win, and history now tells us that no one did. But one man came awfully close, and notched a historical footnote in the process. At the fifth hole in the second round, the Irishman Harry Bradshaw's drive finished against the broken glass of an empty beer bottle. What to do now? What Bradshaw should have done was to wait for an official ruling, which would have decreed a free drop; instead he decided to play on and play the ball as it lay. He moved it about 20 yards and ran up a six.

What gave the incident its fame is that the following day Bradshaw played the golf of his life, and after 72 holes had fin-

Bobby Locke (left) with Harry Bradshaw in 1949

ished tied on the winning score with Locke. Naturally the cry from the Irish was that if only he had waited for a ruling he would have avoided the six and won. As the Irish know only too well, that is far too simplistic an analysis.

Would Bradshaw have played such golf on the final day if he had been that much closer to the lead? The play-off suggests he might have struggled; he shot 147 for two rounds the following day, and lost to Locke by a mammoth 12 shots.

This was the first of three wins in four years for Locke, and the Open had its first dominant champion since Jones and Hagen had carved up the championship between them in the Roaring Twenties. In between there was one celebrated success for Britain as the colourful Max Faulkner won when the Open made its one and, to date, only appearance in Northern Ireland in 1951. It would be 18 years and a different world entirely before another British player would achieve a similar success.

Bleak Carnoustie

One Open Championship stood out in the 1950s, and that was the year in which Ben Hogan was persuaded to cross the Atlantic and make his one and only appearance. The venue was Carnoustie – a bleak, grey setting that made for a suitable backdrop to the dour, grey Hogan. It would be nice to state for the record that Hogan came because he was drawn by the place that the town holds in American golfing history; after all, where would American golf have been without the pioneering skills of the famous sons that left Carnoustie in the final years of the last century to spread the word? Nice, but also completely wrong.

The year was 1953 and Hogan was at his peak. He won the Masters by five shots and the US Open by six; what next? The USPGA Championship was due to take place in the first week in July, but Hogan was unwilling to play 36 holes every day because of the toll such a workload would inevitably take on his legs. Then someone suggested the Open Championship, which was to be played the following week at somewhere called Carnoustie; men with a serious sense of golfing history, men like Gene Sarazen, pointed out that no man could be considered a candidate for true greatness if the only place he ever won was America. Sarazen's argument was: just think what it would do for your career if you won the oldest event in golf, the one that large parts of the globe consider to be the world championship?

Hogan bought the argument, and prepared for the event as only he could. He arrived on the east coast of Scotland a full week before; he played the course in all its different winds and grew accustomed to the slightly different demands of the 1.62-inch ball; he learned about the chip-and-run and how to play off hanging lies; he learned about hitting crisp iron shots from the bone-hard turf. And as he learned so an affinity grew with the people of Carnoustie, who took him to their hearts. While Hogan went out each day to practise, so the number of observers grew each day, to watch a man who struck a ball more cleanly than any man before and, some would say, since.

Bobby Locke, though, played in the pre-qualifying rounds with the confidence of a player who knew how to win the Open. He was fully five strokes clear of the field. Perhaps he played too much of his good golf too early; whatever, he would finish nine strokes adrift of the winning score when the competition began in earnest.

The leader on the first day was Frank Stranahan, the American amateur who had been a faithful supporter of the Open every year when more famous members of his US brethren had chosen to stay away. One stroke behind on 71 was the Scot, Eric Brown, giving the natives some hope of a long-overdue home victory. Hogan, meanwhile, opened with a 73.

The second day belonged to the Celts. Brown continued to keep the home fires alight with a second successive 71, while the Welshman Dai Rees finished with a birdie and an eagle to join him on a 36-hole score of 142. Behind, however, the overseas challenge was gathering. Roberto de Vicenzo, the muscular Argentinian who would challenge for so many years in the Open, was just a stroke behind, while Hogan had followed his 73 with a 71 and was joined on 144 by Stranahan.

On the final day Hogan played with the stamp of authority that makes legends. By now the largest crowds were following his progress as they eagerly snatched at the chance to watch a true genius at work. Perhaps only Arnold Palmer at his first appearance in 1960 has made such an impact at an Open.

He was known among the locals as the "wee ice mon", and on the final day the iceman cometh. In the morning he was round in 70, and now Hogan and de Vicenzo were tied for the lead. But it was close. A stroke behind were Rees, Tony Cerda – another Argentinian, who had finished second to Max Faulkner in 1951 – and the elegant Australian, Peter Thomson. Just three behind were Stranahan and Brown.

Stranahan set the target with a wonderful conclusion to his final round. He single putted each of the last six greens, a sequence that included a holed putt of fully 40 feet on the last for an eagle three. It gave him a score of 286.

In the event, three other players matched it: Cerda, Rees and Thomson. But this was an afternoon when one man stood alone, when one man continued the downward progression that had characterized each of his rounds. The key, perhaps, was the 5th, where Hogan missed his first green and had to chip from an awkward sandy lie. He then demonstrated that his armoury extended well beyond the shots he struck from tee to green, which flew so unerringly straight that it was as if they had been fired from a rifle. He chipped in. At the 6th, Hogan struck two wooden shots on to the green and two putted for another birdie. Three pars to follow and he was out in 34, and by now it was apparent that par golf for the back nine would be good enough to win.

Hogan did better than that. He had a birdie at the short 13th and then passed beyond the menace of the 16th and the 17th with pars on his card. A birdie at the 18th meant a 34 coming home, a new course record of 68, and the Open Championship.

Hogan was so good during this phase of his career that Sarazen was wrong: he would have been considered one of the top three or four golfers of the century even if all his significant wins had been achieved only in America. But there is no doubt that winning the Open at Carnoustie fleshed out his illustrious CV. The victory margin was four, and it meant that his record in the majors in which he played following his car accident in 1949, to this point, read: fifth, win, win, win, seventh, third, win, win, win.

Thomson's revenge

Over the next five years Thomson, runner-up for two Opens in a row, would win four championships while, in the other year, Locke would claim his fourth victory. That Thomson dominated the event at a time when the opposition was not at its strongest should not detract from the quality of his play. He was, in fact, the perfect Open champion, a man who placed the emphasis on strategy and keeping the ball in play. The only golfers who have won five Open Championships this century are James Braid, Tom Watson and Thomson. Of the three, Watson's achievement stands head and shoulders above the other two because it was completed at a time when Jack Nicklaus was still close to his peak and Europeans like Severiano Ballesteros had emerged. But after Watson and Nicklaus, Thomson might be the finest player the Open has seen since the Second World War. His sequence of victories began at Birkdale in 1954 and ended there 11 years later, when he removed all doubts over his qualities as a golfer by overcoming a field that contained every great name. That year he was at his finest, playing calculating golf that eschewed every gamble. It is said that he never took anything more than a three wood off the tee, and the strategy worked.

It is a measure of Thomson's brilliance during the 1950s that from 1952 to 1958 no British player ever finished above him in the Open. One man, however, came terribly close, and that was in 1958 at Lytham. Two others finished just a stroke behind as well.

The golfer who forced Thomson to a play-off was Dave Thomas, and he became a national figure practically overnight. As for the pair who were one shot behind, it would be the story of their Open careers as far as Eric Brown and Christy O'Connor were concerned. At the last O'Connor had needed a par to tie, but he found one of the cluster of dreaded bunkers that dominate the fairway at this fine finishing hole. Brown's finish was even more heartbreaking. He needed a four to win, but he, too, found a bunker off the tee and needed three to reach the green. Then he was far too bold with his first putt and missed the return.

Both Thomas and Thomson played superbly well in the morning of the play-off. The young Briton was round in 69, with Thomson pipping him by one. It was the more experienced man, however, who kept it going after lunch to win by four shots. What a performance, though, from Thomas, at the age of just 23. He seemed a natural star, the player British golf had been waiting for since Henry Cotton. Sadly, he would never fulfil the promise of that performance, but he did finish within a stroke of Jack Nicklaus at Muirfield in 1966. In 2001 and 2002, he will be captain of the Professional Golfers' Association.

In 1959 the Open at Muirfield appeared to be following a familiar script when Peter Thomson led the qualifiers. When the tournament began, things would be startlingly different. Indeed Thomson would turn in his most indifferent performance for a decade, finishing well down the list in 22nd place. Instead it was a young South African who emerged, just as his

Peter Thomson – dominated the tournament in the 1950s

hero, Bobby Locke, was reaching the end of his distinguished career. Gary Player had travelled to Britain four years earlier with little money in his pocket and the derision of many of the players to whom he turned for help. One said the best advice he could offer would be to get the next flight home.

Perversely, it may have been the best advice that Player ever received, for he always enjoyed proving people wrong. He was also never more dangerous than when apparently out of contention. After three rounds he was four shots off the pace, tied with three other players and with nine other golfers ahead of him. In the afternoon Player turned in a magnificent 17 holes. He reached the turn in 34, and then further birdies at the 16th and the 17th meant he needed a par four at the last for a 66.

Player felt that if he could get that regulation figure he would set a target that may well last for the rest of the day. As it was, he bunkered his drive and then needed three putts. A disastrous six and Player could not fight back the tears. He thought he had thrown away the Open.

Behind him, the leaders were desperately trying to prove him wrong. One by one they fell away until there was only the Belgian, Flory van Donck, left. Even he needed a birdie three when he came to the last, and instead succumbed to a bogey five. Player had won his first Open, despite his worst fears.

It was a new name on the trophy at a time when a new generation was beginning to emerge in golf. A new decade would begin the following year, and it would prove to be the most thrilling in the Open Championship's long and dramatic history.

Given that Prestwick was no longer an option, there was only one place at which the centenary Open could be held. All told, 301 golfers gathered for competition over the Old Course, which was a far cry from the eight who had journeyed to the west coast of Scotland in 1860.

Palmer bucks US prejudice

The notable landmark was not sufficient to persuade the Americans to shed their prejudice against the event, but one significant name did make the trip – the 1960 Masters and US Open Champion. Neither had Arnold Palmer needed any persuading. He could not keep a smile off his face as he looked around the "auld grey toun", and greeted its citizens.

Palmer's victory at the Masters was one thing; but he had entranced all golf with his performance at the US Open at Cherry Hills, when he claimed the trophy with a wonderful final-round 65. Now he had arrived in Britain offering his own unique brand of golf; the first time the word "swashbuckling" had been heard around the sport since Walter Hagen was a lad.

It was Roberto de Vicenzo who set the pace over the first two rounds, shooting a pair of 67s for the best 36 holes seen at an Open since Henry Cotton had shot 67, 65 at Royal St George's in 1934. An unassuming Australian by the name of Kel Nagle, meanwhile, was lurking two strokes behind following a 67 of his own on the second day. And where was Palmer? He was reasonably well placed on 141, and then on the morning of the third round he shot 70. This still left him four behind as de Vicenzo faded and Nagle took up the reins, much to the delight of Thomson. He had had a little bet on his fellow Australian, a 35-1 shot, believing he was something of a mirror image of himself: he was straight off the tee, hit the greens in regulation, and he rarely three putted.

Thomson aside, everyone else was hoping for one of those Palmer charges. When he pitched stone dead at both the first and second holes, it was exactly what everyone had come to see. But those were the only birdies he could find on the front nine, and when the unassuming Nagle matched his outward half of 34, the gap was still four.

As they turned for home, it was clear that these two players had the tournament to themselves. At the 13th Palmer finally holed for a birdie to cut the gap to three. At the 15th Nagle dropped a stroke and, with Palmer forcing in a six-foot putt for par at the 16th, the lead was two.

At the 17th Palmer got his par for the first time all week and then, at the last, set up a grandstand finish by pitching to five feet and holing for a 68. It was a wonderful conclusion to his round and now all the pressure was on the 39-year-old Nagle. As the tumultuous roar went up for Palmer at the 18th, Nagle was looking at a seven-foot putt for par at the previous hole to remain in the lead.

It was a brave holed putt in the circumstances and made a heck of a difference; now he needed a par at the easiest finishing hole in all of golf to win, rather than a birdie. And the par was achieved with some comfort. Nagle played the hole in textbook fashion, just as Thomson thought he would. The Open had its most surprising winner for some time; the memories, meanwhile, were of the man who finished second.

It was a hallmark of the 1950s that many Americans would come over for a year, have a near miss, and then – seemingly discouraged by the experience – fail to return. Palmer was of the other kind. Naturally he was disappointed at not winning, but he could not wait to return in 1961. He had been seduced by the magic of the Open, and he spread the word when he got back home.

The venue was Royal Birkdale and would prove a wonderful occasion. Palmer was considered among the favourites, but nothing more than that; there were still some who doubted whether his thrashing style could ever work at an Open. After all, had not the lesson of the previous 10 years been that the championship rewarded a more calculating, precise style of play?

The second round put an end to those doubts. In terms of wind velocity, this was one of the worst days the event had seen; tents were blown down, and players were, metaphorically at least, blown away. Bobby Locke shot 84 to miss the cut; the legendary Irish amateur, Joe Carr, followed him after an 86.

Palmer, meanwhile, started his second round with five birdies in the first six holes. Conquering the elements with those great forearms of his, driving down on the ball to keep it under the worst of the wind, this was supreme golf. Not even Palmer, though, could avoid disaster on such a day, and at the 16th he ran up a seven. His 73, however, was sufficient to take him to within one shot of the lead.

In the third round Palmer demonstrated his remarkable powers of recovery. A seven or eight at the 16th appeared likely when he missed the green to this par five with his third shot; he was in a horrible spot. But Palmer opened the face of his wedge, thrashed the ball skywards, and it came down like a stone next to the hole. It helped him to a 69, and he was a stroke ahead with a round to play.

Dai Rees would prove his nearest challenger, recovering manfully from a disastrous seven at the opening hole on the final day. The Welshman never gave up the fight, even when he trailed by four with five to play. He then birdied the 15th, the key hole of the afternoon play.

Rees clearly needed some help from Palmer, and it looked like he might get it at this hole when the American pushed his drive into the willow scrub. Now he had 140 yards to the green, a seemingly impossible shot given the lie. Palmer, furious with himself at his mistake off the tee, tore into the ball with the ferocity of a man hell-bent upon making amends. Somehow the ball finished on the green and he two putted for his par. When Rees birdied the 16th and got a three down the last, it put the importance of Palmer's second shot at the 15th into perspective. He had won by just one shot.

The hole is now the 16th on the card at Birkdale and a plaque has been erected to commemorate the shot, only the second to be laid to celebrate such a feat: the other was to remember the second shot that Bobby Jones played to the 17th at Lytham in 1926.

American force

The message was getting home to the USA. When Palmer arrived for the 1962 Open at Troon, he brought a lot more of his friends with him. This was the strongest field the championship had seen since 1953. Slowly but surely, it was regaining all its own lustre. This Open was also the first to feature Jack Nicklaus, who had a rather rude introduction to links golf, shooting 80 in the first round, with all the damage coming on one hole, the 11th, where he ran up a 10. With hindsight we can say we got a real inkling of the man's character the following day when he came back and shot 72 to qualify on the mark at 152. Nicklaus would eventually finish in a tie for 32nd place.

This Open, though, was close to being Palmer's finest hour. Opening with a 71, he followed it with a 69 which saw him play the fabled back nine at Troon in just 32 strokes. In the third round he shot 67, and now the classiest field the Open had seen for a while was in danger of being lapped. Palmer was five strokes clear of Kel Nagle, who in turn was three ahead of the man in third place, Bob Charles.

So it continued into the final round. Two early birdies, and Palmer had turned the Open into a one-man show. In the aftermath of his six-stroke victory, one of the great golf correspondents, Pat Ward-Thomas, wrote: "Palmer's qualities as a golfer, a competitor and as a human being are so exceptional that any measure of supremacy is within his phenomenal powers."

Yet, strangely, Palmer was never to win the Open again, never indeed to finish above seventh place despite attending every year until he was well into his 60s.

Jack Nicklaus's first chance of winning came in 1963, and he

Bob Charles – became the first and, to date, only left-handed player to win a major championship, the Open in 1963

kicked himself all the way back to America for failing to do so. For 70 holes of that championship, he confessed in his recent autobiography, he was sure he could not lose. He was two strokes ahead and playing brilliant golf. Then he bogeyed the 17th and stood on the 18th tee trying to calculate what he needed to stay ahead. When he heard no applause coming from the 16th green, he assumed that neither of his closest pursuers had birdied the hole. In fact, both Bob Charles and Phil Rogers had birdied it, but because the wind was blowing in the wrong direction, the noise had not travelled. So Nicklaus played the hole more cautiously than he would have done had the plethora of scoreboards that are around today been in existence, and like Eric Brown and Christy O'Connor before him in 1958, found a bunker and took a bogey. "It was the biggest mental blunder of my career," Nicklaus would say, more than 30 years later. Charles and Rogers both parred in to set up a 36-hole play-off. They had finished a shot ahead of Nicklaus.

In truth, the play-off could have done with the emerging star. The occasion between two uncharismatic men is remembered chiefly for the fact that Charles became the first and, to date, only left-hander to win a major championship. In that calm, composed manner of his, the New Zealander shot 140 for two rounds and prevailed by eight strokes.

Golden Bear

Jack Nicklaus had been waiting a year for the 1964 Open, and his first chance to atone for what had happened at Lytham. The fact that it was to be his first Open at the Old Course made the occasion even more special. It was also the first Open full stop for Tony Lema, although when he pitched up allowing himself barely enough time for one practice round, no one seriously rated his chances.

Not that the practice days were any preparation for the tempest that greeted the players in the opening round. It was a day for an Irishman who was used to controlling the ball in such conditions, and Christy O'Connor duly obliged with a 71. Nicklaus took 76; Lema was handily placed after a 73.

When asked for his opinion of the Old Course, Lema replied: "Amusing and crotchety." On the second day he demonstrated that when it came to conquering its crotchetiness, he was a natural. He shot 68 to be two strokes ahead of Harry Weetman, with Christy O'Connor a further shot adrift. Could Lema keep it going? By 1964 he had become a leading player on the US Tour, but no one had expected this.

In the third round Lema's swing and easy grace took hold of the championship. In the morning he was once more around in 68 and had a seven-stroke lead over Nicklaus, who had moved through the field with a 66. Not even the Golden Bear, however, could make up seven shots against a player as self-confident as Lema. A 68 enabled him to trim the winning margin to five, but Lema had charmed all St Andrews – including the Old Course herself – for a convincing win. As for Nicklaus, it had become obvious by now that here was a player who had all the armoury with which to play links golf. His first big year would be 1966. Sadly, that would be Lema's last Open. With his wife Betty alongside him, the light aircraft in which he was travelling crashed into a golf course just outside Chicago, killing all on board.

Everyone must look back upon their first Open victory with particular fondness, and Nicklaus's triumph at Muirfield in 1966 was no exception. He liked the course so much that when he went into course architecture he called his first creation Muirfield Village.

Nicklaus had prepared more thoroughly for the event than any major championship in which he had yet competed. He had played no fewer than six practice rounds, and while half the field were bitching about the narrow fairways and the other half moaning about the severe rough, Nicklaus felt as comfortable as anyone because he knew intimately where all the worst trouble lay. He opened with a 71 and then followed it with a 67 in the calm of the late afternoon to take the lead on his own for the first time in Britain. Poor third rounds were rarely part of the Nicklaus repertoire, but here was one. After 13 good holes in a difficult wind, during which time he had increased his advantage over Peter Butler to four shots, Nicklaus then gave the rest of the field a chance with four sloppy bogeys over the last five holes.

The effect it had on the tournament was dramatic. Phil Rodgers came home in 30 to make up nine shots in nine holes on Nicklaus and was now the third-round leader, two ahead of the latter. Palmer had made a charge, too, coming home in 32 to pull within two of Nicklaus.

On the final day, normal service was resumed. At the tough first hole, Nicklaus hit a three wood and three iron to 25 feet and rolled in the putt. From being two behind he was now level, as Rodgers ran up a bogey. The pattern for the day was set. By the turn Nicklaus was three shots ahead, but once more he got ahead of himself, missing from 18 inches at the 11th and running up another bogey at the next. Ahead, Dave Thomas and Doug Sanders had both set a target of 283. By the time he came to the 15th, Nicklaus knew he needed to par home just to tie.

After getting regulation figures at the 15th and the 16th, Nicklaus was home in two shots at the par-five 17th to set up a birdie. Now he needed to par the last to win and he did so, a glorious three-iron approach to the middle of the green concluding matters. At the finish Nicklaus wore a smile as wide as the Firth of Forth. As he should, of course – he had just become only the fourth golfer to win all four major championships at least once.

Jack Nicklaus – first success at Muirfield in 1966

Open nerves

In 1967 the Open conjured up a story that was pure romance. Since 1948 Roberto de Vicenzo had been playing in the Open, and few better ball strikers have ever graced the tournament. But while he was the most prolific winner the game had seen, he became a nervous wreck when in contention in the Open. By 1967 he had decided to take a different tack. As he put it himself: "For years I came over trying so hard to win. This year I simply came back to see my friends."

Surely it was that more relaxed approach that lay behind this popular victory, where the 45-year-old Argentinian opened up a two-stroke gap on the field thanks to a wonderful third-round 67. Only one five appeared on his card that day, but still it was not enough to shake off Gary Player, who had recorded a 67 of his own. Nicklaus was only three adrift.

Given the company he was keeping, it was generally expected that de Vicenzo would duly succumb to nerves on the final day, but he played beautifully. Naturally Nicklaus charged, shooting 69, but de Vicenzo held firm, bravely birdieing the 16th. Two pars to finish, and he had won the Open at the 20th time of asking.

What a corker!

Certain types of Open players thrive at Lytham. Like no other course the same names crop up, and so after two rounds in 1969 it was no surprise that the leader was Bob Charles, who had won the Open there in 1963. In second place was Christy O'Connor, who had finished one shot shy of the winning score in 1958. And three behind was the 25-year-old son of a Scunthorpe lorry driver, Tony Jacklin.

In truth Jacklin was not heavily favoured to do well. He had struggled in America in the run-up to the tournament, missing five cuts in six events. The good news was that Jacklin himself felt he was playing well enough to make a challenge, and now he lent substance to the argument.

On the third day the recurring Open scenario of a rampant Golden Bear revealed itself once more. He shot 66, as did the defending champion, de Vicenzo. They were one shot behind Charles, who had lost pole position owing to some erratic driving. The man who had taken up the reins, to mounting excitement in Lancashire, was Jacklin, who had shot 70.

Early on the final day that excitement had grown to hysterical proportions. After five holes Jacklin was five strokes clear

Tony Jacklin – held his nerve for a British victory in 1969

of the field. Surely nothing could stop him now? By the turn Charles had got a stroke back, but still the lead was four. Slowly the shots slipped away, Charles gnawing constantly at the advantage. As the pair stood on the 18th tee, Jacklin held a two-stroke lead.

Naturally, there was some sense of foreboding in British hearts. Was it not here in 1958 that Eric Brown had needed a four for victory and taken six? What if Jacklin found a bunker off the tee and Charles birdied the hole?

It was then that Jacklin calmed all fears with perhaps the best drive of his life. In the BBC commentary booth, Henry Longhurst almost wept with joy: "Oh, it's gone for miles, what a corker!" he jubilantly exclaimed to the nation. Jacklin had but a seven iron to the green, and when that pulled up 20 feet away, victory was in his palm. Two putts later and he closed his fingers around the most famous trophy in golf.

Heartbreak misses

Over the course of this century there have been many, many millions of putts struck in tournament play. But when it comes down to the most heartbreaking missed putt of the last 100 years, three stand out, and of the three there is a clear winner. The other two contenders are Sam Snead's miss from 30 inches to lose the 1947 US Open; and Bernhard Langer's missed six-footer at Kiawah Island that cost Europe the 1991 Ryder Cup; but above all – a long way above all – is Doug Sanders's miss from three feet on the home hole at the home of golf, which caused the 1970 Open Championship to slip away.

What perhaps made the miss so shocking was the play that immediately preceded it. With Nicklaus sitting in the clubhouse on a total of 283, Sanders knew that he had to finish par, par to win. Clearly the difficult part of the task came at the Road Hole, and never more so than when Sanders's approach shot finished in the Road Hole bunker. If Sanders had gone on to win, the sand shot he played to within 12 inches of the hole would surely have been remembered as one of the best the game has seen. As it was it gave him his par, and now he needed but one more regulation figure.

Sanders's approach was caught a touch thin, the ball coming to rest 60 feet from the hole. Two putts needed for victory; the first, alas, was too cautious. If he was going to be three feet away, better past the hole than short. That way he would be putting uphill. But it finished three feet short, and now he had a tricky putt with an all-too-subtle break. As he prepared to putt, a fleck of grass blew across his line and he bent down to pick it up. In that second he betrayed his nerves; in the commentary box, Henry Longhurst spoke with a portentous dread, as if he knew what would happen next.

The putt from Sanders was a tentative prod, and it took the break for which he had never allowed. Nicklaus had been reprieved. Sanders, runner-up in 1966 to the Golden Bear, was in despair. To his credit he came back the next day and made a great fist of the play-off, now reduced to 18 holes. Coming to the last there was just one shot in it, and Nicklaus tried to intimidate his opponent by taking off his sweater and attempting to drive the green. He caught it too well, the ball running through the putting surface. Sanders, meanwhile, pitched to four feet; Nicklaus chipped to about three times that distance and now had that putt for victory.

Nicklaus made no mistake, and when the ball fell below ground he flung his putter high in the air. For a moment both players covered their heads, for fear it would land upon them. When it hit the ground they shook hands, leaving Sanders to contemplate a lifetime of regret. Asked 20 years later if he ever thought about that putt, he replied: "Sometimes I go as long as five minutes without thinking about it."

Centenary Open

The 100th Open Championship was staged in 1971, and by now the event was once more golf's leading light. This would be emphasized by the top 20 that year at Birkdale, which embraced all six continents. This was the year of Liang Huan Lu, the charming man with the porkpie hat from Formosa who captivated the crowds and became known affectionately as Mr Lu. This was also the year in which Lee Trevino became recognized as a great player, the year in which he achieved three "Open" titles in the space of one month. First there was his second victory in the US Open; then he won the Canadian Open. Now, at Birkdale, he shot two rounds of 69 and two of 70 to beat Mr Lu by a single stroke. In third place was Tony Jacklin; the latter would have to get used to dropping on his knee to the former.

The following Open was the pair's big year, the sort of dramatic event that can wreck players' careers. It certainly proved the beginning of the end for poor Jacklin. Both played beautifully for three rounds and at the end of them Trevino was just a stroke ahead, albeit a shade fortuitously, owing to a freak holed bunker shot at the 16th when the thinned trap shot caught the pin flush and dropped into the hole. Still, he had fully capitalized on his fortune, and what a pairing they would now make for the final day. In third place was the luckless Sanders, with Jack Nicklaus six strokes adrift.

For Nicklaus the dream of a Grand Slam was fading. Like Ben Hogan in 1953 and Arnold Palmer in 1960, he had come to the Open with a record for the year in the majors that read: played two, won two. In the final round the dream came alive. Casting aside his previous cautious strategy, Nicklaus took a blowtorch to Muirfield and scorched round in just 38 strokes for 11 holes. From nowhere he had become the championship leader.

Could Nicklaus keep it going? A series of pars followed, but then he dropped his first shot of the day at the 16th. Now he desperately needed a birdie at the 17th; it did not happen, however. A par at the last meant it was "only" a 66. The target was 278.

It was well within the grasp of Trevino and Jacklin as they came to the 17th, with the former one ahead and needing two pars to beat Nicklaus. With the 17th a very birdieable par five, no wonder Nicklaus was disconsolate in the clubhouse, and Jacklin confident of his own prospects. After two shots the situation had changed. Jacklin was now well placed to get his birdie, being 40 yards short of the green, but Trevino was in trouble. He had hooked his drive into a bunker and, having chipped out, now he hooked again. When he put his fourth through the green up a bank, he said: "That's it. I've thrown it away."

Certainly Jacklin ought to have drawn level at worst; the way Trevino was thinking, he should probably have gone ahead. Perhaps such thinking influenced his disappointing chip, which came up 25 feet short. Back to Trevino's shot, which was played with the minimum of care; his self-disgust at throwing away the event was all too evident. The ball ran on and on – and then fell against the flagstick and in for the flukiest five of all time. For Jacklin, it was all too much. Now he had to hole the putt merely to draw level. He struck it three feet by and then missed the return. Another dropped shot at the last and he did not even finish second; a par for Trevino, meanwhile, confirmed his own impression that God, indeed, was a Mexican.

After Tom Weiskopf's sole success in 1973 and Gary Player's third in 1974, an amiable young man arrived at Carnoustie for his first Open carrying a bagful of mental luggage. Tom Watson had always been a wonderfully gifted striker of the ball, but since turning professional had lacked the mental strength to convert that talent into victories. Perhaps his psychology degree was telling against him; perhaps he knew too much.

He arrived at Carnoustie with little preparation, and during the first round his caddie, Alfie Fyles, had to guide him around the course. He was clearly not taking his first Open seriously. Yet for Watson it became love at first sight, indeed the start of a lifelong love affair with links golf that continues to this day.

Suddenly he was relaxed, a golfer in his spiritual home. After three rounds he was just three strokes behind the leader, Bobby Cole, and he followed that with a 72 to set the target of 279. Of those who had stood ahead of him, only the Australian, Jack Newton, could match his total. Newton had actually had a holeable putt at the 18th but, fearful of risking a three-footer coming back, had played safe; perhaps he was mindful that he was taking on a player the following day who had a reputation as a "choker".

Watson buried that reputation for ever in the play-off. It was he who strode tall on the final hole, getting a par four to win by one stroke. The age of Watson had begun.

Seve's second

The 1976 Open was memorable for two reasons. First the majesty of Johnny Miller, who demonstrated – as he had at Oakmont in the 1973 Open – that when he was on song he was all but unbeatable. In blazing sunshine at Birkdale, he went round in 66 on the final day to win by six shots. They say no one remembers who finishes second, but this is often untrue in the Open. Second in Miller's year was a 19-year-old Spaniard called Severiano Ballesteros who either led or was tied for the lead after each of the first three rounds. "His time will come," everyone agreed. In this particular instance, a truer word was never spoken.

Open greats

The greatest Open of all time? There is only one really serious contender. It was Turnberry's first Open in 1977, and it proved unforgettable. The combination of ideal weather, glorious scenery and the two greatest players in the world both performing close to the peak of their powers proved irresistible.

At the halfway stage the lead was held by Roger Maltbie, with Hubert Green, Lee Trevino, Nicklaus and Watson all a shot behind. The latter pair had had identical scores for two rounds, and so were paired together for the third day.

It was a special occasion. One birdie was matched by another, one silky stroke equalized by a similar blow. Nicklaus led early, but back came Watson over the closing holes. At the last Watson almost holed an outrageous birdie putt; Nicklaus practically did likewise with a chip.

For the third day running they had come in with identical scores, only this time the ante had been upped, for both had shot 65s. Only Ben Crenshaw was remotely in touch, three shots behind.

On the fourth day it was Nicklaus who again established an early lead. At the 2nd Watson, for once, played a poor chip and ran up a bogey; Nicklaus, by contrast, rolled in a birdie putt. Suddenly there was daylight between them. And at the 4th another Nicklaus birdie gave him a three-shot cushion.

Watson was far from finished. It was clear that on this day he would have to make things happen rather than rely on a mistake, and he duly birdied three holes out of four from the 5th. He was all square again. Then he bogeyed the 9th. One down again.

Over a series of tense holes at the start of the back nine, Nicklaus clung to his slender lead. Then came the pivotal par-three 15th. Here Nicklaus hit the green with his tee shot while Watson had hooked, and was short and left, some 25 yards away. The possibility of a two-stroke lead with three holes to play must have crossed Nicklaus's mind. Watson chose a putter to play his next shot, despite the distance; he promptly holed. Far from being two ahead, Nicklaus was back to all-square.

Watson and Nicklaus at the end of their 1977 showdown

Both parred the 16th. At the par-five 17th both drove superbly, but only Watson's approach was struck with true authority, finding the target while Nicklaus's came up 20 yards short. His chip was a decent one, finishing four feet away. Watson putted up stone dead, leaving Nicklaus to hole to keep matters level. Or so everyone thought. But the putt was never on line, and for the first time all day Watson was ahead.

At the last he hit another wonderful drive, while Nicklaus, perhaps rattled, drove near to a whin bush. Watson then hit the shot of a champion, a gorgeous seven iron that finished no more than three feet from the hole. Surely that was it?

Nicklaus thought differently. Somehow from his wicked lie he forced the ball on to the green; then with sheer willpower he holed an outrageous putt. Instead of two for it, Watson now had to hole for a birdie, and commendably he did. So Nicklaus had shot 65, 66 for the last two rounds and lost to a man who shot 65, 65.

It was superlative golf, and never let any man decry it by saying the golf course played easily. The fact is that the man in third place, Hubert Green, finished ten shots behind Nicklaus; and he was the only other man to complete 72 holes under par.

Given the amazing number of times he had been in contention to win, it was remarkable that Nicklaus had just two Open titles to his name. He somewhat made amends for that in 1978 by winning his third Open and his second at St Andrews. It was his 15th major championship, and meant that he had won each of them on at least three occasions. When you consider that no one else has ever won each of them twice, it gives a good indication of the measure of his achievement.

European champion

By 1979 the possibility had arisen that the Open might crown its first champion from continental Europe for 72 years. The championship had returned to Lancashire for the first time since Severiano Ballesteros charmed the whole county three years earlier. They were rooting for him almost as much as they were for the home challengers. In the third round it looked as if the Spaniard might let them down. He had shot a 75, but fortunately the second-round leader Hale Irwin had done the same, and so he remained only two shots behind. The field had closed, however. Nicklaus had predictably taken advantage of the slip-ups by the pair to move to within three. Ben Crenshaw was four off the pace; even Watson was only five adrift.

Ballesteros made a decisive move from the start, birdieing the first hole, and when Irwin took six down the second, he was in front. Thereafter the crowd was treated to the full Ballesteros repertoire. At the sixth he struck a tee shot that was fully 90 yards off-line. At the 16th he drove into an area reserved for BBC vehicles. There was brilliance to go with the bizarre; Irwin could not handle it. Frustrated beyond belief, he referred to Ballesteros as the "car park champion" afterwards, a remark that cut the Spaniard to the quick. It was nothing more than sour grapes, and certainly nothing like as fortuitous a victory as that achieved by Trevino eight years earlier.

Tom Watson's form going into the 1980 Open at Muirfield had been positively magisterial. He had already won three times on the US Tour and finished third in the US Open. On top of that he was playing his favourite form of golf. So, mind, was Lee Trevino, and when he opened with rounds of 68 and 67 to stand on 137, three shots ahead of Watson, the thoughts of many must have scanned back three years to wonder whether we were about to see a shoot-out along similar lines to that at Turnberry.

As things turned out, we were not, simply because Watson's golf was so good. In the third round he was at his best, coming home in a scarcely believable 30 strokes for a 64 and a four-stroke lead. Who could give Watson in his prime such a lead on a links course and hope to win? The simple answer, of course, was no one. Watson matched Trevino's 69 in the final round, and so four shots remained the difference between them at the end.

The victory had an amusing interlude. On the Sunday evening Ben Crenshaw and Watson decided to play a match down the 10th and 18th holes using old hickory clubs and guttie balls. When they reached the green the old Muirfield secretary, Paddy Hanmer, was waiting for them. Adding to the club's terrible reputation, Hanmer blasted from both barrels along the lines of, "You may be the Open champion, but that event finished hours ago and now you are trespassing and indulging in totally unacceptable behaviour." The response from the pair is not known, but no doubt they disappeared into the good night, laughing hysterically to themselves at the pompous old fool.

Bill Rogers's time at the top in golf was short and sweet, but during the two years or so that he was there he achieved great things. In 1981 he finished runner-up in the US Open at Merion and then won the Open at Royal St George's, with Bernhard Langer trailing four shots behind in second place. In the months that followed Rogers discovered just how powerful a magnet it is to be Open champion. He played in every event that invited him, and at the end of it he discovered that he did not care much for tournament golf any more. He retired to become head professional at San Antonio Country Club, and that is where he has remained.

After a one-year absence, normal service was resumed at the Open in 1982 and 1983 when Tom Watson won his fourth and fifth titles. The first followed the sad collapse of Bobby Clampett in the third round and Nick Price in the fourth, and meant that his victories had come on four different Scottish courses.

Watson strikes

Naturally it was time he won in England, and 1983 provided the ideal opportunity as the Open travelled to Birkdale. The tournament was won with one of the finest shots that even Watson has ever struck. Appropriately enough it came at the 18th, a wonderful par four into the teeth of a strong breeze that required a two-iron approach for Watson to reach the green. He had no strokes to spare if he was to avoid a play-off with two other golfers, and he did not need any. The two iron left the club like a tracer bullet, and came to rest 12 feet from the hole.

Watson had claimed victory following a second successive 70, accompanying rounds of 67 and 68, and victory by one shot from Hale Irwin and Andy Bean. He was just 33 and now within touching distance of Harry Vardon's record of six wins. He would also surely become just the fifth player to win all four majors when he finally claimed the USPGA. But these two records would forever stand out of reach for Watson and, with his 50th birthday imminent, it is hard to see him claiming either of them now. Nevertheless, his record is there for the ages. Alongside J.H. Taylor, James Braid and Peter Thomson, he is the only player to have won the Open five times. And the greatest of these is Watson, the finest links golfer the game has ever seen.

Why, though, did he not go on to win more Open Championships? One of the reasons came in 1984, when once again he was in a position to win. As usual he was just off the pace coming to the closing holes, getting ever nearer, eliminating mistakes, making inspired plays, putting the heat on those in front of him and forcing mistakes by his presence on the leaderboard. At St Andrews that year everything was going to plan. He had drawn level with Severiano Ballesteros and now he was playing the 17th, and the situation called for a Tom Watson special; one of those heroic long irons to set up an unlikely birdie. But this time it did not happen. This time a shot that Watson had thought looked sweet in the air landed on the green, rolled over the road beyond it, and against the boundary wall. For a moment Watson seemed unable to comprehend what had occurred. There is no doubt that for some time afterwards it would gnaw at his self-belief. At the time it added up to a certain bogey. Just as he holed out, Ballesteros was doing his matador's impression on the final green, a shocking contrast of emotions. The Spaniard had holed from 20 feet for a birdie, and his smile and his reaction lit up St Andrews. For Watson there was nowhere to hide, nowhere to go but to confront the reality of bitter disappointment.

Lyle's moment

The only thing that could compare with a Ballesteros victory as far as the home crowds were concerned was one for a British player, and in 1985 the cup finally runneth over. Sandy Lyle had first played in the Open in 1974 when he was just 16 years old. Now at Sandwich he made his full contribution to a year that European golf will never forget. First Bernhard Langer had won the Masters at Augusta; later both Lyle and Langer would help Europe win back the Ryder Cup. Now it was Lyle's sweetest individual moment. On a brutally tough course where no player matched the par of 280, Lyle made his crucial move with birdies at the tough 14th and 15th holes. At the last, however, there was agony. Lyle's second shot had finished to the left of the green and now he had to play up a shelf to a pin perched practically on top of it. He hit the chip a fraction too soft, and the ball came back to his feet. Lyle slumped to his knees in disappointment. Then he recovered manfully to get down in two at the second attempt. He would still get his chance in a play-off at least.

It turned out better than that because while plenty tried, no one could match his score of 282, two over par. It was not only

Lyle who had found the going tough at the close; everyone else had. And amidst patriotic scenes, a British golfer had claimed the trophy at long last. As Lyle's fans celebrated long into the night, how did the man himself mark the evening of his greatest hour? He went back to his rented house and had a quiet meal, stopping only to wash the dishes before heading off to bed.

Mr Saturday Night

In 1986 Greg Norman rather cruelly became known as Mr Saturday Night, the name of a Billy Crystal film doing the rounds at the time and a reference to him leading every major championship after three rounds but winning only one. At least he won the big one, the Open at Turnberry, and he did so with a bit of a swagger, too, a five-shot triumph that was set up by his second-round 63, achieved in terrible conditions. Tom Watson was so impressed that he later called it "the finest round by any player in any tournament in which I have been a competitor".

Since Tom Watson's demise, no American had stepped into the breach. For the first time since the 1950s their names were not being annually inscribed on the trophy; instead it was mostly Europeans. And if Sandy Lyle was winning the Open then surely it was time for Nick Faldo to do likewise.

Throughout their careers the pair had been spurring each other on, with Faldo usually half a step behind. In 1983 Faldo had taken the brave decision to remodel his swing, after disappointment in that year's Open at Birkdale. When Lyle won in 1985 with a swing that not even his wife would describe as pretty, it looked like a big mistake by Faldo; particularly as he had fallen off the graph.

Faldo provided his answer in 1987, and he did so with one of the most remarkable last rounds in Open history. He parred every single hole, and the best par of all came on the 18th, where he struck a wonderful five iron from the middle of the fairway to the middle of the green. For Faldo, this was confirmation of everything upon which he had worked. One stroke behind Paul Azinger with two holes to play, he had claimed his first major championship with a style that would characterize four of the five majors to follow; by grinding down his opponent, and thriving on the pressure.

A career of two halves

There is no question that one half of Severiano Ballesteros's

Nick Faldo secures victory on the 18th at Muirfield in 1987

career ended on April 13, 1986, and another began. That was the day he lost the Masters when holding a two-shot lead with four holes to play; his sense of *destino* went for ever that day. But there was still one more major to claim, one glorious last hurrah when everything in the world would be right again. Once again it was Lytham, and record crowds descended on the Lancashire course to see him do it.

Ballesteros led after the opening day with a 67, but Nick Price matched that score on the second day for a one-stroke lead. Torrential rain washed out the Saturday play and so the third round took place on the Sunday. Nick Faldo became a factor; he joined Price at the top of the leaderboard. Ballesteros was just two strokes behind.

And so to the first Monday finish in the Open Championship, and it proved suitably climactic. "Once or twice a lifetime does a man get to play that well," Ballesteros would say later, and he was right. You had to feel sorry for Price who shot 69 around Lytham on the final day, and yet found that it was still two strokes short of the winning score. Ballesteros had gone round in 65, a record for the final round of an Open, embellishing the occasion with a wondrous chip from beside the 18th green that nestled softly next to the pin. It was, of course, the Spaniard's second win at Lytham, but achieved in a manner starkly different from the first. Then he had hardly hit a fairway on the last day; this time he hardly missed one. For a day at least, Ballesteros had returned to his very best form, and it was good to have him back.

Four-hole first

The first four-hole play-off in Open history took place in 1989, and it ended up in a surprising win for Mark Calcavecchia, as Greg Norman discovered a new way to lose a major championship. The Australian had been seven shots behind the third-round leader, Wayne Grady, but he made up most of that deficit before the frontmen had even teed off, beginning his round with six successive birdies. Eventually he signed for a course-record 64 and sat back to see what would happen. Grady tied him with a 71. So did Calcavecchia following a 68. Calcavecchia had been the recipient of an extraordinary piece of luck at the 12th hole during his final round. Here he had missed the green with a wild approach and was looking at a bogey at best. He thrashed at his ball in the undergrowth, and watched in amazement as it fell from the sky, landing in the hole and staying there.

In the play-off Norman began as he had done in regulation play; he had two birdies. Calcavecchia matched the second of them, and poor Grady was quickly relegated to the periphery. At the third extra hole Norman bogeyed and so they were level again. At the last Norman hit the dumbest drive of his career, a three wood that finished in the fairway bunker. From there the only score available is five and Norman did not even manage that. He went from there into another bunker and from there out of bounds. Game over.

Faldo on fire

The following year at St Andrews Norman was in the thick of things again, well for two rounds at least. Then he was paired with Nick Faldo. Faldo shot 67. Norman shot 76. This was Faldo at perhaps the peak of his powers. Nothing could disturb his concentration, his wonderful command of all the shots that links golf requires. He had demonstrated as much from the first day, a lovely seven-iron chip and run at the 18th that travelled through the Valley of Sin and dropped into the hole for an eagle two. Now he was destroying Norman by showing that raw talent is never the equal of unfailing nerve. Those dramatic events of the third day gave Faldo a five-shot lead with one round to go, and turned the final day into a glorious coronation. The English may not normally be popular in Scotland, but this was an exception. The crowd on the 18th rose as one to greet an exceptional performance. Faldo's winning score of 270 was the lowest in any major championship since Tom Watson had scorched round Turnberry in 268 in 1977.

It was also Faldo's fourth major championship and two years later, following the strange case of Ian Baker-Finch's win at Birkdale in 1991, he claimed his third Open title at Muirfield. This was perhaps his most heartstopping. For three rounds his golf was simply imperious. He opened with a 66 and then followed it with a 64 to blitz the field. A 69 on the third day meant he had become the first player to break 200 for three rounds at the Open. He was unstoppable.

But leading by a distance is a curious thing. Few players have been able to manage it with complete confidence; Raymond Floyd is one of the few. Now suddenly the shots slipped away from Faldo and John Cook came into the picture. Faldo bogeyed the 11th and then needed three putts at the 13th. At the 14th he drove into a bunker and that was another bogey. Cook, meanwhile, up ahead was holing from 20 feet for a two at the 16th. The leader by four after three rounds was now trailing by two with only four holes to play.

Great champions have wonderful reserves of mental fortitude, however. From somewhere Faldo summoned the strength to birdie the 15th and the 17th. When his nearest challenger, John Cook, missed a terribly short putt for a birdie at the 17th and then followed it with a bogey at the 18th, just as Paul Azinger had done five years earlier, Faldo once more needed a four for the title. He achieved it to become just the second British golfer since the First World War to win the Open on three occasions.

Finest-ever round

Is there another contender to challenge the 1977 Open as the best of all? Well, of course, and none stronger than the 1993 edition, which went ahead at a decidedly parched Royal St George's. What made this Open so special was the calibre of the leaderboard going into the final round, and the quality of golf played on the final day. Having said that, it was pretty special leading up to it as well.

The tone was set on a stunning first day as four players came in with a 66, including those 1989 protagonists, Calcavecchia and Norman. As if to emphasize that this was a far different Sandwich from the one that had dominated all players in 1985, Nick Faldo equalled the lowest-ever score in a major in the second round, a 63, to set the pace at 132. On the third day he shot 70.

Leading the way now were Faldo and Corey Pavin, while Greg Norman and Bernhard Langer were just a stroke behind.

John Daly – the "Wild Thing" came good at St Andrews

In other words, four of the best players in the world would occupy the last two groupings on the last day of the Open.

There is little doubt that if someone had offered Faldo, from this position, a 67 for a total of 269 – one better than his St Andrews total in 1990, remember, one off the record Open score – he would surely have stayed in the clubhouse and waited contentedly for the prize presentation.

Yet that was the score Faldo came in with and still had to accept second best, beaten by two shots. For once it was Norman who fired all the bullets on the final day, answering all the criticism that had come his way. Heaven knows why he has not been able to play well on so many occasions in the last round, but on this day at least he was simply magnificent. He was confronted by probably the three most redoubtable competitors around at the time, and blitzed them all.

After the wonderful tribute Tom Watson paid him regarding his second-round 63 at Turnberry in 1986, now Langer said of Norman's 64: "That is the finest round of golf that I have ever witnessed."

It set a shoalful of records. Not only did it complete the lowest 72-hole total in Open history, indeed major championship history, but it was the lowest final round to win. His prize was the first six-figure cheque to be awarded at the Open, but possibly sweeter were the accolades that came ringing in his ears. And from the side of the 18th green came the biggest one of all. Gene Sarazen, then 91, said: "I never thought I would live to see golf played like this."

Greg Norman's best friend in golf is Nick Price, so there must have been a particular pleasure to hand over the trophy to the Zimbabwean the following year. And what a popular victory it was for the man who had gone so close on two previous occasions. Price had shown, like countless players before him, that winning the Open is invariably a matter of patience, of getting into contention and learning how to win, and then claiming the trophy once the experience has been accumulated. And emphasizing the message was the runner-up, Jesper Parnevik. What a finish he had put into his final round. He had come from some way off the pace to birdie five of the last seven holes. Now he stood on the 18th tee with a two-stroke lead. Only he did not know that. There was no excuse, since a huge scoreboard was clearly visible, but he chose not to look at it. He opted instead to attack the difficult pin position. He gambled and lost and ran up a bogey five. And as he did that Price rolled in a 50-foot eagle putt at the 17th. Price, of course, couldn't wait to look at the leaderboard. It told him he now only needed a par at the last to win. He played safe and got his par. For Parnevik, it was the harshest lesson.

There is another way to victory apart from Price's tried and trusted route, but only one man has attempted it and succeeded. That is the John Daly route. In 1991 he won the USPGA Championship while getting drunk most nights. Now he

Greg Norman – a final-round 64 brought victory in 1993

claimed the claret jug as a recovering alcoholic. When he first played in the Open, Daly had pronounced that he would never get used to the wind; now he showed how much he had learned. On the final day it gusted to 35mph at times to make a mockery of the idea that the Old Course had become too easy. The winning score was 282, one that Costantino Rocca matched in the most unlikely manner imaginable. Needing a birdie at the last to tie with Daly, he completely duffed his chip, so that it finished in the Valley of Sin, some 70 feet from the pin. Rocca was staring at a lifetime of ignominy when the putt sped on its way and dropped into the hole. The amiable Italian dropped to the floor and beat the sacred ground in joy. Even when he comfortably lost the subsequent four-hole play-off, the smile never left his face. He had lost with pride.

Experience counts

The victory was the first of the 1990s for American golf, and signalled the end of a long period of domination by international players. Now the Americans have regained the ascendancy they have held for long periods of the twentieth century. In 1996 there was a fine victory for the popular Tom Lehman, while Justin Leonard endeared himself to millions in 1997 with a victory speech that was immaculate in both its message and delivery. Jesper Parnevik finished second again. In 1998 Mark O'Meara claimed his second major championship of the year with a wonderful win in a classic tournament at Royal Birkdale.

There was dramatic golf from the start. Tiger Woods opened with a 65 to dispute the lead with John Huston. On the second day a little-known American called Brian Watts followed up his opening 68 with a 69, and now he held the lead. But all England was captivated by the player in second place, a 17-year-old amateur called Justin Rose who had shot 66 on the second day and now would go out in the final grouping in the third round.

Naturally everyone expected him to fall off his perch, but what a performance Rose put up. Only in the last few holes did it all get too much on the wildest Open day for some time. Phil Mickelson had no fewer than 13 bogeys on his card – that's how tough it was. Rose shot 75 to be three behind Watts, with O'Meara tied for second with Jim Furyk and the luckless Jesper Parnevik.

When he came to the 18th on the final day, Rose was looking like he would drop outside the top four for the first time since he had been unknown on Friday. Since then countless thousands of Lancastrians had journeyed with him on an epic voyage, but now it appeared he was floundering. He had missed the green at the 18th and was faced with a 50-yard pitch. Three more from there and he would finish seventh, still brilliant for a 17-year-old, but disappointing after what had gone before.

Rose played the shot to perfection, of course, and when it dropped into the hole, the ovation was the loudest that Sir Michael Bonallack, the secretary of the Royal and Ancient, said that he had ever heard in his life.

O'Meara certainly heard it way back at the 16th, where he was closing in on victory. He would eventually set a target of 280 with a flawless last-round 68 that Watts would match, courtesy of a miraculous bunker shot at the last to retrieve par. The Open had its third-ever, four-hole, sudden-death play-off.

Experience told in the end. O'Meara departed the 18th second time around with the trophy while Watts left with a lifetime of memories. So did Rose.

The Open, meanwhile, had shown that in its 138th year its capacity to enthral remained as strong as ever.

October 17, 1860

Prestwick GC, Ayrshire, Scotland

Prestwick was a 12-hole course measuring 3,799 yards with a par of 48.

1	**Willie Park Sr**	55	59	60	174
2	**Tom Morris Sr**	58	59	59	176
3	**Andrew Strath**				180
4	**Robert Andrew**				191
5	**George Brown**				192
6	**Charlie Hunter**				195
	Alexander Smith (score not known)				
	William Steel				232

September 26, 1861

Prestwick GC, Ayrshire, Scotland

1	**Tom Morris Sr**	54	56	53	163
2	**Willie Park Sr**	54	54	59	167
3	**William Dow**	59	58	54	171
4	**David Park**	58	57	57	172
5	**Robert Andrew**	58	61	56	175
6	**Peter McEwan**	56	60	62	178
7	**Wilie Dunn Sr**	61	59	60	180
8	**James Fairlie (a)**				184
9	**George Brown**	60	65	60	185
10	**Robert Chambers Jr (a)**				187
11	**Jamie Dunn**	63	62	63	188
12	**Charlie Hunter**	67	64	59	190

September 11, 1862

Prestwick GC, Ayrshire, Scotland

1	**Tom Morris Sr**	54	56	53	163
2	**Willie Park Sr**	59	59	58	176
3	**Charlie Hunter**	60	60	58	176
4	**William Dow**	60	58	63	181
5	**James Knight (a)**	62	61	63	186
6	**J.F. Johnston (a)**	64	69	75	208
	William Mitchell (a) (score not known)				
	R. Pollock (a) (score not known)				

September 18, 1863

Prestwick GC, Ayrshire, Scotland

1	**Willie Park Sr**	56	54	58	168
2	**Tom Morris Sr**	56	58	56	170
3	**David Park**	55	63	54	172
4	**Andrew Strath**	61	55	58	174
5	**George Brown**	58	61	57	176
6	**Robert Andrew**	62	57	59	178
7	**Charlie Hunter**	61	61	62	184
8	**James Knight (a)**	66	65	59	190
9	**James Miller (a)**	63	63	66	192
10	**James Paxton**	65	65	66	196
=11	**Peter Chalmers (a)**	65	67	65	197
	J.F. Johnston (a)	66	66	65	197
13	**William Mitchell (a)**	70	70	66	206
14	**William Moffat (a)**	75	78	80	233

September 16, 1864

Prestwick GC, Ayrshire, Scotland

1	**Tom Morris Sr**	54	58	55	167
2	**Andrew Strath**	56	57	56	169
3	**Robert Andrew**	57	58	60	175
4	**Willie Park Sr**	55	67	55	177
5	**William Dow**	56	58	67	181
6	**William Strath**	60	62	69	182

September 14, 1865

Prestwick GC, Ayrshire, Scotland

Official printed scorecards were introduced for the first time.

1	**Andrew Strath**	55	54	53	162
2	**Willie Park Sr**	56	52	56	164
3	**William Dow**				171
4	**Bob Kirk**	64	54	55	173
5	**Tom Morris Sr**	57	61	56	174
6	**William Doleman (a)**	62	57	59	178
7	**Robert Andrew**	61	59	59	179
8	**William Strath**	60	60	62	182
9	**William Miller**	63	60	66	189
10	**Tom Hood (a)**	66	66	66	198

September 13, 1866

Prestwick GC, Ayrshire, Scotland

1	**Willie Park Sr**	54	56	59	169
2	**David Park**	58	57	56	171
3	**Robert Andrew**	58	59	59	176
4	**Tom Morris Sr**	61	58	59	178
5	**Bob Kirk**	60	62	58	180
=6	**William Doleman (a)**	60	60	62	182
	Andrew Strath	61	61	60	182
8	**John Allan**	60	63	60	183
9	**Tom Morris Jr**	63	60	64	187
10	**Willie Dunn Sr**	64	63	62	189
11	**Tom Hood (a)**	61	69	61	191
12	**James Hutchison**	63	67	64	194

Date not known, 1867

Prestwick GC, Ayrshire, Scotland

1	**Tom Morris Sr**	58	54	58	170
2	**Willie Park Sr**	58	56	58	172
3	**Andrew Strath**	61	57	56	174
4	**Tom Morris Jr**	58	59	58	175
5	**Bob Kirk**	57	60	60	177
6	**William Doleman (a)**	55	66	57	178
7	**Robert Andrew**	56	58	65	179
=8	**William Dow**	62	57	65	184
	T. Hunter (a)	62	60	62	184
10	**Willie Dunn Sr**	64	63	62	189

September 23, 1868

Prestwick GC, Ayrshire, Scotland

1	**Tom Morris Jr**	50	55	52	157
2	**Robert Andrew**	53	54	52	159
3	**Willie Park Sr**	58	50	54	162
4	**Bob Kirk**	56	59	56	171
5	**John Allan**	54	55	63	172
6	**Tom Morris Sr**	56	62	58	176

	September 23, 1868 continued				
7	**William Dow**	61	58	60	179
8	**William Doleman (a)**	57	63	61	181
9	**Charlie Hunter**	60	64	58	182
10	**Willie Dunn Sr**	60	63	60	183

September 16, 1869

Prestwick GC, Ayrshire, Scotland

1	**Tom Morris Jr**	51	54	49	154
2	**Tom Morris Sr**	54	50	53	157
3	**S. Mure Fergusson (a)**	57	54	54	165
4	**Bob Kirk**	53	58	57	168
5	**Davie Strath**	53	56	60	169
6	**Jamie Anderson**	60	56	57	173
7	**Willie Doleman (a)**	60	56	59	175
8	**G. Mitchell-Innes (a)**	64	58	58	180

September 15, 1870

Prestwick GC, Ayrshire, Scotland

1	**Tom Morris Jr**	47	51	51	149
=2	**Bob Kirk**	52	52	57	161
	Davie Strath	54	49	58	161
4	**Tom Morris Sr**	56	52	54	162
5	**William Doleman (a)**	57	56	58	171
6	**Willie Park Sr**	60	55	58	173
7	**Jamie Anderson**	59	57	58	174
8	**John Allan**	61	58	57	176
=9	**A. Doleman (a)**	61	59	58	178
	Charlie Hunter	58	56	64	178
11	**J. Brown**	66	55	59	180
12	**J. Millar**	66	62	54	182
13	**T. Hunter (a)**	62	63	60	185
14	**F. Doleman**	65	64	60	189
=15	**W. Boyd**	65	59	67	191
	J. Hunter	62	65	64	191
16	**William Dow**	68	64	66	198

1871 – No championship

September 13, 1872

Prestwick GC, Ayrshire, Scotland

1	**Tom Morris Jr**	57	56	53	166
2	**Davie Strath**	56	52	61	169
3	**William Doleman (a)**	63	60	54	177
=4	**Tom Morris Sr**	62	60	57	179
	David Park	61	57	61	179
6	**Charlie Hunter**	60	60	69	189
7	**Hugh Brown**	65	73	61	199
8	**William Hunter (a)**	65	63	74	202

October 4, 1873

Royal & Ancient GC, St Andrews, Fife, Scotland

1	**Tom Kidd**	91	88	179
2	**Jamie Anderson**	91	89	180
=3	**Bob Kirk**	91	92	183
	Tom Morris Jr	94	89	183
5	**Davie Strath**	97	90	187
6	**Walter Gourlay**	92	96	188
7	**Tom Morris Sr**	93	96	189
8	**Henry Lamb (a)**	96	96	192
=9	**Willie Fernie**	101	93	194

	October 4, 1873 continued			
	Bob Martin	97	97	194
=11	**R. Armitage (a)**	96	99	195
	Jas Fenton	94	101	195
	J.O.F. Morris	96	99	195
14	**S. Mure Fergusson (a)**	98	101	199
15	**R. Manzie**	96	104	200
16	**Jack Morris**	106	100	206
=17	**David Ayrton**	111	96	207
	R. Thomson	98	109	207
19	**John Chisholm**	103	105	208
20	**Bob Pringle**	109	102	211
21	**D. Brand**	110	103	213

April 10, 1874

Honourable Co. of Edinburgh Golfers, Musselburgh, Midlothian, Scotland

1	**Mungo Park**	75	84	159
2	**Tom Morris Jr**	83	78	161
3	**George Paxton**	80	82	162
4	**Bob Martin**	85	79	164
5	**Jamie Anderson**	82	83	165
=6	**David Park**	83	83	166
	William Thomson	84	82	166
=8	**Bob Ferguson**	83	84	167
	Tom Kidd	84	83	167
=10	**J. Fergusson**	87	82	169
	G. M'Cachnie	79	90	169
	J.O.F. Morris	88	81	169
13	**Willie Park Sr**	83	87	170
=14	**Tom Hood**	83	88	171
	Bob Pringle	85	86	171
16	**T. Hunter (a)**	88	86	174
17	**T. Brown**	87	88	175
=18	**Tom Morris Sr**	90	86	176
	Davie Strath	86	90	176
=20	**William Cosgrove**	88	89	177
	William Doleman (a)	89	88	177
=22	**R. Cosgrove**	92	86	178
	Willie Dunn Sr	87	91	178
=24	**J. Dow**	88	94	182
	Jas Fenton	90	92	182
26	**William Brown**	91	93	184
27	**W. Hutchison**	90	95	185
28	**Charlie Hunter**	93	94	187
29	**N. Patrick**	98	98	196
30	**D. Clayton**	99	101	200
31	**A. Brown**	96	106	202

September 10, 1875

Prestwick GC, Ayrshire, Scotland

1	**Willie Park Sr**	56	59	51	166
2	**Bob Martin**	56	58	54	168
3	**Mungo Park**	59	57	55	171
4	**Bob Ferguson**	58	56	58	172
5	**James Rennie**	61	59	57	177
6	**Davie Strath**	59	61	58	178
7	**Bob Pringle**	62	58	61	181
=8	**William Doleman (a)**	65	59	59	183
	Hugh Morrison	62	59	62	183
10	**John Campbell**	57	66	63	186
11	**Neil Boon**	67	60	62	189
12	**James Guthrie**	63	64	66	193
13	**Matthew Allan**	67	65	62	194
14	**James Boyd**	67	65	63	195

September 30, 1876

Royal & Ancient GC, St Andrews, Fife, Scotland

Bob Martin won the title after Davie Strath refused to participate in play-off.

Pos	Player	R1	R2	Total
1	Bob Martin*	86	90	176
2	Davie Strath	86	90	176
3	Willie Park Sr	94	89	183
=4	Tom Morris Sr	90	95	185
	Mungo Park	95	90	185
	William Thompson	90	95	185
7	Henry Lamb (a)	94	92	186
=8	Walter Gourlay	98	89	187
	Bob Kirk	95	92	187
	George Paxton	95	92	187
11	Robert Kinsman	88	100	188
=12	Jamie Anderson	96	93	189
	David Lamb (a)	95	94	189
=14	David Anderson Sr	93	97	190
	John Thompson	89	101	190

April 6, 1877

Honourable Co. of Edinburgh Golfers, Musselburgh, Midlothian, Scotland

Pos	Player	R1	R2	R3	R4	Total
1	Jamie Anderson	40	42	37	41	160
2	Bob Pringle	44	38	40	40	162
=3	William Cosgrove	41	39	44	40	164
	Bob Ferguson	40	40	40	44	164
=5	William Brown	39	41	45	41	166
	Davie Strath	45	40	38	43	166
7	Mungo Park					167

October 4, 1878

Prestwick GC, Ayrshire, Scotland

Pos	Player	R1	R2	R3	Total
1	Jamie Anderson	53	53	51	157
2	Bob Kirk	53	55	51	159
3	J.O.F. Morris	50	56	55	161
=4	John Ball Jr (a)	53	57	55	165
	Bob Martin	57	53	55	165
=6	William Cosgrove	55	56	55	166
	Willie Park Sr	53	56	57	166
8	Jamie Allan	62	53	52	167
=9	John Allan	55	55	58	168
	Tom Dunn	54	60	54	168
11	Tom Morris Sr	55	53	63	171
12	Ben Sayers	56	59	58	173
13	Edwin Paxton	58	59	58	175
14	George Strath	63	62	51	176
15	Alex Patrick	62	56	60	178
16	Jack Morris	58	57	64	179
17	Mungo Park	60	58	62	180
18	George Low	57	61	63	181
19	Neil Boon	63	54	66	183
20	William Hunter (a)	67	65	55	187
21	James Moore	62	62	65	189
22	Bob Pringle	62	65	65	192

September 27, 1879

Royal & Ancient GC, St Andrews, Fife, Scotland

September 27, 1879 continued

Pos	Player	R1	R2	Total
1	Jamie Anderson	84	85	169
=2	Jamie Allan	88	84	172
	Andrew Kirkaldy	86	86	172
4	George Paxton			174
5	Tom Kidd			175
6	Bob Ferguson			176
7	David Anderson Sr			178
=8	Tom Dunn			179
	Walter Gourlay	92	87	179
	J.O.F. Morris			179
11	A.W. Smith (a)			180
=12	Willie Fernie			181
	John Kirkaldy			181
	James Rennie			181
=15	Thomas Arundel			184
	David Ayton			184
	Henry Lamb (a)			184
=18	William Doleman (a)			185
	Robert Kinsman			185
	Tom Morris Sr			185
21	Bob Martin			186
22	Ben Sayers			187
=23	D. Corstorphine			189
	Robert Dow			189
	David Grant			189
	Edwin Paxton			189
	Smith (Cambridge)			189
28	Argyll Robertson (a)			190
=29	R. Armitage			191
	George Strath			191

April 9, 1880

Honourable Co. of Edinburgh Golfers, Musselburgh, Midlothian, Scotland

Pos	Player	R1	R2	Total
1	Bob Ferguson	81	81	162
2	Peter Paxton	81	86	167
3	Ned Cosgrove	82	86	168
=4	David Brown	86	83	169
	George Paxton	85	84	169
	Bob Pringle	90	79	169
7	Andrew Kirkaldy	85	85	170
=8	William Brown	87	84	171
	David Grant	87	84	171
=10	Thomas Arundel	86	93	179
	T. Brown	90	89	179
	Willie Campbell	88	91	179
	J. Foreman	92	87	179
14	Willie Park Sr	89	92	181
15	Willie Park Jr	92	90	182
=16	A. Brown	91	92	183
	D. Corstorphine	93	90	183
	George Strath	87	96	183
19	Ben Sayers	91	94	184
20	Mungo Park	95	92	187
=21	R. Drummond	96	94	190
	William Thomson	96	94	190
23	James Beveridge	94	97	191

October 14, 1881

Prestwick GC, Ayrshire, Scotland

Pos	Player	R1	R2	R3	Total
1	Bob Ferguson	53	60	57	170
2	Jamie Anderson	57	60	56	173
3	Ned Cosgrove	61	59	57	177
4	Bob Martin	57	62	59	178
=5	Willie Campbell	60	56	65	181
	Tom Morris Sr	58	65	58	181
	Willie Park Jr	66	57	58	181
8	Willie Fernie	65	62	56	183

September 30, 1882

Royal & Ancient GC, St Andrews, Fife, Scotland

1	**Bob Ferguson**	83	88	171
2	**Willie Fernie**	88	86	174
=3	**Jamie Anderson**	87	88	175
	Fitz Boothby (a)	86	89	175
	John Kirkcaldy	86	89	175
	Bob Martin	89	86	175
=7	**David Ayton**	90	88	178
	James Mansfield (a)	91	87	178
	Willie Park Sr	89	89	178
	James Rennie	90	88	178
=11	**Tom Kidd**	87	93	180
	Henry Lamb (a)	88	92	180
=13	**Andrew Alexander**	93	88	181
	George Low	95	86	181
	Douglas Rolland	88	93	181
=16	**W. Honeyman**	93	89	182
	William Thomson	95	87	182
=18	**Tom Dunn**	93	90	183
	Willie Park Jr	90	93	183
	Ben Sayers	92	91	183
=21	**David Anderson Sr**	91	93	184
	Peter Fernie	94	90	184
=23	**Jack Burns**	97	92	189
	George Forrester	94	95	189
	Bob Pringle	92	97	189
	David Simpson	98	91	189
27	**Thomas Arundel**	97	93	190
28	**James Kirk**	101	90	191
=29	**James Hunter (a)**	92	100	192
	Robert Kinsman	99	93	192

November 16, 1883

Honourable Co. of Edinburgh Golfers, Musselburgh, Midlothian, Scotland

** Won after a play-off.*

1	**Willie Fernie***	75	84	159
2	**Bob Ferguson**	78	81	159
3	**William Brown**	83	77	160
4	**Bob Pringle**	79	82	161
=5	**Willie Campbell**	80	83	163
	George Paxton	80	83	163
7	**Ben Sayers**	81	83	164
8	**Willie Park Jr**	77	88	165
9	**Willie Dunn Jr**	85	81	166
=10	**Ben Campbell**	81	86	167
	Tom Morris Sr	86	81	167
	Peter Paxton	85	82	167
	Douglas Rolland (a)	82	85	167
14	**T. Grossart**	82	86	168
15	**F. Park**	84	85	169
16	**William Cosgrove**	79	91	170
=17	**Tom Dunn**	87	84	171
	Jack Simpson (a)	90	81	171
19	**G. Miller (a)**	80	92	172
20	**D. Leitch (a)**	88	86	174
21	**T. Arundel**	87	88	175
22	**Willie Park Sr**	94	82	176
23	**William Thomson**	90	87	177
=24	**David Brown**	88	91	179
	David Grant	89	90	179
26	**D. Corstorphine**	88	93	181
27	**Mungo Park**	93	89	182
28	**Bob Tait**	89	94	183

November 16, 1883 continued

29	**George Strath**	91	93	184
30	**D. Baldie (a)**	92	93	185

Date not known, 1884

Prestwick GC, Ayrshire, Scotland

1	**Jack Simpson**	78	82	160
=2	**Willie Fernie**	80	94	164
	Douglas Rolland	81	83	164
=4	**Willie Campbell**	84	85	169
	Willie Park Jr	96	93	169
6	**Ben Sayers**	83	87	170
=7	**Tom Dunn**			171
	George Fernie			171
=9	**Peter Fernie**			172
	John Kirkaldy			172
=11	**Matthew Allan**			173
	Willie Dunn Jr			173
=13	**J.O.F. Morris**			174
	Tom Morris Sr			174
15	**Jamie Anderson**			175
=16	**William Cosgrove**			178
	William Doleman (a)			178
18	**James Hunter (a)**			179
19	**David Grant**			180
20	**G. Smith**			183

October 3, 1885

Royal & Ancient GC, St Andrews, Fife, Scotland

1	**Bob Martin**	84	87	171
2	**Archie Simpson**	83	89	172
3	**David Ayton**	89	84	173
=4	**Willie Fernie**	89	85	174
	Willie Park Jr	86	88	174
	Bob Simpson	85	89	174
7	**Jack Burns**	88	87	175
8	**Peter Paxton**	85	91	176
=9	**Willie Campbell**	86	91	177
	J.O.F. Morris	91	86	177
=11	**Horace Hutchinson (a)**	87	91	178
	John Kirkaldy	94	84	178
=13	**Johnny Laidlay (a)**	87	92	179
	Jack Simpson	87	92	179
15	**Ben Sayers**	94	86	180
=16	**Leslie Balfour (a)**	90	91	181
	William Greig	89	92	181
=18	**H.S.C. Everard (a)**	90	92	182
	George Fernie	87	95	182
	James Rennie	90	92	182
21	**David Anderson Sr**	96	87	183
22	**Ben Campbell**	88	96	184
23	**Willie Brown**	91	95	186
=24	**Willie Anderson Sr**	90	97	187
	S. Mure Fergusson (a)	96	91	187
26	**W.H. Goff (a)**	97	91	188
=27	**T.S. Hendry (a)**	94	95	189
	Robert Kinsman	96	93	189
=29	**Jamie Allan**	93	97	190
	William Cosgrove	88	102	190
	Bruce Goff (a)	96	94	190
	Tom Morris Sr	96	94	190

November 5, 1886

Honourable Co. of Edinburgh Golfers, Musselburgh, Midlothian, Scotland

1	**David Brown**	79	78	157
2	**Willie Campbell**	78	81	159
3	**Ben Campbell**	79	81	160
=4	**Bob Ferguson**	82	79	161
	Thomas Gossett	80	81	161
	Willie Park Jr	84	77	161
	Archie Simpson	82	79	161
=8	**Willie Fernie**	79	83	162
	David Grant	86	76	162
	Johnny Lindlay (a)	80	82	162
11	**J.O.F. Morris**	81	82	163
=12	**John Lambert**	78	86	164
	Thomas McWatt	81	83	164
	Jack Simpson	83	81	164
15	**Bob Simpson**	84	81	165
=16	**Tom Dunn**	83	83	166
	Horace Hutchinson (a)	81	85	166
	Bob Pringle	80	86	166
	Ben Sayers	84	82	166
=20	**William Cosgrove**	84	83	167
	Bob Tait	84	83	167
22	**Peter Fernie**	85	83	168
23	**Peter Paxton**	87	82	169
=24	**Jacky Ferguson**	83	87	170
	George Strath	86	84	170
26	**David Simpson**	84	88	172
=27	**Willie Dunn Jr**	85	88	173
	Tom Morris Sr	88	85	173
=29	**Charlie Crawford**	85	89	174
	James Keddie	84	90	174

September 16, 1887

Prestwick GC, Ayrshire, Scotland

1	**Willie Park Jr**	82	79	161
2	**Bob Martin**	81	81	162
3	**Willie Campbell**	77	87	164
4	**Johnny Laidlay (a)**	86	80	166
=5	**Ben Sayers**	83	85	168
	Archie Simpson	81	87	168
=7	**Willie Fernie**	86	87	173
	David Grant	89	84	173
9	**David Brown**	82	92	174
=10	**Ben Campbell**	88	87	175
	Horace Hutchinson (a)	87	88	175
=12	**David Ayton**	89	87	176
	James Kay	89	87	176
	John Kirkaldy	89	87	176
	Jack Simpson	85	91	176
16	**Bob Simpson**	90	89	179
=17	**George Fennie**	92	88	180
	A. Monaghan	90	90	180
19	**Hugh Kirkaldy**	89	92	181
=20	**James Boyd**	95	87	182
	P. Wilson (a)	90	92	182
=22	**Allan Macfie (a)**	94	90	184
	A. Stuart (a)	96	88	184
24	**Peter Fernie**	95	90	185
=25	**J.S. Carrick (a)**	96	90	186
	Jack Morris	93	93	186
27	**David McEwan**	94	93	187

October 6, 1888

Royal & Ancient GC, St Andrews, Fife, Scotland

1	**Jack Burns**	86	85	171
=2	**David Anderson Jr**	86	86	172
	Ben Sayers	85	87	172
4	**Willie Campbell**	84	90	174
5	**Leslie Balfour (a)**	86	89	175
=6	**David Grant**	88	88	176
	Andrew Kirkaldy	87	89	176
8	**Sandy Herd**	93	84	177
9	**David Ayton**	87	91	178
10	**Johnny Laidlay (a)**	93	87	180
=11	**H.S.C. Everard (a)**	93	89	182
	Hugh Kirkaldy	98	84	182
	Willie Park Jr	90	92	182
=14	**Laurie Auchterlonie**	91	92	183
	Willie Fernie	91	92	183
=16	**Bob Martin**	86	98	184
	Archie Simpson	91	93	184
=18	**Jamie Allan**	95	90	185
	Willie Auchterlonie	92	93	185
	John Kirkaldy	92	93	185
	Allan Macfie (a)	94	91	185
	Bob Tait	95	90	185
=23	**William Grieg (a)**	94	92	186
	J.O.F. Morris	96	90	186
25	**N. Playfair (a)**	94	93	187
26	**D. Leitch (a)**	93	96	189
=27	**Willie Anderson Sr**	98	92	190
	Tom Morris Sr	94	96	190
	D.G. Rose (a)	101	89	190
30	**Bob Simpson**	90	101	191

November 8, 1889

Honourable Co. of Edinburgh Golfers, Musselburgh, Midlothian, Scotland

** Willie Park Jr (158) beat Andrew Kirkaldy (163) in the 18-hole play-off.*

1	**Willie Park Jr***	39	39	39	38	155
2	**Andrew Kirkaldy**	39	38	39	39	155
3	**Ben Sayers**	39	40	41	39	159
=4	**David Brown**	43	39	41	39	162
	Johnny Laidlay (a)	42	39	40	41	162
6	**Willie Fernie**	45	39	40	40	162
=7	**Willie Brown**	44	43	41	37	165
	Willie Campbell	44	40	42	39	165
	David Grant	41	41	41	42	165
=10	**Hugh Kirkaldy**	44	39	43	40	166
	William Thomson	43	42	40	41	166
12	**Archie Simpson**	44	45	37	41	167
13	**A.M. Ross (a)**	42	45	42	40	169
14	**Jack Burns**	47	39	42	42	170

September 11, 1890

Prestwick GC, Ayrshire, Scotland

1	**John Ball Jr**	82	82	164
=2	**Willie Fernie**	85	82	167
	Archie Simpson	85	82	167
=4	**Andrew Kirkaldy**	81	89	170
	Willie Park Jr	90	80	170
6	**Horace Hutchinson (a)**	87	85	172
=7	**David Grant**	86	87	173
	Hugh Kirkaldy	82	91	173
9	**W. McEwan**	87	87	174

September 11, 1890 continued

10	**David Brown**	85	90			175
=11	**James Kay**	86	91			177
	Johnny Laidlay (a)	89	88			177
13	**D. Leitch (a)**	86	93			179
14	**David Anderson Jr**	90	90			180
=15	**John Allan**	93	88			181
	Ben Campbell	93	88			181
=17	**D. Anderson (a)**	91	91			182
	David Ayton	97	85			182
19	**Ben Sayers**	90	93			183
20	**A. Wright**	92	92			184
21	**G. Fernie**	92	94			186
22	**R.B. Wilson**	91	96			187
=23	**D.D. Robertson (a)**	94	95			189
	Bob Mearns	96	93			189
25	**Robert Adam (a)**	91	99			190
26	**James Mair (a)**	98	96			194
=27	**James Cunningham**	104	95			199
	Charles Whigham (a)	93	106			199
29	**James McKay**	104	96			200
30	**D.H. Gillan (a)**	100	104			204

October 6, 1891

Royal & Ancient GC, St Andrews, Fife, Scotland

1	**Hugh Kirkladly**	83	83			166
=2	**Willie Fernie**	84	84			168
	Andrew Kirkaldy	84	84			168
4	**R. Mure Fergusson (a)**	86	84			170
5	**W.D. More**	84	87			171
6	**Willie Park Jr**	88	85			173
7	**David Brown**	88	86			174
8	**Willie Auchterlonie**	85	90			175
=9	**Ben Sayers**	91	85			176
	Tom Vardon	89	87			176
=11	**John Ball Jr (a)**	94	83			177
	Archie Simpson	86	91			177
13	**Sandy Herd**	87	91			178
=14	**David Grant**	84	95			179
	James Kay	93	86			179
	John Kirkaldy	90	89			179
	Bob Mearns	88	91			179
=18	**Laurie Auchterlonie**	87	93			180
	Charles Hutchings (a)	89	91			180
	Johnny Laidlay	90	90			180
	David Simpson	91	89			180
=22	**David Anderson Jr**	90	91			181
	David Ayton	94	87			181
	Ernley R.H. Blackwell (a)	90	91			181
	Willie Campbell	94	87			181
	Horace Hutchinson (a)	89	92			181
	George Mason	94	87			181
=28	**H.S.C. Everard (a)**	89	93			182
	William Grieg (a)	95	87			182
	R.H. Johnston (a)	95	87			182
	Freddie Tait (a)	94	88			182

September 22–23, 1892

Honourable Co. of Edinburgh Golfers, Musselburgh, Midlothian, Scotland

The first championship to be spread over two days and 72 holes.

1	**Harold Hilton (a)**	78	81	72	74	305
=2	**John Ball Jr (a)**	75	80	74	79	308
	Sandy Herd	77	78	77	76	308
	Hugh Kirkaldy	77	83	83	85	308

September 22–23, 1892 continued

5	**James Kay**	82	78	74	78	312
	Ben Sayers	80	76	81	75	312
7	**Willie Park Jr**	78	77	80	80	315
8	**Willie Fernie**	79	83	76	78	316
9	**Archie Simpson**	81	81	76	79	317
10	**Horace Hutchinson (a)**	74	78	86	80	318
11	**Jack White**	82	78	78	81	319
12	**Tom Vardon**	83	75	80	82	320
=13	**Edward B.H. Blackwell (a)**	81	82	82	76	321
	Andrew Kirkaldy	84	82	80	75	321
15	**S. Mure Fergusson (a)**	78	82	80	82	322
=16	**David Anderson Jr**	76	82	79	87	324
	R.T. Boothby (a)	81	81	80	82	324
	Ben Campbell	86	83	79	76	324
=19	**F.A. Fairlie (a)**	83	87	79	76	325
	William McEwan	79	83	84	79	325
=21	**W.D. More**	87	75	80	84	326
	G.G. Smith (a)	84	82	79	81	326
	Freddie Tait (a)	81	83	84	78	326
24	**David Brown**	77	82	84	85	328
=25	**George Douglas**	81	83	86	79	329
	Douglas McEwan	84	84	82	79	329
27	**Ernley R.H. Blackwell (a)**	79	81	84	86	330
=28	**Leslie Balfour (a)**	83	87	80	81	331
	Jack Simpson	84	78	82	87	331
30	**Charlie Crawford**	79	85	86	84	333

August 31–September 1, 1893

Prestwick GC, Ayrshire, Scotland

1	**W. Auchterlonie**	78	81	81	82	322
2	**Johnny Laidlay (a)**	80	83	80	81	324
3	**Sandy Herd**	82	81	78	84	325
=4	**Andrew Kirkaldy**	85	82	82	77	326
	Hugh Kirkaldy	83	79	82	82	326
=6	**James Kay**	81	81	80	85	327
	Bob Simpson	81	81	80	85	327
=8	**John Ball Jr (a)**	83	79	84	86	322
	Harold Hilton (a)	88	81	82	81	322
=10	**J.H. Taylor**	75	89	86	83	333
	Jack White	81	86	80	86	333
12	**Ben Sayers**	87	88	84	76	335
13	**Charlie Hutchings (a)**	81	92	80	84	337
14	**Archie Simpson**	84	86	84	85	339
=15	**S. Mure Fergusson (a)**	83	85	85	87	340
	John Hunter	87	85	83	85	340
=17	**David Grant**	86	86	85	84	341
	Joe Lloyd	85	91	84	81	341
=19	**L.S. Anderson (a)**	89	83	86	84	342
	P.C. Anderson (a)	93	84	83	82	342
	Willie Park Jr	82	89	86	85	342
22	**David Anderson Jr**	86	93	83	81	343
=23	**John Allan**	81	88	83	92	344
	T. Carmichael (a)	90	87	82	85	344
	Willie Fernie	86	92	85	81	344
	Bob Mearns	86	84	86	88	344
	Harry Vardon	84	90	88	85	344
=28	**F.A. Fairlie (a)**	82	90	88	85	345
	William McEwan	88	84	90	83	345
	Tom Vardon	85	86	82	92	345

June 11–12, 1894

St George's GC, Sandwich, Kent, England

1	**J.H. Taylor**	84	80	80	81	326
2	**Douglas Rolland**	86	79	84	82	331
3	**Andrew Kirkaldy**	86	79	83	84	332
4	**A.H. Toogood**	84	85	82	82	333
=5	**Willie Fernie**	84	84	86	80	334
	Ben Sayers	85	81	84	84	334
	Harry Vardon	86	86	82	80	334
8	**Alex Herd**	83	85	82	88	338
9	**Freddie Tait (a)**	90	83	83	84	340
=10	**A.D. Blyth (a)**	91	83	83	84	341
	James Braid	91	84	82	84	341
12	**Willie Park Jr**	88	86	82	87	343
=13	**John Ball Jr (a)**	84	89	87	84	344
	David Brown	93	83	81	87	344
	Hugh Kirkaldy	90	85	80	89	344
	Archie Simpson	90	86	86	82	344
17	**Joe Lloyd**	95	81	86	83	345
18	**S. Mure Fergusson (a)**	87	88	84	87	346
19	**Tom Vardon**	87	88	82	91	348
=20	**C.E. Dick (a)**	85	89	89	90	353
	David Grant	91	84	87	91	353
	David Herd	92	93	84	84	353
=23	**Willie Auchterlonie**	96	81	93	85	355
	John Rowe	90	90	84	91	355
=25	**Stuart Anderson (a)**	90	87	91	88	356
	C.E. Hambro (a)	96	90	82	88	356
	Charles Hutchings (a)	93	85	88	90	356
28	**Charles Gibson**	92	94	87	84	357
29	**Rowland Jones**	89	88	93	88	358
30	**A. Lumsden**	90	93	87	89	359

June 12–13, 1895

Royal & Ancient GC, St Andrews, Fife, Scotland

1	**J.H. Taylor**	86	78	80	78	322
2	**Sandy Herd**	82	77	82	85	326
3	**Andrew Kirkaldy**	81	83	84	84	332
4	**George Pulford**	84	81	83	86	334
5	**Archie Simpson**	88	85	78	85	336
=6	**David Anderson Jr**	86	83	84	84	337
	David Brown	81	89	83	84	337
	Willie Fernie	86	79	86	86	337
=9	**Ben Sayers**	84	87	85	82	338
	A.H. Toogood	85	84	83	86	338
	Harry Vardon	80	85	85	88	338
	Tom Vardon	82	83	84	89	338
=13	**Laurie Auchterlonie**	84	84	85	87	340
	J. Robb	89	88	81	82	340
=15	**Hugh Kirkaldy**	87	87	83	84	341
	Freddie Tait (a)	87	86	82	86	341
17	**Johnny Laidlay**	91	83	82	86	342
=18	**John Ball Jr (a)**	85	85	88	86	344
	L. Waters	86	83	85	90	344
20	**David Herd**	85	85	84	91	345
=21	**Albert Tingey Sr**	83	88	87	88	346
	Jack White	88	86	85	87	346
23	**James Kinnell**	84	83	88	92	347
24	**Jack Ross**	87	84	89	88	348
=25	**James Kay**	88	85	92	86	351
	David McEwan	85	90	90	86	351
=27	**Willie Aveston**	89	86	89	89	353
	Douglas McEwan	95	85	92	81	353
	A.M. Ross (a)	92	85	88	88	353
	Walter Toogood	87	91	88	87	353

June 10–11, 1896

Honourable Company, Muirfield, East Lothian, Scotland

** Harry Vardon (157) beat J.H. Taylor (161) in the 36-hole play-off.*

1	**Harry Vardon***	83	78	78	77	316
2	**J.H. Taylor**	77	78	81	80	316
=3	**Willie Fernie**	78	79	82	89	319
	Freddie Tait (a)	83	75	84	77	319
5	**Sandy Herd**	72	84	79	85	320
6	**James Braid**	83	81	79	85	323
=7	**David Brown**	80	77	81	86	324
	Ben Sayers	83	76	79	86	324
	Andrew Scott	83	84	77	80	324
10	**Tom Vardon**	83	82	77	83	325
11	**Peter McEwan**	83	81	80	84	328
=12	**Willie Auchterlonie**	80	86	81	82	329
	Archie Simpson	85	79	78	87	329
=14	**James Kay**	77	88	83	82	330
	Andrew Kirkaldy	84	85	79	82	330
	Willie Park Jr	79	80	83	88	330
17	**A.H. Toogood**	81	85	84	84	334
=18	**John Hunter**	85	79	83	88	335
	Johnny Laidlay (a)	85	82	82	86	335
	David McEwan	83	89	81	82	335
	Jack Ross	83	87	84	81	335
22	**Walter Toogood**	87	84	80	85	336
23	**Harold Hilton (a)**	82	85	85	85	337
=24	**David Anderson Jr**	86	89	83	81	339
	D. Jackson (a)	85	84	82	88	339
	Walter Kirk	85	87	86	82	339
27	**David Herd**	85	87	86	82	340
28	**Albert Tingey Sr**	84	84	88	86	342
29	**J.W. Taylor**	87	83	84	90	344
30	**Peter Paxton**	84	89	86	86	345

May 19–20, 1897

Royal Liverpool GC, Hoylake, Cheshire, England

1	**Harold Hilton (a)**	80	75	84	75	314
2	**James Braid**	80	74	82	79	315
=3	**George Pulford**	80	79	79	79	317
	Freddie Tait (a)	79	79	80	79	317
5	**Sandy Herd**	78	81	79	80	318
6	**Harry Vardon**	84	80	80	76	320
=7	**David Brown**	79	82	80	83	324
	Archie Simpson	83	81	81	79	324
	Tom Vardon	81	81	79	83	324
=10	**Andrew Kirkaldy**	83	83	82	82	330
	J.H. Taylor	82	80	82	86	330
=12	**Ben Sayers**	84	78	85	84	331
	S. Mure Fergusson (a)	87	83	79	82	331
=14	**Peter McEwan**	86	79	85	82	332
	T.G. Renouf	86	79	83	84	332
16	**Andrew Scott**	83	83	84	83	333
17	**John Ball Jr**	78	81	88	87	334
=18	**Willie Auchterlonie**	84	85	85	81	335
	Jack Graham (a)	85	80	87	83	335
=20	**James Kinnell**	82	83	78	93	336
	Joe Lloyd	86	84	82	84	336
=22	**Willie Fernie**	81	82	93	81	337
	Willie Park Jr	91	81	83	82	337
	A.H. Toogood	88	82	84	83	337
25	**James Kay**	86	81	86	85	338
26	**Walter Toogood**	97	89	80	83	339
27	**James Sherlock**	85	86	84	85	340
28	**John Rowe**	84	86	86	86	342
29	**James Laidlay (a)**	82	86	86	89	343

May 19–20, 1897 continued

=30	**John Cuthbert**	89	83	87	85	344
	Charles Gibson	88	90	80	86	344
	C. Ralph Smith	88	82	94	80	344
	J.W. Taylor	87	84	85	88	344
	Albert Tingey Sr	86	86	87	85	344

June 8–9, 1898

Prestwick GC, Ayrshire, Scotland

New restrictions on players' performances were introduced. Competitors who were 20 or more strokes behind the leader at the halfway stage were excluded from the final two rounds.

1	**Harry Vardon**	79	75	77	76	307
2	**Willie Park Jr**	76	75	78	79	308
3	**Harold Hilton (a)**	76	81	77	75	309
4	**J.H. Taylor**	78	78	77	79	312
5	**Freddie Tait (a)**	81	77	75	82	315
6	**David Kinnell**	80	77	79	80	316
7	**Willie Fernie**	79	85	77	77	318
8	**John Hunter**	82	79	81	77	319
9	**T.G. Renouf**	77	79	81	83	320
=10	**James Braid**	80	82	84	75	321
	Philip Wynn	83	79	81	78	321
12	**James Kay**	81	81	77	83	322
=13	**George Pulford**	83	81	78	81	323
	Jack White	82	81	77	83	323
=15	**James Kinnell**	77	81	78	88	324
	Archie Simpson	83	80	82	79	324
=17	**Sandy Herd**	80	79	84	82	325
	Peter McEwan	83	83	77	82	325
=19	**Ben Sayers**	85	78	79	85	327
	Walter Toogood	82	84	83	78	327
=21	**J.R. Gairdner (a)**	84	77	82	85	328
	David Herd	79	81	83	85	328
	James Hutchinson	83	79	84	82	328
	Andrew Kirkaldy	82	84	85	77	328
	Peter Paxton	81	82	86	79	328
	Tom Williamson	86	84	77	81	328
=27	**C. Ralph Smith**	84	78	85	82	329
	J.W. Taylor	83	84	80	82	329
=29	**Fred Butel**	81	84	86	81	332
	Andrew Scott	83	84	78	87	332
	Bob Simpson	84	81	82	85	332

June 7-8, 1899

St George's GC, Sandwich, Kent, England

1	**Harry Vardon**	76	76	81	77	310
2	**Jack White**	79	79	82	75	315
3	**Andrew Kirkaldy**	81	79	82	77	319
4	**J.H. Taylor**	77	76	82	77	320
=5	**James Braid**	78	78	85	81	322
	Willie Fernie	79	83	82	78	322
=7	**James Kinnell**	76	84	80	84	324
	Freddie Tait (a)	81	82	79	82	324
=9	**Albert Tingey Sr**	81	81	79	85	326
	Tom Williamson	76	84	80	86	326
11	**Ben Sayers**	81	79	82	86	328
=12	**Harold Hilton (a)**	86	80	80	83	329
	T.G. Renouf	79	82	84	84	329
14	**Willie Park Jr**	77	79	85	89	330
15	**Willie Aveston**	77	86	82	86	331
=16	**Sandy Herd**	82	81	80	89	332
	Peter Rainford	79	83	83	87	332
	Ted Ray	84	80	84	84	332
	Archie Simpson	84	84	81	83	332

June 7–8, 1899 continued

20	**Walter Toogood**	82	86	81	84	333
21	**C.E. Hambro (a)**	78	86	88	82	334
22	**T. Hutchison**	82	87	82	85	336
23	**A.H. Toogood**	83	85	85	84	337
24	**William McEwan**	84	86	83	85	338
=25	**John Ball Jr (a)**	81	82	90	86	339
	Andrew Scott	86	85	87	81	339
	J.W. Taylor	82	85	86	86	339
28	**David Herd**	80	88	83	89	340

June 6–7, 1900

Royal & Ancient GC, St Andrews, Fife, Scotland

1	**J.H. Taylor**	79	77	78	75	309
2	**Harry Vardon**	79	81	80	77	317
3	**James Braid**	82	81	80	79	322
4	**Jack White**	80	81	82	80	323
5	**Willie Auchterlonie**	81	85	80	80	326
6	**Willie Park Jr**	80	83	81	84	328
=7	**Robert Maxwell (a)**	81	81	86	81	329
	Archie Simpson	82	85	83	79	329
9	**Ben Sayers**	81	83	85	81	330
=10	**Sandy Herd**	81	85	81	84	331
	Andrew Kirkaldy	87	83	82	79	331
	Tom Vardon	81	85	84	81	331
13	**Ted Ray**	88	80	85	81	334
=14	**David Anderson Jr**	81	87	85	84	337
	Tom Simpson	84	86	83	84	337
=16	**William Grieg (a)**	93	84	80	81	338
	Harold Hilton (a)	83	87	87	81	338
18	**J.W. Taylor**	91	81	84	83	339
=19	**John Kirkaldy**	86	85	87	82	340
	Peter Paxton	87	87	79	87	340
21	**Peter McEwan**	85	80	89	87	341
=22	**P.J. Gaudin**	85	88	81	88	342
	James Kay	84	81	87	90	342
	F.M. Mackenzie (a)	88	82	89	83	342
	Andrew Scott	84	84	84	90	342
=26	**George Coburn**	83	88	83	89	343
	W.H. Fowler (a)	86	85	88	84	343
	Johnny Laidlay (a)	85	87	85	86	343
29	**J.M. Williamson**	87	82	88	89	346
=30	**Ted Blackwell (a)**	88	86	86	89	349
	C. Ralph Smith	83	87	88	91	349

June 5–6, 1901

Honourable Company, Muirfield, East Lothian, Scotland

1	**James Braid**	79	76	74	80	309
2	**Harry Vardon**	77	78	79	78	312
3	**J.H. Taylor**	79	83	74	77	313
4	**Harold Hilton (a)**	89	80	75	76	320
5	**Sandy Herd**	87	81	81	76	325
6	**Jack White**	82	82	80	82	326
=7	**James Kinnell**	79	85	86	78	328
	Johnny Laidlay (a)	84	82	82	80	328
=9	**P.J. Gaudin**	86	81	86	76	329
	Jack Graham (a)	82	83	81	83	329
11	**Rowland Jones**	85	82	81	83	331
=12	**Ted Ray**	87	84	74	87	332
	T.G. Renouf	83	86	81	82	332
	Tom Yeoman	85	83	82	82	332
=15	**Fred Collins**	89	80	81	84	334
	S. Mure Fergusson (a)	84	86	82	82	334
	J.H. Oke	91	83	80	80	334
=18	**Andrew Kirkaldy**	82	87	86	81	336

June 5–6, 1901 continued

	Alf Lewis	85	82	83	86	336
	Willie Park Jr	78	87	81	90	336
	Andrew Scott	85	80	81	90	336
=22	**Charles Neaves**	84	87	81	85	337
	L. Waters	86	87	86	78	337
24	**C. Dalziel (a)**	82	84	89	93	338
=25	**David Herd**	90	80	82	87	339
	James Hutchison	84	83	91	81	339
	Jack Ross	84	85	86	84	339
28	**Walter Toogood**	87	86	85	82	340
=29	**Willie Auchterlonie**	86	82	88	86	342
	David McEwan	86	84	86	86	342

June 4–5, 1902

Royal Liverpool GC, Hoylake, Cheshire, England

1	**Sandy Herd**	77	76	73	81	307
=2	**James Braid**	78	76	80	74	308
	Harry Vardon	72	77	80	79	308
4	**Robert Maxwell (a)**	79	77	79	74	309
5	**Tom Vardon**	80	76	78	79	313
=6	**Harold Hilton (a)**	79	76	81	78	314
	James Kinnell	78	80	79	77	314
	J.H. Taylor	81	76	77	80	314
9	**Ted Ray**	79	74	85	80	318
=10	**Andrew Kirkaldy**	77	78	83	82	320
	Arnaud Massy	77	81	78	84	320
=12	**Willie Fernie**	76	82	84	79	321
	Rowland Jones	79	78	85	79	321
14	**S.H. Fry (a)**	78	79	80	85	322
=15	**John Ball Jr (a)**	79	79	84	81	323
	John Rowe	79	78	85	81	323
17	**James Sherlock**	79	84	80	81	324
18	**Jack White**	82	75	82	86	325
19	**Ben Sayers**	84	80	80	82	326
=20	**T.G. Renouf**	84	82	77	84	327
	Walter Toogood	83	83	80	81	327
22	**George Pulford**	81	81	85	81	328
=23	**F. Jackson**	80	81	83	85	329
	Willie Park Jr	79	82	82	86	329
=25	**William McEwan**	83	84	81	82	330
	Tom Yeoman	85	83	79	83	330
27	**C. Ralph Smith**	85	79	85	82	331
=28	**David Herd**	82	81	84	85	332
	Peter Rainford	78	79	88	87	332
=30	**Archie Simpson**	88	79	85	81	333
	Tom Williamson	78	80	90	85	333

June 9–10, 1903

Prestwick GC, Ayrshire, Scotland

1	**Harry Vardon**	73	77	72	78	300
2	**Tom Vardon**	76	81	75	74	306
3	**Jack White**	77	78	74	79	308
4	**Sandy Herd**	73	83	76	77	309
5	**James Braid**	77	79	79	75	310
=6	**Andrew Scott**	77	77	83	77	314
	Robert Thomson	83	78	77	76	314
8	**William Leaver**	79	79	77	80	315
=9	**George Cawsey**	80	78	76	82	316
	J.H. Taylor	80	82	78	76	316
=11	**Andrew Kirkaldy**	82	79	78	78	317
	Tom Williamson	76	80	79	82	317
=13	**Willie Hunter Sr**	81	74	79	84	318
	Robert Maxwell (a)	82	84	76	76	318
=15	**Ernest Gray**	77	83	79	80	319

June 9–10, 1903 continued

	James Kinnell	78	86	76	79	319
	Willie Park Jr	78	86	80	75	319
=18	**David Kinnell**	82	78	80	80	320
	George Pulford	79	86	79	76	320
	A.H. Toogood	86	77	80	78	320
=21	**John Hunter**	77	79	84	81	321
	Ben Sayers	79	84	80	78	321
23	**Ted Ray**	90	78	80	75	323
=24	**Willie Fernie**	78	81	76	89	324
	James Hepburn	78	82	87	77	324
	Harold Hilton (a)	81	79	83	81	324
	Rowland Jones	82	82	81	79	324
	John Milne	81	86	79	78	324
=29	**George Coburn**	81	82	75	87	325
	J.H. Oke	80	81	81	83	325
	Archie Simpson	79	85	80	81	325

June 8–10, 1904

St George's GC, Sandwich, Kent, England

1	**Jack White**	80	75	72	69	296
=2	**James Braid**	77	80	69	71	297
	J.H. Taylor	77	78	74	68	297
4	**Tom Vardon**	77	77	75	72	301
5	**Harry Vardon**	76	73	79	74	302
6	**James Sherlock**	83	71	78	77	309
=7	**Jack Graham (a)**	76	76	78	80	310
	Andrew Kirkaldy	78	79	74	79	310
9	**Sandy Herd**	84	76	76	75	311
=10	**Robert Maxwell (a)**	80	80	76	77	313
	Ben Sayers	80	80	76	77	313
=12	**Willie Park Jr**	84	72	81	78	315
	Ted Ray	81	81	77	76	315
	Robert Thomson	75	76	80	84	315
	A.H. Toogood	88	76	74	77	315
=16	**George Coburn**	79	82	75	80	316
	John Rowe	86	82	75	73	316
18	**John Ball Jr (a)**	83	78	79	78	318
=19	**George Cawsey**	82	80	78	79	319
	Frederick Collins	88	77	75	79	319
	Ernest Gray	84	77	74	84	319
22	**J.S. Worthington (a)**	85	79	78	78	320
23	**T.G. Renouf**	82	79	79	81	321
=24	**P.J. Gaudin**	79	83	80	80	322
	Alf Matthews	85	81	78	78	322
26	**Alec Thomson**	86	81	75	81	323
=27	**Ted Blackwell (a)**	88	77	81	79	325
	George Cawkwell	83	83	79	80	325
	Rowland Jones	89	77	77	82	325
=30	**A.E. Bellworthy**	82	84	83	77	326
	James Hepburn	87	80	79	80	326
	Percy Hills	85	83	80	78	326

June 7–9, 1905

Royal & Ancient GC, St Andrews, Fife, Scotland

1	**James Braid**	81	78	78	81	318
=2	**Rowland Jones**	81	77	87	78	323
	J.H. Taylor	80	85	78	80	323
4	**James Kinnell**	82	79	82	81	324
=5	**Ernest Gray**	82	81	84	78	325
	Arnaud Massy	81	80	82	82	325
7	**Robert Thomson**	81	81	82	83	327
8	**James Sherlock**	81	84	80	83	328
=9	**Tom Simpson**	82	88	78	81	329
	Harry Vardon	80	82	84	83	329

June 7–9, 1905 continued

=11	**Ted Ray**	85	82	81	82	330
	John Rowe	87	81	80	82	330
=13	**Willie Park Jr**	84	81	85	81	331
	Tom Williamson	84	81	79	87	331
15	**Sandy Herd**	80	82	83	87	332
=16	**T.G. Renouf**	81	85	84	83	333
	Alex Smith	81	88	86	78	333
=18	**J.C. Johnstone**	85	86	84	80	335
	Archie Simpson	87	84	81	83	335
	Tom Watt	86	85	79	85	335
	Jack White	86	83	83	83	335
=22	**Fred Collins**	86	86	83	81	336
	Percy Hills	87	84	84	81	336
=24	**Ernest Foord**	85	86	84	83	338
	James Hepburn	84	84	87	83	338
	Willie Hunter Sr	84	85	88	81	338
	Andrew Kirkaldy	83	83	83	89	338
=28	**David Stephenson**	84	86	83	86	339
	Walter Toogood	82	83	87	87	339
30	**James Kay**	85	83	85	87	340

June 13–15, 1906

Honourable Company, Muirfield, East Lothian, Scotland

1	**James Braid**	77	76	74	73	300
2	**J.H. Taylor**	77	72	75	80	304
3	**Harry Vardon**	77	73	77	78	305
4	**Jack Graham (a)**	71	79	78	78	306
5	**Rowland Jones**	74	78	73	83	308
6	**Arnaud Massy**	76	80	76	78	310
7	**Robert Maxwell (a)**	73	78	77	83	311
=8	**George Duncan**	73	78	83	78	312
	Ted Ray	80	75	79	78	312
	T.G. Renouf	76	77	76	83	312
11	**David Kinnell**	78	76	80	79	313
=12	**Willie Hunter Sr**	79	76	80	80	315
	William Leaver	80	76	78	81	315
	Tom Vardon	76	81	81	77	315
=15	**George Cawsey**	79	80	79	78	316
	Thomas Simpson	78	78	81	79	316
	Walter Toogood	83	79	83	71	316
	Robert Whitecross (a)	74	83	80	79	316
=19	**P.J. Gaudin**	77	77	80	83	317
	Harry Hamill	83	78	79	77	317
	Sandy Herd	81	79	77	80	317
	David McEwan	79	79	81	78	317
	Tom Williamson	77	77	78	85	317
=24	**Tom Ball**	78	79	79	82	318
	Ernest Gray	77	77	78	86	318
	Donald Kenny	82	85	83	78	318
	Ernest Riseborough	81	77	80	80	318
=28	**James Kinnell**	81	75	82	81	319
	Alf Matthews	84	77	80	78	319
=30	**Ernest Foord**	78	84	78	80	320
	James Hepburn	81	78	84	77	320
	James Kay	80	79	81	80	320
	George Pulford	80	81	81	78	320
	Robert Thomson	76	78	83	83	320

June 20–21, 1907

Royal Liverpool GC, Hoylake, Cheshire, England

1	**Arnaud Massy**	76	81	78	77	312
2	**J.H. Taylor**	79	79	76	80	314
=3	**George Pulford**	81	78	80	75	317
	Tom Vardon	81	81	80	75	317

June 20–21, 1907 continued

=5	**James Braid**	82	85	75	76	318
	Ted Ray	83	80	79	76	318
=7	**George Duncan**	83	78	81	77	319
	Harry Vardon	84	81	74	80	319
	Tom Williamson	82	77	82	78	319
10	**Tom Ball**	80	78	81	81	320
11	**P.J. Gaudin**	83	84	80	76	323
12	**Sandy Herd**	83	81	81	77	324
=13	**Jack Graham (a)**	83	81	80	82	326
	Walter Toogood	76	86	82	82	326
=15	**John Ball Jr (a)**	88	83	79	77	327
	Frederick Collins	83	83	79	82	327
=17	**Alf Matthews**	82	80	84	82	328
	Charles Mayo	86	78	82	82	328
	T.G. Renouf	83	80	82	83	328
20	**Reg Gray**	83	85	81	80	329
=21	**James Bradbeer**	83	85	82	80	330
	G. Carter	89	80	81	80	330
23	**John Rowe**	83	83	85	80	331
24	**A.H. Toogood**	87	83	85	77	332
=25	**William Horne**	91	80	81	80	333
	Harry Kidd	84	90	82	77	333
	David McEwan	89	83	80	81	333
	Charles Roberts	86	83	84	80	333
	Alex Smith	85	84	84	80	333
=30	**James Kinnell**	89	79	80	86	334
	J.H. Oke	86	85	82	81	334

June 18-19, 1908

Prestwick GC, Ayrshire, Scotland

1	**James Braid**	70	72	77	72	291
2	**Tom Ball**	76	73	76	74	299
3	**Ted Ray**	79	71	75	76	301
4	**Sandy Herd**	74	74	79	75	302
=5	**David Kinnell**	75	73	80	78	306
	Harry Vardon	79	78	74	75	306
=7	**Thomas Simpson**	75	77	76	79	307
	J.H. Taylor	79	77	76	75	307
=9	**P.J. Gaudin**	77	76	75	80	308
	Arnaud Massy	76	75	76	81	308
=11	**James Edmundson**	80	72	76	82	310
	Tom Watt	81	73	78	78	310
=13	**John Ball Jr (a)**	74	78	78	81	311
	Fred Collins	78	77	77	79	311
	Ernest Gray	68	79	83	81	311
	William Leaver	79	79	75	78	311
	Tom Vardon	77	79	76	79	311
=18	**George Duncan**	79	77	80	76	312
	Jack Graham (a)	76	82	76	78	312
	George Pulford	81	77	74	80	312
	Fred Robson	72	79	83	78	312
	A.H. Toogood	82	76	77	77	312
	Walter Toogood	80	75	78	79	312
=24	**George Coburn**	77	79	77	81	314
	James Hepburn	80	79	79	76	314
	Rowland Jones	75	77	83	79	314
27	**R. Andrew (a)**	83	78	77	77	315
=28	**Willie Aveston**	77	77	79	83	316
	T.G. Renouf	78	78	83	77	316
=30	**Charles Mayo**	83	79	80	75	317
	Ben Sayers	74	76	84	83	317
	Albert Tingey Sr	76	82	79	80	317

June 10–11, 1909

Royal Cinq Ports, Deal, Kent, England

1	J.H. Taylor	74	73	74	74	295
=2	Tom Ball	74	75	76	76	301
	James Braid	79	75	73	74	301
4	Charles Johns	72	76	79	75	302
5	T.G. Renouf	76	78	76	73	303
6	Ted Ray	77	76	76	75	304
7	William Horne	77	78	77	74	306
=8	James Hepburn	78	77	76	76	307
	Sandy Herd	76	75	80	76	307
=10	Bertie Lassen (a)	82	74	74	78	308
	Bernard Nicholls	78	76	77	77	308
	George Pulford	81	76	76	75	308
13	Robert Maxwell (a)	75	80	80	74	309
=14	E.P. Gaudin	76	77	77	80	310
	Peter Rainford	78	76	76	80	310
16	George Cawsey	79	76	78	78	311
=17	Ben Sayers	79	77	79	77	312
	Robert Thomson	81	79	75	77	312
=19	C.K. Hutchison (a)	75	81	78	79	313
	Tom Vardon	80	75	80	78	313
=21	Fred Collins	81	78	75	80	314
	George Duncan	77	82	80	75	314
	Ernest Foord	77	80	81	76	314
	Michael Moran	82	81	74	77	314
	Wilfred Reid	77	83	78	76	314
=26	A.E. Bellworthy	76	84	78	78	316
	Arthur Butchart	80	79	80	77	316
	Douglas Edgar	81	81	76	78	316
	Rowland Jones	80	79	79	78	316
	Harry Vardon	82	77	79	78	316

June 22–24, 1910

Royal & Ancient GC, St Andrews, Fife, Scotland

1	James Braid	76	73	74	76	299
2	Sandy Herd	78	74	75	76	303
3	George Duncan	73	77	71	83	304
4	Laurie Ayton Sr	78	76	75	77	306
=5	Ted Ray	76	77	74	81	308
	Fred Robson	75	80	77	76	308
	Willie Smith	77	71	80	80	308
=8	E.P. Gaudin	78	74	76	81	309
	James Kinnell	79	74	77	79	309
	T.G. Renouf	77	76	75	81	309
	Donald Ross	78	79	75	77	309
=12	Tom Ball	81	77	75	78	311
	P.J. Gaudin	80	79	74	78	311
=14	Michael Moran	77	75	79	81	312
	J.H. Taylor	76	80	78	78	312
=16	Fred MacKenzie	78	80	75	80	313
	William Ritchie	78	74	82	79	313
	Harry Vardon	77	81	75	80	313
=19	John Ball Jr (a)	79	75	78	82	314
	James Hepburn	78	82	76	78	314
	Tom Williamson	78	80	78	78	314
=22	Arnaud Massy	78	77	81	79	315
	John Rowe	81	74	80	80	315
=24	William Binnie	80	76	77	83	316
	C.K. Hutchison (a)	82	74	78	82	316
	Wilfred Reid	78	83	77	78	316
	Charles Roberts	81	73	79	83	316
=28	Willie Auchterlonie	79	76	79	83	317
	Ernest Foord	80	77	79	81	317
	Herbert Riseborough	75	81	80	81	317

June 22–24, 1910 continued

	James Sherlock	77	81	80	79	317

June 26–29, 1911

St George's GC, Sandwich, Kent, England

** Harry Vardon (143 after 35 holes) beat Arnaud Massy (148 after 34 holes) when Massy conceded at the 35th hole in the 36-hole play-off.*

1	Harry Vardon*	74	74	75	80	303
2	Arnaud Massy	75	78	74	76	303
=3	Sandy Herd	77	73	76	78	304
	Horace Hilton (a)	76	74	78	76	304
=5	James Braid	78	75	74	78	305
	Ted Ray	76	72	79	78	305
	J.H. Taylor	72	76	78	79	305
8	George Duncan	73	71	83	79	306
9	Laurie Ayton Sr	75	77	77	78	307
=10	James Hepburn	74	77	83	75	309
	Fred Robson	78	74	79	78	309
12	Fred Collins	78	74	79	78	310
=13	J. Piper	78	79	80	74	311
	T.G. Renouf	75	76	79	81	311
15	Tom Ball	76	77	79	80	312
=16	Rowland Jones	80	76	85	72	313
	Charles Mayo	78	78	79	78	313
	Wilfred Reid	78	79	80	76	313
	James Sherlock	73	80	76	84	313
	H.E. Taylor (a)	83	73	76	81	313
=21	Ernest B.H. Blackwell (a)	71	81	72	80	314
	Michael Moran	72	78	83	81	314
	William Watt	76	80	79	79	314
=24	Ernest Jones	77	82	81	75	315
	L.D. Stevens (a)	79	83	77	76	315
	Josh Taylor	79	81	80	75	315
=27	Robert Harris (a)	77	80	76	83	316
	Fred Leach	75	79	87	75	316
=29	Tom R. Fernie	80	78	76	83	317
	J.C. Johnsone	82	79	78	78	317
	A.F. Kettley	79	77	81	80	317
	James Ockenden	75	78	81	83	317
	Robert Thomson	77	76	85	79	317

June 24–25, 1912

Honourable Company, Muirfield, East Lothian, Scotland

1	Ted Ray	71	73	76	75	295
2	Harry Vardon	75	72	81	71	299
3	James Braid	77	71	77	78	303
4	George Duncan	72	77	78	78	305
=5	Laurie Ayton Sr	74	80	75	80	309
	Sandy Herd	76	81	76	76	309
=7	Fred Collins	76	79	81	74	310
	Jean Gassiat	76	80	78	76	310
	Reg Wilson	82	75	75	78	310
10	Arnaud Massy	74	77	82	78	311
=11	Charles Mayo	76	77	78	81	312
	J.H. Taylor	75	76	77	84	312
=13	George Fotheringham	75	78	79	81	313
	Robert Thomson	73	77	80	83	313
=15	Hughie McNeill	76	78	82	78	314
	Michael Moran	76	79	80	79	314
=17	Fred Leach	75	82	81	77	315
	Tom Williamson	80	77	79	79	315
19	T.G. Renouf	77	80	80	79	316
=20	Douglas Edgar	77	81	80	79	317
	William Horne	73	85	82	77	317
	Wilfred Reid	80	79	79	79	317

June 24–25, 1912 continued

23	**P.J. Gaudin**	80	76	82	80	318
=24	**F.H. Frostick**	77	80	81	81	319
	Philip Taylor	76	82	81	80	319
26	**Tom Ball**	75	81	86	78	320
=27	**Jas Batley**	79	86	80	76	321
	Rowland Jones	78	82	84	77	321
	Charles Pope	83	80	77	81	321
	Charles Roberts	82	81	83	75	321

June 23–24, 1913

Royal Liverpool GC, Hoylake, Cheshire, England

1	**J.H. Taylor**	73	75	77	79	304
2	**Ted Ray**	73	74	81	84	312
=3	**Michael Moran**	76	74	89	74	313
	Harry Vardon	79	75	79	80	313
=5	**John McDermott**	75	80	77	83	315
	T.G. Renouf	75	78	84	78	315
=7	**James Bradbeer**	78	79	81	79	317
	Arnaud Massy	77	80	81	79	317
	James Sherlock	77	86	79	75	317
	Tom Williamson	77	80	80	80	317
=11	**Fred Collins**	77	85	79	77	318
	Jack Graham (a)	77	79	81	81	318
	Sandy Herd	73	81	84	80	318
=14	**Bertie Lassen (a)**	79	78	80	82	319
	Charles Roberts	78	79	84	78	319
	Josh Taylor	80	75	85	79	319
17	**Philip Taylor**	78	81	83	78	320
=18	**James Braid**	80	79	82	80	321
	Claude Gray	80	81	79	81	321
	Ernest Jones	75	85	81	80	321
	Hughie McNeill	80	81	81	79	321
=22	**Jean Gassiat**	80	78	86	78	322
	Cyril Hughes	76	78	83	85	322
	Louis Tellier	77	80	85	80	322
25	**T.L. Macnamara**	80	78	85	80	323
26	**Wilfred Reid**	78	82	85	79	324
=27	**Arthur Catlin**	77	81	81	86	325
	Charles Mayo	83	82	78	82	325
	Thomas Simpson	79	83	85	78	325
=30	**Laurie Ayton Sr**	78	83	86	80	327
	Tom Ball	82	83	86	76	327
	G.R. Buckle	81	80	87	79	327
	Jack B. Ross	75	89	84	79	327

June 18–19, 1914

Prestwick GC, Ayrshire, Scotland

1	**Harry Vardon**	73	77	78	78	306
2	**J.H. Taylor**	74	78	74	73	309
3	**Harry Simpson**	77	80	78	75	310
=4	**Abe Mitchell**	76	78	79	79	312
	Tom Williamson	75	79	79	79	312
6	**Reg Wilson**	76	77	80	80	313
7	**James Ockenden**	75	76	83	80	314
=8	**P.J. Gaudin**	78	83	80	74	315
	J.L.C. Jenkins (a)	79	80	73	83	315
=10	**James Braid**	74	82	78	82	316
	George Duncan	77	79	80	80	316
	Arnaud Massy	77	82	75	82	316
	Ted Ray	77	82	76	81	316
=14	**James Bradbeer**	77	80	80	80	317
	Douglas Edgar	79	75	84	79	317
	Jean Gassiat	76	81	80	80	317
=17	**Willie Hunter Sr**	82	77	77	83	319

June 18–19, 1914 continued

	Bertie Lassen (a)	85	78	79	77	319
=19	**Ernest Foord**	82	81	82	76	321
	Cyril Hughes	80	81	80	80	321
=21	**Jas Batley**	78	83	81	80	322
	Ernest Jones	87	81	80	74	322
	Fred Leach	76	86	78	82	322
	C. Ralph Smith	81	79	80	82	322
=25	**Walter Hambleton**	79	75	86	83	323
	Michael Moran	82	83	82	76	323
	Josh Taylor	82	79	84	78	323
	David Watt	84	80	78	81	323
=29	**Sandy Herd**	79	87	79	79	324
	C.K. Hutchison (a)	81	75	82	86	324
	J.C. Lonie	77	84	82	81	324
	Ernest Whitcombe	74	83	84	83	324

1915 – 1919 – No championship

June 30–July 1, 1920

Royal Cinq Ports, Deal, Kent, England

1	**George Duncan**	80	80	71	72	303
2	**Sandy Herd**	72	81	77	75	305
3	**Ted Ray**	72	83	78	73	306
4	**Abe Mitchell**	74	73	84	76	307
5	**Len Holland**	80	78	71	79	308
6	**Jim Barnes**	79	74	77	79	309
=7	**Arthur Havers**	80	78	81	74	313
	Sydney Wingate	81	74	76	82	313
=9	**G.R. Buckle**	80	80	77	78	315
	Archie Compston	79	83	75	78	315
	William Horne	80	81	73	81	315
12	**J.H. Taylor**	78	79	80	79	316
13	**L. Lafitte**	75	85	84	73	317
=14	**Eric Bannister**	78	84	80	76	318
	Harry Vardon	78	81	81	78	318
=16	**A. Gaudin**	81	82	77	79	319
	Charles Johns	82	78	81	78	319
	James Sherlock	82	81	80	76	319
	Philip Taylor	78	84	77	80	319
	Angel de la Torre	84	78	78	79	319
=21	**James Braid**	79	80	80	82	320
	William B. Smith	81	81	77	81	320
	Dick Wheildon	82	78	83	77	320
	Reg Wilson	76	82	78	84	320
25	**Cyril Hughes**	83	81	80	77	321
=26	**Willie Hunter Jr (a)**	81	80	81	80	322
	Tom Williamson	77	86	79	80	322
28	**C. Ralph Smith**	84	80	79	80	323
=29	**Arthur Day**	77	83	84	80	324
	Jean Gassiat	79	82	78	85	324
	D. Grant (a)	83	76	82	83	324
	Fred Leach	83	82	78	81	324
	Arnaud Massy	81	82	80	81	324
	William Ritchie	79	86	81	78	324

June 23–25, 1921

Royal & Ancient GC, St Andrews, Fife, Scotland

** Jock Hutchinson (150) beat Roger Wethered (159) in the 36-hole play-off.*

1	Jock Hutchinson*	72	75	79	70	296
2	Roger Wethered	78	75	72	71	296
3	Tom Kerrigan	74	80	72	72	298
4	Arthur Havers	76	74	77	72	299
5	George Duncan	74	75	78	74	301
=6	Jim Barnes	74	74	74	80	302
	Walter Hagen	74	79	72	77	302
	Sandy Herd	75	74	73	80	302
	Joe Kirkwood Sr	76	74	73	79	302
	Fred Leach	78	75	76	73	302
	Arnaud Massy	74	75	74	79	302
	Tom Williamson	79	71	74	78	302
=13	Abe Mitchell	78	79	76	71	304
	W. Pursey	74	82	74	74	304
15	J.W. Gaudin	78	76	75	76	305
=16	James Braid	77	75	78	76	306
	Len Holland	78	78	76	74	306
	Bill Mehlhorn	75	77	76	78	306
=19	Frank Ball	79	78	74	76	307
	P. Hunter (a)	75	78	76	78	307
	Ted Ray	76	72	81	78	307
	William Watt	81	77	75	74	307
=23	Clarence Hackney	77	75	80	76	308
	Henry Kinch	73	77	81	77	308
	Harry Vardon	77	77	80	74	308
=26	Aubrey Boomer	78	80	72	79	309
	Walter Bourne	78	78	75	78	309
	Arthur Butchart	78	80	77	74	309
	Douglas Edgar	82	76	78	73	309
	Emmett French	79	76	75	79	309
	D.H. Kyle (a)	77	77	81	74	309
	George McLean	76	73	82	78	309
	Hugh Roberts	79	82	74	74	309
	J.H. Taylor	80	80	75	74	309

June 22–23, 1922

Royal St George's GC, Sandwich, Kent, England

1	Walter Hagen	76	73	79	72	300
=2	Jim Barnes	75	76	77	73	301
	George Duncan	76	75	81	69	301
4	Jock Hutchison	79	74	73	76	302
5	Charles Whitcombe	77	79	72	75	303
6	J.H. Taylor	73	78	76	77	304
7	Jean Gassiat	75	78	74	79	306
=8	Harry Vardon	79	79	74	75	307
	Thomas Walton	75	78	77	77	307
10	Percy Alliss	75	78	78	77	308
11	Charles Johns	78	76	80	75	309
=12	George Gadd	76	81	76	77	310
	Arthur Havers	78	80	78	74	310
	Len Holland	79	81	74	76	310
	F.C. Jewell	75	80	78	77	310
	Ernest R. Whitcombe	77	78	77	78	310
=17	Aubrey Boomer	75	80	76	80	311
	Dick Wheildon	80	80	76	75	311
19	Abe Mitchell	79	79	78	76	312
=20	Joe Kirkwood Sr	79	76	80	78	313
	Herbert Osborne	80	81	76	76	313
	Michael Scott (a)	77	83	79	74	313
=23	Willie Hunter Jr (a)	77	81	75	81	314
	Tom King Sr	83	78	78	75	314
	W. Pursey	77	81	80	76	314

June 22–23, 1922 continued

	William B. Smith	81	78	74	81	314
27	Archie Compston	81	79	75	80	315
=28	Gus Faulkner	74	81	80	81	316
	Arthur Monk	80	78	78	80	316
	William Watt	82	78	79	77	316
	Tom Williamson	83	77	75	81	316

June 14–15, 1923

Troon GC, Ayrshire, Scotland

1	Arthur Havers	73	73	73	76	295
2	Walter Hagen	76	71	74	75	296
3	Macdonald Smith	80	73	69	75	297
4	Joe Kirkwood Sr	72	79	69	78	298
5	Tom Fernie	73	78	74	75	300
=6	George Duncan	79	75	74	74	302
	Charles Whitcombe	70	76	74	82	302
=8	Herbert Jolly	79	75	75	74	303
	J.H. Mackenzie	76	78	74	75	303
	Abe Mitchell	77	77	72	77	303
	William Watt	76	77	72	78	303
=12	Gordon Lockhart	78	71	76	79	304
	Ted Ray	79	75	73	77	304
	Tom Williamson	79	78	73	74	304
	Sydney Wingate	80	75	74	75	304
=16	Frank Ball	76	77	77	75	305
	Tom Barber	78	80	76	71	305
	Fred Collins	76	78	72	79	305
=19	Johnny Farrell	79	73	75	79	306
	Angel de la Torre	78	80	74	74	306
	Thomas Walton	77	74	78	77	306
=22	Sid Brews	77	76	72	82	307
	Sandy Herd	82	75	74	76	307
	R. Scott Jr (a)	74	76	79	78	307
=25	Leo Diegel	80	80	73	75	308
	Len Holland	81	75	73	79	308
	F.C. Jewell	80	78	70	80	308
	James Ockenden	78	79	75	76	308
=29	George Gadd	78	76	79	76	309
	J.W. Gaudin	80	79	76	74	309
	Fred Robson	82	78	74	75	309
	Reg Wilson	78	77	75	79	309

June 26–27, 1924

Royal Liverpool GC, Hoylake, Cheshire, England

1	Walter Hagen	77	73	74	77	301
2	Ernest R. Whitcombe	77	70	77	78	302
=3	Frank Ball	78	75	74	77	304
	Macdonald Smith	76	74	77	77	304
5	J.H. Taylor	75	74	79	79	307
=6	Aubrey Boomer	75	78	76	79	308
	George Duncan	74	79	74	81	308
	Len Holland	74	78	78	78	308
=9	J.M. Barber	78	77	79	75	309
	George Gadd	79	75	78	77	309
	James Sherlock	76	75	78	80	309
	Percy Weston	76	77	77	79	309
=13	Sandy Herd	76	79	76	79	310
	Gilbert Nicholls	75	78	79	78	310
	Tom Williamson	79	76	80	75	310
=16	J.W. Gaudin	79	78	80	76	313
	Charles Johns	77	77	78	81	313
=18	James Braid	80	80	78	76	314
	Albert Tingey Jr	82	81	76	75	314
	Cyril Tolley (a)	73	82	80	79	314

June 26–27, 1924 continued

=21	**Archie Compston**	79	81	76	79	315
	B.S. Weastell	76	82	78	79	315
=23	**Arthur Butchart**	82	75	77	82	316
	Rowland Jones	80	73	82	81	316
	Fred Leach	78	74	86	78	316
	William Robertson	84	75	77	80	316
	Fred Robson	83	80	77	76	316
	Sydney Wingate	79	79	82	76	316
=29	**Arthur Havers**	79	77	86	75	317
	Mark Seymour	74	81	80	82	317

June 25–26, 1925

Prestwick GC, Ayrshire, Scotland

1	**Jim Barnes**	70	77	79	74	300
=2	**Archie Compston**	76	75	75	75	301
	Ted Ray	77	76	75	73	301
4	**Macdonald Smith**	76	69	76	82	303
5	**Abe Mitchell**	77	76	75	77	305
=6	**Percy Alliss**	77	80	77	76	310
	Bill Davies	76	76	80	78	310
	J.W. Gaudin	78	81	77	74	310
	J.H. Taylor	74	79	80	77	310
	Sydney Wingate	74	78	80	76	310
=11	**Robert Harris (a)**	75	81	78	77	311
	Fred Robson	80	77	78	76	311
13	**H.A. Gaudin**	76	79	77	80	312
=14	**Tom Fernie**	78	74	77	85	314
	Sandy Herd	76	79	77	80	314
	Joe Kirkwood Sr	83	79	76	76	314
=17	**J.I. Cruikshank (a)**	80	78	82	75	315
	Jack Smith	75	78	82	80	315
	Harry Vardon	79	80	77	79	315
=20	**Arthur Havers**	77	80	80	79	316
	Duncan McCulloch	76	77	84	79	316
	James Ockenden	80	78	80	78	316
	Reg Whitcombe	81	80	79	76	316
=24	**Frank Ball**	76	78	81	82	317
	Dick May	82	77	78	80	317
=26	**Aubrey Boomer**	79	82	76	81	318
	Ernest R. Whitcombe	81	83	77	77	318
=28	**James Adwick**	81	77	82	80	320
	George Duncan	79	77	83	81	320
	Cedric Sayner	83	80	78	79	320
	Cyril Tolley (a)	82	81	78	79	320

June 22–24, 1926

Royal Lytham and St Anne's GC, Lancashire, England

1	**Bobby Jones (a)**	72	72	73	74	291
2	**Al Waltrous**	71	75	69	78	293
=3	**Walter Hagen**	68	77	74	76	295
	George Von Elm (a)	75	72	76	72	295
=5	**Tom Barber**	77	73	78	71	299
	Abe Mitchell	78	78	72	71	299
7	**Fred McLeod**	71	75	76	79	301
=8	**Emmett French**	76	75	74	78	303
	Jose Jurado	77	76	74	76	303
	Bill Mehlhorn	70	74	79	80	303
=11	**H.A. Gaudin**	78	78	71	77	304
	J.H. Taylor	75	78	71	80	304
13	**Tommy Armour**	74	76	75	80	305
=14	**W.L. Hartley (a)**	74	77	79	76	306
	Harry Walker	74	77	78	77	306
	Reg Whitcombe	73	82	76	75	306
	Tom Williamson	78	76	76	76	306

June 22–24, 1926 continued

=18	**Jim Barnes**	77	80	72	78	307
	Fred Robson	79	76	77	75	307
	Cyril Walker	79	71	80	77	307
=21	**George Duncan**	75	79	80	74	308
	Sandy Herd	81	76	75	76	308
23	**Herbert Jolly**	79	76	79	75	309
=24	**Edward Douglas**	79	78	75	78	310
	George Gadd	80	71	78	81	310
	Joe Kirkwood Sr	81	76	78	75	310
	Charles Whitcombe	79	78	75	78	310
=28	**James Braid**	82	75	75	79	311
	Arthur Havers	75	76	82	78	311
=30	**Fred Boobyer**	79	79	80	74	312
	Charles Corlett	77	80	76	79	312
	Jean Gassiat	78	78	79	77	312
	J. MacDowell	75	82	75	80	312
	Ted Ray	78	80	74	80	312

July 13–15, 1927

Royal & Ancient GC, St Andrews, Fife, Scotland

1	**Bobby Jones (a)**	68	72	73	72	285
=2	**Aubrey Boomer**	76	70	73	72	291
	Fred Robson	76	72	69	74	291
=4	**Joe Kirkwood Sr**	72	72	75	74	293
	Ernest R. Whitcombe	74	73	73	73	293
6	**Charles Whitcombe**	74	76	71	75	296
=7	**Arthur Havers**	80	74	73	70	297
	Bert Hodson	72	70	81	74	297
9	**Henry Cotton**	73	72	77	76	298
=10	**Percy Alliss**	73	74	73	80	300
	Sandy Herd	76	75	78	71	300
	Phil Perkins (a)	76	78	70	76	300
	Phillip H. Rodgers	76	73	74	77	300
	W.B. Torrance	72	80	74	74	300
	R.D. Vickers	75	75	77	73	300
	Tom Williamson	75	76	78	71	300
=16	**Jim Barnes**	76	76	72	77	301
	G.R. Buckle	77	69	77	78	301
	O. Johns	74	78	73	76	301
=19	**Donald Curtis**	73	76	79	74	302
	Jean Gassiat	76	77	73	76	302
	Tom Stevens	76	73	74	79	302
=22	**Archie Compston**	74	78	79	72	303
	Len Holland	75	75	71	82	303
	Henry Kinch	80	73	73	77	303
	Jack Smith	81	73	73	76	303
26	**Duncan McCulloch**	74	77	78	75	304
=27	**Chas Gadd**	74	74	78	79	305
	Tom King Jr	73	74	74	84	305
=29	**James Braid**	75	77	76	78	306
	William Kennett	78	75	75	78	306
	D. Murray	72	78	77	79	306
	Ted Ray	78	73	77	78	306
	W. Tweddell (a)	78	74	78	76	306
	William Twine	75	78	78	75	306

June 9–11, 1928

Royal St George's GC, Sandwich, Kent

1	**Walter Hagen**	75	73	72	72	292
2	**Gene Sarazen**	72	76	73	73	294
3	**Archie Compston**	75	74	73	73	295
=4	**Percy Alliss**	75	76	75	72	298
	Fred Robson	79	73	73	73	298
=6	**Jim Barnes**	81	73	76	71	301

June 9–11, 1928 continued

	Aubrey Boomer	79	73	77	72	301
	Jose Jurado	74	71	76	77	301
9	**Bill Mehlhorn**	71	78	76	77	302
10	**Bill Davies**	78	74	79	73	304
=11	**Fred Taggart**	76	74	77	78	305
	Albert Whiting	78	76	76	75	305
13	**Jack Smith**	79	77	76	74	306
=14	**Phil Perkins (a)**	80	79	76	72	307
	William Twine	75	79	77	76	307
16	**Stewart Burns**	76	74	75	83	308
17	**C.O. Hezlet (a)**	79	76	78	76	309
=18	**Henry Cotton**	77	75	83	75	310
	Duncan McCulloch	78	78	78	76	310
	George Duncan	75	77	78	80	310
=21	**Abe Mitchell**	78	75	82	76	311
	Tom Williamson	77	73	77	84	311
=23	**Bob Bradbeer**	83	76	78	75	312
	George Gadd	83	73	78	78	312
	Jean Gassiat	76	77	81	78	312
	W.L. Hope (a)	84	75	75	78	312
	James Ockenden	80	78	79	75	312
	Reg Whitcombe	79	77	81	75	312
	Reg Wilson	82	73	77	80	312
	Sydney Wingate	75	82	79	76	312

May 8–10, 1929

Honourable Company, Muirfield, East Lothian, Scotland

1	**Walter Hagen**	75	67	75	75	292
2	**Johnny Farrell**	72	75	76	75	298
3	**Leo Diegel**	71	69	82	77	299
=4	**Percy Alliss**	69	76	76	79	300
	Abe Mitchell	72	72	78	78	300
6	**Bobby Cruikshank**	73	74	78	76	301
7	**Jim Barnes**	71	80	78	74	303
=8	**Gene Sarazen**	73	74	81	76	304
	Al Watrous	73	79	75	77	304
10	**Tommy Armour**	75	73	79	78	305
11	**Arthur Havers**	80	74	76	76	306
12	**Archie Compston**	76	73	77	81	307
=13	**Johnny Golden**	74	73	86	75	308
	Jimmy Thomson	78	78	75	77	308
=15	**Aubrey Boomer**	74	74	80	81	309
	Herbert Jolly	72	80	78	79	309
	Macdonald Smith	73	78	78	80	309
=18	**Sid Brews**	76	77	78	79	310
	Bill Davies	79	76	81	74	310
	Ed Dudley	72	80	80	78	310
	Mark Seymour	75	74	78	83	310
22	**George Duncan**	78	76	81	76	311
=23	**William Nolan**	80	76	79	77	312
	Phil Perkins (a)	79	73	80	80	312
=25	**Jose Jurado**	77	73	81	82	313
	W. Willis Mackenzie (a)	80	71	80	82	313
	Cedric Sayner	80	75	78	80	313
	Horton Smith	76	76	84	77	313
	Cyril Tolley (a)	74	76	87	76	313
	Joe Turnesa	78	74	81	80	313
	Tom Williamson	73	78	80	82	313

June 18–20, 1930

Royal Liverpool GC, Hoylake, Cheshire, England

1	**Bobby Jones**	70	72	74	75	291
=2	**Leo Diegel**	74	73	71	75	293
	Macdonald Smith	70	77	75	71	293

June 18–20, 1930 continued

=4	**Fred Robson**	71	72	78	75	296
	Horton Smith	72	73	78	73	296
=6	**Jim Barnes**	71	77	72	77	297
	Archie Compston	74	73	68	82	297
8	**Henry Cotton**	70	79	77	73	299
=9	**Tom Barber**	75	76	72	77	300
	Auguste Boyer	73	77	70	80	300
	Charles Whitcombe	74	75	72	79	300
12	**Bert Hodson**	74	77	76	74	301
=13	**Abe Mitchell**	75	78	77	72	302
	Reg Whitcombe	78	72	73	79	302
=15	**Donald Moe (a)**	74	73	76	80	303
	Phillip H. Rodgers	74	73	76	80	303
=17	**Percy Alliss**	75	74	77	79	305
	William Large	78	74	77	76	305
	Ernest R. Whitcombe	80	72	76	77	305
	Arthur Young	75	78	78	74	305
=21	**H. Crapper**	78	73	80	75	306
	Pierre Hirigoyen	75	79	76	76	306
	Harry Large	79	74	78	75	306
=24	**Stewart Burns**	77	75	80	75	307
	Bill Davies	78	77	73	79	307
	Arthur Lacey	78	79	74	76	307
	Ted Ray	78	75	76	78	307
	Norman Sutton	72	80	76	79	307
29	**Tom Green**	73	79	78	78	308
=30	**Duncan McCulloch**	78	78	79	74	309
	Alf Perry	78	74	75	82	309

June 3–5, 1931

Carnoustie GC, Angus, Scotland

1	**Tommy Armour**	73	75	77	71	296
2	**Jose Jurado**	76	71	73	77	297
=3	**Percy Alliss**	74	78	73	73	298
	Gene Sarazen	74	76	75	73	298
=5	**Johnny Farrell**	72	77	75	75	299
	Macdonald Smith	75	77	71	76	299
=7	**Marcos Churio**	76	75	78	71	300
	Bill Davies	76	78	71	75	300
8	**Arthur Lacey**	74	80	74	73	301
=9	**Henry Cotton**	72	75	79	76	302
	Arthur Havers	75	76	72	79	302
=11	**Gus Faulkner**	77	76	76	74	303
	Tomas Genta	75	78	75	75	303
	Abe Mitchell	77	74	77	75	303
	Horton Smith	77	79	75	72	303
	Tom Williamson	77	76	73	77	303
=16	**Marcel Dallemagne**	74	77	78	75	304
	Willie Hunter Jr	76	75	74	79	304
	William Oke	74	80	75	75	304
	Reg Whitcombe	75	78	71	80	304
=20	**Aubrey Boomer**	76	77	78	77	304
	Fred Robson	80	76	76	74	306
=22	**Len Holland**	80	74	78	75	307
	Mark Seymour	80	79	75	73	307
	Ernest R. Whitcombe	79	76	76	76	307
=25	**Bert Hodson**	77	76	78	77	308
	Joe Kirkwood Sr	75	75	77	81	308
	William Twine	72	78	79	79	308
=28	**Archie Compston**	77	76	75	81	309
	Ernest W.H. Kenyon	75	78	78	78	309
	Duncan McCulloch	76	78	77	78	309
	William McMinn	78	78	79	74	309
	Phillip H. Rodgers	77	74	78	80	309
	Charles Whitcombe	80	76	75	78	309

June 8–10, 1932

Prince's GC, Sandwich, Kent, England

1	**Gene Sarazen**	70	69	70	74	283
2	**Macdonald Smith**	71	76	71	70	288
3	**Arthur Havers**	74	71	68	76	289
=4	**Percy Alliss**	71	71	78	72	292
	Alf Padgham	76	72	74	70	292
	Charles Whitcombe	71	73	73	75	292
=7	**Bill Davies**	71	73	74	75	293
	Arthur Lacey	73	73	71	76	293
9	**Fred Robson**	74	71	78	71	294
=10	**Archie Compston**	74	70	75	76	295
	Henry Cotton	74	72	77	72	295
	Abe Mitchell	77	71	75	72	295
=13	**Syd Easterbrook**	74	75	72	77	298
	H. Prowse	75	75	75	73	298
=15	**C.S. Denny**	73	81	72	73	299
	W.L. Hope (a)	74	79	75	81	299
=17	**Tommy Armour**	75	70	74	81	300
	Bert Hodson	77	73	77	73	300
	Alf Perry	73	76	77	74	300
	Charlie Ward	73	77	77	73	300
	Reg Whitcombe	75	74	75	76	300
=22	**Ernest W.H. Kenyon**	74	73	76	78	301
	Mark Seymour	74	75	81	71	301
	T.A. Torrance (a)	75	73	76	77	301
=25	**Alf Beck**	78	71	74	79	302
	Lister Hartley (a)	76	73	80	73	302
	Phillip H. Rodgers	74	79	75	74	302
	William Twine	80	74	71	77	302
=29	**Pierre Hirigoyen**	79	73	75	76	303
	L.O. Munn (a)	74	75	78	76	303
	W. Purse	76	75	73	79	303
	Cedric Sayner	74	74	79	76	303
	Percy Weston	75	79	76	73	303

July 5–7, 1933

Royal & Ancient GC, St Andrews, Fife, Scotland

** Denny Shute (149) beat Craig Wood (154) in the 36-hole play-off.*

1	**Denny Shute***	73	73	73	73	292
2	**Craig Wood**	77	72	68	75	292
=3	**Leo Diegel**	75	70	71	77	293
	Syd Easterbrook	73	72	71	77	293
	Gene Sarazen	72	73	73	75	293
6	**Olin Dutra**	76	76	70	72	294
=7	**Henry Cotton**	73	71	72	79	295
	Ed Dudley	70	71	76	78	295
	Abe Mitchell	74	68	74	79	295
	Alf Padgham	74	73	74	74	295
	Reg Whitcombe	76	75	72	72	295
=12	**Archie Compston**	72	74	77	73	296
	Ernest R. Whitcombe	73	73	75	75	296
=14	**Auguste Boyer**	76	72	70	79	297
	Arthur Havers	80	72	71	74	297
	Joe Kirkwood Sr	72	73	71	81	297
	Horton Smith	73	73	75	76	297
=18	**Aubrey Boomer**	74	70	76	78	298
	Jack M'Lean (a)	75	74	75	74	298
	Cyril Tolley (a)	70	73	76	79	298
21	**Laurie Ayton Sr**	78	72	76	74	300
=22	**Bert Gadd**	75	73	73	80	301
	Walter Hagen	68	72	79	82	301
	D.C. Jones	75	72	78	76	301
	Fred Robertson	71	71	77	82	301
26	**Alf Perry**	79	73	74	76	302

July 5–7, 1933 continued

27	**Allan Dailey**	74	74	77	78	303
=28	**Ross Somerville (a)**	72	78	75	79	304
	W. Spark	73	72	79	80	304
	Charlie Ward	76	73	76	79	304

June 27–29, 1934

Royal St George's GC, Sandwich, Kent, England

1	**Henry Cotton**	67	65	72	79	283
2	**Sid Brews**	76	71	70	71	288
3	**Alf Padgham**	71	70	75	74	290
=4	**Marcel Dallemagne**	71	73	71	77	292
	Joe Kirkwood Sr	74	69	71	78	292
	Macdonald Smith	77	71	72	72	292
=7	**Bert Hodson**	71	74	74	76	295
	Charles Whitcombe	71	72	74	78	295
=9	**Percy Alliss**	73	75	71	77	296
	Ernest R. Whitcombe	72	77	73	74	296
11	**William Twine**	72	76	75	74	297
12	**John Burton**	80	72	72	74	298
=13	**Bill Davies**	76	68	73	82	299
	Edward Jarman	74	76	74	75	299
	Charlie Ward	76	71	72	70	299
=16	**Allan Dailey**	74	73	78	75	300
	James McDowall	73	74	76	77	300
	Jack M'Lean (a)	77	76	69	78	300
	Reg Whitcombe	75	76	74	75	300
20	**Denny Shute**	71	72	80	78	301
=21	**Alf Beck**	78	72	78	74	302
	Bert Gadd	76	74	74	78	302
	William Nolan	73	71	75	83	302
	Gene Sarazen	75	73	74	80	302
	Percy Weston	72	76	77	77	302
=26	**Jimmy Adams**	73	78	73	79	303
	Tom Green	75	73	74	81	303
	Alf Perry	76	76	74	77	303
=29	**Auguste Boyer**	78	75	77	74	304
	L.T. Cotton	76	73	79	76	304

June 26–28, 1935

Honourable Company, Muirfield, East Lothian, Scotland

1	**Alf Perry**	69	75	67	72	283
2	**Alf Padgham**	70	72	74	71	287
3	**Charles Whitcombe**	71	68	73	76	288
=4	**Bert Gadd**	72	75	71	71	289
	Lawson Little (a)	75	71	74	69	289
6	**Henry Picard**	72	73	72	75	292
=7	**Henry Cotton**	68	74	76	75	293
	Syd Easterbrook	75	73	74	71	293
9	**William Branch**	71	73	76	74	294
10	**Laurie Ayton Sr**	74	73	77	71	295
11	**Auguste Boyer**	74	75	76	71	296
=12	**Aubrey Boomer**	76	69	75	77	297
	Jack Busson	75	76	70	76	297
	Bill Cox	76	69	77	75	297
	Ernest W.H. Kenyon	70	74	74	79	297
=15	**Percy Alliss**	72	76	75	75	298
	J.A. Jacobs	78	74	75	71	298
=17	**W. Laidlaw**	74	71	75	79	299
	Philip H. Rodgers	74	76	74	75	299
	Mark Seymour	75	76	75	73	299
	Macdonald Smith	69	77	75	78	299
	Ernest R. Whitcombe	75	72	74	78	299
=22	**Reg Cox**	75	73	76	76	300
	Sam King	76	74	75	75	300

June 26–28, 1935 continued

	Arthur Lacey	71	75	74	80	300
	Laddie Lucas (a)	74	73	72	81	300
=26	**Frank Ball**	76	75	73	77	301
	Alf Beck	74	76	77	74	301
	Len Holland	72	74	78	77	301
	P.W.L. Risdon (a)	78	74	75	74	301
=30	**Sid Brews**	79	74	75	74	302
	Dai Rees	75	73	77	77	302
	Cyril Thomson	74	76	75	77	302

June 24–26, 1936

Royal Liverpool GC, Hoylake, Cheshire, England

1	**Alf Padgham**	73	72	71	71	287
2	**Jimmy Adams**	71	73	71	73	288
=3	**Henry Cotton**	73	72	70	74	289
	Marcel Dallemagne	73	72	75	69	289
=5	**Percy Alliss**	74	72	74	71	291
	Tom Green	74	72	70	75	291
	Gene Sarazen	73	75	70	73	291
=8	**Arthur Lacey**	76	74	72	72	294
	Bobby Locke (a)	75	73	72	74	294
	Reg Whitcombe	72	77	71	74	294
11	**Dai Rees**	77	71	72	75	295
=12	**Dick Burton**	74	71	75	76	296
	Bill Cox	70	74	79	73	296
14	**Bill Davies**	72	76	73	77	298
=15	**Aubrey Boomer**	74	75	75	75	299
	Wally Smithers	75	73	77	74	299
	Hector Thomson (a)	76	76	73	74	299
	Ted Turner	75	74	76	74	299
=19	**Gordon Good**	75	73	79	73	300
	Charles Whitcombe	73	76	79	72	300
=21	**Max Faulkner**	74	75	77	75	301
	Bert Gadd	74	72	77	78	301
=23	**Ernie Ball**	74	77	72	79	302
	Johnny Fallon	78	73	78	73	302
	Francis Francis (a)	73	72	79	78	302
	Willie Goggin	74	78	73	77	302
	Norman Sutton	75	72	78	77	302
=28	**Sam King**	79	74	75	76	304
	H.R. Manton	76	78	77	73	304
	Jean Saubaber	74	78	75	77	304

July 7–9, 1937

Carnoustie GC, Angus, Scotland

1	**Henry Cotton**	74	73	72	71	290
2	**Reg Whitcombe**	72	70	74	76	292
3	**Charles Lacey**	76	75	70	72	293
4	**Charles Whitcombe**	73	71	74	76	294
5	**Byron Nelson**	75	76	71	74	296
6	**Ed Dudley**	70	74	78	75	297
=7	**Arthur Lacey**	75	73	75	75	298
	W. Laidlaw	77	72	73	76	298
	Alf Padgham	72	74	76	76	298
10	**Horton Smith**	77	71	79	72	299
=11	**Ralph Guldahl**	77	72	74	77	300
	Sam Snead	75	74	75	76	300
13	**Bill Branch**	72	75	73	81	301
14	**Denny Shute**	73	73	76	80	302
=15	**Percy Alliss**	75	76	75	77	303
	Henry Picard	76	77	70	80	303
=17	**Jimmy Adams**	74	78	76	76	304
	Arthur Havers	77	75	76	76	304
	Bobby Locke (a)	74	74	77	79	304

July 7–9, 1937 continued

	Fred Robertson	73	75	78	78	304
=21	**Bill Cox**	74	77	81	73	305
	Dai Rees	75	73	78	79	305
23	**Jack Busson**	74	77	79	76	306
24	**Tom Collinge**	75	75	83	74	307
25	**Douglas Cairncross**	73	76	77	82	308
=26	**Marcel Dallemagne**	78	75	79	77	309
	Walter Hagen	76	72	80	81	309
	Jack M'Lean	78	74	81	76	309
=29	**John Burton**	76	75	82	77	310
	Sam King	79	74	75	82	310
	Ernest E. Whitcombe	76	76	81	77	310

July 6–8, 1938

Royal St George's GC, Sandwich, Kent, England

1	**Reg Whitcombe**	71	71	75	78	295
2	**Jimmy Adams**	70	71	78	78	297
3	**Henry Cotton**	74	73	77	74	298
=4	**Dick Burton**	71	69	78	85	303
	Jack Busson	71	69	83	80	303
	Allan Dailey	73	72	80	78	303
	Alf Padgham	74	72	75	82	303
=8	**Fred Bullock**	73	74	77	80	304
	Bill Cox	70	70	84	80	304
=10	**Bert Gadd**	71	70	84	80	305
	Bobby Locke	73	72	81	79	305
	Charles Whitcombe	71	75	79	80	305
=13	**Sid Brews**	76	70	84	77	307
	Dai Rees	73	72	79	83	307
=15	**J.H. Ballingall**	76	72	83	77	308
	Alf Perry	71	74	77	86	308
17	**Arthur Lacey**	74	72	82	81	309
18	**Bill Shankland**	74	72	84	81	311
19	**Ernest R. Whitcombe**	70	77	83	82	312
=20	**J.L. Black**	72	72	83	86	313
	P.J. Mahon	73	74	83	83	313
22	**Jack M'Lean**	72	74	83	85	314
=23	**Marcel Dallemagne**	70	74	86	85	315
	Willie Hastings	74	74	83	84	315
	Sam King	74	73	83	85	315
=26	**Johnny Fallon**	70	75	82	89	316
	Eustace Storey (a)	77	71	84	84	316
=28	**Ernest W.H. Kenyon**	77	71	86	83	317
	Bob Pemberton	74	72	91	80	317
	Cyril Tolley (a)	77	68	86	86	317

July 5–7, 1939

Royal & Ancient GC, St Andrews, Fife, Scotland

1	**Dick Burton**	70	72	77	71	290
2	**Johnny Bulla**	77	71	71	73	292
=3	**Johnny Fallon**	71	73	71	79	294
	Sam King	74	72	75	73	294
	Alf Perry	71	74	73	76	294
	Bill Shankland	72	73	72	77	294
	Reg Whitcombe	71	75	74	74	294
8	**Martin Pose**	71	72	76	76	295
=9	**Percy Alliss**	75	73	74	74	296
	Ernest W.H. Kenyon	73	75	74	74	296
	Bobby Locke	70	75	76	75	296
12	**Dai Rees**	71	74	75	77	297
=13	**Jimmy Adams**	73	74	75	76	298
	Enrique Bertolino	73	75	75	75	298
	Jimmy Bruen (a)	72	75	75	76	298
	Henry Cotton	74	72	76	76	298

	July 5–7, 1939 continued					
=17	**Bill Anderson**	73	74	77	75	299
	Enrique Serra	77	72	73	77	299
19	**W.H. Green**	75	75	72	78	300
=20	**Bill Davies**	71	79	74	77	301
	Syd Easterbrook	74	71	80	76	301
	Alex Kyle (a)	74	76	75	76	301
=23	**L.G. Crawley (a)**	72	76	80	74	302
	Max Faulkner	70	76	76	80	302
25	**Harry Busson**	70	75	81	77	303
=26	**Laurie Ayton Jr**	72	77	78	77	304
	W.S. Collins	75	74	79	76	304
	Fred Taggert	73	77	76	78	304
29	**Aurelio Castanon**	77	73	80	75	305
=30	**Laurie Ayton Sr**	76	72	82	76	306
	Charlie Ward	71	74	78	83	306

1940 – 1945 – No championship

July 3–5, 1946

Royal & Ancient GC, St Andrews, Fife, Scotland

1	**Sam Snead**	71	70	74	75	290
=2	**Johnny Bulla**	71	72	72	79	294
	Bobby Locke	69	74	75	76	294
=4	**Henry Cotton**	70	70	76	79	295
	Norman von Nida	70	76	74	75	295
	Dai Rees	75	67	73	80	295
	Charlie Ward	73	73	73	76	295
=8	**Fred Daly**	77	71	76	74	298
	Joe Kirkwood Sr	71	75	78	74	298
10	**Lawson Little**	78	75	72	74	299
11	**Harry Bradshaw**	76	75	76	73	300
12	**Dick Burton**	74	76	76	76	302
13	**Bill Shankland**	76	76	77	75	304
=14	**Bill Anderson**	76	76	78	75	305
	Reg Whitcombe	71	76	82	76	305
16	**Laurie Ayton Jr**	77	74	80	75	306
17	**Percy Alliss**	74	72	82	79	307
=18	**Archie Compston**	77	74	77	80	308
	Frank Jowle	78	74	76	80	308
	Arthur Lees	77	71	78	82	308
=21	**G. Knight**	77	75	82	76	310
	Ernest E. Whitcombe	75	79	77	79	310
=23	**R.K. Bell (a)**	81	73	81	77	312
	J.A. Jacobs	76	77	80	79	312
=25	**Alf Perry**	78	77	78	80	313
	J.C. Wilson (a)	78	76	81	78	313
=27	**Flory van Donck**	76	78	83	78	315
	A. Dowie (a)	81	71	80	83	315
	A.M. Robertson	79	75	80	81	315
=30	**Tom Haliburton**	78	76	81	81	316
	Alf Padgham	79	74	76	87	316
	Ronnie White (a)	76	79	84	77	316

July 2–4, 1947

Royal Liverpool GC, Hoylake, Cheshire, England

1	**Fred Daly**	73	70	78	72	293
=2	**Reg Horne**	77	74	72	71	294
	Frank Stranahan (a)	71	79	72	72	294
4	**Bill Shankland**	76	74	75	70	295
5	**Dick Burton**	77	71	77	71	296
=6	**Johnny Bulla**	80	72	74	71	297
	Henry Cotton	69	78	74	76	297
	Sam King	75	72	77	73	297
	Arthur Lees	75	74	72	76	297

	July 2–4, 1947 continued					
	Norman von Nida	74	76	71	76	297
	Charlie Ward	76	73	76	72	297
12	**Jimmy Adams**	73	80	71	75	299
=13	**Alf Padgham**	75	75	74	76	300
	Reg Whitcombe	75	77	71	77	300
=15	**Laurie Ayton Jr**	69	80	74	79	302
	Fred Bullock	74	78	78	72	302
17	**Norman Sutton**	77	76	73	77	303
=18	**Vic Ghezzi**	75	78	72	79	304
	Alf Perry	76	77	71	81	304
	Ernest E. Whitcombe	77	76	74	77	304
=21	**Dai Rees**	77	74	73	81	305
	Flory van Donck	73	76	81	75	305
23	**Alan Waters**	75	78	76	77	306
24	**John Burton**	73	79	76	71	309
=25	**Harry Busson**	80	76	71	83	310
	J.A. Jacobs	75	80	76	79	310
=27	**Ken Bousfield**	78	76	79	78	311
	Arthur Havers	80	76	79	76	311
	N. Quigley	79	77	76	79	311
	B. Shepard	78	78	77	78	311

June 30–July 2, 1948

Honourable Company, Muirfield, East Lothian, Scotland

1	**Henry Cotton**	71	66	75	72	284
2	**Fred Daly**	72	71	73	73	289
=3	**Roberto de Vicenzo**	70	73	72	75	290
	Jack Hargreaves	76	78	73	73	290
	Norman von Nida	71	72	76	71	290
	Charlie Ward	69	72	75	74	290
=7	**Johnny Bulla**	74	72	73	72	291
	Sam King	69	72	74	76	291
	Alf Padgham	73	70	71	77	291
	Flory van Donck	69	73	73	76	291
=11	**Mario Gonzales**	76	72	70	75	293
	E.C. Kingsley (a)	77	69	77	70	293
	Arthur Lees	73	79	73	78	293
	Alan Waters	75	71	70	77	293
=15	**Max Faulkner**	75	71	74	74	294
	Dai Rees	73	71	76	74	294
	Ernest E. Whitcombe	74	73	73	74	294
=18	**Dick Burton**	74	70	74	77	295
	Frank Jowle	70	78	74	73	295
	Reg Whitcombe	77	67	77	74	295
=21	**Ken Bousfield**	76	71	73	76	296
	Johnny Fallon	73	74	74	75	296
=23	**Tom Haliburton**	73	74	76	74	297
	Alf Perry	77	71	76	73	297
	Frank Stranahan (a)	77	71	75	74	297
	Norman Sutton	72	73	77	75	297
27	**Claude Harmon**	75	73	78	72	298
=28	**Otway Hayes**	74	73	75	78	300
	Reg Horne	71	77	73	79	300
=30	**Arthur Clark**	74	71	75	81	301
	Harold Gould	75	73	78	75	301

July 6–8, 1949

Royal St George's, Sandwich, Kent, England

** Bobby Locke (135) beat Harry Bradshaw (147) in the 36-hole play-off.*

1	**Bobby Locke***	69	76	68	70	283
2	**Harry Bradshaw**	68	77	68	70	283
3	**Roberto de Vicenzo**	68	75	73	69	285
=4	**Sam King**	71	69	74	72	286
	Charlie Ward	73	71	70	72	286

July 6–8, 1949 continued

=6	**Max Faulkner**	71	71	71	74	287
	Arthur Lees	74	70	72	71	287
=8	**Jimmy Adams**	67	77	72	72	288
	Johnny Fallon	69	75	72	72	288
	Wally Smithers	72	75	70	71	288
=11	**Ken Bousfield**	69	77	76	67	289
	Bill Shankland	69	73	74	73	289
13	**Frank Stranahan (a)**	71	73	74	72	290
=14	**Bill Branch**	71	75	74	71	291
	Dick Burton	73	70	74	74	291
	J. Knipe	76	71	72	72	291
17	**Walter Lees**	74	72	69	78	293
18	**Alan Waters**	70	76	75	73	294
19	**Norman Sutton**	69	78	75	73	295
=20	**Reg Horne**	73	74	75	74	296
	Arthur Lacey	72	73	73	78	296
	Gregor McIntosh	70	77	76	73	296
	William McMinn	70	75	78	73	296
	E.A. Southerden	69	76	74	77	296
25	**Jim Wade**	71	74	77	75	297
26	**Herbert Osborne**	73	74	75	76	298
27	**Johnny Bulla**	71	73	76	79	299
28	**Ugo Grappasoni**	70	76	77	77	300
29	**Ernest W.H. Kenyon**	72	75	77	77	301
30	**Bill White**	74	71	80	78	303

July 5–7, 1950

Troon GC, Ayrshire, Scotland

1	**Bobby Locke**	69	72	70	68	279
2	**Roberto de Vicenzo**	72	71	68	70	281
=3	**Fred Daly**	75	72	69	66	282
	Dai Rees	71	68	72	71	282
=5	**Max Faulkner**	72	70	70	71	283
	Eric Moore	74	68	73	68	283
=7	**Fred Bullock**	71	71	71	71	284
	Arthur Lees	68	76	68	72	284
=9	**Sam King**	70	75	68	73	286
	Frank Stranahan (a)	77	70	73	66	286
	Flory van Donck	73	71	72	70	286
=12	**Jimmy Adams**	73	75	69	70	287
	Wally Smithers	74	70	73	70	287
=14	**Johnny Bulla**	73	70	71	74	288
	Hector Thomson	71	72	73	72	288
16	**Harry Bradshaw**	73	71	75	70	289
=17	**Reg Horne**	73	75	71	71	290
	James McHale (a)	73	73	74	70	290
	Ernest E. Whitcombe	69	76	72	73	290
=20	**Alf Padgham**	77	71	74	69	291
	John Panton	76	69	70	76	291
	Norman von Nida	74	72	76	69	291
23	**Eric Brown**	73	73	73	73	292
=24	**Trevor Allen**	77	70	75	71	293
	Bill Branch	71	69	78	75	293
	Stewart Field	73	71	73	76	293
	Norman Sutton	71	75	74	73	293
	Bill White	74	74	73	72	293
29	**Fred Allott**	72	71	77	74	294
=30	**David Blair (a)**	72	72	77	74	295
	H. Hassanein	73	72	77	73	295

July 4–6, 1951

Royal Portrush GC, Co. Antrim, Northern Ireland

1	**Max Faulkner**	71	70	70	74	285
2	**Antonio Cerda**	74	72	71	70	287
3	**Charlie Ward**	75	73	74	68	290
=4	**Jimmy Adams**	68	77	75	72	292
	Fred Daly	74	70	75	73	292
=6	**Bobby Locke**	71	74	74	74	293
	Bill Shankland	73	76	72	72	293
	Norman Sutton	73	70	74	76	293
	Peter Thomson	70	75	73	75	293
	Harry Weetman	73	71	75	74	293
11	**John Panton**	73	72	74	75	294
=12	**Dick Burton**	74	77	71	73	295
	Dai Rees	70	77	76	72	295
	Frank Stranahan (a)	75	75	72	73	293
15	**Harry Bradshaw**	80	71	74	71	296
16	**Eric Cremin**	73	75	75	74	297
=17	**Kep Enderby (a)**	76	74	75	73	298
	Alan Waters	74	75	78	71	298
=19	**Ugo Grappasoni**	73	73	77	76	299
	Jack Hargreaves	73	78	79	69	299
	Willie John Henderson	77	73	76	73	299
	Kel Nagle	76	76	72	75	299
	Christy O'Connor Sr	79	74	72	74	299
=24	**Joe Carr**	75	76	73	76	300
	P. Traviani	74	79	73	74	300
	Flory van Donck	72	76	76	76	300
	Ernest E. Whitcombe	74	74	76	76	300
=28	**J. McKenna**	74	76	76	76	302
	Alan Poulton	77	77	73	75	302
	Wally Smithers	75	73	76	78	302

July 9–11, 1952

Royal Lytham and St Anne's GC, Lancashire, England

1	**Bobby Locke**	69	71	74	73	287
2	**Peter Thomson**	68	73	77	70	288
3	**Fred Daly**	67	69	77	76	289
4	**Henry Cotton**	75	74	74	71	294
=5	**Antonio Cerda**	73	73	76	73	295
	Sam King	71	74	74	76	295
7	**Flory van Donck**	74	75	71	76	296
8	**Fred Bullock**	76	72	72	77	297
=9	**Harry Bradshaw**	70	74	75	79	298
	Eric Brown	71	72	78	77	298
	Willie Goggin	71	74	75	78	298
	Arthur Lees	76	72	76	74	298
	Syd Scott	75	69	76	78	298
	Norman von Nilda	77	70	74	77	298
=15	**John Panton**	72	72	78	77	299
	Harry Weetman	74	77	71	77	299
=17	**Max Faulkner**	72	76	79	73	300
	Gene Sarazen	74	73	77	76	300
	Wally Smithers	73	74	76	77	300
20	**Norman Sutton**	72	74	79	76	301
=21	**Fred Allott**	77	71	76	78	302
	Ken Bousfield	72	73	79	78	302
	Jimmy Hines	73	78	74	77	302
	Eddie Noke	72	78	76	76	302
=25	**J.A. Jacobs**	74	72	81	76	303
	Alan Poulton	71	74	76	82	303
=27	**Jack Hargreaves**	75	75	79	75	304
	John Jacobs	73	70	79	77	304
	J.W. Jones (a)	73	70	78	83	304
	Dai Rees	76	74	77	77	304

July 8–10, 1953

Carnoustie GC, Angus, Scotland

1	**Ben Hogan**	73	71	70	68	282
=2	**Antonio Cerda**	75	71	69	71	286
	Dai Rees	72	70	73	71	286
	Frank Stranahan (a)	70	74	73	69	286
	Peter Thomson	72	72	71	71	286
6	**Roberto di Vicenzo**	72	71	71	73	287
7	**Sam King**	74	73	72	71	290
8	**Bobby Locke**	72	73	74	72	291
=9	**Peter Alliss**	75	72	74	71	292
	Eric Brown	71	71	75	75	292
11	**Fred Daly**	73	75	71	75	294
12	**Max Faulkner**	74	71	73	77	295
13	**Arthur Lees**	76	76	72	72	296
=14	**T.H.T. Fairbairn**	74	71	73	79	297
	John Jacobs	79	74	71	73	297
	Harry Weetman	80	73	72	72	297
=17	**H. Hassanein**	78	71	73	76	298
	Eric Lester	83	70	72	73	298
	Charlie Ward	78	71	76	73	298
=20	**Reg Horne**	76	74	75	74	299
	Flory van Donck	77	71	78	73	299
=22	**Syd Scott**	74	74	78	74	300
	Hector Thompson	76	74	74	76	300
=24	**Reg Knight**	74	79	74	74	301
	Lloyd Mangrum	75	76	74	76	301
	Christy O'Connor Sr	77	77	72	75	301
=27	**Ugo Grappasoni**	77	75	72	78	302
	John Panton	79	74	76	73	302
=29	**R. Ferguson**	77	75	74	77	303
	Tom Haliburton	75	76	76	76	303
	Alan Poulton	75	77	75	76	303
	Norman Sutton	76	72	76	79	303

July 7–9, 1954

Birkdale GC, Southport, Lancashire, England

1	**Peter Thompson**	72	71	69	71	283
=2	**Bobby Locke**	74	71	69	70	284
	Dai Rees	72	71	69	72	284
	Syd Scott	76	67	69	72	284
=5	**Jimmy Adams**	73	75	69	69	286
	Antonio Cerda	71	71	73	71	286
	Jim Turnesa	72	72	71	71	286
=8	**Peter Alliss**	72	74	71	70	287
	Sam King	69	74	74	70	287
=10	**Jimmy Demaret**	73	71	74	71	289
	Flory van Donck	77	71	70	71	289
=12	**Alfonso Angelini**	76	70	73	71	290
	Harry Bradshaw	72	72	73	73	290
	J.W. Spence	69	72	74	75	290
=15	**Bobby Halsall**	72	73	73	73	291
	Peter Toogood (a)	72	75	73	71	291
=17	**Ugo Grappasoni**	72	75	74	71	292
	C. Kane	74	72	74	72	292
	Gene Sarazen	75	74	73	70	292
=20	**Norman Drew**	76	71	74	72	293
	Max Faulkner	73	78	69	73	293
	Jack Hargreaves	77	72	77	67	293
	John Jacobs	71	73	80	69	293
	Eric Lester	72	75	73	73	293
	Christy O'Connor Sr	74	72	72	75	293
	Lambert Topping	75	76	69	73	293
=27	**Norman Sutton**	70	80	72	72	294
	E.B. Williamson	76	73	75	70	294

July 7–9, 1954 continued

=29	**Jimmy Hitchcock**	73	72	76	74	295
	Ben Shelton	74	77	71	73	295
	Frank Stranahan (a)	73	75	71	76	295

July 6–8, 1955

Royal & Ancient GC, St Andrews, Fife, Scotland

1	**Peter Thompson**	71	68	70	72	281
2	**Johnny Fallon**	73	67	73	70	283
3	**Frank Jowle**	70	71	69	74	284
4	**Bobby Locke**	74	69	70	72	285
=5	**Ken Bousfield**	71	75	70	70	286
	Antonio Cerda	73	71	71	71	286
	Bernard Hunt	70	71	74	71	286
	Flory van Donck	71	72	71	72	286
	Harry Weetman	71	71	70	74	286
=10	**Romauldo Barbieri**	71	71	73	72	287
	Christy O'Connor Sr	71	75	70	71	287
=12	**Eric Brown**	69	70	73	76	288
	Fred Daly	75	72	70	71	288
	John Jacobs	71	70	71	76	288
=15	**Iain Anderson**	71	72	77	69	289
	Willie John Henderson	74	71	72	72	289
=17	**D.F. Smalldon**	70	69	78	73	290
	Arturo Soto	72	73	72	73	290
=19	**Ed Furgol**	71	76	72	73	292
	Kel Nagle	72	72	74	74	292
	Syd Scott	69	77	73	73	292
=22	**Harry Bradshaw**	72	70	73	78	293
	Bill Branch	75	72	73	73	293
	Joe Conrad (a)	72	76	74	71	293
	Bobby Halsall	71	74	76	72	293
	Reg Horne	72	75	75	71	293
=27	**H. Hassanein**	73	72	76	73	294
	Dai Rees	69	79	73	73	294
	Norman Sutton	71	74	75	74	294

July 4–6, 1956

Royal Liverpool GC, Hoylake, Cheshire, England

1	**Peter Thompson**	70	70	72	74	286
2	**Flory van Donck**	71	74	70	74	289
3	**Roberto de Vicenzo**	71	70	79	70	290
4	**Gary Player**	71	76	73	71	291
5	**John Panton**	74	76	72	70	292
=6	**Enrique Bertolino**	69	72	76	76	293
	Henry Cotton	72	76	71	74	293
=8	**Antonio Cerda**	72	81	68	73	294
	Mike Souchak	74	74	74	72	294
=10	**Christy O'Connor Sr**	73	78	74	70	295
	Harry Weetman	72	76	75	72	295
12	**Frank Stranahan**	72	76	72	76	296
=13	**Bruce Crampton**	76	77	72	72	297
	Angel Miguel	71	74	75	77	297
	Dai Rees	75	74	75	73	297
16	**John Jacobs**	73	77	76	72	298
=17	**Al Balding**	70	81	76	73	300
	Jack Hargreaves	72	80	75	73	300
	Ricardo Rossi	75	77	72	76	300
	Dave Thomas	70	78	77	75	300
	Charlie Ward	73	75	78	74	300
=22	**Ken Bousfield**	73	77	76	75	301
	Gerard de Wit	76	73	74	78	301
	Eric Lester	70	76	77	78	301
=25	**Jimmy Adams**	75	76	76	75	302
	Laurie Ayton Jr	74	78	78	72	302

July 4–6, 1956 continued

	Eric Moore	75	75	78	74	302
=28	**K.W.C. Adwick**	77	76	74	76	303
	Syd Scott	78	74	74	77	303
	D.F. Smalldon	68	79	78	78	303

July 3–5, 1957

Royal & Ancient GC, St Andrews, Fife, Scotland

1	**Bobby Locke**	69	72	68	70	279
2	**Peter Thompson**	73	69	70	70	282
3	**Eric Brown**	67	72	73	71	283
4	**Angel Miguel**	72	72	69	72	285
=5	**Tom Haliburton**	72	73	68	73	286
	Dick Smith (a)	71	72	72	71	286
	Dave Thomas	72	74	70	70	286
	Flory van Donck	72	68	74	72	286
=9	**Antonio Cerda**	71	71	72	73	287
	Henry Cotton	74	72	69	72	287
	Max Faulkner	74	70	71	72	287
=12	**Peter Alliss**	72	74	74	68	288
	Henry Weetman	75	71	71	71	288
14	**Cary Middlecoff**	72	71	74	72	289
=15	**Norman Drew**	70	75	71	74	290
	Eric Lester	71	76	70	73	290
	Sebastian Miguel	71	75	76	68	290
	John Panton	71	72	74	73	290
=19	**Harry Bradshaw**	73	74	69	75	291
	Johnny Fallon	75	67	73	76	291
	Christy O'Connor Sr	77	69	72	73	291
	Frank Stranahan	74	71	74	72	291
23	**Jimmy Hitchcock**	69	74	73	76	292
=24	**Reg Horne**	76	72	72	73	293
	Bernard Hunt	72	72	74	75	293
	Sam King	76	72	70	75	293
	Gary Player	71	74	75	73	293
	Trevor Wilkes	75	73	71	74	293
29	**Harold Henning**	75	73	71	75	294
=30	**Laurie Ayton Jr**	67	76	75	77	295
	Peter Butler	77	71	74	73	295
	Reg Knight	71	73	75	76	295
	Dai Rees	73	72	79	71	295
	Norman Sutton	69	76	73	77	295

July 2–4, 1958

Royal Lytham and St Anne's GC, Lancashire, England

1	**Peter Thompson**	66	72	67	73	278
2	**Dave Thomas**	70	68	69	71	278
=3	**Eric Brown**	73	70	65	71	279
	Christy O'Connor Sr	67	68	73	71	279
=5	**Leopoldo Ruiz**	71	65	72	73	281
	Flory van Donck	70	70	67	74	281
7	**Gary Player**	68	74	70	71	283
=8	**Henry Cotton**	68	75	69	72	284
	Eric Lester	73	66	71	74	284
	Harry Weetman	73	67	73	71	284
=11	**Peter Alliss**	72	70	70	73	285
	Don Swaelens	74	67	74	70	285
13	**Harold Henning**	70	71	72	73	286
=14	**Jean Garialde**	69	74	72	72	287
	Dai Rees	77	69	71	70	287
=16	**Max Faulkner**	68	71	71	78	288
	Bobby Locke	76	70	72	70	288
	Eric Moore	72	72	70	74	288
	Gene Sarazen	73	73	70	72	288
=20	**A.B. Coop**	69	71	75	75	290

July 2–4, 1958 continued

	Fred Daly	71	74	72	73	290
	Norman Drew	69	72	75	74	290
	Christy Greene	75	71	72	72	290
=24	**Harry Bradshaw**	70	73	72	76	291
	Gerard de Wit	71	75	72	73	291
=26	**Antonio Cerda**	72	71	74	75	292
	Sebastian Miguel	74	71	73	74	292
	Trevor Wilkes	76	70	69	77	292
29	**Angel Miguel**	71	70	75	77	293
=30	**Bernard Hunt**	70	70	76	79	295
	Sam King	71	73	76	75	295
	David Snell	72	72	72	79	295

July 1–3, 1959

Honourable Company, Muirfield, East Lothian, Scotland

1	**Gary Player**	75	71	70	68	284
=2	**Fred Bullock**	68	70	74	74	286
	Flory van Donck	70	70	73	73	286
4	**Syd Scott**	73	70	73	71	287
=5	**Reid Jack (a)**	71	75	68	74	288
	Sam King	70	74	68	76	288
	Christy O'Connor Sr	73	74	72	69	288
	John Panton	72	72	71	73	288
=9	**Dai Rees**	73	73	69	74	289
	Leopoldo Ruiz	72	74	69	74	289
=11	**Michael Bonallack (a)**	70	72	72	76	290
	Ken Bousfield	73	73	71	73	290
	Jimmy Hitchcock	75	68	70	77	290
	Bernard Hunt	73	75	71	71	290
	Arnold Stickley	68	74	77	71	290
=16	**Peter Alliss**	76	72	76	67	291
	Harry Bradshaw	71	76	72	72	291
	Antonio Cerda	69	74	73	75	291
	Harry Weetman	72	73	76	70	291
	Guy Wolstenholme (a)	78	70	73	70	291
=21	**Neil Coles**	72	74	71	75	292
	Jean Garaialde	75	70	74	73	292
=23	**Harold Henning**	73	73	72	76	294
	Geoff Hunt	72	73	74	75	294
	Reg Knight	71	71	74	78	294
	Peter Mills	75	71	72	76	294
	J.R. Moss	72	73	73	76	294
	Peter Thompson	74	74	72	74	294
=29	**Jimmy Adams**	71	74	75	75	295
	Tom Haliburton	74	69	74	78	295
	Bobby Locke	73	73	76	73	295
	P.J. Shanks	76	70	75	74	295
	Ernest E. Whitcombe	71	77	74	73	295

July 6–8, 1960

Royal & Ancient GC, St Andrews, Fife, Scotland

1	**Kel Nagle**	69	67	71	71	278
2	**Arnold Palmer**	70	71	70	68	279
=3	**Roberto de Vicenzo**	67	67	75	73	282
	Harold Henning	72	72	69	69	282
	Bernard Hunt	72	73	71	66	282
6	**Guy Wolstenholme (a)**	74	70	71	68	283
7	**Gary Player**	72	71	72	69	284
8	**Joe Carr (a)**	72	73	67	73	285
=9	**David Blair (a)**	70	73	71	72	286
	Eric Brown	75	68	72	71	286
	Dai Rees	73	71	73	69	286
	Syd Scott	73	71	67	75	286
	Peter Thompson	72	69	75	70	286

	July 6–8, 1960 continued					
	Harry Weetman	74	70	71	71	286
15	**Ramon Sota**	74	72	71	70	287
=16	**Fidel de Luca**	69	73	75	71	288
	Reid Jack (a)	74	71	70	73	288
	Angel Miguel	72	73	72	71	288
	Ian Smith	74	70	73	71	288
20	**Peter Mills**	71	74	70	74	289
=21	**Ken Bousfield**	70	75	71	74	290
	Alec Deboys (a)	76	70	73	71	290
	George Low	72	74	71	73	290
	John MacDonald	76	71	69	74	290
	Ralph Moffitt	72	71	76	71	290
=26	**Bill Johnston**	75	74	71	71	291
	Sebastian Miguel	73	68	74	76	291
=28	**Laurie Ayton Jr**	73	69	75	75	292
	Fred Boobyer	74	74	73	71	292
	Geoff Hunt	76	69	72	75	292
	Jimmy Martin	72	72	72	76	292

July 12–14, 1961

Birkdale GC, Southport, Lancashire, England

1	**Arnold Palmer**	70	73	69	72	284
2	**Dai Rees**	68	74	71	72	285
=3	**Neil Coles**	70	77	69	72	288
	Christy O'Connor Sr	71	77	67	73	288
=5	**Eric Brown**	73	76	70	70	289
	Kel Nagle	68	75	75	71	289
7	**Peter Thompson**	75	72	70	73	290
=8	**Peter Alliss**	73	75	72	71	291
	Ken Bousfield	71	77	75	68	291
=10	**Harold Henning**	68	74	75	76	293
	Syd Scott	76	75	71	71	293
12	**Ramon Sota**	71	76	72	76	295
13	**A.B. Coop**	71	79	73	74	297
=14	**Norman Johnson**	69	80	70	79	298
	Reg Knight	71	80	73	74	298
	Angel Miguel	73	79	74	72	298
	Sebastian Miguel	71	80	70	77	298
=18	**Dennis Hutchinson**	72	80	74	73	299
	Paul Runyan	75	77	75	72	299
=20	**Harry Bradshaw**	73	75	78	74	300
	Peter Butler	72	76	78	74	300
	John Jacobs	71	79	76	74	300
	Lionel Platts	70	80	71	79	300
=26	**Jean Garaialde**	69	81	76	75	301
	Brian Huggett	72	77	75	77	301
	Eric Lester	71	77	75	78	301
	Ralph Moffitt	73	80	73	75	301
=30	**David Miller**	69	79	80	74	302
	George Will	74	75	75	78	302

July 11–13, 1962

Troon GC, Ayrshire, Scotland

1	**Arnold Palmer**	71	69	67	69	276
2	**Kel Nagle**	71	71	70	70	282
=3	**Brian Huggett**	75	71	74	69	289
	Phil Rodgers	75	70	72	72	289
5	**Bob Charles**	75	70	70	75	290
=6	**Sam Snead**	76	73	72	71	292
	Peter Thompson	70	77	75	70	292
=8	**Peter Alliss**	77	69	74	73	293
	Dave Thomas	77	70	71	75	293
10	**Syd Scott**	77	74	75	68	294
11	**Ralph Moffitt**	75	70	74	76	295

	July 11–13, 1962 continued					
=12	**Jean Garaialde**	76	73	76	71	296
	Sebastian Miguel	72	79	73	72	296
	Harry Weetman	75	73	73	75	296
	Ross Whitehead	74	75	72	75	296
=16	**Roger Foreman**	77	73	72	75	297
	Bernard Hunt	74	74	75	73	297
	Dennis Hutchinson	78	73	76	70	297
	Jimmy Martin	73	72	76	76	297
	Christy O'Connor Sr	74	78	73	72	297
	John Panton	74	73	79	71	297
22	**A.B. Coop**	76	75	75	72	298
23	**Don Swaelens**	72	79	74	74	299
=24	**Brian Bamford**	77	73	74	76	300
	Lionel Platts	78	74	76	72	300
	Guy Wolstenholme	78	74	76	72	300
=27	**Hugh Boyle**	73	78	74	76	301
	Keith MacDonald	69	77	76	79	301
29	**George Low**	77	75	77	73	302
=30	**Harry Bradshaw**	72	75	81	75	303
	Harold Henning	74	73	79	77	303
	Jimmy Hitchcock	78	74	72	79	303

July 10–12, 1963

Royal Lytham and St Anne's GC, Lancashire, England

** Bob Charles (140) beat Phil Rodgers (148) in the 36-hole play-off.*

1	**Bob Charles***	68	72	66	71	277
2	**Phil Rodgers**	67	68	73	69	277
3	**Jack Nicklaus**	71	67	70	70	278
4	**Kel Nagle**	69	70	73	71	283
5	**Peter Thompson**	67	69	71	78	285
6	**Christy O'Connor Sr**	74	68	76	68	286
=7	**Gary Player**	75	70	72	70	287
	Ramon Sota	69	73	73	72	287
=9	**Jean Garaialde**	72	69	72	75	288
	Sebastian Miguel	73	69	73	73	288
=11	**Bernard Hunt**	72	71	73	73	289
	Alex King	71	73	73	72	289
13	**Sewsunker Sewgolum**	71	74	73	72	290
=14	**Brian Allen**	75	71	71	74	291
	Brian Huggett	73	74	70	74	291
	Hugh Lewis	71	77	69	74	291
	Ian MacDonald	71	71	74	75	291
=18	**Peter Alliss**	74	71	77	80	292
	Frank Phillips	70	73	75	74	292
=20	**Neil Coles**	73	75	72	73	293
	Max Faulkner	77	71	71	74	293
	Harold Henning	76	68	71	78	293
	Malcolm Leeder	76	73	74	70	293
	John MacDonald	73	75	75	70	293
	Brian Wilkes	70	77	74	72	293
=26	**Jimmy Hitchcock**	75	73	70	76	294
	Arnold Palmer	76	71	71	76	294
	Doug Sewell	75	72	73	74	294
	Dave Thomas	74	74	75	71	294
=30	**Ken Bousfield**	73	75	71	76	295
	Tom Haliburton	68	73	77	77	295
	Tony Jacklin	73	72	76	74	295

July 8–10, 1964

Royal & Ancient GC, St Andrews, Fife, Scotland

1	**Tony Lema**	73	68	68	70	279
2	**Jack Nicklaus**	76	74	66	68	284
3	**Roberto de Vicenzo**	76	72	70	67	285
4	**Bernard Hunt**	73	74	70	70	287

July 8–10, 1964 continued

5	**Bruce Devlin**	72	72	73	73	290
=6	**Christy O'Connor Sr**	71	73	74	73	291
	Harry Weetman	72	71	75	73	291
=8	**Harold Henning**	78	73	71	70	292
	Angel Miguel	73	76	72	71	292
	Gary Player	78	71	73	70	292
11	**Doug Sanders**	78	73	74	68	293
12	**Frank Phillips**	77	75	72	70	294
=13	**Jean Garaialde**	71	74	79	72	296
	Christy Greene	74	76	73	73	296
	Ralph Moffitt	76	72	74	74	296
	Dave Thomas	75	74	75	72	296
=17	**Alex Caygill**	77	74	71	75	297
	Bob Charles	79	71	69	78	297
=19	**Malcolm Gregson**	78	70	74	76	298
	John MacDonald	78	74	74	72	298
	A. Murray	77	73	76	72	298
	Phil Rodgers	74	79	74	71	298
	Syd Scott	75	74	73	76	298
=24	**A.B. Coop**	75	72	76	76	299
	Doug Ford	75	76	76	72	299
	Liang-Huan Lu	76	71	78	74	299
	Jimmy Martin	74	72	79	74	299
	Peter Thompson	79	73	72	75	299
29	**George Will**	74	79	71	76	300
=30	**Peter Butler**	78	75	74	75	301
	Geoff Hunt	77	75	74	75	301
	Ramon Sota	77	74	74	76	301

July 7–9, 1965

Royal Birkdale GC, Southport, Lancashire, England

1	**Peter Thomson**	74	68	72	71	285
=2	**Brian Huggett**	73	68	76	70	287
	Christy O'Connor Sr	69	73	74	71	287
4	**Roberto de Vicenzo**	74	69	73	72	288
=5	**Bernard Hunt**	74	74	70	71	289
	Tony Lema	68	72	75	74	289
	Kel Nagle	74	70	73	72	289
=8	**Bruce Devlin**	71	69	75	75	290
	Sebastian Miguel	72	73	72	73	290
=10	**Max Faulkner**	74	72	74	73	293
	John Panton	74	74	75	70	293
=12	**Hugh Boyle**	73	69	76	76	294
	Neil Coles	73	74	77	70	294
	Jack Nicklaus	73	71	77	73	294
	Lionel Platts	72	72	73	77	294
16	**Arnold Palmer**	70	71	75	79	295
=17	**Eric Brown**	72	70	77	77	296
	Tommy Horton	75	73	76	72	296
	Cobie Legrange	76	73	75	72	296
	Guy Wolstenholme	72	75	77	72	296
-21	**Brian Bamford**	72	76	74	75	297
	Christy Greene	72	77	74	74	297
	Dennis Hutchinson	74	72	76	75	297
	George Will	75	69	74	79	297
=25	**Fred Boobyer**	74	73	73	78	298
	Tony Jacklin	75	73	73	77	298
	Doug Sewell	72	75	74	77	298
	Ramon Sota	75	70	78	75	298
=29	**Michael Burgess (a)**	74	73	78	74	299
	Harry Weetman	76	69	80	74	299

July 6–9, 1966

Honourable Company, Muirfield, East Lothian, Scotland

1	**Jack Nicklaus**	70	67	75	70	282
=2	**Doug Sanders**	71	70	72	70	283
	Dave Thomas	72	73	69	69	283
=4	**Bruce Devlin**	73	69	74	70	286
	Kel Nagle	72	68	76	70	286
	Gary Player	72	74	71	69	286
	Phil Rodgers	74	66	70	76	286
=8	**Dave Marr**	73	76	69	70	288
	Sebastian Miguel	74	72	70	72	288
	Arnold Palmer	73	72	69	74	288
	Peter Thomson	73	75	69	71	288
12	**R.H. Sikes**	73	72	73	72	290
=13	**Harold Henning**	71	69	75	76	291
	Christy O'Connor Sr	73	72	74	72	291
15	**Julius Boros**	73	71	76	72	292
=16	**Peter Butler**	73	65	80	75	293
	Alex Caygill	72	71	73	77	293
	Jimmy Hitchcock	70	77	74	72	293
	Ronnie Shade (a)	71	70	75	77	293
=20	**Peter Alliss**	74	72	75	73	294
	Roberto de Vicenzo	74	72	71	77	294
	Doug Sewell	76	69	74	75	294
=23	**Eric Brown**	78	72	71	74	295
	Peter Townsend (a)	73	75	72	75	295
	George Will	74	75	73	73	295
26	**Keith MacDonald**	75	74	70	77	296
=27	**Michael Bonallack (a)**	73	76	75	73	297
	Denis Hutchinson	74	73	73	77	297
	Bob Stanton	73	72	73	79	297
=30	**Fred Boobyer**	72	76	77	73	298
	Bobby Cole (a)	73	75	73	77	298
	Christy Greene	72	76	76	74	298
	Alan Henning	73	73	74	78	298
	Tony Jacklin	74	76	72	76	298
	Tony Lema	71	76	76	75	298

July 12–15, 1967

Royal Liverpool GC, Hoylake, Cheshire, England

1	**Roberto de Vicenzo**	70	71	67	70	278
2	**Jack Nicklaus**	71	69	71	69	280
=3	**Clive Clark**	70	73	69	72	284
	Gary Player	72	71	67	74	284
5	**Tony Jacklin**	73	69	73	70	285
=6	**Harold Henning**	74	70	71	71	286
	Sebastian Miguel	72	74	68	72	286
=8	**Al Balding**	74	71	69	73	287
	Hugh Boyle	74	74	71	68	287
	Bruce Devlin	70	70	72	75	287
	Tommy Horton	74	74	69	70	287
	Peter Thomson	71	74	70	72	287
=13	**Deane Beman**	72	76	68	73	289
	M. Hoyle	74	75	69	71	289
	Stanley Peach	71	75	73	70	289
	Lionel Platts	68	73	72	76	289
	Guy Wolstenholme	74	71	73	71	289
=18	**Barry Coxon**	73	76	71	70	290
	Hedley Muscroft	72	73	72	73	290
	Doug Sanders	71	73	73	73	290
21	**Christy O'Connor Sr**	70	74	71	76	291
=22	**Denis Hutchinson**	73	72	71	76	292
	Peter Mills	72	75	73	72	292
	Kel Nagle	70	74	69	79	292
=25	**Brian Barnes**	71	75	74	73	293

July 12–15, 1967 continued

	Robin Davenport	76	69	75	73	293
	Barry Franklin	70	74	73	76	293
	Brian Huggett	73	75	72	73	293
=29	**Fred Boobyer**	70	71	74	79	294
	Jimmy Hulme	69	72	73	80	294

July 10–13, 1968

Carnoustie GC, Angus, Scotland

1	**Gary Player**	74	71	71	73	289
=2	**Bob Charles**	72	72	71	76	291
	Jack Nicklaus	76	69	73	73	291
4	**Billy Casper**	72	68	74	78	292
5	**Maurice Bembridge**	71	75	73	74	293
=6	**Brian Barnes**	70	74	80	71	295
	Gay Brewer	74	73	72	76	295
	Neil Coles	75	76	71	73	295
9	**Al Balding**	74	76	74	72	296
=10	**Roberto de Vicenzo**	77	72	74	74	297
	Bruce Devlin	77	73	72	75	297
	Arnold Palmer	77	71	72	77	297
=13	**Peter Alliss**	73	78	72	75	298
	Bobby Cole	75	76	72	75	298
	Tommy Horton	77	74	73	74	298
	Brian Huggett	76	71	75	76	298
	Kel Nagle	74	75	75	74	298
=18	**Eric Brown**	76	76	74	73	299
	Tony Jacklin	72	72	75	80	299
	Paddy Skerritt	72	73	77	77	299
=21	**Michael Bonallack (a)**	70	77	74	79	300
	Sebastian Miguel	73	75	76	76	300
	D.L. Webster	77	71	78	74	300
=24	**Alex Caygill**	79	76	71	75	301
	Keith MacDonald	80	71	73	77	301
	Peter Thomson	77	71	78	75	301
=27	**Malcolm Gregson**	77	75	76	74	302
	Bob Shaw	75	76	73	78	302
	Dave Thomas	75	71	78	78	302
	Sandy Wilson	73	81	74	74	302

July 9–12, 1969

Royal Lytham and St Anne's, Lancashire, England

1	**Tony Jacklin**	68	70	70	72	280
2	**Bob Charles**	66	69	75	72	282
=3	**Roberto de Vicenzo**	72	73	66	72	283
	Peter Thomson	71	70	70	72	283
5	**Christy O'Connor Sr**	71	65	74	74	284
=6	**Davis Love Jr**	70	73	71	71	285
	Jack Nicklaus	75	70	68	72	285
8	**Peter Alliss**	73	74	73	66	286
9	**Kel Nagle**	74	71	72	70	287
10	**Miller Barber**	69	75	75	69	288
=11	**Neil Coles**	75	76	70	68	289
	Tommy Horton	71	76	70	72	289
	Cobie Legrange	79	70	71	69	289
	Guy Wolstenholme	70	71	76	72	289
15	**Gay Brewer**	76	71	68	75	290
=16	**Eric Brown**	73	76	69	73	291
	Bruce Devlin	71	73	75	72	291
	Harold Henning	72	71	75	73	291
	Brian Huggett	72	72	69	78	291
	Orville Moody	71	70	74	76	291
	Peter Townsend	73	70	76	72	291
	Bert Yancey	72	71	71	77	291
=23	**Bernard Hunt**	73	71	75	73	292

July 9–12, 1969 continued

	Gary Player	74	68	76	74	292
=25	**Fred Boobyer**	74	70	76	73	293
	Billy Casper	70	70	75	78	293
	Alex Caygill	71	67	79	76	293
=28	**Hedley Muscroft**	68	77	73	76	294
	Peter Tupling (a)	73	71	78	72	293
=30	**Max Faulkner**	71	74	76	74	295
	Jean Garaialde	69	77	76	73	295
	Mike Ingham	73	73	74	75	295
	Don Swaelens	72	73	76	74	295

July 8–11, 1970

Royal & Ancient GC, St Andrews, Fife, Scotland

** Jack Nicklaus (72) beat Doug Sanders (73) in the 18-hole play-off.*

1	**Jack Nicklaus***	68	69	73	73	283
2	**Doug Sanders**	68	71	71	73	283
=3	**Harold Henning**	67	72	73	73	285
	Lee Trevino	68	68	72	77	285
5	**Tony Jacklin**	67	70	73	76	286
=6	**Neil Coles**	65	74	72	76	287
	Peter Oosterhuis	73	69	69	76	287
8	**Hugh Jackson**	69	72	73	74	288
=9	**Tommy Horton**	66	73	75	75	289
	John Panton	72	73	73	71	289
	Peter Thomson	68	74	73	74	289
12	**Arnold Palmer**	68	72	76	74	290
=13	**Maurice Bembridge**	67	74	75	76	292
	Bob Charles	72	73	73	74	292
	J.C. Richardson	67	72	76	77	292
	Bert Yancey	71	71	73	77	292
=17	**Roberto Bernadini**	75	69	74	75	293
	Billy Casper	71	74	73	75	293
	Clive Clark	69	70	77	77	293
	Roberto de Vicenzo	71	76	71	75	293
	Christy O'Connor Sr	72	68	74	79	293
=22	**Walter Godfrey**	71	75	74	74	294
	Tom Weiskopf	70	74	72	78	294
	Guy Wolstenholme	68	77	72	77	294
=25	**Bruce Devlin**	72	76	72	75	295
	Graham Marsh	75	72	74	74	295
	Ronnie Shade	72	75	69	79	295
=28	**Stuart Brown**	73	73	71	79	296
	Bobby Cole	71	76	71	78	296
	Brian Huggett	68	78	73	77	296
	Tom Shaw	73	71	73	79	296

July 7–9, 1971

Royal Birkdale GC, Southport, Lancashire, England

1	**Lee Trevino**	69	70	69	70	278
2	**Liang Huan Lu**	70	70	69	70	279
3	**Tony Jacklin**	69	70	70	71	280
4	**Craig DeFoy**	72	72	68	69	281
=5	**Charles Coody**	74	71	70	68	283
	Jack Nicklaus	71	71	72	69	283
=7	**Billy Casper**	70	72	75	67	284
	Gary Player	71	70	71	72	284
=9	**Doug Sanders**	73	71	74	67	285
	Peter Thomson	70	73	73	69	285
=11	**Harry Bannerman**	73	71	72	71	287
	Roberto de Vicenzo	71	70	72	74	287
	Kel Nagle	70	75	73	69	287
	Ramon Sota	72	72	70	73	287
	Dave Stockton	74	74	68	71	287
	Bert Yancey	75	70	71	71	287

July 7–9, 1971 continued

17	**Dale Hayes**	71	72	70	75	288
=18	**Bob Charles**	77	71	71	70	289
	Peter Oosterhuis	76	71	66	76	289
=20	**Bernard Hunt**	74	73	73	70	290
	Howie Johnson	69	76	72	73	290
=22	**Michael Bonallack (a)**	71	72	75	73	291
	Neil Coles	76	72	72	71	291
	Hugh Jackson	71	73	72	75	291
=25	**Peter Butler**	73	73	73	73	292
	Vincente Fernandez	69	79	73	71	292
	Malcolm Gregson	71	71	73	77	292
	Brian Huggett	73	73	74	72	292
	Bill Large	73	75	73	71	292
	John Lister	74	71	74	73	292
	Doug Sewell	73	74	74	71	292
	Randall Vines	75	71	73	73	292

July 12–15, 1972

Honourable Company, Muirfield, East Lothian, Scotland

1	**Lee Trevino**	71	70	66	71	278
2	**Jack Nicklaus**	70	72	71	66	279
3	**Tony Jacklin**	69	72	67	72	280
4	**Doug Sanders**	71	71	69	70	281
5	**Brian Barnes**	71	72	69	71	283
6	**Gary Player**	71	71	76	67	285
=7	**Guy Hunt**	75	72	67	72	286
	Arnold Palmer	73	73	69	71	286
	David Vaughan	74	73	70	69	286
	Tom Weiskopf	73	74	70	69	286
=11	**Clive Clark**	72	71	73	71	287
	Dave Marr	70	74	71	72	287
=13	**Roberto Bernadini**	73	71	76	68	288
	Peter Townsend	70	72	76	70	288
=15	**Peter Butler**	72	75	73	69	289
	Bob Charles	75	70	74	70	289
	Jan Dorrestein	74	71	72	72	289
	Johnny Miller	76	66	72	75	289
=19	**Harry Bannerman**	77	73	73	67	290
	Frank Beard	70	76	74	70	290
	Maurice Bembridge	73	71	75	71	290
	Bert Yancey	73	72	72	73	290
=23	**Craig DeFoy**	70	75	71	75	291
	Doug McClelland	73	74	72	72	291
	Christy O'Connor Sr	73	74	73	71	291
=26	**Bruce Devlin**	75	70	77	70	292
	Brian Huggett	73	72	79	68	292
=28	**John Garner**	71	71	76	75	293
	Jerry Heard	75	75	71	72	293
	Peter Oosterhuis	75	75	73	70	293

July 11–14, 1973

Troon GC, Ayrshire, Scotland

1	**Tom Weiskopf**	68	67	71	70	276
=2	**Neil Coles**	71	72	70	66	279
	Johnny Miller	70	68	69	72	279
4	**Jack Nicklaus**	69	70	76	65	280
5	**Bert Yancey**	69	69	73	70	281
6	**Peter Butler**	71	72	74	69	286
=7	**Bob Charles**	73	71	73	71	288
	Christy O'Connor Sr	73	68	74	73	288
	Lanny Wadkins	71	73	70	74	288
=10	**Brian Barnes**	76	67	70	76	289
	Gay Brewer	76	71	72	70	289
	Harold Henning	73	73	73	70	289

July 11–14, 1973 continued

	Lee Trevino	75	73	73	68	289
=14	**Tony Jacklin**	75	73	72	70	290
	Doug McClelland	76	71	69	74	290
	Arnold Palmer	72	76	70	72	290
	Gary Player	76	69	76	69	290
=18	**Hugh Baiocchi**	75	74	69	74	292
	Hugh Boyle	75	75	69	73	292
	Bruce Crampton	71	76	73	72	292
	Bruce Devlin	72	78	71	71	292
	Bernard Gallacher	73	69	75	75	292
	D.J. Good	75	74	73	70	292
	Dave Hill	75	74	74	69	292
	Peter Oosterhuis	80	71	69	72	292
	Eddie Polland	74	73	73	72	292
	Peter Wilcock	71	76	72	73	292
=28	**Roberto de Vicenzo**	72	75	74	72	293
	Chi Chi Rodriguez	72	73	73	75	293
	Doug Sanders	79	72	72	70	293

July 10–13, 1974

Royal Lytham and St Anne's GC, Lancashire, England

1	**Gary Player**	69	68	75	70	282
2	**Peter Oosterhuis**	71	71	73	71	286
3	**Jack Nicklaus**	74	72	70	71	287
4	**Hubert Green**	71	74	72	71	288
=5	**Danny Edwards**	70	73	76	73	292
	Liang-Huan Lu	72	72	75	73	292
=7	**Bobby Cole**	70	72	76	75	293
	Don Swaelens	77	73	74	69	293
	Tom Weiskopf	72	72	74	75	293
10	**Johnny Miller**	72	75	73	74	294
=11	**John Garner**	75	78	73	69	295
	David Graham	76	74	76	69	295
=13	**Neil Coles**	72	75	75	74	296
	Al Geiberger	76	70	76	74	296
	John Morgan	69	75	76	76	296
	Alan Tapie	73	77	73	73	296
	Peter Townsend	79	76	72	69	296
=18	**Peter Dawson**	74	74	73	76	297
	Tony Jacklin	74	77	71	75	297
	Gene Littler	77	76	70	74	297
	Dewitt Weaver	73	80	70	74	297
=22	**Ronnie Shade**	78	75	73	72	298
	Lanny Wadkins	78	71	75	74	298
=24	**Bernard Gallacher**	76	72	76	75	299
	Angel Gallardo	74	77	75	73	299
	Hale Irwin	76	73	79	71	299
	Christy O'Connor Jr	78	76	72	73	299
=28	**Ben Crenshaw**	74	80	76	70	300
	David Jagger	80	71	76	73	300
	Doug McClelland	75	79	73	73	300

July 9–12, 1975

Carnoustie GC, Angus, Scotland

** Tom Watson (71) beat Jack Newton (72) in the 18-hole play-off.*

1	**Tom Watson***	71	67	79	72	279
2	**Jack Newton**	69	71	75	74	279
=3	**Bobby Cole**	72	66	66	76	280
	Johnny Miller	71	69	66	74	280
	Jack Nicklaus	69	71	68	72	280
6	**Graham Marsh**	72	67	71	71	281
=7	**Neil Coles**	72	69	67	74	282
	Peter Oosterhuis	68	70	71	73	282
9	**Hale Irwin**	69	70	69	75	283

July 9–12, 1975 continued

=10	**George Burns**	71	73	69	71	284
	John Mahaffey	71	68	69	76	284
=12	**Bob Charles**	74	73	70	69	286
	P. Leonard	70	69	73	74	286
	Andries Oosthuizen	69	69	70	78	286
15	**Tom Weiskopf**	73	72	70	72	287
=16	**Maurice Bembridge**	75	73	67	73	288
	Arnold Palmer	74	72	69	73	288
	Alan Tapie	70	72	67	79	288
=19	**Bernard Gallacher**	72	67	72	78	289
	Lon Hinckle	76	72	69	72	289
	Tommy Horton	72	71	71	75	289
	Sam Torrance	72	74	71	72	289
=23	**Brian Barnes**	71	74	72	73	290
	Hugh Baiocchi	72	72	73	73	290
	Danny Edwards	70	74	71	75	290
	Ray Floyd	71	72	76	71	290
	Martin Foster	72	74	73	71	290
=28	**Roberto de Vicenzo**	71	74	72	74	291
	David Graham	74	70	72	75	291
	Simon Hobday	70	70	76	75	291
	Guy Hunt	73	68	76	74	291

July 7–10, 1976

Royal Birkdale GC, Southport, Lancashire, England

1	**Johnny Miller**	72	68	73	66	279
=2	**Seve Ballesteros**	69	69	73	74	285
	Jack Nicklaus	74	70	72	69	285
4	**Ray Floyd**	76	67	73	70	286
=5	**Hubert Green**	72	70	78	68	288
	Tommy Horton	74	69	72	73	288
	Mark James	76	72	74	66	288
	Tom Kite	70	74	73	71	288
	Christy O'Connor Jr	69	73	75	71	288
=10	**George Burns**	75	69	75	70	289
	Peter Butler	74	72	73	70	289
	Vincente Fernandez	79	71	69	70	289
	Norio Suzuki	69	75	75	70	289
14	**Brian Barnes**	70	73	75	72	290
=15	**Eamonn Darcy**	78	71	71	71	291
	John Fourie	71	74	75	71	291
=17	**Graham Marsh**	71	73	72	76	292
	Jack Newton	70	74	76	72	292
	Tom Weiskopf	73	72	76	71	292
	Guy Wolstenholme	76	72	71	73	292
=21	**Stewart Ginn**	78	72	72	71	293
	David Graham	77	70	75	71	293
	Simon Hobday	79	71	75	68	293
	Chi-San Hsu	81	69	71	72	293
	David Huish	73	74	72	74	293
	Bob Shearer	76	73	75	69	293
	Alan Tapie	74	72	75	72	293
=28	**Neil Coles**	74	77	70	73	294
	Nick Faldo	78	71	76	69	294
	Gary Player	72	72	79	71	294
	Doug Sanders	77	73	73	71	294

July 6–9, 1977

Turnberry GC, Ayrshire, Scotland

1	**Tom Watson**	68	70	65	65	268
2	**Jack Nicklaus**	68	70	65	66	269
3	**Hubert Green**	72	66	74	67	279
4	**Lee Trevino**	68	70	72	70	280
=5	**George Burns**	70	70	72	69	281

July 6–9, 1977 continued

	Ben Crenshaw	71	69	66	75	281
7	**Arnold Palmer**	73	73	67	69	282
8	**Ray Floyd**	70	73	68	72	283
=9	**Mark Hayes**	76	63	72	73	284
	Tommy Horton	70	74	65	75	284
	Johnny Miller	69	74	67	74	284
	John Schroeder	66	74	73	71	284
=13	**Howard Clark**	72	68	72	74	286
	Peter Thomson	74	72	67	73	286
=15	**Seve Ballesteros**	69	71	73	74	287
	Peter Butler	71	68	75	73	287
	Bobby Cole	72	71	71	73	287
	Guy Hunt	73	71	71	72	287
	Graham Marsh	73	69	71	74	287
	Jerry Pate	74	70	70	73	287
	Bob Shearer	72	69	72	74	287
=22	**Peter Dawson**	74	68	73	73	288
	John Fourie	74	69	70	75	288
	Gary Player	71	74	74	69	288
	Tom Weiskopf	74	71	71	72	288
=26	**Gaylord Burrows**	69	72	68	80	289
	Martin Foster	67	74	75	73	289
	Angel Gallardo	78	65	72	74	289
	David Ingram	73	74	70	72	289
	Roger Maltbie	71	66	72	80	289
	Rik Massengale	73	71	74	71	289
	John O'Leary	74	73	68	74	289
	Norio Suzuki	74	71	69	75	289

July 12–15, 1978

Royal & Ancient GC, St Andrews, Fife, Scotland

1	**Jack Nicklaus**	71	72	69	69	281
=2	**Ben Crenshaw**	70	69	73	71	283
	Ray Floyd	69	75	71	68	283
	Tom Kite	72	69	72	70	283
	Simon Owen	70	75	67	71	283
6	**Peter Oosterhuis**	72	70	69	73	284
=7	**Isao Aoki**	68	71	73	73	285
	Nick Faldo	71	72	70	72	285
	John Schroeder	74	69	70	72	285
	Bob Shearer	71	69	74	71	285
=11	**Michael Cahill**	71	72	75	68	286
	Dale Hayes	74	70	71	71	286
	Orville Moody	73	69	74	70	286
=14	**Mark Hayes**	70	75	75	67	287
	Jumbo Ozaki	72	69	75	71	287
	Tom Watson	73	68	70	76	287
=17	**Seve Ballesteros**	69	70	76	73	288
	Bob Byman	72	69	74	73	288
	Guy Hunt	71	73	71	73	288
	Tommy Nakajima	70	71	76	71	288
	Tom Weiskopf	69	72	72	75	288
=22	**Bernard Gallacher**	72	71	76	70	289
	Nick Job	73	75	68	73	289
=24	**Antonio Garrido**	73	71	76	70	290
	Hale Irwin	75	71	76	78	290
	Carl Mason	70	74	72	74	290
	Jack Newton	69	76	71	74	290
	Peter Thomson	72	70	72	76	290
=29	**Tienie Britz**	73	74	72	72	291
	Hubert Green	78	70	67	76	291
	John Morgan	74	68	77	72	291
	Greg Norman	72	73	74	72	291
	Lee Trevino	75	72	73	71	291

July 18–21, 1979

Royal Lytham and St Anne's GC, Lancashire, England

1	**Seve Ballesteros**	73	65	75	70	283
=2	**Ben Crenshaw**	72	71	72	71	286
	Jack Nicklaus	72	69	73	72	286
4	**Mark James**	76	69	69	73	287
5	**Rodger Davis**	75	70	70	72	288
6	**Hale Irwin**	68	68	75	78	289
=7	**Isao Aoki**	70	74	72	75	291
	Bob Byman	73	70	72	76	291
	Graham Marsh	74	68	75	74	291
=10	**Bob Charles**	78	72	70	72	292
	Greg Norman	73	71	72	76	292
	Jumbo Ozaki	75	69	75	72	292
=13	**Wally Armstrong**	74	74	73	72	293
	Terry Gale	71	74	75	73	293
	John O'Leary	73	73	74	73	293
	Simon Owen	75	76	74	68	293
=17	**Peter McEvoy (a)**	71	74	72	77	294
	Lee Trevino	71	73	74	76	294
=19	**Ken Brown**	72	71	75	77	295
	Nick Faldo	74	74	78	69	295
	Sandy Lyle	74	76	75	70	295
	Orville Moody	71	74	76	74	295
	Gary Player	77	74	69	75	295
=24	**Tony Jacklin**	73	74	76	73	296
	Tohru Nakamura	77	75	67	77	296
=26	**Jerry Pate**	69	74	76	78	297
	Ed Sneed	76	75	70	76	297
	Peter Thomson	76	75	72	74	297
	Tom Watson	72	68	76	81	297
=30	**Mark Hayes**	75	75	77	71	298
	Simon Hobday	75	77	71	75	298
	Tom Kite	73	74	77	74	298
	Bill Longmuir	65	74	77	82	298
	Armando Saavedra	76	76	73	73	298
	Bobby Verway	75	77	74	72	298

July 17–20, 1980

Honourable Company, Muirfield, East Lothian, Scotland

1	**Tom Watson**	68	70	64	69	271
2	**Lee Trevino**	68	67	71	69	275
3	**Ben Crenshaw**	70	70	68	69	277
=4	**Carl Mason**	72	69	70	69	280
	Jack Nicklaus	73	67	71	69	280
=6	**Andy Bean**	71	69	70	72	282
	Ken Brown	70	68	68	76	282
	Hubert Green	77	69	64	72	282
	Craig Stadler	72	70	69	71	282
=10	**Gil Morgan**	70	70	71	72	283
	Jack Newton	69	71	73	70	283
=12	**Isao Aoki**	74	74	63	73	284
	Nick Faldo	69	74	71	70	284
	Sandy Lyle	70	71	70	73	284
	Larry Nelson	72	70	71	71	284
=16	**John Bland**	73	70	70	73	285
	Jerry Pate	71	67	74	73	285
	Tom Weiskopf	72	72	71	70	285
=19	**Seve Ballesteros**	72	68	72	74	286
	Bruce Lietzke	74	69	73	70	286
	Bill Rogers	76	73	68	69	286
	Norio Suzuki	74	68	72	72	286
=23	**Gary Cullen**	72	72	69	74	287
	Bill McColl	75	73	68	71	287
	Mark McNulty	71	73	72	71	287

July 17–20, 1980 continued

	Peter Oosterhuis	72	71	75	69	287
=27	**Tom Kite**	72	72	74	70	288
	Nick Price	72	71	71	74	288
=29	**Hugh Baiocchi**	76	67	69	77	289
	Neil Coles	75	69	69	76	289
	David Graham	73	71	68	77	289

July 16–19, 1981

Royal St George's, Sandwich, Kent, England

1	**Bill Rogers**	72	66	67	71	276
2	**Bernhard Langer**	73	67	70	70	280
=3	**Ray Floyd**	74	70	69	70	283
	Mark James	72	70	68	73	283
5	**Sam Torrance**	72	69	73	70	284
=6	**Bruce Lietzke**	76	69	71	69	285
	Manuel Pinero	73	74	68	70	285
=8	**Howard Clark**	72	76	70	68	286
	Ben Crenshaw	72	67	76	71	286
	Brian Jones	73	76	66	71	286
=11	**Isao Aoki**	71	73	69	74	287
	Nick Faldo	77	68	69	73	287
	Lee Trevino	77	67	70	73	287
=14	**Brian Barnes**	76	70	70	72	288
	Eamonn Darcy	79	69	70	70	288
	David Graham	71	71	74	72	288
	Nick Job	70	69	75	74	288
	Sandy Lyle	73	73	71	71	288
=19	**Gordon J. Brand**	78	65	74	72	289
	Graham Marsh	75	71	72	71	289
	Jerry Pate	73	73	69	74	289
	Peter Townsend	73	70	73	73	289
=23	**Hubert Green**	75	72	74	69	290
	Tony Jacklin	71	71	73	75	290
	Mark McNulty	74	74	74	68	290
	Jack Nicklaus	83	66	71	70	290
	Simon Owen	71	74	70	75	290
	Arnold Palmer	72	74	73	71	290
	Nick Price	77	68	76	69	290
	Tom Watson	73	69	75	73	290

July 15–18, 1982

Royal Troon GC, Ayrshire, Scotland

1	**Tom Watson**	69	71	74	70	284
=2	**Peter Oosterhuis**	74	67	74	70	285
	Nick Price	69	69	74	73	285
=4	**Nick Faldo**	73	73	71	69	286
	Masahiro Kuramoto	71	73	71	71	286
	Tom Purtzer	76	66	75	69	286
	Des Smyth	70	69	74	73	286
=8	**Sandy Lyle**	74	66	73	74	287
	Fuzzy Zoeller	73	71	73	70	287
=10	**Bobby Clampett**	67	66	78	77	288
	Jack Nicklaus	77	70	72	69	288
12	**Sam Torrance**	73	72	73	71	289
=13	**Seve Ballesteros**	71	75	73	71	290
	Bernhard Langer	70	69	78	73	290
=15	**Ben Crenshaw**	74	75	72	70	291
	Ray Floyd	74	73	77	67	291
	Curtis Strange	72	73	76	70	291
	Denis Watson	75	69	73	74	291
19	**Ken Brown**	70	71	79	72	292
=20	**Isao Aoki**	75	69	75	74	293
	Tohru Nakamura	77	68	77	71	293
=22	**Jose-Maria Canizares**	71	72	79	72	294

	July 15–18, 1982 continued					
	Johnny Miller	71	76	75	72	294
	Bill Rogers	73	70	76	75	294
=25	**Bernard Gallacher**	75	71	74	75	295
	Graham Marsh	76	76	72	71	295
=27	**David Graham**	73	70	76	77	296
	Jay Haas	78	72	75	71	296
	Greg Norman	73	75	76	72	296
	Arnold Palmer	71	73	78	74	296
	Lee Trevino	78	72	71	75	296

July 14–17, 1983

Royal Birkdale GC, Southport, Lancashire, England

1	**Tom Watson**	67	68	70	70	275
=2	**Andy Bean**	70	69	70	67	276
	Hale Irwin	69	68	72	67	276
4	**Graham Marsh**	69	70	74	64	277
5	**Lee Trevino**	69	66	73	70	278
=6	**Seve Ballesteros**	71	71	69	68	279
	Harold Henning	71	69	70	69	279
=8	**Denis Durnian**	73	66	74	67	280
	Nick Faldo	68	68	71	73	280
	Christy O'Connor Jr	72	69	71	68	280
	Bill Rogers	67	71	73	69	280
=12	**Peter Jacobsen**	72	69	70	70	281
	Craig Stadler	64	70	72	75	281
=14	**Ray Floyd**	72	66	69	75	282
	David Graham	71	69	67	75	282
	Gary Koch	75	71	66	70	282
	Mike Sullivan	72	68	74	68	282
	Fuzzy Zoeller	71	71	67	73	282
=19	**Tienie Britz**	71	74	69	69	283
	Bernard Gallacher	72	71	70	70	283
	Hubert Green	69	74	72	68	283
	Jay Haas	73	72	68	70	283
	Simon Hobday	70	73	70	70	283
	Greg Norman	75	71	70	67	283
	Brian Waites	70	70	73	70	283
=26	**Howard Clark**	71	72	69	72	284
	Eamonn Darcy	69	72	74	69	284
	Rodger Davis	70	71	70	73	284
=29	**Terry Gale**	72	66	72	75	285
	Mark James	70	70	74	71	285
	Tom Kite	71	72	72	70	285
	C.S. Lu	71	72	74	68	285
	Mike McCullough	74	69	72	70	285
	Tohru Nakamura	73	69	72	71	285
	Jack Nicklaus	71	72	72	70	285
	Curtis Strange	74	68	70	73	285
	Hal Sutton	68	71	75	71	285
	Lanny Wadkins	72	73	72	68	285

July 19–22, 1984

Royal & Ancient GC, St Andrews, Fife, Scotland

1	**Seve Ballesteros**	69	68	70	69	276
=2	**Bernhard Langer**	71	68	68	71	278
	Tom Watson	71	68	66	73	278
=4	**Fred Couples**	70	69	74	68	281
	Lanny Wadkins	70	69	73	69	281
=6	**Nick Faldo**	69	68	76	69	282
	Greg Norman	67	74	74	67	282
8	**Mark McCumber**	74	67	72	70	283
=9	**Hugh Baiocchi**	72	70	70	72	284
	Ian Baker-Finch	68	66	71	79	284
	Graham Marsh	70	74	73	67	284

	July 19–22, 1984 continued					
	Ronan Rafferty	74	72	67	71	284
	Sam Torrance	74	74	66	70	284
=14	**Andy Bean**	72	69	75	69	285
	Bill Bergin	75	73	66	71	285
	Ken Brown	74	71	72	68	285
	Hale Irwin	75	68	70	72	285
	Sandy Lyle	75	71	72	67	285
	Peter Senior	74	70	70	71	285
	Lee Trevino	70	67	75	73	285
	Fuzzy Zoeller	71	72	71	71	285
=22	**Ben Crenshaw**	72	75	70	69	286
	Peter Jacobsen	67	73	73	73	286
	Tom Kite	69	71	74	72	286
	Gil Morgan	71	71	71	73	286
	Corey Pavin	71	74	72	69	286
	Paul Way	73	72	69	72	286
=28	**Terry Gale**	71	74	72	70	287
	Jaime Gonzalez	69	71	76	71	287
	Craig Stadler	75	70	70	72	287

July 18–21, 1985

Royal St George's, Sandwich, Kent, England

1	**Sandy Lyle**	68	71	73	70	282
2	**Payne Stewart**	70	75	70	68	283
=3	**David Graham**	68	71	70	75	284
	Bernhard Langer	72	69	68	75	284
	Christy O'Connor Jr	64	76	72	72	284
	Mark O'Meara	70	72	70	72	284
	Jose Rivero	74	72	70	68	284
=8	**Anders Forsbrand**	70	76	69	70	285
	Tom Kite	73	73	67	72	285
	D.A. Weibring	69	71	74	71	285
=11	**Jose-Maria Canizares**	72	75	70	69	286
	Eamonn Darcy	76	68	74	68	286
	Peter Jacobsen	71	74	68	73	286
	Gary Koch	75	72	70	69	286
	Fuzzy Zoeller	69	76	70	71	286
=16	**Simon Bishop**	71	75	72	69	287
	Greg Norman	71	72	71	73	287
	Sam Torrance	74	74	69	70	287
	Ian Woosnam	70	71	71	75	287
=20	**Ian Baker-Finch**	71	73	74	70	288
	Jaime Gonzalez	72	72	73	71	288
	Mark James	71	68	66	73	288
	Graham Marsh	71	75	70	73	288
	Lee Trevino	73	76	68	71	288
=25	**Gordon J. Brand**	73	72	72	72	289
	Michael Cahill	72	74	71	72	289
	David Frost	70	74	73	72	289
	Robert Lee	68	73	74	74	289
	Kristen Moe	70	76	73	70	289
	Jose-Maria Olazabal (a)	72	76	71	70	289
	Philip Parkin	68	76	77	68	289
	Manuel Pinero	71	73	72	73	289

July 17–20, 1986

Turnberry GC, Ayrshire, Scotland

1	**Greg Norman**	74	63	74	69	280
2	**Gordon J. Brand**	71	68	75	71	285
=3	**Bernhard Langer**	72	70	76	68	286
	Ian Woosnam	70	74	70	72	286
5	**Nick Faldo**	71	70	76	70	287
=6	**Seve Ballesteros**	76	75	73	64	288
	Gary Koch	73	72	72	71	288

July 17–20, 1986 continued

=8	**Brian Marchbank**	78	70	72	69	289
	Tommy Nakajima	74	67	71	77	289
	Fuzzy Zoeller	75	73	72	69	289
=11	**Jose-Maria Canizares**	76	68	73	73	290
	David Graham	75	73	70	72	290
	Christy O'Connor Jr	75	71	75	69	290
=14	**Andy Bean**	74	73	73	71	291
	Curtis Strange	79	69	74	69	291
=16	**Ray Floyd**	78	67	73	74	292
	Anders Forsbrand	71	73	77	71	292
	Jose-Maria Olazabal	78	69	72	73	292
=19	**Bob Charles**	76	72	73	72	293
	Manuel Pinero	78	71	70	74	293
=21	**Derrick Cooper**	72	79	72	71	294
	Ben Crenshaw	77	69	75	73	294
	Danny Edwards	77	73	70	74	294
	Vincente Fernandez	78	70	71	75	294
	Robert Lee	71	75	75	73	294
	Philip Parkin	78	70	72	74	294
	Ronan Rafferty	75	74	75	70	294
	Vaughan Somers	73	77	72	72	294
	Sam Torrance	78	69	71	76	294
=30	**Masahiro Kuramoto**	77	73	73	72	295
	Sandy Lyle	78	73	70	74	295
	John Mahaffey	75	73	75	72	295
	Ian Stanley	72	74	78	71	295
	D.A. Weibring	75	70	76	74	295

July 16–19, 1987

Honourable Company, Muirfield, East Lothian, Scotland

1	**Nick Faldo**	68	69	71	71	279
=2	**Paul Azinger**	68	68	71	73	280
	Rodger Davis	64	73	74	69	280
=4	**Ben Crenshaw**	73	68	72	68	281
	Payne Stewart	71	66	72	72	281
6	**David Frost**	70	68	70	74	282
7	**Tom Watson**	69	69	71	74	283
=8	**Nick Price**	68	71	72	73	284
	Craig Stadler	69	69	71	75	284
	Ian Woosnam	71	69	72	72	284
=11	**Mark Calcavecchia**	69	70	72	74	285
	Graham Marsh	69	70	72	74	285
	Mark McNulty	71	69	75	70	285
	Jose-Maria Olazabal	70	73	70	72	285
	Jumbo Ozaki	69	72	71	73	285
	Hal Sutton	71	70	73	71	285
=17	**Ken Brown**	69	73	70	74	286
	Eamonn Darcy	74	69	72	71	286
	Ray Floyd	72	68	70	76	286
	Wayne Grady	70	71	76	69	286
	Bernhard Langer	69	69	76	72	286
	Sandy Lyle	76	69	71	70	286
	Mark Roe	74	68	72	72	286
	Lee Trevino	67	74	73	72	286
25	**Gerard Taylor**	69	68	75	75	287
=26	**Gordon Brand Jr**	73	70	75	70	288
	David Feherty	74	70	77	67	288
	Larry Mize	68	71	76	73	288
=29	**Danny Edwards**	71	73	72	73	289
	Anders Forsbrand	73	69	73	74	289
	Ken Green	67	76	74	72	289
	Lanny Wadkins	72	71	75	71	289
	Fuzzy Zoeller	71	70	76	72	289

July 14–18, 1988

Royal Lytham and St Anne's GC, Lancashire, England

1	**Seve Ballesteros**	67	71	70	65	273
2	**Nick Price**	70	67	69	69	275
3	**Nick Faldo**	71	69	68	71	279
=4	**Fred Couples**	73	69	71	68	281
	Gary Koch	71	72	70	68	281
6	**Peter Senior**	70	73	70	69	282
=7	**Isao Aoki**	72	71	73	67	283
	David Frost	71	75	69	68	283
	Sandy Lyle	73	69	67	74	283
	Payne Stewart	73	75	68	67	283
=11	**Brad Faxon**	69	74	70	71	284
	David J. Russell	71	74	69	70	284
=13	**Larry Nelson**	73	71	68	73	285
	Eduardo Romero	72	71	69	73	285
	Curtis Strange	79	69	69	68	285
=16	**Andy Bean**	71	70	71	74	286
	Ben Crenshaw	73	73	68	72	286
	Don Pooley	70	73	69	74	286
	Jose Rivero	75	69	70	72	286
=20	**Gordon Brand Jr**	72	76	68	71	287
	Bob Charles	71	74	69	73	287
	Rodger Davis	76	71	72	68	287
	Tom Kite	75	71	73	68	287
	Bob Tway	71	71	72	73	287
=25	**Jack Nicklaus**	75	70	75	68	288
	Ian Woosnam	76	71	72	69	288
27	**Mark O'Meara**	75	69	75	70	289
=28	**Tommy Armour III**	73	72	72	73	290
	Chip Beck	72	71	74	73	290
	Jim Benepe	75	72	70	73	290
	Howard Clark	71	72	75	72	290
	Mark McNulty	73	73	72	72	290
	Tom Watson	74	72	72	72	290

July 20–23, 1989

Royal Troon GC, Ayrshire, Scotland

** Mark Calcavecchia (4-3-3-3) beat Wayne Grady (4-4-4-4) and Greg Norman (3-3-4-x) in the four-hole play-off.*

1	**Mark Calcavecchia***	71	68	68	68	275
=2	**Wayne Grady**	68	67	69	71	275
	Greg Norman	69	70	72	64	275
4	**Tom Watson**	69	68	68	72	277
5	**Jodie Mudd**	73	67	68	70	278
=6	**Fred Couples**	68	71	68	72	279
	David Feherty	71	67	69	72	279
=8	**Paul Azinger**	68	73	67	72	280
	Eduardo Romero	68	70	75	67	280
	Payne Stewart	72	65	69	74	280
=11	**Nick Faldo**	71	71	70	69	281
	Mark McNulty	75	70	70	66	281
=13	**Roger Chapman**	76	68	67	71	282
	Howard Clark	72	68	72	70	282
	Mark James	69	70	71	72	282
	Steve Pate	69	70	70	73	282
	Craig Stadler	73	69	69	71	282
	Philip Walton	69	74	69	70	282
=19	**Derrick Cooper**	69	70	76	68	283
	Tom Kite	70	74	67	72	283
	Larry Mize	71	74	66	72	283
	Don Pooley	73	70	69	71	283
=23	**Davis Love III**	72	70	73	69	284
	Jose-Maria Olazabal	68	72	69	75	284
	Vijay Singh	71	73	69	71	284

July 20–23, 1989 continued

=26	**Chip Beck**	75	69	68	73	285
	Stephen Bennett	75	69	68	73	285
	Scott Simpson	73	66	72	74	285
	Lanny Wadkins	72	70	69	74	285
=30	**Ian Baker-Finch**	72	69	70	75	286
	Mark Davis	77	68	67	74	286
	Jeff Hawkes	75	67	69	75	286
	Peter Jacobsen	71	74	71	70	286
	Gary Koch	72	71	74	69	286
	Brian Marchbank	69	74	73	70	286
	Miguel Martin	68	73	73	72	286
	Jack Nicklaus	74	71	71	70	286
	Jumbo Ozaki	71	73	70	72	286

July 19–22, 1990

Royal & Ancient GC, St Andrews, Fife, Scotland

1	**Nick Faldo**	67	65	67	71	270
=2	**Mark McNulty**	74	68	68	65	275
	Payne Stewart	68	68	68	71	275
=4	**Jodie Mudd**	72	66	72	66	276
	Ian Woosnam	68	69	70	69	276
=6	**Ian Baker-Finch**	68	72	64	73	277
	Greg Norman	66	66	76	69	277
=8	**David Graham**	72	71	70	66	279
	Donnie Hammond	70	71	68	70	279
	Steve Pate	70	68	72	69	279
	Corey Pavin	71	69	68	71	279
=12	**Paul Broadhurst**	74	69	63	74	280
	Robert Gamez	70	72	67	71	280
	Tim Simpson	70	69	69	72	280
	Vijay Singh	70	69	72	69	280
=16	**Peter Jacobsen**	68	70	70	73	281
	Steve Jones	72	67	72	70	281
	Sandy Lyle	72	70	67	72	281
	Frank Nobilo	72	67	68	74	281
	Jose-Maria Olazabal	71	67	71	72	281
	Mark Roe	71	70	72	68	281
=22	**Eamonn Darcy**	71	71	72	68	282
	Craig Parry	68	68	69	77	282
	Jamie Spence	72	65	73	72	282
=25	**Fred Couples**	71	70	70	72	283
	Christy O'Connor Jr	68	72	71	72	283
	Nick Price	70	67	71	75	283
	Jose Rivero	70	70	70	73	283
	Jeff Sluman	72	70	70	71	283
	Lee Trevino	69	70	73	71	283

July 18–21, 1991

Royal Birkdale GC, Southport, Lancashire, England

1	**Ian Baker-Finch**	71	71	64	66	272
2	**Mike Harwood**	68	70	69	67	274
=3	**Fred Couples**	72	69	70	64	275
	Mark O'Meara	71	68	67	69	275
=5	**Eamonn Darcy**	73	68	66	70	277
	Jodie Mudd	72	70	72	63	277
	Bob Tway	75	66	70	66	277
8	**Craig Parry**	71	70	69	68	278
=9	**Seve Ballesteros**	66	73	69	71	279
	Bernhard Langer	71	71	70	67	279
	Greg Norman	74	68	71	66	279
=12	**Roger Chapman**	74	66	71	69	280
	Rodger Davis	70	71	73	66	280
	Vijay Singh	71	69	69	71	280
	Magnus Sunesson	72	73	68	67	280

July 18–21, 1991 continued

	David Williams	74	71	68	67	280
=17	**Chip Beck**	67	78	70	66	281
	Paul Broadhurst	71	73	68	69	281
	Nick Faldo	68	75	70	68	281
	Barry Lane	68	72	71	70	281
	Mark Mouland	68	74	68	71	281
	Peter Senior	74	67	71	69	281
	Andrew Sherborne	73	70	68	70	281
	Lee Trevino	71	72	71	67	281
	Ian Woosnam	70	72	69	70	281
=26	**Wayne Grady**	69	70	73	70	282
	Mark James	72	68	70	72	282
	Colin Montgomerie	71	69	71	71	282
	Mike Reid	68	71	70	73	282
	Eduardo Romero	70	73	68	71	282
	Tom Watson	69	72	72	69	282

July 16–19, 1992

Honourable Company, Muirfield, East Lothian, Scotland

1	**Nick Faldo**	66	64	69	73	272
2	**John Cook**	66	67	70	70	273
3	**Jose-Maria Olazabal**	70	67	69	68	274
4	**Steve Pate**	64	70	69	73	276
=5	**Gordon J. Brand**	65	68	72	74	279
	Ernie Els	66	69	70	74	279
	Donnie Hammond	70	65	70	74	279
	Robert Karlsson	70	68	70	71	279
	Malcolm Mackenzie	71	67	70	71	279
	Andrew Magee	67	72	70	70	279
	Ian Woosnam	65	73	70	71	279
=12	**Chip Beck**	71	68	67	74	280
	Ray Floyd	64	71	73	72	280
	Sandy Lyle	68	70	70	72	280
	Mark O'Meara	71	68	72	69	280
	Larry Rinker	69	68	70	73	280
	Jamie Spence	71	68	70	71	280
18	**Greg Norman**	71	72	70	68	281
=19	**Ian Baker-Finch**	71	71	72	68	282
	Hale Irwin	70	73	67	72	282
	Tom Kite	70	69	71	72	282
=22	**Paul Lawrie**	70	72	68	73	283
	Peter Mitchell	69	71	72	71	283
	Tom Purtzer	68	69	75	71	283
=25	**Billy Andrade**	69	71	70	74	284
	Peter Senior	70	69	70	75	284
	Duffy Waldorf	69	70	73	72	284
=28	**Mark Calcavecchia**	69	71	73	72	285
	Russ Cochran	71	68	72	74	285
	Mats Lanner	72	68	71	74	285
	Mark McNulty	71	70	70	74	285
	Jodie Mudd	71	69	74	71	285
	Craig Parry	67	71	76	71	285

July 15–18, 1993

Royal St George's, Sandwich, Kent, England

1	**Greg Norman**	66	68	69	64	267
2	**Nick Faldo**	69	63	70	67	269
3	**Bernhard Langer**	67	66	70	67	270
=4	**Corey Pavin**	68	66	68	70	272
	Peter Senior	66	69	70	67	272
=6	**Ernie Els**	68	69	69	68	274
	Paul Lawrie	72	68	69	65	274
	Nick Price	68	70	67	69	274
=9	**Fred Couples**	68	66	72	69	275

	July 15–18, 1993 continued					
	Wayne Grady	74	68	64	69	275
	Scott Simpson	68	70	71	66	275
12	**Payne Stewart**	71	72	70	63	276
13	**Barry Lane**	70	68	71	68	277
=14	**Mark Calcavecchia**	66	73	71	68	278
	John Daly	71	66	70	71	278
	Tom Kite	72	70	68	68	278
	Mark McNulty	67	71	71	69	278
	Gil Morgan	70	68	70	70	278
	Jose Rivero	68	73	67	70	278
	Fuzzy Zoeller	66	70	71	71	278
=21	**Peter Baker**	70	67	74	68	279
	Howard Clark	67	72	70	70	279
	Jesper Parnevik	68	74	68	69	279
=24	**Rodger Davis**	68	71	71	70	280
	David Frost	69	73	70	68	280
	Mark Roe	70	71	73	66	280
=27	**Seve Ballesteros**	68	73	69	71	281
	Mark James	70	70	70	71	281
	Malcolm Mackenzie	72	71	71	67	281
	Larry Mize	67	69	74	71	281
	Yoshinori Mizumaki	69	69	73	70	281
	Iain Pyman (a)	68	72	70	71	281
	Des Smyth	67	74	70	70	281

July 14–17, 1994

Turnberry GC, Ayrshire, Scotland

1	**Nick Price**	69	66	67	66	268
2	**Jesper Parnevik**	68	66	68	67	269
3	**Fuzzy Zoeller**	71	66	64	70	271
=4	**David Feherty**	68	69	66	70	273
	Anders Forsbrand	72	71	66	64	273
	Mark James	72	67	66	68	273
7	**Brad Faxon**	69	65	67	73	274
=8	**Nick Faldo**	75	66	70	64	275
	Tom Kite	71	69	66	70	275
	Colin Montgomerie	72	69	65	69	275
=11	**Mark Calcavecchia**	71	70	67	68	276
	Russell Claydon	72	71	68	65	276
	Jonathan Lomas	66	70	72	68	276
	Mark McNulty	71	70	68	67	276
	Larry Mize	73	69	64	70	276
	Frank Nobilo	69	67	72	68	276
	Greg Norman	71	67	69	69	276
	Ronan Rafferty	71	66	65	74	276
	Tom Watson	68	65	69	74	276
=20	**Mark Brooks**	74	64	71	68	277
	Peter Senior	68	71	67	71	277
	Vijay Singh	70	68	69	70	277
	Greg Turner	65	71	70	71	277
=24	**Andrew Coltart**	71	69	66	72	278
	Ernie Els	69	69	69	71	278
	Bob Estes	72	68	72	66	278
	Peter Jacobsen	69	70	67	72	278
	Paul Lawrie	71	69	70	68	278
	Tom Lehman	70	69	70	69	278
	Jeff Maggert	69	74	67	68	278
	Terry Price	74	65	71	68	278
	Loren Roberts	68	69	69	72	278
	Mike Springer	72	67	68	71	278
	Craig Stadler	71	69	66	72	278

July 20–23, 1995

Royal & Ancient GC, St Andrews, Fife, Scotland

** John Daly beat Costantino Rocca in the four-hole play-off.*

1	**John Daly***	67	71	73	71	282
2	**Costantino Rocca**	69	70	70	73	282
=3	**Steven Bottomley**	70	72	72	69	283
	Mark Brooks	70	69	73	71	283
	Michael Campbell	71	71	65	76	283
=6	**Steve Elkington**	72	69	69	74	284
	Vijay Singh	68	72	73	71	284
=8	**Bob Estes**	72	70	71	72	285
	Mark James	72	75	68	70	285
	Corey Pavin	69	70	72	74	285
=11	**Ernie Els**	71	68	72	75	286
	Brett Ogle	73	69	71	73	286
	Payne Stewart	72	68	75	71	286
	Sam Torrance	71	70	71	74	286
=15	**Robert Allenby**	71	74	71	71	287
	Ben Crenshaw	67	72	76	72	287
	Brad Faxon	71	67	75	74	287
	Per-Ulrik Johansson	69	78	68	72	287
	Greg Norman	71	74	72	70	287
=20	**Andrew Coltart**	70	74	71	73	288
	David Duval	71	75	70	72	288
	Barry Lane	72	73	68	75	288
	Peter Mitchell	73	74	71	70	288
=24	**Mark Calcavecchia**	71	72	72	74	289
	Bill Glasson	68	74	72	75	289
	Lee Janzen	73	73	71	72	289
	Bernhard Langer	72	71	73	73	289
	Jesper Parnevik	75	71	70	73	289
	Katsuyoshi Tomori	70	68	73	78	289
	Steven Webster (a)	70	72	74	73	289

July 18–21, 1996

Royal Lytham and St Anne's GC, Lancashire, England

1	**Tom Lehman**	67	67	64	73	271
=2	**Ernie Els**	68	67	71	67	273
	Mark McCumber	67	69	71	66	273
4	**Nick Faldo**	68	68	68	70	274
=5	**Mark Brooks**	67	70	68	71	276
	Jeff Maggert	69	70	72	65	276
=7	**Fred Couples**	67	70	69	71	277
	Peter Hedblom	70	65	75	67	277
	Greg Norman	71	68	71	67	277
	Greg Turner	72	69	68	68	277
=11	**Alexander Cejka**	73	67	71	67	278
	Darren Clarke	70	68	69	71	278
	Vijay Singh	69	67	69	73	278
=14	**David Duval**	76	67	66	70	279
	Paul McGinley	69	65	74	71	279
	Mark McNulty	69	71	70	69	279
	Shigeki Maruyama	68	70	69	72	279
=18	**Padraig Harrington**	68	68	73	71	280
	Rocco Mediate	69	70	69	72	280
	Loren Roberts	67	69	72	72	280
	Michael Welch	71	68	73	68	280
=22	**Jay Haas**	70	72	71	68	281
	Mark James	70	68	75	68	281
	Carl Mason	68	70	70	73	281
	Steve Stricker	71	70	66	74	281
	Tiger Woods (a)	75	66	70	70	281
=27	**Paul Broadhurst**	65	72	64	71	282
	Ben Crenshaw	73	68	71	70	282
	Tom Kite	77	66	69	70	282

	July 18–21, 1996 continued					
	Peter Mitchell	71	68	71	72	282
	Frank Nobilo	70	72	68	72	282
	Corey Pavin	70	66	74	72	282

July 17–20, 1997

Royal Troon GC, Troon, Ayrshire, Scotland

1	**Justin Leonard**	69	66	72	65	272
=2	**Darren Clarke**	67	66	71	71	275
	Jesper Parnevik	70	66	66	73	275
4	**Jim Furyk**	67	72	70	70	279
=5	**Stephen Ames**	74	69	66	71	280
	Padraig Harrington	75	69	69	67	280
=7	**Fred Couples**	69	68	70	74	281
	Peter O'Malley	73	70	70	68	281
	Eduardo Romero	74	68	67	72	281
=10	**Robert Allenby**	76	68	66	72	282
	Mark Calcavecchia	74	67	72	69	282
	Ernie Els	75	69	69	69	282
	Retief Goosen	75	69	70	68	282
	Tom Kite	72	67	74	69	282
	Davis Love III	70	71	74	67	282
	Shigeki Maruyama	74	69	70	69	282
	Frank Nobilo	74	72	68	68	282
	Tom Watson	71	70	70	71	282
	Lee Westwood	73	70	67	72	282
=20	**Stuart Appleby**	72	72	68	71	283
	Brad Faxon	77	67	72	67	283
	Mark James	76	67	70	70	283
	Jose-Maria Olazabal	75	68	73	67	283
=24	**Jay Haas**	71	70	73	70	284
	Tom Lehman	74	72	72	66	284
	Peter Lonard	72	70	69	73	284
	Phil Mickleson	76	68	69	71	284
	Colin Montgomerie	76	69	69	70	284
	David A. Russell	75	72	68	69	284
	Tiger Woods	72	74	64	74	284
	Ian Woosnam	71	73	69	71	284

July 16–19, 1998

Royal Birkdale GC, Southport, Lancashire, England

** Mark O'Meara beat Brian Watts in the four-hole play-off.*

1	**Mark O'Meara***	72	68	72	68	280
2	**Brian Watts**	68	69	73	70	280
3	**Tiger Woods**	65	73	77	66	281
=4	**Jim Furyk**	70	70	72	70	282
	Jesper Parnevik	68	72	72	70	282
	Justin Rose (a)	72	66	75	69	282
	Raymond Russell	68	73	75	66	282
8	**Davis Love III**	67	73	77	68	283
=9	**Thomas Bjorn**	68	71	76	71	286
	Costantino Rocca	72	74	70	70	286
=11	**David Duval**	70	71	75	71	287
	Brad Faxon	67	74	74	72	287
	John Huston	65	77	73	72	287
14	**Gordon Brand Jr**	71	70	76	71	288
=15	**Peter Baker**	69	72	77	71	289
	Jose-Maria Olazabal	73	72	75	69	289
	Des Smyth	74	69	75	71	289
	Greg Turner	68	75	75	71	289
=19	**Robert Allenby**	67	76	78	69	290
	Mark James	71	74	74	71	290
	Sandy Lyle	70	73	75	72	290
	Vijay Singh	67	74	78	71	290
	Curtis Strange	73	73	74	70	290

	July 16–19, 1998 continued					
=24	**Stephen Ames**	68	72	79	72	291
	Bob Estes	72	70	76	73	291
	Lee Janzen	72	69	80	70	291
	Peter O'Malley	71	71	78	71	291
	Sam Torrance	69	77	75	70	291
=29	**Scott Dunlap**	72	69	80	71	292
	Ernie Els	73	72	75	72	292
	Sergio Garcia (a)	69	75	76	72	292
	Shageki Maruyama	70	73	75	74	292
	Nick Price	66	72	82	72	292
	Loren Roberts	66	76	76	74	292

THE US OPEN

In the top three

If the Masters and the Open Championships are both all about the values of shot-making and the miraculous recovery, the US Open seeks a winner who embraces the art of precision. No errors are allowed at the US Open, well not ones that go unpunished anyway. It has meant that the tournament has often developed as much into a battle of attrition as a golf event. At the Olympic Golf Club in San Francisco in 1998, the winner was simply the last man standing, and that happened to be Lee Janzen.

That was one instance where the United States Golf Association (USGA) strayed badly from their mandate. By contrast, the previous year at Congressional the merits of their penal layouts were seen to best effect. The course was very long and stringent, but the fairways were wide enough to encourage the most confident players to use their drivers from the tee. It was a full and wonderful test of the game.

At Olympic, however, the fairways slope viciously because the course lies on the San Andreas fault. They were designed to be soft and moist in the cool and foggy San Francisco summers, and so if a member hits a straight drive he knows it will hold the fairway. At the US Open, however, they were – by USGA design – hard and bouncy; in other words, they were tricked up. Many were the players who hit a straight drive, only to see it bounce down a hill and into a savage lie in the rough. It was, basically, unfair.

On too many occasions in recent years the USGA have got it wrong like this, which in turn has led to a number of strange winners. Somewhere along the way, as the players have come to hit the ball ever farther from the tee and have got still better around the greens, the USGA has sought to cancel these improvements by making courses play how they were not meant to be played. The golfers who have suffered have invariably been the artists. Tricked-up golf courses are, by definition, great levellers.

It is no surprise, therefore, to see that the status of the US Open has diminished over the last decade or so. There was a time when all Americans would have chosen it as the tournament they most wanted to win; increasingly, players like Mark O'Meara and Tiger Woods have pointed towards the fairer challenge offered by the Open, or the more exciting one presented at the Masters, and pinpointed those as the game's leading events.

No doubt the USGA will get the message. Their goal is a worthy one: to find the best golfer by means of the most punitive challenge available. But it is only worthy if the test remains a fair one, and the courses play as they were designed to be played. Anything else, and the second major championship of each season becomes a lottery.

The status of the US Open may have dipped slightly in recent years, but everything is relative: it remains, by anyone's reckoning, one of the top-three strokeplay events in world golf. In the final years of the last century, its position was far less secure. Indeed, the United States Amateur Championship was the main event, the Open not much more than an afterthought.

The early days

The first seeds were sown in 1894. Golf had spread to America and a number of clubs had been formed: St Andrew's (note the apostrophe to distinguish it from the original) Golf Club in New York, Newport in Rhode Island, the Chicago Golf Club. With no central body it was perhaps inevitable that a rivalry would begin. In 1894, both the Newport club and St Andrew's held national amateur tournaments. Newport went one further and held an Open event for professionals.

Four accepted the challenge, and on a bright, clear October day Willie Dunn from Musselburgh defeated Willie Campbell to become the first Open champion of the United States. To commemorate the victory, Dunn was given $100 and a gold medal.

Would the result stand, however? Charles Macdonald, the founder of the Chicago club who had lost both the national amateur events run by St Andrew's and Newport, complained that one club could not run a US Open. Dunn replied that Prestwick in Scotland had effectively run the early Open Championships, and those results stood. It seemed a fair argument, but not one that Macdonald and his supporters felt prepared to allow. The game was in turmoil.

Clearly something had to be done, and shortly after the St Andrew's amateur tournament representatives of that club, Newport, and The Country Club near Boston invited delegates from Shinnecock Hills and Chicago to a dinner in New York City. The date was December 22, 1894, the mission being to form what is now known as the United States Golf Association and determine the sites for both the 1895 US Open and Amateur Championships.

In the event they were both scheduled for the same week in October at Newport. The Amateur, a matchplay event, would be decided first, followed by the Open, a strokeplay

Harry Vardon – raised the prestige of the tournament when he entered in 1900

tournament conducted over four circuits of Newport's nine-hole course. Dunn returned to battle for his title that had now been scrubbed from the records, alongside nine other professionals and one amateur. Many of the other amateurs who had competed in their own event – won, incidentally, by Macdonald – stayed behind to serve as markers or indulge in some heavy betting. Who they chose depended upon where they lived: the New Englanders bet on their man, Campbell, trying to make amends for the previous year's defeat to Dunn; those from Chicago, meanwhile, laid their money on Jim Foulis; the New York money was on Dunn.

When Campbell made birdies at both the opening holes it appeared he might run away with it, but he dropped strokes on the next two; then the wind became a factor, a chilly gale off the Atlantic, and Campbell could not cope over the second nine, shooting 48. It added up to an 89, but he still shared pole position with Dunn and Foulis. After lunch, while these three kept fierce eyes on one another, a 21-year-old Englishman named Horace Rawlins moved into contention. After 91 in the first round, he sped to the turn in 41 to move into second place on his own on 132. Still the money went on the leader, Campbell, but he fell apart over the final nine. Rawlins shot another 41 for a total of 173. No one caught him.

Sadly, neither Dunn nor Campbell ever won the US Open, although the former wore his gold medal with pride for the rest of his life, and was happy to debate with anyone that he should be recognized as the first champion. Unhappily for him, the record books have long disagreed. Foulis, however, was rather more successful, winning the following year at Shinnecock Hills as Rawlins had to settle for second place.

English prestige

In 1900, the prestige of the US Open rose considerably as the great British professionals of the age, Harry Vardon and John Henry Taylor, both decided to enter. Not that it was the importance of the event that caused them to make the long journey: Vardon's sponsors, the A.G. Spalding company, had just introduced a new ball, the Vardon Flyer, and they wanted their man to promote it. This meant a tour which lasted virtually the entire year, covered 20,000 miles, and was a roaring personal success for Vardon. By the time he teed up in October 1900 at the Chicago Club he was revered by the Americans, who had never seen anyone strike the ball with such easy grace. Taylor, meanwhile, had formed his own golf-club company with a lifelong friend, George Cann, and both agreed that a promotional trip to America would help the business. Taylor also agreed to write articles for an American golf magazine for the sum of £2,000, a large amount at the time.

An excellent field had gathered, including the famous Carnoustie brothers, Willie and Alex Smith, and the Chicago native Foulis, for an event that was now played over 72 holes. It was Vardon and Taylor who duly dominated, the former winning by two strokes with a total of 313, the lowest yet.

In the early years of the twentieth century, the British professionals continued to rule. Willie Anderson, the son of a greenkeeper from North Berwick, won four US Opens in five years from 1901, the only other player allowed a look-in being Laurie Auchterlonie from St Andrews. In 1906 and 1910, there were also two victories for Alex Smith.

Americans raise the standard

As the century got into its stride, though, things began to change. As the number of entries rose, so did the standard of the Americans. In 1911, at the tender age of 19, Johnny McDermott became the first American-born player to win the tournament and the following August at the Country Club of Buffalo in upstate New York, he successfully defended the title. McDermott was on the verge of greatness. He was a wonderful talent with the true arrogance of a champion. But sometimes that arrogance got the better of him. In his victory speech in 1912, he said: "We hope our foreign visitors had a good time, but we don't think they did, and we are sure they won't win the National Open."

The USGA was appalled, and pointed out to McDermott that his "extreme discourtesy" could well result in his entry for the 1913 event being turned down. This did not happen, but for a year McDermott became a changed man, depressed and broody by turn. And then, just as he appeared to have regained his confidence, he was struck down by a tragic turn of events.

Travelling home from Britain following the 1914 Open Championship – an event, incidentally, in which he did not play owing to a missed rail connection – his ocean liner, the *Kaiser Wilhelm*, was involved in a collision in the English Channel with a grain ship. McDermott was led to a lifeboat and it was some hours later before he was picked up. At first he seemed unharmed, but he quickly became more affected by the experience than anyone realized. The following year he blacked out when he entered a shop in Atlantic City, and had a nervous breakdown from which he never recovered, spending the rest of his days in and out of rest homes.

With hindsight it appears a terrible loss, but it was not the way it was judged at the time. By 1914, McDermott had become a largely forgotten figure anyway; for while he was giving a subdued performance at the 1913 Open, events were taking place that would change the game of golf in America for ever. And at the end of it, a new hero – a new kind of hero at that – had emerged.

One hundred and sixty-five golfers entered for the 1913 US Open, by some distance the highest number yet. It reflected the growing confidence among the American professionals that they could hold their own with anybody. This was the year they would get the chance to prove it.

For Harry Vardon was to make a return trip, and this time he was bringing the more-than-useful Ted Ray along for company. By now Vardon was 43 years old, but he remained the game's complete stylist. His trip was backed by Lord Northcliffe, the owner of *The Times*, who specifically wanted him to win the US Open.

Before it took place, Vardon and Ray took on the cream of the American professional ranks and thrashed them one by one. They played 41 matches in all, and the only players who defeated them were the Smith brothers from Carnoustie; and that was after the Open. American hearts sank. When the US Open began at The Country Club that September, the American pros were mentally three strokes down before they began.

In the first round the pace was set by Alex Ross and Macdonald Smith, who both shot 71. Walter Hagen had a 73, while Vardon could only manage a 75 and Ray a disappointing 79. On day two, Ray recovered wonderfully well to post a 70, while Vardon shot a steady 72 to dispute the lead with Wilfred Reid.

The tension of the occasion was getting to the players. That evening, at the Copley Square Hotel, a discussion between Reid and Ray about the British system of taxation developed into a raging argument that led to the latter bloodying the former's nose with two powerful punches. Fortunately, a brave waiter came between them before Reid's fists could land a suitable reply.

Amateur Ouimet

Meanwhile, back on the golf course, the weather turned miserable. Reid collapsed – perhaps through the elements, perhaps because of Ray's pugilism – and on the final day could only manage rounds of 85 and 86. Ray shot 76, and now was sharing the lead with Vardon and an unknown 20 year old from the host club called Francis Ouimet, the Massachusetts Amateur Champion.

Ouimet was one of the last out on the course, and as he began his final round, Ray finished his, a mediocre 79 for a total of 304 that looked vulnerable. But Vardon could not improve on it, also shooting 79 for 304. What about the Americans? Surely they now had a chance?

Hagen made a run at it, shrugging off a wretched start to have his chance as he came to the last few holes. The 14th did for him, however, where he ran up a seven. He would shoot 80 and finish three adrift. Now only one American could catch the Brits; the unknown amateur named Ouimet.

Not that his chances appeared good. Wracked with nerves, he had gone to the turn in 43 strokes and started the back nine with a double bogey. Now he had to play the last eight in one under simply to tie. In the clubhouse, the Englishmen contemplated the play-off that would be theirs, and theirs alone, the following day.

As he walked to the 11th tee, Ouimet heard a conversation along the same lines between two spectators. "It's too bad Francis has blown up," one said. It was just what Ouimet, a born fighter, needed to hear. Holing an unlikely succession of putts for pars and grabbing the birdie he needed at the 17th, Ouimet came in with a score that matched the two legends. He would get his chance in the play-off.

Ouimet had learned to play golf in the street where he lived, adjacent to The Country Club. His bother Wilfred, a caddie, had introduced him and Francis Ouimet had taken an immediate interest. Soon he thought of little else and would sneak on to The Country Club for a few holes at five in the morning, before a greenkeeper would chase him away.

By 1910 he was good enough to enter for the US Amateur Championship at The Country Club, but he missed qualifying by a stroke. He also missed in 1911 and 1912, but by 1913 he was ready to compete in the best amateur tournaments. The Massachusetts Amateur was quite a feather in his cap.

But how could he play in the Open? He had already taken off more time than he was owed. At the behest of the USGA president he entered, but planned to withdraw, and particularly when the qualifying rounds were published in the local paper and his boss came up and said: "I see you're now going to play in the Open." Suitably embarrassed, Ouimet told him of his plan, but that he would be grateful if he could go and watch Vardon and Ray. "Well," said his boss, with a crafty grin, "Seeing as you have entered, you might as well play."

As Ouimet walked out for the 18-hole play-off and a closer look at the two Brits than he could ever have imagined, Johnny McDermott took his arm and told him: "Forget Vardon and Ray. Play your own game." It proved good advice. The crowd was enormous, a tribute not only to the pulling power of Vardon but also to the incredible interest that Ouimet's performance had generated.

Underestimated by his opponents, Ouimet drew enormous cheers from the gallery as he pulled two clear of Vardon by the 12th. Vardon, meanwhile, could hardly believe what was happening; he thought his only competition would be Ray. He got one back at the 13th. Ray, though, was out of it following a six at the 15th; he was now four behind. Vardon, too, was struggling to catch the upstart. He remained one behind as he came to the 17th and, in trying for a birdie, attempted to cut the corner of this dog-leg par four with his drive. To no avail. It caught the bunker and settled up near the face. Now he had no chance of making the green in two, let alone a three overall.

Ouimet, by contrast, struck two wonderful shots into the

Francis Ouimet – on the way to a victory in 1913 which changed the face of the game in his native America

heart of the green and, just as he had during the last round of regulation play, dropped the putt. When Vardon registered a bogey, the 10,000-strong crowd realized that they were witnessing history. The final scores were Ouimet 72, Vardon 77 and Ray 78.

Playing explosion

In the weeks that followed, Ouimet became a national hero and the national exposure introduced the sport to a new audience. In 1913, it is estimated that 350,000 Americans played golf. Ten years later, that number had grown to two million. While Europe became embroiled in war the Americans honed their skills, and by the time hostilities had ended the latter would never be considered inferior golfers again.

In the years that followed, Walter Hagen twice got his name on the trophy; Chick Evans, the finest striker of a ball in American golf, also won and there was a victory, too, for a young man of Italian descent who changed his name from Eugene Saracenio to Gene Sarazen. Ted Ray won as well, when he returned to play in the event in 1920. Vardon, then aged 50, finished tied for second.

In his qualifying rounds for that tournament at Inverness, OH, Vardon – the oldest man in the field – was paired with the youngest, a 19-year-old amateur from Atlanta, GA, who went by the name of Robert Tyre Jones, or Bob Jones to his friends. Vardon could see the young man's potential: "Some of his recovery shots were the longest I have ever seen," he said. But Jones had still to learn about course management. He shot 77 in the final round and finished fifth.

The following year he finished fifth again and, with the impatience that was a hallmark of his early career, he was beginning to wonder whether he would ever win the event when he turned up in 1922. This time he finished runner-up, and to make matters worse the winner, someone named Sarazen, was younger than him.

The entry had risen to 360 when Jones teed it up for the 1923 Open at Inwood, NY. By now Jones had entered Harvard to study English literature, which occupied most of his year. His Open preparations therefore were foreshortened, to say the least. In practice he was having trouble breaking 80 around the narrow layout.

Once the tournament started, however, he found some of his best form. He shot opening rounds of 71 and 73 and found himself trailing the leader, Jock Hutchinson, by two. The field was spreadeagled: only one other player had broken 150.

In the third round, Hutchinson ballooned to an 82. Jones shot 76 to lead by three from Bobby Cruickshank. Could he now set all the previous disappointments from his mind to claim the national Open? Jones thought even a 75 might be good enough to win. That was easily within his capabilities as he came to the closing holes, but once more nerves appeared to consume him. His approach to the 17th sailed out of bounds, and it was only following a timely piece of luck that he managed a bogey five. Now he needed a four at the last for a 74. That would surely be good enough. But Jones was not up to it. He took six, and Cruickshank had a chance. When he finished par, birdie to force a play-off, Jones contrasted it with his own miserable finish. He was convinced he would have to confront another failure the following day.

A fine crowd of around 8,000 had gathered by the first tee for the 2pm start. Jones looked drawn and depressed; he had good reason to be after six holes, as he fell two behind to some inspired play from his opponent. Through the green there was no comparison between the players, since Jones was by far and away the superior shotmaker, but Cruickshank hung on with some inspired golf around the greens. When Jones dropped a shot at the 17th it meant they were level once more, with a hole to play.

A theory has been propounded that had that last hole not worked out for Jones he may well have retired from golf without having won anything. There is no doubt the disappointments were taking their toll, and one more may well have pushed him over the edge. As it was, Cruickshank drove poorly, and needed four shots more to make the putting surface; Jones, off a fine drive, struck one of the great mid-iron shots to six feet. He was a major champion at last, and what wonders lay in store.

Keeping up with the Joneses

By 1926, any remaining doubts over whether the American golfer was superior to his British counterpart had evaporated. Jess Sweetser had become the first native American to win the Amateur Championship, the United States won the Walker Cup (it would be another year before the Ryder Cup was founded) and Americans dominated the Open at Royal Lytham, taking seven of the first ten places. The winner was Bobby Jones.

Now he had to dash back on the *Aquitania* to make it to Scioto Country Club in Columbus, OH, in time for the US Open. For the first time the event would be played over three days. The entries had swollen to 694, of which 147 would qualify to play 18 holes on each of the first two days, followed by 36 on the last. The prize money had grown to $2,145, to be shared by 20 players.

Jones opened brightly with a 70, but seemed tired and fatigued in compiling a second-round 79. With two rounds to come on one day and trailing Bill Mehlhorn by six strokes, his prospects appeared slim. He recovered, however, the following morning to shoot 71; it left him three behind Joe Turnesa, in third place, with Mehlhorn second following a 75.

Bobby Jones – the first man to win both the US and Open Championships in the same year in 1926, did so again in 1930

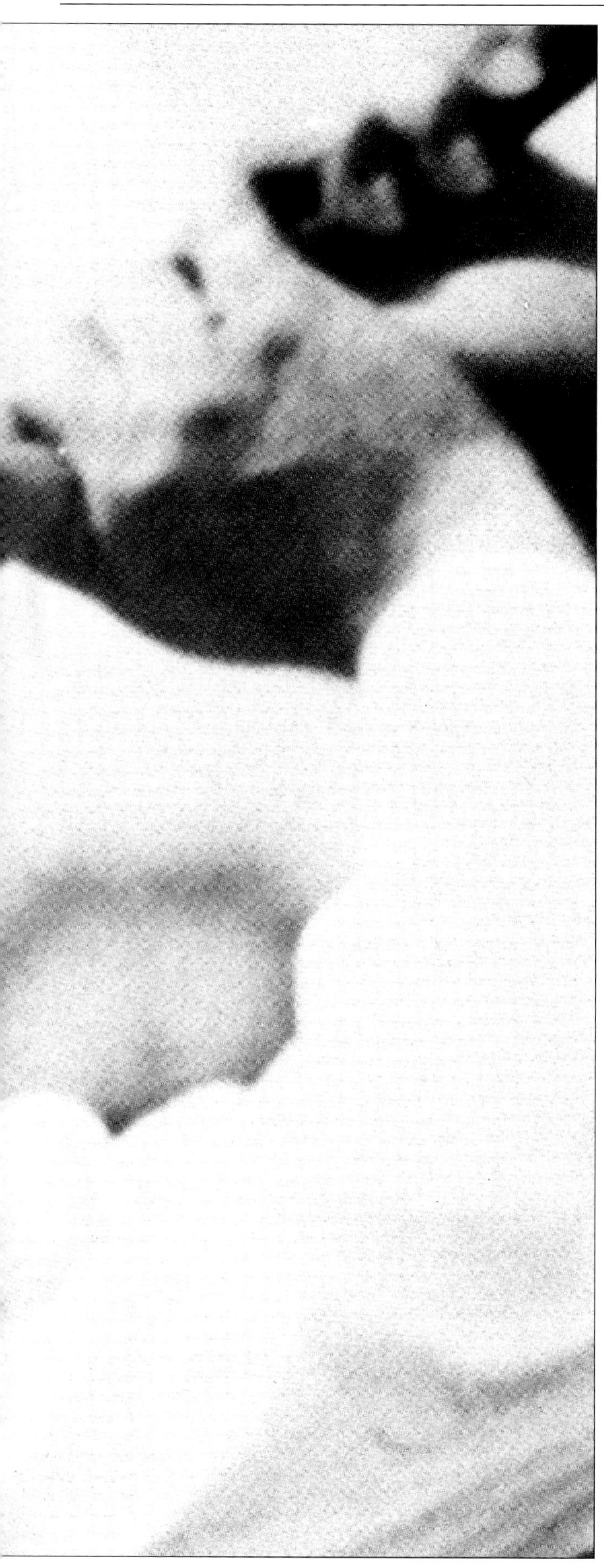

The conditions were hardly conducive to good scoring after lunch. A humid, bothersome wind was blowing across the course, bringing occasional showers with it. Mehlhorn quickly dropped from contention, and Jones was struggling to stay in touch as well. With seven holes left to play, Turnesa was four strokes to the good, and playing fine golf. The turning point came at the 12th, where Turnesa ran up an unlucky bogey and Jones holed from eight feet for a birdie. Turnesa lost another stroke at the 13th and now was clearly rattled; another went at the 16th and the pair were level. A fourth bogey in six holes went down on Turnesa's card at the 17th, but he recovered manfully to birdie the par-five 18th to set Jones the target of equalling that four to win.

This was a different, more composed Jones than the impetuous youth of old. No longer plagued by self-doubt, he ripped into two marvellous shots, leaving the ball just 10 feet from the hole in two. Two putts more, and he had become the first man to hold both the US and Open Championships in the same year.

Jones now had the game in thrall. By 1929 he was but 27 with a host of trophies to his name. He had won the US Amateur on four occasions, the Open twice, and the US Open twice. A play-off loss to Johnny Farrell for the 1928 US Open had left a nasty taste in the mouth, however, and Jones was particularly determined when he turned up for the 1929 tournament at Winged Foot, NY. He opened with a wonderful 69, but a second-round 75 meant that he trailed Gene Sarazen and Al Espinosa by two. It would be that sort of tournament for Jones. Back he came in round three with a 71 to lead by four. In the final round, however, he had two sevens on his card and came to the last hole needing a 12-foot putt to force a play-off with Espinosa. It tumbled into the cup and so, just as in the previous year, Jones would have to complete 36 holes more in an effort to win the trophy. This, though, was a stroll in the park. Jones played peerless golf while Espinosa was hopeless. The final victory margin after the play-off was no less than 23 shots. Jones had his third US Open.

In 1930 the tournament travelled to Interlachen, and took place just three weeks after the completion of the Open at Hoylake. Jones had won that and also the Amateur Championship at his beloved St Andrews. Naturally, interest surrounding his attempt at the third leg of the Grand Slam was intense.

Yet Jones was in the groove. His game had always responded to practice and now he was at his confident peak. He opened with a 71, which left him just a stroke behind the leaders, Mac Smith and the 1927 champion, Tommy Armour. Also in touch were Joe Turnesa and Walter Hagen, adding up to a formidable quartet of adversaries.

Smith led after the second round, but this time it was Horton rather than Mac – the same Horton Smith who four years later would win the inaugural Augusta National Invitational. Jones, meanwhile, kept in touch with a 71 that left him two behind.

On day three, the tournament continued to be all about Smith and Jones, but this time it was the latter who made the decisive move. Off early on a beautiful Minnesota summer's day, Jones was never better than when he did not have to worry about pacemaking. For 16 holes he played peerless golf, and came to the last two holes needing a pair of pars to become the first man in US Open history to shoot a 66. Alas, the strain became too much and he had two bogeys instead. Nevertheless, the 68 took him five clear of the field, with the afternoon round to come.

If Jones had one weakness, it was that he was never a great front-runner. After lunch he started with three straight bogeys, and with Mac Smith playing the stretch in one under, the seemingly comfortable interval advantage he enjoyed had evaporated. Smith, seven behind three holes ago, was now only three adrift. At the 13th he picked up two more, a par to Jones's nervous-looking double bogey. Could Jones recover his momentum?

He did. At the par-four 14th he ripped a three iron to within 10 feet of the flag and holed; another birdie followed at the 15th and then a third in a row at the 16th. It was a wonderful riposte, just as he was in danger of falling to a stunning defeat. Now he was three ahead, but there was still drama, not to mention controversy, to come.

At the monstrous 262-yard, par-three 17th, Jones swung as hard as he could but the ball missed the green on the right, hit a tree, and was never seen again. "What shall I do?" Jones asked the referee, Prescott Bush. "The ball went into the parallel water hazard, and so you are permitted to drop a ball in the fairway opposite the point where the ball crossed the margin of the hazard," Bush replied. So Jones did as he was told, and pitched and two-putted for a five.

But was it the right call? If the ball definitely went into the water hazard it was, but that was a matter of considerable debate. As far as anyone can tell, no one saw the ball go into it, and in that instance Bush made a crucial error. Jones should have been told to go back to the tee and play another ball. Given that he never made a par on that hole all week, he was staring a triple-bogey six in the face. In a newspaper column shortly afterwards, Gene Sarazen said the ruling tainted Jones's victory. It is certainly easy to understand why there was such strength of feeling.

Back to the tournament, for even with the five, Jones was only a shot to the good against Smith. Now he needed a birdie at the last to ensure victory. Jones hit a fine drive, a three iron to 40 feet, and then rolled in the putt. It meant a 75, and a two-stroke triumph.

Not long afterwards, Jones won the US Amateur to complete the "Impregnable Quadrilateral". In Britain J.H. Taylor remarked: "I just don't know how he keeps it up." Neither did Jones. In 11 years, beginning in 1920 and ending in 1930, he had played in 15 US Opens and Open Championships and won seven of them. He had also won five US Amateurs and one Amateur. What could he do for an encore? There was no answer to that one. Added to the strain he was undoubtedly feeling, and the desire to cash in on all his success, Jones announced his retirement from competitive golf. The 1931 US Open, somehow, would have to go on without him.

Longest in history

If it seemed a long tournament, it was not just because Jones was not there. Indeed, it ended up being the longest US Open in history, setting a record that will stand for all time. After 72 holes at Inverness, Billy Burke and George von Elm were tied on eight-over-par scores of 292. That meant 36 holes the following day, and when von Elm birdied the last of them to tie things up again, another 36 resulted. Even that one was close, with Burke prevailing by a single stroke. If he had not, it would have meant another 36. As it was, the two leading protagonists had played 144 holes to determine the winner. It was clearly too much; thereafter, play-offs would be 18 holes.

The following year Gene Sarazen made a welcome return to winning ways, but the Depression years in America were reflected in the US Open tournaments of the time. Most of them were won by men whom time would quickly forget. The 1930s were almost drawing to a close when a new generation of players began to emerge. First, Ralph Guldahl won at Oakland Hills in 1937, and then successfully defended the trophy the following year at Cherry Hills in Denver. But while Guldahl was a very good player, he did not excite the crowds. That was left to an old southern hill-billy called Sam Snead, and his rivalry with first Byron Nelson and then Ben Hogan electrified the sport.

With a swing that was even more powerful and controlled than Bobby Jones's, a first US Open win for Snead appeared merely a matter of time. "I don't know how he ever shoots above 70 with that method," Jones remarked. In 1939 Snead's big moment arrived. The venue was Philadelphia Country Club and Snead opened in confident mood, shooting 68 to take the lead. A second-round 71 meant he led by two, while a 73 the following day left him trailing Johnny Bulla by one. But Bulla fell apart during the final round and now the tournament was between four players: Snead, Nelson, the hapless Craig Wood and Denny Shute. It was Snead who they all had to catch. He had returned to the form of his opening two rounds.

As he came to the 17th tee Snead was in control. Nelson was in the clubhouse with a total of 284, but Snead could afford to finish bogey, par, and still beat that score. Behind him, though he did not know it, Wood and Shute were trying hard to stay in touch.

Ralph Guldahl – winner in 1937 and 1938

A nervous Snead helped them at the 17th. He went through the green with his approach and then chipped to five feet, but left the putt short in the jaws of the hole. Still, a par five at the last – a hole he could reach in two – and he would beat Nelson. But Snead was rattled, and when he heard the cheers behind it certainly did not help. With no scoreboards, Snead thought he now needed a birdie four and he consequently ripped into his drive. He hooked it into the rough. It was here that Snead's decision-making process went awry. He thought he could still get a three wood at it, still make the green or, if not, leave himself an easy pitch.

How he paid for being too aggressive. From the awkward lie he stone-cold topped the ball into a bunker, the ball running high up the face. Now he had 110 yards to go and was struggling to make the green in three. Snead remained positive. He tried an eight iron. The ball embedded itself into the top of the bunker's face; furious, Snead tore at the ball, but only succeeded in putting it into another bunker. From there he did manage to find the green, but now he had played five and was 40 feet away. He needed to hole to tie with Nelson. He knocked it three feet by and left the return putt short. Snead staggered off the green looking like he had been in a car crash. To make matters worse, the pair behind did no better than tie with Nelson. A three-way play-off would take place on the morrow, and it would go ahead without the man who up to that point had dominated the tournament.

Wood, of course, lost – which meant that he had finished second in every major championship; but only after a second 18 holes, for he and Nelson had tied with 68s. The following day Nelson shot 70 to Wood's 73. Snead, meanwhile, was licking his wounds. One observer was heard to remark that he would never win a major championship after what had happened. Thankfully, that did not prove to be the case, but the experience did leave its scars. For this was the second time that Snead had had his chance – in 1937 he had led with a round to play – and it had slipped through his fingers. It would become a recurring, heartbreaking theme. Indeed not even Arnold Palmer's fruitless pursuit of the one major that remained outside his grasp, the USPGA Championship, can match for poignancy Snead's failure to win the US Open. In all he would finish second four times, third once and fifth twice, and during that time he would win the Masters three times, the USPGA three times and the Open the only time he played in it; he also won 78 other US Tour events. But no US Open.

"If I could have shot 69 in the last round every time [the worst score, of course, that Bobby Jones thought he should ever shoot], I would have won nine US Opens," Snead remarked bitterly a few years ago. Alas, he never came close to that mark.

Three years after collecting that unexpected US Open win, Nelson would prevail again. Happily, the defending champion that year was Wood, who had finally learned how to win the big ones, having collected the Masters as well two months earlier.

It was the last US Open before the war and it was held at the Colonial Country Club in Fort Worth, TX. It was an appropriate venue, since it was where Ben Hogan learned to play golf. He finished in a tie for third that year. When the US Open resumed after the war and Hogan was out of uniform, he would dominate the event as completely as Jones had done a generation earlier.

If 1939 was the year in which Sam Snead had the US Open snatched from the palm of his hand, 1947 was the year he let it slip through his fingers. The venue was St Louis Country Club, a none-too-difficult course where Lew Worsham was seen at his best. He opened with two rounds of 70 and followed them with a 71 on the morning of the last day. After lunch he breezed to the turn in 33. A level-par 36 for the back nine would certainly give him the championship, but Worsham took 38, and now Snead had a chance.

When he birdied the 15th he was level with Worsham; one more birdie would give him the elusive Open. Alas, for his watching legion of fans, after scrambling a par at the 16th, Snead dropped a shot at the next. Now he needed to birdie the last to tie. A much harder hole than the previous one, Snead's lovely rhythmical swing smacked the ball straight down the middle, some 290 yards from the tee. Now he had a mid-iron to the green and again he played it well, the ball coming to rest 18 feet from the hole. In the gallery, Worsham watched and waited. Snead's putt fell in to force the fourth play-off in five US Opens. Worsham wandered over and shook Snead's hand.

It was a rather friendlier atmosphere than would prevail on the same green 24 hours later. Both men had played superbly to create a classic play-off, the lead changing hands on several occasions. When they stood on the 18th tee they were all square; when they had played three shots there was still little to separate them – both lay just over two feet from the hole.

Snead wanted to get it over with, get his putt in and put pressure on his man. So, too, did Worsham. Snead had played a little chip to the distance he now had left, and rushed on to the green to take his putt. As he stood over the ball, Worsham said: "Wait a minute, Sam. Are you sure it's your turn?" Snead stopped. A referee was called for, with Snead insistent he should continue putting. "Not unless you're furthest away," the official replied. A tape measure was called for: it revealed that Snead was 30.5 inches from the hole; Worsham was exactly an inch nearer. Snead was right: he would putt first. But he did so in a different frame of mind from before.

A tricky putt with a sharp break, Snead did not hit it with the firmness the putt demanded. It took the break and dribbled away from the hole. Worsham tapped in, and once more the US Open had brought only pain at the 18th for Snead.

Post-war legends

Riviera, the club of Hollywood stars in Beverly Hills, CA, has long been known as "Hogan's Alley", and a considerable slice of the legend was built upon his performance there in 1948. That summer saw Hogan near his best. He had demolished Mike Turnesa in the final of the USPGA Championship a month earlier, and now he continued that remorselessness in the Hollywood Hills. His closest pursuer was also one of his closest friends - Jimmy Demaret – but Demaret had not been able to stop him at the USPGA, losing in the semi-finals, and he could not live with him here either. Hogan shot three rounds in the 60s and one of 72 for a total of 276, a new record for the US Open and one that would not be lowered until Jack Nicklaus conquered Baltusrol in 1967.

Hogan's comeback

A year later, the US Open went on without the defending champion, who was laid up in a Texas hospital. By now the threat to his life following his car accident had receded: Hogan had even posted a poignant entry to the USGA. "I hope and pray that I may see you in June," the accompanying letter read. But June came and Hogan could barely walk, much less play golf. Cary Middlecoff emerged the winner, the luckless Snead being second once more, again a shot shy.

Hogan's comeback began at Riviera and the Los Angeles Open in January, 1950. He had already demonstrated his intention to return to golf by captaining the United States side that won the previous year's Ryder Cup at Ganton. By January, playing golf was no longer the problem; but walking was. Still, he found a way to cope – so well, indeed, that he shot a four-round total of 280, and Snead needed to birdie the last two holes to tie. The fact Snead won the subsequent play-off was of little lasting significance to Hogan. He had shown he could play again. Now he looked forward, first to the Masters where he finished fourth, then on to the US Open, which was held at Merion, one of his favourite courses.

What happened over five days at that historic venue may well be the most dramatic scenes that golf has ever witnessed. After 12 holes of the final round, Hogan had a three-stroke lead; that was the good news. The bad was that the pain in his legs was so overpowering that there were grave doubts as to whether he could continue to put one foot in front of the other. After his drive on that hole Hogan clung to the shoulder of a friend, Harry Radix. "My God, Harry, let me cling to you, I don't think I can finish," he gasped.

And so Hogan tried desperately to concentrate over those final seven holes while inside he was dying. At times he simply had to wait while the pain subsided. On a number of occasions he thought he was going to pass out. When he came to the last his lead had slipped away. Now he needed a par on this awesome finishing hole simply to force a tie. Hogan's one-iron approach has entered golf folklore, a stunning blow that ensured he finished on the same 287 mark as Lloyd Mangrum and George Fazio. They would play off the following day.

Yet how would Hogan cope? As he unwrapped his bandages that night and soaked his aching limbs for hours, the very same thought went through his head. There must have been a moment when he wondered whether it might have been better had he lost.

It had gone by the morning. He wrapped his legs up once more and cajoled them into 18 more holes. Once more it was close. Hogan was playing beautifully, but so was Mangrum, with Fazio out of it. At the 16th Hogan was just a shot ahead. Mangrum, with an eight-foot putt for par, addressed the ball. As he did, an insect landed, and instinctively Mangrum marked his ball with his putter head, picked it up, and blew the bug away. Then he holed the putt.

As he digested the thought that he had escaped, still just a stroke adrift, rules official Ike Grainger came running up to inform him that by cleaning the ball on the green he had infringed the rules, and would be penalized two shots. Mangrum glared at him: "You mean I had a six instead of a four," he enquired. "Yes," Grainger replied. For a moment Mangrum gave him a withering stare. Then he softened. "Well," he said, "I guess we will still all eat tomorrow."

For Hogan, there was a welcome breathing space. His comeback was complete. The week had shown him that he could still win, and that was while in excruciating pain. If he paced himself better, and cut out some of the lesser tournaments to ease the strain on his suffering legs, how much more could he achieve?

Oakland Hills in 1951 may have been the first time that the players began complaining about the way the USGA set up courses. Robert Trent Jones had been brought in to toughen up the Detroit layout, and there was no question that he succeeded on that score. But was it any good? More than that, was it fair?

Ben Hogan did not think so. All his life he had played attacking golf, believing that the man who hit it straightest and truest would gain his reward. But at Oakland Hills even he was forced into a defensive strategy, and the result was opening rounds of 76 and 73. Watching, the veteran Walter Hagen grumbled: "The course is playing the players instead of the players playing the course."

Under these circumstances it was hardly surprising that the greatest putter of his day held the half-way lead; Bobby Locke was practically the only person in the field who had the weapon to compensate for all the problems that he, like everyone else, was experiencing from tee to green.

Soaking his legs that evening, Hogan decided that instead of joining in the continual moaning about the course, he would revise his strategy the following day. He would have to attack,

Ben Hogan – won the first of his four US Open titles at Riviera CC in 1948

and suffer the inevitable consequences if the ploy failed. In the morning third round he shot 71, and passed 10 players. Locke still held the lead, but this time he had been joined out in front by Jimmy Demaret, the only player to match the par of 70. Hogan was not too disappointed. He was only two adrift after all. "I am going to defeat this course this afternoon," he told the referee, Ike Grainger, on the first tee.

It did not look the case on the front nine, as he scrambled his way to an outward half of 35. The key thereafter was probably the 10th, perhaps the hardest hole on the course, and Hogan played it just as Locke was teeing off from the first in his final round. Hogan hit a drive and two iron that finished six feet from the hole. The putt fell. He was under par for the first time in the tournament. Another birdie at the 13th was followed by a bogey at the 14th, but at the next hole Hogan hit a lovely six-iron approach to four feet to go back to two under.

He was now at his imperious best, and the monster that Oakland Hills had been labelled was looking, for one man at least, to be a fairly tame beast. At the 16th two more splendid shots gave Hogan another four-foot birdie putt, but he misread that one. At the 17th a two iron to this long par three found the green, and two putts gave him a par. On to the 18th, a wonderful finishing hole. Hogan negotiated the two bunkers that guard the angle of this dog-leg with a fine, straight drive. It was so long that it left him with but a six iron to the hole. That nestled down 15 feet from the flag, and when the putt disappeared Hogan knew that no one could catch him; he had tamed the monster with a 67 to claim his third US Open in three starts. Years later, he would consider this his finest round of golf.

Hogan led at the half-way stage the following year at Northwood in Dallas, but two indifferent rounds of 74 on the final day dropped him to third. Instead the title went to the sweet-swinging Julius Boros, who made up four shots on Hogan with rounds of 68 and 71 to win by four from Ed Oliver.

Two years stand out in golf this century when players have recorded feats of singular achievement. One belonged to Bobby Jones in 1930; the other to Ben Hogan in 1953. Because of his legs, he only played in six 72-hole tournaments that year and won five of them. He entered three major championships and won them all. Remember, these were the days when the modern Grand Slam had failed to enter the lexicon. The USPGA finished on the day before the Open Championship began. Hogan chose the latter for the first time, partly because the former involved two matches a day, and he did not want to inflict such torture on his legs.

Hogan was simply imperious in the majors, and perhaps even more untouchable than Jones had been 23 years earlier. He did not just win the three greatest tournaments he entered, but he claimed the trophies by convincing margins. In the Masters he was five ahead of the runner-up; at the Open at Carnoustie he won by four; and at the US Open at Oakmont the gap between himself and the luckless Sam Snead in second place was no fewer than six shots.

Hogan led in every round, opening with a 67 to immediately put three shots between himself and the field. But Snead made a closer contest of it than the final result would suggest. He actually led for long periods of the third round, and in the fourth he was within one shot of Hogan going to the 12th tee. Then he did his usual US Open collapse, dropping no fewer than five strokes to par over the last seven holes. Hogan had become the third man to win four US Opens and, more remarkably still, he had achieved it in his last five attempts.

After winning at Carnoustie the following month, Hogan came home to a ticker-tape parade on Broadway, the first golfer to receive the accolade since Jones in 1930.

The following year at Baltusrol saw the US Open broadcast nationwide on television for the first time. Once more Hogan was in the thick of things after two rounds, but he faded away on the closing day and Ed Furgol enjoyed his 15 minutes of fame. The 1955 US Open saw the first of two extraordinary near misses for Hogan. The venue was the Olympic Club and although he was now 43 years old, he was still considered the overwhelming favourite. He justified that tag when he hit the front following the third round on the morning of the final day. Off early in the afternoon, the crowd roared their approval as Hogan overcame the brutally tough layout with a last-round 70; they were certain they had just witnessed his fifth US Open victory.

In the clubhouse, the early finishers were equally certain. Gene Sarazen proffered his hand in congratulatory fashion. Still, Hogan was not sure. He felt in his heart he had won, but as long as there were competitors on the course he could not fully relax.

As he showered and dressed, so those competitors gave up the pursuit until only one was left, a little-heralded pro called Jack Fleck. And even he was two off the pace with four to play. Most of the spectators gave up on him at that point, but Fleck hit a nerveless six-iron approach to 10 feet at the 15th and holed for a birdie. Now the fans came rushing back.

Fleck could not get a birdie at the par-five 16th, but did manage a par four on the toughest hole on the course, the 17th. That left him needing a birdie at the 18th. Fleck's drive went off to the left, but he got lucky with his lie in the rough from which he could hit an unimpeded seven iron to the pin. Fleck played it perfectly, the ball finishing seven feet away. That putt for a play-off: to great roars of approval, he made it.

Naturally, most people thought the award of the trophy had simply been delayed a day. Fleck had come in with a 67 and, given his modest level of performance, he could not be expected to maintain that standard. Then he was up against the greatest professional the game had seen up to that point. What chance did he stand? Hogan's fifth US Open was still in the bag.

What these soothsayers overlooked was the fact that Hogan

Arnold Palmer – ran out winner in 1960 in perhaps the greatest major championship of them all

had mentally wrapped up this tournament the previous afternoon. "Here's my ball for Golf House," he had said to Joe Dey, of the USGA. It is very difficult to crank up the gears once more after such a mental peak. And so it proved that afternoon. Hogan shot a 72, which was respectable enough; Fleck shot 69. It meant that since his year of years in 1953 Hogan had played in four majors, and his sequence read: 2, 6, 2, 2. He would finish runner-up in the US Open the following year as well, missing a three-foot putt on the 71st hole as Middlecoff claimed the title for the second time.

And that was almost it for the great man. As the irascible Tommy Bolt claimed his sole major championship in 1958, as Billy Casper strode on to the world stage a year later at Winged Foot, Hogan was bedevilled by putting woes. But just look again at that record from 1942 to 1956. He played in 11 US Opens over the period and finished first on four occasions, second twice, third twice, fourth once and sixth twice.

Meeting of eras

There was one final swansong, one last reminder of all the glory that had gone before. It came in the epochal US Open of 1960, perhaps the greatest major championship of all.

In the years that followed people would look back on it and describe it as the moment when three eras collided: the past of Hogan, the present of Arnold Palmer and the face of golf's future, present in Jack Nicklaus's chubby features. The venue was Cherry Hills Country Club in Denver, CO. All three would have their chance of victory. And, in the wildest shoot-out golf had ever seen, so would a cast of others. But it was this trio who concentrated the mind. Hogan, 47 years old, and needing an oxygen canister in the rarefied air to aid his breathing, would finish poorly – a man who finally accepted that his winning days were over; Nicklaus would put in the best performance seen by an amateur since Johnny Goodman won in 1933; above all, there was Palmer – then the Masters champion – giving the performance of his life.

For three rounds, the tournament had been about none of these things. Mike Souchak shot 68, 67, 73, and led after every round. At lunchtime on the final day he was on 208, just one stroke ahead of Nicklaus and three in front of Hogan. Palmer, meanwhile, appeared hopelessly adrift at seven off the pace, with no fewer than 14 players between him and Souchak. In the clubhouse he ate a cheeseburger with Ken Venturi, Bob Rosburg and Bob Drum, golf correspondent for Palmer's local paper, the *Pittsburgh Press*. Venturi was speculating on whether Souchak could hold on, and Rosburg said he did not see why not. Then Palmer turned up the heat. "What if I shot 65 this afternoon?" he speculated aloud, "What would that do?" Drum replied: "Nothing. You're too far back."

No one liked a challenge more than Arnie. "The hell I am,"

he said, his eyes ablaze. "That would give me 280, and 280 wins Opens." And with that he got up and left, fired with all the motivation he needed.

What happened over the next seven holes was one of the most remarkable sequences ever seen in golf. At the 1st Palmer drove the green 346 yards away and two putted for a birdie. At the 2nd he holed from off the green for another birdie. At the 3rd, his approach shot finished 12 inches from the hole. At the 4th, an 18-foot putt – another birdie; at the 5th, a wild tee shot, but an excellent recovery to save par. At the par-three 6th, a 25-foot putt for a birdie. And at the 7th, a wedge shot to six feet for another birdie. Do you think he was keen to prove Drum wrong?

Palmer's charge electrified the field. Now the pacemakers could hear the continuous cheers and knew exactly what was happening. In just seven holes Palmer had made up six of the strokes that separated him from Souchak. The leaderboard was in chaos. At 2.45pm Souchak was still in front at five under par, one ahead of Julius Boros, Dow Finsterwald and Nicklaus. Hogan was two behind and Jack Fleck, Jerry Barber and Palmer three adrift. But Palmer kept on charging. And Souchak and one or two others cracked. Seventy-five minutes later and Souchak fell into a three-way tie for the lead. Then a bogey at the 9th left Nicklaus out in front on his own.

Three putts at the 13th, though, meant Nicklaus now shared the lead with Fleck, Boros and Palmer. Another 30 minutes, and the three men in front were Fleck, Hogan and Palmer. Then Fleck's putting went awry.

Finally, two men were left standing: the ageing king and his heir apparent. Could Hogan stop the march of time at one last big tournament? He could not. For 34 holes on that final day he had played some of his finest golf. He had never missed so much as a green in regulation, but his putting was not just pitiful – it was worse than that. And now his long game cracked.

Attacking the course at the 17th as he always did, he got not the birdie he was after but a bogey; his spirit broken with the realization that he had come up short, he followed it with a sad triple bogey at the last. Palmer, meanwhile, finished with two pars for his cherished 65, and he was spot on: a score of 280 does win Opens – in this case, by two shots from Nicklaus.

The collision of three eras had resulted in a suitably momentous occasion. Hogan would slip quietly away after this event; Palmer would dominate the game. As for Nicklaus, his playing partner on that last day, Hogan himself had but one final comment to make: "Hell, I'm disappointed, but I tell you this – I have just played with a kid who would have won this thing by 10 shots if he had been two years older."

Two years on and Nicklaus did indeed win, although not by 10 shots. Indeed he needed a play-off to prevail, and for Palmer the occasion brought bitter disappointment. The Masters champion, he would also go on to win the Open at Troon the following month. Sandwiched in between was the US Open at his beloved Oakmont, just a few miles from where he was born. Naturally he was the favourite, not just in terms of winning, but with the crowd, too. A very partisan crowd, it has to be said. "Nicklaus is a pig," one placard said. "Miss it, fat gut," another proclaimed.

The action was watched by 72,000 fans, 25,000 more than the previous record. And they got their money's worth. In the final round, Nicklaus made up two strokes on the local boy to force a play-off the following day.

What an occasion this would be. First Nicklaus got off to a wonderful start, and threatened to run away with it when he went four ahead after eight holes. Then came a familiar Palmer charge. A birdie on the 9th; a birdie on the 10th; a birdie on the 11th. Now Nicklaus's lead was one. "I thought: 'Uh oh, here he comes,'" Nicklaus said later. He also told himself not to be intimidated, to concentrate on his own play. Which, of course, is easier said than done when the man doing the charging is Palmer. But Nicklaus held on. Palmer bogeyed the 13th and now the lead was two again. It stayed that way until the 18th, where a gambling Palmer dropped another shot.

There is a dramatic photograph of Palmer as he stares disbelievingly at a putt over the crucial closing holes that has failed to drop. In his stance and demeanour there is the look of a man who knows that the game is up; in years to come he would admit what the photo all too clearly reveals – that it was among the most painful losses of his career.

At Congressional in 1964 Palmer led after the first round, but uncharacteristically went backwards after that. Nicklaus finished well down the field. Instead the third-round lead was held by Ken Venturi, who had known hard times since experiencing two heartbreaking failures in major championships. Both had come at the Masters: as an amateur in 1956 he had led all the way through three rounds, and with 18 to go his lead was four – he then shot 80 to lose by one; four years later, Palmer birdied both the last two holes and again Venturi was a shot shy.

Now he was just thankful to be leading the US Open having not even been invited to that year's Masters. Could he hold on this time? It was highly unlikely. Venturi was sick with fever and had finished the morning third round feeling light-headed, as the temperature in his body climbed to match the 100 degrees outside. How would he walk 18 holes after lunch, much less maintain his concentration?

He had a 50-minute break for lunch, and saw a doctor who prescribed some fluids, and that at least brought some respite. Over the front nine he played peerless golf. He passed the fading John Jacobs; he was two in front of him and four ahead of everyone else. For the first time he was playing like a winner. But the fever was returning. Now he concentrated on conserving his energy, registering the pars that he knew would bring him victory.

Over the back nine Venturi's pace slowed to a crawl, but somehow he maintained his standard of play. He knew he was safe if he could do that, for Jacobs was falling apart.

At the 18th Venturi's approach found a bunker, but he played out to 10 feet and holed for victory. He almost collapsed on the spot. "My God," he gasped, "I've won the US Open." His playing partner, Raymond Floyd, lifted his ball from the cup, and when he handed it to him Venturi's face was wet with tears.

Player's triumph

In 1965, the first year the tournament was played over four days, Gary Player's victory at the Bellerive club in St Louis meant that he became just the third golfer to win all four major championships at least once. Furthermore, he had completed it in the shortest span of time, having taken just six years. Even Ben Hogan had needed seven to win all four, while Gene Sarazen had required 13 years. Player was also still a few months short of his 30th birthday. He may have been the junior partner in the golfing firm known as "The Big Three", but what a junior partner.

In the Press room after his victory, Player came over all spiritual. He revealed that he had had a vision, and had seen his name in gold lettering on top of the leaderboard. It had filled him all week with the confidence that he could not lose. Fortunately he kept the vision to himself until he had won the tournament, otherwise he might have been dismissed as a fruitcake. In the aftermath of victory, however, it made good copy.

In 1966 the US Open returned to the Olympic Club where once more the favourite would experience a crushing disappointment every bit as debilitating as that suffered by Ben Hogan 11 years earlier.

Prior to this major, few people had questioned Arnold Palmer's all-out style of aggression. How could they? He had the trophies on the sideboard and more fans than every other player combined. By now he was loved and revered all around the world. But at Olympic the King collapsed in a manner unprecedented in major championship golf, and the reason was his style of play.

That style, mind you, had carried him into a seven-stroke lead with just nine holes to play. Palmer had gone out in 32 to leave his playing partner, Billy Casper, trailing hopelessly in his wake. Palmer felt that Olympic's outward half was more difficult than the inward nine and now, like Hogan before him, he thought the tournament won and he could concentrate on breaking Hogan's record US Open score of 276. It was certainly attainable on paper; a level-par back nine of 35 would have given him a total of 274.

Yet these are thoughts that should never go through a golfer's mind. If breaking the record comes along, fine, but winning the tournament has to be the sole goal. At the 10th Palmer bogeyed, but he retrieved the stroke at the 12th, which Casper also birdied. Hogan remained in sight; and he was six ahead, with six to play.

The lead was five when Palmer bogeyed the 13th, and now he had to play the last five in level par to break Hogan's record. That plan survived the 14th, but began to go pear-shaped at the short 15th, where he ran up a four. Casper got a two, and now was three behind and sniffing a ghost of a chance. At the long 16th Palmer lashed at his tee shot and put it into trouble. The result was a six; Casper had a four. One ahead with two to play.

By now Palmer had forgotten all about Hogan because Casper was proving more than enough for one man to worry about. At the desperately difficult 17th, Palmer had another bogey, while Casper – one of the great putters – made a crucial 10-footer for his par. He had made up five shots in just three holes, and would have won in regulation play but for a brave six-foot putt that Palmer holed at the last.

Now, just as in 1955, the favourite and the outsider would play off. Casper, however, was a better player than Fleck, and certainly much better around the greens. He had lost a lot of weight, and took the game very seriously. And he proved more than a match for Palmer, who shot 73 to his opponent's 69. So Palmer's attacking style, the one that had brought him fame and so many major championships, had badly let him down. Would he tone it down at all in years to come, and forsake it for caution if the occasion demanded? Would he, heck. And the people loved him all the more for the decision.

Given Palmer's desperate desire to break Ben Hogan's 72-hole record total, it was rather ironic that someone would do just that the very next year. Perhaps inevitably it was Jack Nicklaus who did so, cruising around Baltusrol in just 275 shots to win by four from Palmer. At just 27 he had won his seventh major, and clearly there would be more to come. The following year, however, he would have to settle for the runners-up spot as a Mexican called Lee Trevino appeared from nowhere to win at Oak Hill. What is more, he did so with some style, equalling Nicklaus's total from the previous year and becoming the first man to win a major championship with four rounds in the 60s.

The following year Trevino demonstrated he had his finger firmly on the pulse in his Press conference before the championship began. Asked who he thought would win if he did not, he replied: "Sarge Moody." It certainly made the Press sit up and take notice, for few up to that point had seriously considered the claims of the former army sergeant, Orville Moody. "Why him?" they asked Trevino. "Because he is a helluva player," he replied. He was certainly a heck of a player that week at the Champions club in Houston, winning by a stroke from Deane Beman and Al Geiberger.

Gary Player – winner in 1965, the first time the tournament was played over four days

Playing on a cornfield

Few courses in major championship history have received as much flak as Hazeltine, the venue for the 1970 US Open. A Robert Trent Jones design, Jack Nicklaus said it was a poor course when you had one hole where the line from the tee was a chimney, and another someone's house. As ever, though, the most stinging words came from the outspoken Dave Hill. "What does it lack?" he was asked in the Press room. "Eighty acres of corn and a few cows," came back the reply. "What do you recommend they do with it?" "Plough it up and start again." This hilarious interlude took place after the second round, and no one could accuse Hill of sour grapes. He had followed up a 75 with a 69 to stand on 144, three shots off the lead. He would not, however, get any closer, although this had less to do with his own golf than the astonishing play of a 25-year-old Englishman called Tony Jacklin.

The previous year at Lytham, Jacklin had charmed all Britain by winning the Open. Now he waltzed away with the US Open with a still more extraordinary performance. No Englishman had won the event for 49 years; but here he was, the leader by two shots after one round, three after two, four after three, and then no fewer than seven in front after 72 holes. It was the biggest win since the last Englishman to triumph, the Cornishman Jim Barnes who prevailed by nine in 1921.

Merry Mex

Jack Nicklaus's greatness as a golfer was never based purely on the tournaments he won. His sportsmanship was most apparent in 1969 when he conceded a putt to Tony Jacklin to ensure the Ryder Cup was tied, but a little under two years later there was another example. It concerned the Merry Mex Lee Trevino, or the not-so-merry Mex that he had become. Trevino had taken to prolonged bouts of drinking and indulging in behaviour that generally squandered his talent. He went a year without a victory, which was an age for a player who at the US Open in the summer of 1968 had seemed a golfer of almost boundless potential. Step forward, Nicklaus.

"I hope you continue to go right on clowning and never realize how good you could become, because if you ever did the rest of us might as well go home," he said. Trevino never forgot those words. Coming from a man who by that stage had established himself as a formidable presence, their shock value was considerable. Trevino cut down his drinking and took better care of himself.

What happened next was perhaps inevitable. Trevino started winning tournaments. Then he shot 280 in the US Open at Merion and found himself in a play-off with, well, who else but Nicklaus? If the Golden Bear had been that sort of golfer, he might have cursed his earlier intervention. As it was he saw his own words turn into a prophecy as Trevino shot 69 to win the play-off by two strokes. A month later the now-merry-again Mex completed the magical summer double when he collected the Open at Birkdale.

In 1972 the US Open visited Pebble Beach for the first time. No one was happier than Jack Nicklaus. From the first occasion he set eyes on its location he had considered it his favourite course. But the conditions that greeted the players were hardly typical mid-summer weather. The wind turned the links into a bear, so much so that no player was even level par at the end of the championship. The best score was two over; its holder was Nicklaus. It was his third US Open and his 11th major championship in all, putting him level on the all-time list with Walter Hagen.

In seventh place that year was the California boy himself, Johnny Miller. At the Masters the following April he improved on that position by one placing. At 26, Miller was reaching his prime, a player capable of playing the game as well as anyone had played it when he had a good day with his putter. At Oakmont in 1973, he demonstrated that gift to the world.

Miller opened with rounds of 71 and 69, a good start that left him just three shots adrift of Gary Player. A third-round 76, however, appeared to have ended his chances. By now all the attention was on the local boy, Arnold Palmer, who had rekindled memories of old with a third-round 68 to be one of four players tied for the lead. Miller, meanwhile booked a plane reservation for Sunday afternoon. He knew after his botched third round that he would be out reasonably early on the final day and playing for place money.

To reach the top he would, in fact, have to go past 12 men and make up no fewer than six strokes. After three holes, Miller began to think again about that plane reservation. He had birdied all three, and when he came up with another at the 4th, the thought that he could win crossed his mind for the first time. Not that anyone was paying much attention to him, so tightly bunched was the field. When he followed three pars with a bogey, he had fallen four behind.

A birdie at the 9th, however, revived his spirits. Then more birdies at the 10th, the 12th and the 13th. Fabled Oakmont had seen nothing like it; Miller was seven under par for the round and closing fast on the lead. And he kept on charging. Another birdie at the 15th, one of the hardest holes in American golf; a real bonus, the one that made all the difference. He parred in for a 63, the lowest round ever seen in a major, and one that has still to be beaten all these years on. It gave him a total of 279, five under par, and though 12 men tried, none would beat it. Not 43-year-old Palmer, who looked crest-fallen from the moment out on the course that he was told Miller had gone to five under; he would finish tied alongside Nicklaus and Trevino for fourth place, the last time he would seriously challenge for a major. For Miller, meanwhile, it was onwards and upwards.

Scott Simpson – won at the Olympic Club in 1987

The rest of the 1970s meandered to no great effect, with no dominant personality taking the US Open by the scruff of the neck. There were a couple of victories for that redoubtable competitor, Hale Irwin, and Jerry Pate – in his first season as a pro – became the youngest winner since Bobby Jones in 1923 with a victory at Atlanta in 1976. But what the golf world really wanted to know was what had happened to Nicklaus? Not since the 1978 Open at St Andrews had he looked like winning a major. Was he finished at the age of 40? The return to Baltusrol, the scene of his 1967 US Open win, would surely provide the answer, people thought. The omens did not look good when the week before, in the Atlanta Classic, Nicklaus missed the cut.

Nicklaus's revenge

Of the 18 major championship victories that Nicklaus would amass, the two that undoubtedly stand out are those achieved when people had written him off. One was the 1986 win at Augusta. The other was this US Open triumph, at Baltusrol.

Once a golfer that caused people to hold up placards saying, "Miss it, fat gut," here the metamorphosis to beloved icon was complete.

Nicklaus signalled his intentions from the start, equalling Miller's record 18-hole mark with a 63. He followed it with a 71 to remain in the lead, but after a third-round 70 he had been caught by the most talented Japanese player ever, Isao Aoki. Now we would really discover whether Nicklaus continued to have what it took to win.

Paired together for the fourth consecutive day, Aoki and Nicklaus played what amounted to matchplay golf. First one would slip ahead, and then the other. However, when they came to the two par fives to finish, Nicklaus had a little daylight: he was two shots to the good. Aoki refused to concede. He played a gorgeous pitch at the 17th that settled down five feet from the hole for a birdie. Now Nicklaus had to match it. His pitch, though, was disappointing, finishing 22 feet away. With all the concentration and determination he could muster Nicklaus examined the line, and stroked one of the sweetest putts of his career.

Still two ahead, Nicklaus knew a five would be good enough to win at the last. In the event he got another birdie four, as did Aoki. "Jack is back," said the scoreboard at the end. He was indeed. Nicklaus had proven the "horses-for-courses" theory to devastating effect. Now, when the Open returned to Pebble Beach in 1982, could he do so again?

It would prove to be one of the great championships, and a finish as dramatic as the course's location. On the final day it came down to this: Nicklaus had put together a familiar charge and sat in the scorer's hut with a fine total of 284, four under par. Only one player still out on the course had a chance of catching him, and that was his old nemesis, Tom Watson. Yet Watson had bogeyed the 16th after driving into a bunker, and now needed two pars to tie.

Given the pair of holes in front of him, this would be no easy task. The 17th is a daunting par three at the best of times, and never more so than on this day, when it plays into the prevailing wind. Then there was the treacherous par-five 18th, around the rocky Monterey shore. First the 17th, and a bad start. Watson hit a two iron, his rhythm awry, and the ball missed the green on the left and plunged into the murky depths of the rough.

Watson walked grim-faced to the ball. The pin was cut on the side of the green where his ball lay, and a par seemed an impossible task. By this stage of his career he had three Open titles to his name and two Masters; would the US Open always hang out of reach? When he got to the ball, his expression changed. He had been the victim of outrageous good fortune. The ball was not completely buried as he imagined it would be, indeed he felt he could work his sand wedge underneath it. Now he thought he could make his par, and perhaps even better.

"Get it close," his caddie said. "I'm going to do better than get it close, I am going to hole it," he replied. Watson chopped into the grass with his sand wedge, the ball popped up, rolled across the green and, just as it was gathering pace down the slope, collided with the flagstick and dropped into the hole. He set off on a dance of jubilation. He birdied the last as well, and the first person to congratulate him was Nicklaus. "You son of a bitch, you're something else, I am so proud of you," Nicklaus told him.

At Winged Foot in 1984 there came the first of Greg Norman's plethora of near misses in major championships. At the 72nd hole he retrieved some scrappy play with a 45-foot putt for par across the final green. The roar that greeted the putt was tumultuous and for Fuzzy Zoeller, standing back in the middle of the 18th fairway, it appeared very grave news indeed. For by that stage the pair had turned the event into a matchplay contest, and there was nothing in it as they came to the final hole; now Zoeller thought Norman had birdied, and held up a white handkerchief in mock surrender. He was walking to the green when he found the truth of the matter, and his own par meant an 18-hole play-off.

This proved as one-sided as the previous day's encounter had been thrilling. Zoeller was at his best that day, reducing the fabled Mamaroneck course to just 67 strokes. Norman, meanwhile, could do little right and finished with a 75.

In 1985, Oakland Hills's curious reputation as a place where journeymen thrive was underlined when Andy North somehow won the title for a second time. For a while on the final day it looked as if the first player from the Far East would win a major. The Taiwanese T.C. Chen was four strokes to the good with 14 holes to play. All that changed at the 5th as he ran up a disastrous eight. He would eventually shoot 77 and finish a shot adrift.

A year later the tournament returned to Shinnecock Hills after a 90-year absence, and no one was happier than Raymond Floyd, who outstared his playing partner Payne Stewart to win by two strokes.

In 1987 the Olympic Club did it again, confirming its reputation as the graveyard of favourites. Fleck over Hogan; Casper over Palmer; now it was the turn of Scott Simpson over Tom Watson. The latter, emerging from a long slump, had a putt to tie at the 18th, but to groans of anguish it stopped inches short of the hole.

After Tony Jacklin's amazing victory in 1970 the Europeans had reverted to type, with hardly a challenge to be seen. The courses invariably got the blame; the more adventurous venues at Open Championships and Augusta more favoured their style. Or so the excuse, sorry theory, went.

One player who had shown he could play anywhere, anytime, was Nick Faldo and in 1988 he got into a play-off with Curtis Strange at The Country Club. Yes, the same Country Club where Francis Ouimet had repelled the English invaders in 1913. Strange did the same on this occasion as Faldo

Ernie Els – two-time winner of the US Open by 1997, with surely more to come

bogeyed three of the last four holes to lose the play-off by four shots. A year later, Strange completed a successful defence at Oak Hill, following what had become by now a statutory major championship collapse by Tom Kite. Simpson became just the fifth player, after Johnny McDermott, Bobby Jones, Ralph Guldahl and Ben Hogan, to win back-to-back US Opens.

At Medinah in 1990 Hale Irwin completed the most unlikely of triumphs. True, he had won the event on two previous occasions, but by now he was 45. He was also a changed man. Gone were the glasses in favour of contact lenses. The dour personality appeared to have been jettisoned as well. Take the last hole of regulation play, for instance. Nick Faldo had seen a putt lip out here to finish one shot behind the winning score. Irwin, meanwhile, had a putt from all of 60 feet. It broke several different ways before it smashed into the back of the cup and fell below ground. The old Irwin would have taken off his visor and gently acknowledged the roaring crowd. This one recalled the good college footballer he was in his youth; he high-fived his caddie, a marshall, then he went on a lap of honour, high-fiving all the members of his considerable gallery as well.

That outrageous putt had earned him a play-off against Mike Donald, and the following day they still could not be separated after 18 holes. But Irwin was not to be parted from his fate, prevailing at the first extra hole. He had his third US Open, achieved over a time span of 16 years. Only Nicklaus ever won over a longer period.

It was a good start to the 1990s, but in truth the US Opens since have not always lived up to that standard, for the reasons stated in the introduction to this piece. In 1996 there was even the curious sight of a qualifier winning the tournament, as Steve Jones won by a stroke from Tom Lehman and Davis Love at, yes, you've guessed it, Oakland Hills.

There have also been two wins each this decade for Lee Janzen, in 1993 and 1998, and Ernie Els, the latter winning first in a play-off at Oakmont in 1994 with Colin Montgomerie and Loren Roberts and then, most memorably, at Congressional in 1997.

There he showed what a good player he had become, indeed surely the best of the decade alongside Tiger Woods. Level with Montgomerie and Tom Lehman with two holes to play, Els played a three wood off the tee at the desperately difficult 17th because he wanted to play his second shot to the green first. The resultant five iron was the shot of the tournament; it finished eight feet away and put intolerable pressure on his playing partner, Montgomerie. When Lehman, like Montgomerie before him, bogeyed the hole soon after, Els had his second major title.

For Lehman and Montgomerie, the US Open has only brought heartache to date. From 1995, Lehman led going into the last round for three successive years, but came up empty each time. Montgomerie, meanwhile, had cause to regret not only the presence of Els at Oakmont and Congressional. In 1992, in the winds of Pebble Beach, he matched the par of 288 and sat in the television gantry confident that no one would beat it. Jack Nicklaus even came over and proffered his congratulations. Both had reckoned without Jeff Sluman, who beat it by one, but most of all Tom Kite, who finally collected his first major with a 72 for a total of 285.

Centenary Open

And then there was the centenary US Open in 1995, played at wonderful Shinnecock Hills, one of the founding member clubs. What a century of tumultuous change both the tournament and the course had witnessed. When the event was first played there in 1896, 35 players entered. The number of golfers who played the game in America was around 100,000. In 1995 those figures had risen, respectively, to 6,001 and 24.3 million. Prize money in 100 years had grown from $335 to $2 million. And the attendance went from a few hundred to a daily sell-out audience of 40,000.

They witnessed a tournament that, if historical record is anything to go by, was played in better spirit than existed a century ago. Now we had an Australian challenging for the title, alongside two Americans. After two rounds the tournament was all about the former, Greg Norman, who opened with scores of 67 and 68. In the third round he was caught by Lehman, with Corey Pavin three adrift.

How could Pavin hope to compete alongside two behemoths? In the final round he was paired with Ian Woosnam, who outdrove him by 70 yards on some holes. Pavin showed how. Shaping the ball this way and that, he conjured up a series of magnificent shots and topped them all with sure putting. No stroke he played was better than his approach to the 18th, one of the great shots in major championship golf. Pavin had just taken the lead for the first time and now needed to consolidate. Yet he had a four wood for his approach to this daunting par four, with all manner of difficulty in his way. No matter. Pavin struck a wonderfully controlled blow, the ball hopping and skipping over the rolling turf before finishing six feet away. It was, dare one say it, a blow worthy of winning such a significant US Open.

And what of the future? The venues look promising. In 1999 Pinehurst played host for the first time; for the millennium the tournament returns to Pebble Beach, while in 2002 the US Open again breaks new ground, going to the splendid Black course in Bethpage State Park on Long Island, NY.

Let us just hope the USGA play fair and that no player needs to recall Walter Hagen's grumble from long ago – "The course is playing the players, rather than the players playing the course."

Corey Pavin – a major winner at last in the Centenary US Open of 1995

October 4, 1895

Newport GC, Newport, RI						
1	Horace Rawlins	45	46	41	41	173
2	Willie Dunn Jr	43	46	44	42	175
=3	James Foulis	46	43	44	43	176
	A.W. Smith (a)	47	43	44	42	176
5	Willie Davis	46	49	42	42	178
6	Willie Campbell	41	48	42	48	179
=7	John Harland	45	48	43	47	183
	John Patrick	46	48	46	43	183
9	Samuel Tucker	49	48	45	43	185
10	John Reid	49	51	55	51	206

July 18, 1896

Shinnecock Hills GC, Southampton, NY				
1	James Foulis	78	74	152
2	Horace Rawlins	79	76	155
3	Joe Lloyd	76	81	157
=4	George Douglas	79	79	158
	A.W. Smith (a)	78	80	158
=6	John Shippen	78	81	159
	H.J. Whigham (a)	82	77	159
8	Willie Tucker	78	82	160
9	Robert Wilson	82	80	162
10	Alfred Ricketts	80	83	163
11	W.H. Way	83	81	164
12	Willie Dunn Jr	78	87	165
13	Willie Davis	83	84	167
14	Willie Campbell	85	85	170
15	W.T. Hoare	90	81	171
=16	J.N. Mackrell	89	83	172
	Alex Patrick	86	86	172
	John Reid	88	84	172
=19	Tom Gourley	82	91	173
	John Patrick	88	85	73
21	Oscar Bunn	89	85	174
=22	John I'Anson	88	92	180
	George Strath	91	89	180
24	John Harrison	92	91	183
25	W.W. Campbell	91	93	184
26	Willie Norton	87	98	185
27	R. Anderson	92	95	187
28	T. Warrender	97	93	180

September 17, 1897

Chicago GC, Wheaton, IL				
1	Joe Lloyd	83	79	162
2	Willie Anderson Jr	79	84	163
=3	Willie Dunn Jr	87	81	168
	James Foulis	80	88	168
5	W.T. Hoare	82	87	169
=6	Bernard Nicholls	87	85	172
	Alfred Ricketts	91	81	172
=8	David Foulis	86	87	173
	Horace Rawlins	91	82	173
	H.J. Whigham (a)	87	86	173
=11	Charles Macdonald (a)	85	89	174
	William Marshall	87	87	174
	Robert Wilson	83	91	174
14	Harry Turpie	85	90	175
=15	Willie Davis	88	89	177
	Robert Foulis	88	89	177
	Willie Tucker	90	87	177
	J.A. Tyng (a)	86	91	177
19	Findlay Douglas (a)	89	91	180

September 17, 1897 continued

20	W.G. Stewart (a)	91	90	181
=21	R. Leslie	90	92	182
	R.G. McAndrews	90	92	182
	George Pearson	93	89	182
24	John Harrison	97	87	184
=25	Samuel Tucker	87	98	185
	W.H. Way	89	96	185
27	R. White	89	97	186
28	Devereux Emmett (a)	98	90	188
29	W.B. Smith (a)	98	91	189
30	A.C. Tolifson	91	100	191

June 17–18, 1898

Myopia Hunt Club, South Hamilton, MA						
1	Fred Herd	84	85	75	84	328
2	Alex Smith	78	86	86	85	335
3	Willie Anderson Jr	81	82	87	86	336
4	Joe Lloyd	87	80	86	86	339
5	Willie Smith	82	91	85	82	340
6	W.V. Hoare	84	84	87	87	342
7	Willie Dunn Jr	85	87	87	84	343
=8	John Jones	83	84	90	90	347
	H.C. Leeds (a)	81	84	93	89	347
	R.G. McAndrews	85	90	86	86	347
	Bernard Nicholls	86	87	88	86	347
12	Harry Turpie	85	87	86	91	349
13	Alex Findlay	89	88	84	89	350
=14	John Lister	92	88	90	85	355
	Willie Tucker	90	89	87	89	355
16	J.F. Curtis (a)	87	88	88	93	356
17	John Harland	84	93	93	87	357
18	Willie Davis	91	88	95	85	359
=19	Horace Rawlins	91	90	92	88	361
	J.A. Tyng (a)	92	91	88	90	361
=21	Q.A. Shaw (a)	88	85	93	98	364
	Jack Youds	92	90	92	90	364
=23	J.H. Mercer	85	95	93	93	366
	Gilbert Nicholls	91	92	91	92	366
25	John Dunn	91	88	91	97	367
26	Willie Campbell	93	91	97	101	382
27	H.R. Sweeney (a)	92	97	96	99	384
28	W. Rutherford (a)	100	99	98	91	388
29	W.E. Stoddart	103	95	97	96	391

September 14–15, 1899

Baltimore CC, Baltimore, MD						
1	Willie Smith	77	82	79	77	315
=2	Val Fitzjohn	85	80	79	82	326
	George Low	82	79	89	76	326
	W.H. Way	80	85	80	81	326
5	Willie Anderson Jr	77	81	85	84	327
6	Jack Park	88	80	75	85	328
7	Alex Smith	82	81	82	85	330
8	Henry Gullane	81	86	80	84	331
=9	Laurie Auchterlonie	86	87	82	78	333
	Peter Walker	84	86	77	86	333
11	A.H. Findlay	88	86	79	81	334
12	Alex Campbell	83	80	79	94	336
=13	H.M. Harriman (a)	87	88	85	79	339
	Alex Patrick	82	83	84	90	339
	Horace Rawlins	81	85	86	87	339
16	Alfred Ricketts	87	85	88	80	340
17	Bernard Nicholls	86	88	85	84	343
=18	David Foulis	83	86	91	85	345
	Harry Turpie	91	88	83	83	345
=20	James Foulis	94	84	88	80	346

September 14–15, 1899 continued

	Gilbert Nicholls	90	83	86	87	346
22	**Dan Leitch**	87	85	85	90	347
23	**Ernest Way**	85	87	87	89	348
24	**W. Thompson**	82	90	87	90	349
=25	**Fred Herd**	85	86	93	86	350
	John Shippen	86	88	88	88	350
=27	**Robert Braid**	85	90	86	90	351
	R.S. Patrick	85	92	88	86	351
	Willie Tucker	89	91	87	84	351
=30	**William Donovan**	88	89	91	96	354
	David Hunter	89	86	89	90	354

October 4–5, 1900

Chicago GC, Wheaton, IL

1	**Harry Vardon**	79	78	76	80	313
2	**J.H. Taylor**	76	82	79	78	315
3	**David Bell**	78	83	83	78	322
=4	**Laurie Auchterlonie**	84	82	80	81	327
	Willie Smith	82	83	79	83	327
6	**George Low**	84	80	85	82	331
7	**Tom Hutchinson**	81	87	81	84	333
8	**Harry Turpie**	84	87	79	84	334
9	**Stewart Gardner**	85	78	84	89	336
10	**Val Fitzjohn**	84	83	89	82	338
=11	**Willie Anderson Jr**	83	88	79	89	339
	Alex Campbell	86	77	93	83	339
13	**Alex Smith**	90	84	82	84	340
=14	**James Foulis**	86	88	87	82	343
	Robert Simpson	84	84	88	87	343
=16	**Frank Herd**	85	89	84	86	344
	Arthur Smith	89	85	85	85	344
	W.H. Way	88	85	84	87	344
=19	**Willie Norton**	87	87	84	87	345
	Harry Rawlins	86	84	90	85	345
21	**Ernest Way**	89	92	81	84	346
22	**J.B. Schlotman**	85	94	83	88	350
=23	**R.G. McAndrews**	87	93	87	84	351
	Joe Mitchell	88	96	82	85	351
=25	**Henry Gullane**	89	89	92	82	352
	A.C. Tolifson	93	87	88	84	352
=27	**W.V. Hoare**	90	87	91	85	353
	John Shippen	94	87	89	83	353
29	**Robert Foulis**	85	89	90	90	354
30	**Charles Macdonald (a)**	86	90	90	89	355

June 14–16, 1901

Myopia Hunt Club, South Hamilton, MA

** Willie Anderson Jr (85) beat Alex Smith (86) in the 18-hole play-off.*

1	**Willie Anderson Jr***	84	83	83	81	331
2	**Alex Smith**	82	82	87	80	331
3	**Willie Smith**	84	86	82	81	333
4	**Stewart Gardner**	86	82	81	85	334
=5	**Laurie Auchterlonie**	81	85	86	83	335
	Bernard Nicholls	84	85	83	83	335
7	**David Brown**	86	83	83	84	336
8	**Alex Campbell**	84	91	82	82	339
=9	**George Low**	82	89	85	85	341
	Jack Park	87	84	85	85	341
11	**James Foulis**	88	85	85	89	347
=12	**Val Fitzjohn**	86	86	89	87	348
	John Jones	87	84	87	80	348
=14	**Gilbert Nicholls**	87	87	88	87	349
	Robert Simpson	88	87	87	87	349
16	**Isaac Mackie**	87	88	85	90	350
=17	**A.H. Fenn**	87	90	87	87	351
	A.G. Lockwood (a)	82	89	89	91	351

June 14–16, 1901 continued

	Horace Rawlins	90	84	88	89	351
20	**Joe Lloyd**	90	87	86	89	352
21	**Donald Ross**	94	86	91	84	355
=22	**Walter Clark**	88	90	92	87	357
	Alex Taylor	94	84	92	87	357
	Harry Turpie	92	87	88	90	357
=25	**David Hunter**	91	92	89	87	359
	R.S. Patrick	90	91	87	91	359
27	**Willie Davis**	88	91	92	89	360
=28	**John Dingwall**	89	96	89	87	361
	Ed Fitzjohn	90	86	92	93	361
	John Harland	92	92	93	84	361
	Willie Hunter Sr	88	96	91	86	361
	L.C. Servas	94	83	91	93	361

October 10–11, 1902

Garden City GC, Garden City, NY

1	**Laurie Auchterlonie**	78	78	74	77	307
=2	**Stewart Gardner**	82	76	77	78	313
	Walter Travis (a)	82	82	75	74	313
4	**Willie Smith**	82	79	80	75	316
=5	**Willie Anderson Jr**	79	82	76	81	318
	John Shippen	83	81	75	79	318
7	**Charles Thom**	80	82	80	77	319
8	**Harry Turpie**	79	85	78	78	320
9	**Donald Ross**	80	83	78	81	322
10	**Alex Ross**	83	77	84	79	323
11	**Willie Norton**	83	82	79	81	325
=12	**David Brown**	80	88	82	76	326
	George Low	83	84	78	81	326
=14	**Jack Campbell**	77	87	79	85	328
	Jack Hobbens	85	82	80	81	328
=16	**A.S. Griffiths**	79	86	82	83	330
	Horace Rawlins	89	83	79	79	330
=18	**Gilbert Nicholls**	88	86	73	84	331
	Alex Smith	79	86	80	86	331
=20	**Alex Campbell**	88	82	83	79	332
	James Foulis	81	88	82	81	332
	John Harland	82	82	83	85	332
	Willie Hunter Sr	82	79	83	89	332
24	**Fred Herd**	82	79	83	89	333
25	**Jack Park**	79	89	85	81	334
=26	**George Braid**	85	81	84	85	335
	James Campbell	88	84	82	81	335
28	**Bernard Nicholls**	89	84	84	79	336
29	**John Mackie**	88	82	84	84	338
=30	**Alex Findlay**	85	81	87	86	339
	David Hunter	83	81	91	84	339
	R.S. Patrick	85	87	84	83	339

July 8–9, 1903

Baltusrol GC, Springfield, NJ

** Willie Anderson Jr (82) beat David Brown (84) in the 18-hole play-off.*

1	**Willie Anderson Jr***	73	76	76	82	307
2	**David Brown**	79	77	75	76	307
3	**Stewart Gardner**	77	77	82	79	315
4	**Alex Smith**	77	77	81	81	316
5	**Donald Ross**	79	79	78	82	318
6	**Jack Campbell**	76	83	83	77	319
7	**Laurie Auchterlonie**	75	79	84	83	321
8	**Findlay Douglas (a)**	77	79	82	84	322
=9	**Jack Hobens**	76	81	82	84	323
	Alex Ross	83	82	78	80	323
	Willie Smith	80	81	83	79	323
12	**Horace Rawlins**	82	77	78	87	324
=13	**Isaac Mackie**	83	80	78	84	325

July 8–9, 1903 continued

	F.O. Reinhart (a)	81	75	89	80	325
=15	**Alex Campbell**	79	84	80	83	326
	Gilbert Nicholls	86	82	78	80	326
	Walter Travis (a)	83	80	81	82	326
	W.H. Way	84	79	82	81	326
19	**Bernard Nicholls**	85	78	82	83	328
=20	**Willie Norton**	78	81	83	87	329
	David Ogilvie	81	86	81	81	329
22	**George Cummings**	83	86	77	84	330
23	**Harry Turpie**	86	82	81	82	331
=24	**Joe Lloyd**	84	85	80	83	332
	John Reid	82	82	84	84	332
=26	**George T. Brokaw (a)**	78	82	86	87	333
	James Campbell	81	84	82	86	333
	Fred McLeod	83	80	79	91	333
	Arthur Smith	80	87	83	83	333
30	**A.H. Fenn**	82	83	83	86	334

July 8–9, 1904

Glen View GC, Golf, IL

1	**Willie Anderson Jr**	75	78	78	72	303
2	**Gilbert Nicholls**	80	76	79	73	308
3	**Fred MacKenzie**	76	79	74	80	309
=4	**Laurie Auchterlonie**	80	81	75	78	314
	Bernard Nicholls	80	77	79	78	314
=6	**Percy Barrett**	78	79	79	80	316
	Stewart Gardner	75	76	80	85	316
	Robert Simpson	82	82	76	76	316
9	**James Foulis**	83	84	78	82	317
10	**Donald Ross**	80	82	78	78	318
=11	**Jack Hobens**	77	82	80	80	319
	Charles Murray	84	81	76	78	319
13	**Alex Murray**	81	87	80	82	320
14	**Horace Rawlins**	79	76	86	81	322
=15	**George Braid**	82	76	85	81	324
	Alex Ross	87	78	80	79	324
	George Thomson	78	87	81	78	324
18	**Alex Smith**	78	81	82	85	326
19	**David Robertson**	82	78	80	88	328
=20	**Jack Campbell**	80	88	79	82	329
	H. Chandler Egan (a)	84	79	83	83	329
	Harry Turpie	81	82	86	80	329
=23	**Robert Hunter (a)**	83	85	79	84	331
	George Low	89	81	82	79	331
	Alex Taylor	85	83	83	80	331
=26	**Kenneth Edwards**	84	83	80	85	332
	W.H. Way	88	83	79	82	332
28	**George Cummings**	83	83	82	85	333
=29	**Tom McDeever**	81	82	88	83	334
	Fred McLeod	86	88	81	79	334
	Peter Robertson	82	87	85	80	334
	James Watson	83	83	82	86	334

September 21–22, 1905

Myopia Hunt Club, South Hamilton, MA

1	**Willie Anderson Jr**	81	80	76	77	314
2	**Alex Smith**	76	80	80	80	316
=3	**Percy Barrett**	81	80	77	79	317
	Peter Robertson	79	80	81	77	317
5	**Stewart Gardner**	78	78	85	77	318
6	**Alex Campbell**	82	76	80	81	319
=7	**Jack Hobens**	82	80	81	78	321
	Gilbert Nicholls	82	76	84	79	321
9	**George Cummings**	85	82	75	81	323
10	**Arthur Smith**	81	77	80	86	324
=11	**A.G. Lockwood (a)**	84	85	76	80	325

September 21–22, 1905 continued

	Walter Travis (a)	81	80	80	84	325
=13	**Alex Ross**	79	86	78	83	326
	Willie Smith	86	81	76	83	326
15	**George Low**	83	82	81	81	327
=16	**Joe Lloyd**	75	86	83	84	328
	Fred McKenzie	81	85	80	82	328
18	**Walter Clark**	86	81	82	80	329
19	**Frank McLeod**	80	84	80	86	330
=20	**Tom McNamara**	81	79	82	89	331
	Bernard Nicholls	80	82	85	84	331
	George Turnbull	81	88	81	81	331
	W.H. Way	81	89	84	77	331
24	**Laurie Auchterlonie**	85	82	79	86	332
25	**Donald Ross**	83	83	86	81	333
=26	**Jack Jolly**	82	83	85	85	335
	James Maiden	80	86	83	86	335
28	**Robert Peebles**	81	81	86	88	336
=29	**Isaac Mackie**	82	82	83	90	337
	Charles Murray	84	85	83	85	337

June 28–29, 1906

Onwentsia Club, Lake Forest, IL

1	**Alex Smith**	73	74	73	75	295
2	**Willie Smith**	73	81	74	74	302
=3	**Laurie Auchterlonie**	76	78	75	76	305
	James Maiden	80	73	77	75	305
5	**Willie Anderson Jr**	73	76	74	84	307
6	**Alex Ross**	76	79	75	80	310
7	**Stewart Gardner**	80	76	77	78	311
=8	**H. Chandler Egan (a)**	79	78	76	80	313
	Gilbert Nicholls	76	81	77	79	313
10	**Jack Hobens**	75	84	76	79	314
=11	**George Low**	79	82	76	79	316
	Bernard Nicholls	79	77	79	81	316
13	**Harry Turpie**	80	80	76	83	319
=14	**Walter Fovargue**	77	84	78	81	320
	Jack Jolly	78	82	79	81	320
	Peter Robertson	79	78	80	83	320
17	**Alex Baxter**	83	81	81	86	321
=18	**Fred Brand**	78	78	85	81	322
	Alex Campbell	76	84	76	86	322
	George Cummings	79	76	84	83	322
	George Smith	79	76	82	85	322
=22	**James Foulis**	83	86	79	76	324
	Otto Hackbarth	82	82	82	78	324
	W.R. Lovekin	77	85	78	84	324
	D. McIntosh	79	79	81	85	324
	William Marshall	85	77	81	81	324
=27	**James Watson**	76	80	81	88	325
	Ernest Way	83	81	80	81	325
=29	**George O'Neill**	84	82	82	78	326
	David Robertson	82	79	81	84	326

June 20–21, 1907

Philadelphia Cricket Club, Chestnut Hill, PA

1	**Alex Ross**	76	74	76	76	302
2	**Gilbert Nicholls**	80	73	72	79	304
3	**Alex Campbell**	78	74	78	75	305
4	**Jack Hobens**	76	75	73	85	309
=5	**George Low**	78	76	79	77	310
	Fred McLeod	79	77	79	75	310
	Peter Robertson	81	77	78	74	310
=8	**David Brown**	75	80	78	78	311
	Bernard Nicholls	76	76	81	78	311
10	**Donald Ross**	78	80	76	78	312
=11	**Laurie Auchterlonie**	77	77	83	76	313

June 20–21, 1907 continued

	Fred Brand	78	80	73	82	313
13	**David Robertson**	80	78	75	81	314
14	**Tom McNamara**	82	79	78	76	315
15	**Willie Anderson Jr**	81	77	81	77	316
=16	**Mike Brady**	76	77	84	80	317
	David Hunter	77	75	85	80	317
	Martin O'Loughlin	81	81	77	78	317
19	**Jack Campbell**	78	79	82	80	319
20	**G.J. Bouse**	78	78	86	78	320
21	**Stewart Gardner**	81	79	78	83	321
=22	**James Campbell**	76	85	81	80	322
	Walter Clark	78	81	79	84	322
	Isaac Mackie	82	83	79	78	322
25	**Jack Jolly**	78	86	81	78	323
=26	**David Ogilvie**	82	81	81	80	324
	Horace Rawlins	82	76	83	83	324
	W.D. Robinson	82	84	80	78	324
	Jerome Travers (a)	81	84	80	79	324
=30	**W.C. Gaudin**	80	86	82	77	325
	W. Ogilvie	80	83	82	80	325

August 27–29, 1908

Myopia Hunt Club, South Hamilton, MA

** Fred McLeod (77) beat Willie Smith (83) in the 18-hole play-off.*

1	**Fred McLeod***	82	82	81	77	322
2	**Willie Smith**	77	82	85	78	322
3	**Alex Smith**	80	83	83	81	327
4	**Willie Anderson Jr**	85	86	80	79	330
5	**John Jones**	81	81	87	82	331
=6	**Jack Hobens**	86	81	85	81	333
	Peter Robertson	89	84	77	83	333
=8	**Percy Barrett**	94	80	86	78	338
	Jock Hutchinson	82	84	87	85	338
=10	**Richard Kimball**	84	86	83	86	339
	Tom McNamara	85	82	86	86	339
=12	**Donald Ball**	90	81	86	83	340
	Alex Campbell	85	83	89	83	340
	George Low	92	80	84	84	340
	Robert Peebles	85	85	85	85	340
16	**David Hunter**	87	87	84	83	341
=17	**H.H. Barker**	84	85	88	86	343
	Mike Brady	86	87	87	83	343
	Orrin Terry	86	87	83	87	343
20	**David Robertson**	89	83	86	86	344
=21	**Laurie Auchterlonie**	85	83	83	95	346
	Harry Rawlins	85	89	88	84	346
=23	**Isaac Mackie**	94	88	84	81	347
	Alex Ross	89	85	91	82	347
	Walter Travis (a)	90	83	87	87	347
26	**Jack Campbell**	91	89	87	82	349
=27	**David Brown**	87	86	91	86	350
	David Ogilvie	91	89	87	83	350
=29	**Arthur Smith**	97	85	85	85	352
	Herbert Strong	91	89	88	84	352
	W.H. Way	92	88	87	85	352

June 24–25, 1909

Englewood Golf Club, Englewood, NJ

1	**George Sargent**	75	72	72	71	290
2	**Tom McNamara**	73	69	75	77	294
3	**Alex Smith**	76	73	74	72	295
=4	**Willie Anderson Jr**	79	74	76	70	299
	Jack Hobens	75	78	72	74	299
	Isaac Mackie	77	75	74	73	299
=7	**Tom Anderson Jr**	78	74	75	73	300
	H.H. Barker	75	79	73	73	300

June 24–25, 1909 continued

	Andrew Campbell	71	75	77	77	300
	Tom Peebles	76	73	73	78	300
	Walter Travis (a)	72	78	77	73	300
12	**Mike Brady**	76	77	74	75	302
=13	**Alex Campbell**	75	73	81	74	303
	Fred McLeod	78	76	74	75	303
=15	**Orrin Terry**	78	80	73	73	304
	F.R. Upton Jr (a)	72	79	78	75	304
17	**Gilbert Nicholls**	73	75	79	79	306
=18	**Walter Fovargue**	80	76	77	74	307
	David Ogilvie	76	78	79	74	307
=20	**Peter Robinson**	79	72	78	79	308
	Charles Rowe	74	77	76	81	308
22	**Jack Campbell**	74	79	75	81	309
=23	**Laurie Auchterlonie**	78	75	77	71	311
	Findlay Douglas (a)	82	76	78	75	311
	Jock Hutchison	79	76	77	79	311
	Tom Vardon	80	75	82	74	311
=27	**John Dingwall**	79	74	77	72	312
	George Low	78	75	74	85	312
	James Maiden	76	78	80	78	312
=30	**Jack Burke Sr**	75	78	81	79	313
	David Hunter	68	84	84	77	313
	Charles Murray	77	75	77	84	313

June 17–18, 20, 1910

Philadelphia Cricket Club, Chestnut Hill, PA

** Alex Smith (71) beat John McDermott (75) and Macdonald Smith (77) in the 18-hole play-off.*

1	**Alex Smith***	73	73	79	73	298
2	**John McDermott**	74	74	75	75	298
3	**Macdonald Smith**	74	78	75	71	298
4	**Frank McLeod**	78	70	78	73	299
=5	**Tom McNamara**	73	78	73	76	300
	Gilbert Nicholls	73	75	77	75	300
7	**Jack Hobens**	74	77	74	76	301
=8	**Tom Anderson Jr**	72	76	81	73	302
	H.H. Barker	75	78	77	72	302
	Jock Hutchison	77	76	75	74	302
11	**Willie Anderson Jr**	74	78	76	75	303
=12	**George Low**	75	77	79	74	305
	Charles Thom	80	72	78	75	305
=14	**Tom Bonnar**	78	78	71	80	307
	George Cummings	78	73	79	77	307
=16	**Alex Campbell**	79	76	80	74	309
	George Sargent	77	81	74	77	309
=18	**Jack Campbell**	77	77	81	75	310
	James Thomson	74	80	80	76	310
20	**Fred Herreshoff (a)**	76	77	79	79	311
21	**George Smith**	76	78	79	80	313
22	**Alex Ross**	78	84	73	79	314
=23	**Otto Hackbarth**	79	82	78	76	315
	Martin O'Loughlin	77	82	80	76	315
25	**A.W. Tillinghast (a)**	80	81	79	76	316
26	**W.D. Robinson**	83	81	78	75	317
27	**Jack Burke Sr**	81	77	77	84	319
=28	**James Donaldson**	80	78	87	75	320
	David Honeyman	83	79	79	79	320
	Irving Stringer	83	77	82	78	320

June 23–24, 1911

Chicago GC, Wheaton, IL

** John McDermott (80) beat Mike Brady (82) and George Simpson (86) in the 18-hole play-off.*

1	**John McDermott***	81	72	75	79	307
2	**Mike Brady**	76	77	79	75	307

June 23–24, 1911 continued

3	**George Simpson**	76	77	79	75	307
4	**Fred McLeod**	77	72	76	83	308
=5	**Jock Hutchison**	80	77	73	79	309
	Gilbert Nicholls	76	78	74	81	309
=7	**H.H. Barker**	75	81	77	78	311
	George Sargent	76	77	84	74	311
=9	**Peter Robertson**	79	76	78	79	312
	Alex Ross	74	75	81	82	312
11	**Albert Seckel (a)**	78	80	80	75	313
=12	**Alex Campbell**	81	77	72	84	314
	Harry Turpie	77	76	82	79	314
14	**C.P. Nelson**	79	85	74	77	315
=15	**James Donaldson**	78	81	83	74	316
	George Low	80	78	82	76	316
17	**R.L. Simpson**	81	82	75	79	317
=18	**John Burke**	79	77	78	85	319
	D.E. Sawyer (a)	84	79	77	79	319
=20	**Grange Alves**	82	80	73	85	320
	George Cummings	82	80	79	79	320
	Mason Phelps (a)	78	78	78	86	320
=23	**H. Chandler Egan (a)**	81	80	77	83	321
	Robert Gardner (a)	81	78	79	83	321
	J.B. Simpson	81	82	78	80	321
	Alex Smith	76	78	82	85	321
	R.C. Watson (a)	82	79	78	82	321
28	**Walter Fovargue**	83	81	80	78	322
=29	**T.J. Foulis**	79	80	82	83	324
	Otto Hackbarth	78	74	83	89	324
	Robert McDonald	80	82	75	87	324
	Tom McNamara	77	87	79	81	324

August 1–2, 1912

Country Club of Buffalo, Buffalo, NY

1	**John McDermott**	74	75	74	71	294
2	**Tom McNamara**	74	80	73	69	296
=3	**Mike Brady**	72	75	73	79	299
	Alex Smith	77	70	77	75	299
5	**Alex Campbell**	74	77	80	71	302
6	**George Sargent**	72	78	76	77	303
=7	**Jack Dowling**	76	79	76	74	305
	Otto Hackbarth	77	77	75	76	305
9	**Charles Murray**	75	78	77	76	306
=10	**Tom Anderson Jr**	75	76	81	75	307
	Frank Peebles	73	76	83	75	307
	Walter Travis (a)	73	79	78	77	307
=13	**Fred McLeod**	79	77	75	77	308
	George Simpson	79	73	77	79	308
15	**Percy Barrett**	74	73	83	79	309
=16	**John G. Anderson (a)**	80	79	78	73	310
	David Ogilvie	74	83	73	80	310
=18	**Jim Barnes**	77	73	79	82	311
	John Dingwall	77	77	78	79	311
	Willie McFarlane	77	81	73	80	311
=21	**Jack Croke**	74	81	78	79	312
	Tom Vardon	74	83	79	76	312
=23	**Jack Campbell**	74	75	83	81	313
	George Cummings	78	79	77	79	313
	Jock Hutchison	78	77	82	76	313
26	**A.H. Murray**	78	79	79	78	314
27	**Charles Rowe**	77	78	79	81	315
=28	**Dave Robertson**	80	82	77	77	316
	Peter Robertson	77	82	81	76	316
=30	**David Black**	78	77	78	84	317
	David Honeyman	80	82	79	76	317
	David Livie	82	80	76	79	317

September 18–20, 1913

The Country Club, Brookline, MA

** Francis Ouimet (72) beat Harry Vardon (77) and Ted Ray (78) in the 18-hole play-off.*

1	**Francis Ouimet (a)***	77	74	74	79	304
2	**Harry Vardon**	75	72	78	79	304
3	**Ted Ray**	79	70	76	79	304
=4	**Jim Barnes**	74	76	78	79	307
	Walter Hagen	73	78	76	80	307
	Macdonald Smith	71	79	80	77	307
	Louis Tellier	76	76	79	76	307
8	**John McDermott**	74	79	77	78	308
9	**Herbert Strong**	75	74	82	79	310
10	**Pat Doyle**	78	80	73	80	311
=11	**W.C. Fownes Jr (a)**	79	75	78	80	312
	Elmer Loving	76	80	75	81	312
13	**Alex Campbell**	77	80	76	80	313
14	**Mike Brady**	83	74	78	80	315
15	**Matt Campbell**	83	80	77	76	316
=16	**Fred Herreshoff (a)**	75	78	83	82	318
	Jock Hutchinson	77	76	80	85	318
	Tom McNamara	73	86	75	84	318
	Wilfred Reid	75	72	85	86	318
	Alex Smith	82	75	82	79	318
=21	**Robert Andrews (a)**	83	73	83	80	319
	Jack Croke	72	83	83	81	319
	Charles Murray	80	80	80	79	319
	Peter Robertson	79	80	78	82	319
	George Sargent	75	76	79	89	319
=26	**Jack Dowling**	77	77	82	85	321
	Charles Thom	76	76	84	85	321
=28	**Bob MacDonald**	80	79	84	79	322
	Jerome Travers (a)	78	78	81	85	322
=30	**Frank Bellwood**	79	83	80	81	323
	James Donaldson	79	76	85	83	323
	J.H. Taylor	81	80	78	84	323

August 20–21, 1914

Midlothian CC, Blue Island, IL

1	**Walter Hagen**	68	74	75	73	290
2	**Charles Evans Jr (a)**	76	74	71	70	291
=3	**Fred McLeod**	78	73	75	71	297
	George Sargent	74	77	74	72	297
=5	**Mike Brady**	78	72	74	74	298
	James Donaldson	72	79	74	73	298
	Francis Ouimet (a)	69	76	75	78	298
8	**Louis Tellier**	72	75	74	78	299
=9	**John McDermott**	77	74	74	75	300
	Arthur Smith	79	73	76	72	300
=11	**W.M. Rautenbusch (a)**	76	75	75	75	301
	James Simpson	76	71	77	77	301
=13	**Jim Barnes**	73	76	80	73	302
	Charles Hoffner	77	76	77	72	302
	Tom McNamara	72	71	76	83	302
	Joe Mitchell	77	69	77	79	302
	J.J. O'Brien	74	72	77	79	302
	Robert Peebles	78	75	74	75	302
	George Simpson	73	76	76	77	302
=20	**Dan Kenny**	76	75	76	76	303
	Tom Kerrigan	76	73	77	77	303
=22	**Alex Ross**	72	75	82	76	305
	Warren Wood (a)	77	73	77	78	305
24	**Walter Fovargue**	81	71	77	77	306
=25	**Jack Munro**	83	74	75	75	307

August 20–21, 1914 continued

	R.M. Thompson	79	75	78	75	307
27	**Otto Hackbarth**	82	75	77	75	309
=28	**Fred Brand**	78	74	76	82	310
	Jack Burke Sr	75	77	77	81	310
	C.P. Nelson	77	81	77	75	310

June 17–18, 1915

Baltusrol GC, Springfield, NJ

1	**Jerome Travers (a)**	76	72	73	76	297
2	**Tom McNamara**	78	71	74	75	298
3	**Bob MacDonald**	72	77	73	78	300
=4	**Jim Barnes**	71	75	76	79	301
	Louis Tellier	75	71	76	79	301
6	**Mike Brady**	76	71	75	80	302
7	**George Low**	78	74	76	75	303
=8	**Jock Hutchison**	74	79	76	76	305
	Fred McLeod	74	76	76	79	305
=10	**Alex Campbell**	76	75	74	81	306
	Emmett French	77	79	75	75	306
	Walter Hagen	78	73	76	79	306
	Tom Kerrigan	78	75	76	77	306
	Gilbert Nicholls	78	81	73	74	306
	Jack Park	77	77	75	77	306
	Wilfred Reid	77	78	75	76	306
	George Sargent	75	77	79	75	306
18	**Charles Evans Jr (a)**	71	81	80	75	307
=19	**James Donaldson**	83	79	76	70	308
	Max Marston (a)	77	77	80	74	308
21	**A.J. Sanderson**	77	76	77	79	309
=22	**Jack Dowling**	75	79	80	77	311
	Alex Smith	78	76	78	79	311
=24	**H.H. Barker**	77	78	80	77	312
	Charles Hoffner	79	79	79	75	312
=26	**Joe Mitchell**	76	80	74	83	313
	Herbert Strong	83	76	78	76	313
28	**George Sayers**	76	80	81	77	314
=29	**Otto Hackbarth**	80	75	79	81	315
	David Ogilvie	75	78	83	79	315
	Ben Sayers	80	79	79	77	315

June 29–30, 1916

Minikahda Club, Minneapolis, MN

1	**Charles Evans Jr (a)**	70	69	74	73	286
2	**Jock Hutchison**	73	75	72	68	288
3	**Jim Barnes**	71	74	71	74	290
=4	**Gilbert Nicholls**	73	76	71	73	293
	Wilfred Reid	70	72	79	72	293
	George Sargent	75	71	72	75	293
7	**Walter Hagen**	73	76	75	71	295
8	**Bob MacDonald**	74	72	77	73	296
=9	**Mike Brady**	75	73	75	74	297
	J.J. O'Brien	76	72	73	76	297
	Tom Vardon	76	72	75	74	297
12	**Jack Dowling**	71	76	75	76	298
=13	**Walter Fovargue**	76	74	74	75	299
	Louis Tellier	74	75	72	78	299
=15	**Herbert Lagerblade**	77	78	72	73	300
	Tom McNamara	75	79	73	73	300
	Robert Peebles	73	72	76	79	300
	J.B. Simpson	75	76	76	73	300
=19	**Otto Hackbarth**	77	80	69	75	301
	George McLean	77	76	74	74	301
=21	**James Donaldson**	79	75	75	73	302
	Joe Mitchell	75	75	76	76	302
	George Turnbull	83	73	72	74	302

June 29–30, 1916 continued

=24	**Bert Battell**	76	75	75	77	303
	Arthur Fotheringham	78	78	74	73	303
	Fred McLeod	74	75	77	77	303
	George Simpson	76	76	77	74	303
28	**Alex Campbell**	75	75	75	79	304
=29	**Alex Cunningham**	79	75	75	77	306
	James Ferguson	74	75	80	77	306
	Tom Kerrigan	79	72	78	77	306

1917–1918 – No Championship

June 9–12, 1919

Brae Burn CC, West Newton, MA

** Walter Hagen (77) beat Mike Brady (78) in the 18-hole play-off.*

1	**Walter Hagen***	78	73	75	75	301
2	**Mike Brady**	74	74	73	80	301
=3	**Jock Hutchison**	78	76	76	76	306
	Tom McNamara	80	73	79	74	306
=5	**George McLean**	81	75	76	76	308
	Louis Tellier	73	78	82	75	308
7	**John Cowan**	79	74	75	81	309
=8	**George Bowden**	73	78	75	86	312
	Fred McLeod	78	77	79	78	312
10	**Charles Evans Jr (a)**	77	76	82	78	313
=11	**Jim Barnes**	77	78	79	81	315
	Harry Hampton	79	81	77	78	315
=13	**Clarence Hackney**	83	78	81	74	316
	Charles Hoffner	72	78	77	89	316
	Isaac Mackie	82	75	78	81	316
=16	**Gilbert Nicholls**	81	78	82	77	318
	Alex Ross	77	78	77	86	318
=18	**Pat Doyle**	78	82	76	83	319
	Francis Ouimet (a)	76	79	79	85	319
	James West	79	82	80	78	319
=21	**Alex Cunningham**	79	81	79	81	320
	Douglas Edgar	80	78	82	80	320
	Wilfred Reid	82	78	80	80	320
=24	**Jesse Guildford (a)**	79	78	84	80	321
	J. Sanderson	85	79	83	74	321
=26	**Otto Hackbarth**	77	79	82	84	322
	Tom Kerrigan	80	79	82	81	322
	Herbert Lagerblade	79	80	82	81	322
=29	**George Fotheringham**	81	82	79	81	323
	Bob MacDonald	81	78	80	84	323
	George Sargent	84	79	82	78	323

August 12–13, 1920

Inverness Club, Toledo, OH

1	**Ted Ray**	74	73	73	75	295
=2	**Jack Burke Sr**	75	77	72	72	296
	Leo Diegel	72	74	73	77	296
	Jock Hutchison	69	76	74	77	296
	Harry Vardon	74	73	71	78	296
=6	**Jim Barnes**	76	70	76	76	298
	Charles Evans Jr (a)	74	76	73	75	298
=8	**Bobby Jones (a)**	78	74	70	77	299
	Willie MacFarlane	76	75	74	74	299
10	**Bob MacDonald**	73	78	71	78	300
11	**Walter Hagen**	74	73	77	77	301
12	**Clarence Hackney**	78	74	74	76	302
13	**Fred McLeod**	75	77	73	79	304
=14	**Mike Brady**	77	76	74	78	305
	Frank McNamara	78	77	76	74	305
	Charles Rowe	76	78	77	74	305
=17	**Laurie Ayton Sr**	75	78	76	77	306

August 12–13, 1920 continued

	John Golden	77	80	74	75	306
	Eddie Loos	75	74	73	84	306
=20	**Douglas Edgar**	73	82	74	78	307
	James West	80	77	75	75	307
22	**Harry Hampton**	79	76	74	79	308
=23	**Tom Kerrigan**	77	81	74	77	309
	Gilbert Nicholls	77	82	75	75	309
	J.J. O'Brien	82	77	73	77	309
	D.K. White	78	75	79	77	309
=27	**Bill Mehlhorn**	78	74	79	79	310
	Peter O'Hara	84	74	74	78	310
	Alex Ross	80	76	77	77	310
=30	**George Bowden**	74	80	76	81	311
	Charles Hall	77	80	76	80	311
	Willie Kidd	77	81	76	77	311
	George McLean	83	76	73	79	311
	Gene Sarazen	79	79	76	77	311

July 21–22, 1921

Columbia CC, Chevy Chase, MD

1	**Jim Barnes**	69	75	73	72	289
=2	**Walter Hagen**	79	73	72	74	298
	Fred McLeod	74	74	76	74	298
4	**Charles Evans Jr (a)**	73	78	76	75	302
=5	**Emmett French**	75	77	74	77	303
	Bobby Jones (a)	78	71	77	77	303
	Alex Smith	75	75	79	74	303
=8	**George Duncan**	72	78	78	77	305
	Clarence Hackney	74	76	78	77	305
10	**Emil Loeffler**	74	77	74	81	306
11	**Alfred Hackbarth**	80	76	82	69	307
12	**Eddie Loos**	76	79	75	78	308
13	**Cyril Walker**	78	76	76	79	309
=14	**Mike Brady**	77	80	78	75	310
	Jess Sweetser (a)	78	78	77	77	310
	Louis Tellier	76	74	78	82	310
17	**Gene Sarazen**	83	74	77	77	311
=18	**Laurie Ayton Sr**	81	74	74	83	312
	Jock Hutchison	75	83	77	77	312
	Peter O'Hara	81	82	76	73	312
21	**Charles Murray**	75	73	82	83	313
=22	**John Golden**	77	77	82	78	314
	Otto Hackbarth	79	76	80	79	314
	Harry Hampton	80	78	79	77	314
	Charles Mothersole	81	78	79	76	314
=26	**Tom Boyd**	81	79	79	76	315
	Bobby Cruikshank	75	77	80	83	315
	Leo Diegel	75	82	83	75	315
	Jesse Guildford (a)	79	75	78	83	315
=30	**P.O. Hart**	83	80	76	77	316
	Pat O'Hara	77	78	79	82	316

July 14–15, 1922

Stokie CC, Glencoe, IL

1	**Gene Sarazen**	72	73	75	68	288
=2	**John Black**	71	71	75	72	289
	Bobby Jones (a)	74	72	70	73	289
4	**Bill Mehlhorn**	73	71	72	74	290
5	**Walter Hagen**	68	77	74	72	291
6	**George Duncan**	76	73	75	72	296
7	**Leo Diegel**	77	76	73	71	297
=8	**Mike Brady**	73	75	74	76	298
	John Golden	73	77	77	71	298
	Jock Hutchison	78	74	71	75	298
=11	**Laurie Ayton Sr**	72	76	78	73	299
	Johnny Farrell	73	76	75	75	299

July 14–15, 1922 continued

=13	**Joe Kirkwood Sr**	77	74	75	74	300
	Bob MacDonald	73	76	75	76	300
15	**Eddie Loos**	75	76	73	77	301
16	**Charles Evans Jr (a)**	72	76	74	80	302
=17	**George Hackney**	74	78	74	77	303
	Abe Mitchell	79	75	76	73	303
=19	**Emmett French**	76	74	77	78	305
	Jesse Guildford (a)	74	77	76	78	305
	Harry Hampton	76	75	77	77	305
	Charles Hoffner	79	76	77	73	305
	Willie Ogg	79	72	78	76	305
=24	**Jim Barnes**	74	75	77	80	306
	Cyril Hughes	81	74	77	74	306
	Willie Hunter Jr (a)	75	75	76	80	306
	Fred Wright Jr (a)	76	77	73	80	306
=28	**Jack Burke Sr**	76	77	81	73	307
	Bobby Cruikshank	82	74	74	77	307
	Lloyd Gullickson	77	70	83	77	307

July 13–15, 1923

Inwood CC, Inwood, NY

** Bobby Jones (76) beat Bobby Cruikshank (78) in the 18-hole play-off.*

1	**Bobby Jones (a)***	71	73	76	76	296
2	**Bobby Cruikshank**	73	72	78	73	296
3	**Jock Hutchison**	70	72	82	78	302
4	**Jack Forrester**	75	73	77	78	303
=5	**Johnny Farrell**	76	77	75	76	304
	Francis Gallett	76	72	77	79	304
	W.M. Reekie (a)	80	74	75	75	304
=8	**Leo Diegel**	77	77	76	76	306
	Bill Mehlhorn	73	79	75	79	306
	Al Watrous	74	75	76	81	306
11	**Cyril Hughes**	74	76	80	77	307
=12	**Jim Barnes**	78	81	74	75	308
	Joe Kirkwood Sr	77	77	79	75	308
=14	**Charles Evans Jr (a)**	79	80	76	74	309
	Joe Turnesa	76	81	74	78	309
=16	**Charles Mothersole**	77	80	71	82	310
	Gene Sarazen	79	78	73	80	310
=18	**Walter Hagen**	77	75	73	86	311
	Willie Ogg	74	76	80	81	311
=20	**Mike Brady**	74	81	76	81	312
	Macdonald Smith	77	76	81	78	312
22	**Emmett French**	79	78	77	79	313
23	**Cyril Walker**	76	78	80	80	314
=24	**P.O. Hart**	79	80	78	78	315
	Joe Sylvester	77	80	79	79	315
=26	**John Black**	82	76	78	80	316
	William Creavy	73	81	77	85	316
	Eddie Held (a)	80	75	79	82	316
=29	**Hutt Martin**	78	78	76	85	317
	Francis Ouimet (a)	82	75	78	82	317
	George Sargent	77	77	81	82	317

June 5–6, 1924

Oakland Hills CC, Birmingham, MI

1	**Cyril Walker**	74	74	74	75	297
2	**Bobby Jones (a)**	74	73	75	78	300
3	**Bill Mehlhorn**	72	75	76	78	301
=4	**Bobby Cruikshank**	77	72	76	78	303
	Walter Hagen	75	75	76	77	303
	Macdonald Smith	78	72	77	76	303
=7	**Abe Espinosa**	80	71	77	77	305
	Peter O'Hara	76	79	74	76	305
9	**Mike Brady**	75	77	77	77	306
=10	**Charles Evans Jr (a)**	77	77	76	77	307

June 5–6, 1924 continued

	Eddie Loos	73	81	75	78	307
	Dave Robertson	73	76	77	81	307
=13	**Tommy Armour**	78	76	75	80	309
	Clarence Hackney	81	72	78	78	309
=15	**Willie Ogg**	75	80	76	79	310
	Joe Turnesa	76	78	78	78	310
=17	**Walter Bourne**	78	76	79	80	313
	Gene Sarazen	74	80	80	79	313
=19	**Johnny Farrell**	79	76	77	82	314
	Tom Kerrigan	77	74	89	74	314
	Jack Rogers	82	77	77	78	314
=22	**Emmett French**	79	79	78	79	315
	Joe Kirkwood Sr	77	80	80	78	315
	James West	81	72	78	84	315
=25	**Laurie Ayton Sr**	77	79	84	86	316
	Leo Diegel	78	78	82	78	316
	John Golden	75	83	78	80	316
	Jack Stait	79	77	81	79	316
=29	**Wiffy Cox**	82	76	81	78	317
	Jesse Guildford (a)	80	78	79	80	317

June 3–5, 1925

Worcester CC, Worcester, MA

** Willie MacFarlane (75, 72) beat Bobby Jones (75, 73) after the second 18-hole play-off.*

1	**Willie MacFarlane***	74	67	72	78	291
2	**Bobby Jones (a)**	77	70	70	74	291
=3	**Johnny Farrell**	71	74	69	78	292
	Francis Ouimet (a)	70	73	73	76	292
=5	**Walter Hagen**	72	76	71	74	293
	Gene Sarazen	72	72	75	74	293
7	**Mike Brady**	74	72	74	74	294
8	**Leo Diegel**	73	68	77	78	296
=9	**Laurie Ayton Sr**	75	71	73	78	297
	Al Espinosa	72	71	74	80	297
=11	**Macdonald Smith**	73	79	72	75	299
	Joe Turnesa	76	74	71	78	299
=13	**Willie Hunter Jr**	75	77	75	73	300
	Al Watrous	78	73	74	75	300
=15	**Bob MacDonald**	75	77	77	72	301
	Bill Mehlhorn	78	72	75	76	301
17	**Clarence Hackney**	78	72	73	79	302
=18	**John Golden**	76	75	82	70	303
	Tom Kerrigan	75	79	74	75	303
=20	**Tom Boyd**	73	79	75	77	304
	Jack Forrester	71	76	76	81	304
	Emmett French	77	74	77	76	304
	Francis Gallett	73	70	84	77	304
	Harry Hampton	79	75	76	74	304
	Bob Shave	81	72	77	74	304
26	**Charles Mayo**	75	74	78	78	305
=27	**Jock Hutchison**	78	78	79	71	306
	Wilfred Reid	79	75	73	79	306
=29	**Jim Barnes**	75	76	71	85	307
	George Heron	75	77	77	78	307

July 8–10, 1926

Scioto CC, Columbus, OH

1	**Bobby Jones (a)**	70	79	71	73	293
2	**Joe Turnesa**	71	74	72	77	294
=3	**Leo Diegel**	72	76	75	74	297
	Johnny Farrell	76	79	69	73	297
	Bill Mehlhorn	68	75	76	78	297
	Gene Sarazen	78	77	72	70	297
7	**Walter Hagen**	73	77	74	74	298
8	**Willie Hunter Jr**	75	77	69	79	300
=9	**Tommy Armour**	76	76	74	75	301

July 8–10, 1926 continued

	Willie Klein	76	74	75	76	301
	Macdonald Smith	82	76	68	75	301
	Dan Williams	72	74	80	75	301
=13	**Al Espinosa**	71	79	78	74	302
	Charles Evans Jr (a)	75	75	73	79	302
	Jack Forrester	76	73	77	76	302
=16	**Laurie Ayton Sr**	76	78	76	76	306
	Mike Brady	77	82	76	71	306
	George McLean	74	74	79	79	306
	Jimmy Thomson	77	82	73	74	306
=20	**Willie MacFarlane**	72	79	75	81	307
	Jock Rogers	80	79	75	73	307
22	**Clarence Hackney**	77	77	74	80	308
=23	**Arthur De Mane**	76	80	78	75	309
	P.O. Hart	76	81	76	76	309
	Harrison Johnston (a)	79	76	77	77	309
	Tom Stevens	79	78	76	76	309
=27	**Emmett French**	74	79	76	81	310
	Harry Hampton	81	75	78	76	310
	Tom Harmon Jr	73	81	76	80	310
	Bob MacDonald	77	79	77	77	310
	Eddie Murphy	74	77	80	79	310

June 14–17, 1927

Oakmont GC, Oakmont, PA

** Tommy Armour (76) beat Harry Cooper (79) in the 18-hole play-off.*

1	**Tommy Armour***	78	71	76	76	301
2	**Harry Cooper**	74	76	74	77	301
3	**Gene Sarazen**	74	74	80	74	302
4	**Emmett French**	75	79	77	73	304
5	**Bill Mehlhorn**	75	77	80	73	305
6	**Walter Hagen**	77	73	76	81	307
=7	**Archie Compston**	79	74	76	79	308
	Johnny Farrell	81	73	78	76	308
	John Golden	83	77	75	73	308
	Harry Hampton	73	78	80	77	308
=11	**Bobby Cruikshank**	77	78	76	78	309
	Leo Diegel	78	74	80	77	309
	Bobby Jones (a)	76	77	79	77	309
	Eddie Loos	78	75	79	77	309
=15	**Fred Baroni**	80	72	79	79	310
	Perry Del Vecchio	79	79	76	76	310
	Arthur Havers	79	77	74	80	310
=18	**Al Espinosa**	83	80	79	69	311
	Harrison Johnston (a)	73	74	87	77	311
	Willie MacFarlane	82	76	80	73	311
	Macdonald Smith	78	76	81	76	311
	Al Watrous	82	74	78	77	311
23	**Jock Hutchison**	80	77	77	78	312
=24	**Jim Barnes**	78	75	81	79	313
	P.O. Hart	77	77	86	73	313
	Larry Nabholtz	75	81	78	79	313
=27	**Ted Ray**	76	83	77	78	314
	Joe Turnesa	81	79	78	76	314
=29	**Tom Harmon Jr**	79	77	80	79	315
	Bob MacDonald	77	83	78	77	315

June 21–23, 1928

Olympia Fields CC, Matteson, IL

** Johnny Farrell beat Bobby Jones in the 18-hole play-off.*

1	**Johnny Farrell***	77	74	71	72	294
2	**Bobby Jones (a)**	73	71	73	77	294
3	**Roland Hancock**	74	77	72	72	295
=4	**Walter Hagen**	75	72	73	76	296
	George von Elm (a)	74	72	76	74	296
=6	**Harry Ciuci**	70	77	72	80	299

June 21–23, 1928 continued

	Waldo Crowder	74	74	76	75	299
	Ed Dudley	77	79	68	75	299
	Bill Leach	72	74	73	80	299
	Gene Sarazen	78	76	73	72	299
	Denny Shute	75	73	79	72	299
	Macdonald Smith	75	77	75	72	299
	Joe Turnesa	74	77	74	74	299
=14	**Al Espinosa**	74	74	77	75	300
	Willie MacFarlane	73	74	73	80	300
16	**Tommy Armour**	76	75	77	73	301
17	**Jack Forrester**	77	76	75	74	302
=18	**Billy Burke**	74	79	73	77	303
	Neil Christian	80	78	74	71	303
	Leo Diegel	72	79	75	77	303
	Charles Hilgendorf	76	77	79	71	303
=22	**Frank Ball**	70	81	78	75	304
	Archie Compston	76	81	75	72	304
	Harrison Johnston (a)	77	75	79	73	304
=25	**Harry Hampton**	77	76	72	80	305
	Leonard Schmutte	71	81	75	78	305
27	**Frank Walsh**	74	74	80	78	306
=28	**Willie Hunter Jr**	73	83	73	78	307
	Felix Serafin	75	76	77	79	307
	Horton Smith	72	79	76	80	307

June 27–30, 1929

Winged Foot GC, Mamaroneck, NY

** Bobby Jones beat Al Espinosa in the 36-hole play-off.*

1	**Bobby Jones (a)***	69	75	71	79	294
2	**Al Espinosa**	70	72	77	75	294
=3	**Gene Sarazen**	71	71	76	78	296
	Denny Shute	73	71	76	76	296
=5	**Tommy Armour**	74	71	76	76	297
	George von Elm (a)	79	70	74	74	297
7	**Henry Ciuci**	78	74	72	75	299
=8	**Leo Diegel**	74	74	76	77	301
	Peter O'Hara	74	76	73	78	301
10	**Horton Smith**	76	77	74	75	302
=11	**Wiffy Cox**	74	76	80	75	305
	J.E. Rogers	78	76	77	74	305
=13	**P.O. Hart**	76	78	75	77	306
	Charles Hilgendorf	72	79	75	80	306
15	**Billy Burke**	75	80	78	74	307
=16	**Louis Chiapetta**	78	79	72	79	308
	George Smith	77	77	77	77	308
	Craig Wood	79	71	80	78	308
=19	**Walter Hagen**	76	81	74	78	309
	Joe Kirkwood Sr	75	82	76	76	309
=21	**Jim Barnes**	78	78	81	73	310
	Massie Miller	75	82	75	78	310
=23	**Jack Forrester**	77	76	75	83	311
	Ted Longworth	74	82	73	82	311
	Macdonald Smith	77	78	80	76	311
=26	**Jack Burke Sr**	77	80	74	81	312
	Willie Hunter Jr	76	77	76	83	312
	Willie MacFarlane	79	78	76	79	312
	Leonard Schmutte	73	75	89	75	312
=30	**Tom Boyd**	79	80	74	80	313
	Emerick Koscis	79	76	77	81	313

July 10–12, 1930

Interlachen CC, Minneapolis, MN

1	**Bobby Jones (a)**	71	73	68	75	287
2	**Macdonald Smith**	70	75	74	70	289

July 10-12, 1930 continued

3	**Horton Smith**	72	70	76	74	292
4	**Harry Cooper**	72	72	73	76	293
5	**Johnny Golden**	74	73	71	76	294
6	**Tommy Armour**	70	76	75	76	297
7	**Charles Lacey**	74	70	77	77	298
8	**Johnny Farrell**	74	72	73	80	299
=9	**Bill Mehlhorn**	76	74	75	75	300
	Criag Wood	73	75	72	80	300
=11	**Leo Diegel**	75	75	76	75	301
	Johnny Goodman (a)	74	80	72	75	301
	Al Heron (a)	76	78	74	73	301
	Peter O'Hara	75	77	73	76	301
	George Smith	72	81	74	74	301
	George von Elm (a)	80	74	73	74	301
=17	**Ed Dudley**	74	75	78	76	303
	Mortie Dutra	76	80	69	78	303
	Charles Guest	76	73	77	77	303
	Walter Hagen	72	75	76	80	303
	Willie Hunter Jr	76	76	78	73	303
	Bob Shave	76	72	78	77	303
	Joe Turnesa	73	78	78	74	303
	Al Watrous	79	73	73	78	303
=25	**Olin Dutra**	73	79	78	75	305
	Francis Gallett	76	75	74	80	305
	Denny Shute	76	78	77	74	305
=28	**Herman Barron**	77	78	74	77	306
	Billy Burke	76	72	82	76	306
	Jack Forrester	73	75	80	78	306
	Charles Hilgendorf	74	81	76	75	306
	Walter Kozak	74	76	78	78	306
	Gene Sarazen	76	78	77	75	306
	Frank Walsh	75	78	77	76	306

July 2–6, 1931

Inverness GC, Toledo, OH

** Billy Burke (149, 148) beat George von Elm (149, 149) after two 36-hole play-offs.*

1	**Billy Burke***	73	72	74	73	292
2	**George von Elm**	75	69	73	75	292
3	**Leo Diegel**	75	73	74	72	294
=4	**Wiffy Cox**	75	74	74	72	295
	Bill Mehlhorn	77	73	75	71	296
	Gene Sarazen	74	78	74	80	296
=7	**Mortie Dutra**	71	77	73	76	297
	Walter Hagen	74	74	73	76	297
	Phil Perkins (a)	78	76	73	70	297
=10	**Al Espinosa**	72	78	75	74	299
	Johnny Farrell	78	70	79	72	299
	Macdonald Smith	73	73	75	78	299
=13	**Guy Paulsen**	74	72	74	80	300
	Frank Walsh	73	77	75	75	300
=15	**Herman Barron**	71	75	78	77	301
	Harry Cooper	76	75	75	75	301
	Ed Dudley	75	76	76	74	301
	Al Watrous	74	78	76	73	301
=19	**Charles Guest**	71	75	76	80	302
	Tony Manero	74	75	80	73	302
=21	**Olin Dutra**	76	76	76	75	303
	John Kinder	79	72	75	77	303
=23	**Laurie Ayton Sr**	76	79	74	75	304
	Willie Klein	75	80	70	79	304
=25	**Denny Shute**	79	73	77	76	305
	Eddie Williams	71	74	81	79	305
=27	**Johnny Golden**	79	75	78	74	306
	Horton Smith	77	78	75	76	306
=29	**Auguste Boyer**	75	80	72	80	307
	Henry Ciuci	73	79	81	74	307
	Bill Davies	73	83	74	77	307

June 23–25, 1932

Fresh Meadow CC, Flushing, NY

1	Gene Sarazen	74	76	70	66	286
=2	Bobby Cruikshank	78	74	69	68	289
	Phil Perkins	76	69	74	70	289
4	Leo Diegel	73	74	73	74	294
5	Wiffy Cox	80	73	70	72	295
6	Jose Jurado	74	71	75	76	296
=7	Billy Burke	75	77	74	71	297
	Harry Cooper	77	73	73	74	297
	Olin Dutra	69	77	75	76	297
10	Walter Hagen	75	73	79	71	298
11	Clarence Clark	79	72	74	75	300
=12	Vincent Eldred	78	73	77	73	301
	Paul Runyan	79	77	69	76	301
=14	Henry Ciuci	77	74	77	74	302
	Ed Dudley	80	74	71	77	302
	Johnny Goodman (a)	79	78	77	68	302
	Fred Morrison	77	80	69	76	302
	Denny Shute	78	76	76	72	302
	Macdonald Smith	80	76	74	72	302
	Craig Wood	79	71	79	73	302
=21	Tommy Armour	82	73	77	71	303
	George Smith	81	76	72	74	303
=23	Mortie Dutra	77	77	75	75	304
	Joe Kirkwood Sr	76	77	75	76	304
	Charles Lacey	77	76	78	73	304
	Jack Patroni	79	77	77	71	304
=27	John Fischer (a)	81	78	74	73	306
	Bob MacDonald	82	77	74	73	306
	George von Elm	79	73	77	77	306
	Al Zimmerman	79	77	73	77	306

July 8–10, 1933

North Shore CC, Glenview, IL

1	Johnny Goodman (a)	75	66	70	76	287
2	Ralph Guldahl	76	71	70	71	288
3	Craig Wood	73	74	71	72	290
=4	Tommy Armour	68	75	76	73	292
	Walter Hagen	73	76	77	66	292
6	Mortie Dutra	75	73	72	74	294
=7	Olin Dutra	75	71	75	74	295
	Gus Moreland (a)	76	76	71	72	295
=9	Clarence Clark	80	72	72	72	296
	Johnny Farrell	75	77	72	72	296
	Willie Goggin	79	73	73	71	296
	Joe Kirkwood Sr	74	70	79	73	296
=13	Herman Barron	77	77	74	69	297
	Al Watrous	74	76	77	70	297
=15	Henry Ciuci	73	79	74	72	298
	Johnny Revolta	73	76	75	74	298
=17	George Dawson (a)	78	74	71	76	299
	Leo Diegel	78	71	75	75	299
=19	Lester Bolstad (a)	76	74	73	77	300
	Macdonald Smith	77	72	77	74	300
=21	Johnny Golden	79	76	74	72	301
	Archie Hambrick	81	71	75	74	301
	Denny Shute	76	77	72	76	301
=24	Abe Espinosa	76	73	78	75	302
	Horton Smith	75	76	76	75	302
=26	Bob Crowley	75	75	81	72	303
	Ky Laffoon	74	78	79	72	303
	Gene Sarazen	74	77	77	75	303
=29	Harry Cooper	78	76	75	75	304
	Tony Manero	79	73	77	75	304
	Bill Schwartz	75	81	72	76	304
	Frank Walsh	79	73	72	80	304

June 7–9, 1934

Merion Cricket Club, Ardmore, PA

1	Olin Dutra	76	74	71	72	293
2	Gene Sarazen	73	72	73	76	294
=3	Harry Cooper	76	74	74	71	295
	Wiffy Cox	71	75	74	75	295
	Bobby Cruikshank	71	71	77	76	295
=6	Billy Burke	76	71	77	72	296
	Macdonald Smith	75	73	78	70	296
=8	Tom Creavy	79	76	78	76	299
	Ralph Guldahl	78	73	70	78	299
	Jimmy Hines	80	70	77	72	299
	Johnny Revolta	76	73	77	73	299
=12	Joe Kirkwood Sr	75	73	78	74	300
	Ted Luther	78	71	78	73	300
=14	Willie Hunter Jr	75	74	80	72	301
	Alvin Krueger	76	75	75	75	301
16	Mark Fry	79	75	74	74	302
=17	Henry Ciuci	74	74	79	76	303
	Leo Diegel	76	71	78	78	303
	Johnny Golden	75	76	74	78	303
	Horton Smith	74	73	79	77	303
=21	Al Espinosa	76	74	76	78	304
	Phil Perkins	78	74	79	73	304
=23	Hermann Barron	79	72	76	78	305
	Ky Laffoon	76	73	80	76	305
=25	Lawson Little (a)	83	72	76	75	306
	Eddie Loos	76	75	78	77	306
	Orville White	76	79	76	75	306
=28	Rodney Bliss Jr (a)	74	73	82	78	307
	Mortie Dutra	74	77	79	77	307
	Zell Eaton (a)	76	73	78	80	307
	Paul Runyan	74	78	79	76	307
	George Schneitner	76	76	79	76	307
	Bill Schwartz	81	74	73	79	307
	George von Elm	74	76	80	77	307

June 6–8, 1935

Oakmont CC, Oakmont, PA

1	Sam Parks Jr	77	73	73	76	299
2	Jimmy Thomson	73	73	77	78	301
3	Walter Hagen	77	76	73	76	302
=4	Ray Mangrum	76	76	72	79	303
	Denny Shute	78	73	76	76	303
=6	Alvin Krueger	71	77	78	80	306
	Henry Picard	79	78	70	79	306
	Gene Sarazen	75	74	78	79	306
	Horton Smith	73	79	79	75	306
=10	Dick Metz	77	76	76	78	307
	Paul Runyan	76	77	79	75	307
=12	Olin Dutra	77	76	78	77	308
	Vincent Eldred	75	77	77	79	308
=14	Herman Barron	73	79	78	79	309
	Bobby Cruikshank	78	76	77	78	309
	Mortie Dutra	75	77	80	77	309
	Macdonald Smith	74	82	76	77	309
	Ted Turner	80	71	81	77	309
	Al Watrous	75	80	79	75	309
20	Vic Ghezzi	75	78	81	77	311
=21	Sid Brews	76	81	78	77	312
	Ed Dudley	74	83	75	80	312
	Bill Kaiser	78	82	78	74	312
	Gene Kunes	76	79	77	80	312
	Craig Wood	76	80	79	77	312
=26	Ted Luther	80	76	84	73	313
	Frank Walsh	76	82	82	73	313
=28	Harry Cooper	77	81	79	77	314

June 6–8, 1935 continued

	Al Espinosa	75	76	78	85	314
	Willie Hunter Jr	78	80	80	76	314
	Ky Laffoon	75	83	81	75	314

June 4–6, 1936

Baltusrol GC, Springfield, NJ

1	Tony Manero	73	69	73	67	282
2	Harry Cooper	71	70	70	73	284
3	Clarence Clark	69	75	71	72	287
4	Macdonald Smith	73	73	72	70	288
=5	Wiffy Cox	74	74	69	72	289
	Ky Laffoon	71	74	70	74	289
	Henry Picard	70	71	74	74	289
=8	Ralph Guldahl	73	70	73	74	290
	Paul Runyan	69	75	73	73	290
10	Denny Shute	72	69	73	77	291
=11	Herman Barron	73	74	69	76	292
	Tom Kerrigan	70	75	72	75	292
	Ray Mangrum	69	71	76	76	292
=14	Charles Koscis (a)	72	71	73	77	293
	Frank Moore	70	74	75	74	293
	Johnny Revolta	70	71	77	75	293
	Jimmy Thomson	74	73	71	75	293
=18	Billy Burke	72	76	72	74	294
	Vic Ghezzi	70	70	73	81	294
	Willie Goggin	73	73	72	76	294
	Harold McSpaden	75	71	78	70	294
=22	Tommy Armour	74	76	74	71	295
	Johnny Farrell	75	75	70	75	295
	Jerry Gianferante	74	73	71	77	295
	Johnny Goodman (a)	75	73	73	74	295
	Felix Serafin	72	73	74	76	295
	Horton Smith	75	75	72	73	293
=28	Al Brosch	73	75	72	76	296
	Zell Eaton	72	75	72	77	296
	Dick Metz	74	73	73	76	296
	Jack Munger (a)	74	70	76	76	296
	Gene Sarazen	75	72	75	74	296

June 10–12, 1937

Oakland Hills CC, Birmingham, MI

1	Ralph Guldahl	71	69	72	69	281
2	Sam Snead	69	73	70	71	283
3	Bobby Cruikshank	73	73	67	72	285
4	Harry Cooper	72	70	73	71	286
5	Ed Dudley	70	70	71	76	287
6	Al Brosch	74	73	68	73	288
7	Clarence Clark	72	75	73	69	289
8	Johnny Goodman (a)	70	73	72	75	290
9	Frank Strafaci (a)	70	72	77	72	291
=10	Charles Koscis (a)	72	73	76	71	292
	Henry Picard	71	75	72	74	292
	Gene Sarazen	78	69	71	74	292
	Denny Shute	69	76	75	72	292
=14	Ray Mangrum	75	75	71	72	293
	Paul Runyan	76	72	73	72	293
=16	Billy Burke	75	73	71	75	294
	Jimmy Demaret	72	74	76	72	294
	Sam Parks Jr	74	74	72	74	294
	Pat Sawyer	72	70	75	77	294
=20	Vic Ghezzi	72	71	78	74	295
	Jimmy Hines	75	72	76	72	295
	Ky Laffoon	74	74	74	73	295
	Harold McSpaden	74	75	73	73	295
	Fred Morrison	71	76	74	74	295

June 10–12, 1937 continued

	Byron Nelson	73	78	71	73	295
	Bob Stupple	73	73	73	76	295
	Frank Walsh	70	70	78	77	295
=28	Leo Mallory	73	74	76	73	296
	Toney Penna	76	74	75	71	296
	Johnny Revolta	75	73	75	73	296
	Jimmy Thomson	74	66	78	78	296

June 9–11, 1938

Cherry Hills CC, Denver, CO

1	Ralph Guldahl	74	70	71	69	284
2	Dick Metz	73	68	70	79	290
=3	Harry Cooper	76	69	76	71	292
	Toney Penna	78	72	74	68	292
=5	Byron Nelson	77	71	74	72	294
	Emery Zimmerman	72	71	73	78	294
=7	Frank Moore	79	73	72	71	295
	Henry Picard	70	70	77	78	295
	Paul Runyan	78	72	71	74	295
10	Gene Sarazen	74	74	75	73	296
=11	Vic Ghezzi	79	71	75	72	297
	Jimmy Hines	70	75	69	83	297
	Denny Shute	77	71	72	77	297
	George von Elm	78	72	71	76	297
15	Willie Hunter Jr	73	72	78	75	298
=16	Olin Dutra	74	71	77	77	299
	Harold McSpaden	76	67	74	82	299
	Johnny Revolta	74	72	77	76	299
=19	Jim Foulis	74	74	75	77	300
	Horton Smith	80	73	73	74	300
	Al Zimmerman	76	77	75	72	300
22	Charles Lacey	77	75	75	75	302
23	Tommy Armour	78	70	75	80	303
=24	Al Huske	76	79	76	73	304
	Johnny Rogers	71	76	73	84	304
26	Charles Sheppard	79	73	74	79	305
=27	Joe Belfore	75	73	80	78	306
	Stanley Kertes	77	72	82	75	306
	Alvin Krueger	79	69	79	79	306
	Ray Mangrum	77	77	73	79	306

June 6–12, 1939

Philadelphia CC, Philadelphia, PA

** Byron Nelson (68, 70) beat Craig Wood (68, 73) and Denny Shute (76) after two 18-hole play-offs.*

1	Byron Nelson*	72	73	71	68	284
2	Craig Wood	70	71	71	72	284
3	Denny Shute	70	72	70	72	284
4	Bud Ward (a)	69	73	71	72	285
5	Sam Snead	68	71	73	74	286
6	Johnny Bulla	72	71	68	76	287
=7	Ralph Guldahl	71	73	72	72	288
	Dick Metz	76	72	71	69	288
=9	Ky Laffoon	76	70	73	70	289
	Harold McSpaden	70	73	71	75	289
	Paul Runyan	76	70	71	72	289
=12	Harry Cooper	71	72	75	72	290
	Ed Dudley	76	72	73	69	290
	Henry Picard	72	72	72	74	290
15	Horton Smith	72	68	75	76	291
=16	Sam Byrd	75	71	72	74	292
	Olin Dutra	70	74	70	78	292
	Clayton Haefner	73	73	66	80	292
	Wilford Wehrle (a)	71	77	69	75	292
=20	Jimmy Hines	73	74	77	69	293

June 6–12, 1939 continued

	Johnny Rogers	75	70	69	79	293
=22	**Tommy Armour**	70	75	69	80	294
	Jimmy Demaret	72	76	72	74	294
	Johnny Revolta	73	76	71	74	294
=25	**Bobby Cruikshank**	73	74	73	75	295
	Jim Foulis	73	75	77	70	295
	Dutch Harrison	75	72	74	74	295
	Matt Kowal	69	76	75	75	295
=29	**Vic Ghezzi**	73	71	76	76	296
	Ed Oliver	75	77	72	72	296
	Felix Serafin	80	72	71	73	296

June 6–9, 1940

Canterbury GC, Cleveland, OH

** Lawson Little (70) beat Gene Sarazen (73) in the 18-hole play-off.*

1	**Lawson Little***	72	69	73	73	287
2	**Gene Sarazen**	71	74	70	72	287
3	**Horton Smith**	69	72	78	69	288
4	**Craig Wood**	72	73	72	72	289
=5	**Ralph Guldahl**	73	71	76	70	290
	Ben Hogan	70	73	74	73	290
	Lloyd Mangrum	75	70	71	74	290
	Byron Nelson	72	74	70	74	290
9	**Dick Metz**	75	72	72	72	291
=10	**Ed Dudley**	73	75	71	73	292
	Frank Walsh	73	69	71	79	292
=12	**Tommy Armour**	73	74	75	71	293
	Harold McSpaden	74	72	70	77	293
	Henry Picard	73	73	71	76	293
15	**Vic Ghezzi**	70	74	75	75	294
=16	**Jim Foulis**	73	73	77	72	295
	Gene Kunes	76	72	73	74	295
	Johnny Revolta	73	74	72	76	295
	Sam Snead	67	74	73	81	295
=20	**Andrew Gibson**	71	75	77	73	296
	Jimmy Hines	73	74	77	72	296
	Felix Serafin	77	74	71	74	296
=23	**Jock Hutchison Jr**	73	72	75	77	297
	Eddie Kirk	73	77	74	73	297
	Wilford Wehrle (a)	78	73	72	74	297
	Leland Wilcox	75	73	74	75	297
27	**Ray Mangrum**	73	78	75	72	298
28	**Johnny Farrell**	75	77	76	71	299
=29	**Bruce Coltart**	80	72	74	74	300
	Jim Ferrier (a)	73	74	78	75	300
	Al Huske	70	80	76	74	300
	Sam Parks Jr	69	74	79	78	300
	Henry Ransom	75	77	74	74	300
	Jack Ryan	75	75	77	73	300
	Andrew Szwedko	76	77	76	71	300

June 5–7, 1941

Colonial CC, Fort Worth, TX

1	**Craig Wood**	73	71	70	70	284
2	**Denny Shute**	69	75	72	71	287
=3	**Johnny Bulla**	75	71	72	71	289
	Ben Hogan	74	77	68	70	289
=5	**Herman Barron**	75	71	74	71	291
	Paul Runyan	73	72	71	75	291
=7	**Dutch Harrison**	70	82	71	71	294
	Harold McSpaden	71	75	74	74	294
	Gene Sarazen	74	73	72	75	294
=10	**Ed Dudley**	74	74	74	73	295
	Lloyd Mangrum	73	74	72	76	295
	Dick Metz	71	74	76	74	295

June 5–7, 1941 continued

=13	**Henry Ransom**	72	74	75	75	296
	Horton Smith	73	75	73	75	296
	Sam Snead	76	70	77	73	296
	Harry Todd (a)	72	77	76	71	296
=17	**Lawson Little**	71	73	79	74	297
	Byron Nelson	73	73	74	77	297
19	**Vic Ghezzi**	70	79	77	72	298
20	**Gene Kunes**	71	79	74	75	299
=21	**Ralph Guldahl**	79	76	72	73	300
	Clayton Heafner	72	72	78	78	300
	Johnny Palmer	74	76	76	74	300
24	**Jimmy Hines**	74	75	76	76	301
25	**Joe Zarhardt**	74	76	77	75	302
=26	**Sam Byrd**	76	78	75	74	303
	Herman Keiser	74	77	76	76	303
	Johnny Morris	72	73	81	77	303
	Henry Picard	77	79	72	75	303
=30	**Jim Ferrier**	77	71	81	75	304
	Jerry Gianferante	76	77	74	77	304
	Bud Ward (a)	76	77	75	76	304

1942–45 – No Championships

June 13–16, 1946

Canterbury GC, Cleveland, OH

** Lloyd Mangrum (72, 72) beat Vic Ghezzi (72, 73) and Byron Nelson (72, 73) in two 18-hole play-offs.*

1	**Lloyd Mangrum***	74	70	68	72	284
=2	**Vic Ghezzi**	71	69	72	72	284
	Byron Nelson	71	71	69	73	284
=4	**Herman Barron**	72	72	72	69	285
	Ben Hogan	72	68	73	72	285
=6	**Jimmy Demaret**	71	74	73	68	286
	Ed Oliver	71	71	74	70	286
=8	**Chick Harbert**	72	78	67	70	287
	Dick Metz	76	70	72	69	287
=10	**Dutch Harrison**	75	71	72	70	288
	Lawson Little	72	69	76	71	288
=12	**Ed Furgol**	77	69	74	69	289
	Clayton Heafner	75	72	71	71	289
	Henry Picard	71	73	71	74	289
=15	**Claude Harmon**	72	77	70	72	291
	Chandler Harper	76	74	67	74	291
	Steve Kovach	71	72	73	75	291
	Toney Penna	69	77	74	71	291
=19	**Gene Kunes**	74	73	73	72	292
	Sam Snead	69	75	74	74	292
21	**Paul Runyan**	75	72	76	70	293
=22	**Johnny Bulla**	72	74	73	75	294
	Henry Ransom	71	73	73	77	294
	Harry Todd	75	73	70	76	294
	Lew Worsham	73	74	76	71	294
=26	**Leland Gibson**	74	71	78	72	295
	Smiley Quick (a)	75	76	72	72	295
	Mike Turnesa	70	76	74	75	295
	Ellsworth Vines	73	72	75	75	295
	Bud Ward (a)	74	77	72	72	295

June 12–15, 1947

St Louis CC, St Louis, MO

** Lew Worsham (69) beat Sam Snead (70) in the 18-hole play-off.*

1	**Lew Worsham***	70	70	71	71	282
2	**Sam Snead**	72	70	70	70	282
=3	**Bobby Locke**	68	74	70	73	285
	Ed Oliver	73	70	71	71	285

June 12–15, 1947 continued

5	**Bud Ward (a)**	69	72	73	73	287
=6	**Jim Ferrier**	71	70	74	74	289
	Vic Ghezzi	74	73	73	69	289
	Leland Gibson	69	76	73	71	289
	Ben Hogan	70	75	70	74	289
	Johnny Palmer	72	70	75	72	289
	Paul Runyan	71	74	72	72	289
12	**Chick Harbert**	67	72	81	70	290
=13	**Ed Furgol**	70	75	72	74	291
	Dutch Harrison	76	72	70	73	291
	Dick Metz	69	70	78	74	291
	Bill Nary	77	71	70	73	291
	Frank Stranahan (a)	73	74	72	72	291
	Harry Todd	67	75	77	72	291
=19	**Claude Harmon**	74	72	74	72	292
	Gene Kunes	71	77	72	72	292
	George Payton	71	75	75	71	292
	Alfred Smith	70	73	76	73	292
=23	**Sam Byrd**	72	74	70	77	293
	Joe Kirkwood Sr	72	73	70	78	293
	Lloyd Mangrum	77	72	69	75	293
	James McHale Jr (a)	79	72	65	77	293
=27	**Herman Barron**	74	71	75	74	294
	Billy Burke	74	75	71	74	294
=29	**Bob Hamilton**	75	71	75	74	295
	Henry Ransom	67	74	79	75	295

June 10–12, 1948

Riviera CC, Pacific Palisades, CA

1	**Ben Hogan**	67	72	68	69	276
2	**Jimmy Demaret**	71	70	68	69	278
3	**Jim Turnesa**	71	69	70	70	280
4	**Bobby Locke**	70	69	73	70	282
5	**Sam Snead**	69	69	73	72	283
6	**Lew Worsham**	67	74	71	73	285
7	**Herman Barron**	73	70	71	72	286
=8	**Johnny Bulla**	73	72	75	67	287
	Toney Penna	70	72	73	72	287
	Smiley Quick	73	71	69	74	287
11	**Skip Alexander**	71	73	71	73	288
=12	**Charles Congdon**	71	70	71	77	289
	Harold McSpaden	74	69	69	77	289
=14	**Vic Ghezzi**	72	74	74	70	290
	Leland Gibson	71	76	69	74	290
	Otto Greiner	74	73	71	72	290
	Herman Keiser	71	71	73	75	290
	George Schneiter	73	68	75	74	290
	Herschel Spears	72	71	76	71	290
	Ellsworth Vines	75	72	69	74	290
=21	**Joe Kirkwood Jr**	72	70	72	77	291
	Lloyd Mangrum	71	72	74	74	291
	Cary Middlecoff	74	71	73	73	291
	Alfred Smith	73	72	77	69	291
=25	**Art Bell**	72	75	71	74	292
	Pete Cooper	76	72	72	72	292
	George Fazio	72	72	76	72	292
=28	**Marty Furgol**	72	74	73	74	293
	Chick Harbert	72	72	77	72	293
	Joe Kirkwood Sr	73	75	73	72	293
	Frank Moore	73	75	73	72	293

June 9–11, 1949

Medinah CC, Medinah, IL

1	**Cary Middlecoff**	75	67	69	75	286
=2	**Clayton Heafner**	72	71	71	73	287
	Sam Snead	73	73	71	70	287

June 9–11, 1949 continued

=4	**Bobby Locke**	74	71	73	71	289
	Jim Turnesa	78	69	70	72	289
=6	**Dave Douglas**	74	73	70	73	290
	Buck White	74	68	70	78	290
=8	**Pete Cooper**	71	73	74	73	291
	Claude Harmon	71	72	74	74	291
	Johnny Palmer	71	75	72	73	291
=11	**Eric Monti**	75	72	70	75	292
	Herschel Spears	76	71	71	74	292
13	**Al Brosch**	70	71	73	79	293
=14	**Johnny Bulla**	73	75	72	74	294
	Lloyd Mangrum	74	74	70	76	294
	Skee Riegel (a)	72	75	73	74	294
	Harry Todd	76	72	73	73	294
	Ellsworth Vines	73	72	71	78	294
=19	**Fred Haas**	74	73	73	75	295
	Les Kennedy	69	74	79	73	295
	Gene Webb	73	77	70	75	295
22	**Ralph Guldahl**	71	75	73	77	296
=23	**Jim Ferrier**	74	75	74	74	297
	Chick Harbert	70	78	75	74	297
	Jack Isaacs	73	73	74	77	297
	Horton Smith	72	75	74	76	297
=27	**Skip Alexander**	76	72	77	73	298
	Herman Barron	70	78	76	74	298
	Sam Bernadi	80	69	76	73	298
	Jack Burke Jr	74	74	75	75	298
	Charles Farlow	70	77	76	75	298
	James McHale Jr (a)	72	76	74	76	298
	Craig Wood	76	73	76	73	298
	Lew Worsham	71	76	71	80	298

June 8–11, 1950

Merion GC, Ardmore, PA

** Ben Hogan (69) beat Lloyd Mangrum (73) and George Fazio (75) in the 18-hole play-off.*

1	**Ben Hogan***	72	69	72	74	287
2	**Lloyd Mangrum**	72	70	69	76	287
3	**George Fazio**	73	72	72	70	287
4	**Dutch Harrison**	72	67	73	76	288
=5	**Jim Ferrier**	71	69	74	75	289
	Joe Kirkwood Jr	71	74	74	70	289
	Henry Ransom	72	71	73	73	289
8	**Bill Nary**	73	70	74	73	290
9	**Julius Boros**	68	72	77	74	291
=10	**Cary Middlecoff**	71	71	71	79	292
	Johnny Palmer	73	70	70	79	292
=12	**Al Besselink**	71	72	76	75	294
	Johnny Bulla	74	66	78	76	294
	Dick Mayer	73	76	73	72	294
	Henry Picard	71	71	79	73	294
	Skee Riegel	73	69	79	73	294
	Sam Snead	73	75	72	74	294
=18	**Skip Alexander**	68	74	77	76	295
	Fred Haas	73	74	76	72	295
=20	**Jimmy Demaret**	72	77	71	76	296
	Marty Furgol	75	71	72	78	296
	Dick Metz	76	71	71	78	296
	Bob Toski	73	69	80	74	296
	Harold Williams	69	75	75	77	296
=25	**Bobby Cruikshank**	72	77	76	72	297
	Ted Kroll	75	72	78	72	297
	Lee Mackey Jr	64	81	75	77	297
	Paul Runyan	76	73	73	75	297
=29	**Pete Cooper**	75	72	76	75	298
	Henry Williams Jr	69	76	76	77	298

June 14–16, 1951

Oakland Hills CC, Birmingham, MI

1	Ben Hogan	76	73	71	67	287
2	Clayton Heafner	72	75	73	69	289
3	Bobby Locke	73	71	74	73	291
=4	Julius Boros	74	74	71	74	293
	Lloyd Mangrum	75	74	74	70	293
=6	Al Besselink	72	77	72	73	294
	Dave Douglas	75	70	75	74	294
	Fred Hawkins	76	72	75	71	294
	Paul Runyan	73	74	72	75	294
=10	Al Brosch	73	74	76	72	295
	Smiley Quick	73	76	74	72	295
	Skee Riegel	75	76	71	73	295
	Sam Snead	71	78	72	74	295
=14	Jimmy Demaret	74	74	70	78	296
	Lew Worsham	76	71	76	73	296
=16	Charles Koscis (a)	75	74	76	72	297
	Henry Ransom	74	74	76	73	297
	Buck White	76	75	74	72	297
=19	Raymond Gafford	76	74	74	74	298
	Johnny Revolta	78	72	72	76	298
=21	Charles Bassler	79	71	74	75	299
	Joe Kirkwood Jr	74	78	73	74	299
23	Marty Furgol	78	72	74	76	300
=24	Cary Middlecoff	76	73	79	73	301
	Ed Oliver	81	71	77	72	301
	Johnny Palmer	73	78	76	74	301
	Henry Picard	78	73	78	72	301
	Earl Stewart	74	74	78	75	301
=29	Tommy Bolt	77	72	75	78	302
	Roberto de Vicenzo	75	76	74	77	302
	Fred Haas	77	75	77	73	302
	George Kinsman	75	73	75	79	302
	Sam Urzetta (a)	78	71	78	75	302
	Bo Wininger (a)	75	71	77	79	302

June 12–14, 1952

Northwood GC, Dallas, TX

1	Julius Boros	71	71	68	71	281
2	Ed Oliver	71	72	70	72	285
3	Ben Hogan	69	69	74	74	286
4	Johnny Bulla	73	68	73	73	287
5	George Fazio	71	69	75	75	290
6	Dick Metz	70	74	76	71	291
=7	Tommy Bolt	72	76	71	73	292
	Ted Kroll	71	75	76	70	292
	Lew Worsham	72	71	74	75	292
=10	Lloyd Mangrum	75	74	72	72	293
	Sam Snead	70	75	76	72	293
	Earl Stewart	76	75	70	72	293
=13	Clarence Doser	71	73	73	77	294
	Harry Todd	71	76	74	73	294
=15	Al Brosch	68	79	77	71	295
	Jimmy Demaret	74	77	73	71	295
	Milon Marusic	73	76	74	72	295
	Horton Smith	70	73	76	76	295
=19	Doug Ford	74	74	74	74	296
	James Jackson (a)	74	76	75	71	296
	Bill Trombley	72	73	81	70	296
=22	Leland Gibson	73	76	72	76	297
	Paul Runyan	73	78	73	73	297
=24	Chick Harbert	75	75	73	75	298
	Cary Middlecoff	75	74	75	74	298
	Felice Torza	74	76	70	78	298
	Bo Wininger	78	72	69	79	298
=28	Zell Eaton	78	72	69	79	299

June 12–14, 1952 continued

	Raymond Gafford	77	74	75	73	299
	Dick Mayer	74	77	69	79	299
	Stan Mosel (a)	71	77	75	76	299
	P. Patrick	74	76	73	76	299

June 11–13, 1953

Oakmont CC, Oakmont, PA

1	Ben Hogan	67	72	73	71	283
2	Sam Snead	72	69	72	76	289
3	Lloyd Mangrum	73	70	74	75	292
=4	Pete Cooper	78	75	71	70	294
	Jimmy Demaret	71	76	71	76	294
	George Fazio	70	71	77	76	294
=7	Ted Kroll	76	71	74	74	295
	Dick Metz	75	70	74	76	295
=9	Marty Furgol	73	74	76	73	296
	Jay Herbert	72	72	74	78	296
	Frank Souchak (a)	70	76	76	74	296
=12	Fred Haas	74	73	72	78	297
	Bill Ogden	71	78	75	73	297
=14	Jack Burke Jr	76	73	72	77	298
	Dutch Harrison	77	75	70	76	298
	Bobby Locke	78	70	74	76	298
=17	Julius Boros	75	72	76	76	299
	Clarence Doser	74	76	78	71	299
	Bill Nary	76	74	73	76	299
	Jim Turnesa	75	78	72	74	299
=21	Gardner Dickinson	77	73	76	74	300
	Doug Ford	74	77	74	75	300
	Al Mengert	75	71	78	76	300
	Bob Rosburg	76	72	78	74	300
	Frank Stranahan (a)	75	75	75	75	300
=26	Clayton Heafner	75	75	76	75	301
	James McHale Jr (a)	79	74	75	73	301
	Peter Thomson	80	73	73	75	301
	Art Wall	80	72	77	72	301
=30	Louis Barbaro	72	79	74	77	302
	Jerry Barber	72	75	76	79	302
	Toby Lyons	73	78	74	77	302

June 17–19, 1954

Baltusrol GC, Springfield, NJ

1	Ed Furgol	71	70	71	72	284
2	Gene Littler	70	69	76	70	285
=3	Lloyd Mangrum	72	71	72	71	286
	Dick Mayer	72	71	70	73	286
5	Bobby Locke	74	70	74	70	288
=6	Tommy Bolt	72	72	73	72	289
	Fred Haas	73	73	71	72	289
	Ben Hogan	71	70	76	72	289
	Shelley Mayfield	73	75	72	69	289
	Billy Joe Patton (a)	69	76	71	73	289
=11	Cary Middlecoff	72	71	72	75	290
	Sam Snead	72	73	72	73	290
=13	Rudy Horvath	75	72	71	73	291
	Al Mengert	71	72	73	75	291
=15	Jack Burke Jr	73	73	72	75	293
	Claude Harmon	75	72	72	74	293
17	Jay Herbert	77	70	70	77	294
=18	Marty Furgol	73	74	73	75	295
	Leland Gibson	72	77	69	77	295
	Bob Toski	70	74	78	73	295
=21	Dick Chapman (a)	77	67	77	75	296
	Johnny Weitzel	74	76	69	77	296
=23	Julius Boros	78	71	78	70	297
	William Campbell (a)	75	73	73	76	297

	June 17–19, 1954 continued				
	Max Evans	76	74	73	74	297
	Lew Worsham	72	77	77	71	297
=27	George Fazio	74	77	74	73	298
	Ted Kroll	70	79	73	76	298
=29	Jimmy Demaret	79	71	76	73	299
	Dick Metz	75	75	72	77	299
	Johnny Revolta	72	75	73	79	299
	Bob Rosburg	74	77	74	74	299

June 16–19, 1955

Olympic CC, San Francisco, CA

** Jack Fleck (69) beat Ben Hogan (72) in the 18-hole play-off.*

1	Jack Fleck*	76	69	75	67	287
2	Ben Hogan	72	73	72	70	287
=3	Tommy Bolt	67	77	75	73	292
	Sam Snead	79	69	70	74	292
=5	Julius Boros	76	69	73	77	295
	Bob Rosburg	78	74	67	76	295
=7	Doug Ford	74	77	74	71	296
	Bud Holscher	77	75	71	73	296
	E. Harvie Ward Jr (a)	74	70	76	76	296
=10	Jack Burke Jr	71	77	72	77	297
	Mike Souchak	73	79	72	73	297
=12	Shelley Mayfield	75	76	75	72	298
	Frank Stranahan	80	71	76	71	298
14	Walker Inman Jr	70	75	76	78	299
15	Gene Littler	76	73	73	78	300
=16	Al Mengert	76	76	72	77	301
	Smiley Quick	76	74	74	77	301
	Art Wall	77	78	72	74	301
=19	Fred Hawkins	73	78	75	76	302
	George Schneiter	78	74	77	73	302
=21	Bob Harris	77	71	78	77	303
	Cary Middlecoff	76	78	74	75	303
	Arnold Palmer	77	76	74	76	303
	Ernie Vossler	77	76	76	74	303
=25	Marty Furgol	76	77	78	73	304
	Leland Gibson	76	78	76	74	304
27	Billy Maxwell	77	74	75	79	305
=28	Art Bell	74	76	81	75	306
	Max Evans	77	73	76	80	306
	Dow Finsterwald	84	71	74	77	306
	Eric Monti	76	76	78	76	306
	Byron Nelson	77	74	80	75	306
	Charles Rotar	76	75	80	75	306

June 14–16, 1956

Oak Hill CC, Rochester, NY

1	Cary Middlecoff	71	70	70	70	281
=2	Julius Boros	71	71	71	69	282
	Ben Hogan	72	68	72	70	282
=4	Ed Furgol	71	70	73	71	285
	Ted Kroll	72	70	70	73	285
	Peter Thomson	70	69	75	71	285
7	Arnold Palmer	72	70	72	73	287
8	Ken Venturi (a)	77	71	68	73	289
=9	Jerry Barber	72	69	74	75	290
	Wes Ellis Jr	71	70	71	78	290
	Doug Ford	71	75	70	74	290
12	Billy Maxwell	72	71	76	72	291
13	Billy Joe Patton (a)	75	73	70	74	292
=14	Billy Casper	75	71	71	76	293
	Pete Cooper	73	74	76	70	293
	Fred Haas	72	71	72	78	293
=17	Henry Cotton	74	72	73	75	294

	June 14–16, 1956 continued					
	Dutch Harrison	72	76	72	74	294
	Jay Herbert	71	76	73	74	294
	Bill Ogden	76	73	76	69	294
	Bob Toski	76	71	74	73	294
=22	Errie Bell	71	75	73	76	295
	Tommy Bolt	74	71	73	77	295
=24	Johnny Bulla	77	72	73	74	296
	Robert Kay	75	74	76	71	296
	Sam Snead	75	71	77	73	296
=27	Roberto de Vicenzo	76	69	77	75	297
	Doug Higgins	74	75	72	76	297
=29	Walter Burkemo	73	74	76	75	298
	Mike Dietz	73	74	70	81	298
	Shelley Mayfield	75	71	75	77	298
	Mike Souchak	78	71	72	77	298
	Frank Taylor Jr (a)	72	71	80	75	298

June 13–15, 1957

Inverness GC, Toledo, OH

** Dick Mayer (72) beat Cary Middlecoff (79) in the 18-hole play-off.*

1	Dick Mayer*	70	68	74	70	282
2	Cary Middlecoff	71	75	68	68	282
3	Jimmy Demaret	68	73	70	72	293
=4	Julius Boros	69	75	70	70	284
	Walter Burkemo	74	73	72	65	284
=6	Fred Hawkins	72	72	71	71	286
	Ken Venturi	69	71	75	71	286
=8	Roberto de Vicenzo	72	70	72	76	290
	Chick Harbert	68	79	71	72	290
	Billy Maxwell	70	76	72	72	290
	Billy Joe Patton (a)	70	68	76	76	290
	Sam Snead	74	74	69	73	290
=13	Mike Fetchick	74	71	71	75	291
	Dow Finsterwald	74	72	72	73	291
	William Hyndham III (a)	77	73	72	69	291
	Frank Stranahan	72	76	69	74	291
=17	Don Fairfield	78	72	73	69	292
	Jim Ferree	74	74	73	71	292
	Doug Ford	69	71	80	72	292
	Bud Ward	70	74	70	78	292
21	Bo Winninger	70	71	76	76	293
=22	George Bayer	73	77	69	75	294
	Joe Campbell (a)	74	72	73	75	294
	Ed Oliver	74	73	73	74	294
	Peter Thomson	71	72	74	77	294
=26	Jack Fleck	72	76	73	74	295
	Gerald Kesselring	74	71	75	75	295
	Sam Penecale	71	73	73	78	295
	E. Harvie Ward Jr (a)	72	75	74	74	295
=30	Leo Biagetti	73	75	72	76	296
	Johnny Revolta	76	74	74	72	296

June 12–14, 1958

Southern Hills CC, Tulsa, OK

1	Tommy Bolt	71	71	69	72	283
2	Gary Player	75	68	73	71	287
3	Julius Boros	71	75	72	71	289
4	Gene Littler	74	73	67	76	290
=5	Walter Burkemo	75	74	70	72	291
	Bob Rosburg	75	74	72	70	291
=7	Jay Herbert	77	76	71	69	293
	Don January	79	73	68	73	293
	Dick Metz	71	78	73	71	293
=10	Ben Hogan	75	73	75	71	294
	Tommy Jacobs	76	75	71	72	294

June 12–14, 1958 continued

	Frank Stranahan	72	72	75	75	294
=13	**Billy Casper**	79	70	75	71	295
	Charles R. Coe (a)	75	71	75	74	295
	Marty Furgol	75	74	74	72	295
16	**Bob Goetz**	75	75	77	69	296
=17	**Tom Nieporte**	75	73	74	75	297
	Jerry Pittman	75	77	71	74	297
=19	**Jerry Barber**	79	73	73	73	298
	Bruce Crampton	73	75	74	76	298
	Jim Ferree	76	74	73	75	298
	Jerry Magee	76	77	75	70	298
=23	**Dutch Harrison**	76	76	73	74	299
	Dick Mayer	76	74	71	78	299
	Arnold Palmer	75	75	77	72	299
	Earl Stewart	75	74	77	73	299
=27	**Stan Dudas**	76	73	76	75	300
	Don Fairfield	78	75	72	75	300
	Mike Fetchick	78	76	73	73	300
	Labron Harris	74	72	77	77	300
	Billy Maxwell	78	76	76	70	300
	Cary Middlecoff	75	79	75	71	300
	Bo Wininger	78	74	74	74	300

June 11–13, 1959

Winged Foot GC, Mamaroneck, NY

1	**Billy Casper**	71	68	69	74	282
2	**Bob Rosburg**	75	70	67	71	283
=3	**Claude Harmon**	72	71	70	71	284
	Mike Souchak	71	70	72	71	284
=5	**Doug Ford**	72	69	72	73	286
	Arnold Palmer	71	69	72	74	286
	Ernie Vossler	72	70	72	72	286
=8	**Ben Hogan**	69	71	71	76	287
	Sam Snead	73	72	67	75	287
10	**Dick Knight**	69	75	73	73	290
=11	**Dow Finsterwald**	69	73	75	74	291
	Fred Hawkins	76	72	69	74	291
	Ted Kroll	71	73	73	74	291
	Gene Littler	69	74	75	72	291
=15	**Dave Marr**	75	73	69	75	292
	Gary Player	71	69	76	76	292
=17	**Gardner Dickinson**	77	70	71	75	293
	Jay Hebert	73	70	78	72	293
=19	**Jack Fleck**	74	74	69	77	294
	Mac Hunter	75	74	73	72	294
	Don January	71	73	73	77	294
	Cary Middlecoff	71	73	73	77	294
	Johnny Pott	77	72	70	75	294
	Bo Wininger	71	73	72	78	294
25	**Joe Campbell**	73	71	75	76	295
=26	**Chick Harbert**	78	68	76	74	296
	Billy Maxwell	75	75	70	76	296
=28	**Julius Boros**	76	74	72	75	297
	Lionel Herbert	71	74	70	82	297
	Henry Ransom	72	77	71	77	297
	Fred Wampler	74	73	75	75	297

June 16–18, 1960

Cherry Hills CC, Denver, CO

1	**Arnold Palmer**	72	71	72	65	280
2	**Jack Nicklaus (a)**	71	71	69	71	282
=3	**Julius Boros**	73	69	68	73	283
	Dow Finsterwald	71	69	70	73	283
	Jack Fleck	70	70	72	71	283
	Dutch Harrison	74	70	70	69	283

June 16–18, 1960 continued

	Ted Kroll	72	69	75	67	283
	Mike Souchak	68	67	73	75	283
=9	**Jerry Barber**	69	71	70	74	284
	Don Cherry (a)	70	71	71	72	284
	Ben Hogan	75	67	69	73	284
=12	**George Bayer**	72	72	73	69	286
	Billy Casper	71	70	73	72	286
	Paul Harney	73	70	72	71	286
=15	**Bob Harris**	73	71	71	72	287
	Johnny Pott	75	68	69	75	287
=17	**Dave Marr**	72	73	70	73	288
	Donald Whitt	75	69	72	72	288
=19	**Jackson Bradley**	73	73	69	74	289
	Bob Goalby	73	70	72	74	289
	Gary Player	70	72	71	76	289
	Sam Snead	72	69	73	75	289
=23	**Al Feminelli**	75	71	71	73	290
	Lloyd Mangrum	72	73	71	74	290
	Bob Rosburg	72	75	71	72	290
	Ken Venturi	71	73	74	72	290
=27	**Claude Harmon**	73	73	75	70	291
	Lionel Hebert	73	72	71	75	291
	Bob Shave Jr	72	71	71	77	291
	Richard Stranahan	70	73	73	75	291

June 15–17, 1961

Oakland Hills CC, Birmingham, MI

1	**Gene Littler**	73	68	72	68	281
=2	**Bob Goalby**	70	72	69	71	282
	Doug Sanders	72	67	71	72	282
=4	**Jack Nicklaus (a)**	75	69	70	70	284
	Mike Souchak	73	70	68	73	284
=6	**Dow Finsterwald**	72	71	71	72	286
	Doug Ford	72	69	71	74	286
	Eric Monti	74	67	72	73	286
=9	**Jacky Cupit**	72	72	67	76	287
	Gardner Dickinson	72	69	71	75	287
	Gary Player	75	72	69	71	287
=12	**Deane Beman (a)**	74	72	72	70	288
	Al Geiberger	71	70	73	74	288
=14	**Dave Douglas**	72	72	75	70	289
	Ben Hogan	71	72	73	73	289
	Arnold Palmer	74	75	70	70	289
=17	**Billy Casper**	74	71	73	72	290
	Dutch Harrison	74	71	76	69	290
	Kel Nagle	71	71	74	74	290
	Sam Snead	73	70	74	73	290
21	**Bob Rosburg**	72	67	74	78	291
=22	**Tommy Bolt**	70	73	73	76	292
	Bob Brue	69	72	73	78	292
	Bruce Crampton	71	71	74	76	292
	Jim Ferrier	74	72	71	75	292
	Billy Maxwell	73	74	72	73	292
=27	**Jack Fleck**	73	71	79	70	293
	Ted Kroll	78	69	73	73	293
=29	**Edward Brantly**	75	70	72	77	294
	Chick Harbert	75	71	69	79	294
	Robert Harrison	79	70	71	74	294
	Milon Marusic	75	74	71	74	294
	Jerry Steelsmith	74	74	72	74	294

June 14–17, 1962

Oakmont CC, Oakmont, PA

** Jack Nicklaus (71) beat Arnold Palmer (74) in the 18-hole play-off.*

1	**Jack Nicklaus***	72	70	72	69	283

June 14–17, 1962 continued

2	**Arnold Palmer**	71	68	73	71	283
=3	**Bobby Nichols**	70	72	70	73	285
	Phil Rodgers	74	70	69	72	285
5	**Gay Brewer**	73	72	73	69	287
=6	**Tommy Jacobs**	74	71	73	70	288
	Gary Player	71	71	72	74	288
=8	**Doug Ford**	74	75	71	70	290
	Gene Littler	69	74	72	75	290
	Billy Maxwell	71	70	75	74	290
=11	**Doug Sanders**	74	74	74	69	291
	Art Wall	73	72	72	74	291
13	**Bob Rosburg**	70	69	74	79	292
=14	**Deane Beman (a)**	74	72	80	67	293
	Bob Goalby	73	74	73	73	293
	Mike Souchak	75	73	72	73	293
=17	**Jacky Cupit**	73	72	72	77	294
	Jay Herbert	75	72	73	74	294
	Earl Stewart	75	73	75	71	294
	Donald Whitt	73	71	75	75	294
	Bo Wininger	73	74	69	78	294
22	**Miller Barber**	73	70	77	75	295
=23	**Gardner Dickinson**	76	74	75	71	296
	Lionel Hebert	75	72	75	74	296
=25	**Stan Leonard**	72	73	78	74	297
	Edward Meister Jr (a)	78	72	76	71	297
27	**Frank Boynton**	71	75	74	78	298
=28	**Joe Campbell**	78	71	72	78	299
	Dave Douglas	74	70	72	83	299
	Paul Harney	73	73	81	72	299
	Dean Refram	75	73	77	74	299
	Mason Rudolph	74	74	73	78	299

June 20–23, 1963

The Country Club, Brookline, MA

** Julius Boros (70) beat Jacky Cupit (73) and Arnold Palmer (76) in the 18-hole play-off.*

1	**Julius Boros***	71	74	76	72	293
2	**Jacky Cupit**	70	72	76	75	293
3	**Arnold Palmer**	73	69	77	74	293
4	**Paul Harney**	78	70	73	73	294
=5	**Bruce Crampton**	74	72	75	74	295
	Tony Lema	71	74	74	76	295
	Billy Maxwell	73	73	75	74	295
=8	**Walter Burkemo**	72	71	76	77	296
	Gary Player	74	75	75	72	296
10	**Dan Sikes**	77	73	73	74	297
11	**Don January**	72	74	78	75	299
=12	**Dow Finsterwald**	73	69	79	79	300
	Dave Ragan	78	74	74	74	300
=14	**Mike Fetchick**	74	76	75	77	302
	Lionel Hebert	71	79	76	76	302
	Davis Love Jr	71	74	78	79	302
	Bobby Nichols	74	75	75	78	302
	Dean Refram	72	71	80	79	302
=19	**Bob Charles**	74	76	76	77	303
	Ken Still	76	75	78	74	303
=21	**Jack Burke Jr**	75	76	78	75	304
	Gardner Dickinson	76	71	78	79	304
	Gene Littler	75	77	80	72	304
	Dave Marr	75	74	77	78	304
	Bob McAllister	75	77	76	76	304
	Doug Sanders	77	74	75	78	304
=27	**Otto Greiner**	74	75	76	80	305
	Ted Makalena	75	77	76	77	305
	Mason Rudolph	76	75	78	76	305
=30	**Bob Goetz**	79	72	80	75	306
	Bill Ogden	73	76	78	79	306

June 18–20, 1964

Congressional CC, Bethesda, MD

1	**Ken Venturi**	72	70	66	70	278
2	**Tommy Jacobs**	72	64	70	76	282
3	**Bob Charles**	72	72	71	68	283
4	**Billy Casper**	71	74	69	71	285
=5	**Gay Brewer**	76	69	73	68	286
	Arnold Palmer	68	69	75	74	286
7	**Bill Collins**	70	71	74	72	287
8	**Dow Finsterwald**	73	72	71	72	288
=9	**Johnny Pott**	71	73	73	72	289
	Bob Rosburg	73	73	70	73	289
=11	**George Bayer**	75	73	72	71	291
	Don January	75	73	74	69	291
	Gene Littler	73	71	74	73	291
=14	**Bruce Crampton**	72	71	75	74	292
	Terry Dill	73	73	75	71	292
	Ray Floyd	73	70	72	77	292
	Ed Furgol	72	74	72	74	292
	Al Geiberger	74	70	75	73	292
	Bobby Nichols	72	72	76	72	292
20	**Tony Lema**	71	72	75	75	293
=21	**Lionel Hebert**	73	74	72	75	294
	Bill Ogden	73	73	73	75	294
=23	**Ted Makalena**	73	74	75	73	295
	Jack Nicklaus	72	73	77	73	295
	Gary Player	75	74	72	74	295
	Dudley Wysong	74	73	75	73	295
27	**Charles Sifford**	72	70	77	77	296
=28	**Jacky Cupit**	75	71	75	76	297
	Don Fairfield	75	72	74	76	297
	John Farquhar (a)	74	73	77	73	297
	Labron Harris Jr	72	76	74	75	297

June 17–21, 1965

Bellerive CC, St Louis, MO

** Gary Player (71) beat Kel Nagle (74) in the 18-hole play-off.*

1	**Gary Player***	70	70	71	71	282
2	**Kel Nagle**	68	73	72	69	282
3	**Frank Beard**	74	69	70	71	284
=4	**Julius Boros**	72	75	70	70	287
	Al Geiberger	70	76	70	71	287
=6	**Bruce Devlin**	72	73	72	71	288
	Ray Floyd	72	72	76	68	288
=8	**Tony Lema**	72	74	73	70	289
	Gene Littler	73	71	73	72	289
	Dudley Wysong	72	75	70	72	289
=11	**Deane Beman (a)**	69	73	76	72	290
	Mason Rudolph	69	72	73	76	290
	Doug Sanders	77	73	69	71	290
14	**Billy Maxwell**	76	73	71	71	291
15	**Steve Oppermann**	72	77	73	70	292
16	**Gay Brewer**	72	74	71	76	293
=17	**Billy Casper**	73	73	76	72	294
	Charles Huckaby	73	74	73	74	294
	George Knudson	80	69	73	72	294
	Bob Verwey	73	74	75	72	294
=21	**Gardner Dickinson**	77	73	71	74	295
	Eric Monti	76	71	75	73	295
23	**Lou Graham**	70	77	76	73	296
=24	**Wes Ellis Jr**	73	76	77	71	297
	Labron Harris Jr	74	76	74	73	297
	Ted Kroll	76	74	72	75	297
	Sam Snead	75	71	77	74	297
=28	**Dutch Harrison**	78	72	72	76	298
	Tommy Jacobs	76	71	74	77	298

June 17–21, 1965 continued

	Dean Refram	71	79	72	76	298
	Terry Wilcox	74	73	73	78	298

June 16–20, 1966

Olympic GC, San Francisco, CA

** Billy Casper (69) beat Arnold Palmer (73) in the 18-hole play-off.*

1	**Billy Casper***	69	68	73	68	278
2	**Arnold Palmer**	71	66	70	71	278
3	**Jack Nicklaus**	71	71	69	74	285
=4	**Tony Lema**	71	74	70	71	286
	Dave Marr	71	74	68	73	286
6	**Phil Rodgers**	70	70	73	74	287
7	**Bobby Nichols**	74	72	71	72	289
=8	**Wes Ellis Jr**	71	75	74	70	290
	Johnny Miller (a)	70	72	74	74	290
	Mason Rudolph	74	72	71	73	290
	Doug Sanders	70	75	74	71	290
12	**Ben Hogan**	72	73	76	70	291
=13	**Rod Funseth**	75	75	69	73	292
	Rives McBee	76	64	74	78	292
=15	**Bob Murphy (a)**	73	72	75	73	293
	Gary Player	78	72	74	69	293
=17	**George Archer**	74	72	76	72	294
	Frank Beard	76	74	69	75	294
	Julius Boros	74	69	77	74	294
	Don January	73	73	75	73	294
	Ken Venturi	73	77	71	73	294
=22	**Walter Burkemo**	76	72	70	77	295
	Bob Goalby	71	73	71	80	295
	Dave Hill	72	71	79	73	295
	Bob Verwey	72	73	75	75	295
=26	**Miller Barber**	74	76	77	69	296
	Bruce Devlin	74	75	71	76	296
	Al Mengert	67	77	71	81	296
	Bob Shave	76	71	74	75	296
=30	**Tommy Aaron**	73	75	71	78	297
	Deane Beman (a)	75	76	70	76	297
	Al Geiberger	75	75	74	73	297
	Vince Sullivan	77	73	73	74	297

June 15–18, 1967

Baltusrol GC, Springfield, NJ

1	**Jack Nicklaus**	71	67	72	65	275
2	**Arnold Palmer**	69	68	73	69	279
3	**Don January**	69	72	70	70	281
4	**Billy Casper**	69	70	71	72	282
=5	**Lee Trevino**	72	70	72	70	284
	Deane Beman	69	71	71	73	284
	Gardner Dickinson	70	73	68	73	284
	Bob Goalby	72	71	70	71	284
=9	**Dave Marr**	70	74	70	71	285
	Kel Nagle	70	72	72	71	285
	Art Wall	69	73	72	71	285
=12	**Al Balding**	75	72	71	68	286
	Wes Ellis Jr	74	69	70	73	286
	Gary Player	69	73	73	71	286
15	**Tom Weiskopf**	72	71	74	70	287
=16	**Dutch Harrison**	70	76	72	70	288
	Jerry Pittman	72	72	75	69	288
=18	**Miller Barber**	71	71	69	78	289
	Marty Fleckman (a)	67	73	69	80	289
	Paul Harney	71	75	72	71	289
	Dave Hill	76	69	69	75	289
	Bob Verwey	75	71	69	74	289
=23	**Bruce Devlin**	72	68	77	73	290
	Billy Farrell	76	71	73	70	290

June 15–18, 1967 continued

	Howie Johnson	74	73	71	72	290
	Bob Murphy (a)	73	73	75	69	290
	Bobby Nichols	74	71	73	72	290
=28	**Charles Coody**	77	71	75	68	291
	Mike Fetchick	73	71	76	71	291
	Al Geiberger	71	73	73	74	291
	Lou Graham	71	75	76	69	291
	Labron Harris Jr	75	71	72	73	291
	Ken Venturi	74	74	72	71	291

June 13–16, 1968

Oak Hill CC, Rochester, NY

1	**Lee Trevino**	69	68	69	69	275
2	**Jack Nicklaus**	72	70	70	67	279
3	**Bert Yancey**	67	68	70	76	281
4	**Bobby Nichols**	74	71	68	69	282
=5	**Don Bies**	70	70	75	69	284
	Steve Spray	73	75	71	65	284
=7	**Bob Charles**	73	69	72	71	285
	Jerry Pittman	73	67	74	71	285
=9	**Gay Brewer**	71	71	75	69	286
	Billy Casper	75	68	71	72	286
	Bruce Devlin	71	69	75	71	286
	Al Geiberger	72	74	68	72	286
	Sam Snead	73	71	74	68	286
	Dave Stockton	72	73	69	72	286
15	**Dan Sikes**	71	71	73	72	287
=16	**George Archer**	74	72	73	69	288
	Julius Boros	71	71	71	75	288
	Charles Coody	69	71	72	76	288
	Rod Funseth	74	72	69	73	288
	Dave Hill	74	68	74	72	288
	Gary Player	76	69	70	73	288
=22	**Mac McLendon**	72	76	70	71	289
	Hugh Royer Jr	75	72	73	69	289
=24	**Miller Barber**	74	68	78	70	290
	Roberto de Vicenzo	72	76	72	70	290
	Bob Erickson	75	68	72	75	290
	Don January	71	75	71	73	290
	Bob Lunn	74	73	73	70	290
	Pat Schwab	76	70	75	69	290
	Tom Weiskopf	75	72	70	73	290
	Larry Ziegler	71	71	74	74	290

June 12–15, 1969

Champions GC, Houston, TX

1	**Orville Moody**	71	70	68	72	281
=2	**Deane Beman**	68	69	73	72	282
	Al Geiberger	68	72	72	70	282
	Bob Rosburg	70	69	72	71	282
5	**Bob Murphy**	66	74	72	71	283
=6	**Miller Barber**	67	71	68	78	284
	Bruce Crampton	73	72	68	71	284
	Arnold Palmer	70	73	69	72	284
9	**Bunky Henry**	70	72	68	75	285
=10	**George Archer**	69	74	73	70	286
	Bruce Devlin	73	74	70	69	286
	Dave Marr	75	69	71	71	286
=13	**Julius Boros**	71	73	70	73	287
	Charles Coody	72	68	72	75	287
	Dale Douglass	76	69	70	72	287
	Ray Floyd	79	68	68	72	287
	Dave Hill	73	74	70	70	287
	Howie Johnson	72	73	72	70	287
	Dean Refram	69	74	70	74	287
	Phil Rodgers	76	70	69	72	287

June 12–15, 1969 continued

	Kermit Zarley	74	72	70	71	287
=22	**Bob Stanton**	74	70	71	73	288
	Tom Weiskopf	69	75	71	73	288
	Bert Yancey	71	71	74	72	288
=25	**Joe Campbell**	73	74	73	69	289
	Richard Crawford	70	75	73	71	289
	Tony Jacklin	71	70	73	75	289
	Bobby Mitchell	72	74	66	77	289
	Jack Nicklaus	74	67	75	73	289
	Dave Stockton	75	69	72	73	289

June 18–21, 1970

Hazeltine National GC, Minneapolis, MN

1	**Tony Jacklin**	71	70	70	70	281
2	**Dave Hill**	75	68	71	73	288
=3	**Bob Charles**	76	71	75	67	289
	Bob Lunn	77	72	70	70	289
5	**Ken Still**	78	71	71	71	291
6	**Miller Barber**	75	75	72	70	292
7	**Gay Brewer**	75	71	71	76	293
=8	**Billy Casper**	75	75	71	73	294
	Bruce Devlin	75	75	71	73	294
	Lee Trevino	77	73	74	70	294
	Larry Ziegler	75	73	73	73	294
=12	**Julius Boros**	73	75	70	77	295
	Bobby Cole	78	75	71	71	295
	Joel Goldstrand	76	76	71	72	295
	Howie Johnson	75	72	75	73	295
	Gene Littler	77	72	71	75	295
	Bobby Mitchell	74	78	74	69	295
=18	**Al Balding**	75	74	75	72	296
	Paul Harney	78	73	75	70	296
	Johnny Miller	79	73	73	71	296
	Randy Wolff	78	67	76	75	296
=22	**Frank Beard**	75	73	79	70	297
	Richard Crawford	74	71	76	76	297
	Ray Floyd	78	73	70	76	297
	Ted Hayes Jr	79	73	73	72	297
	Bert Yancey	81	72	73	71	297
=27	**Chi Chi Rodriguez**	73	77	75	73	298
	Mason Rudolph	73	75	73	77	298
	Dan Sikes	81	69	72	76	298
=30	**George Archer**	76	73	77	73	299
	Bruce Crampton	79	71	74	75	299
	Bunky Henry	80	68	77	74	299
	Dave Marr	82	69	74	74	299
	Kel Nagle	78	75	73	73	299
	Tom Weiskopf	76	73	78	72	299

June 17–21, 1971

Merion GC, Ardmore, PA

** Lee Trevino (68) beat Jack Nicklaus (71) in the 18-hole play-off.*

1	**Lee Trevino***	70	72	69	69	280
2	**Jack Nicklaus**	69	72	68	71	280
=3	**Jim Colbert**	69	69	73	71	282
	Bob Rosburg	71	72	70	69	282
=5	**George Archer**	71	70	70	72	283
	Johnny Miller	70	73	70	70	283
	Jim Simmons (a)	71	71	65	76	283
8	**Ray Floyd**	71	75	67	71	284
=9	**Gay Brewer**	70	70	73	72	285
	Larry Hinson	71	71	70	73	285
	Bobby Nichols	69	72	69	75	285
	Bert Yancey	75	69	69	72	285
=13	**Bob Charles**	72	75	69	70	286
	Bobby Cole	72	71	72	71	286

June 17–21, 1971 continued

	Jerry Heard	73	71	73	69	286
	Jerry McGee	72	67	77	70	286
	Chi Chi Rodriguez	70	71	73	72	286
	Lanny Wadkins (a)	68	75	75	68	286
=19	**Homero Blancas**	71	71	75	70	287
	Dave Eichelberger	72	72	70	73	287
	Bob Goalby	68	76	74	69	287
	Hale Irwin	72	73	72	70	287
	Ken Still	71	72	69	75	287
=24	**Dick Lotz**	72	72	73	71	288
	Arnold Palmer	73	68	73	74	288
	Bob E. Smith	71	74	71	72	288
=27	**Ben Crenshaw (a)**	74	74	68	73	289
	Bruce Devlin	72	69	71	77	289
	Don January	75	73	71	70	289
	Ralph Johnston	70	75	73	71	289
	Bob Lunn	71	73	71	74	289
	Bobby Mitchell	72	74	72	71	289
	Orville Moody	71	71	76	71	289
	Gary Player	76	71	72	70	289
	John Schroeder	72	73	69	75	289
	Kermit Zarley	74	70	72	73	289

June 15–18, 1972

Pebble Beach GL, Pebble Beach, CA

1	**Jack Nicklaus**	71	73	72	74	290
2	**Bruce Crampton**	74	70	73	76	293
3	**Arnold Palmer**	77	68	73	76	294
=4	**Homero Blancas**	74	70	76	75	295
	Lee Trevino	74	72	71	78	295
6	**Kermit Zarley**	71	73	73	69	296
7	**Johnny Miller**	74	73	71	79	297
8	**Tom Weiskopf**	73	74	73	78	298
=9	**Chi Chi Rodriguez**	71	75	78	75	299
	Caesar Sanudo	72	72	78	77	299
=11	**Billy Casper**	74	73	79	74	300
	Don January	76	71	74	79	300
	Bobby Nichols	77	74	72	77	300
	Bert Yancey	75	79	70	76	300
=15	**Don Massengale**	72	81	70	78	301
	Orville Moody	71	77	79	74	301
	Gary Player	72	74	75	78	301
	Jim Simons (a)	75	75	79	72	301
=19	**Lou Graham**	75	73	75	79	302
	Tom Kite (a)	75	73	79	75	302
=21	**Al Geiberger**	80	74	76	73	303
	Paul Harney	79	72	75	77	303
	Bobby Mitchell	74	80	73	76	303
	Charles Sifford	79	74	72	78	303
=25	**Gay Brewer**	77	77	72	78	304
	Rod Funseth	73	73	84	74	304
	Lanny Wadkins	76	68	79	81	304
	Jim Wiechers	74	79	69	82	304
=29	**Miller Barber**	76	76	73	80	305
	Julius Boros	77	77	74	77	305
	Dave Eichelberger	76	71	80	78	305
	Lee Elder	75	71	79	80	305
	Jerry Heard	73	74	77	81	305
	Dave Hill	74	78	74	79	305
	Tom Watson	74	79	76	76	305

June 14–17, 1973

Oakmont CC, Oakmont, PA

1	**Johnny Miller**	71	69	76	63	279
2	**John Schlee**	73	70	67	70	280
3	**Tom Weiskopf**	73	69	69	70	281

June 14–17, 1973 continued

=4	**Jack Nicklaus**	71	69	74	68	282
	Arnold Palmer	71	71	68	72	282
	Lee Trevino	70	72	70	70	282
=7	**Julius Boros**	73	69	68	73	283
	Jerry Heard	74	70	66	73	283
	Lanny Wadkins	74	69	75	65	283
10	**Jim Colbert**	70	68	74	72	284
11	**Bob Charles**	71	69	72	74	286
12	**Gary Player**	67	70	77	73	287
=13	**Al Geiberger**	73	72	71	72	288
	Ralph Johnston	71	73	76	68	288
	Larry Ziegler	73	74	69	72	288
16	**Ray Floyd**	70	73	75	71	289
17	**Marvin Giles (a)**	74	69	74	73	290
=18	**Gene Littler**	71	74	70	76	291
	Rocky Thompson	73	71	71	76	291
=20	**Rod Funseth**	75	74	70	74	293
	Hale Irwin	73	74	75	71	293
	Denny Lyons	72	74	75	72	293
	Bob Murphy	77	70	75	71	293
	Bobby Nichols	75	71	74	73	293
=25	**Miller Barber**	74	71	71	78	294
	Frank Beard	74	75	68	77	294
	Tom Shaw	73	71	74	76	294
	Bert Yancey	73	70	75	76	294
=29	**Don Bies**	77	73	73	72	295
	Charles Coody	74	74	73	74	295
	John Mahaffey	74	72	74	75	295
	Chi Chi Rodriguez	75	71	75	74	295
	Sam Snead	75	74	73	73	295

June 13–16, 1974

Winged Foot GC, Mamaroneck, NY

1	**Hale Irwin**	73	70	71	73	287
2	**Forrest Fezler**	75	70	74	70	289
=3	**Lou Graham**	71	75	74	70	290
	Bert Yancey	76	69	73	72	290
=5	**Jim Colbert**	72	77	69	74	292
	Arnold Palmer	73	70	73	76	292
	Tom Watson	73	71	69	79	292
=8	**Tom Kite**	74	70	77	72	293
	Gary Player	70	73	77	73	293
=10	**Brian Allin**	76	71	74	73	294
	Jack Nicklaus	75	74	76	69	294
=12	**Frank Beard**	77	69	72	77	295
	John Mahaffey	74	73	75	73	295
	Larry Ziegler	78	68	78	71	295
=15	**Ray Floyd**	72	71	78	75	296
	Mike Reasor	71	76	76	73	296
	Tom Weiskopf	76	73	72	75	296
=18	**Dale Douglass**	77	72	72	76	297
	Al Geiberger	75	76	78	68	297
	David Graham	73	75	76	73	297
=21	**J.C. Snead**	76	71	76	75	298
	Leonard Thompson	75	75	76	72	298
=23	**Bruce Crampton**	72	77	76	74	299
	Larry Hinson	75	76	75	73	299
	Bobby Mitchell	77	73	73	76	299
=26	**Hubert Green**	81	67	76	76	300
	Jim Jamieson	77	73	75	75	300
	Chi Chi Rodriguez	75	75	77	73	300
	Lanny Wadkins	75	73	76	76	300
=30	**Ron Cerrudo**	78	75	75	73	301
	Rod Funseth	73	75	78	75	301
	David Glenz	76	74	75	76	301
	Rik Massengale	79	72	74	76	301
	Jerry McGee	77	72	78	74	301

June 19–23, 1975

Medinah CC, Medinah, IL

** Lou Graham (71) beat John Mahaffey (73) in the 18-hole play-off.*

1	**Lou Graham***	74	72	68	73	287
2	**John Mahaffey**	73	71	72	71	287
=3	**Frank Beard**	74	69	67	78	288
	Ben Crenshaw	70	68	76	74	288
	Hale Irwin	74	71	73	70	288
	Bob Murphy	74	73	72	69	288
=7	**Jack Nicklaus**	72	70	75	72	289
	Peter Oosterhuis	69	73	72	75	289
=9	**Pat Fitzsimons**	67	73	73	77	290
	Arnold Palmer	69	75	73	73	290
	Tom Watson	67	68	78	77	290
=12	**Ray Floyd**	76	71	72	72	291
	Andy North	75	72	72	72	291
=14	**Joe Inman**	72	72	71	77	292
	Rik Massengale	71	74	71	76	292
	Eddie Pearce	75	71	70	76	292
	Jim Wiechers	68	73	76	75	292
=18	**Terry Dill**	72	69	77	75	293
	Hubert Green	74	73	68	78	293
	Gary Groh	73	74	73	73	293
	Jay Haas (a)	74	69	72	78	293
	Grier Jones	69	73	79	72	293
	Jerry Pate (a)	79	70	72	72	293
=24	**Brian Allinn**	76	70	73	75	294
	Miller Barber	74	71	71	78	294
	Dale Douglass	71	77	72	74	294
	Forrest Fezler	73	75	71	75	294
	Kermit Zarley	73	71	75	75	294
=29	**Tommy Aaron**	73	71	82	69	295
	David Graham	71	76	74	74	295
	Jerry Heard	77	67	78	73	295
	Don January	75	71	74	75	295
	Steve Melnyk	75	73	74	73	295
	Ed Sneed	75	74	73	73	295
	Nate Starks	75	72	76	72	295
	Lee Trevino	72	75	73	75	295
	Tom Weiskopf	75	71	74	75	295

June 17–20, 1976

Atlanta Athletic Club, Atlanta, GA

1	**Jerry Pate**	71	69	69	68	277
=2	**Al Geiberger**	70	69	71	69	279
	Tom Weiskopf	73	70	68	68	279
=4	**Butch Baird**	71	71	71	67	280
	John Mahaffey	70	68	69	73	280
6	**Hubert Green**	72	70	71	69	282
7	**Tom Watson**	74	72	68	70	284
=8	**Ben Crenshaw**	72	68	72	73	285
	Lyn Lott	71	71	70	73	285
10	**Johnny Miller**	74	72	69	71	286
=11	**Rod Funseth**	70	70	72	75	287
	Jack Nicklaus	74	70	75	68	287
13	**Ray Floyd**	70	75	71	72	288
=14	**Mark Hayes**	74	74	70	71	289
	Don January	71	74	69	75	289
	Mike Morley	71	71	70	77	289
	Andy North	74	72	69	74	289
	J.C. Snead	73	69	71	76	289
=19	**Danny Edwards**	73	75	70	72	290
	Randy Glover	72	74	76	68	290
=21	**Dave Eichelberger**	73	70	74	74	291
	Larry Nelson	75	74	70	72	291
=23	**Joe Inman**	75	73	74	70	292

	June 17–20, 1976 continued					
	Calvin Peete	76	69	74	73	292
	Gary Player	72	77	73	70	292
=26	**Hale Irwin**	75	72	75	71	293
	Tom Jenkins	72	74	75	72	293
=28	**Lou Graham**	75	74	72	73	294
	Barry Jaeckel	74	77	69	74	294
	Grier Jones	76	69	71	78	294
	Wayne Levi	74	73	74	73	294
	Bob E. Smith	72	75	74	73	294

June 16–19, 1977

Southern Hills CC, Tulsa, OK

1	**Hubert Green**	69	67	72	70	278
2	**Lou Graham**	72	71	68	68	279
3	**Tom Weiskopf**	71	71	68	71	281
4	**Tom Purtzer**	69	69	72	72	282
=5	**Jay Haas**	72	68	71	72	283
	Gary Jacobsen	73	70	67	73	283
=7	**Terry Diehl**	69	68	73	74	284
	Lyn Lott	73	72	71	67	284
	Tom Watson	74	72	71	67	284
=10	**Rod Funseth**	69	70	72	74	285
	Al Geiberger	70	71	75	69	285
	Mike McCullough	73	73	60	70	285
	Jack Nicklaus	74	68	71	72	285
	Peter Oosterhuis	71	70	74	70	285
	Gary Player	72	67	71	75	285
=16	**Wally Armstrong**	71	70	70	75	286
	Joe Inman	70	70	72	74	286
	Steve Melnyk	70	73	70	73	286
=19	**Bill Kratzert**	73	69	75	70	287
	Bruce Lietzke	74	68	71	74	287
	Jerry McGee	76	69	76	66	287
	Arnold Palmer	70	72	73	72	287
=23	**Sam Adams**	70	69	76	73	288
	Andy Bean	71	70	68	79	288
	Ron Streck	73	73	71	71	288
26	**Gay Brewer**	73	72	70	74	289
=27	**George Archer**	73	72	74	71	290
	Tom Kite	71	73	70	76	290
	John Lister	72	73	68	77	290
	Johnny Miller	71	73	70	76	290
	Mike Morley	70	73	74	73	290
	Don Padgett	70	74	66	80	290
	J.C. Snead	72	75	68	75	290
	Lee Trevino	74	70	73	73	290

June 15–18, 1978

Cherry Hills CC, Denver, CO

1	**Andy North**	70	70	71	74	285
=2	**J.C. Snead**	70	72	72	72	286
	Dave Stockton	71	73	70	72	286
=4	**Hale Irwin**	69	74	75	70	288
	Tom Weiskopf	77	73	70	68	288
=6	**Andy Bean**	72	72	71	74	289
	Bill Kratzert	72	74	70	73	289
	Johnny Miller	78	69	68	74	289
	Jack Nicklaus	73	69	74	73	289
	Gary Player	71	71	70	77	289
	Tom Watson	74	75	70	70	289
=12	**Ray Floyd**	75	70	76	70	291
	Joe Inman	72	72	74	73	291
	Mike McCullough	75	75	73	68	291
	Lee Trevino	72	71	75	73	291
=16	**Seve Ballesteros**	75	69	71	77	292

	June 15–18, 1978 continued					
	Artie McNickle	74	75	70	73	292
	Jerry Pate	73	72	74	73	292
	Bob Shearer	78	72	71	71	292
=20	**Wally Armstrong**	73	73	74	73	293
	Phil Hancock	71	73	75	74	293
	Tom Kite	73	73	70	77	293
	Bruce Lietzke	72	73	72	76	293
=24	**Dale Douglass**	74	75	74	72	295
	Tom Purtzer	75	72	72	76	295
	Victor Regalado	74	72	73	76	295
=27	**Jerry McGee**	74	76	71	75	296
	Pat McGowan	74	73	72	77	296
	Peter Oosterhuis	72	72	78	74	296
=30	**Billy Casper**	71	76	73	77	297
	Bobby Clampett (a)	70	73	80	84	297
	Charles Coody	74	76	76	71	297
	Rod Curl	78	72	74	73	297
	Lee Elder	76	73	73	75	297

June 14–17, 1979

Inverness GC, Toledo, OH

1	**Hale Irwin**	74	68	67	75	284
=2	**Jerry Pate**	71	74	69	72	286
	Gary Player	73	73	72	68	286
=4	**Larry Nelson**	71	68	76	73	288
	Bill Rogers	71	72	73	72	288
	Tom Weiskopf	71	74	67	76	288
7	**David Graham**	73	73	70	73	289
8	**Tom Purtzer**	70	69	75	76	290
=9	**Keith Fergus**	70	77	72	72	291
	Jack Nicklaus	74	77	72	68	291
=11	**Ben Crenshaw**	75	71	72	75	293
	Lee Elder	74	72	69	78	293
	Andy North	77	74	68	74	293
	Calvin Peete	72	75	71	75	293
	Ed Snead	72	73	75	73	293
=16	**Bob Gilder**	77	70	69	78	294
	Graham Marsh	77	71	72	74	294
	Jim Simons	74	74	78	68	294
=19	**Al Geiberger**	74	74	69	78	295
	Lee Trevino	77	73	73	72	295
	Lanny Wadkins	73	74	71	77	295
	Bobby Walzel	74	72	71	78	295
	D.A. Weibring	74	76	71	74	295
24	**Hubert Green**	74	77	73	72	296
=25	**Andy Bean**	70	76	71	80	297
	Lou Graham	70	75	77	75	297
	Wayne Levi	77	73	75	72	297
	Bob Murphy	72	79	69	77	297
	Bobby Nichols	76	75	71	75	297
	Mike Reid	74	75	74	74	297
	Bob E. Smith	77	71	69	80	297

June 12–15, 1980

Baltusrol GC, Springfield, NJ

1	**Jack Nicklaus**	63	71	70	68	272
2	**Isao Aoki**	68	68	68	70	274
=3	**Keith Fergus**	66	70	70	70	276
	Lon Hinkle	66	70	69	71	276
	Tom Watson	71	68	67	70	276
=6	**Mark Hayes**	66	71	69	74	280
	Mike Reid	69	67	75	69	280
=8	**Hale Irwin**	70	70	73	69	282
	Mike Morley	73	68	69	72	282
	Andy North	68	75	72	67	282

June 12–15, 1980 continued

	Ed Sneed	72	70	70	70	282
=12	**Bruce Devlin**	71	70	70	72	283
	Joe Hager	72	70	71	70	283
	Lee Trevino	68	72	69	74	283
	Bobby Wadkins	72	71	68	72	283
=16	**Joe Inman**	74	69	69	72	284
	Pat McGowan	69	69	73	73	284
	Gil Morgan	73	70	70	71	284
	Bill Rogers	69	72	70	73	284
	Craig Stadler	73	67	69	75	284
	Curtis Strange	69	74	71	70	284
=22	**Gary Hallberg (a)**	74	68	70	73	285
	Peter Jacobsen	70	69	72	74	285
	Jim Simons	70	72	71	72	285
	J.C. Snead	69	71	73	72	285
=26	**Jay Haas**	67	74	70	75	286
	Mark Lye	68	72	77	69	286
=28	**George Burns**	75	69	73	70	287
	David Edwards	73	68	72	74	287
	John Mahaffey	72	73	69	73	287
	Calvin Peete	67	76	74	70	287

June 18–21, 1981

Merion GC, Ardmore, PA

1	**David Graham**	68	68	70	67	273
=2	**George Burns**	69	66	68	73	276
	Bill Rogers	70	68	69	69	276
=4	**John Cook**	68	70	71	70	279
	John Schroeder	71	68	69	71	279
=6	**Frank Conner**	71	72	69	68	280
	Lon Hinkle	69	71	70	70	280
	Jack Nicklaus	69	68	71	72	280
	Sammy Rachels	70	71	69	70	280
	Chi Chi Rodriguez	68	73	67	72	280
=11	**Isao Aoki**	72	71	71	67	281
	Ben Crenshaw	70	75	64	72	281
	Jim Thorpe	66	73	70	72	281
=14	**Mark Hayes**	71	70	72	69	282
	Calvin Peete	73	72	67	70	282
	Lanny Wadkins	71	68	72	71	282
=17	**Bruce Lietzke**	70	71	71	71	283
	Jack Renner	68	71	72	72	283
	Curtis Strange	71	69	72	71	283
=20	**Tom Kite**	73	74	67	70	284
	Larry Nelson	70	73	69	72	284
	Mike Reid	71	72	69	72	284
=23	**Johnny Miller**	69	71	73	72	285
	Scott Simpson	72	67	71	75	285
	Tom Watson	70	69	73	73	285
=26	**Jim Colbert**	71	69	77	69	286
	Bruce Devlin	73	71	70	72	286
	Rik Massengale	70	75	70	71	286
	Jerry Pate	70	69	72	75	286
	Gary Player	72	72	71	71	286
	Craig Stadler	71	76	68	71	286
	Tom Valentine	69	68	72	77	286

June 17–20, 1982

Pebble Beach GC, Pebble Beach, CA

1	**Tom Watson**	72	72	68	70	282
2	**Jack Nicklaus**	74	70	71	69	284
=3	**Bobby Clampett**	71	73	72	70	286
	Dan Pohl	72	74	70	70	286
	Bill Rogers	70	73	69	74	286
=6	**David Graham**	73	72	69	73	287

June 17–20, 1982 continued

	Jay Haas	75	74	70	68	287
	Gary Koch	78	73	69	67	287
	Lanny Wadkins	73	76	67	71	287
=10	**Bruce Devlin**	70	69	75	74	288
	Calvin Peete	71	72	72	73	288
=12	**Chip Beck**	76	75	69	69	289
	Danny Edwards	71	75	73	70	289
	Lyn Lott	72	71	75	71	289
=15	**Larry Rinker**	74	67	75	74	290
	Scott Simpson	73	69	72	76	290
	J.C. Snead	73	75	71	71	290
	Fuzzy Zoeller	72	76	71	71	290
=19	**Ben Crenshaw**	76	74	68	73	291
	Larry Nelson	74	72	74	71	291
	Hal Sutton	73	76	72	70	291
=22	**Mike Brannan**	75	74	71	72	292
	Joe Hagar	78	72	72	70	292
	Gene Littler	74	75	72	71	292
	John Mahaffey	77	72	70	73	292
	Gil Morgan	75	75	68	74	292
	Andy North	72	71	77	72	292
	Craig Stadler	76	70	70	76	292
29	**Tom Kite**	73	71	75	74	293
=30	**Isao Aoki**	77	74	72	71	294
	Don Bies	73	74	74	73	294
	George Burns	72	72	70	80	294
	Peter Oosterhuis	73	78	67	76	294
	Greg Powers	77	71	74	72	294
	Jack Renner	74	71	77	72	294
	Jim Thorpe	72	73	72	77	294

June 16–20, 1983

Oakmont CC, Oakmont, PA

1	**Larry Nelson**	75	73	65	67	280
2	**Tom Watson**	72	70	70	69	281
3	**Gil Morgan**	73	72	70	68	283
=4	**Seve Ballesteros**	69	74	69	74	286
	Calvin Peete	75	68	70	73	286
6	**Hal Sutton**	73	70	73	71	287
7	**Lanny Wadkins**	72	73	74	69	288
=8	**David Graham**	74	75	73	69	291
	Ralph Landrum	75	73	69	74	291
=10	**Chip Beck**	73	74	74	71	292
	Andy North	73	71	72	76	292
	Craig Stadler	76	74	73	69	292
=13	**Lennie Clements**	74	71	75	73	293
	Ray Floyd	72	70	72	79	293
	Pat McGowan	75	71	75	72	293
	Mike Nicolette	76	69	73	75	293
	David Ogrin	75	69	75	74	293
	Scott Simpson	73	71	73	76	293
	Jim Thorpe	75	70	75	73	293
=20	**Tom Kite**	75	76	70	73	294
	Griff Moody	76	72	73	73	294
	Gary Player	73	74	76	71	294
	D.A. Weibring	71	74	80	79	294
=24	**Gary Koch**	78	71	72	74	295
	Tom Weiskopf	75	73	74	73	295
=26	**Bob Ford**	76	73	75	72	296
	Ken Green	77	73	71	75	296
	Mark Hayes	75	72	74	75	296
	Tommy Nakajima	75	74	74	73	296
	Joey Rassett	72	69	78	77	296
	Curtis Strange	74	72	78	72	296

June 14–18, 1984

Winged Foot GC, Mamaroneck, NY

** Fuzzy Zoeller (67) beat Greg Norman (75) in the 18-hole play-off.*

1	**Fuzzy Zoeller***	71	66	69	70	276
2	**Greg Norman**	70	68	69	69	276
3	**Curtis Strange**	69	70	74	68	281
=4	**Johnny Miller**	74	68	70	70	282
	Jim Thorpe	68	71	70	73	282
6	**Hale Irwin**	68	68	69	79	284
=7	**Peter Jacobsen**	72	73	73	67	285
	Mark O'Meara	71	74	71	69	285
=9	**Fred Couples**	69	71	74	72	286
	Lee Trevino	71	72	69	74	286
=11	**Andy Bean**	70	71	75	71	287
	Jay Haas	73	73	70	71	287
	Tim Simpson	72	71	68	76	287
	Lanny Wadkins	72	71	72	72	287
	Tom Watson	72	72	74	69	287
=16	**Isao Aoki**	72	70	72	74	288
	Lennie Clements	69	76	72	71	288
	Mark McCumber	71	73	71	73	288
	Tom Purtzer	73	72	72	71	288
	Hal Sutton	72	72	74	70	288
=21	**Chip Beck**	72	74	71	72	289
	David Graham	71	72	70	76	289
	Gil Morgan	70	74	72	73	289
	Jack Nicklaus	71	71	70	77	289
=25	**Bill Glasson**	72	75	71	72	290
	Joe Hager	74	73	71	72	290
	Peter Oosterhuis	73	71	71	75	290
	Scott Simpson	72	75	74	69	290
	Mike Sullivan	70	73	70	77	290
=30	**Jim Albus**	77	69	74	71	291
	Seve Ballesteros	69	73	74	75	291
	Hubert Green	68	75	72	76	291
	John Mahaffey	72	74	77	68	291

June 13–16, 1985

Oakland Hills CC, Birmingham, MI

1	**Andy North**	70	65	70	74	279
=2	**Dave Barr**	70	68	70	72	280
	Tze-Chung Chen	65	69	69	77	280
	Dennis Watson	72	65	73	70	280
=5	**Seve Ballesteros**	71	70	69	71	281
	Payne Stewart	70	70	71	70	281
	Lanny Wadkins	70	72	69	70	281
8	**Johnny Miller**	74	71	68	69	282
=9	**Rick Fehr**	69	67	73	74	283
	Corey Pavin	72	68	73	70	283
	Jack Renner	72	69	72	70	283
	Fuzzy Zoeller	71	69	72	71	283
13	**Tom Kite**	69	70	71	74	284
14	**Hale Irwin**	73	72	70	70	285
=15	**Andy Bean**	69	72	73	72	286
	Jay Haas	69	66	77	74	286
	Greg Norman	72	71	71	72	286
	Mark O'Meara	72	67	75	72	286
	Don Pooley	73	69	73	71	286
	Tony Sills	75	70	71	70	286
	Scott Simpson	73	73	68	72	286
	Joey Sindelar	72	72	69	73	286
=23	**Ray Floyd**	72	67	73	75	287
	David Frost	74	68	74	71	287
	Fred Funk	75	70	72	70	287
	David Graham	73	72	74	68	287
	Gil Morgan	71	72	72	72	287
	Mike Reid	69	75	70	73	287

June 13–16, 1985 continued

	Tom Sieckmann	73	73	70	71	287
	Hal Sutton	74	71	74	68	287

June 12–15, 1986

Shinnecock Hills GC, Southampton, NY

1	**Ray Floyd**	75	68	70	66	279
=2	**Chip Beck**	75	73	68	65	281
	Lanny Wadkins	74	70	72	65	281
=4	**Hal Sutton**	75	70	66	71	282
	Lee Trevino	74	68	69	71	282
=6	**Ben Crenshaw**	76	69	69	69	283
	Payne Stewart	76	68	69	70	283
=8	**Bernhard Langer**	74	70	70	70	284
	Mark McCumber	74	71	68	71	284
	Jack Nicklaus	77	72	67	68	284
	Bob Tway	70	73	69	72	284
=12	**Greg Norman**	71	68	71	75	285
	Dennis Watson	72	70	71	72	285
14	**Mark Calcavecchia**	75	75	72	68	287
=15	**David Frost**	72	72	77	67	288
	David Graham	76	71	69	72	288
	Gary Koch	73	73	71	71	288
	Jodie Mudd	73	75	69	71	288
	Joey Sindelar	81	66	70	71	288
	Craig Stadler	74	71	74	69	288
	Scott Verplank	75	72	67	74	288
	Bobby Wadkins	75	69	72	72	288
	Fuzzy Zoeller	75	74	71	68	288
=24	**Seve Ballesteros**	75	73	68	73	289
	Andy Bean	76	72	73	68	289
	Lennie Clements	75	72	67	75	289
	Dave Eichelberger	80	70	72	67	289
	Larry Mize	75	71	73	70	289
	Calvin Peete	77	73	70	69	289
	Don Pooley	75	71	74	69	289
	Mike Reid	74	73	76	66	289
	Larry Rinker	77	71	70	71	289
	Tom Watson	72	71	71	75	289

June 16–19, 1987

Olympic GC, San Francisco, CA

1	**Scott Simpson**	71	68	70	68	277
2	**Tom Watson**	72	65	71	70	278
3	**Seve Ballesteros**	68	75	68	71	282
=4	**Ben Crenshaw**	67	72	72	72	283
	Bernhard Langer	69	69	73	72	282
	Larry Mize	71	68	72	72	283
	Curtis Strange	71	72	69	71	283
	Bobby Wadkins	71	71	70	71	283
=9	**Lennie Clements**	70	70	70	74	284
	Tommy Nakajima	68	70	74	72	284
	Mac O'Grady	71	69	72	72	284
	Dan Pohl	75	71	69	69	284
	Jim Thorpe	70	68	73	73	284
=14	**Isao Aoki**	71	73	70	71	285
	Bob Eastwood	73	66	75	71	285
	Tim Simpson	76	66	70	73	285
=17	**Mark Calcavecchia**	73	68	73	72	286
	David Frost	70	72	71	73	286
	Kenny Knox	72	71	79	74	286
	Jodie Mudd	72	75	71	68	286
	Jumbo Ozaki	71	69	72	74	286
	Nick Price	69	74	69	74	286
	Jim Woodward	71	74	72	69	286
=24	**Jay Don Blake**	70	75	71	71	287
	Danny Edwards	72	70	72	73	287

June 16–19, 1987 continued

	Peter Jacobsen	72	71	71	73	287
	John Mahaffey	72	72	67	76	287
	Steve Pate	71	72	72	72	287
	Don Pooley	74	72	72	69	287
	Craig Stadler	72	68	74	73	287

June 16–20, 1988

The Country Club, Brookline, MA

** Curtis Strange (71) beat Nick Faldo (75) in the 18-hole play-off.*

1	Curtis Strange*	70	67	69	72	278
2	Nick Faldo	72	67	68	71	278
=3	Mark O'Meara	71	72	66	71	280
	Steve Pate	72	69	72	67	280
	D.A. Weibring	71	69	68	72	280
=6	Paul Azinger	69	70	76	66	281
	Scott Simpson	69	66	72	74	281
=8	Bob Gilder	68	69	70	75	282
	Fuzzy Zoeller	73	72	71	66	282
=10	Fred Couples	72	67	71	73	283
	Payne Stewart	73	73	70	67	283
=12	Andy Bean	71	71	72	70	284
	Ben Crenshaw	71	72	74	67	284
	Larry Mize	69	67	72	76	284
	Dan Pohl	74	72	69	69	284
	Lanny Wadkins	70	71	70	73	284
=17	Ray Floyd	73	72	73	67	285
	Hale Irwin	71	71	72	71	285
	Mark McNulty	73	72	72	68	285
	Joey Sindelar	76	68	70	71	285
=21	Chip Beck	73	72	71	70	286
	Bob Eastwood	74	72	69	71	286
	Scott Hoch	71	72	71	72	286
	Peter Jacobsen	76	70	76	64	286
=25	Dave Barr	73	72	72	70	287
	Jay Haas	73	67	74	73	287
	Sandy Lyle	68	71	75	73	287
	Billy Mayfair (a)	71	72	71	73	287
	Craig Stadler	70	73	71	73	287
	Bob Tway	77	68	73	69	287
	Mark Wiebe	75	70	73	69	287

June 15–18, 1989

Oak Hill CC, Rochester, NY

1	Curtis Strange	71	64	73	70	278
=2	Chip Beck	71	69	71	68	279
	Mark McCumber	70	68	72	69	279
	Ian Woosnam	70	68	73	68	279
5	Brian Claar	71	72	68	69	280
=6	Jumbo Ozaki	70	71	68	72	281
	Scott Simpson	67	70	69	75	281
8	Peter Jacobsen	71	70	71	70	282
=9	Paul Azinger	71	72	70	70	283
	Hubert Green	69	72	74	68	283
	Tom Kite	67	69	69	78	283
	Jose-Maria Olazabal	69	72	70	72	283
=13	Scott Hoch	70	72	70	72	284
	Mark Lye	71	69	72	72	284
	Larry Nelson	68	73	68	75	284
	Tom Pernice	67	75	68	74	284
	Payne Stewart	66	75	72	71	284
=18	Jay Don Blake	66	71	72	76	285
	Nick Faldo	68	72	73	72	285
	David Frost	73	72	70	70	285
=21	Fred Couples	74	71	67	74	286
	Steve Elkington	70	70	78	68	286
	Bill Glasson	73	70	70	73	286

June 15–18, 1989 continued

	Nolan Henke	75	69	72	70	286
	D.A. Weibring	70	74	73	69	286
=26	Ray Floyd	68	74	74	71	287
	Don Pooley	74	69	71	73	287
	Robert Wrenn	74	71	73	69	287
=29	Emlyn Aubrey	69	73	73	73	288
	Dan Pohl	71	71	73	73	288
	Hal Sutton	69	75	72	72	288
	Scott Taylor	69	71	76	72	288

June 14–18, 1990

Medinah CC, Medinah, IL

** Hale Irwin (74) beat Mike Donald (74) at the 1st extra hole after the 18-hole play-off was tied.*

1	Hale Irwin*	69	70	74	67	280
2	Mike Donald	67	70	72	71	280
=3	Billy Ray Brown	69	71	69	72	281
	Nick Faldo	72	72	68	69	281
=5	Mark Brooks	68	70	72	73	283
	Greg Norman	72	73	69	69	283
	Tim Simpson	66	69	75	73	283
=8	Scott Hoch	70	73	69	72	284
	Steve Jones	67	76	74	67	284
	Jose-Maria Olazabal	73	69	69	73	284
	Tom Sieckmann	70	74	68	72	284
	Craig Stadler	71	70	72	71	284
	Fuzzy Zoeller	73	70	68	73	284
=14	Jim Benepe	72	70	73	70	285
	John Huston	68	72	73	72	285
	John Inman	72	71	70	72	285
	Larry Mize	72	70	69	74	285
	Larry Nelson	74	67	68	75	285
	Scott Simpson	66	73	73	73	285
	Jeff Sluman	66	70	74	75	285
=21	Steve Elkington	73	71	73	69	286
	Curtis Strange	73	70	68	75	286
	Ian Woosnam	70	70	74	72	286
=24	Paul Azinger	72	72	69	74	287
	Webb Heintzelman	70	75	74	68	287
	Jumbo Ozaki	73	72	74	68	287
	Corey Pavin	74	70	73	70	287
	Billy Tuten	74	70	72	71	287
=29	Chip Beck	71	71	73	73	288
	Brian Claar	70	71	71	76	288
	Mike Hulbert	76	66	71	75	288
	Phil Mickleson (a)	74	71	71	72	288

June 13–17, 1991

Hazeltine National GC, Minneapolis, MN

** Payne Stewart (75) beat Scott Simpson (77) in the 18-hole play-off.*

1	Payne Stewart*	67	70	73	72	282
2	Scott Simpson	70	68	72	72	282
=3	Fred Couples	70	70	75	70	285
	Larry Nelson	73	72	72	68	285
5	Fuzzy Zoeller	72	73	74	67	286
6	Scott Hoch	69	71	74	73	287
7	Nolan Henke	67	71	77	73	288
=8	Ray Floyd	73	72	76	68	289
	Jose-Maria Olazabal	73	71	75	70	289
	Corey Pavin	71	67	79	72	289
=11	Jim Gallagher Jr	70	72	75	73	290
	Hale Irwin	71	75	70	74	290
	Davis Love III	70	76	73	71	290
	Craig Parry	70	73	73	74	290
	D.A. Weibring	76	71	75	68	290
=16	Nick Faldo	72	74	73	72	291

June 13–17, 1991 continued

	Sandy Lyle	72	70	74	75	291
	Tom Watson	73	71	77	70	291
=19	**Mark Brooks**	73	73	73	73	292
	Billy Ray Brown	73	71	77	71	292
	John Cook	76	70	72	74	292
	Peter Persons	70	75	75	72	292
	Nick Price	74	69	71	78	292
	Tom Sieckmann	74	70	74	74	292
	Craig Stadler	71	69	77	75	292
=26	**Rick Fehr**	74	69	73	77	293
	Jodie Mudd	71	70	77	75	293
	Mike Reid	74	72	74	73	293
	Tim Simpson	73	72	76	72	293
	Bob Tway	75	69	75	74	293

June 18–21, 1992

Pebble Beach GL, Pebble Beach, CA

1	**Tom Kite**	71	72	70	72	285
2	**Jeff Sluman**	73	74	69	71	287
3	**Colin Montgomerie**	70	71	77	70	288
=4	**Nick Faldo**	70	76	68	77	291
	Nick Price	71	72	77	71	291
=6	**Billy Andrade**	72	74	72	74	292
	Jay Don Blake	70	74	75	73	292
	Bob Gilder	73	70	75	74	292
	Mike Hulbert	74	73	70	75	292
	Tom Lehman	69	74	72	77	292
	Joey Sindelar	74	72	68	78	292
	Ian Woosnam	72	72	69	79	292
=13	**Ian Baker-Finch**	74	71	72	76	293
	John Cook	72	72	74	75	293
	Mark McCumber	70	76	73	74	293
	Gil Morgan	66	69	77	81	293
=17	**Fred Couples**	72	70	78	74	294
	Andy Dillard	68	70	79	77	294
	Wayne Grady	74	76	81	73	294
	Andrew Magee	77	69	72	76	294
	Tray Tyner	74	72	78	70	294
	Willie Wood	70	75	75	74	294
=23	**Seve Ballesteros**	71	76	69	79	295
	Brad Bryant	71	76	75	73	295
	Jay Haas	70	77	74	74	295
	Donnie Hammond	73	73	73	76	295
	Dudley Hart	76	71	71	77	295
	Jim Kane	73	71	76	75	295
	Bernhard Langer	73	72	75	75	295
	Billy Mayfair	74	73	75	73	295
	Jumbo Ozaki	77	70	72	76	295
	Curtis Strange	67	78	76	74	295

June 17–20, 1993

Baltusrol, Springfield, NJ

1	**Lee Janzen**	67	67	69	69	272
2	**Payne Stewart**	70	66	68	70	274
=3	**Paul Azinger**	71	68	69	69	277
	Craig Parry	66	74	69	68	277
=5	**Scott Hoch**	66	72	72	68	278
	Tom Watson	70	66	73	69	278
=7	**Ernie Els**	71	73	68	67	279
	Ray Floyd	68	73	70	68	279
	Fred Funk	70	72	67	70	279
	Nolan Henke	72	71	67	69	279
=11	**John Adams**	70	70	69	71	280
	David Edwards	70	72	66	72	280
	Nick Price	71	66	70	73	280
	Loren Roberts	70	70	71	69	280

June 17–20, 1993 continued

	Jeff Sluman	71	71	69	69	280
=16	**Fred Couples**	68	71	71	71	281
	Barry Lane	74	68	70	69	281
	Mike Standly	70	69	70	72	281
=19	**Ian Baker-Finch**	70	70	70	72	282
	Dan Forsman	73	71	70	68	282
	Tom Lehman	71	70	71	70	282
	Blaine McCallister	68	73	73	68	282
	Steve Pate	70	71	71	70	282
	Corey Pavin	68	69	75	70	282
=25	**Chip Beck**	72	68	72	71	283
	Mark Calcavecchia	70	70	71	72	283
	John Cook	75	66	70	72	283
	Wayne Levi	71	69	69	74	283
	Rocco Mediate	68	72	73	70	283
	Joe Ozaki	70	70	74	69	283
	Kenny Perry	74	70	68	71	283
	Curtis Strange	73	68	75	67	283

June 16–20, 1994

Oakmont CC, Oakmont, PA

** Ernie Els (74) beat Colin Montgomerie (78) and tied with Loren Roberts (74) in the 18-hole play-off, before winning at the second extra hole.*

1	**Ernie Els***	69	71	66	73	279
=2	**Loren Roberts**	76	69	74	70	279
	Colin Montgomerie	71	65	73	70	279
4	**Curtis Strange**	70	70	70	70	280
5	**John Cook**	73	65	73	71	282
=6	**Tom Watson**	68	73	68	74	283
	Clark Dennis	71	71	70	71	283
	Greg Norman	71	71	69	72	283
=9	**Jeff Maggert**	71	68	75	70	284
	Frank Nobilo	69	71	68	76	284
	Jeff Sluman	72	69	72	71	284
	Duffy Waldorf	74	68	73	69	284
=13	**David Edwards**	73	65	75	72	285
	Scott Hoch	72	72	70	71	285
	Jim McGovern	73	69	74	69	285
=16	**Fred Couples**	72	71	69	74	286
	Steve Lowery	71	71	68	76	286
=18	**Seve Ballesteros**	72	72	70	73	287
	Hale Irwin	69	69	71	78	287
	Scott Verplank	70	72	75	70	287
=21	**Steve Pate**	74	66	71	77	288
	Sam Torrance	72	71	76	69	288
=23	**Bernhard Langer**	72	72	73	72	289
	Kirk Triplett	70	71	71	77	289
=25	**Chip Beck**	73	73	70	74	290
	Craig Parry	78	68	71	73	290
	Mike Springer	74	72	73	71	290
=28	**Lennie Clements**	73	71	73	75	292
	Jim Furyk	74	69	74	75	292
	Davis Love III	74	72	74	72	292
	Jack Nicklaus	69	70	77	76	292
	Jumbo Ozaki	70	73	69	80	292

June 15–18, 1995

Shinnecock Hills GC, Southampton, NY

1	**Corey Pavin**	72	69	71	68	280
2	**Greg Norman**	68	67	74	73	282
3	**Tom Lehman**	70	72	67	74	283
=4	**Bill Glasson**	69	70	76	69	284
	Jay Haas	70	73	72	69	284
	Neal Lancaster	70	72	77	65	284
	Davis Love III	72	68	73	71	284
	Jeff Maggert	69	72	77	66	284

	June 15–18, 1995 continued					
	Phil Mickleson	68	70	72	74	284
=10	**Frank Nobilo**	72	72	70	71	285
	Vijay Singh	70	71	72	72	285
	Bob Tway	69	69	72	75	285
=13	**Brad Bryant**	71	75	70	70	286
	Lee Janzen	70	72	72	72	286
	Mark McCumber	70	71	77	68	286
	Nick Price	66	73	73	74	286
	Mark Roe	71	69	74	72	286
	Jeff Sluman	72	69	74	71	286
	Steve Stricker	71	70	71	74	286
	Duffy Waldorf	72	70	75	69	286
=21	**Billy Andrade**	72	69	74	72	287
	Pete Jordan	74	71	71	71	287
	Brett Ogle	71	75	72	69	287
	Payne Stewart	74	71	73	69	287
	Scott Verplank	72	69	71	75	287
	Ian Woosnam	72	71	69	75	287
	Fuzzy Zoeller	69	74	76	68	287
=28	**David Duval**	70	73	73	72	288
	Gary Hallberg	70	76	69	73	288
	Mike Hulbert	74	72	72	70	288
	Miguel Jimenez	72	72	75	69	288
	Colin Montgomerie	71	74	75	68	288
	Jose-Maria Olazabal	73	70	72	73	288
	Jumbo Osaki	69	68	80	71	288
	Scott Simpson	67	75	74	72	288

June 13–16, 1996

Oakland Hills CC, Birmingham, MI

1	**Steve Jones**	74	66	69	69	278
=2	**Tom Lehman**	71	72	65	71	279
	Davis Love III	71	69	70	69	279
4	**John Morse**	68	74	68	70	280
=5	**Ernie Els**	72	67	72	70	281
	Jim Furyk	72	69	70	70	281
=7	**Ken Green**	73	67	72	70	282
	Scott Hoch	73	71	71	67	282
	Vijay Singh	71	72	70	69	282
=10	**Lee Janzen**	68	75	71	69	283
	Colin Montgomerie	70	72	69	72	283
	Greg Norman	73	66	74	70	283
=13	**Dan Forsman**	72	71	70	71	284
	Frank Nobilo	69	71	70	74	284
	Tom Watson	70	71	71	72	284
=16	**David Berganio**	69	72	72	72	285
	Mark Brooks	76	68	69	72	285
	Stewart Cink	69	73	70	73	285
	John Cook	70	71	71	73	285
	Nick Faldo	72	71	72	70	285
	Mark O'Meara	72	73	68	72	285
	Sam Torrance	71	69	71	74	285
=23	**Billy Andrade**	72	69	72	73	286
	Woody Austin	67	72	72	75	286
	Brad Bryant	73	71	74	68	286
	Peter Jacobsen	71	74	70	71	286
=27	**John Daly**	72	69	73	73	287
	Pete Jordan	71	74	72	70	287
	Jack Nicklaus	72	74	69	72	287
	Payne Stewart	67	71	76	73	287
	Curtis Strange	74	73	71	69	287

June 12–15, 1997

Congressional GC, Bethesda, MD

	June 12–15, 1997 continued					
1	**Ernie Els**	71	67	69	69	276
2	**Colin Montgomerie**	65	76	67	69	277
3	**Tom Lehman**	67	70	68	73	278
4	**Jeff Maggert**	73	66	68	74	281
=5	**Olin Browne**	71	71	69	71	282
	Jim Furyk	74	68	69	71	282
	Tommy Tolles	74	67	69	72	282
	Bob Tway	71	71	70	70	282
=10	**Scott Hoch**	71	68	72	72	283
	Scott McCarron	73	71	69	70	283
	David Ogrin	70	69	71	73	283
=13	**Billy Andrade**	75	67	69	73	284
	Stewart Cink	71	67	74	72	284
	Loren Roberts	72	69	72	71	284
=16	**Bradley Hughes**	75	70	71	69	285
	Davis Love III	75	70	69	71	285
	Jose-Maria Olazabal	71	71	72	71	285
=19	**Nick Price**	71	74	71	70	286
	Paul Stankowski	75	70	68	73	286
	Hal Sutton	66	73	73	74	286
	Lee Westwood	71	71	73	71	286
	Tiger Woods	74	67	73	72	286
=24	**Scott Dunlap**	75	66	75	71	287
	Steve Elkington	75	68	72	72	287
	Edward Fryatt	72	73	73	69	287
	Len Mattiace	71	75	73	68	287
=28	**Paul Azinger**	72	72	74	70	288
	Kelly Gibson	72	69	72	75	288
	Paul Goydos	73	72	74	69	288
	Hideki Kase	68	73	73	74	288
	Mark McNulty	67	73	75	73	288
	Jeff Sluman	69	72	72	75	288
	Payne Stewart	71	73	73	71	288
	Fuzzy Zoeller	72	73	69	74	288

June 18–21, 1998

Olympic Club, San Francisco, CA

1	**Lee Janzen**	73	66	73	68	280
2	**Payne Stewart**	66	71	70	74	281
3	**Bob Tway**	68	70	73	73	284
4	**Nick Price**	73	68	71	73	285
=5	**Tom Lehman**	68	75	68	75	286
	Steve Stricker	73	71	69	73	286
=7	**David Duval**	75	68	75	69	287
	Jeff Maggert	69	69	75	74	287
	Lee Westwood	72	74	70	71	287
=10	**Stuart Appleby**	73	74	70	71	288
	Stewart Cink	73	68	73	74	288
	Phil Mickleson	71	73	74	70	288
	Jeff Sluman	72	74	74	68	288
=14	**Paul Azinger**	75	72	77	65	289
	Jim Furyk	74	73	68	74	289
	Matt Kuchar (a)	70	69	76	74	289
	Jesper Parnevik	69	74	76	70	289
=18	**Frank Lickliter**	73	71	72	74	290
	Colin Montgomerie	70	74	77	69	290
	Jose-Maria Olazabal	68	77	71	74	290
	Loren Roberts	71	76	71	72	290
	Tiger Woods	74	72	71	73	290
=23	**Glen Day**	73	72	71	75	291
	Casey Martin	74	71	74	72	291
=25	**Thomas Bjorn**	72	75	70	75	292
	Mark Carnevale	67	73	74	78	292
	Per-Ulrik Johannson	71	75	73	73	292
	Chris Perry	74	71	72	75	292
	Eduardo Romero	72	70	76	74	292
	Vijay Singh	73	72	73	74	292
	D.A. Weibring	72	72	75	73	292

THE MASTERS

It was despite the misgivings of its creator, Bobby Jones, that the Masters became one of the four major championships, yet surely the great man would have been proud of the tournament's standing as we approach a new millennium. The youngest of the Grand Slam events is frequently the most exciting each year and certainly the most dignified – no advertising hoardings desecrate any tee at Augusta, indeed no billboards of any description are allowed inside the hallowed grounds. Even CBS, the powerful television company that signs over millions of dollars each year for the privilege of broadcasting the event in America, finds itself being dictated to – the normal pattern for American TV of an advert every five minutes or so is not allowed during the Masters. Instead, only three adverts every hour are allowed, and then only advertisers approved by the Masters authorities. Oh, and CBS are not allowed to televise the front nine either. "We like to maintain a little air of secrecy for the benefit of our patrons," the former chairman, Jack Stephens, once explained.

A ticket to drive

It is such autocratic behaviour that has given the tournament a unique feel. The patrons, as Stephens calls them, are the same each year, for every January the letter comes through the post asking whether they would like to buy a season ticket as usual. If they do not, they are required to hand over the privilege to the next person on the waiting list. Furthermore, anyone who buys the season ticket and then sells it on to a tout thinking they can make a swift buck will only ever do it once: each ticket is numbered, and patrons who hand over their right to an unauthorized source are tersely informed they are no longer welcome. As it is only the same spectators – sorry, patrons – who are allowed through the gate each year, and as no one in their right mind gives up that privilege or passes on the ticket to someone outside their close circle of friends and family, it is perhaps hardly surprising that a pass to the Masters has become one of the hottest tickets in sport. Each year people hand over many thousands of dollars to purchase one of the few tickets that bucks the system and makes it on to the black market. The demand so heavily exceeds supply that it has resulted in tragedy. In 1997, a corporate trader who promised tickets for clients and then found he could not deliver committed suicide.

It was in recognition of the vast numbers who wanted to see for themselves the special magic of Augusta at Masters time that the authorities finally approved a relaxation of their policy of exclusivity in the 1990s, and allowed people to come to watch the practice rounds. Still the demand was not satiated and the gates would be closed before 12 noon, with an estimated 75,000 people inside. In the last couple of years the rules have been modified and tickets have been issued for the practice days as well. One thing is for certain: they could sell three times as many if they had the room.

The actual number of tickets is a heavily guarded secret, but it is believed that 60,000 are issued for each of the three practice days, with fewer than half that number for the four days of the tournament itself. Which makes it close to 300,000 for the week; which in turn makes it a far cry from the tournament's formative days, when Jones would wander the sacred acres and often find the greens surrounded by no more than 10 or 15 "patrons".

As the generation who grew up with Bobby Jones dwindles inexorably in number, so it becomes difficult to fully appreciate the scale of the respect and affection he commanded; and why, when he retired from playing the game in 1930 having won the Grand Slam (a term taken from the game of bridge by his faithful biographer, O.B. Keeler), people wondered whether golf would ever be the same again.

Well, perhaps it would not in a way – amateur golf, for example, became less important with each passing year – and certainly it was not until Arnold Palmer came along in the late 1950s that a figurehead emerged who inspired similar reverence.

Yet, equally, could Jones turn his back completely on his beloved game? Winning the Grand Slam may have taken its toll on his fragile health, but could he devote himself totally to his law practice without any golfing outlet? The answer, thankfully, was no, although the decision was not borne purely out of love: Jones wanted to capitalize on his fame and make a deal of money from a series of best-selling instructional films and books. He also set about fulfilling a lifetime's ambition: to build a golf course in Georgia which he could invite his friends to play and join.

A year before his retirement, during the Amateur Championship at Pebble Beach, Jones had struck up a deep conversation on the subject with Dr Alister Mackenzie, who had just finished constructing the neighbouring Cypress Point. It was a discussion that Jones never forgot. From the start, he knew Mackenzie was right for his golf course project.

But where would the backing come from in Depression-hit America? Jones was never short of influential friends. He called upon the assistance of a New York businessman called Clifford Roberts, who had started out as a suit salesman and who thoroughly enjoyed his Georgia trips to play golf with Jones; Thomas Barrett of the Augusta Chamber of Commerce;

Bobby Jones – unwittingly created one of the world's finest tournaments

and the journalist Grantland Rice, and several financiers. The site they visited was one Barrett had recommended to Jones, one of the first nurseries in Georgia which went by the name of "Fruitlands".

Jones fell in love with it at first sight. "It seemed that this land had been lying here for years waiting for someone to lay a golf course upon it," he said. The purchase was underwritten and money flowed in from all over the world to meet building costs. Naturally, when it came to the choice of architect, Jones had only one name on his list.

Dr Alister Mackenzie was hardly a golfer at all, never mind one proficient in the game. He served as a surgeon during the Boer War in South Africa, but whilst there became increasingly fascinated by something at which the Boers were particularly good: camouflage. The art served him well when he returned to Scotland and became involved in golf course design. Disguising pitfalls became a Mackenzie trademark.

His career really took off after he met the prominent designer Harry Colt in 1907. The pair collaborated on the building of Alwoodley near Leeds, where Mackenzie was secretary. Then came the First World War, and Mackenzie served not as a surgeon, but as an expert in camouflage.

After the war he concentrated on golf course architecture, and so his fame spread. It was assured from the moment he finished completing Cypress Point in 1928, which explains why Jones was so keen to talk to him.

Jones was very particular. He struck a great many balls to verify shot values around the Fruitlands layout; Mackenzie designed with generous fairways and greens, little rough, and few bunkers. Instead of these, mounds were used to produce a rolling topography after the style of Jones's beloved St Andrews with its seaside humps and hollows. One of the underlying aims was to produce a course that all of Jones's friends could enjoy, but one that would still test the scratch golfer. He also wanted one that would look more difficult than it really was and Mackenzie, the master of disguise, carried out the instructions to the letter. Sadly, after supervising all of the construction and design, Mackenzie died without seeing it become recognized as one of his true masterpieces, one of the great golf courses of the world.

It was known as Augusta National, and by the time the first Augusta National Invitation was issued in 1934 the final touch had been added; every hole was named after a blossom and decorated with that blossom, among others. Jones's idea was for a jolly spring meeting with his former golfing friends both professional and amateur, but the idea never lasted beyond the first gathering. For one thing, Jones's worldwide reputation was such that the interest in both his tournament and his golf course was considerable; for another Clifford Roberts was not slow when it came to publicizing this new venture. It would be unfair to call him the Don King of his day, but he knew what he was doing: he made a fuss of the Press, which is always a good public-relations move, and he also made sure that they had something to write about. Later, he hit the promotional jackpot by enrolling Eisenhower as a member.

Roberts persuaded Jones to come out of retirement to play in the first and, what would prove to be last, Augusta Invitation. He finished tied for 13th with his old sparring partner, Walter Hagen, 10 shots behind the winner, Horton Smith, and naturally generated more column inches than the victor. Yet Smith was no fluke winner – he had been one of the few players who had managed to beat Jones during his all-conquering year of 1930.

Everyone was delighted with the tournament's success, although Roberts was unhappy over at least one aspect. He had wanted to call the tournament the Masters, but Jones did not like the idea, believing it to be presumptuous. It is not known how the Press got a sniff of Roberts's idea for the Masters title, but, given his shrewd dealings with them, it is not hazarding too wild a guess to believe that he planted the idea.

Whatever, the name caught on immediately, although it would be five years before Jones would officially relent and allow the name on programmes and stationery. By then, though, he probably had no choice. For everyone else, from 1935 onwards, the tournament had become the Masters.

And what an eventful edition that year would prove. The only leading player missing from the field in the first year had been Gene Sarazen, who had been away on a tour of South Africa. How he would make amends for his initial absence.

The first real Masters

The tournament was rapidly drawing to a close when Jones decided to wander down and join the 25 or so patrons who had gathered behind the 15th green to watch the starred pairing of Sarazen and Hagen. The previous year this hole had been the 5th, but, with one of those decisions that later on seems to have been guided by fate, the nines had been reversed the previous autumn.

Now Jones just wanted to see how his former adversaries were faring. In the case of Hagen, the answer was not very well. He would eventually conclude with a 79 and a tie for 15th place with Sam Parks Jnr. But Sarazen still had a sniff of a chance, although nothing more than that. With four holes to play he trailed Craig Wood by three shots, the latter sitting comfortably in the clubhouse on a total of 282.

Sarazen knew that to have any chance of victory he would have to gamble on the par-five 15th. Yet his drive had left him with 220 yards to go to the flag, and that was the very limit of his range with a four wood. If he missed it at all he would finish in the water that protected the green and, in all likelihood, drop out of the frame. Sarazen had only ever thought about winning, and took on the gamble. From the moment he hit it he knew he had cleared the water, and a birdie, possibly even an eagle, was on the cards. He was therefore assured of making inroads into Wood's lead. What he could never have envisaged was what actually happened next. The ball pitched on the front of the green, ran for several yards before, under the astonished gaze of Jones himself, rolling into the hole for an albatross, or a double-eagle as they say in Georgia. Wood's three-shot lead had vanished, literally, at a stroke.

Sarazen parred the last three holes to set up a 36-hole play-off which he won the next day by five after returning a level-par total of 144. All of which, apart from the matter of victory, became incidental. It was the shot that earned the hype – the shot that was heard all round the world.

Hitting the greens

Augusta was on the map and so was the Masters. In 1937 the members began wearing their symbolic green jackets and were particularly encouraged to do so at Masters time. The entry list also included the name of Sam Snead for the first time, one that would make every entry list for the next 44 years. Indeed, a year has never gone by without an appearance from the great man; these days he plays an honorary tee ball from the first in the company of Sarazen and Byron Nelson.

Snead's first year was also one that Nelson will never forget. He strode on to the first tee complete with a set of clubs featuring the new steel shafts that had just been invented. He proceeded to give such a masterly demonstration that it ensured there was no going back. Nelson hit every green in regulation, apart from the four-par fives which he reached in two. He signed for a 66, which was a new course record. A bad third-round 75, however, appeared to have cost him the tournament, for it let in Ralph Guldahl, who now led by four with a round to play. Nelson prevailed, though, a final-round 70 proving good enough as Guldahl faded to a 76.

The pre-war halcyon days

Two years later, with the tournament now officially renamed the Masters, Guldahl got his green jacket, coming home in 33 strokes to beat Snead by one and become the first player to shoot lower than 280 in a major championship. A year on, and Lloyd Mangrum set another record, breaking Nelson's standard

Byron Nelson (right) pipped Ben Hogan by one stroke in the play-off in 1942

with a 64 in the opening round. He paid for such impertinence, however, his three rounds that followed never coming close to such golf, and Jimmy Demaret emerged the winner by four.

In 1941, the erstwhile luckless Craig Wood finally got his reward. He did it the hard way, too, leading in every round to claim his first major championship after years of disappointment. Two months later, having finally discovered the secret, he would win the US Open, too.

For the next edition of the Masters the number of patrons had swollen considerably, to the extent that gallery control and roping was used for the first time. The changes were necessary, too, as Augusta witnessed its first heavyweight clash.

At the time Nelson and Ben Hogan were the biggest names in the game. They were born in the same town, in the same year, but while Nelson was the natural and had been a star for some time, Hogan was just getting to grips with the game after a long struggle fighting a hook. Now he caught up three strokes on Nelson in the final round to force an 18-hole play-off.

The following day the momentum continued to be with Hogan. After five holes he had established a three-stroke lead as Nelson dropped a couple of strokes to par. Clearly Nelson was going to have to put in a sustained stretch of brilliance to stand a chance, and it is a measure of the man that he recovered from such a poor start to do just that. Hogan played those last 13 holes in one under par, and yet found at the end that he had lost by one. Nelson had played them in five under for a 69.

And that was that. The year was 1942 and America had entered the Second World War. The club was wound down for the duration with cattle keeping the grass short, and profit made from turkey farming.

After the battle

The club reopened for play in 1945. Naturally, there was much work to be done, and private contributions were sought from some of the wealthier members to revive both the course and the clubhouse in time for when Jones, Snead, Hogan and company were out of uniform.

In the event the 1946 Masters went ahead on its usual date of the second weekend in April. In truth, it was somewhat anticlimactic. Of all the majors, the Masters has historically produced the fewest number of surprising winners, but Herman Keiser's success certainly falls into that category, and particularly since he was up against Ben Hogan.

The Texan had his chance, too. Trailing from the opening round, where he shot 74 to Keiser's 69, Hogan got to the final hole within sight of the leader, and particularly when Keiser nervously three-putted. Now Hogan, less than 20 feet away, needed one putt to win, and two to tie. That he actually required three was a huge disappointment to his many admirers and again raised doubts about whether he had the mental strength to ever win a major championship. You could say he answered those doubts in the years that followed.

The following year a familiar cast list dominated. In the first round it was Demaret and Nelson who disputed the lead following opening 69s. Once more Hogan started disappointingly with a 75, but revived his hopes with a 68, the lowest score of the second round. Demaret, however, was a model of consistency, becoming the first man to win the Masters by shooting four sub-par rounds. His best round was his first, his worst a 71, and it gave him a two-stroke victory over Nelson and a young amateur named Frank Stranahan, who would challenge for several majors over the next decade.

The amateur impact

In a tradition that recognizes Jones's status as the greatest amateur of all time, amateur golfers have always been welcome at the Masters. Even today, when amateur golf barely gets a mention outside the leading broadsheet newspapers, the amateur champions of both America and Great Britain are duly accorded an invitation, as is the runner-up of the former plus the US mid-amateur champion and Public Links title holder. And they have made their full contribution – three indeed have gone closer than Stranahan and finished one shot shy of the winning score; Billy Joe Patton in 1954, Ken Venturi two years later, and Charles Coe in 1961. Even in more recent times, when they have not challenged for the green jacket, the amateurs have remained a refreshing presence. Reporters have filed countless stories on those who have frozen on their big day, and on amateurs who have risen to the occasion. In 1998, the smiling face of the young amateur Matt Kuchar, a Georgia native, was almost as good a story as that of the winner, Mark O'Meara.

In 1948 history of another kind – which will never be repeated – was made when Claude Harmon won the title, thus becoming the first and last non-tournament-playing professional to triumph. Harmon, the pro at Winged Foot near New York, emulated Demaret's achievement of the previous year, recording three sub-par rounds of 70 and one of 69 to achieve a comfortable victory by five strokes over Cary Middlecoff.

One of the traditions of the Masters has been the awarding of a green jacket to the winner in a ceremony that takes place beside the 18th green, with the previous winner helping him into his prize. As we have seen, it was in 1937 that the members started wearing these coats, as they are known in Georgia. They were purchased from the Brooks Uniform Company in New York and, if truth be told, were not initially very popular. They were a winter style, which was not conducive to warm Augusta afternoons. Within several years, a lightweight, made-to-order jacket was made available from the club's golf shop.

First green

It was in 1949 that the winner was first awarded a green jacket. Single-breasted, it is adorned with an Augusta National Golf Club logo on the left chest pocket, and on the brass buttons.

Traditionally the champion takes his jacket home with him during his year of office, so to speak, but is expected to accord with the spirit of the club's rules. He is allowed to wear it for dinners where he is recognized as the Masters champion, for example, but must not do anything that is remotely commercial, or would demean what the jacket stands for. A few years ago, Nick Faldo wore the jacket to a chat show on BBC television. Not a week had passed before he was informed by the Masters authorities that this was patently an unsuitable occasion on which to wear his prized possession, and it must not happen again.

It was Sam Snead who had the honour of winning the first one to be awarded, and he did so with one of the great comeback victories. After two rounds he trailed the leaders by five shots, but he made up the ground and more with two closing rounds of 67, his final one containing no fewer than eight birdies. It gave him a two-stroke victory over Johnny Bulla and Lloyd Mangrum.

Hogan's run

In 1950 the top six bore an awesome look: Demaret (the first man to win the Masters three times), Jim Ferrier, Snead, Hogan, Nelson and Mangrum. As good as Demaret's achievement was, Hogan's high finish was even more remarkable. For this was his first appearance in a major since his horrific car crash and now, 14 months on from being told that to walk again would be an amazing achievement, there was naturally a public sense of wonder at his feat. Two months later he ensured that golf made not just the back page but the front by winning the US Open at Merion.

It is, of course, for winning three major championships in the same year (1953) that Hogan, in golfing terms, is most famously known. But two years earlier he won three in a row, too. After his 1950 US Open win, he did not play in the final two majors that year owing to the pain in his legs. The following year he completed a successful defence of his US Open title, and in between he finally won his first green jacket after so many near misses.

Hogan was now playing a drastically reduced schedule, but enough, mind, to maintain his sharpness for the events that mattered. This time, he got off to a good start at Augusta, an opening 70 leaving him just two strokes behind George Fazio. A second-round 72 was followed by one of 70, and now he trailed Snead and Skee Riegel by a stroke.

Perhaps surprisingly, Snead was never a factor in the final round and would eventually sign for a horrific score of 80. So

Sam Snead – awarded the first green jacket in 1949

it was between Hogan and Riegel, and it was experience that told in the former's favour. Carding a 68 that contained no bogeys, Hogan was a winner at last by two strokes, his monetary reward being $3,000.

Winner's fare

Another Masters tradition is the champions' dinner, which takes place on the Tuesday before the start of the tournament. Here, the defending champion hosts previous winners, picking up the bill for the meal and choosing the menu. When the British players started to win the tournament in the 1980s, this led to some hilarious selections. Sandy Lyle, for example, chose haggis: what some of the old winners thought of that particular Scottish delicacy is not known.

Anyway, Hogan got first choice with the introduction of the champions' dinner in 1952; the tournament, meanwhile, was won by Snead, who probably still had indigestion from his failure the year before. The event was marred by strong winds over the final two days, and Snead could afford to shoot 77 in the third round and yet still maintain a share of the lead with the defending champion, who shot 74.

In the final round, however, it was Hogan's turn to slip quietly down the field with a 79; Snead matched the par of 72, and that was good enough to win by four from Jack Burke Jnr, who came charging through the field with a last-round 69.

The tone for Hogan's year of years in 1953 was firmly set at Augusta when he collected his second green jacket with a new record 72-hole score of 274. One newspaper described it as "the best 72 holes played by anyone, anywhere, at any time". Certainly the statistics are enormously impressive. Hogan followed an opening round of 70 with two cards of 69 and one of 66 to shave no fewer than five shots from Augusta's previous benchmark and set a total that would stand for 12 years.

Twelve months on and Hogan found himself in the position of defending no fewer than three major titles, although he would choose not to do so at the Open. The best stab he made at the other two came at Augusta, where he was going for four major wins in a row. The weather could hardly have been less clement, given that it was Georgia in April, but, as ever, Hogan looked on top of it for three days at least, carving out a three-shot advantage. Surely no one would catch him now? Someone did – his old adversary Snead to be precise, and so the pair played off the following day over 18 holes. After setting the lowest winning score a year earlier, Hogan now found that a total of 15 shots worse played off for the title. It remains tied for the highest winning score in Masters history.

Before the play-off could commence, there were commiserations to get out of the way. For Billy Joe Patton, the tournament had ended in heartbreak. Patton led after the second round and during the course of the fourth, and a first amateur victory appeared a possibility as he approached the 13th. He took seven. When all the totals were added up, he was one shot shy of the winning score.

Twelve years had now passed since Hogan had been involved in the only other 18-hole play-off for the title. That had been against Nelson; now he was up against Snead in what was, once more, a clash between the two best players of the day. But again it was Hogan who had to give way. He shot 71, while Snead came in with a 70 to emulate Demaret's achievement of winning the Masters on three occasions.

Though no one knew it at the time, Hogan had lost his edge, and had begun the reversal to his former status as a "nearly man". He would finish second again the following year to Cary Middlecoff, and also in the US Open that year at Olympic. He would never again win a major.

Yet his record at Augusta from 1941 to 1955 is worth studying in closer detail, for it is truly astonishing. During that time he played in 11 Masters and finished first on two occasions, second four times, fourth three times, sixth once and seventh once. In other words, he was never outside the top seven despite two prolonged periods when he was unable to play golf – once because of the war, and the other through his car accident. No player before or since has ever achieved anything like it, taking into account the circumstances under which Hogan's extraordinary sequence was compiled.

On the box

The era of Hogan came to an end just as the era of television began. Perhaps it was just as well, for Hogan was far from televisual. He rarely smiled, and wore dark colours or sober grey. Who would be the character to take the game into this brave new world? The answer would appear at the Masters before the decade was out, but in the event the 1956 edition was a dandy in its own right. From the start the amateur, Ken Venturi, looked a special talent. He shot 66 to lead in the first round and then, answering those who wondered whether he would be fazed by it the following day, carded a 69 to maintain his pacemaking position. And after three rounds still no one had caught the front runner, indeed only Lloyd Mangrum was within four shots of his aggregate of 210. Could Venturi hold on for perhaps the most sensational of all Masters victories? Alas, the answer was to be that convention told against him in the end. Venturi shot 80 on the last day and lost by a stroke. The winner was Jack Burke Jnr, who came from eight shots back on the last day to win with a 71, and achieve the major championship success that had proved so elusive to his father.

A 36-hole cut to the leading 40 players plus ties was instigated at Augusta in 1957 where, despite the passing years, some familiar faces were still contending for the first prize. Leading after three rounds was Sam Snead, now aged 45; not

Arnold Palmer – the first of four Masters triumphs came in 1958

far behind was another three-time champion, Jimmy Demaret, who was two years older. Snead was three strokes ahead of Doug Ford with a round to play, but could not maintain his position. Not that he folded on the last day, as he had in 1951 to let in Hogan. Rather, this was a tournament won by Ford as opposed to one lost by Snead, since he carded a 66 to win by three shots. He must have known it was his day at the last, given what happened after he had bunkered his second shot. At that stage there was still a possibility that he could be caught by Snead if he played the sand shot poorly and took a double-bogey six. In the event he played it perfectly, and holed for a birdie three.

And so who was the player who emerged for the television age, as intimated earlier? In fact, his first appearance at the Masters pre-dated television by one year, as he teed it up in 1955 and finished tied for tenth.

But 1958 was the year in which it all began to happen for Arnold Palmer, and Augusta was where he achieved his first Grand Slam title. It was a momentous year all round: not only was television there to record a victory for a character with all the colour of the flowers that decorated the course; Herb Warren Wind, writing a story about the last day's play, first used the words "Amen Corner" to describe the treacherous triangle of holes from the 11th.

Naturally, it was Palmer who inspired the term; Palmer, who never knew the meaning of the words "play safe". He was leading the defending champion, Ford, when he came to the par-three 12th, but he overshot the green and the ball embedded itself when it landed in mud. Palmer called for an official ruling, expecting to be told that he could drop the ball no nearer the hole. The official decreed otherwise, telling him that he had to play it as it lay. Palmer did not argue, doing as he was told. He moved the ball about a foot from the buried lie and needed three more to finish the hole. The result was a double-bogey five, and now he was leading no more.

After finishing the hole, Palmer returned to the spot where the ball had been embedded and played it again, only this time using his interpretation of the rules. This time he chipped close to the hole and sank the putt for a par.

Palmer was not trying to be clever. He felt he was fully within his rights. The previous day had been marked by torrential rain, and a rule had been introduced saying that any ball that finishes in its own pitchmark can be lifted and dropped without penalty, provided it has not finished in a sand trap. Palmer knew the rule; the official did not.

Several holes later Palmer's questioning of the decision was upheld, and he was retrospectively credited with a par three. He finished with a 73, and sat in the clubhouse while 10 other players took a pot at his 72-hole score of 284. Ford came within a stroke of it; Palmer's querying of the rule had gained him two. The Palmer era had begun as it would continue, with drama a constant companion.

The great man would finish third the following year as Art Wall claimed his only major championship. Aside from that victory, Wall's other claim to fame is more holes-in-one than any other player – an astonishing 45 at the last count.

Palmer would return to the winner's circle in 1960 for the second of his four Masters victories. It was, perhaps, the epochal year in the game's history. As Thomas Hauser so beautifully put it in *Arnold Palmer: A Personal Journey*: "In every sport, there are landmark years when the game irrevocably changes. 1927 will always be remembered as the year in which Babe Ruth hit 60 home runs and the New York Yankees were the greatest team ever. In 1958 the Baltimore Colts topped the New York Giants in sudden-death overtime and pro football found new fans by the millions. In 1979, Magic Johnson and Larry Bird entered the NBA and pro basketball was never the same again. But no year ever meant more to a sport than 1960 meant to golf, and the man with the magic wand was Arnold Palmer. He elevated his profession to new heights." And, as Dan Jenkins later wrote, "For a few years we absolutely forgot that anyone else played the game."

At Augusta, Palmer ushered in this new age with a performance that was rivetting theatre and which had the embryonic television audience perched on the edge of their seats. In the weeks leading up to the Masters Palmer had won three events in a row, and now he shot 67 in the first round to be the pacemaker once more. In the second round he was troubled by a blister but, using a torn scorecard, hobbled his way to a 73 to maintain his lead. On day three he shot 72 and was still in pole position. In round four, however, he faltered, and the man who took advantage, ironically enough, was Ken Venturi, who had led for three rounds in 1956 only to do some backing up of his own in the last round. The difference in this case was a dose of pure Palmer magic at the death.

With two holes to play Palmer trailed Venturi by a stroke, but seemed to float on air at the 17th as he rolled in a putt of fully nine yards for an equalizing birdie. Now a par at the last would force a play-off. Not that Palmer looked at the situation like that. Remember, this was the new age in golf, where players – or at least Palmer – did not think in terms of pars. At the 18th, Palmer hit the perfect drive and six iron to five feet. Watching him line up the putt, fellow competitor Bob Rosburg told a reporter: "Arnold will get it in the hole if he has to stare it in. The ball is scared of him." Pity poor Venturi, who had tried so hard to make amends for his earlier failure. But how do you stop the relentless march of fate? The simple answer is that you cannot. Needless to say, the putt dropped.

The Big Three

And for the Masters the good times had truly begun, a golden age that continues to this day. Two more victories would come Palmer's way in the first half of the 1960s, but now he had to share centre stage with two other golfers: Jack Nicklaus and Gary Player. Their agent, Mark McCormack, would later christen them The Big Three, and their dominance of golf at that time was never more secure than it was at the Masters. From 1960 to 1966 no other golfer was allowed so much as a peek at a green jacket. Only at the turn of this century, when the game was a British game and the Great Triumvirate dominated everyone at the Open Championship, have three golfers so monopolized one tournament.

In 1961 it was Player's turn. His first three rounds were bril-

Arnold Palmer – on his way to another Masters success in 1960

liant, and even Palmer could not keep up. Scores of 69, 68 and 69 gave Player a four-stroke cushion over Palmer going into the last day. Then the rains came. And never went away.

Play was held over until the Monday and no one suffered more than Player. Now the last round became a tremendous struggle for the little South African, and as he came to the last it appeared one that he had lost. Bravely he got down in two from a bunker, but it looked like it would not be enough. For Palmer, doing what he does best, had come marching through and had converted a four-stroke deficit into a one-stroke lead. Now he stood in the middle of the 18th fairway with a seven iron in his hands needing just a par for victory. What happened subsequently illustrates that in this game, nothing is ever certain.

All these years on, Palmer lambasts himself for accepting the cheers of the crowd coming up the last fairway. "I had just driven, had still the rest of the hole to finish, and I was thanking the crowd for saluting my success. What audacity!" The seven iron drifted a little and finished in the bunker. "Instead of taking a moment to cool down and study the shot, I went up to it, hurrying to get my win," Palmer recalls. "I figured I could blast out near the cup, and get the ball down with one putt."

But the bunker shot was far too bold; it shot through the green and finished near a television gantry. Now Palmer needed to get down in two merely to tie. It proved beyond him. When the putt for bogey missed, Palmer's face creased into a painful grimace. It was his first devastating loss in a major championship, but not his last.

Still, there appeared no lasting effects when he won the Open at Birkdale three months later, and he was back for more at the Masters in 1962. This was the year the Big Three won all four majors and Palmer chipped in with two. At Augusta, Player was again alongside him and this time the pair had Dow Finsterwald for company.

Player shot 67 in the first round to lead but was overtaken by Palmer, who had a second-round 66. Palmer held the lead through the third round but once again stumbled on the final day. Player came home in a wonderful last nine of 31 strokes to tie with Palmer, who could only manage a 75. Finsterwald shot a 73, and so the Masters had its first-ever three-way tie.

Which Palmer would turn up at the play-off? Would it be the man who had played faultless golf for three rounds, or the all-too-human hero who shot 75 on the fourth day, missing a 20-inch putt into the bargain? In the event, both showed up. After nine holes Palmer trailed by three. Then he had four birdies in the next five holes and led by four. He would eventually finish with a 68 as Finsterwald's putting fell apart and he shot 77. Player fought as hard as ever but carded a 71. In the clubhouse, Bobby Jones observed: "Arnold is good with all the clubs, but he has got that ability to hole the important putts more than anyone that I have ever seen. It is just something in his make-up. Some people play better under pressure and some play worse. He is one who plays better. He's just got it."

Palmer would come within a play-off that year of winning the first three majors, but it was significant who stood in his way: a pudgy son of Ohio named Nicklaus, who defeated him at the US Open. Nine months later, Nicklaus would enjoy the first of what would prove an unprecedented six triumphs at the Masters.

At 23, Nicklaus was the youngest winner yet, emerging victorious following unusually inclement weather. On the one day it relented, the second, Nicklaus shot 66. He won by a stroke from Tony Lema and Jones, now struggling with ill health, opined perhaps the most celebrated of all his quotes: "He plays a game with which I am not familiar."

In 1964 Palmer would win again, to become the first man to win the Masters on four occasions. Nicklaus was second alongside Dave Marr, the victory margin no less than six strokes. Remarkably, it was Palmer's last major championship victory. Nicklaus's reign was about to continue, virtually unfettered.

In 1965 the Big Three occupied the first three spots, with Player and Palmer tying for second. But nine shots up was Nicklaus, who shattered Hogan's 72-hole record score by three to set a total of 271 that would not be beaten until Tiger Woods came along in 1997. There were other records: no one had managed 17 under par in a major before, and neither had anyone won the Masters by so many. It was not only Jones who thought Nicklaus was playing a game with which he was unfamiliar. The scoring suggested everyone was in the same boat.

How would the Masters authorities react? The answer came back the following year. A fairway bunker was placed on the second at just about the area where Nicklaus's drive would pitch; similarly two bunkers were added to the left side of the 18th fairway specifically to stop him hitting without impunity. Did it make any difference? Well, the lead did change hands a remarkable 17 times during the course of the 1966 tournament; but ultimately, only to the extent that Nicklaus won in a play-off rather than by nine shots.

The truth was that the changes may have handicapped him, but Nicklaus was never someone who just went for the big heave off the tee. Strategy was always the most important thing for him; in any case, he was not only longer than anyone else, but he was also straighter than 90 percent of the field. The fairway bunkers might have narrowed the target, but it was still wide enough for the Golden Bear.

Gay Brewer and Tommy Jacobs tied with Nicklaus after 72 holes, and the next day the latter made an interesting contest of the play-off, going round in 72 shots. Nicklaus, though, shot 70, and the Masters had its first champion who had managed to complete a successful defence the following year.

One question remained: who would help Nicklaus into his green jacket, thus maintaining the custom of the previous winner doing the honours? Bobby Jones and Clifford Roberts had a little tête-à-tête, after which it was decided that tradition

Jack Nicklaus – celebrates the first of an unprecedented six Masters titles in 1963

should be maintained, and Nicklaus could put on his own jacket. "It was fine by me," Nicklaus commented.

That play-off must have been a painful experience for Brewer, who had a terrible front nine and so was never a factor, enduring a thoroughly futile afternoon in the sun and eventually carding a 78. It reflects greatly upon him, therefore, that when he next set eyes on Augusta it acted as a motivator, not a destroyer. A final-round 67 in 1967 gave him victory by a stroke over Bobby Nichols, and finally the Big Three monopoly of the Masters had been broken. In fact, it was well and truly snapped: Palmer fared best, but only finished fourth, which was poor by his previous standards. Player was sixth while Nicklaus, whom everyone had tipped to win once more, demonstrated what a humbling game golf can be by shooting 72 and 79 to miss the cut.

A costly mistake

During the course of a long professional career, Roberto de Vicenzo had become one of the most popular players. When he finally won a major championship in 1967, it was Henry Cotton who led the rejoicing gallery down the final fairway at Royal Liverpool, co-ordinating the celebrations. Now, at Augusta the following spring, the Open champion was in prime position to complete a rare double. Rolling in a birdie putt at the 17th, he now needed but a par to tie with Bob Goalby and force a play-off.

That last day featured some of the best final-round golf ever seen at the Masters. Bert Yancey shot a 65 to finish two shots off the winning score in third place. Goalby himself came in with a 66 to set the pace. Now de Vicenzo matched when he secured his par at the final hole. Or so everyone thought.

In hindsight we can now say that it was probably an accident waiting to happen, and that sadly de Vicenzo was the fall guy. In the immediate aftermath of a round, it is a player's responsibility to check the score on every hole and then to sign it to say that it is correct. Once he has done that, he is effectively bound to a contract. Unfortunately, de Vicenzo's playing partner Tommy Aaron marked down a four on the 17th instead of a three, and the Argentinian didn't spot the error until it was pointed out to him following the signing. So while everyone at Augusta saw him gain a birdie three, while millions watching worldwide on television saw him gain a birdie three, the par four that he had signed for had to stand. Which left de Vicenzo on 278, one shot adrift of Goalby.

As he came out of the scorer's tent, de Vicenzo tried his best to conceal his heartache with a smile and, in fractured English, uttered the immortal words: "What a stupid I am." It was, unquestionably, the saddest way to lose a major, and ever since the rules have been changed. For how easy it must be, after the emotions have been stretched taut for four hours or more, to miss a wrong figure on a hole. Now a player can request that his score be double-checked by someone before he signs it, thus eliminating the possibility of such a mistake.

Yet there was not just one loser that day, for in the hour of his greatest triumph Goalby was robbed of a kind of glory, too. As he slipped on the green jacket, the only thing people were concerned about was poor de Vicenzo. And so it has continued in the years that have passed, and the feeling has grown: Goalby did not win

that Masters, but de Vicenzo lost it by the slip of a pen.

It has left Goalby somewhat embittered, and understandably so. After all, he birdied the 13th and 14th and eagled the 15th hole to register his 66. The worst thing that could have happened to him was that he would have been in a play-off the next day; he would still have had his own shot at victory and, after that finish, who is to say that he would not have prevailed? And it was hardly his fault that de Vicenzo signed for a wrong card.

Sadly, de Vicenzo never came so close again at Augusta. He was already in his mid-40s, which added, of course, to the poignancy. Incidentally, an ironic postscript was added five years later when the green jacket was slipped on the shoulders of Tommy Aaron.

After the drama of the wrong scorecard, the Masters went through a humdrum stage for a number of years, as if the

The moment of truth – an error on his scorecard cost Roberto di Vicenzo a play-off chance in 1967

shockwaves from that most dramatic of incidents had left their mark. George Archer won in 1969 and then Billy Casper the following year, after a play-off with Gene Littler. Charles Coody was a two-stroke winner over Johnny Miller in 1971.

A legend passes, and another is inspired...

That was to be the final Masters that the event's creator, Bobby Jones, witnessed. In December that year he passed away peacefully in his sleep at the age of 69. He had seen the event go from being the Augusta Invitational to the golfing rite of spring, a tournament that signalled to most amateurs in the northern hemisphere that the winter months were over and the clubs could be rescued from the attic. Furthermore, he had seen it become recognized among the players as the golfer's golf tournament. It was some accolade, and the Masters some legacy.

When the Masters reconvened the following April there was naturally an air of sadness. There was also an appropriate winner. Jones considered Jack Nicklaus the finest golfer he had ever seen. Now he joined Arnold Palmer as the only four-time winner of the event. It was a victory achieved in the classic manner. Nicklaus opened with a 68, and led throughout to win by three strokes from Bruce Crampton. And among those watching in Britain, snug under the bedclothes and enraptured by his first golf broadcast, was Nick Faldo. He was 13 years old, and the following day he went down to his local golf club at Welwyn Garden City and enquired about lessons. "I want to play at Augusta one day," he said.

A challenger emerges

In the years that followed the tragic death of his father, Tom Weiskopf became a man on a mission. Perhaps the most naturally gifted golfer since Sam Snead, Weiskopf had lacked the dedication to fulfil major championship dreams, and his was a squandered talent until the moment his father died and he became consumed by guilt. Weiskopf was invincible in the summer of 1973 and duly collected the Open Championship at Royal Troon with an inspired show.

At Augusta, he was less fortunate. In 1974 and 1975 he played wonderfully well, but on both occasions was pipped by master strokes from two members of the Big Three, whose appetite had not been diminished by the passing years. First Gary Player hit a spectacular nine-iron shot to within inches of the pin at the 17th on the final day to clinch a two-stroke victory. Then came one of the great Masters tournaments of all time.

It was momentous in many ways: Lee Elder became the first black to tee it up in the tournament; Sam Snead, aged 62, shot an opening-round 71; best of all, there was the Sunday climax featuring the three favourites before the tournament began – Weiskopf, Johnny Miller and Jack Nicklaus.

The first two were in the final pairing, while Nicklaus was immediately in front, and so in the best position to make things happen. Which is, characteristically, what he duly did. At the 15th he hit a one iron that he would later describe as the best shot he ever struck with the club under pressure. It stopped 10 feet beyond the pin for a crucial birdie.

As he walked to the 16th tee, Nicklaus glanced at the leader-board. It showed that the pair behind were having their share of birdies as well. Miller had birdied the 13th to be two adrift, while Weiskopf had carded a three at the 14th to be level with Nicklaus – and he still had the birdieable 15th to come. As he prepared to hit his tee shot to the 16th, Nicklaus heard two roars behind, which indicated to him that both players had cleared the water in two strokes.

The resultant five iron, however, was disappointing. He caught it thin and it spun back 40 feet from the hole. Before attempting the putt, Nicklaus could see Weiskopf get his birdie and now he was a stroke behind. It was now that he got a lucky break. His playing partner, Tom Watson, had hit two shots into the lake at the 16th, but his third tee ball finished just outside Nicklaus's on almost the same line. Nicklaus watched intently as Watson's putt snaked off at the last minute by the hole.

Now it was his turn. Nicklaus had but one thought as he stood over the ball. "Make it," he told himself. Nicklaus knew the putt was going in 12 feet from the hole. His putter raised in the air in salute, when it finally dropped he set off on what can only be described as a victory dance. Watching on the tee, what must have been going through Weiskopf's mind? Whatever it was, it was not positive. He caught his tee shot heavy, finished 70 feet from the hole, and three-putted. Now he was one behind.

There was one further element to the drama. As he prepared to putt out at the 18th, Nicklaus once more heard a roar from behind. Had Weiskopf birdied the 17th? He waited until the scoreboard told him what had happened. It revealed that it was Miller who had registered a three. Instead of going for the putt Nicklaus made sure of his par, and now the other two both needed a birdie at the last to force extra holes.

Miller's approach finished 20 feet away but Weiskopf's was a beauty, stopping seven feet beyond the pin. Nicklaus prepared himself mentally for a play-off, telling himself that one would hole, but that he would still have his chance for victory. In the end, neither did. Weiskopf's putt was too firm and it did not take the break, grazing the edge of the hole. Nicklaus had become the first player to win the Masters on five occasions.

Floyd on fire

The best front-runner in the history of the game may well have been the man with the implacable stare, Raymond Floyd. Whenever he took the lead after an opening round, his fellow competitors always knew that the task of winning had just become infinitely harder. So it was at the 1976 Masters. Floyd opened with a 65 to lead by three. Who could live with him? When he followed that wonderful score with a 66 the following day, it quickly became clear that the answer was "no one". After the drama of the previous year's tournament, when everything had hinged on events at the 72nd hole, now this event was seemingly over at the half-way stage. Tension had given way to brilliant predictability, as one man put on the show of his life.

In the third round Floyd slipped a little: all he could manage was a 70, to smash a host of records. His lead was eight over Nicklaus. Not even Nicklaus could charge to that extent in the final round. Floyd had another 70 on the last day to match Nicklaus's record 72-hole winning score of 271. Nicklaus shot 73 on the last day and slipped to third behind Ben Crenshaw. Floyd's victory margin was eight strokes.

Watson's help

The story of 1977 would be the dominance of Tom Watson over Jack Nicklaus. It happened most memorably at the Open Championship at Turnberry during the summer where Watson triumphed by one stroke, but here in the spring it happened first at Augusta, as Nicklaus discovered that not even a last-round 66 was sufficient to close a three-stroke gap on Watson, since the man from Kansas City closed with a 67. Nicklaus had come to the last hole needing a birdie to tie; in the end he had a bogey. Yet Watson would have his share of disappointments, too, finishing runner-up himself over the following two Masters as first Gary Player claimed a third green jacket and then Fuzzy Zoeller won at his very first attempt, winning the first sudden-death play-off at the Masters at the second extra hole.

Tom Watson – two-time Masters winner in 1977 (above) and 1981

Europe strikes back

In 1980, a very strange thing happened at the Masters: a European held centre stage. Hitherto, European golfers had made hardly any impression at all. True, Peter Oosterhuis led by three going into the final round in 1973, only to fade badly with a 74. And Maurice Bembridge equalled the course record the following year to finish in the top ten. But no one had truly threatened to win the event when the tournament began in earnest over the closing nine holes on Sunday. No one, that is, until Severiano Ballesteros played Augusta like a man inspired. By the last nine holes in 1980 the tournament was over, and the Spaniard was being fitted for a green jacket.

Throughout that event Ballesteros was fuelled by a feeling of injustice. When he had first journeyed to America, he felt that he was not given any respect. On one occasion he was announced on the first tee as "Steve" Ballesteros, which very nearly resulted in the said announcer having a driver wrapped around his neck. The final straw came when he won the Open Championship at Royal Lytham in 1979 and Hale Irwin, on account of a stray drive at the 16th on the final day that finished in a temporary parking area, ungraciously labelled him "the car park champion".

Ballesteros's sense of resentment, however, did not extend to Augusta itself. From the moment he set eyes on the course he fell in love with it, and knew that it was a special place upon which he could weave his magic. Which is what he did. He opened with a 66 to share the lead with David Graham; he followed it with a 69, and now he was out on his own. Then he shot 68 on the third day and the tournament was a procession. When he stood on the 10th tee on the final day, he was no fewer than 10 shots ahead. Some car-park champion.

With the tournament over and won, it was perhaps understandable that Ballesteros lost concentration over the inward half. A level-par back nine would have given him a new record 72-hole total, but as it was he had proved a point. The eventual winning margin was four and, at 23 years old, he had become the event's youngest champion. Asked about his thoughts on his victory, he could not forget the pain caused by Irwin's remark the previous year. "I guess I just got lucky again," he said.

A stellar leaderboard contested the Masters in 1981. Tom Kite finished in a tie for fifth, while fourth place went to a young Greg Norman. Jack Nicklaus and Johnny Miller tied for the runners-up spot, but once again denying the former first place was Tom Watson, claiming his second green jacket by a two-stroke margin. This was the first Masters played on bentgrass greens, which made them even slicker than before. Watson's winning score was five shots worse than Ballesteros's the previous year.

In 1982 the sudden-death play-off between Craig Stadler and Dan Pohl went no further than the first extra hole, when the latter missed from six feet for par. A year later the second Monday finish in the tournament's history produced a second green jacket for Ballesteros, again by a four-shot winning margin. Ben Crenshaw was second again that year, but he finally got his hands on a major championship in 1984. The decisive move came around the turn on the final day, as Crenshaw made three birdies in a row, the climax coming at the 10th when he holed from fully 60 feet. When a man does that, he somehow knows it is going to be his day.

Langer strikes

In 1985 Bernhard Langer showed that the European challenge extended to more than one player. This was a remarkable victory for a player who had had to overcome an attack of the yips earlier in his career; now here he was, winning on the slippiest greens of all. Doubling the satisfaction for Langer was the sight of Ballesteros in second place: the previous year at the World Matchplay he had accused the Spaniard of trying to intimidate him.

What the Masters editions of the first half of the 1980s had illustrated was that golf had become a global game: instead of a winners' board consisting almost exclusively of Americans, now an international contingent had demonstrated that they could both compete and win. As the decade wore on, this would increasingly become the case. But first there was the greatest Masters of all, when the best the internationals could offer had to bend the knee one final time to the finest golfer who ever drew breath.

Premature reports of a demise...

In hindsight it was one of those newspaper pieces that frequently come back to haunt a writer. "Jack Nicklaus is finished," was the gist. For the first time since the early 1960s, the Golden Bear would no longer be a factor. At 46, with arthritic hips and knees, Nicklaus's time at the top was over.

At the time, it was difficult to argue with the writer. A new generation had forced themselves on to the agenda: Norman, Ballesteros, Langer and Kite, while Watson was still only in his mid-30s. How could Nicklaus hope to compete with these people? The player himself, meanwhile, cut out the newspaper clipping from the Atlanta Constitution, and attached it to the refrigerator door of the home he was renting for the week.

The first round followed a familiar pattern; two journeymen called Ken Green and Bill Kratzert led on 68, while Ballesteros, Kite and Norman were all tucked in neatly behind. Nicklaus was well down the pack following a 74. On day two, Ballesteros shot 68 and now he was in the lead. After the third round it was Norman's turn, a 68 giving him a one-

Jack Nicklaus – proved the critics wrong with a sixth Masters triumph in 1986, at the age of 46

shot advantage over the Spaniard. Also one shot behind was Nick Price, who had come in with an extraordinary third-round score of 63, which finally broke the course record that had stood since 1940. Indeed Price had a putt on the final green for a 62 that seemed to disappear below ground, only to come up at the final second, as if gasping for air, and there it stubbornly remained, on the edge of the hole. Perhaps it was punishment from the gods at the impertinence of trying to shoot such a low round. Whatever, Price remained delighted with his score – and delighted, too, with his position.

And what of old man Nicklaus? Well, at least he had improved. He shot 71 in the second round and 69 in the third. But he was still four behind Norman, three behind Ballesteros and Price, and two adrift of Kite. If just one player had stood between him and the lead, then it might have looked possible to make up the deficit. But with so many quality performers standing between him and the green jacket, a sixth win appeared remote. At least, that was how the slightly concerned man from the *Atlanta Constitution* was consoling himself.

After eight holes on day four, he had even less to concern him. Nicklaus was on just level par for the day and had slipped further off the pace. Behind him, all hell was breaking loose. At the 8th, Ballesteros holed an 80-yard pitch for an eagle three; then Tom Kite, his playing partner, did exactly the same from 50 yards. Few were thinking about the hunched figure at the back of the 9th green, who moved away as he heard the roars. "Now let us see if I can set off a roar of my own," Nicklaus told the gallery, before rolling the putt in for a birdie.

At the 10th Nicklaus hit a poor tee shot but got lucky, the ball bouncing off the gallery and back into play. No one ever took more advantage of such moments of kind fate than the Golden Bear. Now he crushed a four iron to 25 feet and rolled in the birdie putt. At the 11th he hit a wonderful drive, and then an eight iron finished 25 feet away. When another long putt disappeared, Nicklaus's caddie, his son Jackie, leapt jubilantly into the air.

There is a wonderful feeling at golf tournaments when Nicklaus is on the prowl. It is almost as if what happens next takes on an air of inevitability. Bobby Jones once talked about Arnold Palmer's ability to stare down putts, and Nicklaus had the same gift – not over six or seven years, like Palmer, but more than 20. And by now the gallery was going bananas.

Any thoughts of witnessing a piece of history did not extend to the short 12th, however, where Nicklaus went through the back of the green and then watched in anguish as his putt for par hit a spike mark and drifted away from the hole. Nicklaus was furious at the lapse, which gave those playing behind some breathing space.

He gave himself a pep talk, which instantly did the trick. Nicklaus safely made the birdie on offer at the 13th and glanced at the leaderboard that showed he had closed to within two strokes of Ballesteros, and one of Kite. He was tied with Norman, who had double-bogeyed the 10th.

After getting a par at the 14th, Nicklaus hit a wonderful drive down the long 15th, which left him with a four iron to the green. "Hit it solid," he told himself, which is exactly what he did. The ball finished 12 feet from the hole. Now if only I could squeeze this into the hole, Nicklaus was telling himself...

When Nicklaus gets into that frame of mind, he usually holes, and so he did on this occasion. Pandemonium. Yet while Nicklaus was making an impression on the scoreboard, one player remained seemingly impervious. Ballesteros was playing brilliant golf of his own, and when he eagled the 13th to neutralize Nicklaus's gain, he still had a two-shot lead.

Ballesteros's father had died a month earlier, and now the Spaniard was playing on sheer adrenalin and determination. Suspended from playing on the US Tour that year, he had hardly played: it did not seem to matter. For all Nicklaus's heroics, the tournament remained his to win or lose. At the 15th, Ballesteros hit another good drive and now had a four iron to the green; a birdie, and his lead over the field would be a surely unassailable three strokes, and four over Nicklaus.

The shot Ballesteros played next has haunted him for the rest of his career. Up to that moment he had always believed in *destino*, that it was his destiny to become the greatest player of all time. But he caught the four iron heavy and there was a look of disbelief across his face as he saw the ball plunge into Rae's Creek that fronts the green. For a moment the spectators were silent, as if they could hardly comprehend such a catastrophic error. Ballesteros could not get down in a chip and putt either; he took seven, and now Nicklaus was just two behind.

Ballesteros looked completely crestfallen as he heard the crowd go wild beside the 16th green; Nicklaus had put the ball to within three feet of the hole, and in went the putt for another birdie. Naturally Nicklaus knew all about what was happening when he stood over his birdie putt at the 17th. You could see it in his eyes as he rolled in the putt, which meant that he had played the last nine holes in seven under par. Just to spell it out, he had gone: birdie, birdie, birdie, bogey, birdie, par, eagle, birdie, birdie. Ballesteros, meanwhile, found the bunker at the 16th and could not get down in two from a wretched lie. He was now one behind.

A par at the last gave Nicklaus a 65, and now he could sit in Bobby Jones's cabin and watch the final stages unfold, to see if anyone could match his total of 279. Poor Ballesteros had three-putted the 17th as well, so his opportunity had gone. Kite had a chance, if he could make a birdie at the 18th. But the ball veered away from the hole at the last. The best chance of all, however, lay with Norman, who had birdied four holes in a row from the 14th to roar back into contention. Now he needed merely a par at the last to tie his boyhood hero, and his tee shot split the fairway.

Norman's career, of course, is littered with poor shots played under pressure, and here was another one. In between clubs for his approach, he missed the green well to the right and could not get down in a chip and a putt.

And so the old man who was finished had won. The party began; the telegrams poured in. Best of all was one from his old adversary, Arnold Palmer. "That was just fantastic," it said. "Do you think there is any chance for a 56-year-old?" In the *Atlanta Constitution* the following day there was a humbling apology.

Twenty-three years after his first victory at the Masters, Nicklaus had claimed his sixth green jacket, and his 18th major in all. It is a total that will stand for all time.

How could the Masters possibly come up with a tournament to match that one? All credit to the players; they tried hard. Ballesteros and Norman were back again, disputing the lead

Ian Woosnam – celebrates his winning putt in 1991

over the closing holes, only this time they did not have Nicklaus or Kite for company, but a rather average professional called Larry Mize, who was having the week of his life. It was quite a story. Mize, the Augusta native who used to peek over the fence as a boy to get a glimpse of the course, was battling away with the two best players of their generation. As he came to the 18th it looked as if he would fall just short. Ballesteros and Norman had tied on totals of 285 and were now set for what would surely prove a titanic play-off. Mize, meanwhile, needed to birdie the final hole to join them. Mize, 28, had a reputation among the Americans as something of a choker. He certainly buried that reputation with his play at the 18th, striking a wonderful drive and mid-iron to six feet and holing the putt to join the other two in extra holes.

Naturally, no one gave him a chance, but it was Ballesteros who was the first to fall, three-putting the first extra hole, the 10th, and he strode back up the steep hill to the clubhouse in tears. On to the 11th: Norman hit two wonderful shots to 20 feet; Mize had pushed his second, and now had a treacherous-looking chip from 140 feet. What increased its difficulty was the fact that the green sloped towards a small lake, and if Mize was at all clumsy that was assuredly where it would finish. How tempting, therefore, to leave it short and so have an all-but-impossible putt. In the event, Mize did neither, the ball bouncing this way and that over the humps and hollows, taking this break and that on the green, before nestling into the hole for the most freakish of birdies. Poor Norman, who had lost the previous major championship to a holed bunker shot. Now this. "Clear the women out of here," was his first comment when he came into the Press room. Little did he know that the Masters would bring even more heartbreak in the decade to come. For Mize, meanwhile, professional life would never get any sweeter.

A new British triumvirate

British golf had little to cheer from Tony Jacklin's all-too-brief time at the top until a modern great triumvirate emerged in the 1980s. It was Sandy Lyle who was their leader in every sense. At 16 he had played in the Open Championship, and in 1985 he won it at Sandwich, the first home winner for 16 long years.

Lyle showed the way at Augusta, too, precipitating what would now be a scarcely believable run of four consecutive wins by three different British golfers. His year was 1988.

They say the hardest trick in the game is to switch momentum when it is sliding in the wrong direction. On the final day Lyle, two shots clear of Mark Calcavecchia and Ben Crenshaw overnight, made mistakes at the 11th, 12th and 13th holes, and now the pursued was doing the pursuing. When Calcavecchia eagled the 15th hole, it meant that Lyle needed one birdie from the final three holes to force a play-off, two to win.

His tee shot to the 16th was a good one, the ball coming to rest some 12 feet from the hole. The putt he had left was far from academic, a curling effort that could quickly get away from him. But Lyle holed it, and the earlier errors were now forgotten. He was sharing the lead with Calcavecchia. A par at the 17th, however, meant he could afford no mistakes at the 18th, which is precisely what happened off the tee. Lyle looked away as his drive bounded on, for he knew where it was heading, the iron for safety finishing in the first of the two fairway bunkers. From there he had 150 yards to the pin, all uphill. The lie was clean, and under normal circumstances Lyle would have expected to have escaped with a par; these were hardly normal circumstances, though.

The stroke Lyle played was later described by America's most respected golf writer, Herb Warren Wind, as the finest bunker shot in Masters history. Few people would argue. It never left the flag from the moment Lyle struck it, pitching 15 feet behind the hole on a tiny incline. From there it rolled nearer, coming to rest eight feet away. Now, instead of looking like he would miss out on a play-off, Lyle's supporters found their rollercoaster ride had left their man with a putt for victory. Lyle's nerve held. The putt was sure and true, and he flung his arms into the air in triumph.

All through his career, Lyle had been involved in a fierce rivalry with Nick Faldo, and it was wonderfully healthy for British golf. Now, after "equalizing" Lyle's victory in the Open with one of his own in 1987, Faldo set off in pursuit of a green jacket. His big chance came the very next year. It seemed to end as well when he completed the delayed third round on Sunday morning in wretched style, a 77 leaving him trailing Crenshaw by five shots.

When he returned to the first tee that afternoon, it was clear that he needed to make early inroads into the advantage held by the queue of players in front of him. A bogey at the 11th, however, left him at only one under par and four behind with only seven holes to play. At the 13th Faldo played two glorious shots, but the 15-foot eagle putt refused to fall. Still, it was a birdie, and another followed at the 14th. He failed to take the one on offer at the 15th but, just like Lyle a year earlier, got one at the 16th.

Faldo was now right in the thick of things. Ballesteros had ruined his chance with a double bogey at the 16th, and Crenshaw was struggling as well. Mike Reid had fallen out of the lead with a seven at the 15th and would never recover. That left Faldo with Scott Hoch for company, and his old adversary, Greg Norman. It was Faldo who birdied the 17th to complete an inspired finish; the target was 283. Norman could not match it, despite only needing a par at the last for the second time in four years. Once more he came up short.

Hoch was playing with Crenshaw, who had just had three

birdies in a row. Now the pair were tied coming to the 18th, needing a par each to force a play-off. It proved beyond Crenshaw, who bunkered his approach; now it was between Hoch and Faldo down the first extra hole.

Neither player could manage a par there, but in Hoch's case that bald statistic does not begin to tell the tale. In fact, he had a putt of no more than two feet for par, but on a tricky green it slid by. There was to be no second chance, Faldo rolling in a birdie putt at the 11th and having the satisfaction of Lyle helping him into the green jacket.

The following year Faldo was again involved in a play-off, this time against the redoubtable Raymond Floyd. Once more, Faldo had played a successful game of catch-up simply to get that far. Seven behind the leader after 18, five behind after 36, three adrift after 54, Faldo started the last round with a double-bogey six. When Floyd birdied the short 12th, he was no fewer than four strokes clear of the defending champion. "I did not think I could lose," he said afterwards. Just as he had done the year before, Faldo put in a sterling finish. He birdied the 13th and the 15th and then again the 16th. When Floyd three-putted the 17th, it was extra holes once more.

At 47 Floyd was trying to become the oldest man to win the event, but age caught up with him at the 11th, scene once more of a Faldo triumph. This time, as darkness descended and a chill lay in the air, Floyd found himself with a three-iron second shot to make the green. It never looked nearly enough club, plunging into the water and taking Floyd's chances with it.

While Lyle and Faldo rose to the top of the world game, a pugnacious little Welshman was determined to keep pace with them. In 1991, Ian Woosnam did more than that. After three rounds Woosnam was 11 under par and had the lead by a stroke from Tom Watson, while Jose-Maria Olazabal and Lanny Wadkins were three adrift. On that final afternoon Woosnam had to contend with some ungracious behaviour from certain Masters patrons, who had clearly got fed up with victories for the Brits. They wanted a victory for "good ole boy" Watson, and cheered when Woosnam ran up a six at the 13th.

Anyone who knew Woosnam, of course, also knew that such behaviour would only make him still more determined. He held on over the closing holes and, with Olazabal dropping a shot at the last and Watson taking six, knew that a par four would be good enough to tie the former. Woosnam's tee shot did not meddle with the bunkers on the left side of the 18th fairway; he simply took out his driver and carried them. That left him with a wedge to the green, which finished five feet from the hole. When he was an amateur, Woosnam had played in the same Shropshire team as Sandy Lyle. Now he emulated Lyle on the 72nd green at the Masters, registering a birdie for his first major championship win. Another British victory. The home country could scarcely believe what was happening.

Ben Crenshaw – a popular winner in 1995

Playing as Couples

Given his talent, Fred Couples should perhaps have won more than one major championship, but when it came at the 1992 Masters it was hugely popular. It was hugely fortunate as well. Couples's tee shot to the 12th seemed bound for Rae's Creek as it pitched on the front of the green before sliding inexorably down the shaved slope that leads to the water. For some reason that only fate can explain, it then stopped on the bank. Not surprisingly, Couples could not get there quickly enough to play it. He chipped virtually stone dead and so a five had been turned into a three. His victory margin over Floyd was those two shots that some unforeseen hand had saved him.

If the Americans thought they had broken the stranglehold the Europeans had placed on the trophy, they were sadly mistaken. In 1993 it was Bernhard Langer's turn again, as he played 72 holes at Augusta with just one three-putt to his name. Langer's victory was made easy for him by Chip Beck. The American had a chance to go for the green on the 15th but elected instead to consolidate second position by playing short. So the German won by four strokes and Beck was left to face a nation's wrath. It is fair to say that, from that moment, his career never recovered.

A victory for Jose-Maria Olazabal had always appeared likely at Augusta. He might not have possessed prodigious length off the tee that gave the big hitters an advantage, but he had a short game that was almost as wondrous as Ballesteros's. In 1994, that short game carried him to victory to make it nine wins by European golfers since Ballesteros waltzed away with the title in 1980. It was an emotional triumph for Olazabal, naturally. But for Augusta itself it was just a warm-up before three extraordinary Masters editions in a row.

Tragedy and triumph

One player who could safely be ruled out of winning the 1995 tournament was Ben Crenshaw. Or so it seemed. For a start, his game had been in turmoil for some time; for another, his mentor, Harvey Penick, had died in the week before the event. On the eve of the Masters, Crenshaw forgot about practice because some things are more important: he flew to Austin, TX to be a pallbearer at Penick's funeral.

He returned in time for his first round and, in the circumstances, 70 was more than creditable. He was only four shots behind the leaders, who included the defending champion, Olazabal. Crenshaw then did something that nobody expected; he put together rounds of 67 and 69, and now he was tied for the lead with Brian Henninger with a round to play.

The latter quickly faded from contention on the final day. Crenshaw assumed the lead, with three players firing pot-shots at him: Davis Love, Jay Haas and our old friend Norman. Love and Norman were in the same group, and seemed to give their gallery something to shout about on every hole. As Haas collapsed with late bogeys, Love and Norman maintained their charge. In the end Love would birdie the 17th and sign for a 66 to set the target on 275; Norman three-putted the 17th to finish with a 68 and a tie with Haas on 277.

That left Crenshaw out on the course, needing three pars to finish to tie with Love. He did better than that. One of the great putters of all time rolled in birdie efforts at the 16th and 17th to take a two-stroke lead. He would need it. He played the 18th sloppily, and in the end he needed to hole from three feet simply for a bogey. "I don't know how I made it," he said later. "I just let it all out. I could not hold it in any longer." Once the business was over, Crenshaw bent over the 18th hole and wept without restraint. Many in the gallery did as well, because they knew exactly what the victory meant to him.

For whom the Bell tolls...

Now in his 40s, people were wondering whether Greg Norman would ever have his shoulders draped in a green jacket. Certainly, far worse players than him had won one, perhaps even more than one. It was his favourite golf tournament, had always been his favourite golf tournament, and yet it had treated him as if he were the bastard son. But not in 1996. Well, not for three days anyway.

For 54 holes Norman's golf was quite simply sublime. He equalled Price's course record in the first round, shot 69 in the second and 71 in the third. He was no fewer than six strokes to the good. No one had ever had such a lead in a major championship and lost. "Surely not even you can mess up now," a British writer who had become a good friend said jocularly to Norman on Saturday night.

Just one small thing nagged at the consciousness. Nick Faldo had sneaked in with a birdie at the 18th in the third round, and this meant he and Norman would be paired together for the final 18 holes. At the time this meant far more to Faldo than it did to Norman: it meant that the Englishman could keep an eye on his only rival for the title, every step of the final day.

Faldo came up with every legal trick in the matchplay book during that last round. He went ahead and holed a second putt from four feet at the first, leaving Norman with a putt from similar length to match him. He missed. Yet any feelings of discomfort did not last long. After five holes Norman still had a five-stroke lead. Everything was going his way.

On the face of it, golf is one of the slowest games – but not when things are going against you. During those occasions time slips away very quickly, and the mind becomes seized with panic. This is what happened to Norman over the next 10 amazing holes, 90 minutes that will live with everyone who ever witnessed it. In Australia the motor-racing driver Damon

Faldo and Norman embrace after their 1996 showdown

Hill, a friend of Norman's and someone who lives with death every day of his working life, said he had to turn away from the television because he could not watch any more.

What did happen was that a man unravelled before our very eyes. At the 6th Norman dropped a stroke and then at the 7th failed to hole from seven feet to restore his five-shot lead. Now he became impatient. He tried to make something happen at the long 8th by going for the green, and hooked the ball into the woods. He chipped out and salvaged par, but Faldo had birdied. Now the lead was three. Norman was again too aggressive at the 9th and ran up another bogey. At the half-way stage his lead, once a seemingly invincible six shots, was now a highly vulnerable two.

At the 10th Norman again missed the green and again ran up a bogey. Down to one. After the remarkable events of the 11th, it became clear that the Australian was about to make history of a most unwanted kind. Ten feet away in two, Norman had a putt to stop the bleeding; instead the ball wandered three feet beyond the pin and he missed the return. What a thing to happen before walking to the short 12th, the treacherous Golden Bell. It was no surprise by now when it tolled for Norman. He wore the air of a beaten man. His tee shot never remotely looked like crossing the water.

Faldo was in front and there was to be no let-up. The Englishman played two marvellous shots on to the 13th green, and what happened from there on in was both at once wonderful but also terribly sad. On one side of the fairway you had a man playing immaculate catch-up golf, never losing patience or control; on the other you had a man who simply did not know how to cope. At the end they embraced, which was a heartening example of sportsmanship. Faldo had shot 67 and Norman 78.

In the days that followed, Norman found he had friends that he never knew about, for everyone was impressed with the manner in which he accepted defeat. For Faldo, meanwhile, it was quite simply the victory of a lifetime.

Just as had been the case a decade before, everyone wanted to know what Augusta could possibly conjure up for an encore. There appeared only two possible scenarios to top the events of 1996. One was a comeback victory for Greg Norman, but instead he missed the cut; the other was a win for a rookie professional playing in his first major championship since joining the paid ranks.

Out of the Woods

Tiger Woods was, of course, no ordinary rookie. He had already won three times on the US Tour in just six months as a pro. *Sports Illustrated* had no hesitation in naming him the favourite. When he took 40 to the turn on the first day it appeared a reckless piece of journalism.

Yet Woods was always more than just a great golfer; his fighting qualities are an important part of his make-up. He shot 30 for the back nine for a 70 that sent a shiver down the rest of the field. On Friday Woods strolled round in 66 and now in 27 holes he had gone from being seemingly bound to miss the cut to taking the half-way lead. One of the few who appeared unperturbed by this was Colin Montgomerie, his closest pursuer. He thought experience would tell in the end.

Poor old Monty received quite an awakening the following day when he was paired with Woods. One of them shot 65, the other 74; it was not Montgomerie who made experience tell. Afterwards the Scot looked like he had just experienced hell on earth. Which, as far as he was concerned, of course, he had. Woods was now nine shots ahead, and when one reporter foolishly asked Montgomerie whether he thought he could be caught he duly received both barrels. "Are you mad? Have you not been watching what has been going on out there? There is no possible way he can be caught," he said. Well, it was certainly more accurate than the answers he had given about Woods the night before.

All America fell in love with the new boy-wonder on that final afternoon. Although it was a stroll around Augusta, more than twice as many viewers tuned in to CBS television than had watched the Norman-Faldo epic the year before. On the lawn in front of the clubhouse, Jack Nicklaus said graciously: "Tell you, if Bob Jones was alive today he could have saved his comments from '63 for this boy, because he certainly plays a game with which we are not familiar."

All that remained to be determined was the winning margin, and when he signed for a 69 to claim the green jacket by 12 shots Woods had collected a plethora of Masters records. They included a new 72-hole record score of 270 and the biggest winning margin in major championship history. Woods was just 21 years old. He was by some distance the youngest winner of the event, indeed he was the youngest winner of a major this century.

Experience threatens to surprise

For a while in 1998 things threatened to get seriously out of hand. Over the first seven holes on the final day Jack Nicklaus put himself in a position where he could once more threaten the leaders. "Any chance for someone aged 56?" Palmer had jocularly said in a telegram 12 years earlier. He had been talking, of course, about himself. Now here was Nicklaus, aged 58. It could not last, and even Nicklaus finally had to acknowledge Old Father Time. Naturally, it was done with extreme reluctance. He eventually finished tied for sixth, and became the oldest player ever to finish in the top 10. The other fairytale story of that year was the Georgia amateur, Matt Kuchar, who smiled his way to a level-par 72-hole total of 288, the best performance by an amateur for a generation.

But after the heroics of Tiger Woods in 1997, this Masters was ultimately about experience and a man almost twice his age. Mark O'Meara's career had been highly successful in terms of monetary reward, but up to that point there were precious few cups in the trophy cabinet. Now, standing on the 17th

tee, he needed a birdie and a par to force a play-off against Fred Couples and David Duval.

Woods and O'Meara had become good friends by this time. Both lived in the same exclusive community just outside Orlando, FL. And some of the competitiveness of the former had clearly rubbed off on the latter. O'Meara birdied the 17th; then he birdied the 18th as well. He seemed almost in shock for a moment, as if he could not believe he had won. Even as Woods helped him into the green jacket he appeared unable to comprehend. Three months later, however, he proved it was no fluke by winning the Open. At 41, his *annus mirabilis* had arrived in the nick of time.

Tiger Woods – made the Masters his own in 1997, winning by a massive 12 strokes

March 22–25, 1934

1	**Horton Smith**	70	72	70	72	284
2	**Craig Wood**	71	74	69	71	285
=3	**Billy Burke**	72	71	70	73	286
	Paul Runyan	74	71	70	71	286
5	**Ed Dudley**	74	69	71	74	288
6	**Willie McFarlane**	74	73	70	74	291
=7	**Al Espinosa**	75	70	75	72	292
	Jimmy Hines	70	74	74	74	292
	Harold McSpaden	77	74	72	69	292
	Macdonald Smith	74	70	74	74	292
=11	**Mortie Dutra**	74	75	71	73	293
	Al Watrous	74	74	71	74	293
=13	**Walter Hagen**	71	76	70	77	294
	Bobby Jones (a)	76	74	72	72	294
	Denny Shute	73	73	76	72	294
=16	**Leo Diegel**	73	72	74	76	295
	Ralph Stonehouse	74	70	75	76	295
=18	**Ky Laffoon**	72	79	72	73	296
	Johnny Revolta	75	72	75	74	296
	W.J. Schwartz	75	72	71	78	296
=21	**Johnny Golden**	71	75	74	77	297
	Charlie Yates (a)	76	72	77	72	297
=23	**John Dawson (a)**	74	73	76	75	298
	Henry Picard	71	76	75	76	298
=25	**Henry Ciuci**	74	73	74	78	299
	Tom Creavy	74	73	80	72	299
	Vic Ghezzi	77	74	74	74	299
=28	**Bobby Cruikshank**	74	74	80	72	300
	Jim Foulis	78	74	76	72	300
	Mike Turnesa	75	74	77	74	300

April 4–8, 1935

** Gene Sarazen (144) beat Craig Wood (149) in the 36-hole play-off.*

1	**Gene Sarazen***	68	71	73	70	282
2	**Craig Wood**	69	72	68	73	282
3	**Olin Dutra**	70	70	70	74	284
4	**Henry Picard**	67	68	76	75	286
5	**Denny Shute**	73	71	70	73	287
6	**Lawson Little**	74	72	70	72	288
7	**Paul Runyan**	70	72	75	72	289
8	**Vic Ghezzi**	73	71	73	73	290
=9	**Bobby Cruickshank**	76	70	73	72	291
	Jimmy Hines	70	70	77	74	291
	Byron Nelson	71	74	72	74	291
	Joe Turnesa	73	71	74	73	291
=13	**Ray Mangrum**	68	71	76	77	292
	Johnny Revolta	70	74	73	75	292
=15	**Walter Hagen**	73	69	72	79	293
	Sam Parks Jr	74	70	74	75	293
=17	**John Dawson (a)**	75	72	72	75	294
	Al Espinosa	76	72	73	73	294
19	**Clarence Clark**	77	75	73	71	296
	Leo Diegel	72	73	74	77	296
	Ed Dudley	73	73	74	76	296
	Harold McSpaden	75	72	75	74	296
	Horton Smith	74	75	74	73	296
	Charlie Yates (a)	75	70	76	75	296
=25	**Harry Cooper**	73	76	74	74	297
	Bobby Jones (a)	74	72	73	78	297
	Mike Turnesa	72	74	75	76	297
=28	**Gene Kunes**	76	72	77	73	298
	Ky Laffoon	76	73	72	77	298
	Phil Perkins	77	71	75	75	298

April 2–5, 1936

1	**Horton Smith**	74	71	68	72	285
2	**Harry Cooper**	70	69	71	76	286
3	**Gene Sarazen**	78	67	72	70	287
=4	**Bobby Cruickshank**	75	69	74	72	290
	Paul Runyan	76	69	70	75	290
=6	**Ed Dudley**	75	75	70	73	293
	Ky Laffoon	75	70	75	73	293
	Ray Mangrum	76	73	68	73	293
=9	**John Dawson (a)**	77	70	7	77	294
	Henry Picard	75	72	74	73	294
=11	**Walter Hagen**	77	74	73	72	296
	Denny Shute	76	68	75	77	296
=13	**Wiffy Cox**	82	69	75	72	298
	Byron Nelson	76	71	77	74	298
=15	**Al Espinosa**	72	73	75	79	299
	Vic Ghezzi	77	70	77	75	299
	Harold McSpaden	77	75	71	76	299
	Jimmy Thomson	76	78	71	74	299
	Orville White	78	73	77	71	299
=20	**Tommy Armour**	79	74	72	75	300
	Chick Chin	76	74	71	79	300
	Lawson Little	75	75	73	77	300
	Sam Parks Jr	76	75	72	77	300
	Craig Wood	88	67	69	76	300
25	**Johnny Revolta**	77	72	76	76	301
26	**Albert Campbell (a)**	82	73	68	79	302
27	**Dick Metz**	79	78	76	70	303
28	**Billy Burke**	74	77	74	79	304
=29	**Johnny Farrell**	78	75	74	78	305
	Joe Kirkwood Sr	81	76	73	75	305
	Torchy Toda	81	84	75	75	305
	Al Watrous	78	76	73	78	305

April 1–4, 1937

1	**Byron Nelson**	66	72	75	70	283
2	**Ralph Guldahl**	69	72	68	76	285
3	**Ed Dudley**	70	71	71	74	286
4	**Harry Cooper**	73	69	71	74	287
5	**Ky Laffoon**	73	70	74	73	290
6	**Jimmy Thomson**	71	73	74	73	291
7	**Al Watrous**	74	72	71	75	292
=8	**Tommy Armour**	73	75	73	72	293
	Vic Ghezzi	72	72	72	77	293
=10	**Leonard Dodson**	71	75	71	77	294
	Jimmy Hines	77	72	68	77	294
12	**Wiffy Cox**	70	72	77	76	295
=13	**Clarence Clark**	77	75	70	74	296
	Tony Manero	71	72	78	75	296
	Johnny Revolta	71	72	72	81	296
	Denny Shute	74	75	71	76	296
17	**Bobby Cruickshank**	79	69	71	78	297
18	**Sam Snead**	76	71	72	79	298
=19	**Lawson Little**	70	79	74	76	299
	Willie MacFarlane	73	76	73	77	299
	Paul Runyan	74	77	72	76	299
	Felix Serafin	75	76	71	77	299
	Horton Smith	75	72	77	75	299
=24	**Ray Mangrum**	71	80	72	77	300
	Gene Sarazen	74	80	73	73	300
=26	**Craig Wood**	79	77	74	71	301
	Charlie Yates (a)	76	73	74	78	301
28	**Francis Francis (a)**	77	74	75	76	302
=29	**Billy Burke**	77	71	75	80	303
	Al Espinosa	72	76	79	76	303

April 1–4, 1937 continued

	Bobby Jones (a)	79	74	73	77	303

April 1–4, 1938

1	**Henry Picard**	71	72	72	70	285
=2	**Harry Cooper**	68	77	71	71	287
	Ralph Guldahl	73	70	73	71	287
4	**Paul Runyan**	71	73	74	70	288
5	**Byron Nelson**	73	74	70	73	290
=6	**Ed Dudley**	70	69	77	75	291
	Felix Serafin	72	71	78	70	291
=8	**Dick Metz**	70	77	74	71	292
	Jimmy Thomson	74	70	76	72	292
=10	**Vic Ghezzi**	75	74	70	74	293
	Jimmy Hines	75	71	75	72	293
	Lawson Little	72	75	74	72	293
=13	**Billy Burke**	73	73	76	73	295
	Gene Sarazen	78	70	68	79	295
15	**Stanley Horne**	74	74	77	71	296
=16	**Bobby Jones (a)**	76	74	72	75	297
	Harold McSpaden	72	75	77	73	297
=18	**Bobby Cruickshank**	72	75	77	74	298
	Johnny Revolta	73	72	76	77	298
	Tommy Taller	74	69	75	80	298
=21	**Chuck Kocsis (a)**	76	73	77	73	299
	Horton Smith	75	75	78	71	299
23	**Sam Parks Jr**	75	75	76	74	300
=24	**Wiffy Cox**	74	78	74	75	301
	Ben Hogan	75	76	78	72	301
=26	**Ky Laffoon**	78	76	74	74	302
	Tony Manero	72	78	82	70	302
	Frank Walsh	74	75	77	76	302
	Al Watrous	73	77	76	76	302

March 30–April 2, 1939

1	**Ralph Guldahl**	72	68	70	69	279
2	**Sam Snead**	70	70	72	68	280
=3	**Billy Burke**	69	72	71	70	282
	Lawson Little	72	72	68	70	282
5	**Gene Sarazen**	73	66	72	72	283
6	**Craig Wood**	72	73	71	68	284
7	**Byron Nelson**	71	69	72	75	287
8	**Henry Picard**	71	71	76	71	289
9	**Ben Hogan**	75	71	72	72	290
=10	**Ed Dudley**	75	75	69	72	291
	Toney Penna	72	75	72	72	291
=12	**Tommy Armour**	71	74	76	72	293
	Vic Ghezzi	73	76	72	72	293
	Harold McSpaden	75	72	74	72	293
15	**Denny Shute**	78	71	73	72	294
=16	**Paul Runyan**	73	71	75	76	295
	Felix Serafin	74	76	73	72	295
=18	**Chick Harbert**	74	73	75	74	296
	Jimmy Thomson	75	71	73	77	296
	Charlie Yates (a)	74	73	74	75	296
21	**Tommy Taller**	78	75	73	71	297
=22	**Jimmy Hines**	76	73	74	75	298
	Ky Laffoon	72	75	73	78	298
	Frank Moore	75	74	75	74	298
25	**Al Watrous**	75	75	74	75	299
=26	**Tony Manero**	76	73	77	74	300
	Horton Smith	75	79	74	72	300
	Willie Turnesa (a)	78	70	79	73	300
=29	**Jess Sweetser**	75	75	75	77	302
	Frank Walsh	76	76	72	78	302

April 4–7, 1940

1	**Jimmy Demaret**	67	72	70	71	280
2	**Lloyd Mangrum**	64	75	71	74	284
3	**Byron Nelson**	69	72	74	70	285
=4	**Harry Cooper**	69	75	73	70	287
	Ed Dudley	73	72	71	71	287
	Willie Goggin	71	72	73	71	287
=7	**Henry Picard**	71	71	71	75	288
	Sam Snead	71	72	69	76	288
	Craig Wood	70	75	67	76	288
=10	**Ben Hogan**	73	74	69	74	290
	Toney Penna	73	73	72	72	290
=12	**Paul Runyan**	72	73	72	74	291
	Frank Walsh	73	75	69	74	291
=14	**Sam Byrd**	73	74	72	73	292
	Johnny Farrell	76	72	70	74	292
	Ralph Guldahl	74	73	71	74	292
=17	**Harold McSpaden**	73	71	74	75	293
	Charlie Yates (a)	72	75	71	75	293
=19	**Lawson Little**	70	77	75	72	294
	Ed Oliver	73	75	74	72	294
=21	**Johnny Bulla**	73	73	74	75	295
	Dick Metz	71	74	75	75	295
	Gene Sarazen	74	71	77	73	295
	Bud Ward (a)	74	68	75	78	295
	Al Watrous	75	70	73	77	295
26	**Jim Ferrier**	73	74	75	74	296
=27	**Jimmy Hines**	75	76	74	72	297
	Johnny Revolta	74	74	74	75	297
=29	**Jim Foulls**	74	75	73	76	298
	Tony Manero	75	75	73	75	298

April 3–6, 1941

1	**Craig Wood**	66	71	71	72	280
2	**Byron Nelson**	71	69	73	70	283
3	**Sam Byrd**	73	70	68	74	285
4	**Ben Hogan**	71	72	75	68	286
5	**Ed Dudley**	73	72	75	68	288
=6	**Vic Ghezzi**	77	71	71	70	289
	Sam Snead	73	75	72	69	289
8	**Lawson Little**	71	70	74	75	290
=9	**Willie Goggin**	71	72	72	76	291
	Harold McSpaden	75	74	72	70	291
	Lloyd Mangrum	71	72	72	76	291
=12	**Jimmy Demaret**	77	69	71	75	292
	Clayton Heafner	73	70	76	73	292
=14	**Harry Cooper**	72	73	75	73	293
	Ralph Guldahl	76	71	75	71	293
17	**Jack Ryan**	73	74	74	74	295
18	**Denny Shute**	77	75	74	70	296
=19	**Dick Chapman (a)**	76	73	70	78	297
	Jimmy Hines	76	74	75	72	297
	Gene Kunes	76	74	76	71	297
	Dick Metz	74	72	75	76	297
	Sam Parks Jr	75	76	75	71	297
	Toney Penna	73	74	80	70	297
	Gene Sarazen	76	72	74	75	297
	Felix Serafin	72	79	74	72	297
	Horton Smith	74	72	77	74	297
28	**Ray Mangrum**	76	70	78	74	298
=29	**Jim Ferrier**	75	76	73	75	299
	Jim Foulis	76	75	71	77	299
	Martin Pose	77	74	76	72	299

April 9–13, 1942

* Byron Nelson (69) beat Ben Hogan (70) in the 18-hole play-off.

1	**Byron Nelson***	68	67	72	73	280
2	**Ben Hogan**	73	70	67	70	280
3	**Paul Runyan**	67	73	72	71	283
4	**Sam Byrd**	68	68	75	74	285
5	**Horton Smith**	67	73	74	73	287
6	**Jimmy Demaret**	70	70	75	75	290
=7	**Dutch Harrison**	74	70	71	77	292
	Lawson Little	71	74	72	75	292
	Sam Snead	78	69	72	73	292
=10	**Chick Harbert**	73	73	72	75	293
	Gene Kunes	74	74	74	71	293
12	**Jimmy Thomson**	73	70	74	77	294
13	**Chandler Harper**	75	75	76	69	295
14	**Willie Goggin**	74	70	78	74	296
=15	**Bobby Cruickshank**	72	79	71	75	297
	Jim Ferrier	71	76	80	70	297
	Henry Picard	75	72	75	75	297
=18	**Harry Cooper**	74	77	76	72	299
	Harold McSpaden	74	72	79	74	299
	Felix Serafin	75	74	77	73	299
21	**Ralph Guldahl**	74	74	76	76	300
22	**Toney Penna**	74	79	73	75	301
=23	**Billy Burke**	71	79	80	72	302
	Herman Keiser	784	74	78	76	302
	Craig Wood	72	75	72	73	302
=26	**Jim Foulis**	75	71	79	78	303
	Johnny Palmer	78	75	75	75	303
=28	**Tommy Armour**	74	79	76	75	304
	Bobby Jones (a)	72	75	79	78	304
	Gene Sarazen	80	74	75	75	304
	Bud Ward (a)	76	73	80	75	304
	Charlie Yates (a)	78	76	74	76	304

1943–45 – No tournaments

April 4–7, 1946

1	**Herman Keiser**	69	68	71	74	282
2	**Ben Hogan**	74	70	69	70	283
3	**Bob Hamilton**	75	69	71	72	287
=4	**Jimmy Demaret**	75	70	71	73	289
	Jim Ferrier	74	72	68	75	289
	Ky Laffoon	74	73	70	72	289
=7	**Chick Harbert**	69	75	76	70	290
	Clayton Heafner	74	69	71	76	290
	Byron Nelson	72	73	71	74	290
	Sam Snead	74	75	70	71	290
11	**Jim Foulis**	75	70	72	74	291
12	**Cary Middlecoff (a)**	72	76	70	74	292
=13	**Vic Ghezzi**	71	79	67	76	293
	George Schneiter	73	73	72	75	293
15	**Fred Haas**	71	75	68	80	294
=16	**Johnny Bulla**	72	76	73	74	295
	Lloyd Mangrum	76	75	72	72	295
18	**Claude Harmon**	76	75	74	71	296
19	**Chandler Harper**	74	76	73	74	297
20	**Frank Stranahan (a)**	76	74	73	75	298
=21	**Lawson Little**	74	74	78	73	299
	Toney Penna	71	73	80	75	299
	Felix Serafin	76	75	79	69	299
	Horton Smith	78	77	75	69	299
=25	**Herman Barron**	74	73	74	79	300
	Henry Picard	79	73	72	77	300
	Denny Shute	79	77	71	73	300

April 4–7, 1946 continued

	Jimmy Thomson	72	70	79	79	300
=29	**Gene Kunes**	76	72	77	76	301
	Harold McSpaden	75	74	75	77	301
	Al Zimmerman	76	76	74	75	301

April 3–6, 1947

1	**Jimmy Demaret**	69	71	70	71	281
=2	**Byron Nelson**	69	72	72	70	283
	Frank Stranahan (a)	73	72	7	68	283
=4	**Ben Hogan**	75	68	71	70	284
	Harold McSpaden	74	69	70	71	284
=6	**Jim Ferrier**	70	71	73	72	286
	Henry Picard	73	70	72	71	286
=8	**Chandler Harper**	77	72	68	70	287
	Lloyd Mangrum	76	73	68	70	287
	Dick Metz	72	72	72	71	287
	Ed Oliver	70	72	74	71	287
	Toney Penna	71	70	75	71	287
13	**Johnny Bulla**	70	75	74	69	288
=14	**Dick Chapman (a)**	72	71	74	72	289
	Lawson Little	71	71	76	71	289
	Bobby Locke	74	74	71	70	289
=17	**Herman Barron**	71	71	74	74	290
	Fred Haas	70	74	73	73	290
	Johnny Palmer	70	73	74	73	290
20	**Denny Shute**	73	75	72	71	291
21	**Vic Ghezzi**	73	77	71	71	292
=22	**Horton Smith**	72	70	76	75	293
	Sam Snead	72	71	75	75	293
=24	**Herman Keiser**	74	75	73	72	294
	Elsworth Vines	75	71	75	73	294
=26	**Claude Harmon**	73	69	76	77	295
	Gene Sarazen	75	76	74	70	295
	George Schneiter	70	75	78	72	295
=29	**Dutch Harrison**	74	71	74	77	296
	Clayton Heafner	75	73	75	73	296
	Cary Middlecoff	71	69	76	80	296
	Harry Todd	74	74	71	77	296

April 8–11, 1948

1	**Claude Harmon**	70	70	69	70	279
2	**Cary Middlecoff**	74	71	69	70	284
3	**Chick Harbert**	71	70	70	67	287
=4	**Jim Ferrier**	71	71	75	71	288
	Lloyd Mangrum	69	73	75	71	288
=6	**Ed Furgol**	70	72	73	74	289
	Ben Hogan	70	71	77	71	289
=8	**Byron Nelson**	71	73	72	74	290
	Harry Todd	72	69	80	71	290
=10	**Herman Keiser**	70	72	76	73	291
	Bobby Locke	71	71	74	75	291
	Dick Metz	71	72	75	73	291
=13	**Johnny Bulla**	74	72	76	71	293
	Dutch Harrison	73	77	73	70	293
	Skee Riegel (a)	71	74	73	75	293
=16	**Al Smith**	73	73	74	74	294
	Sam Snead	74	75	72	73	294
=18	**Jimmy Demaret**	73	72	78	72	295
	Ed Dudley	73	76	75	71	295
	Vic Ghezzi	75	73	73	74	295
	Fred Haas	75	75	76	69	295
	Bob Hamilton	72	72	76	75	295
=23	**Art Bell**	71	74	74	77	296
	Gene Sarazen	77	74	73	72	296

April 8–11, 1948 continued

=25	**Herman Barron**	73	77	71	76	297
	Henry Cotton	72	73	75	77	297
	Henry Picard	73	73	74	77	297
=28	**Johnny Palmer**	75	73	76	74	298
	Elsworth Vines	76	71	77	74	298
=30	**Bud Ward (a)**	74	74	77	74	299
	Lew Worsham	74	78	71	76	299

April 7–10, 1949

1	**Sam Snead**	73	75	67	67	282
=2	**Johnny Bulla**	74	73	69	69	285
	Lloyd Mangrum	69	74	72	70	285
=4	**Johnny Palmer**	73	71	70	72	286
	Jim Turnesa	73	72	71	70	286
6	**Lew Worsham**	76	75	70	68	289
7	**Joe Kirkwood Jr**	73	72	70	75	290
=8	**Jimmy Demaret**	76	72	73	71	292
	Clayton Heafner	71	74	72	75	292
	Byron Nelson	75	70	74	73	292
=11	**Claude Harmon**	73	75	73	72	293
	Herman Keiser	75	68	78	72	293
=13	**Herman Barron**	73	75	71	75	294
	Leland Gibson	71	77	74	72	294
	Bobby Locke	74	74	74	72	294
=16	**Charles R. Coe (a)**	77	72	72	74	295
	John Dawson (a)	78	72	72	73	295
	Jim Ferrier	77	72	67	79	295
=19	**Tony Holguin**	81	70	71	74	296
	Frank Stranahan (a)	70	77	75	74	296
=21	**Pete Cooper**	76	75	72	74	297
	Henry Picard	74	77	73	73	297
=23	**Bob Hamilton**	77	79	69	73	298
	Dutch Harrison	73	78	75	72	298
	Lawson Little	72	77	73	76	298
	Cary Middlecoff	76	77	72	73	298
	Toney Penna	74	76	76	72	298
	Horton Smith	75	72	78	73	298
29	**Fred Haas**	75	70	75	79	299
=30	**Skip Alexander**	74	77	75	74	300
	George Fazio	78	76	71	75	300
	Dick Metz	71	76	76	77	300
	Skee Riegel (a)	75	74	74	77	300

April 6–9, 1950

1	**Jimmy Demaret**	70	72	72	69	283
2	**Jim Ferrier**	70	67	73	75	285
3	**Sam Snead**	71	74	70	72	287
=4	**Ben Hogan**	73	68	71	67	288
	Byron Nelson	75	70	69	74	288
6	**Lloyd Mangrum**	76	74	73	68	291
=7	**Clayton Heafner**	74	77	69	72	292
	Cary Middlecoff	75	76	68	73	292
9	**Lawson Little**	70	73	75	75	293
=10	**Fred Haas**	74	76	73	71	294
	Gene Sarazen	80	70	72	72	294
=12	**Roberto de Vicenzo**	76	76	73	71	296
	Horton Smith	70	79	75	72	296
=14	**Skip Alexander**	78	74	73	72	297
	Vic Ghezzi	78	75	70	74	297
	Leland Gibson	78	73	72	74	297
	Herman Keiser	75	72	75	75	297
	Joe Kirkwood Jr	75	74	77	71	297
	Henry Picard	74	79	73	71	297
	Frank Stranahan (a)	74	79	73	71	297

April 6–9, 1950 continued

=21	**George Fazio**	73	74	78	73	298
	Toney Penna	71	75	77	75	298
	Skee Riegel	69	75	78	76	298
=24	**Chick Harbert**	76	75	73	75	299
	Johnny Palmer	72	76	76	75	299
26	**Eric Monti**	74	79	74	73	300
=27	**Herschel Spears**	70	74	79	78	301
	Norman Von Nida	77	74	74	76	301
=29	**Billy Burke**	80	75	76	71	302
	Pete Cooper	74	77	77	74	302

April 5–8, 1951

1	**Ben Hogan**	70	72	70	68	280
2	**Skee Riegel**	73	68	70	71	282
=3	**Lloyd Mangrum**	69	74	70	73	286
	Lew Worsham	71	71	72	72	286
5	**Dave Douglas**	74	69	72	73	288
6	**Lawson Little**	72	73	72	72	289
7	**Jim Ferrier**	74	70	74	72	290
=8	**Johnny Bulla**	71	72	73	75	291
	Byron Nelson	71	73	73	74	291
	Sam Snead	69	74	68	80	291
11	**Jack Burke Jr**	73	71	74	73	292
=12	**Charles R. Coe (a)**	76	71	73	73	293
	Cary Middlecoff	73	73	69	78	293
	Gene Sarazen	75	74	73	71	293
=15	**Ed Furgol**	80	71	72	71	294
	Dutch Harrison	76	71	76	71	294
17	**Julius Boros**	76	72	74	73	295
=18	**George Fazio**	68	74	74	80	296
	Bob Toski	75	73	73	75	296
=20	**Al Besselink**	76	73	71	77	297
	Dick Chapman (a)	72	76	72	77	297
	Clayton Heafner	74	72	73	78	297
	Joe Kirkwood Jr	73	71	78	75	297
	Roberto de Vicenzo	75	74	74	74	297
=25	**Ted Kroll**	76	75	71	76	298
	Dick Mayer	71	75	79	73	298
	Bill Nary	76	73	73	76	298
	Henry Ransom	74	74	74	76	298
	Sam Urzetta	73	72	78	75	298
=30	**Jimmy Demaret**	76	74	78	71	299
	Johnny Palmer	73	74	77	75	299

April 3–6, 1952

1	**Sam Snead**	70	67	77	72	286
2	**Jack Burke Jr**	76	67	78	69	290
=3	**Al Besselink**	70	76	71	74	291
	Tommy Bolt	71	71	75	74	291
	Jim Ferrier	72	70	77	72	291
6	**Lloyd Mangrum**	71	74	75	72	292
=7	**Julius Boros**	73	73	76	71	293
	Fred Hawkins	71	73	78	71	293
	Ben Hogan	70	70	74	79	293
	Lew Worsham	71	75	73	74	293
11	**Cary Middlecoff**	72	72	72	78	294
12	**Johnny Palmer**	69	74	75	77	295
13	**Johnny Revolta**	71	71	77	77	296
=14	**George Fazio**	72	71	78	76	297
	Claude Harmon	73	74	77	73	297
	Chuck Kocsis (a)	75	78	71	73	297
	Ted Kroll	74	74	76	73	297
	Skee Riegel	75	71	78	73	297
=19	**Joe Kirkwood Jr**	71	77	74	76	298

April 3–6, 1952 continued

	Frank Stranahan (a)	72	74	76	76	298
=21	**Doug Ford**	71	74	79	75	299
	Bobby Locke	74	71	79	75	299
	E. Harvie Ward Jr (a)	72	71	78	78	299
=24	**Arnold Blum (a)**	74	77	77	74	302
	Clayton Heafner	76	74	74	78	302
	Byron Nelson	72	75	78	77	302
27	**Skip Alexander**	71	73	77	82	303
	Smiley Quick	73	76	79	75	303
	Norman Von Nida	77	77	73	76	303
=30	**Dave Douglas**	76	69	81	78	304
	Vic Ghezzi	77	77	76	74	304
	Ed Oliver	72	72	77	83	304
	Horton Smith	74	73	77	80	304

April 9–12, 1953

1	**Ben Hogan**	70	69	66	69	274
2	**Ed Oliver**	69	73	67	70	279
3	**Lloyd Mangrum**	74	68	71	69	282
4	**Bob Hamilton**	71	69	70	73	283
=5	**Tommy Bolt**	71	75	68	71	285
	Chick Harbert	68	73	70	74	285
7	**Ted Kroll**	71	70	73	72	286
8	**Jack Burke Jr**	78	69	69	71	287
9	**Al Besselink**	69	75	70	74	288
=10	**Julius Boros**	73	71	75	70	289
	Chandler Harper	74	72	69	74	289
	Fred Hawkins	75	70	74	70	289
13	**Johnny Palmer**	74	73	72	71	290
=14	**Frank Stranahan (a)**	72	75	69	75	291
	E. Harvie Ward Jr (a)	73	74	69	75	291
=16	**Charles R. Coe (a)**	75	74	72	71	292
	Jim Ferrier	74	71	76	71	292
	Dick Mayer	73	72	71	76	292
	Sam Snead	71	75	71	75	292
	Earl Stewart Jr	75	72	70	75	292
=21	**Jerry Barber**	73	76	72	72	293
	Doug Ford	73	73	72	75	293
=23	**Leland Gibson**	73	71	72	78	294
	Al Mengert	77	70	75	72	294
	Dick Metz	73	72	71	78	294
26	**Fred Haas**	74	73	71	77	295
=27	**Cary Middlecoff**	75	76	68	77	296
	Jim Turnesa	73	74	73	76	296
=29	**Skip Alexander**	72	78	74	73	297
	Byron Nelson	73	73	78	73	297
	Skee Riegel	74	72	76	75	297
	Felice Torza	78	73	72	74	297
	Bo Wininger	80	70	72	75	297

April 8–12, 1954

* *Sam Snead (70) beat Ben Hogan (71) in the 18-hole play-off.*

1	**Sam Snead***	74	73	70	72	289
2	**Ben Hogan**	72	73	69	75	289
3	**Billy Joe Patton (a)**	70	74	75	71	290
=4	**Dutch Harrison**	70	79	74	69	291
	Lloyd Mangrum	71	75	76	69	291
=6	**Jerry Barber**	74	76	71	71	292
	Jack Burke Jr	71	77	73	71	292
	Bob Rosburg	73	73	76	70	292
=9	**Al Besselink**	74	74	74	72	294
	Cary Middlecoff	73	76	70	75	294
11	**Dick Chapman (a)**	75	75	75	70	295
=12	**Tommy Bolt**	73	74	72	77	296

April 8–12, 1954 continued

	Chick Harbert	73	75	75	73	296
	Byron Nelson	73	76	74	73	296
	Lew Worsham	74	74	74	74	296
=16	**Julius Boros**	76	79	68	74	297
	Jay Herbert	79	74	74	70	297
	Peter Thomson	76	72	76	73	297
	Ken Venturi (a)	76	74	73	74	297
=20	**Charles R. Coe (a)**	76	75	73	74	298
	E. Harvie Ward Jr (a)	78	75	74	71	298
=22	**Walter Burkemo**	74	77	75	73	299
	Peter Cooper	73	76	75	75	299
	Marty Furgol	76	79	75	69	299
	Gene Littler	79	75	73	72	299
	Ed Oliver	79	75	73	72	299
	Earl Stewart Jr	78	75	75	71	299
	Bob Toski	80	74	71	74	299
=29	**Jimmy Demaret**	80	75	72	73	300
	Vic Ghezzi	73	79	73	75	300
	Dick Mayer	76	75	72	77	300

April 7–10, 1955

1	**Cary Middlecoff**	72	65	72	70	279
2	**Ben Hogan**	73	68	72	73	286
3	**Sam Snead**	72	71	74	70	287
=4	**Julius Boros**	71	75	72	71	289
	Bob Rosburg	72	72	72	73	289
	Mike Souchak	71	74	72	72	289
7	**Lloyd Mangrum**	74	73	72	72	291
=8	**E. Harvie Ward Jr (a)**	77	69	75	71	292
	Stan Leonard	77	73	68	74	292
=10	**Dick Mayer**	78	72	72	71	293
	Byron Nelson	72	75	74	72	293
	Arnold Palmer	76	76	72	69	293
=13	**Jack Burke Jr**	67	76	71	80	294
	Skee Riegel	73	73	73	75	294
=15	**Walter Burkemo**	73	73	72	77	295
	Jay Herbert	75	74	74	72	295
	Frank Stranahan	77	76	71	71	295
=18	**Joe Conrad (a)**	77	71	74	75	297
	Billy Maxwell (a)	77	72	77	71	297
	Johnny Palmer	77	73	72	75	297
	Peter Thomson	74	73	74	76	297
=22	**Tommy Bolt**	76	70	77	75	298
	Gene Littler	75	72	76	75	298
=24	**Pete Cooper**	73	73	78	75	299
	Ed Furgol	74	72	78	75	299
	Hillman Robbins Jr (a)	77	76	74	72	299
27	**Max Evans**	76	75	75	76	302
=28	**William L. Goodloe Jr (a)**	74	73	81	75	303
	Claude Harmon	77	75	78	73	303
=30	**Don Cherry**	79	75	78	82	304
	Bud Ward	77	73	77	77	304

April 5–8, 1956

1	**Jack Burke Jr**	72	71	75	71	289
2	**Ken Venturi**	66	69	75	80	290
3	**Cary Middlecoff**	67	72	75	77	291
=4	**Lloyd Mangrum**	72	74	72	74	292
	Sam Snead	73	76	72	71	292
=6	**Jerry Barber**	71	72	76	75	294
	Doug Ford	70	72	75	77	294
=8	**Tommy Bolt**	68	74	78	76	296
	Ben Hogan	69	78	74	75	296
	Shelley Mayfield	68	74	80	74	296

April 5–8, 1956 continued

11	**Johnny Palmer**	76	74	74	73	297
=12	**Pete Cooper**	72	70	77	79	298
	Gene Littler	73	77	74	74	298
	Billy Joe Patton (a)	70	76	79	73	298
	Sam Urzetta	73	75	76	74	298
16	**Bob Rosberg**	70	74	81	74	299
=17	**Walter Burkemo**	72	74	78	76	300
	Roberto de Vicenzo	75	72	78	75	300
	Hillman Robbins Jr (a)	73	73	78	76	300
	Mike Souchak	73	73	74	80	300
21	**Arnold Palmer**	73	75	74	79	301
=22	**Frank Stranahan (a)**	72	75	79	76	302
	Jim Turnesa	74	74	74	80	302
=24	**Julius Boros**	73	78	72	80	303
	Dow Finsterwald	74	73	79	77	303
	Ed Furgol	74	75	78	76	303
	Stan Leonard	75	75	79	74	303
	Al Mengert	74	72	79	78	303
=29	**Al Balding**	75	78	77	74	304
	Vic Ghezzi	74	77	77	76	304
	Fred Haas	78	72	75	79	304
	Fred Hawkins	71	73	76	84	304
	Walter Inman Jr	73	75	74	82	304

April 3–6, 1957

1	**Doug Ford**	72	73	72	66	283
2	**Sam Snead**	72	68	74	72	286
3	**Jimmy Demaret**	72	70	75	70	287
4	**E. Harvie Ward Jr (a)**	73	71	71	73	288
5	**Peter Thomson**	72	73	73	71	289
6	**Ed Furgol**	73	71	72	74	290
=7	**Jack Burke Jr**	71	72	74	74	291
	Dow Finsterwald	74	74	73	70	291
	Arnold Palmer	73	73	69	76	291
10	**Jay Herbert**	74	72	76	70	292
=11	**Marty Furgol**	73	74	73	73	293
	Stan Leonard	75	72	68	78	293
=13	**Henry Cotton**	73	73	72	76	294
	Frank M. Taylor Jr (a)	74	74	77	69	294
	Ken Venturi	74	76	74	70	294
=16	**Al Balding**	73	73	73	76	295
	Billy Casper	75	75	75	70	295
	Mike Fetchick	74	73	72	76	295
	Byron Nelson	74	72	73	76	295
=21	**Bruce Crampton**	72	75	78	71	296
	Al Mengert	75	75	71	75	296
	Henry Ransom	75	73	72	76	296
=24	**Johnny Palmer**	77	73	73	74	297
	Gary Player	77	72	75	73	297
=26	**Jerry Barber**	73	77	78	70	298
	Jack Fleck	76	74	75	73	299
	Bill Johnston	77	70	78	74	299
	Lawson Little	76	72	77	74	299
	Lloyd Mangrum	77	71	74	77	299

April 3–6, 1958

1	**Arnold Palmer**	70	73	68	73	284
=2	**Doug Ford**	74	71	70	70	285
	Fred Hawkins	71	75	68	71	285
=4	**Stan Leonard**	72	70	73	71	286
	Ken Venturi	68	72	74	72	286
=6	**Cary Middlecoff**	70	73	69	75	287
	Art Wall	71	72	70	74	287
8	**Billy Joe Patton (a)**	72	69	73	74	288

April 3–6, 1958 continued

=9	**Claude Harmon**	71	76	72	70	289
	Jay Herbert	72	73	73	71	289
	Billy Maxwell (a)	71	70	72	76	289
	Al Mengert	73	71	69	76	289
13	**Sam Snead**	72	71	68	79	290
=14	**Jimmy Demaret**	69	79	70	73	291
	Ben Hogan	72	77	69	73	291
	Mike Souchak	71	75	73	71	291
=17	**Dow Finsterwald**	72	71	74	75	292
	Chick Harbert	69	74	73	76	292
	Bo Wininger	69	73	71	79	292
=20	**Billy Casper**	76	71	72	74	293
	Byron Nelson	71	77	73	71	293
22	**Phil Rodgers**	77	72	73	72	294
=23	**Charles R. Coe (a)**	73	76	69	77	295
	Ted Kroll	73	75	75	72	295
	Peter Thomson	72	74	73	76	295
=26	**Al Balding**	75	72	71	78	296
	Bruce Crampton	73	76	72	75	296
	William Hyndman III (a)	71	76	70	79	296
=29	**George Bayer**	74	75	72	76	297
	Arnold Blum (a)	72	74	75	76	297
	Joe E. Campbell	73	75	74	75	297

April 2–5, 1959

1	**Art Wall**	73	74	71	66	284
2	**Cary Middlecoff**	74	71	68	72	285
3	**Arnold Palmer**	71	70	71	74	286
=4	**Stan Leonard**	69	74	69	75	287
	Dick Mayer	73	75	71	68	287
6	**Charles R. Coe Jr (a)**	74	74	67	73	288
7	**Fred Hawkins**	77	71	68	73	289
=8	**Julius Boros**	75	69	74	72	290
	Jay Herbert	72	73	72	73	290
	Gene Littler	72	75	72	71	290
	Billy Maxwell (a)	73	71	72	74	290
	Billy Joe Patton (a)	75	70	71	74	290
	Gary Player	73	75	71	71	290
=14	**Chick Harbert**	74	72	74	71	291
	Chandler Harper	71	74	74	72	291
	Ted Kroll	76	71	73	71	291
	Ed Oliver	75	69	73	74	291
=18	**Dow Finsterwald**	79	68	73	72	292
	Jack Fleck	74	71	71	76	292
	William Hyndman III (a)	73	72	76	71	292
	Bo Wininger	75	70	72	75	292
=22	**Walter Burkemo**	75	70	71	77	293
	Chuck Kocsis (a)	73	75	70	75	293
	Sam Snead	74	73	72	74	293
=25	**Don Cherry**	77	71	75	71	294
	Doug Ford	76	73	73	72	294
	Paul Harney	75	69	77	73	294
	Angel Miguel	72	72	76	74	294
	Mike Souchak	73	71	74	76	294
=30	**Tommy Bolt**	72	75	72	76	295
	Ben Hogan	73	74	76	72	295
	Bob Rosburg	75	74	73	73	295
	Dave Thomas	73	71	77	74	295

April 7–10, 1960

1	**Arnold Palmer**	67	73	72	70	282
2	**Ken Venturi**	73	69	71	70	283
3	**Dow Finsterwald**	71	70	72	71	284
4	**Billy Casper**	71	71	71	74	287

April 7–10, 1960 continued

5	**Julius Boros**	72	71	70	75	288
=6	**Walter Burkemo**	72	69	75	73	289
	Ben Hogan	73	68	72	76	289
	Gary Player	72	71	72	74	289
=9	**Lionel Herbert**	74	70	73	73	290
	Stan Leonard	72	72	72	74	290
=11	**Jack Burke Jr**	72	72	74	74	292
	Sam Snead	73	74	72	73	292
=13	**Ted Kroll**	72	76	71	74	293
	Jack Nicklaus (a)	75	71	72	75	293
	Billy Joe Patton	75	72	74	72	293
=16	**Bruce Crampton**	74	73	75	72	294
	Claude Harmon	69	72	75	78	294
	Fred Hawkins	69	78	72	75	294
	Mike Souchak	72	75	72	75	294
=20	**Tommy Bolt**	73	74	75	73	295
	Don January	70	72	74	79	295
	Ed Oliver	74	75	73	73	295
	Bob Rosburg	74	74	71	76	295
	Frank M. Taylor Jr (a)	70	74	73	78	295
=25	**Tommy Aaron**	74	75	75	73	297
	Doug Ford	74	72	80	81	297
	Billy Maxwell (a)	70	74	73	78	297
	Dave Ragan	74	73	75	75	297
=29	**George Bayer**	73	73	80	72	298
	Deane Benam (a)	71	72	77	78	298
	Richard Crawford	74	72	75	77	298
	Doug Sanders	73	71	81	73	298

April 6–10, 1961

1	**Gary Player**	69	68	69	74	280
=2	**Charles R. Coe Jr (a)**	72	71	69	69	281
	Arnold Palmer	68	69	73	71	281
=4	**Tommy Bolt**	72	71	74	68	285
	Don January	74	68	72	71	285
6	**Paul Harney**	71	73	68	74	286
=7	**Jack Burke Jr**	76	70	68	73	287
	Billy Casper	72	77	69	69	287
	Bill Collins	74	72	67	74	287
	Jack Nicklaus (a)	70	75	70	72	287
=11	**Walter Burkemo**	74	69	73	72	288
	Robert Gardner (a)	74	71	72	71	288
	Doug Sanders	76	71	68	73	288
	Ken Venturi	72	71	72	73	288
=15	**Stan Leonard**	72	74	72	74	289
	Gene Littler	72	73	72	72	289
	Bob Rosburg	68	73	73	75	289
	Sam Snead	74	73	69	73	289
=19	**Dick Mayer**	76	72	70	73	291
	Johnny Pott	71	75	72	73	291
	Peter Thompson	73	76	68	74	291
=22	**Roberto de Vicenzo**	73	74	71	74	292
	Lew Worsham	74	71	73	74	292
=24	**Antonio Cerda**	73	73	72	75	293
	Fred Hawkins	74	75	72	72	293
	Ted Kroll	73	70	72	78	293
27	**Al Balding**	74	74	70	76	294
=28	**Mason Rudolph**	77	69	72	77	295
	Mike Souchak	75	72	75	73	295
=30	**Jay Herbert**	72	75	69	80	296
	Lionel Herbert	74	69	74	79	296

April 4–7, 1962

** Arnold Palmer (68) beat Gary Player (71) and Dow Finsterwald (77) in the 18-hole play-off.*

1	**Arnold Palmer***	70	66	69	75	280
2	**Gary Player**	67	71	71	71	280
3	**Dow Finsterwald**	74	68	65	73	280
4	**Gene Littler**	71	68	71	72	282
=5	**Jerry Barber**	72	72	69	74	287
	Jimmy Demaret	73	73	71	70	287
	Billy Maxwell (a)	71	73	72	71	287
	Mike Souchak	70	72	74	71	287
=9	**Charles R. Coe (a)**	72	74	71	71	288
	Ken Venturi	75	70	71	72	288
=11	**Julius Boros**	69	73	72	76	290
	Gay Brewer	74	71	70	75	290
	Jack Fleck	72	75	74	69	290
	Harold Henning	75	73	72	70	290
=15	**Billy Casper**	73	73	73	72	291
	Gardner Dickinson	70	71	72	78	291
	Paul Harney	74	71	74	72	291
	Jack Nicklaus	74	75	70	72	291
	Sam Snead	72	75	70	74	291
=20	**Jack Cupit**	73	73	72	74	292
	Lionel Herbert	72	73	71	76	292
	Don January	71	73	74	74	292
	Johnny Pott	77	71	75	69	292
24	**Al Balding**	75	68	78	72	293
=25	**Bob Charles**	75	72	73	74	294
	Bob Goalby	74	74	73	73	294
	Ted Kroll	72	74	72	76	294
	Dave Ragan	70	73	76	75	294
=29	**Bill Collins**	75	70	75	75	295
	Bruce Crampton	72	75	74	74	295
	Cary Middlecoff	75	74	73	73	295
	Lew Worsham	75	70	78	72	295

April 4–7, 1963

1	**Jack Nicklaus**	74	66	74	72	286
2	**Tony Lema**	74	69	74	70	287
=3	**Julius Boros**	76	69	71	72	288
	Sam Snead	70	73	74	71	288
=5	**Dow Finsterwald**	74	73	73	69	289
	Ed Furgol	70	71	74	74	289
	Gary Player	71	74	74	70	289
8	**Bo Wininger**	69	72	77	72	290
=9	**Don January**	73	75	72	71	291
	Arnold Palmer	74	73	73	71	291
=11	**Billy Casper**	79	72	71	70	292
	Bruce Crampton	74	74	72	72	292
	Doug Ford	75	73	75	69	292
	Mike Souchak	69	70	79	74	292
=15	**Bob Charles**	74	72	76	71	293
	Chen Ching-po	76	71	71	75	293
	Billy Maxwell (a)	72	75	76	70	293
	Dick Mayer	73	70	80	70	293
	Mason Rudolph	75	72	72	74	293
	Dan Sikes	74	76	72	71	293
=21	**Stan Leonard**	74	72	73	75	294
	Johnny Pott	75	76	74	69	294
	Art Wall	75	74	73	72	294
=24	**Wes Ellis Jr**	74	72	79	70	295
	Gene Littler	77	72	78	68	295
	Bobby Nichols	76	74	73	72	295
27	**Jay Herbert**	70	70	81	75	296
=28	**George Bayer**	71	75	84	67	297

	April 4–7, 1963 continued					
	Tommy Jacobs (a)	78	74	73	72	297
	Doug Sanders	73	74	77	73	297
	Alvie Thompson	79	72	75	71	297

April 9–12, 1964

1	**Arnold Palmer**	69	68	69	70	276
=2	**Dave Marr**	70	73	69	70	282
	Jack Nicklaus	71	73	71	67	282
4	**Bruce Devlin**	72	72	67	73	284
=5	**Billy Casper**	76	72	69	69	286
	Jim Ferrier	71	73	69	73	286
	Paul Harney	73	72	71	70	286
	Gary Player	69	72	72	73	286
=9	**Dow Finsterwald**	71	72	75	69	287
	Ben Hogan	73	75	67	72	287
	Tony Lema	75	68	74	70	287
	Mike Souchak	73	74	70	70	287
=13	**Peter Butler**	72	72	69	75	288
	Al Geiberger	75	73	70	70	288
	Gene Littler	70	72	78	68	288
	Dan Sikes	76	68	71	73	288
=18	**Don January**	70	72	75	72	289
	Billy Maxwell (a)	73	73	69	74	289
	Mason Rudolph	75	73	69	73	289
=21	**Bruce Crampton**	74	72	73	71	290
	Kel Nagle	69	77	71	73	290
	Chi-Chi Rodriguez	71	73	73	73	290
	Bo Wininger	74	71	69	76	290
=25	**Deane Benam (a)**	74	71	70	76	291
	Gay Brewer	75	72	73	71	291
	Gary Cowan (a)	71	77	72	71	291
	Bobby Nichols	75	71	75	70	291
	Phil Rodgers	75	72	72	72	291
=30	**Jay Herbert**	74	74	69	75	292
	Dean Refram	74	72	73	73	292

April 8–11, 1965

1	**Jack Nicklaus**	67	71	64	69	271
=2	**Arnold Palmer**	70	68	72	70	280
	Gary Player	69	72	72	73	280
4	**Mason Rudolph**	70	75	66	72	283
5	**Dan Sikes**	67	72	71	75	285
=6	**Gene Littler**	71	74	67	74	286
	Ramon Sota	71	73	70	72	286
=8	**Frank Beard**	68	77	72	70	287
	Tommy Bolt	69	78	69	71	287
10	**George Knudson**	72	73	69	74	288
=11	**Tommy Aaron**	67	74	71	77	289
	Bruce Crampton	72	72	74	71	289
	Paul Harney	74	74	71	70	289
	Doug Sanders	69	72	74	74	289
=15	**George Bayer**	69	74	75	72	290
	Bruce Devlin	71	76	73	70	290
	Wes Ellis Jr	69	76	72	73	290
	Tommy Jacobs	71	74	72	73	290
	Kel Nagle	75	70	74	71	290
	Byron Nelson	70	74	72	74	290
=21	**Dow Finsterwald**	72	75	72	72	291
	Ben Hogan	71	75	71	74	291
	Tony Lema	67	73	77	74	291
=24	**Terry Dill**	72	73	75	72	292
	Al Geiberger	75	72	74	71	292
=26	**Bernard Hunt**	71	74	74	74	293
	Tomoo Ishii	74	74	70	75	293

	April 8–11, 1965 continued					
	Billy Maxwell (a)	74	72	76	71	293
	Tom Nieporte	71	73	75	74	293
	Bob Wininger	70	72	75	76	293

April 7–11, 1966

** Jack Nicklaus (70) beat Tommy Jacobs (72) and Gay Brewer (78) in the 18-hole play-off.*

1	**Jack Nicklaus***	68	76	72	72	288
=2	**Gay Brewer**	74	72	72	70	288
	Tommy Jacobs	75	71	70	72	288
=4	**Arnold Palmer**	74	70	74	72	290
	Doug Sanders	74	70	75	71	290
=6	**Don January**	71	73	73	75	292
	George Knudson	73	76	72	71	292
=8	**Ray Floyd**	72	73	74	74	293
	Paul Harney	75	68	76	74	293
=10	**Billy Casper**	71	75	76	72	294
	Jay Herbert	72	74	73	75	294
	Bob Rosburg	73	71	76	74	294
14-	**Tommy Aaron**	74	73	77	71	295
	Peter Butler	72	71	79	73	295
	Ben Hogan	74	71	73	77	295
16	**Ken Venturi**	75	74	73	74	296
=17	**Tommy Bolt**	75	72	78	72	297
	Bruce Crampton	74	75	71	77	297
	Terry Dill	75	72	74	76	297
	Doug Ford	75	73	73	76	297
	Phil Rodgers	76	73	75	73	297
=22	**Frank Beard**	77	71	77	73	298
	Chen Ching-po	75	77	76	70	298
	Roberto de Vicenzo	74	76	74	74	298
	Harold Henning	77	74	70	77	298
	Tony Lema	74	74	74	76	298
	Bobby Nichols	77	73	74	74	298
=28	**Julius Boros**	77	73	73	76	299
	Bruce Devlin	75	77	72	77	299
	Gardner Dickinson	76	75	76	72	299
	James A. Grant (a)	74	74	78	73	299
	Gary Player	74	77	76	72	299

April 6–9, 1967

1	**Gay Brewer**	73	68	72	67	280
2	**Bobby Nichols**	72	69	70	70	281
3	**Bert Yancey**	67	73	71	73	284
4	**Arnold Palmer**	73	73	70	69	285
5	**Julius Boros**	71	70	70	75	286
=6	**Paul Harney**	73	71	74	69	287
	Gary Player	75	69	72	71	287
=8	**Tommy Aaron**	75	68	74	71	288
	Lionel Herbert	77	71	67	73	288
=10	**Roberto de Vicenzo**	73	72	74	71	290
	Bruce Devlin	74	70	75	71	290
	Ben Hogan	74	73	66	77	290
	Mason Rudolph	72	76	72	70	290
	Sam Snead	72	76	71	71	290
15	**Jack Cupit**	73	76	67	75	291
=16	**George Archer**	75	67	72	78	292
	Wes Ellis Jr	79	71	74	68	292
	Tony Jacklin	71	70	74	77	292
	Dave Marr	73	74	70	75	292
	Doug Sanders	74	72	73	73	292
=21	**Jay Herbert**	72	77	68	76	293
	Bob Rosburg	73	72	76	72	293
	Ken Venturi	76	73	71	73	293

	April 6–9, 1967 continued					
=24	Peter Butler	72	73	77	72	294
	Billy Casper	70	74	75	75	294
=26	Frank Beard	74	75	75	71	295
	Tommy Bolt	72	77	72	74	295
	Don January	74	74	76	71	295
=28	Gene Littler	72	74	74	75	296
	Juan Rodriguez	73	73	73	76	296

April 11–14, 1968

1	Bob Goalby	70	70	71	66	277
2	Roberto de Vicenzo	69	73	70	67	278
3	Bert Yancey	71	71	72	65	279
4	Bruce Devlin	69	73	69	69	280
=5	Frank Beard	75	65	71	70	281
	Jack Nicklaus	69	72	72	69	281
=7	Tommy Aaron	68	72	72	69	282
	Ray Floyd	71	71	69	71	282
	Lionel Herbert	72	71	71	68	282
	Jerry Pittman	70	73	70	69	282
	Gary Player	72	67	71	72	282
=12	Miller Barber	75	69	68	71	283
	Doug Sanders	76	69	70	68	283
=14	Don January	71	68	72	73	284
	Mason Rudolph	73	73	72	66	284
=16	Julius Boros	73	71	70	71	285
	Billy Casper	68	75	73	69	285
	Tom Weiskopf	74	71	69	71	285
19	Bob Charles	75	71	70	70	286
=20	Dave Marr	74	71	71	71	287
	Kermit Zarley	70	73	74	70	287
=22	George Archer	75	71	72	70	288
	Gardner Dickinson	74	71	72	71	288
	Martin Giles III (a)	71	72	72	73	288
	Harold Henning	72	71	71	74	288
	Tony Jacklin	69	73	74	72	288
	Art Wall	74	74	73	67	288
=28	Jay Herbert	74	71	71	73	289
	George Knudson	75	71	72	71	289
=30	Charles Coody	76	72	72	70	290
	Al Geiberger	72	70	72	72	290
	Kel Nagle	76	71	72	71	290
	Bobby Nichols	74	73	73	70	290
	Bob Rosburg	74	73	71	72	290

April 10-13, 1969

1	George Archer	67	73	69	72	281
=2	Billy Casper	66	71	71	74	282
	George Knudson	70	73	69	70	282
	Tom Weiskopf	71	71	69	71	282
=4	Charles Coody	74	68	69	72	283
	Don January	74	73	70	66	283
7	Miller Barber	71	71	68	74	284
=8	Tommy Aaron	71	71	73	70	285
	Lionel Herbert	69	73	70	73	285
	Gene Littler	69	75	70	71	285
11	Mason Rudolph	69	73	74	70	286
12	Dan Sikes	69	71	73	74	287
=13	Bruce Crampton	69	73	74	72	288
	Al Geiberger	71	71	74	72	288
	Takaaki Kono	71	75	68	74	288
	Bert Yancey	69	75	71	73	288
18	Dave Stockton	71	71	75	72	289
=19	Frank Beard	72	74	70	74	290
	Deane Beman	74	73	74	69	290

	April 10–13, 1969 continued					
	Bruce Devlin	67	70	76	77	290
	Dale Douglas	73	72	71	74	290
	Lee Trevino	72	74	75	69	290
=23	Jack Burke Jr	73	72	70	76	291
	Dave Hill	75	73	72	71	291
	Jack Nicklaus	68	75	72	76	291
26	Arnold Palmer	73	75	70	74	292
27	Johnny Pott	72	72	71	78	293
=28	Roberto Bernardini	76	71	72	75	294
	Bob Charles	70	76	72	76	294
	Gardner Dickinson	73	74	71	76	294
	Bobby Nichols	78	69	74	73	294

April 9–13, 1970

** Billy Casper (69) beat Gene Littler (74) in the sudden-death play-off.*

1	Billy Casper*	72	68	68	71	279
2	Gene Littler	69	70	70	70	279
3	Gary Player	74	68	68	70	280
4	Bert Yancey	69	70	72	70	281
=5	Tommy Aaron	68	74	69	72	283
	Dave Hill	73	70	70	70	283
	Dave Stockton	72	72	69	70	283
8	Jack Nicklaus	71	75	69	69	284
9	Frank Beard	71	76	68	70	285
=10	Bob Lunn	70	70	75	72	287
	Chi-Chi Rodriguez	70	76	73	68	288
	Bert Green	75	71	70	72	288
	Tony Jacklin	73	74	70	71	288
	Don January	76	73	69	70	288
	Takaaki Kono	75	68	71	74	288
16	Bob Charles	75	71	71	72	289
=17	Howie Johnson	75	71	73	71	290
	Dick Lotz	74	72	72	72	290
	Orville Moody	73	72	71	74	290
=20	Miller Barber	76	73	77	65	291
	Terry Wilcox	79	70	70	72	291
=22	Deane Beman	74	72	72	74	292
	Julius Boros	75	71	74	72	292
	Charles R. Coe (a)	74	71	72	75	292
	Bob Murphy	78	70	73	71	292
	Sam Snead	76	73	71	72	292
	Tom Weiskopf	73	73	72	74	292
=28	Yung-Yo Hsieh	75	75	69	74	293
	Jimmy Wright	75	72	71	75	293

April 8–11, 1971

1	Charles Coody	66	73	73	70	279
=2	Johnny Miller	72	73	68	68	281
	Jack Nicklaus	70	71	68	72	281
=4	Don January	69	69	73	72	283
	Gene Littler	72	69	73	69	283
=6	Gary Player	72	72	71	69	284
	Ken Still	72	71	72	69	284
	Tom Weiskopf	71	69	72	72	284
=9	Frank Beard	74	73	69	70	286
	Roberto de Vicenzo	76	69	72	69	285
	Dave Stockton	72	73	69	72	286
12	Ben Greene	73	73	71	70	287
=13	Billy Casper	72	73	71	72	288
	Bruce Devlin	72	70	72	74	288
	Ray Floyd	69	75	73	71	288
	Hale Irwin	69	72	71	76	288
	Bob Murphy	69	70	76	73	288
=18	Bruce Crampton	73	72	74	70	289

April 8–11, 1971 continued

	Arnold Palmer	73	72	71	73	289
=20	**Dave Eichelberger**	76	71	70	73	290
	Orville Moody	79	69	70	72	290
=22	**Tommy Aaron**	76	72	74	69	291
	Bobby Mitchell	72	70	74	75	291
=24	**Al Geiberger**	73	75	72	72	292
	Dick Lotz	77	72	73	70	292
	Steve Melnyk	73	70	75	74	292
=27	**Dale Douglass**	70	71	76	76	293
	Dave Hill	74	73	74	76	293
	Art Wall	71	76	72	74	293
=30	**Larry Hinson**	75	71	76	72	294
	Yung-Yo Hsieh	75	69	77	73	294
	Juan Rodriguez	73	75	71	75	294
	Larry Ziegler	73	70	77	74	294

April 6–9, 1972

1	**Jack Nicklaus**	68	71	73	74	286
=2	**Bruce Crampton**	72	75	69	73	289
	Bobby Mitchell	73	72	71	73	289
	Tom Weiskopf	74	71	70	74	289
=5	**Homero Blancas**	76	71	69	74	290
	Bruce Devlin	74	75	70	71	290
	Jerry Heard	73	71	72	74	290
	Jim Jamieson	72	70	71	77	290
	Jerry McGee	73	74	71	72	290
=10	**Gary Player**	73	75	72	71	291
	Dave Stockton	76	70	74	71	291
=12	**George Archer**	73	75	72	72	292
	Charles Coody	73	70	74	75	292
	Al Geiberger	76	70	74	72	292
	Steve Melnyk	72	72	74	74	292
	Bert Yancey	72	69	76	75	292
=17	**Billy Casper**	75	71	74	74	294
	Bob Goalby	73	76	72	73	294
=19	**Ben Crenshaw (a)**	73	74	74	74	295
	Takaaki Kono	76	72	73	74	295
	Lanny Wadkins	72	72	77	74	295
=22	**Bob Charles**	72	76	74	74	296
	Roberto de Vicenzo	74	69	76	76	296
	Gardner Dickinson	77	72	73	74	296
	Hubert Green	75	74	74	73	296
	Paul Harney	71	69	75	81	296
=27	**Tony Jacklin**	72	76	75	74	297
	Tom Kite	74	74	76	73	297
	Sam Snead	69	75	76	77	297
30	**J.C. Snead**	74	77	72	75	298

April 5–9, 1973

1	**Tommy Aaron**	68	73	74	68	283
2	**J.C. Snead**	70	71	73	70	284
=3	**Jim Jamieson**	73	71	70	71	285
	Jack Nicklaus	69	77	73	66	285
	Peter Oosterhuis	73	70	68	74	285
=6	**Bob Goalby**	73	70	71	74	288
	Johnny Miller	75	69	71	73	288
=8	**Bruce Devlin**	73	72	72	72	289
	Jumbo Ozaki	69	74	73	73	289
=10	**Gay Brewer**	75	66	74	76	291
	Gardner Dickinson	74	70	72	75	291
	Don January	75	71	75	70	291
	Chi-Chi Rodriguez	72	70	73	76	291
=14	**Hubert Green**	72	74	75	71	291
	Mason Rudolph	72	72	77	71	291

April 5–9, 1973 continued

	Dave Stockton	72	74	71	75	291
=17	**Billy Casper**	75	73	72	73	293
	Bob Dickson	70	71	76	76	293
	Lou Graham	77	73	72	71	293
	Babe Hiskey	74	73	72	74	293
	Gene Littler	77	72	71	73	293
	Kermit Zarley	74	71	77	71	293
23	**Phil Rodgers**	71	75	75	73	294
=24	**Frank Beard**	73	75	71	76	295
	Ben Crenshaw (a)	73	72	74	76	295
	Paul Harney	77	71	74	73	295
	Bobby Nichols	79	72	76	68	295
	Arnold Palmer	77	72	76	70	295
=29	**Bob Charles**	74	70	74	78	296
	Charles Coody	74	73	79	70	296
	David Graham	72	74	77	73	296
	Sam Snead	74	76	73	73	296
	Lanny Wadkins	75	74	71	76	296

April 11–14, 1974

1	**Gary Player**	71	71	66	70	278
=2	**Dave Stockton**	71	66	70	73	280
	Tom Weiskopf	71	69	70	70	280
=4	**Jim Colbert**	67	72	69	73	281
	Hale Irwin	68	70	72	71	281
	Jack Nicklaus	69	71	72	69	281
=7	**Bobby Nichols**	73	68	68	73	282
	Phil Rodgers	72	69	68	73	282
=9	**Maurice Bembridge**	73	74	72	64	283
	Hubert Green	68	70	74	71	283
=11	**Bruce Crampton**	73	72	69	70	284
	Jerry Heard	70	70	73	71	284
	Dave Hill	71	72	70	71	284
	Arnold Palmer	76	71	70	67	284
=15	**Bud Allin**	73	73	70	69	285
	Miller Barber	75	67	72	71	285
	Ralph Johnson	72	71	70	72	285
	Johnny Miller	72	74	69	70	285
	Dan Sikes	69	71	74	71	285
=20	**Chi-Chi Rodriguez**	70	74	71	71	286
	Sam Snead	72	72	71	71	286
=22	**Frank Beard**	69	70	72	76	287
	Ben Crenshaw	75	70	70	72	287
	Ray Floyd	69	72	76	70	287
	Bob Goalby	76	71	72	68	287
=26	**Julius Boros**	75	70	69	74	288
	John Schlee	75	71	71	71	288
	J.C. Snead	73	68	74	73	288
29	**Charles Coody**	68	74	73	74	288

April 10–13, 1975

1	**Jack Nicklaus**	68	67	73	68	276
=2	**Johnny Miller**	75	71	65	66	277
	Tom Weiskopf	69	72	66	70	277
=4	**Hale Irwin**	73	74	71	64	282
	Bobby Nichols	67	74	72	69	282
6	**Billy Casper**	70	70	73	70	283
7	**Dave Hill**	75	71	70	68	284
=8	**Hubert Green**	74	71	70	70	285
	Tom Watson	70	70	72	73	285
=10	**Tom Kite**	72	74	71	69	286
	J.C. Snead	69	72	75	70	286
	Lee Trevino	71	70	74	71	286
=13	**Arnold Palmer**	69	71	75	72	287

April 10–13, 1975 continued

	Larry Ziegler	71	73	74	69	287
=15	**Bobby Cole**	73	71	73	71	288
	Rod Curl	72	70	76	70	288
	Bruce Devlin	72	70	76	70	288
	Allen Miller	68	75	72	73	288
	Art Wall	72	74	72	70	288
=20	**Bud Allin**	73	69	73	74	289
	Ralph Johnston	74	73	69	73	289
=22	**Hugh Baiocchi**	76	72	72	70	290
	Pat Fitzsimmons	73	78	79	70	290
	Gene Littler	72	72	72	74	290
	Graham Marsh	75	70	74	71	290
=26	**Miller Barber**	74	72	72	73	291
	Maurice Bembridge	75	72	75	69	291
	Jerry Heard	71	75	72	73	291
	Dave Stockton	72	72	73	74	291

April 8–11, 1976

1	**Ray Floyd**	65	66	70	70	271
2	**Ben Crenshaw**	70	70	72	67	279
=3	**Jack Nicklaus**	67	69	73	73	282
	Larry Ziegler	67	71	72	72	282
=5	**Charles Coody**	72	69	70	74	285
	Hale Irwin	71	77	67	70	285
	Tom Kite	73	67	72	73	285
8	**Billy Casper**	71	76	71	69	287
=9	**Roger Maltbie**	72	75	70	71	288
	Graham Marsh	73	68	75	72	288
	Tom Weiskopf	73	71	70	74	288
=12	**Jim Colbert**	71	72	74	72	289
	Lou Graham	68	73	72	76	289
	Gene Littler	71	72	74	72	289
=15	**Al Geiberger**	75	70	73	73	291
	Dave Hill	69	73	76	73	291
	Jerry McGee	71	73	72	75	291
	Curtis Strange (a)	71	76	73	71	291
=19	**Bud Allin**	69	76	72	75	292
	Bruce Devlin	77	69	72	74	292
	Hubert Green	71	66	78	77	292
	Dale Hayes	75	74	73	70	292
=23	**Gay Brewer**	75	74	71	73	293
	Rik Massengale	70	72	78	73	293
	Johnny Miller	71	73	74	75	293
	Peter Oosterhuis	76	74	75	68	293
27	**Bruce Crampton**	74	76	71	73	294
=28	**Bob Murphy**	72	74	76	73	295
	Eddie Pearce	71	71	79	74	295
	Gary Player	73	73	70	79	295
	Lee Trevino	75	75	69	76	295
	Art Wall	74	71	75	75	295

April 7–10, 1977

1	**Tom Watson**	70	69	70	67	276
2	**Jack Nicklaus**	72	70	70	66	278
=3	**Tom Kite**	70	73	70	67	280
	Rik Massengale	70	73	67	70	280
5	**Hale Irwin**	70	74	70	68	282
=6	**David Graham**	75	67	73	69	284
	Lou Graham	75	71	69	69	284
=8	**Ben Crenshaw**	70	69	69	76	285
	Ray Floyd	70	72	71	71	285
	Hubert Green	67	74	72	72	285
	Don January	69	76	69	71	285
	Gene Littler	71	72	73	69	285

April 7–10, 1977 continued

	John Schlee	75	73	69	68	285
=14	**Billy Casper**	72	72	73	69	286
	Jim Colbert	72	71	69	74	286
	Rod Funseth	72	67	74	73	286
	Jerry Pate	70	72	74	70	286
	Tom Weiskopf	73	71	71	71	286
=19	**George Archer**	74	74	69	70	287
	Andy Bean	74	70	71	72	287
	Danny Edwards	72	74	68	73	287
	Lee Elder	76	68	72	70	287
	Gary Player	71	70	72	74	287
=24	**Billy Kratzert**	69	71	78	70	288
	Andy North	74	74	71	69	288
	Arnold Palmer	76	71	71	70	288
	Bob Wynn	75	73	70	70	288
=28	**Isao Aoki**	73	76	70	70	289
	Bruce Lietzke	73	71	72	73	289
	Jerry McGee	73	73	72	71	289

April 6–9, 1978

1	**Gary Player**	72	72	69	64	277
=2	**Rod Funseth**	73	66	70	69	278
	Hubert Green	72	69	65	72	278
	Tom Watson	73	68	68	69	278
=5	**Wally Armstrong**	72	70	70	68	280
	Billy Kratzert	70	74	67	69	280
7	**Jack Nicklaus**	72	73	69	67	281
8	**Hale Irwin**	73	67	71	71	282
=9	**David Graham**	75	69	67	72	283
	Joe Inman Jr	69	73	72	69	283
=11	**Don January**	72	70	72	70	284
	Jerry McGee	71	73	71	69	284
	Tom Weiskopf	72	71	70	71	284
=14	**Peter Oosterhuis**	74	70	70	71	285
	Lee Trevino	70	69	72	74	285
=16	**Ray Floyd**	76	71	71	68	286
	Lindy Miller (a)	74	71	70	71	286
=18	**Steve Ballesteros**	74	71	68	74	287
	Tom Kite	71	74	71	71	287
	Gill Morgan	73	73	70	71	287
	Jerry Pate	72	71	72	72	287
	Ed Sneed	74	70	70	73	287
	Lanny Wadkins	74	70	73	70	287
=24	**Miller Barber**	75	67	73	73	288
	Andy Bean	76	68	73	71	288
	Gene Littler	72	68	70	78	288
	Leonard Thompson	72	69	75	72	288
28	**Bobby Cole**	77	70	70	72	289
=29	**Gary Brewer**	73	71	69	77	290
	Mac McLendon	72	72	72	74	290
	Bill Rogers	76	70	68	76	290

April 12–15, 1979

** Fuzzy Zoeller beat Ed Sneed and Tom Watson in the suden-death play-off at the second extra hole.*

1	**Fuzzy Zoeller**	70	71	69	70	280
=2	**Ed Sneed**	68	67	69	76	280
	Tom Watson	68	71	70	71	280
4	**Jack Nicklaus**	69	71	72	69	281
5	**Tom Kite**	71	72	68	72	283
6	**Bruce Lietzke**	67	75	68	74	284
=7	**Craig Stadler**	69	66	74	76	285
	Leonard Thompson	68	70	73	74	285
	Lanny Wadkins	73	69	70	73	285

April 12–15, 1979 continued

=10	**Hubert Green**	74	69	72	71	286
	Gene Littler	74	71	69	72	286
=12	**Seve Ballesteros**	72	68	73	74	287
	Miller Barber	75	64	72	76	287
	Jack Newton	70	72	69	76	287
	Andy North	72	72	74	69	287
	Lee Trevino	73	71	70	73	287
=17	**Lee Elder**	73	70	74	71	288
	Ray Floyd	70	68	73	77	288
	Billy Kratzert	73	68	71	76	288
	Artie McNickel	71	72	74	71	288
	Gary Player	71	72	74	71	288
22	**J.C. Snead**	73	71	72	73	289
=23	**Bobby Clampett**	73	71	73	73	290
	Lou Graham	69	71	76	74	290
	Joe Inman Jr	68	71	76	75	290
	Hale Irwin	72	70	74	74	290
	Jim Simons	72	70	75	73	290
=28	**Tommy Aaron**	72	73	76	70	291
	Andy Bean	69	74	74	74	291
	Graham Marsh	71	72	73	75	291

April 10–13, 1980

1	**Seve Ballesteros**	66	69	68	72	275
=2	**Gibby Gilbert**	70	74	68	67	279
	Jack Newton	68	74	69	68	279
4	**Hubert Green**	68	74	71	67	280
5	**David Graham**	66	73	72	70	281
=6	**Ben Crenshaw**	76	70	68	69	283
	Ed Fiori	71	70	69	73	283
	Tom Kite	69	71	74	69	283
	Larry Nelson	69	72	73	69	283
	Jerry Pate	72	68	76	67	283
	Gary Player	71	71	71	70	283
=12	**Andy Bean**	74	72	68	70	284
	Tom Watson	73	69	71	71	284
=14	**Jim Colbert**	72	70	70	73	285
	Jack Renner	72	70	72	71	285
	J.C. Snead	73	69	69	74	285
=17	**Ray Floyd**	75	70	74	67	286
	Jay Haas	72	74	70	70	286
=19	**Billy Kratzert**	73	69	72	73	287
	Gil Morgan	74	71	75	67	287
	Calvin Peete	73	71	76	67	287
	Jim Simons	70	70	72	75	287
	Fuzzy Zoeller	72	70	70	75	287
24	**Andy North**	70	72	69	77	288
	Arnold Palmer	73	73	73	69	288
=26	**Keith Fergus**	72	71	72	74	289
	Lou Graham	71	74	71	73	289
	Jay Sigel (a)	71	71	73	74	289
	Craig Stadler	74	70	72	73	289
	Dave Stockton	74	70	76	69	289
	Lee Trevino	74	71	70	74	289

April 9–12, 1981

1	**Tom Watson**	71	68	70	71	280
=2	**Johnny Miller**	69	72	73	68	282
	Jack Nicklaus	70	65	75	72	282
4	**Greg Norman**	69	70	72	72	283
=5	**Tom Kite**	74	72	70	68	284
	Jerry Pate	71	72	71	70	284
7	**David Graham**	70	70	74	71	285
=8	**Ben Crenshaw**	71	72	70	73	286

April 9-12, 1981 continued

	Ray Floyd	75	71	71	69	286
	John Mahaffey	72	71	69	74	286
=11	**George Archer**	74	70	72	71	287
	Hubert Green	70	70	74	73	287
	Peter Jacobsen	71	70	72	74	287
	Bruce Lietzke	72	67	73	75	287
=15	**Gay Brewer**	75	68	71	74	288
	Bob Gilder	72	75	69	72	288
	Gary Player	73	73	71	71	288
	Jim Simons	70	75	71	72	288
=19	**Don Pooley**	71	75	72	71	289
	Curtis Strange	69	79	70	71	289
=21	**John Cook**	70	71	72	77	290
	Gil Morgan	74	73	70	73	290
	Calvin Peete	75	70	71	74	290
	Lanny Wadkins	72	71	71	76	290
=25	**Jim Colbert**	73	68	74	76	291
	Hale Irwin	73	74	70	74	291
	Wayne Levi	72	71	73	75	291

April 8–11, 1982

** Craig Stadler beat Dan Pohl in the sudden-death play-off at the first extra hole.*

1	**Craig Stadler***	75	69	67	73	284
2	**Dan Pohl**	75	75	67	67	284
=3	**Seve Ballesteros**	73	73	68	71	285
	Jerry Pate	74	73	67	71	285
=5	**Tom Kite**	76	69	73	69	287
	Tom Watson	77	69	70	71	287
=7	**Ray Floyd**	74	72	69	74	289
	Larry Nelson	79	71	70	69	289
	Curtis Strange	74	70	73	72	289
=10	**Andy Bean**	75	72	73	70	290
	Mark Hayes	74	73	73	70	290
	Tom Weiskopf	75	72	68	75	290
	Fuzzy Zoeller	72	76	70	72	290
14	**Bob Gilder**	79	71	66	75	291
=15	**Yataka Hagawa**	75	74	71	72	292
	Jack Nicklaus	69	77	71	75	292
	Gary Player	74	73	71	74	292
	Jim Simons	77	74	69	72	292
19	**David Graham**	73	77	70	73	293
=20	**Peter Jacobsen**	78	75	70	71	294
	Bruce Lietzke	76	75	69	74	294
	Jodie Mudd (a)	77	74	67	76	294
	Jack Renner	72	75	76	71	294
=24	**Ben Crenshaw**	74	80	70	71	295
	Danny Edwards	75	74	74	72	295
	Morris Hatalsky	73	77	75	70	295
	Wayne Levi	77	76	72	70	295
	Peter Oosterhuis	73	74	75	73	295
	John Schroeder	77	71	70	77	295

April 7–11, 1983

1	**Seve Ballesteros**	68	70	73	69	280
=2	**Ben Crenshaw**	76	70	70	68	284
	Tom Kite	70	72	73	69	284
=4	**Ray Floyd**	67	72	71	75	285
	Tom Watson	70	71	71	73	285
=6	**Hale Irwin**	72	73	72	69	286
	Craig Stadler	69	72	69	76	286
=8	**Gil Morgan**	67	70	76	74	287
	Dan Pohl	74	72	70	71	287
	Lanny Wadkins	73	70	73	71	287
11	**Scott Simpson**	70	73	72	73	288

April 7–11, 1983 continued

=12	**George Archer**	71	73	71	74	289
	Wayne Levi	72	70	74	73	289
	Johnny Miller	72	72	71	74	289
	J.C. Snead	68	74	74	73	289
=16	**Keith Fergus**	70	69	74	79	290
	Tommy Nakajima	72	70	72	76	290
	Jack Renner	67	75	78	70	290
19	**Isao Aoki**	70	76	74	71	291
=20	**Nick Faldo**	70	70	76	76	292
	Mark Hayes	71	73	76	71	292
	Peter Jacobsen	73	71	76	72	292
	Peter Oosterhuis	73	69	78	72	292
	Lee Trevino	71	72	72	77	292
	Tom Weiskopf	75	72	71	74	292
	Fuzzy Zoeller	70	74	76	72	292
=27	**Jay Haas**	73	69	73	78	293
	Scott Hoch	74	69	74	76	293
	Hal Sutton	73	73	70	77	293

April 12–15, 1984

1	**Ben Crenshaw**	67	72	70	68	277
2	**Tom Watson**	74	67	69	69	279
=3	**David Edwards**	71	70	72	67	280
	Gil Morgan	73	71	69	67	280
5	**Larry Nelson**	76	69	66	70	281
=6	**Ronnie Black**	71	74	69	68	282
	David Graham	69	70	70	73	282
	Tom Kite	70	68	69	75	282
	Mark Lye	69	66	73	74	282
10	**Fred Couples**	71	73	67	72	283
=11	**Rex Caldwell**	71	71	69	73	284
	Wayne Levi	71	72	69	72	284
	Larry Mize	71	70	71	72	284
	Jack Renner	71	73	71	69	284
=15	**Nick Faldo**	70	69	70	76	285
	Ray Floyd	70	73	70	72	285
	Calvin Peete	79	66	70	70	285
=18	**Andy Bean**	71	70	72	73	286
	Danny Edwards	72	71	70	73	286
	Jack Nicklaus	73	73	70	70	286
=21	**Jay Haas**	74	71	70	72	287
	Hale Irwin	70	71	74	72	287
	Gary Player	71	72	73	71	287
	Payne Stewart	76	69	68	74	287
=25	**Isao Aoki**	69	72	73	74	288
	George Archer	70	74	71	73	288
	Rick Fehr (a)	72	71	70	75	288
	Peter Jacobsen	72	70	75	71	288
	Greg Norman	75	71	73	69	288
	Tom Purtzer	69	74	76	69	288

April 11–14, 1985

1	**Bernhard Langer**	72	74	68	68	282
=2	**Seve Ballesteros**	72	71	71	70	284
	Ray Floyd	70	73	69	72	284
	Curtis Strange	80	65	68	71	284
5	**Jay Haas**	73	73	72	67	285
=6	**Gary Hallberg**	68	73	75	70	286
	Bruce Lietzke	72	71	73	70	286
	Jack Nicklaus	71	74	72	69	286
	Craig Stadler	73	67	76	70	286
=10	**Fred Couples**	75	73	69	70	287
	David Graham	74	71	71	71	287
	Lee Trevino	70	73	72	72	287

April 11–14, 1985 continued

	Tom Watson	69	71	75	72	287
=14	**Billy Kratzert**	73	77	69	69	288
	John Mahaffey	72	75	70	71	288
=16	**Isao Aoki**	72	74	71	72	289
	Gary Koch	72	70	73	74	289
=18	**Wayne Levi**	75	72	70	73	290
	Mark McCumber	73	73	79	65	290
	Sam Randolph (a)	70	75	72	73	290
	Tim Simpson	73	72	75	70	290
	Jim Thorpe	73	71	72	74	290
	Lanny Wadkins	72	73	72	73	290
24	**Mark O'Meara**	73	76	72	70	291
=25	**Andy Bean**	72	74	73	73	292
	Nick Faldo	73	73	75	71	292
	Sandy Lyle	78	65	76	73	292
	Johnny Miller	77	68	76	71	292
	Corey Pavin	72	75	75	70	292
	Payne Stewart	69	71	76	76	292

April 10–13, 1986

1	**Jack Nicklaus**	74	71	69	65	279
=2	**Tom Kite**	70	74	68	68	280
	Greg Norman	70	72	68	70	280
4	**Seve Ballesteros**	71	68	72	70	281
5	**Nick Price**	79	69	63	71	282
=6	**Jay Haas**	76	69	71	67	283
	Tom Watson	70	74	68	71	283
=8	**Tommy Nakajima**	70	71	71	72	284
	Payne Stewart	75	71	69	69	284
	Bob Tway	70	73	71	70	284
=11	**Donnie Hammond**	73	71	67	74	285
	Sandy Lyle	76	70	68	71	285
	Mark McCumber	76	67	71	71	285
	Corey Pavin	71	72	71	71	285
	Calvin Peete	75	71	69	70	285
=16	**Dave Barr**	70	77	71	68	286
	Ben Crenshaw	71	71	74	70	286
	Gary Koch	69	74	71	72	286
	Bernhard Langer	74	68	69	75	286
	Larry Mize	75	74	72	65	286
=21	**Curtis Strange**	73	73	69	72	287
	Fuzzy Zoeller	73	73	69	72	287
=23	**Tze-Chung Chen**	69	73	75	71	288
	Roger Maltbie	71	75	69	73	288
=25	**Bill Glasson**	72	74	72	71	289
	Peter Jacobsen	75	73	68	73	289
	Scott Simpson	76	72	67	74	289
=28	**Danny Edwards**	71	71	72	76	290
	David Graham	76	72	74	68	290
	Johnny Miller	74	70	77	69	290

April 9–12, 1987

** Larry Mize beat Seve Ballesteros and Greg Norman in the sudden-death play-off at the second extra hole.*

1	***Larry Mize**	70	72	72	71	285
=2	**Seve Ballesteros**	73	71	70	71	285
	Greg Norman	73	74	66	72	285
=4	**Ben Crenshaw**	73	74	66	72	285
	Roger Maltbie	76	66	70	74	285
	Jodie Mudd	74	72	71	69	285
=7	**Jay Haas**	72	72	72	73	289
	Bernhard Langer	71	72	70	76	289
	Jack Nicklaus	74	72	73	70	289
	Tom Watson	71	72	74	72	289

April 9–12, 1987 continued

	D.A. Weibring	72	75	71	71	289
=12	**Chip Beck**	75	72	70	73	290
	Tze-chung Chen	74	69	71	76	290
	Mark McCumber	75	71	69	75	290
	Curtis Strange	71	70	73	76	290
	Lanny Wadkins	73	72	70	75	290
=17	**Paul Azinger**	77	73	69	72	291
	Mark Calcavecchia	73	72	78	68	291
	Sandy Lyle	77	74	68	72	291
	Craig Stadler	74	74	72	71	291
21	**Bobby Wadkins**	76	69	73	74	292
=23	**Gary Koch**	76	75	72	70	293
	Nick Price	73	73	71	76	293
=24	**John Cook**	69	73	74	78	294
	Tom Kite	73	74	74	73	294
	Mark O'Meara	75	74	71	74	294
=27	**David Graham**	73	77	72	73	295
	Donnie Hammond	73	75	74	73	294
	Corey Pavin	71	71	81	72	294
	Scott Simpson	72	75	72	76	294
	Denis Watson	76	74	73	72	294
	Fuzzy Zoeller	76	71	76	72	294

April 7–10, 1988

1	**Sandy Lyle**	71	67	72	71	281
2	**Mark Calcavecchia**	71	69	72	70	282
3	**Craig Stadler**	76	69	70	68	283
4	**Ben Crenshaw**	72	73	67	72	284
=5	**Fred Couples**	75	68	71	71	285
	Greg Norman	77	73	71	64	285
	Don Pooley	71	72	72	70	285
8	**David Frost**	73	74	71	68	286
=9	**Bernhard Langer**	71	72	71	73	287
	Tom Watson	72	71	73	71	287
=11	**Seve Ballesteros**	73	72	70	73	288
	Ray Floyd	80	69	68	71	288
	Lanny Wadkins	74	75	69	70	288
=14	**Nick Price**	75	76	72	66	289
	Doug Tewell	75	73	68	73	289
=16	**Mark McNulty**	74	71	73	72	290
	Dan Pohl	78	70	69	73	290
	Fuzzy Zoeller	76	66	72	76	290
=19	**Tze-Chung Chen**	76	73	72	70	291
	Hubert Green	74	70	75	72	291
=21	**Chip Beck**	73	70	76	73	292
	Jack Nicklaus	75	73	72	72	292
	Curtis Strange	76	70	72	74	292
24	**Mark McCumber**	79	71	72	71	293
=25	**Isao Aoki**	74	74	73	73	294
	Gary Koch	72	73	74	75	294
	Payne Stewart	75	76	71	72	294
	Robert Wrenn	69	75	76	74	294
29	**Roger Davis**	77	72	71	75	295

April 6–9, 1989

** Nick Faldo beat Scott Hoch in the sudden-death play-off at the second extra hole.*

1	**Nick Faldo***	68	73	77	65	283
2	**Scott Hoch**	69	74	71	69	283
=3	**Ben Crenshaw**	71	72	70	71	284
	Greg Norman	74	75	68	67	284
5	**Seve Ballesteros**	71	72	73	69	285
6	**Mike Reid**	72	71	71	72	286
7	**Jodie Mudd**	73	76	72	76	287
=8	**Chip Beck**	74	76	70	68	288

April 6–9, 1989 continued

	Jose-Maria Olazabal	77	73	70	68	288
	Jeff Sluman	74	72	74	68	288
=11	**Fred Couples**	72	76	74	67	289
	Ken Green	74	69	73	73	289
	Mark O'Meara	74	71	72	72	289
=14	**Paul Azinger**	75	75	69	71	290
	Don Pooley	70	77	76	67	290
	Tom Watson	72	73	74	71	290
	Ian Woosnam	74	76	71	69	290
=18	**David Frost**	76	72	73	70	291
	Tom Kite	72	72	72	75	291
	Jack Nicklaus	73	74	73	71	291
	Jumbo Ozaki	71	75	73	72	291
	Curtis Strange	74	71	74	72	291
	Lee Trevino	67	74	81	69	291
=24	**Tom Purtzer**	71	76	73	72	292
	Payne Stewart	73	75	74	70	292
=26	**Bernhard Langer**	74	75	71	73	293
	Larry Mize	72	77	69	75	293
	Steve Pate	76	75	74	68	293
	Lanny Wadkins	76	71	73	73	293
	Fuzzy Zoeller	76	74	69	74	293

April 5–8, 1990

** Nick Faldo beat Ray Floyd in the sudden-death play-off at the second extra hole.*

1	**Nick Faldo***	71	72	66	69	278
2	**Ray Floyd**	70	68	68	72	278
=3	**John Hudson**	66	74	68	75	283
	Lanny Wadkins	72	73	70	68	283
5	**Fred Couples**	74	69	72	69	284
6	**Jack Nicklaus**	72	70	69	74	285
=7	**Seve Ballesteros**	74	73	68	71	286
	Bill Britton	68	74	71	73	286
	Bernhard Langer	70	73	69	74	286
	Scott Simpson	74	71	68	73	286
	Curtis Strange	70	73	71	72	286
	Tom Watson	77	71	67	71	286
13	**Jose-Maria Olazabal**	72	73	68	74	287
=14	**Ben Crenshaw**	72	74	73	69	288
	Scott Hoch	71	68	73	76	288
	Tom Kite	75	73	66	74	288
	Larry Mize	70	76	71	71	288
	Ronan Rafferty	72	74	69	73	288
	Craig Stadler	72	70	74	72	288
=20	**Mark Calcavecchia**	74	73	73	69	289
	Steve Jones	77	69	72	71	289
	Fuzzy Zoeller	72	74	73	70	289
23	**Jumbo Ozaki**	70	71	77	72	290
=24	**Donnie Hammond**	71	74	75	71	291
	Gary Player	73	74	68	76	291
	Lee Trevino	78	69	72	72	291
=27	**Wayne Grady**	72	75	72	73	292
	Andy North	71	73	77	71	292
	Jeff Sluman	78	68	75	71	292

April 11–14, 1991

1	**Ian Woosnam**	72	66	67	72	277
2	**Jose-Maria Olazabal**	68	71	69	70	278
=3	**Ben Crenshaw**	70	73	68	68	279
	Steve Pate	72	73	69	65	279
	Lanny Wadkins	67	71	70	71	279
	Tom Watson	68	68	70	73	279
=7	**Ian Baker-Finch**	71	70	69	70	280
	Andrew Magee	70	72	68	70	280

	April 11–14, 1991 continued					
	Jodie Mudd	70	70	71	69	280
=10	**Hale Irwin**	70	70	75	66	281
	Tommy Nakajima	74	71	67	69	281
=12	**Mark Calcavecchia**	70	68	77	67	282
	Nick Faldo	72	73	67	70	282
	Billy Mayfair	72	72	72	66	282
	Craig Stadler	70	72	71	69	282
	Fuzzy Zoeller	70	70	75	67	282
=17	**Ray Floyd**	71	68	71	73	283
	Jim Gallagher Jr	67	74	71	71	283
	Peter Jacobsen	73	70	68	72	283
	Mark McCumber	67	71	73	72	283
	Larry Mize	72	71	66	74	283
=22	**Seve Ballesteros**	75	70	69	70	284
	Steve Elkington	72	69	74	69	284
	Rocco Mediate	72	69	71	70	284
	Corey Pavin	73	70	69	72	284
	Scott Simpson	69	73	69	73	284
=27	**Jay Don Blake**	74	72	68	71	285
	Mark O'Meara	74	68	72	71	285
=29	**Morris Hatalsky**	71	72	70	73	286
	John Huston	73	72	71	70	286
	Jeff Sluman	71	71	72	72	286

April 9–12, 1992

1	**Fred Couples**	69	67	69	70	275
2	**Ray Floyd**	69	68	69	71	277
3	**Corey Pavin**	72	71	68	67	278
=4	**Mark O'Meara**	74	67	69	70	280
	Jeff Sluman	65	74	70	71	280
=6	**Ian Baker-Finch**	70	69	68	74	281
	Nolan Henke	70	71	70	70	281
	Larry Mize	73	69	71	68	281
	Greg Norman	70	70	73	68	281
	Steve Pate	73	71	70	67	281
	Nick Price	70	71	67	73	281
	Ted Schultz	68	69	72	72	281
=13	**Nick Faldo**	71	72	68	71	282
	Wayne Grady	68	75	71	68	282
	Bruce Lietzke	69	72	68	73	282
	Craig Parry	69	66	69	78	282
	Dillard Pruitt	75	68	70	69	282
	Scott Simpson	70	71	71	70	282
=19	**Billy Ray Brown**	70	74	70	69	283
	John Daly	71	71	73	68	283
	Mike Hulbert	68	74	71	70	283
	Andrew Magee	73	70	70	70	283
	Ian Woosnam	69	66	73	75	283
	Fuzzy Zoeller	71	70	73	69	283
=25	**Bruce Fleisher**	73	70	72	69	284
	Jim Gallagher Jr	74	68	71	71	284
	John Hudson	69	73	3	69	284
	Davis Love III	68	72	72	72	284
	Craig Stadler	70	71	70	73	284
	D.A. Weibring	71	68	72	73	284

April 8–11, 1993

1	**Bernhard Langer**	68	70	69	70	277
2	**Chip Beck**	72	67	72	70	281
=3	**John Daly**	70	71	73	69	283
	Steve Elkington	71	70	71	71	283
	Tom Lehman	67	75	73	68	283
	Lanny Wadkins	69	72	71	71	283
=7	**Dan Forsman**	69	69	73	73	284

	April 8–11, 1993 continued					
	Jose-Maria Olazabal	70	72	74	68	284
=9	**Brad Faxon**	74	70	72	69	285
	Payne Stewart	74	70	72	69	285
=11	**Seve Ballesteros**	74	70	71	71	286
	Ray Floyd	68	71	74	73	286
	Anders Forsbrand	71	74	75	66	286
	Corey Pavin	67	75	73	71	286
	Scott Simpson	72	71	71	72	286
	Fuzzy Zoeller	75	67	71	73	286
=17	**Mark Calcavecchia**	71	70	74	72	287
	Jeff Sluman	71	72	71	73	287
	Howard Twitty	70	71	73	73	287
	Ian Woosnam	71	4	73	69	287
=21	**Russ Cochran**	70	69	73	76	288
	Fred Couples	72	70	74	72	288
	Sandy Lyle	73	71	71	73	288
	Jeff Maggert	70	67	75	76	288
	Larry Mize	67	74	74	73	288
	Mark O'Meara	75	69	73	71	288
=27	**Nolan Henke**	76	69	71	73	289
	Hale Irwin	74	69	74	72	289
	Jack Nicklaus	67	75	76	71	289
	Joey Sindelar	72	69	76	72	289

April 6–9, 1994

1	**Jose-Maria Olazabal**	74	67	69	69	279
2	**Tom Lehman**	70	70	69	72	281
3	**Larry Mize**	68	71	72	71	282
4	**Tom Kite**	69	72	71	71	283
=5	**Jay Haas**	72	72	72	69	285
	Jim McGovern	72	70	71	72	285
	Loren Roberts	75	68	72	70	285
=8	**Ernie Els**	74	67	74	71	286
	Corey Pavin	71	72	73	70	286
=10	**Ian Baker-Finch**	71	71	71	74	287
	Ray Floyd	71	74	71	72	287
	John Huston	72	72	74	69	287
13	**Tom Watson**	70	71	73	74	288
14	**Dan Forsman**	74	66	76	73	289
=15	**Chip Beck**	71	71	75	74	291
	Brad Faxon	71	73	73	74	291
	Mark O'Meara	75	70	76	70	291
=18	**Seve Ballesteros**	70	76	75	71	292
	Ben Crenshaw	74	73	73	72	292
	David Edwards	73	72	73	74	292
	Bill Glasson	72	73	75	72	292
	Hale Irwin	73	68	79	72	292
	Greg Norman	70	70	75	77	292
	Lanny Wadkins	73	74	73	72	292
=25	**Bernhard Langer**	74	74	72	73	293
	Jeff Sluman	74	75	71	73	293
=27	**Scott Simpson**	74	74	73	73	294
	Vijay Singh	70	75	74	75	294
	Curtis Strange	74	70	75	75	294

April 6–9, 1995

1	**Ben Crenshaw**	70	67	69	68	274
2	**Davis Love III**	69	69	71	66	275
=3	**Jay Haas**	71	64	72	70	277
	Greg Norman	73	68	68	68	277
=5	**Steve Elkington**	73	67	67	72	279
	David Frost	66	71	71	71	279
=7	**Scott Hoch**	69	67	71	73	280
	Phil Mickelson	66	71	70	73	280

April 6–9, 1995 continued

9	**Curtis Strange**	72	71	65	73	281
=10	**Fred Couples**	71	69	67	75	282
	Brian Henninger	70	68	68	76	282
=12	**Lee Janzen**	69	69	74	71	283
	Kenny Perry	73	70	71	69	283
=14	**Hale Irwin**	69	72	71	72	284
	Jose-Maria Olazabal	66	74	72	72	284
	Tom Watson	73	70	69	72	284
=17	**Paul Azinger**	70	72	73	70	285
	Brad Faxon	76	69	69	71	285
	Ray Floyd	71	70	70	74	285
	John Huston	70	66	72	77	285
	Colin Montgomerie	71	69	76	69	285
	Corey Pavin	67	71	72	75	285
	Ian Woosnam	69	72	71	73	285
=24	**David Edwards**	69	73	73	71	286
	Nick Faldo	70	70	71	75	286
	David Gilford	67	73	75	71	286
	Loren Roberts	72	69	72	73	286
	Duffy Waldorf	74	69	67	76	286

April 11–14, 1996

1	**Nick Faldo**	69	67	73	67	276
2	**Greg Norman**	63	69	71	78	281
3	**Phil Mickelson**	65	73	72	72	282
4	**Frank Nobilo**	71	71	72	69	283
=5	**Scott Hoch**	67	73	73	71	284
	Duffy Waldorf	72	71	69	72	284
=7	**Davis Love III**	72	71	74	68	285
	Jeff Maggert	71	73	72	69	285
	Corey Pavin	75	66	73	71	285
=10	**David Frost**	70	68	74	74	286
	Scott McCarron	70	70	72	74	286
=12	**Ernie Els**	71	71	72	73	287
	Lee Janzen	68	71	75	73	287
	Bob Tway	67	72	76	72	287
=15	**Mark Calcavecchia**	71	73	71	73	288
	Fred Couples	78	68	71	71	288
17	**John Huston**	71	71	71	76	289
=18	**Paul Azinger**	70	74	76	70	290
	David Duval	73	72	69	76	290
	Tom Lehman	75	70	72	73	290
	Mark O'Meara	72	71	75	72	290
	Nick Price	71	75	70	74	290
=23	**Larry Mize**	75	71	77	68	291
	Loren Roberts	71	73	72	75	291
=25	**Brad Faxon**	69	77	72	74	292
	Ray Floyd	70	74	77	71	292
=27	**Bob Estes**	71	71	79	72	293
	Justin Leonard	72	74	75	72	293

April 10–13, 1997

1	**Tiger Woods**	70	66	65	69	270
2	**Tom Kite**	77	69	66	70	282
3	**Tommy Tolles**	72	72	72	67	283
4	**Tom Watson**	75	68	69	72	284
=5	**Constantino Rocca**	71	69	70	75	285
	Paul Stankowski	68	74	79	74	285
=7	**Fred Couples**	72	69	73	72	286
	Bernhard Langer	72	72	74	68	286
	Justin Leonard	76	69	71	70	286
	Davis Love III	72	71	72	71	286
	Jeff Sluman	74	67	72	73	286
=12	**Steve Elkington**	76	72	72	67	287

April 10-13, 1997 continued

	Per-Ulrik Johannson	72	73	73	69	287
	Tom Lehman	73	76	69	69	287
	Jose-Maria Olazabal	71	70	74	72	287
	Willie Wood	72	76	71	68	287
=17	**Mark Calcavecchia**	74	73	72	69	288
	Ernie Els	73	70	71	74	288
	Fred Funk	74	73	69	72	288
	Vijay Singh	75	74	69	70	288
=21	**Stuart Appleby**	72	76	70	71	289
	John Huston	67	77	75	70	289
	Jesper Parnevik	73	72	71	73	289
=24	**Nick Price**	71	71	75	74	291
	Lee Westwood	77	71	74	73	291
=26	**Lee Janzen**	72	73	74	73	292
	Craig Stadler	77	72	71	72	292
=28	**Paul Azinger**	69	73	77	74	293
	Jim Furyk	74	75	72	72	293

April 9–12, 1998

1	**Mark O'Meara**	74	70	68	67	279
=2	**Fred Couples**	69	70	71	70	280
	David Duval	71	68	74	67	280
4	**Jim Furyk**	76	70	67	68	281
5	**Paul Azinger**	71	72	69	70	282
=6	**Jack Nicklaus**	73	72	70	68	283
	David Toms	75	72	72	64	283
=8	**Darren Clarke**	76	73	67	69	285
	Tiger Woods	71	72	72	70	285
	Justin Leonard	74	73	69	69	285
	Colin Montgomerie	71	75	69	70	285
=12	**Jose-Maria Olazabal**	70	73	71	72	286
	Jay Haas	72	71	71	72	286
	Per-Ulrik Johansson	74	75	67	70	286
	Phil Mickelson	74	69	69	74	286
=16	**Scott Hoch**	70	71	73	73	287
	Ernie Els	75	70	70	72	287
	Ian Woosnam	74	71	72	70	287
	Scott McCarron	73	71	72	71	287
	Mark Calcavecchia	74	74	69	70	287
=21	**Matt Kuchar (a)**	72	76	68	72	288
	Willie Wood	74	74	70	70	288
=23	**Jeff Maggert**	72	73	72	72	289
	Stewart Cink	74	76	69	70	289
	John Huston	77	71	70	71	289
=26	**David Frost**	72	73	74	71	290
	Brad Faxon	73	74	71	72	290
	Steve Jones	75	70	75	70	290
29	**Michael Bradley**	73	74	72	72	291
30	**Steve Elkington**	75	75	71	71	292

April 8–11, 1999

1	**Jose-Maria Olazabal**	70	66	73	71	280
2	**Davis Love III**	69	72	70	71	282
3	**Greg Norman**	71	68	71	73	283
=4	**Bob Estes**	71	72	69	72	284
	Steve Pate	71	75	65	73	284
=6	**David Duval**	71	74	70	70	285
	Carlos Franco	72	72	68	73	285
	Phil Mickelson	74	69	71	71	285
	Nick Price	69	72	72	72	285
	Lee Westwood	75	71	68	71	285
=11	**Steve Elkington**	72	70	71	74	287
	Bernhard Langer	76	66	72	73	287
	Colin Montgomerie	70	72	71	74	287

THE USPGA CHAMPIONSHIP

The fourth major

From its position in the calendar to its priority status among the leading players, the USPGA Championship has long been ranked as the fourth major in every sense. Millions of words have been expounded in recent years theorizing on how it could be elevated to the level of the other three majors; the most popular suggestion has long been to revert to its old format of matchplay, which would at least give it an identity. But with the World Matchplay Championship starting up in California in February 1999, and featuring the top 64 players, that is no longer an option, and the tournament will continue for the foreseeable future as a strokeplay event, set in the dog days of August to avoid any clash with the American football season.

That said, while there cannot be a top player who would rather win the PGA before the other three, there are a number of golfers who would do anything to have the rather large and cumbersome Rodman Wanamaker Cup in their trophy rooms. Arnold Palmer is one; Tom Watson is another. For many years this title was the one glaring omission on their illustrious CVs and, try as they might, they could not break the spell. Both had near things, of which more later.

In recent years the PGA of America have done their level best to put on the best championship they can, and there is no doubt that, like the other three majors, it possesses a certain cachet not available to any other tournament. For a long time the charge was that they aped the United States Golf Association, setting up the course in the same way as the latter organization did for the US Open; then they took it to patently unsuitable venues, where either the weather was too hot or humid, or the golf course had been awarded the event for commercial rather than meritorious reasons. To hold the tournament in Florida in August, as they did in 1987, for example, was frankly stupid.

Those mistakes, however, appear to have been rectified. Some of the recent venues have been many of the classic courses in America: Winged Foot, for example, or Medinah. Skilfully they have interspersed these venues with some hidden gems; Sahalee in 1998 was a positive revelation.

They have also been unwittingly helped by the various professional tours around the world, for the more they clutter the schedules with events the more people turn to the four majors for a yardstick. And the great thing is you cannot buy a major; a sponsor can put up a $10 million first prize if he is daft enough, but what he cannot purchase is history and tradition, the illustrious list of names on Wanamaker's trophy; names like Hagen, Snead, Nelson, Nicklaus and Trevino.

That is why, whatever happens in these money-obsessed times for the game, the PGA will always be part of the Grand Slam, and thus one of the four most cherished events in golf.

Birth of the PGA

Rodman Wanamaker was a highly successful New York salesman who also took a keen interest in both golf and golf administration. As the explosion of clubs continued across America, all with their own professional, it became obvious that they would need organizing into regional bodies under a national umbrella. This led to the formation of the Professional Golfers' Association of America, and Wanamaker presented a trophy for a national championship.

His motives were not entirely altruistic. As a prime mover in the setting-up of the PGA, he got the concession to sell golf merchandise at a cheaper rate than the pros could manage.

The first PGA was held in 1916. It was decided that the event should have a matchplay format, thereby giving the professionals an alternative to the staple diet of strokeplay. The inspiration for this idea came, as ever, from Britain, where the British PGA Matchplay Championship, sponsored by the *News of the World*, was proving a great hit with the players. The first winner of the US version was a naturalized American. Jim Barnes was born in Cornwall but had lived in San Francisco for a decade. His opponent in the final was the Scot, Jock Hutchinson, who had also finished runner-up in the US Open. The match was a close affair, with Barnes edging it on the final hole.

The event was hailed as a great success. Two rounds of strokeplay had been required to whittle down the qualifiers to an even 32, with every match taking place over 36 holes. But just as plans for a second PGA were being made, so America entered the First World War.

It would be three years before the PGA was resurrected at Engineers Country Club on Long Island, NY. The time away had done nothing to blunt Barnes's matchplay skills. In 1919 he demolished the opposition, and never needed to go beyond the 34th hole in any round. His opponent in the final was Fred McLeod, and he was easily disposed of by a six-and-five margin. Barnes's prize was the same as in 1916: $500. In 1920 Hutchinson, from St Andrews, got his name on the trophy, beating Douglas Edgar in the final. Almost unbelievably, it was one of only two victories for British-born golfers in the event.

Three Americans in particular would dominate for the rest of the 1920s. There were two wins each for Leo Diegel and

Leo Diegel – a two-time winner in the 1920s

Gene Sarazen, but above all this became Walter Hagen's tournament, his party piece, and accordingly he put it on the map. In all he would win it on five occasions, including four in a row from 1924 to 1927. Hagen remains the only 20th-century golfer to have won any of the four blue-riband events in four successive years.

Widened entry qualifications

In 1921 the criterion for entry was changed, with the 32 qualifiers comprising the top 31 from the US Open, plus the defending champion, Hutchinson. He departed in round two, losing heavily to the 19-year-old Sarazen. But the two men who had finished first and second in that US Open – Barnes and Hagen – emphasized their shot-making skills by making prodigious progress. Fortunately for the watching spectators, they were in opposite halves of the draw, to set up a truly heavyweight clash in the final. Barnes reached as far by winning his matches by the respective margins of three and two, eight and seven, eleven and nine, and five and four. Hagen conserved his energy as well – he defeated his opponents six and four, six and five, eight and seven, and five and four.

Who would prevail in the final? It was the irrepressible Hagen – reversing their positions at the US Open – although appropriately it was his closest match of the week as Barnes took him to the 16th hole in the afternoon play before succumbing three and two. The following year Sarazen became the first player to win two major championships in the same season, although they were not recognized as such at the time, of course. Still, the two that he won, the US Open and the PGA, were two of the three biggest professional tournaments in America at the time – the other prized trophy being the Western Open – and emphasized the promise of the small, but immensely pugnacious, 20-year-old.

In 1923, the final of the PGA turned out to be one of the great matchplay contests of all time. Sarazen had already emphasized his determination to hang on to the trophy by beating Barnes in a tense quarter-final that went to the 36th hole. Now he was up against Hagen in the final.

For Sarazen this was a wonderful opportunity to quieten some of the criticism that had followed his victory a year earlier. Because Hagen had not entered – he was probably off somewhere raking in lucrative exhibition dollars – some commentators had sniped that it was a hollow victory. Well, no such words could be written were he to win this time.

The match lived up to every expectation, with the lead switching back and forth. What a wonderful contrast of opposites they made; the stylishly flamboyant Hagen against the quietly determined Sarazen. As the match came to the closing stages it was Sarazen who held the upper hand. Three up with a handful of holes to play, he was still two up with just three to go. But the "Haig" clawed his way back into the match. He won both the 34th and 35th holes to square matters, and when the 36th was halved in pars the PGA had its first final that had gone to extra holes.

The 37th was halved as well, and then at the 38th came the sort of dramatic scenario that only matchplay really produces. Hagen had struck an imperious drive while Sarazen had hooked into a savage lie. Now all that Hagen appeared to have to do was put the ball on the green to claim victory; before he could do that, Sarazen gave his approach a ferocious hack. To the amazement of everyone watching, and above all Hagen, the ball flew straight as an arrow towards the pin, stopping no more than two feet from the hole. It was a wondrous blow, and so flummoxed Hagen that he dumped his approach into a bunker and lost the match. Sarazen had completed a successful defence.

Hagen supreme

How would Hagen react to such a devastating loss? A man with a less equable temperament may well have struggled, of course, ever to be a factor in golf again. The "Haig", meanwhile, had probably forgotten the loss a week after it had happened. Certainly, by the time he returned the following year his self-confidence was again unswerving, and would remain so for each of the next four years. First he defeated Barnes once more in the final, this time by a margin of just two holes; then "wild" Bill Mehlhorn was comfortably despatched, followed by Leo Diegel in 1926. The best match of all came in 1927, a close encounter against Joe Turnesa that went down to the final putt on the final green. But once more it was Hagen who prevailed, to create his own unique moment in golfing history.

Not that Hagen was getting too excited about it all, of course. In 1928 he had to be cajoled to enter to try to win it for a fifth time in a row. Apparently an exhibition match called, offering many more dollars than even first prize could summon. Not surprisingly given that frame of mind, Hagen never progressed beyond the quarter-final, although it was a good man who beat him: Leo Diegel, who won the final against Al Espinosa. There was one problem, however. Hagen had lost the trophy. "Where did you last see it?" Diegel wanted to know. "In a taxi?" Hagen ventured. It would be 1930 before it was found in a Detroit sports-goods factory. At least Diegel was still the rightful owner, having completed a successful defence. Once more he had defeated Hagen – well, he had every motivation to do so, didn't he? – and this would be the last year in which the great man would be a factor. Indeed his 1929 Open Championship win would be his last major victory. Still, he had left an indelible imprint on the decade. At a time when Bobby Jones was at his peak, Hagen had averaged a major championship a year for the period from 1919 to 1929. Only Jack Nicklaus would win more.

Denny Shute – back-to-back titles in 1936 and 1937

Byron Nelson holes a putt on the final green in the 1940 championship to deny Snead a victory for the second successive year

In 1930 the professionals must have been pleased that the PGA was not open to amateurs to enter, for otherwise Bobby Jones would probably have walked off with that title as well. This was the year of his Impregnable Quadrilateral, of course, and naturally it dominated all golf talk. Accordingly the PGA that year was a low-key affair, although the final itself was a fine match – albeit a bit of a grudge one – between Tommy Armour and Gene Sarazen. Armour, the "Silver Scot", became the last British-born winner of the event, taking the title on the home green by the slimmest of margins.

Sarazen's swansong

Sarazen, however, did have one more victory left in him. It came in 1933 and it was a sweet moment, for Armour had been shouting his mouth off, claiming that Sarazen was past his best. "Pretty good for a washed-up golfer," was Sarazen's opening remark to the Press, after winning in the final by a margin of five and four against Willie Goggin. It was his sixth major championship, with the 1935 Masters, of course, still to come.

The vagaries of matchplay were amply demonstrated in 1936. By now the event featured the leading 64 players, comprising 63 qualifiers following 36 holes of strokeplay plus the defending champion. Hagen was back, but both he and Diegel did not even make the matchplay stages. Then Sarazen, Armour and another former champion, Paul Runyon, were beaten in the first round. It left the way clear, therefore, for Denny Shute to win the first of back-to-back PGA titles.

In 1938 a young Sam Snead had a demoralizing introduction to the PGA. True, he made it to the final, which was a feat in itself, but once there he was no match for Paul Runyon, who played the golf of his life to win the title for a second time by the astonishing score of eight and seven. It would be the biggest winning margin in all the years that the PGA was a matchplay event.

Snead would lose again in the final in 1940 to Byron Nelson, although this was an altogether much tighter affair, with the latter holing a putt on the home green to win. Two years later Snead finally made his breakthrough in the majors, and just in the nick of time, too. On the day he was due to play in the final, Snead was supposed to sign up for the US Navy, and it needed some special persuasion from the recruiting officer to allow him a few days' extra leave. He made them tell, winning the final two and one against Jim Turnesa. Now, with the majors breakthrough having been made, he joined the US fleet bound for the Second World War.

The PGA resumed after a gap of just one year, with the 1944 event producing a huge upset as the 10–1 outsider, Bob Hamilton, defeated Byron Nelson in the final. Nelson made amends the following year, and while the field remained

Walter Burkemo – a surprise winner in 1953, the year that Ben Hog

e to play in the Open Championship instead

under-strength he still had to beat major champions like the veteran Gene Sarazen, Denny Shute and Claude Harmon before he could claim the title. This, of course, was Nelson's big year, and the PGA was part of his extraordinary sequence when he won every tournament he entered between March and August – 11 in all.

During the war years a more compact format had been used, with just 32 qualifiers, but with everyone out of uniform by 1946 and America demob-happy, the 1941 set-up – with 64 going through to the matchplay stages – was adopted once more. No one appeared happier to be playing golf again than Ben Hogan. He ripped his opponents apart, and collected the title by winning his matches by the margins of, respectively, four and three, five and four, five and four, ten and nine (against Jimmy Demaret, too – that must have tested their friendship), and six and four in the final against Ed Oliver.

No golfer, of course, was more suited to matchplay golf than Hogan. It was not in his nature to betray any facial reaction, whatever the stroke he played, and imagine coming up against a player who seemingly did not notice what you were doing, much less be affected by it. Hogan won again in 1948, this time demolishing Mike Turnesa in the final by seven and six. How many matchplay titles he would have won but for his car accident, heaven only knows. What we do know is that the 36-holes-a-day format was simply too much for him when he returned to golf, which is reflected in the fact that he was never a factor in the event again.

In the decade left to the PGA as a matchplay tournament there were a couple more victories for Sam Snead, but that was about it of any note. In 1953 Hogan elected to play in the Open Championship rather than the PGA, which was an enormous blow to the prestige of the event. So was the victory that year for Walter Burkemo, a journeyman club professional who happened to hit paydirt that week.

Television forces strokeplay

The PGA felt the event was losing lustre when compared with what was happening with the other majors. Doug Ford won the 1955 edition, but his moment of fame came not with that victory but with his remarkable triumph in the 1957 Masters. Then television came along to twist the PGA's arm. Television has always disliked matchplay golf. There is all that uncertainty for one thing. They like to schedule a programme that will last from 2pm to 6pm, and they know that in strokeplay they can almost predict to the minute that they will fill that slot. But matchplay? Dear me, it could be over by four or it could go on until seven. What good is that?

Even in 1958 television was all-powerful, so the PGA made the switch from matchplay to strokeplay at their master's behest. The traditionalists were split in two at the switch. From being the best matchplay tournament in the world it had now become the fourth-most-important strokeplay event – at best. The critics felt the PGA had lost its unique reason for being part of the calendar, and also some of its prestige.

Against that there was the argument that the only fair format for deciding a major champion is 72 holes of strokeplay golf. Under such a regimen, the best golfer invariably wins; contrast that with matchplay, where a man can win one day despite shooting 78.

Even now the arguments rage back and forth, but on balance it has to be said that the PGA Championship has become a more important event because of the change. When someone like Hogan decides to come to Britain for the first time instead of staying put in America, then clearly something is wrong with the event at home. And in the early years of the strokeplay format there was a series of brilliant tournaments that lent credence to the change. The 1960s were not very old before it had been accepted as part of the modern Grand Slam, the fourth of the four majors. It was a leap up in prestige, from the days when Hagen would rather play in an exhibition match than participate, from when Hogan would rather board an ocean liner heading east.

The PGA of America must have felt fully vindicated in their decision following the first seven strokeplay tournaments. All were memorable, for a variety of different reasons. In 1958 Dow Finsterwald claimed the title in a thrilling finish. After three rounds Sam Snead held the lead, a two-shot advantage over Finsterwald. But the latter came through to win at Llanerch Country Club in Pennsylvania with a wonderful last round of 67.

The following year there was another dramatic come-from-behind triumph. Bob Rosburg trailed Jerry Barber by as many as nine shots at the half-way stage, but he made up the deficit with closing rounds of 68 and 66 to win by one. In 1960 the event had romance, as Jay Hebert emulated the achievement of his brother, Lionel, to win the PGA at Firestone.

In 1961 it had sentiment, and surely one of the most enthralling finishes to any major championship. With three holes to play, Jerry Barber appeared destined to finish second once more. He trailed Don January by four shots, with just three holes to play. Then amazing things began to happen. Barber holed from 18 feet for a birdie while January dropped a shot; Barber then holed from 35 feet for a par, while January dropped another shot. So when he came to the last, Barber still found himself in contention, although it was an outside chance given that his approach to the 18th at Olympia Fields was 60 feet from the hole. Remarkably, he sank it for his third big putt in a row, to force a play-off.

January could have been forgiven for thinking the game was up before he even headed out for 18 more holes the following day. He was certainly right if he thought this was a tournament that apparently he could not win. He shot 68 in the play-off, which normally would have been more than good enough to win such an event; Barber, however, fuelled by destiny, shot 67. It was to be the start of a remarkable few months for him. In October that year he captained the American Ryder Cup side and led them to an easy victory at Lytham.

Arrival of the Big Three

For 32 years the PGA Championship had been completely dominated by Americans, but in 1962 that was to change. This would be the year when the Big Three would totally impose themselves on the game, winning all four majors between them: Gary Player's contribution was the PGA at Aronimink, PA.

A week before the event a Player victory appeared to be the last thing that was likely to happen. The Open at Troon had finished just six days before the PGA was about to start and, as he headed for the plane to cross the Atlantic yet again, Player felt exhausted. He had not won a tournament for a while and he phoned his manager, Mark McCormack, to tell him that he did not think he could keep up his hectic jet-setting schedule. When he touched down at the course, a different Gary Player emerged.

Here was a course far removed from the exposed brutalities of Troon. It was exceptionally difficult, but the sun was shining, the fairways were lush, the course was lined with trees; as a consequence Player felt relaxed, and liked his chances from the start.

Scoring was not easy on a course that was over 7,000 yards long and possessed a tough par of 70. Player opened with a 72, but scores of 67 and 69 took him out in front. In the final round he had to contend with Bob Goalby and an excellent contest ensued. As Goalby made up ground with a series of unlikely birdie putts, so Player fended him off with birdies of his own. But by the 16th Goalby had drawn to within one shot. Both players had their chances for birdies on the final two holes, but pars were the scores that went down on their respective cards. Player had become the first non-American to win the PGA since Tommy Armour in 1930. In just four years he had won his third different major championship. He would complete the set with the US Open in 1965.

Dallas heat

Jack Nicklaus arrived at the Dallas Athletic Club for the 1963 PGA Championship feeling every bit as cheesed off with life as Gary Player had been the year before. The reasons were exactly the same. The PGA was once more scheduled too close to the Open to allow the players to fully do themselves justice. One of the reasons why Arnold Palmer would never win the event was that during his purple patch the tournament would run practically back-to-back with the Open – and he always gave everything he had in that event. There was simply not enough recovery time.

It was not the only reason for which Nicklaus arrived in Dallas with a weight on his mind. He had thrown away the Open at Lytham, or so he thought, by committing what he would later describe as his biggest mental blunder during all his years in the game. He was hardly in the right frame of mind to tackle another major so soon afterwards. Added to all that was the Texas heat, with the thermometer rising above 100 degrees every day. Put it this way: Gary Player did not even wear his all-black garb – that's how hot it was.

Again like Player, Nicklaus's attitude changed from the moment he stepped on to the first tee. That's the thing about the majors: they have this unique feel all of their own. Nicklaus shrugged off his fatigue to open with a 69, which left him just three strokes off the pace. For two rounds the front-runner was an unknown assistant professional called Dick Hart who predictably faded in the third round. Taking up the pace was Bruce Crampton, the tour's so-called ironman, on account of the number of tournaments in which he played. Crampton shot a fine third-round 75 to be two ahead of Dow Finsterwald. Nicklaus was three strokes back.

Playing with Crampton in the final round, Nicklaus instantly made inroads into that advantage with what became a statement of intent at the opening hole. A par five of 521 yards, Nicklaus smashed a drive and five iron to within 15 feet of the hole, and sank the putt for an eagle three.

For the first time all week he considered the possibility of winning. The thought pervaded his play all afternoon. Thriving on a piece of good fortune at the 4th, where his third shot ought to have finished in water, only to be luckily deflected on to dry land by a tree, Nicklaus continued to make inroads into Crampton's advantage. Soon he was ahead as they reached the back nine. At the 15th Nicklaus holed his longest putt all week, a 35-foot effort for a birdie. It gave him a two-shot lead.

At the 18th, thoughts of Lytham must have once more zoomed across his mind as he struck a poor drive into the undergrowth. Unlike at Lytham, this time he got his arithmetic right. He took his punishment, marked down a bogey, and won by two shots.

Nicklaus's second year as a professional had ended with his claiming the USPGA to go with the Masters. In just 24 months he had won all three of the American majors, a feat that only three other players before him had managed during the course of their entire lifetimes, let alone two years.

The 1964 PGA Championship saw Nicklaus defend the title in his own backyard. The venue was Columbus Country Club, just down the road from where he had learned to play the game. As ever, he was feeling fatigued following his second

Gary Player – on his way to becoming the first non-American to win the title for 32 years since Tommy Armour in 1930

straight near-thing the week before at the Open Championship. But at least he could now rest and prepare at a place called Home.

Nicklaus opened well, too, with a 67 that left him three shots behind the leader – a gifted sportsman called Bobby Nichols, who had quite a story of his own to tell. Nichols was a talented football and basketball player, when he was travelling in a car as a passenger which failed to take a bend properly and crashed. He suffered a broken pelvis, back injuries, concussion and other internal injuries. Nichols was paralysed from the waist down and lay in a coma for almost two weeks. In all he would spend over three months in hospital recovering from the accident.

At the end of his ordeal it was immediately clear that his career in his previous two sports was over, and now he had to look around for another one. He chose golf, and quickly showed the same aptitude. By 1960 he was good enough to turn professional and make it on to the US Tour. He won tournaments in 1962 and 1963, so when it came to leading the 1964 PGA it was hardly a fluke. Nichols followed his marvellous opening score with rounds of 71 and 69, and still led on a total of 208. Behind him, however, were two other players with good stories to tell. One was Nicklaus, the hometown boy; the other was Arnold Palmer, the most popular figure in golf, trying to win the one major championship that continued to elude him.

On the final day Palmer and Nicklaus did their best to make Nichols crack. Palmer shot 69 while Nicklaus matched his total of 274 with a wonderful 64. But Nichols held firm, returning a 67 of his own, to win by three shots with a new record score for the tournament. What happened to Bobby Nichols, who was then just 28? He continued to win a number of events, until in 1975 he was struck by lightning, along with Lee Trevino and Jerry Heard, while playing in the Western Open. The experience shook him up even more than his earlier car accident, and his form deserted him completely.

In 1967 the tournament produced a touching story as Don January shot 68 in the final round to match the total of 281 set by Don Massingale. And so they set out on an 18-hole play-off, and January would not have been human if the memory of the 1961 PGA had not fleetingly crossed his mind, the one he lost in a play-off to some amazing play from Jerry Barber. Now, at Columbine Country Club in Denver, he shot 69 in the play-off, which was actually a shot worse than the score he recorded and lost with in 1961. This time it was good enough for a two-stroke triumph, and a much-deserved success.

By 1968 people were beginning to have serious doubts about Arnold Palmer. He had not won a major championship for four long years, and more than that he had suffered some crushing losses, most notably his shattering defeat to Billy Casper in the 1966 US Open. He was still as popular as ever,

Gary Player – claimed his sixth major title with victory in 1972

but Palmer craved more than the attention; a true traditionalist, he wanted that PGA title. He had seen his peers, Jack Nicklaus and Gary Player, win all four majors. It was time he emulated them.

At Pecan Valley Country Club in San Antonio he opened with rounds of 71 and 69 to be two strokes off the lead, held by Frank Beard and Marty Fleckman. The same duo were still leading after the third round, having both shot 72s. Palmer, meanwhile, had matched them, and would have his chance on the final day.

This was particularly the case when the leading duo started to fade. Palmer had begun well, and now the challenge was coming from two other players with whom he had been tied after three rounds: Bob Charles and Julius Boros, who at 48 was trying to become the oldest winner of the event.

The trio continued to fight out a close one. For a while it looked as if Palmer would finally get his hands on the cherished Wanamaker trophy, but Boros would not back down. When it came to the last, Palmer needed to birdie the hole to force a play-off. He struck a wonderful approach to eight feet – but there was only anguish when the putt failed to drop. The magic touch of being able to stare down putts had well and truly gone.

Hostile crowds

In later life, Gary Player would describe his performance at the 1969 USPGA as the best of his life. Given that he finished runner-up to Raymond Floyd, it would appear on paper to be the oddest of choices. What bald, black-and-white statistics do not reveal was the demonstrations with which Player had to contend that year. The tournament took place in Dayton, OH at a time when civil rights were very much on the agenda. Player's participation in the event caused outrage when someone found an old cutting, which showed that he had some sympathy with the apartheid cause (he spent the rest of his life both in word and deed proving that he had been wrong). And in the third round, when he was paired with Jack Nicklaus – another target – the activists set to work.

On the 4th tee a programme was lobbed over the heads of some spectators and landed between Player's legs as he addressed the ball; as he walked between the 9th green and the 10th tee a cupful of ice was thrown in his face. When Player cornered the man and asked what he had ever done to him, he replied: "You're a damn' racist."

On the 10th green a man broke free from the crowd and made a beeline for Nicklaus, who protected himself with his putter. Both balls were thrown off the green and it was some time before play could be resumed. Nicklaus would say later that he had never been so scared in his life. Player responded as only he could; he holed the putt.

Player finished with a 71 that day, Nicklaus a 74, and while the latter had dropped from contention the former was a distant five behind the runaway leader, Floyd. In the last round Floyd and Player competed together under police escort. Player would hardly have been human if he had not scanned the faces of the crowd before every shot, trying to spy out the first sign of trouble. In the event there was none. There was, however, some typically defiant play from the South African, who made up four strokes on that day to push Floyd all the way.

For Arnold Palmer, the last big throw of the dice in the PGA would come in 1970. The venue was Southern Hills and on the final day he was charged with the task of trying to catch Dave Stockton. For three days Stockton had played imperious golf; he had shot two rounds of 70 and followed them with a 66 to lead by five. But over the last day he betrayed some signs of nerves and Palmer, now 41, was charging in a manner that was reminiscent of the Palmer of old. Sadly for the great man, the finishing tape came too soon. He had shot 70, Stockton a 73, and for the third and last time in his life he would finish second in the PGA.

In 1971 the tournament was held in February, and so for once became the first major of the year rather than the last. The reason for this was chiefly the venue. The tournament was held at PGA National in Florida to fulfil a contractual obligation, but an August date could not be countenanced on grounds that will be obvious to anyone who has ever spent a day in that state in August. Well, it could not be countenanced until the PGA of America actually went there in 1987 – but that's another story.

One man who was pleased with the change of date was Jack Nicklaus. Instead of having to prepare hurriedly for the tournament on its usual date so soon after the Open, now he had the whole of January and most of February to focus. It did not seem to have done him much good, mind, in the first round as he sprayed the ball everywhere from tee to green. Even when he was playing badly, however, Nicklaus very rarely defeated himself, and usually found a way to keep a score going. On this day he did miraculously well. Holing any number of single putts for pars, including the last three holes, he came in with a 69 and somehow was the first-round leader. He had had just 23 putts in total.

Naturally to play so badly and still to be leading infused Nicklaus with confidence. Instinctively he felt that this was to be his championship, the moment he completed the Grand Slam twice so to speak, for victory would mean that he would have won each of the four majors on at least two occasions.

In the second round Nicklaus shot another 69 and was again leading; when he followed that with a 70, he was four strokes ahead of the field. Perhaps he relaxed over the opening 11 holes of the last round. Whatever the case, he had thrown away all but one shot of his advantage, playing the stretch in a decidedly sloppy three over par. The 12th hole won him the tournament. A par five, Nicklaus used his vast strength to find the green in two blows, and two putted for his birdie. Four pars followed before another birdie at the next par five, the 17th. Billy Casper had finished with two birdies for a 68, but now it was to no avail. A par at the last gave Nicklaus a 73 and victory by two shots.

For Gary Player, the moment of truth in the 1972 PGA at Oakland Hills came with three holes to play in the final round. Player had shot rounds of 71, 71 and 67 to open up a three-stroke lead. But that had all evaporated when he missed a short putt at the 15th, and now there was a host of other golfers who were in with a chance of winning. At the 16th Player tried to erase the thought of the missed putt, the thought of finishing second or worse from his mind, but could not. His drive drifted on the wind, close to a willow tree which rested on the edge of a lake that curves around and protects the green. Now Player was in quite a spot. He knew he could not play too safe because then he would be playing catch-up on the final two holes, and no one can do that given the final pair at Oakland Hills.

The distance was 152 yards, and if it had been lying on the fairway Player would have taken an eight iron. But he needed to get the ball airborne quickly and thrashed at it with a nine iron, hoping against hope that he cleared the water. When he made contact with the ball he knew instinctively that it was going to be his day, that on this occasion all fears of finishing second had been banished. The ball finished four feet from the hole, and he sank it for what proved to be a crucial birdie. He would eventually win by two from Tommy Aaron and Jim Jamieson to claim his sixth major championship.

Nicklaus's milestone

The 1973 PGA was held in Jack Nicklaus's home state of Ohio, at Canterbury. By this stage of his career Nicklaus had won 11 major championships and was tied with Walter Hagen for first place on the all-time list. Yet it was another Columbus resident who began the tournament as favourite: Tom Weiskopf, who had moved there many years ago, was finally fulfilling his immense talent. He was top of the money list in America and had won the Open at Troon the previous month. In practice, Weiskopf had demonstrated he was still in the groove with a pair of rounds in the mid-60s. All of which, of course, gave Nicklaus extra incentive.

He was further motivated by the prospect of achieving such a historical landmark in front of his friends and family. Nicklaus opened with a mediocre 72, but his ball striking, he felt, had been a great deal better than the score suggested. He was sure he would improve as the week progressed and so was not too concerned at instantly falling five strokes off the pace.

Nicklaus proved as good as his thought the following day, shooting 68 to close within a shot of the lead; a third-round 68 left him feeling instinctively that the tournament was in the bag. "Shoot 70 and the title is yours," he told himself. It would have been, too, but Nicklaus did better than that, concluding with a 69 for a four-stroke win.

And so he had passed Hagen's total, and won more majors than any other professional. Naturally, the "greatest of all time" labels started to appear at this point. This may have been a mite premature. The comparison with Bobby Jones, for example, becomes invidious when it is considered that Jones is generally credited with seven majors these days – but then he was not allowed to play in one and only ever played in another, the one he created, when he was long past his best. If the four majors that existed in Jones's day and for which he was eligible are taken into account, his total becomes 13.

What we can say beyond doubt, or at least as far as this author is concerned, is that this great weight of achievement, when added to what he still had subsequently to achieve, makes Nicklaus the greatest golfer of all.

Trevino's curse

Sam Snead was 62 years old when the 1974 PGA reached his home state of North Carolina. The venue was Tanglewood and it would prove to play host to one of the most remarkable performances of all time. Snead's swing was still extraordinarily full and graceful, and he continued to propel the ball a long way. But who could have predicted that he would shoot four rounds under 72 – 69, 71, 71 and 68 – to finish in the frame at his age?

Indeed the only players who would finish above him were young enough to be his children. They were both pretty awesome talents as well: Jack Nicklaus and Lee Trevino. Up to this point in his career, Trevino was the player that Nicklaus most disliked having to tackle. In three previous major championships Nicklaus had played close to his best golf, but each time had come up empty thanks to the unique brand of sorcery that Trevino possessed. And now it would happen again. After opening rounds of 73 and 66, Trevino hit the front with a third-round 68. In the final round he played nerveless golf, always managing to stay one step ahead of his greatest rival. On the final green Nicklaus needed a putt to tie. It was from 20 feet and it looked in all the way. Then, half a ball's turn from the hole, it decided to pull up and inwardly Nicklaus screamed with frustration. The Trevino curse had struck once more.

Could Nicklaus make amends in 1975? The venue was one of his favourite golf courses, Firestone, where he had enjoyed quite a bit of success. He had won the first World Series of Golf to be held there, and also took the title on three subsequent occasions. He could hardly wait to get there. Firestone suited Nicklaus because it placed the emphasis on long, straight driving and unerring long-iron play, which just happened to be his two greatest assets, behind his singular strength of mind.

The course measures almost 7,200 yards and possesses a par of 70, and in the first round Nicklaus matched it to be three strokes behind the South African, Dale Hayes. How often it was that Nicklaus won his tournaments by putting together strong rounds on the second and third days. This time he shot 68 and 67 to be four strokes in front of Bruce Crampton with a round to play. The key had come at the 16th on the third day, a hole long known as "the monster" on account of its measurement of 625 yards. After three strokes, Nicklaus was in deep trouble. His options were to pitch out on to the fairway and then pitch over the water that protected the green and two putt for a seven; gamble and go for the green, knowing that if it dropped into the water it would be a catastrophic eight. At this time in his career Nicklaus had got ever more conservative, but here was a shock: he decided to go for it.

A decision completely out of character it might have been, but he swung as hard as he could, the ball cleared the tree in front of him by a matter of inches, cleared the water, and finished 30 feet from the pin. So he had rescued a six. Or so everyone thought. Instead, Nicklaus holed for a par. "Just your average miracle five," he later told reporters.

In comparison with all that excitement, the last day was a complete anti-climax. Nicklaus was never in trouble, and could even afford a double bogey at the last and still win by two from Crampton. It was his 14th major championship and fourth win in the PGA. Only Walter Hagen, with five, had won more.

Over the next eight years the PGA visited a succession of venues that are rated as American classics. Congressional, Pebble Beach, Oakmont, Oak Hill, Oakland Hills, Southern Hills and Atlanta Athletic Club. All these courses had hosted US Opens at one time or another, and so the accusation began that the tournament was too like that event for its own good.

There was no denying, however, that there were some good events and some tense finishes, and the almost continual presence on the leaderboard of Jack Nicklaus gave the event all the prestige it needed. Indeed, in his recent autobiography, Nicklaus gave the PGA warm praise, considering it above the Masters – "the most enjoyable to play in but the least prestigious because of the quality of the field" – in his ranking of the four majors. Nicklaus went on to say that he always treated the event as first among equals with the other blue-riband tournaments.

In 1976 and 1977 his efforts to tie with Walter Hagen's record of five wins in the event were both narrowly thwarted. First at Congressional there was an uncharacteristically weak final round when in contention to win. After three rounds the leader was Charles Coody, with Nicklaus but a shot behind.

Lanny Wadkins – his only major title came in the first sudden-death play-off in major championship history in 1977

Coody could only manage a final-round 77, while Nicklaus did not do that much better, carding a 74.

The way was clear for someone to emerge from behind, and that man proved to be Dave Stockton, who claimed his second PGA of the decade. Two other PGA champions pushed him to the finish line. Don January and Raymond Floyd shot 72 and 71, respectively, for totals of 282 – a mark that Stockton could beat if he parred the difficult final hole. This was no easy task on a brutally difficult course where no one had managed to equal the 72-hole par of 280. In the end it came down to an awkward 13-foot putt. Stockton, one of the finest short-game exponents of the 1970s, duly holed for his second major championship win.

Pebble Beach was always Nicklaus's favourite golf course, but once more an uninspired last round, this time of 73, denied him victory. He was one shot shy of the totals of Gene Littler and Lanny Wadkins, and these two went back out on to the course for the first-ever sudden-death play-off in major championship history.

For Littler, known as "Gene the machine" on account of his consistency, it was a shattering experience to be out there at all. At the turn on the final day he had led Wadkins by no fewer than five shots, but over the inward half he littered his card with an uncharacteristic series of bogeys, with no fewer than five coming in six holes from the turn. Still, it looked as if he might hang on as Nicklaus dropped a shot at the 17th. Now Nicklaus or Wadkins needed to birdie the 18th to force the play-off; it was Wadkins who did so, with his first birdie of the round - a most timely one, to say the least. The first sudden-death play-off proved not so sudden at all. It went to the third extra hole before Wadkins claimed what surprisingly would prove to be his only major championship.

The 1978 PGA at Oakmont meant that the Pennsylvania course had been used for more major championships than any other course in America outside Augusta National. Five years earlier it had been the stage for one of the great final rounds in majors history as Johnny Miller came firing from out of the pack to shoot 66 in the final round to win.

John Mahaffey may not have possessed Miller's charisma or his innate talent, but here he did something similar. Trailing Tom Watson by seven strokes going into the final day, he shot 66 to make up the leeway with Watson and force another sudden-death play-off, with the 1975 US Open Champion Jerry Pate the third member of the group following a 68. It was Mahaffey whose hot streak continued. He birdied the second extra hole to pull off a shock win.

Jack's back

By the summer of 1980 Jack Nicklaus had had the temerity to go almost two years without a major championship victory, and the fact that he had also reached the age of 40 gave another bunch of writers the excuse to write silly things like: "That's the end of Jack then." Naturally he won the US Open for his 16th major championship victory – "Jack's back," they now proclaimed – and accordingly came to Oak Hill for the PGA in great heart. Walter Hagen's record still hung out of reach, of course, but here was a venue that suited him down to the ground.

Not everybody felt happy about the course. After Lee Trevino had shot 275 for four rounds in winning the US Open in 1968, the United States Golf Association had suggested that the course may no longer be difficult enough to warrant consideration for future championships. That set the Oak Hill officials into quite a tizz. They signed up George and Tom Fazio to toughen it up, and a lot of players were none too happy when they arrived and set eyes on the changes to the Donald Ross design. Tom Weiskopf, as ever, was not afraid to voice his opinions. "I'm going to start an organization called the Classic Golf Course Preservation Society. Members get to carry loaded guns in case they see anybody touching a Donald Ross course," he said.

When the action began it was clear that Weiskopf had more than a case. The action was dull, with players desperate to cling on to or near par. The PGA of America had out-US Opened the US Open. Nicklaus remained contented enough. He matched par on the opening day and then shot 69 to be just a stroke behind the leader Gil Morgan. On the third day Nicklaus did what came naturally in the third round of the majors – he charged. He shot 66 for a three-shot lead. Still, Nicklaus was not getting too excited. At one point he had been seven ahead, before a sloppy finish gave his pursuers a ghost of a chance.

In retrospect it may have been the best thing that could have happened. It sharpened his mind for the final day, which he duly turned into a one-man show. The final winning margin was seven, and his dominance over the field was emphasized by one stunning fact: in a tournament in which no other player finished under par for 72 holes, Nicklaus shot three rounds that broke the par of 70 and one that matched it. What a suitably heroic way in which to match Walter Hagen's PGA record.

"Who does he think he is, Jack Nicklaus... again?" one of the competitors, Ed Sneed, said. "I think what he has done is truly fantastic," Gary Player commented. "I really take my hat off to him. After two dry years, to come back and win two majors in one year – what more can you say?"

Nothing, perhaps, although Dan Jenkins summed up the whole "Jack's finished – Jack's back" nonsense in a few brilliant sentences for *Sports Illustrated*: "With that flying right elbow on his backswing and those small hands that force him to use the unorthodox interlocking grip, and all of

Jack Nickaus – equalled Walter Hagen's record of five USPGA wins with his second major of the year in 1980

ANNUAL
CHAMPIONSHIP
OF THE
PROFESSIONAL
GOLFERS
ASSOCIATION
OF
AMERICA
RODMAN WANAMAKER
TROPHY

that time he takes standing over his putts, the chances are that Jack Nicklaus will never win 30 major championships. It has to catch up with him sooner or later; any golfing expert can see that.

"Yeah, sure Jack turned the PGA Championship into a hunting expedition in which you were supposed to find the rest of the field. But you could see that because of Nicklaus's age, which is 40, his desire and the mechanics of his game were deteriorating at the finish.

"He made a bogey on the next-to-last hole and won his fifth PGA by seven strokes, not eight. Oak Hill was definitely the beginning of the end because the course had been made tougher to prevent anyone from shooting an embarrassing 275, five under par, as Lee Trevino had back in 1968 when he won the US Open. And on this tree-infested, rough-gnarled, water-patrolled layout, which had been carefully, even evilly doctored, the best Jack could do was fire rounds of 70, 69, 66 and 69 for a total of 274."

Some players learn to play golf almost as soon as they can walk, like Tiger Woods and Justin Rose. Larry Nelson first picked up a golf club when he was 22. By that stage he had served in Vietnam and worked as an illustrator at the Lockheed plant near his home in Georgia.

Ho-hum, what to do next? Let's go to the driving range and try out this game they call golf. Nelson liked it so much that he went to work in a professional's shop. So began one of the more unusual careers in golf, one that yielded three major championships. The first came in the 1981 PGA, just down the road at Atlanta Athletic Club from where he was born.

The golf was blistering. Nelson shot 70 and 66 for the first two days and yet was still not the leader; Bob Murphy had followed an opening 66 with a 69. The third day, as it so often proves to be, was crucial. Nelson shot his second successive 66, to the delight of the locals. Murphy could not keep pace, fading to a 73. On the final day the course was a much tougher proposition, which suited Nelson just fine. Now he knew that if he could score somewhere around par, no one would touch him. And that is how it turned out. He shot 71 to win by four from Fuzzy Zoeller.

In 1982 at Southern Hills, ol' Hawkeye was back. Thirteen years had elapsed since his previous PGA victory, but from the moment Raymond Floyd shot 63 in the opening round the rest of the field knew the man who could stare down an elephant was back doing what he did best, and that was leading from the front. No player had ever won two PGAs while leading in every round, but such a statistical nicety did not worry Floyd. He followed his opening salvo with rounds of 69 and 68 to turn the last round into a lap of honour. A 72 meant the winning margin turned out to be three shots.

By 1983 Jack Nicklaus was 43 and once more had had the temerity to go a few majors without winning. "Jack's finished," they said again. At Riviera Country Club in Los Angeles he shot 65 in the second round, and the leader Hal Sutton had good cause to wish reporters would stop provoking him like that. In the third round Sutton shot 72, and now Nicklaus had caught up another stroke. There were still six shots between them, mind. Surely that would be enough...

There again, maybe not. A few weeks earlier Sutton had blown a six-stroke lead in a tournament in Virginia, and although he had now gone to the turn in 32 shots and the PGA seemed over, he started playing the back nine as if he were an 18 handicapper. From the 12th, Sutton bogeyed three holes in a row; Nicklaus, meanwhile, was charging and birdied the 14th and the 16th. Now the lead between them was just a stroke.

Nicklaus would par in for a wonderful 66. Could Sutton for a 71 and the PGA? To his credit he did, and the writers, who could hardly write "Jack's finished" after such a round, claimed instead that Sutton, with his golden hair and coolness under pressure at the end, reminded them of someone... yes, that's it... "Sutton is the next Jack Nicklaus."

Trevino's return

You could not make up the 1984 PGA. It was held at a new course called Shoal Creek in Alabama, and was designed by Jack Nicklaus, who promptly showed how not to play it by shooting 77 in the first round. The leader after three rounds was Lee Trevino, who had not featured for a long while in any major because of the very good reason that he could hardly swing a club, owing to a long-standing back complaint. But here he was, back for a last stab at glory, and chasing him all the way was someone four years older, Gary Player. Also in contention was a man with a bent arm who had not picked up a club until he was in his 20s, Calvin Peete. Quite deliciously, he was black, playing this course that did not allow black members and showing how it should be played.

So what happened on the final day? Well, after a few holes play was stopped for lightning and no one ran for cover quicker than Trevino, who had already been struck by a bolt from God in 1975. Surely that would be the end of him? Ultimately, Severiano Ballesteros would come in with a 70 to finish fifth; Peete closed with a 68 to claim fourth spot; Gary Player, who shot a wonderful 63 in the second round, finished tied for second.

It came down to Lanny Wadkins and Trevino, and at the 16th it was looking very good for the former. He had played a beautiful second shot to 12 feet while Trevino had found a bunker. The best the Mexican could do was to get the ball out to 15 feet and so had to putt first for a par before Wadkins for a

Lee Trevino – in winning the USPGA in 1984, he became the first player to shoot all four rounds in the 60s

John Daly provided the greatest fairy-tale of them all at Crooked Stick in 1991

birdie. It was a classic matchplay situation. It went Trevino's way; not only did he hole but Wadkins missed.

At the 17th Wadkins drove into the trees and needed two shots to find the fairway again. The importance of Trevino's putt at the 16th and the effect it had had on Wadkins were now amply demonstrated. Now, with the trophy in the bag, all that was left for Trevino to do was to hole a 15-foot putt on the final green to become the first man in major championship history to score four rounds in the 60s. Naturally, he did so. "God, I'm so happy," he said afterwards, as he drank beer from two plastic cups. "Get me a funnel, because I don't think I am even going to taste the first four beers," he added.

Trevino was leading at the half-way stage the following year as well, but a third-round 75 caused irreparable damage to his chances. Instead it was the unlikely figure of Hubert Green who stole through with a third-round 70 and then shot 72 on the last day to defeat Trevino by a couple of shots. It was quite a surprise, for Green had put in eight years of anonymous performances following his 1977 US Open win and third-place finish in the Open at Turnberry. And after it, he strode straight back down the road to mediocrity.

Norman blows it

Greg Norman's year of years in 1986 saw him throw away 54 hole leads in the Masters and the US Open, but in the Open at Turnberry he had built upon another position of strength after the third round to record a five-stroke victory. He therefore arrived at the USPGA at Inverness, OH in a relaxed frame of mind. Whatever happened now, the year was a good one, but clearly his golf was currently of such a quality that here was another golden opportunity to follow his first major victory with a second.

Norman's play on the opening day illustrated once more that when at the peak of his form he was an awe-inspiring sight. As the Canadian golf writer, Lorne Rubenstein, put it: "Fred Astaire could not have tip-toed around the flag any better than Norman's ball." His enjoyment was obvious. Norman waved to his three-year-old daughter, Morgan-Leigh, in the gallery; he joked with his playing partners, Hubert Green and Larry Nelson. On the back nine Norman shot 31 for a 65, which on this day was just about the worst he could have scored. It was still a new course record, and inevitably he was the leader.

A second-round 68 followed and now he had a stranglehold on the tournament. A third-round 69 gave him a unique place in the history books; no player had ever led all four majors in one year after 54 holes. For the rest of the field, the only thing they could do was to try to keep hold of Norman's coat-tails and hope for something dramatic to happen on the final day. Bob Tway did just that, breaking Norman's course record with a 64. He was in the clubhouse just four strokes behind.

No one expected Tway to have much of a chance on the final day. In comparison with Norman he was a journeyman after all – and he was starting from a position of four adrift. Surely he would need another 64 to win? After nine holes the expected script was being written. Norman was still four ahead. But he clearly was not as comfortable as he was over the first three days, not as relaxed. At the par-three 3rd Norman so misclubbed that his ball cleared the green. At the 7th he had another bogey.

At the 11th the unthinkable started to close in on the Australian, the start of a series of bad breaks, bad bounces, bad play, that make a golfer believe in fate. Off a perfect drive Norman's ball finished in a divot; he caught his shot fat and it buried itself in a bunker. He barely got it out and took a double-bogey six. His lead had been halved.

Then Tway birdied the long 13th and now the difference between them was down to a stroke. Norman then bogeyed the 14th. All square. From there to the end there was no comparison between the golf the pair played. Norman played some wonderful strokes, Tway's were awful. At the 15th Tway missed the green but got down in a chip and putt; at the 17th he did so again. Surely it could not go on? At the last Norman hit a perfect drive and Tway found the heavy rough; it was as much as he could do to force the ball into the bunker that fronts the green. From the middle of the fairway Norman's pitching wedge looked the perfect stroke. It hit the green by the pin, the crowd roared their approval – but then the backspin kicked in and it finished in the rough at the front of the green. Still, advantage Norman. With the pin cut close to the front, Tway's bunker shot was hellishly awkward. A par would be an achievement.

Tway opened his stance and the wedge cut the sand two inches behind the ball. Up it popped, and settled. It was clearly a good shot. Then it disappeared into the hole and the man who had shown no emotion all day jumped and played in the sand like a kid on the beach. When normality returned, Norman had his chip to tie. It missed. And that was why the year when Norman finally won a major will always leave a slightly bitter taste.

The unknown golfer

That PGA does not come close to being the most far-fetched major championship story of all. Nor does Trevino's win in the 1984 tournament. Instead that accolade belongs to the 1991 edition, which was held at a course called Crooked Stick in a place called Carmel in the state of Indiana. The ninth stand-in for that tournament was a wild-driving, wild-living 25-year-old from the state of Arkansas who was self-taught and was scraping a living playing in any events in which he could enter.

When he heard on the eve of the tournament that eight players had dropped out and he was now next in line for a place in the field, he told his wife Bettye: "Hell, we better get up there." It was long drive, taking all of Wednesday, but when he pulled in to Carmel at 1.30am he discovered that it had all been worth it; Nick Price had pulled out to be with his wife at the birth of their child. "I just hope they have a wonderful baby," the overjoyed stand-in said.

Price lent him not only his spot but his caddie, who proved decidedly useful given that the stand-in had never had a practice round. The next day they went out early and the caddie, Jeff Medlen, who would tragically lose his life to cancer a few years later, found himself giving yardage from places that Nick Price could only think about in his dreams. Suddenly he found himself carrying the bag for a player with more natural talent than he had witnessed before at close quarters. His new charge opened with rounds of 69 and 67 to grab the halfway lead.

The world's Press could hardly believe what was happening. Only a small *côterie* of the American media had heard of John Daly – for it was him – let alone knew anything about him. The lazier hacks consoled themselves with the thought that unknowns who lead after round two are usually gone by round three. Daly was not gone. He shot 69 and was still leading. Furthermore, the quality of his golf was such that the obvious possibility that he could win his first-ever major championship had dawned on everyone. For Daly was driving the ball uncannily straight, and that gave him such a huge advantage over everyone else. On a course measuring over 7,200 yards, with many struggling to reach the longer par fours in two, Daly could reach all the par fives in two and never had more than a seven iron for his second shot to any of the par fours.

In the commentary booth Raymond Floyd sniffed and muttered something about him not lasting the pace; Jack Nicklaus, however, was in his element. When Daly started high-fiving the crowd during his final round the Golden Bear could not keep a smile off his face. Every time Daly went into trouble his apparently nerveless putting saved him. His closest challenger was an experienced and talented pro called Bruce Lietzke, but he was never allowed to get really close. Daly kept him at bay all the way round, and when he came up the last with a three-stroke lead the roar seemed to go on for ever.

By a lovely twist of fate Medlen was back on the bag of Price the following year when the Zimbabwean succeeded Daly as PGA Champion to finally claim his first major championship. This was a reward for patience and tenacity, and it was not the greatest surprise when, having finally learned how to win a big one, he did so again two years later by claiming the Wanamaker Trophy at Southern Hills. In between, the tournament returned to Inverness - yes, the same Inverness where Greg Norman had lost to a holed bunker shot on the 72nd hole by Bob Tway.

And who was this, leading after 54 holes, just as he was that year? Yes, the same Greg Norman. He had banned all questions about Tway – "Seven years ago is seven years ago," he said – but there was an uncanny sense of déjà vu when he started to drop shots on the front nine on Sunday. Then something miraculous happened. The putts started going in. Norman birdied the 8th, the 11th, the 13th and the 16th. Was he finally going to claim his first major in America at Inverness, of all places? Wait a minute, what's this? Paul Azinger is holing a bunch of putts as well. He completes the back nine in 32. Now Greg Norman is standing over a 20-foot putt to avoid a sudden-death play-off against the Zinger. The putt is a beauty. There is nowhere it can go apart from in the hole. Azinger knows it; he is preparing to shake Norman's hand. Norman knows it; so does his ten-year-old daughter. "It's in the hole, it's in the hole," she screams joyfully. And it was in the hole, too. It started to disappear below ground. Then, just as Norman got ready to celebrate, it began to spin out. "Please no. Not again," said Laura Norman, his wife. Again. The ball spun out 270 degrees and stayed above ground. Has golf really, really, known a crueller moment than that? Maybe the play-off at the 11th, when Norman had a five-foot putt to stay alive and the ball hit the hole and lipped out again. It was all too much. Even Azinger, for a moment, did not feel much like celebrating, preferring instead to bow his head before shaking the hand of the luckless victim of circumstance.

Three of the last four PGAs have been won by top-notch players who had to wait rather longer than perhaps they should have done to win their first major championship. All swing the club quite beautifully, and all are capable of winning any tournament when the mood is upon them. In 1995 it was the turn of the Australian, Steve Elkington, who matched the 267 total of Colin Montgomerie – the lowest 72-hole score ever seen in a major – at Riviera and then beat him at the first extra hole of a play-off by holing a 25-foot putt. In 1997 it was the turn of Davis Love, whose father had been a successful teaching professional and a highly respected member of the PGA. It was a poignant moment for the popular Love, because his father had lost his life in an air crash in 1988. He could not help but think of the symmetry, that his first major victory had come in the PGA Championship. It came, too, with golf of a quality rarely seen before; at fabled Winged Foot, Love had three rounds of 66 and one of 71 to win by five. And then in 1998 it was Vijay Singh's moment in the sun, a reward for dedication to his craft, for the man who turns off the lights every night at every practice ground in the land.

Try telling those players that winning the PGA is not one of the great feelings in golf. It may be the fourth major but it is far from second rate.

9–14 October, 1916

Siwanoy CC, Bronxville, New York

MATCHPLAY

32 qualifiers after 36 holes strokeplay. All Rounds 36 holes

Round by Round Details

ROUND 1 (Last 32)

Tom Kerrigan bt Charles Adams 6&4; George McLean bt Tom MacNamara 6&5; Alex Smith bt James Ferguson 4&2; Jim Barnes bt George Fotheringham 8&7; Willie MacFarlane bt Robert McNulty 10&9; Mike Brady bt James West 7&6; Emmett French bt Eddie Towns 3&1; Jack Dowling (bye); J.J. O'Brien bt Wilfred Reid 1 up; George Simpson bt Walter Fovargue 6&5; Bob MacDonald bt Jimmie Donaldson 3&2; Walter Hagen bt J.R. Thomson 7&6; Jock Hutchinson bt Joe Mitchell 11&9; W. Brown bt F. Clarkson (default); Cyril Walker bt Louis Tellier 4&2, Jack Hobens bt Mike Sherman (default)

ROUND 2 (Last 16)

Kerrigan bt McLean 2&1 | Barnes bt Smith 8&7
MacFarlane bt Brady 3&2 | Dowling bt French 1 up (after 37)
O'Brien bt Simpson 3&2 | Hagen bt MacDonald 3&2
Hutchinson bt Brown 11&9 | Walker bt Hobens 5&4

QUARTER FINAL

Barnes bt Kerrigan 3&1 | MacFarlane bt Brady 2&1
Hagen bt O'Brien 10&9 | Hutchinson bt Walker 5&4

SEMI FINAL

Barnes bt MacFarlane 6&5 | Hutchinson bt Hagen 2 up

FINAL Jim Barnes bt Jock Hutchinson 1 up

September 15–20, 1919

Engineers CC, Long Island, NY

MATCHPLAY

32 qualifiers after 36 holes strokeplay All rounds 36 holes

Round-by-Round Details

ROUND 1 (last 32)

Jim Barnes bt Carol Anderson 8&6; Otto Hackbarth bt Joe Sylvester 5&4; Tom Kerrigan bt Bill Mehlhorn 3&2; Emmett French bt Clarence Hackney 7&6; Bob MacDonald bt Tom Boyd 1 up; George Fotheringham bt Eddie Loos 8&6; Tom McNamara bt Louis Martucci 7&6; Jock Hutchison bt John Bredemus 6&5; Harry Hampton bt Jack Hobens 7&6; Douglas Edgar bt Joe Rosman (default); Fred McLeod bt James Rose 9&7; George Gordon bt Dave Wilson 3&2; Wilfred Reid bt Pat Doyle 1 up; Jimmy West bt Willie Kidd (default); Mike Brady bt Louis Teller 7&6; George McLean bt Johnny Farrell 7&6.

ROUND 2 (last 16)

Barnes bt Hackbarth 3&2 | French bt Kerrigan 2 up
MacDonald bt Fotheringham 2&1 | Hutchison bt McNamara 8&6
Edgar bt Hampton 5&4 | McLeod bt Gordon 2 up
West bt Reid 2&1 | McLean bt Brady 6&5

QUARTER FINAL

Barnes bt French 3&2 | MacDonald bt Hutchison 3&2
McLeod bt Edgar 8&6 | McLean bt West 9&7

SEMI FINAL

Barnes bt MacDonald 5&4 | McLeod bt McLean 3&2

FINAL Jim Barnes beat Fred McLeod 6&5

17–21 August, 1920

Flossmor, Chicago, Illinois

MATCHPLAY

32 qualifiers after 36 holes strokeplay. All Rounds 36 holes

Round by Round Details

ROUND 1 (Last 32)

Alex Cunnigham bt Willie MacFarlane 2&1; Peter O'Hara bt Pat Doyle 1 up; George McLean bt George Sayers 6&5; Tom Kennett bt Otto Hackbarth 3&1; Douglas Edgar bt Pat O'Hara 1 up; Joe Sylvester bt Tom Boyd 4&3; Bob MacDonald bt Leo Diegel 4&3; Bill Mehlhorn bt Wallie Nelson 3&2; Harry Hampton bt Jack Gordon 6&5; George Thompson bt Isaac Mackie 3&2; Clarence Hackney bt Phil Hesler 3&2; Jim Barnes bt George Bowden 4&3; Charles Mayo bt Lloyd Gullickson 2&1; Louis Tellier bt Joe Rosman 10&9; Laurie Ayton bt Charles Hoffner 1 up (after 39); Jock Hutchinson bt Eddie Loos 5&3

ROUND 2 (Last 16)

O'Hara bt Cunningham 5&4 | McLean bt Kennett 2&1
Edgar bt Sylvester 11&9 | MacDonald bt Mehlhorn 1 up
Hampton bt Thompson 5&4 | Hackney bt Barnes 5&4
Tellier bt Mayo 4&2 | Hutchinson bt Ayton 5&3

QUARTER FINAL

McLean bt O'Hara 1 up (after 38) | Edgar bt MacDonald 5&4
Hampton bt Hackney 4&3 | Hutchinson bt Tellier 6&5

SEMI FINAL

Edgar bt McLean 8&7 | Hutchinson bt Hampton 6&5

FINAL Jock Hutchinson bt Douglas Edgar 1 up

September 26–October 1, 1921

Inwood CC, Far Rockaway, NY

MATCHPLAY

Field selected from the top 31 PGA available finishers in the 1921 US Open plus the defending champion (Jock Hutchison). All rounds 36 holes

Round-by-Round Details

ROUND 1 (last 32)

Fred McLeod bt Fred Canausa 1 up (after 37); Jack Gordon bt Bill Leach 8&7; Bobby Cruickshank bt Charlie Thom 4&3; Jim Barnes bt Clarence Hackney 3&2; George McLean bt Tom Kerrigan 2&1; Jimmy West bt Jack Pirie 1 up (after 37); Charles Clarke bt Peter O'Hara I up; Emmett French bt Joe Sylvester 8&7; Cyril Walker bt Emil Loeffler 1 up (after 37): Charles Mothersole bt Johnny Farrell 1 up (after 40); Gene Sarazen bt Harry Hampton 4&3; Jock Hutchison bt Pat O'Hara 1 up (after 39); Tom Boyd bt Eddie Towns (default); Walter Hagen bt Jack Forrester 6&4; Laurie Ayton Sr bt T.J. Rajoppi 7&6; John Golden bt Robert Barnett 5&3.

ROUND 2 (Last 16)

McLeod bt Gordon 4&2 | Barnes bt Cruickshank 8&7
McLean bt West 8&7 | French bt Clarke 8&7
Walker bt Mothersole 4&2 | Sarazen bt Hutchison 8&7
Hagen bt Boyd 6&5 | Golden bt Ayton 1 up

QUARTER FINAL

Barnes bt McLeod 11&9 | French bt McLean 5&3
Walker bt Sarazen 5&4 | Hagen bt Golden 8&7
Golden bt Ayton 8&7

SEMI FINAL

Barnes bt French 5&4 | Hagen bt Walker 5&4

FINAL Walter Hagen bt Jim Barnes 3&2

August 12–18, 1922

Oakmont CC, Oakmont, PA

MATCHPLAY

64 qualifiers from strokeplay. Rounds 1 and 2, 18 holes; QF, SF and F, 36 holes

Round-by-Round Details

ROUND 2 (Last 32)

Francis Gallett bt Fred Brand 5&4; Bobby Cruickshank bt Al Watrous 3&2; Jack Burgess bt Peter Walsh 3&2; Charles Rowe bt Tom Boyd 3&1; Frank Sprogell bt Dan Kenny 4&3; Gene Sarazen bt Willie Ogg 2&1; Jock Hutchison bt Dan Goss 6&4; Harry Hampton bt Charles Hoffner 3&2; Tom Kerrigan bt Charles Hilgendorf 5&4; Johnny Farrell bt Jim Barnes 1 up; John Golden bt P.J. Gaudin 8&7; Al Ciuci bt George Stark 4&2; Emil Loeffler bt Dave Robertson 4&3; Eddie Towns bt Matt Duffy 1 up; R.S. Miner bt Fred Baroni 1 up (after 19); Emmett French bt Mike Brady 3&1

ROUND 3 (Last 16)

Cruickshank bt Gallett 7&6 | Rowe bt Burgess 6&5
Sarazen bt Sprogell 9&7 | Hutchison bt Hampton 4&3
Kerrigan bt Farrell 4&3 | Golden bt Ciuci 3&2
Loeffler bt Towns 3&1 | French bt Miner 8&7

QUARTER FINAL

Cruickshank bt Rowe 3&2 | Sarazen bt Hutchison 3&1
Golden bt Kerrigan 4&3 | French bt Loeffler 4&2

SEMI FINAL

Sarazen bt Cruickshank 3&2 | French bt Golden 8&7

FINAL Gene Sarazen bt Emmett French 1 up

September 23–29, 1923

Pelham GC, Pelham Manor, NY

MATCHPLAY

64 qualifiers from strokeplay. All rounds 36 holes

Round-by-Round Details

ROUND 2 (Last 32)

Bobby Cruickshank bt Herbert Obendorf 7&5; Ray Derr bt Frank Coltart 5&4; Willie MacFarlane bt Wilfred Reid 3&2; Jack Stait bt Jack Forrester 1 up; Jim Barnes bt John Cowan 12&11; Cyril Walker bt Harry Cooper 2&1; Alex Campbell bt Willie Klein 4&3; Gene Sarazen bt D.K. White 11&10; Clarence Hackney bt R.S. Miner 7&6; Fred McLeod bt James Meehan 4&3; Walter Hagen bt Jack Elphick 10&9; John Golden bt Robert Barnett 1 up; Joe Kirkwood Sr bt Jimmy West 2 up; Johnny Farrell bt Willie Hunter Jr 4&3; George McLean bt Jimmy Donaldson 6&4; Willie Ogg bt Carl Anderson 12&11

ROUND 3 (Last 16)

Cruickshank bt Derr 1 up — MacFarlane bt Stait 5&4
Barnes bt Walker 8&7 — Sarazen bt Campbell 3&2
McLeod bt Hackney 1 up — Hagen bt Golden 4&3
Kirkwood bt Farrell 1 up — McLean bt Ogg 1 up (after 38)

QUARTER FINAL

Sarazen bt Barnes 1 up — Cruickshank bt MacFarlane 1 up (after 39)
Hagen bt McLeod 5&4 — McLean bt Kirkwood 5&4

SEMI FINAL

Sarazen bt Cruickshank 6&5 — Hagen bt McLean 12&11

FINAL Gene Sarazen beat Walter Hagen 1 up (after 38)

September 15–20, 1924

French Springs, French Lick, IN

MATCHPLAY

32 qualifiers after 36 holes strokeplay. All rounds 36 holes

Round-by-Round Details

ROUND 2 (Last 32)

Willie MacFarlane bt George Dow 5&4; Johnny Farrell bt Neil Christian 2&1; Al Watrous bt George Aulbach 3&1; Walter Hagen bt Tom Harmon Jr 6&5; Al Espinosa bt Arthur Ham 4&2; Francis Gallett bt Bill Mehlhorn 4&3; Bobby Cruickshank bt Willie Ogg 7&5; Ray Derr bt Harry Hampton 2 up; Henry Ciuci bt Charles Hoffner 4&2; Dan Williams bt Fred Baroni 4&2; Gene Sarazen bt Fred McLeod 5&4; Larry Nabholtz bt Jack Forrester 1 up; Mortie Dutra bt Leo Diegel 3&1; Emmett French bt Jock Robertson 6&4; Jim Barnes bt Mike Brady 1 up (after 39); Eddie Towns bt Jock Hutchison 4&3

ROUND 3 (Last 16)

Farrell bt MacFarlane 2&1 — Hagen bt Watrous 4&3
Espinosa bt Gallett 4&3 — Derr bt Cruickshank 2&1
Ciuci bt Williams 4&3 — Nabholtz bt Sarazen 2&1
French bt Dutra 3&1 — Barnes bt Towns 10&9

QUARTER FINAL

Hagen bt Farrell 3&2 — Derr bt Espinosa 2&1
Nabholtz bt Ciuci 5&4 — Barnes bt French 6&4

SEMI FINAL

Hagen bt Derr 8&7 — Barnes bt Nabholtz 1 up

FINAL Walter Hagen beat Jim Barnes 2 up

September 21–26, 1925

Olympia Fields CC, Olympia Fields, Illinois

MATCHPLAY

32 qualifiers after 36 holes strokeplay. All Rounds 36 holes

Round-by-Round Details

ROUND 2 (Last 32)

Walter Hagen bt Al Watrous 1 up (after 39); Mike Brady bt JS Collins 10&9; Leo Diegel bt Laurie Ayton, Sr. 2&1; Bobby Cruickshank bt Bill Leach 4&3: Harry Cooper bt Jack Blakeslee 7&6; Jack Burke, Sr. bt Gene Sarazen 8&7; Johnny Farrell bt William Creavy 6&4; Ray Derr bt Abe Espinosa 4&3; Bill Mehlhorn bt Emmett French 5&4; Al Espinosa bt George Howard 5&3; Tom Kerrigan bt George Smith 5&3; Dan Williams bt Charles Hoffner 4&3; Mortie Dutra bt Willie Ogg 2&1; Ed Dudley bt Mike Patton 3&2; Tommy Armour bt George Griffin 3&1; John Golden bt Dave Robertson 9&8

ROUND 3 (Last 16)

Hagen bt Brady 7&6 — Diegel bt Cruickshank 2&1
Cooper bt Burke 2&1 — Farrell bt Derr 1 up (after 37)
Mehlhorn bt Al Espinosa 1 up — Kerrigan bt Williams 2 up
Dutra bt Dudley 6&5 — Armour bt Golden 6&5

QUARTER FINAL

Hagen bt Diegel 1 up (after 40) — Cooper bt Farrell 2&1
Mehlhorn bt Kerrigan 7&6 — Dutra bt Armour 2 up

SEMI FINAL

Hagen bt Cooper 3&1 — Mehlhorn bt Dutra 8&6

FINAL Walter Hagen bt Bill Mehlhorn 6&5

September 20–25, 1926

Salisbury GL, Westbury, Long Island, NY

MATCHPLAY

32 qualifiers after 36 holes strokeplay. All rounds 36 holes

Round-by-Round Details

ROUND 2 (Last 32)

Marshall Crichton bt Francis Gallett 1 up; Pat Doyle bt Willie Maguire 2&1; Dick Grout bt Jock Hendry 4&3; Walter Hagen bt Joe Turnesa 3&2; Dick Linnars bt Fred McLeod 5&4; Johnny Farrell bt Al Watrous 6&5; Harry Hampton bt Larry Nabholtz 5&4; Tom Harmon Jr bt Al Espinosa 6&4; Abe Espinosa bt Gunnar Nelson 7&6; Mike Brady bt George Aulbach 1 up (after 37); Leo Diegel bt Mike Patton 8&7; Neal McIntyre bt Bobby Cruickshank 4&2; John Golden bt Harry Cooper 5&3; Gene Sarazen bt Jim Barnes 5&4; Bill Leach bt Laurie Ayton Sr 3&2; George Christ bt Leo Shea 3&2

ROUND 3 (Last 16)

Doyle bt Crichton 3&2 — Hagen bt Grout 7&6
Farrell bt Linnars 6&5 — Hampton bt Harmon 6&5
Abe Espinosa bt Brady 1 up — Diegel bt McIntyre 6&5
Golden bt Sarazen 4&3 — Christ bt Leach 1 up (after 38)

QUARTER FINAL

Hagen bt Doyle 6&5 — Farrell bt Hampton 3&1
Diegel bt Abe Espinosa 3&2 — Golden bt Christ 7&6

SEMI FINAL

Hagen bt Farrell 6&5 — Diegel bt Golden 1 up

FINAL Walter Hagen bt Leo Diegel 5&3

October 31–November 5, 1927

Cedar Crest CC, Dallas, TX

MATCHPLAY

32 qualifiers after 36 holes' strokeplay. All rounds 36 holes

Round-by-Round Details

ROUND 1 (Last 32)

Tommy Armour bt Johnny Farrell 4&3; Tom Harmon Jr bt Johnny Perelli 4&3; Tony Manero bt Bobby Cruickshank 4&3; Walter Hagen bt Jack Farrell 3&2; Mortie Dutra bt Albert Alcroft 12&11; Charles Guest bt Roland Hancock 3&2; Al Espinosa bt Mel Smith 5&4; Harry Cooper bt Eddie Murphy 7&6; Ed Dudley bt James Gullane 8&7; Gene Sarazen bt Jack Curley 1 up (after 37); Willie Klein bt Bill Mehlhorn 1 up; Joe Turnesa bt Charles McKenna 5&3; John Golden bt Charles Koontz 2&1; Harold Long bt Willie Kidd 4&3; Francis Gallett bt Bob Shave 4&3; Ralph Beach bt Fred Baroni 1 up

ROUND 2 (Last 16)

Armour bt Harmon Jr 7&6 — Hagen bt Manero 11&10
Dutra bt Guest 2 up — Espinosa bt Cooper 5&4
Sarazen bt Dudley 4&3 — Turnesa bt Klein 1 up
Golden bt Long 1 up (after 37) — Gallett bt Beach 2 up

QUARTER FINAL

Hagen bt Armour 4&3 — Espinosa bt Dutra 1 up
Turnesa bt Sarazen 3&2 — Golden bt Gallett 4&2

SEMI FINAL

Hagen bt Espinosa 1 up (after 37) Turnesa bt Golden 7&6

FINAL Walter Hagen bt Joe Turnesa 1 up

October 1–6, 1928

Five Farms CC, Baltimore, MD

MATCHPLAY

32 qualifiers after 36 holes' strokeplay. All rounds 36 holes

Round-by-Round Details

ROUND 1 (Last 32)

Willie MacFarlane beat Jim Foulis 9&7; Horton Smith bt Billy Burke 2&1; Glen Spencer bt Fred McDermott 8&6; Perry del Vecchio bt Jack Burke Sr 1 up (after 37); Al Espinosa bt John Golden 8&7; Bob MacDonald bt Willie Kidd 2 up; Jock Hutchison bt Willie Klein 3&2; Pat Doyle bt Mortie Dutra 6&4; Jim Barnes bt Tommy Armour 3&2; Gene Sarazen bt Bill Mehlhorn 3&2; Al Watrous bt Olin Dutra 2&1; Ed Dudley bt Wiffy Cox 3&2; George Christ bt Albert Alcroft 1 up (after 38): Leo Diegel bt Tony Manero 10&8; Walter Hagen bt Willie Ogg 4&3; Julian Blanton bt Ed McElligott 9&8

ROUND 2 (Last 16)

Smith bt MacFarlane 1 up
del Vecchio bt Spencer 1 up (after 37)
Hutchison bt Doyle 1 up
Espinosa by MacDonald 1 up (after 37)
Sarazen bt Barnes 3&2
Dudley bt Watrous 3&2
Diegel bt Christ 6&4
Hagen bt Blanton 2 up

QUARTER FINAL

Smith bt del Vecchio 2 up
ESPINOSA bt Hutchison 5&4
Sarazen bt Dudley 7&6
DIEGEL bt Hagen 2&1

SEMI FINAL

ESPINOSA bt Smith 6&5
DIEGEL bt Sarazen 9&8

FINAL Leo Diegel bt Al Espinosa 6&5

December 2–7, 1929

Hillcrest CC, Los Angeles, CA

MATCHPLAY

32 qualifiers after 36 holes strokeplay. All rounds 36 holes

Round-by-Round Details

ROUND 1 (Last 32)

Larry Nabholtz bt Albert Alcroft 1 up; Al Watrous bt Neal McIntyre 4&3; Al Espinosa bt Dave Hackney 5&4; Bill Mehlhorn bt Guy Paulsen 7&6: Neil Christian bt Frank Walsh 7&6; Craig Wood bt Horton Smith 1 up (after37); Henry Ciuci bt Clarence Clark 3&2; Johnny Farrell bt John Golden 1 up; Tony Manero bt Denny Shute 6&5; Eddie Schultz bt Wiffy Cox 5&4; Walter Hagen bt Bob Shave 9&8; Charles Guest bt Mortie Dutra 1 up; Leo Diegel bt P.O. Hart 10&9; Herman Barron bt Clarence Doser 5&4; Gene Sarazen bt Jock Hendry 3&2; Fred Morrison bt Joe Kirkwood Sr 5&4

ROUND 2 (Last 16)

Watrous bt Nabholtz 9&7
Espinosa bt Mehlhorn 1 up (after 40)
Wood bt Christian 3&2
Farrell bt Ciuci 3&1
Manero bt Schultz 6&5
Hagen bt Guest 5&4
Diegel bt Barron 10&9
Sarazen bt Morrison 3&2

QUARTER FINAL

Watrous bt Espinosa 2 up
Farrell bt Wood 1 up (after 37)
Hagen bt Manero 6&5
Diegel bt Sarazen 3&2

SEMI FINAL

Farrell bt Watrous 6&5
Diegel bt Hagen 3&2

FINAL Leo Diegel bt Johnny Farrell 6&4

September 8–13, 1930

Fresh Meadows CC, Flushing Meadows, NY

MATCHPLAY

32 qualifiers after 36 holes' strokeplay. All rounds 36 holes

Round-by-Round Details

ROUND 1 (Last 32)

Al Watrous bt Eric Seavall 3&1; Charles Lacey bt Charles Guest 3&2; Harold Sampson bt Clarence Ehresman 4&3; Leo Diegel bt Henry Ciuci 8&7; Tommy Armour bt Clarence Hackney 11&10; Bob Shave bt Joseph Kenny 1 up; Denny Shute bt Joe Frank 8&6; Johnny Farrell bt Norman Smith 7&5; Gene Sarazen bt Charles Schneider 1 up; Bob Crowley bt Wiffy Cox 4&3; Harry Cooper bt Bill Mehlhorn 2&1; Al Espinosa bt Mark Fry 2&1; Joe Kirkwood Sr bt Gunnar Johnson 8&7; J.S. Collins bt John Golden 5&4; Horton Smith bt Billy Burke 2&1; Laurie Ayton Sr bt Earl Fry 4&3

ROUND 2 (Last 16)

Lacey bt Watrous 5&4
Sampson bt Diegel 1 up (after 38)
Armour bt Shave 7&5
Farrell bt Shute 1 up
Sarazen bt Crowley 7&6
Espinosa bt Cooper 4&3
Horton Smith bt Ayton 5&4
Kirkwood bt Collins 1 up (after 37)

QUARTER FINAL

Lacey bt Sampson 4&3
Armour bt Farrell 2&1
Sarazen bt Espinosa 2&1
Kirkwood bt Horton Smith 1 up

SEMI FINAL

Armour bt Lacey 1 up
Sarazen bt Kirkwood 5&4

FINAL Tommy Armour bt Gene Sarazen 1 up

September 7–14, 1931

Wannamoisett CC, Rumford, RI

MATCHPLAY

31 qualifiers plus the defending champion (Tommy Armour), after 36 holes strokeplay. All rounds 36 holes

Round-by-Round Details

ROUND 1 (Last 32)

Paul Runyan bt Arthur Gusa 3&2; Gene Sarazen bt Al Espinosa 9&8; Willie MacFarlane bt Henry Ciuci 3&2; Horton Smith bt Walter Bemish 7&6; Cyril Walker bt Ed Dudley 3&2; John Golden bt Alfred Sargent 3&2; Peter O'Hara bt Walter Hagen 4&3; Tom Creavy bt Jack Collins 5&4; Bob Crowley bt Pat Circelli 1 up; Billy Burke bt Dave Hackney 5&3; Abe Espinosa bt Vincent Eldred 4&3; Bill Mehlhorn bt Leo Diegel 3&2: Denny Shute bt Tony Butler 2 up (after 38); Jim Foulis bt Johnny Farrell 2 up; Tommy Armour bt Joe Kirkwood Jr 2&1; Walter Murray bt Eddie Schultz 6&5

ROUND 2 (Last 16)

Sarazen bt Runyan 7&6
Smith bt MacFarlane 6&5
Walker bt Golden 5&4
Creavy bt O'Hara 2 up
Burke bt Crowley 5&4
Abe Espinosa bt Mehlhorn 2&1
Shute bt Foulis 2&1
Armour bt Murray 5&3

QUARTER FINAL

Sarazen bt Smith 5&4
Creavy bt Walker 3&1
Burke bt Abe Espinosa 5&3
Shute bt Armour 3&1

SEMI FINAL

Creavy bt Sarazen 5&3
Shute bt Burke 1 up

FINAL Tom Creavy bt Denny Shute 2&1

August 31–September 4, 1932

Keller GC, St Paul, MN

MATCHPLAY

31 qualifiers plus the defending champion (Tom Creavy), after 36 holes strokeplay. All rounds 36 holes

Round-by-Round Details

ROUND 2 (Last 32)

Olin Dutra bt George Smith 9&8; Reggie Myles bt Horton Smith 1 up (after 37); Herman Barron bt Neal McIntyre 8&7; Abe Espinosa bt Eddie Schultz 4&3; Henry Picard bt Charles Lacey 6&4; Ed Dudley bt Joe Turnesa 8&7; Al Collins bt Gunnar Nelson 5&4; John Golden bt Walter Hagen 1 up (after 43); Vincent Eldred bt Paul Runyan 1 up (after 38): Bobby Cruickshank bt Al Watrous 1 up (after 41 holes); Gene Kunes bt Craig Wood 3&2; Frank Walsh bt Ted Longworth 1&6; Ralph Stonehouse bt Vic Ghezzi 6&5; John Kinder bt Joe Kirkwood Sr 1 up; Johnny Perelli bt Denny Shute 3&2; Tom Creavy bt Jimmy Hines 7&6

ROUND 3 (Last 16)

Dutra bt Myles 5&3
Barron bt Espinosa 1 up (after 38)
Dudley bt Picard 10&9
Collins bt Golden 1 up
Cruickshank bt Eldred 3&1
Walsh bt Kunes 9&8
Stonehouse bt Kinder 3&2
Creavy bt Perelli 1 up

QUARTER FINAL
Dutra bt Barron 5&4 | Dudley bt Collins 1 up (after 38)
Walsh bt Cruickshank 8&7 | Creavy bt Stonehouse 3&2
SEMI FINAL
Dutra bt Dudley 3&2 | Walsh bt Creavy 1 up (after 38)
FINAL Olin Dutra bt Frank Walsh 4&3

August 8–13, 1933

Blue Mound CC, Milwaukee, WI

MATCHPLAY
31 qualifiers plus the defending champion (Olin Dutra), after 36 holes strokeplay. All rounds 36 holes
Round-by-Round Details
ROUND 1 (Last 32)
Jimmy Hines bt Mortie Dutra 3&2; Henry Picard bt Willie Klein 2&1; Frank Walsh bt Jack Curley 3&2; Tom Creavy bt Dick Metz 3&2; Al Espinosa bt Charles Schneider 3&2; Willie Goggin bt Leo Diegel 4&3; Paul Runyan bt Al Houghton 6&5; Johnny Revolta bt Alex Gerlak 12&11; Clarence Clark bt Horton Smith 6&5; Ed Dudley bt Ben Pautke 2&1; Gene Sarazen bt Vincent Eldred 8&7; Harry Cooper bt Dave Hackney 6&5; John Golden bt Gunnar Johnson 4&3; Bobby Cruickshank bt Bunny Torpey 3&2; Johnny Farrell bt Vic Ghezzi 1 up; Olin Dutra bt Reggie Myles 4&3
ROUND 2 (Last 16)
Hines bt Picard 5&3 | Creavy bt Walsh 2&1
Goggin bt Espinosa 9&1 | Runyan bt Revolta 2&1
Dudley bt Clark 3&1 | Sarazen bt Cooper 4&3
Golden bt Cruickshank 2&1 | Farrell bt Olin Dutra 1 up
QUARTER FINAL
Hines bt Creavy 4&3 | Goggin bt Runyan 6&5
Sarazen bt Dudley 6&5 | Farrell bt Golden 5&4
SEMI FINAL
Goggin bt Hines 1 up | Sarazen bt Farrell 5&4
FINAL Gene Sarazen bt Willie Goggin 5&4

July 24–29, 1934

Park Club of Buffalo, Williamsville, NY

MATCHPLAY
31 qualifiers plus the defending champion (Gene Sarazen), after 36 holes strokeplay. All rounds 36 holes
Round-by-Round Details
ROUND 1 (Last 32)
Gene Sarazen bt Herman Barron 3&2; Al Watrous bt Errie Ball 8&7; Harry Cooper bt Bill Mehlhorn 4&2; Craig Wood bt Leo Fraser 6&5; Ky Laffoon bt George Smith 12&10; Denny Shute bt Walter Hagen 4&3; Al Houghton bt George Christ 7&6; Fay Coleman bt Leo Diegel 4&2; Dick Metz bt Joe Paletti 6&5; Tommy Armour bt Byron Nelson 4&3;Vic Ghezzi bt Eddie Burke 2&1; Paul Runyan bt Johnny Farrell 8&6; Johnny Revolta bt Jim Foulis 7&6; Gene Kunes bt Orville White 3&2; Ted Turner bt Willie Goggin 1 up (after 31); Bob Crowley bt Eddie Loos 3&2
ROUND 2 (Last 16)
Watrous bt Sarazen 4&3 | Wood bt Cooper 4&3
Shute bt Laffoon 3&2 | Houghton bt Coleman 4&3
Metz bt Armour 3&2 | Runyan bt Ghezzi 2&1
Kunes bt Revolta 2&1 | Crowley bt Turner 1 up
QUARTER FINAL
Wood bt Watrous 2&1 | Shute bt Houghton 6&5
Runyan bt Metz 1 up | Kunes bt Crowley 4&3
SEMI FINAL
Wood bt Shute 2&1 | Runyan bt Kunes 4&2
FINAL Paul Runyan bt Craig Wood 1 up (after 38)

October 18–23, 1935

Twin Hills CC, Oklahoma City, OK

MATCHPLAY
63 qualifiers plus the defending champion (Paul Runyan), after 36 holes strokeplay. Rounds 1 and 2, 18 holes; Round 3, QF, SF and F, 36 holes
Round-by-Round Details
ROUND 2 (Last 32)
Paul Runyan bt Mortie Dutra 3&2; Tony Manero bt Clarence Doser 1 up; Levi Lynch bt Art Bell 4&2; Al Zimmerman bt Vic Ghezzi 2&1; Pat Cicelli bt Orville White 3&2; Johnny Revolta bt Jimmy Hines 1 up; Alvin Krueger bt Gene Sarazen 2&1; Eddie Schultz bt G Slingerland 2&1; Al Watrous bt Harold Sampson 2&1; Sam Parks Jr bt Francis Scheider 1 up; Horton Smith bt Ray Mangrum 1 up; Denny Shute bt Henry Bontempo 4&3; Jimmy Thomson bt J.G. Collins 6&4; Ed Dudley bt Dick Metz 3&1; Ky Laffoon bt Eddie Loos 1 up (after 21); Tommy Armour bt Charles Schneider 3&2
ROUND 3 (Last 16)
Runyan bt Manero 9&8 | Zimmerman bt Lynch 7&6
Revolta bt Circelli 4&2 | Schultz bt Krueger 1 up (after 37)
Watrous bt Parks Jr 4&3 | Smith bt Shute 2&1
Dudley bt Thomson 6&4 | Armour bt Laffoon 3&2
QUARTER FINAL
Zimmerman bt Runyan 3&2 | Revolta bt Schultz 4&2
Watrous bt Smith 1 up | Armour bt Dudley 1 up (after 39)
SEMI FINAL
Revolta bt Zimmerman 4&3 | Armour bt Watrous 2&1
FINAL Johnny Revolta bt Tommy Armour 5&4

November 17–22, 1936

Pinehurst CC, Pinehurst, NC

MATCHPLAY
63 qualifiers plus the defending champion (Johnny Revolta), after 36 holes strokeplay. Rounds 1 and 2, 18 holes; Round 3, QF, SF and F, 36 holes
Round-by-Round Details
ROUND 2 (Last 32)
Harold McSpaden bt Johnny Revolta 1 up (after 19); Leo Walper bt Clarence Hackney 2&1; Jimmy Thomson bt Willie Klein 3&2; Henry Picard bt Alvin Krueger 5&4; Harry Cooper bt Clarence Doser 3&2; Craig Wood bt Frank Walsh 1 up; Bobby Cruickshank bt Errie Ball 2&1; Tony Manero bt Mortie Dutra 6&5; Horton Smith bt Jack Patroni 6&5; Willie Goggin bt Les Madison 5&4; Denny Shute bt Al Zimmerman 3&2; Billy Burke bt Ky Laffoon 4&3; Bill Mehlhorn bt Dick Metz 1 up (after 23); Ed Dudley bt Tom LoPresty 2&1; Jimmy Hines bt Ray Mangrum 2&1; Vic Ghezzi bt Fay Coleman 1 up
ROUND 3 (Last 16)
McSpaden bt Walper 4&3 | Thomson bt Picard 4&2
Wood bt Cooper 2&1 | Manero bt Cruickshank 4&2
Smith bt Goggin 2&1 | Shute bt Burke 2&1
Mehlhorn bt Dudley 6&4 | Hines bt Ghezzi 4&3
QUARTER FINAL
Thomson bt McSpaden 1 up | Wood bt Manero 5&4
Shute bt Smith 3&2 | Mehlhorn bt Hines 4&2
SEMI FINAL
Thomson bt Wood 5&4 | Shute bt Mehlhorn 1 up
FINAL Denny Shute bt Jimmy Thomson 3&2

May 26–30, 1937

Pittsburgh Field Club, Aspinwall, PA

MATCHPLAY
63 qualifiers plus the defending champion (Denny Shute), after 36 holes strokeplay. Rounds 1 and 2, 18 holes; Round 3, QF, SF and F, 36 holes
Round-by-Round Details
ROUND 2 (Last 32)
Denny Shute bt Olin Dutra 3&2; Ed Dudley bt Pat Wilcox 4&3; Paul Runyan bt Willie Goggin 2&1; Jimmy Hines bt Al Espinosa 1 up; Harry Cooper bt Johnny

Revolta 1 up; Jim Foulis bt Gene Sarazen 1 up; Vic Ghezzi bt Sam Parks Jr 1 up; Tony Manero bt Willie MacFarlane 4&3; Byron Nelson bt Craig Wood 4&2; Johnny Farrell bt Charles Schneider 1 up; Ky Laffoon bt Billy Burke 2&1; Jimmy Thompson bt Ralph Guldahl 2&1; Harold McSpaden bt Bunny Torpey 1 up (after 20); Sam Snead bt Alvin Krueger 2 up; Henry Picard bt Sam Bernardi 1 up; Horton Smith bt Al Watrous 1 up (after 19)

ROUND 3 (Last 16)

Shute bt Dudley 3&2 | Hines bt Runyan 2&1
Cooper bt Foulis 5&4 | Manero bt Ghezzi 3&1
Nelson bt Farrell 5&4 | Laffoon bt Thompson 4&3
McSpaden bt Snead 3&2 | Picard bt Smith 4&3

QUARTER FINAL

Shute bt Hines 4&3 | Manero bt Cooper 1 up
Laffoon bt Nelson 2 up | McSpaden bt Picard 1 up (after 39)

SEMI FINAL

Shute bt Manero 1 up | McSpaden bt Laffoon 2&1

FINAL Denny Shute bt Harold McSpaden 1 up

July 10–16, 1938

Shawnee CC, Shawnee-on-Delaware, PA

MATCHPLAY

63 qualifiers plus the defending champion (Denny Shute), after 36 holes strokeplay. Rounds 1 and 2, 18 holes; Round 3, QF, SF and F, 36 holes

Round-by-Round Details

ROUND 2 (Last 32)

Denny Shute bt John Thoren 7&6; Jimmy Hines bt Frank Walsh 2&1; Byron Nelson bt Alvin Krueger 1 up (after 20); Harry Bassler bt Ed Dudley 4&3; Marvin Stahl bt George Whitehead 6&5; Jim Foulis bt Jimmy Thomson 1up; Sam Snead bt Terl Johnson 4&3; Felix Serafin bt Ky Laffoon 3&2; Billy Burke bt Frank Moore 1 up (after 19); Horton Smith bt Leo Diegel 2&1; Ray Mangrum bt Harold McSpaden 1 up (after 20); Paul Runyan bt Tony Manero 3&2; Gene Sarazen bt Harry Nettlebladt 6&5; Jimmy Demaret bt Johnny Revolta 2 up; Henry Picard bt Bob Shave 3&2; Dick Metz bt Ralph Guldahl 1 up

ROUND 3 (Last 16)

Hines bt Shute 2&1 | Nelson bt Bassler 11&14
Foulis bt Stahl 6&5 | Snead bt Serafin 4&3
Smith bt Burke 3&2 | Runyan bt Mangrum 1 up (after 31)
Picard bt Metz 4&3 | Sarazen bt Demaret 1 up (after 38)

QUARTER FINAL

Hines bt Nelson 2&1 | Snead bt Foulis 8&7
Runyan bt Smith 4&3 | Picard bt Sarazen 3&2

SEMI FINAL

Snead bt Hines 1 up | Runyan bt Picard 4&3

FINAL Paul Runyan bt Sam Snead 8&7

July 9–15, 1939

Pomonock CC, Flushing, NY

MATCHPLAY

64 qualifiers after 36 holes strokeplay. Rounds 1 and 2, 8 holes; Round 3, QF, SF and F, 36 holes

Round-by-Round Details

ROUND 2 (Last 32)

Paul Runyan bt Frank Champ 3&2; Ben Hogan bt Abe Espinosa 5&4; Billy Burke bt Herman Barron 2&1; Dick Metz bt Al Brosch 1 up; Tom O'Connor bt Ky Laffoon 2 up; Rod Munday bt Jack Ryan 2 up; Henry Picard bt Joe Zarhardt 2 up; Al Watrous bt Ken Tucker 5&3; Dutch Harrison bt Johnny Farrell 3&2; Bruce Coltart bt Mike Turnesa 1 up (after 21); Clarence Doser bt Ralph Guldahl 2 up; Horton Smith bt Ray Mangrum 3&2; Emerick Kocsis bt Vic Ghezzi 3&1; Denny Shute bt Leo Diegel 3&1; Johnny Revolta bt Tony Manero 3&2; Byron Nelson bt William Francis 3&1

ROUND 3 (Last 16)

Runyan bt Hogan 3&2 | Metz bt Burke 6&4
Munday bt O'Connor 2 up | Picard bt Watrous 8&7
Harrison bt Coltart 10&9 | Smith bt Doser 4&2
Kocsis bt Shute 3&1 | Nelson bt Revolta 6&4

QUARTER FINAL

Metz bt Runyan 2&1 | Picard bt Munday 2&1
Harrison bt Smith 4&3 | Nelson bt Kocsis 10&9

SEMI FINAL

Picard bt Metz 1 up | Nelson bt Harrison 9&8

FINAL Henry Picard bt Byron Nelson 1 up (after 37)

August 26–September 2, 1940

Hershey CC, Hershey, PA

MATCHPLAY

64 qualifiers after 36 holes strokeplay. Rounds 1, 2 and 3, 18 holes; QF, SF and F, 36 holes

Round-by-Round Details

ROUND 2 (Last 32)

Henry Picard bt Alex Gerlak 4&3; Gene Sarazen bt Ray Mangrum 2&1; Jimmy Hines bt Ray Hill 2&1; Sam Snead bt Charles Sheppard 3&2; Ed Dudley bt John Gibson 2&1; Paul Runyan bt Al Watrous 3&2; Walter Hagen bt Vic Ghezzi 2&1; Harold McSpaden bt Herman Keiser 2&1; Dick Metz bt Ky Laffoon 3&2; Byron Nelson bt Frank Walsh 1 up (after 20); Arthur Clark bt Billy Burke 1 up; Eddie Kirk bt Jimmy Demaret 2&1; Al Brosch bt Red Francis 5&4; Ben Hogan bt Harry Nettlebladt 5&4; Ralph Guldahl bt John Kinder 5&5; Jim Foulis bt Craig Wood 1 up (after 19)

ROUND 3 (Last 16)

Sarazen bt Picard 1 up | Snead bt Hines 2&1
Runyan bt Dudley 4&3 | McSpaden bt Hagen 1 up
Nelson bt Metz 2&1 | Kirk bt Clark 5&4
Hogan bt Brosch 3&4 | Guldahl bt Foulis 5&3

QUARTER FINAL

Snead bt Sarazen 1 up | McSpaden bt Runyan 8&6
Nelson bt Kirk 6&5 | Guldahl bt Hogan 3&2

SEMI FINAL

Snead bt McSpaden 5&4 | Nelson bt Guldahl 3&2

FINAL Byeon Nelson bt Sam Snead 1 up

July 7–13, 1941

Cherry Hill CC, Denver, CO

MATCHPLAY

63 qualifiers plus the defending champion (Byron Nelson), after 36 holes strokeplay. Rounds 1 and 2, 18 holes; Round 3, QF, SF and F, 36 holes

Round-by-Round Details

ROUND 2 (Last 32)

Byron Nelson bt William Heinlein 1 up; Ralph Guldahl bt Gene Kunes 2&1; Ben Hogan bt Bud Oakley 2 up; Horton Smith bt Ralph Stonehouse 3&2; Denny Shute bt Jim Foulis 1 up; Leonard Ott bt Jack Ryan (default); Bruce Coltart bt George Fazio 1 up (after 19); Gene Sarazen bt Toney Penna 1 up (after 19); Sam Snead bt Phil Greenwaldt 7&6; Mike Turnesa bt Harry Bassler 4&2; Mark Fry bt Craig Wood 6&5; Lloyd Mangrum bt Charles Sheppard 3&1; Jack Grout bt Fay Coleman 1 up; Vic Ghezzi bt Augie Nordone 1 up; Harold McSpaden bt George Schneiter 3&2; Jimmy Hines bt Ed Dudley 3&2

ROUND 3 (Last 16)

Nelson bt Guldahl 4&3 | Hogan bt Smith 2&1
Shute bt Ott 5&3 | Sarazen bt Coltart 9&7
Snead bt Turnesa 1 up | Mangrum bt Fry 1 up
Ghezzi bt Grout 1 up | Hines bt McSpaden 6&4

QUARTER FINAL

Nelson bt Hogan 2&1 | Sarazen bt Shute 7&6
Mangrum bt Snead 6&4 | Ghezzi bt Hines 6&4

SEMI FINAL

Nelson bt Sarazen 2 up | Ghezzi bt Mangrum 1 up

FINAL Vic Ghezzi bt Byron Nelson 1 up (after 38)

May 23–31, 1942

Seaview CC, Atlantic City, NJ

MATCHPLAY

31 qualifiers plus the defending champion (Vic Ghezzi), after 36 holes strokeplay.

All rounds 36 holes

Round-by-Round Details

ROUND 1 (Last 32)

Jimmy Demaret bt Vic Ghezzi 4&3; Tom Harmon Jr bt Bruce Coltart 3&2; Craig Wood bt Rod Munday 5&4; Leland Gibson bt Jimmy Gauntt 10&9; Sam Snead bt Sam Byrd 7&6; Willie Goggin bt Eddie Burke 2&1; Ed Dudley bt Denny Shute 3&2; Toney Penna bt Jimmy Hines 3&2; Harry Cooper bt Mike Turnesa 3&1; Lloyd Mangrum bt Dick Metz 6&5; Byron Nelson bt Harry Nettlebladt 5&3; Joe Kirkwood Sr bt Jimmy Thomson 4&2; Jim Turnesa bt Dutch Harrison 6&5; Harold McSpaden bt Sam Parks Jr 7&5; Ben Hogan bt Ben Loving 7&6; Ky Laffoon bt Vic Bass 12&11

ROUND 2 (Last 16)

Demaret bt Harmon 3&2 | Wood bt Gibson 7&6
Snead bt Goggin 9&8 | Dudley bt Penna 4&2
Cooper bt Mangrum 1 up | Nelson bt Kirkwood 2&1
Turnesa bt McSpaden | Hogan bt Laffoon 9&8

QUARTER FINAL

Demaret bt Wood 7&6 | Snead bt Dudley 1 up
Nelson bt Cooper 1 up (after 39) | Turnesa bt Hogan 2&1

SEMI FINAL

Snead bt Demaret 3&2 | Turnesa bt Nelson 1 up (after 37)

FINAL Sam Snead bt Jim Turnesa 2&1

1943 – No championship

14–20 August 1944

Manito G7CC, Spokane, Washington

MATCHPLAY

32 qualifiers after 36 holes strokeplay. All Rounds 36 holes

Round by Round Details

ROUND 1 (Last 32)

Byron Nelson bt Mike DeMassey 5&4; Mark Fry bt Neil Christian 2&1; Willie Goggin bt Purvis Ferree 8&7; Tony Manero bt Clayton Aleridge 1 up (after 38); Sam Byrd bt WA Stackhouse 4&3; Chuck Congdon bt Henry Williams Jr 7&6 ; Ed Dudley bt Steve Savel 7&6; Jimmy Hines bt Thurman Edwards 7&6; Harold McSpaden bt Bruce Coltart 7&5; Fred Annon bt Harry Nettlebladt 5&4; Bob Hamilton bt Gene Kunes 6&5; Harry Bassler bt Joe Mozel 6&5; Art Bell bt Joe Zarhardt 1 up (after 37); Craig Wood bt Jimmy D'Angelo 5&4; Toney Penna bt Morrie Gravatt 3&2; George Schneiter bt Ted Longworth 7&6

ROUND 2 (Last 16)

Nelson bt Fry 7&6 | Goggin bt Manero 4&3
Congdon bt Byrd 2&1 | Dudley bt Hines 1 up (after 37)
McSpaden bt Annon 8&7 | Hamilton bt Bassler 6&5
Bell bt Wood 3&2 | Schneiter bt Penna 4&3

QUARTER FINAL

Nelson bt Goggin 4&3 | Congdon bt Dudley 6&5
Hamilton bt McSpaden 2&1 | Schneiter bt Bell 2&1

SEMI FINAL

Nelson bt Congdon 8&7 | Hamilton bt Schneiter 1 up

FINAL Bob Hamilton bt Byron Nelson 1 up

July 9–15, 1945

Moraine CC, Dayton, OH

MATCHPLAY

31 qualifiers plus the defending champion (Bob Hamilton), after 36 holes strokeplay. All rounds 36 holes

Round-by-Round Details

ROUND 1 (Last 32)

Jack Grout bt Bob Hamilton 5&4; Ky Laffoon bt Felix Serafin 4&3; Clarence Doser bt Harold McSpaden 5&4; Toney Penna bt Wayne Timberman 2 up; Johnny Revolta bt Frank Kringle 10&9; Sam Byrd bt Augie Nordone 4&3; Herman Barron bt Harry Nettlebladt 5&3; Vic Ghezzi bt Ed Dudley 7&6; Byron Nelson bt Gene Sarazen 4&3; Mike Turnesa bt John Gibson 5&4; Denny Shute bt Barney Clark 4&3; Bob Kepler bt George Schneiter 2&1; Terl Johnson bt Dutch Harrison 1 up; Ralph Hutchinson bt Ted Huge 6&5; Jim Turnesa bt Byron Harcke 6&5; Claude Harmon bt Verl Stinchcombe 2&1

ROUND 2 (Last 16)

Laffoon bt Grout 5&4 | Doser bt Penna 1 up
Byrd bt Revolta 2&1 | Ghezzi bt Barron 2 up
Nelson bt Mike Turnesa 1 up | Shute bt Kepler 5&4
Hutchinson bt Johnson 6&5 | Harmon bt Jim Turnesa 8&7

QUARTER FINAL

Doser bt Laffoon 2&1 | Byrd bt Ghezzi 7&6
Nelson bt Shute 3&2 | Harmon bt Hutchinson 4&3

SEMI FINAL

Byrd bt Doser 7&6 | Nelson bt Harmon 5&4

FINAL Byron Nelson bt Sam Byrd 4&3

August 19–25, 1946

Portland GC, Portland, OR

MATCHPLAY

63 qualifiers plus the defending champion (Byron Nelson), after 36 holes strokeplay. Rounds 1 and 2, 18 holes; Round 3, QF, SF and F, 36 holes

Round-by-Round Details

ROUND 2 (Last 32)

Byron Nelson bt Larry Lamberger 3&2; Herman Barron bt Fay Coleman 3&2; Ed Oliver bt Dick Metz 3&1; Chandler Harper bt Jimmy Thomson 2&1; Dutch Harrison bt Toney Penna 1 up; Harold McSpaden bt Bob Hamilton 4&3; Chuck Congdon bt Newton Bassler 1 up (after 19); George Schneiter bt Sam Snead 6&5; Jim Ferrier bt Lawson Little 3&2; Jimmy Demaret bt Dave Tinsley 3&2; Jim Turnesa bt Henry Ransom 1 up; Dick Shoemaker bt Vic Ghezzi 1 up; Ben Hogan bt William Heinlein 4&3; Art Bell bt Al Nelson 4&3; Frank Moore bt George Fazio 2&1; Harry Bassler bt Lew Worsham 1 up

ROUND 3 (Last 16)

Nelson bt Barron 3&2 | Oliver bt Harper 5&4
McSpaden bt Harrison 4&3 | Congdon bt Schneiter 2&1
Demaret bt Ferrier 3&2 | Turnesa bt Shoemaker 5&4
Hogan bt Bell 5&4 | Moore bt Harry Bassler 4&3

QUARTER FINAL

Oliver bt Nelson 1 up | McSpaden bt Congdon 5&3
Demaret bt Turnesa 6&5 | Hogan bt Moore 5&4

SEMI FINAL

Oliver bt McSpaden 6&5 | Hogan bt Demaret 10&9

FINAL Ben Hogan bt Ed Oliver 6&4

June 18–24, 1947

Plum Hollow CC, Detroit, MI

MATCHPLAY

63 qualifiers plus the defending champion (Ben Hogan), after 36 holes strokeplay. Rounds 1 and 2, 18 holes; Round 3, QF, SF and F, 36 holes

Round-by-Round Details

ROUND 2 (Last 32)

Ky Laffoon bt Toney Penna 1 up; Gene Sarazen bt Sam Snead 2&1; Dick Metz bt Henry Ransom 1 up; Art Bell bt Johnny Bulla 4&3; Claude Harmon bt Jim Milward 5&3; Jim Ferrier bt Herman Barron 3&2; Mike Turnesa bt Chandler Harper 1 up (after 22); Lloyd Mangrum bt Ed Dudley 4&3; Vic Ghezzi bt Earl Martin 6&5; Jim Turnesa bt Walter Ambo 4&3; Lew Worsham bt Clarence Dowser 5&4; Reggie Myles bt George Schneiter 1 up; Chick Harper bt Clayton Heafner 1 up (after 20); Ed Oliver bt Harry Bassler 4&3; Eddie Joseph bt Lloyd Wadkins 1 up; Leland Gibson bt Jack Smith 3&2

ROUND 3 (Last 16)

Laffoon bt Sarazen 4&3 | Bell bt Metz 1 up (after 37)
Ghezzi bt Jim Turnesa 4&3 | Ferrier bt Harmon 1 up (after 37)
Worsham bt Myles 7&6 | Mangrum bt Mike Turnesa 1 up
Harbert bt Oliver 3&2 | Gibson bt Joseph 1 up

QUARTER FINAL

Bell bt Laffoon 2 up | Ferrier bt Mangrum 4&3
Ghezzi bt Worsham 3&2 | Harbert bt Gibson 2 up

SEMI FINAL

Ferrier bt Bell 10&9 Harbert bt Ghezzi 6&5

FINAL Jim Ferrier bt Chick Harbert 5&4

May 19–25, 1948

Northwood Hills CC, St Louis, MO

MATCHPLAY

63 qualifiers plus the defending champion (Jim Ferrier), after 36 holes strokeplay. Rounds 1 and 2, 18 holes; Round 3, QF, SF and F, 36 holes

Round-by-Round Details

ROUND 2 (Last 32)

Claude Harmon bt Jim Ferrier 1 up; Henry Ransom bt Lloyd Mangrum 3&2; Sam Snead bt Frank Moore 4&3; Leland Gibson bt Pete Cooper 1 up; Johnny Bulla bt Armand Farida 4&3; Ky Laffoon bt Chandler Harper 3&2; Mike Turnesa bt Zell Eaton 1 up (after 21); Al Smith bt Jimmy Hines 4&3; Skip Alexander bt Al Brosch 2 up; Chick Harper bt Eddie Burke 1 up (after 26); Ben Hogan bt Johnny Palmer 1 up; Gene Sarazen bt Jackson Bradley 2&1; Jimmy Demaret bt George Getchell 3&1; Lew Worsham bt Errie Ball 7&6; Ed Oliver bt Sherman Elworthy 3&2; George Fazio bt Henry Williams Jr 7&6

ROUND 3 (Last 16)

Harmon bt Ransom 2&1 — Snead bt Gibson 5&3
Bulla bt Laffoon 6&5 — Turnesa bt Smith 3&2
Harbert bt Alexander 11&10 — Hogan bt Sarazen 1 up
Demaret bt Worsham 3&2 — Fazio bt Oliver 1 up

QUARTER FINAL

Harmon bt Snead 1 up (after 42) — Turnesa bt Bulla 6&5
Hogan bt Harbert 2&1 — Demaret bt Fazio 5&4

SEMI FINAL

Turnesa bt Harmon 1 up (after 42) — Hogan bt Demaret 5&4

FINAL Ben Hogan bt Mike Turnesa 7&6

May 25–31, 1949

Hermitage CC, Richmond, VA

MATCHPLAY

64 qualifiers (the defending champion Ben Hogan was unable to compete), after 36 holes' strokeplay. Rounds 1 and 2, 18 holes; Round 3, QF, SF and F, 36 holes

Round-by-Round Details

ROUND 2 (Last 32)

Ray Hill bt Jack Isaacs 3&2; Walter Romans bt Frank Moore 4&2; Herman Barron bt Jimmy Thomson 2&1; Lloyd Mangrum bt Bob Hamilton 3&2; Johnny Palmer bt Clay Gaddie 8&6; Lew Worsham bt George Schneiter 5&4; Henry Williams Jr bt Jack Harden 1 up; Al Brosch bt Horton Smith 5&4; Sam Snead bt Henry Ransom 3&1; Dave Douglas bt Mike DeMassey 3&2; Jimmy Demaret bt George Fazio 3&1; Jim Turnesa bt Johnny Bulla 1 up; Clayton Heafner bt Claude Harmon 2&1; Jack Patroni bt Jimmy Johnson 1 up; Jim Ferrier bt Skip Alexander 1 up; Marty Furgol bt Eddie Burke 2&1

ROUND 3 (Last 16)

Hill bt Romans 5&4 — Mangrum bt Barron 4&3
Palmer bt Worsham 2&1 — Williams Jr bt Brosch 7&6
Snead bt Douglas 1 up — Demaret bt Turnesa 5&3
Heafner bt Patroni 5&4 — Ferrier bt Furgol 8&6

QUARTER FINAL

Mangrum bt Hill 7&6 — Palmer bt Williams Jr 7&6
Snead bt Demaret 4&3 — Ferrier bt Heafner 3&2

SEMI FINAL

Palmer bt Mangrum 6&5 — Snead bt Ferrier 3&2

FINAL Sam Snead bt Johnny Palmer 3&2

June 17–27, 1950

Scioto CC, Columbus, OH

MATCHPLAY

63 qualifiers plus the defending champion (Sam Snead), after 36 holes strokeplay. Rounds 1 and 2, 18 holes; Round 3, QF, SF and F, 36 holes

Round-by-Round Details

ROUND 2 (Last 32)

Eddie Burke bt Sam Snead 1 up; Ray Gafford bt Leonard Schmutte 1 up; Denny Shute bt Elsworth Vines 4&3; Jimmy Demaret bt Rod Munday 5&3; Lloyd Mangrum bt Skip Alexander 1 up; Chick Harper bt Harold Williams 5&3; Bob Toski bt George Fazio 1 up; Chandler Harper bt Dick Metz 1 up; Claude Harmon bt Al Brosch 2&1; Henry Williams Jr bt Emery Thomas 6&5; Elmer Reed bt Jim Ferrier 5&4; Dave Douglas bt Jimmy Hines 5&4; Jackson Bradley bt George Shafer 4&3; Henry Picard bt Clarence Doser 4&2; Johnny Palmer bt Lew Worsham 4&2; Ted Kroll bt Al Watrous 2&1

ROUND 3 (Last 16)

Gafford bt Burke 4&3 — Demaret bt Shute 4&3
Mangrum bt Harbert 6&5 — Harper bt Toski 2&1
Douglas bt Reed 3&2 — Williams Jr bt Harmon 1 up (after 38)
Picard bt Bradley 1 up — Palmer bt Kroll 1 up

QUARTER FINAL

Demaret bt Gafford 5&4 — Harper bt Mangrum 1 up
Williams Jr bt Douglas 1 up — Picard bt Palmer 10&8

SEMI FINAL (SF)

Harper bt Demaret 2&1 — Williams Jr bt Picard 1 up (after 38)

FINAL Chandler Harper bt Henry Williams Jr 4&3

June 27–July 3, 1951

Oakmont CC, Oakmont, PA

MATCHPLAY

63 qualifiers plus the defending champion (Chandler Harper), after 36 holes strokeplay. Rounds 1 and 2, 18 holes; Round 3, QF, SF and F, 36 holes

Round-by-Round Details

ROUND 2 (Last 32)

Charles Bassler bt Jim Turnesa 5&4; George Bolesta bt Ed Oliver 2&1; Al Brosch bt Lew Worsham 5&4; Jack Harden bt Toney Penna 5&3; Lloyd Mangrum bt Buck White 2&1; Sam Snead bt Marty Furgol 1 up (after 21); Jack Burke Jr bt Gene Sarazen 5&3; Gene Kunes bt Ray Gafford 2&1; Dick Shoemaker bt Lawson little 2&1; Walter Burkemo bt Chick Harper 1 up (after 19); Vic Ghezzi bt Rod Munday 4&3; Reggie Miles bt Mike Pavella 1 up (after 20); Jackson Bradley bt Denny Shute 2&1; Elsworth Vines bt Henry Picard 1 up; Jim Ferrier bt Milton Marusic 3&2; Johnny Bulla bt Bob Hamilton 5&3

ROUND 3 (Last 16)

Bassler bt Bolesta 1 up (after 37) — Brosch bt Harden 6&5
Snead bt Mangrum 3&2 — Burke Jr bt Kunes 4&3
Burkemo bt Shoemaker 2&1 — Myles bt Ghezzi 1 up
Vines bt Bradley 2&3 — Bulla bt Ferrier 9&8

QUARTER FINAL

Bassler bt Brosch 1 up — Snead bt Burke Jr 2&1
Burkemo bt Myles 1 up — Vines bt Bulla 1 up

SEMI FINAL

Snead bt Bassler 9&8 — Burkemo bt Vines 1 up (after 37)

FINAL Sam Snead bt Walter Burkemo 7&6

June 18–25, 1952

Big Spring CC, Louisville, KY

MATCHPLAY

63 qualifiers plus the defending champion (Sam Snead), after 36 holes strokeplay. Rounds 1 and 2, 18 holes; Round 3, QF, SF and F, 36 holes

Round-by-Round Details

ROUND 2 (Last 32)

Ray Hosberger bt Jim Ferrier 1 up; Ted Kroll bt Lloyd Mangrum 2 up; Cary Middlecoff bt Charles Harter 3&2; Al Smith bt Labron Harris 1 up (after 19); Jim Turnesa bt Chandler Harper 3&1; Roberto de Vicenzo bt Jack Burke Jr 1 up; Clarence Doser bt Bob Gajda 3&2; Jack Isaacs bt Marty Furgol 3&2; Fred Haas bt Lew Worsham 1 up; Milon Marusic bt Zell Eaton (default); Henry Williams Jr bt Jack Jones 1 up; Chick Harbert bt Leonard Schmutte 3&2; Frank Champ bt John Trish 2&1; Walter Burkemo bt Dave Douglas 1 up; Vic Ghezzi bt Mel Carpenter 5&3; Bob Hamilton bt Sam Bernardi 3&1

ROUND 3 (Last 16)

Middlecoff bt Smith 4&2 — Kroll bt Honsberger 1 up (after 38)
Turnesa bt de Vicenzo 5&4 — Doser bt Isaacs 1 up
Haas bt Marusic 1 up (after 38) — Harbert bt Williams Jr 6&5
Champ bt Burkemo 3&1 — Hamilton bt Ghezzi 9&8

QUARTER FINAL

Kroll bt Middlecoff 1 up (after 38) — Turnesa bt Doser 2&1
Harbert bt Haas 2&1 — Hamilton bt Champ 2&1

SEMI FINAL

Turnesa bt Kroll 4&2 | Harbert bt Hamilton 2&1

FINAL Jim Turnesa bt Chick Harbert 1 up

July 7–17, 1953

Birmingham CC, Birmingham, MI

MATCHPLAY

63 qualifiers plus the defending champion (Jim Turnesa), after 36 holes strokeplay. Rounds 1 and 2, 18 holes; Round 3, QF, SF and F, 36 holes

Round-by-Round Details

ROUND 2 (Last 32)

Felice Torza bt Jim Turnesa 4&3; Wally Ulrich bt Buck White 2&1; Jimmy Clarke bt Cary Middlecoff 5&4; Henry Williams Jr bt Charles Bassler 3&1; Jack Isaacs bt Fred Haas 1 up; Labron Harris bt Marty Furgol 1 up; Al Smith bt Iverson Martin 3&2; Henry Ransom bt Bob Toski 3&2; Jackson Bradley bt Tommy Bolt 1 up; Dave Douglas bt Sam Snead 1 up (after 19); Walter Burkemo bt Mike Turnesa 3&1; Pete Cooper bt Leonard Dodson 6&5; Bill Nary bt Dutch Harrison 1 up; Jim Browning bt Broyles Plemmons 3&1; Ed Furgol bt Jim Ferrier 3&1; Claude Harmon bt Jack Grout 4&2

ROUND 3 (Last 16)

Torza bt Ulrich 1 up (after 38) | Clark bt Williams Jr 4&3
Isaacs bt Harris 5&4 | Ransom bt Smith 1 up
Nary bt Browning 6&5 | Douglas bt Bradley 1 up (after 37)
Burkemo bt Cooper 3&2 | Harmon bt Furgol 5&3

QUARTER FINAL

Torza bt Clark 1 up | Isaacs bt Ransom 1 up
Burkemo bt Douglas 2 up | Harmon bt Nary 6&5

SEMI FINAL

Torza bt Isaacs 1 up (after 39) | Burkemo bt Harmon 1 up

FINAL Walter Burkemo bt Felice Torza 2&1

July 21–27, 1954

Keller GC, St Paul, MN

MATCHPLAY

63 qualifiers plus the defending champion (Walter Burkemo), after 36 holes strokeplay. Rounds 1 and 2, 18 holes; Round 3, QF, SF and F, 36 holes

Round-by-Round Details

ROUND 2 (Last 32)

Tommy Bolt bt Arthur Doering 2&1; Jim Browning bt Ed Furgol 1 up; Sam Snead bt Jim Milward 4&3; Dutch Harrison bt Johnny Palmer 4&3; Charles Bassler bt Bill Trombley 5&4; Jerry Barber bt Fred Haas 1 up (after 19); Chick Harbert bt John O'Donnell 3&1; Ed Oliver bt Bill Nary (1 up); Walter Burkemo bt Claude Harmon 2&1; Johnny Revolta bt Toby Lyons 5&4; Roberto de Vicenzo bt Henry Ransom 4&3; Elroy Marti bt Henry Williams Jr 2 up; Cary Middlecoff bt Bob Toski 2&1; Ted Kroll bt Max Evans 1 up (after 24); Shelley Mayfield bt Wally Ulrich 5&4; Horton Smith bt Jack Isaacs 3&2

ROUND 3 (Last 16)

Bolt bt Browning 2&1 | Snead bt Harrison 4&3
Barber bt Bassler 1 up (after 38) | Harbert bt Oliver 3&1
Burkemo bt Revolta 4&3 | de Vicenzo bt Marti 8&6
Middlecoff bt Kroll 5&4 | Mayfield bt Smith 3&2

QUARTER FINAL

Bolt bt Snead 1 up (after 39) | Harbert bt Barber 1 up
Burkemo bt de Vicenzo 5&4 | Middlecoff bt Mayfield 3&1

SEMI FINAL

Harbert bt Bolt 1 up | Burkemo bt Middlecoff 1 up (after 37)

FINAL Chick Harbert bt Walter Burkemo 4&3

July 20–26, 1955

Meadowbrook CC, Northville, MI

MATCHPLAY

64 qualifiers after 36 holes strokeplay. Rounds 1 and 2, 18 holes; Round 3, QF, SF and F, 36 holes

Round-by-Round Details

ROUND 2 (Last 32)

Brien Charter bt Lionel Hebert 1 up; Don Fairfield bt Vic Ghezzi 1 up (after 23); Shelley Mayfield bt Gene Sarazen 4&3; Claude Harmon bt Eldon Briggs 2&1; Ed Furgol bt Gus Salerno 1 up (after 20); Fred Hawkins bt Fred Haas 2 up; Wally Ulrich bt Leonard Wagner 2 up; Doug Ford bt Ted Kroll 2&1; Johnny Palmer bt Chick Harbert 1 up; Lew Worsham bt Ray Hill 2&1; Tommy Bolt bt Sam Snead 3&2; Jack Fleck bt Jay Hebert 2&1; Cary Midllecoff bt Bill Nary 3&2; Mike Pavella bt Jim Browning 4&3; Marty Furgol bt Tony Holguin 1 up; Jack Burke Jr bt Dave Douglas 8&6

ROUND 3 (Last 16)

Fairfield bt Charter 2&1 | Mayfield bt Harmon 1 up
Hawkins bt E. Furgol 6&5 | Ford bt Ulrich 12&10
Worsham bt Palmer 6&5 | Bolt bt Fleck 3&1
Middlecoff bt Pavella 8&7 | Burke Jr bt M. Furgol 2&1

QUARTER FINAL

Mayfield bt Fairfield 3&2 | Ford bt Hawkins 5&4
Bolt bt Burke Jr 8&7 | Middlecoff bt Mayfield 1 up (after 40)

SEMI FINAL

Ford bt Mayfield 4&3 | Middlecoff bt Bolt 4&3

FINAL Doug Ford bt Cary Middlecoff 4&3

July 20–24, 1956

Blue Hill G&CC, Canton, MA

MATCHPLAY

128 players Rounds 1 and 2, 18 holes; Round 3, QF, SF and F, 36 holes

Round-by-Round Details

ROUND 2 (Last 32)

Walter Burkemo bt Doug Ford 5&3; Bill Johnson bt Tony Fortino 4&3; Henry Ransom bt Claude Harmon 1 up (after 23); Lew Worsham bt Shelley Mayfield 5&4; Sam Snead bt Bob Toski 4&3; Gene Sarazen bt Mike Krak 3&2; Ted Kroll bt Michael Rooney 3&2; Jim Turnesa bt Jack Fleck 1 up; Charles Harper Jr bt Babe Lichardus 1 up; Jack Burke bt Fred Haas 1 up (after 20); Fred Hawkins bt Art Wall 1 up (after 19); Lionel Hebert bt Skee Riegel 3&1; Toby Lyons bt Charles Lepre 3&2; Terl Johnson bt Charles DuPree 4&2; Robert Kay bt Mike Fetchick 1 up; Ed Furgol bt Jerry Barber 2&1

ROUND 3 (Last 16)

Johnson bt Burkemo 1 up | Ransom bt Worsham 2 up
Snead bt Sarazen 5&4 | Kroll bt Turnesa 1 up
Burke Jr bt Harper Jr 3&2 | Hawkins bt Hebert 4&3
Furgol bt Kay 4&3 | Johnson bt Lyons 1 up (after 19)

QUARTER FINAL

Johnson bt Ransom 3&2 | Kroll bt Snead 2&1
Burke Jr bt Hawkins 4&2 | Furgol bt Johnson 1 up

SEMI FINAL

Kroll bt Johnson 10&8 | Burke Jr bt Furgol 1 up (after 37)

FINAL Jack Burke bt Ted Kroll 3&2

July 17–21, 1957

Miami Valley GC, Dayton, OH

MATCHPLAY

128 players. Rounds 1, 2, 3 and 4, 18 holes; QF, SF and F, 36 holes

Round-by-Round Details

ROUND 3 (Last 32)

Milon Marusic bt Mike Krak 2&1; Donald Whitt bt Ellsworth Vines 4&3; Ted Kroll bt Ewing Pomeroy 4&3; Dick Mayer bt Al Smith 5&3; Warren Smith bt Skee Riegel 3&2; Charles Sheppard bt Buck White 1 up; Sam Snead bt John Thoren 3&2; Dow Finsterwald bt Joe Kirkwood Jr 2&1; Nike Souchak bt Brien Charter 4&3; Lionel Hebert bt Charles Farlow 3&1; Claude Harmon bt Charles Bassler 4&3; Tommy Bolt bt Eldon Briggs 7&6; Henry Ransom bt Herman Keiser 5&3; Walter Burkemo bt Tony Holguin 1 up; Jay Hebert bt Charles Harper Jr 1 up; Doug Ford bt Bob Gajda 3&2

ROUND 4 (Last 16)

Whitt bt Marusic 2&1 | Mayer bt Kroll 1 up
Sheppard bt Smith 4&3 | Finsterwald bt Snead 2&1
L. Hebert bt Souchak 2&1 | Harmon bt Bolt 1 up
Burkemo bt Ransom 5&4 | Hebert bt Ford 3&2

QUARTER FINAL
Whitt bt Mayer 2&1 — Finsterwald bt Sheppard 2 up
L. Hebert bt Harmon 2&1 — Burkemo bt J. Hebert 3&2
SEMI FINAL
Finsterwald bt Whitt 2 up — L. Hebert bt Burkemo 3&1
FINAL Lionel Hebert bt Dow Finsterwald 3&1

July 17–20, 1958

Llanerch CC, Havertown, PA

1	Dow Finsterwald	67	72	70	67	276
2	Billy Casper	73	67	68	70	278
3	Sam Snead	73	67	67	73	280
4	Jack Burke Jr	70	72	69	70	281
=5	Tommy Bolt	72	70	73	70	285
	Julius Boros	72	68	73	72	285
	Jay Hebert	68	71	73	73	285
=8	Buster Cupit	71	74	69	73	287
	Ed Oliver	74	73	71	69	287
	Mike Souchak	75	69	69	74	287
=11	Doug Ford	72	70	70	76	288
	Hob Rosburg	71	73	76	68	288
	Art Wall	71	78	67	72	288
=14	Fred Hawkins	72	75	70	73	290
	Dick Mayer	69	76	69	76	290
=16	John Barnum	75	69	74	73	291
	Walter Burkemo	76	73	66	76	291
	Lionel Hebert	69	73	74	75	291
	Bo Wininger	76	73	69	73	291
=20	Ted Kroll	69	74	75	74	292
	Cary Middlecoff	71	73	76	72	292
	Eric Monti	73	71	73	75	292
	Bob Toski	79	70	71	72	292
	Ken Venturi	72	73	74	73	292
=25	Pete Cooper	74	77	73	69	293
	George Fazio	72	74	73	74	293
	Bob Gajda	75	70	75	73	293
	Billy Maxwell	75	69	74	75	293
=29	Dick Shoemaker	79	72	73	70	294
	Don Whitt	77	72	73	78	294

July 30–August 2, 1959

Minneapolis GC, St Louis Park, MN

1	Bob Rosburg	71	72	68	66	277
2	Jerry Barber	69	65	71	73	278
	Doug Sanders	72	66	68	72	278
4	Dow Finsterwald	71	68	71	70	280
=5	Bob Goalby	72	69	72	69	281
	Mike Souchak	69	67	71	74	281
	Ken Venturi	70	72	70	69	281
=8	Cary Middlecoff	72	68	70	72	282
	Sam Snead	71	73	68	70	282
10	Gene Littler	69	70	72	73	284
=11	Doug Ford	71	73	71	70	285
	Billy Maxwell	70	76	70	69	285
	Ed Oliver	75	70	69	71	285
=14	Paul Harney	74	71	71	70	286
	Tommy Jacobs	73	71	68	74	286
	Arnold Palmer	72	72	71	71	286
=17	Tommy Bolt	76	69	68	74	287
	Jack Burke Jr	70	73	72	72	287
	Walter Burkemo	69	72	73	73	287
	Billy Casper	69	71	73	74	287
	Pete Cooper	78	70	68	71	287
	Buster Cupit	70	72	72	73	287
	Babe Lichardus	71	73	72	71	287

July 30–August 2, 1959 continued

	Ernie Vossler	75	71	72	69	287
=25	Jay Hebert	72	70	69	77	288
	Ted Kroll	72	74	71	71	288
	Art Wall	70	72	73	73	288
=28	Clare Emery	74	74	72	69	289
	Chick Harbert	73	71	71	74	289
	Fred Hawkins	72	69	71	76	289

July 21–24, 1960

Firestone CC, Akron, OH

1	Jay Hebert	72	67	72	70	281
2	Jim Ferrier	71	74	66	71	282
=3	Doug Sanders	70	71	69	73	283
	Sam Snead	68	73	70	72	283
5	Don January	70	70	72	72	284
6	Wes Ellis Jr	72	72	72	69	285
=7	Doug Ford	75	70	69	72	286
	Arnold Palmer	67	74	75	70	286
9	Ken Venturi	70	72	73	72	287
=10	Fred Hawkins	73	69	72	74	288
	Dave Marr	75	71	69	73	288
=12	Bill Collins	71	75	71	73	290
	Ted Kroll	73	71	72	74	290
	Mike Souchak	73	73	70	74	290
=15	Pete Cooper	73	74	74	74	291
	Dow Finsterwald	73	73	69	76	291
	Johnny Pott	75	72	72	72	291
=18	Paul Harney	69	78	73	72	292
	Lionel Hebert	75	72	70	75	292
	Gene Littler	74	70	75	73	292
	Tom Nieporte	72	74	74	72	292
=22	Dave Ragan	75	75	68	75	293
	Mason Rudolph	72	71	76	74	293
=24	Julius Boros	76	73	72	73	294
	Walter Burkemo	72	77	73	72	294
	Billy Casper	73	75	75	71	294
	Billy Maxwell	74	77	72	71	294
	Ernie Vossler	71	77	74	72	294
=29	Jack Burke Jr	73	72	78	72	295
	Cary Middlecoff	73	74	73	75	295
	Bo Wininger	73	77	71	74	295

July 27–31, 1961

Olympia Fields CC, Olympia Fields, IL

1	Jerry Barber	69	67	71	70	277
2	Don January	72	66	67	72	277
3	Doug Sanders	70	68	74	68	280
4	Ted Kroll	72	68	70	71	281
=5	Wes Ellis Jr	71	71	68	72	282
	Doug Ford	69	73	74	66	282
	Gene Littler	71	70	72	69	282
	Arnold Palmer	73	72	69	68	282
	Johnny Pott	71	73	69	71	282
	Art Wall	67	72	73	70	282
=11	Paul Harney	70	73	69	71	23
	Cary Middlecoff	74	69	71	69	283
13	Jay Hebert	68	72	72	72	284
14	Walter Burkemo	71	71	73	70	285
=15	Billy Casper	74	72	69	71	286
	Bob Goalby	73	72	68	73	286
	Ernie Vossler	68	72	71	75	286
	Don Whitt	76	72	70	68	286
=19	Gardner Jackson	71	71	71	74	287
	Jack Fleck	70	74	73	70	287

July 27–31, 1961 continued

	Bob Rosburg	70	71	73	73	287
=22	**George Bayer**	73	71	72	72	288
	Don Fairfield	70	71	74	73	288
	Fred Hawkins	75	73	71	69	288
	Dave Marr	72	74	73	69	288
	Shelley Mayfield	70	74	72	72	288
=27	**Billy Maxwell**	71	72	73	73	289
	Sam Snead	72	71	71	75	289
=29	**Charles Bassler**	73	73	72	72	290
	Bob Keller	72	73	72	73	290
	Al Mengen	72	74	72	72	290
	Gary Player	72	74	71	73	290

July 19–22, 1962

Aronimink GC, Newton Square, PA

1	**Gary Player**	72	67	69	70	278
2	**Bob Goalby**	69	72	71	67	279
=3	**George Bayer**	69	70	71	71	281
	Jack Nicklaus	71	75	69	67	281
5	**Doug Ford**	69	69	73	71	282
6	**Bobby Nichols**	72	70	71	70	283
=7	**Jack Fleck**	74	69	70	77	284
	Paul Harney	70	73	72	69	284
	Dave Ragan	72	74	70	68	284
10	**Jay Hebert**	73	72	70	70	285
=11	**Julius Boros**	73	69	74	70	286
	Dow Finsterwald	73	70	70	73	286
	Chick Harbert	68	76	69	73	286
	Bob McCallister	74	66	70	76	286
=15	**Cary Middlecoff**	73	66	74	74	287
	Doug Sanders	76	69	73	69	287
=17	**Jack Burke Jr**	73	69	71	75	288
	Bruce Crampton	76	73	67	72	288
	Billy Farrell	73	71	73	71	288
	Arnold Palmer	71	72	73	72	288
	Sam Snead	75	70	71	72	288
	Frank Stranahan	69	73	72	74	288
=23	**Fred Haas**	75	71	74	69	289
	Tommy Jacobs	73	73	73	70	289
	Gene Littler	73	75	72	69	289
	Art Wall	72	75	71	71	289
=27	**Joe Campbell**	70	74	74	73	291
	Don January	70	74	72	75	291
	Johnny Pott	71	71	71	72	291
=30	**Tommy Bolt**	72	74	72	74	292
	Pete Cooper	73	71	74	74	292
	Buster Cupit	76	70	76	70	292
	Wes Ellis Jr	75	72	73	72	292
	Dick Hart	70	73	76	73	292
	Ted Kroll	73	70	76	73	292
	Shelley Mayfield	74	70	74	74	292
	Tom Nieporte	75	75	69	73	292
	Don Whitt	74	73	70	75	292

July 18–21, 1963

Dallas Athletic Club, Dallas, TX

1	**Jack Nicklaus**	69	73	69	68	279
2	**Dave Ragan**	75	70	67	69	281
=3	**Bruce Crampton**	70	73	65	74	282
	Dow Finsterwald	72	72	66	72	282
=5	**Al Geiberger**	72	73	69	70	284
	Billy Maxwell	73	71	69	71	284
7	**Jim Ferrier**	73	73	70	69	285
=8	**Gardner Dickinson**	72	74	74	66	286

July 18–21, 1963 continued

	Tommy Jacobs	74	72	70	70	286
	Bill Johnson	71	72	72	71	286
	Gary Player	74	75	67	70	286
	Art Wall	73	76	66	71	286
=13	**Julius Boros**	69	72	73	73	287
	Bob Charles	69	76	72	70	287
	Tony Lema	70	71	77	69	287
	Jack Sellman	75	70	74	68	287
=17	**Manuel de la Torre**	71	71	74	72	288
	Wes Ellis Jr	71	74	71	72	288
	Bob Goalby	74	70	74	70	288
	Dick Hart	66	72	76	74	288
	Dave Hill	73	72	69	74	288
	Doug Sanders	74	69	70	75	288
=23	**Paul Harney**	72	74	71	72	289
	Bobby Nichols	74	73	71	71	289
	Mason Rudolph	69	75	71	74	289
	Mike Souchak	72	72	73	72	289
=27	**Doug Ford**	70	72	71	77	290
	J.C. Goosie	74	74	74	68	290
	Fred Haas	80	70	70	70	290
	Sam Snead	71	73	70	76	290
	Earl Stewart	70	77	70	73	290
	Bert Weaver	76	73	71	70	290
	Bo Wininger	75	71	71	73	290

July 16–19, 1964

Columbus CC, Columbus, OH

1	**Bobby Nichols**	64	71	69	67	271
=2	**Jack Nicklaus**	67	73	70	64	274
	Arnold Palmer	68	68	69	69	274
4	**Mason Rudolph**	73	66	68	69	276
=5	**Tom Nieporte**	68	71	68	72	279
	Ken Venturi	72	65	73	69	279
7	**Bo Wininger**	69	68	73	70	280
8	**Gay Brewer**	72	71	71	67	281
=9	**Billy Casper**	68	72	70	72	282
	Jon Gustin	69	76	71	66	282
	Ben Hogan	70	72	68	72	282
	Tony Lema	71	68	72	71	282
=13	**Ed Furgol**	71	69	72	71	283
	Billy Maxwell	72	71	70	70	283
	Gary Player	70	71	71	71	283
	Mike Souchak	67	73	71	72	283
=17	**Walter Burkemo**	70	71	72	71	284
	Jacky Cupit	72	71	72	69	284
=19	**Bob Charles**	68	71	73	73	285
	Al Geiberger	73	72	72	68	285
=21	**Tommy Aaron**	72	74	70	70	286
	Julius Boros	70	73	71	72	286
=23	**Gardner Dickinson**	74	74	68	71	287
	Mike Fetchick	74	73	74	66	287
	Ed Kroll	75	72	72	68	287
	Ted Kroll	72	73	72	70	287
	Dick Rhyan	71	72	71	73	287
=28	**Bill Bisdorf**	73	72	73	70	288
	Jim Ferree	70	72	75	71	288
	Dick Hart	73	73	72	70	288
	George Knudson	76	69	72	71	288
	Doug Sanders	71	73	76	68	288

August 12–15, 1965

Laurel Valley GC, Ligonier, PA

1	Dave Marr	70	69	70	71	280
=2	Billy Casper	70	70	71	71	282
	Jack Nicklaus	69	70	72	71	282
4	Bo Wininger	73	72	72	66	283
5	Gardner Dickinson	67	74	69	74	284
=6	Bruce Devlin	68	75	72	70	285
	Sam Snead	68	75	74	72	285
=8	Tommy Aaron	66	71	72	78	287
	Jack Burke Jr	75	71	72	69	287
	Jacky Cupit	72	76	70	69	287
	Rod Funseth	75	72	69	71	287
	Bob McCalliscer	76	68	70	73	287
=13	Wes Ellis Jr	73	76	70	69	288
	R.H. Sykes	71	71	71	75	288
=15	Ben Hogan	72	75	72	70	289
	Mike Souchak	70	72	77	70	289
=17	Julius Boros	75	72	73	70	290
	Ray Floyd	68	73	72	77	290
19	Al Geiberger	74	71	71	75	291
=20	Bruce Crampton	77	74	70	71	292
	Jack Fleck	76	71	72	73	292
	Doug Ford	73	70	77	72	292
	Gordon Jones	72	76	71	73	292
	George Knudson	75	69	73	75	292
	Kel Nagle	74	75	71	72	292
	Mason Rudolph	67	76	75	74	292
	Doug Sanders	71	73	74	74	292
=28	Gay Brewer	75	70	73	75	293
	Paul Keily	76	71	75	71	293
	Gene Littler	78	70	70	75	293
	Johnny Pott	76	70	74	73	293

July 21–24, 1966

Firestone CC, Akron, OH

1	Al Geiberger	68	72	68	72	280
2	Dudley Wysong	74	72	66	72	284
=3	Billy Casper	73	73	70	70	286
	Gene Littler	75	71	71	69	286
	Gary Player	73	70	70	73	286
=6	Julius Boros	69	72	75	71	287
	Jacky Cupit	70	73	73	71	287
	Arnold Palmer	75	73	71	68	287
	Doug Sanders	69	74	73	71	287
	Sam Snead	68	71	75	73	287
11	Frank Beard	73	72	69	74	288
=12	Dow Finsterwald	74	70	73	72	289
	Jay Hebert	75	73	70	71	289
	Dow January	69	71	73	76	289
=15	Paul Harney	74	73	71	72	290
	Bill Martindale	73	75	70	72	290
	Ken Venturi	74	75	69	72	290
=18	Gardner Dickinson	74	72	73	72	291
	Ray Floyd	74	72	74	68	291
	Dare Marr	75	75	68	73	291
	Ernie Vossler	77	70	75	69	291
=22	Tommy Aaron	71	72	75	74	292
	Frank Boynton	73	74	73	72	292
	Billy Farrell	73	70	71	78	292
	Jack Nicklaus	75	71	75	71	292
	Mason Rudolph	74	73	76	69	292
27	Gay Brewer	73	73	76	71	293
=28	Butch Baird	73	74	73	74	294
	Bruce Devlin	76	71	71	76	294

July 21–24, 1966 continued

	Ron Howell	76	71	75	72	294
	Don Massengale	74	72	75	73	294
	Dan Sikes	72	76	74	72	294
	R.H. Sikes	75	72	73	74	294

July 20–24, 1967

Columbine CC, Denver, CO

** Don January (69) beat Don Massingale (71) in the 18-hole play-off.*

1	Don January	71	71	70	68	281
2	Don Massingale	70	75	70	66	281
=3	Jack Nicklaus	67	75	69	71	282
	Dan Sikes	69	70	70	73	282
=5	Julius Boros	69	76	70	68	283
	Al Geiberger	73	71	69	70	283
=7	Frank Beard	71	74	70	70	285
	Don Bies	69	70	76	70	285
	Bob Goalby	70	74	68	73	285
	Gene Littler	73	72	71	69	285
=11	Billy Farrell	75	72	69	70	286
	Dave Hill	66	73	74	73	286
	Ken Venturi	73	74	71	68	285
=14	Sam Carmichael	75	71	69	72	287
	Lionel Hebert	75	71	70	71	287
	Bobby Nichols	75	75	67	70	287
	Arnold Palmer	70	71	72	74	287
	R.H. Sikes	72	71	71	73	287
19	Billy Casper	75	70	75	68	288
=20	Tommy Aaron	70	65	76	78	289
	Bill Bisdorf	72	71	77	69	289
	Dick Crawford	76	73	73	67	289
	Ray Floyd	74	69	74	72	289
	Mike Souchak	70	73	70	76	289
25	Wes Ellis Jr	76	71	72	71	290
=26	Bruce Crampton	71	77	74	69	291
	Earl Stewart	77	70	72	72	291
=28	Gay Brewer	75	74	71	72	292
	Gardner Dickinson	75	72	69	76	292
	Phil Rodgers	71	76	72	73	292
	Mason Rudolph	72	73	73	74	292
	Doug Sanders	72	71	76	73	292

July 18–21, 1968

Pecan Valley CC, San Antonio, TX

1	Julius Boros	71	71	70	69	281
=2	Bob Charles	72	70	70	70	282
	Arnold Palmer	71	69	72	70	282
=4	George Archer	71	69	74	69	283
	Marty Fleckman	66	72	72	73	283
=6	Frank Beard	68	70	72	74	284
	Billy Casper	74	70	70	70	284
=8	Miller Barber	70	70	72	73	285
	Frank Boynton	70	73	72	70	285
	Charles Coody	70	77	70	68	285
	Al Geiberger	70	73	71	71	285
	Bob Goalby	73	72	70	70	285
	Lou Graham	73	70	70	72	285
	Doug Sanders	72	67	73	73	285
	Dan Sikes	70	72	73	70	285
	Kermit Zarley	72	75	68	70	285
=17	Dave Hill	72	74	69	71	286
	Mason Rudolph	69	75	70	72	286
	Dave Stockton	75	71	68	72	286
=20	Gay Brewer	71	72	72	72	287
	Al Mengert	71	73	70	73	287

July 18–21, 1968 continued

	Dick Rhyan	72	72	68	75	287
=23	**Bruce Crampton**	71	75	70	72	288
	Lee Trevino	69	71	72	76	288
	Bert Yancey	75	71	70	72	288
=26	**Tommy Aaron**	73	73	73	70	289
	Don Bies	69	73	74	73	289
	Dick Crawford	71	75	73	70	289
	Steve Reid	73	73	71	72	289
=30	**Gardner Dickinson**	74	69	76	71	290
	Lionel Hebert	75	71	70	74	290
	Gene Littler	73	74	74	69	290
	Bob Lunn	72	75	72	71	290

August 14–17, 1969

NCR CC, Dayton, OH

1	**Ray Floyd**	69	66	67	74	276
2	**Gary Player**	71	65	71	70	277
3	**Bert Greene**	71	68	68	71	278
4	**Jimmy Wright**	71	68	69	71	279
=5	**Miller Barber**	73	75	64	68	280
	Larry Ziegler	69	71	70	70	280
=7	**Charles Coody**	69	71	72	69	281
	Orville Moody	70	68	71	72	281
	Terry Wilcox	72	71	72	66	281
10	**Frank Beard**	70	75	68	69	282
=11	**Don Bies**	74	64	71	74	283
	Bunky Henry	69	68	70	76	283
	Larry Mowry	69	71	69	74	283
	Jack Nicklaus	70	68	74	71	283
=15	**Bruce Crampton**	70	70	72	72	284
	Dave Hill	74	75	67	68	284
	Don January	75	70	70	69	284
	Chi Chi Rodriguez	72	72	71	69	284
=19	**Howie Johnson**	73	68	72	72	285
	Johnny Pott	69	75	71	70	285
=21	**Ron Cerrudo**	74	66	70	76	286
	Bobby Cole	72	74	71	69	286
	Bob Lunn	69	74	73	70	286
	Tom Shaw	69	75	73	70	286
=25	**Julius Boros**	72	74	70	71	287
	Gay Brewer	74	71	76	66	287
	Bob Dickson	74	72	70	71	287
	Tony Jacklin	73	70	73	71	287
	George Knudson	70	75	67	75	287
	Fred Marti	73	70	71	73	287
	Dan Sikes	71	74	69	73	287

August 13–16, 1970

Southern Hills CC, Tulsa, OK

1	**Dave Stockton**	70	70	66	73	279
=2	**Bob Murphy**	71	73	71	66	281
	Arnold Palmer	70	72	69	70	281
=4	**Larry Hinson**	69	71	74	68	282
	Gene Littler	72	71	69	70	282
=6	**Bruce Crampton**	73	75	68	67	283
	Jack Nicklaus	68	76	73	66	283
=8	**Ray Floyd**	71	73	65	75	284
	Dick Lotz	72	70	75	67	284
=10	**Billy Maxwell**	72	71	73	69	285
	Mason Rudolph	70	70	73	71	285
=12	**Don January**	73	71	73	69	286
	Johnny Miller	68	77	70	71	286
	Gary Player	74	68	74	70	286
	Sam Snead	70	75	68	73	286

August 13–16, 1970 continued

=16	**Al Geiberger**	72	74	71	71	288
	Mike Hill	70	71	74	73	288
=18	**Billy Casper**	72	70	74	73	289
	Bruce Devlin	75	70	71	73	289
	Al Mengert	76	72	70	71	289
	Dan Sikes	74	70	75	70	289
=22	**Lou Graham**	75	68	74	73	290
	Bob Stanton	71	74	72	73	290
	Bert Yancey	74	69	75	72	290
	Kermit Zarley	73	74	73	70	290
=26	**Julius Boros**	72	71	72	76	291
	Bob Charles	74	73	72	72	291
	Terry Dill	72	71	75	73	291
	Bobby Nichols	72	76	72	72	291
	Lee Trevino	72	77	77	65	291

February 25–28, 1971

PGA National GC, Palm Beach Gardens, FL

1	**Jack Nicklaus**	66	69	70	73	281
2	**Billy Casper**	71	73	71	68	283
3	**Tommy Bolt**	72	74	69	69	284
=4	**Miller Barber**	72	68	75	70	285
	Gary Player	71	73	68	73	285
=6	**Gibby Gilbert**	74	67	72	73	286
	Dave Hill	74	71	71	70	286
	Jim Jamieson	72	72	72	70	285
=9	**Jerry Heard**	73	71	72	71	287
	Bob Lunn	72	70	73	72	287
	Fred Marti	72	71	74	70	287
	Bob Rosburg	74	72	70	71	287
=13	**Frank Beard**	74	71	73	70	288
	Bob Charles	70	75	70	73	288
	Bruce Devlin	71	71	74	72	288
	Larry Hinson	71	73	73	71	288
	Lee Trevino	71	73	75	69	288
=18	**Herb Hooper**	74	71	73	71	289
	Arnold Palmer	75	71	70	73	289
=20	**Johnny Miller**	71	76	72	71	290
	Bob E. Smith	73	70	75	72	290
=22	**Brad Anderson**	71	75	75	70	291
	Chuck Courtney	74	71	74	72	291
	Hale Irwin	73	72	72	74	291
	Jerry McGee	73	74	71	73	291
	John Schroeder	72	74	74	71	291
	Tom Weiskopf	72	70	77	72	291
	Larry Wood	74	71	72	74	291
	Bert Yancey	71	74	70	76	291
=30	**Terry Dill**	75	78	75	74	292
	Gene Borek	72	70	73	77	292
	Rod Funseth	72	77	75	71	292
	Al Geiberger	74	69	77	72	292

August 3–6, 1972

Oakland Hills CC, Birmingham, MI

1	**Gary Player**	71	71	67	72	281
=2	**Tommy Aaron**	71	71	70	71	283
	Jim Jamieson	69	72	72	70	283
=4	**Billy Casper**	73	70	67	74	284
	Ray Floyd	69	71	74	70	284
	Sam Snead	70	74	71	69	284
=7	**Gay Brewer**	71	70	70	74	285
	Jerry Heard	69	70	72	74	285
	Phil Rodgers	71	72	68	74	285
	Doug Sanders	72	72	68	73	285
=11	**Hale Smith**	71	69	75	71	286
	Lee Trevino	73	71	71	71	286
=13	**Jack Nicklaus**	72	75	68	72	287
	Dan Sikes	70	72	73	73	287
15	**Charles Coody**	71	73	70	74	288
=16	**Miller Barber**	73	74	72	70	289
	Hubert Green	75	71	73	70	289
	Arnold Palmer	69	75	72	73	289
	Lanny Wadkins	74	68	72	75	289
=20	**Johnny Miller**	70	76	70	74	290
	Bob Shaw	72	72	74	72	290
	J.C. Snead	72	72	71	75	290
	Larry Wise	74	71	67	78	290
=24	**Bruce Crampton**	73	74	68	76	291
	Lee Elder	73	71	71	76	291
	Chi Chi Rodriguez	71	74	73	73	291
	Bob E. Smith	72	69	76	74	291
	Art Wall	72	71	75	73	291
=29	**Jerry McGee**	73	74	72	73	292
	Mike Souchak	73	73	71	75	292
	Jim Wiechers	70	73	69	80	292
	Bert Yancey	72	74	71	75	292

August 9–12, 1973

Canterbury GC, Cleveland, OH

1	**Jack Nicklaus**	72	68	68	69	277
2	**Bruce Crampton**	71	73	67	70	281
=3	**Manson Rudolph**	69	70	70	73	282
	J.C. Snead	71	74	68	69	282
	Lanny Wadkins	73	69	71	69	282
=6	**Don Iverson**	67	72	70	74	283
	Dan Sikes	72	68	72	71	283
	Tom Weiskopf	70	71	71	71	283
=9	**Hale Irwin**	76	72	68	68	284
	Sam Snead	71	71	71	71	284
	Kermit Zarley	76	71	68	69	284
=12	**Bobby Brue**	70	72	73	70	285
	Jim Colbert	72	70	69	74	285
	Larry Hinson	73	70	71	71	285
	Denny Lyons	73	70	67	75	285
	Dave Stockton	72	69	75	69	285
	Tom Watson	75	70	71	69	285
=18	**Al Geiberger**	67	76	74	69	286
	Gibby Gilbert	70	70	73	73	286
	Bob Goalby	75	70	71	70	286
	Jim Jamieson	71	73	71	71	286
	Johnny Miller	72	71	74	69	286
	Lee Trevino	76	70	73	67	286
=24	**Miller Barber**	73	73	70	71	287
	Bruce Devlin	73	70	74	70	287
	Lee Elder	71	76	70	70	287
	Mike Hill	69	73	75	70	287
	Chi Chi Rodriguez	72	71	74	70	287

August 9–12, 1973 continued

	Bert Yancey	74	72	69	72	287
=30	**Don Bies**	70	72	71	75	288
	Lou Graham	74	71	73	70	288
	John Mahaffey	75	71	72	70	288
	Orville Moody	73	74	70	71	288

August 8–11, 1974

Tanglewood GC, Clemmons, NC

1	**Lee Trevino**	73	66	68	69	276
2	**Jack Nicklaus**	69	69	70	69	277
=3	**Bobby Cole**	69	68	71	71	279
	Hubert Green	68	68	73	70	279
	Dave Hill	74	69	67	69	279
	Sam Snead	69	71	71	68	279
7	**Gary Player**	73	64	73	70	280
8	**Al Geiberger**	70	70	75	66	281
=9	**Don Bies**	73	71	68	71	282
	John Mahaffey	72	72	71	67	282
=11	**Tommy Aycock**	73	68	73	70	284
	Frank Beard	73	67	69	75	284
	Lee Elder	74	69	72	69	284
	Ray Floyd	68	73	74	70	284
	Mike Hill	76	72	68	68	284
	Tom Watson	69	72	68	68	284
=17	**Gay Brewer**	72	72	72	69	285
	Tom Jenkins	70	73	71	71	285
	John Shlee	68	67	75	75	285
	Dan Sikes	71	75	71	68	285
	Leonard Thompson	69	71	70	75	285
=22	**Larry Brion**	71	71	74	70	286
	Bruce Devlin	70	74	70	72	286
=24	**Don Massengale**	74	71	70	72	287
	J.C. Snead	72	72	75	68	287
=26	**Larry Hinson**	74	73	69	72	288
	Dave Stockton	71	73	69	72	288
=28	**Jim Colbert**	70	76	70	73	289
	Gene Littler	76	72	70	71	289
	Arnold Palmer	72	75	70	72	289
	Victor Regalado	70	72	77	70	289

August 7–10, 1975

Firestone CC, Akron, OH

1	**Jack Nicklaus**	70	68	67	71	276
2	**Bruce Crampton**	71	63	75	69	278
3	**Tom Weiskopf**	70	71	70	68	279
4	**Andy North**	72	74	70	65	281
=5	**Billy Casper**	69	72	72	70	283
	Hale Irwin	72	65	73	73	283
=7	**Dave Hill**	71	71	74	68	284
	Gene Littler	76	71	66	71	284
9	**Tom Watson**	70	71	71	73	285
=10	**Buddy Allin**	73	72	70	71	286
	Ben Crenshaw	73	72	71	70	286
	Ray Floyd	70	73	72	71	286
	David Graham	72	70	70	74	286
	Don January	72	70	71	73	286
	John Schlee	71	68	75	72	286
	Leonard Thompson	74	69	72	71	286
=17	**Dale Douglas**	74	72	74	67	287
	Gibby Gilbert	73	70	77	67	287
	Mike Hill	72	71	70	74	287
	Steve Melnyk	71	72	74	70	287
	Gil Morgan	73	71	71	72	287
=22	**Ed Dougherty**	69	70	72	77	288

August 7–10, 1975 continued

	Mark Hayes	67	71	75	75	288
	Chi Chi Rodriguez	73	72	74	69	288
=25	**Jerry Heard**	75	70	70	74	289
	Mac McLendon	73	71	70	75	289
	Bob Murphy	75	68	69	77	289
=28	**Larry Hinson**	68	73	72	77	290
	John Mahaffey	71	70	75	74	290
	J.C. Snead	73	67	75	75	290
	Bob Wynn	69	69	80	72	290

August 12–16, 1976

Congressional CC, Bethseda, MD

1	**Dave Stockton**	70	72	69	70	281
=2	**Ray Floyd**	72	68	71	71	282
	Don January	70	69	71	72	282
=4	**David Graham**	70	71	70	72	283
	Jack Nicklaus	71	69	69	74	283
	Jerry Pate	69	73	72	69	283
	John Schlee	72	71	70	70	283
=8	**Charles Coody**	68	72	67	77	284
	Ben Crenshaw	71	69	74	70	284
	Jerry McGee	68	72	72	72	284
	Gil Morgan	66	68	75	75	284
	Tom Weiskopf	65	74	73	72	284
=13	**Tom Kite**	66	72	73	75	286
	Gary Player	70	69	72	75	286
=15	**Lee Elder**	68	74	70	75	287
	Mark Hayes	69	72	73	73	287
	Mike Hill	72	70	73	72	287
	Mike Morley	69	72	72	74	287
	Arnold Palmer	71	76	68	72	287
	J.C. Snead	74	71	70	72	287
	Tom Watson	70	74	70	73	287
=22	**Lou Graham**	74	70	70	74	288
	Jerry Heard	72	74	69	73	288
	Dave Hill	76	66	75	71	288
	Joe Inman Jr	72	69	74	73	288
	Gene Littler	71	69	73	75	288
	Don Massengale	71	74	73	70	288
	Leonard Thompson	73	69	72	74	288
29	**Joe Porter**	72	71	70	76	289
=30	**Hubert Green**	73	70	73	74	290
	Grier Jones	71	70	75	74	290
	Rik Massengale	71	72	73	74	290
	Bob Zender	69	71	73	77	290

August 11–14, 1977

Pebble Beach Golf Links, Pebble Beach, CA

** Lanny Wadkins beat Gene Littler in a sudden-death play-off at the third extra hole*

1	**Lanny Wadkins***	69	71	72	70	282
2	**Gene Littler**	67	69	70	76	282
3	**Jack Nicklaus**	69	71	70	73	283
4	**Charles Coody**	70	71	70	73	284
5	**Jerry Pate**	73	70	69	73	285
=6	**Al Geiberger**	71	70	73	72	286
	Lou Graham	71	73	71	71	286
	Don January	75	69	70	72	286
	Jerry McGee	68	70	77	71	286
	Tom Watson	68	73	71	74	286
=11	**Joe Inman Jr**	72	69	73	73	287
	Johnny Miller	70	74	73	70	287
=13	**Tom Kite**	73	73	70	72	288
	Lee Trevino	71	73	71	73	288
=14	**George Cadle**	69	73	70	77	289

August 11–14, 1977 continued

	Bruce Lietzke	74	70	74	71	289
	Gil Morgan	74	68	70	77	289
	Leonard Thompson	72	73	69	75	289
=19	**George Archer**	70	73	76	72	291
	George Burns	71	76	70	74	291
	Mark Hayes	68	75	74	74	291
	Arnold Palmer	72	73	73	73	291
	J.C. Snead	76	71	72	72	291
=24	**Miller Barber**	77	68	69	78	292
	Grier Jones	72	74	72	74	292
	Bill Kratzert	71	76	75	70	292
	Lyn Lott	76	75	67	74	292
	Bob Murphy	72	72	69	75	292
	Jim Simons	74	74	69	75	292

August 3–6, 1978

Oakmont CC, Oakmont, PA

** John Mahaffey beat Jerry Pate and Tom Watson in the sudden-death play-off at the second extra hole.*

1	**John Mahaffey***	75	67	68	66	276
=2	**Jerry Pate**	72	70	66	68	276
	Tom Watson	67	69	67	73	276
=4	**Gill Morgan**	76	71	66	67	280
	Tom Weiskopf	73	67	69	71	280
6	**Craig Stadler**	70	74	67	71	282
=7	**Andy Bean**	72	72	70	70	284
	Graham Nash	72	74	68	70	284
	Lee Trevino	69	73	70	74	284
10	**Fuzzy Zoeller**	75	69	73	68	285
11	**Joe Inman Jr**	72	68	69	77	286
=12	**Hale Irwin**	73	71	73	70	287
	Bill Kratzert	70	77	73	67	287
	Larry Nelson	76	71	70	70	287
	John Schroeder	76	69	70	72	287
=16	**Ben Crenshaw**	69	71	75	73	288
	Phil Hancock	70	73	70	75	288
	Grier Jones	70	73	71	74	288
=19	**Willy Armstrong**	71	73	75	70	289
	George Burns	79	68	70	72	289
	Bob Gilder	74	71	70	74	289
	Don January	73	72	75	69	289
	Bobby Nichols	75	67	73	74	289
	Dave Stockton	68	75	74	72	289
	Kermit Zarley	75	71	67	76	289
=26	**George Cadle**	74	74	74	68	290
	Rod Curl	76	72	73	70	290
	Hubert Green	71	71	74	74	290
	Peter Oosterhuis	73	72	72	73	290
	Gary Player	76	72	71	71	290
	Greg Powers	75	70	75	70	290
	Bob Shearer	73	73	71	73	290
	Bob Zender	73	69	74	74	290

August 2–5, 1979

Oakmont Hills CC, Birmingham, MI

** David Graham beat Ben Crenshaw in a sudden-death play-off at the third extra hole.*

1	**David Graham**	69	68	70	65	272
2	**Ben Crenshaw**	69	67	69	67	272
3	**Red Caldwell**	67	70	66	71	274
4	**Ron Streck**	68	71	69	68	276
=5	**Gibby Gilbert**	69	72	68	69	278
	Jerry Pate	69	69	69	71	278
=7	**Jay Haas**	68	69	73	69	279
	Don January	69	70	71	69	279
	Howard Twitty	70	73	69	67	279
=10	**Lou Graham**	69	74	68	69	280
	Gary Koch	71	71	71	67	280
=12	**Andy Bean**	76	69	68	68	281
	Jerry McGee	73	69	71	68	281
	Jack Renner	71	74	66	70	281
	Tom Watson	66	72	69	74	281
=16	**Bob Gilder**	73	71	68	70	282
	Hubert Green	69	70	72	71	282
	Bruce Lietzke	69	69	71	73	282
	Gene Littler	71	71	67	73	282
	Graham Marsh	69	70	71	72	282
=21	**Bob Byman**	73	72	69	69	283
	John Schroeder	72	72	70	69	283
=23	**Frank Conner**	70	73	69	72	284
	Rob Funseth	70	69	76	69	284
	Peter Jacobsen	70	74	67	76	284
	Gary Player	73	70	70	71	284
	Alan Tapie	73	65	76	70	284
=28	**Miller Barber**	73	72	69	71	285
	George Burns	71	74	67	73	285
	Mark McCumber	75	68	70	72	285
	Artie McNickle	69	70	72	74	285
	Gil Morgan	72	73	70	70	285
	Larry Nelson	70	75	70	70	285
	Ed Sneed	77	67	70	71	285

August 7–10, 1980

Oak Hill CC, Rochester, NY

1	**Jack Nicklaus**	70	69	66	69	274
2	**Andy Bean**	72	71	68	70	281
=3	**Lon Hinckle**	70	69	69	75	283
	Gil Morgan	68	70	73	72	283
=5	**Curtis Strange**	68	72	72	72	284
	Howard Twitty	68	74	71	71	284
7	**Lee Trevino**	74	71	69	69	285
=8	**Bill Rodgers**	71	71	72	72	286
	Bobby Walzel	68	76	71	71	286
=10	**Terry Diehl**	72	72	68	76	288
	Peter Jacobsen	71	73	74	70	288
	Jerry Pate	72	73	70	73	288
	Tom Watson	75	74	72	67	288
	Tom Weiskopf	71	73	72	72	288
=15	**John Mahaffey**	71	77	69	72	289
	Andy North	72	70	73	74	289
=17	**George Archer**	70	73	75	72	290
	Ray Floyd	70	76	71	73	290
	Joe Inman Jr	72	71	75	72	290
=20	**Rex Caldwell**	73	70	73	75	291
	Rod Curl	74	71	75	71	291
	Tom Kite	73	70	76	72	291
	Bob Murphy	68	80	72	71	291
	Jack Newton	72	73	73	73	291
	Alan Tapie	74	75	69	73	291

August 7–10, 1980 continued

=26	**Lee Elder**	70	75	74	73	292
	David Graham	69	75	73	75	292
	Gary Player	72	74	71	75	292
	Leonard Thompson	71	75	73	73	292
=30	**Jim Colbert**	73	75	77	68	293
	Bruce Devlin	76	73	71	73	293
	Bob Eastwood	72	73	73	75	293
	David Edwards	73	76	73	71	293
	Hale Irwin	69	76	74	74	293
	Bruce Lietzke	71	75	74	73	293
	Artie McNickle	71	71	76	75	293
	Scott Simpson	74	74	74	71	293
	Mike Sullivan	71	74	75	74	293
	Doug Tewell	73	71	75	74	293
	Lanny Wadkins	76	72	72	73	293

August 6–9, 1981

Atlanta Athletic Club, Duluth, GA

1	**Larry Nelson**	70	66	66	71	273
2	**Fuzzy Zoeller**	70	68	68	71	277
3	**Dan Pohl**	69	67	73	69	278
=4	**Isao Aoki**	75	68	66	70	279
	Keith Fergus	71	71	69	68	279
	Bob Gilder	74	69	70	76	279
	Tom Kite	71	67	69	72	279
	Bruce Lietzke	70	70	71	68	279
	Jack Nicklaus	71	68	71	69	279
	Greg Norman	73	67	68	71	279
=11	**Vance Heafner**	68	70	70	72	280
	Andy North	68	69	70	73	280
	Jerry Pate	71	68	70	71	280
	Tommy Valentine	73	70	71	66	280
15	**J.C. Snead**	70	71	70	70	281
=16	**David Edwards**	71	69	70	72	282
	Hale Irwin	71	74	68	69	282
18	**Bob Murphy**	66	69	73	75	283
=19	**John Cook**	72	69	70	73	284
	Ray Floyd	71	70	71	72	284
	Jay Haas	73	68	71	69	284
	Joe Inman Jr	73	71	67	73	284
	Don January	70	72	70	72	284
	Gil Morgan	70	69	74	71	284
	Don Pooley	74	70	69	71	284
	Tom Purtzer	70	70	73	71	284
=27	**Bobby Clampett**	75	71	70	69	285
	Hubert Green	71	74	71	69	285
	Peter Jacobsen	74	71	71	69	285
	Bill Rodgers	72	75	66	72	285
	Curtis Strange	73	72	74	66	285
	Tom Weiskopf	71	72	72	70	285

August 5–8, 1982

Southern Hills CC, Tulsa, OK

1	**Ray Floyd**	63	69	68	72	272
2	**Lanny Wadkins**	71	68	69	67	275
=3	**Fred Couples**	67	71	72	66	276
	Calvin Peete	69	70	68	69	276
=5	**Jay Haas**	71	66	68	72	277
	Greg Norman	66	69	70	72	277
	Jim Simons	68	67	73	69	277
8	**Bob Gilder**	66	68	72	72	278
=9	**Lon Hinkle**	70	68	71	71	280
	Tom Kite	73	70	70	67	280
	Jerry Pate	72	69	70	69	280

August 5–8, 1982 continued

	Tom Watson	72	69	71	68	280
13	**Seve Ballesteros**	71	68	69	73	281
=14	**Nick Faldo**	67	70	73	72	282
	Curtis Strange	72	70	71	69	282
=16	**Jim Colbert**	70	72	72	69	283
	Dan Halldorsan	69	71	72	71	283
	Bruce Lietzke	73	71	70	69	283
	Jack Nicklaus	74	70	72	67	283
	Tom Purtzer	73	69	73	68	283
	Craig Stadler	71	70	70	72	283
=22	**Danny Edwards**	71	71	68	74	284
	Gil Morgan	76	66	68	74	284
	Peter Oosterhuis	72	72	74	66	284
	Mark Pfeil	68	73	76	67	284
	Ron Streck	71	72	71	70	284
	Doug Tewell	72	70	72	70	284
	Leonard Thompson	72	72	71	69	284
=29	**Mike Holland**	71	73	70	71	285
	Bill Rodgers	73	71	70	71	285
	Hal Sutton	72	68	70	75	285

August 4–7, 1983

Riviera CC, Pacific Palisades, CA

1	**Hal Sutton**	65	66	72	71	274
2	**Jack Nicklaus**	73	65	71	66	275
3	**Peter Jacobsen**	73	70	68	65	276
4	**Pat McGowan**	68	67	73	69	277
5	**John Fought**	67	69	71	71	278
=6	**Bruce Lietzke**	67	71	70	71	279
	Fuzzy Zoeller	72	71	67	69	279
8	**Dan Pohl**	72	70	69	69	280
=9	**Ben Crenshaw**	68	66	71	77	282
	Jay Haas	68	72	69	73	282
	Mike Reid	69	71	72	70	282
	Scott Simpson	66	73	70	73	282
	Doug Tewell	74	72	69	67	282
=14	**Keith Fergus**	68	70	72	73	283
	David Graham	79	69	74	70	283
	Hale Irwin	72	70	73	68	283
	Roger Maltbie	71	71	71	70	283
	Jim Thorpe	68	72	74	69	283
	Lee Trevino	70	68	74	71	283
=20	**John Cook**	74	71	68	71	284
	Danny Edwards	67	76	71	70	284
	Ray Floyd	69	75	71	69	284
=23	**Chip Beck**	72	71	70	72	285
	Fred Couples	71	70	73	71	285
	Jerry Pate	69	72	70	74	285
	Don Pooley	72	68	74	71	285
=27	**Seve Ballesteros**	71	76	72	67	286
	Bobby Wadkins	73	72	74	67	286
	Buddy Whitten	66	70	73	77	286
=30	**Andy Bean**	71	73	71	72	287
	Bob Boyd	70	77	72	68	287
	Johnny Miller	72	75	73	67	287
	Mark Pfeil	73	71	70	73	287
	Jim Simons	69	75	72	71	287
	Tom Weiskopf	76	70	69	72	287

August 16–19, 1984

Shoal Creek CC, Birmingham, AL

1	**Lee Trevino**	69	68	67	69	273
=2	**Gary Player**	74	63	69	71	277
	Lanny Wadkins	68	69	68	672	277
4	**Calvin Peete**	71	70	69	68	278
5	**Seve Ballesteros**	70	69	70	70	279
=6	**Gary Hallberg**	69	71	68	72	280
	Larry Mize	71	69	67	73	280
	Scott Simpson	69	69	72	70	280
	Hal Sutton	74	73	64	69	280
=10	**Russ Cochran**	73	68	73	67	281
	Tommy Nakajima	72	68	67	74	281
	Victor Regalado	69	69	73	70	281
13	**Ray Floyd**	68	71	69	74	282
=14	**Hubert Green**	70	74	66	73	283
	Mark Reid	68	72	72	71	283
=16	**Andy Bean**	69	75	70	70	284
	Donnie Hammond	70	69	71	74	284
=18	**Peter Jacobsen**	70	72	72	71	285
	Craig Stadler	71	73	73	68	285
=20	**Fred Couples**	72	72	75	67	286
	Nick Faldo	69	73	74	70	286
	Keith Fergus	72	72	72	70	286
	John Mahaffey	72	72	72	70	286
	Corey Pavin	73	72	74	67	286
=25	**Chip Beck**	69	77	70	71	287
	Red Caldwell	71	71	74	71	287
	Jim Colbert	71	72	74	70	287
	Hale Irwin	71	70	74	72	287
	Jack Nicklaus	77	70	71	69	287
	Tim Simpson	73	70	72	72	287
	Doug Tewell	72	71	71	73	287

August 8–11, 1985

Cherry Hills CC, Eglewood, CO

1	**Hubert Green**	67	69	70	72	278
2	**Lee Trevino**	66	68	75	71	280
=3	**Andy Bean**	71	70	72	68	281
	Tze-Ming Chen	69	76	71	65	281
5	**Nick Price**	73	73	65	71	282
=6	**Fred Couples**	70	65	76	72	283
	Buddy Garner	73	73	70	67	283
	Corey Pavin	66	75	73	69	283
	Tom Watson	67	70	74	72	283
=10	**Peter Jacobsen**	66	71	75	72	284
	Lanny Wadkins	70	69	73	72	284
=12	**Scott Hoch**	70	73	73	69	285
	Tom Kite	69	75	71	70	285
	Dan Pohl	72	74	69	70	285
	Scott Simpson	72	68	72	73	285
	Payne Stewart	72	72	73	68	285
	Doug Tewell	64	72	77	72	285
=18	**Bob Gilder**	73	70	74	69	286
	Wayne Levi	72	69	74	71	286
	Bruce Lietzke	70	74	72	70	286
	Calvin Peete	69	72	75	70	286
	Craig Stadler	72	73	74	67	286
=23	**T.C. Chen**	73	74	74	66	287
	John Mahaffey	74	73	71	69	287
	Larry Mize	71	70	73	73	287
	Larry Nelson	70	74	71	72	287
	Willie Wood	71	73	74	69	287
=28	**Roger Maltbie**	69	73	72	74	288
	Gil Morgan	69	77	72	70	288

August 8–11, 1985 continued

	Mark O'Meara	71	76	71	70	288
	Joey Sindelar	71	75	71	71	289

August 7–10, 1986

Inverness Club, Toledo, OH

1	Bob Tway	72	70	64	70	276
2	Greg Norman	65	68	69	76	278
3	Peter Jacobsen	68	70	70	71	279
4	D.A. Weibring	71	72	68	69	280
=5	Bruce Lietzke	69	71	70	71	281
	Payne Stewart	70	67	72	72	281
=7	David Graham	75	69	71	67	282
	Mike Hulbert	69	68	74	71	282
	Jim Thorpe	71	67	73	71	282
10	Doug Tewell	73	71	68	71	283
=11	Ben Crenshaw	72	73	72	67	284
	Donnie Hammond	70	71	68	75	284
	Lonnie Nielsen	73	69	72	70	284
	Lee Trevino	71	74	69	70	284
	Lanny Wadkins	71	75	70	68	284
=16	Chip Beck	71	73	71	70	285
	Jack Nicklaus	70	68	72	75	285
	Don Pooley	71	74	69	71	285
	Tony Sills	71	72	69	73	285
	Tom Watson	72	69	72	72	285
=21	Ronnie Black	68	71	74	73	286
	David Frost	70	73	68	75	286
	Wayne Grady	68	76	71	71	286
	Corey Pavin	71	72	70	73	286
	Hal Sutton	73	71	70	72	286
=26	Ken Green	71	72	71	73	287
	Hale Irwin	76	70	73	68	287
	Tom Kite	72	73	71	71	287
	Dan Pohl	71	71	74	71	287
=30	Wayne Levi	68	73	71	76	288
	Calvin Peete	72	73	69	74	288
	Gene Sauers	69	73	69	74	288
	Jeff Sluman	70	71	76	71	288
	Craig Stadler	67	74	73	74	288
	Ian Woosnam	72	70	75	71	288

August 6–9, 1987

PGA National GC, Palm Beach Gardens, FL

** Larry Nelson beat Lanny Wadkins in a sudden-death play-off at the first extra hole.*

1	Larry Nelson*	70	72	73	72	287
2	Lanny Wadkins	70	70	74	73	287
=3	Scott Hoch	74	74	71	69	288
	D.A. Weibring	73	72	67	76	288
=5	Mark McCumber	74	69	69	77	289
	Don Pooley	73	71	73	72	289
=7	Ben Crenshaw	72	70	74	74	290
	Bobby Wadkins	68	74	71	77	290
9	Curtis Strange	70	76	71	74	291
=10	Seve Ballesteros	72	70	72	78	292
	David Frost	75	70	71	76	292
	Tom Kite	72	77	71	72	292
	Nick Price	76	71	70	75	292
=14	Curt Byrum	74	75	68	76	293
	David Edwards	69	75	77	72	293
	Ray Floyd	70	70	73	80	293
	Dan Pohl	71	78	75	69	293
	Tom Watson	70	79	73	71	293
19	Peter Jacobsen	73	75	73	73	294
=20	Jim Hallett	73	78	73	71	295
	Bernhard Langer	70	78	77	70	295
	Gil Morgan	75	74	70	76	295
=23	Ken Brown	73	74	73	76	296
	Jack Nicklaus	76	73	74	73	296
	Gene Sauers	76	74	68	78	296
	Payne Stewart	72	75	75	74	296
=27	Ronnie Black	76	70	76	75	297
	Bobby Clampett	71	72	77	77	297
	Russ Cochran	73	76	69	79	297
	John Cook	76	70	72	79	297
	Brad Fabel	73	73	77	74	297
	Nick Faldo	73	73	77	74	297
	Jay Haas	74	70	76	77	297
	Bruce Lietzke	75	76	74	72	297
	Roger Maltbie	74	72	75	76	297
	Chris Perry	75	75	74	73	297
	Craig Stadler	75	72	75	75	297
	Hal Sutton	73	74	74	76	297

August 11–14, 1988

Oak Tree GC, Edmond, OK

1	Jeff Sluman	69	70	68	65	272
2	Paul Azinger	67	66	71	71	275
3	Tommy Nakajima	69	68	74	67	278
=4	Tom Kite	72	69	71	67	279
	Nick Faldo	67	71	70	71	279
=6	Bob Gilder	66	75	71	68	280
	Dave Rummells	73	64	68	75	280
8	Dan Pohl	69	71	70	71	281
=9	Ray Floyd	68	68	74	72	282
	Steve Jones	69	68	72	73	282
	Kenny Knox	72	69	68	73	282
	Greg Norman	68	71	72	71	282
	Mark O'Meara	70	71	70	71	282
	Payne Stewart	70	69	70	73	282
=15	John Mahaffey	71	71	70	71	283
	Craig Stadler	68	73	75	67	283
=17	Mark Calcavecchia	73	69	70	72	284
	Ben Crenshaw	70	71	69	74	284
	David Graham	70	67	73	74	284
	Mark McNulty	73	70	67	74	284
	Jay Overton	68	66	76	74	284
	Corey Pavin	71	70	75	68	284
	Nick Price	74	70	67	73	284
	Richard Zokol	70	70	74	70	284
=25	Ronnie Black	71	71	70	73	285
	Jay Don Blake	71	73	72	69	285
	David Edwards	71	69	77	69	285
	Scott Hoch	74	69	68	74	285
	Blaine McCallister	73	67	75	70	285
	Lanny Wadkins	74	69	70	72	285

August 10–13, 1989

Kemper Lakes GC, Hawthorn Woods, IL

1	**Payne Stewart**	74	66	69	67	276
=2	**Andy Bean**	70	67	74	66	277
	Mike Reid	66	67	70	74	277
	Curtis Strange	70	68	70	69	277
5	**Dave Rummells**	68	69	69	72	278
6	**Ian Woosnam**	68	70	70	71	279
=7	**Scott Hoch**	69	69	69	73	280
	Craig Stadler	71	64	72	73	280
=9	**Nick Faldo**	70	73	69	69	281
	Ed Fiori	70	67	75	69	281
	Tom Watson	67	69	74	71	281
=12	**Seve Ballesteros**	72	70	66	74	282
	Jim Gallagher Jr	73	69	68	72	282
	Greg Norman	74	71	67	70	282
	Mike Sullivan	76	66	67	73	282
	Mark Wiebe	71	70	69	72	282
=17	**Isao Aoki**	72	71	65	75	283
	Ben Crenshaw	68	72	72	71	283
	Buddy Garner	72	71	70	70	283
	Dave Love III	73	69	72	69	283
	Blaine McCallister	71	72	70	70	283
	Larry Mize	73	71	68	71	283
	Chris Perry	67	70	70	76	283
=24	**Tommy Armour**	70	69	73	72	284
	Dan Pohl	71	69	74	70	284
	Jeff Sluman	75	70	69	70	284
=27	**David Frost**	70	74	69	72	285
	Mike Hulbert	70	71	72	72	285
	Peter Jacobsen	70	70	73	72	285
	Jack Nicklaus	68	72	73	72	285
	Tim Simpson	69	70	73	73	285
	Bryan Tennyson	71	69	72	73	285
	Howard Twitty	72	71	68	74	285

August 9–12, 1990

Shoal Creek CC, Birmingham, AL

1	**Wayne Grady**	72	67	72	71	282
2	**Fred Couples**	69	71	73	72	285
3	**Gil Morgan**	77	72	65	72	286
4	**Bill Britton**	72	74	72	71	289
=5	**Chip Beck**	70	71	78	71	290
	Billy Mayfair	70	71	75	74	290
	Loren Roberts	73	71	70	76	290
=8	**Mark McNulty**	74	72	75	71	292
	Don Pooley	75	74	71	72	292
	Tim Simpson	71	73	75	73	292
	Payne Stewart	71	72	70	79	292
=12	**Hale Irwin**	77	72	70	74	293
	Larry Mize	72	68	76	77	293
=14	**Billy Andrale**	75	72	73	74	294
	Morris Hatalsky	73	78	71	72	294
	Jose-Maria Olazabal	73	77	72	72	294
	Corey Pavin	73	75	72	74	294
	Fuzzy Zoeller	72	71	76	75	294
=19	**Bob Floyd**	74	74	71	76	295
	Nick Faldo	71	75	80	69	295
	Blaine McCallister	75	73	74	73	295
	Greg Norman	77	69	76	73	295
	Mark O'Meara	69	76	79	71	295
	Tom Watson	74	71	77	73	295
	Mark Wiebe	74	73	75	73	295
=26	**Mark Brooks**	78	69	76	73	296
	Peter Jacobsen	74	75	71	76	296

August 9–12, 1990 continued

	Chris Perry	75	74	72	75	296
	Ray Stewart	73	73	75	75	296
	Brian Tennyson	71	77	71	77	296

August 8–11, 1991

Crooked Stick GC, Carmel, IN

1	**John Daly**	69	67	69	71	276
2	**Bruce Lietzke**	68	69	72	70	279
3	**Jim Gallagher Jr**	70	72	72	67	281
4	**Kenny Knox**	67	71	70	74	282
=5	**Bob Gilder**	73	70	67	73	283
	Steve Richardson	70	72	72	69	283
=7	**David Feherty**	71	74	71	68	284
	Ray Floyd	69	74	72	69	284
	John Huston	70	72	70	72	284
	Steve Pate	70	75	70	69	284
	Craig Stadler	68	71	69	76	284
	Hal Sutton	74	67	72	71	284
=13	**Jay Don Blake**	75	70	72	68	285
	Andrew Magee	69	73	68	75	285
	Payne Stewart	74	70	71	70	285
=16	**Nick Faldo**	70	69	71	76	286
	Ken Green	68	73	71	74	286
	Wayne Levi	73	71	72	70	286
	Sandy Lyle	68	75	71	72	286
	Rocco Mediate	71	71	73	71	286
	Gil Morgan	70	71	74	71	286
	Howard Twitty	70	71	75	70	286
=23	**Seve Ballesteros**	71	72	71	73	287
	Chip Beck	73	73	70	71	287
	Mike Hulbert	72	72	73	70	287
	Jack Nicklaus	71	72	73	71	287
=27	**Fred Couples**	74	67	76	71	288
	Rick Fehr	70	73	71	74	288
	Jim Hallett	69	74	73	72	288
	Mark McNulty	75	71	69	73	288
	Loren Roberts	72	74	72	70	288

August 13–16, 1992

Bellerive CC, St Louis, MO

1	**Nick Price**	70	70	68	70	278
=2	**John Cook**	71	72	67	71	281
	Nick Faldo	68	70	76	67	281
	Jim Gallagher Jr	72	66	76	67	281
	Gene Sauers	67	69	70	75	281
6	**Jeff Maggert**	71	72	65	74	282
=7	**Russ Cochran**	69	69	76	69	283
	Dan Forsman	70	73	70	70	283
=9	**Brian Claar**	68	73	73	70	284
	Anders Forsbrand	73	71	70	70	284
	Duffy Waldorf	74	73	68	69	284
=12	**Billy Andrade**	72	71	70	72	285
	Corey Pavin	71	73	70	71	285
	Jeff Sluman	73	71	72	69	285
=15	**Mark Brooks**	71	72	68	75	286
	Brad Faxon	72	69	75	70	286
	Greg Norman	71	74	71	70	286
=18	**Steve Elkington**	74	70	71	72	287
	Rick Fehr	74	73	71	69	287
	John Huston	73	75	71	68	287
=21	**Bill Britton**	70	77	70	71	288
	Fred Couples	69	73	73	73	288
	Lee Janzen	74	71	72	71	288
	Tom Kite	73	73	69	73	288

	August 13–16, 1992 continued					
	Gill Morgan	71	69	73	75	288
	Tommy Nakajima	71	75	69	73	288
	Tom Purtzer	72	72	74	70	288
=28	**Mike Hulbert**	74	74	70	71	289
	Peter Jacobsen	73	71	72	73	289
	Larry Nelson	72	68	75	74	289
	Joe Ozaki	76	72	74	67	289
	Tom Wargo	72	72	73	72	289

August 12–15, 1993

Inverness Club, Toledo, OH

* *Paul Azinger beat Greg Norman in a sudden-death play-off at the second extra hole.*

1	**Paul Azinger***	69	66	69	68	272
2	**Greg Norman**	68	68	67	69	272
3	**Nick Faldo**	68	68	69	68	274
4	**Vijay Singh**	68	63	73	70	274
5	**Tom Watson**	69	65	70	72	276
=6	**John Cook**	72	66	68	71	277
	Bob Estes	69	66	69	73	277
	Dudley Hart	66	68	71	72	277
	Nolan Henke	72	70	67	68	277
	Scott Hoch	74	68	68	67	277
	Hale Irwin	68	69	67	73	277
	Phil Mickelson	67	71	69	70	277
	Scott Simpson	64	70	71	72	277
=14	**Steve Elkington**	67	66	74	71	278
	Brad Faxon	70	70	65	73	278
	Bruce Fleisher	69	74	67	68	278
	Gary Hallberg	70	69	68	71	278
	Lanny Wadkins	65	68	71	74	278
	Richard Zokol	66	71	71	70	278
=20	**Jay Haas**	69	68	70	72	279
	Eduardo Romero	67	67	74	71	279
=22	**Lee Janzen**	70	68	71	72	281
	Jim McGovern	71	67	69	74	281
	Frank Nobilo	69	66	74	72	281
	Gene Sauers	68	74	70	69	281
	Ian Woosnam	70	71	68	72	281
=28	**Peter Jacobsen**	71	67	74	70	282
	Billy Mayfair	68	73	70	71	282
	Loren Roberts	67	67	76	72	282

August 11–14, 1994

Southern Hills CC, Tulsa, OK

1	**Nick Price**	67	65	70	67	269
2	**Corey Pavin**	70	67	69	69	275
3	**Phil Mickelson**	68	71	67	70	276
=4	**John Cook**	71	67	69	70	277
	Nick Faldo	73	67	71	66	277
	Greg Norman	71	69	67	70	277
=7	**Steve Elkington**	73	70	66	69	278
	Jose Maria Olazabal	72	66	70	70	278
=9	**Ben Crenshaw**	70	67	70	72	279
	Tom Kite	72	68	69	70	279
	Loren Roberts	69	72	67	71	279
	Tom Watson	69	72	67	71	279
	Ian Woosnam	68	72	73	66	279
14	**Jay Haas**	71	66	68	75	280
=15	**Glen Day**	70	69	70	72	281
	Mark McNulty	72	68	70	71	281
	Larry Mize	72	72	67	70	281
	Kirk Triplett	71	69	71	70	281
=19	**Bill Glasson**	71	73	68	70	282

	August 11–14, 1994 continued					
	Mark McCumber	73	70	71	68	282
	Craig Parry	70	69	70	73	282
	Craig Stadler	70	70	74	68	282
	Curtis Strange	73	71	68	70	282
	Fuzzy Zoeller	69	71	72	70	282
=25	**Ernie Els**	68	71	69	75	283
	David Frost	70	71	69	73	283
	Barry Lane	70	73	68	72	283
	Bernhard Langer	73	71	67	72	283
	Jeff Sluman	70	72	66	75	283
=30	**Bob Boyd**	72	71	70	71	284
	Lennie Clements	74	70	69	71	284
	Brad Faxon	72	73	73	66	284
	Wayne Grady	75	68	71	70	284
	Sam Torrance	69	75	69	71	284
	Richard Zokol	77	67	67	73	284

August 10–13, 1995

Riviera CC, Pacific Palisades, CA

* *Steve Elkington beat Colin Montgomerie in the sudden-death play-off at the first extra hole.*

1	**Steve Elkington***	68	67	68	64	267
2	**Colin Montgomerie**	68	67	67	65	267
=3	**Ernie Els**	66	65	66	72	269
	Jeff Maggert	66	69	65	69	269
5	**Bob Faxon**	70	67	71	63	271
=6	**Bob Estes**	69	68	68	68	273
	Mark O'Meara	64	67	69	73	273
=8	**Jay Haas**	69	71	64	70	274
	Justin Leonard	68	66	70	70	274
	Steve Lowery	69	68	68	69	274
	Jeff Sluman	69	67	68	70	274
	Craig Stadler	71	66	66	71	274
=13	**Jimmy Furyk**	68	70	69	68	275
	Miguel Jimenez	69	69	67	70	275
	Payne Stewart	69	70	69	67	275
	Kirk Triplett	71	69	68	67	275
=17	**Michael Campbell**	71	65	71	69	276
	Constantino Rocca	70	69	68	69	276
	Curtis Strange	72	68	68	68	276
=20	**Greg Norman**	66	69	70	72	277
	Jesper Parnevik	69	69	70	69	277
	Duffy Waldorf	69	69	67	72	277
=23	**Woody Austin**	70	70	70	68	278
	Nolan Henke	68	73	67	70	278
	Peter Jacobsen	69	67	71	71	278
	Lee Janzen	66	70	72	70	278
	Bruce Lietzke	73	68	67	70	278
	Billy Mayfair	68	68	72	70	278
	Steve Stricker	75	64	69	70	278
	Sam Torrance	69	69	69	71	278

August 8–11, 1996

Valhalla GC, Louisville, KY

* *Mark Brooks beat Kenny Perry in a sudden-death play-off at the first extra hole.*

1	**Mark Brooks***	68	70	69	70	277
2	**Kenny Perry**	66	72	71	68	277
=3	**Steve Elkington**	67	74	67	70	278
	Tommy Tolles	69	71	71	67	278
=5	**Justin Leonard**	71	66	72	70	279
	Jesper Parnevik	73	67	69	70	279
	Vijay Singh	69	69	69	72	279
=8	**Lee Janzen**	69	71	71	70	280
	Per-Ulrik Johannson	73	72	66	69	280

August 8 - 11,1996 continued

	Phil Mickelson	67	67	74	72	280
	Larry Mize	71	70	69	70	280
	Frank Nobilo	69	72	71	68	280
=13	**Mike Brisky**	71	69	69	72	281
	Tom Lehman	71	71	69	70	281
	Joey Sindelar	73	72	69	67	281
=16	**Russ Cochran**	68	72	65	77	282
	David Edwards	69	71	72	70	282
	Brad Faxon	72	68	73	69	282
	Jim Furyk	70	70	73	69	282
	Greg Norman	68	72	69	73	282
	Tom Watson	69	71	73	69	282
	D.A. Weibring	71	73	71	67	282
=23	**Emlyn Aubrey**	69	74	72	68	283
	Miguel Jimenez	71	71	71	70	283
=25	**Fred Funk**	73	69	73	69	284
	Mark O'Meara	71	70	74	69	284
	Corey Pavin	71	74	70	69	284
	Curtis Strange	73	70	68	73	284
	Steve Stricker	73	72	72	67	284

August 14–17, 1997

Winged Foot GC, Mamaroneck, NY

1	**Davis Love III**	66	71	66	66	269
2	**Justin Leonard**	68	70	65	71	274
3	**Jeff Maggert**	69	69	73	65	276
4	**Lee Janzen**	69	67	74	69	279
5	**Tom Kite**	68	71	71	70	280
=6	**Phil Blackmar**	70	68	74	69	281
	Jim Furyk	69	72	72	68	281
	Scott Hoch	71	72	68	70	281
9	**Tom Byrum**	69	73	70	70	282
=10	**Tom Lehman**	69	72	72	70	283
	Scott McCarron	74	71	67	71	283
	Joey Sindelar	72	71	71	69	283
=13	**David Duval**	70	70	71	73	284
	Tim Herron	72	73	68	71	284
	Colin Montgomerie	74	71	67	72	284
	Greg Norman	68	71	74	71	284
	Mark O'Meara	69	73	75	67	284
	Nick Price	72	70	72	70	284
	Vijay Singh	73	66	76	69	284
	Tommy Tolles	75	70	73	66	284
	Kirk Triplett	73	70	71	70	284
	Bob Tway	68	75	72	69	284
=23	**Mark Calcavecchia**	71	74	73	76	285
	John Cook	71	71	74	69	285
	Bernhard Langer	73	71	72	69	285
	Doug Martin	69	75	74	67	285
	Shigeki Maruyama	68	70	74	73	285
	Kenny Perry	73	68	73	71	285
=29	**Ronnie Black**	76	69	71	70	286
	Fred Couples	71	67	73	75	286
	John Daly	66	73	77	70	286
	Paul Goydos	70	72	71	73	286
	Hale Irwin	73	70	71	72	286
	Phil Mickelson	69	69	73	75	286
	Frank Nobilo	72	73	67	74	286
	Don Pooley	72	74	70	70	286
	Payne Stewart	70	70	72	74	286
	Lee Westwood	74	68	71	73	286
	Tiger Woods	70	70	71	75	286

August 13–16, 1998

Sahalee Country Club, Redmond, WA

1	**Vijay Singh**	70	66	67	68	271
2	**Steve Stricker**	69	68	66	70	273
3	**Steve Elkington**	69	69	69	67	274
=4	**Nick Price**	70	73	68	65	276
	Mark O'Meara	69	70	69	68	276
	Frank Lickliter	68	71	69	68	276
=7	**Billy Mayfair**	73	67	67	70	277
	Davis Love III	70	68	69	70	277
=9	**John Cook**	71	68	70	69	278
	Kenny Perry	69	72	70	68	279
	Tiger Woods	66	72	70	71	279
	Skip Kendall	72	68	68	71	279
=13	**Brad Faxon**	70	68	74	68	280
	Fred Couples	74	71	67	68	280
	Bob Tway	69	76	67	68	280
	Paul Azinger	68	73	70	69	280
	Bill Glasson	68	74	69	69	280
	Steve Flesch	75	69	67	69	280
	John Huston	70	71	68	71	280
	Robert Allenby	72	68	69	71	280
=21	**Ernie Els**	72	72	71	66	281
	Andrew Magee	70	68	72	71	281
=23	**Per-Ulrik Johansson**	69	74	71	68	282
	Fred Funk	70	71	71	70	282
	Scott Gump	68	69	72	73	282
	Greg Kraft	71	73	65	73	282
=27	**Jeff Sluman**	71	73	70	69	283
	Hal Sutton	72	68	72	71	283
=29	**Glen Day**	68	71	75	70	284
	Tom Lehman	71	71	70	72	284
	Ian Woosnam	70	75	67	72	284
	Lee Rinker	70	70	71	73	284
	Scott Hoch	72	69	70	73	284

Chapter 3

THE OTHER TOURNAMENTS

THE FOUR MAJOR CHAMPIONSHIPS MAY BE THE MOST IMPORTANT TOURNAMENTS IN GOLF BUT THEY ARE, OF COURSE, FAR FROM THE ONLY ONES. INDEED, THE RYDER CUP NOW STANDS AT LEAST ALONGSIDE THEM IN TERMS OF SPECTATOR INTEREST IN EUROPE. THEN THEIR ARE THE TOURNAMENTS THAT MAKE UP THE SCHEDULES ON THE EUROPEAN AND UNITED STATES TOURS, WOMEN'S AND SENIOR GOLF, AND THE THREE NEW WORLD CHAMPIONSHIP EVENTS WITH THEIR PRIZE FUNDS THAT ENABLE THE TOP PLAYERS TO EARN SALARIES COMFORTABLY INTO SEVEN FIGURES PER ANNUM. WHAT FOLLOWS IS A COMPREHENSIVE ROUND-UP OF WHAT SPORTING COMMENTATORS ARE FOND OF REFERRING TO AS "THE BEST OF THE REST".

THE RYDER CUP

For those who have come to golf over the last 20 years, it must be hard to believe that it is only during that time-span that the Ryder Cup has been anything more than an exhibition contest between successive American sides who became increasingly bored with its one-sidedness and British teams ill-equipped to do anything about it.

It was Jack Nicklaus who changed that mentality in 1977, with one of the more auspicious interventions of even his career. He suggested to Lord Derby, the president of the Professional Golfers' Association, that their cause might be better served with the inclusion in their 12-man team of the best of the European players who were just beginning to make an impact. Without such a move, it is quite possible that the Ryder Cup would not be around today.

Now, on the strength of it, it has become one of sport's great events, a gladiatorial occasion between two teams that still do not always look well-matched in theory, but who invariably prove so in practice. Since Nicklaus was taken up on his suggestion, 10 Ryder Cups have been played and America have won five, Europe four, with one tie.

Furthermore, a closer examination of the scorelines in each instance fully illustrates what a titanic struggle the Ryder Cup has become. Of the eight matches to have been held since 1983, seven have been decided by a margin of two points or less. This is surely unprecedented in team sports over such a period of time. The nature of any game is that one side will usually have a period of dominance over another. But for 16 years now this has happily not been the case with the Ryder Cup, and long may it continue.

It was far different, of course, in the days when Great Britain and Ireland had to go it alone and successes became as rare as precious diamonds. In some matches, America could have fielded a third team and still won. The saving grace was often solely the spirit of the Ryder Cup, fostered long ago in the dim mists of the 1920s, and one which has largely been maintained to the present day.

The one downside of the present operation is the fact that the Ryder Cup has been a victim of its own success. It has become such a money-spinner in Europe that it is blatantly used as a marketing tool by both the PGA and the European Tour, and consequently sold to the highest bidder.

This was true in 1997 when it was outrageously taken to Spain, despite the fact that countries that had been playing in it from the start, like Wales and Ireland, had still to be host. This was because Jaime Patino, the owner of the winning venue, Valderrama, provided the financial wherewithal that made it worth the European Tour's while.

It was a similarly depressing story when The Belfry was awarded the 2001 contest despite having already hosted it three times since 1985, and will be true again when it finally touches down in Ireland in 2005. The vast majority of people would like it to have gone to a true links like Portmarnock, but instead it will go to a new course called the K Club, for the overriding reason that the owner, Michael Smurfit, is exceedingly rich and has agreed to act as munificent benefactor to the European Tour in return.

What Samuel Ryder would have made of such shenanigans one shudders to think, but certainly such overt commercialism was far from his thoughts when he agreed to provide a trophy for competition between teams representing the United States and Great Britain and Ireland.

The Ryder Cup is born

Ryder, the son of a Manchester corn merchant, made his own fortune from the innovative idea of selling penny packets of seeds to the garden lovers of England. He took to golf in 1910 at the age of 50, after the business had become well established and he could afford to spend more time relaxing and indulging in various leisure pursuits.

He quickly became hooked by the game and enthralled by the skill of the professionals. In 1923 he sponsored a tournament at his home club – Verulam, in St Albans, Hertfordshire – which was believed to be the first of its kind. Among the participants was Abe Mitchell, and the pair hit it off so well that Ryder employed him to be his personal tutor at the then exceedingly generous sum of £1,000 a year.

It was through his friendship with Mitchell that Ryder found himself at an unofficial match in 1926 between professionals representing America and Great Britain. The venue was Wentworth, the reason for the match to fill in some time between regional qualifying for the Open Championship and the event itself. Mitchell teamed up with George Duncan to defeat the defending Open champion Jim Barnes and Walter Hagen 9&8. It set the tone, for the home side won by a score of thirteen-and-a-half points to one-and-a-half. As impressed by the atmosphere in the bar afterwards as the golf, Ryder is said to have pronounced: "We must do this again."

Certainly he must have said something that was in keeping with the spirt of this remark, for he was instantly prevailed upon to present a trophy that would ensure that it was done again. Thus the Ryder Cup was born, with its striking gold tro-

Abe Mitchell – a personal tutor to Samuel Ryder who was honoured by being the golfer to adorn the trophy

Walter Hagen (left) – capained the first official US Ryder Cup team in 1927

phy that cost the considerable sum of £250. The golfer that sits on top of the lid is, predictably enough, Abe Mitchell.

The date of the first official Ryder Cup was arranged for June 3 and 4, the venue Worcester Country Club, which intriguingly is less than an hour's drive from the 1999 venue, the Country Club, Brookline.

The professionals, naturally, were wildly enthusiastic at these developments, but such fervour was hardly shared by the golfing public. In Britain an appeal was launched through the magazine, *Golf Illustrated*, to help fund the expenses of the players. It had been hoped to raise £3,000, but in the end there was a shortfall of £500. More than 1,700 clubs were approached for help but only 216 gave it their financial support.

The editor of *Golf Illustrated* was apoplectic. In an editorial, he thundered: "It is disappointing that the indifference or selfishness of the multitude of golfers should have been so marked that what they could have done with ease has been imposed as a burden upon a small number. It is a deplorable reflection on the attitude of the average golfer towards the game. At a very conservative estimate there are at least 500,000 golfers in this country. If only one in every five had given a shilling [5p] – surely not a lot to expect – a sum of £5,000 would have been raised."

Nevertheless the team that was chosen had high hopes of doing well both in the Ryder Cup and the US Open, which would be held a week later. Harold Hilton, writing in *Golf Monthly*, said: "This team is a well-considered blending of experienced skill and rising skill."

It was not long, however, before reality hit home. The side were about to board the *Aquitania* for America when the captain, Abe Mitchell, was struck down with appendicitis. Ted Ray took his place as captain, with Herbert Jolly called in at the last moment to replace him as a player.

The format agreed in advance was the same as had been played in the four Walker Cup matches to have been staged to that point; that is, four foursomes matches followed by eight singles, all matches over 36 holes.

The pattern of Ryder Cups to come was set on the first day. The Americans took the series 3–1, with Ray uttering words that would become a mantra for Great Britain & Ireland captains over the next 50 years: "They were far superior on the greens, and holed out much better than we did."

The only success for the visitors had come from Aubrey Boomer and Charlie Whitcombe, who played impressive par golf to defeat Leo Diegel and Bill Mehlhorn 7&6.

If the foursomes had been one-sided it was as nothing compared with the singles the following day. Again there was only one success for Great Britain and Ireland, that coming from George Duncan. That was in the last match which went to the final green – but by then the American team was heavily into celebratory mood. There were some fearfully large victories: Diegel recovered from the opening day to beat Ray 7&5; Johnny Golden topped even that, beating the decidedly unjolly Jolly 8&7. Whitcombe, however, gained a half against Gene Sarazen, thus to emerge as the only unbeaten player on the GB&I side. It is a measure of the Americans' superiority, however, that while no visiting player managed two points out of two, four US golfers recorded the feat.

If the opening Ryder Cup had been a disappointingly one-sided affair, the second match at Moortown, Leeds, in 1929 amply compensated, offering some of the raw excitement that matchplay can induce. It also introduced partisanship, which may come as quite a surprise to those who thought the phenomenon of cheering a missed putt from the opposition was another example of declining standards in the modern era.

Indeed, in his excellent *History of the Ryder Cup*, the late Michael Williams describes the "definite cheer" that went up when the leading American foursome of Johnny Farrell and Joe Turnesa managed to miss a putt of little more than 12 inches on the opening green.

Nevertheless, the American pair recovered to force a halved match against Charlie Whitcombe and Archie Compston, and the Ryder Cup appeared to be going the way of the first held two years earlier when America won two of the foursomes that followed, and lost one.

Still, the margin going into the singles was a highly recoverable one point, and the home side were in high spirits as the effervescent Fred Robson went through his funny man's routine and the waiter at the Majestic Hotel, Harrogate, plied them with copious amounts of whisky. Imagine what the tabloid newspapers would make of such revelations today!

It never affected the team the next day, that is for sure. Charlie Whitcombe made it three points from four matches, and no losses, when he got the home side off to the perfect start by trouncing Johnny Farrell 8&6 in the top singles.

In the match behind, Hagen was stumbling to an even more comprehensive defeat at the hands of the Great Britain and Ireland captain, George Duncan. Diegel evened things up overall by beating Abe Mitchell, but then Archie Compston defeated Gene Sarazen. The 10,000 crowd who turned up were feverish with excitement as the matches behind reached their conclusion.

Firstly, Aubrey Boomer upset the odds by seeing off the more talented Jim Turnesa, which cancelled out a loss for Robson at the hands of some wonderful golf from Horton Smith. Two matches out on the course... and GB&I one point ahead.

First it looked as if Ernest Whitcombe would secure the trophy when he went two up with two to play against Al Espinosa, but then he had an attack of nerves and lost both holes to finish all square.

So finally it was up to the youngest member of the British team, Henry Cotton, against Al Watrous. At first this looked likely to be a comprehensive success for the American as he won three of the first four holes. But Cotton pegged him back with trademark indefatigability. He squared the match at the 18th by chipping in with his wedge, a wonderful psychological blow with which to end the morning play.

After lunch all the benefits were apparent. He grew in stature the more the match went on, and eventually saw off his opponent 4&3. Great Britain and Ireland had pulled off a notable success.

Home side monopoly

Any prospect that GB&I could build on that success and put up a good performance upon their return to America in 1931 was ended before the team even set sail for America. A Trust Deed agreed between the teams ruled that players had not only to be natives of the country they represented but also resident. This ruled out two leading Britons: Aubrey Boomer because he was the pro at St Cloud, Paris; and Percy Alliss who was attached to the Wansee Club in Berlin. Just to put the tin lid on matters, a fatuous decision by the PGA that all players had to return to Britain directly after the match led to Henry Cotton turning down his invitation. He had no intention of being dictated to by anyone.

Given the absence of such talents, what happened next at Scioto, OH, was all too predictable. The Americans won three of the four foursomes matches, and six of the eight singles, to run out convincing winners.

Despite this, large crowds turned up at Southport and Ainsdale two years later to see if GB&I could square the series at two matches each. The home captain was J.H. Taylor, now 62 but still a revered figure. He was probably a little less revered when he ordered the team on to Southport beach every morning at 6.30 a.m. for a morning run. "The Ryder Cup is not a picnic," he explained.

Once more Henry Cotton was absent, this time because he broke the rules of eligibility as he was stationed at the Royal Waterloo club in Belgium. Of more fascination was the American team, which contained no fewer than five players who were competing for the first time in Britain. The result was two teams that looked evenly matched on paper, and proved so on the course. This was a precursor to all those thrilling Ryder Cups that would dot the 1980s and 1990s.

From the start, things went well for the British; for the first time they took the opening foursomes, establishing a one-point lead going into the second day.

In the top singles Gene Sarazen, the reigning US Open champion, evened matters with a remorseless thrashing of Alf Padgham. This was balanced, however, by a still-more-dominant performance from Abe Mitchell, at 46 the oldest player on either team. He started well against Olin Dutra and just kept pulling away, eventually emerging triumphant by 9&8.

It was not a triumph upon which the home side could build. Behind, Walter Hagen and Craig Wood were both notching victories. With four matches out on the course, Great Britain and Ireland were in dire need of a strong performance from the tail, with three wins necessary for an overall success.

With the Duke of Windsor in attendance, Percy Alliss started the ball rolling, beating Paul Runyon two and one. Then Arthur Havers kept the cheers rolling all over Southport & Ainsdale's picturesque dunes as he ran out a 4&3 winner against Leo Diegel. Could Charlie Whitcombe manage the winning point against Horton Smith? He could not, losing two and one.

So it was all down to Syd Easterbrook against Denny Shute for the Ryder Cup. To say there was not a spare seat in the house as they came to the final hole is not an exaggeration.

Walter Hagen – at the tee in the 1933 clash at Southport & Ainsdale. Amongst the crowd is the Prince of Wales

The momentous nature of the occasion had its effect on the players; both bunkered their approach shots. Neither recovery was a particularly good one, and when Easterbrook putted first and missed, Shute had his chance for the Ryder Cup.

Clearly, this was all that was on his mind. He went for it, too boldly as it turned out, and the ball finished four feet from the hole. Years later, just a couple of miles away, Tony Jacklin would be faced with a slightly shorter putt to achieve what Easterbrook was trying to achieve, and salvage a tie. In that later instance Jack Nicklaus picked up Jacklin's ball and conceded the putt. This, however, was slightly further away, and Shute had to putt. He missed.

That it did not unduly affect him was evident from the fact that later the same month he won the Open Championship at St Andrews. For now, though, there was merely delerium. The cup was back in British hands. It would be almost a quarter of a century before it would be again.

The most interesting thing that can be said for the 1935 match was that the British side featured three brothers: Charles, Reg and Ernest Whitcombe. None was able to prevent a much superior American side from handing out a 9–3 tousing, although Charles and Ernest did combine to produce the visitors' only point from the foursomes. A measure of the massive one-sidedness of the contest came from the other three matches – the winning margin in each instance was, respectively, 7&6, 6&5 and 9&8.

The British Press did not waver in its pungent criticism. In the *Daily Mail* Tom Webster wrote that the away side "could not hole out in a hole the size of the Atlantic". Another verdict was: "The British were content to go for the greens while the Americans always went for the flag."

In 1937 the Americans were determined to do something about their poor record on British soil. Once more the venue was Southport and Ainsdale, but one look at the visiting team suggested that things would be completely different this time.

The non-playing captain was Walter Hagen, while the chosen 10 included a young Sam Snead and Byron Nelson, plus Ralph Guldahl, Horton Smith and the ageless Gene Sarazen. All 10 members would, at some stage in their careers, win at least one major championship.

By contrast the home 10 had just one player who would be so successful, and that was Cotton, who was back in the fold having returned to England from Waterloo.

Yet at lunchtime on the first morning Great Britain & Ireland were ahead in two matches and level in the other two. Alas, it was a false promise; America would recover to win two points and halve a third.

The superior strength in depth of the Americans was obvious on the second day. In practice only Dai Rees and Cotton had appeared to be in good form for the British, and they turned out to be the only singles winners. Sam King did manage a half with Denny Shute, returning to the scene of his worst nightmare, but elsewhere there were only wins for the stronger unit. The final victory margin was 8–4 and America had well and truly snapped the travelling voodoo.

There was some consolation for the British golf audience. From Southport and Ainsdale the two teams headed northward for Carnoustie and the Open Championship, where

The US Ryder Cup team in 1937 set out to defend their trophy and to record a first win on British soil

Henry Cotton scored successively lower in each round to claim a notable triumph. Could things be different in the next Ryder Cup? The two chosen teams never got the chance to find out. The match had been scheduled for November, 1939, at the Ponte Vedra club in Jacksonville, but Britain declared war on Germany two months earlier and it would be eight more years before the Ryder Cup could be staged once again.

Back to business

Even then it was only thanks to one generous benefactor that the Ryder Cup was revived; without his help it is quite possible that the match would quite simply have slipped away.

Robert Hudson was an industrialist who sponsored the Portland Open each year on the US Tour and who placed great value on the Ryder Cup. Without his support there is no way the British team could have made its way to Portland in November, 1947. The British PGA were in an impoverished state and knew they could not launch an appeal fund so soon after the end of the war.

Henry Cotton was captain of the Great Britain and Ireland side that sailed on the *Queen Mary*. Waiting for him was Ben Hogan, captain of one of the strongest American sides ever to have been assembled. Leonard Crawley, writing in the *Daily Telegraph*, confirmed the view. "This is as good a side as any that has ever played against Great Britain, and probably better," he wrote.

Crawley thought the visitors would be lucky to win four games out of the 12 played. In the event they did not come close to even that miserly target, going down by a score of 11–1, the heaviest defeat of all.

To be fair to the British, there were mitigating circumstances. While play had been impossible in Britain during the war, the tour had been kept on the road in America and many of the US Ryder Cup side had consequently retained their competitive edge.

That said, even the ones who did see combat played beautifully. Like Lloyd Mangrum, who was wounded and subsequently decorated in the D-Day landings. He teamed up with Sam Snead to overcome Fred Daly and Charlie Ward 6&5 in the foursomes; on the second day Mangrum recorded the same margin of victory in disposing of Max Faulkner.

Ben Hogan was again the American captain two years later at Ganton, but this time he could not play. This match came just six months after his horrific car accident, and he was still on crutches when he arrived in Yorkshire. Not that the experience softened him in any way. On the eve of the match Hogan expressed himself unhappy with some of the clubs used by a number of the British players, believing that the grooves were too deep.

At first many thought this a tit-for-tat accusation, following Cotton's request to inspect the golf balls the Americans had used in Oregon in 1947, as he believed they had imparted too much backspin. In fact, Hogan was on very solid ground. The clubs did not comply with the rules and the Ganton professional Jock Ballantine worked through the night to file them down so they did meet the specification.

It was not the only bone of contention. With food rationing still in force in Britain, the Americans brought with them their own supply of food, including 600 steaks. A number of British players and officials took this the wrong way, believing that it implied that what the hosts had to offer was not good enough. The jokers in the team, meanwhile, were wondering how the Americans could possibly eat so much food in such a short space of time.

Anyway, with those two grievances to fuel their motivation, plus the memory for no fewer than seven of them of the 11–1 humiliation two years earlier, Great Britain and Ireland gave a wonderful account of themselves on the first day.

From the off they rocked the visitors with a series of sterling strokes. At lunch on the first day Great Britain were three up and two up in the first two foursomes, one down in the third and all square in the fourth.

In the afternoon, Max Faulker and Jimmy Adams maintained the onslaught in the top foursomes, and when they finished off the match on the 17th green they were no less than five under the card. Behind them, Fred Daly and Ken Bousfield had gone round in 69 to earn their lunchtime lead, and when the debutant Bousfield pitched adjacent to the flag at the 14th second time around the match was over.

Jimmy Demaret and Clayton Heafner got a point back for the Americans before Dick Burton and Arthur Lees ensured it was the home side's day with a notable defeat on the home green of the formidable pairing of Snead and Mangrum.

It meant that Great Britain and Ireland needed just three-and-a-half points from the second day's eight singles to win. The morning was not too old, however, before it became clear that this was not going to be as straightforward as it sounded. Dai Rees quickly established a winning advantage against Bob Hamilton, while Adams disposed of Johnny Palmer. But where was the other point-and-a-half to come from? Certainly not Max Faulkner, who was hammered 8&7, while Ward also lost heavily to Sam Snead. So to the final four matches, and the furious wagging of the American tail. All told there were victories for Heafner, Chick Harbert, Demaret and Mangrum, to complete a stunning US fightback.

As disappointing as it was for the home side, credit had to be given to the visitors. Some of the golf was extraordinary, particularly from Mangrum, a magnificent player who never quite got the credit his golf deserved since it came in the era of Snead, Hogan, and Nelson. But it was not just Fred Daly who could not live with him on that second day; it would have been beyond the remit of anyone.

GB&I salvage some pride

Back in America the Ryder Cup was once more a yawn. The venue was Pinehurst, NC, but it did not matter where the match was played – the British on their travels had no answer to the American's superiority. The winning margin was nine-and-a-half, two-and-a-half.

It was clear that it needed the British to have the advantage of home soil to make a contest of the Ryder Cup, and never was this emphasized more than by the two matches that took place in the 1950s. One would result in a famous victory, at Lindrick in 1957. But first there was the shattering heartbreak of a close defeat, one that brought unfair condemnation raining down upon the heads of two young players who did not deserve the criticism that came their way.

The year was 1953, the year that Britain finally stopped looking backwards towards the war and instead cast its eyes forward towards regeneration. There was the coronation of Queen Elizabeth II; and the climbing of Everest by Sir Edmund Hillary and his sherpa, Tensing. Sport played its part as well. England won the Ashes, Gordon Richards the Derby, and Sir Stanley Matthews had his day of days in the FA Cup final.

When it came to the Ryder Cup optimism abounded, principally because the visitors travelled without Ben Hogan, who that year won each of the three major championships he entered. Hogan had decided against playing 36-hole matches, which remained the Ryder Cup's format.

The British captain was Henry Cotton, who exemplified the optimism by leaving out the experienced Dai Rees and Max Faulkner in the foursomes and instead playing all four of his debutants. It was just one aspect of Cotton's captaincy that with hindsight looks seriously awry, and certainly the plan seriously misfired. After the first day, the score was America 3, GB&I 1. "It was gloom and misery everywhere," Desmond Hackett wrote in the *Daily Express*.

It was almost much worse as well. Fred Daly and Harry Bradshaw, three up with nine to play against Walter Burkemo and Cary Middlecoff, were pegged back to one up with one to play. Fortunately they held on, which was just as well because by then the other three games had all been lost.

What made matters worse for the crowd was that two of the matches were lost causes from the start. Eric Brown and John Panton were seven down after nine to the all-conquering Snead and Mangrum, while Ted Kroll and Jack Burke were round the West Course in 66 before lunch to go seven up on Jimmy Adams and Bernard Hunt. The top foursomes were closer, but Dave Douglas and Ed Oliver finished up winners when it ended on the 17th, against Harry Weetman and Peter Alliss.

After Cotton the inveterate gambler on the opening morning we saw Cotton the great motivator on the second day. Rees was put out first in the belief that he could not wait to get at the Americans having not played the first day. Then Daly, then Brown, with the simple instruction: "All I want from you is a point."

To which the irascible Brown replied: "And you are bloody going to get it."

The tactics worked like a charm. Rees went down to Burke, but the next three matches were all won with Brown and Weetman recording particularly worthy victories on the final hole against Mangrum and Snead, respectively. To gathering excitement at Wentworth, the home side were in with a shout.

The out-of-sorts Faulkner lost to Middlecoff but Bradshaw chipped in with a point against Fred Haas, which meant that with two matches still to be decided, the sides were level. The good news for Britain was that they were up in both games as they came to the conclusive holes. Both featured young players, however, and no one knew whether they were as yet equipped to handle the severest pressure.

One up with three to play, Peter Alliss allowed his opponent, Joe Turnesa, to turn a poor drive at the 16th into a win with a par. At the 17th Alliss then drove out of bounds; one down. At the last, it was Turnesa's turn to feel the unbearable tension - he drove into the trees. With Alliss just short of the green in two and Turnesa destined for a six, at least the young Englishman would be able to salvage a half.

Alas for Alliss, he made a mess of the pitch. It came miserably to rest just short of the green but the riposte that followed was defiant, his chip finishing four feet from the hole. When Turnesa missed his putt for a par, Alliss appeared to be off the hook. Then he missed his putt, and the beginning of a lifetime of regret on the greens had begun.

As far as the Ryder Cup was concerned, however, there was still hope in the final match. If Bernard Hunt could win, and he was one up with one to play against Dave Douglas, then the contest would have its first tie. It was the least the home side deserved for its stirring second-day fightback, but it was not to be. Three miserable putts from the back of the green when two would have sufficed meant that Hunt, like Alliss, had taken six on the last. Over such little things can Ryder Cups slip away and this one had, by a single point.

GB&I close the gap

Back in America, all was predictable. No wonder the wider US public treated the Ryder Cup with all the excitement of a grass-growing competition. In 1955 the score at the Thunderbird Ranch and Country Club, CA, was 8–4 to the home side.

Four points, however, was more than Great Britain and Ireland had ever managed before on America soil, and at the closing ceremony Lord Brabazon of Tara took great comfort

Dai Rees holds aloft the Ryder Cup in 1957 – the first time it had been held in British hands since 1933

from it. "We have learned a lot, although we have lost, and we are going back to practise in the streets and on the beaches," he pronounced.

They were to prove prophetic words, for in 1957 GB&I turned in arguably the finest performance in all the contests held before they were amalgamated with the best of the Europeans. Well, the best second-day performance anyway, for after the opening day the natural order of things had taken place as America established a 3–1 lead.

Immediately after play had finished the home captain Dai Rees called a team meeting to decide who would participate in the singles. The matter was settled quickly: Max Faulkner, with trademark honesty, said that his golf was "rubbish" and he should not play; Weetman, too, reacted promptly and said he should stand down.

And so it fell to Eric Brown to lead the counter-attack, with a defiant 4&3 victory over the aptly-named Tommy Bolt in the top singles. "I guess you won, but I did not enjoy it a bit," Bolt said to Brown when it was over. "And nor would I after the licking I have just given you," Brown replied. Bolt was furious.

again," the Golden Bear told his opponent. Then he began birdie, birdie. But Barnes was not intimidated and eventually followed up his 4&2 victory with a 2&1 triumph. What Barnes remembers most of all now is how well Nicklaus took his two defeats. That was always the measure of the man, of course.

It was back to Lytham in 1977, where in 1961 the format of the Ryder Cup had been tampered with for the first time. Now it was tinkered with again. At Laurel Valley the players had complained of playing too much golf, and their criticisms did not go unanswered. Now there was just one series of foursomes and fourballs matches on the first two days, followed by ten singles on the final day. With just 20 points at stake instead of 32, and a maximum of three games instead of five, perhaps GB&I would have a better chance.

It was a disaster. It was the Ryder Cup's Golden Jubilee and the contest plumbed new depths. There was simply not enough golf for the spectators to watch on the first two days, and then when there was enough on the third day the Ryder Cup was over as a contest. Furthermore, for the games over the first two days, the tee-times were 45 minutes apart, so one of the essentials of the Ryder Cup – the way the cheers of the spectators filter down to the matches behind – was completely lost. The final score was twelve-and-a-half seven-and-a-half to the Americans, and now there clearly would need to be a lot of hard thinking as to what to do about the match.

Europe provides the answer

The Americans, indeed, were ready to call a halt to proceedings. It was Jack Nicklaus who suggested a solution. "It is vital to widen the selection procedures if the Ryder Cup is to continue to enjoy its past prestige," he told Lord Derby.

In a book that came out shortly after the Ryder Cup, Nicklaus expanded on this view: "I've played in five Ryder Cup matches and have greatly enjoyed both the camaraderie of the event and the goodwill it promotes. But as far as the Americans are concerned it is very difficult to get charged up for the matches themselves. By saying this I am not trying to put down my British friends, but the fact must be faced that British professional golf in recent years simply has not developed a sufficient depth of good players to make a true contest."

Nicklaus then went on to make the suggestion of an amalgamated European team, or a team comprising the rest of the world, to take on the US. And now once the seed had been planted, it started to grow. The British PGA were at first reluctant but the Americans insisted. And so the change was made. It would be Europe versus America from 1979. And the Ryder Cup was about to enter the golden age.

Few could have suspected that such joyous times would be just around the corner when the two teams gathered at the Greenbrier, WV in September, 1979. John Jacobs, who had been instrumental in the setting-up of the European Tour three years earlier, was given the honour of being captain – although what a dubious honour it appeared to be when two members of his team started behaving like spoilt schoolboys.

Mark James and Ken Brown were the brats in question, which seems astonishing given their standing now with the establishment, to the extent that they are the captain and vice-captain, respectively, for the 1999 match.

Back then they were the mutineers. James turned up for the trip across the Atlantic in a pair of jeans instead of the team uniform. Brown insisted that he would only partner James, and no other player. At one point, at a time when a team meeting was due to take place, the pair were off shopping in the Greenbrier arcade. When the opening ceremony took place, both did not try to disguise their boredom.

In some respects the blame for all this delinquency can be laid at Jacobs's feet, since he was clearly far too lenient with them, and they took full advantage. A stronger captain like Tony Jacklin would have laid the law down to both in no uncertain terms. Indeed the great man remarked later that looking back he would have told both to pack their bags.

Certainly officialdom was ready to take a strong line over what went on. When the pair got home Brown was fined £1,000 and suspended from team golf for a year, while James was fined £1,500.

Did their stupid behavour influence the outcome of the match? After all, Europe only trailed by one point going into the singles. It seems unlikely. James, indeed, only played one match due to injury. Brown, meanwhile, claimed a notable singles scalp in Fuzzy Zoeller, not that many people felt like handing out the warmest congratulations.

The two continentals who had the distinction of being the first to play in the Ryder Cup were Antonio Garrido and Severiano Ballesteros. In truth neither contributed quite as much as hoped. They were partners in all four pairings matches but won only one; both lost their singles as well.

All 12 players were due to compete in the singles for the first time, with six matches scheduled for the morning and six after lunch. In the event James had to withdraw, and Gil Morgan was the unlucky American who dropped out. By the time the afternoon's singles went ahead, the Ryder Cup was all but over. America had won five in the morning session to establish a six-point difference between the teams, which would remain the margin at the end.

Walton Heath was the venue in 1981, a last-minute substitute after the proposed host, The Belfry, had to withdraw because it had still to complete its transformation from a potato field. Walton Heath, in any case, was a much better venue, a glorious traditional course and a worthy setting for the matches.

One look at the scoreline suggests that the assimilation of the continentals had made little difference to the composition

Jack Nicklaus and Tom Watson – part of arguably the best Ryder Cup team of all time in 1981

of the Ryder Cup. Nine points separated the teams at the end of the contest, a massive margin.

Two factors were influential. Much the smallest of the two was the self-inflicted wound of leaving out Severiano Ballesteros, because he had played much of his golf in America and so was deemed to have failed to support the European Tour. It was the first in a whole series of lamentable decisions that have dogged the last 20 years of the contest; decisions have been made on what is best for the European Tour, instead of what is best for the Ryder Cup.

In any event, it would have needed at least half-a-dozen Ballesteroses to have stopped this particular American juggernaut. When people talk about the best Ryder Cup team of all time, then surely this US side must get the vote. All told 11 of the 12 had either won or would win major championships and the twelfth, Bruce Lietzke, would have done so as well if he had possessed an ounce of dedication.

For the Europeans it was like taking on a battleship armed with a dinghy. The whole contest was summed up in a nutshell by the match involving Sandy Lyle and Tom Kite. When it finished on the 16th green of one of England's most formidable venues, Lyle was six under par and shaking hands. Yet, extraordinarily, it was in defeat, for Kite was 10 under.

Plus points? Nick Faldo showed his developing maturity with a 2&1 win over Johnny Miller; a young Bernhard Langer grabbed a half with Lietzke. Europe may have lost this particular battle but it was clear that a young group of players were emerging that would come again, and next time the American challenge would surely not be as formidable. And there was always Ballesteros, if they could get him back on their side.

The Ryder Cup comes of age

The Ryder Cup truly entered the modern era in 1983. Tony Jacklin was appointed captain and what a difference he made. Jacklin had lived through the dog days, and felt that the British and now the Europeans were one down before they started because they thought they were inferior to the Americans. He changed all that. He told the PGA that he would only take on the job if the team travelled across the Atlantic on Concorde, and wore the best suits that money could buy. He was determined to raise their horizons.

The other key factor, he felt, was to get Ballesteros into the fold. He did this by appealing to the great man's pride. He told the Spaniard that he was the most important player in the team, which was hardly an exaggeration since he was a triple major championship winner by this stage. He told him to think of how badly the Americans treated him – how they never got his name right when he stepped on to the first tee; how Hale Irwin had branded him a car-park champion at Lytham in 1979.

Ballesteros took the bait. When he arrived at PGA National at Palm Beach, FL, he was breathing fire. The next masterstroke that Jacklin pulled was to pair Ballesteros with a young Paul Way, believing that being the senior partner would appeal to the Spaniard.

Way and Ballesteros would lose on the first morning but that would prove their only defeat in four matches. Way was so inspired by the experience that he defeated Curtis Strange in the singles. That opening defeat mattered little as Nick Faldo and Bernhard Langer, and Jose-Maria Canizares and Sam Torrance, both gained points. The first series had always proved the most difficult for Britain and Ireland, and now under the guise of Europe they at least lunched on equal terms.

After lunch it got better than that. Brian Waites and Ken Brown joined Ballesteros and Way in the winner's circle, while Torrance and Ian Woosnam gained a half. For the first time ever, the visitors were ahead at the end of the opening day on American soil.

The second day was scintillating, and what mixed emotions it must have wrought in the home captain Jack Nicklaus. It was one thing to suggest to Lord Derby that the Europeans should be assimilated into the British team; but the last thing he wanted was a net result by which he became the first American captain to lose on home soil.

With the singles to come it remained a possibility. America had the better of the second day but only by a single point. That made the teams level with 12 points to be decided. With the pivotal day to come, it was already the best Ryder Cup ever staged in America.

The first match out inevitably featured Ballesteros. Jacklin wanted his star man to give his side the best possible send-off. What a match he had with Fuzzy Zoeller. Three up with seven to play and seemingly cruising, perhaps the effects of a long hard week took their toll on the Spaniard. Whatever, he then lost four holes in a row before winning the 16th.

His cause seemed lost at the par-five 18th when he drove into the deep rough and recovered only into a bunker, some 240 yards from the green, with water threatening the approach. What happened next is part of the Ballesteros legend, and those who saw the ball up near the lip of the sand swear that, given the circumstances, it was the finest shot ever played. Where most players would have taken a mid-iron at most, Ballesteros played a three wood and struck it perfectly, the ball finishing pin high, from where he got down in a chip and putt. He escaped with a half.

Faldo and Langer won the next two matches to put Europe in the driving seat but back came America. They won the next three; then Way came in with his vital point; then Craig Stadler beat Woosnam.

With two matches on the course, the scores were level at 13–13. In one, Lanny Wadkins was one down playing the last against Jose-Maria Canizares; in the other Tom Watson was one up playing the 17th against Bernard Gallacher.

An overall tie, then, appeared likely. But then Wadkins produced a stroke of magic. Both he and Canizares had laid up short at the 18th, where it was the American who produced the killer thrust, a wedge that almost pitched in the hole and finished stone dead, while the Spaniard came up well short. Wadkins had escaped with a half, and it made all the difference.

Now Gallacher had to make up a hole, but it was not to be. At the 17th both players succumbed to the pressure of the moment. Watson gave Gallacher a chance by taking a bogey four, but all the Scot could offer in return was a double-bogey five.

America had escaped with the trophy. Nicklaus kissed the ground from where Wadkins had played his pivotal pitch; for Jacklin, meanwhile, there was only crushing disappointment. As for the Ryder Cup, it had rarely known such excitement, and the fun was only just beginning.

Everything felt right for Europe at The Belfry in 1985. Earlier that spring Bernhard Langer had joined Ballesteros as a major championship winner by collecting a green jacket at the Masters. In the summer, Sandy Lyle had become the first British golfer since Tony Jacklin in 1969 to win the Open. Together with Nick Faldo and Ian Woosnam, this quintet provided a powerful argument for believing that Europe had a team that was every bit the equal of the opposition.

Fuelling that belief was the fact that Tony Jacklin was back for another stint as captain. Helping him was that his opposite number was Lee Trevino, who would prove an uninspiring skipper. Five continentals were among the 12 home players, emphasizing that this was very much a European team.

Being European did not cure the team's old failing – making a poor start in the opening series of foursomes. Only Ballesteros and Manuel Pinero emerged with a point as the home side were thumped 3–1. The afternoon fourballs restored faith. Ballesteros and Pinero were once more inspired, while Paul Way and Ian Woosnam defeated Fuzzy Zoeller and Hubert Green. With Langer and Jose-Maria Canizares gaining a half, the deficit at the end of the first day was a point.

The turning point in this Ryder Cup undoubtedly came with the last match in the morning play on the second day. Two down with two to play, Lyle and Langer got back into it when the former holed a huge eagle putt at the 17th. At the last, however, it appeared the well had run dry. Stadler was left with an 18-inch putt for a half, and a one-hole victory, which would give each side two points apiece, and leave the momentum still with the Americans.

As Stadler surveyed it, there was some disquiet as to why the Europeans had not conceded it, the putt being so tiny. Then the reason was revealed, as Stadler yanked it wide of the hole. From the moment he hit it he knew he had missed, and turned his back instantly.

To say it was a fillip for the Europeans would be the biggest of understatements. Now they were level, now they could not wait to get back out on to the course. In the afternoon fourballs it showed. They won three matches, lost one, and now a historic victory was in sight with 12 singles matches to come.

On that final day there was a brave win for Stadler over Woosnam, but in the Ryder Cup momentum is everything.

Tony Jacklin – an inspirational captain for the Europeans

Pinero, Lyle, Langer and Way all registered victories while Ballesteros got a half against Tom Kite. Now it was up to Sam Torrance against the US Open champion Andy North. North found the water with his drive off the 18th, Torrance was so far down the fairway he had but a nine iron to the green. When he hit it to 20 feet the Ryder Cup was won; when he sank the birdie putt his hands shot up to form an appropriate V for victory, and as he was swamped by his team-mates he promptly broke down and cried with joy.

What partly makes American golf so strong is the bitterness felt in defeat. It was there as Concorde left The Belfry in 1985 and was still present two years later when the team assembled at Muirfield Village to try to reclaim the trophy. Jack Nicklaus was back as the American captain, at the sublime course that he designed. Jacklin was back again as well.

For an American team to ever be the underdogs in a Ryder Cup was unprecedented, but to be unfavoured when playing at home was virtually unthinkable. Yet their players and supporters knew just what a task they had in trying to wrest the trophy from European hands.

The visitors were not only talented, they were also infused with the self-belief that comes from winning Ryder Cups, from winning major championships. As this Ryder Cup was to prove all too conclusively, even the relative journeymen captured the mood of the occasion.

Jacklin was acutely aware that Europe had to avoid the mistake of many Ryder Cups past and not begin slowly. Accordingly he packed his ranks with his best players on the first morning and emerged with a 2–2 scoreline, the points coming from two new pairings that would prove inspirational not only in this Ryder Cup but in future contests: Nick Faldo and Ian Woosnam and, particularly, Ballesteros and Jose-Maria Olazabal.

What a sight these two made. I'll never forget walking all 18 holes of their match against Larry Nelson and Payne Stewart. Over the outward half Olazabal was so nervous that he found it impossible to hit the ball even remotely straight. But time and again Ballesteros saved him, and after every shot he was by his side, encouraging but never criticizing. By the second nine Olazabal had so recouped his confidence that it was him saving Ballesteros.

It was, needless to say, an extraordinary performance from the pair, and all Europe became inspired by it. In the afternoon fourballs the visitors' golf was beyond reproach. The Americans were powerless by comparison as they suffered their first-ever whitewash in a series. At the end of the first day Europe were an implausible 6–2 ahead.

From the second morning's foursomes they added another point to their lead, with Ballesteros and Olazabal making it three out of three. When they halved the afternoon series it now became a matter of not whether they would win an historic first victory on American soil, but by how many points.

The Americans, however, are never more dangerous than when in this situation. They might not have had the best players, but they had more strength in depth, and now they set about making it tell.

Of the first five matches to finish, America claimed three points and a halved match. Even more disturbing for Jacklin was the state of the matches involving Langer and Lyle, two players he had banked on for points. Both were in losing positions.

Never mind. The ever-dependable Ballesteros was in good shape against Curtis Strange. Then there was Eamonn Darcy's match against Ben Crenshaw. This looked like an American formality at the start, but the not-so-gentle Ben had been irritated by his poor start and had broken his putter in a fit of temper at the 6th. Because it was broken in anger, he was not allowed a replacement.

Crenshaw was two down at the time and it seemed curtains. Then a remarkable thing happened. Putting with a one iron or the leading edge of his sand wedge, Crenshaw started to get back in the match. When he made a par at the 16th he actually went into the lead. What a nightmare for Jacklin; it was all going horribly wrong.

At the 17th Darcy proved a real trooper, a six iron setting up a winning birdie to square the match. At the last Crenshaw drove into a ditch and had to take a penalty shot. He then bunkered his third shot; to the groans of the considerable gathering of European supporters, so did Darcy.

In the circumstances, the bunker shots that both players played were brilliant. Both were inside six feet, which from tricky lies in the sand was quite something. Then Crenshaw, with his one iron, rolled in his putt for a remarkable five.

The problem for Darcy was that his five-footer was down a treacherous slope and he knew that if he missed he could leave himself with a putt almost as long as the one Crenshaw had just holed. Somehow he managed to banish such negativism from his mind; he struck the putt true and it rolled into the heart for a par four and a one-hole victory. In that instant he was elevated to the pantheon of Irish heroes.

A few moments later Ballesteros kept his date with destiny and rolled in the putt that meant that Europe had won for the first time on American soil. What scenes of celebration there were. At the closing ceremony Olazabal did an impromptu conga as the 18th green became awash in the colours of Europe.

In the areas where food and drink were available to the general public the singing began. All the players were feted as heroes, a song for each. In the locker-room they could hear the jubilant voices, and it was Woosnam who suggested that they meet their public for one joyous hoolie.

In that moment the Americans finally understood how important the Ryder Cup was to those on the other side of the Atlantic. After years of winning it almost as a matter of course,

Seve Ballesteros and Jose-Maria Olazabal – the greatest partnership in Ryder Cup history?

they also realized that now there was an opposition who could meet them on equal terms. After exactly 60 years it could be said that in that precise moment, the Ryder Cup came of age.

A whole new audience

If the effect of two successive defeats was to galvanize the Americans it was as nothing compared to what happened in Europe. Quite simply a whole continent reacted like it had been kissed on the lips for the first time. Throughout mainland Europe a sport which had hitherto been a backwater pursuit was now a mainstream game and courses were constructed at a feverish rate.

In England, the timing could hardly have been better. Football was still struggling to shake off its hooligan reputation. The comparison with golf was stark indeed. Almost overnight, a huge mass of the population decided they would actually rather spend Saturday afternoons on the tranquil pastures of their local municipal than worrying about thugs at their local football ground.

The result of all this was that when the Ryder Cup returned to The Belfry in 1989, golf in Europe had its first all-ticket, sold-out event. Could the match possibly live up to the hype? After all, one paper billed it "The Match of the Century". The wonder is that it not only lived up to the hype but exceeded it.

On the opening morning the Americans emphasized their determination to leave The Belfry this time with the trophy. From the opening four foursomes matches they won two and halved two to take an instant grip on the match. It was not long before it was dramatically loosened. In 1987 at Muirfield Village, the Europeans had achieved their first ever whitewash in the fourballs on the second day. Now, remarkably, they repeated the feat and the noise from the crowd was deafening. After day one Europe, 3–1 down at lunch, were 5–3 ahead.

On the second morning the star troops came up trumps: Faldo and Woosnam won, and so did Ballesteros and Olazabal. Two points each, therefore, and Europe still two ahead. Now back to the fourballs, where the Americans could only improve on the opening-day shocker. And so they did, with Paul Azinger and Chip Beck, and Tom Kite and Mark McCumber winning the first two matches. Back came Europe, with wins for Howard Clark and Mark James and, just for a change, Ballesteros and Olazabal. By this time the thought of kidnapping the two Spaniards must have crossed American minds.

So to the singles, with Europe two points to the good. What a curious series this would prove to be, with America in control for so long in so many matches, only to come undone at the watery grave that is so often the treacherous 18th.

First Stewart went in the water to lose to Olazabal; then the Open champion Mark Calcavecchia followed him in to lose to Ronan Rafferty. There were wins, however, for Paul Azinger over Ballesteros, and Chip Beck over Bernhard Langer. With Tom Kite demolishing Howard Clark by the record margin of 8&7, Fred Couples against Christy O'Connor had become a pivotal game.

On paper O'Connor had no chance, yet playing the 18th he was all square. After the drives the difference in talent between the players was all too obvious: O'Connor had a two iron to the pin, while Couples had a nine iron.

Before O'Connor played his shot, Jacklin strode over to have a word, and filled him with belief. What followed was one of the great Ryder Cup shots, the two iron of Christy's life, one struck so true that it never left the flag for a second, finishing four feet away. Couples knew at that moment that he was up against forces beyond his control. Suddenly his simple nine-iron shot became a stroke of unfathomable difficulty, and he pushed it to the right. When he could not get down in two he conceded O'Connor's putt. The Irishman had won on the last, and understandably he broke down and wept.

Behind him was another unlikely hero, Canizares, a one-hole winner against Ken Green. With four matches still out on the course, Europe were four points ahead and the Ryder Cup had been retained.

A television interviewer, spying Tom Kite, wandered over and asked his thoughts regarding a European victory. "We have not lost yet," Kite pointed out, unable to control his temper, and then he repeated the words in big, bold capital letters.

And he was right too. What a finish from the Americans. McCumber won on the last; then Tom Watson over Sam Torrance, and Lanny Wadkins over Nick Faldo. And when Curtis Strange finished with four straight birdies the match had ended in an overall tie.

But all the scenes of joy belonged to the home side. They had achieved what they set out to do and that was to retain the Ryder Cup. And in doing so they had unearthed some new heroes. For who could possibly have predicted that Ballesteros, Langer, Faldo, Woosnam and Torrance would all lose in the singles and yet Europe would not lose the trophy that had become so precious to their self-esteem?

Since 1983 the Ryder Cup has been blessed with one Herculean struggle after another, but the one that sticks in the craw is the one that took place at Kiawah Island in 1991. Nothing wrong with the drama, which reached new levels of feverish excitement in the final, dramatic hour. But there was too much wrong with the build-up to this match, and a series of unsavoury incidents that took place along the way, for it to be recalled with the same affection as some of the other contests.

The first difference was in the captains' armchairs. Jacklin had finally decided to quit after four matches in charge, four matches that had changed the entire outlook of not only the Ryder Cup but European golf. His replacement was Bernard Gallacher, who could not hold a candle to Jacklin when it

Christy O'Connor, his wife and Tony Jacklin celebrate the former's sensational win over Fred Couples at The Belfry in 1989

came to charisma, but who was well-liked by the players. His opposite number, meanwhile, was Dave Stockton.

He never made any secret of his ambitions. He wanted the Ryder Cup back on American soil and he did not care what it took to win. A local radio station grasped his meaning by ringing up the European players in the middle of the night. "War on the Shore," was the preview headline in the American magazine, *Golf Digest*, clearly wound up by events going on in the Gulf, where America and its allies were doing their best to liberate Kuwait. Some of the players appeared to take the headline too literally. Corey Pavin turned up in a soldier's cap.

On the first morning it became obvious that Gallacher still had much to learn about captaincy, despite being Jacklin's second-in-command for three matches. One of his foursomes pairings featured two rookies, Colin Montgomerie and David Gilford. Their inexperience was all too painfully revealed when they went up against Lanny Wadkins and Hale Irwin. It was part of yet another disappointing first session for the Europeans, who found themselves staring at a 3–1 deficit.

Once more, they found fourballs much to their liking. The team of Ballesteros and Olazabal, the only winners in the morning, were back once more to haunt the Americans, and Mark James and the rookie Steve Richardson also won. Europe took the series by a point with a half from Sam Torrance and David Feherty.

The second day followed an almost identical pattern. Once more the Americans dominated the foursomes. David Gilford found himself partnered on this occasion by Nick Faldo, which proved another mistake by Gallacher. Faldo was absolutely no help at all to the intimidated rookie, and they were massacred 7&6. Again Ballesteros and Olazabal were the saviours in a 3–1 defeat. They were keeping Europe in the match.

The one pairing that Gallacher had got right was James and Richardson, who again contributed a point in the afternoon fourballs. Once more it was a wonderful session for the Europeans, who only gave up half a point. With 12 singles matches to come, the teams were tied at eight points apiece.

When Gallacher received the pairings sheet for the singles he was thrilled. He had accurately read Stockton's mind and the match-ups were all he wanted. At the team meeting on Saturday evening, he was a very contented man. He slept soundly.

The same could hardly be said of Stockton. He looked down the list and saw a defeat staring him in the face. The following morning, it was all change.

On the Wednesday evening Steve Pate had injured his abdomen in a car accident on the way to the Gala Ball and had had to sit out the first day's play. Happily he had recovered to play on the second day and was hitting the ball, to use Gallacher's words, "a country mile". But Pate had been drawn to play Ballesteros in the singles, just as Gallacher had hoped.

Now Pate, mysteriously, found that he was no longer able to play in the singles. Unforgiveably Stockton never even had the decency to inform Gallacher. He just withdrew him from play. Which meant that when Gallacher arrived at the course on the Sunday morning his buoyancy soon left him. His first task now was to inform poor David Gilford, whose name had been in the envelope to cover just this eventuality, that he would not be playing. Instead of a certain defeat against Ballesteros, Pate was now credited with a half point. It also meant that Ballesteros played Wayne Levi, something Gallacher had been desperate to avoid. He did not want to waste his star man on a journeyman.

And so Stockton had revealed just how badly he wanted to win; in so doing, he had totally contravened what the spirit of the Ryder Cup is all about.

In the 11 matches left, the players did their best to remove that sour taste. It was a sensational day's play, one that saw Colin Montgomerie come back from four down with four to play against Mark Calcavecchia to snatch a half; gutsy wins for Paul Azinger and Corey Pavin; a great win for the European rookie Paul Broadhurst over Mark O'Meara.

With wins for Fred Couples and Lanny Wadkins, in the end it came down to Bernhard Langer against Hale Irwin. What a courageous showing the German put up. Two down with four to play he applied a tourniquet to Irwin's neck. A par four was good enough to win the difficult 15th; at the 17th Irwin missed the sort of short putt he had holed with nonchalant ease earlier in the match. All square.

Now Langer had to win the last and the Ryder Cup would be heading back to Europe following another tie. Clearly, the chance was there. Irwin was clearly affected. His response to a perfect drive from Langer was one that crashed violently into the gallery. It then bounced back on to the fairway; lucky, lucky, Irwin. Both players came up short of the green, from where Irwin chipped to 12 feet. Langer's effort was a good one, but it rolled five feet by. Irwin, completely gone, missed comfortably. Yet Langer had to hole. It was the ultimate pressure situation: a five-foot putt for the Ryder Cup.

Agonizingly for Langer, it missed on the right side. Stockton was jubilant. Ballesteros, who had had his disputes with Langer in the past, was a giant. He swallowed his disappointment and told the Press: "No one could have holed that putt, not Bernhard, not me, not Jack Nicklaus. The pressure was too great." And so the cup was back in American hands.

One American who had been greatly disturbed by the manner in which it had got there was Tom Watson. When he was appointed captain for the 1993 contest he quickly met with Bernard Gallacher, who had been retained as European skipper, and told him the match at The Belfry would be a far different affair. The words came as a relief not only to Gallacher but to all who love the Royal and Ancient game.

It was a wise move by the PGA of America to appoint such a popular figure in Britain to be captain for that match.

Agony – Bernhard Langer misses "that" putt at Kiawah Island in 1991

Watson knew just what to say at the right time and proved an inspired selection. Together with Gallacher he rescued what had become a dangerously inflammatory situation.

And the 1993 Ryder Cup was another beauty as a result. What had looked a strong American side in theory proved so in practice, as they produced an inspired fightback.

After the first day it was advantage Europe. The opening foursomes had been halved with two points apiece, but the fourballs again proved to Europe's liking as wins for Ballesteros and Olazabal and Woosnam and Baker were aided with a half from Nick Faldo and Colin Montgomerie.

On the second morning, Europe increased its advantage. Only Peter Baker and Barry Lane lost. The home side were now three points to the good.

The joy of the supporters, however, was counteracted when the pairings for the afternoon play were revealed. No Bernhard Langer and, worse, Ballesteros was not partnering Olazabal for the first time since 1985. Later it was revealed that both players had asked to be left out and Gallacher had complied. His thinking was to keep both fresh for the singles.

But as we have seen, momentum in the Ryder Cup is everything. Three points ahead, Europe should have sought to press home their advantage. That was Jacklin's secret and now it had not been maintained. And how the Americans loved the sight of their chief tormentor being absent from the course.

Olazabal, now partnered with Joakim Haeggman, found himself four down after just six holes and lost two and one. Indeed only Peter Baker and Ian Woosnam could keep the

Nick Faldo celebrates his one-hole victory over Curtis Strange at Oak Hill in 1995

Americans at bay. Fourballs had been the game where Europe had enjoyed the most success; now they had lost a pivotal series 3–`1. There was just one point between the teams, and the momentum was with the visitors.

In the singles there were some European heroes. Haeggman won while Baker inspired all sorts of punned headlines with a victory over Corey Pavin that completed the most personally satisfying week of his career. But there were two fall guys too, and sadly for them the fate of the Ryder Cup hung around their matches.

First, there was Barry Lane, three up with five to play against Chip Beck. From that dominant position Lane contrived to lose four of the last five holes, completing his decline by dumping his second shot into the water at the 18th. He lost one up.

An even more spectacular snatching of defeat from the jaws of victory came from Costantino Rocca, who was one up with two to play, then lost the long 17th to a par five after three putting from nowhere. At the last he sadly became the object of the crowd's derision with another bogey to lose by one hole to Davis Love.

They were fatal blows to Europe's cause, and as a consequence The Belfry was, for once, not a scene for European triumphalism. The Americans had completed a magnificent fightback under a wonderful captain.

A lot of pessimism surrounded the European team as they made their way to Oak Hill in upstate New York for the 1995 match, but quite why was hard to fathom. All right, there appeared plenty wrong with the European team, but it was not as if the American side was one of their strongest. Indeed, as events would prove it would turn out to be their weakest for at least a generation.

It featured players like Jay Haas, Peter Jacobsen and Ben Crenshaw, while the captain Lanny Wadkins had done Europe a huge favour by inexplicably selecting Curtis Strange over Lee Janzen. All four players were past their sell-by date.

On the first morning there was appropriately nothing to choose between these two evenly matched teams. In the afternoon it was a different story. David Gilford and Severiano Ballesteros proved an inspired pairing by Bernard Gallacher, who was back for a third match in charge, but the other three matches went the way of the Americans. They led 5–3.

The second morning belonged to Europe. Costantino Rocca, the fall guy of two years earlier, who had rescued his reputation in the 1995 Open at St Andrews, now showed what a wonderful ball striker he is. In tandem with Sam Torrance he proved irresistible, and the pair had a hole-in-one on their way to a 6&5 victory. They took the limelight, as Europe took the series 3–1. All square again.

It was American voices that rang out across Oak Hill in the second series of fourballs. Brad Faxon and Fred Couples claimed a point off Torrance and Colin Montgomerie; Haas and Phil Mickelson saw off Ballesteros and Gilford. The critical point appeared to fall in the match between Corey Pavin and Loren Roberts, against Bernhard Langer and Nick Faldo.

Bring four of the slowest players in golf together and the result was a round that took the best part of six hours to complete. Yet it was totally bewitching, with a mesmerizing conclusion, as Pavin chipped in from the back of the green for a precious point.

It left the Americans two points ahead with the singles to come and apparently home and dry. They were jubilant in the Press conferences afterwards. Gallacher, for once, came up with some inspired words. Asked about the day's play he said: "Looking back is for amateurs, professionals only look forward." For a moment he sounded like Tony Jacklin.

The words and the full meaning were picked up by the European team who breathed defiance. Meanwhile, travelling away from the course, Paul Azinger, who had been working as a television commentator, thought for a moment about driving back. "I listened to the words of the American team and it suddenly struck me that they thought the contest was already over. I wanted to go back and tell them that if they thought that they were seriously mistaken."

What prophetic words they would turn out to be. Europe were simply brilliant in the singles, helped it must be said, by some awful American play. This was Gallacher's finest moment.

Remarkably, five games went to the final hole and Europe won four and halved one of them. In those points the match was won and lost. There was Howard Clark beating Jacobsen by one hole; Gilford's win by a similar margin as a man renowned for his putting, Faxon, contrived to miss a straight six-footer uphill; Woosnam gaining a share of the spoils against Couples.

Most of all there was Faldo and Philip Walton. First Faldo got up and down from 90 yards following the gutsiest wedge shot and a six-foot putt. From one down with two to play against the hapless Strange, Faldo had pulled off the win of his career and now it gave Walton a chance to steal the glory.

Three up with three to play, Walton found his throat held in a vice as Haas holed a bunker shot at the 16th; Walton then missed from five feet at the 17th. Fortunately for the Irishman, Haas was every bit as nervous. At the last the American drove wildly into the trees. It meant Walton could take a bogey five and still win, and that is just what he did. When he holed the two-foot putt for his five, Gallacher leapt six feet into the air. Europe had pulled off the most spectacular of comebacks, the most amazing of wins. And in 11 matches first as a player and then a captain, Gallacher had finally managed a first, elusive win.

A move to Spain

There was only one man who could be European captain when the Ryder Cup went to Spain for the first time in 1997, and that was Severiano Ballesteros. This was a captaincy that was unforgettable in every sense, and in particular the sight of Ballesteros driving round Valderrama, with a buggy apparently powered by a Formula One engine, will live with all who witnessed it.

The Costa del Sol they call it, but on the first morning it was the Costa del Worst Storm in the History of Southern Spain. What great timing. It was only due to the impeccable drainage at Valderrama that any play was possible at all.

The opening series was halved, but Europe edged in front in the afternoon fourballs that went on the following morning with wins for Langer and Montgomerie and Faldo and Lee Westwood, with Ignacio Garrido and Jesper Parnevik contributing a half.

On the second day Ballesteros continued to court extreme controversy. Per-Ulrik Johansson, who had teamed up to win his match on the opening morning, never played all day. This followed Ballesteros's decision to leave Ian Woosnam and Darren Clarke out on the opening day. Woosnam, in particular, was furious and in the middle of the match he and Ballesteros had, well, let us describe it as a heated debate.

Yet Woosnam picked the wrong argument. It is impossible to berate a captain when his pairings work, no matter how disappointed you are at being left out, and no one could argue that they worked. Indeed Europe so enjoyed themselves that with the singles to play they enjoyed a giddy ten-and-a-half to five-and-a-half point lead. It was the biggest margin in Europe's favour after two days in Ryder Cup history.

As Ballesteros said: "What did Woosnam want me to say to the other guys? To tell them that actually I was wrong to pick them even though they won?"

Woosnam belittled his case even further by losing his singles match to Couples by a record-equalling 8&7 margin, although to be fair no one could have lived with the American, who was at his very best. Behind, the European points emerged agonizingly slowly. Rocca saw off Tiger Woods with the best win of his career and Johansson made it two points out of two in his matches. Thomas Bjorn, meanwhile, halved with the Open champion Justin Leonard after being four down after four holes.

But where was the other point-and-a-half coming from? It came late in the day – from Bernhard Langer, putting the trauma of Kiawah firmly behind him to claim the point that meant that the Ryder Cup was at least retained. And then from Colin Montgomerie, Europe's best player, who would have defeated Scott Hoch, but for Ballesteros making him concede a 25-foot putt on the last green that gave the American a half.

But Europe had won again, and once more the margin of victory was just a point. They had staved off a stirring American fightback and underlined the unique nature of the contest. The new millennium finds the Ryder Cup in better shape than it has ever been.

Seve Ballesteros – captain marvellous when the Ryder Cup circus

Valderrama, Spain in 1997

THE RYDER CUP STATISTICS

1927

Worcester Country Club, Worcester, MA

Captains: E. Ray (GB), W. Hagen (US)

Great Britain & Ireland		United States	
Foursomes			
E. Ray & F. Robson	0	W. Hagen & J. Golden (2&1)	1
G. Duncan & A. Compston	0	J. Farrell & J. Turnesa (8&6)	1
A.G. Havers & H.C. Jolly	0	G. Sarazen & A. Watrous (3&2)	1
A. Boomer & C.A. Whitcombe (7&5)	1	L. Diegel & W. Mehlhorn	0
Singles			
A. Compston	0	W. Mehlhorn (1 hole)	1
A. Boomer	0	J. Farrell (5&4)	1
H.C. Jolly	0	J. Golden (8&7)	1
E. Ray	0	L. Diegel (7&5)	1
C.A. Whitcombe (halved)	½	G. Sarazen (halved)	½
A.G. Havers	0	W. Hagen (2&1)	1
F. Robson	0	A. Watrous (3&2)	1
G. Duncan (1 hole)	1	J. Turnesa	0
GB	**2½**	**US**	**9½**

1929

Moortown Golf Club, Leeds

Captains: G. Duncan (GB), W. Hagen (US)

Great Britain & Ireland		United States	
Foursomes			
C.A. Whitcombe & A. Compston (halved)	½	J. Farrell & J. Turnesa (halved)	½
A. Boomer & G. Duncan	0	L. Diegel & A. Espinosa (7&5)	1
A. Mitchell & F. Robson (2&1)	1	G. Sarazen & E. Dudley	0
E.R. Whitcombe & T.H. Cotton	0	J. Golden & W. Hagen (2 holes)	1
Singles			
C.A. Whitcombe (8&6)	1	J. Farrell	0
G. Duncan (10&8)	1	W. Hagen	0
A. Mitchell	0	L. Diegel (8&6)	1
A. Compston (6&4)	1	G. Sarazen	0
A. Boomer (4&3)	1	J. Turnesa	0
F. Robson	0	H. Smith (4&2)	1
T.H. Cotton (4&3)	1	A. Watrous	0
E.R. Whitcombe (halved)	½	A. Espinosa (halved)	1
GB	**7**	**US**	**5**

1931

Scioto Country Club, Columbus, OH

Captains: C.A. Whitcombe (GB), W. Hagen (US)

Great Britain & Ireland		United States	
Foursomes			
A. Compston & W.H. Davies	0	G. Sarazen & J. Farrell (8&7)	1
G. Duncan & A.G. Havers	0	W. Hagen & D. Shute (10&9)	1
A. Mitchell & F. Robson (3&1)	1	L. Diegel & A. Espinosa	0
S. Easterbrook & E.R. Whitcombe	0	W. Burke & W. Cox (3&2)	1
Singles			
A. Compston	0	W. Burke (7&6)	1
F. Robson	0	G. Sarazen (7&6)	1
W.H. Davies (4&3)	1	J. Farrell	0
A. Mitchell	0	W. Cox (3&1)	1
C.A. Whitcombe	0	W. Hagen (4&3)	1
B. Hodson	0	D. Shute (8&6)	1
E.R. Whitcombe	0	A. Espinosa (2&1)	1
A.G. Havers (4&3)	1	C. Wood	0
GB	**3**	**US**	**9**

1933

Southport & Ainsdale Golf Club, Southport

Captains: J.H. Taylor (GB), W. Hagen (US)

Great Britain & Ireland		United States	
Foursomes			
P. Alliss & C.A. Whitcombe (halved)	½	G. Sarazen & W. Hagen (halved)	½
A. Mitchell & A.G. Havers (3&2)	1	O. Dutra & D. Shute	0
W.H. Davies & S. Easterbrook (1 hole)	1	C. Wood & P. Runyan	0
A.H. Padgham & A. Perry	0	E. Dudley & W. Burke (1 hole)	1
Singles			
A.H. Padgham	0	G. Sarazen (6&4)	1
A. Mitchell (9&8)	1	O. Dutra	0
A.J. Lacey	0	W. Hagen (2&1)	1
W.H. Davies	0	C. Wood (4&3)	1
P. Alliss (2&1)	1	P. Runyan	0
A.G. Havers (4&3)	1	L. Diegel	0
S. Easterbrook (1 hole)	1	D. Shute	0
C.A. Whitcombe	0	H. Smith (2&1)	1
GB	**6½**	**US**	**5½**

1935

Ridgewood Country Club, Ridgewood, NJ

Captains: C.A. Whitcombe (GB), W. Hagen (US)

Great Britain & Ireland		United States	
Foursomes			
A. Perry & J. Busson	0	G. Sarazen & W. Hagen (7&6)	1
A.H. Padgham & P. Alliss	0	H. Picard & J. Revolta (6&5)	1
W.J. Cox & E.W. Jarman	0	P. Runyan & H. Smith (9&8)	1
C.A. Whitcombe & E.R. Whitcombe (1 hole)	1	O. Dutra & K. Laffoon	0
Singles			
J. Busson	0	G. Sarazen (3&2)	1
R. Burton	0	P. Runyan (5&3)	1
E.R. Whitcombe	0	J. Revolta (2&1)	1
A.H. Padgham	0	O. Dutra (4&2)	1
P. Alliss (1 hole)	1	C. Wood	0
W.J. Cox (halved)	½	H. Smith (halved)	½
E.R. Whitcombe	0	H. Picard (3&2)	1
A. Perry (halved)	½	S. Parks (halved)	½
GB	**3**	**US**	**9**

1937

Southport & Ainsdale Golf Club, Southport

Captains: C.A. Whitcombe (GB), W. Hagen (US)

Great Britain & Ireland		United States	
Foursomes			
A.H. Padgham & T.H. Cotton	0	E. Dudley & B. Nelson (4&2)	1
A.J. Lacey & W.J. Cox	0	R. Guldahl & T. Manero (2&1)	1
C.A. Whitcombe & D.J. Rees (halved)	½	G. Sarazen & D. Shute (halved)	½
P. Alliss & R. Burton (2&1)	1	H. Picard & J. Revolta	0
Singles			
A.H. Padgham & T.H. Cotton	0	E. Dudley & B. Nelson	1
A.H. Padgham	0	R. Guldahl (8&7)	1
S.L. King (halved)	½	D. Shute (halved)	½
D.J. Rees (3&1)	1	B. Nelson	0
T.H. Cotton (5&3)	1	T. Manero	0
P. Alliss	0	G. Sarazen (1 hole)	1
R. Burton	0	S. Snead (5&4)	1
A. Perry	0	E. Dudley (2&1)	1
A.J. Lacey	0	H. Picard (2&1)	1
GB	**4**	**US**	**8**

1939–1945: No Matches played due to World War II

1947

Portland Golf Club, Portland, OR

Captains: T.H. Cotton (GB), B. Hogan (US)

Great Britain & Ireland		United States	
Foursomes			
T.H. Cotton & A. Lees	0	E. Oliver & L. Worsham (10&8)	1
F. Daly & C.H. Ward	0	S. Snead & L. Mangrum (6&5)	1
J. Adams & M. Faulkner	0	B. Hogan & J. Demaret (2 holes)	1
D.J. Rees & S.L. King	0	B. Nelson & H. Barron (2&1)	1
Singles			
F. Daly	0	E.J. Harrison (5&4)	1
J. Adams	0	L. Worsham (3&2)	1
M. Faulkner	0	L. Mangrum (6&5)	1
C.H. Ward	0	E. Oliver (4&3)	1
A. Lees	0	B. Nelson (2&1)	1
T.H. Cotton	0	S. Snead (5&4)	1
D.J. Rees	0	J. Demaret (3&2)	1
S.L. King (4&3)	1	H. Keiser	0
GB	**1**	**US**	**11**

1949

Ganton Golf Club, Scarborough, England

Captains: C.A. Whitcombe (GB), B. Hogan (US)

Great Britain & Ireland		United States	
Foursomes			
M. Faulkner & J. Adams (2&1)	1	E.J. Harrison & J. Palmer	0
F. Daly & K. Bousfield (4&2)	1	R. Hamilton & S. Alexander	0
C.H. Ward & S.L. King	0	J. Demaret & C. Heafner (4&3)	1
R. Burton & A. Lees (1 hole)	1	S. Snead & L. Mangrum	0
Singles			
M. Faulkner	0	E.J. Harrison (8&7)	1
J. Adams (2&1)	1	J. Palmer	0
C.H. Ward	0	S. Snead (6&5)	1
D.J. Rees (6&4)	1	R. Hamilton	0
R. Burton	0	C. Heafner (3&2)	1
S.L. King	0	C. Harbert (4&3)	1
A. Lees	0	J. Demaret (7&6)	1
F. Daly	0	L. Mangrum (4&3)	1
GB	**5**	**US**	**7**

1951

Pinehurst Country Club, Pinehurst, NC

Captains: A.J. Lacey (GB), S. Snead (US)

Great Britain & Ireland		United States	
Foursomes			
M. Faulkner & D.J. Rees	0	C. Heafner & J. Burke (5&3)	1
C.H. Ward & A. Lees (2&1)	1	E. Oliver & H. Ransom	0
J. Adams & J. Panton	0	S. Snead & L. Mangrum (5&4)	1
F. Daly & K. Bousfield	0	B. Hogan & J. Demaret (5&4)	1
Singles			
J. Adams	0	J. Burke (4&3)	1
D.J. Rees	0	J. Demaret (2 holes)	1
F. Daly (halved)	½	C. Heafner (halved)	½
H. Weetman	0	L. Mangrum (6&5)	1
A. Lees (2&1)	1	E. Oliver	0
C.H. Ward	0	B. Hogan (3&2)	1
J. Panton	0	S. Alexander (8&7)	1
M. Faulkner	0	S. Snead (4&3)	1
GB	**2½**	**US**	**9½**

1953

Wentworth Golf Club, Virginia Water

Captains: T.H. Cotton (GB), L. Mangrum (US)

Great Britain & Ireland		United States	
Foursomes			
H. Weetman & P. Alliss	0	D. Douglas & E. Oliver (2&1)	1
E.C. Brown & J. Panton	0	L. Mangrum & S. Snead (8&7)	1
J. Adams & B J. Hunt	0	T. Kroll & J. Burke (7&5)	1
F. Daly & H. Bradshaw (1 hole)	1	W. Burkemo & C. Middlecoff	0
Singles			
D.J. Rees	0	J. Burke (2&1)	1
F. Daly (9&7)	1	T. Kroll	0
E.C. Brown (2 holes)	1	L. Mangrum	0
H. Weetman (1 hole)	1	S. Snead	0
M. Faulkner	0	C. Middlecoff (3&1)	1
P. Alliss	0	J. Turnesa (1 hole)	1
B.J. Hunt (halved)	½	D. Douglas (halved)	½
H. Bradshaw (3&2)	1	F. Haas	0
GB	**5½**	**US**	**6½**

1955

Thunderbird Golf & Country Club, Palm Springs, CA

Captains: D.J. Rees (GB), C. Harbert (US)

Great Britain & Ireland		United States	
Foursomes			
J. Fallon & J.R.M. Jacobs (1 hole)	1	C. Harper & J. Barber	0
E.C. Brown & S.S. Scott	0	D. Ford & T. Kroll (5&4)	1
A. Lees & H. Weetman	0	J. Burke & T. Bolt (1 hole)	1
H. Bradshaw & D.J. Rees	0	S. Snead & C. Middlecoff (3&2)	1
Singles			
C. O'Connor	0	T. Bolt (4&2)	1
S.S. Scott	0	C. Harbert (3&2)	1
J.R.M. Jacobs (1 hole)	1	C. Middlecoff	0
D.J. Rees	0	S. Snead (3&1)	1
A. Lees (3&2)	1	M. Furgol	0
E.C. Brown (3&2)	1	J. Barber	0
H. Bradshaw	0	J. Burke (3&2)	1
H. Weetman	0	D. Ford (3&2)	1
GB	**4**	**US**	**8**

1957

Lindrick Club, Sheffield

Captains: D.J. Rees (GB), J. Burke (USA)

Great Britain & Ireland		United States	
Foursomes			
P. Alliss & B.J. Hunt	0	D. Ford & D. Finsterwald (2&1)	1
K. Bousfield & D.J. Rees (3&2)	1	A. Wall & F. Hawkins	0
M. Faulkner & H. Weetman	0	T. Kroll & J. Burke (4&3)	1
C. O'Connor & E.C. Brown	0	R. Mayer & T. Bolt (7&5)	1
Singles			
E.C. Brown (4&3)	1	T. Bolt	0
R.P. Mills (5&3)	1	J. Burke	0
P. Alliss	0	F. Hawkins (2&1)	1
K. Bousfield (4&3)	1	L. Hebert	0
D.J. Rees (7&6)	1	E. Furgol	0
B.J. Hunt (6&5)	1	D. Ford	0
C. O'Connor (7&6)	1	D. Finsterwald	0
H. Bradshaw (halved)	½	R. Mayer (halved)	½
GB	**7½**	**US**	**4½**

1959

Eldorado Country Club, Palm Desert, CA

Captains: D.J. Rees (GB), S. Snead (US)

Great Britain & Ireland		United States	
Foursomes			
B.J. Hunt & E.C. Brown	0	R. Rosburg & M. Souchak (5&4)	1
D.J. Rees & K. Bousfield	0	J. Boros & D. Finsterwald (2 holes)	1
C. O'Connor & P. Alliss (3&2)	1	A. Wall & D. Ford	0
H. Weetman & D.C. Thomas (halved)	½	S. Snead & C. Middlecoff (halved)	½
Singles			
N.V. Drew (halved)	½	D. Ford (halved)	½
K. Bousfield	0	M. Souchak (3&2)	1
H. Weetman	0	R. Rosburg (6&5)	1
D.C. Thomas	0	S. Snead (6&5)	1
C. O'Connor	0	A. Wall (7&6)	1
D.J. Rees	0	D. Finsterwald (1 hole)	1
P. Alliss (halved)	½	J. Hebert (halved)	½
E.C. Brown (4&3)	1	C. Middlecoff	0
GB	**3½**	**US**	**8**

1961

Royal Lytham & St Annes, St Annes

Captains: D.J. Rees (GB), J. Barber (US)

Great Britain & Ireland		United States	
Foursomes: Morning			
C. O'Connor & P. Alliss (4&3)	1	D. Ford & G. Littler	0
J. Panton & B.J. Hunt	0	A. Wall & J. Herbert (4&3)	1
D.J. Rees & K. Bousfield	0	W. Casper & A. Palmer (2&1)	1
T.B. Haliburton & N.C. Coles	0	W. Collins & M. Souchak (1 hole)	1
Foursomes: Afternoon			
C. O'Connor & P. Alliss	0	A. Wall & J. Hebert (1 hole)	1
J. Panton & B.J. Hunt	0	W. Casper & A. Palmer (5&4)	1
D.J. Rees & K. Bousfield (2&1)	1	W. Collins & M. Souchak	0
T.B. Haliburton & N.C. Coles	0	J. Barber & D. Finsterwald (1 hole)	1
Singles: Morning			
H. Weetman	0	D. Ford (1 hole)	1
R.L. Moffitt	0	M. Souchak (5&4)	1
P. Alliss (halved)	½	A. Palmer (halved)	½
K. Bousfield	0	W. Casper (5&3)	1
D.J. Rees (2&1)	1	J. Hebert	0
N.C. Coles (halved)	½	G. Littler (halved)	½
B.J. Hunt (5&4)	1	J. Barber	0
C. O'Connor	0	D. Finsterwald (2&1)	1
Singles: Afternoon			
H. Weetman	0	A. Wall (1 hole)	1
P. Alliss (3&2)	1	W. Collins	0
B.J. Hunt	0	M. Souchak (2&1)	1
T.B. Haliburton	0	A. Palmer (2&1)	1
D.J. Rees (4&3)	1	D. Ford	0
K. Bousfield (1 hole)	1	J. Barber	0
N.C. Coles (1 hole)	1	D. Finsterwald	0
C. O'Connor (halved)	½	G. Littler (halved)	½
GB	**9½**	**US**	**14½**

1963

East Lake Country Club, Atlanta, GA

Captains: J. Fallon (GB), A. Palmer (US)

Great Britain & Ireland		United States	
Foursomes: Morning			
B. Huggett & G. Will (3&2)	1	A. Palmer & J. Pott	0
P. Alliss & C. O'Connor	0	W. Casper & D. Ragan (1 hole)	1
N.C. Coles & B.J. Hunt (halved)	½	J. Boros & A. Lema (halved)	½
D. Thomas & H. Weetman (halved)	½	G. Littler & D. Finsterwald (halved)	½

Foursomes: Afternoon			
D. Thomas & H. Weetman	0	W. Maxwell & R. Goalby (4&3)	1
B. Huggett & G. Will	0	A. Palmer & W. Casper (5&4)	1
N.C. Coles & G.M. Hunt (2&1)	1	G. Littler & D. Finsterwald	0
T.B. Haliburton & B.J. Hunt	0	J. Boros & A. Lema (1 hole)	1
Foursomes: Morning			
B. Huggett & D. Thomas	0	A. Palmer & D. Finsterwald (5&4)	1
P. Alliss & B.J. Hunt (halved)	½	G. Littler & J. Boros (halved)	½
H. Weetman & G. Will	0	W. Casper & W. Maxwell (3&2)	1
N.C. Coles & C. O'Connor	0	R. Goalby & D. Ragan (1 hole)	1
Fourballs: Afternoon			
N.C. Coles & C. O'Connor	0	A. Palmer & D. Finsterwald (3&2)	1
P. Alliss & B.J. Hunt	0	A. Lema & J. Pott (1 hole)	1
T.B. Haliburton & G.M. Hunt	0	W. Casper & W. Maxwell (2&1)	1
B. Huggett & D. Thomas (halved)	½	R. Goalby & D. Ragan (halved)	½
Singles: Morning			
G.M. Hunt	0	A. Lema (5&3)	1
B. Huggett (3&1)	1	J. Pott	0
P. Alliss (1 hole)	1	A. Palmer	0
N.C. Coles (halved)	½	W. Casper (halved)	½
D. Thomas	0	R. Goalby (3&2)	1
C. O'Connor	0	G. Littler (1 hole)	1
H. Weetman (1 hole)	1	J. Boros	0
B.J. Hunt (2 holes)	1	D. Finsterwald	0
Singles: Afternoon			
G. Will	0	A. Palmer (3 & 2)	1
N.C. Coles	0	D. Ragan (2 & 1)	1
P. Alliss (halved)	½	A. Lema (halved)	½
T.B. Haliburton	0	G. Littler (6 & 5)	1
H. Weetman	0	J. Boros (2 & 1)	1
C. O'Connor	0	W. Maxwell (2 & 1)	1
D. Thomas	0	D. Finsterwald (4 & 3)	1
B.J. Hunt	0	R. Goalby (2 & 1)	1
GB	**9**	**US**	**23**

1965

Royal Birkdale, Southport

Captains: H. Weetman (GB), B. Nelson (US)

Great Britain & Ireland		**United States**	
Foursomes: Morning			
L. Platts & P.J. Butler	0	J. Boros & A. Lema (1 hole)	1
D.C. Thomas & G. Will (6&5)	1	A. Palmer & D. Marr	0
B.J. Hunt & N.C. Coles	0	W. Casper & G. Littler (2&1)	1
P. Alliss & C. O'Connor (5&4)	1	K. Venturi & D. January	0
Foursomes: Afternoon			
D.C. Thomas & G. Will	0	A. Palmer & D. Marr (6&5)	1
P. Alliss & C. O'Connor (2&1)	1	W. Casper & G. Littler	0
J. Martin & J. Hitchcock	0	J. Boros & A. Lema (5&4)	1
B.J. Hunt & N.C. Coles (3&2)	1	K. Venturi & D. January	0
Fourballs: Morning			
D.C. Thomas & G. Will	0	D. January & T. Jacobs (1 hole)	1
L. Platts & P. Butler (halved)	½	W. Casper & G. Littler (halved)	½
P. Alliss & C. O'Connor	0	A. Palmer & D. Marr (6&4)	1
B.J. Hunt & N.C. Coles (1 hole)	1	J. Boros & A. Lema	0
Fourballs: Afternoon			
P. Alliss & C. O'Connor (2 holes)	1	A. Palmer & D. Marr	0
D.C. Thomas & G. Will	0	D. January & T. Jacobs (1 hole)	1
L. Platts & P.J. Butler (halved)	½	W. Casper & G. Littler (halved)	½
B.J. Hunt & N.C. Coles	0	K. Venturi & A. Lema (1 hole)	1
Singles: Morning			
J. Hitchcock	0	A. Palmer (3&2)	1
L. Platts	0	J. Boros (4&2)	1
P.J. Butler	0	A. Lema (1 hole)	1
N.C. Coles	0	D. Marr (2 holes)	1
B.J. Hunt (2 holes)	1	G. Littler	0
D.C. Thomas	0	T. Jacobs (2&1)	1
P. Alliss (1 hole)	1	W. Casper	0
G. Will (halved)	½	D. January (halved)	½

Singles: Afternoon

C. O'Connor	0	A. Lema (6&4)	1
J. Hitchcock	0	J. Boros (2&1)	1
P.J. Butler	0	A. Palmer (2 holes)	1
P. Alliss (3&1)	1	K. Venturi	0
N.C. Coles (3&2)	1	W. Casper	0
G. Will	0	G. Littler (2&1)	1
B.J. Hunt	0	D. Marr (1 hole)	1
L. Platts (1 hole)	1	T. Jacobs	0
GB	**12½**	**US**	**19½**

1967

Champions Golf Club, Houston, TX

Captains: D.J. Rees (GB), B. Hogan (US)

Great Britain & Ireland		**United States**	
Foursomes: Morning			
B.G.C. Huggett & G. Will (halved)	½	W. Casper & J. Boros (halved)	½
P. Alliss & C. O'Connor	0	A. Palmer & G. Dickinson (2&1)	1
A. Jacklin & D.C. Thomas (4&3)	1	D. Sanders & G. Brewer	0
B.J. Hunt & N.C. Coles	0	R. Nichols & J. Pott (6&5)	1
Foursomes: Afternoon			
B.G.C. Huggett & G. Will	0	W. Casper & J. Boros (1 hole)	1
M. Gregson & H. Boyle	0	G. Dickinson & A. Palmer (5&4)	1
A. Jacklin & D.C. Thomas (3&2)	1	G. Littler & A. Geiberger	0
P. Alliss & C. O'Connor	0	R. Nichols & J. Pott (2&1)	1
Fourballs: Morning			
P. Alliss & C. O'Connor	0	W. Casper & G. Brewer (3&2)	1
B.J. Hunt & N.C. Coles	0	R. Nichols & J. Pott (1 hole)	1
A. Jacklin & D.C. Thomas	0	G. Littler & A. Geiberger (1 hole)	1
B.G.C. Huggett & G. Will	0	G. Dickinson & D. Sanders (3&2)	1
Fourballs: Afternoon			
B.J. Hunt & N.C. Coles	0	W. Casper & G. Brewer (5&3)	1
P. Alliss & M. Gregson	0	G. Dickinson & D. Sanders (3&2)	1
G. Will & H. Boyle	0	A. Palmer & J. Boros (1 hole)	1
A. Jacklin & D.C. Thomas (halved)	½	G. Littler & A. Geiberger (halved)	½
Singles: Morning			
H. Boyle	0	G. Brewer (4&3)	1
P. Alliss	0	W. Casper (2&1)	1
A. Jacklin	0	A. Palmer (3&2)	1
B.G.C. Huggett (1 hole)	1	J. Boros	0
N.C. Coles (2&1)	1	D. Sanders	0
M. Gregson	0	A. Geiberger (4&2)	1
D.C. Thomas (halved)	½	G. Littler (halved)	½
B.J. Hunt (halved)	½	R. Nichols (halved)	½
Singles: Afternoon			
B.G.C. Huggett	0	A. Palmer (5&3)	1
P. Alliss (2&1)	1	G. Brewer	0
A. Jacklin	0	G. Dickinson (3&2)	1
C. O'Connor	0	R. Nichols (3&2)	1
G. Will	0	J. Pott (3&1)	1
M. Gregson	0	A. Geiberger (2&1)	1
B.J. Hunt (halved)	½	J. Boros (halved)	½
N.C. Coles (2&1)	1	D. Sanders	0
GB	**8½**	**US**	**23½**

1969

Royal Birkdale, Southport

Captains: E.C. Brown (GB), S. Snead (US)

Great Britain & Ireland		**United States**	
Foursomes: Morning			
N.C. Coles & B.G.C. Huggett (3&2)	1	M. Barber & R. Floyd	0
B. Gallacher & M. Bembridge (2&1)	1	L. Trevino & K. Still	0
A. Jacklin & P. Townsend (3&1)	1	D. Hill & T. Aaron	0
C. O'Connor & P. Alliss (halved)	½	W. Casper & F. Beard (halved)	½

Foursomes: Afternoon			
N.C. Coles & B.G.C. Huggett	0	D. Hill & T. Aaron (1 hole)	1
B. Gallacher & M. Bembridge	0	L. Trevino & G. Littler (1 hole)	1
A. Jacklin & P. Townsend (1 hole)	1	W. Casper & F. Beard	0
P.J. Butler & B.J. Hunt	0	J. Nicklaus & D. Sikes (1 hole)	1
Fourballs: Morning			
C. O'Connor & P. Townsend (1 hole)	1	D. Hill & D. Douglas	0
B.G.C. Huggett & G.A. Caygill (halved)	½	R. Floyd & M. Barber (halved)	½
B. Barnes & P. Alliss	0	L. Trevino & G. Littler (1 hole)	1
A. Jacklin & N.C. Coles (1 hole)	1	J. Nicklaus & D. Sikes	0
Fourballs: Afternoon			
P.J. Butler & P. Townsend	0	W. Casper & F. Beard (2 holes)	1
B.G.C. Huggett & B. Gallacher	0	D. Hill & K. Still (2&1)	1
M. Bembridge & B.J. Hunt (halved)	½	T. Aaron & R. Floyd (halved)	½
A. Jacklin & N.C. Coles (halved)	½	L. Trevino & M. Barber (halved)	½
Singles: Morning			
P. Alliss	0	L. Trevino (2&1)	1
P. Townsend	0	D. Hill (5&4)	1
N.C. Coles (1 hole)	1	T. Aaron	0
B. Barnes	0	W. Casper (1 hole)	1
C. O'Connor (5&4)	1	F. Beard	0
M. Bembridge (1 hole)	1	K. Still	0
P.J. Butler (1 hole)	1	R. Floyd	0
A. Jacklin (4&3)	1	J. Nicklaus	0
Singles: Afternoon			
B. Barnes	0	D. Hill (4&2)	1
B. Gallacher (4&3)	1	L. Trevino	0
M. Bembridge	0	M. Barber (7&6)	1
P.J. Butler (3&2)	1	D. Douglas	0
N.C. Coles	0	D. Sikes (4&3)	1
C. O'Connor	0	G. Littler (2&1)	1
B.G.C. Huggett (halved)	½	W. Casper (halved)	½
A. Jacklin (halved)	½	J. Nicklaus (halved)	½
GB	**16**	**US**	**16**

1971

Old Warson Country Club, St Louis, MO

Captains: E.C. Brown (GB), J. Hebert (US)

Great Britain & Ireland		**United States**	
Foursomes: Morning			
N.C. Coles & C. O'Connor (2&1)	1	W. Casper & M. Barber	0
P. Townsend & P. Oosterhuis	0	A. Palmer & G. Dickinson (1 hole)	1
B.G.C. Huggett & A. Jacklin (3&2)	1	J. Nicklaus & D. Stockton	0
M. Bembridge & P.J. Butler (1 hole)	1	C. Coody & F. Beard	0
Foursomes: Afternoon			
H. Bannerman & B. Gallacher (2&1)	1	W. Casper & M. Barber	0
P. Townsend & P. Oosterhuis	0	A. Palmer & G. Dickinson (1 hole)	1
B.G.C. Huggett & A. Jacklin (halved)	½	L. Trevino & M. Rudolph (halved)	½
M. Bembridge & P.J. Butler	0	J. Nicklaus & J.C. Snead (5&3)	1
Fourballs: Morning			
C. O'Connor & B. Barnes	0	L. Trevino & M. Rudolph (2&1)	1
N.C. Coles & J. Garner	0	F. Beard & J.C. Snead (2&1)	1
P. Oosterhuis & B. Gallacher	0	A. Palmer & G. Dickinson (5&4)	1
P. Townsend & H. Bannerman	0	J. Nicklaus & G. Littler (2&1)	1
Fourballs: Afternoon			
B. Gallacher & P. Oosterhuis (1 hole)	1	L. Trevino & W. Casper	0
A. Jacklin & B.G.C. Huggett	0	G. Littler & J.C. Snead (2&1)	1
P. Townsend & H. Bannerman	0	A. Palmer & J. Nicklaus (1 hole)	1
N.C. Coles & C. O'Connor (halved)	½	C. Coody & F. Beard (halved)	½
Singles: Morning			
A. Jacklin	0	L. Trevino (1 hole)	1
B. Gallacher (halved)	½	D. Stockton (halved)	½
B. Barnes (1 hole)	1	M. Rudolph	0
P. Oosterhuis (4&3)	1	G. Littler	0
P. Townsend	0	J. Nicklaus (3&2)	1
C. O'Connor	0	G. Dickinson (5&4)	1
H. Bannerman (halved)	½	A. Palmer (halved)	½
N.C. Coles (halved)	½	F. Beard (halved)	½

Singles: Afternoon			
B.G.C. Huggett	0	L. Trevino (7&6)	1
A. Jacklin	0	J.C. Snead (1 hole)	1
B. Barnes (2&1)	1	M. Barber	0
P. Townsend	0	D. Stockton (1 hole)	1
B. Gallacher (2&1)	1	C. Coody	0
N.C. Coles	0	J. Nicklaus (5&3)	1
P. Oosterhuis (3&2)	1	A. Palmer	0
H. Bannerman (2&1)	1	G. Dickinson	0
GB	**13½**	**US**	**18½**

1973

Muirfield, Scotland

Captains: B.J. Hunt (GB & I), J. Burke (US)

GB & Ireland		**United States**	
Foursomes: Morning			
B.W. Barnes & B.J. Gallacher (1 hole)	1	L. Trevino & W.J. Casper	0
C. O'Connor & N.C. Coles (3&2)	1	T. Weiskopf & J.C. Snead	0
A. Jacklin & P.A. Oosterhuis (halved)	½	J. Rodriguez & L. Graham (halved)	½
M.E. Bembridge & E. Polland	0	J.W. Nicklaus & A. Palmer (6&5)	1
Fourballs: Afternoon			
B.W Barnes & B.J. Gallacher (5 & 4)	1	T. Aaron & G. Brewer	0
M.E. Bembridge & B.G.C. Huggett (3&1)	1	A. Palmer & J.W. Nicklaus	0
A. Jacklin & P. Oosterhuis (3&1)	1	T. Weiskopf & W.J. Casper	0
C. O'Connor & N.C. Coles	0	L. Trevino & H. Blancas (2&1)	1
Foursomes: Morning			
B.W. Barnes & P.J. Butler	0	J.W. Nicklaus & T. Weiskopf (1 hole)	1
P.A. Oosterhuis & A. Jacklin (2 holes)	1	A. Palmer & D. Hill	0
M.E. Bembridge & B.G.C. Huggett (5&4)	1	J. Rodriguez & L. Graham	0
N.C. Coles & C. O'Connor	0	L. Trevino & W.J. Casper (2&1)	1
Fourballs: Afternoon			
B.W. Barnes & P.J. Butler	0	J.C. Snead & A. Palmer (2 holes)	1
A. Jacklin & P.A. Oosterhuis	0	G. Brewer & W. Casper (3&2)	1
C. Clark & E. Polland	0	J.W. Nicklaus & T. Weiskopf (3&2)	1
M.E. Bembridge & B.G.C. Huggett (halved)	½	L. Trevino & H. Blancas (halved)	½
Singles: Morning			
B.W. Barnes	0	W.J. Casper (2&1)	1
B.J. Gallacher	0	T. Weiskopf (3&1)	1
P.J. Butler	0	H. Blancas (5&4)	1
A. Jacklin (3&1)	1	T. Aaron	0
N.C. Coles (halved)	½	G. Brewer (halved)	½
C. O'Connor	0	J.C. Snead (1 hole)	1
M.E. Bembridge (halved)	½	J.W. Nicklaus (halved)	½
P.A. Oosterhuis (halved)	½	L. Trevino (halved)	½
Singles: Afternoon			
B.G.C. Huggett (4&2)	1	H. Blancas	0
B.W. Barnes	0	J.C. Snead (3&1)	1
B.J. Gallacher	0	G. Brewer (6&5)	1
A. Jacklin	0	W.J. Casper (2&1)	1
N.C. Coles	0	L. Trevino (6&5)	1
C. O'Connor (halved)	½	T. Weiskopf (halved)	½
M.E. Bembridge	0	J.W. Nicklaus (2 holes)	1
P.A. Oosterhuis (4&2)	1	A. Palmer	0
GB & I	**13**	**US**	**19**

1975

Laurel Valley, PA

Captains: B.J. Hunt (GB&I), A. Palmer (US)

GB & Ireland		United States	
Foursomes: Morning			
B.W. Barnes & B.J. Gallacher	0	J.W. Nicklaus & T. Weiskopf (5&4)	1
N. Wood & M.E. Bembridge	0	G. Littler & H. Irwin (4&3)	1
A. Jacklin & P. Oosterhuis	0	A. Geiberger & J. Miller (3&1)	1
T. Horton & J. O'Leary	0	L. Trevino & J.C. Snead (2&1)	1
Fourballs: Afternoon			
P. Oosterhuis & A. Jacklin (2&1)	1	W.J. Casper & R. Floyd	0
E. Darcy & C. O'Connor Jr	0	T. Weiskopf & L. Graham (3&2)	1
B.W. Barnes & B.J. Gallacher (halved)	½	J.W. Nicklaus & R. Murphy (halved)	½
T. Horton & J. O'Leary	0	L. Trevino & H. Irwin (2&1)	1
Fourballs: Morning			
P. Oosterhuis & A. Jacklin (halved)	½	W.J. Casper & J. Miller (halved)	½
T. Horton & N. Wood	0	J.W. Nicklaus & J.C. Snead (4&2)	1
B.W. Barnes & B.J. Gallacher	0	G. Littler & L. Graham (5&3)	1
E. Darcy & G.L. Hunt (halved)	½	A. Geiberger & R. Floyd (halved)	½
Foursomes: Afternoon			
A. Jacklin & B.W. Barnes (3&2)	1	L. Trevino & R. Murphy	0
C. O'Connor Jr & J. O'Leary	0	T. Weiskopf & J. Miller (5&3)	1
P. Oosterhuis & M. Bembridge	0	H. Irwin & W.J. Casper (3&2)	1
E. Darcy & G.L. Hunt	0	A. Geiberger & L. Graham (3&2)	1
Singles: Morning			
A. Jacklin	0	R. Murphy (2&1)	1
P. Oosterhuis (2 holes)	1	J. Miller	0
B.J. Gallacher (halved)	½	L. Trevino (halved)	½
T. Horton (halved)	½	H. Irwin (halved)	½
B.G.C. Huggett	0	G. Littler (4&2)	1
E. Darcy	0	W.J. Casper (3&2)	1
G.L. Hunt	0	T. Weiskopf (5&3)	1
B.W. Barnes (4&2)	1	J.W. Nicklaus	0
Singles: Afternoon			
A. Jacklin	0	R. Floyd (1 hole)	1
P. Oosterhuis (3&2)	1	C. Snead	0
B.J. Gallacher (halved)	½	A. Geiberger (halved)	½
T. Horton (2&1)	1	L. Graham	0
J. O'Leary	0	H. Irwin (2&1)	1
M. Bembridge	0	R. Murphy (2&1)	1
N. Wood (2&1)	1	L. Trevino	0
B.W. Barnes (2&1)	1	J.W. Nicklaus	0
GB & I	**11**	**US**	**21**

1977

Royal Lytham & St Annes, St Annes

Captains: B.G.C. Huggett (GB&I), D. Finsterwald (US)

GB & Ireland		United States	
Foursomes			
B.J. Gallacher & B.W. Barnes	0	L. Wadkins & H. Irwin (3&1)	1
N.C. Coles & P. Dawson	0	D. Stockton & M. McGee (1 hole)	1
N. Faldo & P. Oosterhuis (2&1)	1	R. Floyd & L. Graham	0
E. Darcy & A. Jacklin (halved)	½	E. Sneed & D. January (halved)	½
T. Horton & M. James	0	J.W. Nicklaus & T. Watson (5&4)	1
Fourballs			
B.W. Barnes & T. Horton	0	T. Watson & H. Green (5&4)	1
N.C. Coles & P. Dawson	0	E. Sneed & L. Wadkins (5&3)	1
N. Faldo & P. Oosterhuis (3&1)	1	J.W. Nicklaus & R. Floyd	0
A. Jacklin & E. Darcy	0	D. Hill & D. Stockton (5&3)	1
M. James & K. Brown	0	H. Irwin & L. Graham (1 hole)	1
Singles			
H. Clark	0	L. Wadkins (4&3)	1
N.C. Coles	0	L. Graham (5&3)	1
P. Dawson (5&4)	1	D. January	0
T. Horton	0	D. Hill (5&4)	1
B.J. Gallacher (1 hole)	1	J.W. Nicklaus	0

E. Darcy	0	H. Green (1 hole)	1
M. James	0	R. Floyd (2&1)	1
N. Faldo (1 hole)	1	T. Watson	0
P. Oosterhuis (2 holes)	1	J. McGee	0
B. Barnes	1	H. Green	0
GB & I	**7½**	**US**	**12½**

1979

The Greenbrier, WV

Captains: J. Jacobs (Europe), W. Casper (US)

Europe		**United States**	
Foursomes: Morning			
A. Garrido & S. Ballesteros	0	L. Wadkins & L. Nelson (2&1)	1
K. Brown & M. James	0	L. Trevino & F. Zoeller (3&2)	1
P. Oosterhuis & N. Faldo	0	A. Bean & L. Elder (2&1)	1
B. Gallacher & B. Barnes (2&1)	1	H. Irwin & J. Mahaffey	0
Foursomes: Afternoon			
K. Brown & D. Smyth	0	H. Irwin & T. Kite (7&6)	1
S. Ballesteros & A. Garrido (3&2)	1	F. Zoeller & H. Green	0
A. Lyle & A. Jacklin (halved)	½	L. Trevino & G. Morgan (halved)	½
B. Gallacher & B. Barnes	0	L. Wadkins & L. Nelson (4&3)	1
Foursomes: Morning			
A. Jacklin & A. Lyle (5&4)	1	L. Elder & J. Mahaffey	0
N. Faldo & P. Oosterhuis (6&5)	1	A. Bean & T. Kite	0
B. Gallacher & B. Barnes (2&1)	1	F. Zoeller & M. Hayes	0
S. Ballesteros & A. Garrido	0	L. Wadkins & L. Nelson (3&2)	1
Fourballs: Afternoon			
S. Ballesteros & A. Garrido	0	L. Wadkins & L. Nelson (5&4)	1
A. Jacklin & A. Lyle	0	H. Irwin & T. Kite (1 hole)	1
B. Gallacher & B. Barnes (3&2)	1	L. Trevino & F. Zoeller	0
N. Faldo & P. Oosterhuis (1 hole)	1	L. Elder & M. Hayes	0
Singles: Morning			
B. Gallacher (3&2)	1	L. Wadkins	0
S. Ballesteros	0	L. Nelson (3&2)	1
A. Jacklin	0	T. Kite (1 hole)	1
A. Garrido	0	M. Hayes (1 hole)	1
M. King	0	A. Bean (4&3)	1
B. Barnes	0	J. Mahaffey (1 hole)	1
Singles: Afternoon			
N. Faldo (3&2)	1	L. Elder	0
D. Smyth	0	H. Irwin (5&3)	1
P. Oosterhuis	0	H. Green (2 holes)	1
K. Brown (1 hole)	1	F. Zoeller	0
A. Lyle	0	L. Trevino (2&1)	1
M. James (injured, halved)	½	G. Morgan	½
Europe	**11**	**US**	**17**

1981

Walton Heath, Surrey

Captains: J. Jacobs (Europe), D. Marr (US)

Europe		**United States**	
Foursomes: Morning			
B. Langer & M. Pinero	0	L. Trevino & L. Nelson (1 hole)	1
A. Lyle & M. James (2&1)	1	B. Rogers & B. Lietzke	0
B. Gallacher & D. Smyth (3&2)	1	H. Irwin & R. Floyd	0
P. Oosterhuis & N. Faldo	0	T. Watson & J. Nicklaus (4&3)	1
Fourballs: Afternoon			
S. Torrance & H. Clark (halved)	½	T. Kite & J. Miller (halved)	½
A. Lyle & M. James (3&2)	1	B. Crenshaw & J. Pate	0
D. Smyth & J.M. Canizares (6&5)	1	B. Rogers & B. Lietzke	0
B. Gallacher & E. Darcy	0	H. Irwin & R. Floyd (2&1)	1
Fourballs: Morning			
N. Faldo & S. Torrance	0	L. Trevino & J. Pate (7&5)	1
A. Lyle & M. James	0	L. Nelson & T. Kite (1 hole)	1
B. Langer & M. Pinero (2&1)	1	R. Floyd & H. Irwin	0
J.M. Canizares & D. Smyth	0	J. Nicklaus & T. Watson (3&2)	1

Foursomes: Afternoon			
P. Oosterhuis & S. Torrance	0	L. Trevino & J. Pate (2&1)	1
B. Langer & M. Pinero	0	J. Nicklaus & T. Watson (3&2)	1
A. Lyle & M. James	0	B. Rogers & R. Floyd (3&2)	1
D. Smyth & B. Gallacher	0	T. Kite & L. Nelson (3&2)	1
Singles			
S. Torrance	0	L. Trevino (5&3)	1
A. Lyle	0	T. Kite (3&2)	1
B. Gallacher (halved)	½	B. Rogers (halved)	½
M. James	0	L. Nelson (2 holes)	1
D. Smyth	0	B. Crenshaw (6&4)	1
B. Langer (halved)	½	B. Lietzke (halved)	½
M. Pinero (4&2)	1	J. Pate	0
J.M. Canizares	0	H. Irwin (1 hole)	1
N. Faldo (2&1)	1	J. Miller	0
H. Clark (4&3)	1	T. Watson	0
P. Oosterhuis	0	R. Floyd (1 hole)	1
E. Darcy	0	J. Nicklaus (5&3)	1
Europe	**9½**	**US**	**18½**

1983

PGA National Golf Club, Palm Beach Gardens, FL

Captains: A. Jacklin (Europe), J. Nicklaus (US)

Europe		**United States**	
Foursomes: Morning			
B. Gallacher & A. Lyle	0	T. Watson & B. Crenshaw (5&4)	1
N. Faldo & B. Langer (4&2)	1	L. Wadkins & C. Stadler	0
J. Canizares & S. Torrance (4&3)	1	R. Floyd & B. Gilder	0
S. Ballesteros & P. Way	0	T. Kite & C. Peete (2&1)	1
Fourballs: Afternoon			
B. Waites & K. Brown (2&1)	1	G. Morgan & F. Zoeller	0
N. Faldo & B. Langer	0	T. Watson & J. Haas (2&1)	1
S. Ballesteros & P. Way (1 hole)	1	R. Floyd & C. Strange	0
S. Torrance & I. Woosnam (halved)	½	B. Crenshaw & C. Peete (halved)	½
Fourballs: Morning			
B. Waites & K. Brown	0	L. Wadkins & C. Stadler (1 hole)	1
N. Faldo & B. Langer (4&2)	1	B. Crenshaw & C. Peete	0
S. Ballesteros & P. Way (halved)	½	G. Morgan & J. Haas (halved)	½
S. Torrance & I. Woosnam	0	T. Watson & B. Gilder (5&4)	1
Foursomes: Afternoon			
N. Faldo & B. Langer (3&2)	1	T. Kite & R. Floyd	0
S. Torrance & J.M. Canizares	0	G. Morgan & L. Wadkins (7&5)	1
S. Ballesteros & P. Way (2&1)	1	T. Watson & B. Gilder	0
B. Waites & K. Brown	0	J. Haas & C. Strange (3&2)	1
Singles:			
S. Ballesteros (halved)	½	F. Zoeller (halved)	½
N. Faldo (2&1)	1	J. Haas	0
B. Langer (2 holes)	1	G. Morgan	0
G.J. Brand	0	B. Gilder (2 holes)	1
A. Lyle	0	B. Crenshaw (3&1)	1
B. Waites	0	C. Peete (1 hole)	1
P. Way (2&1)	1	C. Strange	0
S. Torrance (halved)	½	T. Kite (halved)	½
I. Woosnam	0	C. Stadler (3&2)	1
J.M. Canizares (halved)	½	L. Wadkins (halved)	½
K. Brown (4&3)	1	R. Floyd	0
B. Gallacher	0	T. Watson (2&1)	1
Europe	**13½**	**US**	**14½**

1985

The Belfry Golf & Country Club, Sutton Coldfield, West Midlands

Captains: A. Jacklin (Europe), L. Trevino (US)

Europe		**United States**	
Foursomes: Morning			
S. Ballesteros & M. Pinero (2&1)	1	C. Strange & M. O'Meara	0
B. Langer & N. Faldo	0	C. Peete & T. Kite (3&2)	1

A. Lyle & K. Brown	0	L. Wadkins & R. Floyd (4&3)	1
H. Clark & S. Torrance	0	C. Stadler & H. Sutton (3&2)	1
Fourballs: Afternoon			
P. Way & I. Woosnam (1 hole)	1	F. Zoeller & H. Green	0
S. Ballesteros & M. Pinero (2&1)	1	A. North & P. Jacobsen	0
B. Langer & J.M. Canizares (halved)	½	C. Stadler & H. Sutton (halved)	½
S. Torrance & H. Clark	0	R. Floyd & L. Wadkins (1 hole)	1
Fourballs: Morning			
S. Torrance & H. Clark (2&1)	1	T. Kite & A. North	0
P. Way & I. Woosnam (4&3)	1	H. Green & F. Zoeller	0
S. Ballesteros & M. Pinero	0	M. O'Meara & L. Wadkins (3&2)	1
B. Langer & A. Lyle (halved)	½	C. Stadler & C. Strange (halved)	½
Foursomes: Afternoon			
J.M. Canizares & J. Rivero (4&3)	1	T. Kite & C. Peete	0
S. Ballesteros & M. Pinero (5&4)	1	C. Stadler & H. Sutton	0
P. Way & I. Woosnam	0	C. Strange & P. Jacobsen (4&2)	1
B. Langer & K. Brown (3&2)	1	R. Floyd & L. Wadkins	0
Singles:			
M. Pinero (3&1)	1	L. Wadkins	0
I. Woosnam	0	C. Stadler (2&1)	1
P. Way (2 holes)	1	R. Floyd	0
S. Ballesteros (halved)	½	T. Kite (halved)	½
A. Lyle (3&2)	1	P. Jacobsen	0
B. Langer (5&4)	1	H. Sutton	0
S. Torrance (1 hole)	1	A. North	0
H. Clark (1 hole)	1	M. O'Meara	0
J. Rivero	0	C. Peete (1 hole)	1
N. Faldo	0	H. Green (3&1)	1
J.M. Canizares (2 holes)	1	F. Zoeller	0
K. Brown	0	C. Strange (4&2)	1
Europe	**16½**	**US**	**11½**

1987

Muirfield Village, Columbus, OH

Captains: A. Jacklin (Europe), J.W. Nicklaus (US)

Europe		**United States**	
Foursomes: Morning			
S. Torrance & H. Clark	0	C. Strange & T. Kite (4&2)	1
K. Brown & B. Langer	0	H. Sutton & D. Pohl (2&1)	1
N. Faldo & I. Woosnam (2 holes)	1	L. Wadkins & L. Mize	0
S. Ballesteros & J-M Olazabal (1 hole)	1	L. Nelson & P. Stewart	0
Fourballs: Afternoon			
G. Brand Jr & J. Rivero (3&2)	1	B. Crenshaw & S. Simpson	0
A. Lyle & B. Langer (1 hole)	1	A. Bean & M. Calcavecchia	0
N. Faldo & I. Woosnam (2&1)	1	H. Sutton & D. Pohl	0
S. Ballesteros & J-M Olazabal (2&1)	1	C. Strange & T. Kite	0
Foursomes: Morning			
J. Rivero & G. Brand Jr	0	C. Strange & T. Kite (3&1)	1
N. Faldo & I. Woosnam (halved)	½	H. Sutton & L. Mize (halved)	½
A. Lyle & B. Langer (2&1)	1	L. Wadkins & L. Nelson	0
S. Ballesteros & J-M Olazabal (1 hole)	1	B. Crenshaw & P. Stewart	0
Fourballs: Afternoon			
N. Faldo & I. Woosnam (5&4)	1	C. Strange & T. Kite	0
E. Darcy & G. Brand Jr	0	A. Bean & P. Stewart (3&2)	1
S. Ballesteros & J-M Olazabal	0	H. Sutton & L. Mize (2&1)	1
S. Lyle & B. Langer (1 hole)	1	L. Wadkins & L. Nelson	0
Singles			
I. Woosnam	0	A. Bean (1 hole)	1
H. Clark (1 hole)	1	D. Pohl	0
S. Torrance (halved)	½	L. Mize (halved)	½
N. Faldo	0	M. Calcavecchia (1 hole)	1
J-M Olazabal	0	P. Stewart (2 holes)	1
J. Rivero	0	S. Simpson (2&1)	1
A. Lyle	0	T. Kite (3&2)	1
E. Darcy (1 hole)	1	B. Crenshaw	0
B. Langer (halved)	½	L. Nelson (halved)	½
S. Ballesteros (2&1)	1	C. Strange	0
K. Brown	0	L. Wadkins (3&2)	1

G. Brand Jr (halved)	?½	H. Sutton (halved)	½
Europe	**15**	**US**	**13**

1989

The Belfry Golf & Country Club, Sutton Coldfield, West Midlands

Captains: A. Jacklin (Europe), R. Floyd (US)

Europe		United States	
Foursomes: Morning			
N. Faldo & I. Woosnam (halved)	½	T. Kite & C. Strange (halved)	½
H. Clark & M. James	0	L. Wadkins & P. Stewart (1 hole)	1
S. Ballesteros & J-M Olazabal (halved)	½	T. Watson & C. Beck (halved)	½
B. Langer & R. Rafferty	0	M. Calcavecchia & K. Green (2&1)	1
Fourballs: Afternoon			
S. Torrance & G. Brand Jr (1 hole)	1	C. Strange & P. Azinger	0
H. Clark & M. James (3&2)	1	F. Couples & L. Wadkins	0
N. Faldo & I. Woosnam (2 holes)	1	M. Calcavecchia & M. McCumber	0
S. Ballesteros & J-M Olazabal (6&5)	1	T. Watson & M. O'Meara	0
Foursomes: Morning			
I. Woosnam & N. Faldo (3 & 2)	1	L. Wadkins & P. Stewart	0
G. Brand Jr & S. Torrance	0	C. Beck & P. Azinger (4&3)	1
C. O'Connor Jr & R. Rafferty	0	M. Calcavecchia & K. Green (3&2)	1
S. Ballesteros & J-M Olazabal (1 hole)	1	T. Kite & C. Strange	0
Fourballs: Afternoon			
N. Faldo & I. Woosnam	0	C. Beck & P. Azinger (2&1)	1
B. Langer & J.M. Canizares	0	T. Kite & M. McCumber (2&1)	1
H. Clark & M. James (1 hole)	1	P. Stewart & C. Strange	0
S. Ballesteros & J-M Olazabal (4&2)	1	M. Calcavecchia & K. Green	0
Singles			
S. Ballesteros	0	P. Azinger (1 hole)	1
B. Langer	0	C. Beck (3&2)	1
J-M Olazabal (1 hole)	1	P. Stewart	0
R. Rafferty (1 hole)	1	M. Calcavecchia	0
H. Clark	0	T. Kite (8&7)	1
M. James (3&2)	1	M. O'Meara	0
C. O'Connor Jr (1 hole)	1	F. Couples	0
J.M. Canizares (1 hole)	1	K. Green	0
G. Brand Jr	0	M. McCumber (1 hole)	1
S. Torrance	0	T. Watson (3&1)	1
N. Faldo	0	L.Wadkins (1 hole)	1
I. Woosnam	0	C. Strange (2 holes)	1
Europe	**14**	**US**	**14**

1991

Ocean Course, Kiawah Island, SC

Captains: B. Gallacher (Europe), D. Stockton (US)

Europe		United States	
Foursomes: Morning			
S. Ballesteros & J-M Olazabal (2&1)	1	P. Azinger & C. Beck	0
B. Langer & M. James	0	R. Floyd & F. Couples (2&1)	1
D. Gilford & C. Montgomerie	0	L. Wadkins & H. Irwin (4&2)	1
N. Faldo & I. Woosnam	0	P. Stewart & M. Calcavecchia (1 hole)	1
Fourballs: Afternoon			
S. Torrance & D. Feherty (halved)	½	L. Wadkins & M. O'Meara (halved)	½
S. Ballesteros & J-M Olazabal (2&1)	1	P. Azinger & C. Beck	0
S. Richardson & M. James (5&4)	1	C. Pavin & M. Calcavecchia	0
N. Faldo & I. Woosnam	0	R. Floyd & F. Couples (5&3)	1
Foursomes: Morning			
D. Feherty & S. Torrance	0	H. Irwin & L. Wadkins (4&2)	1
M. James & S. Richardson	0	M. Calcavecchia & P. Stewart (1 hole)	1
N. Faldo & D. Gilford	0	P. Azinger & M. O'Meara (7&6)	1
S. Ballesteros & J-M Olazabal (3&2)	1	F. Couples & R. Floyd	0
Fourballs: Afternoon			
I. Woosnam & P. Broadhurst (2&1)	1	P. Azinger & H. Irwin	0
B. Langer & C. Montgomerie (2&1)	1	C. Pavin & S. Pate	0
M. James & S. Richardson (3&1)	1	L. Wadkins & W. Levi	0
S. Ballesteros & J-M Olazabal (halved)	½	P. Stewart & F. Couples (halved)	½

Singles

N. Faldo (2 holes)	1	R. Floyd	0
D. Feherty (2&1)	1	P. Stewart	0
C. Montgomerie (halved)	½	M. Calcavecchia (halved)	½
J-M Olazabal	0	P. Azinger (2 holes)	1
S.R. Richardson	0	C. Pavin (2&1)	1
S. Ballesteros (3&2)	1	W. Levi	0
I. Woosnam	0	C. Beck (3&1)	1
P. Broadhurst (3&1)	1	M. O'Meara	0
S. Torrance	0	F. Couples (3&2)	1
M. James	0	L. Wadkins (3&2)	1
B. Langer (halved)	½	H. Irwin (halved)	½
D. Gilford (halved)	½	S. Pate (halved)	½
		(Pate withdrew through injury)	
Europe	**13½**	**US**	**14 ½**

1993

The Belfry Golf & Country Club, Sutton Coldfield, West Midlands

Captains: B. Gallacher (Europe), T. Watson (US)

Europe		**United States**	
Foursomes: Morning			
S. Torrance & M. James	0	L. Wadkins & C. Pavin (4&3)	1
I. Woosnam & B. Langer (7&5)	1	P. Azinger & P. Stewart	0
S. Ballesteros & J-M Olazabal	0	T. Kite & D. Love III (2&1)	1
N. Faldo & C. Montgomerie (4&3)	1	R. Floyd & F. Couples	0
Fourballs: Afternoon			
I. Woosnam & P. Baker (1 hole)	1	J. Gallagher Jr & L. Janzen	0
B. Langer & B. Lane	0	L. Wadkins & C. Pavin (4&2)	1
N. Faldo & C. Montgomerie (halved)	½	P. Azinger & F. Couples (halved)	½
S. Ballesteros & J-M Olazabal (4&3)	1	D. Love III & T. Kite	0
Foursomes: Morning			
N. Faldo & C. Montgomerie (3&2)	1	L. Wadkins & C. Pavin	0
B. Langer & I. Woosnam (2&1)	1	F. Couples & P. Azinger	0
P. Baker & B. Lane	0	R. Floyd & P. Stewart (3&2)	1
S. Ballesteros & J-M Olazabal (2&1)	1	D. Love III & T. Kite	0
Fourballs: Afternoon			
N. Faldo & C. Montgomerie	0	J. Cook & C. Beck (1 hole)	1
M. James & C. Rocca	0	C. Pavin & J. Gallagher Jr (5&4)	1
I. Woosnam & P. Baker (6&5)	1	F. Couples & P. Azinger	0
J-M Olazabal & J. Haeggman	0	R. Floyd & P. Stewart (2&1)	1
Singles			
I. Woosnam (halved)	½	F. Couples (halved)	½
B. Lane	0	C. Beck (1 hole)	1
C. Montgomerie (1 hole)	1	L. Janzen	0
P. Baker (2 holes)	1	C. Pavin	0
J. Haeggman (1 hole)	1	J. Cook	0
M. James	0	P. Stewart (3&2)	1
C. Rocca	0	D. Love III (1 hole)	1
S. Ballesteros	0	J. Gallagher Jr (3&2)	1
J-M Olazabal	0	R. Floyd (2 holes)	1
B. Langer	0	T. Kite (5&3)	1
N. Faldo (halved)	½	P. Azinger (halved)	½
S. Torrance*	½	L. Wadkins	½
(*S. Torrance retired due to injury; match was halved)			
Europe	**13**	**US**	**15**

1995

Oak Hill Country Club, Rochester, NY

Captains: B. Gallacher (Europe), L. Wadkins (US)

Europe		**United States**	
Foursomes: Morning			
N. Faldo & C. Montgomerie	0	C. Pavin & T. Lehman (1 hole)	1
S. Torrance & C. Rocca (3&2)	1	J. Haas & F. Couples	0
H. Clark & M. James	0	D. Love III & J. Maggert (4&3)	1
B. Langer & P.-U. Johansson (1 hole)	1	B. Crenshaw & C. Strange	0

Europe		US	
Fourballs: Afternoon			
D. Gilford & S. Ballesteros (4&3)	1	B. Faxon & P. Jacobsen	0
S. Torrance & C. Rocca	0	J. Maggert & L. Roberts (6&5)	1
N. Faldo & C. Montgomerie	0	F. Couples & D. Love III (3&2)	1
B. Langer & P.-U. Johansson	0	C. Pavin & P. Mickelson (6&4)	1
Foursomes: Morning			
N. Faldo & C. Montgomerie (4&2)	1	C. Strange & J. Haas	0
S. Torrance & C. Rocca (6&5)	1	D. Love III & J. Maggert	0
I. Woosnam & P. Walton	0	L. Roberts & P. Jacobsen (1 hole)	1
B. Langer & D. Gilford (4&3)	1	C. Pavin & T. Lehman	0
Fourballs: Afternoon			
S. Torrance & C. Montgomerie	0	B. Faxon & F. Couples (4&2)	1
I. Woosnam & C. Rocca (3&2)	1	D. Love III & B. Crenshaw	0
S. Ballesteros & D. Gilford	0	J. Haas & P. Mickelson (3&2)	1
N. Faldo & B. Langer	0	C. Pavin & L. Roberts (1 hole)	1
Singles			
S. Ballesteros	0	T. Lehman (4&3)	1
H. Clark (1 hole)	1	P. Jacobsen	0
M. James (4&3)	1	J. Maggert	0
I. Woosnam (halved)	½	F. Couples (halved)	½
C. Rocca	0	D. Love III (3&2)	1
D. Gilford (1 hole)	1	B. Faxon	0
C. Montgomerie (3&1)	1	B. Crenshaw	0
N. Faldo (1 hole)	1	C. Strange	0
S. Torrance (2&1)	1	L. Roberts	0
B. Langer	0	C. Pavin (3&2)	1
P. Walton (1 hole)	1	J. Haas	0
P.-U. Johansson	0	P. Mickelson (2&1)	1
Europe	**14½**	**US**	**13½**

1997

Valderrama Golf Club, Spain

Captains: S. Ballesteros (Europe), T. Kite (USA)

Europe		**United States**	
Fourballs: Morning			
J-M Olazabal & C. Rocca (1 up)	1	D. Love III & P. Mickelson	0
N. Faldo & L. Westwood	0	F. Couples & B. Faxon (1 up)	1
J. Parnevik & P.-U. Johansson (1 up)	1	T. Lehman & J. Furyk	0
B. Langer & C. Montgomerie	0	T. Woods & M. O'Meara (3&2)	1
Foursomes: Afternoon			
J-M Olazaball & C. Rocca	0	S. Hoch & L. Janzen (1 up)	1
B. Langer & C. Montgomerie (5&3)	1	T. Woods & M. O'Meara	0
N. Faldo & L. Westwood (3&2)	1	J. Leonard & J. Maggert	0
I. Garrido & J. Parnevik (halved)	½	T. Lehman & P. Mickelson (halved)	½
Fourballs: Morning			
C. Montgomerie & D. Clarke (1 up)	1	F. Couples & D. Love III	0
I. Woosnam & T. Bjorn (2&1)	1	J. Leonard & B. Faxon	0
N. Faldo & L. Westwood (2&1)	1	T. Woods & M. O'Meara	0
J-M Olazabal & I. Garrido (halved)	½	P. Mickelson & T. Lehman (halved)	½
Foursomes: Afternoon			
C. Montgomerie & B. Langer (1 up)	1	L. Janzen & J. Furyk	0
N. Faldo & L. Westwood	0	S. Hoch & J. Maggert (2&1)	1
J. Parnevik & I. Garrido (halved)	½	J. Leonard & T. Woods	½
J-M Olazaball & C. Rocca (5&4)	1	D. Love III & F. Couples	0
Singles			
I. Woosnam	0	F. Couples (8&7)	1
P.-U. Johansson (3&2)	1	D. Love III	0
C. Rocca (4&2)	1	T. Woods	0
T. Bjorn (halved)	½	J. Leonard (halved)	½
D. Clarke	0	P. Mickelson (2&1)	1
J. Parnevik	0	M. O'Meara (5&4)	1
J-M Olazabal	0	L. Janzen (1 up)	1
B. Langer (2&1)	1	B. Faxon	0
L. Westwood	0	J. Maggert (3&2)	1
C. Montgomerie (halved)	½	S. Hoch (halved)	½
N. Faldo	0	J. Furyk (3&2)	1
I. Garrido	0	T. Lehman (7&6)	1
Europe	**14½**	**US**	**13½**

THE WALKER CUP

Time was when the Walker Cup, which predates the Ryder Cup by five years, was by some distance the more important of the two in the golfing calendar. The decision to augment the best of the British and Irish golfers with the leading European players in the latter contest, thereby practically ensuring a close match every time, certainly reversed that situation.

The Walker Cup has coped readily enough with its changed circumstances. It remains a glorious reminder of the days when team matches were not written up like they were death-and-glory battles. Each time the Americans record a resounding victory the cry goes up to follow the professionals and have it America versus Europe. Each time it is rejected by both sides, who would rather retain the event's Corinthian ideals, where it is the taking part that matters.

Ironically, the Europeans might have been there from the start if they had shown any interest. In 1920, George Herbert Walker, the president of the United States Golf Association, offered to donate an international Challenge Trophy for a competition involving all countries who wished to send amateur teams to the United States the following year. Nobody turned up.

Plan B was quickly put into operation, whereby William Fownes, the US Amateur champion in 1910, took a team to Hoylake for an informal international on the eve of the 1921 Amateur Championship. Fownes's team, a wonderfully talented unit containing Bobby Jones, Chick Evans and Francis Ouimet, won 9–3.

The following year the Royal and Ancient Golf Club of St Andrews declared that they would send a team to the National Golf Links in Southampton, Long Island, to contest the Walker Cup. Walker himself, who incidentally was the maternal grandfather of the future American president, George Bush, was not sure about his name being given to the trophy. He was a modest man and just wanted to present a trophy.

But the Walker Cup it would be, and at least it was up and running, with the first match setting the format: Great Britain and Ireland versus the USA. It has to be said that the contest did not get off to the best of starts. The British captain Robert Harris fell ill and was unable to play. Who could take his place? The visitors were so desperate that they turned to a journalist covering the match. Fortunately, he was not just any old journalist. Bernard Darwin of *The Times* was a scratch golfer in his own right, and he ensured there was plenty to write home about by defeating his American counterpart Bill Fownes in the singles. This, despite being three down after four holes. Alas for Darwin, the rest of his colleagues were not as successful, and America ran out 8–4 winners.

In a fit of initial enthusiasm the Walker Cup was held the next year and in 1924 as well, before settling into its biennial routine. In 1923, GB&I should have recorded their first victory. Willis Mackenzie was the player whose nerve failed to hold. He was six up after 14 holes of his 36-hole singles match, but somehow contrived to lose. With one point proving the difference between the sides at the close, it was to prove the costliest of lapses.

In 1924 the Americans were comfortable winners, but when the match returned to St Andrews in 1926 there was again just a point between the sides: unfortunately for the home players, it was the Americans who once more had their noses in front.

It was the last time that the Walker Cup would be a meaningful contest for some considerable time. A series of overwhelming American victories followed; this was the golden age of American amateur golf, with players like Ouimet, Johnny Goodman and, of course, the peerless Bobby Jones to call upon.

Jones, in particular, was invincible as far as his British counterparts were concerned. Some of his victory margins were by rugby scores; in 1926 he beat Cyril Tolley 12&11; two years later poor Phil Perkins went down 13&12, while in Jones's Grand Slam year of 1930 Roger Wethered's 9&8 defeat sounds almost respectable. Jones's record in singles at the end of five Walker Cup appearances was peerless: played five, won five.

The Americans as a team were similarly impregnable. After eight successive victories they truly surpassed themselves in 1936 at Pine Valley. Twelve points were on offer and GB&I did not win any of them. They recorded three halves and nine losses, and moved Henry Longhurst to remark: "The British side of the scoreboard looked like a daisy chain, with 12 noughts beneath one another."

A bizarre incident in the 1932 Walker Cup at The Country Club, Brookline, appeared to sum up the British effort. At the 18th Leonard Crawley, later to become golf correspondent of the *Daily Telegraph*, hit a shot so wayward that it struck the trophy that was on show in front of the clubhouse and caused a noticeable dent. It appeared to be the only way in which the British would ever leave their mark on the cup.

Certainly, few people seriously questioned that the Americans would make it 10 wins out of 10 at St Andrews in 1938, but two who did were the Open champion, Henry Cotton, and the captain John Beck. In the months before the contest was due to be held they staged trials, and refined the selection process.

James Bruen from Belfast proved inspirational. On the eve of the match he convinced his team-mates that the Americans could be beaten. They believed him, even more so when news of his top foursomes match filtered back down the course. Paired with Harry Bentley, they were three down at lunch to John Fischer and Charles Kocsis. But in the afternoon they played sterling golf, going round the Old Course in four under par to snatch an unlikely half. It completely reversed the trend of the Walker Cup up to that point. Previously, the only dramatic switch involving British and Irish players had been to snatch defeat from the jaws of victory. That half enabled the home side to cling to a slender one-point lead going into the second day's singles.

Bruen was to lose, but he had worked the oracle on hs colleagues. They won the singles 5–3 to record their first victory in the Walker Cup, and against a side captained by the great Ouimet to boot. The two captains were still *in situ* when GB&I came to defend the trophy. But it would be nine years before they were given the chance to do so. The venue was again St Andrews, the world a far different place.

America resumes its dominance

The aftermath of the Second World War and its attendant problems made it difficult for the British side to travel, which was why they got the chance to defend on home soil. It proved no lucky charm on this occasion. American dominance resumed, and with it another long series of heavy victories had commenced.

The American amateur scene was once more blessed with a number of highly gifted players – competitors like Frank Stranahan, who would finish runner-up at the Open Championship on no fewer than two occasions; Bill Campbell; and the 1947 Amateur Champion, Willie Turnesa.

Any sign of a challenge proved a gesture of tokenism. Ronnie White from Wallasey, Merseyside, had a fine record with six wins from 10 appearances between 1947 and 1955, but the Americans had almost a monopoly of the won–lost credit balances.

Just as GB&I must have thought that things could not get any worse, they did. The American college system was now turning out a superior type of golfer, exemplified by the fat kid with a crew-cut who turned up at Muirfield in 1959. He must have looked anything except a top athlete but, as all the world would learn, Jack William Nicklaus could really play. Their opponents would contain such names as Joe Carr, Michael Bonallack and Michael Lunt, and two years later they could further call upon the servies of Ronnie Shade. All to no avail. The Americans demolished their opponents on both occasions. These two matches were Nicklaus's only appearances in the Walker Cup, and he duly won both his singles and foursomes matches to finish his amateur team days with an unblemished record.

For the 1963 match at Turnberry the number of points on offer was increased from 12 to 24, with matches down from 36 holes to 18. It was the one concession to try to equalize the overwhelming superiority of the Americans, for the shorter distance is undoubtedly a great leveller. Such a theory was borne out on the first day's singles, which GB&I managed to win by the startling margin of 5–1. Normal service may have been resumed on the second day, with the Americans running out four-point winners overall, but at least there had been a hint of better things to come for the perennial underdogs.

At Five Farms, Baltimore, in 1965 this impression was underscored when one of the great Walker Cups was staged, as Great Britain and Ireland finally rose to the occasion in America. Here was a side full of bright new talent... Gordon Cosh, Gordon Clark, Clive Clark, Rodney Foster. Above all there was a wonderfully gifted teenager called Peter Townsend, who fully lived up to his pre-match billing by collecting three points out of four, including a victory in the first day's singles against the great American amateur Billy Joe Patton, who was at the other end of his career.

The opening match on the first day set the tone, a wonderfully tight affair in which Michael Lunt and Gordon Cosh managed to squeeze a verdict on the final hole. With Townsend and Ronnie Shade also winning, and Michael Bonallack and Clive Clark getting a half, Britain had the lead.

In the afternoon, they showed the confidence they had gained. At one stage it looked almost a whitewash. Bill Campbell quickly got ahead of Bonallack, and Deane Beman was edging Foster. But that would prove the only American joy. The six matches that followed all went the way of the visitors, and at the halfway stage GB&I had a five-point lead. When they halved the morning foursomes the following day, it appeared game over. They now needed just two points from the last eight singles to register an historic first victory on American soil. Surely that would be a straightforward task?

It proved anything but. The Americans sent out the heavy artillery early and it worked. The 46-year-old Edgar Tutweiler retained his unbeaten record to beat Shade; Campbell notched a second singles win, this time against Foster. Cosh stopped the rot to leave the visitors needing just a half. But where would it come from? Messrs Saddler, Bonallack, Townsend and Lunt could not equal their earlier heroics. It came down, therefore, to Clive Clark against John Hopkins, and as they surveyed their putts on the final green the mood among the British was utterly abject. Here Clark had to hole from 35 feet simply for a halved match that would mean a tie overall. What a contrast from the mood at lunchtime.

While his colleagues prayed for a miracle, Clark set about ensuring it would happen. He surveyed the putt and then sent it on its way, the ball travelling exactly as he had planned before dropping into the hole. For both sides it was a satisfactory outcome. The British and Irish captain, Joe Carr, must have been disappointed having led for so long, but at least he was the first not to lose on American soil; while for the Americans John Fischer had got out of jail and kept the trophy.

Flushed with their success, Clark and Townsend immediately embarked on moderately successful professional careers. The gap proved too great in 1967 for the Walker Cup selectors to fill, and the Americans were again easy victors. Just two points separated the sides in 1969, however, which proved the prelude to an astonishing home victory, again at St Andrews, in 1971.

Home victory at St Andrews

The American side came, as ever, fully expecting to win. Their ranks included two promising young players, Lanny Wadkins and Tom Kite, both with the steely eye of a true competitor.

The home captain was Michael Bonallack and he led by example in the opening foursomes, as he and Warren Humphreys got Great Britain and Ireland off to a remarkable start. It would prove to be the first of four victories in the morning foursomes, the only time before or since that the Americans have been whitewashed in a series.

You could say that the visitors were quite upset with their performance that morning. By dinner-time they were leading, having conceded just one-and-a-half points from the eight singles after lunch. Most of the matches were closer than the score indicates; no fewer than five, indeed, went to the 18th hole. The Americans did not lose any of them, winning four and halving one. They were back on track towards victory, a trend that continued the following morning when they edged another point in front following the second series of foursomes. Surely it was all over for the home side for another Walker Cup?

The American captain duly put out his young gunslingers, Wadkins and Kite, at the top and bottom of the singles order. Both delivered points, Wadkins defeating Michael Bonallack while Kite saw off Geoffrey Marks. Sandwiched in between, however, was the stuff of sensation.

GB&I had to win five of these six matches and halve the other to win the Walker Cup, a task that appeared impossible on paper; another massacre was more likely. But gradually the impossible scenario unfolded: Stuart and Humphreys delivered victories on the Road Hole; Charlie Green and Roddy Carr were taken to the last but prevailed; so did Charlie Green.

And so it was left to Dr David Marsh, who was up against the formidable Bill Hyndman. As they came to the 17th hole Marsh was one up, and a half there would mean he could not lose his match, and Great Britain and Ireland would be home and dry, having achieved only their second success.

If the odds were in his favour, it had to be remembered whom he was playing. Hyndman was competing in his fifth Walker Cup, and had still to lose a match of any kind; he could be relied upon to scrap to the end.

Marsh's drive was slightly left of centre, and that left him 220 yards to go to the flag with a light breeze in his favour. Marsh knew that he could not play too safe. He selected a three iron and envisaged the ball bouncing short; he hoped it would hop up on to the green. It was hardly the safest play – that would

The flags of Great Britain, the United States and Ireland fly over

have been to elect to go to the right of the green and hope for a pitch and putt – but it proved the correct one. In spite of the awesome pressure and clamorous excitement, he hit just the stroke he intended. The ball pitched 15 yards short of the green and scampered onwards, coming to rest 25 feet from the flag. Two putts from there, and Great and Britain and Ireland had indeed won for a second time.

The excitement was immense, the story making headlines

es for the Walker Cup, although the original intention was that amateur teams from all countries should take part

The Walker Cup – the trophy offered to the United States Golf Association by George Herbert Walker in 1920

around the country. It could not last, although they did make a brave stab at defending the trophy in 1973. Great Britain and Ireland would actually claim nine of the 16 points on offer in the two series of singles. But their play in the foursomes was dire: here, they never won a match, losing the two series by the calamitous margin of 7–1. Just two halved matches was pitiful.

The Walker Cup returned to St Andrews in 1975, but this time the visiting team was full of American heroes. No fewer than six of the 10 players on view would go on to make a very good living on the US Tour; three would win major championships. Jay Haas, Gary Koch, George Burns, Curtis Strange, Jerry Pate and Craig Stadler were the half-dozen, the latter three being the major winners.

Not until 1985 would the Walker Cup, once more, produce a meaningful contest. The reasons why were all too obvious. The American college system, now fully refined, encouraged the most promising players to reach at least 20 years of age before turning pro – unlike their British counterparts, who would make the decision two years earlier. Then there were career amateurs like the venerable Jay Sigel, a positive inspiration to the younger element.

In 1985, however, Great Britain and Ireland had some young talent of their own worth boasting about. Colin Montgomerie, David Gilford and Peter Baker would all turn professional and go on to play in the Ryder Cup, while Peter McEvoy was there as the older head, playing in his fourth match.

In the morning foursomes, McEvoy and Baker teamed to great effect to demolish Randy Sonnier and Jerry Haas, as the visitors won two-and-a-half points from the four available. Naturally the Americans rallied after lunch. McEvoy won again, but there were heavy defeats for Montgomerie and Paul Mayo. At the end of play each side had six points each.

It was turning into a fine Walker Cup, with Pine Valley proving the perfect venue. In the foursomes on the second day there was a remarkable conclusion to the match featuring Montgomerie and Mayo. They were up against the formidable Americans, Scott Verplank and Jay Sigel. When they came to the last, their task was difficult indeed; they had to get down in two from 215 yards to force a half. Remarkably, they did so. Montgomerie struck a wonderful approach over a large pond to 10 feet and Mayo rolled in the putt.

Alas, it was the only bit of good news that the visitors would receive. America won the other three foursomes to make a decisive break. GB&I fought hard after lunch to claim the second series of singles. But it proved too little too late – they could only recoup one point of the deficit and so lost out 13–11.

It was, nevertheless, a performance of great heart and character, and the 10,000 spectators who gathered each day two years later when it was held inland in Britain for the first time were naturally infused with optimism. The words of the home captain Geoffrey Marks had added to the hope. He said that the days when British players felt in awe on the first tee had gone.

He could have fooled everyone who gathered by the first at Sunningdale's wondrous Old Course. Great Britain and Ireland were never in it from the opening blow. On the easiest opening hole in Christendom Montgomerie and Graeme Shaw managed to run up a bogey six. First blood to America. They would win every meaningful contest thereafter. The result was a demolition, the margin between the teams nine points. Goodbye optimism.

Hardly surprisingly, there was not a whole lot of it about two years later. Peachtree was the venue – that venerable masterpiece just outside Atlanta. Even when GB&I took a one-point advantage from the opening foursomes the expectation was that they would probably get whitewashed in the afternoon singles. But no, they came and went with a two-point win for the visitors, so that was now three points to the good.

Marks was once more the captain; had his words about an inferiority complex having now disappeared been delivered two years too early? Whatever, what happened on the morning of the second day was truly remarkable. Everyone turned up to watch the American recovery, but the opposite happened. From the second series of foursomes the Americans were lucky to get a half; that is a mere half point. Now they were six points behind with one series of singles to come; now GB&I needed just one-and-a-half points out of eight to win. "Mathematically, we are not eliminated," said the US captain Fred Ridley before adding, with classic understatement: "But I don't really like our chances a whole lot."

By 4.45p.m., though, he liked his team chances a whole lot more. It was Five Farms, Baltimore, and 1965 all over again. The leaderboard showed that, as every game went through the turn, the Americans were ahead in all eight. A glimmer of hope was provided for the visitors by Andrew Hare, who clawed his way back from three down with seven to play to claim a half against Doug Martin. That left two halves or one victory to find.

It did not come on the 18th green in the top match, where Robert Gamez saw off Stephen Dodd by the slimmest of margins; nor in the third match, where McEvoy went down to the Peachtree member Dan Yates. But the Irishman Eoghan O'Connell, in a tight tussle against Phil Mickelson, managed to get a half at the 18th; now just another half was necessary, with four matches on the course.

The trouble was, America won the first three. One match was left out on the course. It featured an unassuming Scot by the name of Jim Milligan against the best American amateur of his generation, Jay Sigel. After 14 holes, it was all going to type: Sigel was two up. On the 15th Sigel hit his drive down the middle, while Milligan went into the rough. It looked as if the American would be three up with three to play, but Milligan holed a brave ten-footer for par to stay two down. At the 16th he gave himself a glimmer of hope by hitting his approach stone-dead for a winning birdie. By now all the interest was on this match: the veteran Sigel, one up with two to play, needed to win to give America the cup.

The 17th will never be forgotten by anyone who witnessed it. Milligan, through the back in two, then duffed his pitch and sank to his knees; it never even made the putting surface. Amazingly, from the front of the green, Sigel then showed he was not immune to the pressure by doing the same. They were equidistant in three. It was Milligan to play first – another pitch. This one was better – a lot better. As the hole came into view, it was clear that it was well-nigh perfect. Or even better than that. With its last gasp, it dropped into the hole. All square.

At the last, Sigel looked like a broken man. Milligan got the half he needed. After 67 years Great Britain and Ireland had finally won the Walker Cup on American soil. For the first time the Curtis, Walker and Ryder Cup trophies all resided in Britain. "There should be a law against all this silverware leaving the country," said one USGA official.

A move to Ireland

The Walker Cup went to Ireland for the first time in 1991. Phil Mickelson got into a bit of trouble from the start. When his playing partner hit the ball deep into the undergrowth, beyond the spectators, he tried a joke that misfired spectacularly. "The Irish girls may be pretty but they're not that good-looking," he said to his colleague. Some sensitive soul reported it back to an Irish tabloid, and by the next morning Mickelson discovered over his breakfast cereal that he had actually said, in bold black and white letters to boot, that Irish women were ugly.

Like the top pro he would become, he never let it bother him. He won both his matches on the opening day as America laid a grip on the trophy that they would never relinquish. The final winning margin was four, the abiding memory the wonderful fervour of the Irish golfing fraternity.

At Interlachen two years later the British gathered in fine spirits. After all, they had won their last match in America and lost the one before that by only two points. This one, though, was little short of a disaster. The opening foursomes was washed out by rain but, even so, the visitors managed to lose the other three series by the combined margin of 14 points.

From the American perspective, the match was a complete triumph for Jay Sigel, yes, the same Sigel who had looked all washed up at Peachtree in 1989. Since that debacle, he had played in two more Walker Cup matches, winning four games and losing two.

His overall record of playing in nine Walker Cups overtook that of Francis Ouimet, who participated in eight, and tied with Joe Carr's achievement for appearances for Britain and

The Walker Cup has played host to a number of the game's great names, among them Tiger Woods in 1995

Justin Rose (putting), watched here by Gary Wolstenholme, became the youngest-ever Walker Cup player in 1997

Ireland. Sigel played in 33 games, won 18 and halved five. Perhaps the fullest indication of just how good that record is comes when it is considered that the next best number of victories compiled by any player is 11. Joe Carr played in 20 games and won just five. True, the greats like Bobby Jones only played in two matches each Walker Cup rather than the four in which Sigel was eligible to compete, and so would definitely have got nearer his landmark. Nevertheless, it remains a wonderful achievement.

And after it was over Sigel gave up his life insurance business and in 1994, at the age of 50, turned professional and joined the US Senior Tour. Against players who had done nothing else but play competitive golf all their lives, Sigel still made a decisive impression. Over the next five seasons he averaged a shade over $1 million a season. Truly, an extraordinary player.

So that was the American perspective from Interlachen. In Britain there was no such positive aspect. It was a humiliating loss without any redeeming factors, and led to huge cries to alter the format to include the best of the Europeans on the GB&I side.

Those noises were made to look premature two years later when the Walker Cup followed up its first trip to Ireland with a similar one to Wales. This contest attracted enormous publicity, not least because of the leading personalities on both sides. The British and Irish had Gordon Sherry, who had delighted us all that summer by finishing fourth in the Scottish Open and then outplaying his playing partners Tom Watson and Greg Norman the following week in the Open Championship at St Andrews.

The American equivalent was Tiger Woods, the starriest amateur the game had seen since Jack Nicklaus, who had just retained his US Amateur Championship.

Yet the match proved much more than just Woods against Sherry. There was the preparation for a start. After the Interlachen calamity, two squad visits were organized to Royal Porthcawl to ensure that the British and Irish players were well acquainted with the links before they tackled it in earnest. Furthermore, the Ryder Cup captain, Bernard Gallacher, was employed to guide the players on how best to manage themselves.

The start, though, was not promising. The Americans claimed a point advantage after the morning foursomes, which was quite a coup given that in one match they had salvaged a half having been three down with four to play. The afternoon singles – played in sunny, breezy weather – was a different script. Sherry won, as did Stephen Gallacher, the nephew of Bernard. With one match still out on the course, the contest overall was level. In that last match Woods was up against Gary Wolstenholme.

This was such an uneven contest in terms of length that at the 18th Wolstenholme had a wood for his second shot while Woods had a short iron. Remarkably the tortoise, so to speak, prevailed. Wolstenholme found the green to put the pressure on Woods. He responded by airmailing his approach out of bounds. Instead of being all square at the halfway stage, GB&I were two points ahead, and Wolstenholme had a story that he will dine out on for ever.

It would prove to be the decisive breakthrough. The second series of foursomes would be halved two points each, with Woods losing again, but in the afternoon the home side took a firm grip on the match.

The weather was as doleful as it can be when the elements envelop the Bristol Channel. The top members of the British and Irish batting order were, however, exultant. Naturally, the exuberant Sherry led the way. He won the top match, and he was followed home by David Howell. Gallacher won as well, as did the Irishman Jody Flanagan. When Barclay Howard claimed a half from the fifth singles, Great Britain and Ireland had won the Walker Cup with three matches still out on the course.

As was to be expected, given the chance of a rematch against Wolstenholme, Woods duly won four and three. Lightning rarely strikes twice. But the damage had been done 24 hours earlier, and how the underdogs seized their chance on the second day.

At Quaker Ridge, NY, in 1997 it was back to the old story of complete American domination. The pattern was all too familiar: the greens were too slick for the visitors, the rough too severe. The preparation had been so complete that perhaps it was too thorough. The away side travelled to America fully eight days before the match began. The only consolation was the performance of Justin Rose, who at 17 became the youngest player ever to compete in the Walker Cup. He claimed two points out of four.

But the truth of the matter was, and remains, that on most occasions the Americans will prove too strong - and sometimes, as in 1997, it will be to an embarrassing degree. How can it be otherwise, when they have so many more players from which to choose, and the opposition have so few?

There is, however, a kinder way of looking at this: after just one win in the first 22 Walker Cups, Great Britain and Ireland have now won three of the last 12, and two of the last five. It might not be worth getting on to a rooftop to brag about, but it is progress, and it does help to keep interest in the contest alive. The gap is closing.

Whatever happens, all calls to restructure the format should be severely resisted. This is amateur golf at its purest, and as long as the players regard it as the benchmark by which they can judge themselves – the highest honour they can attain before succumbing to the temptations of professionalism – then it must continue. As the players prepared to gather for the latest contest in Nairn in September, 1999, there is no evidence that the Walker Cup means any less at the end of the century than it did when it began all those years ago.

THE WALKER CUP STATISTICS

1922

National Golf Links of America, New York

Captains: W.C. Fownes Jr (US), R.. Harris (GB & Ire)

United States		Great Britain and Ireland	
Foursomes			
J.P. Guilford and F.D. Ouimet (8&7)	1	C.J.H. Tolley and B. Darwin	0
C. Evans Jr and R.A. Gardner	0	R.H. Wethered and C.C. Aylmer (5&4)	1
R.T. Jones Jr and J.W. Sweetser (3&2)	1	W.B. Torrance and C.V.L. Hooman	0
M.R. Marston and W.C. Fownes Jr (2&1)	1	J. Caven and W.W. Mackenzie	0
Singles			
J.P. Guilford (2&1)	1	C.J.H. Tolley	0
R.T. Jones Jr (3&2)	1	R.H. Wethered	0
C. Evans Jr (5&4)	1	J. Caven	0
F.D. Ouimet (8&7)	1	C.C. Aylmer	0
R.A. Gardner (7&5)	1	W.B. Torrance	0
M.R. Marston	0	W.W. Mackenzie (6&5)	1
W.C. Fownes Jr	0	B. Darwin (3&1)	1
J.W. Sweetser	0	C.V.L. Hooman (37th)	1
United States	**8**	**Great Britain and Ireland**	**4**

1923

St Andrews

Captains: R.A. Gardner (US), R. Harris (GB & Ire)

United States		Great Britain and Ireland	
Foursomes			
F.D. Ouimet and J.W. Sweetser	0	C.J.H. Tolley and R.H. Wethered (6&5)	1
R.A.. Gardner and M.R. Marston (7&6)	1	R. Harris and C.V.L. Hooman	0
G.V. Rotan and S.D. Herron	0	E.W.E. Holderness and W.L. Hope (1 hole)	1
H.R. Johnston and J.F. Neville	0	J. Wilson and W.A. Murray (4&3)	1
Singles			
F.D. Ouimet	0	R.H. Wethered	0
J.W. Sweetser	0	C.J.H. Tolley (4&3)	1
R.A. Gardner (1 hole)	1	R. Harris	0
G.V. Rotan (5&4)	1	W.W. Mackenzie	0
M.R. Marston (6&5)	1	W.L. Hope	0
F.J. Wright Jr (1 hole)	1	E.W.E. Holderness	0
S.D. Herron	0	J. Wilson (1 hole)	1
O.F. Willing (2&1)	1	W.A. Murray	0
United States	**6**	**Great Britain and Ireland**	**5**

1924

Garden City, New York

Captains: R.A. Gardner (US), C.J.H. Tolley (GB & Ire)

United States		Great Britain and Ireland	
Foursomes			
M.R. Marston and R.A. Gardner (3&1)	1	E.F. Storey and W.A. Murray	0
J.P. Guilford and F.D. Ouimet (2&1)	1	C.J.H. Tolley and C.O. Hezlet	0
R.T. Jones Jr and W.C. Fownes	0	Hon M. Scott and R. Scott Jr (1 hole)	1
J.W. Sweetser and H.R. Johnston (4&3)	1	T.A. Torrance and O.C. Bristowe	0
Singles			
M.R. Marston	0	C.J.H. Tolley (1 hole)	1
R.T. Jones Jr (4&3)	1	C.O. Hezlet	0
C. Evans Jr (2&1)	1	W.A. Murray	0
F.D. Ouimet (1 hole)	1	E.F. Storey	0
J.W. Sweetser	0	Hon M. Scott (7&6)	1
R.A. Gardner (3&2)	1	W.L. Hope	0
J.P. Guilford (2&1)	1	T.A. Torrance	0

United States		Great Britain and Ireland	
O.F. Willing (3&2)	1	D.H. Kyle	0
United States	**9**	**Great Britain and Ireland**	**3**

1926

St Andrews

Captains: R.A. Gardner (US), R. Harris (GB & Ire)

United States		Great Britain and Ireland	
Foursomes			
F.D. Ouimet and J.P. Guilford	0	R.H. Wethered and E.W.E. Holderness (4&5)	1
R.T. Jones Jr and W. Gunn (4&3)	1	C.J.H. Tolley and A. Jamieson Jr	0
G. Von Elm and J.W. Sweetser (8&7)	1	R. Harris and C.O. Hezlet	0
R.A. Gardner and R.R. MacKenzie (1 hole)	1	E.F. Storey and Hon W.G.E. Brownlow	0
Singles			
R.T. Jones Jr (12&11)	1	C.J.H. Tolley	0
J.W. Sweetser (4&3)	1	E.W.E. Holderness	0
F.D. Ouimet	0	R.H. Wethered (5&4)	1
G. Von Elm	0	C.O. Hezlet	0
J.P. Guilford	0	R. Harris (2&1)	1
W. Gunn (9&8)	1	Hon W.G.E. Brownlow	0
R.R. MacKenzie	0	E.F. Storey (2&1)	1
R.A. Gardner	0	A. Jamieson Jr (5&4)	1
United States	**6**	**Great Britain and Ireland**	**5**

1928

Chicago, Illinois

Captains: R.T. Jones Jr (US), W. Twedell (GB & Ire)

United States		Great Britain and Ireland	
Foursomes			
J.W. Sweetser and G. Von Elm (7&6)	1	T.P. Perkins and W. Tweddell	0
R.T. Jones Jr and C. Evans Jr (5&3)	1	C.O. Hezlet and W.L. Hope	0
F.D. Ouimet and H.R. Johnston (4&2)	1	T.A. Torrance and E.F. Storey	0
W. Gunn and R.R. MacKenzie (7&5)	1	J.B. Beck and G.N.C. Martin	0
Singles			
R.T. Jones Jr (13&12)	1	C.J.H. Tolley	0
G. Von Elm (3&2)	1	R.H. Wethered	0
F.D. Ouimet (8&7)	1	R.W. Hartley	0
J.W. Sweetser (5&4)	1	E.W.E. Holderness	0
H.R. Johnston (4&2)	1	R. Harris	0
C. Evans Jr	0	T.A. Torrance (1 hole)	1
W. Gunn (11&10)	1	J.A. Stout	0
R.R. MacKenzie (2&1)	1	W. Campbell	0
United States	**11**	**Great Britain and Ireland**	**1**

1930

Sandwich, Royal St George's

Captains: R.T. Jones Jr (US), R. Harris (GB & Ire)

United States		Great Britain and Ireland	
Foursomes			
G. Von Elm and G.J. Voigt	0	C.J.H. Tolley and R.H. Wethered (2 holes)	1
R.T. Jones Jr and O.F. Willing (8&7)	1	R.W. Hartley and T.A. Torrance	0
R.R. MacKenzie and D.K. Moe (2&1)	1	E.W.E. Holderness and J.A. Stout	0
H.R. Johnston and F.D. Ouimet (2&1)	1	W. Campbell and J.N. Smith	0
Singles			
H.R. Johnston (5&4)	1	C.J.H. Tolley	0
R.T. Jones Jr (9&8)	1	R.H. Wethered	0
G. Von Elm (3&2)	1	R.W. Hartley	0
G.J. Voigt (10&8)	1	E.W.E. Holderness	0
O.F. Willing (2&1)	1	R. Harris	0
F.D. Ouimet	0	T.A. Torrance (7&6)	1
D.K. Moe (1 hole)	1	J.A. Stout	0
R.R. MacKenzie (6&5)	1	W. Campbell	0
United States	**10**	**Great Britain and Ireland**	**2**

1932

Brookline, Massachusetts

Captains: F.D. Ouimet (US), T.A. Torrance (GB & Ire)

United States		Great Britain and Ireland	
Foursomes			
J.W. Sweetser and G.J. Voigt (7&6)	1	R.W. Hartley and W.L. Hartley	0
C.H. Seaver and G.T. Moreland (6&5)	1	T.A. Torrance and J.G. De Forest	0
F.D. Ouimet and G.T. Dunlap Jr (7&6)	1	J.A. Stout and J. Burke	0
D.K. Moe and W. Howell (5&4)	1	E.W. Fiddian and E.A. McRuvie	0
Singles			
F.D. Ouimet	0	T.A. Torrance	0
J.W. Sweetser	0	J.A. Stout	0
G.T. Moreland (2&1)	1	R.W. Hartley	0
J. Westland	0	J. Burke	0
G.J. Voigt	0	L.G. Crawley (1 hole)	1
M.J. McCarthy Jr (3&2)	1	W.L. Hartley	0
C.H. Seaver (7&6)	1	E.W. Fiddian	0
G.T. Dunlap Jr (10&9)	1	E.A. McRuvie	0
United States	**8**	**Great Britain and Ireland**	**1**

1934

St Andrews

Captains: F.D. Ouimet (US), Hon M. Scott (GB & Ire)

United States		Great Britain and Ireland	
Foursomes			
J.G. Goodman and W.L. Little Jr (8&6)	1	R.H. Wethered and C.J.H. Tolley	0
G.T. Moreland and J. Westland (6&5)	1	H.G. Bentley and E.W. Fiddian	0
H.C. Egan and M.R. Marston (3&2)	1	Hon M. Scott and S.L. McKinley	0
F.D. Ouimet and G.T. Dunlap Jr	0	E.A. McRuvie and J. McLean (4&2)	1
Singles			
J.G. Goodman (7&6)	1	Hon M. Scott	0
W.L. Little Jr (6&5)	1	C.J.H. Tolley	0
F.D. Ouimet (5&4)	1	L.G. Crawley	0
G.T. Dunlap Jr (4&3)	1	J. McLean	0
J.W. Fisher (5&4)	1	E.W. Fiddian	0
G.T. Moreland (3&1)	1	S.L. McKinley	0
J. Westland	0	E.A. McRuvie	0
M.R. Marston	0	T.A. Torrance	1
United States	**9**	**Great Britain and Ireland**	**2**

1936

Pine Valley, New Jersey

Captains: FD Ouimet (US), W Tweddell (GB & Ire)

United States		Great Britain and Ireland	
Foursomes			
J.G. Goodman and A.E. Campbell (7&5)	1	H. Thomson and H.G. Bentley	0
R. Smith and E. White (8&7)	1	J. McLean and J.D.A. Langley	0
C.R. Yates and W. Emery	0	G.B. Peters and J.M. Dykes	0
H.L. Givan and G.J. Voigt	0	G.A. Hills and R.C. Ewing	0
Singles			
J.G. Goodman (3&2)	1	H. Thomson	0
A.E. Campbell (5&4)	1	J. McLean	0
J.W. Fisher (8&7)	1	R.C. Ewing	0
R. Smith (11&9)	1	G.A. Hill	0
W. Emery (1 hole)	1	G.B. Peters	0
C.R. Yates (8&7)	1	J.M. Dykes	0
G.T. Dunlap Jr	0	H.G. Bentley	1
E. White (6&5)	1	J.D.A. Langley	0
United States	**9**	**Great Britain and Ireland**	**1**

1938

St Andrews

Captains: J.B. Beck (GB & Ire), F.D. Ouimet (US)

Great Britain and Ireland | **United States**

Foursomes			
H.G. Bentley and J. Bruen Jr	0	J.W. Fisher and C.R. Kocsis	0
G.B. Peters and H. Thomson (4&2)	1	J.G. Goodman and M.H. Ward	0
A.T. Kyle and C. Stowe	0	C.R. Yates and R.E. Billows (3&2)	1
J.J.F. Pennink and L.G. Crawley (3&1)	1	R. Smith and F. Haas Jr	0
Singles			
J. Bruen Jr	0	C.R. Yates (2&1)	1
H. Thomson (6&4)	1	J.G. Goodman	0
L.G. Crawley	0	J.W. Fisher (3&2)	1
C. Stowe (2&1)	1	C.R. Kocsis	0
J.J.F. Pennink	0	M.H. Ward (12&11)	1
R.C. Ewing (1 hole)	1	R.E. Billows	0
G.B. Peters (9&8)	1	R. Smith	0
A.T. Kyle (5&4)	1	F. Haas Jr	0
Great Britain and Ireland	**7**	**United States**	**4**

1947

St Andrews

Captains: F.D. Ouimet (US), J.B. Beck (GB & Ire)

United States		**Great Britain and Ireland**	
Foursomes			
S.E. Bishop and R.H. "Skee" Riegel (3&2)	1	J.B. Carr and R.C. Ewing	0
M.H. Ward and S.L. Quick	0	L.G. Crawley and P.B. Lucas (5&4)	1
W.P. Turnesa and A.F. Kramer Jr (5&4)	1	A.T. Kyle and J.C. Wilson	0
F.R. Stranahan and R.D. Chapman	0	R.J. White and C. Stowe (4&3)	1
Singles			
M.H. Ward (5&3)	1	L.G. Crawley	0
S.E. Bishop	0	J.B. Carr (5&3)	1
R.H. "Skee" Riegel (6&5)	1	G.H. Micklem	0
W.P. Turnesa (6&5)	1	R.C. Ewing	0
F.R. Stranahan (2&1)	1	C. Stowe	0
A.F. Kramer Jr	0	R.J. White (4&3)	1
S.L. Quick (8&6)	1	J.C. Wilson	0
R.D. Chapman (4&3)	1	P.B. Lucas	0
United States	**8**	**Great Britain and Ireland**	**4**

1949

Winged Foot, New Jersey

Captains: F.D. Ouimet (US), P.B. Lucas (GB & Ire)

United States		**Great Britain and Ireland**	
Foursomes			
R.E. Billows and W.P. Turnesa	0	J.B. Carr and R.J. White (3&2)	1
C.R. Kocsis and F.R. Stranahan (2&1)	1	J. Bruen Jr and S.M. McCready	0
S.E. Bishop and R.H. "Skee" Riegel (9&7)	1	R.C. Ewing and G.H. Micklem	0
J.W. Dawson and B.N. McCormick (8&7)	1	K.G. Thom and A.H. Perowne	0
Singles			
W.P. Turnesa	0	R.J. White (4&3)	1
F.R. Stranahan (6&5)	1	S.M. McCready	0
R.H. "Skee" Riegel (5&4)	1	J. Bruen Jr	0
J.W. Dawson (5&3)	1	J.B. Carr	0
R.C. Coe (1 hole)	1	R.C. Ewing	0
R.E. Billows (2&1)	1	K.G. Thom	0
C.R. Kocsis (4&2)	1	A.H. Perowne	0
J.B. McHale Jr (5&4)	1	G.H. Micklem	0
United States	**10**	**Great Britain and Ireland**	**2**

1951

Birkdale

Captains: W.P. Turnesa (US), R. Oppenheimer (GB & Ire)

United States		**Great Britain and Ireland**	
Foursomes			
F.R. Stranahan and W.C. Campbell	0	R.J. White and J.B. Carr	0
C.R. Coe and J.B. McHale Jr	0	R.C. Ewing and J.D.A. Langley	0
R.D. Chapman and R.W. Knowles Jr (1 hole)	1	A.T. Kyle and I. Caldwell	0
W.P. Turnesa and S. Urzetta (5&4)	1	J. Bruen Jr and J.L. Morgan	0

Singles			
S. Urzetta (4&3)	1	S.M. McCready	0
F.R. Stranahan	0	J.B. Carr (2&1)	1
C.R. Coe	0	R.J. White (2&1)	1
J.B. McHale Jr (2 holes)	1	J.D.A. Langley	0
W.C. Campbell (5&4)	1	R.C. Ewing	0
W.P. Turnesa	0	A.T. Kyle (2 holes)	1
H.D. Paddock Jr	0	I. Caldwell	0
R.D. Chapman (7&6)	1	J.L. Morgan	0
United States	**6**	**Great Britain and Ireland**	**3**

1953

Kittansett, Massachusetts

Captains: C.R. Yates (US), A.A .Duncan (GB & Ire)

United States		**Great Britain and Ireland**	
Foursomes			
S. Urzetta and K. Venturi (6&4)	1	J.B. Carr and R.J. White	0
M.H. Ward Jr and J. Westland (9&8)	1	J.D.A. Langley and A.H. Perowne	0
J.G. Jackson and G.A. Littler (3&2)	1	J.C. Wilson and R.C. McGregor	0
W.C. Campbell and C.R. Coe	0	G.H. Micklem and J.L. Morgan (4&3)	1
Singles			
M.H. Ward Jr (4&3)	1	J.B. Carr	0
R.D. Chapman	0	R.J. White (1 hole)	1
G.A. Littler (5&3)	1	G.H. Micklem	0
J. Westland (7&5)	1	R.C. McGregor	0
D.R. Cherry (9&7)	1	N.V. Drew	0
K. Venturi (9&8)	1	J.C. Wilson	0
C.R. Coe	0	J.L. Morgan (3&2)	1
S. Urzetta (3&2)	1	J.D.A. Langley	0
United States	**9**	**Great Britain and Ireland**	**3**

1955

St Andrews

Captains: W.C. Campbell (US), G.A. Hill (GB & Ire)

United States		**Great Britain and Ireland**	
Foursomes			
M.H. Ward Jr and D.R. Cherry (1 hole)	1	J.B. Carr and R.J. White	0
W.J. Patton and R.L. Yost (2&1)	1	G.H. Micklem and J.L. Morgan	0
J.W. Conrad and D. Morey (3&2)	1	I. Caldwell and E.B. Millward	0
B.H. Cudd and J.G. Jackson (5&4)	1	D.A. Blair and J.R. Cater	0
Singles			
M.H. Ward Jr (6&5)	1	R.J. White	0
W.J. Patton (2&1)	1	P.F. Scrutton	0
D. Morey	0	I. Caldwell (1 hole)	1
D.R. Cherry (5&4)	1	J.B. Carr	0
J.W. Conrad	0	D.A. Blair (1 hole)	1
B.H. Cudd (2 holes)	1	E.B. Millward	0
J.G. Jackson (6&4)	1	R.C. Ewing	0
R.L. Yost (8&7)	1	J.L. Morgan	0
United States	**10**	**Great Britain and Ireland**	**2**

1957

Minikahda, Minnesota

Captains: C.R. Coe (US), G.H. Micklem (GB & Ire)

United States		**Great Britain and Ireland**	
Foursomes			
R. Baxter Jr and W.J. Patton (2&1)	1	J.B. Carr and F.W.G. Deighton	0
W.C. Campbell and F.M. Taylor Jr (4&3)	1	A.F. Bussel and P.F. Scrutton	0
A.S. Blum and C.R. Kocsis	0	R.R. Jack and D. Sewell (1 hole)	1
H. Robbins Jr and E.M. Rudolph	0	A.E. Shepperson and G.B. Wolstenholme	0
Singles			
W.J. Patton (1 hole)	1	R.R. Jack	0
W.C. Campbell (3&2)	1	J.B. Carr	0
R. Baxter Jr (4&3)	1	A. Thirlwell	0
W. Hyndman III (7&6)	1	F.W.G. Deighton	0

W.C. Campbell	0	A.F. Bussel (2&1)	1
F.M. Taylor Jr (1 hole)	1	D. Sewell	0
E.M. Rudolph (3&2)	1	P.F. Scrutton	0
H. Robbins Jr	0	G.B. Wolstenholme (2&1)	1
United States	**8**	**Great Britain and Ireland**	**3**

1959

Honourable Company, Muirfield

Captains: CR Coe (US), GH Micklem (GB & Ire)

United States		**Great Britain and Ireland**	
Foursomes			
M.H. Ward Jr and F.M. Taylor Jr (1 hole)	1	R.R. Jack and D.N. Sewell	0
W. Hyndman III and T.D. Aaron (1 hole)	1	J.B. Carr and G.B. Wolstenholme	0
W.J. Patton and C.R. Coe (9&8)	1	M.F. Bonallack and A.H. Perowne	0
H.W. Wettlaufer and J.W. Nicklaus (2&1)	1	M.S.R. Lunt and A.E. Shepperson	0
Singles			
C.R. Coe	0	J.B. Carr (2&1)	1
M.H. Ward Jr (9&8)	1	G.B. Wolstenholme	0
W.J. Patton	0	R.R. Jack (5&3)	1
W. Hyndman III (4&3)	1	D.N. Sewell	0
T.D. Aaron	0	A.E. Shepperson (2&1)	1
D.R. Beman (2 holes)	1	M.F. Bonallack	0
H.W. Wettlaufer (6&5)	1	M.S.R. Lunt	0
J.W. Nicklaus (5&4)	1	W.D. Smith	0
United States	**9**	**Great Britain and Ireland**	**3**

1961

Seattle, Washington

Captains: J. Westland (US), C.D. Lawrie (GB & Ire)

United States		**Great Britain and Ireland**	
Foursomes			
D.R. Beman and J.W. Nicklaus (6&5)	1	J. Walker and B.H.G. Chapman	0
C.R. Coe and D.R. Cherry (1 hole)	1	D.A. Blair and M.J. Christmas	0
W. Hyndman III and R.W. Gardner (4&3)	1	J.B. Carr and G. Huddy	0
R.E. Cochran and E.S. Andrews (4&3)	1	M.F. Bonallack and R.D.B.M. Shade	0
Singles			
D.R. Beman (3&2)	1	M.F. Bonallack	0
C.R. Coe (5&4)	1	M.S.R. Lunt	0
F.M. Taylor Jr (3&2)	1	J. Walker	0
W. Hyndman III (7&6)	1	D.W. Frame	0
J.W. Nicklaus (6&4)	1	J.B. Carr	0
C.B. Smith	0	M.J. Christmas (3&2)	1
R.W. Gardner (1 hole)	1	R.D.B.M. Shade	0
D.R. Cherry (5&4)	1	D.A. Blair	0
United States	**11**	**Great Britain and Ireland**	**1**

1963

Turnberry

Captains: R.S. Tufts (US), C.D. Lawrie (GB & Ire)

First Series

United States		**Great Britain and Ireland**	
Foursomes			
W.J. Patton and R.H. Sikes	0	M.F. Bonallack and S.W.T. Murray (4&3)	1
A.D. Gray Jr and L.E. Harris Jr (2 holes)	1	J.B. Carr and C.W. Green	0
D.R. Beman and C.R. Coe (5&3)	1	M.S.R. Lunt and D.B. Sheahan	0
R.W. Gardner and E.R. Updegraff	0	J.F.D. Madeley and R.D.B.M. Shade	0
Singles			
D.R. Beman	0	S.W.T. Murray (3&1)	1
W.J. Patton (3&2)	1	M.J. Christmas	0
R.H. Sikes	0	J.B. Carr (7&5)	1
L.E. Harris Jr	0	D.B. Sheahan (1 hole)	1
R.D. Davies	0	M.F. Bonallack (1 hole)	1
C.R. Coe	0	S. Sadler	0
A.D. Gray Jr	0	R.D.B.M. Shade (4&3)	1
C.B. Smith	0	M.S.R. Lunt	0

Second Series

United States		Great Britain and Ireland	
Foursomes			
W.J. Patton and R.H. Sikes (1 hole)	1	M.F. Bonallack and S.W.T. Murray	0
A.D. Gray and L.E. Harris Jr (3&2)	1	M.S.R. Lunt and D.B. Sheahan	0
R.W. Gardner and E.R. Updegraff (3&1)	1	C.W. Green and S. Saddler	0
D.R. Beman and C.R. Coe (3&2)	1	J.F.D. Madeley and R.D.B.M. Shade	0
Singles			
W.J. Patton (3&2)	1	S.W.T. Murray (3&1)	1
R.D. Davies	0	D.B. Sheahan (1 hole)	0
E.R. Updegraff (4&3)	1	J.B. Carr	0
L.E. Harris Jr (3&2)	1	M.F. Bonallack	0
R.W. Gardner (3&2)	1	M.S.R. Lunt	0
D.R. Beman	0	S. Saddler	0
A.D. Gray Jr	0	R.D.B.M. Shade (2&1)	1
C.R. Coe (4&3)	1	C.W. Green	0
United States	**12**	**Great Britain and Ireland**	**8**

1965

Five Farms, Maryland

Captains: J.W. Fisher (US), J.B. Carr (GB & Ire)

First Series

United States		Great Britain and Ireland	
Foursomes			
W.C. Campbell and A.D. Gray Jr	0	M.S.R. Lunt and G. Cosh (1 hole)	1
D.R. Beman and D.C. Allen	0	M.F. Bonallack and C.A. Clark	0
W.J. Patton and E.M. TutWiler (5&4)	1	R. Foster and G. Clark	0
J.M. Hopkins and D. Eichelberger	0	P. Townsend and R.D.B.M. Shade (2&1)	1
Singles			
W.C. Campbell (6&5)	1	M.F. Bonallack	0
D.R. Beman (2 holes)	1	R. Foster	0
A.D. Gray Jr	0	R.D.B.M. Shade (3&1)	1
J.M. Hopkins	0	C.A. Clark (5&3)	1
W.J. Patton	0	P. Townsend(3&2)	1
D. Morey	0	S. Sadler (2&1)	1
D.C. Allen	0	G. Cosh(2 holes)	1
E.R. Updegraff	0	M.S.R. Lunt (2&1)	1
Second Series			
W.C. Campbell and A.D. Gray Jr (4&3)	1	A.C. Saddler and R. Foster	0
D.R. Beman and D. Eichelberger	0	P. Townsend and R.D.B.M. Shade (2&1)	1
W.J. Patton and E.M. TutWiler (2&1)	1	M.S.R. Lunt and G. Cosh	0
D.C. Allen and D. Morey	0	M.F. Bonallack and C.A. Clark (2&1)	1
Singles			
W.C. Campbell (3&2)	1	M.F. Bonallack	0
D.R. Beman (1 hole)	1	R. Foster	0
E.M. Tutwiler (5&3)	1	R.D.B.M. Shade (3&1)	1
D.C. Allen	0	C.A. Clark (5&3)	1
A.D. Gray Jr (1 hole)	1	P. Townsend(3&2)	1
J.M. Hopkins	0	S. Sadler (2&1)	1
D. Eichelberger (5&3)	0	G. Cosh(2 holes)	1
W.J. Patton (4&2)	0	M.S.R. Lunt (2&1)	1
United States	**9**	**Great Britain and Ireland**	**15**

1967

Sandwich, Royal St George's

Captains: J.W. Sweetser (US), J.B. Carr (GB & Ire)

First Series

United States		Great Britain and Ireland	
Foursomes			
R.J. Murphy and R.J. Cerrudo	0	R.D.B.M. Shade and P.A. Oosterhuis	0
W.C. Campbell and J.W. Lewis Jr (1 hole)	1	R. Foster and A.C. Saddler	0
A.D. Gray Jr and E.M. Tutwiler (5&4)	1	M.F. Bonallack and M.F. Attenborough	0
R.B. Dickson and J.A. Grant (3&1)	1	J.B. Carr and T. Craddock	1

Singles

United States		Great Britain and Ireland	
W.C. Campbell (2&1)	1	R.D.B.M. Shade	0
R.J. Murphy (2&1)	1	R. Foster	0
A.D. Gray Jr	0	M.F. Bonallack	0
R.J. Cerrudo (4&3)	1	M.F. Attenborough	0
R.B. Dickson (6&4)	1	P.A. Oosterhuis	0
J.W. Lewis Jr (2&1)	1	T. Craddock	0
D.C. Allen	0	A.K. Pirie	0
M.A. Fleckman	0	A.C. Saddler (3&2)	1

Second Series

United States		Great Britain and Ireland	
Foursomes			
R.J. Murphy and R.J. Cerrudo	0	M.F. Bonallack and T. Craddock (2 holes)	1
W.C. Campbell and J.W. Lewis Jr (1 hole)	1	A.C. Saddler and A.K. Pirie	0
A.D. Gray Jr and E.M. Tutwiler	0	R.D.B.M. Shade and P.A. Oosterhuis (3&1)	1
D.C. Allen and M.A. Fleckman	0	R. Foster and D.J. Millensted (2&1)	1
Singles			
W.C. Campbell (3&2)	1	R.D.B.M. Shade	0
R.J. Murphy	0	M.F. Bonallack (4&2)	1
A.D. Gray Jr	0	A.C. Saddler (3&2)	1
R.J. Cerrudo	0	R. Foster	0
R.B. Dickson (4&3)	1	A.K. Pirie	0
J.W. Lewis Jr	0	T. Craddock (5&4)	1
J.A. Grant (1 hole)	1	P.A. Oosterhuis	0
E.M. Tutwiler (3&1)	1	D.J. Millensted	0
United States	**13**	**Great Britain and Ireland**	**8**

1969

Milwaukee, Wisconsin

Captains: W.J. Patton (US), M.F. Bonallack (GB & Ire)

First Series

United States		Great Britain and Ireland	
Foursomes			
M. Giles III and S. Melnyk (3&2)	1	M.F. Bonallack and T. Craddock	0
B. Fleisher and A. Miller III	0	P. Benka and B. Critchley	0
L. Wadkins and R.L. Siderowf	0	C. Green and A. Brooks (3&2)	1
W. Hyndman III and J. Inman Jr (2&1)	1	R. Foster and G. Marks	0
Singles			
B. Fleisher	0	M.F. Bonallack	0
M. Giles III (1 hole)	1	C. Green	0
A. Miller III (1 hole)	1	B. Critchley	0
R.L. Siderowf (6&5)	1	P. Tupling	0
S. Melnyk	0	P. Benka (3&1)	1
L. Wadkins	0	G. Marks (1 hole)	1
J. Bohmann (2&1)	1	M.G. King	0
E.R. Updegraff (6&5)	1	R. Foster	0

Second Series

United States		Great Britain and Ireland	
Foursomes			
M. Giles III and S. Melnyk	0	C. Green and A. Brooks (3&2)	0
B. Fleisher and A. Miller III	0	P. Benka and B. Critchley (2&1)	1
L. Wadkins and R.L. Siderowf (6&5)	1	R. Foster and M.G. King	0
E.R. Updegraff and J. Bohmann	0	M.F. Bonallack and P. Tupling (4&3)	1
Singles			
B. Fleisher	0	M.F. Bonallack (5&4)	1
R.L. Siderowf	0	B. Critchley	0
A. Miller III (1 hole)	1	M.G. King	0
M. Giles III	0	T. Craddock	0
J. Inman Jr (2&1)	1	P. Benka	0
J. Bohmann	0	A. Brooks (4&3)	1
W. Hyndman III	0	C. Green	0
E.R. Updegraff	0	G. Marks (3&2)	1
United States	**10**	**Great Britain and Ireland**	**8**

1971

St Andrews

Captains: M.F. Bonallack (GB & Ire), J.M. Winters Jr (US)

First Series

Great Britain and Ireland		United States	
Foursomes			
M.F. Bonallack and W. Humphreys (1 hole)	1	L. Wadkins and J.B. Simons	0
C.W. Green and R.J. Carr (1 hole)	1	S. Melnyk and M. Giles III	0
D.M. Marsh and G. Macgregor (2&1)	1	Al Miller III and J. Farquar	1
J.S. Macdonald and R. Foster (2&1)	1	W.C. Campbell and T.O. Kite Jr	0
Singles			
C.W. Green	0	L. Wadkins (1 hole)	1
M.F. Bonallack	0	M. Giles III (1 hole)	1
G.C. Marks	0	Al Miller III (1 hole)	1
J.S. Macdonald	0	S. Melnyk (3&2)	1
R.J. Carr	½	W. Hyndman III	½
W. Humphreys	0	J.R. Gabrielsen (1 hole)	1
H.B. Stuart (3&2)	1	J. Farquar	0
R. Foster	0	T.O. Kite Jr (3&2)	1

Second Series

Great Britain and Ireland		United States	
Foursomes			
G.C. Marks and C.W. Green	0	S. Melnyk and M. Giles III (1 hole)	1
R.J. Carr and H.B. Stuart (1 hole)	1	L. Wadkins and J.R. Gabrielsen	0
D.M. Marsh and M.F. Bonallack	0	Al Miller III and J. Farquar (5&4)	1
J.S. Macdonald and R. Foster	½	W.C. Campbell and T.O. Kite Jr	½
Singles			
M.F. Bonallack	0	L. Wadkins (3&1)	1
H.B. Stuart (2&1)	1	M. Giles III	0
W. Humphreys (2&1)	1	S. Melnyk	0
C.W. Green (1 hole)	1	Al Miller III	0
J.B. Carr (2 holes)	1	J.B. Simons	0
G. Macgregor	1	J.R. Gabrielsen	0
D.M. Marsh (1 hole)	0	W. Hyndman III	0
G.C. Marks	1	T.O. Kite Jr (2&1)	1
Great Britain and Ireland	**13**	**United States**	**12**

1973

Brookline, Massachusetts

Captains: J.W. Sweetser (US), D.M. Marsh (GB & Ire)

First Series

United States		Great Britain and Ireland	
Foursomes			
M. Giles and G. Koch	½	M.G. King and P. Hedges	½
R. Siderowf and M. Pfeil (5&4)	1	H.B. Stuart and J. Davies	0
D. Edwards and J. Ellis (2&1)	1	C.W. Green and W.T. Milne	0
M. West and D. Ballenger (2&1)	1	R. Foster and T.W.B. Homer	0
Singles			
M. Giles (5&4)	1	H.B. Stuart	0
R. Siderowf (4&2)	1	M.F. Bonallack	0
G. Koch(1 hole)	1	J. Davies (1 Hole)	1
M. West	0	H.K. Clark(2&1)	1
D. Edwards (2 holes)	1	R. Foster	0
M. Killian	0	M.G. King (1 hole)	1
W. Rodgers	0	C.W. Green (1 hole)	1
M. Pfeil	0	W.T. Milne (4&3)	1

Second Series

United States		Great Britain and Ireland	
Foursomes			
M. Giles and G. Koch (7&5)	1	R. Foster and T.W.B. Homer	0
R. Siderowf and M. Pfeil	½	H.K. Clark and J. Davies	½
D. Edwards and J. Ellis (2&1)	1	M.G. King and P. Hedges	0
W. Rodgers and M. Killian (1 hole)	1	W.T. Milne and H.B. Stuart	0
Singles			
J. Ellis	0	H.B. Stuart (5&3)	1

R. Siderowf	0	J. Davies (3&2)	1
D. Edwards (2&1)	1	T.W.B. Homer	0
M. Giles	½	C.W. Green	½
M. West (1 hole)	1	M.G. King	0
M. Killian	0	W.T. Milne (2&1)	1
G. Koch	½	P. Hedges	½
M. Pfeil (1 hole)	1	H.K. Clark	0
United States	**15**	**Great Britain and Ireland**	**10**

1975

St Andrews

Captains: E.R. Updegraff (US), Dr D.M. Marsh (GB & Ire)

First Series

United States		**Great Britain and Ireland**	
Foursomes			
J. Pate and R. Siderowf	0	M. James and G.R.D. Eyles (1 hole)	1
G.F. Burns and C. Stadler (5&4)	1	J.C. Davies and M.A. Poxon	0
J. Haas and C. Strange (2&1)	1	C.W. Green and H.B. Stuart	0
M.M. Giles and G. Koch (5&4)	1	G. Macgregor and I.C. Hutcheon	0
Singles			
J. Pate	½	M. James	½
C. Strange	½	J.C. Davies	½
R.L. Siderowf	0	P. Mulcare (1 Hole)	1
G. Koch (3&2)	1	H.B. Stuart	0
J. Grace (3&1)	1	M.A. Poxon	0
W.C. Campbell	½	I.C. Hutcheon	½
J. Haas (2&1)	1	G.R.D. Eyles	0
M.M. Giles (5&4)	1	G. Macgregor	0

Second Series

United States		**Great Britain and Ireland**	
Foursomes			
J. Pate and R. Siderowf	0	P. Mulcare and I.C. Hutcheon (1 hole)	1
G.F. Burns and C. Stadler (1 hole)	1	C.W. Green and H.B. Stuart	0
W.C. Campbell and J. Grace	0	M. James and G.R.D. Eyles (5&3)	1
J. Haas and C. Strange (3&2)	1	J.C. Davies and P. Hedges	0
Singles			
J. Pate	0	I.C. Hutcheon (3&2)	1
C. Strange (4&3)	1	P. Mulcare	0
G. Koch (5&4)	1	M. James	0
G.F. Burns	0	J.C. Davies (2&1)	1
J. Grace (2&1)	1	C.W. Green	0
C. Stadler (3&2)	1	G. Macgregor	0
W.C. Campbell (2&1)	1	G.R.D. Eyles	0
M.M. Giles	½	P. Hedges	½
United States	**16**	**Great Britain and Ireland**	**8**

1977

Shinnecock Hills, New York

Captains: L.W. Oehmig (US), S.C. Saddler (GB & Ire)

First Series

United States		**Great Britain and Ireland**	
Foursomes			
J. Fought and V. Heafner (4&3)	1	A.W.B. Lyle and P. McEvoy	0
S. Simpson and L. Miller (5&4)	1	J.C. Davies and M.J. Kelley	0
R.L. Siderowf and G. Hallberg	0	I.C. Hutcheon and P. Deeble (1 hole)	1
J. Sigel and M. Brannan (1 hole)	1	A. Brodie and S. Martin	0
Singles			
L. Miller (2 holes)	1	P. McEvoy	0
J. Fought (4&3)	1	I.C. Hutcheon	0
S. Simpson (7&6)	1	G.H. Murray	0
V. Heafner (4&3)	1	J.C. Davies	0
B. Sander	0	A. Brodie (4&3)	1
G. Hallberg	0	S. Martin (3&2)	1
F. Ridley (2 holes)	1	A.W.B. Lyle	0
J. Sigel (5&3)	1	P. McKellar	0

Second Series

United States		Great Britain and Ireland	
Foursomes			
J. Fought and V. Heafner (4&3)	1	I.C. Hutcheon and P. Deeble	0
S. Simpson and L. Miller (2 holes)	1	J.C. Davies and P. McEvoy	0
R.L. Siderowf and B. Sander	0	A. Brodie and S. Martin (6&4)	1
F. Ridley and M. Brannan	0	G.H. Murray and M.J. Kelley (4&3)	1
Singles			
L. Miller (1 hole)	1	S. Martin	0
J. Fought (2&1)	1	J.C. Davies	0
B. Sander	0	A. Brodie (2&1)	1
G. Hallberg (4&3)	1	P. McEvoy	0
R.L. Siderowf	0	M.J. Kelley (2&1)	1
M. Brannan	0	I.C. Hutcheon (2 holes)	1
F. Ridley (5&3)	1	A.W.B. Lyle	0
J. Sigel (1 hole)	1	P. Deeble	0
United States	**16**	**Great Britain and Ireland**	**8**

1979

Honourable Company, Muirfield

Captains: R.L. Siderowf (US), R. Foster (GB & Ire)

First Series

United States		Great Britain and Ireland	
Foursomes			
S. Hoch and J. Sigel (1 hole)	1	P. McEvoy and B. Marchbank	0
M. West and H. Sutton	0	G. Godwin and I.C. Hutcheon (2 holes)	1
D. Fischesser and J. Holtgrieve (1 hole)	1	G. Brand and M.J. Kelley	0
G. Moody and M. Gove	0	A. Brodie and I. Carslaw (2&1)	1
Singles			
J. Sigel	½	P. McEvoy	½
D. Clarke (8&7)	1	J.C. Davies	0
S. Hoch (9&7)	1	J. Buckley	0
J. Holtgrieve (6&4)	1	I.C. Hutcheon	0
M. Peck	0	B. Marchbank (1 hole)	1
G. Moody	0	G. Godwin (3&2)	1
D. Fischesser	0	M.J. Kelley (3&2)	1
M. Gove (3&2)	1	A. Brodie	0

Second Series

United States		Great Britain and Ireland	
Foursomes			
S. Hoch and J. Sigel (4&3)	1	G. Godwin and G. Brand	0
J. Holtgrieve and D. Fischesser	0	P. McEvoy and B. Marchbank (2&1)	1
M. West and H. Sutton	½	I.C. Hutcheon and M.J. Kelley	½
D. Clarke and M. Peck	½	A. Brodie and I. Carslaw	½
Singles			
S. Hoch (3&1)	1	P. McEvoy	0
D. Clarke (2&1)	1	G. Brand	0
M. Gove (3&2)	1	G. Godwin	0
M. Peck (2&1)	1	I.C. Hutcheon	0
M. West	0	A. Brodie (3&2)	1
G. Moody (2&2)	1	M.J. Kelley	0
H. Sutton (3&1)	1	B. Marchbank	0
J. Sigel (2&1)	1	I. Carslaw	0
United States	**15½**	**Great Britain and Ireland**	**8½**

1981

Cypress Point, California

Captains: J. Gabrielson (US), R. Foster (GB & Ire)

First Series

United States		Great Britain and Ireland	
Foursomes			
H. Sutton and J. Sigel	0	P. Walton and R. Rafferty (4&2)	1
J. Holtgrieve and F. Fuhrer (1 hole)	1	R. Chapman and P. McEvoy (2 holes)	0
B. Lewis and D. von Tacky (2&1)	1	I.C. Hutcheon and I.C. Hutcheon	0
R. Commans and C. Pavin (5&4)	1	D. Evans and P. way	0
Singles			
H. Sutton (3&1)	1	R. Rafferty	0

J. Rasset (1 hole)	1	C. Dalgleish	0
R. Commans	0	P. Walton (1 hole)	1
B. Lewis	0	R. Chapman (2&1)	1
J. Mudd (1 hole)	1	G. Godwin	0
C. Pavin (4&3)	1	I.C. Hutcheon	0
D. von Tacky	0	P. Way (3&1)	1
J. Sigel (4&2)	1	P. McEvoy	0

Second Series

United States		**Great Britain and Ireland**	
Foursomes			
H. Sutton and J. Sigel	0	R. Chapman and P. Way (1 hole)	1
J. Holtgrieve and F. Fuhrer	0	P. Walton and R. Rafferty	0
B. Lewis and D. von Tacky	0	D. Evans and C. Dalgleish	0
J. Rasset and J. Mudd (5&4)	1	I.C. Hutcheon and G. Godwin	0
Singles			
H. Sutton	0	R. Chapman (1 hole)	1
J. Holtgrieve (2&1)	1	R. Rafferty	0
F. Fuhrer (4&3)	1	P. Walton	1
J. Sigel (6&5)	1	P. Way	1
J. Mudd (7&5)	1	C. Dalgleish	0
R. Commans	½	G. Godwin	½
J. Rasset (4&3)	1	P. Deeble	0
C. Pavin	½	D. Evans	½
United States	**15**	**Great Britain and Ireland**	**9**

1983

Hoylake, Royal Liverpool

Captains: J. Sigel (US), C.W. Green (GB & Ire)

First Series

United States		**Great Britain and Ireland**	
Foursomes			
J. Sigel and R. Fehr	0	G. Macgregor and P. Walton (3&2)	1
W. Wood and B. Faxon (3&1)	1	S. Keppler and A. Pierse	0
B. Lewis Jr and J. Holtgrieve (7&6)	1	M. Lewis and M. Thomson	0
W. Hoffer and D. Tentis	0	L. Mann and A. Oldcorn (5&4)	1
Singles			
J. Sigel	0	P. Walton (1 hole)	1
R. Fehr (1 hole)	1	S. Keppler	0
W. Wood	½	G. Macgregor	½
B. Faxon (3&1)	1	D. Carrick	0
B. Tuten	0	A. Oldcorn (4&3)	1
N. Crosby	0	A. Parkin (5&4)	1
B. Lewis Jr (3&1)	1	A. Pierse	0
J. Holtgrieve (6&5)	1	L. Mann	0

Second Series

United States		**Great Britain and Ireland**	
Foursomes			
N. Crosby and W. Hoffer (2 holes)	1	G. Macgregor and P. Walton	0
W. Wood and B. Faxon	0	A. Parkin and M. Thomson (1 hole)	1
B. Lewis Jr and J. Holtgrieve	0	L. Mann and A. Oldcorn (1 hole)	1
J. Sigel and R. Fehr	½	S. Keppler and A. Pierse	½
Singles			
W. Wood	0	P. Walton (2&1)	1
B. Faxon (3&2)	1	A. Parkin	0
R. Fehr (2&1)	1	G. Macgregor	0
B. Tuten (3&2)	1	M. Thomson	0
D. Tentis	½	L. Mann	½
B. Lewis Jr (6&5)	1	S. Keppler	0
J. Holtgrieve	0	A. Oldcorn (3&2)	1
J. Sigel (3&2)	1	D. Carrick	0
United States	**13½**	**Great Britain and Ireland**	**10½**

1985

Pine Valley, New Jersey

Captains: J. Sigel (US), C.W. Green (GB & Ire)

First Series

United States		**Great Britain and Ireland**	
Foursomes			
S. Verplank and J. Sigel (1 hole)	1	C. Montgomerie and G. Macgregor	0
D. Waldorf and S. Randolph	0	J. Hawksworth and G. McGimpsey (4&3)	1
R. Sonnier and J. Haas	0	P. Baker and P. McEvoy (6&5)	1
M. Padolak and D. Love	½	C. Bloice and S. Stephen	½
Singles			
S. Verplank (2&1)	1	G. McGimpsey	0
S. Randolph (5&4)	1	P. Mayo	0
R. Sonnier	½	J. Hawksworth	½
J. Sigel (5&4)	1	C. Montgomerie	0
B. Lewis	0	P. McEvoy (2&1)	1
C. Burroughs	0	G. Macgregor (2 holes)	1
D. Waldorf (4&2)	1	D. Gilford	0
J. Haas	0	S. Stephen (2&1)	1

Second Series

United States		**Great Britain and Ireland**	
Foursomes			
S. Verplank and J. Sigel	½	C. Montgomerie and P. Mayo	½
S. Randolph and J. Haas (3&2)	1	J. Hawksworth and G. McGimpsey	0
B. Lewis and C. Burroughs (2&1)	1	P. Baker and P. McEvoy	0
M. Padolak and D. Love (3&2)	1	C. Bloice and S. Stephen	0
Singles			
S. Randolph	½	G. McGimpsey	½
S. Verplank (1 hole)	1	C. Montgomerie	0
J. Sigel	0	J. Hawksworth (4&3)	1
D. Love (5&3)	1	P. McEvoy	0
R. Sonnier	0	P. Baker (5&4)	1
C. Burroughs	0	G. Macgregor (3&2)	1
B. Lewis (4&3)	1	C. Bloice	0
D. Waldorf	0	S. Stephen (2&1)	1
United States	**13**	**Great Britain and Ireland**	**11**

1987

Sunningdale, Berkshire

First Series

Great Britain and Ireland		**United States**	
Foursomes			
C. Montgomerie and G. Shaw	0	B. Alexander and B. Mayfair (5&4)	1
D. Curry and P. Mayo	0	C. Kite and L. Mattice (2&1)	1
G. Macgregor and J. Robinson	0	B. Lewis and B. Loeffler (2&1)	1
J. McHenry and P. Girvan	½	J. Sigel and B. Andrade	½
Singles			
D. Curry (2 holes)	1	B. Alexander	0
J. Robinson	0	B. Andrade (7&5)	1
C. Montgomerie (3&2)	1	J. Sorenson	0
R. Eggo	0	J. Sigel (3&2)	0
J. McHenry	0	B. Montgomerie (1 hole)	1
P. Girvan	0	B. Lewis (3&2)	1
D. Carrick	0	B. Mayfair (2 holes)	1
G. Shaw (1 hole)	1	C. Kite	0

Second Series

Great Britain and Ireland		**United States**	
Foursomes			
D. Curry and D. Carrick	0	B. Lewis and B. Loeffler (4&3)	1
C. Montgomerie and G. Shaw	0	C. Kite and L. Mattice (5&3)	1
P. Mayo and G. Macgregor	0	J. Sorenson and B. Montgomerie (4&3)	1
J. McHenry and J. Robinson (4&2)	1	J. Sigel and B. Andrade	0

Singles			
D. Curry	½	B. Alexander	½
C. Montgomerie (4&2)	1	B. Andrade	1
J. McHenry (3&2)	1	B. Loeffler	0
G. Shaw	½	J. Sorenson	½
J. Robinson (1 hole)	1	L. Mattice	1
D. Carrick	0	B. Lewis (3&2)	1
R. Eggo	0	B. Mayfair (2 holes)	1
P. Girvan	½	C. Kite	½
Great Britain and Ireland	**9**	**United States**	**15**

1989

Peachtree, Atlanta

First Series

Great Britain and Ireland		United States	
Foursomes			
R. Claydon and D. Prosser	0	R. Gamez and D. Martin (3&2)	1
S. Dodd and G. McGimpsey	½	D. Yates and P. Mickelson	½
P. McEvoy and E. O'Connell (6&5)	1	D. Lesher and J. Sigel	0
J. Milligan and A. Hare (2&1)	1	D. Eger and K. Johnson	0
Singles			
J. Milligan	0	R. Gamez (7&6)	1
R. Claydon (5&4)	1	D. Martin	0
S. Dodd	½	E. Meeks	½
E. O'Connell (5&4)	1	R. Howe	0
P. McEvoy (2&1)	1	D. Yates	0
G. McGimpsey	0	P. Mickelson (4&2)	1
C. Cassells (1 hole)	1	D. Lesher	0
R.N. Roderick	½	J. Sigel	½

Second Series

Great Britain and Ireland		United States	
Foursomes			
P. McEvoy and E. O'Connell	½	R. Gamez and D. Martin	½
R. Claydon and C. Cassells (3&2)	1	D. Lesher and J. Sigel	0
J. Milligan and A. Hare (2&1)	1	D. Eger and G.K. Johnson	0
G. McGimpsey and S. Dodd (2&1)	1	D. Yates and P. Mickelson	0
Singles			
S. Dodd	0	R. Gamez (1 hole)	1
A. Hare	½	D. Martin	½
R. Claydon	0	D. Lesher (3&2)	1
P. McEvoy	0	D. Yates (4&3)	1
E. O'Connell	½	P. Mickelson	½
R.N. Roderick	0	D. Eger (4&2)	1
C. Cassells	0	G.K. Johnson (4&2)	1
J. Milligan	½	J. Sigel	½
Great Britain and Ireland	**12½**	**United States**	**11½**

1991

Portmarnock, Dublin

First Series

Great Britain and Ireland		United States	
Foursomes			
J. Milligan and G. Hay	0	P. Mickelson and B. May (5&3)	1
J. Payne and G. Evans	0	D. Duval and S. Sposa (1 hole)	1
G. McGimpsey and R. Willison	0	V. Voges and D. Eger (1 hole)	1
P. McGinley and P. Harrington	0	J. Sigel and A. Doyle (2&1)	1
Singles			
A. Coltart	0	P. Mickelson (4&3)	1
J. Payne (2&1)	1	L. Langham	0
G. Evans (2&1)	1	D. Duval	0
R. Willison	0	B. May (2&1)	1
G. McGimpsey (1 hole)	1	S. Sposa	0
P. McGinley	0	A. Doyle (6&4)	1
G. Hay (1 hole)	1	T. Scherrer	0
L. White	0	J. Sigel (4&3)	1

Second Series

Great Britain and Ireland		United States	
Foursomes			
J. Milligan and G. McGimpsey (2&1)	1	V. Voges and D. Eger	0
J. Payne and R. Willison	0	D. Duval and S. Sposa (1 hole)	1
G. Evans and A. Coltart (4&3)	1	L. Langham and T. Scherrer	0
L. White and P. McGinley (1 hole)	1	P. Mickelson and B. May	0
Singles			
J. Milligan	0	P. Mickelson (1 hole)	1
J. Payne (3&1)	1	A. Doyle	0
G. Evans	0	L. Langham (4&2)	1
A. Coltart (1 hole)	1	J. Sigel	0
R. Willison (3&2)	1	T. Scherrer	0
P. McGinley	0	D. Eger(3&2)	1
G. McGimpsey	0	B. May (4&3)	1
G. Hay	0	V. Voges (3&1)	1
Great Britain and Ireland	**14**	**United States**	**10**

1993

Interlachen, Minnesota

First Series

Great Britain and Ireland		United States	
Singles			
I. Pyman	0	A. Doyle (1 hole)	1
S. Stanford (3&2)	1	D. Berganio	0
D. Robertson (3&2)	1	J. Sigel	0
S. Cage	½	K. Mitchum	½
P. Harrington	0	T. Herron (1 hole)	1
P. Page	0	D. Yates (2&1)	1
R. Russell	0	T. Demsey (2&1)	1
R. Burns	0	J. Leonard (4&3)	1
V. Phillips (2&1)	1	B. Gay	0
B. Dredge	0	J. Harris (4&3)	1

Second Series

Great Britain and Ireland		United States	
Foursomes			
I. Pyman and S. Cage	0	A. Doyle and J. Leonard (4&3)	1
S. Stanford and P. Harrington	0	D. Berganio and T. Demsey (3&2)	1
B. Dredge and V. Phillips	0	J. Sigel and K. Mitchum (3&2)	1
R. Russell and D. Robertson	0	J. Harris and T. Herron (1 hole)	1
Singles			
D. Robertson	0	A. Doyle (4&3)	1
I. Pyman	0	J. Harris (3&2)	1
S. Cage	0	D. Yates (2&1)	1
P. Harrington	½	B. Gay	½
P. Page	0	J. Sigel (5&4)	1
V. Phillips	0	T. Herron (3&2)	1
R. Russell	0	K. Mitchum (4&2)	1
R. Burns (1 hole)	1	D. Berganio	0
B. Dredge	0	T. Demsey (3&2)	1
S. Stanford	0	J. Leonard (5&4)	1
Great Britain and Ireland	**5**	**United States**	**19**

1995

Royal Porthcawl, Wales

First Series

Great Britain and Ireland		United States	
Foursomes			
G. Sherry and S. Gallacher	0	J. Harris and T. Woods (4&3)	1
M. Foster and D. Howell	½	A. Bratton and C. Riley	½
G. Rankin and B. Howard	0	N. Begay and T. Jackson (4&3)	1
P. Harrington and J. Fanagan (5&3)	1	K. Cox and T. Kuehne	0
Singles			
G. Sherry (3&2)	1	N. Begay	0
L. James	0	K. Cox (1 hole)	1
M. Foster (4&3)	1	B. Marucci	0

S. Gallacher (4&3)	1	T. Jackson	0
P. Harrington (2 holes)	1	T. Courville	0
B. Howard	½	A. Bratton	½
G. Rankin	0	J. Harris (1 hole)	1
G. Wolstenholme (1 hole)	1	T. Woods	0

Second Series

Great Britain and Ireland		**United States**	
Foursomes			
G. Sherry and S. Gallacher	0	A. Bratton and C. Riley (4&2)	1
M. Foster and L. James (3&2)	1	K. Cox and T. Kuehne	0
G. Wolstenholme and B. Howard	0	B. Marucci and T. Courville (6&5)	1
P. Harrington and J. Fanagan (2&1)	1	J. Harris and T. Woods	0

Great Britain and Ireland		**United States**	
Singles			
G. Sherry (2 holes)	1	C. Riley	0
D. Howell (2&1)	1	N. Begay	0
S. Gallacher (3&2)	1	T. Kuehne	0
J. Fanagan (3&2)	1	T. Courville	0
B. Howard	½	T. Jackson	½
M. Foster	½	B. Marucci	½
P. Harrington	0	J. Harris (3&2)	1
G. Wolstenholme	0	T. Woods (4&3)	1
Great Britain and Ireland	**14**	**United States**	**10**

1997

Quaker Bridge, New York

First Series

Great Britain and Ireland		**United States**	
Foursomes			
B. Howard and S. Young	0	B. Elder and J. Kribel (4&3)	1
J. Rose and M. Brooks	0	J. Courville and B. Marucci (5&4)	1
G. Wolstenholme and K. Nolan	0	J. Gore and J. Harris (6&4)	1
R. Coughlan and D. Park	0	R. Leen and C. Wollmann (1 hole)	1

Great Britain and Ireland		**United States**	
Singles			
S. Young (5&4)	1	D. Delcher	0
C. Watson (1 hole)	1	S. Scott	0
B. Howard	0	B. Elder (5&4)	1
J. Rose (1 hole)	1	J. Kribel	0
K. Nolan	0	R. Leen (3&2)	1
G. Rankin	0	J. Gore (3&2)	1
R. Coughlan	½	C. Wollmann	½
G. Wolstenholme (1 hole)	0	J. Harris (1 hole)	1

Second Series

Great Britain and Ireland		**United States**	
Foursomes			
C. Watson and S. Young	0	B. Elder and J. Harris (3&2)	1
B. Howard and G. Rankin	0	J. Courville and B. Marucci (5&4)	1
R. Coughlan and D. Park	0	D. Delcher and S. Scott (1 hole)	1
G. Wolstenholme and J. Rose (2&1)	1	R. Leen and C. Wollmann	0
Singles			
S. Young (2&1)	1	J. Kribel	0
C. Watson	½	J. Gore (3&2)	½
J. Rose	0	J. Courville (3&2)	1
K. Nolan	0	B. Elder (2&1)	1
M. Brooks	0	J. Harris (6&5)	1
D. Park	0	B. Marucci (4&3)	1
G. Wolstenholme	0	D. Delcher (2&1)	1
R. Coughlan	0	S. Scott (2&1)	1
Great Britain and Ireland	**6**	**United States**	**18**

THE PGA EUROPEAN TOUR

In 2001 the PGA European Tour will celebrate its 30th anniversary. It will deservedly be some party. In that relatively short space of time the tour has gathered up a selection of national Open events and integrated them into a structure so lucrative that before the end of the millennium a player will become a sterling millionaire simply on the back of one season's earnings.

The European Tour is the second most powerful tour in the world after America, although the name has become something of a misnomer. Indeed the 1999 tour was eight tournaments old before it even touched down in Europe. By that stage play had been conducted in three other continents, by way of tournaments co-sanctioned with other tours. Perhaps one day all these tours will amalgamate, but if they do it will be the European Tour that will remain the dominant voice, the driving force.

Its extraordinary development has been overseen by Ken Schofield, its Executive Director since 1975. Schofield was once the youngest bank manager in Scotland. For the past 25 years he has applied a keen mind to the task of getting the best possible deal for European professionals. Schofield's mantra has been to "maximize opportunity and incentive". If this means treading on some of the game's traditionalist views, then so be it. Schofield sees no problem with taking the Ryder Cup to an average venue, for example, if the net result is extra tournaments elsewhere for his members to play in, thanks to some munificent benefactor.

The European Tour evolved in much the same way as the PGA Tour, with touring professionals becoming increasingly restless at being under the umbrella of the Professional Golfers' Association, which looked after the interests of the club pros. On October 1, 1971, the breakaway was finally made. John Jacobs was made Tournament Director-General of the PGA, marking the official birth of the European Tour.

When Schofield took over in 1975 there were 17 tournaments on the schedule with total prize money of £42,917. It was his brief both to raise the number of opportunities to play and the amounts they were playing for, and in both tasks he succeeded spectacularly. Eight years later there were ten more tournaments and prize money had shot up to a shade under £2.5 million.

Schofield would be the first to admit that he was helped in his task by an extraordinary stroke of luck. Soon after he took

Severiano Ballesteros – in the late 1970s he was one of the best possible adverts for European golf

Nick Faldo at the Emirates Course in Dubai, one of the many courses that play host to a European Tour covering four continents

FALDO

over it became clear that European golf was in for some exciting times. In 1976 a young 19-year-old Spaniard called Severiano Ballesteros electrified all Birkdale in finishing runner-up in the Open, before winning the Dutch Open in his next tournament outing. And there was not just Ballesteros. From Germany there emerged Bernhard Langer. Two countries that had never considered golf anything more than a game for the bourgeoisie suddenly had modern, working-class heroes.

There was more. From Wales came Ian Woosnam, from Scotland Sandy Lyle, and from England Nick Faldo. All not only combined an innate skill for the game with a champion's winning mentality, but all were photogenic too. Here were five players upon whom you could hang any tour.

And soon they started winning major championships. It was Severiano Ballesteros who set the ball rolling with the 1979 Open and then Langer at the Masters. Then Lyle at the Open. Now Schofield could go to every potential sponsor in the land and say legitimately: here in Europe we have some of the very best players in the world, where's your dosh?

These five quickly captured the public's imagination. Their images hung from bedroom walls where previously there had only been football stars. And there were not only the major championships, but their performances in European Tour events. Then came the 1985 Ryder Cup.

That contest put the tin lid on the best year of all time for European golf. Wins in the Masters for Langer and the Open for Lyle were accompanied by the first win over the Americans for 28 years. And a win in Europe to boot.

When Europe repeated the trick at Muirfield Village two years later, golf was riding an amazing wave of popularity. All over the continent courses were built to satisfy the new audience. Most of all, of course, these people wanted to watch their new heroes in the flesh.

Countries like Germany, France and Spain, instead of having just one event, now had two or three, or even more. Now, instead of going to sponsors, Schofield found them coming to him. He was in the wonderful position of having more potential benefactors than slots in the calendar. He could drive up the price.

The best deal he will ever sign came in 1988 when Volvo approached him. The car manufacturer was fed up with the brattish behaviour of some tennis players and wished to switch their sponsorship funds to a sport with a more pristine image. The deal still goes on. So far, it has been worth well over £100 million to the European Tour.

One problem for Schofield during this time was the fact that the Ryder Cup was still owned by the PGA. This irked him immensely. As it began to rake in huge profits – with his members, the people who play in it after all, not seeing a cent – so he got hotter under the collar.

The Johnny Walker Classic kicks off the European Tour year

Costantino Rocca – a Challenge Tour graduate who has gone on to Ryder Cup success and near-major glory

The problem was that the PGA refused to back down, and its Chief Executive John Lindsey would not be intimidated. Faced with threats from the players that they would refuse to play in the event, Lindsey bravely countered: "Fine. We'll enter a team of whose who do wish to play."

Two stubborn men played out their drama in front of the Press, which was great from a story point of view, but excruciating when the game of golf was considered. The last thing the sport needed at the height of its popularity was its two leading officers behaving like football folk.

Yet taking sides was not easy because the reasons for such intransigence were obvious too. The Schofield point of view – that the Ryder Cup is nothing without the players, so why should their organization not be entitled to see some of the rewards – was reasonable enough; but then so was Lindsey's claim that the PGA had stuck with the Ryder Cup through thick and thin, and were not just interested in it in the good times, like the glory hunters.

Clearly something had to give and in the end it was Lindsey. He was forced out by his board of directors. If Schofield allowed himself a quiet smile of satisfaction, it must have become a broad grin the moment he saw who would replace Lindsey. For in came Sandy Jones, a fellow Scot and an old friend. The pair had no trouble brokering an agreement. And so the ownership of the Ryder Cup was split between the two bodies: every time it was held in Europe they would be entitled to choose the venue on an alternate basis, and keep the profits. There came peace in our time.

For a few years, all was exceedingly well. The players continued to win trophies at the highest level. Europe's record at the Masters became a thing of beauty, with seven wins in 10 years from 1985. The schedule took on a settled, prestigious look, the prize money continuing to rise so rapidly as to make a mockery of inflation.

Then something happened. Someone took a pin to the golfing miracle and it was inevitable that the European Tour should feel some of the effects. The boom came to an end in the early 1990s and thereafter Schofield discovered that once more he would have to go out and find sponsorship deals; with a seven-figure sum needed to both fund a tournament and run it, he found that they were not queuing up to bite off his hand.

This is where the Ryder Cup slush fund came in handy. Tournaments with no title sponsor were supported. In return for the Ryder Cup going to Spain in 1997 the European Tour got an agreement from the Spanish Tourist Board that they would run a number of events. The same arrangement exists with DeVere Hotels, who will host the 2001 contest at The Belfry, and Bord Failte, the Irish tourist board which will underwrite events between now and 2005, when the Ryder Cup goes to Kildare. Without this arrangement the tour could well have collapsed completely. As it is, the number of official tournaments was down from 38 in 1993 to 32 in 1998.

There was another short-sighted decision made during this sticky period that has caused the game as a whole to repent at leisure. In 1995 Sky Television agreed to pay the tour an undisclosed amount for the right to televise the Ryder Cup exclusively plus 26 European Tour events, including a number that hitherto had been the preserve of the BBC.

Schofield knew more than anyone that it was after watching the gripping events at the 1985 and 1987 Ryder Cups that millions of people took up the game. Now the contest was being confined to a small audience on cable and satellite who were all golf fanatics anyway.

It was a decision that has had catastrophic effects, in that the number of people playing golf has fallen dramatically. Since it can be traced back to a number of events being taken away from the BBC, meaning that golf is only on national television seven or eight weekends a year, it can hardly be said to be a coincidence. Is this Schofield's concern? Perhaps he can argue that his only priority is his members, and they have clearly benefited from Sky's patronage – in their wallets anyway.

And so we come to the present. Thirty-two events may sound like quite a fall from 38 in 1993, but on the plus side they are of a better overall standard. The venues are better and so is their conditioning. Five years ago, at least half-a-dozen of the tournaments should not have been held. In particular, holding events in Spain in February and March, when the weather remains unpredictable, proved a particular non-starter.

The tour have rightly abandoned the practice and sought fresher pastures. The Dubai Desert Classic was a wonderful step in the right direction and the Emirates Course, its venue for all but one year, a classic place to play golf. The tour now also visits Australia and South Africa, and while this provokes a mixed reaction among the membership, no one can dispute that the courses are a good deal better than those in Europe at that time of year.

As the tour has grown so, naturally, has the number of players who wish to be members. Apeing the American tour, a challenge circuit was created to give non-members a place to play and hone their skills. Now it comprises 27 events in 14 different countries.

It is a hard circuit to play. It costs a lot and the rewards are small. But the incentive is there, and the message from its survivors is clearly that if you can make it there you can make it on to the regular tour. Flying the beacon for the Challenge Tour in recent years have been Thomas Bjorn and Costantino Rocca who are two of many who have made the graduation. Both of those, of course, have gone on to become Ryder Cup stalwarts.

Another imitation of the American circuit has been the setting up of a Senior Tour, which is holding its own. It is hard to visualize it developing dramatically until some showcase names reach the age of 50, like Sam Torrance, or better still Ballesteros, Langer and company. The other thing that would give it a notable boost is a Senior Ryder Cup, which Schofield has been keen to set up. At the time of writing, the Americans refuse to bite.

With close to 100 tournaments spread over three tours, Schofield can be proud of his tempestuous 25 years at the head of European golf. Over that spread of time he has seen European players reach the pinnacle of the game before slipping back a little; it is probably not a coincidence that the fortunes of the tour itself have mirrored both this dramatic progression, and small blip.

Walking on water – Colin Montgomerie has finished top of the European Tour Order of Merit for the last six years

THE PGA EUROPEAN TOUR STATISTICS

JOHNNIE WALKER CLASSIC

1992	I. Palmer
1993	N. Faldo
1994	G. Norman
1995	F. Couples
1996	I. Woosnam
1997	E. Els
1998	T. Woods

HEINEKEN CLASSIC

1996	I. Woosnam
1997	M. Martin
1998	T. Bjorn

SOUTH AFRICAN OPEN

1997	V. Singh
1998	E. Els

ALFRED DUNHILL SOUTH AFRICAN PGA CHAMPIONSHIP

Formerly known as the Lexington Championship (1995); Alfred Dunhill (1996)

1995	E. Els
1996	S. Strüver
1997	N. Price
1998	T. Johnstone

DUBAI DESERT CLASSIC

Formerly known as the Emirates Airline Classic (1990); Dubai Classic (1992). Tournament not played in 1991.

1989	M. James
1990	E. Darcy
1991	*Not played*
1992	S. Ballesteros
1993	W. Westner
1994	E. Els
1995	F. Couples
1996	C. Montgomerie
1997	R. Green
1998	J-M. Olazabal

MOROCCAN OPEN

Tournament not played 1988–1991

1987	H. Clark
1988–91	*Not played*
1992	D. Gilford
1993	D. Gilford
1994	A. Forsbrand
1995	M. James
1996	P. Hedblom
1997	C. Whitelaw
1998	S. Leaney

PORTUGUESE OPEN

Formerly known as Quinto do Lago (1984–86). Tournament not played 1957, 1965, 1980–81.

1953	E.C. Brown
1954	A. Miguel
1955	F. van Donck
1956	A. Miguel
1957	*Not played*
1958	P. Alliss
1959	S. Miguel
1960	K. Bousfield
1961	K. Bousfield
1962	A. Angelini
1963	R. Sota
1964	A. Miguel
1965	*Not played*
1966	A. Angelini
1967	A. Gallardo
1968	M. Faulkner
1969	R. Sota
1970	R. Sota
1971	L. Platts
1972	G. Garrido
1973	J. Benito
1974	B.G.C. Huggett
1975	H. Underwood
1976	S. Balbuena
1977	M. Ramos
1978	H. Clark
1979	B. Barnes
1980–81	*Not played*
1982	S. Torrance
1983	S. Torrance
1984	A. Johnstone
1985	W. Humphreys
1986	M. McNulty
1987	R. Lee
1988	M. Harwood
1989	C. Montgomerie
1990	M. McLean
1991	S. Richardson
1992	R. Rafferty
1993	D. Gilford
1994	P. Price
1995	A. Hunter
1996	W. Riley
1997	M. Jonzon
1998	P. Mitchell

QATAR OPEN

1998	A. Coltart

CANNES OPEN

Formerly known as Compagnie de Chauffe (1984–85), Suze (1986–87), Crédit Lyonnaise (1989–92), Air France (1993–96), Europe 1 (1997)

1984	D. Frost
1985	R. Lee
1986	J. Bland
1987	S. Ballesteros
1988	M. McMulty
1989	P. Broadhurst
1990	M. McNulty
1991	D. Feherty
1992	A. Forsbrand
1993	R. Davis
1994	I. Woosnam
1995	A. Bossert
1996	R. Russell
1997	S. Cage
1998	T. Levet

PEUGEOT OPEN DE ESPANA

Formerly known as Benson & Hedges (1980–85), Peugeot (1986–87). Tournament not played 1913–15, 1918, 1920, 1922, 1924, 1931, 1936–40, 1962, 1965.

1912	A. Massy
1913–15	*Not played*
1916	A. de la Torre
1917	A. de la Torre
1918	*Not played*
1919	A. de la Torre
1920	*Not played*
1921	E. Lafitte
1922	*Not played*
1923	A. de la Torre
1924	*Not played*
1925	A. de la Torre
1926	J. Bernardino
1927	A. Massy
1928	A. Massy
1929	E. Lafitte
1930	J. Bernardino
1931	*Not played*
1932	G. Gonzalez
1933	G. Gonzalez
1934	J. Bernadino
1935	A. de la Torre
1936–40	*Not played*
1941	M. Provencio
1942	G. Gonzalez
1943	M. Provencio
1944	N. Sargardia
1945	C. Celles
1946	M. Morcillo
1947	M. Gonzalez (a)
1948	M. Morcillo
1949	M. Morcillo
1950	A. Cerda
1951	M. Provencio
1952	M. Faulkner
1953	M. Faulkner
1954	S. Miguel
1955	H. de Lamaze (a)
1956	P. Alliss
1957	M. Faulkner
1958	P. Alliss
1959	P. Thomson

1960	S. Miguel
1961	A. Miguel
1962	*Not played*
1963	R. Sota
1964	A. Miguel
1965	*Not played*
1966	R. de Vicenzo
1967	S. Miguel
1968	R. Shaw
1969	J. Garaialde
1970	A. Gallardo
1971	D. Hayes
1972	A. Garrido
1973	N. Coles
1974	J. Heard
1975	A. Palmer
1976	E. Polland
1977	B. Gallacher
1978	B. Barnes
1979	D. Hayes
1980	E. Polland
1981	S. Ballesteros
1982	S. Torrance
1983	E. Darcy
1984	B. Langer
1985	S. Ballesteros
1986	H Clark
1987	N. Faldo
1988	M. James
1989	B. Langer
1990	R. Davis
1991	E. Romero
1992	A. Sherborne
1993	J. Haeggman
1994	C. Montgomerie
1995	S. Ballesteros
1996	P. Harrington
1997	M. James
1998	T. Bjorn

CONTE OF FLORENCE ITALIAN OPEN

Formerly known as Lancia (1987–89), Lancia-Martini (1990–93), Tisettanta (1994), Conte of Florence (1997–). Tournament not played 1933, 1939–46, 1961–70.

1925	F. Pasquali
1926	A. Boyer
1927	P. Alliss
1928	A. Boyer
1929	R. Golias
1930	A. Boyer
1931	A. Boyer
1932	A. Boomer
1933	*Not played*
1934	N. Nutley
1935	P. Alliss
1936	H. Cotton
1937	M. Dallemagne
1938	F. van Donck
1939–46	*Not played*
1947	F. van Donck
1948	A. Casera
1949	H. Hassenain
1950	U. Grappasonni
1951	J. Adams
1952	E. Brown
1953	F. van Donck
1954	U. Grappasonni
1955	F. van Donck
1956	A. Cerda
1957	H. Henning
1958	P. Alliss
1959	P. Thomson
1960	B. Wilkes
1961–70	*Not played*
1971	R. Sota
1972	N. Wood
1973	A. Jacklin
1974	P. Oosterhuis
1975	W. Casper
1976	B. Dassu
1977	A. Gallardo
1978	D. Hayes
1979	B. Barnes
1980	M. Mannelli
1981	J-M. Canizares
1982	M. James
1983	B. Langer
1984	A. Lyle
1985	M. Pinero
1986	D. Feherty
1987	S. Torrance
1988	G. Norman
1989	R. Rafferty
1990	R. Boxall
1991	C. Parry
1992	A. Lyle
1993	G. Turner
1994	E. Romero
1995	S. Torrance
1996	J. Payne
1997	B. Langer
1998	P. Sjöland

TURESPANA MASTERS

Formerly known as Turespana Masters Open de Andalucia (1992–95), Turespana Masters Open Communitat Valenciana Paradores de Turismo (1996), Turespana Masters – Open de Canarias (1997)

1992	V. Singh
1993	A. Oldcorn
1994	C. Mason
1995	A. Cejka
1996	D. Borrego
1997	J-M. Olazabal
1998	M.A. Jimenez

BENSON & HEDGES INTERNATIONAL OPEN

Formerly known as the Benson & Hedges Festival (1971–75)

1971	A. Jacklin
1972	J. Newton
1973	V. Baker
1974	P. Toussaint
1975	V. Fernandez
1976	G. Marsh
1977	A. Garrido
1978	L. Trevino
1979	M. Pembridge
1980	G. Marsh
1981	T. Weiskopf
1982	G. Norman
1983	J. Bland
1984	S. Torrance
1985	A. Lyle
1986	M. James
1987	N. Ratcliffe
1988	P. Baker
1989	G. Brand Jr
1990	J-M. Olazabal
1991	B. Langer
1992	P. Senior
1993	P. Broadhurst
1994	S. Ballesteros
1995	P. O'Malley
1996	S. Ames
1997	B. Langer
1998	D. Clarke

VOLVO PGA CHAMPIONSHIP

Restricted to UK and Irish professionals until 1966. Formerly known as the Schweppes PGA Championship (1967–69), Viyella PGA Championship (1972–74), Penfold PGA Championship (1975–77), Colgate PGA Championship (1978–79), Sun Alliance PGA Championship (1980–83), Whyte & Mackay PGA Championship (1984–87). Tournament not played 1970–71. In 1967 and 1968 the PGA "open" (o) and "closed" (c) tournaments were contested. Tournament not played 1970–71.

1955	K. Bousfield
1956	C.H. Ward
1957	P. Alliss
1958	H. Bradshaw
1959	D.J. Rees
1960	A.F. Strickley
1961	B.J. Bamford
1962	P. Alliss
1963	P.J. Butler
1964	A.G. Grubb
1965	P. Alliss
1966	G. Wolstenholme
1967	B.G.C. Huggett (c)
1967	M.E. Gregson (o)
1968	P.M. Townsend (c)
1968	D. Talbot (o)
1969	B. Gallacher
1970–71	*Not played*
1972	A. Jacklin
1973	P. Oosterhuis
1974	M. Bembridge
1975	A. Palmer
1976	N. Coles
1977	M. Pinero
1978	N. Faldo
1979	V. Fernandez
1980	N. Faldo
1981	N. Faldo
1982	A. Jacklin
1983	S. Ballesteros
1984	H. Clark
1985	P. Way
1986	R. Davis
1987	B. Langer
1988	I. Woosnam
1989	N. Faldo
1990	M. Harwood
1991	S. Ballesteros
1992	T. Johnstone
1993	B. Langer
1994	J-M. Olazabal

1995	B. Langer
1996	C. Rocca
1997	I. Woosnam
1998	C. Montgomerie

DEUTSCHE BANK – SAP OPEN – TPC OF EUROPE

Formerly known as SOS Talisman (1979), Haig Whisky (1980–82), St Mellion Timeshare (1983–84), Portuguese Open (1989–90). Tournament not played, 1985, 1987–88, 1991–94.

1977	N. Coles
1978	B. Waites
1979	M. King
1980	B. Gallacher
1981	B. Barnes
1982	N. Faldo
1983	B. Langer
1984	J. Gonzalez
1985	*Not played*
1986	I. Woosnam
1987–88	*Not played*
1989	C. Montgomerie
1990	M. McLean
1991–94	*Not played*
1995	B. Langer
1996	F. Nobilo
1997	R. McFarlane
1998	L. Westwood

THE NATIONAL CAR RENTAL ENGLISH OPEN

Formerly known as the Lada English Open (1979), State Express English Open (1981–83), NM English Open (1989–91), Murphy's English Open (1992–95), Alamo English Open (1996–97). Tournament not played 1984–87.

1979	S. Ballesteros
1980	M. Pinero
1981	R. Davis
1982	G. Norman
1983	H. Baiocchi
1984–87	*Not played*
1988	H. Clark
1989	M. James
1990	M. James
1991	D. Gilford
1992	V. Fernandez
1993	I. Woosnam
1994	C. Montgomerie
1995	P. Walton
1996	R. Allenby
1997	P-U. Johansson
1998	L. Westwood

COMPAQ EUROPEAN GRAND PRIX

Formerly known as the Slaley Hall Northumberland Challenge (1996), Compaq European Grand Prix (1997).

1996	R. Goosen
1997	C. Montgomerie
1998	*Cancelled*

MADEIRA ISLAND OPEN

1993	M. James
1994	M. Lanner
1995	S. Luna
1996	J. Sandelin
1997	P. Mitchell
1998	M. Lanner

PEUGEOT OPEN DE FRANCE

Formerly known as Paco Rabane Open de France (1980–83). Tournament not played 1915–19, 1940–45

1906	A. Massy
1907	A. Massy
1908	J.H. Taylor
1909	J.H. Taylor
1910	J. Braid
1911	A. Massy
1912	J. Gassiat
1913	G. Duncan
1914	J.D. Edgar
1915–19	*Not played*
1920	W. Hagen
1921	A. Boomer
1922	A. Boomer
1923	J. Ockenden
1924	C.J.H. Tolley
1925	A. Massy
1926	A. Boomer
1927	G. Duncan
1928	C.J.H. Tolley
1929	A. Boomer
1930	E.R. Whitcombe
1931	A. Boomer
1932	A.J. Lacey
1933	B. Gadd
1934	S.F. Brews
1935	S.F. Brews
1936	M. Dallemagne
1937	M. Dallemagne
1938	M. Dallemagne
1939	M. Pose
1940–45	*Not played*
1946	T.H. Cotton
1947	T.H. Cotton
1948	F. Cavalo
1949	U. Grappasonni
1950	R. de Vicenzo
1951	H. Hassenein
1952	A.D. Locke
1953	A.D. Locke
1954	F. van Donck
1955	B. Nelson
1956	A. Miguel
1957	F. van Donck
1958	F. van Donck
1959	D.C. Thomas
1960	R. de Vicenzo
1961	K. Nagle
1962	A. Murray
1963	B. Devlin
1964	R. de Vicenzo
1965	R. Sota
1966	D.J. Hutchinson
1967	B.J. Hunt
1968	P.J. Butler
1969	J. Garaialde
1970	D. Graham
1971	Lu Liang Huan
1972	B. Jaeckel
1973	P. Oosterhuis
1974	P. Oosterhuis
1975	B. Barnes
1976	V. Tshabalala
1977	S. Ballesteros
1978	D. Hayes
1979	B. Gallacher
1980	G. Norman
1981	A. Lyle
1982	S. Ballesteros
1983	N. Faldo
1984	B. Langer
1985	S. Ballesteros
1986	S. Ballesteros
1987	J. Rivero
1988	N. Faldo
1989	N. Faldo
1990	P. Walton
1991	E. Romero
1992	M.A. Martin
1993	C. Rocca
1994	M. Roe
1995	P. Broadhurst
1996	R. Allenby
1997	R. Goosen
1998	S. Torrance

MURPHY'S IRISH OPEN

Formerly known as the Carrolls Irish Open (1975–93). Tournament not played 1940–45, 1951–52, 1954–74

1927	G. Duncan
1928	E. Whitcombe
1929	A. Mitchell
1930	C. Whitcombe
1931	E. Kenyon
1932	A. Padgham
1933	E. Kenyon
1934	S. Easterbrook
1935	E. Whitcombe
1936	R. Whitcombe
1937	B. Gadd
1938	A. Locke
1939	A. Lees
1940–45	*Not played*
1946	F. Daly
1947	H. Bradshaw
1948	D. Rees
1949	H. Bradshaw
1950	H. Pickworth
1951–52	*Not played*
1953	E. Brown
1954–74	*Not played*
1975	C. O'Connor Jr
1976	B. Crenshaw
1977	H. Green
1978	K. Brown
1979	M. James
1980	M. James
1981	S. Torrance
1982	J. O'Leary
1983	S. Ballesteros
1984	B. Langer
1985	S. Ballesteros
1986	S. Ballesteros
1987	B. Langer
1988	I. Woosnam
1989	I. Woosnam
1990	J.-M. Olazabal
1991	N. Faldo
1992	N. Faldo
1993	N. Faldo
1994	B. Langer

1995	S. Torrance
1996	C. Montgomerie
1997	C. Montgomerie
1998	D. Carter

STANDARD LIFE LOCH LOMOND

Formerly known as Loch Lomond World Invitational from 1996–97.

1996	T. Bjorn
1997	T. Lehman
1998	L. Westwood

TNT DUTCH OPEN

Formerly known as KLM (1981–90), Heineken (1991–95), Sun Microsystems (1996–97). Until 1934 played over 36 holes. Tournament not played 1940–45.

1919	D. Oosterveer
1920	H. Burrows
1921	H. Burrows
1922	G. Pannell
1923	H. Boomer
1924	H. Boomer
1925	H. Boomer
1926	H. Boomer
1927	P. Boomer
1929	J.J. Taylor
1930	J. Oosterveer
1931	F. Dyer
1932	A. Boyer
1933	M. Dallemagne
1934	S.F. Brews
1935	S.F. Brews
1936	F. van Donck
1937	F. van Donck
1938	A.H. Padgham
1939	A.D. Locke
1940–45	*Not played*
1946	F. van Donck
1947	G. Ruhl
1948	C. Denny
1949	J. Adams
1950	R. de Vicenzo
1951	F. van Donck
1952	C. Denny
1953	F. van Donck
1954	U. Grappasonni
1955	A. Angelini
1956	A. Cerda
1957	J. Jacobs
1958	D. Thomas
1959	S. Sewgolum
1960	S. Sewgolum
1961	B.B.S. Wilkes
1962	B.G.C. Huggett
1963	R. Waltman
1964	S. Sewgolum
1965	A. Miguel
1966	R. Sota
1967	P. Townsend
1968	J. Cockin
1969	G. Wolstenholme
1970	V. Fernandez
1971	R. Sota
1972	J. Newton
1973	D. McClelland
1974	B. Barnes
1975	H. Baiocchi
1976	S. Ballesteros
1977	R. Byman
1978	R. Byman
1979	G. Marsh
1980	S. Ballesteros
1981	H. Henning
1982	P. Way
1983	K. Brown
1984	B. Langer
1985	G. Marsh
1986	S. Ballesteros
1987	G. Brand Jr
1988	M. Mouland
1989	J-M. Olazabal
1990	S. McAllister
1991	P. Stewart
1992	B. Langer
1993	C. Montgomerie
1994	M. A. Jimenez
1995	S. Hoch
1996	M. McNulty
1997	S. Strüver
1998	S. Leaney

VOLVO SCANDINAVIAN MASTERS

Formerly known as Volvo (1995–97).

1991	C. Montgomerie
1992	N. Faldo
1993	P. Baker
1994	V. Singh
1995	J. Parnevik
1996	L. Westwood
1997	J. Haeggman
1998	J. Parnevik

CHEMAPOL TROPHY CZECH OPEN

1994	P-U. Johansson
1995	P. Teravainen
1996	J. Lomas
1997	B. Langer

SMURFIT EUROPEAN OPEN

Formerly known as the Dixcel Tissues (1981), Panasonic (1983–90), General Accident (1991–93), Smurfit (1995).

1978	B. Wadkins
1979	A. Lyle
1980	T. Kite
1981	G. Marsh
1982	M. Pinero
1983	I. Aoki
1984	G. Brand Jr
1985	B. Langer
1986	G. Norman
1987	P. Way
1988	I. Woosnam
1989	A. Murray
1990	P. Senior
1991	M. Harwood
1992	N. Faldo
1993	G. Brand Jr
1994	D. Gilford
1995	B. Langer
1996	P-U. Johansson
1997	P-U. Johansson
1998	N. Grönberg

BMW INTERNATIONAL OPEN

1989	D. Feherty
1990	P. Azinger
1991	A. Lyle
1992	P. Azinger
1993	P. Fowler
1994	M. McNulty
1995	F. Nobilo
1996	M. Farry
1997	R. Karlsson
1998	R. Claydon

CANON EUROPEAN MASTERS (INCORPORATING SWISS OPEN)

Played over 36 holes 1923–38. Formerly known as European Masters (1983), Ebel (1982–90), Canon (1991–97). Tournament not played 1927–28, 1932–33, 1940–47).

1923	A. Ross
1924	P. Boomer
1925	A. Ross
1926	A. Ross
1927–28	*Not played*
1929	A. Wilson
1930	A. Boyer
1931	M. Dallemagne
1932–33	*Not played*
1934	A. Boyer
1935	A. Boyer
1936	F. Francis (a)
1937	M. Dallemagne
1938	J. Saubaber
1939	F. Cavalo
1940–47	*Not played*
1948	U. Grappasonni
1949	M. Dallemagne
1950	A. Casera
1951	E.C. Brown
1952	U. Grappasonni
1953	F. van Donck
1954	A. D. Locke
1955	F. van Donck
1956	D. J. Rees
1957	A. Angelini
1958	K. Bousfield
1959	D. J. Rees
1960	H. Henning
1961	K.D.G. Nagle
1962	R.J. Charles
1963	D.J. Rees
1964	H.R. Henning
1965	H.R. Henning
1966	A. Angelini
1967	R. Vines
1968	R. Bernardini
1969	R. Bernardini
1970	G. Marsh
1971	P. M. Townsend
1972	G. Marsh
1973	H. Baiocchi
1974	R. J. Charles
1975	D. Hayes
1976	M. Pinero
1977	S. Ballesteros
1978	S. Ballesteros

1979	H. Baiocchi
1980	N. Price
1981	M. Pinero
1982	I. Woosnam
1983	N. Faldo
1984	J. Anderson
1985	C. Stadler
1986	J-M. Olazabal
1987	A. Forsbrand
1988	C. Moody
1989	S. Ballesteros
1990	R. Rafferty
1991	J. Hawkes
1992	J. Spence
1993	B. Lane
1994	E. Romero
1995	M. Grönberg
1996	C. Montgomerie
1997	C. Rocca
1998	S. Strüver

ONE TO ONE BRITISH MASTERS

Formerly known as the Dunlop Masters (1946–82), Silk Cut Masters (1983), Dunhill (1985–94), Collingtree (1995), One 2 One (1996–97). Tournament not played 1984.

1946	A.D. Locke
	J. Adams
1947	A. Lees
1948	N. von Nida
1949	C. Ward
1950	D. Rees
1951	M. Faulkner
1952	H. Weetman
1953	H. Bradshaw
1954	A.D. Locke
1955	H. Bradshaw
1956	C. O'Connor
1957	E. Brown
1958	H. Weetman
1959	C. O'Connor
1960	J. Hitchcock
1961	P. Thomson
1962	D. Rees
1963	B. Hunt
1964	C. Legrange
1965	B. Hunt
1966	N. Coles
1967	A. Jacklin
1968	P. Thomson
1969	C. Legrange
1970	B.G.C. Huggett
1971	M. Bembridge
1972	R.J. Charles
1973	A. Jacklin
1974	B. Gallacher
1975	B. Gallacher
1976	B. Dassu
1977	G. Hunt
1978	T. Horton
1979	G. Marsh
1980	B. Langer
1981	G. Norman
1982	G. Norman
1983	I. Woosnam
1984	*Not played*
1985	L. Trevino
1986	S. Ballesteros
1987	M. McNulty
1988	A. Lyle
1989	N. Faldo
1990	M. James
1991	S. Ballesteros
1992	C. O'Connor Jr
1993	P. Baker
1994	I. Woosnam
1995	S. Torrance
1996	R. Allenby
1997	G. Turner
1998	C. Montgomerie

TROPHEE LANCOME

1970	A. Jacklin
1971	A. Palmer
1972	T. Aaron
1973	J. Miller
1974	W. Casper
1975	G. Player
1976	S. Ballesteros
1977	G. Marsh
1978	L. Trevino
1979	J. Miller
1980	L. Trevino
1981	D. Graham
1982	D. Graham
1983	S. Ballesteros
1984	A. Lyle
1985	N. Price
1986	S. Ballesteros
	and B. Langer
1987	I. Woosnam
1988	S. Ballesteros
1989	E. Romero
1990	J-M. Olazabal
1991	F. Nobilo
1992	M. Row
1993	I. Woosnam
1994	V. Singh
1995	C. Montgomerie
1996	J. Parnevik
1997	M. O'Meara
1998	M.A. Jimenez

LINDE GERMAN MASTERS

Formerly known as Mercedes (1990–95).

1987	A. Lyle
1988	J-M. Olazabal
1989	B. Langer
1990	S. Torrance
1991	B. Langer
1992	B. Lane
1993	S. Richardson
1994	S. Ballesteros
1995	A. Forsbrand
1996	D. Clarke
1997	B. Langer
1998	C. Montgomerie

OPEN NOVOTEL PERRIER

1996	J. Lomas
	S. Bottomley
1997	A. Forsbrand
	M. Jonzon
1998	C. Montgomerie

VOLVO MASTERS

1988	N. Faldo
1989	R. Rafferty
1990	M. Harwood
1991	R. Davis
1992	A. Lyle
1993	C. Montgomerie
1994	B. Langer
1995	A. Cejka
1996	M. McNulty
1997	L. Westwood
1998	D. Clarke

SUBARU SARAZEN WORLD OPEN

1994	E. Els
1995	F. Nobilo
1996	F. Nobilo
1997	M. Calcavecchia
1998	D. Hart

GERMAN OPEN

Formerly known as Braun (1978–80), Lufthansa (1982–88), Volvo (1990–97). Tournament not played 1913–25, 1940–50.

1911	H. Vardon
1912	J.H. Taylor
1913–25	*Not played*
1926	P. Alliss
1927	P. Alliss
1928	P. Alliss
1929	P. Alliss
1930	A. Boyer
1931	R. Golias
1932	A. Boyer
1933	P. Alliss
1934	A.H. Padgham
1935	A. Boyer
1936	A. Boyer
1937	T.H. Cotton
1938	T.H. Cotton
1939	T.H. Cotton
1940–50	*Not played*
1951	A. Cerda
1952	A. Cerda
1953	F. van Donck
1954	A.D. Locke
1955	K. Bousfield
1956	F. van Donck
1957	H. Weetman
1958	F. de Luca
1959	K. Bousfield
1960	P.W. Thomson
1961	B.J. Hunt
1962	R. Verwey
1963	B.G.C. Huggett
1964	R. de Vicenzo
1965	H.R. Henning
1966	R. Stanton
1967	D. Swaelens
1968	B. Franklin
1969	J. Garaialde
1970	J. Garaialde
1971	N.C. Coles
1972	G. Marsh
1973	F. Abreu
1974	S. Owen

1975	M. Bembridge
1976	S. Hobday
1977	T. Britz
1978	S. Ballesteros
1979	A. Jacklin
1980	M. McNulty
1981	B. Langer
1982	B. Langer
1983	C. Pavin
1984	W. Grady
1985	B. Langer
1986	B. Langer
1987	M. McNulty
1988	S. Ballesteros
1989	C. Parry
1990	M. McNulty
1991	M. McNulty
1992	V. Singh
1993	B. Langer
1994	C. Montgomerie
1995	C. Montgomerie
1996	I. Woosnam
1997	I. Garrido
1998	S. Allan

PGA EUROPEAN TOUR QUALIFYING SCHOOL

From 1984, six rounds; from 1994, four rounds only

1976	D.A. Russell
1977	A. Lyle
1978	S. Evans
	G. Ralph
1979	C. Cox
	K. Williams
1980	P. Carrigill
	M. Montes
1981	G. Brand Jr
	R. Mann
1982	J. Rivero
	G. Turner
1983	D. Ray
	A. Oldcorn
	F. Regard
1984	R. Wrenn Jr
1985	J-M. Olazabal
1986	W. Smith
1987	M. Smith
1988	J. Parnevik
1989	H-P. Thül
1990	D. Silva
1991	A. Hare
1992	R. Goosen
1993	B. Nelson
1994	D. Carter
1995	S. Webster
1996	N. Fasth
1997	C. van der Velde
1998	R. Drummond

PAST CHAMPIONS – FORMER EVENTS

AGF OPEN

Known as AGF Biarritz Open (1988).

1988	D. Llewellyn
1989	M. James
1990	B. Ogle

ANDERSEN CONSULTING WORLD CHAMPIONSHIP OF GOLF

1995	B. Lane
1996	G. Norman
1997	C. Montgomerie

ASAHI GLASS FOUR TOURS CHAMPIONSHIP

Known as Nissan Cup (1985–86), Kirin Cup (1987–88), Asahi Glass Four Tours (1989–91).

1985	1-US PGA Tour
	2-PGA European Tour
	3-PGA Japan Tour
	4-Australia/New Zealand Tour
1986	1-PGA Japan Tour
	2-PGA European Tour
	3-Australia/New Zealand Tour
	4-US PGA Tour
1987	1-US PGA Tour
	2-PGA European Tour
	3-Australia/New Zealand Tour
	4-PGA Japan Tour
1988	1-US PGA Tour
	2-PGA European Tour
	3-Australia/New Zealand Tour
	4-PGA Japan Tour
1989	1-US PGA Tour
	2-PGA European Tour
	3-PGA Japan Tour
	4-Australia/New Zealand Tour
1990	1-Australia/New Zealand Tour
	2-US PGA Tour
	3-PGA European Tour
	4-PGA Japan Tour
1991	1-PGA European Tour
	2-Australia/New Zealand Tour
	3-PGA Japan Tour
	4-US PGA Tour

AUSTRIAN OPEN

Known as Mitsubishi and Denzel (1991), Mitsubishi (1992), Hohe Brücke (1993–1996).

1990	B. Langer
1991	M. Davis
1992	P. Mitchell
1993	R. Rafferty
1994	M. Davis
1995	A. Cejka
1996	P. McGinley

VINHO VERDE ATLANTIC OPEN

1990	S. McAllister

TURESPANA OPEN CANARIAS

Known as Turespana (1992, 1994–95), Turespana Iberia (1993). Tournament not played 1991.

1989	J-M. Olazabal
1990	V. Fernandez
1991	*Not played*
1992	J-M. Olazabal
1993	M. James
1994	D. Gilford
1995	J. Sandelin

TURESPANA OPEN BALEARES

Mallorca (1988), Renault (1989-90), Turespana (1992-95) Turespana Iberia (1993).

1988	S. Ballesteros
1989	O. Sellberg
1990	S. Ballesteros
1991	G. Levenson
1992	S. Ballesteros
1993	J. Payne
1994	B. Lane
1995	G. Turner

BELGIAN OPEN

1910–27, 36 holes. Known as Volvo (1987–89), Peugeot-Trends (1990), Renault (1991), PIAGET (1992), Alfred Dunhill Open (1993–94). Tournament not played 1915–19, 1940–45, 1959–77, 1980–86.

1910	A. Massy
1911	C.H. Mayo
1912	G. Duncan
1913	T. Ball
1914	T. Ball
1915–19	*Not played*
1920	R. Jones
1921	E. Lafitte
1922	A. Boomer
1923	A. Boomer
1924	W. Hagen
1925	E. Lafitte
1926	A. Boomer
1927	M. Dallemagne
1928	A. Tingey Jr
1929	S.F. Brews
1930	T.H. Cotton
1931	A. Lacey
1932	A. Lacey
1933	A. Boyer
1934	T.H. Cotton
1935	W.J. Branch
1936	A. Boyer
1937	M. Dallemagne
1938	T.H. Cotton
1939	F. van Donck
1940–45	*Not played*
1946	F. van Donck
1947	F. van Donck
1948	W.S. Forrester
1949	J. Adams
1950	R. de Vicenzo
1951	A. Pelissier
1952	A. Cerda
1953	F. van Donck
1954	D.J. Rees

1955	D.C. Thomas
1956	F. van Donck
1957	B.J. Hunt
1958	K. Bousfield
1959–77	*Not played*
1978	N. Ratcliffe
1979	G. Levenson
1980–86	*Not played*
1987	E. Darcy
1988	J-M. Olazabal
1989	G.J. Brand
1990	O. Sellberg
1991	P-U. Johansson
1992	M.A. Jimenez
1993	D. Clarke
1994	N. Faldo

BARCELONA OPEN

Known asTorras Hostench (1988).

1988	D. Whelan

BENSON & HEDGES TROPHY

1988	M. McNulty/ M. L. de Lorenzi
1989	M. A. Jimenez/ X. Wunsch-Ruiz
1990	J. M. Canizares/ T. Abitbol
1991	A. Forsbrand/ H. Alfredsson

CACHAREL WORLD UNDER 25s

1976	E. Darcy
1977	*Not played*
1978	J. Nelford
1979	B. Langer
1980	J. Renner
1981	T. Simpson
1982	I. Woosnam
1983	M. McLean

CALLERS OF NEWCASTLE OPEN

1977	J. Fourie

CAR CARE PLAN INTERNATIONAL

1982	B. Waites
1983	N. Faldo
1984	N. Faldo
1985	D.J. Russell
1986	M. Mouland

CARROLLS INTERNATIONAL

Known as the Carrolls Sweet Afton (1963–65), Carrolls International (1966–74).

1963	B.J. Hunt
1964	C. O'Connor
1965	N.C. Coles
1966	C. O'Connor
1967	C. O'Connor
1968	J. Martin
1969	R.D. Shade
1970	B.G.C. Huggett
1971	N.C. Coles
1972	C. O'Connor
1973	P. McGuirk
1974	B. Gallacher

OPEN CATALONIA

Known as Heineken (1993–94), Turespana (1995). Tournament not played 1990.

1989	M. Roe
1990	*Not played*
1991	J-M. Olazabal
1992	J. Rivero
1993	S. Torrance
1994	J. Coceres
1995	P. Walton
1996	P. Lawrie

CLASSIC INTERNATIONAL

1970	H. Muscroft
1971	P. Butler

COCA-COLA YOUNG PROFESSIONALS

1968	P. Townsend
1969	B. Barnes
1970	P. Oosterhuis
1971	J. Garner
1972	P. Oosterhuis
1973	B. Gallacher
1974	D. Hayes

DIMENSION DATA PRO-AM

1996	M. McNulty
1997	N. Price

THE DAKS GOLF TOURNAMENT

1950	N. Sutton
1951	J. Panton
1952	F. Daly
1953	D. Rees
1954	P. Alliss
1955	J.D. Pritchett
1956	T. Wilkes
1957	A.D. Locke
1958	P. Thomson H. Henning
1959	C. O'Connor
1960	P. Thomson
1961	B. Hunt
1962	D. Rees R.J. Charles
1963	N.C. Coles P. Alliss
1964	N.C. Coles
1965	P. Thomson
1966	H. Boyle
1967	M. Gregson
1968	M. Gregson
1969	B.G.C. Huggett
1970	N.C. Coles
1971	N.C. Coles B.G.C. Huggett

DOUBLE DIAMOND INTERNATIONAL

Known as the Double Diamond International (1971–75), Double Diamond Golf Classic (1976–77).

1971	England
1972	England
1973	Scotland
1974	England
1975	Americas
1976	England
1977	United States

DOUBLE DIAMOND STROKE PLAY

1974	M. Bembridge
1975	P. Dawson
1976	S. Owen

EL BOSQUE OPEN

1990	V. Singh

EL PARADISO OPEN

1974	P. Oosterhuis

EPSON GRAND PRIX OF EUROPE

1986–89 Matchplay, 1990–91 Strokeplay.

1986	O. Sellberg
1987	M. Lanner
1988	B. Langer
1989	S. Ballesteros
1990	I. Woosnam
1991	J-M. Olazabal

EQUITY & LAW CHALLENGE

1987	B. Lane
1988	R. Rafferty
1989	B. Ogle
1990	B. Marchbank
1991	B. Marchbank
1992	A. Forsbrand

EUROPEAN PRO-CELEBRITY TOURNAMENT

Known as Bob Hope (1980–83), Four Stars (1985), London Standard Four Stars (1986–87), Wang Four Stars (1988–90). Tournament not played 1984.

1980	J.M. Canizares
1981	B. Langer
1982	G. Brand Jr
1983	J.M. Canizares
1984	*Not played*
1985	K. Brown
1986	A. Garrido
1987	M. McNulty
1988	R. Davis
1989	C. Parry
1990	R. Davis
1991	P. Broadhurst

OPEN DE EXTREMADURA

1994 P. Eales

FNB PLAYERS CHAMPIONSHIP

1996 W. Westner

GALLAHER ULSTER

1965 B. Hunt
1966 C. O'Connor
1967 B. Hunt
1968 C. O'Connor
1969 C. O'Connor
1970 J. Lister
1971 T. Horton

GEVACOLOR FILM

Known as Gevacolor Film (1963–64), Agfa-Gevaert (1965–67 and 1971), Agfacolor Film (1968–70).

1963 B. Hunt
1964 A. Miguel
1965 J. Hitchcock
1966 A. Miguel
1967 P. Alliss
1968 C. Clark
1969 B. Barnes
1970 B. Hunt
1971 P. Oosterhuis

GIRONA OPEN

1991 S. Richardson

GLASGOW OPEN

Known as the Glasgow Golf Classic (1983); Glasgow Open (1984).

1983 B. Langer
1984 K. Brown
1985 H. Clark

GREATER MANCHESTER OPEN

Known as the Cold Shield (1980-81).

1976 J. O'Leary
1977 E. Darcy
1978 B. Barnes
1979 M. McNulty
1980 D. Smyth
1981 B. Gallacher

GSI-L'EQUIPE OPEN

1974 GB & Ireland
1976 GB & Ireland
1978 GB & Ireland
1980 GB & Ireland
1982 GB & Ireland
1984 England

HONDA OPEN

1992 B. Langer
1993 S. Torrance
1994 R. Allenby

JERSEY OPEN

Known as British Airways/Avis (1978–79), Avis (1980), Billy Butlin (1981), BNP (1988), Jersey European Airways (1989, 91–94), DHL (1995). Tournament not played 1990.

1978 B.C.G. Huggett
1979 A. Lyle
1980 J.M. Canizares
1981 A. Jacklin
1982 B. Gallacher
1983 J. Hall
1984 B. Gallacher
1985 H. Clark
1986 J. Morgan
1987 I. Woosnam
1988 D. Smyth
1989 C. O'Connor Jr
1990 *Not played*
1991 S. Torrance
1992 D. Silva
1993 I. Palmer
1994 P. Curry
1993 A. Oldcorn

JOHNNY WALKER WORLD CHAMPIONSHIP

1991 F. Couples
1992 N. Faldo
1993 L. Mize
1994 E. Els
1995 F. Couples

KERRYGOLD INTERNATIONAL CLASSIC

1975 G. Burns
1976 A. Jacklin
1977 L. Higgins

KRONENBOURG OPEN

1993 S. Torrance

LANCIA D'ORO OPEN

1972 J. M. Canizares

LAWRENCE BATLEY INTERNATIONAL

1981 A. Lyle
1982 A. Lyle
1983 N. Faldo
1984 J. Rivero
1985 G. Marsh
1986 I. Woosnam
1987 M. O'Meara

LORD DERBY'S UNDER-23 PROFESSIONAL TOURNA-MENT STROKE-PLAY

Known as the Under-25 Matchplay (1972-74), combined with Ladbroke 1974. Strokeplay 1968–71.

1968 G. Hunt
1969 C. Defoy
1970 P. Oosterhuis
1971 D. Vaughan
1972 S. Torrance
1973 B. Thompson
1974 R. Jewell

OPEN DE LYON

1992-94 V33

1992 D. J. Russell
1993 C. Rocca
1994 S. Ames

MADRID OPEN

Formerly known as Cepsa (1983-90); Iberia (1992)

1968 G. Garrido
1969 R. Sota
1970 M. Cabrera
1971 V. Barrios
1972 J. Kinsella
1973 G. Garrido
1974 M. Pinero
1975 R. Shearer
1976 F. Abreu
1977 A. Garrido
1978 H. Clark
1979 S. Hobday
1980 S. Ballesteros
1981 M. Pinero
1982 S. Ballesteros
1983 A. Lyle
1984 H. Clark
1985 M. Pinero
1986 H. Clark
1987 I. Woosnam
1988 D. Cooper
1989 S. Ballesteros
1990 B. Langer
1991 A. Sherborne
1992 D. Feherty
1993 D. Smyth

MARTINI INTERNATIONAL (CLUB)

1961 B. Hunt
1962 P. Thomson
1963 C. O'Connor
N.C. Coles
1964 C. O'Connor
1965 P. Butler
1966 P. Alliss
W. Large
1967 M. Gregson
B.G.C. Huggett
1968 B.G.C. Huggett
1969 G. Henning
A. Caygill
1970 D. Sewell
P. Thomson
1971 B. Gallacher
1972 B. Barnes
1973 M. Bembridge
1974 S. Ginn
1975 I. Stanley
C. O'Connor
1976 S. Torrance
1977 G. Norman
1978 S. Ballesteros

1979	G. Norman
1980	S. Ballesteros
1981	G. Norman
1982	B. Gallacher
1983	N. Faldo

MERSEYSIDE INTERNATIONAL

1980	I. Mosey

MONTE CARLO OPEN

Known as the Johnnie Walker (1985–1987), Torras (1989–1991), The European Newspaper (1992).

1984	I. Mosey
1985	S. Torrance
1986	S. Ballesteros
1987	P. Senior
1988	J. Rivero
1989	M. McNulty
1990	I. Woosnam
1991	I. Woosnam
1992	I. Woosnam

MOTOROLA CLASSIC

Combined with PGA Southern Open (1988).

1988	D. Williams
1989	D. Llewellyn
1990	P. Broadhurst

MURPHY'S CUP

1989	H. Baiocchi
1990	A. Johnstone
1991	A. Johnstone

NEWCASTLE BROWN "900" OPEN

1980	D. Smyth

PARMECO GOLF CLASSIC

1971	E. Polland

PENFOLD

Known as PENFOLD-SWALLOW/ SWALLOW-PENFOLD alternate years from 1955. Penfold-Bournemouth (1971–73).

1932	P. Alliss
1933	J. Burton
1934	R. Whitcombe
1935	P. Alliss
1936	J. Adams
1939	T.H. Cotton
1946	N. Sutton
1947	D. Rees
	R. Whitcombe
	N. Von Nida
1948	F. Daly
1949	J. Burton & M. Faulkner
1950	N. Sutton (& Mrs Gee)
1951	A. Lees
1952	E. Brown
1953	A. Lees
1954	T.H. Cotton
1955	C. O'Connor
1956	E. Lester
1957	H. Weetman
1958	H. Weetman
1959	P. Butler
1960	H. Weetman
1961	K. Bousfield
1962	H. Weetman
1963	B. Hunt
1964	P. Alliss
1965	A. Miguel
1966	D. Thomas
1967	J. Cockin
1968	P. Butler
1969	A. Caygill
1970	B. Hunt
1971	N. Coles
1972	P. Oosterhuis
1973	E. Polland
1974	T. Horton

PGA MATCHPLAY TOURNAMENT

Known as the News of the World (1903–1969), Long John Whisky (1970), Benson & Hedges (1972–1974), Sun Alliance (1975–1979). Tournament not played 1914–18, 1941–44, 1971.

1903	J. Braid
1904	J.H. Taylor
1905	J. Braid
1906	A. Herd
1907	J. Braid
1908	J.H. Taylor
1909	T. Ball
1910	J. Sherlock
1911	J. Braid
1912	H. Vardon
1913	G. Duncan
1914–18	*Not played*
1919	A. Mitchell
1920	A. Mitchell
1921	B. Seymour
1922	G. Gadd
1923	R. G. Wilson
1924	E. Whitcombe
1925	A. Compston
1926	A. Herd
1927	A. Compston
1928	C. Whitcombe
1929	A. Mitchell
1930	C. Whitcombe
1931	A. Padgham
1932	H. Cotton
1933	P. Alliss
1934	J. Busson
1935	A. Padgham
1936	D. Rees
1937	P. Alliss
1938	D. Rees
1940	H. Cotton
1941–44	*Not played*
1945	R. Horne
1946	H. Cotton
1947	F. Daly
1948	F. Daly
1949	D. Rees
1950	D. Rees
1951	H. Weetman
1952	F. Daly
1953	M. Faulkner
1954	P. Thomson
1955	K. Bousfield
1956	J. Panton
1957	C. O'Connor
1958	H. Weetman
1959	D. Snell
1960	E. Brown
1961	P. Thomson
1962	E. Brown
1963	D. Thomas
1964	N.C. Coles
1965	N.C. Coles
1966	P. Thomson
1967	P. Thomson
1968	B.G.C. Huggett
1969	M. Bembridge
1970	T. Horton
1971	*Not played*
1972	J. Garner
1973	N.C. Coles
1974	J. Newton
1975	E. Polland
1976	B. Barnes
1977	H. Baiocchi
1978	M. James
1979	D. Smyth

PHILIP MORRIS INTERNATIONAL TEAM

1976	United States

PICCADILLY MEDAL

1962–67, 72 holes strokeplay; 1968 matchplay (fourball); 1969–75 matchplay decided on strokes (1969–72, 36-hole final); 1976 72 holes strokeplay. "Medal" in title from 1969. Tournament not played 1963.

1962	P. Thomson
1963	*Not played*
1964	J. Martin
1965	P. Butler
1966	B. Hunt
1967	P. Butler
1968	H. Jackson
	R. Emery
1969	P. Alliss
1970	J. Lister
1971	P. Oosterhuis
1972	T. Horton
1973	P. Oosterhuis
1974	M. Bembridge
1975	B. Shearer
1976	S. Torrance

JOHN PLAYER CLASSIC

1970	C. Clark
1971	*Not played*
1972	R. J. Charles
1973	C. Coody

JOHN PLAYER TROPHY

1970	C. Clark
1971	*Not played*
1972	R. Whitehead

PLM OPEN

1986	P. Senior
1987	H. Clark
1988	F. Nobilo
1989	M. Harwood
1990	R. Rafferty

PRINGLE OF SCOTLAND

Known as 1969–74 Seniors

1964	H. Henning
1965	C. Legrange
1966	N. Coles
1967	A. Jacklin
1969	J. Panton
1970	M. Faulker
1971	K. Nagle
1972	K. Bousfield
1973	K. Nagle
1974	E. Lester

ROMA MASTERS

1992	J-M. Canizares
1993	J. Van de Velde

SANYO OPEN

1982	N. Coles
1983	D. Smyth
1984	S. Torrance
1985	S. Ballesteros
1986	J.-M. Olazabal

SCANDINAVIAN ENTERPRISE OPEN

1973	R.J. Charles
1974	A. Jacklin
1975	G. Burns
1976	H. Baiocchi
1977	B. Byman
1978	S. Ballesteros
1979	A. Lyle
1980	G. Norman
1981	S. Ballesteros
1982	B. Byman
1983	S. Torrance
1984	I. Woosnam
1985	I. Baker-Finch
1986	G. Turner
1987	G. Brand Jr
1988	S. Ballesteros
1989	R. Rafferty
1990	C. Stadler

THE SCOTTISH OPEN

Known as Bells (1986–94)

1986	D. Feherty
1987	I. Woosnam
1988	B. Lane
1989	M. Allen
1990	I. Woosnam
1991	C. Parry
1992	P. O'Malley
1993	J. Parnevik
1994	C. Mason
1995	W. Riley
1996	I. Woosnam

SKOL LAGER INDIVIDUAL

1977	N. Faldo

SUMRIE CLOTHES

Known as Sumrie Clothes (1968–73); Better-ball from 1969; Sumrie-Bournemouth (1974–78). Tournament not played 1971, 1977.

1968	B.G.C. Huggett
1969	M. Bembridge
	A. Gallardo
1970	B. Hunt
	N. Coles
1971	*Not played*
1972	B.G.C. Huggett
	M. Gregson
1973	N. Coles
	B. Hunt
1974	C. Clark
	P. Butler
1975	J. Newton
	J. O'Leary
1976	E. Darcy
	C. O'Connor Jr
1977	*Not played*
1978	E. Darcy
	C. O'Connor Jr

SUNBEAM ELECTRIC

Combined with the Scottish Open (1972–73).

1971	P. Oosterhuis
1972	N. Coles
1973	G. Marsh

TIMEX OPEN

1983	S. Ballesteros
1984	M. Clayton

TOURNOI PERRIER DE PARIS

1994	P. Baker and
	D.J. Russell
1995	J-M. Olazabal and
	S. Ballesteros

TPD YOUNG PROFESSIONALS

Known as TPD Under-25 1976

1975	D. Hayes
1976	H. Clark

TURESPANA OPEN MEDITERRANIA

Known as Amex (1990), Fujitsu (1991), Turespana (1993–95).

1990	I. Woosnam
1991	I. Woosnam
1992	J-M. Olazabal
1993	F. Nobilo
1994	J-M. Olazabal
1995	R. Karlsson

TUNISIAN OPEN

1982	A. Garrido
1983	M. James
1984	S. Torrance
1985	S. Bennett

UAP UNDER 25s EUROPEAN OPEN

1988	J. Van de Velde
1989	S. Hamill
1990	P. Baker
1991	P. McGinley
1992	P. Lawrie
1994	P. Talbot

UNIROYAL INTERNATIONAL

1976	T. Horton
1977	S. Ballesteros

VOLVO OPEN DI FIRENZE

Known as Volvo Open (1989).

1989	V. Singh
1990	E. Romero
1991	A. Forsbrand
1992	A. Forsbrand

WELSH GOLF CLASSIC

Known as Coral (1980–82).

1979	M. James
1980	A. Lyle
1981	D. Smith
1982	G. Brand Jr

W. D. & H.O. WILLS

1968	P. Butler
1969	B. Gallacher
1970	A. Jacklin
1971	B. Hunt
1972	P. Thomson
1973	C. Coody
1974	N. Coles

UNITED STATES PGA TOUR

Written off at the start of the decade as a colourless product full of faceless personalities, the United States PGA Tour is now the chic place to be in sport, its protagonists feted wherever they go. It is a startling transformation, one for which the players – and one golfer in particular – are entirely responsible.

It was the US Tour's extreme good fortune that when the television contracts came up for renewal in 1996, Tiger Woods had just exploded on to the golf scene. After his victory in the 1997 Masters in his first tournament as a professional, the game crossed the final frontier, appealing to minorities in a way that had never happened before. The resultant television deals have provoked an extraordinary rise in prize money, which has doubled in just four years. To think, as recently as 1977 the players were competing for total purses of under $10 million. Now that figure has risen to a mind-boggling $132 million.

In 1999 it is estimated that the top 40 players on the money list will all earn in excess of $1 million. That is just for one season, by the way. Roughly 75 golfers will make over $620,000, which just happens to be the figure that the US Tour's most prolific winner of all time, Sam Snead, made over the course of his entire career.

It was, as they say, an entirely different ball game back in the early, cash-strapped, play-it-by-ear days when the players needed to possess the spirit of pioneers. There were huge distances to cover, usually by car, cheap lodgings to find if prize money had been elusive of late, and even if it had not in most cases. Tournaments were loosely organized (golfers who got there first teed off first) and players had to have other sources of income because prize money was small and the available cash did not go far down the list of also-rans.

Contrast that with the modern tour event, which is run with military precision. These days the players will go bananas if their luxury courtesy car is five minutes late in picking them up from the airport, or alternatively the local airfield if they have arrived in their own jet. Accommodation is booked in the best hotels money can buy, while at the tournaments themselves all the finest medical attention is available. Before or after a round a player can then relax in the tour's own gymnasium.

This is progress on a grand scale, and it is continued on the golf course. Where once players were simply happy to pitch up anywhere, now they play at venues which are nearly always in impeccable condition. At some courses the fairways are so smooth they are better than the greens 40 years ago. The idea of having to fashion a shot from a divot, once commonplace, is now so rare as to be virtually unknown.

Back in the early days the players used to combine club duties with playing. Since the tour began with winter events in Florida, Texas, and other southern states, they could also hold down a club job in the north during the months when play was difficult or impossible, and custom at professional shops correspondingly light. The tournaments, often at tourist resorts, were usually sponsored by the local chamber of commerce, for the results would be reported in the great cities of the north-eastern seaboard and mid-west, giving publicity at a reasonable rate to the fact that where the golfers were there was sun. In this way chilly northerners were made well aware of the best places to take vacations.

There is a restless quality about many Americans, the constant drive to take to the road and see if life is better in the next town. The early pros embodied this frontier spirit. "Wild" Bill Mehlhorn – whose father had left Germany rather than join the ranks of Kaiser Wilhelm's army – kept dollars in his pocket by giving lessons en route to the winter tour and selling magazine subscriptions.

This desire to constantly keep on the move was no doubt fuelled by the fact that the living to be made from a pro shop was often not all that great. The players may have possessed the ability to teach the game but their marketing skills were primitive, to say the least that side of the game was left to the suppliers of golf clubs, clothing and the rest. These middlemen made it a hard life for many club professionals, and clubs were only too ready to claim profits on ball sales, the pro's main stock-in-trade.

It was because of this blatant exploitation that the United States Professional Golfers' Association came into being in 1916. It was, and remains, an organization to protect the interests of the club professional.

A good many British prejudices still ruled in America, inimical to professional golf, for the amateur was still king, and the paid man looked down upon. Professionals in England commanded a good deal more respect (though not as far as permitting entrance to clubhouses) partly due to the mighty reputations, in technique and competitive drive, of players such as Harry Vardon and J.H. Taylor, first and second in the 1900 US Open, and the excitement of watching money matches. What a treat, for example, for the Scottish islanders of Islay to watch Vardon and Taylor take on James Braid and Alex Herd in an international fourball on the newly built Machrie course.

In the United States, tournament life took a different route. The PGA gave the professionals a peg to hang their season on with the USPGA, for which the first winner in 1916,

Jim Barnes, received $500 – about what Vardon would get in a big-money challenge match in the Old Country.

The USPGA and the US Open, however, were far from developing into the central events in a well-ordered tour, the growth of which began haphazardly in the Sunbelt of the south immediately around the turn of the century, with prize money reaching three figures in Florida resorts. No detailed chronology exists of how it began, except to say that winter tournaments in California, Texas and Florida in the early 1920s were key elements.

Amateur events were held at the resorts long before the First World War, and pro tournaments grew up alongside, usually provoking less interest from the Press.

It was clear that what the professional game needed was a heroic figure everyone could look up to. Amateurs in particular and US golf in general certainly found one at the 1913 US Open – Francis Ouimet. Walter Hagen almost achieved that status in the same championship, but fell just short of the epochal play-off in which Ouimet beat Vardon and Ted Ray. Such was Hagen's confidence that he might well have surprised all three; 12 months later Hagen was Open champion, and became leader in the considerable task of transforming

Walter Hagen – one of the earliest pioneers of Pro Tour golf

Sam Snead – the US Tour's most prolific winner of all time whose career spanned three decades

the golf pro into an envied (though not always prosperous) and admired (if not entirely respected) pillar of society.

Hagen's role contrasted greatly with the touring pro of today. He depended less on prize money and more on exhibition matches. Instead of defending his first USPGA title he played in just such a match, and attracted thousands of spectators to his one-day appearances, charging admission of one dollar. He had the happy knack of being able not only to impress the galleries with his golf but to entertain them with a line of chat that would have probably led him to the music-hall stage if he had not made it on the golfing version.

Instead this natural comedian created his own lucrative theatre of the open air, aided by such players as Gene Sarazen, just out of his teens and winner of the US Open and USPGA titles in 1922. This was the PGA Hagen had passed up to play in an exhibition, so another exhibition – a challenge match between the two – was set up, expansively billed as being for the Golf Championship of the World. Hype may be a new word, but it is assuredly not a new phenomenon.

Sarazen, two down after the first two rounds at Oakmont, was in pain before the final holes at the palatial Westchester-Biltmore Country Club in New York. In wind and rain he struggled on, overtook Hagen, and then the following day had an emergency operation to have his appendix removed. His prize was $2,000, and Hagen received half that amount. It was huge money at the time – winning the US Open was not worth $1,000 until 1929.

One pillar upon which the PGA Tour was built was the Texas Open, founded in 1923 by businessmen in San Antonio. The total purse was a record $5,000. Another was erected three years later when the Los Angeles Open was created by the city's Junior Chamber of Commerce; this one was worth $10,000. A year later other Californian cities organized pro events. The tour was now acquiring some form of order, the players starting in the west early in the New Year, moving east to Texas and Florida, then up the east coast for spring and summer events. The total prize money on offer in 1928 came to $77,000. This supported a growing band of men who depended almost entirely on their playing, rather than their club pro skills. And so Walter Hagen was no longer a unique species of touring pro.

Regarding central organization, though, there remained none until a succession of newspapermen, who had every reason to want the tour to expand, played their part. Of these, the most influential was Bob Harlow, son of a Congregationalist minister. He also just happened to be Walter Hagen's manager.

No man has a better claim than Harlow to be the chief innovator of the PGA Tour although he had his running battles with the PGA themselves. Like those before him who had tried to bring order to the tour, he wanted to supplement his income from newspaper articles, and as agent for Hagen and other leading players, with a salary or commission for putting tournaments together and persuading sponsors to part with cash.

After lengthy discussions he got a $100-a-week salary but in 1932 the PGA sacked him because, they claimed, he was spending too much time on his activities outside tour business. Some officials, however, were upset at the growing image of the players, who they looked upon as a pampered, footloose gang of opportunists, who unjustly commanded too many choice club pro jobs on the basis of their playing prowess.

Perhaps there was an element of truth in this but that was hardly Harlow's problem. It was he who rationalized the tour with a showman's flair. He used every contemporary method of advertising to publicize tournaments, issued lists of tournament pairings and tee-times (no first-come, first-served with Harlow), got golf clothing manufacturers to supplement the prize fund when local sponsors were short on dollars, issued orders of merit, encouraged club volunteers to help in running tournaments (a thriving activity today) and in his first year almost doubled the tour purses.

It was hardly surprising, therefore, that the PGA were forced to rethink, and the following year Harlow was back on the payroll. By this stage the American economy had been flattened by the Depression, yet Harlow invented the minimum purse and worked out a system by which the best players were exempt from qualifying. Already the players, eager for more cash and freedom from the PGA and its fixation with club professionals, were looking at ways to set up a rival organization. This would reach a head in the 1960s when the rift widened to such an extent as to involve threats of boycott.

Golf had moved on quite a way by the time another journalist, Fred Corcoran, became involved in 1936. His salary was $5,000 a year. A natural publicist, he improved information services for the public with coloured scoreboards and brought a greater range of sponsors, including financial firms and airlines, into play.

Though the sums pocketed by the leading performer on tour had declined radically at times in the depressed 1930s, better times, looser corporate purse-strings and the sheer quality of professionals such as Ben Hogan, Sam Snead and Byron Nelson made life easier for tour managers as peace broke out in 1945.

Golf was gaining a profile that transcended the game. Nelson's amazing achievements in 1945, when he won 11 consecutive tournaments and 19 overall, saw him recognized as the Male Athlete of the Year by the Associated Press. Then there was Ben Hogan's extraordinary comeback from his horrific car accident, which even attracted the attention of Hollywood.

The introduction of Arnold Palmer, the greatest crowd-pleaser since Hagen, taken together with the advent of televised golf, changed many things. Television began with local coverage of the 1947 US Open at St Louis, MO, and soon progressed to a national broadcast under the influence of George May, promoter of the Tam O'Shanter National Open in Chicago.

Arnold Palmer – his arrival onto the professional golf scene coincided with the advent of televised golf

May's tournament in particular and golf in general had a golden stroke of luck in 1953. May was not present when ABC television offered national coverage for $32,000. Chet Posson, May's assistant, took a chance and accepted. May, a management consultant, said when he heard what Posson had done: "I don't care if it costs us a million. Do it!"

So more people – an estimated two million – saw the Tam O'Shanter of 1953 than had witnessed any previous event in history. So that was one piece of good fortune; what placed the tin lid on things was the drama of the finish. Lew Worsham won it with a 135-yard wedge shot to the final green that disappeared into the hole for an eagle two. One minute the commentators were congratulating Chandler Harper on at least making a play-off for the $25,000 first prize, since Worsham needed a birdie to tie; the next the luckless Harper had lost by a stroke.

Naturally the shot was the talk of television, and it made Worsham a wealthy man. In addition to his winnings, he also won a contract to do 25 exhibitions at $1,000 each.

It was television that gave golf the Midas touch, and continues to fuel the phenomenal growth. Prize money doubled in 10 years from $6.7 million in 1970 and this had tripled by 1990. Sponsors could now use golf to reach consumers across the nation. In 1955 the World Championship of Golf offered the first $100,000 prize in PGA history. Arnold Palmer, the game's top man in 1963, took home winnings of $128,230. The first recorded leading money winner, Paul Runyon in 1934, had won $6,767.

The leading post-war players would soon be thinking aeroplane instead of automobile. The younger ones, many of whom were not long out of college, had no knowledge of mending clubs and selling chocolate bars across the counter. Once television rights began to swell, tour pros could not see why the PGA should get much of what their skill alone, as they saw it, was channelling into the prize pot.

Boycott threats by the touring professionals in 1967 were followed by an overt move for independence – and an announcement that the breakaway American Professional Golfers had a $3.5 million tour programme for 1969. In this particular poker game the PGA had two pairs, the tournament players a royal flush. Without the leading players, which now included Jack Nicklaus – a prime mover in the negotiations with Gardner Dickenson – television and sponsors did not fancy PGA golf at all; only Sam Snead stuck by the old regime.

So the players became free men, their Magna Carta granted unconditionally under what was no more than a convenient fiction, the creation of a new PGA division. Harlow would have enjoyed this moment but sadly he had died in 1954, still wedded to his reporting career. He would have been totally at ease with the fact that golf is the only sport whose professionals run their own events. In recent years the PGA Tour players have even built their own courses. They are known as Tournament Players Championship (TPC) courses, and in 1999 no fewer than 10 of them were of sufficiently high standard to host tour events. The TPC network now includes facilities in Japan, Thailand and China, as well as all over the United States.

The result of this ownership is that the game has managed to avoid the sort of "them and us" situation that has been so costly in other big American sports in recent years. It was exactly that sort of schism that led to the loss of the 1994 World Series in baseball, and it needed several years of patient diplomacy and some remarkable achievements by a number of players and the New York Yankees team before the game's fans forgave both the employers and employees in 1998. A similar rift led to the start of the 1998–99 basketball season being delayed for several months.

Yet the division in golf was not without bitterness, and the club players were sore for some years afterwards at what they believed to be the greed of the tournament professionals. Clubmaker MacGregor, it was reported, got requests from club pros to remove Jack Nicklaus's name from their products. This was an extreme reaction, one that overlooked the fact that it was almost certainly the feats of Nicklaus, Palmer and company that dragged the amateurs into the club shops in the first place.

Joseph Dey was the tour's first Commissioner, taking up the post in 1968. The modern PGA Tour was born. In 1974 he was succeeded by a former professional, Deane Beman, who proved an astute businessman. He stayed in the post for almost 20 years and under his shrewd eye the PGA Tour developed at an extraordinary rate. When he took over its assets were $730,000; when he left in 1993 they were more than $200 million.

Beman presided over a number of landmarks, including the relocation of the PGA Tour's headquarters from Washington to Ponte Vedra Beach in Florida. In 1980 he oversaw the foundation of the Senior Tour, and in 1986 the first $1 million prize fund offered at an event. That was the Las Vegas Invitational. In 1999 there is not an event that has a purse less than two-and-a-half times that amount.

In 1990 the Ben Hogan Tour was set up, to recognize the huge increase in the numbers of players wanting to join the tour. This became an invaluable nursery slope where players could learn their trade and graduate to the regular tour. In 1993 it was taken over by clothing manufacturer Nike, and has continued to evolve. Among the players who have come through the Nike Tour are John Daly, Stuart Cink and David Duval.

One downside of Beman's reign was the xenophobia that he allowed to go unchecked among certain American professionals. In the mid-1980s there was no doubt that Europe had the best players in the world and naturally the sponsors of American tournaments wanted to see them in action. So did the sponsors in Europe.

A number of American players saw this as cherry-picking

Tiger Woods – his appearance to the professional ranks saw an unprecedented boom in the game's popularity

John Daly – two-time major winner and a successful graduate of the Nike Tour

and made their feelings known. The better American players tried to make their voices heard, because they saw it as jealousy on the part of their compatriots.

Sadly, Beman sided with the xenophobes. He drafted in legislation that said that all foreign players had to play in at least 15 tournaments to keep their US Tour cards, otherwise they were restricted just to the majors. It was an outrageous decision, one that deservedly attracted the wrath of all fair-minded citizens.

It needed the more rounded mind of Tim Finchem, appointed in 1994, to work out a more equable solution. Foreign players can now play in the three major championships in America, the Players' Championship, the two new World Championship events in the States, and accept six tournament invites without having a US Tour card. It is a fair compromise, one that recognizes the responsibilities that these players have to their home tours as well as to America.

In the 1990s the lot of the tournament professional, as we have seen, has reached new heights of luxury. Occasionally there are grumblings of discontent, however, usually from the rank and file. In 1998 a group of players got together to campaign for prize money to be paid regardless of whether they made the cut or not. They argued that they still had expenses to pay to get to a tournament – should this not be recognized with cheques for all?

But this is surely the first step down the road to madness. Many sports fans look at the guaranteed cheques in sports such as baseball and basketball and get angry at the sheer greed of the players.

Golf needs to avoid being tarred by this brush. One of its lasting virtues is the fact that its players get paid solely on the quality of their performances in the present, not in the past. In 1988 Chip Beck made almost a million dollars as he turned in performances of consistent quality. Ten years later he made just $10,000, precisely because he could not hit his hat.

By retaining this system the players deserve to avoid all accusations of greed. Yes, the top performers are unbelievably well paid, but inasmuch as any sportsman deserves to earn seven-figure cheques they should be at the top of the list because their income depends upon performing day-in, day-out, not on their batting average for the previous season. And if they run up an injury, or play badly, they don't get paid at all.

It is easy, at first glance, to look from the outside and declare that the modern professional has things all his own way. But it is a high-wire act, with many distractions, and many other performers eager for their share of the action.

The future? Five years ago it looked as if the US Tour might relinquish its position as the powerhouse of world golf as Greg Norman's proposed World Tour took centre stage. This would have involved ten events for 40 players with guaranteed purses of $3 million at each event.

How ironic it would have been if this had got off the ground. After the tour players had left the club pros behind, now the world's elite would have parted company from the rest of their tour brethren. Clearly, it would have left many US Tour events looking like second-division tournaments, and no wonder Commissioner Tim Finchem moved swiftly to try to kill it at birth.

He was helped by the imminent television deal mentioned above. What a wonderful bargaining position to be in, to go into negotiations with Tiger Woods as the ultimate marketing tool. And what a deal it was with which Finchem emerged. In April 1997 he was able to announce that in four years revenue would quadruple to $200 million. In 1997 the average prize money per tournament was $2 million. Just two years later it was $3.5 million. But all this would only work, Finchem said, if the new World Tour was abandoned.

Furthermore, the advent of three new World Championship events countered Norman's stance that the players did not meet enough in top competition. No wonder all this became sufficient to cut Norman's proposed tour off at the first corner.

And so the PGA Tour goes from strength to strength. It is Finchem's express intention to make the top players as wealthy as basketball stars. He counters the argument that they have much longer careers and so many more years to earn their money with the statistic that between 1993 and 1998 there was a turnover of 50 percent in players who obtained tour cards.

Finchem's tour is now so successful that in February, 1999, when the first World Championship of Golf event was held for the top 64 players in California, he was still able to put on another tournament for the rest in Tucson, AZ, with a prize fund of $2 million.

So it continues. In 1998 the World Golf Village was opened in north Florida, just 40 minutes from the PGA Tour's headquarters in Jacksonville. It was Beman who envisaged this project in 1987; now it has blossomed into a $350 million mega-project occupying no less than 6,300 acres. It houses the World Golf Hall of Fame, and honours all the influential figures the sport has seen, from Old and Young Tom Morris, through to Severiano Ballesteros, who was inducted in 1999. All told there are 73 members in the Hall of Fame, and they are honoured in a 75,000 sq. ft centrepiece of the World Golf Village.

Spread around the lake in front of the Hall of Fame, the other elements of the World Golf Village have developed. There is a 300-room resort hotel and convention centre, residential areas in the Village, a World Golf Library and Resource centre, and a huge shopping facility.

There is also – of course – a golf course. Named The Slammer and The Squire, it honours two of the pioneers who set the ball rolling for the PGA Tour all those years ago: Gene Sarazen and Sam Snead.

When they opened it in 1998, the wheel, in a way, had turned full circle.

US PGA TOUR STATISTICS

Mercedes Championships

Formerly known as the Mercedes Tournament of Champions (1953–1974), Mony Tournament of Champions (1975–1989), Infiniti Tournament of Champions (1990-1993).

Year	Winner
1953	Al Besselink
1954	Art Wall
1955	Gene Littler
1956	Gene Littler
1957	Gene Littler
1958	Stan Leonard
1959	Mike Souchak
1960	Jerry Barber
1961	Sam Snead
1962	Arnold Palmer
1963	Jack Nicklaus
1964	Jack Nicklaus
1965	Arnold Palmer
1966	Arnold Palmer
1967	Frank Beard
1968	Don January
1969	Gary Player
1970	Frank Beard
1971	Jack Nicklaus
1972	Bobby Mitchell
1973	Jack Nicklaus
1974	Johnny Miller
1975	Al Geiberger
1976	Don January
1977	Jack Nicklaus
1978	Gary Player
1979	Tom Watson
1981	Lee Trevino
1980	Tom Watson
1982	Lanny Wadkins
1983	Lanny Wadkins
1984	Tom Watson
1985	Tom Kite
1986	Calvin Peete
1987	Mac O'Grady
1988	Steve Pate
1989	Steve Jones
1990	Paul Azinger
1991	Tom Kite
1992	Steve Elkington
1993	Davis Love III
1994	Phil Mickelson
1995	Steve Elkington
1996	Mark O'Meara
1997	Tiger Woods
1998	Phil Mickelson

Phoenix Open Invitational

1935	Ky Laffoon
1936–38	*Not played*
1939	Byron Nelson
1940	Ed Oliver
1941–43	*Not played*
1944	Harold McSpaden
1945	Byron Nelson
1946	Ben Hogan
1947	Ben Hogan
1948	Bobby Locke
1949	Jimmy Demaret
1950	Jimmy Demaret
1951	Lew Worsham
1952	Lloyd Mangrum
1953	Lloyd Mangrum
1954	Ed Furgol
1955	Gene Littler
1956	Cary Middlecoff
1957	Billy Casper
1958	Ken Venturi
1959	Gene Littler
1960	Jack Fleck
1961	Arnold Palmer
1962	Arnold Palmer
1963	Arnold Palmer
1964	Jack Nicklaus
1965	Rod Funseth
1966	Dudley Wysong
1967	Julius Boros
1968	George Knudson
1969	Gene Littler
1970	Dale Douglas
1971	Miller Barber
1972	Homero Blancas
1973	Bruce Crampton
1974	Johnny Miller
1975	Johnny Miller
1976	Bob Gilder
1977	Jerry Pate
1978	Miller Barber
1979	Ben Crenshaw
1980	Jeff Mitchell
1981	David Graham
1982	Lanny Wadkins
1983	Bob Gilder
1984	Tom Purtzer
1985	Calvin Peete
1986	Hal Sutton
1987	Paul Azinger
1988	Sandy Lyle
1989	Mark Calcavecchia
1990	Tommy Armour III
1991	Nolan Henke
1992	Mark Calcavecchia
1993	Lee Janzen
1994	Bill Glasson
1995	Vijay Singh
1996	Phil Mickelson
1997	Steve Jones
1998	Jesper Parnevik

AT&T Pebble Beach National Pro-Am

Formerly known as Bing Crosby Professional Amateur (1937–52), The Bing Crosby Professional Amateur Invitational (1953–55), The Bing Crosby National Professional-Amateur Golf Championship (1956–58), Bing Crosby National (1960–63), Bing Crosby National Professional-Amateur (1964–85).

1937	Sam Snead
1938	Sam Snead
1939	Dutch Harrison
1940	Ed Oliver
1941	Sam Snead
1942	John Dawson
1943–46	*Not played*
1947	Tie-Ed Furgol, George Fazio
1948	Lloyd Mangrum
1949	Ben Hogan
1950	Tie: Sam Snead, Jack Burke Jr, Smiley Quick, Dave Douglas
1951	Byron Nelson
1952	Jimmy Demaret
1953	Lloyd Mangrum
1954	Dutch Harrison
1955	Cary Middlecoff
1956	Cary Middlecoff
1957	Jay Hebert
1958	Billy Casper
1959	Art Wall, Gene Littler
1960	Ken Venturi
1961	Bob Rosburg
1962	Doug Ford
1963	Billy Casper
1964	Tony Lema
1965	Bruce Crampton
1966	Don Massengale
1967	Jack Nicklaus
1968	Johnny Pott
1969	George Archer
1970	Bert Yancey
1971	Tom Shaw
1972	Jack Nicklaus
1973	Jack Nicklaus
1974	Johnny Miller
1975	Gene Littler
1976	Ben Crenshaw
1977	Tom Watson
1978	Tom Watson
1979	Lon Hinkle
1980	George Burns
1981	John Cook
1982	Jim Simons
1983	Tom Kite
1984	Hale Irwin
1985	Mark O'Meara
1986	Fuzzy Zoeller
1987	Johnny Miller
1988	Steve Jones

1989	Mark O'Meara
1990	Mark O'Meara
1991	Paul Azinger
1992	Mark O'Meara
1993	Brett Ogle
1994	Johnny Miller
1995	Peter Jacobsen
1996	*Not played*
1997	Mark O'Meara
1998	Phil Mickelson

Buick Invitational

Formerly known as the San Diego Open (1952–54), Convair-San Diego Open (1955–56), San Diego Open Invitational (1957–67), Andy Williams-San Diego Open Invitational (1968–80), Wickes-Andy Williams San Diego Open (1981–82), Isuzu/Andy Williams San Diego Open (1983–85), Shearson Lehman Brothers Andy Williams Open (1986–87), Shearson Lehman Hutton Andy Williams Open (1988), Shearson Lehman Hutton Open (1989–90), Shearson Lehman Brothers Open (1991), Buick Invitational of California (1992–95).

1952	Ted Kroll
1953	Tommy Bolt
1954	Gene Littler
1955	Tommy Bolt
1956	Bob Rosburg
1957	Arnold Palmer
1958	No Tournament
1959	Marty Furgol
1960	Mike Souchak
1961	Arnold Palmer
1962	Tommy Jacobs
1963	Gary Player
1964	Art Wall
1965	Wes Ellis
1966	Billy Casper
1967	Bob Goalby
1968	Tom Weiskopf
1969	Jack Nicklaus
1970	Pete Brown
1971	George Archer
1972	Paul Harney
1973	Bob Dickson
1974	Bobby Nichols
1975	J.C. Snead
1976	J.C. Snead
1977	Tom Watson
1978	Jay Haas
1979	Fuzzy Zoeller
1980	Tom Watson
1981	Bruce Lietzke
1982	Johnny Miller
1983	Gary Hallberg
1984	Gary Koch
1985	Woody Blackburn
1986	Bob Tway
1987	George Burns
1988	Steve Pate
1989	Greg Twiggs
1990	Dan Forsman
1991	Jay Don Blake
1992	Steve Pate
1993	Phil Mickelson
1994	Craig Stadler
1995	Peter Jacobsen
1996	Davis Love III
1997	Mark O'Meara
1998	Scott Simpson

United Airlines Hawaiian Open

Formerly known as the Hawaiian Open (1965–90), United Hawaiian Open (1991).

1965	Gay Brewer
1966	Ted Makalena
1967	Dudley Wysong
1968	Lee Trevino
1969	Bruce Crampton
1970	No Tournament
1971	Tom Shaw
1972	Grier Jones
1973	John Schlee
1974	Jack Nicklaus
1975	Gary Groh
1976	Ben Crenshaw
1977	Bruce Lietzke
1978	Hubert Green
1979	Hubert Green
1980	Andy Bean
1981	Hale Irwin
1982	Wayne Levi
1983	Isao Aoki
1984	Jack Renner
1985	Mark O'Meara
1986	Corey Pavin
1987	Corey Pavin
1988	Lanny Wadkins
1989	Gene Sauers
1990	David Ishii
1991	Lanny Wadkins
1992	John Cook
1993	Howard Twitty
1994	Brett Ogle
1995	John Morse
1996	Jim Furyk
1997	Paul Stankowski
1998	John Huston

Tucson Chrysler Classic

1945	Ray Mangrum
1946	Jimmy Demaret
1947	Jimmy Demaret
1948	Skip Alexander
1949	Lloyd Mangrum
1950	Chandler Harper
1951	Lloyd Mangrum
1952	Henry Williams Jr
1953	Tommy Bolt
1954	*Not played*
1955	Tommy Bolt
1956	Ted Kroll
1957	Dow Finsterwald
1958	Lionel Hebert
1959	Gene Littler
1960	Don January
1961	Dave Hill
1962	Phil Rogers
1963	Don January
1964	Jack Cupit
1965	Bob Charles
1966	Joe Campbell
1967	Arnold Palmer
1968	George Knudson
1969	Lee Trevino
1970	Lee Trevino
1971	J.C. Snead
1972	Miller Barber
1973	Bruce Crampton
1974	Johnny Miller
1975	Johnny Miller
1976	Johnny Miller
1977	Bruce Lietzke
1978	Tom Watson
1979	Bruce Lietzke
1980	Jim Colbert
1981	Johnny Miller
1982	Craig Stadler
1983	Gil Morgan
1984	Tom Watson
1984	Gene Littler
1985	Jim Thorpe
1985	Harold Henning
1986	Don January
1987	Mike Reid
1988	David Frost
1989	*Not played*
1990	Robert Gamez
1991	Phil Mickelson
1992	Lee Janzen
1993	Larry Mize
1994	Andrew Magee
1995	Phil Mickelson
1996	Phil Mickelson
1997	Jeff Sluman
1998	David Duval

Nissan Open

Formerly known as the Glen Campbell Los Angeles Open (1971–83), Los Angeles Open (1984–86), Los Angeles Open Presented by Nissan (1987–88), Nissan Los Angeles Open (1989–94).

1926	Harry Cooper
1927	Bobby Cruickshank
1928	Mac Smith
1929	Mac Smith
1930	Densmore Shute
1931	Ed Dudley
1932	Mac Smith
1933	Craig Wood
1934	Mac Smith
1935	Vic Ghezzi
1936	Jimmy Hines
1937	Harry Cooper
1938	Jimmy Thomson
1939	Jimmy Demaret
1940	Lawson Little
1941	Johnny Bulla
1942	Ben Hogan
1943	No Tournament
1944	Harold McSpaden
1945	Sam Snead
1946	Byron Nelson
1947	Ben Hogan
1948	Ben Hogan
1949	Lloyd Mangrum
1950	Sam Snead
1951	Lloyd Mangrum
1952	Tommy Bolt

1953	Lloyd Mangrum
1954	Fred Wampler
1955	Gene Littler
1956	Lloyd Mangrum
1957	Doug Ford
1958	Frank Stranahan
1959	Ken Venturi
1960	Dow Finsterwald
1961	Bob Goalby
1962	Phil Rodgers
1963	Arnold Palmer
1964	Paul Harney
1965	Paul Harney
1966	Arnold Palmer
1967	Arnold Palmer
1968	Billy Casper
1969	Charles Sifford
1970	Billy Casper
1971	Bob Lunn
1972	George Archer
1973	Rod Funseth
1974	Dave Stockton
1975	Pat Fitzsimons
1976	Hale Irwin
1977	Tom Purtzer
1978	Gil Morgan
1979	Lanny Wadkins
1980	Tom Watson
1981	Johnny Miller
1982	Tom Watson
1983	Gil Morgan
1984	David Edwards
1985	Lanny Wadkins
1986	Doug Tewell
1987	Tze-Chung Chen
1988	Chip Beck
1989	Mark Calcavecchia
1990	Fred Couples
1991	Ted Schulz
1992	Fred Couples
1993	Tom Kite
1994	Corey Pavin
1995	Corey Pavin
1996	Craig Stadler
1997	Nick Faldo
1998	Billy Mayfair

Doral-Ryder Open

Formerly known as the Doral CC Open Invitational (1962–69), Doral-Eastern Open Invitational (1970–86).

1962	Billy Casper
1963	Dan Sikes
1964	Billy Casper
1965	Doug Sanders
1966	Phil Rodgers
1967	Doug Sanders
1968	Gardner Dickinson
1969	Tom Shaw
1970	Mike Hill
1971	J.C. Snead
1972	Jack Nicklaus
1973	Lee Trevino
1974	Brian Allin
1975	Jack Nicklaus
1976	Hubert Green
1977	Andy Bean
1978	Tom Weiskopf
1979	Mark McCumber
1980	Raymond Floyd
1981	Raymond Floyd
1982	Andy Bean
1983	Gary Koch
1984	Tom Kite
1985	Mark McCumber
1986	Andy Bean
1987	Lanny Wadkins
1988	Ben Crenshaw
1989	Bill Glasson
1990	Greg Norman
1991	Rocco Mediate
1992	Raymond Floyd
1993	Greg Norman
1994	John Huston
1995	Nick Faldo
1996	Greg Norman
1997	Steve Elkington
1998	Michael Bradley
1999	Steve Elkington

Bob Hope Chrysler Classic

1960	Arnold Palmer
1961	Billy Maxwell
1962	Arnold Palmer
1963	Jack Nicklaus
1964	Tommy Jacobs
1965	Billy Casper
1966	Doug Sanders
1967	Tom Nieporte
1968	Arnold Palmer
1969	Billy Casper
1970	Bruce Devlin
1971	Arnold Palmer
1972	Bob Rosburg
1973	Arnold Palmer
1974	Hubert Green
1975	Johnny Miller
1976	Johnny Miller
1977	Rik Massengale
1978	Bill Rogers
1979	John Mahaffey
1980	Craig Stadler
1981	Bruce Lietzke
1982	Ed Fiori
1983	Keith Fergus
1984	John Mahaffey
1985	Lanny Wadkins
1986	Donnie Hammond
1987	Corey Pavin
1988	Jay Haas
1989	Steve Jones
1990	Peter Jacobsen
1991	Corey Pavin
1992	John Cook
1993	Tom Kite
1994	Scott Hoch
1995	Kenny Perry
1996	Mark Brooks
1997	John Cook
1998	Fred Couples

Honda Classic

Formerly known as Jackie Gleason's Inverrary Classic (1972, 1974–80), Jackie Gleason's Inverrary National Airlines Classic (1973), American Motors Inverrary Classic (1981), Honda Inverrary Classic (1982–83).

1972	Tom Weiskopf
1973	Lee Trevino
1974	Leonard Thompson
1975	Bob Murphy
1976	*Not played*
1977	Jack Nicklaus
1978	Jack Nicklaus
1979	Larry Nelson
1980	Johnny Miller
1981	Tom Kite
1982	Hale Irwin
1983	Johnny Miller
1984	Bruce Lietzke
1985	Curtis Strange
1986	Kenny Knox
1987	Mark Calcavecchia
1988	Joey Sindelar
1989	Blaine McCallister
1990	John Huston
1991	Steve Pate
1992	Corey Pavin
1993	Fred Couples
1994	Nick Price
1995	Mark O'Meara
1996	Tim Herron
1997	Stuart Appleby
1998	Mark Calcavecchia

Bay Hill Invitational

Formerly known as the Florida Citrus Open Invitational (1966–78), Bay Hill Citrus Classic (1979), Bay Hill Classic (1980–84), Hertz Bay Hill Classic (1985–88), The Nestle Invitational (1989–95).

1966	Lionel Hebert
1967	Julius Boros
1968	Dan Sikes
1969	Ken Still
1970	Bob Lunn
1971	Arnold Palmer
1972	Jerry Heard
1973	Brian Allin
1974	Jerry Heard
1975	Lee Trevino
1976	Hale Irwin
1977	Gary Koch
1978	Mac McLendon
1979	Bob Byman
1980	Dave Eichelberger
1981	Andy Bean
1982	Tom Kite
1983	Mike Nicolette
1984	Gary Koch
1985	Fuzzy Zoeller
1986	Dan Forsman
1987	Payne Stewart
1988	Paul Azinger
1989	Tom Kite
1990	Robert Gamez
1991	Andrew Magee

1992	Fred Couples
1993	Ben Crenshaw
1994	Loren Roberts
1995	Loren Roberts
1996	Paul Goydos
1997	Phil Mickelson
1998	Ernie Els

The Players Championship

Formerly known as the Tournament Players Championship (1974–87).

1974	Jack Nicklaus
1975	Al Geiberger
1976	Jack Nicklaus
1977	Mark Hayes
1978	Jack Nicklaus
1979	Lanny Wadkins
1980	Lee Trevino
1981	Raymond Floyd
1982	Jerry Pate
1983	Hal Sutton
1984	Fred Couples
1985	Calvin Peete
1986	John Mahaffey
1987	Sandy Lyle
1988	Mark McCumber
1989	Tom Kite
1990	Jodie Mudd
1991	Steve Elkington
1992	Davis Love III
1993	Nick Price
1994	Greg Norman
1995	Lee Janzen
1996	Fred Couples
1997	Steve Elkington
1998	Justin Leonard

Entergy Classic

Formerly known as the Greater New Orleans Open Invitational (1938–74), First NBC New Orleans Open (1975–79), Greater New Orleans Open (1980), USF&G New Orleans Open (1981), USF&G Classic (1982–91), Freeport-McMoran Classic (1992–95), Freeport-McDermott Classic (1996–).

1938	Harry Cooper
1939	Henry Picard
1940	Jimmy Demaret
1941	Henry Picard
1942	Lloyd Mangrum
1943	No Tournament
1944	Sammy Byrd
1945	Byron Nelson
1946	Byron Nelson
1947	No Tournament
1948	Bob Hamilton
1949–57	*Not played*
1958	Billy Casper
1959	Bill Collins
1960	Dow Finsterwald
1961	Doug Sanders
1962	Bo Wininger
1963	Bo Wininger
1964	Mason Rudolphtuart
1965	Dick Mayer
1966	Frank Beard
1967	George Knudson
1968	George Archer
1969	Larry Hinson
1970	Miller Barber
1971	Frank Beard
1972	Gary Player
1973	Jack Nicklaus
1974	Lee Trevino
1975	Billy Casper
1976	Larry Ziegler
1977	Jim Simons
1978	Lon Hinkle
1979	Hubert Green
1980	Tom Watson
1981	Tom Watson
1982	Scott Hoch
1983	Bill Rogers
1984	Bob Eastwood
1985	Severiano Ballesteros
1986	Calvin Peete
1987	Ben Crenshaw
1988	Chip Beck
1989	Tim Simpson
1990	David Frost
1991	Ian Woosnam
1992	Chip Beck
1993	Mike Standly
1994	Ben Crenshaw
1995	Davis Love III
1996	Scott McCarron
1997	Brad Faxon
1998	Lee Westwood

MCI Classic – The Heritage of Golf

Formerly known as the Heritage Classic (1969–70), Sea Pines Heritage Classic (1971–86), MCI Heritage Classic (1987–94).

1969	Arnold Palmer
1970	Bob Goalby
1971	Hale Irwin
1972	Johnny Miller
1973	Hale Irwin
1974	Johnny Miller
1975	Jack Nicklaus
1976	Hubert Green
1977	Graham Marsh
1978	Hubert Green
1979	Tom Watson
1980	Doug Tewell
1981	Bill Rogers
1982	Tom Watson
1983	Fuzzy Zoeller
1984	Nick Faldo
1985	Bernhard Langer
1986	Fuzzy Zoeller
1987	Davis Love III
1988	Greg Norman
1989	Payne Stewart
1990	Payne Stewart
1991	Davis Love III
1992	Davis Love III
1993	David Edwards
1994	Hale Irwin
1995	Bob Tway
1996	Loren Roberts
1997	Nick Price
1998	Davis Love III

Greater Greensboro Chrysler Classic

Formerly known as the Greater Greensboro Open (1938–87), Greater Greensboro Open (1988–95).

1938	Sam Snead
1939	Ralph Guldahl
1940	Ben Hogan
1941	Byron Nelson
1942	Sam Byrd
1943–44	*Not played*
1945	Byron Nelson
1946	Sam Snead
1947	Vic Ghezzi
1948	Lloyd Mangrum
1949	Sam Snead
1950	Sam Snead
1951	Art Doering
1952	Dave Douglas
1953	Earl Stewart
1954	Doug Ford
1955	Sam Snead
1956	Sam Snead
1957	Stan Leonard
1958	Bob Goalby
1959	Dow Finsterwald
1960	Sam Snead
1961	Mike Souchak
1962	Billy Casper
1963	Doug Sanders
1964	Julius Boros
1965	Sam Snead
1966	Doug Sanders
1967	George Archer
1968	Billy Casper
1969	Gene Littler
1970	Gary Player
1971	Bud Allin
1972	George Archer
1973	Chi Chi Rodriguez
1974	Bob Charles
1975	Tom Weiskopf
1976	Al Geiberger
1977	Danny Edwards
1978	Seve Ballesteros
1979	Raymond Floyd
1980	Craig Stadler
1981	Larry Nelson
1982	Danny Edwards
1983	Lanny Wadkins
1984	Andy Bean
1985	Joey Sindelar
1986	Sandy Lyle
1987	Scott Simpson
1988	Sandy Lyle
1989	Ken Green
1990	Steve Elkington
1991	Mark Brooks
1992	Davis Love III
1993	Rocco Mediate
1994	Mike Springer
1995	Jim Gallagher Jr
1996	Mark O'Meara
1997	Frank Nobilo
1998	Trevor Dodds

Shell Houston Open

Formerly known as the Tournament of Champions (1946–49), Houston Open (1950–58, 1972–79, 1985–86), Houston Classic (1959–65), Houston Champions International (1966–71), Michelob Houston Open (1980–82), Houston Coca-Cola Open (1983–84), Big-I Houston Open (1987), Independent Insurance Agent Open (1988–91).

1946	Byron Nelson
1947	Bobby Locke
1948	*Not played*
1949	John Palmer
1950	Cary Middlecoff
1951	Marty Furgol
1952	Jack Burke Jr
1953	Cary Middlecoff
1954	Dave Douglas
1955	Mike Souchak
1956	Ted Kroll
1957	Arnold Palmer
1958	Ed Oliver
1959	Jack Burke Jr
1960	Bill Collins
1961	Jay Hebert
1962	Bobby Nichols
1963	Bob Charles
1964	Mike Souchak
1965	Bobby Nichols
1966	Arnold Palmer
1967	Frank Beard
1968	Roberto de Vicenzo
1969	No Tournament
1970	Gibby Gilbert
1971	Hubert Green
1972	Bruce Devlin
1973	Bruce Crampton
1974	Dave Hill
1975	Bruce Crampton
1976	Lee Elder
1977	Gene Littler
1978	Gary Player
1979	Wayne Levi
1980	Curtis Strange
1981	Ron Streck
1982	Ed Sneed
1983	David Graham
1984	Corey Pavin
1985	Raymond Floyd
1986	Curtis Strange
1987	Jay Haas
1988	Curtis Strange
1989	Mike Sullivan
1990	Tony Sills
1991	Fulton Allem
1992	Fred Funk
1993	Jim McGovern
1994	Mike Heinen
1995	Payne Stewart
1996	Mark Brooks
1997	Phil Blackmar
1998	David Duval

Bell South Classic

Formerly known as the Atlanta Classic (1967–81), Georgia-Pacific Atlanta Golf Classic (1982–88), BellSouth Atlanta Golf Classic (1989–91).

1967	Bob Charles
1968	Bob Lunn
1969	Bert Yancey
1970	Tommy Aaron
1971	Gardner Dickinson
1972	Bob Lunn
1973	Jack Nicklaus
1974	No Tournament
1975	Hale Irwin
1976	No Tournament
1977	Hale Irwin
1978	Jerry Heard
1979	Andy Bean
1980	Larry Nelson
1981	Tom Watson
1982	Keith Fergus
1983	Calvin Peete
1984	Tom Kite
1985	Wayne Levi
1986	Bob Tway
1987	Dave Barr
1988	Larry Nelson
1989	Scott Simpson
1990	Wayne Levi
1991	Corey Pavin
1992	Tom Kite
1993	Nolan Henke
1994	John Daly
1995	Mark Calcavecchia
1996	Paul Stankowski
1997	Scott McCarron
1998	Tiger Woods

GTE Byron Nelson Golf Classic

Formerly known as Texas Victory Open (1944), Dallas Open (1945, 1957–67), Dallas Invitational (1946), Dallas Centennial Open (1956), Texas Invitational Open (a) (1956), Byron Nelson Golf Classic (1968–87).

1944	Byron Nelson
1945	Sam Snead
1946	Ben Hogan
1947–55	*Not played*
1956	Don January
1956(a)	Peter Thomson
1957	Sam Snead
1958	Sam Snead
1959	Julius Boros
1960	Johnny Pott
1961	Earl Stewart Jr
1962	Billy Maxwell
1963	No Tournament
1964	Charles Coody
1965	No Tournament
1966	Roberto de Vicenzo
1967	Bert Yancey
1968	Miller Barber
1969	Bruce Devlin
1970	Jack Nicklaus
1971	Jack Nicklaus
1972	Chi Chi Rodriguez
1973	Lanny Wadkins
1974	Brian Allin
1975	Tom Watson
1976	Mark Hayes
1977	Raymond Floyd
1978	Tom Watson
1979	Tom Watson
1980	Tom Watson
1981	Bruce Lietzke
1982	Bob Gilder
1983	Ben Crenshaw
1984	Craig Stadler
1985	Bob Eastwood
1986	Andy Bean
1987	Fred Couples
1988	Bruce Lietzke
1989	Jodie Mudd
1990	Payne Stewart
1991	Nick Price
1992	Billy Ray Brown
1993	Scott Simpson
1994	Neal Lancaster
1995	Ernie Els
1996	Phil Mickelson
1997	Tiger Woods
1998	John Cook

Mastercard Colonial

Formerly known as the Colonial National Invitation Tournament (1946–88), Southwestern Bell Colonial (1989–94).

1946	Ben Hogan
1947	Ben Hogan
1948	Clayton Heafner
1949	No Tournament
1950	Sam Snead
1951	Cary Middlecoff
1952	Ben Hogan
1953	Ben Hogan
1954	Johnny Palmer
1955	Chandler Harper
1956	Mike Souchak
1957	Roberto de Vicenzo
1958	Tommy Bolt
1959	Ben Hogan
1960	Julius Boros
1961	Doug Sanders
1962	Arnold Palmer
1963	Julius Boros
1964	Billy Casper
1965	Bruce Crampton
1966	Bruce Devlin
1967	Dave Stockton
1968	Billy Casper
1969	Gardner Dickinson
1970	Homero Blancas
1971	Gene Littler
1972	Jerry Heard
1973	Tom Weiskopf
1974	Rod Curl
1975	No Tournament
1976	Lee Trevino
1977	Ben Crenshaw
1978	Lee Trevino
1979	Al Geiberger
1980	Bruce Lietzke
1981	Fuzzy Zoeller
1982	Jack Nicklaus
1983	Jim Colbert
1984	Peter Jacobsen

1985	Corey Pavin
1986	Dan Pohl
1987	Keith Clearwater
1988	Lanny Wadkins
1989	Ian Baker-Finch
1990	Ben Crenshaw
1991	Tom Purtzer
1992	Bruce Lietzke
1993	Fulton Allem
1994	Nick Price
1995	Tom Lehman
1996	Corey Pavin
1997	David Frost
1998	Tom Watson

Memorial Tournament

1976	Roger Maltbie
1977	Jack Nicklaus
1978	Jim Simons
1979	Tom Watson
1980	David Graham
1981	Keith Fergus
1982	Raymond Floyd
1983	Hale Irwin
1984	Jack Nicklaus
1985	Hale Irwin
1986	Hal Sutton
1987	Don Pooley
1988	Curtis Strange
1989	Bob Tway
1990	Greg Norman
1991	Kenny Perry
1992	David Edwards
1993	Paul Azinger
1994	Tom Lehman
1995	Greg Norman
1996	Tom Watson
1997	Vijay Singh
1998	Fred Couples

Kemper Open

1968	Arnold Palmer
1969	Dale Douglas
1970	Dick Lotz
1971	Tom Weiskopf
1972	Doug Sanders
1973	Tom Weiskopf
1974	Bob Menne
1975	Raymond Floyd
1976	Joe Inman
1977	Tom Weiskopf
1978	Andy Bean
1979	Jerry McGee
1980	John Mahaffey
1981	Craig Stadler
1982	Craig Stadler
1983	Fred Couples
1984	Greg Norman
1985	Bill Glasson
1986	Greg Norman
1987	Tom Kite
1988	Morris Hatalsky
1989	Tom Byrum
1990	Gil Morgan
1991	Billy Andrade
1992	Bill Glasson
1993	Grant Waite
1994	Mark Brooks
1995	Lee Janzen
1996	Steve Stricker
1997	Justin Leonard
1998	Stuart Appleby

Buick Classic

Formerly known as the Westchester Classic (1967–75), American Express Westchester Classic (1976–78), Manufacturers Hanover Westchester Classic (1979–89).

1967	Jack Nicklaus
1968	Julius Boros
1969	Frank Beard
1970	Bruce Crampton
1971	Arnold Palmer
1972	Jack Nicklaus
1973	Bobby Nichols
1974	Johnny Miller
1975	Gene Littler
1976	David Graham
1977	Andy North
1978	Lee Elder
1979	Jack Renner
1980	Curtis Strange
1981	Raymond Floyd
1982	Bob Gilder
1983	Seve Ballesteros
1984	Scott Simpson
1985	Roger Maltbie
1986	Bob Tway
1987	J.C. Snead
1988	Seve Ballesteros
1989	Wayne Grady
1990	Hale Irwin
1991	Billy Andrade
1992	David Frost
1993	Vijay Singh
1994	Lee Janzen
1995	Vijay Singh
1996	Ernie Els
1997	Ernie Els
1998	J.P. Hayes

Motorola Western Open

Formerly known as Western Open (1899–1986), Beatrice Western Open (1987–89), Centel Western Open (1990–92), Sprint Western Open (1993).

1899	Willie Smith
1900	*Not played*
1901	Laurie Auchterlonie
1902	Willie Anderson
1903	Alex Smith
1904	Willie Anderson
1905	Arthur Smith
1906	Alex Smith
1907	Robert Simpson
1908	Willie Anderson
1909	Willie Anderson
1910	Charles Evans Jr
1911	Robert Simpson
1912	Mac Smith
1913	John McDermott
1914	Jim Barnes
1915	Tom McNamara
1916	Walter Hagen
1917	Jim Barnes
1918	*Not played*
1919	Jim Barnes
1920	Jock Hutchison
1921	Walter Hagen
1922	Mike Brady
1923	Jock Hutchison
1924	Bill Mehlhorn
1925	Mac Smith
1926	Walter Hagen
1927	Walter Hagen
1928	Abe Espinosa
1929	Tommy Armour
1930	Gene Sarazen
1931	Ed Dudley
1932	Walter Hagen
1933	Mac Smith
1934	Harry Cooper
1935	John Revolta
1936	Ralph Guldahl
1937	Ralph Guldahl
1938	Ralph Guldahl
1939	Byron Nelson
1940	Jimmy Demaret
1941	Ed Oliver
1942	Herman Barron
1943–45	*Not played*
1946	Ben Hogan
1947	Johnny Palmer
1948	Ben Hogan
1949	Sam Snead
1950	Sam Snead
1951	Marty Furgol
1952	Lloyd Mangrum
1953	Dutch Harrison
1954	Lloyd Mangrum
1955	Cary Middlecoff
1956	Mike Fetchick
1957	Doug Ford
1958	Doug Sanders
1959	Mike Souchak
1960	Stan Leonard
1961	Arnold Palmer
1962	Jacky Cupit
1963	Arnold Palmer
1964	Chi Chi Rodriguez
1965	Billy Casper
1966	Billy Casper
1967	Jack Nicklaus
1968	Jack Nicklaus
1969	Billy Casper
1970	Hugh Royer
1971	Bruce Crampton
1972	Jim Jamieson
1973	Billy Casper
1974	Tom Watson
1975	Hale Irwin
1976	Al Geiberger
1977	Tom Watson
1978	Andy Bean
1979	Larry Nelson
1980	Scott Simpson
1981	Ed Fiori
1982	Tom Weiskopf
1983	Mark McCumber
1984	Tom Watson
1985	Scott Verplank
1986	Tom Kite
1987	D.A. Weibring
1988	Jim Benepe

1989	Mark McCumber
1990	Wayne Levi
1991	Russ Cochran
1992	Ben Crenshaw
1993	Nick Price
1994	Nick Price
1995	Billy Mayfair
1996	Steve Stricker
1997	Tiger Woods
1998	Joe Durant

Canon Greater Hartford Open

Formerly known as Insurance City Open (1952–66), Greater Hartford Open Invitational (1967–72), Sammy Davis Jr Greater Hartford Open (1973–84), Canon Sammy Davis Jr Greater Hartford Open (1985–88).

1952	Ted Kroll
1953	Bob Toski
1954	Tommy Bolt
1955	Sam Snead
1956	Arnold Palmer
1957	Gardner Dickinson
1958	Jack Burke Jr
1959	Gene Littler
1960	Arnold Palmer
1961	Billy Maxwell
1962	Bob Goalby
1963	Billy Casper
1964	Ken Venturi
1965	Billy Casper
1966	Art Wall
1967	Charlie Sifford
1968	Billy Casper
1969	Bob Lunn
1970	Bob Murphy
1971	George Archer
1972	Lee Trevino
1973	Billy Casper
1974	Dave Stockton
1975	Don Bies
1976	Rik Massengale
1977	Bill Kratzert
1978	Rod Funseth
1979	Jerry McGee
1980	Howard Twitty
1981	Hubert Green
1982	Tim Norris
1983	Curtis Strange
1984	Peter Jacobsen
1985	Phil Blackmar
1986	Mac O'Grady
1987	Paul Azinger
1988	Mark Brooks
1989	Paul Azinger
1990	Wayne Levi
1991	Billy Ray Brown
1992	Lanny Wadkins
1993	Nick Price
1994	David Frost
1995	Greg Norman
1996	D.A. Weibring
1997	Stewart Cink
1998	Olin Browne

Quad City Classic

Formerly known as the Quad Cities Open (1972–74, 1980-1981), Ed McMahon-Jaycees Quad City Open (1975–79), Miller High-Life Quad Cities Open (1982–84), Lite Quad Cities Open (1985), Hardee's Golf Classic (1986–94).

1972	Deane Beman
1973	Sam Adams
1974	Dave Stockton
1975	Roger Maltbie
1976	John Lister
1977	Mike Morley
1978	Victor Regalado
1979	D.A. Weibring
1980	Scott Hoch
1981	Dave Barr
1982	Payne Stewart
1983	Danny Edwards
1984	Scott Hoch
1985	Dan Forsman
1986	Mark Wiebe
1987	Kenny Knox
1988	B. McCallister
1989	Curt Byrum
1990	Joey Sindelar
1991	D.A. Weibring
1992	David Frost
1993	David Frost
1994	Mark McCumber
1995	D.A. Weibring
1996	Ed Fiori
1997	David Toms

Deposit Guaranty Golf Classic

Formerly known as Magnolia State Classic (1968–85).

1968	B.R. McLendon
1969	Larry Mowry
1970	Chris Blocker
1971	Roy Pace
1972	Mike Morley
1973	Dwight Nevil
1974	Dwight Nevil
1975	Bob Wynn
1976	Dennis Meyer
1977	Mike McCullough
1978	Craig Stadler
1979	Bobby Walzel
1980	Roger Maltbie
1981	Tom Jones
1982	Payne Stewart
1983	Russ Cochran
1984	Lance Ten Broeck
1985	Jim Gallagher Jr
1986	Dan Halldorson
1987	David Ogrin
1988	Frank Conner
1989	Jim Boros
1990	Gene Sauers
1991	Larry Silveira
1992	Richard Zokol
1993	Greg Kraft
1994	Brian Henninger
1995	Ed Dougherty
1996	Willie Wood
1997	Billy Ray Brown
1998	Fred Funk

CVS Charity Classic

Formerly known as the Carling World Open (1965), Kemper Open (1968), AVCO Golf Classic (1969-1970), Massachusetts Classic (1971), USI Classic (1972-1973), Pleasant Valley Classic (1974-1977), American Optical Classic (1978-1979), Pleasant Valley Jimmy Fund Classic (1980-1981), Bank of Boston Classic (1982-1990), New England Classic (1991-1994), Ideon Classic at Pleasant Valley (1995), CVS Charity Classic (1996-)

1965	Tony Lema
1968	Arnold Palmer
1969	Tom Shaw
1970	Billy Casper
1971	Dave Stockton
1972	Bruce Devlin
1973	Lanny Wadkins
1974	Victor Regalado
1975	Roger Maltbie
1976	Bud Allin
1977	Raymond Floyd
1978	John Mahaffey
1979	Lou Graham
1980	Wayne Levi
1981	Jack Renner
1982	Bob Gilder
1983	Mark Lye
1984	George Archer
1985	George Burn
1986	Gene Sauers
1987	Sam Randolph
1988	M. Calcavecchia
1989	B. McCallister
1990	Morris Hatalsky
1991	Bruce Fleisher
1992	Brad Faxon
1993	Paul Azinger
1994	Kenny Perry
1995	Fred Funk
1996	John Cook
1997	Loren Roberts
1998	Steve Pate

Fedex St Jude Classic

Formerly known as the Memphis Invitational Open (1958–69), Danny Thomas Memphis Classic (1970–84), Jude Memphis Classic (1985), Federal Express St Jude Classic(1986–94).

1958	Billy Maxwell
1959	Don Whitt
1960	Tommy Bolt
1961	Cary Middlecoff
1962	Lionel Hebert
1963	Tony Lema
1964	Mike Souchak
1965	Jack Nicklaus
1966	Bert Yancey
1967	Dave Hill
1968	Bob Lunn
1969	Dave Hill
1970	Dave Hill
1971	Lee Trevino

1972	Lee Trevino
1973	Dave Hill
1974	Gary Player
1975	Gene Littler
1976	Gibby Gilbert
1977	Al Geiberger
1978	Andy Bean
1979	Gil Morgan
1980	Lee Trevino
1981	Jerry Pate
1982	Raymond Floyd
1983	Larry Mize
1984	Bob Eastwood
1985	Hal Sutton
1986	Mike Hulbert
1987	Curtis Strange
1988	Jodie Mudd
1989	John Mahaffey
1990	Tom Kite
1991	Fred Couples
1992	Jay Haas
1993	Nick Price
1994	Dicky Pride
1995	J. Gallagher Jr
1996	John Cook
1997	Greg Norman
1998	Nick Price

Buick Open

Formerly known as the Buick Open Invitational (1958–71), Vern Parsell Buick Open (1972), Lake Michigan Classic (1973), Flint Elkes Open (1974–77), Buick Goodwrench Open (1978–80.

1958	Billy Casper
1959	Art Wall
1960	Mike Souchak
1961	Jack Burke Jr
1962	Bill Collins
1963	Julius Boros
1964	Tony Lema
1965	Tony Lema
1966	Phil Rodgers
1967	Julius Boros
1968	Tom Weiskopf
1969	Dave Hill
1970–71	*Not played*
1972	Gary Groh
1973	Wilf Homenuik
1974	Bryan Abbott
1975	Spike Kelley
1976	Tie: Ed Sabo, Randy Erskine
1977	Bobby Cole
1978	Jack Newton
1979	John Fought
1980	Peter Jacobsen
1981	Hale Irwin
1982	Lanny Wadkins
1983	Wayne Levi
1984	Denis Watson
1985	Ken Green
1986	Ben Crenshaw
1987	Robert Wrenn
1988	Scott Verplank
1989	Leonard Thompson
1990	Chip Beck
1991	Brad Faxon
1992	Dan Forsman
1993	Larry Mize
1994	Fred Couples
1995	Woody Austin
1996	Justin Leonard
1997	Vijay Singh
1998	Billy Mayfair

Sprint International

Formerly known as The International (1986–93).

1986	Ken Green
1987	John Cook
1988	Joey Sindelar
1989	Greg Norman
1990	Davis Love III
1991	Jose-Maria Olazabal
1992	Brad Faxon
1993	Phil Mickelson
1994	Steve Lowery
1995	Lee Janzen
1996	Clarence Rose
1997	Phil Mickleson
1998	Vijay Singh

NEC World Series of Golf

From 1962 to 1975, the World Series of Golf was played as a four-man, 36-hole exhibition

1962	Jack Nicklaus
1963	Jack Nicklaus
1964	Tony Lema
1965	Gary Player
1966	Gene Littler
1967	Jack Nicklaus
1968	Gary Player
1969	Orville Moody
1970	Jack Nicklaus
1971	Charles Coody
1972	Gary Player
1973	Tom Weiskopf
1974	Lee Trevino
1975	Tom Watson
1976	Jack Nicklaus
1977	Lanny Wadkins
1978	Gil Morgan
1979	Lon Hinkle
1980	Tom Watson
1981	Bill Rogers
1982	Craig Stadler
1983	Nick Price
1984	Denis Watson
1985	Roger Maltbie
1986	Dan Pohl
1987	Curtis Strange
1988	Mike Reid
1989	David Frost
1990	Jose Maria Olazabal
1991	Tom Purtzer
1992	Craig Stadler
1993	Fulton Allem
1994	Jose Maria Olazabal
1995	Greg Norman
1996	Phil Mickelson
1997	Greg Norman
1998	David Duval

Greater Vancouver Open

1996	Guy Boros
1997	Mark Calcavecchia
1998	David Duval

Greater Milwaukee Open

1968	Dave Stockton
1969	Ken Still
1970	Deane Beman
1971	Dave Eichelberger
1972	Jim Colbert
1973	Dave Stockton
1974	Ed Sneed
1975	Art Wall
1976	Dave Hill
1977	Dave Eichelberger
1978	Lee Elder
1979	Calvin Peete
1980	Bill Kratzert
1981	Jay Haas
1982	Calvin Peete
1983	Morris Hatalsky
1984	Mark O'Meara
1985	Jim Thorpe
1986	Corey Pavin
1987	Gary Hallberg
1988	Ken Green
1989	Greg Norman
1990	Jim Gallagher Jr
1991	Mark Brooks
1992	Richard Zokol
1993	Billy Mayfair
1994	Mike Springer
1995	Scott Hoch
1996	Loren Roberts
1997	Scott Hoch
1998	Jeff Sluman

Bell Canadian Open

Formerly known as the Canadian Open (1904–93).

1904	John H. Oke
1905	George Cumming
1906	Charles Murray
1907	Percy Barrett
1908	Albert Murray
1909	Karl Keffer
1910	Daniel Kenny
1911	Charles Murray
1912	George Sargent
1913	Albert Murray
1914	Karl Keffer
1915–18	*Not played*
1919	J. Douglas Edgar
1920	J. Douglas Edgar
1921	W.H. Trovinger
1922	Al Watrous
1923	C.W. Hackney
1924	Leo Diegel
1925	Leo Diegel
1926	Macdonald Smith
1927	Tommy Armour
1928	Leo Diegel
1929	Leo Diegel
1930	Tommy Armour
1931	Walter Hagen
1932	Harry Cooper

1933	Joe Kirkwood
1934	Tommy Armour
1935	Gene Kunes
1936	Lawson Little
1937	Harry Cooper
1938	Sam Snead
1939	Harold McSpaden
1940	Sam Snead
1941	Sam Snead
1942	Craig Wood
1943–44	*Not played*
1945	Byron Nelson
1946	George Fazio
1947	Bobby Locke
1948	C.W. Congdon
1949	Dutch Harrison
1950	Jim Ferrier
1951	Jim Ferrier
1952	John Palmer
1953	Dave Douglas
1954	Pat Fletcher
1955	Arnold Palmer
1956	Doug Sanders
1957	George Bayer
1958	Wesley Ellis Jr
1959	Doug Ford
1960	Art Wall Jr
1961	Jacky Cupit
1962	Ted Kroll
1963	Doug Ford
1964	Kel Nagle
1965	Gene Littler
1966	Don Massengale
1967	Billy Casper
1968	Bob Charles
1969	Tommy Aaron
1970	Kermit Zarley
1971	Lee Trevino
1972	Gay Brewer
1973	Tom Weiskopf
1974	Bobby Nichols
1975	Tom Weiskopf
1976	Jerry Pate
1977	Lee Trevino
1978	Bruce Lietzke
1979	Lee Trevino
1980	Bob Gilder
1981	Peter Oosterhuis
1982	Bruce Lietzke
1983	John Cook
1984	Greg Norman
1985	Curtis Strange
1986	Bob Murphy
1987	Curtis Strange
1988	Ken Green
1989	Steve Jones
1990	Wayne Levi
1991	Nick Price
1992	Greg Norman
1993	David Frost
1994	Nick Price
1995	Mark O'Meara
1996	Dudley Hart
1997	Steve Jones
1998	Billy Andrade

B.C. Open

1971	Claude Harmon Jr
1972	Bob Payne
1973	Hubert Green
1974	Richie Karl
1975	Don Iverson
1976	Bob Wynn
1977	Gil Morgan
1978	Tom Kite
1979	Howard Twitty
1980	Don Pooley
1981	Jay Haas
1982	Calvin Peet
1983	Pat Lindsey
1984	Wayne Levi
1985	Joey Sindelar
1986	Rick Fehr
1987	Joey Sindelar
1988	Bill Glasson
1989	Mike Hulbert
1990	Nolan Henke
1991	Fred Couples
1992	John Daly
1993	Blaine McCallister
1994	Mike Sullivan
1995	Hal Sutton
1996	Fred Funk
1997	G. Hjertstedt
1998	Chris Perry

LA CANTERA TEXAS OPEN

Formerly known as the Texas Open (1922–69, 1981–85, 1994), San Antonio Texas Open (1970-1980), Vantage Championship (1986–87), Texas Open presented by Nabisco (1988–89), H-E-B Texas Open (1990–93).
** Nabisco Championship of Golf in 1977 became the current day Tour Championship.*

1922	Bob MacDonald
1923	Walter Hagen
1924	Joe Kirkwood
1925	Joe Turnesa
1926	Mac Smith
1927	Bobby Cruickshank
1928	Bill Mehlhorn
1929	Bill Mehlhorn
1930	Denny Shute
1931	Abe Espinosa
1932	Clarence Clark
1933	*Not played*
1934	Wiffy Cox
1935–38	*Not played*
1939	Dutch Harrison
1940	Byron Nelson
1941	Lawson Little
1942	Chick Harbert
1943	*Not played*
1944	Johnny Revolta
1945	Sam Byrd
1946	Ben Hogan
1947	Ed Oliver
1948	Sam Snead
1949	Dave Douglas
1950	Sam Snead
1951	Dutch Harrison
1952	Jack Burke Jr
1953	Tony Holguin
1954	Chandler Harper
1955	Mike Souchak
1956	Gene Littler
1957	Jay Hebert
1958	Bill Johnston
1959	Wes Ellis
1960	Arnold Palmer
1961	Arnold Palmer
1962	Arnold Palmer
1963	Phil Rodgers
1964	Bruce Crampton
1965	Frank Beard
1966	Harold Henning
1967	Chi Chi Rodriguez
1968	*Not played*
1969	Deane Beman
1970	Ron Cerrudo
1971	*Not played*
1972	Mike Hill
1973	Ben Crenshaw
1974	Terry Diehl
1975	Don January
1976	Butch Baird
1977	Hale Irwin
1978	Ron Streck
1979	Lou Graham
1980	Lee Trevino
1981	Bill Rogers
1982	Jay Haas
1983	Jim Colbert
1984	Calvin Peete
1985	John Mahaffey
1986	Ben Crenshaw
1987	Tom Watson*
1988	Corey Pavin
1989	Donnie Hammond
1990	Mark O'Meara
1991	Blaine McCalister
1992	Nick Price
1993	Jay Haas
1994	Bob Estes
1995	Duffy Waldorf
1996	David Ogrin
1997	Tim Herron
1998	Hal Sutton

Buick Challenge

Formerly known as the Green Island Open Invitational (1970), Southern Open Invitational (1971–89), Buick Southern Open (1990–94).

1970	Mason Rudolph
1971	Johnny Miller
1972	DeWitt Weaver
1973	Gary Player
1974	Forrest Fezler
1975	Hubert Green
1976	Mac McLendon
1977	Jerry Pate
1978	Jerry Pate
1979	Ed Fiori
1980	Mike Sullivan
1981	J.C. Snead
1982	Bobby Clampett
1983	Ronnie Black
1984	Hubert Green
1985	Tim Simpson
1986	Fred Wadsworth
1987	Ken Brown

1988 David Frost
1989 Ted Schulz
1990 Kenny Knox
1991 David Peoples
1992 Gary Hallberg
1993 John Inman
1994 Steve Elkington
1995 Fred Funk
1996 Michael Bradley
1997 Davis Love III
1998 Steve Elkington

Michelob Championship at Kingsmill

Formerly known as Kaiser International Open Invitational (1968–76), Anheuser-Busch Golf Classic (1977–95).
** Second tournament, same year.*

1968 Kermit Zarley
1969 Miller Barber
1969 Jack Nicklaus*
1970 Ken Still
1971 Billy Casper
1972 George Knudson
1973 Ed Sneed
1974 Johnny Miller
1975 Johnny Miller
1976 J.C. Snead
1977 Miller Barber
1978 Tom Watson
1979 John Fought
1980 Ben Crenshaw
1981 John Mahaffey
1982 Calvin Peete
1983 Calvin Peete
1984 Ronnie Black
1985 Mark Wiebe
1986 Fuzzy Zoeller
1987 Mark McCumber
1988 Tom Sieckmann
1989 Mike Donald
1990 Lanny Wadkins
1991 Mike Hulbert
1992 David Peoples
1993 Jim Gallagher Jr
1994 Mark McCumber
1995 Ted Tryba
1996 Scott Hoch
1997 David Duval
1998 David Duval

Las Vegas Invitational

Formerly known as Panasonic Las Vegas Invitational (1984–88).

1983 Fuzzy Zoeller
1984 Denis Watson
1985 Curtis Strange
1986 Greg Norman
1987 Paul Azinger
1988 Gary Koch
1989 Scott Hoch
1990 Bob Tway
1991 Andrew Magee
1992 John Cook
1993 Davis Love III
1994 Bruce Lietzke
1995 Jim Furyk
1996 Tiger Woods
1997 Bill Glasson
1998 Jim Furyk

Walt Disney World/Oldsmobile Classic

Formerly known as the Walt Disney World Invitational Open (1971–73), Walt Disney World National Team Championship (1974–81), Walt Disney World Golf Classic (1982–84).

1971 Jack Nicklaus
1972 Jack Nicklaus
1973 Jack Nicklaus
1974 Hubert Green/Mac McLendon
1975 Jim Colbert/Dean Refram
1976 Woody Blackburn/Bill Kratzert
1977 Gibby Gilbert/Grier Jones
1978 Wayne Levi/Bob Mann
1979 George Burns/Ben Crenshaw
1980 Danny Edwards/David Edwards
1981 Vance Heafner/Mike Holland
1982 Hal Sutton
1983 Payne Stewart
1984 Larry Nelson
1985 Lanny Wadkins
1986 Ray Floyd
1987 Larry Nelson
1988 Bob Lohr
1989 Tim Simpson
1990 Tim Simpson
1991 Mark O'Meara
1992 John Huston
1993 Jeff Maggert
1994 Rick Fehr
1995 Brad Bryant
1996 Tiger Woods
1997 David Duval
1998 John Huston

The Tour Championship

Formerly known as the Nabisco Championships of Golf (1987), Nabisco Golf Championships (1988), Nabisco Championships (1989–90).

1987 Tom Watson
1988 Curtis Strange
1989 Tom Kite
1990 Jodie Mudd
1991 Craig Stadler
1992 Paul Azinger
1993 Jim Gallagher Jr
1994 Mark McCumber
1995 Billy Mayfair
1996 Tom Lehman
1997 David Duval
1998 Hal Sutton

Subaru Sarazen World Open Championship

1994 Ernie Els
1995 Frank Nobilo
1996 Frank Nobilo
1997 Mark Calcavecchia
1998 Dudley Hart

The Franklin Templeton Shark Shootout

1989 Curtis Strange and Mark O'Meara
1990 Fred Couples and Raymond Floyd
1991 Tom Purtzer and Lanny Wadkins
1992 Tom Kite and Davis Love III
1993 Steve Elkington and Raymond Floyd
1994 Fred Couples and Brad Faxon
1995 Mark Calcavecchia and Steve Elkington
1996 Jay Haas and Tom Kite
1997 Scott McCarron and Bruce Lietzke
1998 Greg Norman and Steve Elkington

J.C. Penney Classic

1977 Jerry Pate and Hollis Stacy
1978 Lon Hinkle and Pat Bradley
1979 Dave Eichelberger and Murle Breer
1980 Curtis Strange and Nancy Lopez
1981 Tom Kite and Beth Daniel
1982 John Mahaffey and JoAnne Carner
1983 Fred Couples and Jan Stephenson
1984 Mike Donald and Vicki Alvarez
1985 Larry Rinker and Laurie Rinker
1986 Tom Purtzer and Julie Inkster
1987 Steve Jones and Jane Crafter
1988 John Huston and Amy Benz
1989 Bill Glasson and Pat Bradley
1990 Davis Love III and Beth Daniel
1991 Billy Andrade and Kris Tschetter
1992 Dan Forsman and Dottie Pepper
1993 Mike Springer and Melissa McNamara
1994 Brad Bryant and Marta Fig.-Dotti
1995 Davis Love III and Beth Daniel
1996 Mike Hulbert and Donna Andrews
1997 Clarence Rose and Amy Fruhwirth
1998 Steve Pate and Meg Mallon

THE BRITISH AMATEUR CHAMPIONSHIPS

It should be the passport to fame and fortune. It has certainly proved the case for many winners of the US Amateur Championship. But look down the names of the winners of the Amateur Championship over the past 20 years and the only thing that unites most of them is their consequent failure as professionals. The one glowing exception is Jose-Maria Olazabal, the two-time Masters champion, who defeated Colin Montgomerie, six-time PGA European Tour Order of Merit winner, in a classic final in 1984 at Formby.

Otherwise the winners appear to have disappeared into a black hole, buried by the weight of expectation. Why this should be the case is something of a mystery, but my own theory is that it is the Masters at Augusta that is to blame.

Or rather the automatic invitation that the winner of the Amateur continues to receive. This invitation is a throwback to the early days of the Masters when Bobby Jones, the tournament's founder and the finest amateur of them all, recognized that to win the Amateur was one of the greatest prizes and so the winner should be present at Augusta.

To my mind it has proven a poison chalice, well, for anyone with aspirations of becoming a professional, that is. The problem lies in the fact that the Amateur is in June and the Masters is in April. The normal order of things is to turn professional when in the peak of form.

But who can turn down a chance to play at the Masters? So all amateurs wait that extra nine months, often while their friends have turned pro and in some fortunate cases, won their cards at the qualifying school. The Augusta invitee, meanwhile, is usually struggling to find things to play in and places to practise in the winter months. As Peter McEvoy, who played at the Masters on three occasions in the 1970s, says: "One year my competitive preparation consisted of one appearance in the Copt Heath monthly medal."

Is it any surprise that the Amateur champion fails to do himself justice when playing at the Masters? Then what happens is he turns professional after this debilitating experience. Instead of joining the paid ranks with his confidence high, he signs up with his confidence somewhere around his knees. Then the vicious circle continues to spin. He misses a cut or two in the professional ranks, and his confidence falls again. Given that 90% of top-class golf is played between the ears, is it any wonder that so many fail to prosper thereafter? That is my theory anyway, as to why so many end up on the regional professional circuits, making a living as club professionals. Of course, it could just be that winning the Amateur was their pinnacle as golfers, and they simply never improved thereafter.

The saddest example that lends credence to my theory, however, is poor Gordon Sherry. Remember him? His golden year was 1995. He won the Amateur, and then finished fourth in the European Tour event, the Scottish Open at Carnoustie. On the first two days of the Open at St Andrews he was paired with Tom Watson and Greg Norman. After two rounds, he was ahead of both.

Sherry stood 6ft 7in. tall and his head was in the clouds. He had everything going for him. The Walker Cup that year was billed as the clash between Sherry and Tiger Woods. It was Sherry's team that finally won out as convincing winners by 14–10.

So what happened? Sherry found little to play in between that Walker Cup in the September and the Masters the following April. His confidence remained high. In one unfortunate interview he even said he thought he was going to win, which produced a rash of arrogant headlines. Then he arrived at Augusta with his competitive edge blunted through the months of inactivity and he crashed out of the tournament at the halfway stage after rounds of 78, 77. In the clubhouse, he described it as "the worst experience of my life".

Is that any frame of mind in which to turn pro? Yet that is what Sherry did, had to do, and what has happened since has been a litany of broken dreams as everything has gone against him: luck, health, golf, the works. At the time of writing, he is struggling to make an impression on the Challenge Tour. One can only wonder what might have happened had he turned pro when confidence was running high in the wake of that golden July fortnight in the summer of 1995.

Allan MacFie was the first British Amateur champion, but never attained the fame of Horace Hutchinson, whom he beat in the inaugural final at Royal Liverpool. Hutchinson won the second and third finals, the third against John Ball. The latter, also from Hoylake, was accounted the greatest of them all long before 1912 when he won his eighth title, which will remain a record for all eternity.

It was at the instigation of Royal Liverpool that the first Amateur was held in 1885, although for a long time it was not accorded that distinction. That belonged to the 1886 event at St Andrews. It was only after the Royal and Ancient took over sole running of the competition in 1920 that it was duly recognized.

Jose-Maria Olazabal – a rare Amatuer Championship winner who went on to major success

Gordon Sherry – a winner of the British Amateur Championship but little else

By then the tournament was firmly established in the minds of amateurs up and down the land. Before the turn of the century, more than 100 golfers were regularly filing entries, a number that had grown to almost 500 by 1958. Lower and lower handicaps were demanded to keep the numbers of competitors down to manageable proportions. Now, only a scratch golfer has a chance of surviving even into the 36-hole strokeplay qualifying, which was introduced in 1983, and from which the leading 64 then progress through to the matchplay stages.

In this context Michael Bonallack's record of five titles in ten years from 1961 is surely at least the equal of Ball's eight in the days when there was little competition by comparison. Bonallack won three in a row from 1968–70, the latter triumph coming at Royal County Down, his favourite course, and where the Amateur Championship returned for the first time since his victory in 1999. It also happened to be Bonallack's penultimate Amateur before stepping down as secretary of the Royal and Ancient.

In the late 19th century, meanwhile, John Ball and Johnny Laidlay practically carved up the event between them, with one or the other reaching every final between 1887 and 1895. During this time Ball's sphere of influence extended beyond the amateur game. In 1900 he became the first Englishman to win the Open, while two years later another Royal Liverpool amateur, Harold Hilton, also won the tournament.

Freddie Tait, a long hitter who managed to play golf with an extraordinary regularity considering his position as an officer in the Black Watch, might well have emulated Hilton but in 1900, aged 30, he was killed leading his men against the Boers at Koodoosberg in South Africa.

Throughout the twentieth century the Amateur was to attract a growing number of Americans but the first to win, Walter Travis in 1904, did nothing to improve transatlantic golf relations. Ironically, the cause of the rift was that Travis, a triple US Amateur champion, won with a new putter, adopted in desperation for the Amateur at Royal St George's, after his greatest strength had suddenly become his leading weakness.

Trouble was, the instrument he chose to induce a remedy was looked upon by the British establishment as unfair. It was called a Schenectady putter, invented and patented by Arthur Knight of that particular New York town, and had its shaft attached to the middle of a mallet-shaped head.

No one had ever seen such a putter as Travis now deployed as he waltzed past one opponent after another, beating Hilton and Hutchinson in turn to reach the final, where he won at the 33rd hole against Ted Blackwell, who towered above him and outdrove him throughout. Travis relished the victory, which was received with a minimum of applause, which cannot have surprised him, for he felt he had not been accorded the usual

Michael Bonallack – won five titles in ten years from 1961

courtesies, particularly in the matter of clubhouse facilities and an effective caddie.

The Travis Schenectady, centre-shafted wand of victory, although approved by the United States Golf Association, was banned by the R&A, though not – contrary to popular legend – directly as a result of Travis's 1904 win. The ban was imposed in 1910, and even then only after Nga Mutu Golf Club, New Zealand, asked if a small croquet mallet was legal. No, said the R&A. Not until mid-century was the ban on the centre-shafted putter lifted. Ben Hogan used the same type in his one triumphant tilt at the Open in 1953.

From 1920, when the Amateur resumed after the war, it became far more difficult to put together even as few as two wins, and Ball's eight began to look as unbeatable as time has proved it to be. Cyril Tolley, an England international for a quarter of a century, managed two, the first coming upon the resumption in an epic final against Robert Gardner. Both men had survived war service – Tolley, who won a Military Cross, was a POW. The stage for the golf was Muirfield, and it was the 37th hole before they could be separated.

A crowd of around 3,000 cheered as Tolley birdied the first extra hole, for despite the long war years amateur golf had retained its fashionable kudos. This would become even more so as Bobby Jones left his indelible mark on the game in the 1920s. He would only win the Amateur once, though, this success coming in his Grand Slam year, of course, and at his beloved St Andrews to boot, as he defeated Roger Wethered in the final. His closest call had come a round earlier, against Tolley, who could not find an ounce of luck at the first extra hole on this occasion. He went out with the aid of a stymie which was, as Jones himself acknowledged, a "cruel way to lose".

William Lawson Little followed Jones's Grand Slam with two "Little Slams" in 1934 and 1935, capturing both the US Amateur and Amateur titles in both years. Six American victories in the Amateur between the wars was followed by five more in seven years immediately following the resumption in 1946. Even when the Irishman James Bruen, who would go on to become a Ryder Cup player, won it in 1946 he had to beat an American to do so. So did Sam McCready in 1949, holding off Willie Turnesa, the 1947 champion, 2&1 in an historic Amateur at Portmarnock in Ireland – the one time the event has been held outside the United Kingdom.

The best American amateur at the time was undoubtedly the body-builder Frank Stranahan, who loved playing in Britain. On two occasions he finished runner-up in the Open Championship, and on two occasions he went one better in the Amateur, winning at St George's in 1948 and St Andrews in 1950.

Thereafter, until Michael Bonallack came along, the only player to win the event on more than one occasion was Joe Carr, the legendary Irish amateur who would win it three times and boldly carry the tradition of his countrymen that Bruen and McCready had begun after the war.

The strength of American amateur golf, however, was reinforced every four years when the visiting Walker Cup team would play in it and one of them would walk off with the title. This happened every fourth year from 1947 to 1983 and on six occasions both finalists were American. It was Philip Parkin who broke the mould at Turnberry in 1983. It looked to be the preface of one of the great professional careers. Parkin was blessed with a wonderful swing, and an infectious personality. Alas, he disappeared down that aforementioned black hole, and now makes a living doing on-course analysis for satellite television.

The greatest British amateur since Bonallack is undoubtedly Peter McEvoy, who won the title on two successive occasions in 1977-78, and was the Great Britain and Ireland Walker Cup captain for the match against the Americans at Nairn in 1999.

McEvoy's two triumphs were followed by one for a player often seen as his American equivalent, Jay Sigel, but thereafter there have been no more American successes. The main reason for this is the fact the Walker Cup, when it is held in Britain, is no longer back-to-back with the Amateur, and few top Americans come over for it otherwise because the event no longer holds such transatlantic allure.

Instead the Americans have been replaced by a number of continental invaders. Since Sigel beat Scott Hoch in the final, there have been winners from France (1981), Sweden (1988), Holland (1990), and Spain on two occasions (in 1984 and 1998).

The two Spaniards have been the pick of the winners in the last 20 years. First Olazabal, but his successor, Sergio Garcia, will also surely break free of the Amateur Championship hoodoo and become one of the great European players in the early years of the 21st century.

And who knows, perhaps some of the other recent Amateur winners will manage to break free of the ties that bind and prove themselves in the professional arena. Garcia has pointed the way to fill the nine months that separate the winning of the Amateur from the precious invite to Augusta, accepting the invites to professional events that have come his way and gaining experience, so that when the day came to join the paid ranks there was no great chasm to cross - a bridge had already been built.

For Garcia, the invite to play at Augusta, plus the one to tee it up at the Open, became what they should be: two great perks to winning the Amateur Championship. For good or ill, they remain powerful reasons why the event will continue to be held in reverence by all who participate at the highest amateur level.

Sergio Garcia – the 1998 champion seems to be destined for far greater things

BRITISH AMATEUR CHAMPIONSHIPS STATISTICS

Year	Course	Finalists	Score
1885	Hoylake, R Liverpool	A Macfie beat H Hutchinson	7&6
1886	St Andrews	H Hutchinson beat H Lamb	7&6
1887	Hoylake, R Liverpool	H Hutchinson beat J Ball	1 hole
1888	Prestwick	J Ball beat J Laidley	5&4
1889	St Andrews	J Laidlay beat L Melville	2&1
1890	Hoylake, R Liverpool	J Ball beat J Laidley	4&3
1891	St Andrews	J Laidlay beat H Hilton	37th
1892	Sandwich, R St George's	J Ball beat H Hilton	3/1
1893	Prestwick	P Anderson beat J Laidley	2 holes
1894	Hoylake, R Liverpool	J Ball beat S Fergusson	1 hole
1895	St Andrews	L Melville beat J Ball	37th
1896	Sandwich, R St George's	F Tait beat H Hilton	8&7
1897	Muirfield	A Allen beat J Robb	4&2
1898	Hoylake, R Liverpool	F Tait beat S Fergusson	7&5
1899	Prestwick	J Ball beat F Tait	37th
1900	Sandwich, R St George's	H Hilton beat J Robb	8&7
1901	St Andrews	H Hilton beat J Low	1 hole
1902	Hoylake, R Liverpool	C Hutchings beat S Fry	1 hole
1903	Muirfield	R Maxwell beat H Hutchison	7&5
1904	Sandwich, R St George's	W Travis (USA) beat E Blackwell	4&3
1905	Prestwick	A Barry beat Hon O Scott	3&2
1906	Hoylake, R Liverpool	J Robb beat C Lingen	4&3
1907	St Andrews	J Ball beat C Palmer	6&4
1908	Sandwich, R St George's	EALassen beat H Taylor	7&6
1909	Muirfield	R Maxwell beat Capt C Hutchison	1 hole
1910	Hoylake, R Liverpool	J Ball beat C Aylmer	10&9
1911	Prestwick	H Hilton beat E Lassen	4&3
1912	WestwardHo!, R N Devon	J Ball beat A Mitchell	38th
1913	St Andrews	H Hilton beat R Harris	6&5
1914	Sandwich, R St George's	J Jenkins beat C Hezlet	3&2
1915-19	*No Championships*		
1920	Muirfield	C Tolley beat R Gardner (USA)	37th
1921	Hoylake, R Liverpool	W Hunter beat A Graham	12&11
1922	Prestwick	E Holderness beat J Caven	1 hole
1923	Deal, R Cinque Ports	R Wethered beat R Harris	7&6
1924	St Andrews	E Holderness beat E Storey	3&2
1925	Westward Ho!, R N Devon	R Harris beat K Fradgley	3/12
1926	Muirfield	J Sweetser (USA) beat A Simpson	6&5
1927	Hoylake, R Liverpool	Dr W Tweddell beat D Landale	7&6
1928	Prestwick	T Perkins beat R Wethered	6&4
1929	Sandwich, R St George's	C Tolley beat J Smith	4&3
1930	St Andrews	R Jones beat R Wethered	7&6
1931	Westward Ho!, R N Devon	E Smith beat J de Forest	1 hole
1932	Muirfield	J de Forest beat E Fiddian	3&1
1933	Hoylake, R Liverpool	Hon M Scott beat T Bourn	4&3
1934	Prestwick	W Lawson Little (USA) beat J Wallace	14&13
1935	R Lytham & St Annes	W Lawson Little (USA) beat Dr W Tweddell	1 hole
1936	St Andrews	H Thomson beat J Ferrier (Aus)	2 holes
1937	Sandwich, R St George's	R Sweeny jnr (USA) beat L Munn	3&2
1938	Troon	C Yates (USA) beat R Ewing	3&2
1939	Hoylake, R Liverpool	A Kyle beat A Duncan	2&1
1940-45		No Championships	
1946	Birkdale	J Bruen jnr beat R Sweeny jnr	4&3
1947	Carnoustie	W Turnesa (USA) beat R Chapman	3&2
1948	Sandwich, R St George's	F Stranahan (USA) beat C Stowe	5&4
1949	Portmarnock	S McCready beat W Turnesa (USA)	2&1

Year	Course	Finalists	Score
1950	St Andrews	F Stranahan (USA) beat R Chapman (USA)	8&6
1951	Royal Porthcawl	R Chapman (USA) beat C Coe (USA)	5&4
1952	Prestwick	E Ward (USA) beat F Stranahan (USA)	6&5
1953	Hoylake, R Liverpool	J Carr beat E Harvie Ward (USA)	2 holes
1954	Muirfield	D Bachli (Aus) beat W Campbell (USA)	2&1
1955	R Lytham & St Annes	J Conrad (USA) beat A Slater	3&2
1956	Troon	J Beharrell beat L Taylor	5&4
1957	Formby	R Reid Jack beat H Ridgley (USA)	2&1
1958	St Andrews	J Carr beat A Thirlwell	3&2
1959	Sandwich, R St George's	D Berman (USA) beat W Hyndman (USA)	3&2
1960	Royal Portrush	J Carr beat B Cochran (USA)	8&7
1961	Turnberru	M Bonallack beat J Walker	6&4
1962	Hoylake, R Liverpool	R Davies (USA) beat J Povall	1 hole
1963	St Andrews	M Lunt beat J Blackwell	2&1
1964	Ganton	G Clark beat M Lunt	39th
1965	Royal Porthcawl	M Bonallack beat C Clark	2&1
1966	Carnoustie (18 holes)	R Cole (SA) beat R Shade	3&2
1967	Formby	R Dickson (USA) beat R Cerrudo (USA)	2&1
1968	Troon	M Bonallack beat J Carr	7&6
1969	Hoylake, R Liverpool	M Bonallack beat W Hyndman (USA)	3&2
1970	Newcastle, R Co Down	M Bonallack beat W Hyndman (USA)	8&7
1971	Carnoustie	S Melnyk (USA) beat J Simons (USA)	3&2
1972	Sandwich, R St George's	T Homer beat A Thirlwell	4&3
1973	Royal Porthcawl	R Siderowf (USA) beat P Moody	5&3
1974	Muirfield	T Homer beat J Gabrielsen (USA)	2 holes
1975	Hoylake, R Liverpool	M Giles (USA) beat M James	8&7
1976	St Andrews	R Siderowf (USA) beat J Davies	37th
1977	Ganton	P McEvoy beat H Campbell	5&4
1978	Royal Troon	P McEvoy beat P McKeller	4&3
1979	Hillside	J Sigel (USA) beat S Hoch (USA)	3&2
1980	Royal Porthcawl	D Evans beat D Suddards (SA)	4&3
1981	St Andrews	P Ploujoux (Fra) beat J Hirsch (USA)	4&2
1982	Deal, R Cinque Ports	M Thompson beat A Stubbs	4&3
1983	Turnberry	A Parkin beat J Holtgrieve (USA)	5&4
1984	Formby	JM Olazabal (Spa) beat C Montgomerie	5&4
1985	R Dornoch	G McGimpsey beat C Homewood	8&7
1986	R Lytham & St Annes	D Curry beat G Birtwell	11&9
1987	Prestwick	P Mayo beat P McEvoy	3&1
1988	R Porthcawl	C Hardin beat B Fouchee (USA)	1 hole
1989	R Birkdale	S Dodd beat C Cassells	5&3
1990	Muirfield	R Muntz (Neth) beat A Macara	7&6
1991	Ganton	G Wolstenholme beat B May (USA)	8&6
1992	Carnoustie	S Dundas beat B Dredge	7&6
1993	R Portrush	I Pyman beat P Page	37th
1994	Nairn	L James beat G Sherry	2&1
1995	Hoylake, R Liverpool	G Sherry beat M Reynard	7&6
1996	Turnberry, Ailsa & Arran	W Bladon beat R Bearnes	1 hole
1997	Sandwich, R St George's	C Watson beat T Immelman	3&2
1998	Muirfield	S Garcia beat C Williams	7&6

US AMATEUR CHAMPIONSHIPS

It was described as the best match that amateur golf had ever seen – and that was by the loser. The venue was Pumpkin Ridge, OR, the year 1996, the two finalists Steve Scott and a 20-year-old who was about to rip up the record book, Tiger Woods.

It was to be Woods's last act as an amateur, a career in the Corinthian ranks that had already seen him win an unprecedented three consecutive US Junior Championship titles, and now he had the chance to claim an unprecedented three successive US Amateurs.

How unlikely this had seemed at the halfway stage as Woods, completely out of sorts, trailed five down. Yet the legend was such that, even then, his schoolmate Jake Poe declared: "He was so far behind and yet I would have bet my life that he was going to win it, although I had no idea how he could."

As for Scott, as he waltzed around the merchandise tent looking for souvenirs, he was smart enough to realize that they were not yet guaranteed mementoes of a famous victory. "If I was 10 up maybe, but I have seen what he can do in the past," he said.

As the holes slipped away from Scott in the afternoon he was not surprised. The 3rd, 4th and 5th holes all went Woods's way and then when he won the 9th there was just a hole between them. Among the excited gallery was Phil Knight, head honcho at Nike, who would present Woods with a $40 million endorsement contract at the end of the proceedings.

At the par-three 10th, Scott managed to achieve what is always so difficult to do in matchplay, and reverse the momentum. It had looked as if he had left himself an impossible chip, but it hit the flagstick dead centre and dropped into the hole for a welcome two.

That remained the way of things with three holes to play, and Woods's brave recovery appeared destined to end in failure. At the 15th Woods had missed from 10 feet for a birdie. At the 16th he had another chance, this time from eight feet. This one really had to go in. As so often when Woods is in such a position, it did. One down, two to play.

At the 17th Woods was 30 feet away. By this stage, golf fans who had been tuned in to the prestigious World Series on another channel, featuring such names as Greg Norman, Nick Price and Phil Mickelson, switched over and watched two college kids instead. They arrived just in time to watch Woods's putt dive into the hole. "Unbelievable," Scott whispered, under his breath.

It was the 38th hole before Scott gave in to the immovable object called destiny. He bogeyed the hole and Woods had achieved what had proved beyond Bobby Jones, Jack Nicklaus and all the other great amateurs that had coveted this distinguished prize. He had won it three years in a row.

The first US Amateur was played almost back-to-back with the first US Open. It began three days before and lasted three times as long, and in terms of importance completely demolished the professional event. It was a pecking order that was not disturbed until Jones retired, and with his passing went the golden age of the amateurs.

Across the Atlantic, things were somewhat different. The Open pre-dated the Amateur by a quarter of a century, and rapidly became the Holy Grail for all golfers.

There is a direct personal link between the US Amateur and the Open. Old Tom Morris, winner of four Opens, coached the first winner of the American amateur, a well-built, self-willed Chicagoan by the name of Charles Blair Macdonald. He had first fallen in love with golf in Scotland as a student at St Andrews in the 1870s, and in the early 1890s built the Chicago club, then a much-improved 18 holes in the suburb of Wheaton.

Macdonald first came to public notice in his campaign to become American Amateur champion. Since golf lacked a national authority, the clubs of Newport, RI, and St Andrew's, NY, put on "Championships" in 1893 and 1894. Macdonald was runner-up in both, but discounted both the quality of the venues and his opponents. He was an influential man, a stockbroker on the New York exchange, but the game was clearly in need of leadership a little less egotistical than this.

The United States Golf Association came into being at the end of 1894, and the first President, Theodore Havemeyer (a sugar baron), gave an extra veneer of authority to the inaugural Amateur starting on September 1, 1895, by donating a championship trophy.

Macdonald won it easily. His victim in the final at Newport was Charles Sands, who preferred lawn tennis and, to judge by the scoreline, played as if with racquets rather than golf clubs. He lost 12&11. Although Macdonald went on to perform great service both as a USGA committee man and an unpaid course designer, his fame was nothing compared to that of Walter J. Travis, the champion in 1900, 1901 and 1903.

Travis came from Australia as a child and did not take up golf until he was 35. At 37 he reached the semi-final of the US Amateur, and the following year, in 1900, he won it. He was also second in the 1902 US Open.

Travis was a short hitter but a devastating putter. His most celebrated single feat was his British Amateur title – his last major win – in 1904. Ever present was his trademark, a black cigar.

Travis's victory on foreign soil was answered seven years later by the immensely talented British amateur Harold Hilton, who had two Open Championships to his credit. Having won the Amateur in 1911, he went for the transatlantic

Tiger Woods – the only man to win three consecutive US Amateur Championships

Bobby Jones – a consistent winner and original Grand Slam winner

double at the age of 42. At first no one could give him a game, let alone beat him, as he strolled through the early rounds. The final against Fred Herreshoff, however, was a classic, and went to the 37th hole before Hilton completed his cherished double.

Hilton's success came during the Jerry Travers era, when he notched up a record four US Amateur wins in the space of just seven years. Travers's speciality was the Houdini-like recovery, although such feats were not needed in the finals themselves. Each of his victories there was by a comfortable margin, his opponents perhaps intimidated by clubhouse tales of the

deeds that Travers had completed to get so far.

Francis Ouimet's victory in the 1914 US Amateur was in most respects an anti-climax after his epochal victory in the 1913 US Open, but not to the man himself. His dearest wish was to win the amateur, the thing that had driven him when he was a caddie at The Country Club, Brookline. For players like Ouimet and Chick Evans, who graduated to the Stock Exchange to finance his golf, the Amateur remained very much the trophy to win.

In 1916 Evans came up with what at the time was a unique double. First he recorded a total of 286 to win the US Open at Minikhada, MN, a figure not beaten for 22 years. Then three months later he defeated Bob Gardner in the final of the Amateur at Merion in Pennsylvania. Gardner had got into the last four by virtue of a 5&3 victory over a 14-year-old from Georgia who was playing in his first USGA Championship. This was Bobby Jones, who would go on to be a winner on five occasions between 1924 and 1930. Intriguingly, when Jones equalled Evans's double of US Open and Amateur successes in the same year in 1930, the latter victory was also achieved at Merion.

That has to stand as the most emotional Amateur of them all. Not so much for the final, which became a glorified lap of honour as Jones demolished his opponent Eugene Homans 8&7, but for what it meant for golf: the completion of the Grand Slam. And in the nick of time too, before that particular Grand Slam disappeared into the mists of time with the development of the professional game.

And with that Jones stopped playing, with no worlds left to conquer. As O.B. Keeler and Grantland Rice wrote in The *Bobby Jones Story*: "So it was goodbye at Merion, as, long ago, it had been good morning there. It was at Merion in 1916 that Bobby had first played in his first national championship; it was there in 1924 he had won his first [US] Amateur Championship; and there he finished. The chunky schoolboy had grown into the calm and poised young man, whom the world called the master of golf – and who was no less truly master of himself."

Only one man had two wins in the 1930s. That was Lawson Little, who also won the Amateur in the same years as well, the only man ever to achieve that particular feat.

With Jones's retirement, and the fitful but sure growth of the professional tour, the fascination of the amateur game began to fade. After the war, the names of the outstanding professional players like Ben Hogan, Byron Nelson and Sam Snead dominated the sports pages, and with the coming of television the process accelerated.

Gene Littler, Arnold Palmer and Jack Nicklaus used the Amateur as a stepping-stone to wealth, yet the continuing high standards of the amateur game in America were never more clearly demonstrated than at Broadmoor, CO, in 1959 when Charles Coe (at 35 twice a winner) took Jack Nicklaus (then a student at Ohio State University) to the 36th hole of the final. The winner was about to begin a run in the US Open that would see him finish second, fourth and first in successive years. At 19 years and eight months, Nicklaus was the second youngest Amateur champion, three months older than Robert

Phil Mickelson – left-handed master of the short game

Gardner when he collected the trophy half a century earlier.

In 1965 the USGA made the catastrophic mistake of changing the format to strokeplay. This had become all the rage in America, following the conversion of the PGA Championship in 1958. But changing a professional event for television was one thing; there was absolutely no reason for the USGA to walk down that road.

Fortunately, the disastrous experiment lasted just eight years, and when the tournament reverted to matchplay in 1973 it quickly became clear that there was no lasting damage. The entry numbered 2,110 players and the winner was a young man who was already carrying too much weight: Craig Stadler.

He would be followed into the winner's circle by Jerry Pate, who would go on to win the US Open in his first year as a professional just two seasons later. This was a vintage period for the Amateur, with three further champions in a row from 1978 who would go on to leave their mark on the professional game: John Cook, Mark O'Meara and Hal Sutton.

In 1981 a stir was caused by a famous name from quite another sphere: Crosby. The singer's son – Nathanial, aged 19 – won at the Olympic Club, San Francisco, close to his home. Nathanial Crosby, of course, had the pedigree to be a good golfer as well as a decent crooner. His father not only gave his name to the Crosby Pro-am but was a one-handicap golfer for many years. One year he tried to win the Amateur at St Andrews, attracting a huge crowd. Alas, he did not live to see his son's greatest moment. He died in 1977 after playing a round in Spain in the company of Manuel Pinero.

Any list of the great US Amateur Champions would have to include the name of Jay Sigel. He won in 1983 and 1984 and compiled a wonderful CV in the great amateur events in America. Sigel had been dissuaded from joining the professional ranks at the age of 18 and instead made a living selling insurance.

He might well have become one of the great professionals but for that misfortune, a verdict reinforced by his deeds since he did turn pro, at the age of 50, and joined the US Senior Tour. In the five years since he made that decision Sigel has been one of the leading lights and made a shade under $5 million. You'd have to sell a lot of insurance policies to make that kind of money.

The golden age of amateur golf may have been in the 1920s, but a golden age of sorts has come to pass in the 1990s. It began with a victory for Phil Mickelson in 1990. He gave the amateur game a national profile not just because of his dark good looks and the fact he was left-handed. Mickelson could play shots around the greens that took the art of the short game to another level. In so doing he raised the standard of amateur golf – a fact underlined when, within a year, he won the PGA tour event, the Tucson Open, while still an amateur. Mickelson, of course, has gone on to become one of the very best American professionals.

In 1992 the best player in the 36-hole qualifying that sorts out who is eligible for the matchplay stages was a promising young talent called David Duval. The winner, however, was Justin Leonard, illustrating just how much the professional game relies on the amateur ranks to infuse it with new talent.

And then, of course, came Tiger Woods. It is not only his victory against Steve Scott that has entered US Amateur Championship lore. All three finals have. None finished before the 36th hole and all were epics in their own right.

Indeed the first against Trip Kuehne featured an even more remarkable comeback than the last against Scott, since Woods was five down with just 12 holes to play. Gradually he eroded that lead until he went ahead for the first time with a birdie at the last hole. Woods did his trademark pumped-action-fist routine, and no wonder. He had been six down at one point.

He was the youngest US Amateur Champion of all time, and it earned him a letter of congratulations from the First Golfer. Bill Clinton wrote:

"Dear Tiger,

Congratulations on your outstanding achievement as the youngest winner of the 1994 US Amateur golf tournament. You can take great pride in this remarkable accomplishment and in your efforts to give your best performance. In succeeding at this level of competition you have demonstrated your personal dedication to excellence.

I commend you for the sportsmanship, discipline and perseverance that earned you this great honor."

The following year, Woods was down in the final again, this time against Buddy Marucci. Three in arrears after 12, Woods once more clawed back the deficit to stand two up with two to play. But Marucci won the 17th to take the match down to the last. As Woods stood over his wedge approach to the 18th, the television commentator Johnny Miller said: "I would not be surprised if he puts this a foot from the hole." He was wrong. But only by six inches.

In 1997 Matt Kuchar proved a more-than-worthy successor to Woods. The following year at Augusta he showed what a great champion he was when he became the star of the Masters for three days, eventually finishing with a wonderful top-10 finish. In 1998 the winner was Hank Huehne, the family finally claiming the trophy that had seemed Trip's for certain just three years before.

Such is the quality of golf needed now to triumph in the US Amateur, it seems certain that the winners will continue to make headlines worldwide. Mickelson, Leonard and Woods have shown what is possible in just a few short years. Long gone are the days when such amateurs looked at the stars in the professional game and felt in awe. Make no mistake: these boys can play.

Justin Leonard – winner of the 1992 US Amateur Championship

US AMATEUR CHAMPIONSHIPS STATISTICS

Year	Winner	Venue
1895	C.B. Macdonald	Newport, RI
1896	H.J. Whigham	Shinnecock Hills, NY
1897	H.J. Whigham	Chicago, IL
1898	F.S. Douglas	Morris County, NJ
1899	H.M. Harriman	Onwentsia, IL
1900	W.J. Travis	Garden City, NY
1901	W.J. Travis	Atlantic City, NJ
1902	L.N. James	Glen View, IL
1903	W.J. Travis	Nassau, NY
1904	H. Chandler Egan	Baltusrol, NJ
1905	H. Chandler Egan	Wheaton, IL
1906	E.M. Byers	Englewood, NJ
1907	J.D. Travers	Cleveland, OH
1908	J.D. Travers	Garden City, NJ
1909	R. Gardner	Wheaton, IL
1910	W.C. Fownes Jnr	Brookline, MA
1911	H.H. Hilton	Apawamis, NY
1912	J.D. Travers	Wheaton, IL
1913	J.D. Travers	Garden City, NY
1914	F. Ouimet	Ekwanok, VT
1915	R. Gardner	Detroit, MI
1916	C. Evans	Merion, PA
1917–18	*No championship*	
1919	S.D. Herron	Oakmont, PA
1920	C. Evans	Engineers Club, NY
1921	J. Guilford	Clayton, MO
1922	J. Sweetser	Brookline, MA
1923	M.R. Marston	Flossmoor, IL
1924	R.T. Jones Jnr	Merion, PA
1925	R.T. Jones Jnr	Oakmont, PA
1926	G. von Elm	Baltusrol, NJ
1927	R.T. Jones Jnr	Minikahda, MN
1928	R.T. Jones Jnr	Brae Burn, MA
1929	H.R. Johnson	Del Monte, CA
1930	R.T. Jones Jnr	Merion, PA
1931	F. Ouimet	Beverley, IL
1932	C.R. Somerville	Baltimore, NJ
1933	G.T. Dunlap	Kenwood, OH
1934	W. Lawson Little	Brookline, MA
1935	W. Lawson Little	Cleveland, OH
1936	J.W. Fischer	Garden City, NY
1937	J. Goodman	Portland, OR
1938	W P Turnesa	Oakmont, PA
1939	M.H. Ward	Glen View, IL
1940	R. Chapman	Winged Foot, NY
1941	M.H. Ward	Omaha, NE
1942–45	*No championship*	
1946	S.E. Bishop	Baltusrol, NJ
1947	R.H. Riegel	Pebble Beach, CA
1948	W.P. Turnesa	Memphis, TN
1949	C.R. Coe	Rochester, NY
1950	S. Urzetta	Minneapolis, MN
1951	W.J. Maxwell	Saucon Valley, PA

Year	Winner	Venue
1952	J. Westland	Seattle, WA
1953	G. Littler	Oklahoma City, OK
1954	A. Palmer	Detroit, MI
1955	E. Harvie Ward	Richmond, VA
1956	E. Harvie Ward	Lake Forest, IL
1957	H. Robbins	Brookline, MA
1958	C.R. Coe	San Francisco, CA
1959	J. Nicklaus	Broadmoor, CO
1960	D.R. Beman	St Louis, MO
1961	J. Nicklaus	Pebble Beach, CA
1962	L.E. Harris Jnr	Pinehurst No. 2, NC
1963	D.R. Beman	Des Moines, IO
1964	W.C. Campbell	Canterbury, OH
1965–73 Decided by stroke play		
1965	R. Murphy	Southern Hills, OK
1966	G. Cowan	Merion, PA
1967	R. Dickson	Broadmoor, CO
1968	B. Fleisher	Columbus, OH
1969	S.N. Melnyk	Oakmont, PA
1970	L. Wadkins	Portland, OR
1971	G. Cowan	Wilmington, DE
1972	M.M. Giles	Charlotte, NC
Championship reverted to match play		
1973	C. Stadler	Inverness, OH
1974	J. Pate	Ridgewood, NJ
1975	F. Ridley	Richmond, VA
1976	B. Sander	Bel-Air, CA
1977	J. Fought	Aronomink, PA
1978	J. Cook	Plainfield, NJ
1979	M. O'Meara	Canterbury, OH
1980	H. Sutton	Pinehurst, NC
1981	N. Crosby	Olympic, CA
1982	J. Sigel	Brookline, MA
1983	J. Sigel	North Shore, IL
1984	S. Verplank	Oak Tree, OK
1985	S. Randolph	Montclair, NJ
1986	S. Alexander	Shoal Creek, AL
1987	W. Mayfair	Jupiter Hills, FL
1988	E. Meeks	Hot Springs, VA
1989	C. Patton	Merion, PA
1990	P. Mickelson	Cherry Hills, CO
1991	M. Voges	Honours Course, TN
1992	J. Leonard	Muirfield Village, OH
1993	J. Harris	Houston, TX
1994	T. Woods	Sawgrass, FL
1995	T. Woods	Newport, RI
1996	T. Woods	Portland, OR
1997	M. Kuchar	Lemont
1998	H. Kuehne	Oak Hill

THE PRESIDENT'S CUP

The men in control of the US Tour have never been slow to captialize on a commercial opportunity if one arises. Thus, when the Ryder Cup went from being a backwater golf event to a tournament that captured the imagination of the entire sports world, what they wanted to know was this: why is it only played every two years?

Clearly, they felt, there was room in the calendar for a team event played in alternate Ryder Cup years. And so the President's Cup was born, featuring an American side against a non-European International team.

The format is similar to the Ryder Cup, with 12 men on either side. The chief difference is that five fourballs and foursomes matches are played on each of the first two days, as against four in the Ryder Cup.

The first match was played in 1994 at Lake Manassas, VA, where the Internationals were no match for the home side. The pattern of the contest was set on the first morning, with America winning all five fourballs matches. No team has ever recovered from such a deficit, and the Internationals were not about to set a precedent – although they did perform creditably thereafter.

Indeed in the other three series of fourballs and foursomes they actually won a point more than the Americans. The singles, however, were almost as one-sided as the opening series. America won the first three matches out on the course and the trophy was won, with only the winning margin to be decided. As Fred Couples and Davis Love won their matches on the final hole against Nick Price and Steve Elkington, respectively, it turned out to be by the hefty verdict of 20–12.

The President's Cup returned to Lake Manassas in 1996, and a similarly one-sided match appeared on the cards when the opening morning's fourballs again went heavily in America's favour, this time 4–1. The Internationals managed only a half-point more in the afternoon, leaving themselves seemingly hopelessly five points adrift after the first day's play.

The second day, however, was a completely different matter. The Internationals began brightly. The key in fourballs is to do well in the opening two matches to establish some momentum for the players coming up behind. Price and Elkington did this with a stirring final-hole victory over Justin Leonard and Tom Lehman. Then the all-Australian pairing of Greg Norman and Robert Allenby won another match that went to the 18th, this one against Corey Pavin and Steve Stricker.

With Jumbo Ozaki and Vijay Singh scoring a notable success against the leading American pairing, Couples and Love, the Internationals had gained a point back, but, more importantly, had recovered their confidence.

This was shown during a memorable afternoon session for the visitors, when they shocked the Americans with a series of dazzling successes.

First Corey Pavin and Phil Mickelson were despatched 3&2 by Peter Senior and David Frost; then Davis Love and Mark Brooks were beaten by Robert Allenby and Frank Nobilo. The two Zimbabweans, Nick Price and Mark McNulty, teamed up to beat Kenny Perry and Justin Leonard 3&1.

With two matches out on the course, the Internationals were now trailing by a single point. Both were too close to call. The first featured Greg Norman and Ernie Els against Lehman and Stricker. Once more it was the Internationals who came up with the vital putts. Amazingly, the overall scores were now level.

Could the Americans salvage anything from the afternoon session? Step forward Mark O'Meara and Scott Hoch, who sneaked a point on the final green against Elkington and Singh that in the final analysis would prove absolutely vital.

So to the singles, with just one point between the teams. It was a wonderful day's golf, with two big wins for Craig Parry and David Frost, plus one for Steve Stricker making the teams level again. Back and forth the lead went until finally there was only one match out on the course, featuring Fred Couples against Vijay Singh.

The teams could not be separated, so whoever won this match would take the trophy. After 15 holes it was looking good for Couples, who was two up. Then Singh hit his tee shot to the par-three 16th stone dead to cut the deficit. After each had played two shots to the 17th it was again advantage Singh. Couples lay 30 feet from the hole after his approach, while the Fijian was barely half that distance away.

Clearly Couples needed to do something to reverse the momentum, but only in his wildest dreams could he have imagined what came next. For the birdie putt was a beauty, never straying for a moment from its intended line before dropping into the hole. Couples was ecstatic, leaping around the green with joy, and accepting the congratulations of his team-mates. It meant that whatever happened to Singh's putt, America would retain the trophy. When Singh missed, it meant they not only retained it, but had won the match as well by a single point.

The scenes around the 18th green, as the American captain Arnold Palmer dissolved into tears, appeared to firmly establish the President's Cup on the golfing calendar.

Two years later, however, the contest travelled overseas for

The Tiger and the Shark – Tiger Woods ran out the winner by one hole in their 1998 President's Cup clash

Shigeki Maruyama – maximum points in the 1998 President's Cup established him as a player of true force on the world stage

the first time, to Royal Melbourne, where the Americans gave such a pallid performance.

The greatest player of all time, Jack Nicklaus, did nothing to alter his reputation as one of the worst captains of all time by picking a singles line-up that defied all logic. By then, however, the match was virtually all over anyway.

The Internationals were four up after the first day's play, and no fewer than nine points ahead after two days. The final winning margin remained nine points, fully compensating the Internationals for the heartbreaking loss two years earlier.

But will the President's Cup survive as a meaningful event if the Americans display such a half-hearted approach every time it leaves the United States? Only time will tell.

Already, however, the event has made some players. In 1996, the stars of the American team were Mark O'Meara and David Duval, whose careers went up several notches in the years that followed due to the confidence they had gained from their performances.

Similarly, the Japanese Shigeki Maruyama, who gained five points out of five at Melbourne, established himself as the most intriguing player to emerge from Japan since Isao Aoki, and one perhaps capable of becoming the first player from that land to win a major championship.

In this respect, therefore, the President's Cup is a more than valid event. But there must be a danger further down the line of this proving to be one team event too many.

1994

Venue: Robert Trent Jones GC, Lake Monassas, VA

Captains: Hale Irwin (USA), David Graham (International)

USA		International	
Fourball			
C. Pavin & J. Maggert (2&1)	1	S. Elkington & V. Singh	0
J. Haas & S. Hoch (6&5)	1	F. Allem & D. Frost	0
D. Love III & F. Couples (1 up)	1	N. Price & B. Hughes	0
J. Huston & J. Gallagher Jr (4&2)	1	C. Parry & R. Allenby	0
T. Lehman & P. Mickelson (3&2)	1	F. Nobilo & P. Senior	0
Foursomes			
H. Irwin & L. Roberts (3&1)	1	D. Frost & F. Allem	0
J. Haas & S. Hoch (4&3)	1	C. Parry & T. Watanabe	0
C. Pavin & J. Maggert	0	F. Nobilo & R. Allenby (2&1)	1
P. Mickelson & T. Lehman	0	S. Elkington & V. Singh (2&1)	1
N. Price & M. McNulty (halved)	½	D. Love III & J. Gallagher Jr (halved)	½
Fourball			
J. Gallagher Jr & J. Huston	0	F. Allem & M. McNulty (4&3)	1
J. Haas & S. Hoch	0	T. Watanabe & V. Singh (3&1)	1
L. Roberts & T. Lehman	0	C. Parry & B. Hughes (4&3)	1
F. Couples & D. Love III (7&5)	1	F. Nobilo & R. Allenby	0
P. Mickelson & C. Pavin (halved)	½	N. Price & S. Elkington (halved)	½
Foursomes			
H. Irwin & J. Haas	0	D. Frost & P. Senior (6&5)	1
C. Pavin & L. Roberts (1 up)	1	C. Parry & F. Allem	0
J. Maggert & J. Huston	0	V. Singh & S. Elkington (3&2)	1
D. Love III & J. Gallagher Jr (7&5)	1	F. Nobilo & R. Allenby	0
P. Mickelson & T. Lehman (3&2)	1	B. Hughes & M. McNulty	0
Singles			
H. Irwin (1 up)	1	R. Allenby	0
J. Haas (4&3)	1	M. McNulty	0
J. Gallagher Jr (4&3)	1	T. Watanabe	0
P. Mickelson (halved)	½	F. Allem (halved)	½
T. Lehman (halved)	½	V. Singh (halved)	½
J. Huston	0	P. Senior (3&2)	1
S. Hoch (halved)	½	D. Frost (halved)	½
J. Maggert (2&1)	1	B. Hughes	0
L. Roberts (halved)	½	F. Nobilo (halved)	½
F. Couples (1 up)	1	N. Price	0
D. Love III (1 up)	1	S. Elkington	0
C. Pavin	0	C. Parry (1 up)	1
United States	**20**	**International**	**12**

1996

Venue: Robert Trent Jones GC, Lake Manassas, VA

Captains: Arnold Palmer (USA), Peter Thomson (International)

USA		International	
Fourball			
F. Couples & D. Love III (2&1)	1	G. Norman & R. Allenby	0
S. Hoch & M. Brooks	0	E. Els & M. McNulty (2 up)	1
P. Mickelson & C. Pavin (2&1)	1	V. Singh & J. Ozaki	0
M. O'Meara & D. Duval (3&2)	1	S. Elkington & F. Nobilo	0
T. Lehman & S. Stricker (4&2)	1	N. Price & P. Senior	0
Foursomes			
M. O'Meara & D. Duval (2&1)	1	C. Parry & F. Nobilo	0
K. Perry & J. Leonard	0	N. Price & D. Frost (3&2)	1
T. Lehman & S. Stricker	0	S. Elkington & V. Singh (2 up)	1
P. Mickelson & C. Pavin (halved)	½	E. Els & M. McNulty (halved)	½
F. Couples & D. Love III (1 up)	1	G. Norman & R. Allenby	0
Four-Ball			
J Leonard & T Lehman	0	N Price & S Elkington (2 up)	1
S Stricker & C Pavin	0	G Norman & R Allenby (1 up)	1
K Perry & S Hoch (2&1)	1	C Parry & F Nobilo	0
D Love III & F Couples	0	J Ozaki & V Singh (2&1)	1
M O'Meara & D Duval (4&3)	1	E Els & M McNulty	0
Foursomes			
P. Mickelson & C. Pavin	0	P. Senior & D. Frost (3&2)	1
D. Love III & M. Brooks	0	F. Nobilo & R. Allenby (3&2)	1
K. Perry & J. Leonard	0	N. Price & M. McNulty (3&1)	1
T. Lehman & S. Stricker	0	G. Norman & E. Els (1 up)	1
M. O'Meara & S. Hoch (1-up)	1	S. Elkington & V. Singh	0
Singles			
Mark Brooks	0	C. Parry (5&4)	1
D. Duval (3&2)	1	P. Senior	0
M. O'Meara (1 up)	1	N. Price	0
K. Perry	0	D. Frost (7&6)	1
S. Stricker (6&5)	1	R. Allenby	0
S. Hoch (1 up)	1	M. McNulty	0
D. Love III (5&4)	1	J. Ozaki	0
J. Leonard	0	S. Elkington (1 up)	1
P. Mickelson	0	E. Els (3&2)	1
C. Pavin	0	G. Norman (3&1)	1
T. Lehman	0	F. Nobilo (3&2)	1
F. Couples (2&1)	1	V. Singh	0
US	**16 ½**	**International**	**15½**

1998

Venue: Royal Melbourne GC, Australia

Captains: Jack Nicklaus (USA), Peter Thomson (International)

USA		International	
Fourball			
M. O'Meara & J. Furyk	0	G. Norman & S. Elkington (2&1)	1
M. Calcavecchia & J. Huston	0	S. Maruyama & J. Ozaki (4&3)	1
D. Duval & P. Mickelson (halved)	½	E. Els & N. Price (halved)	½
F. Couples & D. Love III (1 up)	1	C. Parry & C. Franco	0
J. Leonard & T. Woods	0	S. Appleby & V. Singh (2&1)	1
Foursomes			
M. O'Meara & D. Duval	0	F. Nobilo & G. Turner (1 up)	1
J. Furyk & J. Huston	0	G. Norman & S. Elkington (2 up)	1
L. Janzen & S. Hoch	0	S. Maruyama & C. Parry (3&2)	1
T. Woods & F. Couples (5&4)	1	E. Els & V. Singh	0
D. Love III & J. Leonard (halved)	½	S. Appleby & N. Price (halved)	½
Fourball			
M. O'Meara & S. Hoch (1 up)	1	F. Nobilo & G. Turner	0
T. Woods & J. Huston	0	E. Els & V. Singh (1 up)	1
D. Duval & P. Mickelson	0	S. Maruyama & J. Ozaki (3&2)	1
L. Janzen & M. Calcavecchia (3&2)	1	N. Price & C. Franco	0
F. Couples & D. Love III	0	G. Norman & S. Elkington (2&1)	1
Foursomes			
D. Love III & J. Leonard	0	F. Nobilo & G. Turner (2 up)	1
L. Janzen & M. Calcavecchia (halved)	½	G. Norman & S. Elkington (halved)	½
T. Woods & F. Couples	0	S. Maruyama & C. Parry (1 up)	1
D. Duval & P. Mickelson	0	S. Appleby & N. Price (1 up)	1
S. Hoch & J. Furyk	0	E. Els & V. Singh (6&4)	1
Singles			
J. Leonard	0	C. Parry (5&3)	1
D. Duval	0	N. Price (2&1)	1
J. Furyk (4&2)	1	F. Nobilo	0
P. Mickelson (halved)	½	C. Franco (halved)	½
J. Huston	0	S. Maruyama (3&2)	1
S. Hoch (4&3)	1	J. Ozaki	0
M. Calcavecchia (halved)	½	G. Turner (halved)	½
L. Janzen (halved)	½	S. Elkington (halved)	½
D. Love III	0	E. Els (1 up)	1
F. Couples (halved)	½	V. Singh (halved)	½
T. Woods (1 up)	1	G. Norman	0
M. O'Meara (1 up)	1	S. Appleby	0
United States	**1½**	**International**	**20½**

PLAYERS' CHAMPIONSHIP

Mark McCumber – the Jacksonville native triumphed in 1988

In the quest to be considered golf's fifth major, The Players' Championship has tried everything. It used to be known as the TPC – Tournament Players' Championship – but then some marketing whizzkid decided they needed a definite article in there somewhere, *à la* The Masters, and The Open. Hence the name change.

Then they looked at the fact that none of the four major championships has a pro-am on the day before the event, so that was

Fred Couples – a huge slice of fortune handed him victory in 1996

dropped. The result of all this tinkering is that the event has come to be considered as the leading tournament to win outside the grand-slam events. Which is not quite what the US Tour wanted, but not a bad consolation prize either.

In fact it is a wonderfully run tournament that annually attracts as good a field as any event all year. It began life in 1974 at Atlanta Country Club, but since 1977 has always been played in Jacksonville, FL, and since 1982 at the US Tour's own course, the fabled TPC at Sawgrass.

Like the event, the venue has improved with age. When it first opened, the players could hardly believe what they were seeing. The designer, Pete Dye, had always had a reputation for devilishly difficult courses, but now he had built one that was not only daunting, but unfair too. After Jerry Pate collected the trophy he earned himself a chorus of approval from his fellow pros by diving into the lake that runs alongside the 18th – and taking the demon Dye with him.

Yet gradually, over the years, the rough edges have been smoothed, without losing the ethos of what Dye was attempting to create. The result is a splendid layout that accords nicely with its surroundings.

Jack Nicklaus did what came naturally when the TPC started, and completed a two-stroke victory over J.C. Snead. Indeed, Nicklaus would win the event three times in the first five years - an achievement that, like so many of his, remains unequalled.

Other great names who appeared on the trophy during its early years were Lee Trevino, Raymond Floyd and Lanny Wadkins. In 1987, Sandy Lyle became the first non-American to win, emerging triumphant at the third play-off hole against Jeff Sluman.

The following year the event became The Players' Championship, and the first winner was a Jacksonville native, Mark McCumber, who defeated Mike Reid by a stroke.

In 1991 Steve Elkington achieved the first of his two victories. In 1997 he would play exemplary golf and win at a canter, but this first triumph came in far different circumstances as Fuzzy Zoeller was in hot pursuit. A last-round 68 gave Elkington victory by a stroke and he said afterwards: "This is a big event to win, and one day it will be a huge event to win."

It was in 1994 that it probably became just that. Here Greg Norman turned in one of those performances that probably only he can. From first to last his golf was majestic, and it says much for the luckless Zoeller that he stayed within four shots of him at the end for a second runners-up spot. An indication of the quality of golf on offer is that Zoeller's 72-hole total of 268 remains the second-best total ever recorded in the tournament since it moved to Sawgrass.

Zoeller is not the only player to have finished second on two occasions. Bernhard Langer was the luckless bridesmaid in both 1993 and 1995, although in the first of those two years he achieved ample compensation by going on to win his second Masters title shortly afterwards.

In 1996 it was Fred Couples's turn to win, profiting from an amazing piece of luck at the 16th. Going for the green in two at this hazardous par five, he sliced his approach; it was heading, with one bounce, straight for the water on the right of his hole. For some reason, however, the bounce defied the laws of physics and instead of spinning into the hazard, turned sharply the other way and dry land. Couples went on to win from Colin Montgomerie and Tommy Tolles.

Will The Players' Championship ever be considered the fifth major? There is no chance. For one thing, the date is wholly wrong. It is always held just a fortnight before the Masters, to accommodate the demands of television. But that does not sit well with the demands of the very best players. They are already focused on Augusta: Nick Faldo and Tiger Woods have both said that they regard Sawgrass as the ideal warm-up for the Masters. Which is fine in itself, but hardly the stuff of a grand-slam tournament.

THE PLAYERS' CHAMPIONSHIP STATISTICS

Formerly known as Tournament Players Championship (1974–87).

1974	Jack Nicklaus
1975	Al Geiberger
1976	Jack Nicklaus
1977	Mark Hayes
1978	Jack Nicklaus
1979	Lanny Wadkins
1980	Lee Trevino
1981	Raymond Floyd
1982	Jerry Pate
1983	Hal Sutton
1984	Fred Couples
1985	Calvin Peete
1986	John Mahaffey
1987	Sandy Lyle
1988	Mark McCumber
1989	Tom Kite
1990	Jodie Mudd
1991	Steve Elkington
1992	Davis Love III
1993	Nick Price
1994	Greg Norman
1995	Lee Janzen
1996	Fred Couples
1997	Steve Elkington
1998	Justin Leonard

WORLD GOLF CHAMPIONSHIPS

Greg Norman – shook the establishment with his proposals for a world tour

The idea for a world tour for golf, which was first mooted in the late 1960s, was given momentum 15 years later during the golden age for European golf, before finally reaching the drawing board in the mid-1990s with a proposal from Greg Norman that rocked the game's establishment.

Norman, with apparent backing from some big-money players including Rupert Murdoch's global television network, was advocating 10–12 tournaments a year around the world for the top 40 players; in other words, a grand prix circuit similar to that in place in Formula One. He believed he had the backing of most of the golfers necessary to make such a project work, and duly went public.

To say the heads of the various tours were appalled at the idea would be an understatement. Ken Schofield, the Executive Director for the European Tour, was rendered virtually speechless with rage, believing it would wreck the game. It would certainly have wrecked the tour he had worked so hard to put into place.

Thus, he had a cogent point. Norman's circuit might have been a gravy train for the 40 souls on it, but what about the other talented players who compete every week on various tours around the world? Who would want to sponsor tournaments outside Norman's chosen few when they would become second-division events?

And so evolution, not revolution, became the mantra of the heads of the various tours as they used force and diplomacy to render Norman's project stillborn. The golfers who had hinted to Norman face-to-face that they would join him retreated from such a stance when told they would be putting their bread-and-butter earnings gained from their home tour in danger.

The tactic worked. A few weeks after announcing that the tour would take place, Norman was forced into a humiliating retreat.

Four years on, US Tour commissioner Tim Finchem acknowledges that Norman's World Tour idea concentrated minds, to urgently explore ways to meet the requirement of the top golfers to play more often in direct competition.

The result is three World Golf Championship events which got underway in 1999 and will be joined by a fourth in 2000. Given that two of the first three in the first year took place in America, it was not quite what Norman had in mind – he wanted tournaments around the world.

But it is conceivable that before the new millennium is very old, there will be two or three more World Championship events, with one each taking place perhaps in Australia, South Africa and Japan every year.

The three that led the way in 1999 were a matchplay tournament held at La Costa, CA, in February; a strokeplay event for current Ryder and President's Cup golfers in Akron, OH, in August; and a strokeplay tournament for the top 70 golfers at Valderrama in November. The prize money at each was $5 million, with $1 million going to the winner.

On paper at least the matchplay was by far the most interesting. The top 64 players from the world ranking were eligible, and it is a measure of how the tournament had captured everyone's imagination that only Jumbo Ozaki turned down the invitation.

Sadly the event did not live up to the hype. Matchplay is the most capricious of formats, and the scattering of the favoured players over the first two days led to a severe reduction in interest. Most people had hoped that David Duval and Tiger Woods would go head-to-head in the 36-hole final. Instead they got Jeff Maggert versus Andrew Magee, and a final that barely appealed to golfers of the anorak persuasion, let alone those with a passing acquaintance in the game.

It was a troubled start, therefore, to the World Golf Championships series, because this was the one event of the three that people were genuinely excited about before it began: if this did not live up to the hype, what hope for the other two?

Magee also raised the question of whether all the players would support the event when it goes to Melbourne in 2001. It is scheduled to take place on January 4–7, which means the Europeans and Americans leaving home on January 1. Will they be bothered? And if they are not bothered, what is the point of the tournament?

The meaning of the second event in the series is also highly questionable. It is not being too cynical to consider this just a back-door method of paying the participants who compete in the Ryder and President's Cups. In recent years a number of players have complained about not being paid to play in the Ryder Cup. Now they can stop whingeing. The Akron event guaranteed them a cheque for $35,000, with the prospect of earning $1 million.

As for the strokeplay championship at Valderrama, few players are happy with the timing of this tournament. For a number of years now the European Tour has finished each year with the Volvo Masters, and the US Tour with the Tour Championship, after which the prizes are handed out.

Now there will be another event the following week, where the respective prize money lists will be decided, the World Strokeplay Championship, which has left many players wondering, whither the Volvo Masters and the Tour Championship? Certainly it is a terrible slap in the face for both events, and immediately downgrades their status. Which leads to another question: wasn't it precisely to avoid such demotion and the harm it would cause that Norman's World Tour was given such short shrift?

So, clearly, there are teething problems with the new events. One suggestion I would make would be to swap the dates of the strokeplay and matchplay events, and make the latter a non-counting event as far as the orders of merit are concerned. It has enough appeal to stand on its own, and in Europe would find a home where the format is better appreciated. The fourth WGC event, incidentally, is to replace the World Cup, although the format had still to be decided at the time of writing.

Teething problems or not, it will be surprising if the World Golf Championships do not make a significant impact on the game in the next century. Over the last 20 years golf has become a worldwide game: in 1998 a player from Fiji, of all places, won a major championship.

It is only right that this trend is recognized, with more important events being played internationally. This is where Greg Norman was spot on, and why his part in the globalization of the game should not go unrecognized.

WORLD GOLF CHAMPIONSHIPS

February 18–21, 1999: La Costa Resort, Carlsbad, CA

	Rank	Player	Eliminated by
1	24	Jeff Maggert	
2	50	Andrew Magee	Maggert 38th hole
3	27	John Huston	
4	61	Steve Pate	Huston 5&4
T5	1	Tiger Woods	Maggert 2&1
T5	30	Jose-Maria Olazabal	Huston 2&1
T5	32	Shigeki Maruyama	Magee 1 up
T5	60	Eduardo Romero	Pate 3&2
T9	12	Phil Mickelson	Romero 2&1
T9	13	Fred Couples	Pate 1up
T9	25	Bernhard Langer	Maggert 1up
T9	34	Bill Glasson	Magee 1up
T9	39	Loren Roberts	Maruyama 2&1
T9	8	Stewart Cink	Woods 2&1
T9	51	Steve Jones	Olazabal 1 up
T9	54	Patrik Sjöland	Huston 1 up
T17	2	David Duval	Glasson 2&1
T17	8	Vijay Singh	Langer 2&1
T17	9	Nick Price	Maggert 1 up
T17	10	Justin Leonard	Maruyama 4&3
T17	20	Scott Hoch	Couples 1 up
T17	21	Lee Janzen	Mickelson 2&1
T17	28	Greg Norman	Romero 21st
T17	33	Bob Tway	Woods 1 up
T17	36	Brandt Jobe	Pate 1 up
T17	43	Carlos Franco	Sjöand 1 up
T17	46	Scott Verplank	Jones 5&4
T17	47	Thomas Bjørn	Magee 2&1
T17	49	Craig Parry	Cink 3&2
T17	58	Paul Azinger	Roberts 2&1
T17	59	Craig Stadler	Huston 2&1
T17	62	Michael Bradley	Olazabal 2&1

Players defeated in the first round:

Mark O'Meara (3) lost to Bradley 2&1; Davis Love III (4) lost to Pate 1 up; Lee Westwood (5) lost to Romero 3&2; Colin Montgomerie (6) lost to Stadler 5&3; Ernie Els (7) lost to Azinger 1 up; Jim Furyk (11) lost to Sjöland 5&3; Steve Elkington (14) lost to Jones 2&1; Darren Clarke (15) lost to Magee (1 up); Jesper Parnevik (16) lost to Parry 1 up; Payne Stewart (17) lost to Cink 3&2; Brian Watts (18) lost to Bjorn 1 up; Tom Lehman (19) lost to Verplank 3&1; Mark Calcavecchia (22) lost to Franco 2&1; Steve Stricker (23) lost to Maruyama (3&2); Hal Sutton (26) lost to Roberts (5&4); Jeff Sluman (29) lost to Jobe 3&2; Stuart Appleby (31) lost to Glasson 2&1; Tom Watson (32) lost to Tway 6&4; Billy Mayfair (35) lost to Olazabal 5&3; John Cook (37) lost to Norman (3&2); Bob Estes (38) lost to Huston 3&2; Brad Faxon (40) lost to Langer 4&2; Fred Funk (41) lost to Maggert 2 up; Glen Day (44) lost to Janzen 3&2; Ian Woosnam (45) lost to Hoch 3&2; Dudley Hart (52) lost to Couples 2 up; Joe Ozaki (53) lost to Mickelson 3&2; Miguel Angel Jimenez (55) lost to Leonard 4&3; Frankie Minoza (56) lost to Price (4&3); Rocco Mediate (57) lost to Singh 5&3; Stephen Leaney (63) lost to Duval 3&1; Nick Faldo (64) lost to Woods 4&3

WORLD MATCHPLAY CHAMPIONSHIP

There is a considerable body of opinion that still regards the Masters and the World Matchplay Championship at Wentworth as the traditional bookends to the season. This hardly survives a cursory analysis, given the fine tournaments that now run prior to Augusta and follow the matchplay, but it is also testament to the enduring value of these two events and, in the case of the latter, the lasting appeal of the oldest format in golf.

The World Matchplay each autumn was Mark McCormack's first idea for golf, and he has still to surpass it. Why not draw together the best eight players of the season and have them battle head-to-head over 36 holes each day? Given that McCormack managed the top three players at the time, there was never any difficulty in attracting the cream of the crop.

Thirty years later the world had changed. By the 1990s the event was struggling to live up to its title. The four major champions were ritually invited, but there was always one at least who had a prior commitment. Just as the event looked as if it would die a death, however, it came up with a tournament in 1998 that was a timely reminder of all the glories that the World Matchplay can offer.

In the semi-finals there was a clash between two of the best young players, Tiger Woods and Lee Westwood. This gave way to a final between Woods and his good friend and neighbour, Mark O'Meara. This is what matchplay golf is all about, the meetings between friends and rivals with no pencil and score-card to divide them – only their respective wits and talents.

The first matchplay was held in 1964, and the tournament got off to a rousing start. In one semi-final Arnold Palmer took on Gary Player. Palmer began in trademark swashbuckling fashion: he opened with an eagle [the first, now a par four, was then a five] a par, and four birdies. After six holes he was five up, and there was no way back for Player, who eventually lost 8&6.

Palmer's opponent in the final was Neil Coles, the perfect match-up for the sponsors: on the one hand the greatest draw in golf; on the other a homegrown talent. Palmer would win it 2&1; the crowd would have to wait 22 years for a British success.

In matchplay one golfer will occasionally hit top form on the day and run away with a match. More frequently, however, and most excitingly, it will come down to a battle of wills. In this respect Gary Player had few equals, and so it was hardly surprising that he put behind him that first-year loss to compile a record in the event that has still not been surpassed.

In particular he was involved in 1965 in a match of which

Graham Marsh – defeated Ray Floyd in the 1977 final

reputations and tournaments are made. Player was up against Tony Lema, and at lunch the match seemed to be going the way of his previous encounter against Palmer: he was six down. When Player lost the first hole after lunch as well, the crowd naturally began to drift away.

They had returned by the time a remarkable comeback began to unfold. Yet with nine holes to go Player was still five down. Still he refused to concede defeat. Gradually he clawed back the deficit. He won the 10th, the 11th and the 13th. Game on. Player won the 16th as well, and then holed a wonderful putt at the 17th to keep the match alive. At the 18th he drew level for the first time since the fourth hole in the morning.

So to the 37th, where Player clinched victory. That was the start of his matchplay legend. He went on to win the final and

Mark O'Meara – his victorious encounter with Tiger Woods in the 1998 final has helped to bring the tournament back to life

then the following year successfully defended the trophy, defeating Arnold Palmer and Jack Nicklaus along the way. The little South African would end up with five titles to his credit before his skills began to ebb.

As Player's hold over the event began to diminish, so the winner's circle emphasized its international appeal. Two victories for Hale Irwin were followed by one each for the Australians David Graham and Graham Marsh. In 1978 the Japanese Isao Aoki triumphed, and helped himself to a house at Gleneagles as well, courtesy of a hole in one.

If the early years belonged to Player, then the 1980s were seized by the tournament's second dominant personality, Severiano Ballesteros. He won it on four occasions out of five from 1981, and invariably the finals would be tense, exciting affairs. Victory over Ben Crenshaw on the home green the first year was followed by an extra-holes marathon against Sandy Lyle. Ballesteros then defeated his great rival, Bernhard Langer, in two successive finals.

The German took a long time to get to grips with the differing demands of matchplay golf. At one point he came out and accused Ballesteros of trying to intimidate him. But that is precisely the point of matchplay – it is man against man, not man against the course, and a player can legitimately make his reputation count.

When Ballesteros did not win, it was Greg Norman whose talents flourished: he would claim the title on three occasions. On each occasion he defeated a British golfer in the final, and it appeared that one would never win.

As the decade reached its close, however, the tournament found it increasingly hard to attract the best overseas, or more specifically, American players. Certainly this probably contributed to a six-year run in which five tournaments were won by British golfers, while Ballesteros equalled Player's total of five victories. There again, at the time, Messrs Faldo, Lyle and Woosnam, together with the Spaniard, were all among the top half-dozen players in the world. They may well have won anyway.

Certainly it is a feature of the tournament down the years that the best player of the year usually rounds off his special season with victory in the matchplay. The 36-hole distance suits the form golfer; whereas anything can happen over one round, over two this is rarely the case. In 1998, Mark O'Meara proved this point to the letter, nicely rounding off his *annus mirabilis* in memorable fashion.

Three successive victories for Ernie Els in the 1990s also ensured that the South African legacy lived on, 30 years after Player helped put the event on the map. As long as the event can continue to attract enough of the top players to justify its grandiose title, then it will have a part to play as one of the top events in world golf.

WORLD MATCHPLAY CHAMPIONSHIP STATISTICS

1964	A. Palmer beat N. Coles 2&1
1965	G. Player beat P. Thomson 3&2
1966	G. Player beat J. Nicklaus 6&4
1967	A. Palmer beat P. Thomson 2 up
1968	G. Player beat B. Charles 1 up
1969	B. Charles beat G. Littler 37th
1970	J. Nicklaus beat L. Trevino 2&1
1971	G. Player beat J. Nicklaus 5&4
1972	T. Weiskopf beat L. Trevino 4&3
1973	G. Player beat G. Marsh at 40th
1974	H. Irwin beat G. Player 3&1
1975	H. Irwin beat A. Geiberger 4&2
1976	D. Graham beat H. Irwin 38th
1977	G. Marsh beat R. Floyd 5&3
1978	I. Aoki beat S. Owen 3&2
1979	B. Rogers beat I. Aoki 1 up
1980	G. Norman beat S. Lyle 1 up
1981	S. Ballesteros beat B. Crenshaw 1 up
1982	S. Ballesteros beat S. Lyle at 37th
1983	G. Norman beat N. Faldo 4&2
1984	S. Ballesteros beat B. Langer 2&1
1985	S. Ballesteros beat B. Langer 6&5
1986	G. Norman beat S. Lyle 2&1
1987	I. Woosnam beat S. Lyle 1 up
1988	S. Lyle beat N. Faldo 2&1
1989	N. Faldo beat I. Woosnam 1 up
1990	I. Woosnam beat M. McNulty 4&2
1991	S. Ballesteros beat N. Price 3&2
1992	N. Faldo beat J. Sluman 8&7
1993	C. Pavin beat N. Faldo 1 up
1994	E. Els beat C. Montgomerie 4&2
1995	E. Els beat S. Elkington 3&1
1996	E. Els beat V. Singh 3&2.
1997	V. Singh beat E. Els 1 up
1998	M. O'Meara beat T. Woods 1 up

THE WORLD CUP OF GOLF

The new millennium will see a new era for the World Cup. The tournament is to come under the umbrella of the World Golf Championships, which should ensure that it returns to its former status as one of the most prestigious events in the calendar.

This has not been the case for over a decade now. In an increasingly congested schedule it has struggled to breathe, and many of the leading players have long given it a miss. In 1998, for example, the United States were represented by Scott Verplank and John Daly. One shudders to think how many rejections the organizers received before they settled upon that unlikely pairing.

Way back in an altogether less-complicated golf world, the event was welcomed with open arms. It was the American industrialist John Jay Hopkins who felt the sport was ready for a team competition involving all nations. In 1953 he launched the Canada Cup, and countries were invited to send two-man teams to represent them in Montreal. The first winners were the formidable Argentinian pairing of Antonio Cerda and Roberto de Vicenzo. Twelve months on Peter Thomson and Kel Nagle won the trophy for Australia.

The format has always been the same: 72 holes of strokeplay, with both scores counting. An individual trophy is awarded, but it is the team prize that dominates proceedings.

An indication of the event's stature in those early years is that even Ben Hogan and Sam Snead were prepared to travel to play in it. They turned up at Wentworth in 1956 and predictably saw off the opposition, Hogan winning the individual trophy with a total of 277.

The organizers were determined to take the event around the world, and in 1957 they brought the excellent Japanese course Kasumigaseki to global attention. Not surprisingly, perhaps, the native pairing of Torakichi "Pete" Nakamura and Koichi Ono proved too strong for the rest.

Their success provoked a manic obsession with the game in Japan that continues to this day. This was one of the lofty aims of the competition – to spread the gospel and extend the hand of friendship to places basically untouched by golf's appeal. In the case of Japan, it worked spectacularly.

The Irish developed a strong affinity with the event following the unexpected success of Christy O'Connor and Harry Bradshaw in the heat of Mexico City in 1958. The triumph provoked wild celebrations and formed part of the legend of both men. Two years later the event came to Portmarnock, and the locals had the privilege of watching a vintage Sam Snead and a young Arnold Palmer defeat all-comers.

This was the start of a run of seven victories for the Americans in just eight years. Given the players they called upon, perhaps this was inevitable. Snead was a member of three of those teams, while on four occasions the partnership the United States relied upon was Jack Nicklaus and Arnold Palmer. During that run of success Snead and Palmer would claim one individual award each, and Nicklaus two.

The only break in that American run of victories came at Olgiata, Rome, in 1968 when Canada caused one of the great upsets. Ironically, the name of the trophy had been changed from the Canada Cup to the World Cup just a year earlier. Now Al Balding and George Knudson did something no one expected of them, holding off a strong challenge from Lee Trevino and Julius Boros – the key moment coming at the 71st where Trevino drove into the trees.

In Palm Springs, CA, in 1976 there was early evidence of the genius of Severiano Ballesteros, as he and Manuel Pinero captured the trophy for the first time for Spain. Twelve months on and Ballesteros, this time in tandem with Antonio Garrido, completed a successful defence in Manila. Spain remain the only country ever to keep the trophy for two years – apart from the United States, of course, who have come to regard it on occasions as part of the nation's silverware.

By the early 1980s the event was beginning to lose some of its lustre. The leading players came to look upon it as one they could miss. Never one to miss an opportunity, Mark McCormack began the Dunhill Nations Cup for three-man teams in 1985, with the added attractions that it would be held at St Andrews every year and that the prize money was huge. In its first year, the Dunhill Cup offered $1.2 million, which was twice the prize fund of the World Cup.

These were dark days indeed for the older event. McCormack not only promoted the Dunhill Cup, but managed most of the top players: it could hardly be put down to coincidence that these same players suddenly started turning up at St Andrews, but were largely unavailable for the World Cup.

Despite this, the tournament still produced some occasions to savour. In 1987 in Kapalua, Hawaii, Sandy Lyle and Ian Woosnam, who had grown up together in Shropshire, but whose parents were Scottish and Welsh respectively, found themselves in opposite teams in a sudden-death play-off.

It was the Welsh who prevailed: David Llewellyn enjoyed the sweetest moment of his journeyman's career, while Woosnam rounded off the season of his life. He claimed no fewer than five European events as well, and began 1988 as the undisputed world number one.

Fred Couples and Davis Love – the formidable pairing won for four successive years between 1992 and 1995

Nick Faldo and David Carter celebrate England's first World Cup success in 1998

At the start of the 1990s those great friends Fred Couples and Davis Love teamed up to represent the United States. They set a record that will surely never be beaten. For four consecutive years they travelled the world, and wherever the World Cup touched down they could not be beaten. Spain, Florida, Puerto Rico, China: it made no difference to these troubadours. They won the tournament every time.

Kiawah Island was the scene of an unhappy Ryder Cup loss for Europe in 1991, but six years on it resulted in triumph for a second time for Ireland, with Padraig Harrington and Paul McGinley afforded the full treatment when they returned home.

In the last years of the century the event has continued to try to fulfil the ideals that Hopkins once outlined. In 1998 it travelled down to New Zealand, while the Mines Club in Malaysia will host the last tournament before the World Golf Championships step in.

At the time of writing there is still some dispute as to whether the format that has served the event so well will be retained. Let us hope that not only is that the case, but that the event as a whole survives and prospers. Tradition is the thing that all tournaments crave, and the World Cup has one that imitators like the Dunhill Cup can only dream about.

WORLD CUP OF GOLF STATISTICS

Year	Country	Winners
1953	Argentina	Antonio Cerda, Roberto de Vicenzo
1954	Australia	Peter Thomson, Kel Nagle
1955	United States	Chick Harbert, Ed Furgol
1956	United States	Ben Hogan, Sam Snead
1957	Japan	Torakichi Nakamura, Koichi Ono
1958	Ireland	Harry Bradshaw, Christy O'Connor
1959	Australia	Peter Thomson, Kel Nagle
1960	United States	Sam Snead, Arnold Palmer
1961	United States	Sam Snead, Jimmy Demaret
1962	United States	Sam Snead, Arnold Palmer
1963	United States	Arnold Palmer, Jack Nicklaus
1964	United States	Arnold Palmer, Jack Nicklaus
1965	South Africa	Gary Player, Harold Henning
1966	United States	Arnold Palmer, Jack Nicklaus
1967	United States	Arnold Palmer, Jack Nicklaus
1968	Canada	Al Balding, George Knudson
1969	United States	Orville Moody, Lee Trevino
1970	Australia	Bruce Devlin, David Graham
1971	United States	Jack Nicklaus, Lee Trevino
1972	Taiwan	Hsieh Min Nan, Lu Liang Huan
1973	United States	Jack Nicklaus, Johnny Miller
1974	South Africa	Bobby Cole, Dale Hayes
1975	United States	Johnny Miller, Lou Graham

Year	Country	Winners
1976	Spain	Seve Ballesteros, Manuel Pinero
1977	Spain	Seve Ballesteros, Antonio Garrido
1978	United States	John Mahaffey, Andy North
1979	United States	John Mahaffey, Hale Irwin
1980	Canada	Dan Halldorson, Jim Nelford
1981	*Not played*	
1982	Spain	Manuel Pinero, J-M Canizares
1983	United States	Rex Caldwell, John Cook
1984	Spain	Jose Maria Canizares, Jose Rivero
1985	Canada	Dan Halldorson, Dave Barr
1986	*Not played*	
1987	Wales	Ian Woosnam, David Llewellyn
1988	United States	Ben Crenshaw, Mark McCumber
1989	Australia	Wayne Grady, Peter Fowler
1990	Germany	Bernhard Langer, Torsten Gideon
1991	Sweden	Anders Forsbrand, P-U Johansson
1992	United States	Fred Couples, Davis Love III
1993	United States	Fred Couples, Davis Love III
1994	United States	Fred Couples, Davis Love III
1995	United States	Fred Couples, Davis Love III
1996	South Africa	Ernie Els, Wayne Westner
1997	Ireland	Padraig Harrington, Paul McGinley
1998	England	Nick Faldo, David Carter

THE US WOMEN'S OPEN

Hope Seignious founded the US Women's Open in 1946, and the first championship took place at the Spokane Country Club in Washington, under the auspices of the Women's Professional Golf Association and the Spokane Athletic Round Table. The latter made a lot of money from slot machines, put up $19,700 in war bonds and Patty Berg, the champion, won $5,600 worth.

Berg, still a tireless promoter of the women's game all these years later, was the leading qualifier, and defeated Betty Jameson by 5&4 in the final. That tournament remains an oddity in that every championship since has been strokeplay, and in 1947 in Greensboro, NC, Jameson – one of many outstanding players honed in Texas – took the title with a score of 295. The received wisdom is that it was the first time any woman had broken 300 in a 72-hole event. There was no bonus for such record-breaking, and in the absence of profitable slot machines the prize money was reduced to $7,500.

At least the championship was up and playing – and its run has been unbroken, whatever difficulties the women professionals have encountered over the years. It quickly acquired the status and mystique that all proper championships have and Babe Zaharias – who won in 1948, 1950 and, most memorably and emotionally of all, by 12 shots in 1954 after an operation for cancer – added greatly to that. She might not have been the best golfer of her generation, but she was an astounding athlete and was the biggest draw by far, a show-woman – and a show-off – down to her spikes. Zaharias was not an easy person, but she injected the flair and flamboyance that all new ventures need, and she was surrounded by an illustrious supporting cast.

Louise Suggs, a slim, stylish Georgian, who kept her own counsel but gave the impression of caring little for the antics of Zaharias, beat the defending champion by a distance in 1949. Suggs won by 14 shots, which is still the biggest winning margin, with a score of 291 to the 305 of Zaharias. Betsy Rawls was another who quickly left the chorus line. Trained in Texas, she was still an amateur when she was runner-up to Zaharias in 1950, but in 1951, having turned professional, she won her first championship.

Rawls, a pupil of the revered Harvey Penick, went on to prove that her performances were not beginner's luck. She became the first player to win the title four times, and so far the only other person to match that tally is Mickey Wright, widely regarded as a player without peer at any time. Rawls won the championship again in 1953 in a play-off with Jackie Pung, and then twice more in 1957 and 1960. Pung, a Hawaiian who won the US Women's Amateur in 1952, had turned professional by 1953 and she and Rawls tied on 302, with the latter winning the play-off by six shots, 71 to 77. It was the first time the championship had gone to extra holes, and the first time it had been run by the USGA (United States Golf Association), which has been in charge ever since.

At Winged Foot in 1957, Pung came in with the best score of 298, one better than Rawls, but instead of winning the title, the Hawaiian was disqualified because she had failed to notice that her marker (Betty Jameson) had written down a five at the 4th hole instead of the six Pung had taken. The total was correct, but the Rules are clear and immutable: the competitor is solely responsible for the correctness of the score recorded at each hole; Pung was undone and obliterated from the record. At least 21 years later at Augusta, Roberto de Vicenzo signed for a higher score rather than a lower score, and was merely relegated to second place instead of a tie for first. Rawls received the trophy and the winner's cheque of $1,800, but Pung was given over $3,000 after members, spectators and officials took a collection in sympathy. On a lighter note, all competitors had been asked to wear skirts instead of shorts, to conform to the host club's dress code.

The 1950s were also notable for the first foreign champion: Fay Crocker, of Montevideo in Uruguay. She had moved to America and turned professional in 1953, presumably in need of a fresh challenge after winning the Uruguayan Women's Amateur championship 20 times. At the Wichita Country Club in Kansas, in winds that reached up to 40mph, she showed masterly control, especially with her long irons, and won by four strokes.

In 1956 there was another first when an amateur called Barbara McIntire tied for top spot with Kathy Cornelius. There were nearly as many amateurs as professionals in the entry of 46, but professional honour was saved when Cornelius won the play-off with a 75 to McIntire's 82. It wasn't until 1967 that the remarkable Catherine Lacoste became the first, and to date only amateur, to win the title. McIntire, who had offers but never turned professional, won the US Women's Amateur twice and played on six Curtis Cup teams. She was also captain twice, in 1976 and again in 1998, when the United States were desperate to end a losing streak. They won.

At the end of the decade, Wright's name started to make its appearance on the trophy. In 1958, at the age of 23, the tall, sweet-swinging Californian, who was to win 82 tournaments as a professional, defeated Suggs by five shots after leading from start to finish. In 1959 it was the same one-two, with Wright winning by two despite putting problems, which she sorted out with a few telephone calls to the short-game maestro, Paul Runyan.

Babe Zaharias – winner of the US Women's Open in 1948, 1950 and, most memorably, in 1954

Mickey Wright – became the first player to win consecutive championships in 1958 and 1959

Wright was the first player to win consecutive championships, and she was on course for an unprecedented hat-trick at Worcester Country Club, but blew up in the last round, and Rawls won her fourth Open. Tied for the lead with Rawls after 54 holes, Wright subsided to fifth place with a round of 82, undone by the weight of expectation. It was her worst moment on a golf course, and she later recalled that she seemed to have no control over what she was doing, that nothing went right no matter how hard she tried. A select few have suffered similarly since, and so far no one has managed to win three championships in a row. Donna Caponi, Susie Berning, Hollis Stacy, Betsy King and Annika Sorenstam have all faced the challenge and come up short.

Wright did not fret for long. Less than 12 months later she won the title for the third time in four years, with a majestic victory at Baltusrol, leaving Rawls six strokes adrift with rounds of 72, 80, 69 and 72. A well-nigh flawless performance on the last day – when she shot 141, three under par – spread-eagled the field. Wright found her length an advantage on a course that measured 6,372 yards; she played the four par-fives in seven under par, and was in no doubt that this was her "most satisfying victory, as it transpired on such a marvellous test of the game". Nearly 10,000 spectators turned up over the three days, a new USGA record.

The old guard of Wright and Rawls – between them they had won every championship since 1957 – was overthrown in 1962 by Murle Lindstrom, who came from five strokes behind after three rounds to record her first victory as a professional. It was to become a bit of a trend of the swinging sixties: in 1963 Mary Mills was a first-time winner; in 1966 it was Sandra Spuzich; in 1969 Donna Caponi had her turn. In 1964, however, Wright ruled again, although she had to work hard to win her fourth and last championship. She got up and down in two from a bunker at the last hole to tie with Ruth Jessen on 290, three under par, then won the high-class play-off 70 to 72.

There were a couple of innovations in 1965, the year in which Carol Mann became the tallest champion, at 6ft 3in. The last two rounds were spread over two days instead of being crammed into one, and the final round was televised nationally for the first time. Two years later the professionals weren't so sure that this exposure was such a good thing because they, supposedly the best women players in the world, were embarrassed by an amateur. What's more, she was just 22 and French. It was a sensation.

Catherine Lacoste, a member of the most famous sporting family in France, became the youngest champion at the appropriately named Virginia Hot Springs Golf and Tennis Club – a distinction she held for over 30 years until 20-year-old Se Ri Pak won in 1998. Catherine's father was the tennis champion René Lacoste, and her mother was a golfer of note, the first Frenchwoman to win the British Amateur championship, in 1927. Their daughter travelled to Virginia on her own and showed that she meant business with an opening 71, one stroke behind the leader, Sandra Haynie. Lacoste moved in front – for good, as it turned out – with a second round of 70 that left her four strokes clear of Susie Maxwell and Margie Masters. The Lacoste lead increased to five despite a 74 in the third round, and at one stage in the last round she led by seven shots.

It looked all over but, as is often the Open way, there was drama to come. Lacoste started to falter and, as the shots leaked away, the opposition crept closer and closer. Louise Suggs, twice champion and five-times runner-up, was an infrequent competitor by this time, but she led the charge. Nine shots behind after 54 holes, she was only one behind after 69. At the 16th, a par five, Suggs misjudged her third shot a fraction and it fell short of the green, embedding itself in the bank of a water hazard. The result was a championship-wrecking double bogey. Suggs tied for fourth on 297, and it was Beth Stone and Maxwell who set the target with 296, both shooting 74 in the fourth round.

It was the 17th that decided matters. Lacoste, with trademark aggression, rallied with two superb shots to 10 feet and rammed home the birdie putt. She parred the last for a 79, a total of 294 and a famous victory. Then she put in a call to France.

Two years later Lacoste won the US Amateur and became the fifth player to win both championships (the others being Berg, Jameson, Zaharias and Suggs, while JoAnne Carner was to become the sixth). Typically contrary, the Frenchwoman was the only one to win the Open first. She put up a stout defence of her title, without threatening to humiliate the professionals again, and finished tied for 13th place, 13 shots behind the newly married Susie Berning, *née* Maxwell. It was the first of three Open titles for Berning, who led all the way after an opening 69 and kept her nerve with a level-par last round of 71. She finished three shots ahead of quadruple champion Mickey Wright, whose closing 68 was the lowest last round ever.

That year, 1968, was the first time in Open history that the entry had topped three figures, and of the 104 entrants 65 were professionals (another record). The professional count was up to 70 the following year when Donna Caponi, a redhead with a slow, sweet swing, but no wins in five seasons on the Tour, kept her nerve in tense circumstances. She eagled the par-five 15th to take the lead, but after she drove off the 18th play was suspended because of an electrical storm. Caponi was confined to the clubhouse for 15 minutes before proceedings recommenced; then she birdied the hole, to win by a shot from Peggy Wilson.

Caponi had another narrow victory in 1969, beating Sandra Haynie and 1966 champion Sandra Spuzich by a shot. Until Caponi's final putt went in, Wright had been the only champion to defend the title successfully. Caponi's bid for the fabled hat-trick foundered in the third and fourth rounds – she shot 77 twice – and she finished a distant third, 11 shots behind JoAnne Carner. In fact, everyone at the Kahkwa Club in Erie, PA, was left in the distance by Carner, who was seven shots clear of the runner-up, Kathy Whitworth. Carner, who had won the US Women's Amateur five times, had not turned professional until late in 1969, aged 30, and was anxious not to waste any time. The Open was her second victory as a professional, and she was to win the championship again in 1976. Whitworth, who won a record 88 tournaments in a distinguished career, never won an Open; in fact, this second-place finish was the nearest she came.

Susie Berning was champion in 1972 and 1973, taking her tally of titles to three alongside Zaharias, Rawls and Wright. For the 1972 championship, Winged Foot was so wet that there had been talk of postponing the championship, and the course played every inch of its 6,226 yards. Berning started with a 79, but in a week when only eight players either matched or bettered the par of 72, she closed with a 71. The key hole was the 17th, a 200-yard par three, which Berning birdied and Pam Barnett bogeyed to tie for second with Kathy Ahern and Judy Rankin, a shot behind the winner.

Berning's cheque for $6,000 was a new record, as was the prize fund of $38,350, but it was made to look like loose change by the purse at the Dinah Shore Colgate Winners Circle, a new, much-hyped event that had taken place at Mission Hills Country Club in California in April. The brainchild of David Foster, the CEO of Colgate-Palmolive, the Dinah Shore was hosted by the singer and entertainer of that name – Foster had persuaded her to transfer her affections from tennis to golf – and celebrities galore were on hand for the Pro-Am. The purse was a massive $110,000 and Jane Blalock, the winner, received $20,050 – for three rounds. The Open had a little way to go yet. It raised the total prize money to $39,490 at the Country Club of Rochester, NY, in 1973 and Berning's share remained $6,000. She had won by five shots from Gloria Ehret and Shelley Hamlin, a relatively untroubled victory after Pam Higgins, who had shared the lead with Berning after three rounds, three-putted from three feet at the sixth and subsided to a 79 and fifth place.

Sandra Haynie, another talented Texan, took the title in 1974 at La Grange Country Club, IL, when she birdied the last two holes to beat Carol Mann and Beth Stone by a shot. It was a startling effort because in the first 70 holes, Haynie had managed only three birdies. At the 17th she holed a monstrous putt of 70 feet and at the 18th she knocked in a relative tiddler of 15 feet, the stuff of Open legend. Fourteen amateurs made the cut, including all eight of the US Curtis Cup team, and one of them, Debbie Massey, won the gold pin for the leading amateur. After two rounds she shared the lead on 144 with Kathy Ahern and Caponi, and eventually tied for seventh place with Caponi.

In a foretaste of things to come, another amateur caught the attention at Atlantic City Country Club the following year when she tied for second, four shots behind the petite Sandra Palmer. The amateur was Nancy Lopez, who was to be runner-up in three more Opens but, come 1999, was still trying to win the championship. Palmer started with an unpromising 78 but, going into the last round, shared the lead with Sally Little of South Africa and Sandra Post of Canada. It had been windy all week, but conditions were particularly difficult on the last day and Palmer, under 5ft 2in. in height and raised in Texas, where it can be breezy, was one of only three players to match the par of 72.

The Open was starting to expand at a rapid rate and in 1976, when the entry topped 200 for the first time, sectional qualifying was introduced. Carner beat Palmer, the defending champion, by two shots in a play-off with a 76, receiving just over $9,000 of the record purse of $60,000. By the end of the decade there were 335 entries, and prize money had soared to $125,000. Jerilyn Britz, the champion in 1979, won $19,000 and her total of 284 equalled the record set by Louise Suggs way back in 1952. Even better, there was a record number of spectators (41,200) over the four days. The Women's Open was looking up, and there were other bright young things out there with Lopez, queuing up to topple the old guard.

Hollis Stacy was one of them. The Georgian had won three successive US Girls' Junior championships between 1969 and 1971, and confirmed her successful transition from prodigy to professional with back-to-back victories in the Open in 1977 and 1978. At Hazeltine in 1977 Stacy led from the off, her 70 being the only sub-par round on the opening day; she won by two shots from Lopez, who was playing her first tournament as a professional. Stacy's defence of the title at the Country Club of Indianapolis developed into a see-saw battle with the redoubtable Carner, but the 24-year-old youngster came out on top to become the fourth, and youngest, player to win successive championships.

In 1984, to show that her double had been no youthful indiscretion, Stacy won the title for a third time, at Salem Country Club in Massachusetts. She shot 69 in the last round – holing a seven-iron for an eagle two at the 13th – for a total of 290, and beat Rosie Jones by a stroke to become the fifth three-time champion. In one of those magical Open quirks of fate, the first had been the legendary Zaharias, who had won her third title at Salem in 1954.

Stacy's success in the 1970s had inspired others of her generation, and in 1980 Amy Alcott, a 24-year-old Californian who had won the US Girls' Junior championship seven years earlier, became Open champion in record-breaking style. Her total of 280 was the best in the championship's history, four better than the mark of Suggs and Britz. At Richland Country Club in Nashville, TN, in temperatures that exceeded 100 degrees, Alcott put together rounds of 70, 70, 68 and 72 to leave Stacy trailing by nine shots in runner-up spot. The champion could not have been more deserving of her record cheque of $20,047.50.

Alcott's record stood for a year. At La Grange Country Club, IL, Pat Bradley returned a total of 279, finishing with a six-under-par 66 to hold off Beth Daniel by a shot. They had a ding-dong battle on the last day, and the championship swung Bradley's way when she holed a birdie putt of 70 feet at the 15th to lead by a shot. Daniel dropped a shot at the 16th to fall two behind, but had a birdie two at the 17th to crank up the tension again. They both birdied the 18th, Bradley holing from two feet for the title. Whitworth, playing in her twenty-third Open, was third on 284 and the cheque for $9,500 made her the first woman to win more than $1 million in her career. It took her 23 years. These days, a player can win that much in one summer.

Janet Alex, who had never won before in her professional career, came from behind to run away with the 1982 Open. A last round of 68 left her five shots clear of the quartet of Carner, Haynie, Daniel and Donna White. Carner was runner-up again the following year, despite the handicap of a first round of 81, and matched Suggs's total of four second places. Carner and Patty Sheehan finished just one shot behind Jan Stephenson, who was the first Australian to win the Open and the first foreign champion since Lacoste in 1967. The wait for the next one was considerably shorter.

In 1985 Kathy Baker, who had been the leading amateur in 1981 and 1982, won the title (her first as a professional) and in 1986 Jane Geddes followed suit, surviving an earthquake, toxic fumes from a derailed tanker, thunderstorms and a play-off (against Sally Little, 71 shots to 73) to win at NCR Country Club in Dayton, OH. Almost unnoticed in the mayhem, a young Englishwoman called Laura Davies tied for 11th on her debut, and a few weeks later she won the British Women's Open at Royal Birkdale. She had given notice that she was a force to be reckoned with.

The following year Davies, aged 23, became the first Englishwoman to win the US Women's Open, at Plainfield Country Club in New Jersey, one of the most protracted championships of all time. The weather was so bad on Sunday that the last round was postponed until Monday, and then there was a three-way play-off on Tuesday featuring Davies, Carner and Ayako Okamoto, the Japanese who was to finish the season as leading money winner on the US Tour and Player of the Year. It was the least experienced member of the trio who triumphed, with a one-under-par 71; this was two shots better than Okamoto and three ahead of Carner, who was runner-up for a record fifth time at the age of 48. The veteran American was a great fan of the new champion's rather cavalier, all-out approach, and couldn't help watching her hit over the closing holes. "My curiosity got me," she smiled. "You'll be hearing a lot from this girl."

Carner was right, and Davies even caused the US LPGA tour to revise their rules. She was not a member when she won

Lisalotte Neumann – her first win in America came at the 1988 US Women's Open

the title, the most important in women's golf, and there were those who insisted that the new US Women's Open champion would have to go through the qualifying school if she wanted to join the Tour. Fortunately, sense prevailed and there is now a clause allowing for the Davies factor. Less sensibly, the Open is not included in Davies's growing list of LPGA victories, an idiotic omission that Davies treats with the contempt it deserves: "I know I won it," she said, "and I know it counts."

She has yet to win the championship again, but her victory proved an inspiration to her fellow Europeans, and the knock-on effect was such that it is no longer a rarity to hail a foreign champion. On the contrary, it has become the norm. There have been four since Davies – they have won five titles between them – and the last American to win her national Open was Patty Sheehan in 1994.

Liselotte Neumann, the Swedish standard-bearer, who learned to play at a nine-hole course called Finspang (it's now 18 holes), followed Davies as champion. It was her first win in America, too, but not her last as she later established herself as one of the world's best players. She started with a 67 and added rounds of 72, 69, 69 to beat Sheehan by three shots. The 22-year-old Swede was the second youngest champion – Lacoste remained the youngest – and her total of 277 was the lowest ever. Her *sang froid* was awesome. Even when she four-putted for a double bogey at the 7th to fall behind Sheehan she did not crumble, but gathered herself and stormed to the title with birdies at the 10th, 11th, 12th, 15th and 17th.

Fears about the state of American golf were allayed over the next few years as the Americans struck back. Betsy King was champion in 1989 and 1990, the fifth player to win the title in successive years. At Indianwood she won her first title relatively comfortably, taking charge on the last day with four birdies in the first nine holes and finishing four shots ahead of Lopez. Things were a little more fraught at Atlanta Athletic Club, when the weather was so bad that 36 holes were played on the last day. King was steadiness personified with rounds of 72, 71, 71 and 70, and Sheehan slithered from the sublime (opening rounds of 66 and 68) to the hideous (rounds of 75 and 76) to lose by a shot.

Meg Mallon kept the Stars and Stripes flying in 1991, adding the Open to the LPGA Championship that she had won earlier in the year, and in 1992 Sheehan showed that she had the mental resilience of a champion when she won at Oakmont, defeating her good friend Juli Inkster in a play-off, 72 to 74. In the final round, Inkster had been two ahead with two to play when a thunderstorm stopped play. She parred the last two holes, but Sheehan birdied them to tie and Inkster, US Women's Amateur champion in 1980, 1981 and 1982, is still waiting to win the Open. Sheehan, the demons of Atlanta well and truly exorcized, won again in 1994, equalling Neumann's total of 277 and confirming herself as a player of the highest quality.

That was the year in which Helen Alfredsson, an exuberant Swede, had done the collapsing. In 1993 she had been pipped at the post by Lauri Merten, who had come from next-to-nowhere to birdie two of the last three holes at Crooked Stick and beat an astonished Alfredsson by one shot. At Indianwood in 1994, the Swede opened up with a 63, the lowest first round ever recorded in the Open, and followed that with a 69 for a 36-hole total of 132, another record. Alfredsson was 13 under par for the first 43 holes and leading by eight shots. Then the slide began, and she played the last 29 holes in 14 over par, finishing eight shots behind Sheehan in a tie for ninth.

There was more of a fairy-tale Swedish finish at the 50th championship at The Broadmoor in Colorado Springs the following year, when a host of former champions turned up to party and reminisce. Annika Sorenstam, who had not won before in America, finished with a 68 to beat Mallon by one shot after the American had come back to the pack with a triple-bogey six at the tiny fourth hole. The 24-year-old Swede admitted that her nerves were jangling on the closing holes and breathing was difficult in the thin mountain air, but her confidence soared after her victory. She won two more tournaments to be number one on the money list, and Player of the Year.

At Pine Needles Sorenstam proved that there was nothing fluky about her Open performance with a majestic defence of her title. She won by six shots with a record total of 272 (eight under par). A wobble at the end of the third round went unpunished by opponents, who regarded the Swede as the epitome of consistency. She missed only two fairways in the last 36 holes, and gave the impression that she could win the Open in perpetuity. The hat-trick jinx dictated otherwise. Sorenstam missed the cut at Pumpkin Ridge in 1997 and Callaway, whose clubs she played, had to ditch the advertisement they'd made to celebrate the "three-peat", as the Americans insisted on calling it.

Sorenstam's successor was another European, the Swede's Solheim Cup team-mate, Alison Nicholas – a born-again

Annika Sorenstam – winner in 1995 and 1996, but she couldn't break the tournament's hat-trick jinx in 1997

Christian from England who was a revelation in Oregon. Nicholas, all five foot of her, finished on 274, 10 under par and one shot ahead of the great Nancy Lopez, who put her heart and soul into winning the championship for the first time and was urged on by thousands of devoted fans – millions, if you include the enthralled television viewers. It was an amazing week, with drama, emotion and outstanding golf at every turn. Lopez produced rounds of 69, 68, 69, 69 – the first time that anyone had had four rounds in the 60s in the Open – but Nicholas, whose total of 10 under par was the first in double figures, held firm.

The Englishwoman started with a 70 and moved into the lead with a 66, followed by a 67 that took her to 10 under par, three ahead of Lopez and five ahead of compatriot Lisa Hackney. Such scoring led to an emergency call-out for the Miracle Sign Company, because the leaderboard at the 18th green had only red 9s. Miracle delivered some 10s, 11s and 12s, and after four holes on Sunday Nicholas was 13 under. Lopez had had three birdies in the first four holes, but made no inroads because Nicholas had countered with a birdie at the 3rd and an eagle three at the 4th, where she pitched in from 56 yards. The excitement and the tension were raised another notch when Nicholas had a double bogey at the 14th and bogeyed the 17th, but Lopez also made a couple of mistakes and the title headed overseas again.

There was no such euphoria for Lopez and Nicholas at Blackwolf Run in Wisconsin, where some windy weather protected an already daunting layout. They both missed the cut, but the 1998 championship came up trumps again, producing another dramatic finish with a play-off between two 20-year-olds, one a rookie professional from South Korea, the other an amateur from Maryland. Too exaggerated a script? Strange, perhaps, but true.

Jenny Chuasiriporn, the unexpected American hope (her father is from Thailand, hence the surname), had been leading amateur the year before tied for 56th and was in the Curtis Cup team, but even she was amazed when she holed a 35-foot putt at the 72nd hole and ended up tied for first with Se Ri Pak, the Korean sensation who had won the LPGA Championship in May. Their score of 290, six over par, was the highest winning total since 1984. They both shot 73 in the play-off – Chuasiriporn led by four shots after five holes, but lost control with a six at the par-three 6th and missed a 12-foot par putt for the title at the last because her hands were shaking so badly. Se Ri, who had paddled barefoot into the water to play her second shot at the 18th, won two holes later courtesy of a 20-foot birdie putt.

Se Ri, the youngest US Women's Open champion ever, is a national heroine in her homeland, and her victory highlighted the cosmopolitan nature of a championship that started in such a small way in 1946. The demands of fame are greater now and so are the rewards – the first prize of $267,500 was more than Patty Berg, the first champion, won in a long and distinguished career. But the object of the exercise remains the same: to win what has become the greatest championship in women's golf.

Se Ri Pak – the tournament's youngest-ever winner

1946

Spokane CC, Spokane, WA
Tournament played as matchplay

1	**Patty Berg**	5&4
2	**Betty Jameson**	

1947

Starmount Forest CC, Greensboro, NC
Tournament changed to stroke-play

1	**Betty Jameson**	300
=2	**Sally Sessions (a)**	301
	Rolly Riley (a)	301

1948

Atlantic City CC, Northfield, NJ

1	**Babe Zaharias**	300
2	**Betty Hicks**	308

1949

Prince Georges CC, Landover, MD

1	**Louise Suggs**	291
2	**Babe Zaharias**	305

1950

Rolling Hills CC, Wichita, KS

1	**Babe Zaharias**	291
2	**Betsy Rawls (a)**	300

1951

Driud Hills GC, Atlanta, GA

1	**Betsy Rawls**	294
2	**Louise Suggs**	298

1952

Bala GC, Philadelphia, PA

1	**Louise Suggs**	284
=2	**Marlene Hagge**	291
	Betty Jameson	291

June 25–28, 1953

Country Club of Rochester, Rochester, N.Y
** Betsy Rawls (71) beat Jacqueline Pung (77) in the 18-hole play-off.*

1	**Betsy Rawls***	75	78	74	75	302
2	**Jacqueline Pung**	80	72	76	74	302
3	**Patty Berg**	71	73	80	79	303
4	**Betty Jameson**	79	76	77	80	312
5	**Marilynn Smith**	78	74	82	79	313
6	**Betty Bush**	80	78	76	81	315
=7	**Beverly Hanson**	79	80	77	79	315
	Patricia Ann Lesser (a)	82	75	78	80	315
9	**Alice Bauer Hagge**	83	79	78	76	316
10	**Louise Suggs**	75	81	79	82	317
11	**Mae Murray (a)**	79	83	78	78	318
12	**Marlene Bauer**	80	83	78	79	320
=13	**Betty Hicks**	81	79	84	78	322
	Peggy Kirk	75	78	85	84	322
15	**Patricia O'Sullivan (a)**	82	79	84	78	323
16	**Betty MacKinnon**	82	82	80	81	225
=17	**Polly Martin (a)**	80	79	82	86	327
	Shirley G. Spork	74	84	84	85	327
19	**Bonnie Randolph**	77	86	84	82	329
20	**Patricia Devany (a)**	81	89	80	81	331
21	**Mrs Herbert O. Breault**	87	79	83	85	334
22	**Shirley Anne Smith (a)**	80	85	88	82	335
=23	**Mrs Harrison F. Flippin**	86	79	85	86	336
	Mrs George M. Trainor (a)	79	89	84	84	336
25	**Ann Rutherford (a)**	84	87	82	89	342
26	**Ethel Benson (a)**	81	57	87	58	343
=27	**Jean Hopkins (a)**	85	86	84	91	346
	Anne Richardson (a)	84	88	93	81	346
29	**Mrs Herbert Astmann (a)**	80	97	89	88	354
30	**Mrs Charles Keating (a)**	84	93	88	94	359

July 1–3, 1954

Salem Country Club, Peabody, Mass

1	**Babe Zaharias**	72	71	73	75	291
2	**Betty Hicks**	75	76	75	77	303
3	**Louise Suggs**	76	77	78	76	307
=4	**Betsy Rawls**	77	73	78	90	308
	Mickey Wright (a)	74	79	79	76	308
6	**Jacqueline Pung**	91	77	78	73	309
=7	**Beverly Hanson**	77	80	78	75	310
	Patricia Ann Lesser (a)	79	73	78	80	310
=9	**Fay Cocker**	77	82	79	73	311
	Claire Doran (a)	72	79	80	80	311
11	**Mrs Hugh B. Jones (a)**	79	81	74	78	312
12	**Patty Berg**	78	76	78	81	313
13	**Betty Dodd**	77	77	78	82	314
=14	**Mary Lena Faulk (a)**	77	76	84	79	316
	Bonnie Randolph	82	81	74	79	316
	Betty Bush	79	79	83	75	316
	Betty Jameson	78	78	80	80	316
=18	**Patricia O'Sullivan**	76	79	81	82	318
	Joyce Ziske (a)	78	82	78	80	318
20	**Marilynn Smith**	83	75	79	82	319
21	**Betty MacKinnon**	78	80	82	80	320
22	**Helen Segel Wilson (a)**	80	82	84	76	322
23	**Jean Hopkins (a)**	78	79	83	86	326
24	**Mrs Edward McAuliffe (a)**	82	83	81	84	330
25	**Bettye Mims Danoff**	81	81	84	85	331
26	**Ellen H. Gery (a)**	86	80	84	85	335
=27	**Virginia Dennehy (a)**	85	85	85	81	336
	Barbara Bruning (a)	83	84	88	81	336

July 1–3, 1954 continued

29	**Mrs Donald McClusky (a)**	83	84	87	84	338
30	**Gloria Armstrong (a)**	89	83	84	85	341

June 30–July 2, 1955

Wichita Country Club, Wichita, KA

1	**Fay Crocker**	74	72	79	74	299
=2	**Louise Suggs**	79	77	72	75	303
	Mary Lena Faulk	77	77	72	77	303
4	**Jacqueline Pung**	79	76	76	75	305
5	**Patty Berg**	78	80	78	71	307
=6	**Polly Riley (a)**	80	78	74	77	309
	Jacqueline P. Yates (a)	76	79	76	78	309
8	**Patricia Ann Lesser (a)**	81	76	79	75	311
=9	**Beverley Hanson**	87	76	77	72	312
	Betty Jameson	83	77	76	76	312
=11	**Betty Hicks**	81	81	72	79	313
	Marilynn Smith	80	79	79	75	313
	Marlene Bauer	85	75	76	77	313
14	**Peggy Kirk Bell**	84	80	75	75	314
15	**Alice Bauer Hagge**	81	80	74	80	315
16	**Betty Bush**	87	76	78	81	322
17	**Mickey Wright**	86	76	78	83	323
18	**Wiffi Smith (a)**	81	85	77	82	325
=19	**Ann Casey Johnstone (a)**	81	86	76	83	326
	Betsy Rawls	84	81	84	77	326
21	**Virginia Dennehy (a)**	86	79	74	88	327
22	**Natasha Matson (a)**	84	79	82	84	329
=23	**Gloria Armstrong**	79	84	81	86	330
	Bettye Mims Danoff	83	81	78	88	330
	Gloria J. Fecht (a)	86	83	77	84	330
=26	**Jean Ashley (a)**	83	85	78	85	331
	Vonnie Colby	89	83	80	79	331
28	**Ruth Jessen (a)**	83	79	90	80	332
=29	**Betty MacKinnon**	84	83	80	86	333
	H.T. Williford (a)	84	84	80	85	333

July 26–28, 1956

Northland Country Club, Duluth, MI

** Kathy Cornelius (75) beat Barbara McIntire (82) in the 18-hole play-off.*

1	**Kathy Cornelius***	73	77	73	79	302
2	**Barbara McIntire (a)**	75	79	77	71	302
=3	**Marlene Bauer Hagge**	74	74	75	80	303
	Patty Berg	78	75	76	74	303
5	**Joyce Ziske**	76	74	79	76	305
6	**Marilynn Smith**	76	78	78	74	306
=7	**Louise Suggs**	76	73	80	78	307
	Betty Jameson	77	75	78	77	307
9	**Mickey Wright**	77	80	78	13	308
=10	**Fay Crocker**	82	80	76	71	309
	Mary Lena Faulk	75	75	81	78	309
12	**Beverly Hanson**	74	77	79	80	310
=13	**Betsy Rawls**	82	77	78	77	314
	Peggy Kirk Bell	79	78	78	79	314
15	**Ruth Jessen (a)**	85	77	81	74	317
=16	**Patricia Ann Lesser (a)**	77	81	81	80	319
	Betty Dodd	80	85	76	78	319
18	**Judy Bell (a)**	83	77	80	80	320
19	**Gloria Armstrong**	79	81	80	82	322
20	**Bonnie Randolph**	82	77	83	81	323
21	**Wanda J. Sanches (a)**	80	88	76	81	325
22	**Phyllis O. Germain**	83	81	84	78	326
=23	**Nan Berry (a)**	84	80	80	83	327
	Gloria J. Fecht	80	87	82	78	327

July 26–28, 1956 continued

=25	**Jacqueline P. Yates (a)**	84	78	79	87	328
	Mary Patton Janssen (a)	80	84	80	84	328
27	**Ann Casey Johnstone (a)**	82	81	85	82	330
28	**Beverly Gammon (a)**	85	86	79	81	331
29	**Vonnie Colby**	83	80	84	85	332
=30	**Virginia Dennehy (a)**	90	83	79	87	339
	Diana Garrett	89	84	86	80	339

July 21–29, 1957

Winged Foot Golf Club, Mamaroneck, N.Y.

1	**Betsy Rawls**	74	74	75	76	299
2	**Patty Berg**	80	77	73	75	305
=3	**Betty Hicks**	75	77	76	80	308
	Louise Suggs	76	81	75	76	308
5	**Betty Dodd**	74	78	76	82	310
=8	**Marlene Bauer Hagge**	72	81	81	77	311
	JoAnn Prentice	75	78	84	74	311
	Alice Bauer	72	73	87	79	311
=9	**Beverly Hanson**	78	76	79	79	312
	Fay Crocker	78	81	75	78	312
=11	**Wiffi Smith**	81	76	79	77	313
	Mary Lena Faulk	76	79	83	75	313
	Barbara McIntire (a)	78	77	82	76	313
14	**Marlene Stewart Streit (a)**	79	79	75	82	315
=15	**Judy Frank (a)**	80	79	81	76	316
	Anne Richardson (a)	78	76	83	79	316
=17	**Peggy Kirk Bell**	78	78	78	83	317
	Bonnie Randolph	78	83	75	81	317
=19	**Gloria Armstrong**	73	85	84	78	320
	Marilynn Smith	77	80	79	84	320
21	**Mrs Philip J. Cudone (a)**	80	80	82	79	321
=22	**Mickey Wright**	79	82	81	80	322
	Joyce Ziske	80	80	80	82	322
24	**Meriam H. Bailey (a)**	81	80	79	84	324
=25	**Ruth Jessen**	85	83	80	77	325
	Vonnie Colby	78	86	80	81	325
	Gloria J. Fecht	83	81	81	80	325
=28	**Helen Sigel Wilson (a)**	77	80	89	81	327
	Mary Patton Janssen (a)	81	79	84	83	327
30	**Kathy Cornelius**	81	79	83	85	328

June 26–28, 1958

Forest Lake Country Club, Bloomfield Hills, MI

1	**Mickey Wright**	74	72	70	74	290
2	**Louise Suggs**	75	74	75	71	295
3	**Fay Crocker**	79	68	76	74	297
4	**Alice Bauer**	75	77	75	72	300
5	**Betty Jameson**	75	80	74	74	303
6	**Betsy Rawls**	79	82	73	70	304
=7	**Wiffi Smith**	81	76	73	75	305
	Jacqueline Pung	75	77	77	76	305
=9	**Vonnie Colby**	77	76	75	78	306
	Patty Berg	78	78	77	73	306
=11	**Mary Lena Faulk**	79	76	79	73	307
	Beverly Hanson	79	77	75	76	307
	Anne Quast (a)	82	73	76	76	307
14	**Marlene Bauer Hagge**	76	79	76	77	308
15	**Kathy Cornelius**	80	74	77	78	309
16	**Joyce Ziske**	78	79	75	77	310
17	**Barbara McIntire**	83	76	77	76	312
18	**Peggy Kirk Bell**	82	79	73	79	313
19	**Marilyn Smith**	82	79	82	73	316
20	**Betty Dodd**	79	80	80	78	317
21	**Bonnie Randolph**	79	78	80	81	318

June 26–28, 1958 continued

22	**JoAnn Prentice**	78	82	78	81	319
=23	**Gloria J. Fecht**	82	79	80	80	321
	Ruth Jessen	83	81	81	76	321
=25	**Mrs Paul Dye Jr. (a)**	84	79	79	80	322
	Murle MacKenzie	82	79	81	80	322
27	**Betty Bush**	86	76	80	82	324
28	**Judy Bell (a)**	84	76	83	82	325
29	**Gloria Armstrong**	83	81	81	81	326
30	**Jon Snyder**	85	80	78	84	327

June 25–27, 1959

Churchill Valley Country Club, Pittsburgh, PA

1	**Mickey Wright**	72	75	69	71	287
2	**Louise Suggs**	71	74	75	69	289
=3	**Joyce Ziske**	75	73	72	72	292
	Ruth Jessen	75	74	72	71	292
	Marlene Bauer Hagge	71	76	73	72	292
6	**Patty Berg**	72	75	75	74	296
7	**Betsy Rawls**	76	73	72	76	297
8	**Murle MacKenzie**	77	75	75	71	298
9	**Anne Quast (a)**	75	76	75	73	299
10	**JoAnn Prentice**	77	74	77	74	302
=11	**Joanna Goodwin (a)**	80	78	72	73	303
	Barbara McIntire (a)	76	77	74	76	303
13	**Mary Lena Faulk**	76	77	76	75	304
14	**Wanda Senches**	75	73	77	80	305
=15	**Beverly Hanson**	79	75	78	74	306
	Betty Hicks	78	76	76	76	306
	Kathy Cornelius	75	17	76	78	306
	Marilynn Smith	76	74	78	78	306
	Fay Crocker	77	74	75	80	306
	Betty Jameson	76	75	81	74	306
21	**Wiffi Smith**	77	79	78	73	307
=22	**Gloria Armstrong**	81	76	73	81	311
	Barbara Williams (a)	76	77	80	78	311
	Betty Bush	77	79	79	76	311
25	**Betty Kerby**	75	79	80	78	312
26	**Barbara Romack**	81	79	75	78	313
=27	**Sherry Wheeler (a)**	81	75	77	82	315
	Betty Mims Danoff	79	77	78	81	315
=29	**Phyllis Preuss (a)**	81	80	77	78	316
	Judy Bell (a)	79	81	78	78	316

July 21–23, 1960

Worcester Country Club, Worcester, MA

1	**Betsy Rawls**	76	73	68	75	292
2	**Joyce Ziske**	75	74	71	73	293
3	**Marlene Bauer Hagge**	74	74	75	75	298
	Mary Lena Faulk	75	72	76	75	298
5	**Mickey Wright**	71	71	75	82	299
6	**Wiffi Smith**	75	76	73	76	300
7	**Beverly Hanson**	75	77	77	72	301
8	**Fay Crocker**	74	76	76	76	302
=9	**Louise Suggs**	78	77	72	77	304
	Marilynn Smith	72	72	83	77	304
	Kathy Whitworth	75	73	80	76	304
=12	**Betty Jameson**	78	74	77	77	306
	Barbara Romack	80	78	73	75	306
	Ruth Jessen	76	77	78	75	306
15	**Murle MacKenzie**	75	80	76	78	309
16	**Gloria Armstrong**	78	78	80	77	313
17	**Patty Berg**	80	76	78	80	314
18	**Wanda Sanches**	77	77	81	81	316
19	**Mary Ann Reynolds**	81	78	79	79	317

July 21–23, 1960 continued

=20	**Betty Bush**	83	79	77	79	318
	Peggy Kirk Bell	79	77	81	81	318
22	**Jacqueline N. Pung**	81	80	80	79	320
23	**Bonnie Randolph**	77	77	87	80	321
24	**Judy Torluemke (a)**	85	81	80	80	326
25	**Gloria Fecht**	86	79	82	81	328
26	**Sally Carroll (a)**	88	81	77	85	329
27	**Claudette A. LaBonte**	82	83	79	86	330
28	**Mrs Edward Stumpp (a)**	83	83	81	85	332
=29	**Mrs Donald K. McClusky (a)**	83	81	87	82	333
	JoAnn Prentice	80	85	81	87	333

June 29–July 1, 1961

Baltusrol Golf Club, Springfield, N.J.

1	**Mickey Wright**	72	80	69	72	293
2	**Betsy Rawls**	74	76	73	76	299
3	**Ruth Jessen**	75	73	77	75	300
4	**Louise Suggs**	78	74	76	73	301
5	**Marilynn Smith**	77	74	77	75	303
6	**JoAnn Prentice**	72	76	80	76	304
=7	**Barbara Romack**	77	77	78	74	306
	Marlene Stewart Streit (a)	74	77	77	78	306
=9	**Mary Lena Faulk**	78	77	80	73	308
	Shirley Englehorn	80	73	78	77	308
	Mrs Philip J. Cudone (a)	77	76	75	80	308
=12	**Fay Crocker**	76	83	77	73	309
	Murle MacKenzie	78	79	78	74	309
=14	**Kathy Cornelius**	76	80	73	82	311
	Carol Mann	80	75	77	79	311
16	**Kathy Whitworth**	81	81	77	74	313
17	**Sybil Griffin**	82	77	77	79	315
18	**Patty Berg**	82	83	77	74	316
=19	**Gerda Whalen**	80	82	77	78	317
	Marlene Hagge	80	84	75	78	317
=21	**Betty Jameson**	81	81	79	77	318
	Barbara E. Greene	80	80	81	77	318
	Anne Richardson (a)	75	76	83	84	318
24	**Helen Sigel Wilson**	74	81	81	83	319
=25	**Beverly Hanson**	83	80	78	79	328
	Judy Torluemke (a)	83	78	78	82	320
	Judy Kimball	78	79	85	78	320
28	**Beth Stone**	82	81	77	81	321
=29	**Marianne Gable (a)**	81	79	80	82	322
	Peggy Kirk Bell	86	78	78	80	322
	Wanda J. Sanches	82	82	79	79	322

June 28–30, 1962

Dunes Golf and Beach Club, Myrtle Beach, SC.

1	**Marie Lindstrom**	78	74	76	73	301
=2	**Ruth Jessen**	72	76	75	80	303
	JoAnn Prentice	75	77	73	78	303
=4	**Louise Suggs**	80	77	74	75	306
	Mickey Wright	75	73	81	77	308
=6	**Shirley Englehorn**	81	72	79	75	307
	Mary Lena Faulk	78	74	78	77	307
=8	**Marlene Bauer Hagge**	76	75	81	76	308
	Shirley G. Spork	77	77	79	75	308
=10	**Mary Mills**	78	79	77	75	309
	Kathy Whitworth	80	78	73	78	309
12	**Barbara Romack**	76	76	81	78	311
=13	**Petty Berg**	85	75	75	77	312
	Kathy Cornelius	79	79	78	76	312
=15	**Marilynn Smith**	79	77	80	77	313
	JoAnne Gunderson (a)	82	74	77	80	313

June 28–30, 1962 continued

17	**Clifford Ann Creed**	79	78	75	84	318
18	**Carol Mann**	82	79	80	76	317
=19	**Peggy Kirk Bell**	80	82	79	77	318
	Jacqueline N. Pung	76	83	75	84	318
=21	**Betsy Rawls**	86	74	80	79	319
	Sandra Haynie	77	83	83	76	319
=23	**Mary Anne Lopez (a)**	77	81	82	80	320
	Nancy Roth (a)	78	83	79	80	320
	Judy Kimball	78	77	75	90	320
=26	**Polly Riley (a)**	81	75	87	79	322
	Judy Torluemke	79	81	82	80	322
	Mrs Paul Dye Jr (a)	78	78	84	82	322
	Beth Stone	82	81	82	78	323
30	**Lesbia Lobo**	82	82	78	83	325

July 18–20, 1963

Kenwood Country Club, Cincinnati, OH

1	**Mary Mills**	71	70	75	73	289
=2	**Sandra Haynie**	75	72	73	72	292
	Louise Suggs	72	72	75	73	292
4	**Clifford Ann Creed**	71	75	79	74	299
=5	**Ruth Jessen**	72	78	77	75	302
	Kathy Whitworth	75	74	80	73	302
=7	**Mary Lena Faulk**	75	73	76	79	303
	Kathy Cornelius	76	75	77	75	303
	Patsy Hahn	74	73	78	78	303
	Murle Lindstrom	83	75	74	71	393
=11	**Betsy Rawls**	75	77	72	80	304
	Judy Kimball	72	78	79	75	304
=13	**Carol Mann**	75	76	78	76	305
	Marlene B. Hagge	80	72	77	76	305
	Phyllis Preuss (a)	76	73	79	77	305
16	**Sandra A. Spuzich**	79	77	75	75	306
17	**Jacqueline N. Pung**	76	73	79	79	307
=18	**Shirley G. Spork**	79	73	77	79	308
	Marilynn Smith	75	76	76	81	308
20	**Betty Jameson**	75	79	80	75	309
21	**Sally Carroll (a)**	77	78	80	75	310
=22	**Shirley Englehorn**	77	79	78	77	311
	Sybil J. Griffin	79	76	78	78	311
	Gail Davis	78	72	84	77	311
=25	**Helen Sigel Wilson (a)**	81	72	79	80	312
	Margaret Jones (a)	81	76	75	80	312
	Sandra McClinton	82	75	76	79	312
28	**JoAnn Prentice**	77	75	83	79	314
=29	**Patty Berg**	77	79	78	81	315
	Beth Stone	75	81	80	79	315
	Andrea Cohn	75	78	86	76	315

July 9–11, 1964

San Diego Country Club, Chula Vista, CA

** Mickey Wright (70) beat Ruth Jessen in the 18-hole play-off.*

1	**Mickey Wright***	71	71	75	73	290
2	**Ruth Jessen**	72	73	74	71	290
=3	**Shirley Englehorn**	71	78	68	74	291
	Marilynn Smith	75	70	72	74	291
5	**Sandra Haynie**	78	73	70	74	295
6	**Peggy Wilson**	73	77	72	74	296
=7	**JoAnn Prentice**	78	73	76	71	298
	Marlene B. Hagge	71	76	74	77	298
9	**Kathy Whitworth**	76	76	75	73	300
10	**Patty Berg**	76	74	77	75	302
=11	**Mary Mills**	79	75	75	75	304

July 9–11, 1964 continued

	Barbara McIntire	76	76	77	75	304
13	**Jacqueline N. Pung**	73	79	76	78	306
14	**Judy Belt (a)**	79	78	67	83	307
=15	**Beverly Hanson**	78	80	76	74	308
	Sandra McClinton	72	78	75	83	308
	Nancy Roth (a)	74	78	75	81	308
=18	**Kathy Cornelius**	80	75	76	78	309
	Barbara Fay White	80	75	72	82	309
	Susan Lance (a)	74	79	79	77	309
21	**Susan O'Connor**	75	77	80	78	310
22	**Betsy Rawls**	81	77	76	77	311
=24	**Barbara Romack**	79	76	81	80	316
	Betty Hicks	82	79	79	76	316
	Wanda J. Sanches	78	83	77	78	316
27	**Alice Bauer Hovey**	76	79	80	82	317
=28	**Linda C. Maurer (a)**	80	79	80	82	321
	Jean Ashley (a)	78	81	80	82	321
	Janis Ferraris (a)	77	77	82	85	321

July 1–4, 1965

Atlantic City CC, Northfield, NJ

1	**Carol Mann**	78	70	70	72	290
2	**Kathy Cornelius**	71	75	77	69	292
3	**Marilynn Smith**	75	74	74	71	294
4	**Mary Mills**	76	76	70	73	295
=5	**Susie Maxwell**	75	75	75	71	296
	Helen Sigel (a)	78	72	75	71	296
7	**Ruth Jessen**	77	76	71	75	299
8	**Louise Suggs**	76	77	71	76	300
9	**Margie Masters**	81	74	79	67	301
=10	**Cliffird Ann Creed**	77	76	76	73	302
	Judy Torluemke	76	74	72	80	302
=12	**Sandra Haynie**	80	76	77	70	303
	Marlene Bauer Hagge	72	82	72	77	303
14	**Catherine Lacoste (a)**	79	73	77	75	304
=15	**Andrea Cohn**	78	80	75	72	305
	Sandra Palmer	76	81	77	71	305
	Nancy Roth (a)	79	77	80	69	305
=18	**Barbara Romack**	79	74	74	79	306
	Kathy Whitworth	79	74	81	72	306
20	**Donna Caponi**	78	79	75	75	307
21	**Anne Quast Welts (a)**	74	79	76	79	308
=22	**Patty Berg**	79	77	80	73	309
	Marlene Stewart Streit (a)	79	73	80	77	309
	Mrs Scott Probasco Jr (a)	80	74	76	79	309
25	**Peggy Kirk Bell**	81	77	77	75	310
=26	**Judy Kimball**	82	75	78	76	311
	Gail Davis	79	76	79	77	311
	JoAnn Prentice	80	77	74	80	311
	Betsy Rawls	75	79	74	83	311
30	**Ann Casey Johnstone**	82	76	77	78	313

June 30–July 3, 1966

Hazeltine National Golf Club, Minneapolis, MI

1	Sandra Spuzich	75	74	76	72	297
2	Carol Mann	73	78	75	72	298
3	Mickey Wright	71	78	77	73	299
4	Clifford Ann Creed	76	75	76	76	303
=5	Sandra Haynie	79	75	78	74	306
	Kathy Whitworth	80	74	76	76	306
7	Judy Torluemke	77	78	79	73	307
8	Mary Mills	79	73	76	80	309
=9	Shirley Englehorn	83	77	75	76	311
	Barbara Romack	80	77	77	77	311
	Susie Maxwell	80	79	75	77	311
	Peggy Wilson	76	76	81	78	311
	Gloria Ehret	82	75	75	79	311
	Shelley Hamlin (a)	81	74	80	76	311
=15	Sharon K. Miller	75	77	77	84	313
	Anne Quest Welts	79	78	77	79	313
17	JoAnn Prentice	78	78	80	78	314
=18	Patty Berg	80	81	80	74	315
	Sandra Palmer	83	78	79	75	315
	Donna M. Caponi	74	82	81	78	315
	Jan Ferraris	78	81	76	80	315
	Joyce Kazmierski (a)	75	77	82	81	315
	Roberta Albers (a)	75	82	81	77	315
24	Piggy S. Conley (a)	77	83	80	76	316
=25	Marlene B. Hagge	78	83	77	79	317
	Cynthia Sullivan	79	83	75	80	317
	Judy Kimball	82	75	79	81	317
=28	Margie Masters	81	79	82	76	318
	Lena Faulk	85	77	79	77	318
	Candy Phillips	81	77	79	81	318

June 29–July 2, 1967

Hot Springs Golf and Tennis Club, Hot Springs, VA

1	Catherine Lacoste (a)	71	70	74	79	294
=2	Susie Maxwell	71	75	76	74	296
	Beth Stone	75	76	71	74	296
=4	Sandra Haynie	70	79	77	71	297
	Murle Lindstrom	75	74	73	75	297
	Louise Suggs	76	74	74	73	297
7	Margie Musters	73	73	74	80	300
=8	Sharon K. Miller	76	80	74	71	301
	Clifford Ann Creed	75	75	76	75	301
	Marilynn Smith	75	77	72	77	301
=11	Judy Torluemke	78	81	70	73	302
	Shirley Englehorn	73	74	76	79	302
	Dorothy Germain (a)	75	78	79	70	302
14	Sybil Griffin	71	79	75	78	303
=15	Betsy Rawls	73	82	75	75	305
	Kathy Whitworth	81	76	73	75	305
	Judy Kimball	78	76	73	78	305
	Lesley Holbert	79	73	74	79	305
	Nancy Roth Syms (a)	76	75	78	76	305
=20	Marlene Bauer Hagge	79	80	73	74	306
	Carol Mann	77	72	82	75	306
	Peggy Wilson	80	72	79	75	306
=23	Gerda Whalen	80	76	79	72	307
	Sandra Palmer	80	76	76	75	307
	Donna M. Caponi	74	76	76	81	307
26	Anne Quast Welts (a)	78	78	75	77	308
=27	Sandra Spuzich	77	79	77	76	309
	Mary Mills	84	75	73	77	309
	Betty Cohen	72	79	77	81	309
	Kathy Ahern	78	74	74	83	309

July 4–7, 1968

Moselem Spring Golf Club, Fleetwood, PA

1	Susie Maxwell	69	73	76	71	289
2	Mickey Wright	70	78	76	68	292
=3	Marilynn Smith	72	76	74	73	295
	Carol Mann	71	76	73	75	295
=5	Kathy Whitworth	75	74	73	74	296
	Murle Lindstrom	73	73	75	75	296
7	Clifford Ann Creed	77	73	76	71	297
8	Gerda Whalen	75	72	79	73	299
=9	Sandra Spuzich	75	75	78	72	300
	Judy Torluamke	75	76	74	75	300
	Phyllis Preuss (a)	73	76	73	78	300
12	Sandra Post	73	76	77	75	301
=13	Pam Barnett	77	75	74	76	302
	Judy Kimball	77	76	70	79	302
	Shelley Hamlin (a)	79	77	74	72	302
	Catherine Lacoste (a)	74	78	77	73	302
=17	Sharron Morgan	78	73	78	74	303
	Mary Mill	80	74	73	76	303
	Ruth Jessen	72	77	77	77	303
	Nancy Roth Syms (a)	77	79	75	72	303
=21	Sandra Palmer	76	77	76	75	304
	Dorothy Porter (a)	79	77	76	72	304
=23	Jane Woodworth	75	80	78	72	305
	Betty Cullen	77	76	78	74	305
	Donna Caponi	76	79	76	74	305
	JoAnn Prentice	74	75	81	75	305
	Mary Lou Daniel	82	73	73	77	305
	Sandra Haynie	78	78	72	77	305
=28	Gail Davis	75	76	82	73	306
	Patty Berg	75	77	78	76	306
	Sybil Griffin	75	75	79	77	306
	Louise Suggs	75	76	77	78	306
	Margie Masters	77	73	74	82	306
	Ann Quest Welts	78	74	76	78	306

June 26–29, 1969

Scenic Hills Country Club, Pensacola, FLA

1	Donna Caponi	74	76	75	69	294
2	Peggy Wilson	71	76	75	73	295
3	Kathy Whitworth	76	78	69	73	296
=4	JoAnn Prentice	73	71	79	75	298
	Sybil Griffin	73	76	77	72	298
	Ruth Jessen	73	72	75	78	298
7	Shirley Englehorn	72	76	77	76	301
=8	Mary Mills	75	80	71	76	302
	Murle Lindstrom	74	79	74	75	302
	Mickey Wright	76	79	76	71	302
	Clifford Ann Creed	76	76	75	75	302
	Louise Suggs	76	78	75	73	302
=13	Sandra Spuzich	76	72	79	76	303
	Kathy Cornelius	80	74	76	73	303
	Sandra Haynie	76	73	74	80	303
=16	Beth Stone	77	74	74	79	304
	Susie Maxwell Berning	78	78	75	73	304
	Marilynn Smith	80	74	77	73	304
	Phyllis Preuss (a)	79	77	79	69	304
=20	Gerda Whalen	78	78	76	73	305
	Betsy Rawls	77	80	76	72	305
	Susan Little	74	78	77	76	305
=23	Sharon K. Miller	75	79	75	77	306
	Sherry Wilder	78	75	76	77	306
	Shelley Hamlin (a)	86	72	76	72	306
=26	Carol Mann	77	78	77	75	307

June 26–29, 1969

	Marlene B. Hagge	80	75	76	76	307
28	**Jane Blalock**	77	76	81	75	309
=29	**Betsy Cullen**	78	77	76	79	310
	Sharron Moran	82	76	76	76	310
	Signa Jean Quandt	78	80	75	77	310

July 2–5, 1970

Muskogee Country Club, Muskogee, OK

1	**Donna Caponi**	69	70	71	77	287
=2	**Sandra Haynie**	71	72	71	74	288
	Sandra Spuzich	72	72	70	74	288
=4	**Sandra Palmer**	73	71	71	74	289
	Kathy Whitworth	71	71	76	71	289
6	**Sharon K. Miller**	70	77	74	69	290
7	**JoAnn Prentice**	72	75	70	74	297
8	**Carol Mann**	69	70	77	76	292
=9	**Shirley Englehorn**	70	74	74	75	293
	Clifford Ann Creed	73	73	74	73	293
=11	**Peggy J. Wilson**	71	75	75	73	294
	Marilynn Smith	72	73	77	72	294
	Cynthia Hill (a)	72	70	75	77	294
=14	**Gerda Whalen**	71	74	75	75	295
	Kathy Ahern	71	74	76	74	295
	Betsy Rawls	72	75	77	71	295
=17	**Mrs Michael J. Skala**	72	74	79	71	296
	Jane Fassinger (a)	71	73	78	74	296
=19	**Jane Blalock**	73	74	77	73	297
	Pam Barnett	77	68	80	72	297
=21	**Judy Kimball**	75	74	73	76	298
	Murle Lindstrom	73	76	73	76	298
	Susan M. Little	74	74	79	71	298
	Joanne Gunderson Carner	73	74	78	73	298
	Jane Bastanchury (a)	74	74	75	75	298
=26	**Betsy Cullen**	71	77	76	75	299
	Gloria Ehret	74	75	74	76	299
	Althea Gibson Darben	73	75	74	77	299
	Marlene B. Hagge	72	76	74	77	299
	Shelley Hamlin (a)	73	75	76	75	299

June 24–27, 1971

Kahkwa Club, Erie, PN

1	**JoAnne Gunderson Carner**	70	73	72	73	288
2	**Kathy Whitworth**	73	77	73	72	295
=3	**Jane Blalock**	75	73	74	77	299
	Donna Caponi	70	75	77	77	299
	Mickey Wright	73	75	75	76	299
	Jane Bestanchury (a)	72	77	76	74	299
=7	**Kathy Cornelius**	73	78	73	76	300
	Lesley Holbert	71	75	81	73	300
=9	**Shelley Hamlin (a)**	77	76	73	75	301
	Martha Wilkinson (a)	74	78	77	72	301
=11	**Murle Lindstrom Breer**	75	72	77	78	302
	Mary Mills	75	72	73	82	302
=13	**Gerda Whalen Boykin**	77	75	78	73	303
	Betsy Cullen	76	76	76	75	303
=15	**Sandra Post Elliott**	79	77	76	72	304
	Marlene B. Hagge	74	78	75	77	304
	Carol Mann	75	77	76	76	304
	Pam Higgins	77	77	76	74	304
	Beth Stone	74	77	73	80	304
	Sandra Haynie	75	78	78	73	304
=21	**Mary Lou Daniel**	74	79	76	77	306
	Marilynn Smith	74	77	79	76	306
23	**JoAnn Prentice**	77	74	77	79	307

June 24–27, 1971

=24	**Pam Barnett**	71	80	75	76	308
	Sharon K. Miller	74	82	73	79	308
	Marlene Stewart Streit (a)	76	78	77	77	308
=27	**Susie Maxwell Berning**	80	76	77	76	309
	Judy Kimball	77	77	76	79	309
=29	**Kathy Ahern**	78	79	74	79	310
	Debbie Austin	78	80	78	74	310
	Hisako Higuchi	79	79	77	75	310
	Barbara Myers	78	81	73	78	310
	Sandra Spuzich	78	81	75	76	310

June 29–July 2, 1972

Winged Foot Golf Club, Mamaroneck, NY

1	**Susie Maxwell Berning**	79	73	76	71	299
=2	**Kathy Ahern**	74	80	76	70	300
	Pam Barnett	73	76	75	76	300
	Judy Torluemke Rankin	76	75	76	73	300
5	**Betty Burfeindt**	75	78	74	75	302
=6	**Mickey Wright**	77	80	76	71	304
	Jane Bastanchury Booth (a)	79	75	78	72	304
	Gloria Ehret	74	74	80	76	304
=9	**Carol Mann**	79	77	78	71	305
	Carol Semple (a)	79	79	74	73	305
	Jocelyne Bourassa	76	75	78	76	305
=12	**Sharon K. Miller**	79	74	79	74	306
	Betsy Cullen	73	78	78	77	306
=14	**Hisako Higuchi**	78	77	79	73	307
	Janie Blalock	78	78	77	74	307
	JoAnn Prentice	79	78	75	75	307
	Sandra Haynie	83	76	73	75	307
	Shirley Englehorn	72	75	.82	78	307
=19	**Shelley Hamlin**	78	74	79	77	308
	Sandra Palmer	78	76	77	77	308
	Sue Roberts	77	78	76	77	308
	Kathy Whitworth	79	79	72	78	308
	Kathy Cornelius	74	80	75	79	308
	Betsy Rawls	77	76	74	81	308
=25	**Gerda Whalen Boykin**	81	76	81	71	309
	Donna Caponi Young	80	75	75	79	309
27	**Marlene B. Hagge**	78	79	80	73	310
28	**Peggy Wilson**	78	75	82	76	311
=29	**Mary Mills**	80	78	78	76	312
	Debbie Austin	80	76	79	77	312
	JoAnne Gunderson Carner	79	79	75	79	312
	Clifford Ann Creed	79	74	78	81	312

July 19–22, 1973

Country Club of Rochester, Rochester, NY

1	**Susie Maxwell Berning**	72	77	69	72	290
=2	**Gloria Ehret**	75	75	74	71	295
	Shelley Hamlin	76	70	75	74	295
4	**Anne Quast Sander (a)**	74	72	76	74	296
5	**Pam Higgins**	72	76	70	79	297
=6	**Judy Torluemke Rankin (a)**	77	72	75	74	298
	Mary Mills	74	73	75	76	298
	Sandra Palmer	76	72	74	76	298
=9	**Janie Blalock**	78	76	72	73	299
	Sue Roberts	71	81	73	74	299
	Mary Lou Crocker	75	78	69	77	299
=12	**Sandra Spuzich**	75	79	74	72	300
	Carole Jo Skala	78	74	74	74	300
=14	**Beth Barry (a)**	74	74	78	75	301
	Margie Masters	74	75	78	74	301
	Sharon K. Miller	73	69	78	81	301

July 19–22, 1973 continued

=17	**Mary Budke (a)**	77	76	76	73	302
	Murle Lindstrom Breer	76	75	75	76	302
	Susie McAllister	77	75	76	74	302
	Kathy Cornelius	74	77	76	75	302
	Mary Dwyer Homer	75	76	76	75	302
	Marilynn Smith	75	76	75	76	302
=23	**Liana Zambresky (a)**	75	78	75	75	303
	Jane Bastanchury Booth (a)	73	74	77	79	303
=25	**Hollis Stacy (a)**	77	77	73	77	304
	Marlene Stewart Streit (a)	72	76	78	78	304
	Amie Amizich	75	78	76	75	304
	Donna Caponi Young	78	73	76	77	304
	Laura Baugh	73	79	77	75	304
30	**Jan Ferraris**	78	71	78	78	305
	Barbara White Boddie	70	81	79	75	305
	Kathy Whitworth	78	74	76	77	305

July 18–21, 1974

La Grange Country Club, La Grange, IL.

1	**Sandra Haynie**	73	73	74	75	295
=2	**Beth Stone**	75	74	76	71	296
	Carol Mann	72	72	77	75	296
=4	**Kathy Whitworth**	75	77	74	71	297
	JoAnne Carner	77	72	71	77	297
6	**Sandra Post**	81	72	71	74	298
=7	**Donna Caponi Young**	71	76	79	73	299
	Deborah Massey (a)	71	73	80	75	299
=9	**Ruth Jessen**	77	71	71	81	300
	Jane Bastanchury Booth (a)	76	74	76	74	300
11	**Susie Maxwell Berning**	73	77	75	76	301
=12	**Sandra Spuzich**	74	74	72	82	302
	Bonnie Lauer (a)	74	72	80	76	302
=14	**Bonnie Bryant**	77	78	81	67	303
	Murle Lindstrom Breer	77	77	76	73	303
	Sue Roberts	82	72	72	77	303
	Hollis Stacy	77	75	72	79	303
=18	**Carole Jo Skala**	77	74	79	74	304
	Gail Denenberg	77	74	78	75	304
	Mary Mills	78	76	75	75	304
	Anne Quast Sander (a)	74	78	76	76	304
	Nancy Lopez (a)	77	73	77	77	304
23	**Lancy Smith (a)**	73	82	75	75	305
=24	**Clifford Ann Creed**	77	75	81	73	306
	Gloria Ehret	78	75	79	74	306
	Maria E. Astrologes	75	76	74	81	306
	Carol Semple (a)	81	74	74	77	306
=28	**Mary Lou Crocker**	75	76	82	74	307
	Kathy Cornelius	76	75	79	77	307
	Debbie Austin	76	73	80	78	307
	Kathy Ahern	68	76	81	82	307
	Judith J. Oliver	78	82	79	78	307

July 17–20, 1975

Atlantic City Country Club, Northfield, NJ

1	**Sandra Palmer**	78	74	71	72	295
=2	**Sandra Post**	74	73	76	76	299
	JoAnne Carner	73	77	74	75	299
	Nancy Lopez (a)	73	74	77	75	299
5	**Susie McAllister**	79	75	74	72	300
6	**Sandra Haynie**	74	77	74	76	301
7	**Kathy Whitworth**	76	76	75	75	302
8	**Debbie Austin**	76	76	72	79	303
=9	**Sally Little**	80	70	73	81	304
	Judy F. Rankin	72	77	79	76	304

July 17–20, 1975 continued

	Jocelyne Bourassa	77	76	75	76	304
=12	**Gerda Boykin**	78	78	75	74	305
	Maria Astrologes	81	73	79	72	305
=14	**Laura Baugh**	76	74	76	80	306
	Jane Blalock	75	76	80	75	306
=16	**Diane Patterson**	75	74	79	79	307
	Pat Bradley	78	77	78	74	307
	Donna Caponi Young	81	74	77	75	307
=19	**Amy Alcott**	75	76	74	83	308
	Mary Lou Crocker	79	76	73	80	308
	Beth Stone	76	75	77	80	308
	Kathy McMullen	80	76	75	77	306
=23	**Kathy Postlewait**	75	76	62	76	309
	Barbara Ann Barrow (a)	79	76	76	78	309
=25	**Sue Roberts**	78	79	76	77	310
	Marilyn J.S. Smith	79	78	75	78	310
	Silvia Bertolaccini	77	78	79	76	310
	Gloria Ehret	81	76	79	74	310
	Deborah A. Massey (a)	81	72	75	82	310
=30	**Judy Kimball**	73	83	79	76	311
	Peggy S. Conley (a)	78	80	74	79	311

July 8–11, 1976

Rolling Green Golf Club, Springfield, Delaware County, PN

** Joanne Carner (76) beat Sandra Palmer (78) in the 18-hole play-off.*

1	**JoAnne Carner***	71	71	77	73	292
2	**Sandra Palmer**	70	74	73	75	292
3	**Jane Blalock**	75	72	73	76	296
4	**Susie McAllister**	76	78	70	73	297
=5	**Amy Alcott**	72	75	78	74	299
	Sharon K. Miller	75	75	77	72	299
7	**Silvia Bertolaccini**	78	73	74	75	300
=8	**Susie Berning**	73	76	79	75	303
	Mary-Beth C. King (a)	76	74	76	77	303
=10	**Carole Jo Skala**	78	77	72	78	305
	Deborah Massey (a)	75	74	74	82	305
	Carol Semple (a)	71	77	82	75	305
=13	**V. Joyce Kazmierski**	74	75	81	76	306
	Gloria Ehret	77	75	76	78	306
	Hisako Higuchi	72	77	78	79	306
	JoAnn Washam	75	77	74	80	306
=17	**Peggy Conley**	74	80	77	76	307
	Judy T. Rankin	79	75	79	74	307
	Jan Stephenson	79	76	75	77	307
	Sandra Spuzich	76	78	74	79	307
	Pat Bradley	74	71	81	81	307
	Betty Burfeindt	77	74	76	80	307
=23	**Hollis Stacy**	75	80	75	78	308
	Bonnie Lauer	73	80	77	78	308
	Ai-Yu Tu	79	77	76	76	308
=26	**Judy Kimball**	76	76	76	81	309
	Mary Lou Crocker	70	80	81	78	309
	Marlene B. Hagge	76	78	77	78	309
	Sandra Post	74	80	77	78	309
30	**Mary Mills**	75	77	77	81	310
	Connie Chillemi	69	84	78	79	310

July 21–24, 1977

Hazeltine National Golf Club, Chaska, MN

Pos	Player	R1	R2	R3	R4	Total
1	Hollis Stacy	70	73	75	74	292
2	Nancy Marie Lopez	73	72	75	74	294
3	JoAnne Carner	74	72	76	73	295
=4	Amy Alcott	72	77	75	74	298
	Pat Bradley	77	72	79	70	298
	Jan Stephenson	72	75	72	79	298
7	Susie McAllister	76	80	73	70	299
8	Donna Caponi Young	76	77	77	70	300
9	Jane Blalock	72	78	77	74	301
=10	Sally Little	81	75	72	74	302
	JoAnn Prentice	77	76	77	72	302
	Judy T. Rankin	75	77	78	72	302
	Kathy Whitworth	74	76	79	73	302
14	Sandra Post	73	80	72	78	303
=15	Sandra Spuzich	76	78	75	75	304
	Mary Lou Crocker	77	74	81	72	304
=17	Betsy Cullen	80	74	73	78	305
	Carol Mann	76	76	77	76	305
	Peggy Conley	74	76	78	77	305
	Debbie Austin	74	75	78	78	305
21	Laura Baugh	77	80	75	74	306
=22	Debbie Massey	76	79	76	76	307
	Pam Higgins	75	74	83	75	307
=24	Bonnie Lauer	76	80	80	72	308
	Beth Daniel (a)	76	77	81	74	308
=26	Marlene Floyd	79	76	80	74	309
	Janet A. Coles	79	78	73	79	309
=28	Sandra Palmer	74	81	78	77	310
	Joyce Kazmierski	72	83	80	75	310
	Beth Stone	80	73	80	77	310
	Silvia Bertolaccini	78	75	80	77	310
	Susan O'Connor	75	81	75	79	310
	Michelle Walker	75	76	79	80	310

July 20–23, 1978

Country Club of Indianapolis, Indianapolis, IN

Pos	Player	R1	R2	R3	R4	Total
1	Hollis Stacy	70	75	72	72	289
=2	JoAnne Carner	73	72	73	72	290
	Sally Little	75	75	75	65	290
=4	Pam Higgins	74	73	75	71	293
	Jane Blalock	74	74	71	74	293
=6	Donna Horton White	72	72	79	71	294
	Kathy Martin	76	74	71	73	294
	Donna Caponi Young	68	78	73	75	294
=9	Sandra Post	78	73	74	70	295
	Nancy Lopez	71	73	79	72	295
	Peggy Conley	75	76	70	74	295
=12	Amy Alcott	75	75	75	71	296
	Mrs Robert C. Meyers	75	73	76	72	296
	Janet A. Coles	71	80	72	73	296
	Jo Ann Washam	72	77	73	74	296
=16	Pat Bradley	76	75	76	70	297
	Marlene B. Hagge	76	75	75	71	297
	Murle Breer	75	77	73	72	297
	Carol Semple (a)	73	71	77	76	297
=20	Betsy King	74	74	79	71	298
	Jan Stephenson	75	72	77	74	298
	Mary Dwyer	75	77	71	75	298
=23	Mickey Wright	74	77	77	71	299
	Laura Baugh	73	74	76	76	299
	Kathy McMullen	78	76	74	71	299
	Bonnie Lauer	73	76	76	74	299
	Juli Simpson	80	72	72	75	299

July 20–23, 1978 continued

Pos	Player	R1	R2	R3	R4	Total
=28	Jerilyn Britz	74	73	78	75	300
	Sharon K. Miller	72	76	77	75	300
	Mary B. Mills	76	76	73	75	300

July 12–15, 1979

Brooklawn Country Club, Fairfield, CO

Pos	Player	R1	R2	R3	R4	Total
1	Jerilyn Britz	70	70	75	69	284
=2	Sandra Palmer	73	69	74	70	286
	Deborah Massey	70	72	70	74	286
4	Sally Little	71	71	74	71	287
=5	Susie Berning	79	66	71	73	289
	Mary Dwyer	73	71	74	71	289
	Jo Ann Washam	76	74	72	67	289
	Joyce Kazmierski	76	72	72	70	290
	Laura Baugh	73	72	77	68	290
	Donna C. Young	72	74	74	70	291
11	Amelia Rorer	73	73	77	69	292
=12	Sandra Post	72	75	74	71	292
	Nancy Lopez	73	73	73	73	292
	Jane Blalock	71	73	74	74	292
=15	Murle Breer	76	74	70	73	293
	Hollis Stacy	71	75	74	73	293
	Penny Pulz	73	72	75	73	293
	Sandra Spuzich	71	73	74	75	293
19	Silvia Bertolaccini	75	74	71	74	294
=20	Shelly Hamlin	78	70	80	67	295
	Lori Garbacz	76	74	74	71	295
	Beth Daniel	78	70	72	75	295
	Janet Coles	75	71	74	75	295
	Pam Higgins	71	72	77	75	295
	Donna H. White	74	74	71	76	295
=26	Jan Stephenson	75	74	74	73	296
	Judy Rankin	76	68	78	74	296
	Pat Bradley	77	70	74	75	296
	Alexandra Reinhardt	74	76	68	78	296
	Cathy Morse	71	75	72	78	296

July 10–13, 1980

Richland Country Club, Nashville, TN

Pos	Player	R1	R2	R3	R4	Total
1	Amy Alcott	70	70	68	72	280
2	Hollis Stacy	75	71	70	73	289
3	Kathy McMullen	74	73	71	73	291
=4	Judy Clark	75	73	73	71	292
	Donna Caponi Young	72	72	75	73	292
=6	Louise Bruce	73	74	73	73	293
	Lori Garbacz	72	76	75	71	294
	Jane Blalock	76	71	71	76	294
	Nancy Lopez-Melton	74	72	71	77	294
=10	Patty Hayes	75	72	74	74	295
	JoAnne Carner	74	72	74	75	295
	Eva Chang	74	74	72	75	295
	Beth Daniel	76	72	69	78	295
14	Penny Pulz	72	72	77	75	296
15	Shelly Hamlin	78	73	71	75	297
=16	Marlene Floyd	72	76	76	74	298
	Dorothy Germain	75	76	72	75	298
	Pat Bradley	74	74	74	76	298
	Cathy Morse	74	74	72	78	298
=20	Sally Little	74	76	76	73	299
	Bonnie Lauer	76	73	75	75	299
	Barbara Moxness	70	74	75	80	299
=23	Pat Meyers	75	73	77	75	300
	Alison Sheard	77	73	75	75	300
	Ai-Yu Tu	75	73	72	80	300

July 10–13, 1980 continued

	Sandra Post	79	68	70	83	300
=27	**Mary Dwyer**	76	75	77	73	301
	Laura Baugh	81	71	73	76	301
	Janet Alex	72	74	77	78	301
=30	**Debbie Austin**	76	75	78	73	302
	Gail Hirata	75	76	78	73	302
	Sandra Spuzich	78	72	75	77	302
	Barbara Barrow	78	73	72	79	302
	Becky Pearson	77	76	76	73	302

July 23–26, 1981

La Grange Country Club, La Grange, IL

1	**Pat Bradley**	71	74	68	66	279
2	**Beth Daniel**	69	74	69	68	280
3	**Kathy Whitworth**	69	70	71	74	284
=4	**Cynthia Hill**	76	70	69	72	287
	Bonnie Lauer	72	67	72	76	287
=6	**Donna Caponi**	71	74	72	73	290
	Marlene Floyd	71	72	73	74	290
	JoAnne Carner	73	71	72	70	290
	Patty Sheehan	74	74	72	74	290
=10	**Amelia Rorer**	73	77	69	.73	292
	Sally Little	74	72	76	70	292
	Hollis Stacy	73	75	71	73	292
	Debbie Massey	71	72	72	77	292
	Sandra Haynie	75	73	73	71	292
	Shelley Hamlin	70	75	75	72	292
=16	**Cathy Sherk**	76	69	76	72	293
	Louise Parks	72	75	72	74	293
18	**Dorothy Germain**	71	76	71	76	294
=19	**Julie Stanger**	74	75	74	72	295
	Amy Alcott	75	73	72	75	295
=21	**Betsy King**	75	75	73	73	296
	Kyle O'Brien	75	69	73	79	296
	Marlene Hagge	74	75	72	75	296
=24	**Vickie Fergon**	77	73	72	76	298
	Dale Lundquist	73	72	74	79	298
=26	**Judy Clark**	74	76	71	78	299
	Janet Alex	77	74	73	75	299
	Kathy Baker (a)	75	77	74	73	299
=29	**Penny Pulz**	80	68	72	80	300
	Sandra Palmer	77	75	74	74	300
	Jan Stephenson	76	70	77	77	300

July 22–25, 1982

Del Paso Country Club, Sacramento, CA

1	**Janet Alex**	70	73	72	68	283
=2	**JoAnne Carner**	69	70	75	75	289
	Beth Daniel	71	71	71	76	289
	Donna White	70	74	73	72	289
	Sandra Haynie	70	74	74	71	289
6	**Susie McAllister**	77	70	75	71	293
=7	**Carole Jo Callison**	76	69	72	77	294
	Nancy Lopez	78	73	74	69	294
	Vicki Tabor	70	76	75	70	294
=10	**Beverley Cooper**	73	72	76	74	295
	Stephanie Farwig	75	76	72	72	295
	Muffin Spencer-Devlin	76	71	76	72	295
=13	**Amy Alcott**	75	74	71	76	296
	Dale Eggeling	72	74	76	74	296
	Sally Little	71	77	75	73	296
	Alexandra Reinhardt	73	75	71	77	296
	Kathy Baker (a)	75	70	72	76	296
=18	**Sandra Palmer**	78	71	75	73	297

July 22–25, 1982 continued

	Lynn Adams	71	76	77	73	297
	Amy Benz	79	70	72	76	297
=21	**Jeannette Kerr**	74	77	71	76	298
	Pat Bradley	77	74	72	75	298
	Donna Caponi	73	76	78	71	298
	Janet Coles	77	77	74	70	298
=25	**Yuko Moriguchi**	73	74	77	75	299
	Jane Blalock	77	77	72	73	299
	Kathy Postlewait	76	73	75	75	299
	Betsy King	75	77	76	71	299
=29	**Carol Semple (a)**	76	72	74	78	300
	Bonnie Lauer	73	71	78	78	300
	Juli Inkster (a)	75	77	77	71	300
	Terry Moody	73	79	72	76	300
	Nancy Rubin	74	78	76	72	300
	Kathy Whitworth	74	75	75	76	300
	Patty Sheehan	78	75	76	71	300

July 28–31, 1983

Cedar Ridge Country Club, Tulsa, OK

1	**Jan Stephenson**	72	73	71	74	290
=2	**JoAnne Carner**	81	70	72	68	291
	Patty Sheehan	71	71	76	73	291
4	**Patti Rizzo**	75	74	73	70	292
5	**Cathy Morse**	76	71	77	69	293
=6	**Dorothy Germain**	73	72	76	73	294
	Myra Van Hoose	77	72	72	73	294
=8	**Ayako Okomoto**	77	73	75	70	295
	Jane Lack	75	73	72	75	295
	Pat Bradley	72	76	71	76	295
=11	**Judy Clark**	79	76	70	71	296
	Rosie Jones	76	74	73	73	296
	Heather Farr (a)	78	69	73	76	296
	Amy Alcott	75	74	71	76	296
=15	**Muffin Spencer-Devlin**	78	76	70	73	297
	Janet Coles	72	75	75	75	297
	Jane Blalock	77	75	70	75	297
	Lauren Howe	72	73	74	78	297
=19	**Valerie Skinner**	79	71	75	73	298
	Sherrin Golbraith	75	75	73	75	298
=21	**Dale Eggeling**	79	73	74	73	299
	Juli Inkster	72	79	74	74	299
	Lori Garbacz	73	79	73	74	299
	Donna White	77	74	73	75	299
	Cynthia Hill	79	71	73	76	299
	Becky Pearson	72	75	75	77	299
	Sandra Haynie	74	74	74	77	299
28	**Stephanie Farwig**	73	75	75	77	300
=29	**Barbara Mizrahie**	79	74	73	75	301
	Martha Nause	79	71	74	77	301
	Debbie Meisterlin	72	73	73	83	301

July 12–15, 1984

Salem Country Club, Peabody, MA

1	**Hollis Stacy**	74	72	75	69	290
2	**Rosie Jones**	73	71	75	72	291
=3	**Amy Alcott**	71	74	73	74	292
	Lori Garvacz	74	76	72	70	292
=5	**Betsy King**	74	72	75	73	294
	Penny Pulz	75	69	78	72	294
	Patty Sheehan	73	77	74	70	294
=8	**Donna White**	75	71	72	77	295
	Ayoko Okamoto	72	74	74	75	295
=10	**Beth Daniel**	76	76	73	72	297

July 12–15, 1984 continued

	Kathy Whitworth	73	75	75	74	297
12	**Susan Fogleman**	74	77	74	73	298
=13	**Patti Rizzo**	75	71	78	75	299
	Pat Bradley	76	77	70	76	299
	Jo Ann Washam	71	78	77	73	299
	Vicki Alvarez	80	74	76	69	299
=17	**Cathy Hanlon Marino**	76	73	74	77	300
	Lauri Peterson	74	79	72	75	300
	Silvia Bertolaccini	74	75	76	75	300
=20	**Alice Miller**	73	77	76	75	301
	JoAnne Carner	77	79	73	72	301
=22	**Amy Benz**	73	79	80	70	302
	Heather Drew	73	75	76	78	302
	Debbie Massey	77	78	75	72	302
	Jerilyn Britz	76	75	77	74	302
	Dorothy Pepper (a)	77	75	75	75	302
=27	**Juli Inkster**	80	76	73	74	303
	Jan Stephenson	72	81	71	79	303
	Jody Rosenthal (a)	79	72	74	78	303
	Marta Figueras-Dotti	77	74	80	72	303

July 11–14, 1985

Baltusrol Golf Club, Springfield, NJ

1	**Kathy Baker**	70	72	68	70	280
2	**Judy Clark**	71	75	65	72	283
3	**Vicki Alavarez**	72	69	71	75	287
=4	**Janet Coles**	72	69	71	76	288
	Nancy Lopez	70	70	71	77	288
=6	**Penny Pulz**	75	74	70	70	289
	Sally Little	73	70	74	72	289
=8	**Ayako Okamoto**	72	74	73	71	290
	Jane Geddes	74	75	69	72	290
	Betsy King	71	73	71	75	290
11	**Amy Alcott**	72	72	74	74	292
=12	**Chris Johnson**	77	73	73	70	293
	Alice Miller	75	75	71	72	293
	Patty Sheehan	73	73	74	73	293
	Pat Bradley	74	75	71	73	293
	Jan Stephenson	71	747	73	75	293
	Cathy Morse	73	74	69	77	293
18	**Muffin Spencer-Devlin**	73	72	75	74	294
19	**Barb Bunkowsky**	76	73	73	73	295
=20	**Lori Garbacz**	71	76	76	73	296
	Stephanie Farwig	78	71	74	73	296
	Marlene Floyd	76	70	76	74	296
	Silvia Bertolaccini	76	72	74	74	296
	Cathy Marino	75	70	74	77	296
	Janet Anderson	70	73	75	78	296
=26	**Kathleen McCarthy (a)**	71	79	73	74	297
	Vickie Fergon	75	75	73	74	297
	Valerie Skinner	73	74	73	77	297
	Danielle Ammaccapane (a)	74	71	73	79	297
30	**Pat Meyers**	75	72	77	74	298

July 10–13, 1986

NCR Country Cub. Kettering, OH

** Jane Geddes (71) beat Sally Little (73) in the 18-hole play-off.*

1	**Jane Geddes***	74	74	70	69	287
2	**Sally Little**	73	72	72	70	287
=3	**Ayoko Okamoto**	76	69	69	74	288
	Betsy King	72	71	70	75	288
=5	**Pat Bradley**	76	71	74	69	290
	Jody Rosenthal	72	76	71	71	290

July 10–13, 1985 continued

	Amy Alcott	75	69	74	72	290
	Judy Dickinson	72	71	74	73	290
=9	**Cathy Morse**	75	71	75	70	291
	Deb Richard	76	69	72	74	291
=11	**Laura Davies**	75	73	73	72	293
	Jan Stephenson	72	78	70	73	293
	Hollis Stacy	73	72	73	75	293
=14	**Tammie Green**	72	79	71	72	294
	Silvia Bertolaccini	71	77	73	73	294
	Ok-Hee Ku	74	74	72	74	294
	Lauren Howe	74	75	70	75	294
	Joan Pitcock (a)	77	69	72	76	294
=19	**Chris Johnson**	76	71	73	75	295
	Nancy Scranton	78	71	71	75	295
=21	**Charlotte Montgomery**	75	74	75	72	296
	Sherri Turner	72	73	78	73	296
	Kathy Baker	74	72	77	73	296
	Beth Daniel	70	76	75	75	296
	Laurie Rinker	77	71	73	75	296
	Val Skinner	74	75	71	76	296
=27	**Patti Rizzo**	76	75	74	72	297
	Muffin Spencer-Delvin	77	76	70	74	297
	Lenore Muraoka	73	73	75	76	297
=30	**Michele Redman (a)**	71	77	79	71	298
	Lori Garbacz	73	79	74	72	298
	Martha Nouse	72	75	72	79	298
	Debbie Massey	75	73	71	79	298
	Penny Hammel	76	74	69	79	298

July 23–28, 1987

Plainfield Country Club, Plainfield, NJ

** Laura Davies (71) beat Ayaka Okamoto (73) and JoAnne Carner (74) in the 18-hole play-off.*

1	**Laura Davies***	72	70	72	71	285
=2	**Ayaka Okamoto**	71	72	70	72	285
	JoAnne Carner	74	70	72	69	285
=4	**Betsy King**	75	73	70	71	289
	Jody Rosenthal	71	72	74	72	289
=6	**Debbie Massey**	76	69	74	71	290
	Deedee Roberts	74	73	69	74	290
8	**Martha Nause**	76	69	70	76	291
=9	**Kathy Postlewait**	70	79	73	70	292
	Sally Quinlan	75	71	71	75	292
	Rosie Jones	75	71	71	75	202
=12	**Dottie Mochrie**	73	72	77	71	293
	Marta Figueras-Dotti	77	70	74	72	293
	Amy Alcott	72	71	76	74	293
=15	**Alice Ritzman**	76	74	73	71	294
	Tammie Green	72	74	72	76	294
=17	**Deb Richard**	72	73	75	75	295
	Sandra Palmer	71	72	75	77	295
=19	**Michele Berteotti**	73	74	79	70	296
	Cindy Rarick	74	71	76	75	296
=21	**Patty Sheehan**	74	74	77	72	297
	Denise Strebig	74	78	73	72	297
	Sherri Turner	77	73	74	73	297
	Donna White	77	72	74	74	297
	Michiko Hattori (a)	78	73	71	71	297
	Nancy Lopez	73	71	77	76	297
	Amy Benz	74	73	74	76	297
=28	**Lori Garbacz**	77	72	77	72	298
	Jerilyn Britz	70	71	76	72	298
	Bonnie Lauer	69	76	76	77	298
	Kathleen McCarthy (a)	74	78	69	77	298
	Anne-Marie Palli	74	73	77	74	298

July 21–24, 1988

Baltimore Country Club (East Course), Baltimore, MA

1	**Liselotte Neumann**	67	72	69	69	277
2	**Patty Sheehan**	70	72	68	70	280
=3	**Dottie Mochrie**	70	69	76	68	283
	Colleen Walker	70	74	68	71	283
5	**Jan Stephenson**	72	72	71	69	284
=6	**Michele Berteotti**	75	71	68	71	285
	Amy Benz	70	72	71	72	285
=8	**Kristi Albers**	73	70	72	71	286
	Juli Inkster	71	68	75	72	286
=10	**Vicki Fergon**	70	71	75	71	287
	Beth Daniel	77	71	66	73	287
=12	**Betsy King**	76	74	71	67	288
	Ayako Okamoto	75	73	71	69	288
	Kris Hanson	73	72	73	70	288
	Nancy Lopez	72	74	71	71	288
=16	**JoAnne Carner**	69	73	76	71	289
	Nancy Brown	71	73	72	73	289
	Kay Cockerill	73	70	72	74	289
=19	**Christa Johnson**	73	74	73	70	290
	Mei Chi Cheng	74	76	70	70	290
	Rosie Jones	74	70	74	72	290
	Marta Figueras-Dotti	77	71	69	73	290
	Tammie Green	71	70	71	78	290
=24	**Robin Hood**	77	72	71	71	291
	Sally Quinlan	69	75	74	73	291
	Deedee Lasker	73	71	74	73	291
	Judy Dickinson	71	76	71	73	291
	Donna White	72	70	73	76	291
=29	**Carol Semple Thompson (a)**	79	71	70	72	292
	Kathy Baker-Guadagnino	72	72	75	73	292
	Sherri Turner	73	72	73	74	292
	Jody Rosenthal	74	73	71	74	292

July 13–16, 1989

Indianwood Golf and Country Club, Lake Orion. MI

1	**Betsy King**	67	71	72	68	278
2	**Nancy Lopez**	73	70	71	68	282
=3	**Penny Hammel**	74	73	69	67	283
	Pat Bradley	73	74	68	68	283
=5	**Dottie Mochrie**	72	70	75	67	284
	Lori Garbacz	71	70	73	70	284
=7	**Laura Davies**	73	71	75	66	285
	Vicki Fergon	72	74	69	70	285
=9	**Jane Geddes**	70	72	72	72	286
	Colleen Walker	72	69	71	74	286
=11	**Ayaka Okamoto**	76	72	74	65	287
	Danielle Ammaccapane	73	70	74	70	287
	Myra Blackwelder	76	68	71	72	287
	Marie-Laure Delorenzi-Taya	68	74	71	74	287
=15	**Kim Bauer**	72	72	73	71	288
	Marta Figueras-Dotti	75	70	70	73	288
=17	**Gina Hull**	74	72	72	71	289
	JoAnne Carner	76	69	71	73	289
	Patty Sheehan	74	67	69	79	289
=20	**Shirley Furlong**	74	75	73	68	299
	Liselotte Neumann	71	71	75	73	290
	Caroline Keggi	71	73	73	73	290
	Beth Daniel	73	73	71	73	290
	Kathy Postlewait	77	70	70	73	290
	Donna Cusano-Wilkins	71	72	71	76	290
=26	**Sally Quinlan**	78	71	73	69	291
	Kim Shipman	74	69	74	74	291
	Amy Alcott	73	71	73	74	291

July 13–16, 1989 continued

=29	**Donna White**	75	73	74	70	292
	Chris Johnson	73	73	75	71	292
	Nancy Taylor	74	73	73	72	292
	Patrice Rizzo	77	69	73	73	292
	Debbie Massey	71	72	75	74	292

July 12–15, 1990

Atlanta Athletic Club (Riverside Course), Duluth, GA

1	**Betsy King**	72	71	71	70	284
2	**Patty Sheehan**	66	68	75	76	285
=3	**Danielle Ammaccapane**	72	73	70	71	286
	Dottie Mochrie	74	74	72	66	286
5	**Mary E. Murphy**	70	74	69	74	287
=6	**Elaine Crosby**	71	74	73	70	288
	Tammie Green	70	74	73	71	288
	Beth Daniel	71	71	74	72	288
=9	**Colleen Walker**	69	75	73	72	289
	Amy Alcott	72	72	72	73	289
	Sherrie E. Turner	74	72	71	72	289
	Hollis Stacy	71	72	77	69	289
	Caroline S. Keggi	67	75	73	74	289
	Meg Mallon	71	71	77	70	289
	Cathy Gerring	70	78	70	71	289
=16	**Missie McGeorge**	72	74	72	72	290
	Rose Jones	72	70	74	74	290
18	**JoAnne Carner**	73	71	70	77	291
=19	**Jody Anschutz**	72	73	74	73	292
	Nancy Lopez	68	76	75	73	292
	Pat Bradley	74	70	75	73	292
	Alice Ritzman	77	70	73	72	292
	Donna Andrews	75	72	73	72	292
	Jane Geddes	66	74	79	73	292
	Cindy Rarick	73	74	70	75	292
=26	**Barbara Mucha**	74	72	75	72	293
	Laura Davies	73	73	74	73	293
	Cindy Figg Currier	76	72	73	72	293
=29	**Allison Finney**	73	73	71	77	294
	Debbie Massey	70	73	75	76	294
	Kathy Postlewait	75	74	75	70	294

July 11–14, 1991

Colonial Country Club, Fort Worth, TX

1	**Meg Mallon**	70	75	71	67	283
2	**Pat Bradley**	69	73	72	71	285
3	**Amy Alcott**	75	68	72	71	286
4	**Laurel Kean**	70	76	71	70	287
=5	**Dottie Mochrie**	73	76	68	71	288
	Chris Johnson	76	72	68	72	288
7	**Joan Pitcock**	70	72	72	75	289
=8	**Kristi Albers**	76	70	71	73	290
	Jody Anschultz	73	72	72	73	290
	Brandie Burton	75	71	69	75	290
=11	**Beth Daniel**	75	76	75	66	291
	Tina Barrett	74	74	72	71	291
	Debbie Massey	72	72	75	72	291
	JoAnne Carner	73	72	73	73	291
=15	**Adele Lukken**	75	76	70	71	292
	Patty Sheehan	74	75	72	71	292
	Liselotte Neumann	74	72	74	74	292
	Alice Ritzman	72	71	77	72	292
	Ayako Okamoto	76	72	71	73	292
	Kris Tscheller	77	72	67	76	292
=21	**Colleen Walker**	72	77	74	70	293
	Mitzi Edgo	75	76	71	71	293

	Tracy Hanson (a)	75	76	71	71	293
	Cathy Gerring	76	70	76	71	293
	Nancy Scranton	72	75	73	73	293
	Judy Dickinson	72	74	74	73	293
	Caroline Keggi	74	72	73	74	293
=28	**Betsy King**	74	78	74	68	294
	Vicki Goetze (a)	76	75	71	72	294
	Jane Geddes	71	74	76	73	294
	Alison Nicholas	77	72	71	74	294

July 23–26, 1992

Oakmont CC, Pakmont, PA

** Patty Sheehan (72) beat Juli Inkster (74) in the 18-hole play-off.*

1	**Patty Sheehan***	69	72	70	69	280
2	**Juli Inkster**	72	68	71	69	280
3	**Donna Andrews**	69	73	72	70	284
4	**Meg Mallon**	73	72	72	70	287
5	**Dawn Coe**	71	71	72	74	288
=6	**Gail Graham**	72	71	71	75	289
	Dottie Mochrie	70	74	72	73	289
	Michelle McGann	72	73	70	74	289
9	**Tammie Green**	72	75	70	73	290
=10	**Jane Geddes**	73	70	78	70	291
	Pam Wright	70	68	76	76	291
12	**Mitzi Edge**	73	74	72	73	292
=13	**Amy Alcott**	76	74	73	70	293
	Helen Alfredsson	71	79	72	71	293
15	**Liselotte Neumann**	76	72	72	74	294
=16	**Nancy Lopez**	75	76	71	73	295
	Suzanne Strudwick	75	73	73	74	295
	Ok-Hee Ku	73	74	74	74	295
	Betsy King	74	73	73	75	295
	Nina Foust	73	74	74	74	295
	Michelle Estill	74	74	73	74	295
=22	**Amy Benz**	73	71	73	79	296
	Alice Ritzman	74	69	77	76	296
	Lisa Walters	74	72	72	78	296
=25	**Vicki Fergon**	74	73	75	75	297
	Kris Monaghan	75	72	75	75	297
	Judy Dickinson	75	72	74	76	297
	Rosie Jones	73	75	73	76	297
=29	**Marti Figueras-Dotti**	74	77	74	73	298
	Tracy Kerdyk	69	77	76	76	298
	Pat Bradley	74	74	78	72	298
	Akiko Fukushima	77	72	78	71	298
	Nancy Ramsbottom	69	75	77	77	298
	Tina Barrett	73	75	75	75	298
	Baro Mucha	78	71	75	74	298

July 22–25, 1993

Crooked Stick, Carmel, IN

1	**Lauri Merten**	71	71	70	68	280
=2	**Donna Andrews**	71	70	69	71	281
	Helen Alfredsson	68	70	69	74	281
=4	**Pat Bradley**	72	70	68	73	283
	Hiromi Kobayashi	71	67	71	74	283
6	**Patty Sheehan**	73	71	69	71	284
=7	**Betsy King**	74	70	72	69	285
	Michelle McGann	70	66	78	71	285
	Nancy Lopez	70	71	70	74	285
	Ayako Okamoto	68	72	71	74	285
=11	**Laura Davies**	73	71	69	73	286
	JoAnne Carner	71	69	73	73	286
=13	**Tina Barrett**	73	73	70	71	287

July 22–25, 1993 continued

	Chris Johnson	71	75	69	72	287
	Sherri Steinhauer	73	67	75	72	287
	Nina Foust	71	71	71	74	287
=17	**Dottie Mochrie**	72	71	74	71	288
	Gail Graham	72	73	70	73	288
	Barb Mucha	75	69	71	73	288
	Kris Tschetter	73	71	69	75	288
21	**Meg Mallon**	73	72	69	75	289
=22	**Danielle Ammaccapane**	73	74	73	70	290
	Allison Finney	74	72	73	71	290
	Michele Redman	75	71	72	72	290
	Dawn Coe-Jones	69	72	76	73	290
=26	**Lori West**	73	73	73	72	291
	Alice Miller	73	68	78	72	291
	Laurie Brower	73	73	72	73	291
	Julie Larsen	76	71	70	74	291
	Amy Alcott	70	74	73	74	291
	Cindy Mah-Lyford	73	73	70	75	291
	Shelley Hamlin	74	68	73	76	291
	Kelly Robbins	71	70	74	76	291
	Dina Ammaccapane	71	70	70	80	291
	Debbi Miho Koyama (a)	70	74	72	75	291

July 18–24, 1994

Indianwood Golf and Country Club, Lake Orion, MI

1	**Patty Sheehan**	66	71	69	71	277
2	**Tammie Green**	66	72	69	71	278
3	**Liselotte Neumann**	69	72	71	69	281
=4	**Tania Abilbol**	72	68	73	70	283
	Alicia Dibos	69	68	73	73	283
=6	**Amy Alcott**	71	67	77	69	284
	Meg Mallon	70	72	73	69	284
	Betsy King	69	71	72	72	284
=9	**Kelly Robbins**	71	72	70	72	285
	Donna Andrews	67	72	70	76	285
	Helen Alfredsson	63	69	76	77	285
=12	**Lauri Merten**	74	68	75	69	286
	Dottie Mochrie	72	72	71	71	286
	Lisa Grimes	72	73	69	72	286
	Michelle Estill	69	68	75	74	286
	Judy Dickinson	66	73	73	74	286
	Laura Davies	68	68	75	75	286
=18	**Michelle McGann**	71	70	77	69	287
	Juli Inkster	75	72	69	71	287
	Beth Daniel	69	74	71	73	287
	Joan Pitcock	74	72	67	74	287
=22	**Stephanie Mayner**	73	70	76	69	288
	Lisa Walters	72	73	72	71	288
	Sherri Steinhauer	68	72	74	74	288
=25	**Kristen Tschetter**	71	73	72	73	289
	Deb Richard	68	74	72	75	289
	Patricia Bradley	72	69	70	78	289
	Pamela Wright	74	65	71	79	289
=29	**Karen Lunn**	72	72	77	69	290
	Vicki Goetze	71	73	73	73	290

July 13–16, 1995

Broadmoor, Colorado Springs, CO

1	**Annika Sorenstam**	67	71	72	68	278
2	**Meg Mallon**	70	69	66	74	279
=3	**Pat Bradley**	67	71	72	67	280
	Betsy King	72	69	72	70	280
=5	**Leta Lindley**	70	68	74	69	281
	Rosie Jones	69	70	70	72	281
=7	**Tammie Green**	68	70	75	69	282
	Dawn Coe-Jones	68	70	74	70	282
	Julie Larsen	68	71	68	75	282
=10	**Marianne Morris**	73	73	70	67	283
	Patty Sheehan	70	73	71	69	283
	Val Skinner	68	72	72	71	283
=13	**Dottie Mochrie**	73	70	69	72	284
	Kris Tschetter	68	74	69	73	284
	Kelly Robbins	74	68	68	74	284
=16	**Chris Johnson**	71	70	74	70	285
	Jill Briles-Hinton	66	72	74	73	285
	Dale Eggeling	70	68	73	74	285
	Tania Abitbol	67	72	72	74	285
=20	**Michele Redman**	70	75	71	70-	286
	Liselotte Neumann	70	71	75	71	287
	Ayako Akamoto	70	73	71	73	287
	Alice Ritzman	75	69	69	74	287
=24	**Joan Pitcock**	72	73	72	71	288
	Carolyn Hill	74	73	70	71	288
	Laura Davies	72	73	69	74	288
	Mary Beth Zimmerman	72	72	68	76	288
=28	**Nancy Lopez**	72	73	74	70	289
	Brandie Burton	72	73	74	70	289
	Amy Fruhwirth	75	72	72	70	289
	Colleen Walker	69	73	75	72	289
	Mayumi Hirase	70	74	73	72	289
	Pamela Wright	72	73	71	73	289
	Jean Bartholomew	67	71	77	74	289
	Debbi Koyami	74	68	73	74	289
	Gail Graham	71	72	71	75	289

May 30–June 2, 1996

Pine Needles Lodge and Country Club, Southern Pines, NC

1	**Annika Sorenstam**	70	67	69	66	272
2	**Kris Tschetter**	70	74	68	66	278
=3	**Pat Bradley**	74	70	67	69	280
	Jane Geddes	71	69	70	70	280
	Brandie Burton	70	70	69	71	280
6	**Laura Davies**	74	68	70	69	281
7	**Catrin Nilsmark**	72	73	68	69	282
=8	**Cindy Rarick**	73	70	72	68	283
	Val Skinner	74	68	71	70	283
	Liselotte Neumann	74	69	70	70	283
	Tammie Green	72	70	69	72	283
12	**Jenny Lidback**	70	76	68	70	284
13	**Alison Nicholas**	74	70	74	67	285
=14	**Patty Sheehan**	74	71	72	69	286
	Stefania Croce	72	70	74	70	286
	Cindy Schreyer	74	70	70	72	286
	Maggie Will	71	72	70	73	286
	Michele Redman	70	73	69	74	286
=18	**Cathy Johnston-Forbes**	72	75	71	69	287
	Meg Mallon	77	68	72	70	287
	Karrie Webb	74	73	68	72	287
	Beth Daniel	69	78	68	72	287
	Mayumi Hirase	74	69	69	75	287
=23	**Michiko Hattori**	74	71	74	69	288

May 30 – June 2, 1996 continued

	Kim Williams	69	78	69	72	288
	Becky Iverson	73	71	71	73	288
	Nancy Harvey	72	71	69	76	288
=27	**Karen Weiss**	74	72	73	70	289
	Rosie Jones	71	70	76	72	289
	Susie Redman	73	73	71	72	289
	Tracy Kerdyk	73	72	69	75	289
	Emilee Klein	71	69	73	76	289

July 10–13, 1997

Pumpkin Ridge Golf Club, Cornelius, OR

1	**Alison Nicholas**	70	66	67	71	274
2	**Nancy Lopez**	69	68	69	69	275
3	**Kelly Robbins**	68	69	74	66	277
4	**Karrie Webb**	73	72	65	68	278
=5	**Stefania Croce**	72	69	71	67	279
	Lisa Hackney	71	70	67	71	279
=7	**Tammie Green**	74	70	71	65	280
	Michele Redman	74	67	70	69	280
=9	**Patty Sheehan**	72	71	71	68	282
	Chris Johnson	72	68	73	69	282
	Dawn Coe-Jones	72	67	73	70	282
	Akiko Fukushima	71	71	69	71	282
	Donna Andrews	74	71	66	71	282
=14	**Juli Inkster**	72	66	76	70	284
	Dottie Pepper	72	70	72	70	284
	Brandie Burton	73	72	69	70	284
	Liselotte Neumann	67	70	76	71	284
	Deb Richard	68	70	73	73	284
=19	**Trish Johnson**	69	74	71	71	285
	Kim Williams	71	71	67	76	285
	Kelli Kuehne	72	73	74	67	286
	Karen Weiss	74	72	72	68	286
	Se Ri Pak	68	74	75	69	286
	Luciana Bemvenuti	73	71	72	70	286
	Pat Hurst	72	74	70	70	286
	Caroline Pierce	71	71	73	71	286
27	**Catriona Matthew**	76	69	70	72	287
=28	**Sherrin Smyers**	71	71	75	71	288
	Pat Bradley	72	71	73	72	288
	Kathryn Marshall	72	71	73	72	288
	Joan Pitcock	71	69	75	73	288
	Betsy King	74	72	69	73	288

July 2–6, 1998

Blackwolf Run Golf Course, Kohler, WI

** Se Ri Pak beat Jenny Chuasiriporn at the second hole of sudden the death play-off after both shot 73 in an 18-hole play-off.*

1	**Se Ri Pak***	69	70	75	76	290
2	**Jenny Chuasiriporn**	72	71	75	72	290
3	**Liselotte Neumann**	70	70	75	76	291
=4	**Danielle Ammaccapane**	76	71	74	71	292
	Pat Hurst	69	75	75	73	292
	Chris Johnson	72	70	76	74	292
=7	**Stefania Croce**	74	71	76	72	293
	Tammie Green	73	71	76	73	293
	Mhairi McKay	72	70	73	78	293
10	**Trish Johnson**	73	71	77	73	294
=11	**Laura Davies**	68	75	78	74	295
	Dottie Pepper	71	71	78	75	295
=13	**Carin Koch**	72	74	77	73	296
	Helen Alfredsson	75	75	73	73	296
=15	**Hollis Stacy**	76	68	82	71	297

July 2–6, 1998 continued

	Anna Acker-Macosko	74	74	76	73	297
	Dina Ammaccapane	75	70	78	74	297
	Brandie Burton	74	72	77	74	297
=19	**Lorie Kane**	74	72	82	70	298
	Jenny Lidback	71	73	79	75	298
	Akiko Fukushima	72	71	79	76	298
	Rosie Jones	74	74	74	76	298
	Wendy Ward	76	69	75	78	298
	Donna Andrews	70	75	75	78	298
	Lisa Walters	76	70	74	78	298
=26	**Dana Dormann**	72	76	79	72	299
	Nancy Scranton	76	72	78	73	299
	Michelle Estill	75	74	76	74	299
	Helen Dobson	71	75	77	76	299
	Laurie Rinker-Graham	75	71	77	76	299

June 3–6, 1999

Old Waverly GC, West Point, MI

1	**Juli Inkster**	65	69	67	71	272
2	**Sherri Turner**	69	69	68	71	277
3	**Kelli Kuehne**	64	71	70	74	279
4	**Lorie Kane**	70	64	71	75	280
=5	**Carin Koch**	72	69	68	72	281
	Meg Mallon	70	70	69	72	281
7	**Karrie Webb**	70	70	68	74	282
=8	**Helen Dobson**	71	70	73	69	283
	Maria Hjorth	73	69	70	71	283
	Catriona Matthew	69	68	74	72	283
	Grace Park (a)	70	67	73	73	283
=12	**Helen Alfredsson**	72	68	70	74	284
	Becky Iverson	72	64	73	75	284
=14	**Michele Redman**	72	71	75	67	285
	Se Ri Pak	68	70	74	73	285
	Dottie Pepper	68	69	72	76	285
=17	**Liselotte Neumann**	73	71	69	73	286
	A.J. Eathorne	69	71	71	75	286
	Catrin Nilsmark	69	71	70	76	286
=20	**Cindy McCurdy**	72	72	74	69	287
	Leta Lindley	72	72	73	70	287
	Sophie Gustafson	72	72	70	73	287
	Donna Andrews	69	71	72	75	287
	Akiko Fukushima	69	70	71	77	287
=25	**Kim Saiki**	70	71	73	74	288
	Stefania Croce	71	71	71	75	288
	Rosie Jones	71	70	72	75	288
	Lisa Kiggens	71	67	73	77	288
	Sherri Steinhauer	68	69	73	78	288
=30	**Mardi Lunn**	72	71	74	72	289
	Jean Zedlitz	75	67	75	72	289
	Mhairi McKay	73	68	76	72	289
	Nancy Scranton	69	72	75	73	289
	Dawn Coe-Jones	73	71	71	74	289
	Anna Acker-Macosko	73	71	71	74	289
	Kelly Robbins	70	70	74	75	289

Tournament Records

Record	Score	Player	Year
9 Hole	30	**Pam Wright**	1994
18 Hole (Par 71)	63 (-8)	**Helen Alfredsson**	1994
18 Hole (Par 72)	64 (-8)	**Kelli Kuehne, Becky Iverson, Lorie Kane**	1999
36 Hole (Par 71)	132 (-10)	**Helen Alfredsson**	1994
36 Hole (Par 72)	134 (-10)	**Patty Sheehan**	1990
54 Hole (Par 72)	201 (-15)	**Juli Inkster**	1999
72 Hole (Par 71)	274 (-10)	**Alison Nicholas**	1997
72 Hole (Par 72)	272 (-16)	**Juli Inkster**	1999

BRITISH WOMEN'S OPEN

One of the proudest moments of Laura Davies's career was winning the Women's British Open Championship at Royal Birkdale in 1986. "This is the moment I have been longing for since I first started to play," she said in the immediate aftermath of the biggest win of her fledgling career. Several years and numerous championships later, she had still not changed her mind. "It was magnificent," she reiterated. "Even then, when it wasn't as big as it is now, it was the big one. For me it's easily the most important tournament of the year. The US Open, the Dinah Shore and the McDonald's LPGA Championship are close behind, but every year I envy the person walking up the 18th at the British with the championship won, and I don't often envy people in golf."

Davies is a staunch Englishwoman, and she has played a substantial part in the growth of the women's professional game in Europe. As she has grown in status, so has an Open Championship that started in a very small way in 1976 under the auspices of the Ladies' Golf Union (LGU) with prize money of £200. There wasn't a women's professional tour in Europe at the time, and the first champion was Jenny Lee Smith, an amateur, who finished a shot ahead of Mary McKenna, another amateur, at Fulford in York.

Janet Melville (also an amateur) was champion in 1978, and at Birkdale in 1982 Marta Figueras-Dotti of Spain became the third and last amateur to win the title – and the first continental European. She finished a shot ahead of Lee Smith, who had turned professional the year before. Amateurs were such a force to be reckoned with in the early days because they often played more competitive golf than the home-based professionals and, not to put too fine a point on it, were the best players in the country. It was to be some years before the leading amateurs automatically looked to turn professional.

Fittingly, the first professional to win the title, at Lindrick in 1977, was Vivien Saunders, a pioneer who fought so hard to make it possible for women to play the game for a living at a time when it was regarded as something only Americans did. In those days being a woman professional required a thick skin and an honours degree in determination and stubbornness – on reflection, perhaps some things never change – as people were inclined to carp and criticize rather than encourage. The whole thing was regarded as rather quaint. Still, the Open acquired a sponsor in Pretty Polly, and when Alison Sheard – a rookie professional from South Africa – won the championship at Southport and Ainsdale, there were plenty of spectators to create an atmosphere.

The next big step was that the Americans arrived, mainly in the shape of Deborah Massey, who won the championship in 1980 and 1981, and encouraged her compatriots to make the trip across the Atlantic. She is still the only player to win the title two years in a row. At Wentworth in 1980 Massey finished a shot ahead of the amateurs Belle Robertson and Figueras-Dotti (who dropped three shots in the last three holes), and was overjoyed to receive the trophy from Lady Heathcoat-Amory, the legendary Joyce Wethered. The American, who played in two Curtis Cup matches (the second at Royal Lytham and St Annes in 1976), loved Britain and British courses, and not only had a feel for the traditions of the game but also a romantic streak that gave her a sense of purpose in promoting the Women's British Open. In an emotional speech at the presentation, she said, "I came with a mission and I intend to carry it out. You British brought golf to the United States, and now I feel that we can repay you for all that you have done. I intend to do all in my power to stimulate interest in this championship. It's a great challenge."

She was right. In 1983 there was no championship at all because Hitachi, the new sponsors, pulled out when the television contracts were not settled in time. Saunders, by this time a practising solicitor, offered £1,000 of her own money to help rescue the championship, but it was a blank year. However, Hitachi were placated, the BBC was brought in and the championship resumed in 1984 at Woburn with prize money an unprecedented £140,000. Things were finally looking up. Or so it seemed.

In fact, the event turned out to be a fiasco. It was October, and the weather was so bad that everyone was wrapped up to the eyeballs; even Jan Stephenson, the eye-catching Australian who had won the US Women's Open the previous year, had her work cut out to look or play well. To add to the problems, the greens were not at their best, and the pin positions were widely condemned as fearsome. The critics had a field day, slamming the overall scoring as pathetic and blasting the slow pace of play that resulted in television having to cover what one viewer described as "anonymous girls on anonymous fairways". The only person to rise above it all made matters worse because she killed the championship as a contest. Ayako Okamoto shot a seven-under-par 289, and won by 11 shots. One of the best players in the world, the Japanese girl failed to receive due credit for an outstanding performance and, unwittingly, helped set the Open back years. Hitachi withdrew for good and television retired hurt.

There were some hopeful signs, though. The fact that the crowds totalled in the region of 25,000 indicated a willingness to come out and watch the women. Dale Reid, a home-grown Scot, tied for second place with Betsy King of the United States. Reid's caddie had forecast that no Briton had a chance of finishing in the top ten – Mary McKenna, the great amateur from Ireland, was also in the top six – and his player remained downbeat afterwards. She said that she had scrambled a lot and had been very lucky, and that she did not think that she was good enough to play on the US Tour. Kathy Whitworth, nearing the end of a career in which she won 88 tournaments, thought otherwise, but Reid's reaction suggested that the British and European players would lag behind the Americans for some time yet.

There were far-sighted beings who believed that there was no tournament in the world with more potential, and the Open survived as the R&A came to the LGU's rescue and enabled them to put up prize money of £60,000 in the next two years. King, who was just starting to hoover up titles back home, came back and was champion in 1985 at Moor Park. Hers is the sort of name that should be on an Open trophy; she was to win the US Women's Open twice and become a member of the Hall of Fame, and there was even better to come.

Laura Davies had turned professional in 1985, and so had Liselotte Neumann, whose achievements played a large part in Sweden's emergence as a golfing power, inspiring the likes of Helen Alfredsson and Annika Sorenstam to great heights. All four were to raise the profile of women's golf in Europe and banish the inferiority complex that had dogged the early years of professionalism. The blonde and carefree Davies, who had given notice of an exceptional talent by finishing 11th on her debut in the US Women's Open in July, made a start at Birkdale in 1986. It was October again, but conditions were benign, there was a generous par of 75 and the tiger tees were given the week off. Twenty-three women were to finish under par, and there were those who felt that the LGU, undoubtedly mindful of the debacle at Woburn, had been too lenient this time. Certainly, one member was apoplectic when he overheard Debbie Massey – who had stuck to her promise and persuaded several Americans to make the journey – say after the first practice round: "There, didn't I tell you this was a cute little course?" He was probably even more incensed when Martha Nause, from Sheyboygan, birdied the last six holes in the first round of the championship proper.

Davies, just 23, demonstrated her capacity for the spectacular when she finished her second round with an eagle and a birdie, to be five shots behind Peggy Conley, an American based in Europe. The following day the Englishwoman three-putted the last for a par and a 69 that left her in second place, three shots adrift of Conley. Then the fun began. Davies started the final round with a birdie and an eagle and Conley, who had started with two pars, was undone. Davies did not take the lead until a birdie at the 7th, but she had done the crucial, psychological damage at the beginning, and went on to win by four shots from Conley and Figueras-Dotti. Conley commented that she would wear blinkers and ear-plugs the next time she encountered the ferocious force that is Davies in full flow. "Laura is so powerful that to see her hit the ball is as bad as seeing it fly. I knew she was clicking and I just couldn't dig up anything to put pressure on her. She had a terrific game plan – to play aggressively and take charge – and it worked." Davies had rounds of 71, 73, 69 and 70 for a total of a 17-under-par 283, a championship record.

In its way it was a turning point. The home supporters, and the Press, were now convinced that they had someone worth talking and writing about, a real talent to lift the spirits and breathe life into the women's game and the championship. At last there was optimism in the air. Weetabix took over the sponsorship, put up £100,000 in prize money and took the championship to St Mellion in Cornwall, the first big test for the course that Jack Nicklaus built. The unexpected bonus, the boost that no money could buy, was that Davies won the US Women's Open, undoubtedly the biggest women's event in the world, in a dramatic play-off in Plainfield, NJ, just two days

Laura Davies – revitalized European women's golf

before she was to defend her British title. It was manna from heaven for Weetabix boss Richard George. He was knighted a few years later for his services to the food industry, but deserves recognition for the support that he has given to women's and junior golf over the years. St Mellion attracted all the attention as Davies tried to complete a unique double. The place was agog.

Davies arrived at Heathrow on the Wednesday morning, went home to Ottershaw to see her grandmother, gathered up some clean clothes and drove herself to Cornwall where a party ensued. It was the continuation of a memorable week and Davies, who had to play the course sight unseen (not something that she was unused to, as she was not one of the world's great practisers), made a valiant defence of the championship despite the euphoria. She started with a level-par 73, four shots behind the leader, Sally Little, a US citizen who was born in South Africa and had been beaten in a play-off for the US Women's Open the year before. She was at pains to stress just how amazing Davies's victory in New Jersey had been: "I don't think everybody in Britain quite realizes what an incredible thing Laura has done. I know how difficult it is to win in America at all, let alone to come over and win the premier title. I tell you, what she's done is incredible. You cannot praise her too highly."

Things began to look even more remarkable when Little suffered more than her fair share of bad bounces in the second round and slipped back with an 80, while Davies moved into the lead with a 72. She was two shots clear of Muffin Spencer-Devlin, an eccentric American who returned a course-record 68 and then had a little go at Jack Nicklaus, the course designer: "I think he must have seen that hollow in front of the 18th green at St Andrews, decided to make it his trademark and gone overboard," she said. "This course is lovely to look at, but there are too many hollows." Undaunted, Spencer-Devlin moved into the lead with a third round of 75, one shot ahead of Little and little Alison Nicholas – an Englishwoman with six second places, but no wins to her name – and two ahead of Davies, who had slumped to a 79.

The last round was tense enough and close enough to live up to all that had gone before. Spencer-Devlin had two birdies in the first three holes, but it was Davies who set the target. She finished with a 73 for a total of 297, and watched as Nicholas and Spencer-Devlin came to the 18th needing a par five to tie or a birdie to win. The American three-putted for a par and Nicholas, jelly-kneed but iron-nerved, chipped up to four feet and holed the putt for the birdie that set her career rolling at last. "Time and again I had been in a position to win and lost it," she said. "I was determined it would not happen again. I knew that round would be one of the most important tests of

Helen Alfredsson – announced herself to the golfing world in 1990 with victory at the fourth extra hole

my career, because I knew that if I could win the British Open I could win anything. My knees were trembling as I stood over that last putt, but the crowds and the cameras seemed a million miles away and I just knocked it in."

There was general disappointment that Davies had just failed to pull off the double, but British and European golf profited because Nicholas proved herself to be a player of substance and won the US Women's Open ten years later. In 1988 at Lindrick she made a bold late bid to retain her British title. Nine strokes behind the leaders with 11 holes to play, Nicholas unleashed a run of seven birdies in nine holes to post a level-par total of 296. It was not quite enough and she finished a shot behind Little and Corinne Dibnah of Australia, who won with a birdie at the second extra hole. It was an outstanding coup for the Queenslander, who was coached by Charlie Earp (the man who taught Greg Norman); Little had won the du Maurier Classic, one of the women's major championships, the previous month.

There was every sign that the championship was developing into a big event, if not yet a major. At a sunbaked Ferndown the following year, Jane Geddes, US Women's Open champion in 1986, gave the British her seal of approval when she courted a fine by competing because she had used up the ungenerous quota of one release that a player was allowed by the US LPGA Tour. She said that she regarded the event as a major championship and felt that it should be recognized as such, an opinion that would gain more credence in the years to come. At least Geddes returned home well able to pay any fine because she won the title and a first prize of £18,000 after leading from start to finish. Rounds of 67, 67, 72 and 68 gave her a total of 274, two shots better than 20-year-old Belgian Florence Descampe, who proved a crowd favourite after scorching round in 66 on the second day, with what was to be the best score of the week. Marie-Laure de Lorenzi of France was third on 278.

The championship moved up to Woburn the following year and stayed there for seven years, during which time it built up a solid reputation and produced champions of quality. An unfortunate trend for runaway winners *à la* Okamoto developed, but that was not apparent in 1990 when the effervescent Swede, Helen Alfredsson, announced herself to the golfing world by beating Jane Hill of Zimbabwe at the fourth extra hole, after they had tied on 288. It was Alfredsson's first win as a professional but, like Nicholas, she went on to prove that it was no fluke, that here was a player capable of world-class performances, a name that added lustre to the championship roll.

Richard George said that he was "moderately pleased" with the way the Open was progressing, and continued his whispering campaign to persuade the LPGA to recognize the championship as an event that their players could play in without restriction. Were that to happen, he would double the prize money immediately to £300,000 – no small matter, even on the lucrative US circuit. The championship was promoted at the breakfast table on packets of Weetabix, with a free admission offer inside the box.

In 1991 the winner came from an unexpected quarter. She was one of the pre-qualifiers, had a 22-month-old son, a husband who was unemployed – he caddied for her during the Open – and a sister who kicked her up the backside and told her to work harder and stop wasting her talent. Thus it came to pass that Penny Grice-Whittaker, who had won £1,206 that season and had won only once since turning professional in 1985, picked up the biggest title in Europe and a cheque for £25,000. It was fairy-tale stuff. Grice-Whittaker started 69, 69, then threw in a 77 that included a nine at the 13th, where she incurred a two-shot penalty for grounding her club in a bunker. Instead of crumbling, she played the last five holes in two under par, and a final round of 69 left her three shots clear of Alfredsson and Diane Barnard. Laura Davies, desperate to win the championship again, was tied for fourth on 288, four shots behind.

To date, Grice-Whittaker is the last British-born champion. She was succeeded by Patty Sheehan of the United States, who became the first woman to win both the US and British Women's Opens in the same season. For the first time the championship was reduced to 54 holes, as rain washed out Friday's play. But 20,000 or so spectators turned out, and there was even talk of the event being the fifth women's major. The BBC ventured into some live coverage for the first time since the debacle of 1984, and Sheehan's last round of 67 (six birdies, no bogeys) was worth watching. The doom-and-gloom mongers said it bode ill for the Solheim Cup at Dalmahoy the following week, but Europe beat the United States in one of the great sporting upsets.

The trouble with the Open of 1993 was that Karen Lunn, the amiable Australian who won, did it too easily. She was five shots ahead of Brandie Burton of the USA and Kathryn Marshall of Scotland after three rounds, and after a largely sleepless night shot 67 in the last round to win by eight shots from Burton; Marshall was third a further three shots behind. Lunn's total of 275 was 17 under par, and she completed an Aussie Open double because Greg Norman had won at Royal St George's in July. Jane Geddes, still travelling, fired a championship-record 64, nine under par, in the final round. She had 10 birdies, an eagle, a double bogey, a bogey and 23 putts, including 13 singles. "I felt as though I holed everything out there," she said. One footnote: Marshall, whose enthusiasm was infectious, had her father caddying for her and they got a lot of airtime – as did her father's trolley. As a result trolleys were banned from future championships, because the powers-that-be thought they looked unprofessional...

The following year marked an even more significant breakthrough in that the Weetabix Women's British Open appeared on the LPGA schedule for the first time, leaving players free to

Karrie Webb – took women's golf by storm when she became the youngest-ever winner, aged 20, in 1995

play without the fear of fines if they had used up their releases. Also, the money they won – and the first prize was a substantial £52,500 – would count on the US money list. Admittedly, the Americans did not appear in droves first time out, but Laura Davies was her usual forthright self: "If they want to play, that's great, but if they regard it as a bit of a chore – as some of them do – well, it's not that I think we need them." The champion was Lotta Neumann, the Swede who had succeeded Davies as US Women's Open champion in 1988, and she won by a comfortable three shots from compatriot Annika Sorenstam and American Dottie Mochrie (*née* Pepper).

A new era was heralded in 1995 when Karrie Webb, a 20-year-old from Ayr in Australia, showed scant respect to a distinguished field that included the legendary Nancy Lopez. Webb became the youngest champion, and was another first-time winner who proved herself a genuine star, taking the US Tour to the cleaners the following season and winning over $1 million as she topped the money list in her rookie year. Webb continued the trend of runaway champions; one ahead of Val Skinner after three rounds, she was six clear of Sorenstam and Jill McGill by the finish, to the relief and disbelief of her parents and friends hanging on to the phone back home in Queensland.

Players from 22 countries competed in a genuinely international championship in 1996 and Emilee Klein, a petite American who had won in Massachusetts the week before, swept them aside, winning by seven shots. Her total of 277 was one better than Webb's, but the Australian set new records at Sunningdale in 1997 when the championship at last felt established enough to start roaming again. Webb never led by fewer than three shots after an opening 65, but it was a scintillating 63 in the third round that clinched matters – a championship record. It left her eight shots clear of all pursuers, and that was how it finished. Her 19-under-par total of 269 was a championship record.

The weather was wet and windy at Royal Lytham and St Annes in 1998 – Betsy King described it as "a classic Open" – and Sherri Steinhauer looked an unlikely champion when she started with a nine-over-par 81. Rock-solid rounds of 72 and 70, capped by an outstanding 69, repaired the damage and the 35-year-old American won by a shot from Burton and Sophie Gustafson, another promising Swede. Janice Moodie, a Scot with great potential, was fourth, two shots behind Steinhauer, who won £100,000. The record sum reflected the championship's growing prestige at a time when the European tour is ailing, even though its players are some of the best in the world.

The addition of new, more traditional venues has enhanced the championship's status, and has added to the interest. It is back to Woburn in 1999, then Royal Birkdale in 2000, where Laura Davies will have the chance to bring things back full circle.

Sherri Steinhauer – a surprise winner in 1998

						1984 continued
	Silvia Bertolaccini	81	77	74	78	310
	Jane Ceddes	75	76	80	79	310
	Alison Nicholas	74	78	77	81	310

1985

1	**Betsy King**	75	76	76	73	300
2	**Marta Figueras Dotti**	77	73	78	74	302
=3	**M. Spencer Devun**	81	80	70	73	304
	Marie Wennersten	75	76	77	76	304
	Sapphire Young	78	74	74	78	304
6	**Jane Forrest**	74	78	78	75	305
=7	**Alison Nicholas**	75	76	77	78	306
	Debbie Dowling	74	78	76	78	306
	Tiru Fernando	77	78	73	78	306
=10	**Lori Garbacz**	77	77	78	75	307
	Barb Thormas	78	70	81	78	307
=12	**Kitrina Douglas**	79	77	80	72	308
	Jill Thornhill (A)	76	78	77	77	308
=14	**Jane Connachan**	76	81	78	75	310
	Peggy Conley	78	80	77	75	310
	Belle Robertson (a)	78	76	80	76	310
=17	**Beth Boozer**	79	78	80	74	311
	Gillian Stewart	82	80	14	75	311
=19	**Dale Reid**	74	77	78	83	312
	Lori Castillo	74	78	77	83	312
=21	**Corinne Dibnah**	77	78	81	77	313
	Vanessa Marvin	77	78	81	77	313
	Maxine Burton	80	78	76	79	313
=24	**Heather Farr**	83	80	75	76	314
	Beverley New	78	81	78	77	314
	Laura Davies	75	82	74	83	314
=27	**Federica Dassu**	80	79	78	78	315
	Suzanne Strudwick	83	77	76	79	315
=29	**Angela Uzielli (A)**	84	78	78	76	316
	Debbie Massey	81	81	75	79	316
	Rae Hast	82	75	78	81	316
	Susan Moorcraft (a)	81	78	73	74	316

1986

1	**Laura Davies**	71	73	69	70	283
=2	**Marta Figueras Dotti**	68	72	74	73	287
	Peggy Conley	70	69	71	77	287
4	**Beverley New**	69	77	76	66	288
5	**Vicki Thomas(a)**	75	73	71	70	289
6	**Betsy King**	73	71	72	74	290
7	**Debbie Dowling**	70	70	75	76	291
8	**Liselotte Neumann**	71	73	74	74	292
9	**Debbie Massey**	76	71	72	74	293
=10	**Penny Grice-Whittaker**	75	74	75	70	294
	Claire Duffy (a)	73	73	73	75	294
=12	**Muriel Thomson**	73	77	73	72	295
	Dale Reid	73	73	74	75	295
	Alison Sheard	73	72	75	75	295
	Suzanne Strudwick	78	69	73	75	295
	Kitrina Douglas	72	74	70	79	295
17	**Catherine Panton**	69	75	73	79	296
=18	**Martha Nause**	70	76	77	74	297
	Alison Nicholas	72	72	78	75	297
=20	**Elizabeth Glass**	75	76	71	76	298
	Jane Connachan	76	71	69	82	298
=22	**Jane Forrest**	75	70	77	77	299
	Beverly Huke	71	75	71	82	299
=24	**Christine Sharp**	73	76	75	76	300
	Barb Thomas	75	75	73	77	300

						1986 continued
=26	**Nicola McCormack**	76	74	74	77	301
	Gillian Stewart	74	72	77	78	301
=28	**Janet Collingham(a)**	76	74	76	76	302
	Rae Hast	75	78	72	77	302
	Meredith Marshall	75	75	75	77	302
	Sonja Van Wyk	73	79	72	78	302
	Susan Moorcraft (a)	78	71	75	78	302
	Rica Comstock	77	73	72	80	302

1987

1	**Alison Nicholas**	74	76	73	73	296
=2	**Laura Davies**	73	72	79	73	297
	Muffin Spencer-Devlin	79	68	75	75	297
4	**Sally Little**	69	80	74	75	298
=5	**Corinne Dibnah**	77	74	78	71	300
	Jane Connachan	77	74	75	74	300
7	**Dale Reid**	75	74	76	76	301
=8	**Marta Figueras Dotti**	78	72	78	74	302
	Beth Boozer	81	74	71	76	302
10	**Dennise Hutton**	76	73	77	77	303
=11	**Natalie Jeanson**	77	77	76	74	304
	Claire Waite	78	71	79	76	304
	Kitrina Douglas	76	75	73	80	304
=14	**Joanne Furby (a)**	80	78	71	76	305
	Vanessa Marvin	79	78	71	77	305
=16	**Maxine Burton**	77	76	78	75	306
	Pat Smillie	74	77	77	78	306
=18	**Susan Shapcott (a)**	81	78	76	72	307
	Rae Hast	80	79	75	73	307
	Gillian Stewart	75	74	80	78	307
=21	**Karinne Espinasse**	80	75	79	74	308
	Julie Brown	80	75	77	76	308
	Debbie Dowling	79	78	75	76	308
	Catherine Panton	79	76	77	76	308
	Peggy Conley	74	75	81	78	308
	Vicki Thomas (a)	76	77	76	79	308
=27	**Meredith Marshall**	79	72	80	78	309
	Helen Wadsworth (a)	80	73	75	81	309
=29	**Marie Laure de Taya**	77	76	80	77	310
	Judy Statham	76	81	73	80	310

1988

=1	**Corinne Dibnah**	73	73	74	75	295
	Sally Little	73	77	69	76	295
3	**Alison Nicholas**	76	73	75	72	296
4	**Karen Lunn**	72	79	75	73	299
5	**Janet Soulsby**	75	77	75	73	300
=6	**Kitrina Douglas**	76	70	78	77	301
	Kathryn Imne (a)	76	72	77	76	301
=8	**Laura Davies**	72	78	79	73	302
	Marie Wennersten	72	82	72	76	302
=10	**Debbie Dowling**	76	80	75	73	304
	Laurette Maritz	77	76	77	74	304
	Dale Reid	78	76	74	76	304
	Gillian Stewart	73	77	77	77	304
	Nicola Way (a)	78	79	70	77	304
	Diana Heinicke	75	79	70	80	304
=16	**Tina Yarwood (a)**	76	79	77	73	305
	Marie Laure de Taya	73	79	74	79	305
=18	**Dennise Hutton**	76	79	80	71	3.06
	Catherine Panton	73	81	76	76	306
	Karine Espinasse	76	81	72	77	306
=21	**Muriel Thomson**	75	80	76	76	307
	Suzanne Strudwick	73	80	77	77	307

1988 continued

	Lori Pianos	75	76	77	79	307
=24	**Joanne Morley (a)**	80	77	76	75	308
	Denise Hermida	74	79	79	76	308
	Pia NIsson	77	80	75	76	308
	Sandra Palmer	74	80	76	78	308
	Beverley New	75	79	76	78	308
	Maureen Garner	74	82	74	78	308
	Tracy Chadman	76	73	77	82	308

1989

1	**Jane Geddes**	67	67	72	68	274
2	**Florence Descampe**	73	66	70	67	276
3	**Marie Laure de Lorenzi**	68	71	67	72	278
=4	**Patti Rizzo**	71	69	68	71	279
	Muffin Spencer-Devlin	72	69	67	71	279
6	**Peggy Conley**	70	67	76	67	280
7	**Xonia Wunsch-Ruiz**	69	73	72	67	281
8	**Kitrina Douglas**	71	70	71	70	282
9	**Alicia Dibos**	67	75	72	69	283
=10	**Ray Bell**	71	68	74	72	285
	Marta Figueras-Dotti	69	71	72	73	285
	Helen Alfredsson	73	70	69	73	285
13	**Laurette Maritz**	67	74	71	74	286
=14	**Laura Davies**	76	71	69	71	287
	Rae Hast	73	71	73	70	287
	Alison Nicholas	71	69	71	76	287
	Melissa McNamara	73	70	72	72	287
	Cindy Scholefield	75	72	71	69	287
=19	**Debbie Dowling**	69	76	72	71	288
	Joanne Furby	71	72	70	75	288
=21	**Patricia Johnson**	72	75	69	73	289
	Suzanne Strudwick	70	74	69	76	289
	Karen Davies	73	70	72	74	289
24	**Nicole Lowien**	71	70	79	70	290
=25	**Jane Connachan**	72	75	69	75	291
	Federica Dassu	74	72	73	72	291
	Susan Moon	75	71	77	68	291
	Alison Munt	73	70	73	75	291
=29	**Marjorie Jones**	74	75	70	73	292
	Liselotte Neumann	71	72	75	74	292

1990

1	**Helen Alfredsson**	70	71	74	73	288
2	**Jane Hill**	77	74	69	68	288
=3	**Laura Davies**	75	73	73	70	291
	Kitrina Douglas	69	71	75	76	291
	Dana Lofland	73	70	75	73	291
=6	**Marie-Laure De Lorenzi**	72	70	72	79	293
	Trish Johnson	71	74	73	75	293
	Myra Blackwelder	73	70	78	72	293
=9	**Diane Barnard**	75	70	73	76	294
	Alison Nicholas	75	75	68	76	294
11	**Pearl Sinn**	70	74	77	74	295
12	**Allison Shapcott**	73	74	76	73	296
=13	**Claire Duffy**	76	74	74	73	297
	Li Wen-Lin	73	69	76	79	297
	Michelle Estill	77	70	76	74	297
=16	**Tiru Fernando**	74	73	74	77	298
	Alicia Dibos	76	73	72	77	298
=18	**Janice Arnold**	79	73	74	73	299
	Corinne Dibnah	71	81	74	73	299
	Beverly Huke	76	76	74	73	299
	Suzanne Strudwick	79	71	71	78	299
=22	**Jane Connachan**	74	75	76	75	300

1990 continued

	Dennise Hutton	77	76	74	73	300
	Tern Luckhurst	74	72	76	78	300
=25	**Tania Abitbol**	74	75	75	77	301
	Dale Reid	76	70	77	78	301
	Mami Sugimoto	76	74	79	72	301
	Tracey Craik	76	76	75	74	301
=29	**Alison Sheard**	72	80	77	73	302
	Gillian Stewart	74	73	77	78	302
	Xonia Wunsch-Ruiz	72	78	75	77	302
	Susan Shapcott	72	75	76	79	302
	Sarah Bennett (a)	75	77	78	72	302

1991

1	**Penny Grice-whittaker**	69	69	77	69	284
=2	**Helen Alfredsson**	73	69	76	69	287
	Diane Barnard	73	72	71	71	287
=4	**Stefania Croce**	75	74	70	69	288
	Laura Davies	71	74	71	72	288
	Helen Wadsworth	68	75	72	74	289
=7	**Marie-Laure de Lorenzi**	73	70	76	71	290
	Trish Johnson	71	72	76	71	290
	Evelyn Orley	75	71	72	72	290
	Kristal Parker	73	69	75	73	290
=11	**Alison Nicholas**	75	73	70	73	291
	Julie Forbes	74	73	71	73	291
	Kelley Markette	72	69	77	73	291
14	**Kitrina Douglas**	73	75	71	73	292
=15	**Corinne Soules**	74	77	72	70	293
	Rica Comstock	71	75	76	71	293
	Julie Larsen	77	72	72	72	293
	Jan Stephenson	74	73	71	75	293
19	**Suzanne Strudwick**	69	75	74	76	294
=20	**Karen Pearce**	76	70	74	75	295
	Federica Dassu	73	70	75	77	295
22	**Lora Fairclough**	72	78	77	69	296
	Akiko Fukushima	73	73	78	72	296
	Karine Espinasse	76	75	73	72	296
	Patricia Gonzalez	73	79	72	72	296
	im Gregg	72	78	76	71	297
=27	**Debbie Dowling**	72	77	77	71	297
	Dennise Button	72	78	76	71	297
	Sally Prosser	73	77	76	71	297
	Beverley New	73	76	75	76	297

1992

1	**Patty Sheehan**	68	72	67	207
=2	**Corinne Dibnah**	70	69	71	210
	Marie-Laure de Lorenzi	71	71	70	212
4	**Liselotte Neumann**	69	74	70	213
=5	**Helen Alfredsson**	74	72	68	214
	Patrice Rizzo	72	70	72	214
	Dottie Mochrie	74	68	73	215
	Suzanne Strudwick	75	72	69	216
	Evelyn Orley	70	75	71	216
	Malin Burstrom	72	73	71	216
	Florence Descampe	71	73	72	216
	Janice Arnold	70	74	72	216
=13	**Pamela Wright**	73	76	69	218
	Kristal Parker	72	74	72	218
	Karen Davies	75	70	73	218
	Jane Geddes	78	69	72	219
=17	**Alicia Dibos**	75	75	70	220
	Valerie Michaud	71	76	73	220
	Dale Reid	73	73	74	220

1992 continued

=20	Federica Dassu	73	77	71	221
	Carin Hjalmarsson	74	75	72	221
	Cindy Figg-Currier	71	77	73	221
	Kathryn Marshall	74	73	74	221
	Patricia Johnson	73	73	75	221
	Li Wen-Lin	74	70	77	221
	Tania Abitbol	72	71	78	221
=27	Stefania Croce	79	73	70	222
	Corinne Soules	78	73	71	222
	Debbie Petrizzi	76	72	74	222

1993

1	Karen Lunn	71	69	68	67	275
2	Brandie Burton	75	70	68	70	283
3	Kathryn Marshall	73	71	69	73	286
=4	Jane Geddes	76	75	72	64	287
	Li Wen-Lin	70	71	74	72	287
6	Patty Sheehan	75	70	72	72	289
=7	Marie-Laure. de Lorenzi	73	77	72	68	290
	Catrin Nusmark	76	71	74	69	290
	Laura Davies	69	76	75	70	290
	Suzanne Strudwick	72	71	73	74	290
11	Alison Nicholas	74	73	70	74	291
=12	Dale Reid	76	75	74	68	293
	Patricia Johnson	72	75	77	69	293
	Helen Alfredsson	77	71	74	71	293
	Carin Hjalmarsson	77	74	68	74	293
=16	Sofia Gronberg	76	70	79	69	294
	Karma Orum	75	72	73	74	294
	Sarah Gautrey	76	75	69	74	294
=19	Claire Duffy	75	76	71	73	295
	Rae Hast	77	71	72	75	295
=21	Janet Soulsby	76	75	73	72	296
	Cindy Figg Currier	75	75	72	74	296
=23	Patricia Meunier	73	76	77	71	297
	Joanne Morley	77	74	74	72	297
	Gillian Stewart	74	75	76	72	297
	Valerie Michaud	79	73	70	75	297
=27	Tania Abitbol	77	74	74	73	298
	Kim Cathrein	74	76	73	75	298
	Xonia Wunsch	73	79	71	75	298
	Nikki Buxton	74	74	74	76	298
	Asa Gottmo	77	70	74	77	298
	Federica Dassu	70	75	75	78	298
	Debbie Hanna	74	73	73	78	298

1994

1	Liselotte Neumann	71	67	70	72	280
=2	Dottie Mochne	73	66	74	70	283
	Annika Sorenstam	69	75	69	70	283
=4	Laura Davies	74	66	73	71	284
	Corinne Dibnah	75	70	67	72	284
6	Cindy Figg Currier	69	74	68	74	285
7	Helen Alfredsson	71	76	71	68	286
8	Tracy Hanson	74	73	66	74	287
=9	Caroline Fierce	70	75	71	72	288
	Val Skinner	77	71	66	74	288
	Suzanne Strudwick	71	71	71	75	288
12	Hiromi Kobayashi	73	73	69	74	289
13	Sarah Gautrey	69	74	72	75	290
=14	Marnie McGuire	71	73	78	69	291
	Penny Grice-Whittaker	77	72	72	70	291
	Tania Abitbal	76	68	75	72	291
=17	Estefania Knuth	78	69	72	73	292

1994 continued

	Jane Geddes	74	72	72	74	292
	Li Wen-Lin	73	70	73	76	292
	Sofia Gronberg	71	69	74	78	292
=21	Pamela Wright	68	75	78	72	293
	Karen Pearce	70	74	75	74	293
	Kne Tschetter	68	76	75	74	293
=24	Amy Allcott	74	74	75	71	294
	Kay Cockerill	71	77	73	73	294
	Alice Ritzman	69	76	75	74	294
	Betsy King	73	74	69	78	294
=28	Susan Moon	72	78	74	71	295
	Mardi Lunn	73	75	75	72	295
	Kathryn Marshall	76	72	75	72	295
	Dale Reid	76	72	75	72	295
	Susan Redman	74	71	76	74	295
	Lora Fairciough	75	72	72	76	295
	Alison Nicholas	72	73	70	80	295

1995

1	Karrie Webb	69	70	69	70	278
=2	Jill McGill	71	73	71	69	284
	Annika Sorenstam	70	72	71	71	284
=4	Michele Serteotti	73	71	71	70	285
	Caroline Pierce	70	70	72	73	285
	Valerie Skinner	74	68	67	76	285
=7	Suzanne Strudwick	73	68	71	74	286
=8	Marie-Laure de Lorenzi	68	74	73	73	298
	Nancy Lopez	71	73	70	74	288
	Wendy Doolan	73	71	70	74	288
	Liselotte Neumann	67	74	71	76	288
=12	Kris Tschetter	73	75	74	67	289
	Catriona Matthew	74	71	73	71	289
	Victoria Goetze	73	72	71	73	289
	Patricia Meunier	73	71	71	74	289
=16	Julie Forbes	69	73	77	71	290
	Sally Prosser	70	74	74	72	290
	Hirorni Kobayashi	72	70	74	74	290
=19	Lynnette Brooky	69	74	76	72	291
	Åsa Gottmo	70	73	74	74	291
	Karen Pearce	74	71	72	74	291
	Brandie Burton	72	70	74	75	291
=23	Rachel Hetherinyton	74	76	76	66	292
	Joanne Morley	72	72	74	74	292
	Evelyn Orley	71	73	74	74	292
=26	Valerie Michaud	76	73	75	69	293
	Alison Nicholas	73	72	76	72	293
	Stephanie Dallongeville	76	72	72	73	293
	Tina Fischer	76	66	77	74	293
	Marnie MaGuire	68	78	73	74	293
	Lisa Hackney	74	74	70	75	293
	Lora Fairclough	76	68	72	77	293
	Mardi Lunn	73	67	73	80	293

1996

1	Emilee Klein	68	66	71	72	277
=2	Penny Hamniel	71	70	72	71	284
	Amy Alcott	72	70	70	72	284
=4	Jane Geddes	72	73	70	70	285
	Lisa Hackney	71	69	73	72	285
	Alison Nicholas	68	71	74	72	285
=7	Barb Whitehead	76	70	71	69	286
	Deb Richard	71	73	71	71	286
	Marie-Laure De Lorenzi	74	72	68	72	286
	Pat Bradley	70	75	69	72	286

1996 continued

	Chris Johnson	72	69	73	72	286
	Rosie Jones	69	71	73	73	286
	Tracy Kerdyk	70	70	72	74	286
=14	**Barbara Mucha**	73	71	74	69	287
	Dale Eggeling	69	77	71	70	287
	Catrin Nusmark	72	76	68	71	287
	Karrie Webb	69	70	74	74	287
	Annika Sorenstam	69.	70	73	75	287
=19	**Donna Andrews**	80	65	74	69	288
	Laura Davies	72	75	71	70	288
	Dale Reid	68	74	74	72	288
	Kiyoe Yamazaki	71	70	74	73	288
	Jenny Lidback	68	73	73	74	288
	Helen Alfredsson	69	76	69	74	288
=25	**Joanne Morley**	72	71	74	72	289
	Kathryn Marshall	71	72	73	73	289
	Tania Abitbol	70	75	70	74	289
	Tina Barrett	71	74	69	75	289
	Maria Hjorth	70	70	71	78	289
=30	**Sofia Gronberg-Whitmore**	75	73	71	71	290
	Charlotta Sorenstam	76	70	71	73	290
	Akiko Fukushima	74	74	69	73	290
	Vicki Goetze	74	70	72	74	290
	Julie Piers	68	73	72	77	290

1997

1	**Karrie Webb**	65	70	63	71	269
2	**Rosie Jones**	70	70	66	71	277
3	**Annika Sorenstam**	72	70	69	67	278
4	**Brandie Burton**	73	69	71	67	280
=5	**Lisa Hackney**	74	69	67	71	281
	Catriona Matthew	70	70	70	71	281
=7	**Wendy Doolan**	74	70	68	70	282
	Tina Barrett	70	72	70	70	282
9	**Chris Johnson**	71	71	73	68	283
=10	**Charlotta Sorenstam**	71	70	72	71	284
	Betsy King	71	72	68	73	284
=12	**Mayurni Hirase**	76	65	74	70	285
	Jenny Lidback	71	74	70	70	285
	Liselotte Neumann	68	75	71	71	285
	Juli Inkster	69	71	73	72	285
	Barb Mucha	72	67	73	73	285
	Helen Dobson	73	69	69	74	285
	Kathryn Marshall	70	68	73	74	285
=19	**Carin Koch**	76	71	71	68	286
	Loraine Lambert	70	73	73	70	286
	Corinne Dibnah	72	71	70	73	286
	Alicia Dibos	71	72	70	73	286
=23	**Rachel Hetherington**	75	70	71	71	287
	Laura Davies	74	73	69	71	287
	Kris Tschetter	73	70	72	72	287
26	**Emilee Klein**	69	74	70	75	288
=27	**Susan Farron**	72	75	75	67	289
	Barb Whitehead	71	74	77	67	289
	Joanne Morley	75	69	76	69	289
	Lynnette Brooky	72	73	72	72	289
	Helen Alfredsson	69	76	72	72	289
	Janice Moodie	74	71	71	73	289

1998

1	**Sherri Steinhauer**	81	72	70	69	292
=2	**Sophie Gustafson**	78	71	74	70	293
	Brandie Burton	71	74	77	71	293
4	**Janice Moodie**	75	72	72	75	294

1998 continued

5	**Karrie Webb**	76	76	71	73	296
=6	**Leslie Spalding**	76	70	75	76	297
	Wendy Ward	76	71	74	76	297
	Smriti Mehra	73	77	71	76	297
	Betsy King	71	77	72	77	297
10	**Catrin Nusmark**	77	77	69	75	298
=11	**Trish Johnson**	72	77	77	73	299
	Juli Inkster	75	75	76	73	299
	Marie-Laure De Lorenzi	79	70	76	74	299
	Annika Sorenstam	75	73	77	74	299
=15	**Mhairi McKay**	75	74	75	76	300
=16	**Myra Murray**	81	76	69	75	301
	Helen Wadsworth	79	74	72	76	301
	Dale Reid	73	79	73	76	301
=19	**Hiromi Kobayashi**	77	74	75	76	302
=20	**Maria Hjorth**	82	73	76	72	303
	Kris Tschetter	79	75	73	76	303
	Jackie Gallagher-Smith	76	74	74	79	303
	Kathryn Marshall	79	74	71	79	303
=24	**Donna Andrews**	81	72	76	75	304
	Joanne Morley	79	74	74	77	304
	Pat Hurst	76	77	70	81	304
=27	**Cathy Johnston-Forbes**	78	76	79	72	305
	Suzanne Strudwick	75	72	75	83	305
=29	**Kim Saiki**	80	76	73	77	306
	Carin Koch	79	74	76	77	306

Note: Tournament not played in 1983

SENIOR GOLF

It has been called the most successful professional sports venture of the last 20 years, and with good reason. In 1980 Don January was the leading money-winner on the US Senior Tour with a grand total of $44,100. In 1998 Hale Irwin topped the money list – with $2,861,945.

Those two figures underscore the extraordinary growth in popularity in seniors' golf in America. Once a place where tournament players, laid out to pasture, grazed and chatted with their friends, is now a circuit where the in-form have replaced the infirm and helped themselves in turn to the pension fund of their dreams. To think, Irwin made more money last year than the leading earner on the regular circuit, David Duval.

One intriguing feature of the tour has been how players who were little better than average in their prime have suddenly become demons in their later years. Gil Morgan is perhaps the leading example. In a 20-year career on the regular Tour, he made $4 million and won seven tournaments.

Not bad by most people's standards, of course, but it is chickenfeed compared with the standards he has set since reaching 50. In just three years on the senior tour he has outstripped

Hale Irwin – topped the money list in 1998 with a massive $2,861,945

what he achieved on the regular tour both in terms of winning tournaments and earnings. In 1997 alone, he won six tournaments. In 1997 and 1998 combined he made $4.5 million.

John Bland is not far behind. An honest toiler for a generation on the European Tour, he was expected to make a solid living once he turned 50, but nothing more. Bland soon made a nonsense of that prediction, the fact he never gave up competing in his forties standing him in excellent stead. In his first two full seasons, 1996 and 1997, he made $2.7 million.

These achievements were completely beyond the comprehension of the six elder statesmen who met in the boardroom of the US Tour on January 16, 1980. Up to that point there were just one or two organized tournaments for seniors, like the Legends of Golf and the PGA Seniors' Championship.

The six founder members were Sam Snead, Gardner Dickinson, Bob Goalby, Don January, the late Dan Sikes and Julius Boros. All six recognized that if the Senior Tour was to be a success the veterans would have to trade both on their achievements in their prime and also give their benefactors a chance to meet them at close quarters through the channels of the Pro-Am. Thus, each tournament would have two Pro-Ams, one of which would count for scoring purposes for the tournament. Two events were held that first year, Don January winning one in Atlantic City, NJ, and Charlie Sifford the other in Melbourne, FL.

Over the next few years the circuit expanded rapidly. Five events were held in 1981 and then 11 in 1982. By 1983 there were 18 tournaments for those players aged 50 and over, with prize money exceeding $3 million. The dominant players were January and his fellow Texan, Miller Barber, who each won two money titles.

The dominant personality, however, was – as ever – Arnold Palmer. It was not purely chance that the setting-up of the Senior Tour coincided with his reaching 50. Palmer may no longer have been competitive on the regular Tour, but there were still many thousands of people up and down America who wanted to watch him play.

Palmer, who has never lost his love of competition, gave the Senior Tour his enthusiastic backing, and turned up everywhere that his other commitments allowed. With Palmer on board, selling the tour became an easy proposition.

And so the expansion and growth continued into 1984, with 24 tournaments now worth $5 million. That prompted January to state publicly: "If you had told me back in 1980 that we would have this many events and be playing for this much money, I would have said you were crazy."

By 1985 the Senior Tour was large enough – 27 tournaments worth more than $6 million – to stand on its own two feet as a division of the US Tour, becoming a distinct operating and financial entity.

The confidence was not misplaced. That year the cable television network ESPN came on board, agreeing to broadcast nationally seven tournaments. Then there were the players: Gary Player had reached 50; so had Chi Chi Rodriguez.

As a new entrant Player won the final event of 1985, and capped a good year for the international contingent. Peter Thomson had committed himself for the first time in his career to play full-time for a season in America and, as ever when he dedicated himself completely to a project, he made a complete success of it. Thomson won nine events in 1985, and 10 in a 12-month stretch.

Rodriguez, meanwhile, was arguably the success story of 1986. Seniors' golf was made for the little Puerto Rican. On the ultra-serious regular Tour, he had made a few enemies over the years with his constant chatter. Now, such a golf routine had found its perfect home.

In the Pro-Ams everyone wanted to partner him, and how

Arnold Palmer – selling and promoting the US Senior Tour was no problem with him on board

they loved his act – he used his putter like a sword, taking it from its imaginary sheath, duelling with it, before returning it to the sheath – which accompanied the holing of any putt that could not be described as routine.

In 1988 the Senior Tour had grown to 37 events, with enough golf for anyone who was eligible. Bob Charles became the first player to win more than $500,000 in a single season.

Given the levels of prize money offered, it was inevitable that matters would become a little more serious than before. The size of fields was expanded to 72 to take into account the higher standard of play, and the Pro-Am format was altered slightly.

Now, for standard events, the two day Pro-Am was a separate matter, with professionals only competing for 54 holes from Friday to Sunday. It is a format that remains in place today.

Charles was again the leading money-winner in 1989, but now his earnings had climbed dramatically to a shade below three-quarters of a million.

All this prefaced the introduction to the tour in 1990 of Jack Nicklaus and Lee Trevino. Alongside Player and Palmer, the tour now had four players who made the galleries feel warm and nostalgic about their youth. A contrast to the nameless personalities that were dominating the regular tour at the time was stark. Many people preferred to watch the seniors.

What a decade it had been. The small beginnings of six veteran golfers chinwagging about a circuit to rekindle old memories had mushroomed into a circuit that was now the second most lucrative in the world – and one that was fast closing in on the first.

It mattered little that Nicklaus chose not to play every week. Indeed it added drama to his ten or so appearances each season, and guaranteed even more publicity because of the rare nature of his visits. And when he was not there, Trevino made up for his absence.

As with Rodriguez, so Trevino. On the course the Merry Mex of legend more than lived up to the moniker. In his first year he had plenty to smile about. He won seven tournaments and collected more than $1.1 million, making him that year's leading money-winner in all of golf.

Yet just as appealing were the stories of the lesser lights who came from nowhere to make their fortune. Few had a better tale to tell than Jim Albus. He turned professional in 1968 and joined the regular tour for a while. He found he could not hit his hat. His best finish ever was tied for 26th at the 1982 Westchester Classic; his career earnings on the US Tour amounted to $16,279.

Naturally, Albus gave it up after a while and became a club professional. And there he stayed, tending to his members' needs, fixing his clubs and selling them the shirt on their backs, until he came within sight of his 50th birthday and discovered itchy feet.

In 1992 Albus so enjoyed life on the Senior Tour that he played in every round in every official event. He finished 16th that year and won over $400,000. Two years later he finished third on the money list and won over a million. In his first eight years on the tour he won over $4 million. You could say he had made up for lost time.

Then there was the heartening story of Bob Murphy, who stepped off the regular tour in 1987 with what appeared at the time to be a sprained ankle, but which developed into a battle with arthritis. At one point his hands were so badly swollen he could not grip the club.

It was Lee Trevino who coaxed him out of a television commentary booth and talked him into playing golf again. By then Murphy had found something that kept his arthritis in check. He joined the Senior Tour in 1993, and in his first five years won 11 tournaments and $4.6 million in prize money.

And what about the career amateurs, Jay Sigel and Allen Doyle? Sigel was arguably the best amateur America had seen since Bobby Jones, but after nine Walker Cups and a houseful of trophies and awards he decided on his 50th birthday to turn professional. Would he be able to compete alongside players who had never stopped competing, while he had combined selling insurance with his golfing pleasures?

At the start of the 1999 season, after five years as a senior, Sigel had emphatically answered the question in the affirmative; he averaged $1 million in winnings per annum. Doyle, meanwhile, turned pro at the age of 46 because, he says, he "was about $10,000 short on his daughter's college tuition fees".

He competed for a couple of years on the Nike Tour to get in shape, won three tournaments, and in 1999 became the first player to win both on that circuit and the Senior Tour.

Another good story is that of Bob Duval, father of David. Here was another player who had failed to make a go of the regular tour and who had opted for the solid, relatively successful living of the club pro. It was David Duval who persuaded him that his golf was better than regional PGA events. Bob Duval took the chance, and is exceedingly glad that he did. His first full season came in 1997, and he made over half a million dollars. The following year he made over three-quarters of a million. It may not match his son's mega-salary, but they are sums he could only have dreamed about as a club pro.

The Senior Tour is full of dreams like these, and in the early 1990s they combined intoxicatingly with the marquee names. It was all so much fun as well. In the 1994 Ford Senior Championship, the Big Three – Player, Palmer, and Nicklaus - were paired together for the first time since they turned 50. What entertainment they provided. On the first day on one hole they typified all the years that they have accumulated playing golf.

The 11th at the TPC of Michigan is a difficult par four with a split fairway, where you can either take your life in your hands for the possible reward of a short-iron second shot, or play

Gary Player – along with Palmer and Nicklaus he made a huge impact on the Senior Tour

conservatively. Palmer, it hardly needs relating, took out his driver, and smashed it gloriously down the middle. As did Player.

Nicklaus? Given that this was day one, again it hardly needs stating that he chose the conservative route with an iron. What was most odd was that he hooked it. It was at this stage that Player walked from his side of the tee to Nicklaus, and, to smiles from an eagerly earwigging gallery, said: "That, Jack, was a crap decision and it deservedly resulted in a crap shot."

The Golden Bear looked at him, and 30 years of friendship dissolved into a shared fit of laughter. It was, of course, golf that we could all relate to, just two players saying what they think and enjoying each other's company.

And it summed up, in essence, one of the cornerstones of the success of the Senior Tour. What about the others? One of the keys was that when golf enjoyed a surge in popularity in the 1980s it was invariably among the over-50s set. As if ready-made, they had a set of sepia-tinted heroes who just happened to be their age. No wonder they became groupies of the Senior rather than the regular Tour.

Then there is the Pro-Am format and the size of the fields. Even now only 78 players take part in a standard event. After two days partnering corporate America, they play their own game in a setting far intimate than on the regular tour with its unwieldy fields of 156.

There is also the point that golf is the businessman's game. Hyatt Hotels in America once did a survey that showed that more business deals were done playing golf than in the boardroom. And who makes the decisions on behalf of the corporations, be they in the boardroom or out on the golf course? Yes, it is the over-50s set once more, and when it comes to trying to find the right sponsorship for their product, what could be more ideal than the game played by the heroes they grew up with, and with whom their clients could play alongside? As they say in America: dead solid perfect.

"I have long said it is a success story of which everyone in golf should be proud, but it really has gone beyond one's imagination now," Gary Player said in 1995.

And so it appeared back then, when Arnie was still a force, and Player and Nicklaus and Trevino were still relatively young.

As the nineties wore on, however, they all got old and lost a little of their popularity. Their replacements, if anything, raised the standard of play, but Hale Irwin and Gil Morgan did it in an expressionless manner that contrasted vividly with what had gone before. Where was a Trevino of the late 1990s, or a Rodriguez come to that?

It was bad news for the seniors that this lull coincided with the arrival on the regular tour of Tiger Woods. Suddenly the next explosion of interest in golf came from the young end of the market, and they were not much interested in players old enough in some cases to be their grandfathers, let alone their fathers. Suddenly it seemed ludicrous to theorize, as many people did in 1995, that the Senior Tour would take over from the regular tour as golf's number-one circuit.

The Senior Tour remains buoyant, however, if not quite the stellar place it was for a while. Certainly, in tournaments when Woods and Duval are at their best, it does pale by comparison. But sponsors remain more than faithful: 44 events dot the calendar, and there would be more but for the inconvenient fact that there are only 52 weeks in a year.

In 1999 it also receives the boost of three more charismatic names to lift it again into the twenty-first century: in August Tom Watson turned 50, to be followed in December by two other former Ryder Cup captains in Lanny Wadkins and Tom Kite.

And it will always produce heartening against-the-odds stories, if only because it is so hard to get close to the honey-pot these days. Yes, the money may be good, but grabbing hold of it is the devil.

A typical field these days comprises: the top 31 players from last year's money list; the top 31 players from the all-time career money list (regular and senior earnings combined); the top eight players from the Qualifying School; winners of Senior Tour events held in the previous 12 months.

In addition, there are four sponsors' invitations, and the scraps that are left to make up a field of 78, which usually amounts to four places, are fed to the 100 or so scavengers who turn up every Monday for an open qualifying event in an effort to make the starting field.

Players like Bland and Brian Barnes came through this most hazardous of routes, and perhaps it is not surprising that, having survived, they went on to prosper.

It seems unlikely that the Senior Tour will ever recapture the glory days of the early 1990s, but it will remain a wonderful place for the over-50s who have retained their games in sufficient good order to be competitive.

And the senior pond is widening too. In 1992 a European version began, with similar modest beginnings to those in America. Yet five years later it too had become a place for ripe pickings, with Tommy Horton the dominant player with six-figure winnings each season.

Nineteen events were established on the schedule for 1999, and this was achieved without one household name to project the tour. By the time famous names like Bernhard Langer, Nick Faldo and Severiano Ballesteros reach 50, perhaps the tour will be well enough established to gain their interest, instead of playing in America or not playing at all.

And perhaps there will be a Senior Ryder Cup by then, to keep the momentum flowing, and pick up another generation of viewers. The possibilities for seniors' golf, therefore, have still to be exhausted, and as long as the game continues to be played by a high percentage of people over 50, then it is hard to see it doing anything but thrive.

SENIOR GOLF STATISTICS

US SENIOR TOUR:

MASTERCARD CHAMPIONSHIP

1997	Hale Irwin
1998	Gil Morgan
1999	John Jacobs

ROYAL CARIBBEAN CLASSIC

Formerly known as Gus Machado Senior Classic (1987–89). Tournament not played in 1989.

1987	Gene Littler
1988	Lee Elder
1989	*Not played*
1990	Lee Trevino
1991	Gary Player
1992	Don Massengale
1993	Jim Colbert
1994	Lee Trevino
1995	J.C. Snead
1996	Bob Murphy
1997	Gibby Gilbert
1998	David Graham
1999	Bruce Fleisher

AMERICAN EXPRESS INVITATIONAL HISTORY

1996	Hale Irwin, 197
1997	Bud Allin, 205
1998	Larry Nelson, 203
1999	Bruce Fleisher, 203

GTE CLASSIC

Formerly known as GTE Suncoast Seniors Classic (1988–89), GTE Suncoast Classic (1990–96).

1988	Dale Douglass
1989	Bob Charles
1990	Mike Hill
1991	Bob Charles
1992	Jim Colbert
1993	Jim Albus
1994	Rocky Thompson
1995	Dave Stockton
1996	Jack Nicklaus
1997	David Graham
1998	Jim Albus

ACE GROUP CLASSIC

1988	Gary Player
1989	Gene Littler
1990	Lee Trevino
1991	Lee Trevino
1992	Jimmy Powell
1993	Mike Hill
1994	Mike Hill
1995	Bob Murphy
1996	Al Geiberger
1997	Hale Irwin
1998	Gil Morgan

LIBERTY MUTUAL LEGENDS OF GOLF

1978	Sam Snead/Gardner Dickinson, Kel Nagle
1979	Julius Boros/Roberto de Vicenzo, Art Wall
1980	Tommy Bolt/Art Wall, Don January
1981	Gene Littler/Bob Rosburg, Kel Nagle
1982	Sam Snead/Don January
1983	Rod Funseth/Roberto de Vicenzo, Paul Harney
1984	Billy Casper/Gay Brewer, Julius Boros
1985	Don January/Gene Littler
1986	Don January/Gene Littler

1987	Bruce Crampton/Orville Moody
1988	Bruce Crampton/Orville Moody
1989	Harold Henning/Al Geiberger
1990	Dale Douglass/Charles Coody
1991	Lee Trevino/Mike Hill
1992	Lee Trevino/Mike Hill
1993	Harold Henning
1994	Dale Douglass/Charles Coody
1995	Lee Trevino/Mike Hill
1996	Lee Trevino/Mike Hill
1997	John Bland/Graham Marsh
1998	Charles Coody, Dale Douglass

EMERALD COAST CLASSIC

1995	Ray Floyd
1996	Lee Trevino
1997	Isao Aoki
1998	Dana Quigley

THE TRADITION PRESENTED BY COUNTRYWIDE

Formerly known as The Tradition at Mountain Desert (1989–1991).

1989	Don Bies
1990	Jack Nicklaus
1991	Jack Nicklaus
1992	Lee Trevino
1993	Tom Shaw
1994	Raymond Floyd
1995	Jack Nicklaus
1996	Jack Nicklaus
1997	Gil Morgan
1998	Gil Morgan

PGA SENIORS' CHAMPIONSHIP

Tournament not played 1939, 1943–44. Formerly known as General Foods PGA Championship (1984–89).

1937	Jock Hutchison
1938	Fred McLeod
1939	*Not played*
1940	Otto Hackbarth
1941	Jack Burke Sr
1942	Eddie Williams
1943	*Not played*
1944	*Not played*
1945	Eddie Williams
1946	Eddie Williams
1947	Jock Hutchison
1948	Charles McKenna
1949	Marshall Crichton
1950	Al Watrous
1951	Al Watrous
1952	Ernest Newnham
1953	Harry Schwab
1954	Gene Sarazen
1955	Mortie Dutra
1956	Pete Burke
1957	Al Watrous
1958	Gene Sarazen
1959	Willie Goggin
1960	Dick Metz
1961	Paul Runyan
1962	Paul Runyan
1963	Herman Barron
1964	Sam Snead
1965	Sam Snead
1966	Freddie Haas
1967	Sam Snead
1968	Chandler Harper
1969	Tommy Bolt
1970	Sam Snead
1971	Julius Boros
1972	Sam Snead
1973	Sam Snead
1974	Roberto de Vicenzo
1975	Charlie Sifford
1976	Pete Cooper
1977	Julius Boros
1978	Joe Jimenez
1979	Jack Fleck
1979	Don January
1980	Arnold Palmer
1981	Miller Barber
1982	Don January
1983	No event
1984	Arnold Palmer
1984	Peter Thomson
1985	No event
1986	Gary Player
1987	Chi Chi Rodriguez
1988	Gary Player
1989	Larry Mowry
1990	Gary Player
1991	Jack Nicklaus

1996	Dave Stockton
1997	Graham Marsh
1998	Hale Irwin

AMERITECH SENIOR OPEN

1989	Bruce Crampton
1990	Chi Chi Rodriguez
1991	Mike Hill
1992	Dale Douglass
1993	George Archer
1994	John Paul Cain
1995	Hale Irwin
1996	Walter Morgan
1997	Gil Morgan
1998	Hale Irwin

COLDWELL BANKER BURNET CLASSIC

Formerly known as Burnet Senior Classic (1993–97).

1993	Chi Chi Rodriguez
1994	Dave Stockton
1995	Raymond Floyd
1996	Vicente Fernandez
1997	Hale Irwin
1998	Leonard Thompson

FRANKLIN QUEST CHAMPIONSHIP

formerly known as The Shootout at Jeremy Ranch (1982–85), Showdown Classic (1986–91), Franklin Showdown Classic (1992)

1982	Billy Casper
1983	Bob Goalby
1984	Don January
1985	Miller Barber
1986	Bobby Nichols
1987	Miller Barber
1988	Miller Barber
1989	Tom Shaw
1990	Rives McBee
1992	Orville Moody
1993	Dave Stockton
1994	Tom Weiskopf
1995	Tony Jacklin
1996	Graham Marsh
1997	Dave Stockton
1998	Gil Morgan

NORTHVILLE LONG ISLAND CLASSIC

Formerly known as The Northville Invitational (1988).

1988	Don Bies
1989	Butch Baird
1990	George Archer
1991	George Archer
1992	George Archer
1993	Raymond Floyd
1994	Lee Trevino
1995	Lee Trevino
1996	John Bland
1997	Dana Quigley
1998	Gary Player

FIRST OF AMERICA CLASSIC

Formerly knownn as Greater Grand Rapids Open (1986–90).

1986	Jim Ferree
1987	Billy Casper
1988	Orville Moody
1989	John Paul Cain
1990	Don Massengale
1991	Harold Henning
1992	Gibby Gilbert
1993	George Archer
1994	Tony Jacklin
1995	Jimmy Powell
1996	Dave Stockton
1997	Gil Morgan
1998	George Archer

BANK OF BOSTON SENIOR CLASSIC

Formerly known as Marlboro Classic (1981–83), Digital Middlesex Classic (1984), Digital Seniors Classic (1985–92).

1981	Bob Goalby
1982	Arnold Palmer
1983	Don January
1984	Don January
1985	Lee Elder
1986	Chi Chi Rodriguez
1987	Chi Chi Rodriguez
1988	Chi Chi Rodriguez
1989	Bob Charles
1990	Bob Charles
1991	Rocky Thompson
1992	Mike Hill
1993	Bob Betley
1994	Jim Albus
1995	Isao Aoki
1996	Jim Dent
1997	Hale Irwin
1998	Hale Irwin

AT&T CANADA SENIOR OPEN CHAMPIONSHIP

Formerly known as Du Maurier Champions (1996–97).

1996	Charles Coody
1997	Jack Kiefer
1998	Brian Barnes

SAINT LUKE'S CLASSIC

Formerly known as Silver Pages Classic (1987), Southwestern Bell Classic (1988–94), VFW Senior Championship (1995–96.

1987	Chi Chi Rodriguez
1988	Gary Player
1989	Bobby Nichols
1990	Jimmy Powell
1991	Jim Colbert
1992	Gibby Gilbert
1993	Dave Stockton
1994	Jim Colbert
1995	Bob Murphy
1996	Dave Eichelberger
1997	Bruce Summerhays
1998	Larry Ziegler

COMFORT CLASSIC AT THE BRICKYARD

Formerly known as GTE North Classic (1988–93), Brickyard Crossing Championship (1994–96).

1988	Gary Player
1989	Gary Player
1990	Mike Hill
1991	George Archer
1992	Ray Floyd
1993	Bob Murphy
1994	Isao Aoki
1995	Simon Hobday
1996	Jimmy Powell
1997	David Graham
1998	Hugh Baiocchi

KROGER SENIOR CLASSIC

1990	Jim Dent
1991	Al Geiberger
1992	Gibby Gilbert
1993	Simon Hobday
1994	Jim Colbert
1995	Mike Hill
1996	Isao Aoki
1997	Jay Sigel
1998	Hugh Baiocchi

VANTAGE CHAMPIONSHIP

Formerly known as RJR Championship (1989).

1987	Al Geiberger
1988	Walt Zembriski
1989	Gary Player
1990	Charles Coody
1991	Jim Colbert
1992	Jim Colbert
1993	Lee Trevino
1994	Larry Gilbert
1995	Hale Irwin
1996	Jim Colbert
1997	Hale Irwin

1998	Gil Morgan

THE TRANSAMERICA

Formerly known as TransAmerica Senior Golf Championship (1989–92).

1989	Billy Casper
1990	Lee Trevino
1991	Charles Coody
1992	Bob Charles
1993	Dave Stockton
1994	Kermit Zarley
1995	Lee Trevino
1996	John Bland
1997	Dave Eichelberger
1998	Jim Colbert

RALEY'S GOLD RUSH CLASSIC

Formerly known as Rancho Murieta Senior Gold Rush (1987–89), Gold Rush at Rancho Murieta (1990), Raley's Senior Gold Rush (1991–95).

1987	Orville Moody
1988	Bob Charles
1989	Dave Hill
1990	George Archer
1991	George Archer
1992	Bob Charles
1993	George Archer
1994	Bob Murphy
1995	Don Bies
1996	Jim Colbert
1997	Bob Eastwood
1998	Dana Quigley

HYATT REGENCY MAUI KAANAPALI CLASSIC

Formerly known as GTE Kaanapali Classic (1987–90), First Development Kaanapali Classic (1991), Kaanapali Classic (1992), Ping Kaanapali Classic (1993).

1987	Orville Moody
1988	Don Bies
1989	Don Bies
1990	Bob Charles
1991	Jim Colbert
1992	Tommy Aaron
1993	George Archer
1994	Bob Murphy
1995	Bob Charles
1996	Bob Charles
1997	Hale Irwin
1998	Jay Sigel

PACIFIC BELL SENIOR CLASSIC

Formerly known as Security Pacific Bell Classic (1990–91), Ralphs Senior Classic (1992–97).

1990	Mike Hill
1991	John Brodie
1992	Ray Floyd
1993	Dale Douglass
1994	Jack Kiefer
1995	John Bland
1996	Gil Morgan
1997	Gil Morgan
1998	Joe Inman

US SENIORS ALL-TIME CAREER MONEY WINNERS (TOP 100)

Rank	*Player*	
1	Hale Irwin	$13,974,663
2	Lee Trevino	$11,823,356
3	Ray Floyd	$11,803,960
4	Gil Morgan	$10,002,111
5	Jim Colbert	$9,959,860
6	Dave Stockton	$9,082,723
7	George Archer	$8,526,494
8	Bob Charles	$8,326,867
9	Jack Nicklaus	$8,280,576
10	Isao Aoki	$7,399,972
11	Mike Hill	$7,297,154
12	Chi Chi Rodriguez	$7,270,053
13	J.C. Snead	$7,168,745
14	Bob Murphy	$7,135,144
15	Gary Player	$6,842,715
16	Jim Dent	$6,828,304
17	Larry Nelson	$6,351,622
18	Dale Douglass	$6,343,028
19	Bruce Crampton	$6,028,877
20	Al Geiberger	$5,857,498
21	Miller Barber	$5,476,058
22	Jay Sigel	$5,142,619
23	Graham Marsh	$4,874,887
24	Gibby Gilbert	$4,864,656
25	Charles Coody	$4,762,537
26	Jim Albus	$4,664,212
27	John Mahaffey	$4,575,322
28	Tom Wargo	$4,573,481
29	David Graham	$4,414,038
30	Don January	$4,363,864
31	Kermit Zarley	$4,175,945
32	Dave Eichelberger	$4,100,200
33	Rocky Thompson	$4,016,166
34	Tom Weiskopf	$3,994,972
35	Hubert Green	$3,958,715
36	Harold Henning	$3,841,982
37	Gene Littler	$3,800,689
38	Orville Moody	$3,766,096
39	Simon Hobday	$3,695,802
40	Arnold Palmer	$3,549,881
41	Jimmy Powell	$3,545,503
42	Leonard Thompson	$3,510,619
43	Dave Hill	$3,498,831
44	Bruce Summerhays	$3,435,756
45	Billy Casper	$3,406,779
46	Tommy Aaron	$3,361,094
47	Terry Dill	$3,331,463
48	Bob Eastwood	$3,303,515
49	John Bland	$3,260,903
50	Don Bies	$3,249,442
51	Jack Kiefer	$3,189,158
52	Calvin Peete	$3,187,928
53	DeWitt Weaver	$3,106,120
54	Vicente Fernandez	$3,041,128
55	Jerry McGee	$3,028,773
56	Tom Shaw	$2,995,460
57	Walter Zembriski	$2,983,075
58	Walter Morgan	$2,886,422
59	Bobby Nichols	$2,880,013
60	Howard Twitty	$2,831,978
61	Butch Baird	$2,788,965
62	Johnny Miller	$2,759,200
63	Gay Brewer	$2,739,329
64	John Jacobs	$2,722,350
65	Larry Ziegler	$2,674,113
66	Lee Elder	$2,599,840
67	Jim Ferree	$2,591,683
68	Larry Laoretti	$2,573,268
69	Bruce Fleisher	$2,562,866
70	Bud Allin	$2,503,465
71	Frank Conner	$2,489,365
72	Bob Dickson	$2,337,853
73	Hugh Baiocchi	$2,306,060
74	Mike McCullough	$2,281,508
75	Jim Thorpe	$2,185,577
76	Lou Graham	$2,129,991
77	Dick Hendrickson	$2,064,561
78	Dana Quigley	$2,064,214
79	Larry Mowry	$2,062,039
80	Bruce Devlin	$2,031,887
81	Ben Smith	$1,971,591
82	Homero Blancas	$1,963,692
83	John Paul Cain	$1,836,557
84	Ed Dougherty	$1,834,790
85	Frank Beard	$1,798,126
86	Rives McBee	$1,787,176
87	Bob Duval	$1,716,055
88	John Schroeder	$1,701,238
89	Brian Barnes	$1,673,573
90	Dick Rhyan	$1,673,031
91	Joe Inman	$1,613,610
92	Jose Maria Canizares	$1,580,338
93	Bob E. Smith	$1,519,234
94	Tony Jacklin	$1,453,027
95	Don Massengale	$1,447,818
96	Ken Still	$1,415,068
97	Joe Jimenez	$1,342,262
98	Bob Goalby	$1,341,884
99	Ed Sneed	$1,329,210
100	Doug Sanders	$1,310,874

EUROPEAN SENIOR TOUR

BEKO CLASSIC

Formerly known as Beko Turkish Senior Open (1996–97).

1996 B. Verwey
1997 T. Horton
1998 B. Lendizon

AIB IRISH SENIORS OPEN

1997 T. Horton
1998 J. McDermott

PHILIPPS PFA GOLF CLASSIC

1997 D. Simon
1998 N. Coles

JERSEY SENIORS OPEN

1996 M. Bembridge
1997 T. Horton
1998 B. Shearer

DE VERE HOTELS SENIORS CLASSIC

1995 T. Horton
1996 R. Campagnoli
1997 T.R. Jones
1998 T. Horton

RYDER SENIORS CLASSIC

Formerly known as Collingtree Park Seniors (1992–93), Joe Powell (1994), Collingtree Seniors (1995), Ryder Collingtree Seniors Classic (1996).

1992 N. Coles
1993 T. Horton
1994 L. Higgins
1995 N. Coles
1996 D. Huish
1997 N. Coles
1998 B. Hardwick

LAWRENCE BATLEY SENIORS

1992 P. Verwey
1993 P. Butler
1994 J. Morgan
1995 A. Croce
1996 M. Gregson
1997 A. Garrido
1998 B. Verwey

CREDIT SUISSE PRIVATE BANKING SENIORS OPEN

1997 B. Waites
1998 B. Verwey

WENTWORTH SENIORS MASTERS

Formerly known as Shell Wentworth Senior Masters (1997).

1997 G. Player
1998 B. Huggett

SENIOR BRITISH OPEN

Formerly known as Volvo Senior British Open (1988–90).

1987 N. Coles
1988 G. Player
1989 R. Charles
1990 G. Player
1991 B. Verwey
1992 J. Fourie
1993 R. Charles
1994 T. Wargo
1995 B. Barnes
1996 B. Barnes
1997 G. Player
1998 B. Huggett

THE BELFRY PGA SENIORS CHAMPIONSHIP

Formerly known as Teachers PGA Seniors Classic (1957–68), Pringle PGA Seniors Championship (1969–74), Ben Sayers & Allied Hotels PGA Seniors Championship (1975–76), Cambridgeshire PGA Seniors Championship (1977–80), Forte PGA Seniors Championship (1981–95).

1957	J. Burton
1958	N. Sutton
1959	A. Lees
1960	R. Horne
1961	S. King
1962	S. King
1963	G. Evans
1964	S. Scott
1965	C. Ward
1966	D. Rees
1967	J. Panton
1968	M. Faulkner
1969	J. Panton
1970	M. Faulkner
1971	K. Nagle
1972	K. Bousfield
1973	K. Nagle
1974	E. Lester
1975	K. Nagle
1976	C. O'Connor
1977	C. O'Connor
1978	P. Skerritt
1979	C. O'Connor
1980	P. Skerritt
1981	C. O'Connor
1982	C. O'Connor
1983	C. O'Connor
1984	E. Jones
1985	N. Coles
1986	N. Coles
1987	N. Coles
1988	P. Thomson
1989	N. Coles
1990	B. Waites
1991	B. Waites
1992	T. Horton
1993	B. Huggett
1994	J. Morgan
1995	J. Morgan
1996	T. Gale
1997	W. Hall
1998	T. Horton

GOLDEN CHARTER PGA SCOTTISH SENIORS OPEN

Formerly known as Shell Scottish Seniors Open (1993–95), Scottish Seniors Open (1996–97).

1993	T. Horton
1994	A. Garrido
1995	B. Huggett
1996	J. Morgan
1997	T. Horton
1998	D. Huish

TOURNAMENT OF CHAMPIONS

Formerly known as Tournament of Champions (1996).

1996	T. Horton
1997	T. Horton
1998	J. Garner

EL BASQUE SENIORS OPEN

1998	T. Horton

SWEDISH SENIORS

1998	M. Bembridge

WEST OF IRELAND SENIORS CHAMPIONSHIP

1998	J. Garner

EFLING EUROPEAN TROPHY

1998	P. Leonard

Chapter 4

THE TOP 200 PLAYERS

GIVEN THE WEALTH OF TALENT THAT HAS GRACED THE SPORT OF GOLF OVER THE LAST ONE HUNDRED YEARS IT IS QUITE SOMETHING TO SIT DOWN TO PICK THE GOLFER OF THE CENTURY AND FIND THAT THE FIRST THREE ACTUALLY SELECT THEMSELVES.

ONCE WE'VE DECIDED THE ORDER IN WHICH TO PLACE MESSRS NICKLAUS, HOGAN, AND JONES, HOWEVER, THINGS GET A LITTLE COMPLICATED...

THE CRITERIA USED HERE IS TO WEIGH THE NUMBER OF MAJOR CHAMPIONSHIPS THAT A PLAYER WON AGAINST THE ERA IN WHICH THEY WERE ASSEMBLED. THEN THE IMPACT THAT A GOLFER HAD ON THE GAME IS FACTORED IN, SO THAT PLAYERS LIKE ARNOLD PALMER AND SEVERIANO BALLESTEROS CAN BE PROPERLY RECOGNISED.

LIKE GENE SARAZEN, I'M OF THE OPINION THAT THE GAME AS IT IS PLAYED NOW IS OF AN IMMEASURABLY HIGHER STANDARD, SO THE MODERN PLAYERS DOMINATE THE LIST. HAVING SAID THAT, NO PLAYER CAN DO MORE THAN BE THE BEST IN HIS ERA, AND THAT HAS BEEN TAKEN INTO ACCOUNT.

ONE OF THE MAJOR DIFFICULTIES WAS WITH PLAYERS WHOSE TALENTS OVERLAP EITHER END OF THE CENTURY. PLAYERS LIKE HARRY VARDON, WHO WON SOME OF HIS MAJOR CHAMPIONSHIPS IN THE PREVIOUS CENTURY, AND ERNIE ELS, WHO WILL SURELY WIN MORE IN THE YEARS TO COME. SINCE IT IS SUPPOSED TO BE THE DEFINING LIST OF THE TWENTIETH CENTURY, ONLY FEATS ACHIEVED DURING THAT TIME SPAN CAN BE CONSIDERED.

ONE EXCEPTION WAS ALLOWED, HOWEVER. IN WINNING HIS FIRST MAJOR CHAMPIONSHIP AS A PROFESSIONAL, AND BY A RECORD MARGIN TO BOOT, TIGER WOODS DESERVES TO STAND OUT FROM THE CROWD. COME THE DAWN OF THE NEW CENTURY HE WILL HAVE JUST TURNED 24. I HAVE NO DOUBT THAT HE WILL BE FEATURED PROMINENTLY IN A SIMILAR TOME IN ONE HUNDRED YEARS' TIME.

John Bland 200

FULL NAME: John Louis Bland

BORN: Johannesburg, South Africa, September 22, 1945

Who could ever have predicted the amazing success that befell John Bland the moment he turned 50 and joined the US Senior Tour? Equally, who would have thought life would be so cruel as to rob him of much of its pleasure when his wife died so tragically in 1998? The happier side of the story is that a solid if unspectacular performer on the European Tour reached his milestone birthday in late 1995, and the following season could not stop winning. He played with Arnold Palmer for the first time and scored a hole-in-one. Since his initial victory at the Ralph's Senior Classic in 1995, he has claimed nearly $3 million in prize money and has passed seven figures in the last two seasons. He was also voted Rookie of the Year in 1996 on the strength of four wins.

Vic Ghezzi 199

Full Name: Victor Ghezzi

BORN: Johannesburg, South Africa, September 22, 1945

MAJOR CHAMPIONSHIPS: USPGA 1941

Vic Ghezzi had been competing in the USPGA Championship for some years without any real distinction. Then came 1941. He beat Lloyd Mangrum on the home hole in the semi-final, and that brought him a match-up against Byron Nelson. This 36-hole match was a tight and tense affair that finally necessitated extra holes to decide it; and in the end it was Ghezzi who gained the upper hand to deny Nelson a successful defence of the title he had won the previous year against Sam Snead. It was to be Ghezzi's one real moment in the spotlight, and not a bad one it was, all things considered.

Hugh Baiocchi 198

FULL NAME: Hugh John Baiocchi

BORN: Johannesburg, South Africa, August 17, 1946

Hugh Baiocchi was a popular and successful visitor to the European Tour for almost 20 years. From 1972 to 1987 he displayed a remarkable level of consistency, only once finishing outside the top 30 in the money list in all that time, and that was a decidedly non-calamitous 39th. Like his good friend, John Bland, his career has reached an even greater peak since he turned 50. In all those years in Europe he had total winnings of £537,000. In just two years on the senior tour, he comfortably doubled that amount, and among his successes were back-to-back wins during the summer of 1998.

Sam Parks 197

FULL NAME: Sam Parks

BORN: Pennsylvania, July 23, 1909

MAJOR CHAMPIONSHIPS: US Open 1935

If ever a horse was made for a certain course, it was Sam Parks at Oakmont. The 1935 US Open was the only tournament he ever won, and he did so by being the only man to break 300 over the daunting Pennsylvania venue. "I'm the dark horse champion," he joyously declared afterwards.

He had certainly been a 20–1 outsider, but what the bookmakers forgot was that Parks knew the course well, and how to cope with its viciously sloping greens. He stayed a pro for only 10 years before becoming a salesman for US Steel – joining Oakmont as a member.

Lee Elder 196

FULL NAME: Robert Lee Elder

BORN: Dallas, TX, July 14, 1934

They hoped that no black golfer would ever sully their tournament, but in 1975 Lee Elder qualified to play at the Masters and walked with head high through the Augusta gates. A barrier had been broken, and 23 years later Tiger Woods smashed it down – hopefully for all time – and what's more Elder made the trip to Augusta on the final Sunday to witness it all. Elder won four times in all on the US Tour, and played in the 1979 Ryder Cup. Later on he was a wonderfully consistent player on the senior tour; between 1984 and 1988 his worst finish on the money list was 19th, while his best was second. His last Senior Tour victory came at the 1988 Gus Machado Classic almost a year to the day after he suffered a mild heart attack

Scott Hoch 195

FULL NAME: Scott Mabon Hoch

BORN: Raleigh, NC, November 24, 1955

Many a player has disappeared without trace after making the sort of error that Scott Hoch made in 1989, when he missed from two foot for the Masters. A few years later he threw away another tournament and said: "Now you know why Hoch rhymes with choke." Yet here we are ten years on and Hoch is still around, still playing great golf, still making stacks of money... And still getting up everybody's nose, like he always did. Noted for always staying away from the Open, he finally turned up in 1998 "because my sponsors made me". A real charmer, that boy. A better golfer than he gets credit for, however, and the record books will prove it.

Chip Beck 194

FULL NAME: Charles Henry Beck
BORN: Fayetteville, NC, September 12, 1956

As Chip Beck went from missed cut to missed cut in 1997 and 1998, it was hard to reconcile that player with the one who was capable of such spectacular golf that in 1991 in Las Vegas he became just the second player on the US Tour to shoot a 59. Beck had 13 birdies and no bogeys that day, as he continued a run that saw him finish in the top 10 in the money list every year from 1987 to 1992. What happened to him? In 1993 he was pilloried for ensuring second place at the Masters when he had a shot at glory. Since then he has been to hell and Beck.

Tom Creavy 193

FULL NAME: Thomas Creavy
BORN: 1910
MAJOR CHAMPIONSHIPS: USPGA 1930

No one could accuse Tom Creavy of an easy ride to victory in the 1931 USPGA Championship. From the quarter-final onwards he defeated Cyril Walker, Gene Sarazen and then Denny Shute in the final. He was just 20 at the time and seemingly destined for a life at the top. What or who could stop him? Well, it turned out to be what rather than who. After doing quite well in the next USPGA or two and featuring in the top 10 of a US Open, he was struck down by a debilitating illness and faded into obscurity.

Peter Jacobsen 193

FULL NAME: Peter Erling Jacobsen
BORN: Portland, OR, March 4, 1954

For over 20 years now Peter Jacobsen has plied a successful trade on the US Tour, racking up prize money that has now passed the $5 million mark. Unusually, his two most successful seasons were 11 years apart: in 1984 he won three tournaments and then, at the start of 1995, back-to-back events in California. One of those wins was the Pebble Beach Pro-Am, the tournament where all the Hollywood stars turn up. It is an event for which the popular Jacobsen is ideally suited, given that he has his own rock band and a top mimic's talent for impersonations.

Mike Souchak 191

FULL NAME: Michael Souchak
BORN: Berwick, PA, May 10, 1927

Mike Souchak was a leading college football player, and accordingly an immense bear of a man. He could hit the ball huge distances, and when everything was in harmony he was capable of prodigious feats; in winning the 1955 Texas Open he set a 72-hole record score of 257 that stands to this day. Yet despite having the talent to nail down 15 tournament wins, he never managed to notch up a major. The closest he came was two third-place finishes in the US Opens of 1959 at Winged Foot and Cherry Hills the following year.

Lee Elder – the first player to truly break the "race" barrier

Herman Keiser 190

FULL NAME: Herman Keiser
BORN: October 7, 1914
MAJOR CHAMPIONSHIPS: Masters 1946

Herman Keiser may be the least recognized of all Masters champions. For a start there was the nervous way he played the last hole in 1946, culminating in a three putt. This led to the exciting prospect of Ben Hogan winning the first post-war tournament at Augusta, and he duly had a 12ft birdie putt on the last to make this happen. But then he missed, missed again... and, well, it was "after you Herman", after all. It is always slightly unfair when champions are regarded in this way, because don't you have to play pretty well to get into a position to win in the first place?

Jay Hebert 189

FULL NAME: Jay Junius Hebert
BORN: New Orleans, LA, February 14, 1923
MAJOR CHAMPIONSHIPS: USPGA 1960

Jay Hebert was well into his thirties when he followed his brother Lionel into the professional ranks. He had been a marine during the Second World War and was wounded at Iwo Jima. Now he made up for lost time, winning seven tournaments between 1957 and 1961, one of which was the USPGA Championship, where a final round 70 saw him to the title by one stroke ahead of Jim Ferrier – it was a title his brother had also won. Hebert would probably have won more but for a weakness around the greens, a problem that cost him a number of trophies. Indeed he would finish second on 16 occasions between 1955 and 1960.

Dick Mayer 188

FULL NAME: Richard Mayer
BORN: Stamford, CT, August 29, 1924
MAJOR CHAMPIONSHIPS: US Open 1957

Dick Mayer's year of years was 1957, when he won the US Open after completely outplaying Cary Middlecoff (who was chasing back-to-back victories) in an 18-hole play-off at Inverness, OH, by the massive margin of seven strokes. Then he won the World Championship event, where the prize money was so huge that he was the leading money-winner for that season by a long way. Just to round off the campaign, he was unbeaten when he played in the Ryder Cup at Lindrick. Alas for Mayer, his luck for the year had clearly run out by then: he might have been undefeated, but that was more than could be said for America, who went down seven-and-a-half to four-and-a-half.

Bob Hamilton 187

FULL NAME: Robert Hamilton
BORN: Indiana, January 10, 1916
MAJOR CHAMPIONSHIPS: USPGA 1944

The criticism of matchplay golf and the early years of the USPGA Championship is that it was possible perhaps to fluke a victory: draw a couple of relative journeymen and progress, hoping the best players would all knock each other out. No one could accuse Bob Hamilton of being undeserving of his 1944 success in the event – he beat the two best American players of the day, Jug McSpaden and Byron Nelson, the latter in the final, with victory coming on the final hole. A personable man with a penchant for cigars almost as big as himself, Hamilton's best finish in a major apart from this was third in the 1946 Masters, five shots behind the champion, Herman Keiser.

Jerry Travers 186

FULL NAME: Jerome Travers
BORN: New York, May 19, 1887
MAJOR CHAMPIONSHIPS: US Open 1915

Jerry Travers may well have been the first player to appreciate the importance of putting. While most golfers in the early part of the century concentrated on the long game, he practised hard on minimizing his errors on the greens. It will come as no surprise to those of us following through generations later to learn that the strategy was a total success. Travers won four US Amateur titles and also won the US Open, by one stroke over Tom McNamara in 1915. And having been there and done that, Travers decided not to play in the event again, concentrating instead on his Wall Street career.

Rodger Davis 185

FULL NAME: Rodger Miles Davis
BORN: Sydney, Australia, May 18, 1951

Rodger Davis was always easily identified on the courses of Europe and Australia by his trademark plus-twos. His career brought him to public attention as well. He won more than 20 times in Australia and New Zealand, and notched up two very prestigious titles in Europe in the PGA Championship and the Volvo Masters. The big one, however – the Open – always got away. In 1979 at Lytham he held the lead with five to play but was overtaken by Severiano Ballesteros, and eventually finished fifth, five shots behind the Spaniard. Eight years later at Muirfield he tied for second place with Paul Azinger, one shot behind Nick Faldo.

David Frost 184

FULL NAME: David Laurence Frost

BORN: Cape Town, South Africa, September 11, 1959

David Frost certainly knows which titles to win. Three of his 18 victories have come in the Million Dollar Challenge in South Africa, helping to make him one of the richest players ever to play the game. In America he has 10 titles to his name, an impressive tally for a foreigner. Certainly the most spectacular of them was his win in the New Orleans Classic in 1990, when he holed a bunker shot on the last hole to beat – yes, you guessed it – Greg Norman by one stroke. He was a member of the International team in both the 1994 and 1996 Presidents Cup and played his part in South Africa's triumph in the 1997 Dunhill Cup at St Andrews. The only continent on which he has not won is Australia.

Orville Moody 183

FULL NAME: Orville Moody

BORN: Chickasha, OK, 1933

MAJOR CHAMPIONSHIPS: US Open 1969

Prior to the 1969 US Open at the Champions Club, Texas, Lee Trevino said to Orville Moody: "If I don't win this week, Sarge, I think you will." It was quite a testament of faith in his friend by Trevino, given that he had never won a tournament. What was even more bizarre was that he was proved right. Moody, the former career soldier, made up three strokes on the third-round leader, Jerry Barber. In the event Trevino would only have to wait two years to win the title himself; Moody, meanwhile, waited a lifetime for another win.

Claude Harmon 182

FULL NAME: Claude Harmon

BORN: Savannah, GA, July 14, 1916

MAJOR CHAMPIONSHIPS: Masters 1948

Claude Harmon was not a tournament professional, but he was so good as a player that no one could tell the difference. When he took on Ben Hogan at the latter's club at Seminole, he beat him as often as the other way round. While club pro at Winged Foot he shot 62. So when he walked the 1948 Masters by five shots over Cary Middlecoff (the biggest winning margin in the tournament to date), playing golf of which any touring pro would have been proud, no one was entirely surprised. Harmon remained true to his teaching code, passing on his secrets to his son Butch – former teacher of Ben Hogan, and the current coach of the phenomenon that is Tiger Woods.

Tony Manero 181

FULL NAME: Anthony Manero

BORN: April 4, 1905

MAJOR CHAMPIONSHIPS: US Open 1936

In winning the US Open at Baltusrol in 1936, Tony Manero set a new record 72-hole total of 282 that emphatically beat the old mark by no fewer than four strokes. At the time Manero was unknown, to the extent that people were congratulating Harry Cooper in the clubhouse on winning because no one could believe his score of 284 would be beaten. This, however, was a case of the tortoise beating the hare. Manero, who was notoriously slow, shot 67 in the final round to come in late in the day and beat the man known as "Lighthorse Harry" because of how fast he played.

Orville Moody – his only major came in the 1969 US Open

Johnny Goodman 180

FULL NAME: John Goodman
BORN: Omaha, 1909
MAJOR CHAMPIONSHIPS: 1. US Open 1933

Though it was not known at the time, Johnny Goodman's victory in the 1933 US Open could be said to have heralded the end of the golden age for amateurs. It followed Bobby Jones's four victories in the event but it would prove the last by any amateur in any major championship. Goodman, an orphan with nine brothers and sisters, did not let poverty prevent him from becoming an outstanding player. He was six clear after three rounds and when he started the last round 4,3,2 a rout seemed likely. But he lost concentration and needed 67 blows for the last 15 holes. Fortunately for him he still had one stroke to spare over Ralph Guldahl.

Calvin Peete 179

FULL NAME: Calvin Peete
BORN: Detroit, MI, July 18, 1943

Calvin Peete's story is an excellent example of how, for all its reputation as a bourgeois sport, great golfers come from all sorts of backgrounds. Peete had 18 brothers and sisters, and did not take up the game until he was 23. And what chance did he have with a left elbow broken in his youth that had not been set properly? Peete found a way; desire always does. For 10 years in a row he led the US Tour statistics for finding the middle of the fairway, and he won his share of titles and his share of money. Only shoulder and lower-back problems towards the end of the mid-1980s prevented him from winning still more, and he now plays with some success on the Senior Tour.

Alf Perry 178

FULL NAME: Alfred Perry
BORN: Leatherhead, England, October 8, 1904
MAJOR CHAMPIONSHIPS: Open 1935

Alf Perry was another example of how in golf the scorecard does not take into account how well or badly you swing a club. Perry was from the inelegant school and displeased the purists, but he won the Open at Muirfield in 1935 with a record-equalling score. All eyes were on the likes of Henry Cotton and Lawson Little, but Perry set up his victory with a fine first-round 69 and an even better third-round 67 – scores that justified his golfing philosophy to constantly attack the pin. Incidentally, this was the year another Perry, Fred, won the Wimbledon Lawn Tennis Championships. They were not related, more's the pity.

Arnaud Massy 177

FULL NAME: Arnaud Massy
BORN: La Boulie, France
MAJOR CHAMPIONSHIP: Open 1907

Only one Frenchman has ever won the Open Championship, and that was Arnaud Massy way back in 1907. Indeed it was not until Severiano Ballesteros won at Lytham in 1979 that there was another winner from continental Europe. Massy earned his £50 first prize by outplaying J.H. Taylor over the closing holes at Royal Liverpool to win by two strokes. Then he dashed back to his home in La Boulie to be with his wife, who had given birth to a daughter while he was winning the Open. Massy wanted to call her Hoylake. Fortunately, Madame Massy thought otherwise.

Jack White 176

FULL NAME: Jack White
MAJOR CHAMPIONSHIPS: Open 1904

Jack White won the Open at Sandwich in 1904 with a performance that set new standards. Mind you, he had to do so in order to break the stranglehold of the Great Triumvirate on the championship – all of whom were, predictably, bunched behind him, with J.H. Taylor and James Braid tied for runner-up and Harry Vardon coming in fifth. This was the Open where the 300 barrier was broken for the first time, and White did so by no fewer than four strokes. He, Braid and Taylor were also the first men to shoot a score in the 60s in any major, White's 69 proving particularly significant since it came in the last round.

Billy Burke 175

FULL NAME: William Burke
BORN: Greenwich, CT, December 14, 1902
MAJOR CHAMPIONSHIPS: US Open 1931

Billy Burke was involved in the US Open that looked like it would never end. After 72 holes he and George von Elm were tied and so played off over 36 holes the next day. That solved nothing; they were still tied. So they played another 36 the following day. Even then there was only one shot separating them, with Burke getting the verdict. It earned him a spot in that year's Ryder Cup at the Scioto Country Club, Colombus, OH, and he responded to representing his country by claiming two points out of two, including a notable singles victory over Archie Compston, by the resounding margin of seven and six, as the home side romped to victory.

Mark Brooks 174

FULL NAME: Mark David Brooks
BORN: Fort Worth, TX, March 25, 1961
MAJOR CHAMPIONSHIPS: USPGA 1996

Mark Brooks has earned over $5 million from tournament golf – and he's still counting. His great year came in 1996 when he won three tournaments, including the USPGA Championship where he birdied the 72nd hole to force a sudden-death play-off with Kenny Perry, and then birdied it again to win. It followed a top-five finish at the Open, and established him as yet another fine player from the Fort Worth, TX, area. Unlike some of his predecessors from that neck of the woods, however, Brooks has subsequently found it difficult to live up to that success.

Harold Hilton 173

FULL NAME: Harold Horsfall Hilton
BORN: West Kirby, England, January 12, 1869
MAJOR CHAMPIONSHIPS: Open 1892, 1897

It is close to sacrilege to have Harold Hilton languishing towards the foot of this list, however distinguished it may be. The fact is, however, that only deeds completed in this century are permitted, and that rules out both of Hilton's Open wins. It still leaves us, however, with four Amateur Championships and a rare British success in the US Amateur. That last triumph came in 1911, the year he took up the post of editor of *Golf Monthly*, the world's oldest monthly golf magazine. He is therefore a talented student of the game, both in playing and writing about it.

Frank Stranahan 172

FULL NAME: Frank Stranahan
BORN: Toledo, OH, August 5, 1922

Frank Stranahan's name crept back into the news in 1998, 45 years after one of his greatest achievements. It was Justin Rose's year at the Open, and today's scribes were eager to find the last time an amateur had seriously contended for the world's number-one golf prize. Stranahan finishing runner-up to Ben Hogan at Carnoustie was the answer. Indeed, Stranahan finished second in 1947 as well, and also won the Amateur on two occasions and reached the final once. Strangely, in his homeland he was less successful, being beaten in his only appearance in the final of the US Amateur, at the 39th hole.

Reg Whitcombe 171

FULL NAME: Reginald Whitcombe
BORN: Burnham, Somerset, April 10, 1898
MAJOR CHAMPIONSHIPS: Open 1938

Some judges have termed Reg the least gifted of the three Whitcombe brothers who all played Ryder Cup golf. Nevertheless, he immortalized the family name by winning the Open at Sandwich in 1938. After finishing runner-up to Henry Cotton the previous year, Whitcombe survived the gales that pounded the Kent coastline on the final day to shoot 75, 78 for a two-shot victory. Perhaps it was a day made for an uncomplicated man with an uncomplicated swing, and Whitcombe was certainly that. "*Golf's No Mystery*" was what he called his instruction book – and to him it was not.

Mark Brooks – one of a host of major winners to emerge from Fort Worth, Texas

Cyril Walker 170

FULL NAME: Cyril Walker

MAJOR CHAMPIONSHIPS: US Open 1924

There was nothing on Cyril Walker's CV before he emigrated to America to suggest that he could challenge the likes of Bobby Jones for a US Open. Yet Oakland Hills would prove a place where surprises happen, and the die was cast in 1924 when Walker took the title in eye-catching fashion. Perhaps he was helped by the strong winds on the first day, for he had learned the game on the Lancashire coastline. Going into the last round Walker was tied with Jones, and he kept his nerve commendably shooting a 75 over the final day for a three-stroke margin of victory.

Howard Clark 169

FULL NAME: Howard Keith Clark

BORN: Leeds, England, August 26, 1954

No less a luminary than Peter Alliss believes the big five of European golf in the 1980s – Lyle, Woosnam, Langer, Ballesteros and Faldo – should have been a big six. Certainly Howard Clark had the talent to join that famous quintet, but he was lacking in the temperament department, and when he followed in Faldo's footsteps and went to see the coach David Leadbetter, he fell apart altogether. The most significant of his 11 European victories came in the PGA Championship at Wentworth in 1984. A year later, while playing for England in the World Cup, he took first prize in the individual section. He also made six appearances in the Ryder Cup.

Jerry Barber 168

FULL NAME: Carl Jerome Barber

BORN: Woodson, IL, April 25, 1916

MAJOR CHAMPIONSHIPS: USPGA 1961

Jerry Barber had a reputation as an unrivalled short-game artist, forged partly on his remarkable success in the 1961 USPGA Championship. It seemed for all the world to be Don January's title to win, but Barber finished birdie-par-birdie, sinking respective putts of 25, 40 and 52ft to force a play-off the following day. He won that by a stroke following a 67. Barber, who played left-handed for two years while growing up, passed on his putting knowledge to all who wanted it in his retirement. Among his customers was Tom Watson, who for a while became unquestionably the best putter in the world.

Dave Marr 167

FULL NAME: David Marr

BORN: Houston, TX, December 23, 1933

MAJOR CHAMPIONSHIPS: USPGA 1965

Dave Marr made the successful transition from player to commentator, indeed he was one of the few in the latter field who have proved a hit on both sides of the Atlantic. Tragically, he lost his life to cancer in 1998. Marr's most memorable moment on the course came in 1965 when he won the USPGA Championship, despite the close attentions of Billy Casper and Jack Nicklaus. In the end, a last-round 71 was good enough to do the trick at Laurel Valley, PA, by two strokes. In 1981 he had the honour of being captain of the best American team ever to play in the Ryder Cup.

David Marr – highly successful as both player and commentator

Gay Brewer 166

FULL NAME: Gay Robert Brewer

BORN: Middletown, OH, March 19, 1932

MAJOR CHAMPIONSHIPS: Masters 1967

Easily the biggest thrill in Gay Brewer's career came when he won the 1967 Masters. Just a year earlier he had been involved in a three-way play-off for the green jacket with Jack Nicklaus and Tommy Jacobs, but he was never a factor, scoring a 78 that left him well behind the other pair. What a difference a year makes. This time Brewer fought tooth and nail with Bobby Nichols over the closing holes before coming out on top by a single stroke, courtesy of a marvellous last-round 67. Brewer won 11 US Tour titles in total, and was a member of the USA Ryder Cup team in both 1967 and 1971.

Jim Turnesa 165

FULL NAME: James Turnesa

BORN: December 12, 1913

MAJOR CHAMPIONSHIPS: USPGA 1952

You could say the Turnesa family was born to play golf. There were seven brothers in all and six of them became professionals. The seventh, meanwhile, won the US Amateur twice, the Amateur once, and was a Walker Cup captain. Jim Turnesa was the most successful, and won the USPGA Championship in 1952. It was a classic duel against Chick Harbert, one in which Turnesa was never ahead until the decisive 36th hole. His one Ryder Cup appearance was a crucial one, in 1953: when Peter Alliss stumbled on the 18th at Wentworth, Turnesa was waiting to claim the point to take the trophy back home.

Arthur Havers 164

FULL NAME: Arthur Havers

BORN: June 10, 1898

MAJOR CHAMPIONSHIPS: Open 1923

Arthur Havers first entered the Open at Prestwick at the age of 16, and managed to qualify for the strokeplay stage. That was in 1914. His big year came after the war at nearby Troon, when he was chased all the way for the Open by Walter Hagen. The American needed a birdie three at the 72nd hole to tie with Havers, which seemed unlikely when he bunkered his approach. The resultant sand shot, however, looked as if it might go in at one point before stopping inches short of the hole. Another Havers highlight came during one trip to America when he beat Bobby Jones over 36 holes and Gene Sarazen over four rounds.

Chandler Harper 163

FULL NAME: Chandler Harper

BORN: March 10, 1935

MAJOR CHAMPIONSHIPS: USPGA 1950

The USPGA's widely held reputation as the fourth of the four majors is based on the fact that the overwhelming majority of golfers who win just one grand-slam event usually win that one. Here's another who enjoyed his glory day in the event, the big year being 1950 when he defeated Henry Williams in the final at Scioto Country Club, OH, four and three. The big wins had come in the earlier rounds: Harper saw off Lloyd Mangrum and Jimmy Demaret in the quarter- and semi-finals, respectively. Harper, who won eight US Tour events in all, rarely practised; indeed he ran his own finance business during his time away from the game.

Lionel Hebert 162

FULL NAME: Lionel Hebert

BORN: New Orleans, LA

MAJOR CHAMPIONSHIPS: USPGA 1957

To say 1957 was something of a bitter-sweet year for this Louisiana native is an understatement. First he won the USPGA Championship in its last year as a matchplay contest, defeating Dow Finsterwald in the final by a margin of three and one. Then he took part in his only Ryder Cup and lost his only match, which just happened to be the crucial one that allowed Great Britain and Ireland to record their first victory since 1933. Three years after his win Hebert's brother Jay also collected the USPGA when it was staged at the Firestone Country Club, Akron, OH. They remain the only brothers to complete this particular double.

Johnny Revolta 161

FULL NAME: John Revolta

BORN: Wisconsin, April 5, 1911

MAJOR CHAMPIONSHIPS: USPGA 1935

With a name like his, Johnny Revolta should surely have been a top-line movie star of the 1930s alongside Humphrey Bogart rather than a top-line golfer. Just to complete the image, he was described by journalists of the time as having the face of a movie gangster "with a jaw like the prow of a battleship". He could play. Walter Hagen considered him one of the finest of short iron players, and got first-hand evidence for the verdict when Revolta defeated both him and Tommy Armour on his way to winning the 1935 USPGA Championship. He won 18 US Tour titles in all.

Alex Smith 160

FULL NAME: Alex Smith
MAJOR CHAMPIONSHIPS: US Open 1906, 1910

Alex Smith was one of four brothers from Carnoustie who made their way to America in the early years of the century to help with the development of the game on the other side of the Atlantic. He won the US Open on two occasions; in the first in 1906 brother Willie finished in the runner's-up spot, while George Smith finished tied for 18th. Four years later it was almost a family affair once more when Alex Smith was joined by Macdonald Smith and Johnny McDermott in a three-way play-off. Smith shot a 71 and won from McDermott by four shots, with Macdonald, who had only just emigrated, a further two strokes adrift.

Harry Cooper 159

FULL NAME: Harold Cooper
BORN: Leatherhead, England, August 4, 1904

Harry Cooper is one of those players whom history has decided is one of the contenders to wear the dreaded "Best golfer never to win a major" mantle. Naturally, he came close. In the 1936 Masters he finished one shot behind Horton Smith after leading going into the final round; in the US Open the same year he broke the tournament record score, but found that Tony Manero had shaved two more strokes off it. The 1927 US Open was even more disappointing. Cooper three-putted the final green while Tommy Armour holed a good one to force a play-off which he won by three shots.

Miller Barber 158

FULL NAME: Miller Westford Barber Jnr
BORN: Shreveport, LA, March 31, 1931

Miller Barber was known as "X" because of his dark glasses and his dislike of publicity. As far as major championship victories are concerned he can remain in obscurity. His golf, however, was deserving of wider recognition. In 1969 he registered top-ten finishes in each of the grand-slam events, and had excellent opportunities to win both the Masters and the US Open, where he led the field after three rounds only to collapse to a 78 on the final day. In all he had 11 victories with the pick of them, perhaps, the 1973 World Open which, at the time, carried a record first prize of $100,000. He was also a member of the USA Ryder Cup teams in both 1969 and 1971. Going into the 1999 season, he had made 491 starts in the Senior Tour – more than any other player, and has won the US Senior Open on three occasions.

Bob Rosberg 157

FULL NAME: Robert Reginald Rosburg
BORN: San Francisco, CA, October 21, 1926
MAJOR CHAMPIONSHIPS: USPGA 1959

Bob Rosburg played on the US Tour for almost 20 years and won seven titles, including the USPGA in 1959. It was the year in which he proved the old adage that a man who can putt is a match for anyone. After finishing runner-up in the US Open at Winged Foot to another great putter, Billy Casper, Rosburg collected his sole major at Minneapolis by virtue of a storming finish. Trailing Jerry Barber by nine at the halfway stage and six shots going into the final round, he putted his rivals into place money with a 66 to win by one shot.

Mark James 156

FULL NAME: Mark Hugh James
BORN: Manchester, England, October 28, 1953

From leading mutineer to captain of the ship is quite a transformation, but one that Mark James made in the Ryder Cup. In 1979 he was almost sent home in disgrace; in 1999 he selects the pairings for the Europeans. It is a deserved honour, too, for not only has he matured as a person, but he has left his imprint as a player who never gives less than his best on the course. It has earned him a wonderful living, a few important titles – most notably the Irish and English Opens on two occasions each, the British Masters and the B&H Invitational – and the complete respect of his peers.

Wayne Grady 155

FULL NAME: Wayne Desmond Grady
BORN: Brisbane, Australia, July 26, 1957
MAJOR CHAMPIONSHIPS: USPGA 1990

One near miss and one glorious victory in major championships constitute the pinnacles in the career of this popular Australian. The former came in the 1989 Open at Troon, when he took part in the first four-hole play-off in Championship history. He was quickly left behind by Greg Norman and the eventual winner Mark Calcavecchia, for this was a play-off where the two pars that Grady opened up with were not good enough. A year later he enjoyed sweet redemption at the USPGA at Shoal Creek, beating Fred Couples by three shots and becoming just the third Australian to lift that title.

In recent times his most successful moment came when Peter Thomson appointed him as Captain's Assistant for the victorious International team in the 1998 Presidents Cup.

Wayne Grady – the 1990 USPGA champion

Charles Coody 154

FULL NAME: Charles Coody
BORN: Stamford, TX, July 13, 1937
MAJOR CHAMPIONSHIPS: Masters 1971

Charles Coody was a consistent money earner rather than a prolific winner, collecting just three tournament victories during a long career on the US Tour. One of them was a major, however, the 1971 Masters, where for four days at least he proved that he could not only live with the best but he could occasionally beat them, too. His rivals that year were none other than Jack Nicklaus and Johnny Miller, and Coody additionally had to ward off the haunting memory of a late collapse in the same tournament two years earlier. He held firm on this occasion, birdieing two of the last four holes to win by two.

Thomas Aaron 153

FULL NAME: Thomas Aaron
BORN: Gainesville, GA, February 22, 1937
MAJOR CHAMPIONSHIPS: Masters 1973

With a name like that, he will for ever be first in any alphabetical list of the top players; his record was good enough also to do pretty well in a compilation of this kind, too. Aaron made headlines in two very different ways at the Masters. In 1968 he marked down a four instead of a three for Roberto De Vicenzo at the 17th, a shot that cost the Argentinian a play-off for the title because he failed to spot the error before signing his card. Five years later Aaron shot a final-round 68 to win the title for himself by one stroke.

Joseph Carr 152

FULL NAME: Joseph B. Carr
BORN: Dublin, Ireland, February 18, 1922

Certainly the finest Irish amateur of all time and one of the top five from the British Isles, Joe Carr was also one of the few to do well in the US Amateur, reaching the semi-final in 1961. The Dubliner won the Amateur Championship on three occasions, and played in every Walker Cup team from 1947 until 1965. As for the titles he won in Ireland, it would need practically a book of this size to list them all: the pick of them was the Irish Amateur on six occasions and the Irish Open Amateur four times.

Jock Hutchinson 151

FULL NAME: Jock Hutchinson
BORN: St Andrews, Scotland, 1884
MAJOR CHAMPIONSHIPS: Open 1921; USPGA 1920

Jock Hutchinson was one of the many Scottish professionals who emigrated to America at the start of the century and found fame and fortune. He started to make his mark with good finishes in the US Open from 1910 onwards, and reached the final of the 1916 USPGA, only to lose out to Jim Barnes. His first major success came in the same event in 1920 when he defeated Douglas Edgar in the final by one hole. A year later he completed a glorious homecoming, claiming the Open Championship at St Andrews after a fine last round of 70 forced a 36-hole play-off which he went on to win by a massive nine strokes from the amateur Roger Wethered.

Bobby Nichols 150

FULL NAME: Robert Herman Nichols
BORN: Louisville, KY, April 14, 1936
MAJOR CHAMPIONSHIPS: USPGA 1964

Bobby Nichols had two golden years. In 1962 he won two tournaments, finished third behind Jack Nicklaus and Arnold Palmer in the US Open, and sixth in the USPGA. In 1964 he again showed he kept the right company when once more he, Palmer and Nicklaus occupied the top three positions in a major. This time, and certainly something to tell the grandchildren about, Nichols's name was at the top of the USPGA leaderboard.

And all in the Golden Bear's lair, to boot – Columbus Country Club, Columbus, OH. What a fairytale for Nichols, who had been paralysed for 13 days and kept in hospital for three months as a youngster following a car accident.

Steve Jones 149

FULL NAME: Steven Glen Jones
BORN: Artesia, NM, December 27, 1958
MAJOR CHAMPIONSHIPS: US Open 1996

Losing three years of his career made Steve Jone's 1996 US Open victory all the sweeter – a qualifier who came good to win the title by one shot over Tom Lehman and Davis Love.

To be fair, Jones was no ordinary journeyman pro. He was having to qualify because of the time he lost owing to ligament and joint damage to his left ring finger after a dirt-bike accident. But that merely added to the melodrama.

Before his accident, Jones was a contender. He had a top-10 finish in the 1988 USPGA Championship, and then won three tournaments the following season. Then, in 1991, cruel fate struck.

If his US Open victory was the highlight since his return, then it is far from the only one. In 1997, for example, he won the Phoenix Open by no fewer than 11 strokes.

Scott Simpson – not the most popular US Open winner

Scott Simpson 148

FULL NAME: Scott William Simpson
BORN: San Diego, CA, September 17, 1955
MAJOR CHAMPIONSHIPS: US Open 1987

It is difficult to imagine a more unpopular US Open win than that managed by Scott Simpson to deny Tom Watson at the Olympic Club in 1987. What is beyond dispute is that Simpson merited his victory. He birdied three holes in a row from the 14th, but the shot that won him the championship was from a bunker to save par at the 17th – undoubtedly one of the great ones.

The US Open was always going to be Simpson's event, with its emphasis on keeping the ball in play, and that victory was followed by a four-year sequence in which he finished sixth on two occasions,and, in 1992, where he lost out to Payne Stewart in a play-off.

Simpson has seven tour victories to his name, the most recent being an emotional triumph in 1998 at the Buick Invitational, which is held in his home town of San Diego.

Chi Chi Rodriguez 147

FULL NAME: Juan Rodriguez
BORN: Rio Piedras, PR, October 23, 1935

Perhaps Chat Chat would have been a more appropriate nickname, for this exuberant Puerto Rican certainly knew how to talk. For many years he was known as the clown prince on the US Tour, but not everyone was enamoured of some of his antics. Among this group he was known as "the four-shot penalty", because that was how many shots they felt he cost them during a round.

Given his entertaining style, it was hardly surprising that Rodriguez proved a particularly big hit upon turning 50. In seven glorious years in senior golf he won 22 titles and his reward came in tournament winnings that have now passed more than $7 million.

On the regular US Tour, though one of the great crowd attractions, he was not a prolific victor, managing only eight triumphs between 1963 and 1979.

Lew Worsham 146

FULL NAME: Lew Worsham
BORN: Alta Vista, VA, October 5, 1917
MAJOR CHAMPIONSHIPS: US Open 1947

It is Lew Worsham's considerable misfortune, as far as his place in history is concerned, that his greatest hour coincided with Sam

Snead's worst nightmare. These were the circumstances: Snead was trying to win the one major title that would always elude him, and when he holed a long putt on the 72nd hole to force a play-off, it seemed that good fortune was smiling on him.

Yet as the pair approached the 18th green of the play-off, they could still not be separated. Snead missed a 30-inch putt and Worsham duly tapped in to claim his only major title.

Outside that victory Worsham's biggest win was in the 1953 World Championship, where he holed from 100 yards on the 18th to win by one. The victory was worth a fortune both in prize money and exhibition fees.

Bob Tway 145

FULL NAME: Robert Raymond Tway

BORN: Oklahoma City, OK, May 4, 1959

MAJOR CHAMPIONSHIPS: USPGA 1986

In 1986 Bob Tway did something that no golfer had ever managed to do in a major championship for 29 years, and that is claim the trophy by holing a bunker shot. He was up against the hapless Greg Norman, who had led that year's USPGA by three with six holes to play, but now the pair were level coming to the final hole. After their approach shots it was advantage Norman: Tway had come up short into the bunker, while Norman was in the semi-rough around the green. When the ball disappeared below ground Tway trampled the sand beneath his feet in joy. It was his fourth victory of the season and a glittering future appeared assured. But despite plenty of money in the intervening years – in 1998 alone he won more than seven figures for the first time in his career – there has been nothing to touch that amazing afternoon when fate kissed him firmly on the lips and left Greg Norman to rue yet another lost opportunity.

Walter Burkemo 144

FULL NAME: Walter Burkemo

BORN: Birmingham, MI, October 9, 1918

MAJOR CHAMPIONSHIPS: USPGA 1953

Here is a terrific quiz question: name two golfers who won major championships in 1953? Ben Hogan, who won three majors that year. But who won the USPGA, the one that Hogan did not enter, because it finished the day before the Open started? The answer is Walter Burkemo, who over several years established a reputation for himself as an accomplished matchplay golfer. In addition to winning the USPGA, he was a beaten finalist on two occasions and a semi-finalist once.

His victory was a popular one, for the event was played in his home town of Birmingham, MI.

Burkemo's other final appearance came as part of a wonderfully spirited defence of his title in 1954, when, after defeating Harmon, Revolta, de Vicenzo and Middlecoff in succession the final against Chick Harbert proved a round too far.

Lou Graham 143

FULL NAME: Louis Krebs Graham

BORN: Nashville, TN, January 7, 1938

MAJOR CHAMPIONSHIPS: US Open 1975

Lou Graham's time came in the mid-1970s, and particularly 1975 when he won the US Open at Medinah. Dropping a shot at the last to fall into a play-off is not usually the portent for glory the next day, but Graham managed it with a level-par round of 71 to beat John Mahaffey by two strokes. Later that year he teamed up with Johnny Miller to win the World Cup for America in Bangkok.

Two years later Graham mounted a wonderful weekend charge to almost secure a second US Open title. Playing the last 36 holes at Southern Hills in 136 shots, equalling the record for the event, he placed tremendous pressure on Hubert Green, who just managed to stave off the onslaught to claim the title by one shot. Three more titles in the space of just eight weeks came two years later. He eventually joined the senior tour, where he enjoyed three productive years, including six top-five finishes in 1989 earning him more than $240,000, before a wrist injury curtailed his play.

Jim Ferrier 142

FULL NAME: James Ferrier

BORN: Sydney, Australia, February 24, 1915

MAJOR CHAMPIONSHIPS: USPGA 1947

Jim Ferrier was one of the most successful players ever to leave the shores of Australia. Turning professional in 1940, he immediately looked east to America. It was the mid-1940s before he became fully attuned to the different demands of American golf, but he compiled an excellent record thereafter, winning 21 tournaments in all, right up to 1961.

His only major championship success came in the 1947 USPGA, when he defeated Chick Harbert in the final by a margin of five and four.

He had a golden opportunity to win a second major in 1950 when he took a five-stroke lead over Jimmy Demaret into the final six holes of the Masters. There then followed one of the most dramatic collapses of all time as he played the stretch in five over par. Demaret, meanwhile, played them in two under par to secure the unlikeliest of two-stroke victories.

Dick Burton 141

FULL NAME: Richard Burton

BORN: Darwen, England, October 11, 1907

MAJOR CHAMPIONSHIPS: Open 1939

It has the feel of a trick sports riddle. Question: which golfer has had the longest reign as Open Champion, and for how long? Answer: Dick Burton, who won the last Open to be played before the Second World War in 1939, and so kept hold of the trophy for seven years until the Championship resumed after hostilities.

Without the war, Burton may well have won the Open again, because when he harnessed his considerable length he was a formidable player. He was also just 31 when first crowned champion, and so had most of his best years in front of him.

Burton won the Open with a touch of style. He needed a par four down the last to clinch the title, which is hardly the most onerous task at St Andrews, but not for Burton the safety-first drive in the direction of the first tee. He took on the bold line down the railings that separate the fairway from the road and offers the easiest route to the pin. A pitch to holeable distance was followed by a perfect putt: Burton was so convinced it was going in that he had tossed his putter to his caddie in jubilation before the ball met the back of the hole.

Burton came close in two other Opens. The previous year he had been one stroke off the lead going into the final round but could not cope with the Sandwich gales, which saw the exhibition tent ripped from its moorings.

Ten years later at Hoylake, Burton finished with a 71 and a tie for fifth place, three strokes adrift of the Irishman Fred Daly.

John Ball 140

FULL NAME: John Ball Jnr

BORN: Hoylake, Cheshire, December 24, 1862

MAJOR CHAMPIONSHIPS: Open 1890

It was unfortunate for John Ball that for the purposes of this book his finest years came in the 1890s, when he won five of his eight Amateur Championships, a record that will never be beaten, and his only Open success. But he was still a force in the first decade of the twentieth century, and in his prime well capable of tackling any professional. Even aged 58, when he entered the Amateur for the final time in 1921, he still reached the fifth round.

The discrepancy between Ball's success in the Open and the Amateur is probably accounted for by his preference for the format and camaraderie of matchplay. Ball was not renowned as a great putter, but he made up for it with a wonderful accuracy with his long shots to the flag. In this respect he was a pioneer, because before he came along players were content to aim for the green.

Given his approach it was hardly surprising that Ball drew an enormous following, and particularly in his home area of Hoylake, where he was considered unbeatable. Ball's father was also a first-class player who owned the Royal Hotel, situated next to the land that was soon to become the links of the Royal Liverpool Golf Club. It was the finest of training grounds for a young player, and Ball made the most of it. From an early age he made his mark, playing in the Open Championship in 1878 at the age of 15, and finishing fourth. Ball had begun a dalliance at the highest level that would last over 30 years.

Peter Alliss – for many he has become the voice of golf

Peter Alliss 139

FULL NAME: Peter Alliss

BORN: Berlin, Germany, February 28, 1931

The doleful sense of humour Peter Alliss exhibited when he bought the registration mark "PUT 3" for his Rolls-Royce will be familiar to anyone who has ever tuned into his golf commentaries in Britain and America. In that sphere at least he is the number one, and has been since Henry Longhurst sadly passed away.

As for his golf, Alliss had everything it took to make as big a mark as he went on to do in television, but for that weakness so blatantly hinted at on his car registration plate.

It did not prevent him from winning some 20 important events in Europe during the 1950s and 1960s, including three in a row in 1958. He was selected for every Ryder Cup team bar one between 1953 and 1969, and also played ten times for England in the World Cup.

He was 22 when he made his Ryder Cup debut, and perhaps he never quite fully recovered from what proved a traumatic experience. He and another debutant, Bernard Hunt, were the last players on the course, and par-fives from both on the final hole at Wentworth would have given Great Britain and Ireland victory. Alas, neither player managed it, Alliss taking four from just 40 yards short of the hole. Great Britain and Ireland lost by a point.

Alliss remains convinced to this day that he was passed over for the 1955 match because of what happened, a shabby to-do if true. For questions have to be asked as well of the 1953 captain Henry Cotton: who else would have placed someone as young as Alliss, who had still to win so much as a tournament, in a position where the fate of the Ryder Cup rested on his shoulders?

Jeff Sluman 138

FULL NAME: Jeffrey George Sluman

BORN: Rochester, NY, September 11, 1957

MAJOR CHAMPIONSHIPS: USPGA 1988

Jeff Sluman has earned more than $6.5 million during the course of his 15-year professional career, which is a tribute to his tenacity and determination. Somewhat surprisingly, he has just three US Tour victories to his name, with the pick being the 1988 USPGA at Oak Tree.

Sluman trailed Paul Azinger by three shots going into the final round but reversed that with a wonderful closing 65. His doggedness has served him particularly well in the major championship arena, and he can count himself slightly unfortunate not to win the 1992 US Open at Pebble Beach.

This was the Open where the wind rose in intensity throughout the final day and Colin Montgomerie, who finished two hours before the leaders went off, was congratulated by Jack Nicklaus when he came off the course because he thought the Scot's level-par total would be good enough.

But Sluman beat it, with a last-round 71. Unfortunately for him, so did Tom Kite, finally flying high in a major. And so it added up to yet another second-place finish for Sluman, who has it down to a fine art. Another notable runner's-up spot was in the 1988 Players' Championship at Sawgrass, where he lost a play-off to Sandy Lyle.

The other time he looked destined for major championship glory was at Augusta in 1992, where he led after an opening round of 65. But he could not manage any more rounds in the 60s, and eventually had to settle for fourth.

At 5ft 7in. and 140lb, Sluman was never going to be a golfing heavyweight, but he has made a name for himself by always being there and thereabouts; on eight occasions he has finished among the leading 30 money winners.

John Mahaffey 137

FULL NAME: John Drayton Mahaffey

BORN: Kerrville, TX, May 9, 1948

MAJOR CHAMPIONSHIPS: USPGA 1978

The classic progression to winning a major championship is to be in contention first before going on to victory, and John Mahaffey followed this trail without any diversions. His first near-miss came in 1975, when he lost a play-off to Lou Graham for the US Open at Medinah; a year later he was again in contention in the same event, but this time he could only stand and admire as Jerry Pate conjured up his miracle birdie at Atlanta to win.

When Mahaffey's moment did arrive, however, Pate was among those who had a front-row seat. The occasion was the 1978 USPGA at Oakmont, a fearsome course well set up for Mahaffey's straight hitting and solid putting.

When the final round began, though, it was Tom Watson who was well in control, indeed he was fully seven shots ahead of Mahaffey. A 66 from the challenger completely changed matters and Watson's 73 meant a sudden-death play-off, with Pate also involved after a last-round 68.

Watson had led from the opening day, but it was Mahaffey who birdied the second extra hole to claim the title. And there might have been more majors but for a battle with a series of injuries, and an even more difficult battle at the start of the 1980s with the booze. At least Mahaffey won the latter contest, to the extent that he returned to win a number of prestigious tournaments, including the 1986 Players' Championship.

A fine striker of the ball, Mahaffey also won the World Cup for America on two occasions, in 1978 in partnership with Andy North, and a year later with Hale Irwin.

Bruce Lietzke 136

FULL NAME: Bruce Alan Lietzke

BORN: Kansas City, MO, July 18, 1951

The package of things that go together to make a superstar may vary in composition – for example, a player to some extent can put in through hard work what nature left out in terms of natural talent – but one thing that is always present is desire. No player can reach the top without it, and Bruce Lietzke is living proof.

For if Lietzke had been consumed by desire he would surely have become one of the very best players to grace the game. As it was he was still able to win 13 times on the US Tour, still able to make the 1981 US Ryder Cup team, by common consent the greatest side that has ever been assembled in the history of that fabled event.

But what would that career sheet have been like if Lietzke had liked fishing a little less and golf a little more? What if the Open had not coincided with his summer hiatus, when he spent quality time with his family and coached children's football teams?

The one thing that playing little each year did give Lietzke was a longer career at the top than might otherwise have happened; given his temperament and an apparent lack of deep affection for the game, he would surely have packed it in at the first sign of a deep slump.

Lietzke will at least return a little to the public eye in 1999 when he will be the assistant to the US Ryder Cup captain, Ben Crenshaw, for the match at Brookline in September. Presumably he will rouse himself sufficiently to hang around for the whole week.

Art Wall 135

FULL NAME: Arthur Jonathan Wall

BORN: Honesdale, PA, November 25, 1923

MAJOR CHAMPIONSHIPS: Masters 1959

Art Wall may not be considered among the very elite of his profession but he has, by most considerations, enjoyed a remarkable life. He won the Masters with one of the great finishes even that tournament has seen and then, over the course of a long career, was still winning events on the regular tour at the age of 51. Oh, and he has also had a few holes-in-one – 45 at the last count. Given that Harry Vardon only ever managed one, it will not come as any surprise to learn that that amazing total is believed to be a world record.

Wall's big year was undoubtedly 1959, when he won four times on the US Tour, including an unforgettable Masters triumph. There appeared little hope for him as he came to the 13th hole on the final day, the last leg of Amen Corner. All his prayers were answered from there on in, however, as he played the sequence in no less than five under par to win by a stroke from Cary Middlecoff, with Arnold Palmer a further shot behind.

Wall turned professional in 1949, and once he had notched his first victory in 1953 he managed a regular stream of victories thereafter until 1966. Given that he was 42 years old at that point, it seemed that time had caught up with him, but there was still to be one more victory no fewer than nine years later in the Greater Milwaukee Open.

Wall played in three Ryder Cup matches, the pick of them coming in 1961 at Royal Lytham, when he claimed three points out of three, including a singles victory by one hole over Henry Weetman.

Gil Morgan 134

FULL NAME: Gilmer Bryan Morgan II

BORN: Wewoka, OK, September 25, 1946

Gil Morgan did not turn professional until completing his degree in optometry, and he still holds a licence to practise. But in a similar tale to Cary Middlecoff's a generation before – his degree was in dentistry – Morgan realized that life in a darkened room examining people's eyes did not remotely compare with life in the open, with all eyes trained on you.

It has been an exceptionally long career in the spotlight. He has been a professional for over 25 years now, and has made the sort of money that even the most successful optometrists could only dream about.

Morgan has enjoyed some of his most lucrative years in recent times, for since joining the US Senior Tour in 1996 he has, quite simply, cleaned up. He won his first title within 11 days of turning 50 at the 1996 Ralphs Senior Classic to become the youngest-ever winner on the Seniors Tour and, together with Hale Irwin, has set new prize records every year since, to the extent that in three seasons he has racked up nearly $5 million in prize money – including prize money of $2 million for two years in succession in 1997 and 1998, notching up 12 victories in the process, one of which was the 1998 Ford Senior Players Championship.

Morgan first came to prominence in 1977 when he won the BC Open, and continued the good work the following year with a significant victory in the World Series, beating Hubert Green in a play-off.

Perhaps his best chance of victory in a major championship came in the 1992 US Open at Pebble Beach, when he became the first player ever to reach 10 under par in that event. Indeed Morgan was 12 under at one point and well clear. Then he woke up, collapsing dramatically to 13th place. It must have been one of the few times when he had wished he had opted for that darkened room.

Jack Fleck 133

FULL NAME: Jack Fleck
BORN: Bettendorf, IA, November 8, 1921
MAJOR CHAMPIONSHIPS: US Open 1955

Everyone shall be famous for 15 minutes, Andy Warhol once famously pronounced, and we don't have to look hard to discover Jack Fleck's quarter-of-an-hour flirtation with the high life.

It came in the 1955 US Open at Olympic, San Francisco. Picture the scene: Hogan is in the locker room accepting the congratulations of anyone who can get near him; he has won a record-breaking fifth Open title. Or so everyone thinks. They are going by a scoreboard that shows no one else who has finished has got within five shots of him. While out on the course only someone called Fleck has a chance; someone who has never won an event, someone who shot 87 in a practice round. In other words, someone with no chance.

But as he came to the last hole Fleck did have a chance, albeit a slim one, since he had to birdie the hole to force a play-off. After the perfect drive Fleck hit a fine pitch to eight foot and calmly holed.

It was a shock, but if truth be told, not a massive one. Surely it only delayed Hogan's fifth amendment by a day, for how was Fleck going to beat him in a play-off over 18 holes? But beat him he did, and with some style, too, keeping his nerve down the final hole as Hogan's failed.

And as he received the trophy, Fleck's 15 minutes all but ended. True he did win a couple more titles, but nothing to remotely compare with that moment in the sun.

Michael Bonallack 132

FULL NAME: Michael Bonallack
BORN: Chigwell, England, December 31, 1934

The top British amateur golfer of the century? There are only three legitimate contenders, and given that many of the finest achievements of Harold Hilton and John Ball came in the previous century, our vote goes to Michael Bonallack, the soon-to-be-retiring secretary of the Royal and Ancient Golf Club of St Andrews.

His contribution to golf has been absolutely immense both in that role and in the example he set as a player, and this was rightly recognized in 1998 when he received a knighthood. His particular forte was matchplay, for which he was ideally suited, since he had the two most precious qualities any player can have for that form of the game: an equable temperament and an imperious short game. This was most obvious during one of his five wins in the English Amateur Championship, a final in 1963 against Alan Thirwell that saw him get down in two from off the green on no fewer than 22 occasions to leave his hapless opponent wondering what on earth he had to do to win.

Bonallack also won the Amateur on three consecutive occasions from 1968 to 1970, a unique achievement beyond even that of Hilton or Ball in the less competitive age in which they compiled their records. He also won it twice more, in 1961 and 1965.

Bonallack became secretary of the R&A in 1983 and has carried out the role with consummate skill. During his time the Open has gone from strength to strength, and he retires with its position as the number-one event in golf not seriously disputed.

Michael Bonallack – the finest British amateur golfer of the century?

Hal Sutton 131

FULL NAME: Hal Evan Sutton
BORN: Shreveport, LA, April 28, 1959
MAJOR CHAMPIONSHIPS: USPGA 1983

Yet another player apparently struck by the curse of being called "the next Jack Nicklaus". That was in 1983 when the glittering promise that Hal Sutton had shown during his amateur days had been realized with a USPGA Championship victory at, of all places, Hollywood Country Club, better known as Riviera.

To be fair, all the hype was understandable. There were not only his amateur days, when Sutton had played in the Walker Cup and been the leading amateur in the Open Championship. There was his first season as a pro in 1982, when he finished rookie of the year.

The following season he won the Players' Championship in Florida and then rounded off a memorable campaign in an epic USPGA, which saw Nicklaus himself emerge from the pack with a wonderful last round of 66. Sutton withstood it all, however, defeating the golden bear by one. At 25 he had his first major, and was seemingly set to become one of the elite.

Quite why it has not happened is something of a mystery. Perhaps marital upheaval has had something to do with it. Equally, perhaps it is not a coincidence that glimpses of his finest form were seen in 1998, now that he has found domestic happiness.

Sutton completed the year with a wonderful win in the Tour Championship, beating Vijay Singh with a birdie at the first extra hole of a sudden-death play-off. It gave him fifth spot in the season-ending order of merit – his best placing since that golden summer of 1983, when he was number one in every sense. It was also the first time that he had won twice in a season since 1986.

Don January 130

FULL NAME: Donald Ray January
BORN: Plainview, TX, November 20, 1929
Major Championships: USPGA 1967

Don January was a successful figure in American golf for over 40 years. He had his first victory in 1956, while in 1996 he matched his age for the first time while playing in a US Senior Tour event. In between he won 10 times on the regular tour, 22 times in the senior arena (leaving him tied in fourth place on the all-time money list with Chi Chi Rodriguez), top of the Senior Tour money list in both 1983 and 1984, with the pick of his career being his victory in the 1967 USPGA Championship in Colorado.

January had lost this title six years earlier in traumatic circumstances. With only three holes to play, he had led Jerry Barber by no fewer than four strokes. But in golf what looks an impregnable lead can turn in the blink of an eye, and two long putts from Barber, added to two dropped shots from January, equalled an 18-hole play-off. January did awfully well to recover sufficiently from his ordeal to shoot 68; the trouble was, Barber shot 67...

He might have been forgiven feelings of deja vu in 1967 when he shot 68 in the final round of the USPGA and still did not win, because Don Massingale had gone round in 66 to force a play-off. This time, however, a three-under-par 69 was good enough for a two-stroke victory.

January was always one of the most consistent players. On 20 occasions he finished among the leading 60 money-winners, despite giving many tournaments a miss. Not for January the long haul from the start of the season to the finish; when he thought he had earned enough to last him the rest of the year, he put the golf clubs away until the start of the next campaign.

Chick Harbert 129

FULL NAME: Melvin Harbert
BORN: Dayton, OH, February 20, 1915
MAJOR CHAMPIONSHIPS: USPGA 1954

With his ability to hit the ball vast distances, and a sure touch on the greens, it was not surprising that Chick Harbert proved particularly adept at matchplay. Accordingly, his finest performances in the majors were reserved for the USPGA Championship, in which he was runner-up once and the victor in 1954 at Keller Country Club in St Paul, MN.

Two years earlier Harbert had lost in the final to Jim Turnesa, a hard defeat to bear since the match went all the way to the home green. Now he enjoyed his moment in the sun, beating Walter Burkemo in the final, having seen off Tommy Bolt a round earlier.

Harbert had shown early promise when he won the Michigan Open in 1937 while still an amateur. He would win it on two more occasions when he joined the professional ranks, together with five other titles. In tandem with Ed Furgol, he also helped America lift the 1955 World Cup.

A belief has grown that the Ryder Cup was of little interest to the Americans for many years because they kept winning it. Perhaps this was true as the seventies came to a close, but in the fifties it was a different matter. Harbert played in two Ryder Cup matches and won both of them, and when asked to describe what the occasion was like, he said: "When I stood on the first tee and they played the "Star Spangled Banner", you couldn't have driven a nail into my ass with a sledgehammer." I think we can take it as read, therefore, that the Ryder Cup meant something to him.

Jumbo Ozaki 128

FULL NAME: Masashi Ozaki

BORN: Tokushima, Japan, January 24, 1947

There are plenty of reasons why Japanese players have made so little impact outside their native land. Chief among them is their reluctance to travel, be it through homesickness, diet or the fact that the best players can earn untold wealth without ever using their passports.

The leading example of this is Jumbo Ozaki, who has achieved superstar status in Japan and earnt more money than he could spend if he lived to be 1,000. Furthermore, he has clocked up more than 65 victories. But outside Japan? He has done little to justify his place throughout the nineties as one of the top ten players in the world rankings.

Yet with a little more ambition there is every chance that he could have become the first player from his country to win a major championship. He has proved this time and again in the Japanese tournaments that regularly attract the best players from around the globe: when the world comes to Jumbo, he has invariably beaten the world.

Ozaki's penchant for colourful silk shirts and outrageous golf bags makes him instantly recognizable. What a shame that he has never exploited his talents to the hilt, and now, aged over 50, he clearly has no desire whatsoever to do so. Invited to take part in the International President's Cup team for the historic first match outside America, at Royal Melbourne in 1998, Ozaki said thanks but no thanks.

Ozaki is the leading member of a trinity of brothers who have all made an impact in Japan, all becoming multi-millionaires through their golfing exploits. It is quite a collective achievement.

Ed Furgol 127

FULL NAME: Edward Furgol

BORN: New York, March 22, 1917

MAJOR CHAMPIONSHIPS: US Open 1954

Ed Furgol's story is one of complete triumph over adversity. While in childhood he broke his arm and it was badly set, and so permanently bent rigid. Consequently, in the golf swing it was of little use to him except to guide the club towards the ball.

Furgol compensated for his disability in a number of ways: he built up the left hand-grip on his clubs so that they were the thickness of a tennis racket; by necessity he had a short swing, but he made amends by thrashing hard at the ball.

Accordingly he was able to hit the ball very powerfully, and enjoyed a distinguished amateur career. His most successful year as a professional came in 1954 when he won the US Open at Baltusrol and was named the USPGA's player of the year. His Open triumph came in a close contest with the then first-year professional, Gene Littler. What a contrast they made; on this occasion the verdict went to the manufactured play of Furgol over the cultured swing of Littler, the margin being just one shot.

The following year Furgol demonstrated it was no fluke by taking the World Cup for America in partnership with Chick Harbert, collecting the individual title as well. Having reached the highest level, however, Furgol appeared to grow tired of the lifestyle soon afterwards, retreating to become a club professional. He remained a formidable competitor, though, as he demonstrated at the 1963 Masters, where he finished a highly creditable fifth, trailing the winner Jack Nicklaus by just two strokes.

Jumbo Ozaki – with more ambition he could have been the first Japanese major champion

Bernard Gallacher 126

FULL NAME: Bernard Gallacher
BORN: Bathgate, Scotland, February 9, 1949

There was no disguising Bernard Gallacher's delight when he captained Europe to the most unexpected of Ryder Cup victories at Oak Hill in 1995. In ten previous matches both as a player and captain he had never tasted the joy of winning, and so it was no wonder the moment was sweet indeed.

It was certainly through little fault of Gallacher's that he had to wait so long to emerge triumphant. While it is true that he never had the magic touch or charisma of Tony Jacklin as a player or captain, he compensated with sheer bloody-mindedness and determination.

Trailing by two points going into the final day's singles, Gallacher marched defiantly into the Press room. Asked about what had happened, he said memorably: "Looking back is for amateurs. Professionals look forward, and we can still win."

Max Faulkner once said that Gallacher was the worst driver of a golf ball that he had ever seen in the professional ranks. That Gallacher overcame such a handicap to hold his own, and much more, at the highest level speaks volumes for both the rest of his play and his tenacity.

His finest years came in the seventies, when he invariably finished in the top 15 in the European order of merit and won a number of prestigious titles, including the Dunlop Masters two years in a row, the Spanish and French Opens, and the Tournament Players' Championship.

It was in the Ryder Cup arena, however, that his battling qualities were seen to best effect. During the decade Gallacher played singles matches against the likes of Lee Trevino, Al Geiberger, Jack Nicklaus, and Lanny Wadkins – and never lost any of them.

Dow Finsterwald 125

FULL NAME: Dow Henry Finsterwald
BORN: Athens, OH, September 6, 1929
MAJOR CHAMPIONSHIPS: USPGA 1958

There was not much dash about Dow Finsterwald's golf. Although he executed his shots with plenty of panache, it was always with one eye on the consequences, and accordingly he invariably settled for being 25 feet from the flag rather than attacking a pin.

Such course management invariably led to consistent finishes every week rather than winning a few tournaments and losing a few. For many years he held the record for the most events played without missing a cut.

It was on the greens that Finsterwald had few peers and, allied to his ultra-safe strategy, it led to him compiling an excellent record in the major championships, although he won only one.

Mark Calcavecchia – 1989 Open champion

That was in the 1958 USPGA Championship at Llanerch Country Club in Pennsylvania. The previous year, the last under the matchplay format, he lost in the final to Lionel Hebert. Now he showed he could adapt to any form of golf by winning the first running of the USPGA as a strokeplay championship. Going into the final round Finsterwald trailed Sam Snead by two strokes but made up the deficit and more, courtesy of a wonderful final round of 67.

Finsterwald won his first tournament in memorable style,

chipping in from 70 feet on the 70th hole to collect the Fort Wayne Open. In 1962 he tied with Arnold Palmer and Gary Player for the Masters, but it was Palmer who comfortably won the 18-hole play-off the following day.

Finsterwald played in four Ryder Cup teams and was also the non-playing captain in 1977. When his career came to a halt he served on the USPGA's Rules Committee.

Mark Calcavecchia 124

FULL NAME: Mark John Calcavecchia
BORN: Laurel, New England, June 12, 1960
MAJOR CHAMPIONSHIPS: Open 1989

It seemed Mark Calcavecchia's lot to be remembered among the most fortunate of Open Champions, partly because he fell from grace after winning in 1989 but mostly because his talents were seen in a far less flattering light at the Ryder Cup in 1991, where he contrived to halve a singles match against Colin Montgomerie having been four up with four holes to play.

It says much about his levels of determination, however, that he put those travails behind him to finish in the top 12 in the American money list in 1998. All told he has won more than $9 million. No golfer can win that sort of money without masses of ability.

Calcavecchia first came to prominence at the 1988 Masters when for a while towards the end of the final afternoon he seemed likely to be crowned champion. Only Sandy Lyle could beat him but he needed to par the final hole, a prospect that seemed remote when he drove into a fairway bunker. Lyle, however, pulled off the shot of his career and a winning birdie.

The American of Italian extraction took it in his stride to enjoy his own moment of glory 15 months later, when he defeated the Australians Wayne Grady and Greg Norman in the first four-hole play-off in Open history, sealing victory with a five-iron shot to within seven feet on the final hole.

The 1991 Ryder Cup undoubtedly had a disastrous effect on Calcavecchia's career for much of the decade, but his good placing in 1998 was a dogged response, and perhaps his CV will be fleshed out still further before he is through.

Jack Newton 123

FULL NAME: Jack Newton
BORN: Sydney, Australia, January 30, 1950

Golf lost a true competitor when Jack Newton tangled with the propeller of a Cessna aeroplane at Sydney's Mascot airport in 1983. He suffered devastating injuries to the right side of his body, losing both an arm and an eye. It is typical of the man, however, that he never bemoaned his lot, and now covers all the major golf tournaments working for Australian television.

During his years at the top Newton won tournaments all over the world – in America, Australia, Africa and Europe – but success in major championships, alas, always remained elusively out of his reach.

He was second on two occasions, most famously at the Open at Carnoustie in 1975. Newton shot 65 in the third round to lead going into the final day but was caught by a young man called Tom Watson, and so had to play-off over 18 holes the following day.

Since Watson was playing in his first Open and had a reputation back home in America as something of a choker, Newton was fully expected to win. It was Watson who prevailed, however, scoring 71 to Newton's 72. History has since proved that being runner-up to Watson was no disgrace.

Five years later Newton was second again, this time at the Masters, although on this occasion he had no chance of winning. He would eventually finish four behind Severiano Ballesteros, but the lead was no less than ten shots with the back nine to play.

Newton continued to play golf after his accident, and in so doing became an inspiration to disabled golfers everywhere.

Tommy Nakajima 122

FULL NAME: Tsuneyuki Nakajima
BORN: Gunma, Japan, October 20, 1954

Only two Japanese golfers have managed to achieve international success outside their native land, and Tsuneyuki Nakajima – or Tommy, as he became affectionately known – is one of them. During the 1970s he became popular wherever he travelled, not only for the quality of his play but for the way he treated the game's vicissitudes with forbearance.

He hardly deserves to be remembered for two disasters that befell him in the same year, but that may well be his fate. The first came at the Masters, where he managed to run up a 13 at the 13th, something even the most humble of amateurs would struggle to do since it may well be the easiest hole on the course.

If that were not bad enough, worse lay in store at the Open when he was challenging for the lead towards the close of the third round. Just short of the 17th green in two, a par four would have taken Nakajima into such a position. Alas, his putt lacked strength and curved inexorably back into a horrible lie in the Road Hole bunker.

The next time Nakajima had sight of the green was four shots later, and his Open chance had come and gone. Thus "the Sands of Nakajima" has entered the golfing phrase-book, a cruel judgement on a player who was actually a noted sand exponent.

Nakajima had another chance in the 1986 Open but was blown away by Greg Norman on the final day. Nevertheless he had made his mark, while in Japan he became a legend with victories in more than 50 events, and in particular four Opens, three PGAs, and three Matchplays to his name.

Sandy Herd 121

FULL NAME: Alexander Herd

BORN: St Andrews, Scotland, April 24, 1868

MAJOR CHAMPIONSHIPS: Open 1902

Sandy Herd was always a notch below the Great Triumvirate of Braid, Taylor and Vardon, but where he outscored them all was in terms of longevity. Herd first played in the Open in 1895 and was still competing in it when the war broke out. The Second World War, that is, not the First.

His long professional career began in 1892 at Huddersfield Golf Club. Herd won three tournaments that year and also performed well at the Open Championship at Muirfield, finishing second behind Harold Hilton.

His finest hour came at Hoylake in 1902 when he won the Open by a stroke from Vardon and Braid. That victory accelerated a revolution in the sport, for it was the first Open win achieved with a modern rubber-core ball instead of the guttie. After Herd's win, no one was interested in playing the old ball any more.

The guttie might have been finished but the century was well advanced before Herd was. In 1920 he was second again in the Open, carding a last-round 75 to lose the lead he held after the third round.

In 1926, at the age of 58, he achieved one of the great feats by a golfer in his sunset years when he won the *News of the World* Matchplay Championship, at a time when it was ranked second only to the Open in terms of prestige.

Raised in St Andrews, Herd made such an impression over his years in the game that Bernard Darwin wrote: "The number of his waggles is only exceeded by that of his friends. I cannot conceive that Sandy ever had an enemy."

Lee Westwood 120

FULL NAME: Lee John Westwood

BORN: Worksop, England, April 24, 1973

Here is another player whose finest achievements will surely fall in the next century, rather than in this one. Nevertheless, Lee Westwood deserves his rating here, if only for the prolific season he enjoyed in 1998 – one which saw him win eight tournaments on four different tours, a success rate that few players over the last 100 years have managed to achieve.

The rise and rise of Westwood actually began the previous year, when he made it into the Ryder Cup team by right and then played as if to the manor born. Westwood has that precious gift of always feeling comfortable, whatever the surroundings. This is reflected in his play-off record. Not for him any nervousness at the thought of going so close and perhaps missing out. "The worst thing that can happen to me is that I will finish second, and I can handle that," he says. Naturally, armed with such a relaxed frame of mind, he usually finishes first.

After a sterling Ryder Cup Westwood had a five-week spell where he won tournaments in Japan, Spain and Australia, and finished second in America. In 1998 he proved he could win all around the world by collecting the New Orleans Open.

The 1999 Masters saw him in contention for a major for the first time, and although he fell away on this occasion, it can only be a matter of time before he puts that right. At the time of writing, he seems to have everything: the game, the temperament, and above all, a desire to reach the top that has not been corrupted by two years of earning silly money.

Dave Hill 119

FULL NAME: James David Hill

BORN: Jackson, MO, May 20, 1937

In a game where the authorities frown upon plain-speaking, it was inevitable that the ever-candid and outspoken Dave Hill would find himself in the middle of any number of controversies. His shining moment came at Hazeltine and the 1970 US Open.

Many of the professionals were unhappy at the then new and immature course, but few were prepared to take on board the inevitable fine that would accompany making such thoughts public. Hill had no such reservations. Taking one look at the venue, he pronounced: "All the course needs now is 80 acres of corn and four cows."

Hill came out of the same mould as Ben Hogan and Gary Player. He saw golf as a game where perfection could be achieved. "You paint pictures out there," he once remarked, "and each good shot is a deft stroke."

Each bad stroke, however, was sufficient to induce the red mist. "I have buried a few clubs in the ground," he admitted. "It took two men to get one of them out!"

In his prime he was an outstanding ball striker who would surely have won more than 13 titles but for that fragile temperament. Hill joined the US Tour in 1959 and was consistently placed among the top money-winners for the next 16 seasons. Perhaps his best year came in 1969, when he achieved three of his 13 Tour wins and had an outstanding Ryder Cup.

Oddly enough, the nearest he came to winning a major was at the Hazeltine National and that infamous US Open. He finished second but, even so, was a distant seven shots behind Tony Jacklin.

Joining the Senior Tour in 1987, he currently has six victories to his name – the last of them coming in 1989.

Macdonald Smith 118

FULL NAME: Macdonald Smith

BORN: Carnoustie, Scotland, 1890

Bing Crosby may have made his name on the silver screen, but it was not the only field in which his knowledge commanded respect. For 30 years he was a low-handicap golfer and he knew a good swing when he saw one. Macdonald Smith's he rated as the best-looking of all.

Smith won over 30 times on the US Tour, but when it came to the majors he always came up short, on several occasions agonizingly so. As early as 1910, for example, at the age of 20, he tied for the US Open only to lose the subsequent play-off.

Larry Mize – a wonder shot saw a 1987 Masters triumph

He had only been in the country for a short while after following in the footsteps of his brothers, Willie and Alex, and leaving Carnoustie for the promise of America's east coast. He wasted little time in making his mark, firing a last-round 71 to tie with Johnny McDermott and his elder sibling, Alex. With no play on Sunday back in those days, the play-off was held over until Monday and by then the magic had gone as far as Macdonald Smith was concerned, leaving Alex to collect the title with a 71.

Macdonald Smith's most famous failure came in the infamous Open at Prestwick in 1925, where he held what appeared an impregnable five-stroke lead going into the final round. Thousands travelled over from Carnoustie in expectation of seeing their man win, but Smith, clearly hampered by poor crowd control which necessitated him playing several shots "blind" over the spectators, ballooned to a final-round 82 when a 76 would have been good enough to lift the title.

Larry Mize 117

FULL NAME: Larry Hogan Mize

BORN: Columbus, GA, September 23, 1958

MAJOR CHAMPIONSHIPS: Masters 1987

Can one shot make a career? It can certainly make a name, and Larry Mize is living proof. His shot of shots, of course, came in the 1987 Masters when he found himself in a sudden-death play-off alongside two of the game's titans, Severiano Ballesteros and Greg Norman.

Mize was the local boy, who used to peek over the fence at Augusta wondering what all the fuss was about. Now he found himself the object of the crowd's affections, but even so not many people gave him much of a chance considering the company he was keeping.

At the first extra hole, however, it was Ballesteros who bogeyed to fall from contention. At the 11th Norman safely found the middle of the green with his second shot, while Mize pushed his approach to the right. The shot he had left was treacherous, to say the least. The lightning-fast green slopes sharply away to the water, so if Mize had been a touch too aggressive he would lose his ball; a touch short, however, and he would leave himself an impossible putt.

In the event, Mize left himself neither of these precarious options, as the ball flew first over hummocks and hollows, next this borrow and that, before dropping gently into the hole. Mize leapt 10 feet into the air, and when Norman missed his birdie putt the title was his.

A year later Mize tried the shot ten times for a magazine feature and never came close once. In truth he could try it a thousand times and never hole it. But he did when it mattered, and that is all that matters.

Brian Barnes 116

FULL NAME: Brian William Barnes

BORN: Addington, England, June 3, 1945

One of the most colourful players of all time, and certainly among the most controversial. The sight of Brian Barnes, wearing shorts, pipe in one hand, beer can in another as he weighed up a shot, is an image that will live for ever.

It suggests a golfer who did not take the game completely seriously, and Barnes would probably agree with that assessment. But no one could deny his exceptional talent, not even the man himself as he tried to squander it on too many late nights and not enough time spent on the practice ground.

He still won 29 tournaments and will always be remembered for his feats at the 1975 Ryder Cup at Laurel Valley, PA. It was back in the days when there were two singles matches on the final day, and Barnes was drawn to play Jack Nicklaus both morning and afternoon.

After losing before lunch, Nicklaus had every motivation to take his revenge in the rematch. But once more Barnes was too good for him on the day. In the Ryder Cup foursomes and fourballs matches Barnes was invariably paired with Bernard Gallacher and, despite being two complete opposites away from the course, they complemented each other perfectly on it.

It was not until he came within sight of his 50th birthday that Barnes truly dedicated himself to his profession. He stopped drinking and concentrated instead on the US Senior Tour. His goal was to make $1 million in five years and it stands as a testimony to his talent that he achieved it with quite a bit of surplus cash to spare.

George Archer 115

FULL NAME: George William Archer

BORN: San Francisco, CA, October 1, 1939

MAJOR CHAMPIONSHIPS: Masters 1969

Like a lot of tall men, George Archer was a wonderful putter, crouching low over the ball with his hands well down the grip of the putter in a trademark style. For a long time he held the US Tour record for the least number of putts in a tournament, taking just 94 to complete his week's work at the Heritage Classic in 1980.

He only came to prominence in major championships in 1968, finishing fourth at the USPGA Championship as Julius Boros collected the title with his usual panache.

In the very next major, the 1969 Masters, Archer showed what he had learned. It was the year that Billy Casper led from round one, but he ran out of steam over the closing holes and Archer slipped stealthily into pole position to collect the title by a stroke.

In all he would win 12 events on the US Tour between 1965 and 1984, and then became one of the first to benefit from the development of the US Senior Tour. Between 1989 and 1995 he racked up 17 victories with earnings that nudged the $7 million mark – nice work if you can get it.

Brian Barnes – added a touch of colour to the world of golf

Archer would have won considerably more on both tours but for a number of major injuries throughout his career. All told he has had seven major pieces of surgery.

His daughter was a pioneer of sorts at Augusta when she became the first female caddie at the Masters, carrying the bag for her father. Since then she has swapped trying to save shots for saving souls and life as a Presbyterian Minister.

Abe Mitchell 114

FULL NAME: Henry Abraham Mitchell

BORN: East Grinstead, England, January 19, 1887

Was Abe Mitchell the best British golfer never to win the Open Championship? Maybe Colin Montgomerie is now pushing him close. In the 1920s, Mitchell achieved a similar status to that of Monty now, as he ruled British golf with an iron hand.

When the Ryder Cup began, Mitchell was the player the Americans feared. And quite right, too, for he had a formidable matchplay reputation. On three occasions he won the PGA Matchplay title, and in the Ryder Cup finished up with four points out of six, a level of success that stands comparison with virtually every player who has turned out in the event. Perhaps his most notable win came in 1933, a comprehensive nine and eight thrashing of Olin Dutra, who was then the USPGA champion.

But while Dutra went on to win another major, Mitchell always fell short. Perhaps his most heartbreaking loss came in 1920 when he led everyone after two rounds and the eventual winner, George Duncan, by no fewer than 13 strokes. Then, overcome by nerves, he three-putted the first three greens on his way to a calamitous 84. At the time Mitchell was considered the natural successor to the Great Triumvirate, whose time at the top was rapidly drawing to a close. Such a defeat put paid to that kind of talk.

Perhaps he lacked the killer instinct in the final analysis, but all who witnessed Mitchell in his prime testified to his wonderful ability. Indeed Henry Longhurst once wrote that his ball striking was infinitely superior to that of every other golfer: "Mitchell hammers courses into submission," he wrote.

Jerry Pate 113

FULL NAME: Jerome Kendrick Pate

BORN: Macon, GA, September 16, 1953

MAJOR CHAMPIONSHIPS: US Open 1976

Consider the two years that Jerry Pate enjoyed in 1975 and 1976, when he won the US Amateur, collected his card from the US Tour qualifying school, and then won the US Open in his first season as a professional. Why did he not go on to become one of the giants of the game? Sadly, his career was hit by injury just as he reached his prime years.

Pate, however, can always look back and say he made it to the mountain top. Ater winning the national amateur title, he won the US Open by virtue of a shot that has passed into golf folklore. Needing a par at the last hole at the Atlanta Athletic Club to defeat Al Geiberger and Tom Weiskopf, Pate had a long carry over water from a good lie in the rough. Rather than play short and make certain of a play-off, he went for the gutsy play and it paid off. His spectacular five iron finished three feet from the hole, and the resultant birdie gave him a dramatic triumph. He was 22.

Pate may well have been the first in what became a very long line of "next Nicklaus" figures, and like all who came after him he never lived up to the billing. He lost the 1978 USPGA in a play-off, and then won the 1982 Tournament Players' Championship in unforgettable style; after collecting the trophy he dived into the water that surrounds the 18th, taking the then commissioner Deane Beman and the course designer Pete Dye with him. Then came that disc problem.

Alf Padgham 112

FULL NAME: Alfred Harry Padgham

BORN: Caterham, England, July 2, 1906

Alf Padgham's prime years came in the 1930s and, in particular, a wonderful three-year run from 1934, when he never finished outside the top three in the Open Championship. A tall, slim figure with a full, natural swing, Padgham's success depended on whether or not he was having one of his occasional hot streaks with his putter.

In 1936 it seemed to last all year long; he carried all before him that season and duly collected the Open as his ultimate prize. Consistent golf enabled him to succeed in his quest for the auld claret jug, where rounds of 73, 72, 71 and 71 saw him ease past Jimmy Adams at Hoylake.

Part of Padgham's problems on the greens surely stemmed from a putting style that was bizarre, to say the least, and certainly contrasted sharply with the elegance of his long game.

Padgham would stand very upright, with his hands away from his body. He said that he pictured a putt just like a drive in miniature and what you can say about the theory is that when it worked he was as good as anyone.

He finished third in the 1934 Open at Sandwich behind Henry Cotton, and then runner-up to Alf Perry the following year, before continuing this natural progression at Royal Liverpool in 1936. Padgham was another golfer who would surely have won more but for the advent of the Second World War.

As it was, in addition to that Open triumph, he won the 1931 PGA matchplay tournament, as well as the Irish, Dutch and German Opens.

Olin Dutra 111

FULL NAME: Olin Dutra

BORN: Los Angeles, CA, January 17, 1901

MAJOR CHAMPIONSHIPS: US Open 1934; USPGA 1932

Olin Dutra carved out his place in golfing history over the first half of the 1930s. A tall, heavy-set man with a fine touch on the greens, he won two major championships in three years and also served as chairman of the USPGA Tournament Committee in 1935.

His first major success came in the 1932 USPGA, which he won in the most impressive manner imaginable. First he led the 32 qualifiers by posting a 36-hole score of 140; then he demolished anyone who stood in his way in the matchplay stages.

Only in his semi-final against Ed Dudley was Dutra extended as far as the 17th green; in the first round he handed out a fearful nine and eight hammering to George Smith, before rounding it all off with a four and three final victory over Frank Walsh.

His win in the 1934 US Open was achieved under starkly contrasting circumstances. This time he had to come from behind, making up no fewer than eight strokes on the half-way leader, Bobby Cruickshank, with two final rounds of 71 and 72 at Merion. What made the achievement still more remarkable is that Dutra had not played golf for 10 days prior to the tournament owing to bowel problems. But there was no rustiness at the death as he overtook Gene Sarazen to claim the title by one stroke.

Dutra's family were among the original Spanish landholders in California, and his success owed everything to hard graft. Dutra started work in a hardware store, but got up every morning as soon as it was light to practise and realized his ambition to be a top professional.

Douglas Edgar 110

FULL NAME: John Douglas Edgar

BORN: Newcastle-upon-Tyne, September 30, 1884

A now largely forgotten figure in golfing history, Douglas Edgar was another whom the gods touched, only for him to be struck down in his prime.

Edgar became a name to be reckoned with when he defeated Harry Vardon by six strokes to collect the French Open in 1914. His greatest achievement followed his emigration to America following the onset of war. Playing in the Canadian Open, he managed to rack up a victory by the almost inconceivable margin of 16 shots. It remains a record to this day in a national Open against a full field, and while some may immediately question the calibre of players he was up against, the names of the golfers who tied for second – Bobby Jones and Jim Barnes – should end any arguments on that score.

There seemed to be no limit to what Edgar could achieve. He successfully defended his Canadian Open title and reached the final of the USPGA Championship in 1920, where he lost to Jock Hutchinson losing out on the title on the very last hole. Tommy Armour described him as "the best golfer I ever saw", while Jones

Harry Bradshaw – but for a broken bottle the 1949 Open could have been his

himself said that he was a "magician with a golf club". Praise indeed.

Sadly, his full potential was never close to being realized, as he died in very mysterious circumstances the following year. The fatal blow was a small but deep wound in his thigh, but what caused it was never known. Was he the victim of a mugging, a hit-and-run driver, a murderer? The story made headlines for a while before, like Edgar himself, fading into obscurity.

Harry Bradshaw 109

FULL NAME: Harry Bradshaw

BORN: Delgany, Co. Wicklow, October 9, 1913

As long as golf is played in Ireland people will talk about Harry Bradshaw and what might have been at the 1949 Open at Sandwich. In the build-up to the championship Bradshaw had worked up a fine head of steam, and when he opened with a 68 many believed that this would be his year.

Then came the second round. At the fifth hole his drive finished in a broken beer bottle. What to do next? These days, of course, a pro would just call for an official ruling. Bradshaw played it as it lay, with his eyes firmly shut. Glass went everywhere, indeed some pieces may have gone further than the ball, which went only 25 yards. Instead of a four, Bradshaw took six and, with his composure disturbed, went on to return a 77.

That was bad enough, but the bizarre incident was placed in another perspective the following day when Bradshaw recovered nobly to shoot rounds of 68 and 70 to force a tie with the South African, Bobby Locke. He was overwhelmed, however, in the play-off.

Perhaps Bradshaw's greatest achievement was winning the World Cup with Christy O'Connor, at a time when it was considered among the top events in golf.

In Ireland he will always be a legend. In the 1940s and 1950s he had something of a monopoly on the Irish Professional Championship, winning it on no fewer than 10 occasions. It was a long time before he finally won in Britain, but it was a significant tournament when he did, the Dunlop Masters in 1953. Just for good measure, he won it again two years later.

Jay Sigel 108

FULL NAME: Robert Jay Sigel

BORN: Narberth, PA, November 13, 1943

In just five lucrative seasons on the US Senior Tour Jay Sigel has won more than $5 million, but what makes this level of performance all the more astonishing is that he did not turn professional until his 50th birthday.

In other words, he never tested himself against the best competition through all his prime years. Instead Sigel sold insurance policies and concentrated on compiling the finest amateur record of the modern era.

No one comes close to his achievements. He won the US Amateur on two successive occasions and also the 1979 British Amateur; he won three US mid-Amateur Championships and also played in seven American teams that contested the World Amateur Team Championship.

It was for his feats at the Walker Cup, however, that he will perhaps be most remembered. In all he played in seven Walker Cup teams and won more points than any other player. He signed off in 1993 by winning both his matches on the second day in an overwhelming American victory.

What to do next? It must have always grated with Sigel that people doubted his playing abilities because they had never been tested at the very highest level. So on his 50th birthday he joined the ranks of the US Senior Tour and conclusively demonstrated that there was no need to have been a success on the regular tour in order to compete successfully. In both 1997 and 1998 he finished fourth on the money list, collecting a combined $3 million for his efforts. You'd have to sell a lot of insurance policies to match that.

David Duval 107

FULL NAME: David Robert Duval

BORN: Jacksonville, FL, November 9, 1971

In the entire history of golf, there cannot be another player who has compiled a record similar to that of David Duval: who has gone from weekly loser to a regular winner in such a short space of time.

Consider the facts. Duval played in 86 US Tour events and never won one of them. His profile was set: he was a good, consistent young golfer who would clearly win a lot of money. But a winner? No sir.

Well, as soon as that little verdict had been cast in stone Duval set about erasing it. His 87th US Tour event resulted in a victory, and once he had achieved the breakthrough he clearly did not want to stop. He won his 88th as well, and his 89th... perhaps it was a good job for the rest of the tour that that event was the last of the year, otherwise no one else might have got a look-in.

Not that he let up much the following year, anyway. In 1998, Duval won four more times and in four different seasons of the year, too. He had proved he could win under any conditions, in any time zone, at any point of the season. He finished the year as the number-one player in the money list by some distance, and collected the Vardon Trophy for the best stroke average.

And still the best was to come, Duval one four more times in the first three months of 1999, including the Bobe Hope Classic with a last-round 59, to overtake Tiger Woods at the top of the world rankings.

Ian Baker-Finch 106

FULL NAME: Ian Baker-Finch
BORN: Nambour, Australia, October 24, 1960
MAJOR CHAMPIONSHIPS: Open 1991

Ian Baker-Finch was a hard player to judge for this guide to the 200 best golfers this century. At his best he was easily worth a place, for this tall Australian was capable of winning anywhere in the world. But, sadly, he has become even better known for always finishing last everywhere in the world.

In happier times this was completely inconceivable, and when he won the Open at Royal Birkdale in 1991 he was arguably the best player on the planet. Certainly the future dawned with inviting possibilities. After all, he had served his time. He had been preciously close to winning the Open in 1984 and now, seven years on, he had shown us what he had learned.

It was then that Baker-Finch, the kindest of souls, started opening his ears to the thoughts of others: "If you do this, Ian, you will hit the ball as far as Norman," that sort of thing. He may well have started hitting it as far as Norman, but the trouble was it would be constantly 40 yards off-line.

As the years passed so Baker-Finch slipped deeper into the mire. In particular there were two crushing experiences in the Open. In 1995, in the company of Arnold Palmer at St Andrews, Baker-Finch achieved the impossible: he drove out of bounds in the first round to the left, and then the following day repeated the feat – only this time to the right. In 1997 at Troon he shot 92 in the first round and realized it was time to give up and take refuge from the entourage of journalists keen to get hold of the inside story. For all the wrong reasons he became one of the most talked-about golfers on the planet. Those of us who are old enough will remember instead the good times, and during that spell Baker-Finch was very good indeed.

Bob Goalby 105

FULL NAME: Robert George Goalby
BORN: Belleville, IL, March 14, 1929
MAJOR CHAMPIONSHIPS: Masters 1968

History has been decidedly unkind to Bob Goalby. The record book states that he won the Masters by virtue of one of the great last rounds, a wonderful 66 that included birdies at the 13th and the 14th and an eagle three at the 15th. But all the credit was snatched away from him through no fault of his own.

For the year was 1968, the year that Roberto de Vicenzo walked into the scorer's tent and signed for a card that showed a four on the 17th instead of the three which he had actually had. Under the rules the higher score stood and Goalby won by one.

The popular de Vicenzo was naturally accorded a huge outpouring of sympathy, and the perception grew that the grumpy Goalby was a lucky champion, that he had been given a green jacket by default. Seeing as it was the only major championship he ever won, it became a hard cross for Goalby to bear.

It is impossible not to feel a little sorry for him, for to put in a finish like that and to have the acclaim deflected is harsh indeed. After all, he had played a great tournament and even if de Vicenzo had marked his card correctly Goalby would still have had his chance to win the play-off.

Goalby was named the rookie of the year on the US Tour in 1958. In all he would win 11 events, while in other majors he came close at the 1961 US Open and also the USPGA the following year, but finished runner-up each time.

This Illinois native was the archetypal streak player. With a notorious temper and a draw that often became an uncontrollable hook, he could be either brilliant or mediocre, but rarely somewhere in between.

Lou Diegel 104

FULL NAME: Louis Diegel
BORN: Detroit, MI, April 27, 1899
MAJOR CHAMPIONSHIPS: USPGA 1928, 1929

"They keep trying to give me the championship, but I won't take it," said Lou Diegel, the Greg Norman of his day, after yet another title had been cast to the winds.

It might have been all so different if he could have translated a strong performance at the 1920 US Open into a victory; alas, a last-round 77 allowed Ted Ray to snatch the title by one, and the die was cast.

And so Diegel was on his way to becoming one of the great under-achievers. There is no question he was blessed with talent, but he was never quite able to fulfil it.

His main problem was that he was never able to get over the trauma of that first major championship loss, and his nerve continued to crack at crisis points. In the 1933 Open at St Andrews, for example, he needed only a par four at one of the easiest last holes in golf to tie, but his putting let him down.

It often did. Despite endless experiments with different putters, a revolutionary method that involved crouching low over the ball, club grip almost touching his chin with both elbows jutting outwards, Diegel never did come up with a full solution.

And yet everything is relative: he may not have fulfilled his potential but he still put trophies on the sideboard. There were 30 in all, including two USPGA Championships in 1928 and 1929 – the first of which ended Walter Hagen's great run of four successive victories.

Norman von Nida 103

FULL NAME: Norman von Nida
BORN: Strathfield, Australia, 1914

It was after a poor first round 77 in the 1998 Australian Open that a wizened old native approached Nick Faldo with an offer of help. It was a reflection of the esteem in which the hunched figure is held that Faldo could not wait to hear what he had to say.

It was in the 1930s that Norman von Nida first emerged, back in the days when Australian golf was in its infancy, and he had to content himself with winning state titles and money games with wealthy amateurs.

Having tried the Far East tour, then also an embryonic circuit, and finished runner-up in the 1939 Australian Open, von Nida decided to go to America. Then war broke out.

It was 1946 and in Europe that he finally found a place to play. He arrived with total reserves of £17 in his pockets, but immediately began winning money, including a decent amount for fourth place in the Open. The following year he dominated the tournament scene, winning four of the first six events, and finishing as leading money-winner with over £3,000. That year he also shared the lead in the Open Championship after three rounds, but fell away badly in the last to finish sixth.

Von Nida was never to recapture the form he showed in 1947, but remained a considerable player for some years to come. He won the Australian Open three times in all and the Australian PGA on four occasions.

And the tip he gave Faldo? "You're gripping the club too hard," he told him. Over the next three days Faldo tried the lighter grip; he rose dramatically through the field to finish fourth, his best performance in a difficult year.

Peter Oosterhuis 102

FULL NAME: Peter Arthur Oosterhuis
BORN: London, May 3, 1948

For four years from 1971, Peter Oosterhuis enjoyed a level of success in Europe that mirrors that of Colin Montgomerie in more recent times. He won the order of merit on each occasion and then decided, with no worlds east of the Atlantic left to conquer, that the only way he could satisfy his ambition would be to follow Tony Jacklin's example and head west. Big mistake. In the US Oosterhuis found himself a rather vulnerable fish in a shark-infested ocean, and his only US Tour victory came not in America at all, but at the Canadian Open.

By the time he decided to leave Britain, Oosterhuis had played in 200 tournaments and finished in the top ten in more than half. He had also won 10 per cent of them, a remarkable success rate, and furthermore had been runner-up in 26 more.

Peter Oosterhuis – success in America eluded him

Perhaps his best performance during this run of form was not in Europe at all, however, but at the 1973 Masters, where he led the field by three strokes going into the final round. Alas, in a portent for future years in America, he fell back with a last-round 74 to finish third.

Oosterhuis will be remembered as well for his sterling Ryder Cup performances over many years. He played in 28 matches spread over six contests, and won exactly half of them. His record in the singles was even better, and for a while he appeared unbeatable. Even Arnold Palmer could not hold a candle to him. All told, Oosty played in nine singles games, collecting six-and-a-half points.

Neil Coles 101

FULL NAME: Neil Chapman Coles

BORN: London, September 26, 1934

Neil Coles has enjoyed a career remarkable more for its longevity than for its landmark achievements. He was never a serious contender for a major championship, for instance, which is quite a blight given how long he was around. Why is he ranked among the top 100, the young may ask? Chiefly because he was the most consistent performer that Europe had seen until Colin Montgomerie came along; from 1961 to 1980 Coles was never lower than 12th in the money list, winning it twice and finishing in the top six on 12 occasions.

And he had his share of victories, too. At a time when the tournament schedule was limited and based largely in Britain, he notched up 28 triumphs, including winning the *News of the World* Matchplay Championship on three occasions, the Dunlop Masters, and the PGA Championship.

Having tied for third in the Open as early as 1961 – albeit a distant four shots behind the winner, Arnold Palmer – Coles was naturally expected to become the first British player since Max Faulkner to win the grand prize.

In 1975 he had perhaps his best chance. Rounds of 72, 69 and 67 had put him strongly in contention, but he fell away badly in the final round, shooting 74 and missing the total that saw Tom Watson and Jack Newton play off for the title by three strokes.

Coles was a prime mover in the formation of a Senior Tour in Europe, and still plays in most of its tournaments while overseeing its development in his capacity as chairman of the European Tour's board of directors.

Flory van Donck 100

FULL NAME: Flory van Donck

BORN: Tervueren, Belgium, June 23, 1912

Until Severiano Ballesteros blazed a trail across Europe, the finest golfer the continent produced was Flory van Donck. Based at that Belgian jewel, Royal Waterloo, van Donck achieved many successes across virtually the whole of mainland Europe, and came close on a number of occasions in the Open as well.

In his native land, there was simply no one who could touch him for several generations. From 1935 to 1968 he won the Belgian Professional Championship on no fewer than 16 occasions and in 1979, at the age of 67, he was still representing his country at the World Cup. One of his finest moments also occurred in that competition at the height of its prestige in 1960, when he finished as the individual winner.

Van Donck's trophy cabinet simply bulges with trophies. He won the Belgian and Dutch Opens on five occasions each, the Italian four times, the Swiss and the German twice, and the French three times. He also won the Opens of Portugal, Uruguay and Venezuela.

The toughest competition then outside the United States, however, was to be found in the British Isles, where he also won five times. In the Open he was seldom out of the top ten for nearly a dozen years from 1950, and twice finished second, to Peter Thomson at Hoylake in 1956, and Gary Player at Muirfield in 1959.

Van Donck had a smooth and rhythmical swing but was less composed on the greens: he liked to putt Aoki-style, with the top of the putter high off the ground.

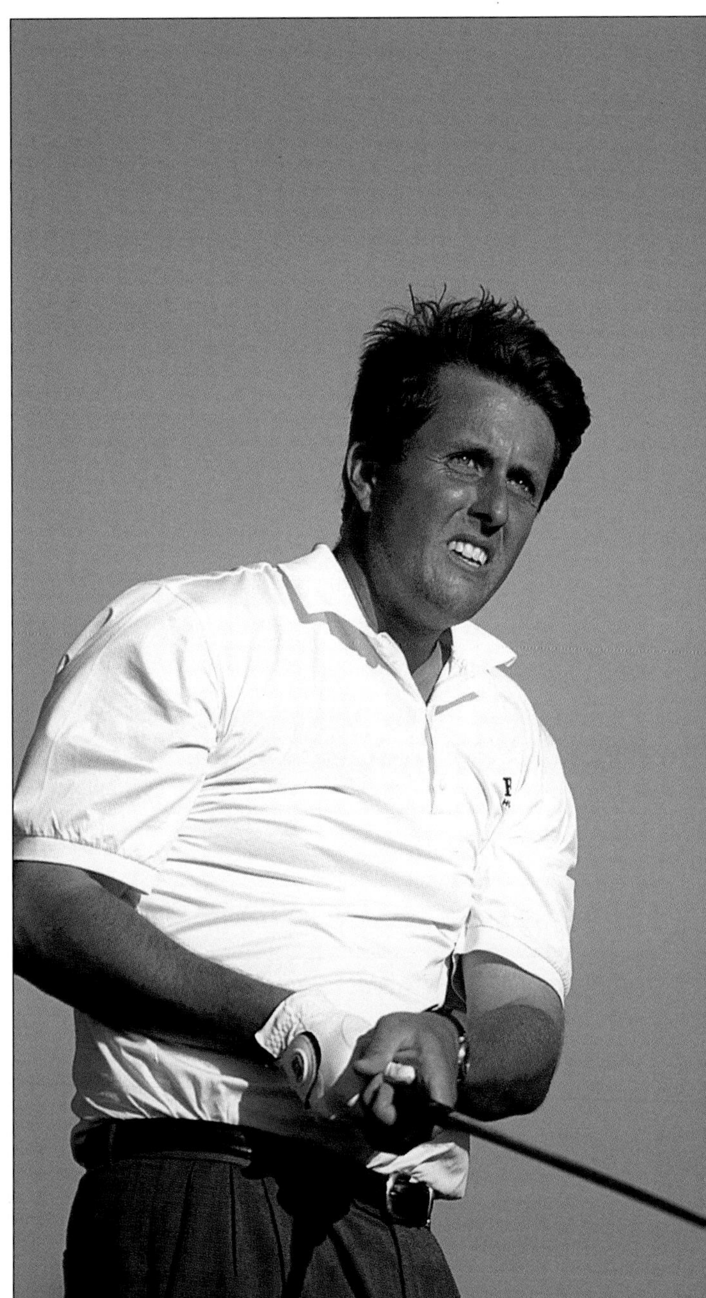

Phil Mickelson – still waiting for a major success

Phil Mickelson 99

FULL NAME: Philip Alfred Mickelson

BORN: San Diego, CA, June 16, 1970

Even though he is only just 29 with theoretically all his best years still to come, Phil Mickelson should nevertheless figure higher up this list. For much of his twenties, he has been the American superstar-in-waiting; the trouble is, with his thirties beckoning, we are still waiting.

It is a source of frustration both to Mickelson and to his many admirers that he has not become the second left-hander in history to win a major. Certainly it has nothing to do with talent or application, but probably the few inches that lie between his ears.

Winning regular tournaments in America would appear to be no problem. Even when an amateur he managed this, capturing the 1991 Northern Telecom Open, to become the first amateur to win a PGA Tour event since Scott Verplank in 1985. Twelve more titles have followed in just seven full seasons on tour, leaving Mickelson with more money than he could ever spend, but also with a nagging feeling that by now one of them should have been a grand-slam event.

When he is on form, Mickelson has it all. He is long from the tee and fearless when it comes to attacking the pins. Then there is a fabled short game, built on a touch and feel around and on the greens the like of which the world has not seen since a young Severiano Ballesteros burst on to the scene.

Like Ballesteros, Mickelson can play shots that others would not even dare to. One shot that he did innovate, however, has now become fairly standard practice: the lobbed wedge, played from around the greens with a full backswing, where the ball travels vertically before stopping on a sixpence.

Johnny Farrell 98

FULL NAME: John Farrell

BORN: White Plains, NY, April 1, 1901

MAJOR CHAMPIONSHIPS: US Open 1928

The 1928 US Open at Olympia Fields came down to a clash between two heavyweights. On the one hand was Bobby Jones, who needs no further introduction; on the other was Johnny Farrell, who perhaps does.

At the time the New Yorker was at the peak of his time as a prolific winner. In 1926 he had won five tournaments and followed that with eight victories the next year, including the stupendous feat of seven wins in a row.

He also had a fine record in the US Open. He had never finished lower than seventh in any of the previous five championships, including missing a play-off for the 1925 US Open by a stroke. He was clearly ready to win a major, and this is exactly what he achieved in 1928.

In the end it all came down to a play-off, the first 36-hole play-off the United States Golf Association had yet held. Farrell, the son of Irish immigrants, donned his lucky green sweater for the occasion.

It served him well. He led Jones by three at lunch after a 70, but the greatest amateur of all predictably fought back thereafter. In the end it all came down to a seven-foot putt on the final green; Farrell holed it, to win by one.

He might have been expected to win more majors following such a momentous achievement, but the nearest he came was to finish second in the Open and the USPGA Championship the following season. An elegant player, and very straight from the tee, Farrell was selected for the inaugural Ryder Cup in 1927 by the American captain Walter Hagen, and won both his matches by a wide margin.

Bruce Devlin 97

FULL NAME: Bruce William Devlin

BORN: Armidale, Australia, October 10, 1937

Another Australian who proved he could win all around the world, Bruce Devlin provided all the evidence he required that he was cut out for the professional game when he won the 1959 Australian Open while still an amateur. It set him on the globetrotting path that would see him finish as the leading money winner in Europe in 1966, and enjoy a highly lucrative life on the US Tour.

It is surprising that a player with so many qualities failed to win a major championship, but Devlin's increasing interest in golf-course design from his mid-thirties onwards may have had something to do with that. Over the past 30 years, he has designed more than 150 courses from his base in Houston and thus has left his thumbprint all around the world.

Devlin turned professional in 1961 and quickly got into winning ways, in the New Zealand and French Opens. In 1964 he won for the first time in America and then two years later won the Carling World Tournament at Royal Birkdale. In 1970, in partnership with David Graham, he carried off the World Cup for Australia.

One of his best performances in a major came in the 1982 US Open at the age of 44. At the half-way stage he led the field by two at Pebble Beach, but he could not sustain the momentum over the weekend, eventually finishing six strokes adrift of the winner, Tom Watson.

In more recent times he has competed on the US Senior Tour since 1987, where, despite a limited schedule owing to his architect's duties, he has still amassed career earnings in excess of $2 million.

Justin Leonard — 96

FULL NAME: Justin Charles Garret Leonard
BORN: Dallas, TX, June 15, 1972
MAJOR CHAMPIONSHIPS: Open 1997

Justin Leonard received a lot of good-natured ribbing when Brad Faxon revealed to the world his obsession with tidiness: apparently, it even extends to Leonard having a sock drawer with the pairs lined up neatly alongside one another.

Leonard's approach to golf is similar. Not for this Texan any wild thrashes from the tee. The strength of his game is course management, with any risks receiving careful calculation before being taken on.

His other great virtue is a competitive streak that recalls other tough Texans such as Hogan and Nelson. When in contention Leonard is clearly so focussed that it is not surprising that his two most memorable victories were achieved by sterling play when the pressure was at its height.

The first came in 1997 at the Open Championship at Troon, where Leonard trailed Jesper Parnevik by six going into the last round but made up most of the margin with a wonderful front nine of 31, and then eroded the rest of it by holing all the crucial putts on the inward half. It added up to a 65, a score Leonard repeated at Winged Foot a month later in the USPGA. This time, however, he had to settle for second place as Davis Love put in the performance of his life.

If 1998 was disappointing for the most part, it did contain a fine victory in the prestigious Players' Championship. It illustrated that while Leonard will not win titles with the frequency of a Phil Mickelson, the difference is that he will win ones that truly matter.

Justin Leonard – at his best under pressure

Paul Runyan — 95

FULL NAME: Paul Runyan
BORN: July 12, 1908
MAJOR CHAMPIONSHIPS: 2, USPGA 1934, 1938

Paul Runyan never had any difficulty proving the old addage that size isn't everything. Dimunitive in stature, short off the tee, the experts who gave him a chance to beat Sam Snead in the final of the 1938 USPGA Championship would surely have been counted on the thumbs of one hand. Suffice to say, the bookmakers made Snead 10-1 on to win, which in a two horse race is quite something.

But most importantly, the man who believed Runyan could win was Runyan himself. Despite being outdriven by 70 yards off the tee, he plugged the gap in skill by exhibiting his remarkable skills from 80 yards in. "Little Poison" he was nicknamed because of his talents on and around the greens and gradually it seeped into Snead's system. Never the most patient of golfers, he eventually could not cope and Goliath was toppled by the overwhelming margin of eight and seven.

Matchplay was the perfect format for Runyan, and it is not a surprise to learn that his other major success also came in the USPGA when he defeated that perennial runner-up Craig Wood at the 38th hole.

Yet Runyan could play the strokeplay game too: all told he won 20 US Tour events. His career lasted longer than most because it was built around his imperious short game qualities which did not diminish until he was well past middle age. Indeed Runyan enjoyed great success as a senior, winning both the US and World Senior titles. By then he had become known worldwide as an outstanding golf teacher, passing on some of the secrets that made him such a master of the black art of chipping and putting.

Andy North 94

FULL NAME: Andrew Stewart North
BORN: Thorp, WI, March 9, 1950
MAJOR CHAMPIONSHIPS: US Open 1978, 1985

What to make of the career of Andy North? On the one hand, he did win two major championships, and if these events are considered the be-all and end-all then he would have to be ranked among the top 50 golfers of all time. The fact he only managed one other tournament victory (the 1977 American Express Westchester Classic), however, has to count against him; indeed he is probably the least regarded double major winner of the modern era.

Everything, however, is relative, and North can say "yah boo, sucks" to all of us, for he has those two US Open mementoes in his trophy cabinet that tell of his considerable prowess. The first came in 1978 at Cherry Hills, and befitting a man unused to the thin air at the top of a major championship leader board, he struggled for breath. North was four shots ahead with five to play, but needed to get down in two from a green-side bunker on the last to secure victory over JC Snead and Dave Stockton.

A sensation appeared to be unfolding in 1985 at Oakland Hills, when TC Chen from Taiwan was four shots ahead with 14 holes to go. Were we about to see the first major championship winner from the Far East? Alas, Chen took eight at the 5th, and it was North who held his nerve over the closing holes while all around were losing theirs. It looked like the Wisconsin native may even win with a degree of style, but this being North, we should have known better – he bogeyed the last.

Dave Stockton 93

FULL NAME: David Knapp Stockton
BORN: San Bernadino, CA, November 2, 1941
MAJOR CHAMPIONSHIPS: USPGA 1970, 1976

Dave Stockton's two victories in the USPGA Championship were the highlights of a long career on the US Tour, during which he won nine other tournaments. But it may be for what has happened to him since his 50th birthday that he may be best remembered: for a start, there was a controversial captaincy of the 1991 American Ryder Cup team; then there has been his highly successful play on the US Senior Tour, where he has been one of the leading lights.

He never quite achieved that sort of fame on the regular tour, where he struggled for length, the consequence of a back injury in his early teens which prevented him from hitting flat out. His strength was around the greens, and particularly putting.

This was in evidence during his second USPGA victory at Congressional in 1976, when he needed to hole from 10 feet at the last to avoid a play-off and did so to win from Ray Floyd and Don January. His earlier victory, at Southern Hills in 1970, saw Arnold Palmer's last serious attempt to win the one major that always hung elusively out of reach. On this occasion he tied for runner-up position with Bob Murphy, with Stockton two in front.

In 1991, Stockton did nothing to discourage some dubious American tactics at the Ryder Cup. He was determined to win back the trophy, seemingly at any cost, and in that goal at least he was successful. But it was a style of captaincy that won him no new admirers.

The Senior Tour is a different matter. Since becoming eligible in 1991 he has been a popular figure, and certainly with his bank manager: so far he has accumulated more than $8 million, and counting, topping the million-dollars-in-a-season mark four times.

Chick Evans 92

FULL NAME: Charles Evans
BORN: Indianapolis, IN, July 18, 1890
MAJOR CHAMPIONSHIPS: US Open 1916

Chick Evans was undoubtedly one of the top three amateur golfers of the twentieth century, his battle to win the US Amateur being an enduring and epic struggle that would eventually be successfully completed. Along the way he took on the best professionals of the age and beat them, his victories in that arena including one in the 1916 US Open, having finished as the runner-up two years earlier.

He did it in the grand manner too, with a total of 286 for a two-shot victory over Jock Hutchinson and a record aggregate 72-hole total that would last for another 20 years. It underscored his reputation as the finest ball striker of his generation.

It was his efforts to win the US Amateur for which he will be best remembered. At a time when many of the top players elected not to turn professional – his US Open win was the third in four years by an amateur – Evans reached the semi-finals on three occasions in a row from 1909, but could get no further.

He played in the Western Open, then the most important professional event in America outside the national Open, and he won that; he went abroad for the first time and won the French Amateur. Still no US Amateur.

His luck finally changed in 1916 when he became the first man to win that title and the US Open in the same year – only Bobby Jones has equalled the feat, and no one else will now.

Once conquered, Evans won the US Amateur again in 1920. He then reached the final in 1922 and 1927, and still qualified to play in it 26 years later at the age of 63! In all, a truly Herculean effort.

George Duncan 91

FULL NAME: George Duncan

BORN: Methlick, Scotland, September 16, 1883

MAJOR CHAMPIONSHIPS: Open 1920

George Duncan was a fine golfer to watch – quick of thought and deed, complemented by an elegant technique. It was surprising that he won only one Open Championship, even allowing for the fact that the First World War disrupted his career.

Before the conflict he finished in the top ten on six occasions before finally winning the event at Deal in 1920. Two years later, again on the Kent coast, he almost tied with Walter Hagen but his putt on the final green at Royal St George's to secure a play-off stubbornly refused to drop.

His sole success came despite two opening rounds of 80, which appeared to leave him with no hope. Concluding scores of 71 and 72 on the final day fully compensated, however: he was the champion golfer by a margin of two strokes.

Duncan, the son of a village policeman, was playing for Scotland by 1906, indeed some of his finest performances would come while playing for teams. He competed in the first three Ryder Cups, for example, winning all his singles matches.

Two of these victories were particularly notable in that they came against the matchplay wonder of the age, Walter Hagen. In 1929, Duncan defeated him in a 36-hole match by the resounding margin of ten and eight. It fully illustrated that when he was in the mood, anything was possible.

Towards the end of his career Duncan was more than happy to pass on his wisdom to all who asked, and he quickly developed an expert reputation in diagnosing the faults of others.

Sam Torrance 90

FULL NAME: Samuel Robert Torrance

BORN: Largs, Scotland, August 24, 1953

Few players who have picked up a club have ever had more talent than Sam Torrance, and what a shame it is that the man himself never realized this until beyond his 40th birthday. His father, the fabled coach Bob Torrance, always said that his son would play some of his best golf after that landmark, and so it proved.

With a wife determined that her husband would fulfil his potential, and a loving family, Torrance embarked on the second half of his career with renewed gusto and in 1995 enjoyed arguably his best season.

He visited the winner's circle on three occasions and came close to winning the European order of merit for the first time. It was only at the death that Colin Montgomerie edged him out.

Torrance has always been one of the most popular European players, and he is held in particular affection by the public. This stems partly from his Ryder Cup performances, some of which have been epic indeed.

None was greater than in 1985, when he had the singular honour of winning the match that signalled the Ryder Cup would be won for the first time by a team that was European rather than one comprising just players from Great Britain and Ireland.

He did it in the grand manner too, sinking a 20-foot birdie putt

Golfing life truly began at 40 for Sam Torrance

on the hardest finishing hole in tournament golf and raising his arms to create an unwitting, but highly appropriate, V for Victory.

Ten years on and Torrance, in his eighth Ryder Cup, played a key role again as Europe once more upset the odds to win back the trophy at Oak Hill.

Paul Azinger 89

FULL NAME: Paul William Azinger
BORN: Holyoke, MA, January 6, 1960
MAJOR CHAMPIONSHIPS: USPGA 1993

Paul Azinger's career was blossoming so nicely that by 1994 he had one major championship to his credit and a string of other notable successes. He had never been outside the top 11 in the US money list since 1987 and his reputation as a tough, determined character was well established; he was on the verge of becoming the next American superstar.

Then Azinger went to see his doctor over a lump in his shoulder that refused to go away. Eventually it was diagnosed as Hodgkin's Disease, a curable form of cancer.

Perhaps it is not surprising that Azinger has struggled to live up to previous form in the years since his recovery. Happily, he won the main battle, for his yearly check-ups have always given him the all-clear, but the winner's circle that he visited frequently pre-cancer has stubbornly remained out of reach.

Azinger first came to prominence when he appeared on the brink of an astonishing Open victory at Muirfield. That was in 1987, when he led Nick Faldo by a stroke with two holes to play. He finished with two bogeys, however, and had to be content with the runner's-up spot.

Like every great champion, the setback merely steeled his resolve. He won nine times on the US Tour in the years until he was in contention to win the 1993 USPGA, and on that occasion he showed how much he had learned, defeating Greg Norman in a sudden-death play-off.

His most dramatic win came at the Memorial Tournament earlier that year, when he holed out from a green-side bunker to win by a stroke from Corey Pavin.

Al Geiberger 88

FULL NAME: Allen Lee Geiberger
BORN: Red Bluff, CA, September 1, 1937
MAJOR CHAMPIONSHIPS: USPGA 1966

Al Geiberger carved a unique niche for himself in golfing history on June 10, 1977. Playing in the Memphis Classic, he carded 11 birdies and one eagle during his second round, and when it was all added up it came to a 59.

Naturally he became known as "Mr 59", but while the four-minute mile, once broken, became over time a feat that any common-or-garden athlete could accomplish, Geiberger's achievement has since been equalled only twice on the US Tour – and never in Europe – and has still not been surpassed.

What gave the feat a slightly ironic feel is that Geiberger made his reputation on tough courses, not by making the most of easy venues. In all he won 11 times on the regular tour, including one major championship.

That total would probably have been more but for stomach problems that persisted throughout his career. The cure for a long while was to eat little but often, and he would snack regularly on a peanut-butter sandwich; indeed, so much so that the peanut-butter company approached him to be their spokesman.

His sole major success illustrated his fondness for stringent layouts. The 1966 USPGA was played at the fearsome Firestone course in Ohio, and it duly lived up to its reputation: only one player, Geiberger, achieved par, and Palmer, Nicklaus, and the rest were left in his wake as he collected the Wannamaker Trophy by a four-shot margin.

Bruce Crampton 87

FULL NAME: Bruce Sidney Crampton
BORN: Sydney, Australia, September 28, 1935

Bruce Crampton was nicknamed "The Iron Man" after playing in 38 consecutive events one year on the US Tour. It was well earned, given that most players today plead exhaustion if they play more than four in a row.

Crampton just loves playing golf. Even at the age of 55 he was still playing in 34 events on the US Senior Tour. And he is a winner, too. In 1997, he achieved his twentieth win on the oldies circuit aged 62.

In all, Crampton notched up 14 wins on the regular tour, and it is surprising that given his skills and his commitment to playing in America that he never won a major championship. He came close on a number of occasions, finishing runner-up twice in the USPGA, once in the Masters and once in the US Open. Perhaps he was slightly unfortunate that his best year coincided with Jack Nicklaus at his absolute prime: in 1972 Crampton followed the Golden Bear home in each of the first two majors.

He first came to prominence in 1956 when he won the Australian Open. The following year he travelled to America and instantly fell in love with travelling the circuit. His first victory followed four years later and thereafter they came in a steady line.

Crampton retired from tournament golf in 1977 and that appeared to be that, as he worked for eight years as an independent gas operator in Texas. Then came the burgeoning US Senior Tour and Crampton leapt right on board, back to his old iron-man ways. With Senior Tour career earnings of $6 million, it was clearly the wisest of decisions.

Kel Nagle 86

FULL NAME: Kelvin David George Nagle
BORN: Sydney, Australia, December 21, 1920
MAJOR CHAMPIONSHIPS: Open 1960

Kel Nagle had to stop playing golf late into his sixties because of persistent back pains. He bowed out in the grand manner, shooting four rounds of par figures in the Australian Seniors Championship. Naturally, he had more than his share of single putts.

For Nagle was one of the great putters – so good, in fact, that Sam Snead once said: "If I could putt like Kel, no one would ever beat me." It earned the Australian more than his share of victories. In addition to the centenary Open at St Andrews, Nagle won no fewer than 88 tournaments around the world, spread over four decades. His outstanding curriculum vitae included wins in the Opens of Australia, Canada, Hong Kong, Ireland, France, Switzerland and New Zealand.

Nagle had to wait until after the Second World War to make an impression, which may actually have helped him. Hitherto wild off the tee and impatient with it, he mellowed considerably, and during his thirties set about accumulating the bulk of the victories that make up his marvellous portfolio.

His Open victory was testament to his prowess on the greens. Chased hard by Arnold Palmer, Nagle was looking over a 10-foot putt for a par at the 17th just as an enormous roar saluted an Arnie birdie at the last. Now, if Nagle missed, they would be level. But he calmly holed, and a par at the last held off a typical Palmer charge. Now in retirement from golf, Nagle looks after a fine stable of horses.

Doug Ford 85

FULL NAME: Douglas Michael Ford Snr
BORN: West Haven, CT, August 6, 1922
MAJOR CHAMPIONSHIPS: Masters 1957; USPGA 1955

Here is another player who would have won nothing if artistic impression had anything to do with golf. Doug Ford's swing was short and ugly, and this was reflected in the length of his drives. Ford was not bothered. He was happy to keep the ball on the straight and narrow, safe in the knowledge that his short game would make up for any shortcomings in the long-driving department.

And at a time when Snead, Hogan and Nelson were in their prime, Ford won two major championships, with 17 victories in other US Tour events and seven play-off defeats. His peak years were from 1951 to 1960, when he was never lower than tenth on the money list, and was twice second.

Ford's victory at the Masters was achieved following a spectacular denouement. With a round to play he trailed Sam Snead by three, but this looked his day from the moment he started accumulating birdies over the front nine. Sure enough he came to the last hole needing a par four for a wonderful 67 and a two-stroke victory margin. However, he dumped his second shot into a green-side bunker, and now he found himself under a bit of pressure; a thinned sand shot, and he might yet throw away his lead and find himself in a play-off.

Ford, however, played the shot perfectly, the ball finishing in the hole for a dramatic birdie, a 66, and victory by three.

His other major championship success came in the 1955 USPGA, where he defeated Cary Middlecoff in the final by a four and three margin.

Ted Ray 84

FULL NAME: Edward Ray
BORN: Jersey, Channel Islands, March 28, 1877
MAJOR CHAMPIONSHIPS: US Open 1920; Open 1912

Ted Ray was unfortunate in some ways that his time at the top coincided with the era of the Great Triumvirate: Vardon, Braid and Taylor. It meant that instead of being under a spotlight the glare that beamed down on him had all the power of a table lamp. But there is another way of looking at it: he succeeded in finding his own place in the record books, despite the close attentions of three of the great golfers of the century. It was no mean achievement.

Indeed he remains one of only three British players to have won both the Open and the US Open. The latter achievement occurred when he was on the second of his popular tours with his fellow Jersey native, Harry Vardon. The first had been in 1913 when the pair were involved in a play-off for the title with the then unheralded local amateur, Francis Ouimet. Both lost.

Ray was quite a draw in his own right. He hit the ball with prodigious power, and it is said that even Bobby Jones was in awe of him. His power was shown to good effect in his US Open victory. On one par four the carry over a ravine was 270 yards, but Ray was able to make it and each time birdied the hole.

His breakthrough victory in the majors came at the 1912 Open at Muirfield, when he was finally able to get the better of the Great Triumvirate, beating Vardon into second place by a comfortable four strokes.

Jack Burke 83

FULL NAME: Jack Burke Jnr
BORN: Fort Worth, TX, January 29, 1923
MAJOR CHAMPIONSHIPS: Masters 1956; USPGA 1956

It was Jack Burke's ambition to go one step beyond his

father, who had missed out on the US Open in 1920 by a single stroke. He never managed to triumph in that event, but he did achieve two major championship victories, and memorable ones at that.

The year was 1956, the year in which a young amateur named Ken Venturi dominated the Masters from the first hole to the 71st. That was when Burke, having been in his rear-view mirror for much of the back nine, moved first alongside him and then past him to win by one.

While much of the sympathy went naturally to Venturi, who had staggered in with an 80, it was a well-deserved success for Burke, who had been runner-up himself in 1952, his first golden year.

That season he won three out of four events to become the talk of the circuit. Burke hailed from the same Fort Worth area as Byron Nelson and Ben Hogan, and everyone wanted to know whether the Texas town had unearthed another golfer of similar star quality.

The answer became swiftly apparent, as in the years that followed Burke failed to live up to that high promise. Until, that is, his second golden year, when he proved that the Masters was no fluke by taking the year's final major as well.

The USPGA was into its penultimate year as a matchplay event and Burke got better as the rounds progressed, coming from behind in both the semi-final and the final, where he putted Ted Kroll over the Blue Hill Country Club course to win by three and two.

Graham Marsh 82

FULL NAME: Graham Vivian Marsh

BORN: Kalgoorlie, Western Australia, January 14, 1944

Another Australian who has toured the world and demonstrated that he can win events on every continent. Graham Marsh, the brother of the legendary Australian wicket-keeper Rodney, enjoyed his most important successes in Europe, including a victory in the 1977 World Matchplay Championship at Wentworth.

In his side of the draw that year were two redoubtable competitors in Hale Irwin and Raymond Floyd, yet Marsh defeated both by conclusive margins.

It was the crown jewel in a year that saw him win six times on three different tours, including the Heritage Classic in America, where he pipped Tom Watson by a stroke.

It was after competing in the 1967 Australian Amateur that Marsh was persuaded by Peter Thomson to turn professional. He soon enjoyed success in Europe, winning the Swiss Open in 1970. It was the prelude to a string of victories, a large proportion of which came in Japan, where he enjoyed extraordinary success for many seasons.

During his prime years Marsh had to put up with some criticism that he could not win against the very best fields, but if it was valid – and the evidence is only partly persuasive – it ceased to be once he turned 50.

Since passing that landmark, Marsh has competed on the US Senior Tour and been among its most successful performers, his victories including its most glittering prize, the US Senior Open, in 1997.

The pension is looking good, too: in five years of senior golf, he has amassed more than $4 million in winnings.

Graham Marsh – the other half of a successful sporting family

Bill Rogers 76

FULL NAME: William Charles Rogers
BORN: Waco, TX, September 10, 1951
MAJOR CHAMPIONSHIPS: Open 1981

The 1981 American Ryder Cup team is widely considered to be the finest of all time. Practically every one of the 12 was a household name, and 11 of them had either won or would go on to win major championships.

But a photograph taken of the team at the time is instructive insofar as it gives a clue as to the mysterious disappearance from public life of one of their number. For almost hidden from view in the corner is Bill Rogers, then Open Champion, but apparently uncomfortable with the trappings and lifestyle that go with being a world-class golfer; he appears desperate to escape the limelight.

It was, in fact, what he ended up doing several years later. Bored by the ceaseless travelling chasing the mighty dollar, he packed it all in and became Head Professional in San Antonio, TX, a position he still holds.

Rogers has some of the memorabilia still stacked away in his office of the time when he was a considerable player on the world stage. There was not only his victory in the Open at Royal St George's, but a triumph in the 1979 World Matchplay Championship at Wentworth, where he defeated Isao Aoki in the final.

It was 1981 that proved to be his year of years, however. In addition to winning the Open and that Ryder Cup showing, he won three times on the US Tour and was named Player of the Year. He also had five victories from six showings worldwide.

It was never the same for Rogers thereafter. His motivation fell and his scores ballooned. At least his tale comes with an in-built "Happy Ever After".

Francis Ouimet 75

FULL NAME: Francis de Sales Ouimet
BORN: Brookline, MA, May 8, 1893
MAJOR CHAMPIONSHIPS: US Open 1913

Francis Ouimet's triumph in the 1913 US Open deserves to rank among the epochal moments in sport in the twentieth century, for it represented no less than the dawning of a new age for golf in America. The victory by a young, unheralded amateur from a humble background over two of the great British players of the day captured the imagination of the public, and set in motion the rise in the game's popularity in the USA that continues to this day.

It was a victory, too, that demonstrated that golf was a game of endless possibilities. Picture the scene: Ouimet did not even expect to get leave from his boss to play in the US Open, despite it being played on the Brookline course next to which he had lived all his life. His boss, however, was insistent and as Ouimet stood on the 13th tee in the final round he must have felt handsomely rewarded, for a good finish would place his employee among the top six.

Instead Ouimet played the six holes of his life, recording figures of two under par. Far from having the event sewn up between them, Ted Ray and Harry Vardon suddenly found themselves with company in the 18-hole play-off the following day. Neither could they subdue the upstart when proceedings reconvened; it was Ouimet who prevailed.

Perhaps inevitably, Ouimet's career was something of an anti-climax thereafter. But he did win the US Amateur on two occasions, and in 1951 he became the first American to be elected as captain of the Royal and Ancient Golf Club of St Andrews.

Tony Lema 74

FULL NAME: Anthony David Lema
BORN: Oakland, CA, February 25, 1934
MAJOR CHAMPIONSHIPS: Open 1964

Tony Lema's time at the top was tragically brief, but during the course of a couple of marvellous seasons he achieved more than most players manage in a lifetime; certainly enough to justify his place among the top 100 golfers of the century.

His first visit overseas showed what a natural talent he possessed. It was to the Open at St Andrews in 1964, and Lema took to it as if he had been placed on the earth to play links golf. The sight of him playing a chip and run through the Valley of Sin on the 72nd hole to clinch victory must have warmed the hearts of all Scotsmen who watched, for not even a native could have played it better.

Lema won by five shots that year from Jack Nicklaus and instantly found friendship in the Press centre by sending bottles of champagne to share out among all the journalists covering the championship. Thus he earnt himself the sobriquet "Champagne Tony".

When he returned the following year to Birkdale and played so majestically to lead at the half-way stage, the writers must have been licking their lips once more. This time, however, Lema fell away with rounds of 75 and 74 to finish fifth, four shots behind the champion, Peter Thomson.

His next visit to Britain was memorable for all the wrong reasons, when he lost to Gary Player in the World Matchplay Championship from a position of six holes up at lunch.

Sadly that defeat was put into a desperate perspective towards the end of 1966 when Lema lost his life in a plane crash. It was one of life's bitter ironies that the plane came down on a golf course.

Dai Rees 73

FULL NAME: David James Rees
BORN: Barry, Wales, March 31, 1913

Dai Rees's career was extraordinary not only for the breadth of its achievements but also its longevity. In 1936 he defeated Ernest Whitcombe to win his first British PGA Matchplay Championship; 37 years on he was still competing, finishing second at the age of 60 in the Martini International. If not literally then figuratively, he was a true giant of a man.

Indeed, it was thought among his contemporaries that he was the finest British player never to win an Open Championship. He certainly came close. In 1946 he was tied for the lead with Sam Snead going into the final round, but it was the American who prevailed with Rees ending up four shots behind the leader, tied in fourth place. Rees also tied for second place in 1953 and 1954, behind Ben Hogan and Peter Thomson respectively, and really ought to have won in 1961 at Royal Birkdale. That year he showed his fighting qualities, bouncing back from the horrors of an opening triple-bogey seven on a rainswept day to post a 72, with three birdies coming in the last four holes. But it was still one stroke shy of Arnold Palmer's total.

Rees's ever-varied life included military service in Africa during the Second World War, when he kept his hand in by smashing boot-polish tins with any old club he could lay his hands on.

In all he would muster 28 tournament victories, but his finest moment had to be the 1957 Ryder Cup. Rees not only captained that winning team, but contributed fully as a player too; he was in the only winning pairing and then, on the second day, trounced the 1954 US Open Champion Ed Furgol, seven and six.

Max Faulkner 72

FULL NAME: Max Faulkner
BORN: Bexhill, England, July 29, 1916
MAJOR CHAMPIONSHIPS: Open 1951

With his long game in a terrible state – in the practice rounds his fellow professionals could not wait to play him because he was afflicted by a terrible slice – Max Faulkner was not among the favourites to win the 1951 Open at Royal Portrush. As the saying goes, however, driving is only for show, and as the putts started to go in from all over the shop so his confidence and self-belief started to rise.

With three holes to play, Faulkner was well clear of the field but then finished with six, five and five: three over par. Even so, his rivals could not take advantage. Faulkner might have lost money in practice, but he had had the last laugh.

Faulkner did not make for easy viewing on the golf course. For a start, a pair of sunglasses was advisable because he would insist on wearing some of the most garish outfits imaginable. But he was a wonderful stylist, with the ability to shape shots both to the left and right.

On the greens, however, was a different story. The Portrush victory might have suggested a magician with a putter, but the facts were rather different. Faulkner would often turn up at tournaments with several home-made putters to try. In all it is said that his garage at home contained over 300 putters. Some magician.

Seventeen years after his unlikely Open victory Faulkner was still a winner, taking the Portuguese Open at the age of 52; he remains the oldest man ever to win a Tour event.

In a nice postscript to his Portrush triumph, his son-in-law, Brian Barnes, won the Senior British Open over the fabled Dunluce links in 1995 and 1996.

Max Faulkner – the oldest-ever player to win a European Tour event

Craig Stadler 71

FULL NAME: Craig Robert Stadler

BORN: San Diego, CA, June 2, 1953

MAJOR CHAMPIONSHIPS: Masters 1982

Over the last 20 years Craig Stadler has been one of the most entertaining figures to watch in world golf. Whether it has been deliberate is uncertain, but few things can equal striding with the Walrus as he goes through the full gamut of emotions.

The innocent will see him turn his back on shots and think, "Oh well, he must have missed the green." But experienced Walrus watchers know their man has actually hit it to about 30 feet from the flag; if he had really missed the green, he would have tossed his club to his caddie without looking, whereupon the caddie, the most experienced Walrus watcher of all, would be in a perfect position to catch it.

Stadler's best years came at the start of the 1980s, when there was rarely any reason for him to toss a club. In 1980 he won twice on the US Tour and finished eighth in the money list. Two years later he won four times, including the Masters in a sudden-death play-off against Dan Pohl.

Things started to turn sour for Stadler at the 1985 Ryder Cup, when he was involved in a pivotal fourballs match against Bernhard Langer and Sandy Lyle on the second morning. He missed a two-foot putt at the 18th and so instead of being 7–5 ahead the Americans were pegged at 6–6. Europe went on to an historic victory.

After that it would be six long years before Stadler would win again, but when he did it was big, the prestigious Tour Championship. In 1998 he took his career earnings beyond the $7 million mark to stand in the top 15 on the all-time list.

Vijay Singh 70

FULL NAME: Vijay Singh

BORN: Lautoka, Fiji, February 22, 1963

MAJOR CHAMPIONSHIPS: USPGA 1998

One thing became true about golf in the last decade of the twentieth century: winners came from all parts of the globe. No island was too small to produce a champion, even those for whom golf was nothing more than a four-letter word.

Fiji is one such island, yet in 1998 one of its inhabitants became the USPGA Champion, and undoubtedly one of the prime exponents of the game of his generation.

Singh has one of the sweetest swings currently to be seen on tour, and while it looks so natural, everyone who follows the game knows that the exact opposite is the case. Not since Gary Player has anyone spent so many hours fine-tuning on the practice ground as this man; it is practically a nightly occurrence that the range on tour closes when he decides to go home.

He always stands in the same place if he can, on the end of a row, beating balls but not aimlessly. The concentration is obvious, and as he enters his prime years it is clear that the toil has found its reward.

Perhaps it was as a result of his victory over Ernie Els in the final of the 1997 World Matchplay Championship that this man from the humblest of beginnings realized he could live with the best. In one golden month in August 1998 he did better than that, winning first the USPGA and then the International tournament the following week. He would finish second on the money list with $2.2 million earned and passed the million-dollars-in-a-season mark for the third time in his career. One thing is for sure: he will still be the last each night to leave the practice ground.

Fred Daly 69

FULL NAME: Fred Daly

BORN: Portrush, Northern Ireland, October 11, 1911

MAJOR CHAMPIONSHIPS: Open 1947

Another player who would surely have achieved much more but for the advent of the Second World War. As it is he stands as the only Irishman to have won the Open Championship, his success coming during his peak years which arrived just after the declaration of peace.

With his cheerful personality and jaunty walk, Daly was the archetypal Irishman, and would whistle quietly to himself as he waltzed down each fairway. He was 30 and winning all over Ireland when play was suspended in Britain and Europe for five years.

Once the war was over he quickly made up for lost time. The biggest victory of his career came in the 1947 Open at Royal Liverpool. Daly began with rounds of 73 and 70 in testing conditions, before slumping to a 78 on the morning of the final day. He was now down the field, and although he shot a 72 after lunch it was thought an unlikely total to trouble the later starters. However, fate was on his side. The weather deteriorated considerably and all in front of him found the target too much; Daly was champion by a stroke from Reg Horne and Frank Stranahan.

The following year he was second and then third in 1950. In 1952 he was third again, having led after two rounds, but he fell away badly on the final day.

Daly played every Ryder Cup match between 1947 and 1953, with his best performance coming in the latter contest, where he claimed two points out of two, including a comprehensive nine and seven singles victory over Ted Kroll.

Lee Janzen 68

FULL NAME: Lee MacLeod Janzen
BORN: Austin, MN, August 28, 1964
Major Championship: US Open 1993, 1998

Lee Janzen is an accomplished if unspectacular golfer who seems to relish the pressure moments. Accordingly, two of his eight victories on the US Tour have come in major championships, and he also showed his mettle in the 1997 Ryder Cup, birdieing the final two holes of his singles match against Jose-Maria Olazabal to come back from one behind with two to play to win.

Janzen's first win in the US Open in 1993 followed four successive rounds in the sixties that enabled him to tie Jack Nicklaus's 72-hole record for the event. On that occasion it was Payne Stewart whom he defeated to the finishing line, and oddly enough it was the same player who again duelled with him for the title five years later at the Olympic Club in San Francisco.

Stewart was no more successful on that occasion, when fate certainly decided to lend Janzen a hand. On the fifth hole, following a slow start, Janzen had whacked his drive into the trees, and could not find it. He was just about to walk back to the tee when a ball became dislodged from the branches of one tree and dropped to the ground; it was Janzen's.

The sign of a great player is the ability to take advantage of such moments of providence. Janzen did just that, playing the remainder of the holes in one under par – no mean feat over an Olympic course that had been tricked up by the United States Golf Association – to join the select group of players who have won America's national Open on more than one occasion.

Lee Janzen – two-time US Open champion

Johnny McDermott 67

FULL NAME: John McDermott
BORN: 1891
MAJOR CHAMPIONSHIPS: US Open 1911, 1912

Johnny McDermott would have featured higher in this list of the great golfers of the century if the gods had smiled at all benevolently on his meteoric life. Just consider the facts: having lost a play-off at the age of 18 for the 1910 US Open against Alex Smith, he came back the following year and again he was in a play-off. This time his opponents were George Simpson and Mike Brady, and now he was successful. Thus he became the first native-born American to win his national Open, and the youngest winner of a major championship this century.

The following year McDermott went out and won the tournament again, this time by two strokes over Tom McNamara. In 1913 McDermott took on the touring Harry Vardon and Ted Ray in a US tournament, fully aware that until then the pair of legendary British professionals were all-conquering, McDermott thrashed them.

Much encouraged by this, he caught the boat to Britain for the Open Championship at Royal Liverpool. He finished fifth.

So, what happened next? Why did McDermott not go on to become one of the great names in golfing history? He entered the 1914 Open but never played in it, after the boat in which he was sailing was involved in a collision. He was led to a lifeboat and duly rescued, but the experience preyed on his mind. So did his stock losses. In 1915 he had a nervous breakdown and never entered another tournament. As more than one golf writer has remarked, Johnny McDermott could have been the greatest of them all.

Payne Stewart 66

FULL NAME: William Payne Stewart

BORN: Springfield, MO, January 30, 1957

MAJOR CHAMPIONSHIPS: US Open 1991; USPGA 1989

Payne Stewart was hardly the first golfer to find that his powers of motivation dwindled as the dollar mountain that was his bank balance rose to Everestian proportions. What singles him out from the majority of such golfers is that he recaptured the feeling to win another mountain of money in 1998, and almost a major championship as well.

Stewart, of course, will mostly be remembered for his clothes, which were not quite so ludicrous when you took into account he was getting paid $330,000 a year to wear them. And underneath the clown's outfits there was a considerable golfer, good enough to win two major championships, and one who might have won at least a couple more had he been able to keep his nerve under the severest pressure.

In this regard, Stewart said it all when he faded over the closing holes of the 1986 US Open at Shinnecock Hills, and the title went to Raymond Floyd. "I just got intimidated by the look in Raymond's eye," he said. Full marks for honesty, yes, but it was hardly what a top player in his own right should have been worrying about.

Nevertheless, Stewart has had his own golden moments. The first came in 1989 when he shot 67 in the final round to make up seven shots on Mike Reid and take the USPGA Championship. Two years later he wrote his name on the US Open trophy, beating Scott Simpson in an 18-hole play-off. There were other chances, and not just at Shinnecock. He was also a contender on several occasions at the Open. It was all indicative of the game he possessed, but like Greg Norman there is a touch of the 'what-might-have-beens' about this career.

David Graham 65

FULL NAME: Anthony David Graham

BORN: New South Wales, Australia, May 23, 1946

MAJOR CHAMPIONSHIPS: US Open 1981; USPGA 1979

In 1981 David Graham became the first Australian to win the US Open, and he did so at Merion with a final round that must have warmed the cockles of the collective hearts of the members of the United States Golf Association.

For this was textbook US Open golf. Graham missed only one fairway on that final day and no greens. With 33 putts he totalled up a 67 to beat George Burns and Bill Rogers by three shots.

It was his second major championship success, for he also took the 1979 USPGA title at Oakland Hills. For 17 holes on the final day Graham's golf was even more peerless than it would prove to be under similar circumstances at Merion; he stood on the last tee needing a four for a 63. However, he took six and Ben Crenshaw seized his chance to force a play-off. Graham's anxiety continued through the first two extra holes before he finally claimed the title at the third.

Those two majors were the highlights of a career in which Graham proved he could win all around the world. In Britain his most memorable victory came in the World Matchplay Championship at Wentworth, where he defeated Hale Irwin at the 38th hole of a wonderful final.

It was all impressive stuff from a player who did not even think about golf until he was 14 – and even then he played left-handed. He was 17 before he switched to right-handed clubs and set out on what proved a very successful quest to make up for lost time.

Isao Aoki 64

FULL NAME: Isao Aoki

BORN: Akibo, Japan, August 31, 1942

Selected Career Highlight: World Matchplay 1978

In attempting to illustrate that in golf it is not a matter of how, but of how many, Isao Aoki must come close to being the defining example. With an ugly swing and a putting stroke that breaks every rule in the book, Aoki would have been on the first plane back to Japan if technical merit had anything to do with matters. As it is, he is unquestionably the best player to emerge from his country.

Only the magic of Jack Nicklaus at his best prevented him from becoming the first Japanese player to win a major championship. Aoki's near-miss happened in the US Open at Baltusrol in 1980 when Nicklaus, at 40, was supposed to be washed up. If he was, this represented some resurrection, because although Aoki finished with two birdies, so did Nicklaus for a two-stroke margin of victory.

Perhaps Aoki's finest achievement was in winning the World Matchplay Championship in 1978. The following year he came close to completing a successful defence, losing out on the 36th green to Bill Rogers.

In the Open the nearest he got to winning was seventh place on two occasions, the first at St Andrews where he led after the first round and shared pole position at half-way.

Aoki was a pioneer for the insular Japanese. He demonstrated that they could compete abroad, and several fine players followed his example – most notably Tommy Nakajima.

The years have not diminished his liking for travelling. Since turning 50 in 1992, Aoki has been wildly successful on the US Senior Tour, where he competes full-time. Indeed he is averaging earnings of over seven figures a year for his six seasons to date.

Doug Sanders 63

FULL NAME: Douglas George Sanders

BORN: Cedartown, GA, July 24, 1933

They say no one ever remembers who finishes second, but the story of Doug Sanders proves the falsity of that statement. For who could ever forget his miss from three feet on the final green at St Andrews to lose the 1970 Open, the most heartbreaking error in the history of major championship golf?

Sanders was once asked whether he ever thought about that miss and he memorably replied: "Not all the time. Sometimes I even go several minutes without thinking about it."

It meant a play-off with Jack Nicklaus, which Sanders duly lost the next day, and it took its place at the head of a queue of near things in the majors for the American.

For Sanders was runner-up in the 1959 USPGA, runner-up in the 1961 US Open, both by the margin of just one stroke, and fourth in the Masters in 1966. He was also second in the Open at Muirfield in 1966 – again to Nicklaus and yet again by one shot.

Yet while his name might not be on any of the sport's leading trophies, it cannot be said that he failed to leave his mark on the game. From the poorest of southern backgrounds, he rose to become one of the leading lights of his generation, and certainly the most colourful. Even now, well into his sixties, he still favours the garish colours of his pomp, and at home he has wardrobes full of clothes that most people would not even wear for a bet. Still worse is his shoe collection: he has hundreds of pairs in such tasteful colours as purple and yellow.

Yet that was Sanders: he wanted to be seen, he wanted to be noticed, and in that respect he continued a tradition begun by his hero Walter Hagen.

Corey Pavin 62

FULL NAME: Corey Allen Pavin

BORN: Oxnard, CA, November 16, 1959

MAJOR CHAMPIONSHIPS: US Open 1995

For the first half of the 1990s, Corey Pavin was just about the worst golfer you wanted battling you for a title. Or worse still, opposing you in matchplay. For Pavin had all the things that always gnaw at an opponent: he would be outdriven by at least 50 yards, but he would always make up for it around the greens. If he was within 100 yards of the putting surface, it was front-page news if he did not get down in two. Sometimes he did better than that.

Take the 1992 Honda Open. Fred Couples thought he had the thing won, sitting in the scorer's tent with what appeared an unbeatable score: the only man with any chance was Pavin, who had to hole an eight-iron shot to tie. That, however, is what Pavin did, and he then birdied the third extra hole to win the play-off.

In the 1994 US Open at Shinnecock Hills, Pavin's drive at the 18th only covered barely half the hole's length, leaving him a four wood to the green. No matter. He simply knocked it to four feet to seal victory.

That triumph was perhaps the ultimate in his successes over the Goliaths of the circuit, since his chief opponent was Greg Norman, who could lap him several times over when it came to natural talent.

The problem for the Pavins of this world comes when their desire becomes corrupted either by age or money or the demands of families or, in this particular case, by all three. They start occasionally taking three shots from 100 yards instead of two, and the four shots or so extra needed to complete a tournament means oblivion. And that is why Pavin disappeared from trace for the second half of the 1990s.

Corey Pavin – a master around the greens

Davis Love 61

FULL NAME: Davis Milton Love III
BORN: Charlotte, NC, April 13, 1964
MAJOR CHAMPIONSHIPS: USPGA 1997

Davis Love's reputation as a supremely gifted shotmaker without the necessary mental toughness to win a major championship ended in no uncertain fashion at the 1997 USPGA.

At Winged Foot, Love came close to reducing it to pitch-and-putt status with some breathtaking play. In all he would manage three rounds of 66 and, attached to a 71, it gave him a victory by no fewer than five shots. In an emotional scene on the 18th green, Love embraced his mother, and both knew what the other was thinking.

For Love had been taught the game by his father, who had a noted tournament career – he was a contender for the 1964 Masters shortly before Love was born – but who really made his name as a teaching professional. He certainly taught his son well, for Love is one of the best swingers of a golf club of his generation.

Love Snr was just watching his son come to worldwide prominence when he was tragically killed in a plane crash in 1988. It took Love quite some time to come to terms with his loss, but in the 1990s he has proved a regular winner on the US Tour.

The major championship near-misses were beginning to rack up, however - his three-putt from 20 feet on the 18th green at Oakland Hills to lose the 1996 US Open by a shot was but one example - when he ended all talk for ever of his being a 'nearly man'. A long-standing back problem permitting, more majors should follow before he is through.

Tom Lehman 60

FULL NAME: Thomas Edward Lehman
BORN: Austin, MN, March 7, 1959
MAJOR CHAMPIONSHIPS: Open 1996

Tom Lehman had just completed his first million-dollar year on the US Tour when he was asked about his taste in clothes. He revealed that the most that he had ever spent on a pair of trousers was $75. "I just could not bring myself to spend more than that," he said, "It would just not be me."

Thus "blue-collar man", golf's working-class hero, revealed that success would not be changing him. And neither has it, even when he became the best golfer of the year in 1996. Lehman was as approachable as ever, a true ambassador for the game.

His story is one of the best the sport has come up with, from being so hard up playing mini-tours that he once took a shower in a rainstorm to save on a hotel bill, to becoming the first American professional to win the Open at Lytham, with all the attendant riches that followed.

That was the week of Lehman's life, when he displayed a sorcerer's touch on the greens to spreadeagle the field. He also won the Loch Lomond tournament in Scotland by a street in 1997.

Colin Montgomerie – out of luck in the majors?

Yet despite victories in his native land as well, there have been disappointments. For three successive years from 1995 he had his chance to win the US Open, but each time failed to get the job done. However, given that a decade ago he was reduced to contemplating a coaching job in Minnesota, which would have involved some skiing duties in the winter, he can reflect overall that his career has taken a glorious leap forward.

Colin Montgomerie 59

FULL NAME: Colin Stuart Montgomerie
BORN: Glasgow, Scotland, June 23, 1963

When Colin Montgomerie saw off the challenge of Lee Westwood in the final round of the Volvo Masters in 1998, he had achieved something that will surely stand the test of time. It meant that he had won the European order of merit for a sixth year in a row, and it is hard to imagine anyone beating that.

That is the good news. The bad is that while dominating Europe on the one hand, Montgomerie has found it difficult to expand his portfolio. In America he managed to play in 50 tournaments without ever winning one, which for a player of his undoubted qualities is verging on the ridiculous.

It hints at a flaw in his character which his record in the Open Championship substantiates. One top-ten finish and five missed cuts in eight appearances is the stuff of journeymen, not one of the game's great players.

Yet when he is concentrating on the task in hand and not allowing his mind to wander and his notorious temper to heat up, he has few rivals. He has been unlucky in major championships too, and particularly in 1995 when he birdied the last three holes at Riviera to reach a play-off for the USPGA Championship, only to be floored by a birdie from Steve Elkington at the first extra hole.

He has also come close on three occasions in his favourite event, the US Open, most notably in 1994 when he lost in another play-off, this time of the 18-hole variety, to Ernie Els.

Bob Charles 58

FULL NAME: Robert James Charles
BORN: Carterton, New Zealand, March 14, 1936
MAJOR CHAMPIONSHIPS: Open 1963

It seems amazing that in the final year of the twentieth century there has still been only one winner of a major championship who is left-handed. Bob Charles carved out his own unique niche of golfing history in 1963 when he won the Open Championship at Royal Lytham.

The New Zealander placed great store on accuracy rather than length, and on a truly magical touch on the greens. The best putter ever? There are plenty of people who witnessed Charles in his prime prepared to make such a judgement.

Ironically enough, Charles is not left-handed by nature at all. He only played that way round because his parents did and he borrowed their clubs. He won the New Zealand Open in 1954, but it would be another six years before he turned professional. Thereafter he was soon winning in both Europe and America.

In 1963 Jack Nicklaus needed two pars to claim his first Open title, but bogeyed both of them to go one stroke adrift of Charles and the burly American, Phil Rogers. In the 36-hole play-off that followed Rogers was never a factor, Charles shooting a total of 140 to triumph by eight shots. He had averaged just 30 putts per round for the tournament.

Charles always looked after himself. A tall, slim figure, he was always obsessed with health supplements and nutrients, and that probably explains why he did so well for so long on the US Senior Tour. By 1998 he had racked up $8 million from this circuit alone.

John Daly 57

FULL NAME: John Patrick Daly
BORN: Carmichael, CA, April 28, 1966
MAJOR CHAMPIONSHIPS: Open 1995; USPGA 1991

The unlikeliest major championship victory this century? To discover the winner of that prize, we need only cast our minds back as far as 1991, when Nick Price pulled out on the eve of the USPGA Championship to be with his wife at the birth of their child.

The PGA of America called up several alternatives, but none felt they could get there on time to do themselves justice. Eventually the ninth reserve answered the call, driving through the night to take his place on the first tee.

John Daly had not even played a practice round, indeed he was probably stuck into a six-pack of beers when the call came. But he found Crooked Stick set up perfectly for his occasionally crooked driving and prodigious length off the tee. Opening with a 69, he took the lead after a second-round 67 and was never headed thereafter, claiming the trophy by three strokes. It was his first win on the US Tour.

All through the final round he high-fived the crowd, as golf discovered it had a popular new champion. But what a flawed hero. By the time he was 30, Daly had been married three times, and had also been in an alcohol rehabilitation centre three times.

During his second drying-out session he found time to win the Open at St Andrews, displaying his wonderfully natural gifts that combine ferocious hitting from the tee with a deftness of touch around the greens that makes him compelling to watch.

At the time of writing, Daly is coming up to his second year without touching a drink. Perhaps, finally, the man who seemed interested only in death or glory has found some middle ground.

Eric Brown 56

FULL NAME: Eric Chalmers Brown
BORN: Edinburgh, Scotland, February 15, 1926

If they ever selected an all-time European Ryder Cup team from all the players who have ever participated in the contest, then a place would have to be found for this combative Scot. He may not have the major championships of some of his peers, but he possessed a grit and determination that was seen at its best in the rough and tumble of matchplay.

Perhaps his finest moment came in Great Britain and Ireland's glorious victory in the 1957 contest at Lindrick. The captain, Dai Rees, put Brown out first in the singles in the hope that he would meet the ever-erupting volcano that was Tommy Bolt. Rees guessed right, and Brown duly beat him four and three.

Afterwards, they exchanged words. "You won Eric, but I did not enjoy the game," Bolt said. "No, of course you didn't," Brown replied, "Because you were ******* licked, that's why." Do you think Brown would have got on well with Severiano Ballesteros?

His great times were not just confined to beating Americans. He won a host of tournaments all over Europe and was second in the Los Angeles Open in 1960. He always came up short in the Open, however, finishing third in 1957 and 1958. The latter was particularly hard to bear since he took six at the last, when a par four would have given him the title.

Brown's final act in the spotlight was, appropriately enough, as Ryder Cup captain of the Great Britain and Ireland side that shared the spoils in the famous halved match at Birkdale in 1969.

Mark O'Meara 55

FULL NAME: Mark Francis O'Meara
BORN: Goldsboro, NC, January 13, 1957
MAJOR CHAMPIONSHIPS: Masters 1998, Open 1998

In his own words Mark O'Meara was a "nice golfer". Nice career, nice lifestyle – and so what, if he was one step down from the best players of his generation? O'Meara was happy with things as they were. And that seemed to be that as he entered his forties.

Then came a friendship with a young player named Tiger Woods who was just making a name for himself. Soon they became inseparable, and for the first time in his life O'Meara saw the game in a different light. Something, you see, in the young man's approach rubbed off, and it generally goes by the name of ambition. Put simply, O'Meara found himself infected by new goals, new ideals and, welded to a fine swing and a golden putting touch, he set about achieving the Indian summer to end them all.

Birdies on the final two holes to win the Masters? No problem: O'Meara's putts disappeared dead centre into the middle of the cup to edge out Freddie Couples and David Duval. A four-hole play-off for the Open? No sweat: his opponent, Brian Watts, never stood a chance.

O'Meara came close to winning a third major in the summer

1998 was most definitely Mark O'Meara's year

of 1998 as well when he challenged for the USPGA. But two was more than enough to bathe his career in a new glow that had nothing to do with niceness.

Just for good measure he rounded off the year by winning the World Matchplay Championship at Wentworth. And his opponent in the final? Why, it had to be Tiger Woods, didn't it?

Horton Smith 54

FULL NAME: Horton Smith

BORN: Springfield, MA, May 22, 1908

MAJOR CHAMPIONSHIPS: Masters 1934, 1936

Horton Smith had a curious career. He first came to prominence in the winter of 1928, and over the course of the following four months won no fewer than eight out of the nine events he played. Naturally, he was the wonder of the age. But while no one could keep up that sort of pace, it is surprising that in subsequent years Smith's foot slipped so far from the accelerator pedal.

He did win two major championships, however, and in particular will for ever be immortalized as the inaugural winner of what was then known as the Augusta National Invitational, but which we now refer to, of course, as the Masters.

The event aroused great interest because Bobby Jones, who had retired from all competitive golf four years earlier in 1930, had decided to play. But it was Smith who prevailed (Jones finished 13th) over the ever-hapless Craig Wood, the crucial hole being the 17th where the champion-to-be rolled in a 20-foot birdie putt. Two years later Smith won again, this time from another player, Harry Cooper, who seemed able to do anything in golf bar put a grand-slam pot in the trophy cabinet. Smith trailed by four at one point during the final round, but a freakish chip-in at the 14th set him on his way.

Smith came close on other occasions to adding to his majors haul. He was twice third in the US Open and once in the Open. In all he won some 30 tournaments and played in three Ryder Cups.

Gene Littler 53

FULL NAME: Eugene Alex Littler

BORN: San Diego, CA, July 21, 1930

MAJOR CHAMPIONSHIPS: US Open 1961

It was one of those quotes that sticks like glue to a player, and helps to define his career. "Here's a kid with a perfect swing, like Sam Snead's...," Gene Sarazen said of Gene Littler, before adding the little rider that made everyone sit up and take notice, "...only better."

That swing like liquid gold earned Littler the nickname "Gene the machine", and as he mopped up trophies in the second half of the 1950s and followed them up with victory in the 1961 US Open following a fine closing round of 68, it seemed that here was a player to challenge Arnold Palmer in his prime and Jack Nicklaus on the cusp of greatness.

Yet Littler lacked the one thing that separates great players from legends: desire. He had a passion for driving, but it was fast cars not golf balls. He seemed content to make a good start to the season and then take things relatively easy.

Littler first emerged in 1953 by winning the US Amateur, before achieving the rare feat the following year of winning a professional event while still a member of the non-paid ranks.

On turning professional he continued to be successful, with 1959 probably his best year as he collected five trophies. In addition to his sole major championship success Littler later lost play-offs for the 1970 Masters to Billy Casper and the 1977 USPGA to Lanny Wadkins. All told he won 29 times on the US Tour, eight times on the Senior Tour, and also made seven Ryder Cup appearances.

Lanny Wadkins 52

FULL NAME: Jerry Lanston Wadkins

BORN: Richmond, VA, December 5, 1949

MAJOR CHAMPIONSHIPS: USPGA 1977

Lanny Wadkins almost defined the term "streak player". That is, when the inspiration was upon him, no golfer was a more thrilling sight. Wadkins attacked the flags at every opportunity, and gets brownie points for the fact that he got on with it, but when his rather untidy swing was out of kilter, there was little he could do about it except retreat for the weekend following another missed cut.

He ought really to have won more than one major championship: perhaps his good weeks simply did not coincide with enough grand-slam events. Certainly there was no questioning his nerve when he was on his knock. The other thing that Wadkins will be remembered for was as a redoubtable competitor, and he won no fewer than 21 times on the US Tour.

He also played in seven Ryder Cup teams and was captain of the losing American team in 1995. That hit Wadkins hard, and his golf has not been the same since. Now approaching 50, it is likely that he will return to prominence on the US Senior Tour.

Perhaps his most memorable Ryder Cup was in 1983, when America barely managed to hold off the improving Europeans and Wadkins played his part over the weekend, winning two matches and halving the other.

His victory in the USPGA was also a memorable one, if only for the fact that it came at Pebble Beach. It also featured the first sudden-death play-off in major championship history, as Wadkins drew level with Gene Littler with his only birdie of the round at the 18th, and then defeated him on the third extra hole.

Henry Picard 51

FULL NAME: Henry Picard

BORN: Plymouth, MA, November 28, 1907

MAJOR CHAMPIONSHIPS: Masters 1938; USPGA 1939

After Bobby Jones and before Ben Hogan, Sam Snead and Byron Nelson there came the sweet-swinging Henry Picard, who made up for not winning his first decent event until he was 27 with a host of victories thereafter. Picard demonstrated his character by defeating that master psychologist, Walter Hagen, once in a play-off. He also has two major championships to his name.

In addition, he helped the next generation in two interesting ways. The first was when he fell into poor health and gave his driver to Snead, who promptly won practically every tournament going with it. The second footnote occurred in 1937, when he bared his big heart by promising a talented but penniless professional a few dollars' sponsorship. It proved a good call, given that the penniless one went by the name of Hogan.

Picard won his first major in 1938 with four very consistent rounds at Augusta of 71, 72, 72 and 70 to win by two strokes from Harry Cooper and Ralph Guldahl. It made up for his disappointment in the inaugural Masters three years earlier, when he had led by four at the half-way stage, only to fall away badly finishing in fourth place, four shots adrift of the champion, Gene Sarazen. In 1939, his golden year, he won the USPGA, defeating Byron Nelson in the final by birdieing the last hole and then repeating the feat at the 37th. It was one of five victories he had that season.

Picard had six years at the top before illness virtually halted his career. By that time he had won 27 tournaments and had been the leading money-winner – with a little over $10,000.

Lloyd Mangrum 50

FULL NAME: Lloyd Mangrum

BORN: Trenton, NJ, August 1, 1914

MAJOR CHAMPIONSHIPS: US Open 1946

With his centre parting, thin moustache and a cigarette eternally dangling from between his lips, Lloyd Mangrum had something of the air of a Mississippi river-boat gambler. He played up to the image, too, and on the course was fearless and cool, as you would expect from a scratch poker player. He also formed the most-feared partnership in Ryder Cup history with Sam Snead... well, until Ballesteros and Olazabal came along, anyway.

Mangrum was indeed a hard man, hard enough to win two Purple Hearts while under the command of General Patton during the 1944 Battle of the Bulge. Apparently undeterred by his wounds, he went off to recuperate at St Andrews and won a GI tournament there before returning to America in time for the 1946 season.

He had already made his mark, causing a sensation in 1940 by setting what was then an Augusta record score of 64 at the Masters. In the end, he finished second to Jimmy Demaret. In 1946 he won his only major championship, a marathon US Open. Mangrum was tied with Byron Nelson and Vic Ghezzi, and in the 18-hole play-off all three had 72s. So the next day they went out and played it again. Mangrum again shot 72, and this time it proved good enough by a stroke.

This was the beginning of his great years, when he twice won the Vardon Trophy, topped the money list, and was always up near the top. By the time his career was over he had won 34 US Tour events. And his Ryder Cup record with Snead? Played four, won three, lost one – the only loss coming in the 1939 at Ganton at the hands of Lees and Burton.

Denny Shute 49

BORN: Densmore Shute

BORN: Cleveland, OH, October 25, 1904

MAJOR CHAMPIONSHIPS: Open 1933; USPGA 1936, 1937

To those who believed that Bernhard Langer's victory in the German Masters one week after missing a six-foot putt for the Ryder Cup represented the supreme act of recovery, we offer Denny Shute's performance some 48 years earlier as an equally good example of overcoming adversity.

All right, the Ryder Cup in 1933 did not have the same death-or-glory resonance to it that existed at Kiawah Island in 1991. Nevertheless, you can imagine how Shute felt at Southport and Ainsdale when he had a putt for the Ryder Cup, ran it four feet past, and then missed that one as well for the tie.

And the next time he went on a golf course it was not for something as run-of-the-mill as the German Masters. It was the Open itself and, what is more, at St Andrews. And Shute went on to claim victory in a 36-hole play-off against the man who always lost play-offs, Craig Wood, after scoring four rounds of 73 during regulation play.

It was perhaps the highlight of a career that had far more ups than downs. In his homeland Shute was practically unbeatable in Ryder Cup play, handing out fearful hammerings in several matches. He also enjoyed success in the major championship arena, claiming back-to-back USPGA titles in 1936 and 1937 – the last player to do so.

Perhaps the pick of the two was the latter, and a thrilling triumph in the 36-hole final against Harold "Jug" McSpaden that went to the first extra hole.

Julius Boros 48

FULL NAME: Julius Boros

BORN: Fairfield, CT, March 3, 1920

MAJOR CHAMPIONSHIPS: US Open 1952, 1963; USPGA 1968

You could say that Julius Boros was a late developer. He never entered the professional ranks until he was 30, and never played Ryder Cup golf until he was 40. But he made an indelible impression nevertheless, ambling nonchalantly along the fairways, as if in a trance. His peers underestimated him at their peril, however: Boros would win three major championships and a lot more else besides before he was through.

It was his love of accountancy that kept him away from pro golf until a relatively late age. When he committed himself, however, he made an immediate impact, and within three seasons had reached the peak of his new career, winning the US Open by four shots over "Porky" Oliver.

His national Open was to prove Boros's baby. He would finish in the top ten on no fewer than nine occasions, and was second twice. He also claimed one more victory, a most unexpected one in 1963 at Brookline following a play-off with Jacky Cupit and Arnold Palmer. Boros did not even expect to get that far following final rounds of 76 and 72. But he seemed to cast a spell over his opponents; Cupit dropped three shots over the last two holes while Palmer missed from two feet at the 17th. Destiny seemed to be dragging Boros to the title, and so it proved in the play-off, which he won with a fine round of 70 to beat Cupit by three and Palmer by six.

Boros's other major championship success came in the USPGA in 1968. At 48, he remains the oldest winner of any grand-slam event.

Jose-Maria Olazabal – triumph over adversity

Jose-Maria Olazabal 47

FULL NAME: Jose-Maria Olazabal

BORN: Fuenterrabia, Spain, February 2, 1966

MAJOR CHAMPIONSHIPS: Masters 1994, 1999

A sporting story more heartwarming than that of Jose-Maria Olazabal would be hard to find. Tragically struck down at the age of 29 with a back ailment that caused problems in his feet, Olazabal returned to the game after an 18-month absence and promptly shot 65 in the week of his return in Dubai. "Once a competitor, always a competitor," Greg Norman said in admiration. A month later, Olazabal returned to the winning circle.

During his youth he had been saddled with the label "the second Seve", but that quickly became disrespectful as he compiled a litany of achievements of his own. A wonderful amateur career was quickly superseded by a string of professional victories, including a truly remarkable 12-shot win in the World Series. The event was held at Firestone, one of America's toughest courses. Olazabal went round it in just 61 shots.

Even more memorable was his Ryder Cup partnership with Ballesteros, the most evocative in the history of the event. In 15 matches together spread over four Ryder Cups, they only ever lost one - an extraordinary record.

Such was his talent around the greens that his first major championship victory, at the 1994 Masters, seemed almost overdue when it finally arrived at the age of 28.

Darkness fell just as he threatened to become the world's leading light. He capped the year of his return with a winning part in the 1997 Ryder Cup at Valderrama and went one further in 1999 – by winning the Masters for the second time.

Ben Crenshaw 46

FULL NAME: Ben Daniel Crenshaw
BORN: Austin, TX, January 11, 1952
MAJOR CHAMPIONSHIPS: Masters 1984, 1995

Did Ben Crenshaw really once say that he did not think he could live with himself if he thought he could not win an Open? Perhaps he has now changed the last word to Masters: let us hope so, anyway. Whatever, this keen golf historian can rest assured that his place in the game's folklore is secure. After all, who could ever forget someone who, when it came to the black art of putting, was a positive Grand Master?

Crenshaw grew up in the same town and at the same time as Tom Kite, both were tutored by the legendary coach, Harvey Penick, and their career achievements are broadly similar. As golfers, however, they could hardly be more different. Kite worked at his game all the hours he could to put in what nature left out; Crenshaw had all nature had to give and more.

The one thing he could never do, in common with many artists, is groove a shot from the tee that could regularly find the fairway. So it was that US Opens and USPGAs came and went without any challenge from Crenshaw, because the fairways were too narrow.

But he won the Masters in 1984, and then again 11 years later in one of the most emotional triumphs of all time: on the eve of the event, Crenshaw was a pall-bearer at Penick's funeral.

He twice came close to his cherished Open goal, in 1978 and 1979, finishing runner-up on each occasion. In 1999 he will be back in the spotlight, as US Ryder Cup captain. Europe will be thankful it is not a putting contest.

Ben Crenshaw – a putting Grand Master

Curtis Strange 45

FULL NAME: Curtis Northrup Strange
BORN: Norfolk, VA, January 20, 1955
MAJOR CHAMPIONSHIPS: US Open 1988, 1989

Curtis Strange's two peak years were 1988 and 1989, during which he became only the sixth player to win consecutive US Opens, and also hauled America back from the brink of defeat in the Ryder Cup. It established his reputation as a player to turn to when the pressure was at its most intense, but cushioned by all the money he could ever hope to spend – in 1988 he became the first player to win more than $1 million in a single season on the US Tour – the fire inside went out in the 1990s.

His first US Open triumph was particularly satisfying, since it came against Nick Faldo, who at the time appeared to be his European equivalent. Both wore formidable game masks, but on this occasion it was Strange who came out on top in the 18-hole play-off at The Country Club.

A year later Strange completed a successful defence at Oak Hill, the first player to do so since Ben Hogan in 1951. This time he had a little more to spare; indeed he could afford the three putts he had on the 18th green and still win by one. Four months later at The Belfry he answered his captain Raymond Floyd's rallying call, as America was in severe danger of losing the Ryder Cup for a third successive match.

Strange was up against Ian Woosnam in the final singles match and was one down with four holes to play, knowing that only victory would suffice. Over the toughest stretch at The Belfry Strange finished with four straight birdies to win on the home green. The trophy stayed in Europe, as they were the holders, but Strange had enabled America to tie that particular Ryder Cup, and thus climb on board Concorde for the journey home with honour intact.

Christy O'Connor 44

FULL NAME: Christy O'Connor

BORN: Galway, Ireland, December 21, 1924

SELECTED CAREER HIGHLIGHTS: Member of ten Ryder Cup teams, including victorious Great Britain and Ireland side at Lindrick in 1957. Winner of the Irish Professional Championship on 10 occasions

It is only natural for following generations to judge players solely by the record books, to look at the major championships won and assess accordingly. Christy O'Connor is one glaring example of why this method can be badly flawed.

Perhaps the best player ever to come out of Ireland, O'Connor would surely have won majors had he lived in today's age, where the price of a first-class flight to America is but loose change to a top player. Contrast that with O'Connor who, despite his many successes in Europe, felt he could not afford to charge over to the States three times every year.

Instead the only major open to him on a regular basis was the Open Championship, and it became a cherished goal to win it. Sadly he always fell short, on three occasions by heartbreaking margins. In 1965 he was two strokes shy of Peter Thomson's winning score and twice he finished third, at Lytham in 1958 and again at Birkdale in 1961.

He was, however, a prolific winner, and a popular champion, his easy grace and effortless charm adding considerably to his substantial qualities as a golfer. In Ireland he is a legend, fuelled partly by his ten victories in the Irish Professional Championship, but mostly by his winning nature.

O'Connor played in no fewer than ten consecutive Ryder Cup matches, which remained a record until 1997, when Nick Faldo surpassed it. He also won the World Cup for Ireland in 1958, in partnership with Harry Bradshaw.

Now into his mid-seventies, O'Connor breaks his age regularly – often with several shots to spare.

Ian Woosnam 43

FULL NAME: Ian Harold Woosnam

BORN: Oswestry, Shropshire, March 2, 1958

MAJOR CHAMPIONSHIPS: Masters 1991

Ian Woosnam's name remains on the pursed lips of every young hopeful who travels down each November to the European Tour's Qualifying School in Spain. For Woosnam's is the classic rags-to-riches golf tale: from travelling the circuit in an old camper-van feasting on cold baked beans to his own private jet and a mansion on the tax-friendly island of Jersey.

Woosnam certainly did it the hard way, and it was splendid watching him do so. Armed with a textbook swing and a compelling pugnacity, if Woosnam's putter was also in tune then neither the game nor his opponents held any fears.

For a year at least, he was indisputably the best player in world golf. In 1987 he won four times on the European Tour, finished number one in the order of merit, and then, just to round off the season, won the World Matchplay Championship and the World Cup of Golf for Wales, taking the individual title in the latter event for his sterling efforts.

But will he remember that year with more affection than 1991? It is unlikely. The latter saw him win twice in America, including success at the Masters when he was at his best. The locals, horrified at the thought of a fourth successive British win, started barracking him, and screaming in favour of his playing partner, Tom Watson. Of course, that just made him even more motivated, and all but guaranteed a memorable Welsh victory. Woosnam completed the task in the grand manner, too, a brave seven-foot putt on the final green giving him a richly deserved green jacket.

Fred Couples 42

FULL NAME: Frederick Steven Couples

BORN: Seattle, WA, October 3, 1957

MAJOR CHAMPIONSHIPS: Masters 1992

The most popular American player of his generation, Fred Couples took a long time to fulfil his potential. He was 30 years old when he stood in the middle of the 18th fairway in a vital Ryder Cup match in 1989, his opponent with a three iron in his hand and Couples with a nine iron. Yet it was Christy O'Connor Jnr who marched to an unforgettable victory, and Couples to tearful ignominy. That Couples recovered from that position to leave his mark in the 1990s says much not only about his talent but also his determination.

Indeed, his languid swing has become one of the trademarks of the decade. With seemingly little effort he is able to propel the ball vast distances, and his putting – particularly under pressure – has improved beyond all recognition.

The 1991 Ryder Cup at Kiawah Island was the making of him. Couples played in all five matches that year and lost just once. Six months later he claimed his first major championship at Augusta, albeit thanks to a huge dollop of good fortune.

At the short 12th, Couples's tee shot finished a yard short of where it should have, and as it slithered down the bank and towards Rae's Creek, a watery grave appeared the only outcome. Inexplicably, the ball stopped on the shaved bank. Understandably, Couples could not get to it fast enough, and took full advantage of his outrageous fortune, chipping and putting for a three. He went on to win by two strokes.

Ironically the man who finished second was the man who guided him around Kiawah six months earlier and showed him how to win under pressure – Raymond Floyd. Perhaps Floyd reflected later that he had taught Couples too well.

Ralph Guldahl 41

FULL NAME: Ralph Guldahl

BORN: Dallas, TX, November 22, 1912

MAJOR CHAMPIONSHIPS: Masters 1939; US Open 1937, 1938

Here is another golfer who, for an all-too-brief period, found golf a simple game and beat the living daylights out of everyone else. In three years he won two US Opens and one Masters. What happened after that? Well, one answer would be to say: who cares? Most players spend their lifetime hoping to win one third as much.

Indeed, that was pretty much Guldahl's attitude as well. "I have done it all in competitive golf," he said, and he did not just mean the good times either.

For Guldahl learned the hard way how to enjoy success at the highest level. In 1933 he had a four-foot putt to force an 18-hole play-off in the US Open – and missed. In 1936 he finished second on the US Tour money list, and then the following spring was firmly in contention to win at Augusta. That is, until he tripped himself up around Amen Corner on the final day, taking a disastrous 11 strokes to play the 12th and 13th, as against the par of eight.

His time was coming, however. Just as the word "choker" was forming on sportswriters' lips, so he won the US Open two months later, followed by a rare successful defence. Then came a cherished victory at the Masters, where he became the first man in major championship history to score less than 280 for four rounds. He was also the first to reach the heady heights of nine under.

What to do for an encore after that little lot? Guldahl wrote an instruction book and retreated into mediocrity.

Larry Nelson 40

FULL NAME: Larry Gene Nelson

BORN: Fort Payne, AL, September 10, 1947

MAJOR CHAMPIONSHIPS: US Open 1983; USPGA 1981, 1987

It is true that if all professionals played the game like Larry Nelson, then the number of spectators paying through the gate would not fill a taxi. Nevertheless, boring Larry was a player of considerable distinction, and the circumstances behind his rise to the top were anything but laborious.

Nelson, indeed, never struck a golf ball until he was 21, and never had a lesson, unless Ben Hogan's legendary book *The Modern Fundamentals of Golf* counts as one. Nelson learned it off by heart; he gripped the club as Hogan advised, stood like him, and swung just as he counselled. The great man must have been as proud as punch when Nelson rose to the game's highest peaks.

Not only did Nelson go on to win major championships – three in all – he also proved to be one of the most redoubtable Ryder Cup competitors. In 1979 and 1983 he played in a total of nine matches and won them all.

In the major championship arena he won the USPGA by four strokes from Fuzzy Zoeller in 1981, and then two years later achieved victory with a dramatic comeback in the US Open. Trailing by seven at the half-way stage, he shot 65 in the third round to close within one of Tom Watson. In the final round the pair could not be separated until the 16th hole, where Nelson drained a 60-footer for a conclusive birdie. In 1987 Nelson won the USPGA for a second time, beating Lanny Wadkins at the first hole of a sudden-death play-off.

In 1998, his second year on the Seniors Tour, he pocketed over $1.4 million, nearly three times his finest earings on the PGA Tour.

Tom Weiskopf 39

FULL NAME: Thomas Daniel Weiskopf

BORN: Massilon, OH, November 9, 1942

MAJOR CHAMPIONSHIPS: Open 1973

In terms of achievement commensurate with a player's talent, Tom Weiskopf has the dubious distinction of finishing bottom of the pile. After all, this is a man who once turned down a place in the American Ryder Cup team because he wanted to go on a hunting trip; this is a man who once missed only four greens in 72 holes at Augusta and yet still managed to finish runner-up; this is also the man who once ran up a 13 on the 12th hole at the Masters.

Yet we can be too harsh on the player nicknamed "terrible Tom" by the Press, because, for all that, his legacy remains considerable. For a start, he had arguably the finest swing of any golfer apart from Sam Snead – a swing that many players from future generations have used as a model, including Steve Elkington.

Then there is his work in the field of design. To this author's mind, of all the players who have gone on to indulge in golf-course architecture on the side, Weiskopf has been the most successful, creating by some distance the most imaginative venues (perhaps his best-known work is Loch Lomond).

We can also be too harsh on him as a golfer, because the bottom line is that at his best he was close to being unbeatable. Inevitably, his finest period of play arrived when he finally became motivated. This was in mid-summer in 1973, shortly after the death of his father. Wracked with guilt at the thought of a talent squandered, Weiskopf went out and won five tournaments in eight weeks, including his sole major championship success at the Open at Troon, which he won by three shots from Neil Coles and Johnny Miller.

1992 brought the long-awaited major for Tom Kite

Tom Kite 38

FULL NAME: Thomas Oliver Kite

BORN: Austin, TX, December 9, 1949

MAJOR CHAMPIONSHIPS: US Open 1992

Tom Kite's career is something of an enigma. Only one major championship came his way which, given his remorseless consistency, hints at a fallibility under pressure. Yet put Kite in a Ryder Cup polo shirt, which is supposed to be the most pressure a golfer can play under, and he became almost invincible.

In 1981 he took part in what is probably, in terms of quality, the greatest singles match ever played. He was up against Sandy Lyle, who played out of his skin, and after 16 holes the Briton was six under par. Given that the venue was the daunting Walton Heath, it was no surprise that Lyle should find himself shaking hands with his opponent at that point. Yet astonishingly it was in defeat not victory, for Kite was an incredible ten under par.

Four years on, and a first victory for Europe since the continentals were assimilated into the team was not achieved with any help from Kite. Indeed, he demolished Howard Clark eight and seven, which remains a record margin of victory in the singles, albeit equalled by Fred Couples against Ian Woosnam in 1997.

Kite's sole major championship success came in the infamous winds at Pebble Beach in the US Open in 1992, and it was a victory that stands as a testimony to one man's determination. Just as Jack Nicklaus was congratulating Colin Montgomerie on winning – he did not believe that anyone still out on the course could master the 40mph winds on the back nine – so Tom Kite held steady to claim a two-shot triumph.

Craig Wood 37

FULL NAME: Craig Wood

BORN: Lake Placid, NY, November 11, 1901

MAJOR CHAMPIONSHIPS: Masters 1941, US Open 1941

Craig Wood is perhaps best known as the player who was on the receiving end when Gene Sarazen had his albatross two at the 15th hole in the 1935 Masters. Up to that point, Wood was cruising along nicely with a three-stroke lead, and apparently destined to win his first major championship. Then he found himself in a play-off that he would go on to lose.

If any of the above sounds like the sort of thing that you thought only happened to Greg Norman in major championships, you might like to know that anything the Australian did, Wood did first. Like Norman, Wood lost play-offs for all four major championships. Again like Norman, he would finally win a couple to rescue something from the wreckage.

Unlike Norman, Wood finally did manage to win at the Masters, in 1941. A decade of disappointment in the grand-slam events was at an end, and just to emphasize the point, Wood won the US Open two months later, despite intimating that he would like to pack up half-way through the first round with a bad back. He was persuaded to carry on, and went on to win by three shots. Talk about "beware the injured golfer".

The triumphs came just in time. Before the end of the year, America would be at war and, although Wood did defend his Masters title in 1942, few people had their minds on anything so trivial as golf. Accordingly, the US Open was not staged, and with the disappearance of big-time golf for several years went Wood's time at the top.

Jim Barnes 36

FULL NAME: Jim Barnes
BORN: Lelant, Cornwall, 1887
MAJOR CHAMPIONSHIPS: US Open 1921; Open 1925; USPGA 1916, 1919

Nicknamed "Long Jim" because of his height, 6ft 4in, Barnes won four major championships, including the last Open to be played at Prestwick in 1925. The triumph he treasured most was his victory in the 1921 US Open, when the trophy was presented by the incumbent President, Warren Harding.

That last Prestwick victory, however, has gone down in golf folklore as among the most controversial. Barnes was up against Macdonald Smith from Carnoustie, and thousands of Scots travelled across the country to see their man win.

As it was, they probably proved more of a hindrance than a help. Crowd control at the time was almost non-existent. Smith is said to have had to have played several shots "blind" over the heads of his supporters. He carded an 82 when a 76 would have given him the title.

Barnes emigrated in 1906 from his native Cornwall to San Francisco. In 1913 he tied for fourth place in the US Open, and the following year achieved the first of three victories in the Western Open, which at the time was the second most important event on the calendar for professionals in the USA.

Even more significant was his win in the first-ever USPGA Championship in 1916. He also won the first post-war event in 1919, and reached the final on two more occasions, losing out each time to Walter Hagen.

As for his US Open triumph, Barnes opened with a 69 and drew away from the rest round by round, eventually finishing up with a nine-stroke winning margin that remains a record in the event to this day.

Roberto de Vicenzo 35

FULL NAME: Roberto de Vicenzo
BORN: Buenos Aires, Argentina, April 14, 1923
MAJOR CHAMPIONSHIPS: Open 1967

This popular Argentinian achieved one of the most emotional major championship victories and also the most heartbreaking defeat. The first came at the 1967 Open at Hoylake, when he became the oldest winner of the event since Old Tom Morris.

De Vicenzo was 44 at the time and was playing in his nineteenth Open. He had been a professional for 29 years and had enjoyed success all over the globe. He had won the national Opens of five different European countries. But his main ambition, The Open, had always hung elusively out of reach. Now, with Henry Cotton leading the cheering crowds, he claimed a two-stroke triumph over Jack Nicklaus. It was the last Open to be held at Royal Liverpool; no one could have asked for a finer curtain call.

The reigning Open Champion looked in a position to add the Masters as well the following spring, when he finished on the same score as Bob Goalby to force what everyone thought would be a play-off. What no one knew at the time was that de Vicenzo had signed for a wrong score. He had marked down a four at the 17th instead of the birdie three he had actually scored and, under the rules of the game, the higher score had to stand. Asked shortly afterwards about the error, de Vicenzo uttered the immortal words: "What a stupid I am."

Nevertheless, his contribution to golf will never be forgotten, particularly in South America where he is, quite simply, a legend. And quite right, too. He remains a true ambassador for his sport.

Fuzzy Zoeller 34

FULL NAME: Frank Urban Zoeller
BORN: New Albany, IN, November 11, 1951
MAJOR CHAMPIONSHIPS: Masters 1979; US Open 1984

Who knows how many major championships Fuzzy Zoeller would have won had he not been plagued by back problems throughout his professional career? As it is he won two, and even from a limited schedule brought pleasure to millions of spectators.

Even in later years, when he was hardly in contention, he was rarely out of the news. First there was his celebrated friendship with John Daly, and Zoeller must have recognized a blood brother, for he knew how to raise a storm or two himself in his youth.

And speaking of a storm, there followed one which developed into a hurricane once the PC police in America got hold of his now notorious "collard greens" comments, regarding what he expected Tiger Woods to choose as the champions' dinner at Augusta.

As for his major victories, both were notable. The first was at the Masters when he achieved that rarest of feats: a victory for a rookie at Augusta. He did it the hard way, too, in a sudden-death play-off with Ed Sneed and Tom Watson – the latter being at his peak at the time.

Five years on at Winged Foot, Zoeller thought he was about to lose the US Open to Greg Norman when the Australian, playing ahead, sank a long putt on the final green. Zoeller held up a white handkerchief in mock surrender. What he did not know was that Norman's putt was for par, not birdie.

Zoeller duly forced a play-off with Norman, which he won quite easily the following day.

Zoeller has eight other Tour titles to his name and three Ryder Cup appearances. He is also famous for wearing dark glasses, whatever the weather, and his on-course whistling.

Bernhard Langer 33

FULL NAME: Bernhard Langer

BORN: Anhausen, Germany, August 27, 1957

MAJOR CHAMPIONSHIPS: Masters 1985, 1993

A more courageous player than Bernhard Langer never struck a golf ball. On at least three occasions he was so afflicted by the yips that he had desperate problems holing putts from 12 inches. But each time he forced his way back to the top and into the annals of the great names who have played the game.

Like so many who came before him, Langer's first taste of the sport was through caddying. Once he turned professional it was the strength of his iron play that singled him out, and on the few occasions when his putting displayed a similar quality, the rest were invariably playing for second place.

Bernhard Langer – "Mr Courageous"

After the first bout of the yips, he came back to win the 1985 Masters; after the second episode in 1988 he returned to win the 1993 version at Augusta, which was arguably his greatest triumph since it contained just a single three-putt; and then after toiling in 1995 with his career seemingly in decline, he returned to play a pivotal role in Europe's Ryder Cup victory at Valderrama in 1997.

For one of the game's true gentleman it was sweet success indeed. Six years earlier, in perhaps the most famous missed putt in Ryder Cup history, Langer had seen a six-footer at Kiawah Island slide by on the 18th hole, which meant the trophy returned to American hands after six years' residence in Europe.

His most cherished goal has always been to win the Open and he has been close on several occasions. Now, at approaching 42, time would appear to be ebbing away but, given the man's stoicism, do not rule him out just yet.

Jimmy Demaret 32

FULL NAME: Jimmy Demaret

BORN: May 10, 1910

MAJOR CHAMPIONSHIPS: Masters 1940, 1947, 1950

Jimmy Demaret won the Masters on three occasions, and the first time at Augusta in 1940 was his sixth tournament win in succession. It was once said that the Texan had more fun and practised less than any other golfer, spending more time looking for clothes than beating balls. Yet, together with his trio of wins at Augusta, his Ryder Cup record of played six, won six, adequately demonstrates his prowess.

Demaret carried on from where Walter Hagen left off. Hagen had been the first golfer to attire himself in two-tone shoes and a bow tie with matching slacks. That was far too conservative for Demaret, who often took to the course looking like a traffic light, with clothes of vivid colours topped off by a tam-o'shanter.

This may seem an odd person for the stern, grey Ben Hogan to choose as a best friend, but Demaret was an excellent competitor. He was the first man to win three times at Augusta, and once shot 30 for the back nine, which stood as the record for over 40 years until broken by Mark Calcavecchia in 1992.

Demaret also left his mark in the shotmaking department. The wisdom of the age was to strike the ball with a draw, thus gaining yardage by applying top-spin that caused the ball to roll upon landing. But Demaret cottoned on to the fact that this often caused the ball to roll into trouble. So he struck his shots with a fade, thus employing a side-spin that enabled the ball to hold both fairways and greens more effectively. An overwhelming number of the top professionals now strike their shots with a fade.

Willie Anderson 31

FULL NAME: William Anderson
BORN: North Berwick, Scotland, c.1880
MAJOR CHAMPIONSHIPS: 4. US Open 1901, 1903, 1904, 1905

In the US Open Willie Anderson set two records shortly after the turn of the century that will not be surpassed now we are about to end it. In 1905 he won his fourth championship, a record that has since been equalled only by Bobby Jones, Ben Hogan and Jack Nicklaus – exalted company indeed.

He also won three of his titles in a row, something no one has managed, although Hogan might have but for his car accident in 1949 (he won the championship in 1948, 1950 and 1951). Anderson competed at a time when it was almost unheard of for players to play in both the US Open and the Open – hence his lop-sided record.

An immigrant Scot from North Berwick, it was not just his victories in the US Open that give him a prominent place in golf history, but also his overall performance level. In addition to his victories he had one second place, one third, two fourths and three fifths. In other words, he had 11 top-five finishes, which is quite something given that he died tragically young at 30.

Anderson enjoyed numerous successes in local tournaments, most of which have disappeared into unrecorded history, as well as a remarkable four wins in the Western Open, which in those days ranked second only to the US Open.

He is unusual in that his victories came with two different kinds of ball, the gutta percha and the rubber core. He had a flat swing, with a good deal of bend in his left arm, and opponents thought his greatest strength was his unflappable temperament.

Sandy Lyle 30

FULL NAME: Alexander Walter Barr Lyle
BORN: Shrewsbury, Shropshire, February 9, 1958
MAJOR CHAMPIONSHIPS: Masters 1988; Open 1985

When Severiano Ballesteros was asked in 1990 who was the most talented player in European golf, he said: "Sandy Lyle: the rest of us are not even close." History will almost certainly proffer a different judgement, but no one should seek to deny Lyle his place among the elite.

For a while in 1988, he was the best golfer in the world, and as far as British players are concerned he was the pioneer, being both the first for a generation to win the Open and then paving the way for four consecutive British successes at the Masters.

The two major championship victories could hardly have been achieved in more contrasting ways, and yet between them they sum up Lyle both good and bad. The first at Sandwich he won at the death almost in spite of himself, a clumsy bogey at the final hole proving insignificant because his closest challengers stumbled as well.

What a difference at the Masters three years later. Standing on the 18th tee needing a four to force a play-off, Lyle appeared to have blown it when he drove into a bunker. The resultant sand shot, however, was later described by the distinguished golf writer Herb Warren Wind as the finest bunker stroke in the history of the game. It finished eight feet from the hole, and Lyle sank the birdie putt for the most memorable of victories.

We sat back and waited for more major successes. But Lyle made the grave mistake of listening to coaches who told him that he would become a still better player if he changed his ugly swing. The only thing that did change was that his scores became ugly instead. Indeed, he slumped tp 183rd on the US money list in 1998, and has to rely on invites to tournaments in an attempt to regain his card – a long way away from the past glories.

Johnny Miller 29

FULL NAME: John Lawrence Miller
BORN: San Francisco, CA, April 29, 1947
MAJOR CHAMPIONSHIPS: US Open 1973; Open 1976

Johnny Miller only won two major championships, but both were achieved with such style and grace as to leave a lasting memory. The first was the 1973 US Open at Oakmont, supposedly the toughest course in America, but brought to its knees by Miller with a final round of 63.

It was a new record for the lowest score achieved in a major championship and, although equalled on many occasions since, at the time of writing (the start of the 1999 season) it has never been bettered. The second was the 1976 Open at Birkdale, and another major claimed with an astonishing final round, this time of 66.

The two victories highlight the fact that when Miller was in what the professionals are fond of referring to as "the zone", nothing was beyond him. No score was out of reach, no course immune to his inestimable gifts. In 1974 he won no fewer than eight events on the US Tour.

Why did he not win more majors? Miller's putting was always streaky, and quickly declined. He also became bored with the lifestyle of a top golfer, and the monotonous travelling. A strict Mormon with six children, there was always another life for Miller, and early in his thirties its lure became all-powerful.

In the 1990s he has remained in the public eye, however, with his insightful commentary work for NBC television in America. Not for Miller the easy way out, making sure he never offends any professional with anything remotely resembling the truth. Rather he will tell it like it is. If someone chokes, he refers to it as such, and accordingly has been a breath of fresh air.

Ernie Els – destined to be one of the sport's true greats

Ernie Els 28

FULL NAME: Theodore Ernest Els
BORN: Johannesburg, South Africa, October 17, 1969
MAJOR CHAMPIONSHIPS: US Open 1994, 1997

For a player who has all his best years in front of him, he must be a sublime talent to reach the top 30 in this list. No one would dispute that label being placed on this classy South African, who is surely destined to become one of the sport's immortals.

Already he has two major championships to his name, and by the time he has finished he should achieve his goal of winning all four of the game's grand-slam events at least once.

Certainly there is no course that is unsuited to his exquisite talents when he is on form. In addition to his two US Open titles, he has also gone close in the Open and the USPGA, while Augusta sets up perfectly for his prodigious left-to-right drives and his dextrous touch on the greens.

Els's breakthrough victory in the majors came at Oakmont in 1994, when he won a three-man play-off against Colin Montgomerie and Loren Roberts. Three years later he would again deny Montgomerie, this time in a classic finish in regulation play. With nothing to choose between the two, Els deliberately played a three wood from the 17th in order to be behind Montgomerie off the tee, and therefore playing his second shot first. It was a psychological master stroke, for he hit his five-iron approach perfectly, the ball finishing six feet from the hole. It completely unnerved Montgomerie, and the one-stroke margin Els opened up on that hole proved the difference in the end.

Such a ploy is more usually used in the matchplay arena, where Els has also established himself as the most formidable of performers. In his first three appearances at the World Matchplay Championship, he walked off with the title.

Hale Irwin 27

FULL NAME: Hale S. Irwin
BORN: Joplin, MO, June 3, 1945
MAJOR CHAMPIONSHIPS: US Open 1974, 1979, 1990

At the time of writing Hale Irwin has just completed the most successful season, in financial terms, in the history of professional golf. His reward for sweeping up on the US Senior Tour was $2,861,000, and it is clear that as he approaches his mid-fifties he is ageing most gracefully.

He always was the most stylish of players, and the years have improved his personality, too. Once unbearably arrogant, Irwin gained a huge army of new admirers with the manner of his third US Open title at Medinah in 1990. Needing to hole a tramliner on the final green to force a play-off, nobody, not even Irwin himself, truly expected him to sink the putt.

But the ball broke this way and that before toppling into the hole on its final breath and Irwin, a college footballer in his youth, remembered those days as he set off on a lap of honour, high-fiving the crowd. The contrast with the dour figure of old was marked.

The three US Opens were the extent of his majors haul, and while that in itself is memorable, it also hints at under-achievement, for here was a player with virtually every faesible attribute.

Perhaps a temper that bubbled just below the surface held him back. Certainly it cost him a play-off for the 1983 Open. In the third round Irwin, furious at missing a putt, missed the ball completely from an inch as he tried to tap it into the hole, and so had to add a stroke. The next day he shot 67 and the missed one-inch putt was to prove the difference between his total and that of the winner, Tom Watson.

J. H. Taylor 26

FULL NAME: John Henry Taylor

BORN: Northam, England, March 19, 1871

MAJOR CHAMPIONSHIPS: Open 1894, 1895, 1900, 1909, 1913

For ever immortalized as part of the Great Triumvirate that dominated golf at the start of the century, J.H. Taylor was the first of the three – James Braid and Harry Vardon were the others – to come to prominence, winning the Open in 1894 and then successfully defending it the following year. He also won it three times after the turn of the century, and would finish runner-up on no fewer than six occasions.

Taylor grew up close to the links at Westward Ho, and worked there as a youngster. By the time he left his teenage years behind, he had blossomed into a fine player and, after a short period at Winchester, moved to Royal Mid-Surrey where he was the resident professional for 47 years until his retirement in 1946.

His victory in the 1894 Open came in only his second appearance in the event, and led to him becoming the most famous professional in Britain. This Open, at Sandwich, was the first to be staged outside Scotland and Taylor won by five strokes to end the domination of the championship by the Scots.

Like Braid, Taylor was instrumental in the founding of the Professional Golfers' Association; so much so that Bernard Darwin, in applauding his contribution, wrote that he had "turned a feckless company into a self-respecting and respected body of men".

In addition to his qualities as a golfer, Taylor had a rare charm, which was recognized when he was made an honorary member of the Royal and Ancient Golf Club in 1947. Ten years later, the Royal North Devon Club bestowed on him their highest honour by electing him President.

Thomas Armour 25

FULL NAME: Thomas Armour

BORN: Edinburgh, Scotland, September 24, 1895

MAJOR CHAMPIONSHIPS: US Open 1927; Open 1931; USPGA 1930

The Silver Scot won three of the four major championships, and may well have completed the set but for the bothersome fact that the Masters was not around when he was in his prime. His victory in the USPGA Championship in 1930, where he had a last-gasp final-hole victory over Gene Sarazen in the final, remains the last time a British-born golfer collected that trophy.

Armour developed into one of the great players of the 1920s, despite losing an eye in France during the First World War, and when he retired he became that rare creature: somebody who could teach as well as he could play.

His first major title came in 1927 at Oakmont. All eyes were on Bobby Jones, but for once he failed to live up to his billing, and two British players contested the trophy; Armour came out on top over Harry Cooper in a duel that needed an 18-hole play-off to separate them, with a round of 76 being good enough for the title.

The title he always wanted, however, was the Open, and after his victory in the USPGA it became something of an obsession. He did not have long to wait, mind, for at Carnoustie the following year he claimed the glittering prize with a wonderful last round of 71, while others blew their chances.

Armour is immortalized for one other reason: he invented the term "the yips" for an afflicted putting stroke. And he knew what he was talking about. Shortly after that Carnoustie victory the dreaded disease struck him, and he retired to become a highly-paid teacher and author of several best-selling instruction books.

Cary Middlecoff 24

FULL NAME: Dr Cary Middlecoff

BORN: Halls, TN, January 6, 1921

MAJOR CHAMPIONSHIPS: Masters 1955; US Open 1949, 1956

He was the finest dentist ever to play golf, although it has to be said that watching him was about as exciting as having a tooth pulled. Middlecoff was so slow he made Bernhard Langer appear a hare, and it is because of examples such as his that tournament golf ground to the snail's pace on show today. Even Bobby Jones was moved to say something critical. But the record books show three major championships to his name, and during the 1950s he also won more events on the US Tour than any other player.

Middlecoff was a serious analyst of the golf swing, and among the first to grasp the importance of set-up. But what an age it took him to align himself to the ball! In a play-off for the 1957 US Open, Dick Mayer was so fed up with the ever-so-deliberate routine of Middlecoff that he took out a camping stool and sat on it while his opponent played his shots. If this was a psychological ploy, it worked: Mayer shot 72 to Middlecoff's 79.

It was a rare lapse from the dentist, however, and he did win his national Open on two occasions, first taking advantage of Ben Hogan's absence in 1949 and then emerging triumphant again in 1957. In 1955 he also won the Masters by an overwhelming margin of seven shots, largely thanks to a blistering second round of 65. Like so many great players, Middlecoff's career at the top came spluttering to a close amidst a flurry of missed short putts, and he retired in 1961.

Nick Price 23

FULL NAME: Nicholas Raymond Liege Price

BORN: Durban, South Africa, January 28, 1957

MAJOR CHAMPIONSHIPS: Open 1994; USPGA 1992, 1994

Certain years have become unequivocally identified with certain players, and just as 1998 was undoubtedly Mark O'Meara's *annus mirabilis*, so 1994 will always be remembered as the season in which Nick Price confirmed all his undoubted potential.

This had been evident from as long ago as the 1982 Open at Troon, when he duelled with Tom Watson for the title, only to display his inexperience over the closing holes. Six years on and Price was once more in contention, this time at Lytham.

On this occasion he demonstrated just what he had learned on the final day, only for Severiano Ballesteros to put together one of the great last rounds in Open history. The Zimbabwean was second again.

In 1992, however, he claimed his first glittering prize, the USPGA, remaining calm despite a final-round charge from the then Open champion Nick Faldo.

Then came 1994, as he emerged from out of the shadow of his peers – players such as Faldo, Norman and Ballesteros. Price won no fewer than six tournaments that year, including an Open-USPGA Championship double that had been completed only once before since Walter Hagen managed it in 1924.

Just as impressive was the manner of his feat. In all, Price was a remarkable 23 under par for the two events, and while the Open was a cliff-hanger at Turnberry – he did not go ahead until he rolled in a 60-foot putt for an eagle at the 17th – the USPGA emphasized his superiority as he waltzed off with the trophy by a six-shot margin.

Tony Jacklin 22

FULL NAME: Anthony Jacklin

BORN: Scunthorpe, England, July 7, 1944

MAJOR CHAMPIONSHIPS: US Open 1970; Open 1969

For a generation of Britons the name of Tony Jacklin will always be held in unrivalled affection. He came along at a time when British golf was in the doldrums and he raised it to such an extent, that despite the attentions of a vintage Jack Nicklaus and a prime-time Lee Trevino, he was, for a time, unquestionably the best golfer in the world.

Jacklin played the game with consummate style. He was not tall, but his swing was a model of technique and he always possessed a touch of charisma. And he had a year of living imperiously.

It started with the Open at Royal Lytham in 1969, and a victory characterized by Henry Longhurst's immortal words describing Jacklin's drive down the 18th hole: "Oh, he's struck it for miles," he said, and there was such joy in his voice that it brooked no argument about who was going to win. Later that year Jacklin returned to the Lancashire coastline to be involved in the famous halved match with Nicklaus that ensured a shared Ryder Cup.

The following June he walked away with the US Open at Hazeltine, practically lapping the field. Who could stop him? Nature found a way. A month on at the Open at St Andrews and Jacklin raced to the turn in 29 shots before lightning halted his progress, as if the gods were upset at his impertinence. When he returned the following day the momentum had gone, and he finished fifth. Two years later Lee Trevino ended it completely, with the luckiest Open win of all time. Jacklin, the victim, was a broken man.

There was some measure of revenge as his European team ended a Ryder Cup famine lasting 28 years, beating Trevino's American side at The Belfry in 1985. It was the second of four wonderful stints as captain, and no one before or since – on either side – has come close to matching his brilliance in the role.

Tony Jacklin – for a time he was the best in the business

Billy Casper 21

FULL NAME: William Earl Casper Jnr

BORN: San Diego, CA, June 24, 1931

MAJOR CHAMPIONSHIPS: Masters 1970, US Open 1959, 1966

SELECTED CAREER HIGHLIGHTS: Winner of 51 US Tour events; member of eight Ryder Cup teams and never on a losing side

It was perhaps Billy Casper's misfortune that his prime years as a golfer coincided with the time of the Big Three, which meant that whatever he achieved was bound to be overshadowed. Add that to his large, unattractive frame, and a style of play so methodical it bordered on the boring, and one can easily see why he is usually considered outside the elite group of American golfing legends.

Nothing, indeed, was impressive about Casper until he waddled on to the greens. Ben Hogan once said: "If he could not putt, he would be selling hot dogs behind the tee." It was, though, a fatuous comment. The fact is, Casper could putt, and because almost half the shots that any professional takes are expended on the greens, any player who can putt is bound to cover up a multitude of sins.

The other quality Casper had in abundance was a tranquillity on the course that stemmed from his Mormon beliefs. Long before it became fashionable among the American pros, Casper spread the gospel, speaking at over 200 church meetings every year.

This came about after a pact he made with his God at the 1966 US Open at the Olympic Club, one of the most dramatic major championships ever staged.

With nine holes to play, Casper trailed Arnold Palmer by seven shots and appeared to be playing for second place. But Palmer foolishly chased the tournament record rather than securing the trophy, and gradually expended shots through unnecessary aggression. Casper, meanwhile, played the nine holes of his life, totally undermining the argument of his detractors that he could not play. And after 72 holes he had drawn level.

Before the 18-hole play-off the following day, Casper drove to a Mormon church to give a lecture. He said afterwards that he had made a covenant with God that if he could win he would teach His Word. The next day Casper shot 69 to Palmer's 73. Clearly, God knew a good bargain when he saw one.

Casper's deadly putting stroke stemmed from his days as an indolent teenager. Not for him hours of toil in the San Diego sun beating balls. He stood under the shelter of a tree and practised his putting.

His father was an itinerant labourer and the young Casper followed him around for a year before spending some time on his grandfather's ranch in New Mexico. After his parents divorced, Casper went to live with his mother in San Diego.

His obesity made him the butt of every joke, and it also gave him an inner toughness that would serve him well in his chosen profession. He also had superb hand-to-eye co-ordination, which he demonstrated not only on the world's putting greens but also with a rifle. He was a scratch player with that, too.

He is also off scratch in the family stakes: Casper has 11 children and a dozen grandchildren.

The facts speak for themselves. In a time of American heroes, Casper carved out a fine record of his own: three major championships, 51 US Tour victories, five times winner of the Harry Vardon Trophy that goes to the player with the season's best stroke average, plus no fewer than eight consecutive Ryder Cup appearances. Make no mistake about it: history should judge that he was a true heavyweight in every sense of the word.

Billy Casper – a true heavyweight in every sense

Henry Cotton 20

FULL NAME: Sir Thomas Henry Cotton

BORN: Holmes Chapel, England, January 26, 1907

MAJOR CHAMPIONSHIPS: Open 1934, 1937, 1948

Henry Cotton was surely born 50 years too early, for how he would have loved the pampered lifestyle enjoyed by today's top professionals, the weekly six-figure cheques that are the reward for winning a tournament.

Cotton lived like a millionaire in the days when professionals were not paid in kind. He was Walter Hagen's most faithful disciple, and accordingly played his part in assuring that those who came after him were afforded the respect they deserved.

He never made any attempt to disguise the fact that he worked all hours at the game to earn money. He was once handed a cheque for £52 for finishing runner-up in the French Open, and told the organizers: "It is almost an insult to give such a ridiculously small sum of money to some of the world's best golfers. You've got to pay if you want the best."

That was Cotton: he would embarrass anyone who denied him what he felt he was worth and, such were his talents both for the game and repartee, the tactics worked. By 1931 he had built a £10,000 house, kept five servants, and even topped the bill at the Coliseum Theatre for £400 a week demonstrating his golf swing.

On the course he played several rounds that have become part of golf folklore, and none more so than at the 1934 Open at Sandwich, where he led the field after three rounds by ten shots. That was largely courtesy of an astonishing 65, a score that would remain the championship record for 43 years. Dunlop, his sponsors, were so impressed that they named a ball after it. Indeed the Dunlop 65 is probably the most famous golf ball to have been manufactured this century.

Cotton was born in 1907, the son of a prosperous iron founder. Whereas most professionals scrimped and saved during their early years, Cotton went to Alleyn's public school and gained his taste for privilege.

He excelled at cricket, but was banned from playing after refusing a caning. Asked what he would do while his peers were competing, Cotton replied: "I'll play golf, sir."

He turned professional at the age of 16, and four years later finished ninth in the Open at St Andrews. Cotton was so impressed by the technique of the winner, a certain Bobby Jones, that he decided to go to America "to find out what made them tick".

Whilst there he marvelled at how well the American professionals were treated, making for a stark contrast with the disdain that was shown toward them at home.

In all he would win three Open Championships, and, among British players who have taken up the game since the First World War, only Nick Faldo can match that. Cotton would surely have won more if the Second World War had not robbed him of some of his best years.

At the end of his career Cotton became involved in both journalism and golf-course architecture; his designs included Penina in Portugal, while in the print game he became the golf correspondent of the *News of the World*, a position he would hold for more than 30 years.

It is an indication of the respect in which he continues to be held that at Arnold Palmer's Bay Hill club in Florida, a Cotton report on one of Palmer's Open wins holds pride of place in the men's locker room.

Henry Cotton – the British player whose record only Nick Faldo can match

Harry Vardon 19

FULL NAME: Harry Vardon

BORN: Jersey, Channel Islands, May 9, 1870

MAJOR CHAMPIONSHIPS: US Open 1900; Open 1896, 1898, 1899, 1903, 1911, 1914

SELECTED CAREER HIGHLIGHTS: Leading member of the Great Triumvirate of Vardon, Braid and Taylor

Harry Vardon was golf's first supreme stylist, his swing a study in effortless grace. No one has ever managed to equal his haul of six Open Championships that straddled either side of the last century. He also won the US Open in 1900.

It was Vardon who popularized the overlapping grip, although it is a common misconception to think he invented it; it might be known as the Vardon grip, but the concept belonged to another. Vardon used it to such devastating effect, however, that even today it is the grip favoured by most professionals.

In addition his name is immortalized through the award of two prestigious trophies on either side of the Atlantic that both carry his moniker. The Harry Vardon Trophy goes to the player with the leading stroke average on the US Tour, and the winner of the Order of Merit on the European Tour.

Vardon was introduced to the game in Jersey, where he worked as a caddie. When his brother, Tom, went to England and made some money at the game, Harry soon followed.

His first job was at a nine-hole course at Ripon in Yorkshire, but it was as the professional at Ganton that he first made his name. When he arrived, J.H. Taylor was the great name of the day, but the members were so confident that their man could defeat the then Open Champion that they raised the money to stage an exhibition match. Vardon did not let them down. He won eight and six.

The confidence that victory gave him was obvious a month later when he succeeded Taylor as Open Champion. Together with James Braid, this pair would dominate the Open for an era, and they became known as the Great Triumvirate.

Vardon was the best of the three, with ball striking so pure that he saw no need to take a divot. From 1896 to 1903 he was absolutely at the peak of his powers, and with four Open titles under his belt already anything seemed possible.

But just as the future dawned with inviting possibilities, Vardon was struck down by tuberculosis, from which he never completely recovered, although there were two more Open victories, in 1911 and 1914.

There was also one memorable showing at the US Open in 1913 that would mark the awakening of interest in golf in America. Over the closing holes, Vardon was disputing the title with Ted Ray, before a little-known American amateur from the host club of Brookline called Francis Ouimet tied both of them with the back nine of his life. The next day it was Ouimet who won the play-off. A country erupted.

Vardon's play through the greens in that championship was as good as ever – but he suffered some pathetic putting lapses. They would get worse, too, and he would become one of the first sufferers of that dreadful affliction now known as the yips.

In his book *This Game of Golf*, Henry Cotton recalled "the unbelievable jerking of the clubhead in an effort to make contact with the ball from two feet or less from the hole".

Amazingly for such an accomplished ball striker, it was not until well into his retirement that Vardon managed his first hole-in-one. He died in 1937, and is buried in a churchyard close to the South Herts club where he was the professional for many years.

Harry Vardon – an unprecedented six Open titles

James Braid 18

FULL NAME: James Braid

BORN: Elie, Fife, February 6, 1870

MAJOR CHAMPIONSHIPS: Open 1901, 1905, 1906, 1908, 1910

James Braid's legacy is considerable. He was a founding member of the Professional Golfers' Association, which will celebrate its centenary with much pomp and circumstance, not to mention a Ryder Cup at its headquarters, in 2001; he was also a notable course architect, with perhaps the King's Course at Gleneagles his most well-known design – and where a hole, Braid's Brawest, is named after him. He also helped enhance and develop the reputation of the two marvellous courses at the club that became his first love, Walton Heath.

First and foremost, however, he deservedly ranks among the finest 20 golfers who ever lived. Braid won the Open five times in the space of just ten years, from 1901 to 1910, and although the century is about to draw to its close, no one else has managed to win more during it.

Even in retirement he remained a considerable golfer. "This tall, stooping ruddy-complexioned Scot is one of the wonders of the golfing world," Henry Cotton wrote. "Despite his years, his recent golfing exploits seem to increase his game, for he beats his age by an ever-increasing margin; at 78 he celebrated his birthday with a 74. I write in 1948 and he still plays a round every day it is fine, on occasions going round twice – and he was born in 1870."

As the last sentence indicates, Braid devoted his life completely to his sport. In childhood he never spent any time playing football like his peers, because that was time wasted from the links. In his biography of Braid, Bernard Darwin wrote: "Some readers may complain that there is too much golf in this book. To them I must reply that this is inevitable, since golf was James's life."

Braid showed promise from an early age on the links at Elie. He was a joiner by trade and used to practise every evening, despite a walk of several miles. Braid was a long hitter, but, like his great rival Harry Vardon, it was on the greens that he betrayed what weakness he had.

Still, word about his prowess spread, and his apprenticeship as a joiner stood him in good stead when he was offered the post as clubmaker at the Army and Navy Stores in London in 1893.

He found time to continue to practise his golf, and in 1894 entered for the Open at Royal St George's, finishing tenth. Two years later, at Muirfield, he finished sixth. One year on and he was runner-up to Harold Hilton over the latter's home course, Hoylake.

In the early years of the new century it was Braid who dominated as J.H. Taylor's powers waned and Vardon struggled with tuberculosis.

In summing up this most worthy of lives, Darwin, as ever, found the right words. "I think everyone recognized in him modesty, dignity, reticence, wisdom, and a deep and essential kindliness," he wrote. "They would also call him almost instinctively a great man. Great is one of those adjectives which we are unable to define, and if we are wise, we shall resolutely decline to try. We know what we mean by it; we naturally and unhesitatingly apply it to some people, and James was one of them."

James Braid – no one has won more Open titles this century

Greg Norman 17

FULL NAME: Gregory John Norman

BORN: Queensland, Australia, February 10, 1955

MAJOR CHAMPIONSHIPS: Open 1986, 1993

SELECTED CAREER HIGHLIGHTS: Winner of 18 US Tour events and 55 tournaments worldwide

What to make of Greg Norman has become one of golf's classic debates. Is he the Great White Shark, or the Great White Flag? Was he supremely unlucky under pressure, or supremely foolish? Was he one of the great players of all time, or simply a sheep in wolf's clothing? As ever in these matters, the truth in each instance probably lies somewhere in between.

Certainly there is a fatal flaw present, which is the only possible explanation for all the endless failures to win a major championship in America when in contention to win. Simply put, Norman is vulnerable when placed under extreme pressure.

But equally the positives should not be overlooked, and those centre around a sublime talent and the pleasure that he has given during his years at the top. Only Severiano Ballesteros of his generation can rival him on that score.

Norman has been responsible for some of the great rounds of golf that have ever been played. Three in particular stand out. The first was in 1986 at Turnberry, when he conquered atrocious conditions and an awesomely difficult course to shoot 63, a card that Tom Watson later described as "the finest round by any player in any tournament in which I have been a competitor".

Seven years later, at Sandwich, Norman came close to such perfection again when he shot 64 in the final round to hold off the challenge of many of the most redoubtable competitors, Faldo, Langer and Pavin among them. Langer afterwards described it as the finest round he had seen, while by the side of the 18th green the wise old denizen Gene Sarazen said he never thought he would live to see such golf played.

Yet Norman played it again at Augusta in 1996 when he equalled the course record with a 63. This time, however, the round proved meaningless in the final analysis as he concluded with a 78 to blow a six-stroke lead.

His detractors would say that this sums Norman up: brilliant one minute, hopeless when it really matters. Certainly the line of failures has been spectacular, with countless pushed shots on the 18th hole at Augusta costing him glory.

But he has been unlucky, too. Bob Tway holed a bunker shot to beat him for the 1986 USPGA Championship; nine months later Larry Mize holed a freak chip to steal a green jacket off his back.

Norman's other weakness is also his drawing card. Like Arnold Palmer before him, he would often go for the daring play rather than the sensible one. Unlike Palmer, though, he has enjoyed a remarkably long career at the highest level. Even after missing almost the whole of 1998 with a shoulder injury, Norman still rebounded with a win in his first tournament back and gained a creditable third place in the first major of 1999, the Masters.

Like many a man when he reaches 40, Norman looked around and found other interests. These days he is as actively involved in his many business ventures as in playing the game, and some spectacular successes have helped pay for a line of trappings that used to be the preserve of Hollywood movie stars, not golfers.

So, what to make of Norman? A great life, and an all-time great golfer - just. But such was his talent and the opportunities he had to join the immortals that this story will probably always be regarded as golf's ultimate tale of what might have been.

Greg Norman – a sublime talent dogged by what could have been

Peter Thomson 16

FULL NAME: Peter William Thomson

BORN: Melbourne, Australia, August 23, 1929

MAJOR CHAMPIONSHIPS: Open 1954, 1955, 1956, 1958, 1965

SELECTED CAREER HIGHLIGHTS: Between 1952 and 1958, in addition to winning the Open four times, he was runner-up on the other three occasions

than just his exploits on the course. Indeed, one might have to go back to Bobby Jones to find another player with such a diverse spread of interests. Painter, television commentator, newspaper columnist, parliamentary candidate, student of wine, classical literature, and classical music; sometimes it is a wonder that he ever found the time to squeeze in playing golf.

unsuccessful in America. From 1953 to 1959 he amassed no fewer than 42 top-ten finishes, and this despite leaving every July to return to Australia. Furthermore, the fifth of his Open titles was claimed at Royal Birkdale against a field that contained every great name of the day: Palmer, Nicklaus and all.

It is true, however, that his style of play was particularly suited to links golf, where a player has to think his way around to make a score. While many a great golfer would rage at an unfair lie and lose the plot for a couple of holes, Thomson would always remain serene, retaining his unshakeable self-belief.

The one time he did commit himself completely to America Thomson proved practically unbeatable. This was in 1985, and the US Senior Tour. He shelved his other interests and devoted himself to playing there, winning ten times. But at the end of it he was bored.

Now he travels the world in his various capacities in the game,

Peter Thomson – in more recent times the true master of the links

Given that range of other pursuits, it follows that Thomson played the game in a cerebral fashion. He was no fan of Arnold Palmer's smash-and-find-it tactics, believing instead in the simple virtues of finding the fairways, locating the greens and, above all, preparing thoroughly and remaining cool at all times. He once said that he could tell a top player simply by meeting him and seeing him under pressure: "The great player has one vital quality: calmness," he said.

His record shows such a level of success in Britain and Ireland in the 1950s as to lead to the conclusion that the decade could best be summed up as "the Thomson era". But what about America? Why no joy there when confronted with players of the quality of Hogan and Snead? It has led some to conclude that Thomson was one step down from the very highest calibre of player. It is a harsh judgement. For a start, he was not completely

most notably as one of the great architects around today. Not for Thomson some of the modern obsessions with water, water, everywhere. "I have come to the conclusion that a great golf course can be judged by the number of balls that a reasonable player needs to finish it," he said recently. "If it is a one-ball course, with all the usual features in place, then it must be a great course. If you need a dozen balls to play it, like some of these courses where fairways are surrounded by man-made lakes, then it is rubbish."

Thomson was perfectly suited to golf. He was not a loner, but he enjoyed his own company, and would often whistle Beethoven's Appassionata while making his way around the course. No golfer proved more the words of the old saying: "If you can keep a level head while all around are losing theirs..."

One of the most fascinating things about sport is to wonder how

Bobby Locke 15

FULL NAME: Arthur D'Arcy Locke

BORN: Germiston, South Africa, November 20, 1917;

MAJOR CHAMPIONSHIPS: Open 1949, 1950, 1952, 1957

SELECTED CAREER HIGHLIGHTS: Winning the South African Open on nine occasions

players who dominated their own era would have fared if placed among another generation. Clearly players like Jack Nicklaus and Ben Hogan would have succeeded, whatever the time frame. But what about Arnold Palmer, whose years of success seemed particularly suited to the optimism that abounded in the early 1960s? In particular, what about Bobby Locke?

One can only think that he would surely have had to change his style completely to have stood a chance. For in these days of dauntingly narrow fairways and snooker-table greens, how could Locke have hoped to compete with a hook that was so pronounced he often aimed right of the target by as much as 45 degrees before winging the ball back towards the flag?

Even with the balata balls on the market these days, no player could hope to stop the ball with such a shape of shot to a flag cut on the right of the green behind a bunker.

Having said that, Locke was so good on the greens he would probably have just played to 20ft and holed more than his share of putts. Uncannily, even those seemed to go into the hole from the right, which led some pros to speculate that he even hooked his putts.

Locke was a golfer from the time he could walk. By the age of eight he was playing off 14 and competing in events from nine. Six years later he was down to scratch, and soon after was dominating the golf scene in his native South Africa. He won his first tournament, the Transvaal Open, in 1934 and thereafter made the South African Open practically his own.

Locke turned professional in 1938 at the age of 20 and quickly made his presence felt in Britain. The war intervened, however, and when it ended he went to the USA. He was not popular. He was slow and deliberate and talked little. Still worse, he was a winner. In two-and-a-half seasons he played in 59 tournaments, winning 13 of them. The insular Americans were not best pleased.

When Locke decided to stay in Britain the year after winning the 1949 Open, it was alleged that he had broken various contracts to play in America and he was barred from the US Tour. Nothing to do with the fact that the Americans were jealous of his success, of course, and regarded it almost as an act of trespass. Nothing at all...

Locke contented himself with playing in Europe and enjoyed many successes, most notably in the Open. For a decade he and the Australian Peter Thomson dominated the Championship, Locke collecting the trophy on four occasions.

His reputation as a loner did not stand four-square with his great passion, which was playing the ukulele. He even played it once on stage at a Southport nightclub!

In February 1960, Locke was on his way to visit his wife when his car was struck by a train on a level crossing. He was in a coma for several days and virtually lost the sight of one eye. But for that accident, his supporters believe he would have gone on at least to match Peter Thomson's record of five Open Championships.

Bobby Locke – nine-time winner of the South African Open

Raymond Floyd 14

FULL NAME: Raymond Loran Floyd

BORN: Fort Bragg, NC, September 4, 1942

MAJOR CHAMPIONSHIPS: Masters 1976; US Open 1986; USPGA 1969, 1982

SELECTED CAREER HIGHLIGHTS: Winner of 22 US Tour events

Everything you ever needed to know about Raymond Floyd was present on the day he collected the US Open trophy at Shinnecock Hills in 1986. It was present in his own golf, as he mastered one of the world's great links courses with a supreme variety of shots. Mostly, it was there in the Press conference that Payne Stewart gave afterwards by the side of the 18th green.

Stewart and Floyd had been partners on the final day, and it was the former who leapt out of the blocks with a wonderful front nine of 33. He then birdied the 11th, a scary par three. From there on in, however, Stewart could not quite shake the feeling that a pair of malevolent eyes was burning a hole in the back of his head. "I could not quite escape the Raymond Floyd stare," he admitted.

In fact, he had been like a rabbit caught in headlights when confronted by the formidable game face of a true competitor. Floyd had a swing for which, had you seen it on the practice ground, you would have told him to find a good coach. But from 70 yards in he was brilliant and, as far as mind games were concerned, he had few equals.

This was seen to best effect when he was on his knock and in front. Most players regard leading for a long time as the most difficult part of the game, because it uses up mental reserves. Floyd, meanwhile, was a front-runner *par excellence*; three of his four major championships were won in this manner, including the 1982 USPGA at Southern Hills, where he opened with a round of 63, which he considers the finest 18 holes he ever played.

His skills at front-running were perhaps seen to best effect, however, in the 1976 Masters, where he opened with a 65 to top the leader board. Would he be nervous? You must be joking. He followed it with a 66 to lap the field. There would be no respite. He went on to equal Jack Nicklaus's then-record 72-hole score of 271 to win by no fewer than eight shots.

What Floyd would have won had he dedicated himself to his sport in his early years one can only imagine. But our Raymond was a party animal, at one time managing an all-girl rock band called the Ladybirds. No one could say he did not make up for it in his later years, indeed at 49 he was still playing Ryder Cup golf, and a valuable role at that.

At the time of the 1991 match in Kiawah Island, Fred Couples was an enormously skilful player whose brain scrambled when confronted by a pressure situation. Floyd asked to be his partner, because he believed he could bring the best out of him, and on the first day the pair were invincible. Couples went on to play in all five matches, losing only one. It proved the making of him.

Some players have games that are suited to various courses, but only at the US Open did Floyd feel less than comfortable. It is surprising, too, that he never won an Open because he was a wonderful improviser. But the prize that would have enabled him to become only the fifth player to win all four major championships always eluded his grasp and, given the competitor he was, one fancies there will be one of two regrets lingering toward the back of his mind about that.

Raymond Floyd – only the Open championship evaded his grasp

Byron Nelson 13

FULL NAME: John Byron Nelson Jnr

BORN: Fort Worth, TX, February 4, 1912

MAJOR CHAMPIONSHIPS: Masters 1937, 1942; US Open 1939; USPGA 1940, 1945

SELECTED CAREER HIGHLIGHTS: Winner of 11 consecutive tournaments in 1945, 54 US Tour events in total

No golfer before or since has amassed a winning streak quite like that of Byron Nelson in 1945. All right, it is fair to point out that the fields were not as strong as they might have been because many of the best American professionals were still in military service. Ben Hogan was serving in the Army Air Force, for example. Even so, 11 tournament victories in a row deservedly earn Nelson a place among the giants who have played the game.

Backing up this judgement are some of the statistics amassed during the streak. Nine of the victories came in strokeplay tournaments, and Nelson played them in 113 under par for a barely credible stroke average of 67.92 shots per round. By all means place an asterisk against the record, but only a fool would dismiss it out of hand.

Nelson was born in the same year and brought up in the same postal district as Hogan, and for years both toiled to make a living. It was Nelson who struck gold first, winning the Masters in 1937, the US Open in 1939, and the USPGA in 1940. Indeed, it would be 1946 before Hogan won his first major, and by that time the haemophilia that had exempted Nelson from war duties was preventing him from being in peak condition on the course. He retired from full-time golf to his Texas ranch shortly after, paid for by the war bonds that he received for his victories the previous year, cash being in short supply at the time. He still lives on the ranch to this day.

Nelson may have been only 34 when he took that course of action, but he left a great deal to remember him by. There was another victory in the Masters in 1942, beating his great adversary Byron Nelson in the play-off – the last before it was halted for the war. Then came 1945, the year golf became locked in a full Nelson.

In all, he won 18 of the 30 tournaments he entered, and finished second in seven others. In strokeplay events, his average lead over those who finished second measured out at 6.3 strokes.

There is a tendency to dismiss Nelson as a lightweight when compared with the overwhelming achievements of his peers at the time, Hogan and Sam Snead. Certainly he cannot match them for longevity. But he made his contribution all the same to an American triumvirate who dominated golf in the period.

It was Nelson who first seized upon the opportunities that the invention of steel shafts opened up in the 1930s, and while many players liked to hit the ball with a soft draw or a fade, he preferred to concentrate on the straight blow.

Byron Nelson – 11 successive tournament victories in 1945

One player who appreciated the contribution that Nelson made to the game was Tom Watson, and the pair have remained lifelong friends. It was Nelson who became an important force behind Watson's development both as a golfer and a man, who guided him during his early years as a pro and told him not to fret, that the victories would come.

Since 1968 the Byron Nelson Classic has been a staple fixture of the US Tour, and Nelson himself has actively promoted it every year. It says something about his standing in the game that while the courses it is now played upon are hardly from the top drawer, the field always is.

Nick Faldo 12

FULL NAME: Nicholas Alexander Faldo

BORN: Welwyn Garden City, England, July 18, 1957

MAJOR CHAMPIONSHIPS: Masters 1989, 1990, 1996; Open 1987, 1990, 1992

SELECTED CAREER HIGHLIGHTS: Eleven consecutive Ryder Cup appearances 1977–1997

Nick Faldo's status as the greatest golfer to emerge from the British Isles was assured in the most dramatic manner imaginable, as he scaled back the six-stroke lead that Greg Norman had held with a round to play to win the 1996 Masters. It was his sixth major championship victory, and it took him to another level on the pantheon. In terms of majors won, Harry Vardon remains the most successful Briton with seven. But even his most fanatical supporter would surely concede that his collection of titles compiled in a far less demanding era does not compare with the feats of Faldo.

Unlike his great rival for so long, Sandy Lyle, Faldo was not born into golf. Indeed, his parents never picked up a club, and it was only because he loved to watch sport that he tuned in to the 1972 Masters. What unfolded before his eyes had an electrifying effect: here was a sport where you were totally in control of your own destiny and did not have to rely on team-mates to succeed. It awoke the competitor within, and the next morning Faldo was inquiring about lessons at Welwyn Garden City Golf Club.

If Severiano Ballesteros has been the most charismatic of the clutch of great Europeans who emerged in the 1980s, then Faldo's contribution has been equally influential in other respects. He became the role model for the Swedes, for example, who agreed with his approach that what happens away from the course has a direct bearing on it. For the last 20 years, for example, Faldo has worked out most days in the gymnasium.

It was following the 1983 Open at Birkdale that Faldo made the decision that would contribute so much to his success. Frustrated with his swing after it had crumbled under pressure on the final day, he sought counsel from a young instructor called David Leadbetter, who was just starting to make a name for himself.

Taking on Faldo was quite a gamble for Leadbetter. He knew that if it worked it would help make his reputation, but if it failed he would struggle to recover. For two years it appeared the latter would be the case. Faldo dropped from contention, and the Press leapt up and down, wanting to know what he was doing entrusting his fate to a guru with no record of success.

Over the following 11 years the pair certainly answered their critics, and both reaped all the benefits. Both are now multi-millionaires, with best-selling books and videos to their names. They pioneered the new approach, where seemingly a player cannot go anywhere without his coach trailing behind.

Faldo's best year was in 1990 when he won both the Masters and the Open, the first European to win two majors in the same year. He did it by showing a steady nerve under pressure, and by now he had an intimidating reputation among his peers of a player who became inspired when the going got tough. It was apparent once more when John Cook handed Faldo the 1992 Open, and most spectacularly at Augusta in 1996. Alongside the majors, Faldo is most proud of his 11 consecutive appearances in the Ryder Cup, which is a record.

In 1997 there was a blip on his CV, and a poor year was followed by what became an inevitable split after 14 seasons from Leadbetter. And so the future remains uncertain. But the desire is still there for more successes and while that remains, together with the best nerve of any player of his generation, then further major championship successes cannot be discounted.

Nick Faldo – a record 11 Ryder Cup appearances

Lee Trevino 11

FULL NAME: Lee Buck Trevino

BORN: Dallas, TX, December 1, 1939

MAJOR CHAMPIONSHIPS: US Open 1968, 1971; Open 1971, 1972; USPGA 1974, 1984

SELECTED CAREER HIGHLIGHTS: Winner of 27 US Tour events

Lee Trevino's story is one of the most colourful ever told. From the humblest of backgrounds he rose to win three Open Championships – of Britain, the United States and Canada – in the space of one month. He lost two fortunes during his lifetime, but fortunately made three, and all the time he played golf with a style that made him a popular favourite with galleries all over the world.

What most people never realized, however, was that this was all an act. Away from the course Trevino was a loner, preferring room service to nights spent at the bar. In a role reversal compared with most players, the only jokes that Trevino ever cracked were inside the ropes, not outside.

Trevino was born the illegitimate son of an immigrant Mexican grave-digger, into a house that had neither electricity nor running water. That he became one of the top dozen players ever to play the game makes his tale the personification of the American dream.

His swing looked exactly what it was: home made, and home grown. How he made it work for him, though – shaping the ball this way and that – and he harnessed it to a ferocious competitive streak honed while betting at golf for money that he did not own. Once asked during an Open about pressure, he replied: "Pressure is playing for $10 when you've only got $3 in your pocket."

Trevino did a bit of caddying while he was growing up, but it was not until he joined the marines at the age of 17 that he expressed any interest in playing the game. When asked if he would like to try the sport to show them what he could do, Trevino promptly responded with a round of 66.

When he returned home to Texas in 1961, Trevino found plenty of locals who were perfect prey for a hustler. Which is just as well, because he struggled during his first seven years as a professional.

Indeed it was not until 1967 that he came to public notice, finishing fifth in the US Open, and being named rookie of the year. It was enough to persuade him to join the tour full-time, and the following year he caused a sensation, defeating Jack Nicklaus to win the US Open, in the process becoming the first player to break 70 in all four rounds of the championship.

Trevino was in his prime in the early years of the 1970s. He won the aforementioned trio of events in 1971, and then returned to Muirfield the following year to complete a remarkable defence of the Open Championship. For all the world it looked Tony Jacklin's title to win, but Trevino holed unlikely chip shots and

Lee Trevino – the ultimate hustler

mesmerizing putts – "God is a Mexican," he later exclaimed.

Back injuries prevented him from fully capitalizing on his talents and self-belief, but there was still one more remarkable victory in the 1984 USPGA Championship at the age of 44.

Six years later Trevino retired to the US Senior Tour and the most lucrative stage of his career. Over the course of the following seven seasons, he won no fewer than 27 tournaments and nearly $11 million in prize money. It is safe to assume his current house has both electricity and running water.

Gene Sarazen 10

FULL NAME: Eugene Sarazen
BORN: Harrison, NY, February 27, 1902
MAJOR CHAMPIONSHIPS: Masters 1935; US Open 1922, 1932; Open 1932; USPGA 1922, 1923, 1933
SELECTED CAREER HIGHLIGHTS: Winner of 18 US Tour events; inventor of the sand wedge

Gene Sarazen's fulsome contribution to the development of golf is apparent every time a player steps into a bunker. In the early 1930s he developed a club with a heavy sole that transformed the playing of these shots, and which became known as the sand wedge. Naturally he became an expert with it, although it was perhaps Gary Player who has most cause to thank Sarazen for his invention.

The little American of Italian stock (he was born Eugene Saraceni) was the first player to win each of the four major championships at least once, and he completed the quartet by virtue of one of the most famous shots ever played.

It was at the 1935 Masters, and he trailed Craig Wood by three shots when he came to the 15th. Sarazen knew he had to be bold, and duly went for the green at this par five with a four wood. The ball rolled into the hole for an albatross, and Sarazen won the subsequent play-off. At the time the Masters was only in its second edition, but Sarazen's shot introduced the event to the world.

Like many great players born in the first half of the twentieth century, Sarazen came into golf as a caddie. His father was a carpenter, and at first it seemed he would join him in that profession. Health reasons forced him to find an outdoor pursuit, and so he took to golf. And by the age of 21 he had three major championships to his name.

Sarazen's great hero when he came into the game was Walter Hagen. He loved his style, his flamboyance – and he took great delight in beating him. After winning the 1922 USPGA Championship, some of the gloss was taken from Sarazen's victory because Hagen had not been present. So a "World Championship" exhibition match was organized between the two. Hagen was five up at one stage, but Sarazen showed all the tenacious qualities for which he was renowned; he ended up winning three and two.

Sarazen has lived for all but two years of this century, and his name has been prevalent in golf for much of that time. In 1973, at the age of 71, he was invited back to the Open at Troon for a sentimental appearance. He still stole some of the headlines, playing the famous 8th hole, the Postage Stamp, in just three shots for two rounds: holing in one with a five iron in the first round, and then holing a bunker shot for a birdie two the next day.

In 1993 Sarazen returned again to the Open, 70 years after he had first played in the event. The grand old man of golf was there by the side of the 18th green as Greg Norman played one of the finest rounds of all time to collect the trophy. Sarazen was suitably magnanimous in his praise: "I never thought I would live to see golf played like this," he said.

He was known as "The Squire" because of his love of farming. Until his death this year he lived in quiet retirement on Marco Island in Florida. In these days when most professionals live behind steel gates and high walls in enclosed communities, Sarazen's telephone number was listed in the local directory.

Gene Sarazen – the first man to win all of the four majors

Tiger Woods 9a

FULL NAME: Eldrick Tiger Woods
BORN: Stanford, CA, December 30, 1975
MAJOR CHAMPIONSHIPS: Masters 1997
SELECTED CAREER HIGHLIGHTS: Twelve-stroke win at Augusta is a record victory margin in a major championship

Lest we forget – and sometimes it is quite easy, given what he has achieved – Tiger Woods is still some way short of his twenty-fourth birthday. This is no place, therefore, to assess his position among the great players of the century; rather, we should acknowledge the unique contribution he has already made to today's game, and wonder what he might realize in the years to come.

Certainly, we do not need any years to pass to appreciate that 1997 stands as a milestone year in the annals of the game. It was enough that a young man, in his first start in a major championship as a professional, waltzed off with the green jacket at the Masters with a record victory margin of 12 shots tucked into his top pocket. But the impact that victory had was simply astonishing, as Woods held not only golf in thrall but large parts of the sporting world.

It is estimated that two million people under the age of 18 tried golf for the first time in America in the week that followed Woods's win. Television viewing figures showed that more than twice as many people followed his progress compared with the epic shootout the year before involving Nick Faldo and Greg Norman.

A month later, Woods turned up at the Byron Nelson Classic, and so did half of Texas. This is one of the US Tour's most revered events, and every player who has ever achieved anything has played in it. Still, the record attendance for the week before Woods showed up was 200,000. In 1997 it was a 350,000 sellout. Indeed, organizers estimated that 500,000 would have turned up during the week had tickets been available.

It was a pattern that was repeated for the rest of the year as Woods became the hottest sporting ticket in America. In a period of 12 months, the average age of spectators at golf tournaments must have dropped by 20 years. They changed colour, too. Golf was no longer an all-white sport.

The eerie thing is that Tiger Woods's father, Earl, practically foresaw all this happening. The photographs of Woods almost from the year dot are revealing, not to mention frightening: at nine months he was sitting in a high-chair watching his father hit golf balls; at 18 months he was climbing down from the said high-chair, and picking up a small plastic club and replicating his father's swing; at two he was entering a competition for those aged 10 and under; at three he broke 50 for the first time for nine holes, albeit with one concession allowed for his age – he was allowed to tee up every shot. At three he appeared on television and was asked why he was so good. "Pwactice," he said. "Pwactice."

The world, therefore, had plenty of notice as to what would happen next. What did happen is that the prodigy continued to achieve feats far beyond what was supposed to happen for his age, something we could say is still happening to this day.

Woods won the US Junior Championship three years in a row, when no one before had won more than one, and he went straight from there to the US Amateur, which he also collected three years in succession, again an unprecedented feat.

During these golden amateur years, Woods played in six major championships and made the cut in four of them. In the 1996 Open Championship at Lytham, he equalled the 18-hole amateur record with a 66 and also the 72-hole record of 281.

One performance in the 1996 US Amateur, however, emphasized his qualities. In the final he was up against Steve Scott, and at lunch in the 36-hole match he was five down. Even with four to play, he was still two adrift. But under the watchful eye of Nike President Phil Knight Woods, he continued the uncanny trick he shares with all the great players – the ability to seemingly "will" putts into the hole when it really matters.

Woods went on to win at the first extra hole against Scott, and it proved a fitting end to his amateur career. He turned pro, was awarded contracts worth $60 million from Nike and Titleist, and now had to live up to the hype.

It is fair to say he managed it. He was permitted seven starts on the US Tour at the end of the 1997 season, from which he had to make enough to gain his card if he were to avoid the qualifying school. Woods did more than that. He won two events to finish the year in twenty-fourth place on the money list with earnings of $790,594. *Sports Illustrated* featured him on its cover. "One month that changed golf for ever," was the headline.

At the first event of 1997, Woods defeated Tom Lehman for the Tournament of Champions. Lehman, then Open Champion, could see the writing on the wall. "I may have been the player of last year, but Tiger is the player of the next two decades," he memorably said. "I'm holding off the inevitable, like I'm trying to bail water out of a sinking boat."

Woods would win three more tournaments in America that year, including his Masters success, to finish first in the order of merit. What could he possibly do in 1998 that would provide an encore?

If anything, he was more consistent, showing especially what he had learned at Royal Birkdale. In an Open marked by high winds, Woods played a wonderful series of improvised shots to finish third, one shot off the winning score held by his great friend, Mark O'Meara.

Woods has certainly learned much about the game from the veteran O'Meara. The result has been that he has carried the burden of expectation with a lightness of touch that makes him a wonderful ambassador for his sport.

In a biography that was written as recently as 1992, the black golfer Charlie Sifford wrote, with clear bitterness: "There is no place for a black man in professional golf. I'm 69 years old and

Tiger Woods – has opened golf up to a whole new audience

I've been playing this game since I was a little kid in North Carolina. I played for 15 years on the US Tour and I've been a regular on the Senior Tour since its inception. And I still don't see room for a black in golf."

Those words illustrate just how much Woods has changed the perception of his sport. As Tom Watson suggests: "Tiger Woods is the most important thing that has happened in golf in 50 years."

Seve Ballesteros 9

FULL NAME: Severiano Ballesteros Sota

BORN: Pedrena, Spain, April 9, 1957

MAJOR CHAMPIONSHIPS: Masters 1980, 1983; Open 1979, 1984, 1988

SELECTED CAREER HIGHLIGHTS: Winner of 48 European Tour events, and 72 tournaments worldwide

European golf was not in a strong position in 1976. Tony Jacklin and Peter Oosterhuis, the two leading British players of their generation, were making only fleeting visits to their home circuit having long since decamped to America. The USA, indeed, was the only place to be.

That is, until a charming boy with a disarming smile turned up on the doorstep at Royal Birkdale in time for the Open Championship. People had trouble pronouncing his name, much less know who he was as he drove off down the first.

But something singled him out from the start, if only for the fact he had a driver in his hands rather than the iron that practically everyone else used for safety. Ballesteros drove 25 yards left of where everybody else aimed that day; he cut the corner and his ball finished in the middle of the fairway. A star, as they say, was born.

Four days later, of course, the world knew his name, even if for some years later they would insist on calling him Steve in some parts of America. And if his first shot was true Ballesteros, so was his parting shot, an imaginative chip threaded through bunkers to four feet, setting up the par that enabled the boy from Pedrena in northern Spain to finish runner-up to Johnny Miller.

Over the next 15 years Ballesteros set the game alight. Was there ever a more natural artist to play the sport? Certainly not around the greens, where his hands conjured up shots that came close to sorcery.

In the process he became Europe's answer to Arnold Palmer. Vast tracts of the continent began to take an interest in a sport they had hitherto thought as being purely for the elite; for the first time, young children had posters of a golfer hanging from their wall; in Britain he was a hero long after the country came up with heroes of its own.

There was more. In tandem with Tony Jacklin, Ballesteros breathed new life into the Ryder Cup, and this pair are primarily responsible for the multi-million-pound extravaganza that the event has become.

Virtually all the Spanish professionals who have distinguished themselves in Europe have done so via one of two routes: they are either sons of professionals or have worked as caddies. Ballesteros emerged through the latter route. His first club was a three iron, with which he learned to strike an amazing variety of shots on the beach near his home. It was here that he laid the foundations for the unique set of strokes that would form part of his repertoire.

When he emerged on to the professional stage, it was like Palmer had been reincarnated. Ballesteros hit the ball, found it, and then hit it again. Naturally he found himself in some troublesome spots, but such was his sense of destiny that Ballesteros never thought them beyond him. He believed he had been placed on this earth to become the greatest player of all time.

At just 22 he claimed his first major championship, the Open at Lytham. To say some of the Americans, and particularly Hale Irwin, were not happy is an understatement. One American journalist christened him the "car-park champion", on account of a tee shot at the 16th that had finished in a temporary car park. Ballesteros responded that he had played to there knowing he would get a free drop, and thus open up a clear avenue to the green – a cheeky answer that, it has to be said, does not bear close scrutiny.

Whatever the case, Ballesteros took his festering sense of resentment to America determined to gain respect. When he was announced on the tee as Steve Ballesteros, it only heightened his motivation. And in 1980, at Augusta, he had the last laugh. With nine holes to play, he was no fewer than ten shots clear of the field. "I was lucky," he told the American Press afterwards.

They took the hint, and four years later accorded him due recognition for a second Masters triumph. It was not enough for

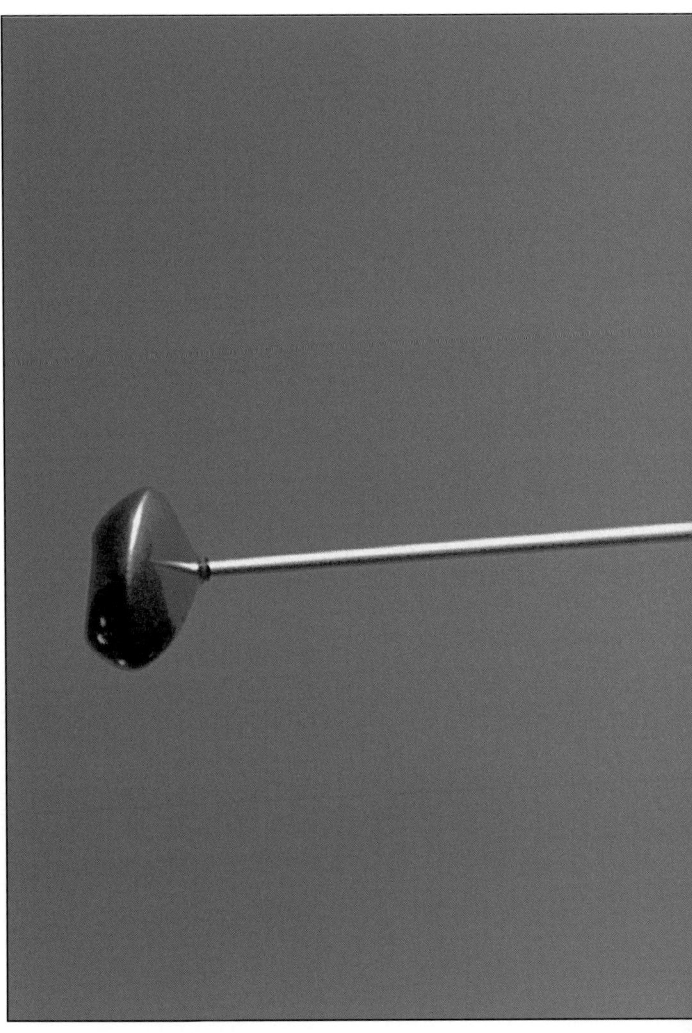

Severiano Ballesteros – was there ever a more natural artist to pla

Ballesteros, and it was Jacklin's genius to recognize this when the latter was named captain for the 1983 Ryder Cup.

Jacklin took Ballesteros aside and made him appreciate that here was the perfect arena not only for his talents but also his emotional grievance.

And how Ballesteros made the Americans pay and pay for their sleights! First with Paul Way, and then in a celebrated partnership with Jose-Maria Olazabal, he came close to appearing invincible in these matches.

In the process he became the unspoken leader of a new generation of Europeans who finally looked upon the Americans not with awe, but as peers who could be beaten. Nick Faldo, Sandy Lyle, Bernhard Langer, Ian Woosnam, Olazabal – all followed Ballesteros across the Atlantic and registered major championship victories.

And what of Ballesteros himself in this area? In 1984 there was one of the great Open victories over Tom Watson at St Andrews, where he holed for a birdie at the last and celebrated with a matador's thrust to all corners of the Old Course.

In 1986, however, came an episode that changed his life. Standing in the middle of the 15th fairway at Augusta on the final day, all was well; he had struck the perfect drive and now he was looking for the birdie four that would set up his third Masters triumph in just seven years. So what that an ageing Jack Nicklaus was charging behind, or that Greg Norman was in the picture? Ballesteros had destiny on his side.

One stroke was sufficient to alter such thinking for ever. The resultant four iron was struck "fat" and did not come close to clearing the water in front of the green. Instead of a four he took six; the green jacket went to Nicklaus instead.

There was one last glorious hurrah for Ballesteros in major championships – at Lytham in 1988, where he finished with a round of 65, one he would later describe thus: "Only once or twice in a lifetime does a man get to play that well."

There were still Ryder Cup victories to come as well, plus one memorable stint as captain at Valderrama in 1997, where some of his motivational tactics were reminiscent of Jacklin at his best.

But Ballesteros the golfer has been a sad sight for much of the past decade. With a sore back and priorities changed by the growth of a lovely family on whom he dotes, we are now left only with occasional glimpses of the innate genius that changed the face of European golf for ever.

Walter Hagen 8

FULL NAME: Walter Charles Hagen

BORN: Rochester, NY, December 21, 1892

MAJOR CHAMPIONSHIPS: US Open 1914, 1919; Open 1922, 1924, 1928, 1929; USPGA 1921, 1924, 1925, 1926, 1927

Heaven knows what Walter Hagen would make of golf today. Certainly he would love the lifestyle of today's modern professionals, with all its Hollywood-style paraphernalia. After all, he pioneered it. But imagine what the tabloids would make of a pro who turned up, as Hagen once did, on the first tee in a dinner suit, having been out on the town all night? Then there was his womanizing and gambling. Wherever he travelled, Hagen's black address book followed, filled – as he so beautifully put it – "with the names of friendly natives".

Imagine the fines that would follow from the sober authorities on the US and European tours at outbreaks of such behaviour? For Hagen, that would certainly go against the grain.

As for the public, there is absolutely no question that they would have loved this ultimate showman, as they did in his heyday, the 1920s. For here was Gatsby brought to life.

It was Hagen who took to the course in silk shirts, his plus-fours immaculately pressed. He always had an enormous golf bag, which immediately placed his opponent at a psychological disadvantage. He also insisted that professional golfers should not be treated like second-class citizens, and although he loved coming to Britain, he railed against the snobbery that he felt existed.

When he came to Deal in 1921, he was appalled to discover that the professionals were not allowed to change in the clubhouse, but had to use a room adjacent to the professional's shop. Hagen had voyaged to Britain in a first-class suite; he had left his belongings in a room at the Savoy and travelled down in a chauffeur-driven Daimler that also had a footman. Not change his shoes in the clubhouse?

Since there was no way around the rule, he insisted on his limousine being parked outside the clubhouse so that he could use the vehicle to change in.

He had made his point, as he did during the 1923 Open at Troon, when he and the winner, Arthur Havers, were invited inside the clubhouse for the presentation. Hagen said that he had been regally entertained in a pub all week, and that if the Royal and Ancient's officials wanted to present him with something for finishing runner-up they would find him there with his supporters.

The fact that somebody was prepared to stand up to the odious wisdom that prevailed at the time accelerated the pace of change toward professionals. These days, of course, they are looked up to as gods, rather than down upon.

Hagen learned his golf as club professional at Oakland Hills in Detroit. This was the playground of the lords of the car industry, men who had made great fortunes out of the first revolution with four wheels. They came largely from humble stock, and never forgot their roots; they treated Hagen very much as their equal – perhaps more than that, given that he had conquered a game they could not hope to master.

It left Hagen with a feeling that no one was better than him, and his great bargaining tool was his skill as a golfer. Hagen simply could not be ignored because his name alone drew the crowds.

Like a lot of great golfers, his forte was the recovery shot, and no one, not even Severiano Ballesteros, pulled it off with more panache. Hagen would march into the woods, and size up a shot from this angle and that. A frown would crease his features, then a smile; finally the shot itself, which invariably lived up to the build-up.

His skills from positions of difficulty, and his game around the greens, made him the complete matchplay golfer. Five of his 11 major championships came in the USPGA, back in the days when it was a matchplay tournament. Four of those successes were achieved consecutively.

This was his golden age, the 1920s, when his form in the Open was almost as good. After finishing sixth in 1921 at St

Walter Hagen – helped to pave the way for the modern game

Andrews, he won in 1922 at Sandwich, and then lost by a stroke the following year to Havers. In 1924 he won again, at Hoylake, but did not complete a defence the following year. He returned in 1926, however, to finish third at Lytham. After another absent year, he was back in 1928 to win at Sandwich and again in 1929 at Muirfield. Thus his record from seven appearances in the Open during that decade reads: four wins, one second, one third, one sixth.

Naturally, they were splattered with many memorable moments. One of them came in 1926, when he needed an eagle at the par-four 18th to tie with Bobby Jones. Hagen drove straight down the middle and then marched straight to the green to survey the shot that was left. Before he completed the long march back, he asked the referee if he could kindly have the flag removed.

Such arrogance would have been absurd if it had not been backed up by deed. Yet Hagen delivered. In that instance, the ball finished just a couple of feet from the hole.

One of his finest performances away from the major championship arena came in an exhibition match with his great rival, Bobby Jones. The match was played over 72 holes, with 36 taking place at Jones's summer retreat in Sarasota, FL, and the final 36 at Hagen's summer home elsewhere in the state at Pasadena.

For Hagen, the match represented something of a gamble. He demanded large sums for these exhibitions, and clearly a heavy defeat would have affected his market price. As it was, he did not have to worry. He gave an inspired performance, and won 12 and 11. It earned him a prize of $7,500.

At his peak Hagen was earning more than $250,000, which hardly equates to today's riches, but was a fortune for a professional at the time. Yet he never saw much of it. As he wrote on the front cover of his autobiography: "I never wanted to be a millionaire – I just wanted to live like one."

Bobby Jones once wrote of Hagen: "He goes along chin-up, smiling away, never grousing about his luck, playing the ball as he finds it."

Perhaps it is too much to ask today's professionals to play in such a fashion, given how much is now at stake. But they could learn much from Hagen's most famous saying: "In life, always take time to smell the flowers along the way." Indeed, we could all learn from it.

Sam Snead 7

FULL NAME: Samuel Jackson Snead

BORN: Ashwood, VA, May 27, 1912

MAJOR CHAMPIONSHIPS: Masters 1949; Open 1946; USPGA 1942, 1949, 1951

SELECTED CAREER HIGHLIGHTS: Winner of 84 US Tour events, and 182 tournaments all told, with 388 top-ten finishes

Sam Snead won more events on the US Tour than any other golfer. He is also the only player to win tournaments in six different decades, and was the first golfer to shoot 59 in competition. He also made 34 career holes-in-one, and is reckoned to have shot below his age on more than a thousand occasions. Even at 62, he was still good enough to finish third in the USPGA Championship behind Lee Trevino and Gary Player.

What do all these things tell us? That Samuel Jackson Snead was probably the most naturally talented golfer who ever lived. He certainly had the most graceful swing. But he was not without his flaws, and most of them were from the neck upwards. If Snead were around today, he would probably be called Greg Norman.

In all he won seven major championships but never the US Open, which continues to rankle even now, when he is well into his eighties. He played in it on no fewer than 26 occasions, but never came closer than his excruciating loss in 1939, when he made a triple-bogey eight on the 71st hole at Spring Hill in Philadelphia to blow a two-shot lead.

"I have figured it," he said years later. "If I had shot 69 in the last round, I would have won nine US Opens. I can go back to places and you won't believe what happens."

Small wonder, therefore, that history has placed an asterisk next to his name. Indeed it has been said of him that he would never have lost a tournament if Ben Hogan's head had been placed on his shoulders.

Endearingly, Snead is aware of his shortcomings. He blames the distribution of his genes, which saw him get more from his father than his mother. "My daddy was a naughty man," he said. "He would speak to you in passing with only a 'Howdy'. And if you touched his head you had a fight on your hands. He'd go to the barbershop and say: 'Hurry up and get this over with; I don't want you to fool with my head.' Boy, I never saw a man so touchy. I suppose I got a lot of that from him, but I'd like to have had all my characteristics and character from my mother. She was easy-going, and one of the few people I ever saw who had 'front sight' as well as hindsight."

Snead was the youngest son of five and grew up in the backwoods of Virginia. Legend has it that he carved his first club from a branch that had broken off while he was climbing down from a tree. The truth is not quite so lyrical, but still remarkable; he did carve out clubs from the limbs of swamp maple.

His swing was all his own work, too, inspired by the sight of his brother Homer flashing huge drives across the farms near their homestead. Soon Sam Snead graduated to a set of cast-off clubs and then a caddying job, which later led to an assistant's post at the Greenbrier, the club with which he has long been associated. It was while there that he was invited to make up a four with Lawson Little, the former British and US amateur champion, and two past US Open winners, John Goodman and Billy Burke. Snead shot 61.

It was so good that the members immediately carried out a whip-round to raise some funds to allow him to try his hand at the professional circuit. He went to California with $300 in his pocket and with the intention of finding, as he called it, "a real job when the money ran out". It never did. He won $600 the first week and then, in his third start, the $1,200 first prize in the Oakland Open. Snead won on four further occasions that year, and finished runner-up in the US Open.

So began a long and winding road that never came to a dead-end until his forced retirement. "Only time I ever went home was at the end of every year to do my taxes," he laughed.

"Slammin' Sam" became his moniker, and he was quickly a popular figure with spectators, who had not had anyone to idolize since the retirement of Bobby Jones. The down-to-earth Snead – with his perfect swing, laconic dry humour and a hill-billy image that was part real, part cultivated – fitted the bill.

His one appearance in the Open came at St Andrews in 1946. It is said that as he came towards the Old Course, he pronounced: "Why the hell have they built a golf course on this cow pasture?" Snead remained unimpressed to the end, railing against the austere accommodation and the food that was prevalent in a country still picking itself up following a long war. It did not stop him winning, however, his final-day rounds of 74 and 75 giving him a four-stroke victory margin over fellow American Johnny Bulla and South African Bobby Locke.

In 1949 Snead won the Masters and the USPGA in his home state of Virginia. But perhaps his best year came in 1950 when he won no fewer than 11 tournaments and earnings of £35,758. It was not without its disappointments, however. Ben Hogan returned following his car accident, won the US Open, and was declared golfer of the year.

To say that hurt Snead would be an understatement. He never did play a full US Tour schedule thereafter, becoming further embroiled instead in something he has enjoyed all his life: hustling.

"I used to play a $25 nassau against everybody in a group," he recalled recently. "The trick was always to play as good as it took to win. Never wear them out, because they won't come back. It was like pickin' up corn."

Snead was a founder member of the US Senior Tour, and naturally cleaned up on it for years. He still turns up at the odd tournament and the competitor is still there, as he curses every bad shot. He remains one of the honorary starters at the Masters, driving off from the first, and he never fails to dissect the fairway, the ball usually travelling 200 yards in the process, even in his mid-eighties.

In terms of career longevity, no one will surely ever come close to Snead. He is also close to being out on his own in the field of story-telling, something learned from his youth when the family would sit around the fireside for supper.

His achievements, therefore, stand comparison with virtually every golfer who ever lived. But they will always beg the question as to just how good he could have been, had he been blessed with a few more genes from his mother.

Sam Snead – the only player to have won tournaments in six different decades

Tom Watson 6

FULL NAME: Thomas Sturges Watson
BORN: Kansas City, MO, September 4, 1949
MAJOR CHAMPIONSHIPS: Masters 1977, 1981; US Open 1982; Open 1975, 1977, 1980, 1982, 1983
SELECTED CAREER HIGHLIGHTS: Winner of 34 US Tour events; US Player of the year five times

At both the start of his career and towards its close, Tom Watson was a man who struggled under pressure. But for nine glorious years in between, no one could touch him, not even a rampant Jack Nicklaus. In particular Watson dominated the Open Championship, winning five times at five different venues. He also won the US Open along the California shore at Pebble Beach. He was, truly, the master of the links.

In all he won eight major championships, including two that fully deserve the use of the word "epic" to describe them. The first was the Open at Turnberry in 1977, when Watson and Nicklaus staged a shootout that could not have been more potent had it been held at the OK Corral.

This one became known as the "Duel in the Sun" and perhaps Hubert Green, who finished a distant third, summed it up best. "Well, I won the Open in which everyone bar two people were playing," he said.

Only three players broke par in the Open that year and yet one of them, Nicklaus, would shoot 65 and 66 for the last two rounds and still find that it was not good enough. Watson, who never led at any stage until the 71st hole, carded two 65s.

This event saw him at his imperious best, a wonderful confidence in his putting method allowing him to go boldly for the hole in the sure knowledge that if he knocked it three feet past, he would still hole the return.

A victory that was almost its equal came at the US Open at Pebble Beach in 1982, and again it was Nicklaus who was left with the runners-up spoils. This seemed highly unlikely when he sat in the scoring cabin knowing that Watson would need to par the last two holes to tie, and the prospect for the first of these had surely disappeared when he hooked wildly from the tee to this perilously difficult short hole.

When he found his ball, Watson knew that what confronted him was a death-or-glory shot. There was no hope of stopping the ball on the fast, sloping green, so the pitch from thick rough either had to disappear into the hole or roll 20ft past the pin. So Watson took dead aim – and holed. It was one of the great major championship shots, and just for good measure he birdied the last as well. A month later he won his fourth Open title, this time at Troon.

Watson turned professional in 1971 after a good amateur record. He did not go to Stanford University on a golf scholarship, however, like so many who eventually turn up in the professional ranks these days. Watson was a psychology student, and he had to study to graduate.

His professional life soon made him a textbook case. He clearly had a rare talent, but he seemed frightened of winning. Any solutions, doc?

Watson came up with his own. Rather than being frightened of winning, he soon demonstrated simply that he had not learned how to win. American sportswriters had labelled him a choker, but that perception began to change when he collected the 1974 Western Open, and was altered for ever when he won the Open at his first attempt at Carnoustie in 1975.

Thus began his much-celebrated love affair with the links courses of the British Isles. Even to this day he will come over early for the Open and practise on some of the links in Ireland or Scotland.

One of his favourite venues is Ballybunion, that jewel on Ireland's West Coast, and last year Watson described it as one of the great thrills of his life when he returned there to play with his son for the first time.

And once he had acquired the knack of winning, Watson became intoxicated by it. Other players became intimidated at the thought of him lurking just a stroke or two behind. In 1982 a young Nick Price struggled over the closing holes at Troon to hand victory to Watson.

When he won again at Birkdale the following year it seemed certain that Watson, then just 34, would go on to tie and then surpass Harry Vardon's record of six Opens, achieved in a much less demanding era.

What lent strength to such feeling was the manner of his fifth triumph, where he concluded matters with a raking long iron into the heart of Birkdale's 72nd green. It was struck with such commanding authority that little seemed beyond him.

Twelve months later, at St Andrews, Watson was once more lurking, history within his grasp. This was the one he dearly wanted to win, not just for Vardon's record, but because none of his Open wins had yet come at the home of golf.

When he came to the 71st hole, Watson knew he needed a par to keep pace with Severiano Ballesteros, who was playing ahead. His long iron was struck with his usual unerring accuracy when faced with such pressure situations, but this time, however, the shot was not perfectly judged. The ball bounced on the green and over it, over the road, and against the wall that frames the back of this celebrated hole.

There was no way he could get down in two from there, and the resulting bogey occurred just as Ballesteros holed from 15ft on the last for a birdie. For the first time, Watson had gone head to head in the Open and lost.

It had a dramatic effect on his career. Now doubts appeared where before there had been none. He had all the money he could ever wish to have, and it corrupted his desire. It would be several years before the hunger returned, and by that time his putting was shot. Watson consoled himself in drink, and as ever it made things worse. In 1996 his long marriage to his college sweetheart Linda was dissolved.

And so making history at the Open remained elusively out of reach. So did his goal of winning the USPGA, and therefore becoming the fifth player to win all four of golf's major championships. Hard times, therefore, had come to the master of the links but, as ever, he took control of his own destiny. In 1997 he showed that he could still be a contender, winning on the US Tour at the age of 48.

Now Watson is happy again. Now the desire has returned for one last glorious Indian summer, before the sunset claims him, as it does every golfer.

Tom Watson – victorious in the epic Open at Turnberry in 1977

Gary Player 5

FULL NAME: Gary Jim Player

BORN: Johannesburg, South Africa, November 1, 1935

MAJOR CHAMPIONSHIPS: Masters 1961, 1974, 1978; US Open 1965; Open 1959, 1968, 1974; USPGA 1962, 1972

SELECTED CAREER HIGHLIGHTS: Winner of more than 100 tournaments worldwide, including 21 in America, and five World Matchplay titles

They were known as the Big Three, which might be the only time that anyone ever referred to Gary Player as big. But no one ever played golf with more heart and resilience than the little man from South Africa, no one ever worked harder to put in what nature left out. The result is a CV that speaks for itself: more than 100 tournament wins worldwide, including nine major championships.

That he is the finest-ever golfer not to have carried an American passport is really beyond dispute. From tee to green he was good enough, and around the greens he was magical. In truth he was probably the junior partner of the Big Three – the other two members were Arnold Palmer and Jack Nicklaus – but that was more a reflection of the company he was keeping than any sleight on his own play.

And in the sixties the Big Three dominated golf. For six straight years, no one else was allowed a look-in at the Masters, and no fewer than 10 other major championships came their way during that golden decade. Player contributed handsomely to the total, to the extent that by the age of 30 he had become just the third player, alongside Ben Hogan and Gene Sarazen, to win all of the majors at least once. Nicklaus, of course, would later sign up.

Yet Player was more than just a one-decade golfer. What singles him out for true greatness is the span over which his triumphs were achieved. Indeed Player would win major championships in four different decades, a feat of longevity which is a tribute not only to his dedication to his sport, but also to his fanatical pursuit of fitness. Now well into his sixties, Player is still lean and trim, still does hundreds of stomach exercises every morning, and still wins occasionally on the US Senior Tour.

Such heady riches hardly seemed likely when he first arrived in Britain in 1955 after his father Harry, a mining engineer, had financed his trip courtesy of an overdraft from a kindly bank manager.

The leading British players took one look at his strong grip, his puny frame, and a backswing that seemed to rise vertically, and advised him to take the next plane back home and pursue another career that would not leave him penniless. Thus began a professional life of always proving people wrong – within 10 years he had become a dollar millionaire.

How he managed this wonderful feat was not just through his own talents and sacrifice. Player was smart, too. He looked at the top British pros and learned from their swings. He was pushy, always seeking advice, and sometimes the answers were less polite than "sorry Gary, not today". But Player never stopped pushing himself, and never took no for an answer. He put up with every discomfort. The first time he went to St Andrews for the Open he was so short of money that he slept the first night in one of the course's many pot-hole bunkers.

But the first of his victories followed in the Dunlop Masters at Sunningdale in 1956, when he shot two 64s in a 72-hole winning total of 270; no one underestimated him thereafter.

That victory earned him his first invitation to the definitive version of the Masters at Augusta, and thus began a love affair with the place that continues to this day.

When he joined the US Tour, Player applied the same principles that had got him thus far. He studied the teachings of Ben Hogan and practised as diligently as the great man. When he was not practising, he was exercising. His arms became so strong that he could do over a hundred press-ups with a suitcase full of clothes on his back.

Before the fifties were through, Player won his first major championship, the Open at Muirfield. Two years later, at the age of 25, he became the first non-American to win at Augusta, signalling to the runner-up – a gentleman by the name of Palmer – that he was not about to have things all his own way. The following year Player collected his first USPGA Championship, defeating Kel Nagle in a play-off, and then, in 1965, his only US Open title. So, in the space of seven years, he had won all four majors.

Practically every player, of course, would have been happy with such a litany of achievement, and particularly those who spend so many days of the year travelling. Not Player. He just looked around for other worlds to conquer.

He found one glittering target in the newly formed World Matchplay Championship at Wentworth. Here, perhaps, he found the perfect format for all his many talents, and what a shame it was that he was never able to utilize them in the context of the Ryder Cup.

At the time, however, the World Matchplay arguably carried more kudos. There were only eight invitees and none was refused. But Player was indisputably the king, right from the moment of his first triumph against Tony Lema in 1965.

This match has gone down in the annals as characterizing everything that anyone ever needed to know about Gary Player, the hallmark of a life lived against the odds. Seven down after 19 holes, he clawed his way back to win at the 37th; in the final he beat Peter Thomson for the first of five victories, a total that only Severiano Ballesteros has matched.

Player's time in golf has not been without controversy. During his twenties he was a supporter of Verwoerd's policy of apartheid, which led to problems at the 1969 USPGA Championship, when he was targeted by black militants. On the 10th tee, he had a cup of ice thrown in his face, and was labelled a racist. He still went

Gary Player – came a long way since spending his first night at St Andrews in one of the courses bunkers

on to finish second, a performance that he rates as highly as any of his major successes.

These days Player calls Nelson Mandela the "finest human being on this earth", and funds a black school near his home. He says he supported Verwoerd because he thought paternalism of whites towards blacks was the only hope for progress. He happily admits his mistake.

Player's love of the game remains as strong as the day he arrived in Britain for the first time, courtesy of his father's monetary gift. Now the wheel has turned full circle: now it is today's young players, like Lee Westwood, who come to him for advice.

Player, then, has witnessed all the changes, the enormous growth in popularity, and the way in which the game has clung fiercely to its core ideals. He can be proud of the part he has played.

Arnold Palmer 4

FULL NAME: Arnold Daniel Palmer

BORN: Latrobe, PA, September 10, 1929

MAJOR CHAMPIONSHIPS: Masters 1958, 1960, 1962, 1964; US Open 1960; Open 1961, 1962

SELECTED CAREER HIGHLIGHTS: Winner of 61 US Tour events; US Player of the Year 1960, 1962

Anyone seeking a definitive answer to the explosion of interest that occurred in golf in the latter half of the twentieth century would have to begin with Arnold Palmer. He is nothing less than the modern game's patriarch.

It has been said so often that Palmer took a black and white sport and splashed it with colour that it has become almost a cliche. Yet how else to explain the detonation that occurred in the late 1950s when grey men with a grey approach suddenly found among their midst a man who stood on the tee and whacked the ball as hard as he could, found it, and then whacked it once more?

In an introduction that would mirror Tiger Woods's almost 40 years later, Palmer brought with him a new audience comprising both men and women, thus paving the way for golf to move away from its closed, elitist image.

Palmer has been such an inspiration that ever since his first appearance at the Masters in 1958, several patrons have returned every year and not watched anyone else play.

Never once, however, has he lost his sense of humility. At Augusta, Palmer does not walk down the middle of the fairway as is customary, but by the ropes in order to shake hands with people he now regards not as fans but friends.

At Bay Hill Golf Club in Orlando, FL, where he lives, and which has become irrevocably associated with his name, Palmer still turns up every day when at home to play with the members.

When he retired from the US Open in 1994 at the Oakmont course just a few miles from where he was raised, Palmer did not indulge in any backslapping on the eve of the event. He did not attend any celebration dinners in his honour. Instead he was to be found nearby at Latrobe Golf Club, where his father taught him to play the game, repairing the binding on a broken old driver. No wonder he has always been regarded as the professional's professional.

The son of a pro, Palmer took to the game from an early age, marrying plenty of natural ability with an innate aggression. He learned a valuable lesson early on, however, that aggression was fine so long as it was controlled. It came during a junior match when, following a muffed shot, he hurled a club over some trees in a fit of rage. On the way home his father, Deacon, let him know what he thought. "He said that it was a gentlemen's game and that he was ashamed of me," Palmer recalled years later. "He told me that if he ever saw me do such a thing again, he was through with me as a golfer."

Palmer enlisted in the US Coast Guard while a teenager, but still managed to win the Ohio State Amateur when on leave. After his discharge in 1954 he collected the US Amateur title. Already, the agents were queuing up to sign the new kid on the block.

Eventually a new entrepreneur by the name of Mark McCormack would secure his signature. Forty years on they are still together, and still making money. Palmer remains one of the most highly paid golfers, even if little of it these days comes through prize money.

When Palmer first captured the imagination in the professional game, it was McCormack who came up with the deals that would be the forerunner to the multi-million contracts that are around today.

Not that he was difficult to sell. Wherever he went, people wanted to watch Arnold Palmer. The Open Championship was dying on its feet in the late 1950s, as the top Americans such as Ben Hogan and Sam Snead kept giving it a miss, thus undermining its credibility. Palmer came over and loved it from the start. The people loved him back.

Over the next few years he persuaded his peers to keep returning with him and so, single-handedly, breathed new life into the event.

Palmer adored the crimpled fairways, the different shots he was required to play, the deep knowledge of the spectators.

He won the Open at Troon in 1961 and then again at Royal Birkdale the following year with a triumph that added fuel to the legend. One ahead of Dai Rees coming down the stretch on the final day, Palmer drove wildly at the 15th (now the 16th). It seemed that his thrashing style had caught up with him, particularly after spying his ball, which had nestled deep into the rough. Surely his only option was to chip back to the fairway?

Palmer thought otherwise. He took a six iron and delivered a blow to the turf so hard that the divot was almost the size of a cricket pitch. To the amazement of all the spectators, the ball bounded on to the front of the green. Palmer secured his par and won by one. In the crater that was caused by the removal of Palmer's ball a plaque was laid, commemorating one of the great blows in Open history. It still stands today.

And what a run of form continued. In 1960 Palmer had stood on the 17th tee at Augusta needing two birdies to win the Masters, and he duly achieved them; later that year he was seven strokes behind the leader in the US Open, but he caught him with a devastating final round of 65.

Nothing seemed beyond him. He won seven major championships between 1958 and 1964. Then, extraordinarily, the star that had arrived before our eyes dimmed almost as quickly.

Palmer found himself overshadowed by Jack Nicklaus, and then he started to lose as spectacularly as he had once won. Now his aggressive style was hindering him. In the 1966 US Open he had a seven-shot lead with nine holes left, and had only to play sensibly over the inward half to claim the title. But he went instead for a tournament record, and not only lost out on that, but the title as well. Each year he set his sights on winning the USPGA and thus becoming just the fifth player to win each of the four major championships once. Each year it remained beyond him.

Not that his audience deserted him. He never did win another major championship of any kind but even in old age, when his swing is a caricature of its former glory, the galleries still turn up.

As for today's professionals, for whom seven-figure annual earnings have become commonplace, they should thank the Lord for the day he put Arnold Palmer on this earth. For without Palmer, it is doubtful they would have had the opportunity to earn a fraction of their wealth.

Arnold Palmer – came to be regarded as the professionals' professional

Bobby Jones 3

FULL NAME: Robert Tyre Jones Jnr

BORN: Atlanta, GA, March 17, 1902

MAJOR CHAMPIONSHIPS: US Open 1923, 1926, 1929, 1930; US Amateur 1924, 1925, 1927, 1928, 1930; Open Championship 1926, 1927, 1930; Amateur Championship 1930

The life and times of Bobby Jones have left a gilded legacy that assures his name will never be forgotten as long as golfers draw breath. He only played in 31 major championships, for example, and yet somehow won 13 of them; he remains the only player ever to have completed a grand slam; each year the Masters is held over the Augusta course he imagined and cherished; and every year, too, countless thousands of golfers make pilgrimages to the Old Course at St Andrews where the 10th hole carries his name.

Several generations have now passed that never saw him play a shot, and yet he continues to have more selfless devotees than any other player. Only Arnold Palmer comes close to Jones in terms of the reverence with which his name is mentioned.

Jones grew up at East Lake Golf Club, in a suburb of Atlanta. By the 1970s the place had fallen into a state of disrepair; the wealthy middle class moved out and, when the city put up subsidized housing, the problems really began.

It is entirely a tribute to Jones that one Atlanta property developer went into this area infested with crime and drugs and restored East Lake, so that today it stands as a shrine to the man and what he stood for.

Why does Jones remain such a compelling figure, that people would risk millions of pounds in the name of his memory? He was perhaps the game's most fascinating player because he had an equally full life away from the course as on it.

Jones could write like an angel and, when he retired from competitive golf at the age of 38 with no worlds left to conquer, he became a first-class lawyer.

Yet it would be wrong to paint him as some sort of saint. For much of his golfing life he had to cope with a terrible temper that would today cause him never to be off the back pages of the newspapers. One unforgettable episode occurred during his first visit to St Andrews for the 1921 Open Championship. Frustrated by a course full of hidden pot bunkers and uneven lies on the fairways, Jones tore up his card after 11 holes and, legend has it, drove his ball into the River Eden.

It was an action that he would always regret. Jones not only made his peace with the Old Course, he came to love it. In 1958, when he was made a freeman of the city, he famously said: "I could take out of my life everything except my experiences at St Andrews, and I'd still have had a rich, full life."

The son of an Atlanta lawyer, Jones was an infirm child and for a while there was a fear that he would not survive infancy. He was introduced to golf when he was just five, an East Lake member cutting down an old long iron for him.

At 14 he was the archetypal prodigy, playing in the 1916 US Amateur and reaching the quarter-finals. He made a name for himself from the first round, when he defeated a former champion, Eben Byers, who was also noted for his volatile temper. It is said they made for quite a scene, these two club throwers, and afterwards Jones explained blithely that he had won because Byers ran out of clubs first.

It was perhaps not a coincidence that while he learned to cure his temper, Jones did not win anything of significance. Seven years would pass before he collected his first US Open. Having said that, Jones was also studying hard for the bar during this period.

One thing Jones never fully came to terms with was the stress of competitive play. During one championship it is said that his weight dropped by no less than 18lb. When the galleries flocked to watch him, Jones would often ask a friend to walk along each fairway. They never exchanged a word; it was as if Jones simply required insulation from the crowd.

But once he had learned how to win, he learned how to cope. For eight glorious years from 1923 he would prove to be the greatest player of his era. All of it was preparation for 1930, the finest year that any golfer has enjoyed before or since.

As an amateur, the grand slam available for Jones consisted of the US Open and US Amateur Championships, and the Open and Amateur Championships in Britain. It was his declared aim to win all four before he retired.

The first of these was the Amateur, which just so happened to mean a return to St Andrews. Jones displayed what he had learned, and eventually defeated Roger Wethered seven and six in the final. Now he had a fortnight to prepare for the Open at Hoylake and, despite never being at his best, he claimed the title.

The third leg of the grand slam was at Interlachen, near Minneapolis. Again he had a fortnight to rehearse, and the confidence he had gained in the UK was obvious as he swaggered five strokes clear of the field with a third-round 68. Although he dropped six shots at three short holes in the final round, a 40-foot birdie on the last gave him title number three. Now for the long wait until the autumn and the US Amateur.

The venue was Merion, where Jones's career had begun 14 years earlier. In the time before the championship, he contemplated how close he had now come to his goal, and if he did not win it this time then there would be no further chances. By now, however, he was at the height of his powers, and the final was no contest. He completely outplayed Gene Homans to win eight and seven.

It is fair to say that Jones did not have the same depths of competition to overcome as someone trying the modern grand slam; hence the fact that this is a feat that will now never be completed.

Bobby Jones – the Masters is his legacy

All the same, he still had to rise above the same mental demons, the self-doubts. And among the professionals of the day were Walter Hagen and Gene Sarazen, who were hardly two mugs.

Retirement allowed him to cash in on his new-found fame, something that would have been impossible had he stayed an amateur. He also bought a piece of nursery land near Augusta and turned it into America's most famous golf course.

In 1934 Jones decided to host an invitational tournament for his friends, but rejected suggestions to call it "The Masters" on account of it being pretentious. But wiser counsel prevailed, and though in declining health and wheelchair-bound in his later years, Jones lived long enough to see the event establish itself as one of today's grand-slam events, and both venue and tournament remain a lasting testament to his genius.

Ben Hogan 2

FULL NAME: William Benjamin Hogan
BORN: Dublin, TX, 1912
MAJOR CHAMPIONSHIPS: Masters 1951, 1953; US Open 1948, 1950, 1951, 1953; Open 1953; USPGA 1946, 1948
SELECTED CAREER HIGHLIGHTS: Winner of 57 US Tour events; USPGA player of the year four times; US leading money winner five times

No one ever made indomitable courage and sheer force of will go as far as Ben Hogan. At the age of 25 he had still to record his first win as a professional, and he would be 34 before he finally claimed his first major championship. But what he lacked in innate talent he compensated for with other human qualities that make this the most remarkable golf story of all.

Picture him, for example, a frail and crumpled wreck, in a critical condition after a horrific car accident in 1949. He had a fractured pelvis, shoulder, leg and ankle, and internal injuries so serious that for a time it was thought he would not live. Then a blood clot caused complications that resulted in him being bound in a plaster cast from his neck downwards.

Now remember him as the golfer who came back from that parlous state, not only to walk again but to enjoy his greatest years; who four years on would become the only golfer before or since to win three major championships in the same year.

And so although, on the surface, his tally of nine majors is only half that compiled by Jack Nicklaus, what makes the life story of Hogan so compelling is just what he went through to achieve that number.

Furthermore, how many majors would Hogan have won but for the debilitating effects of that accident, plus the onset of war just as he was making a name for himself?

Equally destructive as far as his quest to be the greatest golfer of all was concerned was his loathing for overseas travel, which meant he made but one appearance in the Open Championship at Carnoustie in 1953. Yet it says much about the man that, all these years on, his appearance is still mentioned in that part of Tayside in whispered reverence.

In many ways, it was a performance that encapsulated Hogan the golfer. He arrived at Carnoustie a week before the championship began, to grow accustomed both to the different shots he would be required to play and to the weather.

It must have come as quite a culture shock. Two US journalists who were present likened playing at Carnoustie to golf on the moon. Hogan, meanwhile, opined nothing, instead relying on constant practice to teach him the parts of the fairways that would allow him easier access to the flags.

For a fortnight he conducted a masterclass. After the most thorough preparation by any player for any major championship, he proceeded to shoot lower in each round than the one before, beginning with a 73 and concluding with a 68. To the delight of many in the stampeding galleries, he won the title by a massive six strokes from Sam Snead to add to the US Open at Oakmont and the Masters already claimed that year.

No golfer before or since has managed the feat of three majors in the same season, and what makes it still more impressive is that Hogan competed in only three: he did not get home in time from the Open to play in the USPGA. When he did make it to America, it was to a ticker-tape parade and a chat with President Dwight D. Eisenhower.

Who would have thought this would happen to the youthful professional who struggled with a hook, and consequently struggled to make a dime? Hogan never lost faith, nor his practice-ground ethic. In 1938 he claimed his first professional title, and then dominated the US Tour money list from 1940 onwards. In 1948 he won no fewer than 13 tournaments, including the US Open and the USPGA. Then came the unkindest of fates.

On February 2, 1949, Hogan was driving east of Pecos, TX, in thick fog when the car in which he and his wife Valerie were travelling collided with a Greyhound bus. In order to protect his wife, Hogan leant across – an action which almost certainly saved his life, since the impact was so forceful that the engine ended up in the back seat. The news of his critical condition was flashed all over America, and prayers were said in churches throughout the land. They were answered.

Hogan lived, and slowly and painfully rebuilt his shattered life. He defied the doctors and learned how to walk again. Then he started hitting golf balls, venturing on to the course in a motor scooter. He built up his body with constant exercise.

His first shots were a caricature of him at his best, and it was not only in recognition of his achievements that Hogan was named as the 1949 non-playing Ryder Cup captain. Most officials also thought his career was at an end.

Yet 11 months on, Hogan was ready to play golf again, and interest in his appearance at the Los Angeles Open at Riviera in 1950 reached unprecedented levels. When he was introduced on to the first tee, the crowd roared their approval. Despite being in obvious pain, Hogan carded a 73; he was back.

Indeed, he eventually finished in a tie on 280 with Sam Snead, which necessitated a play-off he would lose. Still, for those watching in the gallery, it was a performance beyond concern; Hogan would soon be back winning again.

The problem for the player, however, was that the operation to stem the blood clot caused by his accident had had serious implications for the use of his legs. Hogan was in agony – so much so that rather than have to face a play-off, he expressed the hope that Snead would beat him during normal play. How would he ever get round this problem?

And so it was that Hogan learned to conserve his energies and concentrate instead on the major championships. The following spring he won the Masters and later the US Open. Three years later he enjoyed arguably the greatest professional year of all.

But the constant striving took its toll, as did the countless hours on the practice ground. For Hogan was a loner, at times chillingly cold and aloof.

Several years ago he made a rare public appearance to attend a "Golfer of the Century" award run by *Golf* magazine. Hogan thought he had been invited because he was the winner; imagine the shock, therefore, when Nicklaus's name was read out instead. It was too much for Hogan, who refused to join in the applause. He was nicknamed the "wee ice mon" by the Scots at Carnoustie, and so he remained until his death.

But his legend is secure, as is his legacy. It is contained in his book, *The Five Fundamentals of Golf*. As far as how to play the game is concerned, it is golf's bible, and even after all these years it remains unsurpassed.

Ben Hogan – the only player to have won three majors in a year

Jack Nicklaus 1

FULL NAME: Jack William Nicklaus
BORN: Columbus, OH, January 21, 1940
MAJOR CHAMPIONSHIPS: Masters 1963, 1965, 1966, 1972, 1975, 1986; US Open 1962, 1967, 1972, 1980; Open 1966, 1970, 1978; USPGA 1963, 1971, 1973, 1975, 1980
SELECTED CAREER HIGHLIGHTS: Winner of 71 US Tour events; USPGA Player of the Year five times

It is a measure of the man and the scale of his achievements that at the end of this momentous century he stands tall as unquestionably the greatest golfer of all time.

Such is the depth of his record and the manner in which it was compiled that if a straw poll of every player worldwide were conducted tomorrow on the subject, there is no doubt that support for him would run at more than 80 per cent of the vote. Any politician would kill for such popularity.

Simply put, Jack Nicklaus did it his way. Truly great sportsmen are supposed to come from impoverished backgrounds, their desire fuelled by years of deprivation. Nicklaus was the son of a wealthy pharmacist and was brought up in a prosperous suburb just outside Ohio.

Similarly, golf is supposed to be the game where supreme sacrifices are made, where families are jettisoned in the pursuit of greatness, where no time is available for anything else. Nicklaus has been married to the same person all his professional life, and they have raised five children. The Golden Bear had time for them all. Indeed Lee Trevino once said: "Heaven knows what Jack would have achieved if he had put the game first all those years instead of his family."

A record of 18 major championships will have to suffice, one that will surely stand the test of all time. Almost as impressive, however, was the number of times he finished second, third or fourth: a total of 36 in all.

And so Nicklaus was not only the greatest winner of all time but its most prolific runner-up, too, and every disappointment showed him at his ambassadorial best. In 1982 there looked like there would be victory in a memorable US Open at Pebble Beach, when Tom Watson, his nearest rival, hooked his tee shot wildly to the 17th.

But Watson holed the unlikeliest of pitch shots, and birdied the last as well to beat Nicklaus by two. Who was the first out of the scoring cabin to shake his hand, to put a congratulatory arm around his shoulder? Nicklaus could have been forgiven for thinking it was personal, given that Watson had claimed an even more epic contest between the two, at the Open at Turnberry in 1977.

Such envy, however, was never part of his make-up. "You son of a gun, you've done me again," he said, with the broad smile of one with total respect for his conqueror.

Nicklaus, in fact, rewrote the book on sportsmanship, and it is hard to pick his greatest achievement: showing the world how to win, or the fact that in golf there is only one way to win, and that is fairly.

Whatever the case, for as long as the game is played, people will talk about the moment in the 1969 Ryder Cup at Birkdale, when the destiny of the contest boiled down to a singles match between Nicklaus and Tony Jacklin.

At the time Jacklin was the darling of the home crowd. He had just ended an 18-year wait for a home winner of the Open, down the road at Lytham. But when he got to the final green, he raced his birdie putt three feet past the hole, and now he had to sink it to secure the tie.

As he waited for Jacklin to putt, Nicklaus looked around at the scene. He thought about the great disappointment that would follow should Jacklin miss, and he wondered if the Ryder Cup should be decided on such a mistake. He concluded that it should not. He walked over, picked up Jacklin's ball marker, and said to him: "I don't think you would have missed it, but I did not want to give you the chance."

In the clubhouse, the American captain Sam Snead seethed afterwards at the gesture, but in the years that have passed the game as a whole has proffered a different judgement. Jacklin himself has no doubts, calling it recently the greatest act of sportsmanship in the history of golf.

That Nicklaus would be remembered with such reverence and fondness seemed unlikely when he first came to national prominence. Unhealthily overweight, he was instantly cast as the villain, while Arnold Palmer played John Wayne. Matters came to a head during one tournament in New York, when Nicklaus spotted a banner in the crowd being held by a spectator who was standing in thick rough. "Put it here fat boy," it said. Nicklaus went home and lost three stones in weight. The transformation in his popularity had begun.

What was never in doubt was his ability as a golfer. The 1960 US Open is considered epochal, as the best golfers of three different generations converged on the final afternoon at the head of the leaderboard. Appropriately enough, it was the present in the shape of Palmer who won out over the past (Ben Hogan) and the future (Nicklaus). In the locker room afterwards, however, Hogan had no doubts as to what would happen next. "I tell you, I have just played with a kid who, if he had been a couple of years older, would have won this thing by 10 shots," he said, to anyone who cared to listen.

He was right, too. Nicklaus did have it all. He hit the ball longer than anyone else, and with unerring accuracy. On the greens he seemed to have an uncanny ability to "will" the ball into the hole. By 1963 Bobby Jones, the founder of the Masters, was famously pronouncing: "He plays a game with which I am not familiar."

Unlike Palmer, Nicklaus's style was built to last. Even in 1998, at the remarkable age of 58, with hips that were rapidly coming

Jack Nicklaus – with 18 major titles to his name, he is undoubtedly the greatest of them all

to the end of their useful life, he was still notching a top-ten finish in the Masters.

That was Nicklaus to a tee. Every time someone thought he was finished, he came back to prove them wrong with his indomitable will. It happened in the 1980 US Open at Baltusrol, but perhaps his most evocative triumph came at the 1986 Masters at the age of 46.

"Nicklaus is all washed up," said a cutting in the local paper on the eve of the tournament. Nicklaus pasted it to his refrigerator door. Four days later he surged past the two greatest players of the day, Greg Norman and Severiano Ballesteros, to win a sixth green jacket.

In his dotage, Nicklaus has been extremely generous with his time and his comments to those who seek to follow in his path. When he first saw Tiger Woods play at Augusta, for example, he said: "I tell you, Bob Jones could have saved his comments from '63 for this kid; he really does play a game with which we're not familiar."

It was typical of the golfer of the century to come up with such a remark. And his legacy is a testament to his qualities not only as a player but also as a human being: for, to take one of the baseball player Yoggi Berra's most famous sayings, Nicklaus showed us that while winning may be everything, it is far from the only thing.

Chapter 5

TOP 50 WOMEN

IT WAS, NATURALLY, NO EASY MATTER DECIDING ON THE TOP-50 WOMEN GOLFERS OF THE 20TH CENTURY. THE CRITERIA USED WAS THE SAME AS THE MEN: WEIGHT WAS GIVEN NOT ONLY TO MAJOR CHAMPIONSHIPS WON AND OTHER PLAYING ACHIEVEMENTS, BUT TO HOW THE GOLFER WAS SEEN BY HER CONTEMPORARIES AND THE EFFECT, IF ANY, THAT SHE HAD ON THE WOMEN'S GAME.

ULTIMATELY, OUR TOP THREE HAS A PLEASING SYMMETRY, COMPRISING AS IT DOES OF ONE PLAYER FROM THE THIRTIES, ONE FROM THE SIXTIES AND ONE FROM THE NINETIES. FEEL FREE TO DISAGREE, OF COURSE, BUT NO-ONE CAN DISPUTE THEIR LASTING LEGACY.

Kelly Robbins 50

FULL NAME: Kelly Robbins
BORN: Mount Pleasant, MI, September 29, 1969
MAJOR CHAMPIONSHIPS: LPGA Championship 1995

Kelly Robbins is something of an enigmatic figure on the women's tour. She is an intensely private person performing in a very public place, and she occasionally finds it difficult to reconcile the two. She is, nevertheless, an extremely talented player who has the greatest gift of all in, length.

When she is playing well it seems that nothing is beyond her, and in one of her better seasons – 1997, when she finished third on the money list – this was reflected statistically: she produced more birdies (383) and eagles (17) than anyone else on tour. While this was not altogether surprising, given that she was hitting tee shots miles and therefore having shorter shots to the green, the putts still had to be holed.

She also had more rounds in the 60s (46 out of 96) than anyone else, and it all added up to two victories, in the Diet Dr Pepper National Pro-Am and the Jamie Farr Kroger Classic.

But, of course, long drives have to hit fairways to be of any use, and in 1998 the Robbins record showed an extraordinary tendency to fluctuation. She won the first event of the year, the HealthSouth, an achievement which normally gives the victor the confidence to have an outstanding season. And while Robbins did well enough, and went on to win the Aflac Tournament of Champions later in the year, she finished only 17th on the money list.

This was because although she had eight top-10 finishes in her 25 events, she also missed the cut in seven tournaments. She has played in three Solheim Cup teams between 1994 and 1998, and has been on the winning side each time.

Donna Andrews 49

FULL NAME: Donna Andrews
BORN: Lynchburg, VA, April 12, 1967
MAJOR CHAMPIONSHIPS: Dinah Shore 1994

The popular belief on the women's tour in America is that the greatest walk in golf is down the 18th at Mission Hills when in a position to win what is the first major championship of every year, the Dinah Shore.

But at the time Donna Andrews did not quite see it like that. It was 1994, the year in which Laura Davies was to sweep all before her and win three tournaments, including a major, plus the money list. She was the woman to beat, and on the 18th tee she had not just a one-stroke lead, but the advantage of being able to hit 30–40 yards further than her opponent off the tee.

Andrews could have panicked, but didn't. She had already been a good player for a long time, winning five consecutive Virginia State championships before turning professional, and she had improved quite dramatically in every year of her career. In 1989, her rookie year, she finished 75th on the money list; the following year 65th, then 13th, then 9th.

In fact, it was Davies who was to take the uncharacteristic step of deciding to play conservatively and not going for the green of this 526-yard-long hole in two. She took an iron off the tee, and eventually hit her third on to the green, but 60 feet away. Andrews, with great character, hit a six-iron for her third, and saw it roll to six feet. Davies three-putted, Andrews holed, and had her first major championship.

She won two other events that year, and has twice challenged for the US Women's Open. In 1992 she was third, and the following year was runner-up at Crooked Stick to the shock winner, Lauri Merten. Andrews lives in Pinehurst, NC, surrounded by her twin passions: golf and horses.

Helen Alfredsson 48

FULL NAME: Helen Alfredsson
BORN: Gothenburg, Sweden, April 9, 1965
MAJOR CHAMPIONSHIPS: Dinah Shore 1993

Helen Alfredsson, a player who could hardly be further removed from the dour Swedish archetype, brings a touch of glamour to any golf tournament in which she is involved. Tall at 5ft 10in, she was once a model in Paris, until the demanding lifestyle turned her away. "That was 20lb ago," she will joke these days, but the need to be slim to survive on the catwalk turned her anorexic, although it was not until she woke one morning to find her pillow covered in handfuls of hair that she realized the extent of the problem.

She decided there and then to return to the other love of her life, golf, which she had never completely given up. She came to realize that it was better to be judged on her scores rather than her appearance.

Golf is fortunate that she did so, for there is a compelling quality about her play. Not for her the safe lay-up, or the shot to the safe part of the green. She goes for the pin, and if the shot succeeds she whoops with joy. There is never a danger of not knowing about it if Alfie is playing well. "Those people who react the same way whether they have taken 10, or holed a 30-footer for a birdie, they make you go to sleep," she says.

Runner-up in the US Women's Open of 1993, she should have won in 1994. She started with a 63 – still a first-round record – and established a 36-hole record with a second round of 69. Amazingly, she three-putted from three and four feet on successive holes in that 69, leading to a collapse of confidence and rounds of 76 and 77.

She did win the Dinah Shore in 1993, has won the Weetabix British Women's Open (1990) and has played on all five Solheim Cup teams.

Helen Alfredsson – from catwalk to fairway

Gloria Minoprio 47

FULL NAME: Gloria Minoprio
BORN: 1907

All right, so Gloria Minoprio was not one of the world's great golfers, but she was one of the most mysterious. Furthermore, she was the revolutionary who introduced trousers to women's championship golf in Britain, and created more of a stir than many a worthy champion. Her name should be a legend.

Minoprio first surfaced in 1933 at the English women's championship at Westward Ho!, and everything about her appearance was wonderfully dramatic. She arrived in the nick of time in a large yellow car and walked calmly to the tee, apparently oblivious to the sensation she was causing. She was wearing a navy cap, sweater, white gloves and the offending trousers, beautifully cut and fitted. Her face was white, her lips red and she used only one club, which handicapped her somewhat. She lost, and disappeared until the following year.

The hierarchy was appalled, and "deplored any departure from the traditional costume of the game", but Henry Longhurst saw it differently. He called it the day of the "Great Revolution", and described Minoprio – a slim, trim figure – as "the best-dressed woman golfer I ever saw".

Longhurst also coined the phrase "Sic transit Gloria Monday", because Minoprio usually lost in the first round. One year, when she reached the second round, still observing the one-club rule, it became "Sic transit Gloria Tuesday".

To add to the air of mystery, Minoprio was also a magician, and when the British championship was held at Royal Portrush in 1939, she apparently held parties at the house she rented and demonstrated her conjuring skills.

Ada Mackenzie 46

FULL NAME: Ada Mackenzie
BORN: 1891

Ada Mackenzie played numerous sports when she was young, but she excelled at golf and was Canada's best woman player between the wars. She gave every encouragement to juniors, and founded the Ladies' Golf and Tennis Club of Toronto in 1924, so that women had a place at which to play at times that suited them. It is still in existence, minus the tennis, and is her most lasting legacy.

Mackenzie, who once said that she started golf "when women were supposed to know more about a cook stove than a niblick", was a prolific winner on home turf. She won the Canadian women's open title five times, in 1919, 1925, 1926, 1933 and 1935, and the national closed title five times between 1926 and 1933.

She was good enough to reach the semi-finals of the US Women's Amateur twice. In 1927, when she was the leading qualifier with a record-equalling 77, she lost by 2 and 1 to Maureen Orcutt, and in 1932 she lost by 5 and 4 to Glenna Collett Vare, who had already been champion five times.

In 1925, Mackenzie lost to the then Miss Collett by one hole, after a thunderstorm played havoc with the knitted suit she was wearing. The sleeves almost doubled in length and the skirt got so long that it dragged along the ground. The Canadian went into the sportswear business a few years later and recommended tweed or flannel for skirts.

In 1971 Mackenzie and Marlene Streit were the first women inducted into the Canadian Golf Hall of Fame.

Vivien Saunders 45

FULL NAME: Vivien Inez Saunders
BORN: November 24, 1946

Vivien Saunders – intelligent, outspoken and determined – is a non-conformist who does things her way. She was a pioneering professional, the first European to qualify for the US LPGA tour, the first woman to qualify through the PGA training school and the founder and first chairman of the WPGA in Europe. She is a woman of many parts: golfer, teacher, author, businesswoman and a qualified solicitor, not forgetting the degrees in psychology and business administration.

As an amateur Saunders was a talented player. She was runner-up in the British women's championship in 1966, was a member of the Commonwealth and Vagliano teams in 1967 and played in the Curtis Cup in 1968.

The following year she made an enquiry about turning professional, and on Christmas Eve the Ladies' Golf Union (LGU) rang to say that simply by asking she had relinquished her amateur status and was now a professional.

Stunned, Saunders discovered that there wasn't much of a place for the woman professional at home, so she set to work to change the established view. It wasn't easy, but she refused to take no for an answer and she had her rewards. In 1977 she won the second women's British Open, at Lindrick, and in 1987 she was named Sports Coach of the Year.

Ever resourceful, Saunders bought herself a golf club for her 40th birthday – it's called Abbotsley, and is a thriving 36-hole complex, the base for her golf school business – and in 1998 she bought another course, Cambridge Meridian. Best of all, she's on the executive committee of the PGA.

Alexa Stirling 44

FULL NAME: Alexa Stirling

BORN: 1896

MAJOR CHAMPIONSHIPS: US Amateur 1916, 1919, 1920

Alexa Stirling was raised in Atlanta, GA, and learned her golf at the East Lake Club, alongside Bobby Jones, who was a few years younger. Stewart Maiden taught them both in a straightforward, no-nonsense style, and produced two champion golfers of great grace and style.

In 1915 Stirling reached the semi-finals of the US Women's Amateur, losing at the 22nd, and in 1916 she won the title for the first time. She was the first southerner to do so, and it was three years before she could prove her victory was no fluke because the championship was not played again until 1919 because of the war.

In 1917, Stirling, Jones, Perry Adair and Elaine Rosenthal toured the eastern states playing exhibition matches in aid of the Red Cross, and raised the huge sum of $150,000.

Stirling retained her US Amateur title when the championship resumed in 1919 and Glenna Collett, who had been inspired by the wartime exhibitions, played for the first time and won her first match.

In 1920 Stirling completed a hat-trick of titles when she defeated Dorothy Hurd (née Campbell) five and four in the final. Stirling also won the Canadian Amateur that year, and in 1921 she travelled to Turnberry to play in the British championship. She met the redoubtable Cecil Leitch, the defending champion, in the first round and in filthy weather lost at the 16th. In the semi-finals of the French, Stirling lost to Joyce Wethered.

Stirling, an unflappable competitor, was runner-up in the US Amateur in 1921, 1923 and 1925, and won the Canadian again in 1934 (as Mrs Fraser) .

Brandie Burton 43

FULL NAME: Brandie Burton

BORN: San Bernardino, CA, January 8, 1972

MAJOR CHAMPIONSHIPS: du Maurier 1993, 1998

Brandie Burton first hit a golf ball at the age of nine, and quickly made a name for herself. In 1987 and 1989, aged 15 and 17 respectively, she won the San Diego Junior World Championship. Later she won the US Girls Championship, became the number-one-ranked college golfer in the nation and in 1990 played on the Curtis Cup team that annihilated Great Britain and Ireland at Somerset Hills, NY.

All seemed set fair for her to become one of the most accomplished professionals on the US Tour, and in her opening years that promise was fulfilled. She turned professional in October 1990, was a runner-up in her first season, won in her second season and then, in her third, won two regular tour events plus the du Maurier Classic – her first major.

That season, at 21, she became the youngest woman to earn a million dollars on the LPGA. Her career did not progress as might have been expected, however, and it was to be 1998 before she returned to the winner's circle, collecting the du Maurier Classic once more.

She always had the gift of length, and when she was put out at the top of the order in the singles series of the 1992 Solheim Cup match at Dalmahoy, it seemed perfect that her opponent was Laura Davies, the biggest hitter on either side. The American hung on, and was still all square after 11 holes. Then Davies had three birdies in the next four holes and Burton, in exactly the right spirit, waved her white baseball cap in surrender.

Dottie Pepper 42

FULL NAME: Dottie Pepper

BORN: Saratoga Springs, NY, August 17, 1965

MAJOR CHAMPIONSHIPS: Dinah Shore 1992

Few people play the game with the intensity that Dottie Pepper brings to the course. She is a fiercely determined competitor, and this is shown at its best, or worst, in match play and during the Solheim Cup.

She has played in all five editions of the match against Europe, bringing an enthusiasm that, in the eyes of her opponents, sometimes spills over into poor etiquette. At Muirfield Village in 1998, she was accused by Laura Davies and others on the European team of urging the crowd to cheer and shout while her opponents still had crucial putts to study. Pepper trenchantly rejected such criticism.

Previously, in 1994, she had refused to shake hands with her opponents after a match fuelled by ill-feeling, but all her captains have supported her, seeing her as the soul of the American side.

She had an impressive amateur career, three times gaining All-American honours while at college, although it is perhaps significant that while all her wins are recorded in the LPGA media guide, the fact that she played in the 1986 Curtis Cup team, which became the first-ever to lose in America, is curiously omitted.

Since turning professional she has become one of America's leading players, one not afraid to turn contention into victory, and in her first nine years on tour won 14 official victories and three more unofficial. Her sheer consistency meant that in 1995 she set the all-time record for passing the $3 million mark, in just seven-and-a-half years.

Strangely, for such a fired-up competitor, she has won only one major championship, the 1992 Dinah Shore.

Alison Nicholas 41

FULL NAME: Alison Nicholas

BORN: Gibraltar, March 6, 1942

MAJOR CHAMPIONSHIPS: US Open 1997

Alison Nicholas – 1997 US Open champion

Alison Nicholas took up golf at the age of 17 because she decided that, at five feet tall, she was too tiny to make the grade in tennis. She was easy to pass on the court, but achieved big things on the fairway, the biggest of all being a memorable victory in the US Women's Open championship in 1997.

Born in Gibraltar and brought up in Yorkshire, Nicholas was a small, dark bundle of determination and won the British Strokeplay championship in 1983.

She turned professional in 1984 and recorded the first of her 11 tour victories in 1987, in the Weetabix Women's British Open at St Mellion. She won by a shot from Laura Davies, the defending champion, who had won the US Open title a few days earlier, and Muffin Spencer-Devlin.

Nicholas was number two on the European order of merit from 1988 to 1990, and was number one in 1997. She has played in every Solheim Cup from 1990 to 1998, and in 1992 she and Davies formed an inspirational partnership as Europe won.

In 1995, Nicholas won twice in America, and in 1997 the diminutive Englishwoman confirmed herself as a competitor of stature when she won the US Open at Pumpkin Ridge. She defeated the legendary Nancy Lopez, who was looking for her first Open win, by a shot.

In the last round, Lopez, three shots behind, electrified the huge partisan crowd with three birdies in the first four holes. Nicholas, solid as her native Rock, gave no ground, countering with a birdie and an eagle three at the fourth. It was unforgettable.

Lotta Neumann 40

FULL NAME: Liselotte Neumann

BORN: Finspang, Sweden, May 20, 1966

MAJOR CHAMPIONSHIPS: US Open 1988

Born in the small Swedish town of Finspang, south-west of Stockholm, Lotta Neumann was a successful amateur and turned professional at the age of 18. She inspired a generation of golfers and became one of the world's best players, with 25 victories worldwide by the end of 1998.

In 1985, her first season on the European tour, she won twice and was 12th on the order of merit with £14,058. The following year, she was number two with £37,006, just £494 behind Laura Davies, after one victory, four seconds and three thirds.

In 1988, Neumann was rookie of the year in America. She started at the top, her maiden victory being the US Women's Open at Baltimore Country Club in Maryland. She was 22 and showed remarkable composure – her trademark throughout her career – as she led from the first round. Even when she four-putted in the final round she didn't panic, and recovered to win by three shots from Patty Sheehan to succeed Davies as champion.

Neumann did not win again until 1991 – she conceded that the Open and the attendant publicity had been too much too soon – but in 1994 she recorded three wins on each tour, including the Weetabix Women's British Open, which featured on both the US and the European schedule. She was number one in Europe with £102,750 and number three in America with $505,701.

Neumann concentrates her efforts on the US Tour, and since 1996 has won at least twice a season. She has played in all five Solheim Cup matches from 1990 to 1998.

Lady Margaret Scott 39

FULL NAME: Lady Margaret Scott

BORN: 1875

CHAMPIONSHIPS: British Amateur 1893, 1894, 1895

Lady Margaret Scott, a gentle soul with perfect manners, was a demon performer on the golf course, with a level of skill that was too much for her contemporaries. She could hit the ball 130 or 140 yards from the tee, and won the first three Ladies' British Amateur Championships by sizeable margins before retiring from the fray. Later, as Lady Hamilton-Russell, she won three Swiss championships.

Lady Margaret developed her elegant, long-swinging style playing with her three brothers, all good golfers. The best of them was Michael, whose longevity was such that he won the Amateur Championship in 1933, at the age of 55. She also played with the professional Andrew Kirkcaldy on family holidays at St Andrews, receiving a stroke a hole. When Kirkcaldy won, he would receive an extra half-sovereign from Lady Margaret's father, Lord Eldon.

In 1893 in the first British women's championship at St Anne's, there were fewer than 40 entries and Lady Margaret, aged 18, was not extended. She beat Issette Pearson, the secretary of the fledgling Ladies' Golf Union, by seven and five in the final. Lord Eldon made the victory speech.

There were 63 entrants at Littlestone in 1894, including Lottie Dod, famous for winning the Wimbledon Tennis Championships five times. The championship was on the up. Miss Pearson, an indomitable administrator and no mean golfer, lost again in the final, by five and four, and at Portrush the following year Lady Margaret beat Miss E. Lythgoe by the same margin. Lord Eldon suggested that his daughter should keep the trophy, but his proposal was turned down.

Juli Inkster 38

FULL NAME: Juli Inkster

BORN: Santa Cruz, CA, June 24, 1960

MAJOR CHAMPIONSHIPS: Dinah Shore 1984, 1989; du Maurier 1984

When Juli Inkster won the US Women's Amateur Championship in 1980 – on her honeymoon – it seemed that no goal in golf was beyond her. She had married golf professional Brian, who promptly became her caddie, and this formidable partnership went on to win the Amateur in each of the next two years.

Three wins in a row in that Championship were not quite unprecedented, Virginia Van Wie having done the same thing in 1932–34, but it signalled the presence of a major talent.

Inkster's golf as a professional at first looked as if it might break all records. Having turned professional in 1983, she won on the Tour in her fifth event, the Safeco Classic. The following year – her first full season as a professional and, hence, her rookie year – she won two major championships, the Dinah Shore and the du Maurier.

She was the first rookie to achieve that feat, and the last until Se Ri Pak emulated it in 1998.

In 1986 she won four tournaments to finish third on the money list, in 1988 she won three and in 1989 she won the third of her majors, another Dinah Shore.

In February 1990 she had a daughter, and the remainder of

Julie Inkster – the first rookie to win two majors

that season was necessarily curtailed and, indeed, her career began to level off.

There have been only four official victories during the 1990s, including the Samsung World Championship of Women's Golf in 1997 and 1998, and in the latter year she played well enough not only to get into the winning Solheim Cup team, but also to have her most successful year financially, winning $656,012 to finish sixth on the money list.

Ayako Okamoto 37

FULL NAME: Ayako Okamoto
BORN: Hiroshima, Japan, April 2, 1951
MAJOR CHAMPIONSHIPS:

Born in Hiroshima, Ayako Okamoto was a softball pitcher who represented her country before concentrating on golf. From 1975 to 1998, she won 43 times on the Japanese tour and in 1981 – when she won eight times and was second on six occasions – she also played eight events in the USA, with fourth her best finish.

In 1982, she played 14 US events and won the Arizona Copper Classic after a play-off, the first of 17 LPGA victories. Unlike her male compatriots, she did not shy away from competing overseas, and proved that she could live with the best anywhere.

She started playing the bulk of her golf in America, and in 1984 she won three LPGA events, including a nine-shot triumph in the Ladies' British Open at Woburn. It confirmed that the imperturbable Japanese could play – "My personality is not to be upset or short-tempered" – but did the championship, which was televised live, no favours.

In 1987, Okamoto reached the pinnacle of her career. She won four times and the only thing missing was a major championship. She was runner-up in two, the US Women's Open (she and JoAnne Carner were beaten in a play-off by Laura Davies) and the du Maurier, and was tied for third in the LPGA Championship. She was the first non-American to be player of the year and led the money list with $466,034.

A cult figure in Japan, with her own television show every week, Okamoto had made her point – she could play with the best.

Judy Bell 36

FULL NAME: Judy Bell
BORN: Wichita, KS, September 23, 1936

Born in Wichita, KS, Judy Bell has been devoted to the game since the age of seven. She was a very good player, but hit the heights as an administrator, and in 1996 became the first woman to be elected president of the United States Golf Association, one of the game's governing bodies, founded in 1894. "Our job is to look after the game and to try to get people to understand its traditions and history, and have fun when they play it," she said.

Bell's first clubs were a cut-down, hickory-shafted collection given to her by an aunt, and her mother drilled into her the importance of etiquette and fair play. In her first tournament she shot 72 and won the girls' division, but pointed out that she was no prodigy: it was over nine holes and she was the only girl.

In an amateur era dominated by JoAnne Gunderson, Barbara McIntire and the much-married Anne Quast-Decker-Welts-Sander, Bell did not win championships – she learned how to run them – but did well enough to play in the Curtis Cup in 1960 and 1962. In 1964, in the third round of the US Women's Open, she shot 67, equalling the championship record.

Bell was Curtis Cup captain in 1986 and 1988 – the US lost on both occasions – but the match was regenerated. In 1986, at Prairie Dunes in Kansas, it was the first US defeat for 30 years and the first time any American team, male or female, amateur or professional, had been beaten on home turf.

Lally Segard 35

FULL NAME: Lally Segard
BORN: Paris, France, April 4, 1921
CHAMPIONSHIPS: British Amateur 1950

Lally Segard, who was born in Paris, was not only an excellent player but also a visionary administrator who worked tirelessly with the European Golf Association to promote the game throughout continental Europe.

She was the British girls' champion in 1937, the second French winner of the title, and won her first French championship in 1939. After the Second World War, she went on to win a host of titles at home and abroad. A peripatetic competitor, she won in Switzerland, Luxembourg, Italy, Spain and the Low Countries, spreading the gospel of golf.

In 1950, as the Vicomtesse de Saint Sauveur, she won the British championship at Royal County Down, where her compatriot Simone Thion de la Châme had won the title in 1927. The Vicomtesse, an elegant stylist who hit the ball a fair distance, defeated the experienced Scot Jessie Valentine by three and two, and the Frenchwoman's style and charm won many Irish hearts. In 1963, the next time the championship was held at Newcastle, it was won by Brigitte Varangot, one of the Vicomtesse's protegées.

Lally was the inspiration behind several international competitions: the Vagliano Trophy, presented by her father, was originally for an annual match between France and Great Britain and Ireland, but is now GB & I against the Continent of Europe and is held every two years; the European team championships, also biennial; and the Espirito Santo, the world team championship. It was first played in 1964 in Paris under Lally's chairmanship, and France won, with Lally as non-playing captain.

Bunty Smith 34

FULL NAME: Frances Smith

BORN: 1924; died 1978

CHAMPIONSHIPS: British Amateur 1949, 1954

Frances Smith, née Stephens, was so popular and talented that she was universally known by her nickname. To mention the name "Bunty" in the 1950s and 1960s was to refer to one of the great amateur golfers, with a very deliberate swing and a most marvellous temperament.

She won three English and two British championships, and in 1954 brought forth a burst of scoring, the like of which has rarely been seen from a woman. She played the front nine holes at Woodhall Spa, that great tract of gorse, heather and bomb-crater bunkers, in 30 shots. The outward half measures 3,200 yards and has a woman's par of 39.

Bunty was the daughter of Fred, the professional at Bootle, and in the immediate post-war days, when snobbery in golf still abounded, this was held against her to the extent that she was not selected for the 1948 Curtis Cup. Once in the team two years later, though, she was a sensation, and was never to lose a singles match.

Her record was played five, won four, halved one, and on two occasions she was directly responsible for the Cup going to Great Britain and Ireland. In 1956 she was playing Polly Riley, it was the last match, it came down to the last green, and Smith holed from 20 feet to win the Curtis Cup. History then all but repeated itself in 1958 when the same two players, again in the last match, were playing each other. Smith had to win in order for the match to be a tie and for GB & I to retain the Cup – and she did. It was the first time any team representing the British Isles in the Ryder, Walker or Curtis Cups had not been defeated in America.

Bunty Smith, OBE, died young and much mourned in 1978 at the age of 53.

Meg Mallon 33

FULL NAME: Meg Mallon

BORN: Natick, MA, April 14, 1963

MAJOR CHAMPIONSHIPS: US Open 1991; LPGA 1991

Not many professional golfers would agree to let a journalist with little experience of golf caddy for them in a tournament, but Meg Mallon did – and won. What is more it was the first victory of her career, and led to a season that she has yet to match, including as it did two major championships.

Sonja Steptoe, the caddying journalist, had selected Mallon because of her equable temperament, and they both had plenty to smile about at the end of the 1991 Oldsmobile Classic, which Mallon won by a shot. By the end of the season, Mallon (*sans* Steptoe) had also won the LPGA Championship, the US Women's Open and the Daikyo World Championship. She finished number two on the money list with $633,802.

A former Michigan amateur champion, Mallon elevated herself from steadily improving, fifth-year professional to potential superstar in the space of three weeks in June and July. That's when she won the two majors, beating Pat Bradley and Ayako Okamoto in the LPGA and finishing with a 67 in the last round of the Open at Colonial for a total of 283, two shots ahead of Bradley.

Meg Mallon – winner of two majors in 1991

"It's overwhelming," Mallon said, "but I want to remain a good person and not get caught up in it." She's been consistent enough to qualify for every US Solheim Cup team since 1992, and on the 18th green at Muirfield Village in 1998, with the trophy already won, conceded the hole to her opponent Sophie Gustafson so that they halved their match. That's Mallon: a very good golfer who has always played the game in the right spirit.

Judy Rankin 32

FULL NAME: Judy Rankin

BORN: St Louis, MO, February 18, 1945

Born in St Louis, Judy Torluemke started the game at the age of six and won the Missouri Women's Amateur title when she was 14. The following year, she became the youngest leading amateur in the US Women's Open and by 17 she was playing professionally. When she retired in 1983 with back trouble, she had won 26 tournaments.

In 1962, her first year on tour, she won $701, was 41st on the money list and had a stroke average of 79.08. She improved steadily on all counts and in 1966, playing double the number of tournaments, she won $15,180, was seventh on the money list and averaged 74.52 strokes a round.

She married Yippy Rankin, a Texan, in 1967 and in 1968 she won for the first time. In 1970 she won three times, and from then until 1979 she won at least once every year. In 1973 she won four times, was second on the money list with $72,989 and won her first Vare Trophy with a stroke average of 73.08.

In 1976 and 1977, Rankin – quiet, determined and lethal with the fairway woods – was the best player in the world. She won 11 times in all, was number one on the money list, player of the year and winner of the Vare Trophy.

She never won a major, but Yippy is not alone in thinking that she has done more than enough to be in the Hall of Fame. An insightful on-course commentator for ABC television, she was a thoughtful, meticulous and successful Solheim Cup captain in 1996 and 1998.

Ann Sander 31

FULL NAME: Ann Sander

BORN: Everett, WA, 1937

CHAMPIONSHIPS: British Amateur 1980; US Amateur 1958, 1961, 1963

Few players have proved as enduring as Anne Sander, who has been competing in championships (and winning them) throughout five decades.

Born in Everett, near Seattle, she grew up on a golf course built and run by her parents and in 1952, aged 14, she was the youngest qualifier in the history of the US Women's Amateur. It was the start of her long love affair with competition.

In 1958 she was the leading amateur in the US Women's Open, then won her first US Amateur. She also played in the Curtis Cup at Brae Burn, the first of eight appearances over five decades. The last was in 1990, when she was 52, the oldest player ever selected, and she never played on a losing team. She played in the Espirito Santo three times: 1966, 1968 and 1988.

In 1959 she was the first amateur to break 300 in the Open, and in 1961 she won the Amateur again, by a record margin of 14 and 13. She was nine under par for 112 holes played and lost only six holes. She won her third and last US Amateur in 1963, and was runner-up in 1965, 1968 and 1973.

In 1980 she at last won the British title, and since turning 50 years old in 1987 has been the US Women's Senior champion four times. Since she collected husbands as well as titles, she may be the only person to win championships under four different names: Quast, Decker, Welts and Sander.

Marlene Streit 30

FULL NAME: Marlene Streit

BORN: Cereal, Alberta, Canada, March 9, 1934

CHAMPIONSHIPS: British Amateur 1953; US Amateur 1956

Born in Cereal, Alberta, the diminutive Marlene Streit stood tall as one of the world's great amateurs. She was twice Canada's outstanding athlete of the year and her accuracy, consistency and determination more than made up for a lack of length. Her pitching was lethal. She would hit the ball, head firmly down, then turn to her bag for her putter, certain that the ball would be near the pin.

In 1953, she won the British women's amateur championship at Royal Porthcawl, beating Ireland's Philomena Garvey by seven and six in the final, and in 1956 won the US Women's Amateur. She defeated JoAnne Gunderson, who had just won the US Girls' Junior championship, by two and one. In 1966, the two met again in the final, and the big-hitting American prevailed at the 41st hole – it's still the longest US Women's Amateur final to date.

Streit was the Canadian champion between 1951 and 1957, and is the only woman to win the Canadian, Australian, British and US championships. She married in 1957 and had two daughters, but her game and her competitive edge were enduring. In 1961, she was the leading amateur in the US Women's Open, finishing in a tie for seventh place, and in 1966 she was the leading individual in the Women's World Amateur Team Championship in Mexico City, where Canada were second behind the United States.

Streit also excelled as a senior, winning the US Senior Women's Open in 1985 and 1994 and being runner-up five times.

Catherine Lacoste 29

FULL NAME: Catherine Lacoste

BORN: Paris, France, June 27, 1945

CHAMPIONSHIPS: US Amateur 1969; British Amateur 1969

MAJOR CHAMPIONSHIPS: US Open 1967

Catherine Lacoste, of the eminent sporting family, proved herself a formidable competitor in her own right, and her victory in the US Women's Open of 1967 still stands as a unique achievement: she is the only amateur to win the title. Her father, René, was a world-famous tennis champion and her mother, Simone Thion de la Chaûme, was one of France's best golfers, winner of the British Girls' Championship in 1924 and British Women's champion in 1927.

Their daughter first came to prominence when France won the inaugural women's World Amateur Team Championship in Paris in 1964. Lacoste, less experienced than her team-mates Brigitte Varangot and Claudine Cros, was the leading individual alongside the American Carol Sorenson.

Always a non-conformist, Lacoste missed the European team championship of 1967 to play in the US Open at the Virginia Hot Springs Golf and Tennis Club, and returned home with the trophy, having stunned the professionals. Rounds of 71, 70 and 74 gave her a five-stroke lead, and even with a nervous 79 in the final round, the 22-year-old Frenchwoman won by two shots. She was the youngest champion, and a relieved one: "All of a sudden I feel I am someone myself, not just the daughter of the Lacostes," she said.

However, her real *annus mirabilis* was 1969, when she won the Spanish, French, British and US Amateur titles, a unique grand slam. The victory in the British at Royal Portrush was particularly special because her mother, who had won at Royal County Down 42 years previously, was there.

Sally Little 28

FULL NAME: Sally Little

BORN: Cape Town, South Africa, October 12, 1951

MAJOR CHAMPIONSHIPS: LPGA 1980; du Maurier 1988

Born in Cape Town, Sally Little became South Africa's premier woman golfer, with two major championships to her name. It might have been even more if she had not had to undergo abdominal and knee surgery in her prime.

In 1970 Little was the leading individual in the women's WATC, and in 1971 she won the South African matchplay and strokeplay championships. She turned professional that year and played seven events on the US Tour. She won $1,670, was 51st on the money list and rookie of the year.

Little had a beautiful swing, but it wasn't until 1976 that she won for the first time, holing a bunker shot of nearly 30 yards at the last to win by a shot.

From 1977 to 1982, she was never out of the top ten on the money list. In 1978, she was joint runner-up in the US Women's Open, with a 65 in the last round. In 1980 she won her first major, the LPGA Championship, and in 1982 (her best season) she won four times, including the Dinah Shore, shooting 64 in the last round; she was also third on the money list with $228,941.

In 1983, she missed the bulk of the season because of illness and injury and never quite recovered her form of old, although she was beaten in a play-off for the US Open in 1986; in 1988 she won the du Maurier Classic – her second major and the last of her 15 victories.

Sally Little – double major winner

Susie Berning 27

FULL NAME: Susie Berning (née Maxwell)
BORN: Pasadena, CA, July 22, 1941
MAJOR CHAMPIONSHIPS: US Open 1968, 1972, 1973; Western Open 1965

Susie Berning became a US Women's Open specialist – she won the championship three times – and four of her 11 professional victories were in major championships.

Berning was the first woman to be given a golf scholarship by Oklahoma City University, and competed on the men's team before graduating with a degree in business. She turned professional in 1964 and was Rookie of the Year.

She won twice in 1965, including the Western Open (then a major), and twice in 1967, but limited her schedule from 1968 onward. In 1968 she played in only nine tournaments and still won the Open. Married for less than two months, she led from start to finish with rounds of 69, 73, 76 and 71, and won by three shots from Mickey Wright.

In 1972, Berning won the title again, at Winged Foot, despite starting with a 79 – still the worst start by an eventual champion. However, she finished with a 71, one of only five sub-par rounds that week, to win by a shot from Kathy Ahern, Pam Barnett and Judy Rankin. The first prize was $6,000, which was a record.

In 1973 Berning won again, by five shots, to join an Open elite. By then Wright and Betsy Rawls had each won the title four times, and Babe Zaharias was the only other three-time champion.

Berning later concentrated on teaching, but in 1989 she and her daughter Robin played in the Konica San Jose Classic, the first time a mother and daughter had competed in the same LPGA event.

Carol Mann 26

FULL NAME: Carol Mann
BORN: Buffalo, NY, February 3, 1941
MAJOR CHAMPIONSHIPS: US Open 1965; Western Open 1964

Carol Mann stood head and shoulders above her contemporaries in the literal sense, because she was 6ft 3in tall; and her career, which spanned 22 seasons from 1961 to 1981, hit the heights often enough for her to be inducted into the Hall of Fame in 1977.

Mann, who was born in Buffalo, NY, turned professional at the age of 19. She had to wait until 1964 for the first of her 38 victories, but in the next five seasons she won 27 times, and was never lower than fourth on the money list.

In 1965, she won the US Women's Open, beating Kathy Cornelius by two shots. It was Mann's only major title, although she was runner-up the following year and again in 1974, and tied for third in 1968.

In 1968, Mann was positively prolific, winning ten times – a tally matched by Kathy Whitworth. She also took the Vare Trophy with a stroke average of 72.04, a record that stood for 10 years until it was broken by Nancy Lopez with 71.76. Mann compiled 23 rounds in the 60s, a record that stood until 1980, when Amy Alcott surpassed it with 25.

Mann added eight more victories to her list in 1969, and topped the money list for the one and only time with $49,152, a record that stood until 1972.

Intelligent and articulate, Mann's business activities have ranged across a broad spectrum, from course design to coaching, to writing to corporate outings, to television analysis to motivational speaking, to name but a few.

The Curtis Sisters 25

FULL NAME: Harriot Curtis
BORN: June 30, 1881
CHAMPIONSHIPS: US Amateur 1906

FULL NAME: Margaret Curtis
BORN: 1880
CHAMPIONSHIPS: US Amateur 1907, 1911, 1912

Margaret and Harriot Curtis, both winners of the US Women's Amateur championship, were the instigators of one of the great international team competitions, the Curtis Cup. The sisters, regular visitors to the United Kingdom to play in the competitions available, saw early on that a match between the two countries would be beneficial. In 1905, when both were in England for the British Ladies' Championship at Cromer, they organized a match and labelled it "America versus England".

The "English" team, which contained Scots and Irish players, won 6–1, and six years later when another match – this time called "American and Colonial versus Great Britain", and played at Royal Portrush – was organized, the home team won again, 7–2.

The First World War was to interrupt efforts, and Margaret Curtis became chief of the Paris bureau of the Red Cross. She remained in Europe after the ceasefire, working with a Quaker organization to re-settle French villages destroyed during the war, and was eventually awarded the Légion d'Honneur for her efforts.

It was to be 1932 before the first Curtis Cup match was played, at Wentworth in Surrey, after Margaret had guaranteed $5,000 per match for the first 10 matches for the "defraying" of expenses. America won, 5½ to 3½, so setting a pattern that was to continue for decades (the 1950s apart) until Great Britain and Ireland, in the late 1980s and 1990s, were finally able to give their opponents as much – and occasionally more – than they could handle.

Jan Stephenson 24

FULL NAME: Jan Stephenson

BORN: Sydney, Australia, December 22, 1951

MAJOR CHAMPIONSHIPS: US Open 1983; LPGA 1982; du Maurier 1981

When considering the career of Jan Stephenson, there is a serious danger of regarding her as just a pretty face. That she was, but also a great deal more. Born in Sydney, Australia, she has had a long and enduring career on the US Tour, starting in 1974, and has won three major championships: the US Open, the LPGA Championship and the du Maurier Classic.

She also notched up 16 victories on the US Tour plus seven others around the world. Make no mistake, this slim and vivacious golfer could really play.

She turned professional in 1973 after the Australian authorities ridiculously left her out of the national team, and went on to be Rookie of the Year in America the following year. But it was not just her golf that was causing a sensation in the United States. As Jim Murray, one of the great sportswriters, said in the *Los Angeles Times*: "She led the Ladies' Tour in pulchritude."

She was stunningly photogenic, with a propensity for colourful clothes, and also a willingness to wear flimsy ones, too. She posed for lingerie calendars, was once the centrefold for a men's magazine, and her attractiveness – although resented by many of her colleagues – brought the Tour some much-needed publicity.

Despite the much higher purses of the late 1990s, compared with when she was winning in the 1970s and 1980s, she is still in the top 20 on the all-time money list. Her career, though, took a downward turn when she was mugged in 1990. The attacker tried to wrench her rings off her finger, twisting it and bending it so that there was a spiral fracture that has never properly healed.

Pam Barton 23

FULL NAME: Pamela Barton

BORN: 1917; died 1943

CHAMPIONSHIPS: British Amateur 1936, 1939; US Amateur 1936

The darling of British golf in the 1930s, Pam Barton – who was killed in a plane crash in Kent in 1943 at the age of 26 – packed a lifetime of achievement into a few years.

Strong and sturdy, with a winning smile, she was taught to give the ball a good belt by Archie Compston, and allied that power to great concentration and a fighting spirit. She reached the final of the British championship three years in a row, losing in 1934 and 1935 but winning the title at Southport and Ainsdale in 1936.

She then travelled to Canoe Brook Country Club in New Jersey for the US Women's Amateur, practised assiduously and won that as well, defeating Maureen Orcutt by four and three in the final. The only other woman to win both championships in the same year had been Dorothy Campbell (later Mrs Hurd) in 1909.

Barton, whose sister Mervyn also played for England, competed in the Curtis Cup teams of 1934 and 1936 and won the British title again in 1939 at Royal Portrush. A crowd of 500 watched the Englishwoman defeat Jean Marks – a gallant local, who was flabbergasted that she kept the match going for so long – by two and one.

In her winning speech, Barton paid tribute to her late uncle, Sir Dunbar Plunket Barton, a former president of Royal Portrush, who had started her on her golfing career. The tragedy was that it was so short. She was a gracious opponent, always encouraging and charmed young and old alike.

Hollis Stacy 22

FULL NAME: Hollis Stacy

BORN: Savannah, GA, March 16, 1954

MAJOR CHAMPIONSHIPS: US Open 1977, 1978, 1984; du Maurier 1983

Born into a golfing family in Savannah, GA, Hollis Stacy developed a talent for the big occasion and started winning championships early. As a professional she won 18 times, including four majors.

In 1969, aged 15, she became the youngest winner of the US Girls' Junior, the first of an unprecedented hat-trick of victories in the event. The first two finals went to the 18th and the third, against Amy Alcott, ended at the 19th, with Stacy four under par.

Stacy played in the Curtis Cup in 1972 and turned professional in 1974. It took her until 1977 to win, but she won three times that year, including the US Women's Open at Hazeltine, where she led from the first round and beat Nancy Lopez by two shots. Stacy was fifth on the money list – a position she has never bettered – with $89,155.

In 1978 Stacy retained her Open title, beating JoAnne Carner and Sally Little by a shot. In the last round, which was disrupted by thunder and lightning, Carner and Stacy exchanged the lead six times before the 24-year-old Georgian became the youngest player to win the championship twice.

In 1983 Stacy won her third major, the Peter Jackson Classic (later the du Maurier), and in 1984 she became the fifth player to win the Open three times. She beat Rosie Jones by a shot with a last round of 69, having holed a seven-iron for an eagle two at the 13th.

Between 1977 and 1985 she notched up at least one victory each season.

Cecil Leitch 21

FULL NAME: Charlotte Cecilia Pitcairn Leitch
BORN: Silloth, Cumbria, England 1891; died 1977
CHAMPIONSHIPS: British Amateur 1914, 1920, 1921, 1926

Charlotte Cecilia Pitcairn Leitch grew up with her four sisters and two brothers at remote Silloth in Cumbria and Cecil, as she was always known, compiled a formidable record in championships. She won 12 national titles – four British, two English, five French and one Canadian – and it might have been many more had it not been for the First World War.

Leitch, with her wide stance and hard, fast rhythm, gave the ball a good thump, and scared the daylights out of many opponents. She won the English and British titles in 1914, and retained the former when it was played again in 1919 and the latter when it resumed in 1920.

That year, in the final of the English at Hunstanton, a newcomer called Joyce Wethered beat Leitch, and their subsequent encounters made headlines. In 1921 Leitch got her revenge, beating Wethered in the finals of the French and the British, but it was Wethered who won their remaining encounters, ending Leitch's supremacy.

In 1922 Leitch lost by nine and seven to Wethered in the final of the British at Prince's – the referee, a great supporter of the defending champion, got so upset that he had to leave the course – and in 1925 they had a titanic struggle in the final at Troon. Leitch lost at the 37th, but Wethered was so exhausted that she retired from competition for a few years.

Ever resilient, Leitch won the British again in 1926, but that was the end of her winning run. Her sister Edith, Mrs Guedalla, won the English in 1927.

Glenna Collett Vare 20

FULL NAME: Glenna Collett Vare
BORN: June 20, 1903; died February 3, 1989
CHAMPIONSHIPS: US Amateur 1922, 1925, 1928, 1929, 1930, 1935

Glenna Collett Vare was, by achievement, the greatest woman amateur that America has produced. She won the US Women's Amateur championship six times, an unprecedented feat, and she brought to golf a style and a grace that caused her to be labelled "the female Bobby Jones".

Her successes in the Amateur ran from 1922, when she was only 19, through to 1935, with a spell in the middle when she won successively (1928, 1929 and 1930). She played in the inaugural Curtis Cup match in 1932 at Wentworth, Surrey, and in every succeeding match until 1948. In 1950 she was non-playing captain.

Although she worked hard at the game, she was gifted with a natural sense of timing. When aged 18, only 5ft 6in tall and weighing only 9st, she hit a measured drive of 307 yards, an extraordinary feat with the equipment of the day. She employed a big overswing, *à la* John Daly, to do it, but her irons were hit with a much more compact action.

She played in what was, by common consent, one of the great matches in golf history: the 1929 final of the British Ladies' Championship at St Andrews. Her opponent was Joyce Wethered, and after the first nine holes of the 36-hole final, the home player was five down. Collett had gone out in 34, a pace she could not maintain, and she was only two up at lunch.

Then Wethered went out in 34 as well, won six of the nine holes and, eventually, the match on the 35th green. Wethered paid her gracious tribute, for Collett was a true sportswoman. "Those who are so generous in defeat," said Wethered, "are the people most to be envied."

Glenna Collett Vare – America's greatest woman amateur?

Karrie Webb 19

FULL NAME: Karrie Webb

BORN: Ayr, Queensland, Australia, December 21, 1974

As a teenager Karrie Webb once spent a week with Greg Norman at his home in Florida, living as one of the family, working out with the Great White Shark, hitting balls, playing golf, the lot. She kept up with Norman, a notoriously hard worker, every step of the way and he was impressed, describing her as the most promising young player, male or female, that he had ever seen. She is well on the way to living up to his expectations.

Born in Ayr, a small town in Queensland, Webb tried as many sports as she could when growing up, but golf proved to be her forte. She represented Australia between 1992 and 1994, and won the national strokeplay championship in the latter year. She turned professional that October after the World Amateur Team Championship, and set off to find fame and fortune.

Neither was too long in arriving. In August 1995, still just 20, she won the Weetabix Women's British Open at Woburn by an emphatic six shots from Annika Sorenstam and Jill McGill. Webb was the youngest-ever champion, and one of the most impressive. Pia Nilsson, the Swede who is one of the world's most respected coaches, summed up the Webb way: "She's got a very good swing with so much feel to it, and her shot-making ability is exceptional."

Webb played 12 events in Europe and was Rookie of the Year, finishing third on the money list with £90,556. Then she turned her attention to America, and in October was second at the LPGA final qualifying tournament despite a fractured bone in her wrist.

The Americans quickly discovered just what a cool, determined customer had landed on their fairways when Webb achieved one victory and two second-place finishes in her first three tournaments. The stir she created was not quite Nancy Lopez-like – the Aussie is a more reserved character – but it was considerable. She went on to win three more tournaments and posted a total of 12 top-five finishes. Webb, Rookie of the Year, became the first player to top the million-dollar mark in a season, winning $1,002,000.

In 1997, Webb was marginally less awesome. She won three times, including an eight-shot victory in the British Open at Sunningdale, where she shot 63 in the third round and was relegated to second place on the money list with $987,606. However, she won the Vare Trophy with a record scoring average of 70.00 – a tribute to her consistency.

In 1998, Webb was a little quieter, winning twice, including a win at home in Australia for the first time as a professional and slipping to fourth in the money list with $704,477. She was overshadowed by Se Ri Pak and world number one Annika Sorenstam, who relishes the friendly rivalry with competitors who can push her to her limits.

Webb, world number two and already rich, now wonders why she ever wanted to be famous – she doesn't envy Tiger Woods a bit – but she wants to "be remembered as one of the great women golfers". She will be around for a while yet.

Karrie Webb – the Australian sensation who took women's golf by storm in 1996

Amy Alcott 18

FULL NAME: Amy Alcott

BORN: Kansas City, MO, February 22, 1956

MAJOR CHAMPIONSHIPS: US Open 1980; Dinah Shore 1983, 1988, 1991; du Maurier 1979

Amy Alcott grew up in California, where she sank empty baked-bean cans into the lawn so that she could practise her chipping and putting. Ultimately it has earned her a place in the Hall of Fame, and at an induction ceremony in 1999. Alcott spoke movingly about what it meant to her. "I've waited a long time for this, and I'm going to savour it for a long time," she said.

Alcott revealed a taste for the big occasion and the dramatic when she reached the final of the US Girls' Junior Championship at Augusta Country Club in 1971, losing to Hollis Stacy at the 19th in a memorable match. They had nine birdies between them and Stacy, who became the first player to win the title three years in a row, was four under par for the holes played. Two years later, Alcott won the championship herself.

In 1975 Alcott joined the LPGA tour and settled in quickly, winning her third tournament of the season, the Orange Blossom Classic in Florida. It was the start of a winning streak that lasted 12 years without a break.In 1979 she won four times, including the first of her major titles, the Peter Jackson Classic (later the du Maurier) in Montreal, and was third on the money list with $144,838.

The following season was the best of her career. She had four more victories and won the US Women's Open in Nashville, TN, with a record total of 280, in temperatures that exceeded 100 degrees every day. Rounds of 70, 70, 68 and 72 (the par was 71) were a tribute to Alcott's resilience, and she finished nine strokes ahead of the runner-up, her long-time rival Stacy. Alcott ended the season at number three on the money list with a haul of $219,887 and won the Vare Trophy with a stroke average of 71.51. She had 25 rounds under 70 and was *GOLF* magazine's Player of the Year.

In 1983, Alcott won the Dinah Shore for the first time, and it was a love affair that endured as she took the title again in 1988 and 1991, making quite a splash each time and setting a trend. In 1988, spurred on by her caddie Bill Kurre, the champion jumped into the lake surrounding the 18th green. "Everyone went crazy," Alcott said, "and I soon realized that I'd started something. It added a little colour and excitement to the Tour."

In 1991, when Alcott and her short, compact swing routed the opposition to win by eight shots, Dinah Shore, carefully clad in black slacks instead of her usual white, kept her pre-championship promise and dived into the drink with her good buddy. Shore, the singer and entertainer who had worked tirelessly to give the tournament the highest of profiles and raised the status of the players in the process, was made an honorary member of the LPGA in 1994, the year she died.

Alcott continued to play well in 1991 – she tied for second in the Atlantic City Classic and was third in the Open – but she just could not clinch an elusive 30th victory

Amy Alcott – the five-time major winner has made quite a splash at the Dinah Shore over the years

Beth Daniel 17

FULL NAME: Elizabeth Daniel

BORN: Charleston, SC, October 14, 1956

MAJOR CHAMPIONSHIPS: LPGA Championship 1990

Beth Daniel, born in Charleston, SC, comes from a golfing family and was a star as an amateur before she starred as a professional. She won the US Women's Amateur Championship twice, in 1975 and 1977, and was a member of the Curtis Cup teams of 1976 and 1978. She delayed turning professional to play in the Women's World Amateur Team Championship in Fiji in 1978.

The progression to the paid ranks appeared seamless, with a victory in her first season and 10th place on the money list. Daniel was the 1979 Rookie of the Year and in 1980, when she won four times, she was Player of the Year and number one on the money list with $231,000. She won twice in 1981 and led the money list again; in 1982, she won five times.

The helter-skelter progress slowed a little, with one win in 1983 and one in 1985. Between 1985 and 1989 there were no wins at all, although Daniel was second nine times in that period. She also suffered from mononucleosis in 1988, and missed 13 weeks of the season.

Normal service was resumed in 1989 when the tall, elegant southerner notched four wins and won the Vare Trophy with a stroke average of 70.38, a figure not bettered until Karrie Webb averaged 70.00 in 1997. "The Vare Trophy means a lot to me," Daniel said, "because I've never been considered a consistent player, and scoring average reflects consistency."

Daniel, an aggressive, go-for-broke matchplayer, was learning to play the percentages more as she matured, and in 1990 she had a season to dream of, winning seven times and earning $863,578, a record that stood for six years. Lee Trevino, who won $1 million on the Senior Tour, joked that all he tried to do was keep ahead of Daniel. She was Player of the Year again and won another Vare Trophy.

It was also the season in which Daniel, who had been runner-up in all four major championships, broke her duck, winning the LPGA Championship with a last round of 66. She also won $150,000, the largest first prize ever on the LPGA tour, but in the post-championship Press conference, the cheque didn't rate a mention from Daniel.

"In order to be considered a great player, you have to win major championships," she said. "It shows you can play your best golf under pressure. It shows you can be patient. It shows you can be lucky."

Undoubtedly one of the outstanding golfers of her generation, Daniel is still waiting for her second major title, and it is an omission that is keeping her out of the Hall of Fame. She has 32 victories to her name, but needs another three (or a major championship) to join the elite. Few of her peers doubt that she should be there, but she has not won since 1995, and had to have shoulder surgery in 1997.

The encouraging news was that she played a full schedule of 23 events in 1998, and although she missed six cuts in her first 11 outings, she did not miss another all season. There was only one finish in the top 10, a third place in the Betsy King Classic (her last tournament) an indication that Daniel is far from finished.

Beth Daniel – one of the outstanding golfers of her generation

Donna Caponi 16

FULL NAME: Donna Caponi

BORN: Detroit, MI, January 29, 1945

MAJOR CHAMPIONSHIPS: US Open 1969, 1970; LPGA Championship 1979, 1981; Dinah Shore 1980

There can surely be no more nerve-wracking situation than to arrive at the last hole of a tournament knowing that you need to birdie it to win. Not only that, the tournament is a championship, the US Women's Open, and it would be your first win as a professional golfer.

All that would be bad enough, but imagine that you then hit a good drive, and before you can get to your second, an electrical storm breaks, play has to be halted and for 15 minutes all there is to do is worry about what has still to be done.

But Donna Caponi, who found herself in precisely that situation at the Scenic Hills Country Club in Pensacola, FL, in 1969, did not let it bother her. She managed to keep herself calm throughout the delay, to go on and get the required birdie and become one of only 13 players to make their first professional win the US Women's Open.

The birdie gave her a round of 69, at that time the lowest-ever last round by a winner, and showed that there was nothing lacking in the temperament department. In fact, Caponi was to go on and defend her championship the following year at the Muskogee Country Club in Oklahoma, the first woman to achieve that feat since Mickey Wright had won in 1958–59.

Furthermore she equalled Wright's record total of 287 set in 1959, but the manner of Caponi's second win could hardly have been more different from that of the first. This time she finished with a round of 77, and from having a substantial lead after 54 holes found herself only one ahead after 71. She then double-bogeyed the last, but her challengers could not do much better.

Caponi operated off an exceedingly deliberate – not to say slow – rhythmic swing, but its effectiveness was shown in the 1979 US LPGA. She did not drop a shot for the first 50 holes of the event, and although records of such things are not kept, this is thought to be the best a woman professional has done.

Caponi, a striking woman who lists a love of music and dancing among her recreations, went on to win five major championships and record 24 wins in all on the LPGA tour. She is remembered in Europe because she also won the Colgate European Open, the tournament that was created by the then boss of Colgate, David Foster, and featured a full cast from the American Tour flown over especially for that one event.

Five of her Tour wins came in 1980 although, remarkably, she did not top the money list that year. She came second to Beth Daniel who, while winning only four times, was slightly more consistent in the other tournaments. In a career that effectively lasted from 1965 to 1988, she became the third player after JoAnne Carner and Kathy Whitworth to win more than $1 million in her career. She was nine times in the top 10 of the money list, twice runner-up, once third and a further four times in the top five – but has still not made the Hall of Fame. The LPGA has an extremely demanding set of qualifications, and although she has ample majors – the strictest requirement is only two – she did not win sufficient regular events to qualify.

Despite that, she has become one of the best-known faces in the golf world in America because of her regular appearances on television. She works as an on-course commentator for NBC, and is an analyst for The Golf Channel.

Donna Caponi – her first tour victory came at the 1969 US Open

Sandra Haynie 15

FULL NAME: Sandra Jane Haynie

BORN: Fort Worth, TX, June 4, 1943

MAJOR CHAMPIONSHIPS: US Open 1974; LPGA 1965, 1974; du Maurier Classic 1982

If it is the definition of a champion that they do what they have to do when they have to do it, then Sandra Haynie is a deserving champion. She was not playing as well as she could in the 1974 US Women's Open at La Grange Country Club in Illinois, nor did she convert the birdie chances that came her way.

Remarkably for such a good player, she had only three birdies in the first 70 holes of the championship, and it was a tribute to her short game and her sheer determination that she was still in contention. But other quality players were crowding around, sensing a win in a major – players of the calibre of JoAnne Carner, Kathy Whitworth, Beth Stone and Carol Mann.

Sandra Haynie – a true champion

Haynie knew that if all of them were to be shaken off, something would have to be done about the putting that had so far denied her. One behind playing the 71st hole, her shot to the green was much as many of its predecessors had been, and left her firmly in the two-, possibly three-putt area, some 70 feet from the hole.

But by now she realized that it was no good lagging the putt, no good ensuring that she didn't three-putt: she knew she had to hole it, so she did. That tied her for the lead, so there was still work to be done if a play-off was to be avoided. Her approach to the 18th was better by far than her effort at the 17th, leaving her with a chance from 15 feet, a chance that was eagerly accepted. Three birdies in the first 70 holes, with two in the last two to win by one.

Her rounds of 73, 73, 74, 75 reflected her consistency, and throughout her career, which ran from 1961 to 1989, she was a factor to be reckoned with. Four major championships were allied to no fewer than 42 tournament wins, and that combination was easily good enough to see her elected as a member of the Hall of Fame – one of only 16 players so honoured.

A tally of 42 tournament wins also places her fifth in the all-time list of winners behind Whitworth, Mickey Wright, Betsy Rawls and Louise Suggs.

Haynie was only 18 when she joined the Tour in 1961, and in her rookie year managed to finish 21st. In 1962 she won for the first time, taking the Austin Civitan Open and the Cosmopolitan Open, and from 1963 to 1975 she was in the top three of the money list no fewer than six times. In 1974 she joined Wright as only the second woman to win the LPGA Championship and the US Women's Open in the same season.

But the game was taking its toll both physically and mentally. From 1977 to 1980 she played only a very limited schedule, in part to protect a hurting back and in part because she enjoyed various business ventures, and during that period won a total of less than $18,000.

However, by 1981, rested and with appetite restored, she re-joined the Tour, playing a full schedule of 25 events. She even won one of them, her first tournament win since 1975, the Henredon Classic. She finished 13th in the rankings, and the following year did far, far better.

Although by now almost 40, she won first the Rochester International and then the Peter Jackson Classic, at that time a designated "major" on the LPGA Tour. Her comeback was complete, and the following year she again finished 13th in the rankings.

But by 1984 the old physical problems were returning. She slumped to 75th in the rankings and did not play the Tour in 1985. She underwent electrode treatment to deaden the sensitivity in her lower back and also had knee surgery, and although she played a few events in 1988, going through the $1 million barrier for career earnings in the process, her career was effectively over.

Patty Sheehan 14

FULL NAME: Patricia Sheehan
BORN: Middlebury, VT, October 27, 1956
MAJOR CHAMPIONSHIPS: US Open 1992, 1994; LPGA 1983, 1984, 1993; Dinah Shore 1996

At 5ft 3in, Patty Sheehan is not tall, but she has a big heart, which she tends to wear on her sleeve, and it has carried her to fame and fortune on the world's fairways.

Born in Vermont, she was first and foremost a skier – one of the best juniors in the country as a 13-year old – but she started to excel at golf and the pinnacle of her amateur career was being selected for the Curtis Cup in 1980. A bundle of energy and enthusiasm, she won all four of her matches at St Pierre, Chepstow.

Sheehan turned professional immediately afterwards and was Rookie of the Year in 1981, her first full season, winning once and finishing 11th on the money list with $118,463. In the next 12 seasons, she was formidably consistent, and never finished worse than eighth on the money list. She was second five times but, curiously, has never topped the rankings despite amassing over $5 million in prize money.

In 1983, Sheehan won four times; this included the LPGA Championship, the first of six major titles. She was also Player of the Year for the first, and so far only, time. In 1984, she retained her LPGA title and won the Vare Trophy with a stroke average of 71.40. Such honours have yet to come Sheehan's way again, but she has kept on chalking up victories – 35 at the last count – and overcoming setbacks.

In late 1989, her house was badly damaged in the San Francisco earthquake and she had no insurance. It concentrated her mind wonderfully and in 1990 she had by far the best financial season of her life, just when she really needed it. She won five times and earned $732,618, which was not enough to overhaul a rampant Beth Daniel at the top of the money list, but was a triumph for Sheehan.

She also showed rare strength of character to come back after a potentially soul-destroying collapse during the rain-disrupted 1990 US Women's Open in Atlanta. There were 36 holes on the last day and Sheehan, six shots ahead of Betsy King with nine holes to play, subsided, dizzy and exhausted, suffering from hypocglycemia, to lose out by a shot. It was the second time that King had pipped Sheehan to a major title; they had been in a play-off for the Dinah Shore in 1987. It was also the third time that Sheehan had been runner-up in the Open, 1983 and 1988 being the other occasions.

Many people feared that Sheehan would be scarred for life by that experience, but in 1992 she won the coveted title at Oakmont, defeating her old friend and rival Juli Inkster in a play-off, 72 to 74, after birdieing the 71st and 72nd holes to force the extra day. The demons exorcized, Sheehan won the championship again in 1994 and added the Dinah Shore in 1996.

In between, in 1993, she forced her way into the Hall of Fame with victory in the Standard Register Ping tournament in Phoenix, and added another LPGA championship to her résumé.

Patty Sheehan – a winner who overcame the setbacks

Pat Bradley 13

FULL NAME: Patricia Bradley

BORN: Weatford, MA, March 24, 1951

MAJOR CHAMPIONSHIPS: US Open 1981; LPGA 1986; Dinah Shore 1986; du Maurier Classic 1980, 1985, 1986

Pat Bradley, a quiet, earnest New Englander, prides herself on being the ultimate professional. She has certainly compiled a career to be proud of, with 31 victories, six of them coming in major championships.

An outstanding skier in her youth, Bradley joined the LPGA in 1974 and won her first tournament in 1976. She developed a reputation for hard work, determination and perseverance, and became renowned for her consistency, accumulating money and tournaments with a rare concentration and earnestness.

"I am very, very serious," she conceded. "Even crossing the street I'm extremely serious in my actions, but I'm out here for business." It developed into big business, too. In 1974, her rookie season, she won $10,839, but nearly a quarter of a century later she had taken her career earnings to over $5.5 million. She was the second player on the Tour to pass $5 million and the fourth to win over $1 million. In between, from 1986 to 1991, she was the first player to reach the $2, $3 and $4 million landmarks.

A money-making machine Bradley certainly was, but she also developed a knack for the big occasion, and is the only player so far to have won all four of the modern majors: the US Women's Open, the LPGA Championship, the Dinah Shore and the du Maurier Classic. In fact, in 1986, she won three of them and shared fifth place in the other, the Open, succumbing to the frenzy that inevitably surrounds a grand-slam bid.

Bradley won the first two majors, the Dinah Shore and the LPGA Championship, and got an inkling of the strain involved when she missed the cut the week after winning the LPGA title. That was nearly as newsworthy as the victories, because the consistent Bradley had missed only two cuts in the previous nine seasons. "I did not realize how much the LPGA had taken out of me emotionally and physically," she confessed.

The Open, the third leg of the slam, was much worse and even Bradley, skilled at cocooning herself in concentration, suffered. "There is no way you can close out the hype," she conceded. "They won't let you close it out. When the grand slam is building, no one will let you not think about it. The emotional strain is intense." At least she already had an Open title to her name, won in 1981.

Bradley, who was the defending champion, won the du Maurier a couple of weeks later and added the World Championship for good measure, the fifth win of a scintillating season. For the first time, she was Player of the Year, winner of the Vare Trophy and number one on the money list with earnings of $492,021. The grinder was established as a star, and her parents had been kept busy ringing the bell on the porch back home, the signal that there had been another Bradley win.

There was no bell ringing in 1988, when she was diagnosed with a thyroid condition called Graves Disease. However, it was back to business in 1989, and in 1991 Bradley was number one again, Player of the Year, Vare Trophy winner and leading money winner with $763,118. Best of all, the 30th victory of her career, in the last US event of the year, made her eligible for the Hall of Fame. It was the perfect way to cap a superb season.

Pat Bradley – the only woman to date to have won all four of the modern majors

JoAnne Carner 12

NAME: JoAnne Carner
BORN: Kirkland, WA, April 4, 1939
MAJOR CHAMPIONSHIPS: US Open 1971,76

When she was approaching 50, JoAnne Carner joked that she was putting the word out that after 20 years as a professional she was applying for reinstatement as an amateur so that she could terrorize all her old buddies again as a veteran. Ten years on, at 60, the irrepressible Carner was still playing on the LPGA tour, albeit with a much reduced schedule because of her husband's ill health.

Carner, née Gunderson, a droll extrovert, has been a fierce competitor all her golfing life. In 1955, she was runner-up in the US Girls' Junior championship, and in 1956 she won that title and was runner-up to Marlene Stewart of Canada in the US Women's Amateur. The Great Gundy, as she became known, went on to win the Amateur five times, in 1957, 1960, 1962, 1966 – when she beat Marlene Streit, née Stewart, at the 42nd hole of the final – and 1968. She played on four Curtis Cup teams and in 1969, still an amateur, she won the Burdine's Invitational professional tournament in Miami. The following season, at the advanced age of 30, she was a professional herself.

"When I turned pro, they told me I should figure to retire at 35," Carner recounted in her laconic style. "When I got to 35 and was still winning, they said I'd be through at 40. At 40 I was still going and at 44 I was leading money winner, so I guess they gave up on me."

She was Rookie of the Year in 1970 and won the first of 42 tournaments. In 1971 she won the US Women's Open to become the first – and so far only – person to win the Girls' Junior, Women's Amateur and Women's Open titles. She won the Open again in 1976, beating Sandra Palmer in a play-off, 76 to 78, and picking up the nickname "Big Momma" from her diminutive opponent. She had now won eight USGA championships, and only Bobby Jones had won more with nine.

In 1974, the big-hitting Carner swept the board with six victories, led the money list with $87,094, was Player of the Year and won the Vare Trophy for the first of five times. She showed no signs of retiring, and for the next 10 years she was never out of the top 10 on the money list, and was out of the top five only twice. The fans loved her uninhibited style and personality, and she adored the competition. She won the Vare Trophy again in 1975 and the Golf Writers of America Player of the Year award three years in a row from 1981. She was also Player of the Year in 1981 and 1982, and was leading money winner in 1982 and 1983, at the age of 44.

One of her proudest moments was when she won the World Championship of Women's Golf in 1982, the victory that gained her a place in the Hall of Fame. She was only the 10th member of what remains a very elite group.

In 1994, Carner captained the US Solheim Cup team to victory against Europe at The Greenbrier, and sported a sequinned baseball cap depicting the Stars and Stripes. She wore it with a jaunty swagger that made even the opposition smile, and it summed up the Big Momma philosophy: get among 'em and have fun.

JoAnne Carner – two-time US Open winner

Se Ri Pak 9a

FULL NAME: Se Ri Pak

BORN: Taejon, South Korea, September 28, 1977

MAJOR CHAMPIONSHIPS: US Open 1998; LPGA Championship 1998

It is a little early to tell if Se Ri Pak, the Korean sensation who has become the women's answer to Tiger Woods, will be enduring enough as a competitor to rank among the greatest players in the world, but she merits selection as a wild card simply because her start was so explosive and the impact on her home country so overwhelming.

The impact of her countrymen's expectations on the sturdy 21-year old, who won two major championships in her rookie season on the LPGA Tour, is another factor that will affect her longevity – and her physical and emotional well-being. When she went home at the end of the season, the demands upon her were so great that she collapsed from exhaustion and was admitted to hospital for a few days. Then there were reports of ructions within the Se Ri camp, and David Leadbetter stepped down as her coach, not long after his much-publicized split with Nick Faldo. It was all high-profile stuff, and it was little wonder that Se Ri, so unflappable on the golf course and such a cheerful giggler off it, was knocked sideways.

Quite simply, South Korea, the former economic miracle suffering from severe economic depression, went Se Ri crazy. The reaction was wild enough when she won the McDonald's LPGA Championship in Delaware in May after leading from start to finish, but her victory in the US Women's Open in Wisconsin in July caused euphoria on a nationwide scale. The girl from Taejon, south of Seoul – just 20 years old at the time – was seen as a morale-booster of mammoth proportions.

The president, Kim Dae-jung, sent her a telegram after the Open win, saying, "With all the Korean people, I express my joy over your victory. You are the hero of this era and our hope." The ambasssador in Washington said that she was the best news that the country had had all year, and her fellow citizens went around smiling. Se Ri made them proud to be Korean. Samsung, the conglomerate that signed Se Ri to a multi-million dollar, 10-year deal when she turned professional in 1996, were revelling in the exposure, and the newspapers took to calling the prodigy "the most competitive product South Korea has ever shipped abroad".

What no one should forget is that this is a person, not a product; a human being – and a very young one at that – not an icon. That might be difficult, however. The Se Ri phenomenon is in full swing.

She certainly has the game and the competitive nerve after some ferocious – not to say controversial – training by her father, Joon-Chul Pak, by his own admission a man with a criminal past. He was also a keen golfer and when Se Ri, aged 11, showed an interest and exceptional talent, he put her to work and kept pushing her to practise and improve, ignoring any tears.

He also devised the cemetery drill to "develop her bravery". His teenage daughter had to spend nights camping in the graveyard after he assured her that he would not let the ghosts get her. Se Ri coped, and has developed into an implacable opponent on the golf course, unfazed by anything. "I have no nerves," she replies to questions about the pressures of leading a major championship.

In fact, Se Ri became as obsessed as her father – if she hit a bad shot, she would spend hours working to erase the fault – and won a reported 30 tournaments as an amateur. At the 1994 World Amateur Team Championship in Paris, she shot 65 in the fourth round as her side finished second to the United States. When she turned professional in 1986, Se Ri played 12 tournaments on the Korean LPGA tour, won four times and was second seven times.

In 1997, she was sent to Florida to train under David Leadbetter – Samsung paid him a fee of $120,000 – and he recognized an exceptional talent. "The only problem I have," he said, "is stopping her from working too hard." She won two more tournaments when she went home to Korea, and was joint leading qualifier at the LPGA Qualifying School. Then came 1998.

In the LPGA Championship, Se Ri was paired with all-time greats JoAnne Carner and Nancy Lopez in the first two rounds, and impressed them both with the quality of her striking as she outscored them. Lopez, a player Se Ri admires greatly for her demeanour and durability, summed up: "She hits the ball long and she's very aggressive on the greens. She has a really great swing." At 5ft 7in, Se Ri is strong of body and of mind and she carried serenely on to her maiden LPGA victory, the youngest winner of the championship. "Nothing flusters her," confirmed Jeff Cable, her caddie.

The rookie's next four results were ordinary – a tie for 26th place was the best – but the US Women's Open at Blackwolf Run was a sensational championship with drama at every turn, and it eventually came down to a play-off between two 20-year-olds with an oriental flavour, Se Ri and Jenny Chuasiriporn, an American amateur whose father was born in Thailand. It took 20 extra holes to separate them (they were tied after the designated 18 holes, and it then became sudden death) and it was Se Ri, who had taken off her shoes and socks to play her second shot from the edge of the water at the 18th to keep her championship hopes afloat, who prevailed. "It was last chance, last day, last hole," she said, explaining why she had decided to risk the shot.

Even the stoic Se Ri, who shows little emotion on the course, but smiles a lot off it and has named her beagle puppy Happy, was moved to tears. The following week she won the Jamie Farr

Se Ri Pak – women's golf's answer to Tiger Woods

Kroger Classic by nine shots, scattering the opposition with a second round of 61, 10 under par, the lowest single round on the LPGA tour. She followed it up with a 63 and a 66. Two weeks later she won the Giant Eagle Classic, her third victory in four outings. She was Rookie of the Year by miles, won $872,170 and was second on the money list, behind Player of the Year Annika Sorenstam, who finished the season strongly.

"I want to be the best," said Se Ri, who is also working hard at her English. "That is my dream. I'm just starting – but it is a good start."

Annika Sorenstam 9

FULL NAME: Annika Sorenstam

BORN: Stockholm, Sweden, October 9, 1970

MAJOR CHAMPIONSHIPS: US Open 1995, 1996

Annika Sorenstam, a quiet, articulate Swede from Stockholm, is a phenomenon in a hurry. Neat, precise and unpretentious, she wins golf tournaments with a regularity that suggests she wants to have her career done and dusted by the time she is 30.

Firmly entrenched as the world number one at the end of 1998, but a professional for only six years, Sorenstam has compiled a record that is beginning to stand comparison with the very best, with 16 wins in the last four seasons on the LPGA tour. Her contemporaries are in awe of her consistency – "I do not make many mistakes," she agreed – and it is no accident. Sorenstam paces herself carefully and studies her statistics closely, entering them on her computer and assessing her strengths and weaknesses, so that she can work on improving. That is her main goal: to become a better player.

It is one of the few goals left to the woman who crammed a career's worth of achievements into one spectacular season, and then did it all again – and again. That makes life a little difficult for her younger sister Charlotta, a talented player who wants to be number one herself some day, but has to come to terms with the fact that whatever she does, another Sorenstam is likely to have done it first.

Nurtured by the Swedish system that has turned out a stream of good golfers, Sorenstam attended the University of Arizona, and was College Player of the Year in 1991 and the NCAA champion. In 1992, she was runner-up in the US Women's Amateur Championship and leading individual in the Women's World Amateur Team Championship in Vancouver before turning professional.

She was second on her first outing on the European tour, the Ford Classic at Woburn, and finished second three more times to end her rookie season in third place on the money list. She played quickly and with an admirable lack of fuss, intriguing everyone with her habit of lifting her head as she hit the ball. "I wouldn't recommend it," she said, but it has not impeded her progress.

In 1994, she was Rookie of the Year in America, a respectable 39th on the money list but without a win. The breakthrough came when she won the Australian Open at Royal Adelaide at the end of the year, but what happened in 1995 was the stuff of dreams and surprised even Sorenstam, whose goal for the season was to do well in Europe. She managed rather more than that, becoming the first player to top the money lists in Europe and the US in the same season.

Romantically, the run that made it all possible started in the third week of June, the week in which she announced her engagement to David Esch (they married in January 1997). Sorenstam won the OVB Damen Open in Austria – her maiden victory in Europe – and from then on she was virtually unstoppable. "I had no fear," she said. "I felt I could see no limits." Two weeks later, she won the Hennessy Cup, the second-richest event on the European tour, to take over the number-one spot from Laura Davies, and two weeks after that Sorenstam started touching the heights in America, winning the US Women's Open at The Broadmoor in Colorado Springs.

"I felt as though the nerves were swinging me at the end," Sorenstam confessed after beating Meg Mallon by a shot, but even though all the attention was so overwhelming that it made her ill, her golf showed little reaction, and she moved to the top of the US money list when she won the GHP Heartland Classic by 10 strokes. She made sure that she couldn't be overtaken when she won the World Championship of Women's Golf in dramatic fashion, chipping in to beat Davies at the first hole of a play-off.

Sorenstam became the second foreign player – following Ayako Okamoto – to be the LPGA's Player of the Year and the first to win the Vare Trophy, the award for the lowest scoring average. She was the Athlete of the Year in Sweden, the first golfer to win that honour, and then she sat back to think about what she would do for an encore, having moved the goalposts in no uncertain manner.

In 1996, she slipped to third on the US money list despite winning three times, including the US Women's Open again, when she blew the opposition off the fairways with closing rounds of 69 and 66 to win by six shots. She also won the Vare Trophy again, reducing her stroke average from 71.00 to 70.47, a statistic that told her that she was still getting better. She played only three European tournaments, winning one at home in Sweden, and was the only unbeaten member of Europe's Solheim Cup team; this was small consolation, though, as the US won handily after dominating the singles.

In 1997, Sorenstam scarcely made a false swing, winning six LPGA events and the money list with record earnings of $1,236,789. She was also player of the year again, and lowered her stroke average to 70.04. She was pipped to the Vare Trophy by Karrie Webb, who averaged 70.00, but the big disappointment was missing the cut at the US Women's Open, overwhelmed by the hype and hassle involved in attempting a hat-trick that had eluded everyone else.

If there's anything that Sorenstam dislikes about her celebrity status, it's the attention. There's nothing flamboyant about her game – although the results are little short of sensational – or her personality, and she does her best to keep herself to herself. The world number one is a very private person – even some Swedes accuse her of being boring, which is unfair; but she's also a persistent competitor with a mental toughness given to few. "I love to play. I love to grind. I love to compete," she says. To be true to herself, she has to give of her best, with the inevitable consequence that she keeps on attracting attention.

In 1998, she did it again. She won four times in the US, topped the money list with over a million dollars, was Player of the Year and became the first player to clinch the Vare Trophy with a stroke average of under 70.00. It was 69.99, and Sorenstam had to par her last round of the season to do it. She led the greens-in-regulation statistics – 78.1 percent – and in 21 starts she finished out of the top10 just four times. In a word, phenomenal – again.

Annika Sorentsam – became the first player to top both the US and European money lists in the same year

Betsy King 8

FULL NAME: Elizabeth King
BORN: Reading, PA, August 13, 1955
MAJOR CHAMPIONSHIPS: US Open 1989, 1990; LPGA Championship 1992; Dinah Shore 1987, 1990, 1997

Someone who knows her well once said that Betsy King burns inside, but few would guess: there is no steam coming out of the ears to hint at internal combustion. On the outside all seems cool and calm, for King, from Pennsylvania, has a reputation as golf's own ice maiden, always controlled and self-possessed. Active in the Fellowship of Christian Athletes, King is a perfectionist who goes to church most Sundays and also wins golf tournaments. It was 31 on the LPGA tour at the last count, including six major championships.

A graduate of Furman University, King – billed as Mary-Beth – finished tied for eighth in the US Women's Open while still an amateur in 1976, and was sufficiently encouraged to turn professional the following year. She was not immediately successful, and at the beginning of the 1980s she rebuilt her swing with the help of Ed Oldfield, a great believer in sound mechanics and hard work. "There's no magic to golf," Oldfield said. "The best players are the ones who are best co-ordinated and work hardest."

He warned King, who had once been driven to such despair by her putting that she visited a hypnotist, that things would get worse before they got better; but she worked diligently, her scoring average started improving and, at last, she won for the first time in 1984, at the Women's Kemper Open in Hawaii. It was the start of something very big because it opened the floodgates to a run of victories – at least two a year until 1993 – that took her into the Hall of Fame, a select body that has just 16 members. King became the 14th, gaining her place in 1995.

In 1984, King won three times in all, topped the money list with $266,771 and was Player of the Year for the first time. From 1984 to 1989 she won 20 times, more than anyone else during that period. That total does not include her victory in the Women's British Open at Moor Park in 1985, a time when the championship was just starting to build up its reputation and did not figure on the LPGA's official schedule.

All victories help, however, and King's confidence in herself and her game was growing all the time. In 1987 she won four tournaments, including the Dinah Shore – her first major championship – which she won in dramatic style, beating Patty Sheehan in a play-off after holing a bunker shot at the 70th hole to level the scores. Even the phlegmatic Pennsylvanian looked a bit excited when that went in.

She won the Vare Trophy that year and was second on the money list, less than $6,000 behind Ayako Okamoto, who also pipped her as Player of the Year. In 1988, King chalked up three more wins, but in 1989 she was outstanding and had the season of her career.

It started early, with victory in the Jamaica Classic – the first tournament of the year. King went on to win six times, holding off the challenges of Nancy Lopez and Beth Daniel, a team-mate at Furman, to finish as Player of the Year for the second time. King, who finished in the top five 16 times in 25 outings, topped the money list by a distance, with a record $654,132. Most coveted of all, she was US Women's Open champion for the first time, beating Lopez by four strokes at Indianwood Golf and Country Club in Michigan, having led from start to finish. "It was," King said, "the best golf of my career to that point."

In 1990, she confirmed her star status with victory in the Dinah Shore again, her third major championship, and she also retained her Open title in the most trying conditions at Atlanta Athletic Club. Torrential rain meant that the last 36 holes were squeezed into one day and King, nine shots behind Patty Sheehan after two rounds, squelched her way to victory by a shot as Sheehan was submerged by rounds of 75 and 76. At one stage in the third round, Sheehan had extended her lead to 12, but King was steadiness personified and stayed afloat with rounds of 71 and 70. "It was just a case of being in the right place at the right time," she said modestly.

She added another major championship (her fifth) to the list in 1992, when she won the LPGA Championship with a record total of 267, 17 under par. All four rounds were in the 60s (another first) and by some margin. Scores of 68, 66, 67 and 66 left little room for argument.

King finished the season in second place on the money list with $551,320. However, she and her much-vaunted team-mates were surprisingly defeated by Europe in the Solheim Cup at Dalmahoy. There was some sniping between the sides, with King and Daniel in the middle of it during their foursomes match (the first of the contest) against Laura Davies and Alison Nicholas. The Americans lost to set the tone but since those tetchy, rather un-Christian exchanges, King and Nicholas have travelled to Romania together, to work with an orphan relief organization, and the US (King included) have won the Solheim Cup three more times.

In 1993, King was a runner-up five times, but her only victory – in the Toray Queens Cup, the last event of the season – was invaluable. It meant that she was number one again: leading money winner, Player of the Year and Vare Trophy winner. It also meant that she needed only one more win to qualify for the Hall of Fame.

It took an unexpectedly long time – 594 days, to be exact – but she birdied the last two holes to win the Shoprite Classic in June 1995, and she was in. "Relief was the first feeling," she admitted. That season, she also became the first LPGA player to pass $5 million in career earnings, announced the inaugural

Betsy King – golf's own ice maiden

Betsy King Classic in her hometown of Reading and received the Samaritan Award, which is in recognition of a player's humanitarian and charitable efforts, for the second time. As well as visiting orphanages in Romania, King has done a lot of work for Habitat for Humanity, helping to build houses for the poor, hammering in nails with the best of them.

Hardly surprisingly, things have slowed down a bit since that momentous year, but King, who increased rather than reduced her schedule, won the Dinah Shore again in 1997 at the age of 41 to indicate that the competitive fires are still glowing.

Patty Berg 7

FULL NAME: Patricia Jane Berg

BORN: Minneapolis, MN, February 13, 1918

MAJOR CHAMPIONSHIPS: US Open 1946; Titleholders 1937, 1938, 1939, 1948, 1953, 1955, 1957; Western Open 1941, 1943, 1948, 1951, 1957, 1958

Patty Berg, one of the greatest ambassadors golf has ever had and a pioneer of the women's professional game, was once asked what she would change if she had the chance to live her life again. "Not a thing," Berg said. "I couldn't be this lucky twice."

The daughter of a grain merchant in Minneapolis, Berg learned to play at Interlachen, where Bobby Jones won the US Open in 1930, the year of the Impregnable Quadrilateral. Berg was running in the 30-yard dash at school (she won) and missed the action, but was aware of the excitement. "We were so happy that he won at our club," she said.

A red-haired, freckle-faced bundle of energy, Berg graduated to speed skating then golf after a spell as quarterback for the 50th Street Tigers. Bud Wilkinson, the football captain, who went on to play and coach professionally, told her that she was too slow and that there was no future for her in the game. "We only had one signal – 22," Berg said, "and everyone ran every which way. We didn't have wide ends or tight ends, just a lot of loose ends, but we never lost a game, just teeth." Berg's mother, tired of patching up knees and clothes and no doubt in fear of her daughter's dental bills, also had some say in the retirement.

Berg's first tournament, at the age of 15, was the Minneapolis city championship, and she scraped into the matchplay stages with a round of 122: "It should have been 140," she admitted – and was duly hammered. That set her off. For the next year she devoted herself to practice day in, day out, and won the city title in 1934, the first of many victories.

It was not all plain sailing, however. In 1935, Berg played in an exhibition with a distinguished group that included Walter Hagen, and she was so tense that she hit nothing but people – five in all – on the first nine. "I don't know about that girl," Hagen said. "She's dangerous." Later that year, when Berg reached the final of the US Women's Amateur at Interlachen, Hagen sent her a telegram. "Congratulations," it read. "All is forgiven. Best wishes and good luck."

Berg lost that final and was beaten again in 1937, but she won the title in 1938. She also played in the Curtis Cup sides of 1936 and 1938 before turning professional in 1940, signed up by the Wilson Sporting Goods company. There were only three tournaments open to professionals, with prize money totalling $500, but Berg – outgoing and enthusiastic – was a tireless giver of clinics and exhibitions. Her quick-fire delivery, barked out like a sergeant major so that the people at the back would be sure to hear, was famous; she had a stream of jokes and one-liners that she delivered with all the timing and aplomb of a practised comedian. As an amateur, encouraged by her father who did the organizing, she had played in numerous exhibitions for charity. Being on the road and giving of herself was ingrained in her.

In 1941, the day after Pearl Harbor, Berg was involved in a car crash, broke her knee in three places and was out of action for 18 months. The knee wasn't set properly and had to be broken again, but the indomitable Berg worked her way back to fitness, and in 1943 she won the Western Open and the All-American Open at Tam O'Shanter. Then she joined the Marines, and served for two years in public relations and recruiting until the end of the war.

In 1946, Berg won the first US Women's Open title, which was two rounds of qualifying followed by matchplay. She beat Betty Jameson by five and four in the 36-hole final at Spokane Country Club, and won $5,600 in bonds. In all, Berg won 57 tournaments as a professional, and tops the list of major championship winners with 15 victories: one in the Open, seven in the Titleholders Championship and seven in the Western Open. Three times, in 1948, 1955 and 1957, she won two of the three majors. She also won an event called the Hardscrabble Open three times, and scrabble hard is what the pioneering professionals had to do a lot of the time, with their fields filled out by amateurs as they barnstormed their way around the country.

The Women's Professional Golf Association, founded in 1944 by Hope Seignious on a wing and a vision more than anything else, struggled on until it was superseded at the end of the decade by the Ladies' Professional Golf Association, which had the financial backing of Wilson and appointed Fred Corcoran as tournament director, a role he'd had on the men's tour. Berg was the LPGA's first president, and she went on to be the leading money winner in 1954, 1955 and 1957 for a total of $48,775, and won the Vare Trophy (the benchmark of consistency established in 1953) in 1953, 1955 and 1956. Her averages were 75.00, 74.47 and 74.57.

Courses were long (6,400 yards on average) and varied from championship venues to scrub. Berg once shot 64 at Richmond Country Club, a tough course in California, and Betsy Rawls still reckons it is one of the best rounds she has witnessed. Berg, who like everyone else was overshadowed by Babe Zaharias, was an outstanding player, and the smooth-swinging Mickey Wright, recognized by many good judges as the best woman player of all time, nominated Berg as the finest woman golfer she ever saw, commenting that she knew more golf shots than anyone else.

What is more, she taught those shots to others. Wilson would send its new recruits to Berg and she would put them through their paces, teaching them how to give clinics, how to hit shots to order, how to give speeches, how to conduct themselves as professionals and people. She herself would give a clinic or a speech at a moment's notice – anything to promote the LPGA and the game itself. Nothing daunted her. A woman with a strong religious faith, she fought her way back from cancer surgery with vim and vigour, adding another cause to her long list. She probably has more awards for her charitable endeavours than for her golf, which is no mean feat for a player who is in every Hall of Fame going.

A friend once described her as a frustrated actress, but in fact Berg has been on the professional stage for nigh on 60 years, always keeping the show on the road.

Patty Berg – more major championship titles to her name than any other woman golfer

Kathy Whitworth – a career with 88 LPGA tour victories

Kathy Whitworth 4

FULL NAME: Kathrynne Ann Whitworth

BORN: Monahans, TX, September 27, 1939

MAJOR CHAMPIONSHIPS: LPGA Championship 1967, 1971, 1975; Titleholders Championship 1965, 1966; Western Open 1967

One thing that can never be said for Kathy Whitworth is that she had a classic golf swing. There was not much in the ease and grace department as far as this superb American golfer was concerned, but she certainly made it work.

Kathy Whitworth won more events on the LPGA tour than anyone before or since, and the figure of 88 that she established seems certain to stand for all time. She did it with a method that seemed tortuous, working its way back slowly, inside the line and then making an unhurried way back to the ball.

But Whitworth's great gift was not only that she could make it work consistently. It was a swing that repeated, time and again, in situations of the greatest pressure, and it gave her a record of which any golfer – man or woman – would be proud.

In a playing career that spanned 24 years, she was leading money winner eight times between 1961 and 1973, and for 15 years was never out of the top 10. She was Player of the Year seven times, Vare Trophy winner for the lowest stroke average on seven occasions, and won three LPGA championships, two Titleholder's victories and the Dinah Shore championship.

There was only one blip: she did not win the US Women's Open, although when she came third in 1981 it took her past the $1 million mark in career earnings, the first woman to accomplish such a feat. And if the Open passed her by, she did win six events designated at the time by the LPGA as "majors". In 1967, a year in which the women's tour had three majors, she won two of them: the LPGA Championship and the Western Open.

It was a terrific record, one that got her elected to the Hall of Fame in 1975 and named "Golfer of the Decade" by *GOLF* Magazine for the years 1968–1977.

Whitworth joined the tour in 1958, won her first tournament in 1962 and had the first crisis of her professional career that same year. "I was in Salt Lake City and I had been playing really well," she recalls. "I was going out to the practice tee and hitting a lot of balls great, and then I'd go to the first tee and I could hardly get the club back. You know, paralysis set in and I just stood there and thought, 'Oh my Lord, I can't play'."

To try to get over it, Whitworth did what a great many people on the Tour did in those days. She went to the fount of all knowledge, Mickey Wright, and said: "I go to the practice tee and hit it just great, so good that I don't know what else there can be to work on, and then I get to the first tee and can't even get the club back. Is there such a thing as being too swing conscious?"

Wright told her that yes, there was, and so Whitworth abandoned the practice ground for that week. "I never thought about the game. I went to the movies, anything to get my mind off the game and off the swing. I realized that when I got to the course I had to trust my swing, and that's when I really began to get into course management. I never thought about my swing again that week, and I finished second and went on to win another tournament that year.

"That was a big turning point for me. I wasn't a great striker, but I would put my course management against anybody's."

That week in 1962 apart, Whitworth was actually a great worker at the game. She was one of the pupils of that great teacher, Harvey Penick, the man who also taught Ben Crenshaw, Tom Kite and Betsy Rawls, and would visit Penick for days at a time.

"I would drive over," she says, "and stay near Harvey's club for about three days. I'd take lessons from him all day and then, when he was done, I'd go to a driving range and practise what he'd been saying."

The end result was a golfer who knew about her swing, a player who understood just what had to be done to score well. She had a mastery of all the shots, and there were times when she actually had to prove this to order.

"We used to do exhibitions for Wilson Sporting Goods," she says, "and we had to demonstrate all these different shots and we'd have to talk about how to do 'em – and then do 'em. If we wanted to hook the ball, well, this is how you hook it and you stand up and hook it. If we wanted to slice a ball, then we'd slice it, or a high ball, or a punch shot; we'd have to demonstrate all these shots, and so we used to practise them all the time.

"We'd do about 40 or 50 of these exhibitions every year, so when we got into trouble on the golf course – and everyone's going to get into trouble 'cos no one's that perfect – we could manufacture shots and get out of it. I learned bunker shots at those exhibitions; Patty Berg taught me. I was the worst trap player in the world, but she was the one who taught me how to get out, and because of those exhibitions I became very proficient at trap play.

"But a player still has to manage herself on the course. Someone like Mickey Wright was so technically great that she just had to go out there and execute, but I needed to manage myself, and I think that I did that just about as well as anybody can."

Whitworth learned an invaluable lesson in the middle of her career. In 1963 she won eight tournaments, but in 1964 she struggled all year, winning nothing. As the season drew to its close she had dinner with her first teacher, Hardy Loudermilk, and, as she puts it, "I was poormouthing to Hardy about all my woes for that year when he suddenly said, 'Well, it sounds like you have the big head to me.' Well, that hurt my feelings so much at first, but then I realized he wouldn't say it if it wasn't true.

"I went out on the golf course the next day and sure enough the bounce didn't go my way and I was starting to think, 'Why does it happen to me?...' and then I thought, 'Oops, there it is...,' and it just hit me right between the eyes. So I worked really hard to get my mind back straight, and I won the tournament.

"But that was such a big lesson for me that I thought, 'I will never, ever, ever take for granted winning again.'"

Lessons like that, plus a mental resilience given to few, ensured her career thereafter. A gracious woman and golfer, she nevertheless gave the outward appearance of a toughie, so much so that the celebrated Atlanta journalist, Furman Bisher, once wrote of her that she was the type of person who, when the Indians attacked, you would hand the rifle to and say: "Here, you hold 'em off while I go for help."

However, she did not quite achieve her earliest, and continuing, ambition. "All I ever wanted," she would say, "was to be the greatest-ever woman golfer." That accolade lies elsewhere, but without a doubt she was the most successful.

Babe Zaharias 5

FULL NAME: Mildred Ella Didrickson Zaharias

BORN: Port Arthur, TX, November 26, 1911

MAJOR CHAMPIONSHIPS: US Open 1948, 1949, 1954; Titleholders Championship 1947, 1950, 1952; Western Open 1940, 1944, 1945, 1950

It is sometimes hard to separate fact from fiction when it comes to the exploits of Mildred Didrickson Zaharias, universally known as Babe – after Babe Ruth, because of her ability to hit home runs in baseball games as a girl. Rough, tough and immodest, the Texan was an athlete overflowing with talent, and performed unlikely, jaw-dropping feats with such regularity that people believed her capable of anything. In a poll conducted by the Associated Press, she was voted the Woman Athlete of the First Half of the Twentieth Century.

If it involved running, jumping, throwing or hitting, the Babe excelled. She could also knit, type, play the harmonica and blow her own trumpet. At one particular athletics championship in 1932, she was allowed to enter eight events – the previous limit was three – and in the space of three hours she won six gold medals and broke four world records, a one woman team. Later that year, at the Olympics in Los Angeles, she won gold in the hurdles and the javelin, but was disqualified in the high jump. This was the stuff of headlines.

Babe took up golf seriously in 1933 and she won the Texas Women's Championship in 1935, but someone complained to the United States Golf Association (USGA) and she was barred from amateur events because she was a professional athlete, earning her living from basketball and baseball tours – and vaudeville. She added golf to the list, and played exhibitions with the likes of Gene Sarazen and Joyce Wethered, who later reflected graciously that she was lucky to play her championship golf before the Babe exploded on the scene, shaking up what was rather a genteel, privileged game.

Sarazen remained adamant that Wethered was the best woman golfer of them all, but said that once the Babe – who was not a big woman but was remarkably strong and supple – stopped trying to belt a seven iron as far as a two iron, she started to develop "a grooved swing and a glorious golf game". The general consensus was that if she had taken up the game earlier, she would have been still more sensational; as it was, she made quite an impact.

In 1938, she married George Zaharias, a large, ebullient wrestler who arranged tours to far-flung places such as Australia and New Zealand, but an exhibition was not competition, and in 1940 Babe applied for reinstatement as an amateur. This came through in 1943 and after the Second World War the Zaharias legend swung into overdrive, with some sources crediting her with 17 successive victories in 1946 and 1947. Others made the total 13, but one fact was indisputable: she was hard to beat.

She won the 1946 US Women's Amateur with ease, hammering Clara Sherman by 11 and 9 in the 36-hole final, and in 1947 George dispatched Babe to Gullane in Scotland to compete in the Ladies' British Open Amateur Championship. Not everyone approved of her extrovert ways, but dull she was not. One day she turned up in red and white checked shorts, and was sent back to change into something more decorous; when asked how she hit the ball so far, she replied, rather shockingly: "I just loosen my girdle and let it fly." She smashed the ball and the opposition out of sight, and became the first American to win the title when she defeated Jacqueline Gordon by five and four in the final. She returned to New York in triumph aboard the Queen Mary, and was met by a whole posse of sportswriters in a tug organized by George.

Babe promptly turned professional again – there was a film offer that she couldn't turn down – and rumour had it that she received more for her exhibitions than Ben Hogan or Sam Snead. She was managed by Fred Corcoran, who also managed Snead, so the rumour may not be entirely correct, but between them they made a few bob. Babe, who was always quick with a quip and liked the last word, was never one to undervalue herself.

In 1948, when Babe won the first of her three US Women's Open titles, the entire prize fund was $7,500, but when she won it for the second time, in 1950, the money had fallen to $5,000, as the fledgling LPGA tour struggled to find its feet. That it survived was due in no small measure to Babe's flamboyance and pulling power, a fact readily acknowledged by Patty Berg, whose energy and showmanship were unflagging and who harboured no resentment towards her limelight-hogging peer. "We needed her," Berg said. "She had so much flair and colour."

Others were less charitable, and disliked the star turn's domineering ways. She hated losing at anything, even cards, and would walk into the locker room and ask who was going to be second. That sort of behaviour didn't endear her to her peers, but she just kept on winning – until 1953, when she went into hospital with stomach pains and was diagnosed with cancer of the bowel. The doctors said that she would never play championship golf again, but they reckoned without Babe's strength and fortitude, and she was back on the tournament trail less than four months after a colostomy.

Even her detractors were impressed when she won the US Women's Open again in 1954, dominating the championship, at the Salem Country Club in Massachusetts, with rounds of 72, 71, 73 and 75, to win by 12 shots from Betty Hicks. On a difficult course, the Babe had nothing worse than a five on her card over the four rounds, even on the last day when she had to play 36 holes and her game became a little ragged with fatigue towards the end. She sliced her drive into the trees at the last but, ever the show-woman, ignored the safe option and fired a long iron through a tiny gap on to the green. The crowd loved it all and

Babe Zaharias – the greatest woman athlete of all time?

so did the Babe. It was probably her finest hour.

She won five tournaments that year and the Vare Trophy with a stroke average of 75.48, and also earned $11,437 in prize money. She was the Associated Press Woman Athlete of the Year for the sixth time in what was her last full season of golf.

In 1955, she won twice to take her official tally of professional victories to 31, but she was unable to defend her Open title because of another operation, as the cancer took over and she was in and out of hospital until her death in September 1956, at the age of 45.

Nancy Lopez 4

FULL NAME: Nancy Marie Lopez

BORN: Torrance, CA, January 6, 1957

MAJOR CHAMPIONSHIPS: LPGA Championship 1978, 1985, 1989

Nancy Lopez, with dark good looks, flashing smile and a competitive instinct second-to-none, became a golfing legend in no time at all, drawing unprecedented attention to the women's game and having the same sort of effect that Arnold Palmer had had in the early 1960s. She had the same charisma, the same rapport with the fans and also played the game in a slightly unorthodox, no-holds-barred style.

Her sunny disposition is probably a reflection of a piece of advice her father Domingo gave her when she got frustrated with the game: "You can't see the ball when you're crying. Be happy and play happy," he said.

Lopez took to the game quickly, winning the New Mexico Women's Amateur Championship at the age of 12, and she came to wider notice when she won the US Girls' Junior Championship at her first attempt in 1972. She had an awful grip and a big slice, but she putted fearlessly and revealed a gift to win. She won the title again in 1974 and, still an amateur, was joint runner-up in the US Women's Open in 1975. In 1976, she played in the Curtis Cup and was the leading individual as the United States won the Espirito Santo, the Women's World Amateur Team Championship. She turned professional in 1977.

In 1978, her rookie season, Lopez was sensational, phenomenal, incredible; pick your own superlative. She had a wonderful rhythm, hit the ball far and high, and putted boldly, with no fear of the three-footers back. In all she smiled her way to a staggering nine victories. Even better, five of those wins were in consecutive outings – a tour record, and a dream come true for Ray Volpe, commissioner of the LPGA, a marketing man to the soles of his shoes. The tour and its beaming bombshell were big news, the talk of the nation.

There were carpers, those who resented all the attention lavished on a player whose style was far from classical – the takeaway certainly had too many hitches for the purists – but they were drowned out by the devotees as Lopez took everyone's breath away. She led the money list, was Player of the Year, won the Vare Trophy and was, by some distance, Rookie of the Year.

Lopez slipped a little in 1979, winning a mere eight times, but she was again Player of the Year, winner of the Vare Trophy and leading money winner and proved that she could cope with the celebrity status, even though it puzzled her. A couple of decades on, she said, "I felt like they were just worshipping me for the way I was playing, and to me I was just playing golf. You look at people and wonder what they see."

They continued to see Lopez win tournaments – although in more modest quantities – and act in the gracious, dignified manner that endeared her to an army of fans all over the world. She dominated the public consciousness and inspired spectators and players alike. Few role models were more deserving of the title.

She married Ray Knight, a baseball player, in 1982 and they have three daughters. Ashley, the oldest, was born in 1983 and it was thought that motherhood would be the end of Lopez as a competitive force, but Knight encouraged his wife to keep competing and in 1985 she was number one again, topping the money list, winning Player of the Year and the Vare Trophy. She played 25 tournaments and was in the top 10 a total of 21 times, winning on five occasions including the LPGA Championship, one of the four majors.

In the LPGA, a title she has won three times so far in her career, Lopez demonstrated the mental resilience that is the hallmark of all true champions. In the first round, she was penalized two shots for slow play – "It's not a cross-country race," she protested – and a 63 became a 65. She followed up with rounds of 71, 72 and 65 to win by eight shots. To date the LPGA, which she has won three times, is her only major championship, although she won the Dinah Shore a couple of seasons before it was designated a major.

In 1987, Lopez became the 11th player to be inducted into the LPGA's Hall of Fame at a glittering ceremony in Tiffany's on Fifth Avenue in New York, with tributes paid by golfing greats and golfing presidents. The following year, *GOLF* magazine named her "Golfer of the Decade" for the years 1978–1987.

Her family was now her priority but Knight, who was named MVP when the New York Mets came from behind to win the World Series in 1986, made sure that it was not all domesticity. A great motivator, he wanted Lopez to make the most of her talent while she could, and in 1988 she won three times and was Player of the Year for the fourth time. She also passed the $2 million mark in career earnings.

For someone with a supposedly suspect method, Lopez has been remarkably enduring and has 48 victories to her name so far, the last coming in 1997 after three seasons without a win. The thought of being fat and 40 concentrated her mind wonderfully and she took herself in hand, working out with a personal trainer to become instead fit and 40. She had tired of playing golf that she found embarrassing – it was knuckle down or quit, she decided – and the transformation was such that she was little short of outstanding in the US Women's Open of 1997.

It is a championship that Lopez has never won – she has been runner-up four times – and as time goes on it inevitably gets harder to overcome the psychological challenge, let alone the physical one. At Pumpkin Ridge, Lopez became the first player to break 70 in each round of the championship, with huge, emotional galleries and a vast television audience willing her on. It was compelling stuff. The only problem was that Alison

Nancy Lopez – a glittering role model and an inspiration to thousands

Nicholas, a tenacious Englishwoman, produced the performance of her career and finished one shot better.

Like Sam Snead, perhaps Lopez is destined never to win the US Open, but she has won so many hearts that in 1998 the United States Golf Association presented her with its highest honour, the Bob Jones Award, in recognition of her sportsmanship and devotion to the spirit of the game. Not to mention a smile that lit up the golfing world.

Laura Davies 3

FULL NAME: Laura Jane Davies

BORN: Coventry, England, October 5, 1963

MAJOR CHAMPIONSHIPS: US Women's Open 1987; LPGA Championship 1994, 1996; du Maurier Classic 1996

Laura Davies's penchant for giving the ball an almighty clout – drives of 300 yards plus have been known – has earned her a worldwide reputation. For 15 years now she has been exciting galleries as far apart as Tokyo, Tucson and Tunbridge Wells.

More or less self-taught, she played in the Curtis Cup in 1984 and turned professional in 1985, having borrowed her stake from her mother, Rita. It proved a sound investment and the loan was quickly repaid when Laura won one tournament and the order of merit – earning £21,736 – in her rookie season in Europe. By the end of 1998, the sports-mad girl whose headmaster told her that she wouldn't make any money from golf had earned in the region of $7 million in prize money and won 54 tournaments all over the world.

In 1986, Davies gave the first indication that she was not just a big-hitting fish in a small pond when she finished 11th in the US Women's Open, and a few months later she won the British Women's Open at Royal Birkdale, starting the last round birdie, eagle and eclipsing the field by four shots. The sight and sound of her towering shots intimidated the opposition and captivated the crowd. She was Europe's number one for the second time, and the Tour had found itself a superstar.

Even so, the golfing world was shocked when the 23-year-old Englishwoman, sublimely talented but still raw, won the US Women's Open at Plainfield, NJ, in July 1987, defeating the legendary American JoAnne Carner and Japanese idol Ayako Okamoto, who was US number one that season, in an 18-hole play-off. Davies's length and easy-going attitude impressed Carner immensely, and Okamato was so overwhelmed that she described Davies as "a player from another dimension". At home, Davies made the front pages, not a regular habitat for women golfers.

In America, the Ladies' Professional Golf Association (LPGA) changed its constitution so that Davies was granted automatic membership without having to plough through the qualifying school, and she was widely expected to take the States by storm. In 1988 she won twice, finished 15th on the money list and was beaten to the Rookie of the Year title by Liselotte Neumann, who, inspired by Davies's example, won the US Women's Open that season.

Davies, a true globetrotter, refused to concentrate solely on the American circuit and also won three times in Europe, where she was second on the money list, and once in Japan. However, the going was tougher in the US, where the competition was stronger and the players more mature and battle-hardened, and at first Davies did not dominate as predicted. A free spirit, she had no time for technical niceties and spent little time on the practice ground, preferring shopping or gambling or a game of football, tennis or cricket – indeed anything – to beating balls.

Any coaching she had was of the informal variety, the odd tip from a friend or from the television, where she loved watching and learning from the likes of Seve Ballesteros and Fred Couples. In essence, she just went with the flow, mixing the inconsistent with the incredible, always exciting and unpredictable to watch, never dull and boring, ever willing to take a risk – a crowd-puller, doing things her way.

Offering her advice remains a delicate business. She once partnered Andy Bean in the JC Penney Classic, and didn't take kindly to his suggestions to lay up short of the water on occasion. She's now paired with John Daly. As Beth Daniel put it: "You can't make Laura play conservatively. It is not part of her nature. She is a freewheeler." She is not stupid, however, and she will listen to people she respects on matters ranging from her diet to her putting, the aspect of her game that caused her untold frustration as she got older.

There were low times – in 1990, the worst year of her career, she won only once – but in 1992, she was Europe's number one again and inspired Europe to an unexpected victory over the Americans in the Solheim Cup at Dalmahoy. It was one of the great sporting upsets and Davies, a woman possessed, won all three of her matches and was the Ballesteros-like totem for her side. "If Laura played like that every week, she'd win half a dozen tournaments a year and millions of dollars," an American remarked. "If I played like that every week I'd be in the loony bin," Davies replied.

Even so, Dalmahoy boosted European confidence and self-belief, and Davies was one of four Europeans to win on the LPGA tour in 1993. She also won in England, Thailand and Australia, but surpassed that in 1994, when she became the first player – man or woman – to win on five tours in one calendar year, and realized her dream of being the world number one. She was the leading money winner in the US – another long-held ambition – with $687,201 and won three tournaments, including her second major championship. She won twice in Europe, once in Thailand, once in Japan and once in Australia.

In 1995, Davies won six times worldwide, but had to settle for the number-two spot in Europe and America behind the Swedish sensation Annika Sorenstam. It was a double top that the Englishwoman had coveted, and losing out hurt, but she bounced back in 1996 with the best season of her career (nine wins) and regained the world number-one spot. She was Europe's number one for the fourth time and was Player of the Year in the US, winning three events – two of them majors – and earning $927,302, which would have won the money list easily in every previous year. In 1996, however, Karrie Webb, a rookie from Australia, won over $1 million.

Laura Davies – the first player, man or woman, to win on five tours in a calander year

A streak of 23 wins in three seasons is hard to follow, and in 1997 Davies won a mere three times, once in the US. Typically, there was nothing low-key about it. It was the fourth year in succession that she had won the event, the Standard Register Ping in Phoenix, AZ, to set a tour record and put her alongside Gene Sarazen and Walter Hagen as the only other players to manage the feat. It was also the 50th victory of a career that has established her as both one of the most gifted players of all time and one of the most successful – and the crowds still flock to see her.

Mickey Wright – the most technically proficient swing the women's game has ever seen

Mickey Wright 2

FULL NAME: Mary Kathryn Wright

BORN: San Diego, CA, February 14, 1935

MAJOR CHAMPIONSHIPS: US Open 1958, 1959, 1961, 1964; LPGA Championship 1958, 1960, 1961, 1963; Titleholders' Championship 1961, 1962; Western Open 1962, 1963, 1966

It is a measure of the true greatness of Mickey Wright that there was hardly a professional – man or woman – who did not look up to her. Most good judges are agreed that she possessed the most technically proficient swing that the women's game has ever seen, and 82 career wins (including four US Opens) testify to the fact that she had a temperament to match. It is estimated that she won over a quarter of the tournaments she entered.

Of those 82 victories, 44 came between 1961 and 1964, her

invincible period when she averaged 11 wins per season. It was a time when she achieved an impregnable mix; she knew she was going to win, her opponents knew she was going to win, and she knew that her opponents knew that she was going to win.

Not that she would ever have let on. Miss Wright was, even during her days of public performances, essentially a shy person – a golfer who, after the round was played, would retire rapidly to her hotel. Her idea of a good night out was dinner with some friends, when the talk would preferably be about something other than golf.

That would be difficult, though, if there were other golfers around, for she did so many remarkable things on the golf course that they all wanted to know the secret. There wasn't one, of course, except that, just like Severiano Ballesteros, she had an instinctive understanding of what to do in impossible situations. The difference between her and the Spaniard was that she got on with the job in hand with a minimum of fuss and a complete absence of the dramatics that always accompanied a Ballesteros special.

Kathy Whitworth played lots of golf with Wright, and could only wonder at some of the things she did. "We were playing one hole, a par 5," said Whitworth, "and I had to lay up short of the green. Mickey is behind some trees after her drive and although she could get over them, the problem was to get over them with a club long enough to reach the green.

"Well, I think she hit a four-iron, and nobody in the world could have lifted a four-iron up as quickly as Mickey did, and she hit it about three feet from the hole. And you know, I'm laughing and having the best time because some of the other competitors have come out to watch her play, and I say, 'This is the sort of thing I have to put up with.' Of course, she holed the three-footer for an eagle, and I told her, 'You know Mickey, what is so sad about that is very few people will know how great a golf shot you've just hit.'"

Whitworth, herself one of the great players, needs little encouragement to go on and on about Wright. She recalls the time that Wright's ball was just behind a tree, which meant that although she had a backswing, any suggestion of a follow-through would mean either a broken club or broken knuckles, or both.

"It's probably about a 160-yard shot, and she's taking these huge practice backswings and coming through as hard as she can and stopping the club dead, and it is all so fascinating that I sidle over, thinking, 'I gotta see this.' Anyway, she takes this huge swing, the ball just explodes off the clubhead, and of course it just sails right up there on the green, and I'm thinking, 'No way could I play a shot like that.'

"But it was something she had practised, something she had taught herself how to do, so that was not a phenomenal shot to her, but to me, oh, it just blew my mind."

One of the reasons that Wright is not perhaps as well-known or as properly recognized as she certainly should be is that the height of her career, in the early 1960s, clashed directly with the time that Arnold Palmer and Jack Nicklaus were breathing fire at each other and dominating the golf coverage. It was the time, too, of fledgling television coverage, and the cameras concentrated almost exclusively on the men.

This was a pity, because Wright was more than just a good golf swing. She was both attractive and intelligent, and had an aura about her that instantly appealed. Added Whitworth: "People have always just loved her. They feel special when they're around her. There's an easy grace about Mickey, a charm. She has charisma, and when she walks in a room you just know that you're in the presence of somebody that is a little bit special."

What was it about her golf, though, that made her special? The leading American golf writer Herb Warren Wind felt that her technique was much as a man would play.

In *The Story of American Golf*, Wind says: "She struck the ball with the same decisive hand action that the best men players use, she fused her hitting action smoothly with the rest of her swing, which was like Hogan's in that all the unfunctional moves had been pared away, and like Jones's in that its cohesive timing disguised the effort that went into it."

Perhaps the most instructive part of that commentary is the players that Wind uses as comparisons, although Wright herself thought of her swing slightly differently. Once, when it was pointed out to her that people had said she had the perfect golf swing, Wright replied: "There's no such thing. But I think that because I used to watch Gene Littler, the idea of swinging the club well and swinging it prettily was always important to me – to my detriment.

"You know, you don't score well just by swinging it nicely and hitting it well, but that was always extremely important to me. A good golf swing has always been much more important to me than scoring well."

She went on: "Of course you have to learn everything in golf. That's what makes it such an outstanding challenge. But my strength was my good golf swing which allowed me to be a fine long-iron player. I was able to hit the ball high, carry it a long way. Jackie Burke Jnr (a Ryder Cup player and captain) watched me hit a few balls back in the 50s. He said: 'That's very good young lady. I'll give you one tip. You hit the ball high. Learn to hit it higher. Don't ever forget that.'

"I thought that was one of the keys that helped make me a good player. You cannot hit the golf ball high with a bad golf swing. It's impossible, you cannot do it."

Nor, of course, with a swing like Wright's do you hit many bad shots, and during her career she held just about every record available on the women's tour. Once, in 1964, she remarked on this to Leonard Wirtz, then the LPGA tournament director, who called her attention to the fact that there was one she didn't hold: the lowest score for 18 holes.

The very next tournament she went out and shot 62, a score that was not to be beaten for 34 years, in an altogether different era.

Joyce Wethered 1

FULL NAME: Joyce Wethered

BORN: November 17, 1901

CHAMPIONSHIPS: British Amateur 1922, 1924, 1925, 1929

One of the best-known remarks ever made about any woman golfer was that of Bobby Jones about Joyce Wethered, later to become Lady Heathcoat-Amory. Jones, who could be said to be something of an authority on the subject, said of Wethered that she had the best swing of any golfer, male or female, that he had ever seen. He added: "I have never played with anyone, man or woman, amateur or professional, who made me feel so outclassed."

Outclassed! Bobby Jones! The man who, in 1930, became the only man ever to win the Grand Slam, the Open and Amateur Championships of the USA and the United Kingdom. And yet it was that same year that he played a match against Wethered at St Andrews, with both hitting from the very back of the back tees, and with Wethered, by then retired from championship golf, going round in 75. It was after that match that Jones gave that considered opinion, which has gone into golfing folklore.

Nor was the great man alone in his opinion. Gene Sarazen, looking back at the age of 95 in 1997, said emphatically: "Joyce Wethered was the greatest woman golfer who ever lived." That two Americans could ignore the claim to that latter title of players like Mickey Wright and Babe Zaharias perhaps tells you all you need to know about the excellence of the English player.

Despite the difficulty of travel in those days, Jones knew Wethered well, and on one occasion managed to prevail on her to play an exhibition match at his home club, East Lake, in Atlanta. Charlie Yates, who won the British Amateur in 1938 and, 60 years later, was still going strong as the longest-serving member of Augusta National Golf Club, partnered Wethered. Jones played with Dorothy Kirby who was four times a Curtis Cup player and won the US Women's Amateur in 1951.

It was a sensational match, principally because no one could believe the prodigious hitting – with the smoothest and most rhythmical of swings – of Wethered. The tale is told in *The Bobby Jones Story*, by O.B. Keeler and Grantland Rice.

The authors say: "Miss Wethered played well – but that is no way to say it. Miss Wethered played magnificently. Bobby played with all the verve and debonair abandon of the brave days when he was the d'Artagnan of golf... In sheer power, Miss Wethered's game was bewildering. She picked up a birdie four at the 565-yard 5th and another at the 506-yard 9th.

"At the 14th tee a sudden gale came up to blow full against their drives, and Miss Wethered played a low, raking shot that landed beyond the beautifully struck tee shots of both Jones and Yates."

At the 17th, it seems, Yates hit a drive of which he said afterwards that he had never bettered it in his life. When he got to it, he was a mere 12 yards ahead of Wethered. Yates was flabbergasted: "I don't believe it," he said, "No girl can hit a ball that far."

Yates was also somewhat flustered. He had played 14 holes with this slip of an English girl before he had figured on the card. "Reckon I should have been pretty embarrassed," he said afterwards, "but I was sort of hypnotized watching her play."

Part of that hypnotic effect came about because Wethered did not look as if she should hit the ball miles. It was all done by timing, the swing itself looking effortless, particularly with the irons. She never raised the club higher than her shoulder on either the backswing or the follow-through, and yet propelled it further than any other woman, and many a man.

Wethered was playing her best golf in the 1920s, winning the English championship five times in a row starting in 1920, and also winning the British championship on four occasions. Such was her pre-eminence that Sir Henry Cotton said of her: "In my time, no golfer has stood out so far ahead of his or her contemporaries."

That was a judgement endorsed, even in those chauvinistic times, by a general recognition that had the Walker Cup team been open to players of both sexes, then Wethered would not only have been an automatic choice, she would probably have played no lower than four in the order.

Part of the secret of her success was her intense concentration, something that came to her naturally. Her first English championship was won at Sheringham, that lovely, clifftop north-Norfolk golf course which is sandwiched between the sea and a railway line running the length of the coast.

Nowadays only holiday specials use the line, but then it was in regular use and golfers commonly had to wait until a train had passed in order to play. This was particularly so at the 17th, where the green is only a few yards from the line and where, in one of her matches in the championship, Wethered faced a crucial putt.

She studied it, went briskly to it, and holed it – despite the fact that at that precise moment a train was thundering past, all smoke and sparks. Afterwards Wethered was asked if she had considered waiting for the train to pass before attempting the putt and replied famously: "What train?"

She won 33 successive matches in the English championship, largely thanks to her ability to shut out extraneous matters, and always looked in complete charge both of the situation and of herself. The latter, though, was not always the case. She once said: "I was very nervous and used to shake tremendously. I used to feel very unwell. I don't think you can help it. But I was quite all right the moment the match was over."

Or she was, usually. It was after her epic victory against Cecil Leitch in the British at Troon in 1925 that Wethered decided to retire. The reason? She wrote: "A yard putt to win faced me on the 37th hole, a thing I had always prayed not to have. It went in, and I went and sat down on a hillock by the beach and everyone came and stared at me as though I was something in a zoo.

"I was dead tired. My legs had left me. Usually when you won the elation would carry you on, but not that time."

The retirement lasted until St Andrews in 1929, when she was lured back for the British championship by the fact of the venue. "There is a magic about St Andrews," she said, "and I couldn't resist it."

It was there that she won her fourth title, beating Glenna Collett (later Mrs Vare) in one of the classic matches of all time. Bernard Darwin, golf correspondent of *The Times*, summed it up thus: "It was a great match, greatly played. As to Miss Wethered, if she prefers now once more to retire into private golf she can do so with the knowledge that she has given as complete proof of surpassing greatness as any game player of either sex that ever lived."

Joyce Wethered – even the great Bobby Jones was overawed

RYDER CUP
RYDER CUP
EUROPE 13
15 USA
HOLE
PAR
V COUPLES
V BECK
MONTGOMERIE V JANZEN
BAKER V PAVIN
5 HAEGGMAN V COOK
6 TORRANCE V WADKINS
CONGRATULATIONS USA
7 JAMES V STEWART
8 ROCCA V LOVE
9 BALLESTEROS V GALLAGHER
V FLOYD
V KITE
V AZINGER

Chapter 6

THE TOP 100 COURSES

Given that the planet is decorated with several thousand new courses every year, trying to come up with a definitive list of the top 100 is clearly impossible.

Come to think of it, the task is impossible anyway: who is to say definitively that St Andrews, for example, is a better course than Muirfield? At the end of the day it is a subjective judgement.

So bear that in mind when you are looking through this list and thinking: ha, how can anyone be daft enough to rate the King's Course at Gleneagles as low as 92nd? In fact, the answer is simple: I think the place is overrated. Great views – shame about the golf course.

This, then, is my definitive list, based on 16 years of travelling the world at someone else's expense and being fortunate enough to play not just the courses that are always so highly rated but also some hidden gems and some virtually unknown diamonds as well. It fully reflects my bias towards both links golf and traditional courses. None of the top ten, for example, was built after the Second World War – and no fewer than seven of them come with sea views.

St Enodoc 100

St Enodoc is one of those links courses that, once seen, is never forgotten. It has all the characteristics of the great seaside venues, but possesses its own distinct virtues, too. It measures less than 6,300 yards, but feels much longer, owing to the nature of the challenge. The Church course takes its name from the tiny structure at the far end of the course, where the Poet Laureate, Sir John Betjeman, is buried in the graveyard.

It would be wrong to say that Betjeman put St Enodoc on the map, but by extolling the virtues of the place in verse he certainly brought it to the attention of a much larger audience. A copy of his verse hangs proudly in the clubhouse.

The test begins with one of the classic opening holes, a long par five that winds its way hither and yon through the dunes. At the 6th a player comes face to face with "the Himalayas", about which Bernard Darwin once wrote: "The highest sandhill, to the best of my belief, that I have ever seen on a golf course."

The par-four 13th is a hole that inspired Betjeman's most famous lines, commemorating a rare success – "It lay content, two paces from the pin; A steady putt and then it went oh most securely in. The very turf rejoiced to see that quite unprecedented three." But the best hole is undoubtedly the 10th, a truly fearsome four where the best shots a man can deliver are necessary to secure an orthodox par.

Sea Island 99

The oceanside course at Sea Island was laid out in the late 1920s on an old cotton plantation by the English architects Harry Colt and Charles Alison. The Seaside is the front nine and was considered by Bobby Jones as among the finest halves of golf that he had ever seen. Set among the dunes, it rolls over the broad, undulating fairways, edged by the ocean and surrounded by waterways and marshland. Several of the holes draw near to St Simons Sound.

The Plantation nine, by contrast, weaves its way through great forests of pine and oak, occasionally touching the marsh and often crossing or playing alongside the lagoons. The greens are well elevated and heavily bunkered.

The 7th hole, known as White Heron, is wonderful, offering two options from the tee: the harder drive has to carry a broad marsh inlet, a test made still more stringent should a breeze be blowing; the other alternative is to play to a thin peninsula of fairway – but this leaves a second shot blind over two large bunkers with the marsh threatening on the left.

The two other nines at Sea Island, the Retreat nine designed by Dick Wilson in 1960 and the Marshside, are also notable.

It was Bobby Jones who first brought Sea Island to national attention; these days it is Davis Love III, the course's touring professional.

Spyglass Hill 98

For all the plaudits that always come the way of Pebble Beach and Cypress Point, the title of hardest course on the Monterey Peninsula probably belongs to Spyglass Hill. Designed by Robert Trent Jones in 1966, it makes heavy demands on the mental and physical resources of those who tackle it. Trent Jones was so proud of the finished article that he considers it among the five best courses that he has ever built. "Knowlegeable people have come up to me and told me it is the best course on the Monterey Peninsula," he says.

It is not that, but it does offer immense variety. For five holes, it is a pure links and vicious with it. The 1st, in particular, is a fearsome introduction of what is to follow, a 600-yard par five that dog-legs to the left and where par is a cherished number.

The 2nd and 4th may be relatively short par fours, but demand sound strokemaking to achieve regulation figures.

After six holes, the course changes character completely, towards fairways lined with windswept cypress trees and Californian pines liberally laced with areas of gleaming white sand.

Now the course drops its guard a little and pars become easier to visualize. The short 12th is played across a pond to a small, undulating green, while water also has to be dealt with for the approach to the 555-yard par-five 14th.

The Cascades at The Homestead 97

Tucked in the foothills of the Allegheny Mountains in Virginia, the Cascades course at The Homestead resort is considered by its followers to be the finest mountain layout in America. It is even better since it has been refurbished in readiness for the US Mid-Amateur Championship in 2000.

Under consultation with the United States Golf Association, many changes were instigated, including a series of new tees to make the stringent design more playable for the holiday golfer.

The course was opened in 1924 and had seven of its holes ranked in a recent survey of Virginia's top 18. This was the course where Sam Snead created probably the most elegant swing that the world has ever seen, while, in 1967, Catherine Lacoste became the first non-American, the first amateur and the youngest winner of the US Women's Open.

The first nine holes are extremely tight through dense but tranquil woodland. Then the course opens out with more emphasis on length from the tee. Perhaps the most memorable hole is the 12th, which plunges down a valley from its elevated tee, although the two holes to finish are both visually striking.

The small greens give this imaginatively designed course a further cutting edge. The resort's hotel is a National Historic Landmark dating back to 1766.

Royal St David's 96

Royal St David's was designed with the brief that it should prove a match for the splendour of Royal St George's in England. A tough task, assuredly, but one that was close to being achieved. Certainly Harlech, as it is more generally known, is a wonderful place to play golf, with a regal setting all of its own. Overlooking the reclaimed land of links-like character that is separated from the sea by sandhills is the magnificent Harlech Castle, which stands as a dramatic reminder of turbulent times past.

Nor do the visual splendours end there: on one side of the course lies Tremedog Bay, while the imposing Snowdon and its accompanying peaks in the Snowdonia National Park stand guard on the other.

The course is renowned not just for its beauty but also its large greens, which are almost always in excellent condition. Two of the best holes come late on. Oddly enough, the 15th and the 17th both measure 427 yards, but require markedly contrasting strategies to play them. The 15th has no bunkers to worry about but the fairway, which dog-legs slightly to the right, winds between sandhills and narrows towards a hollow just short of the putting surface. The 17th, meanwhile, requires great accuracy to avoid both the bunkers on the right of the meagre fairway, and cross-bunkers that guard the green.

Royal St David's – with Harlech Castle and Snowdon in the background, it has a setting all of its own

Swinley Forest 95

Swinley Forest is the golf course of choice for dukes and earls, lords and judges. It probably has not held a tournament because the last thing its membership would want would be to draw attention to themselves.

It lies not far from Ascot in the glorious stretch of heathland where Sunningdale and The Berkshire are also housed. In character it most resembles the latter, and in early spring, when nature has awoken from its long slumber, it is a wonderful place to be.

The holes are full of character and variety. All forms of golf course life are here: treacherous short holes, daunting long par fours, delightful short par fours, and par fives that provide a breather.

The 3rd is rather like the equivalent hole on the Old Course at Sunningdale, a fine short par four where the approach pitch has to be sweetly struck to the hold the green which falls away to the rear. The 4th is a wonderful par three, requiring a solid long-iron stroke to find the plateau green. Then comes a par five where the big hitters will fancy their chances.

So it continues, the mix and match of tempting and difficult. The 8th, another fine par three which requires nothing more than a mid-iron, is followed by the stringent par four 9th, where any player is simply glad to find the putting green in two.

The back nine is equally pleasurable, concluding with a splendid par four which reaches away into the distance, towards the stately clubhouse that lies behind the green. In short, a course that one certainly does not need to be a nobleman to enjoy.

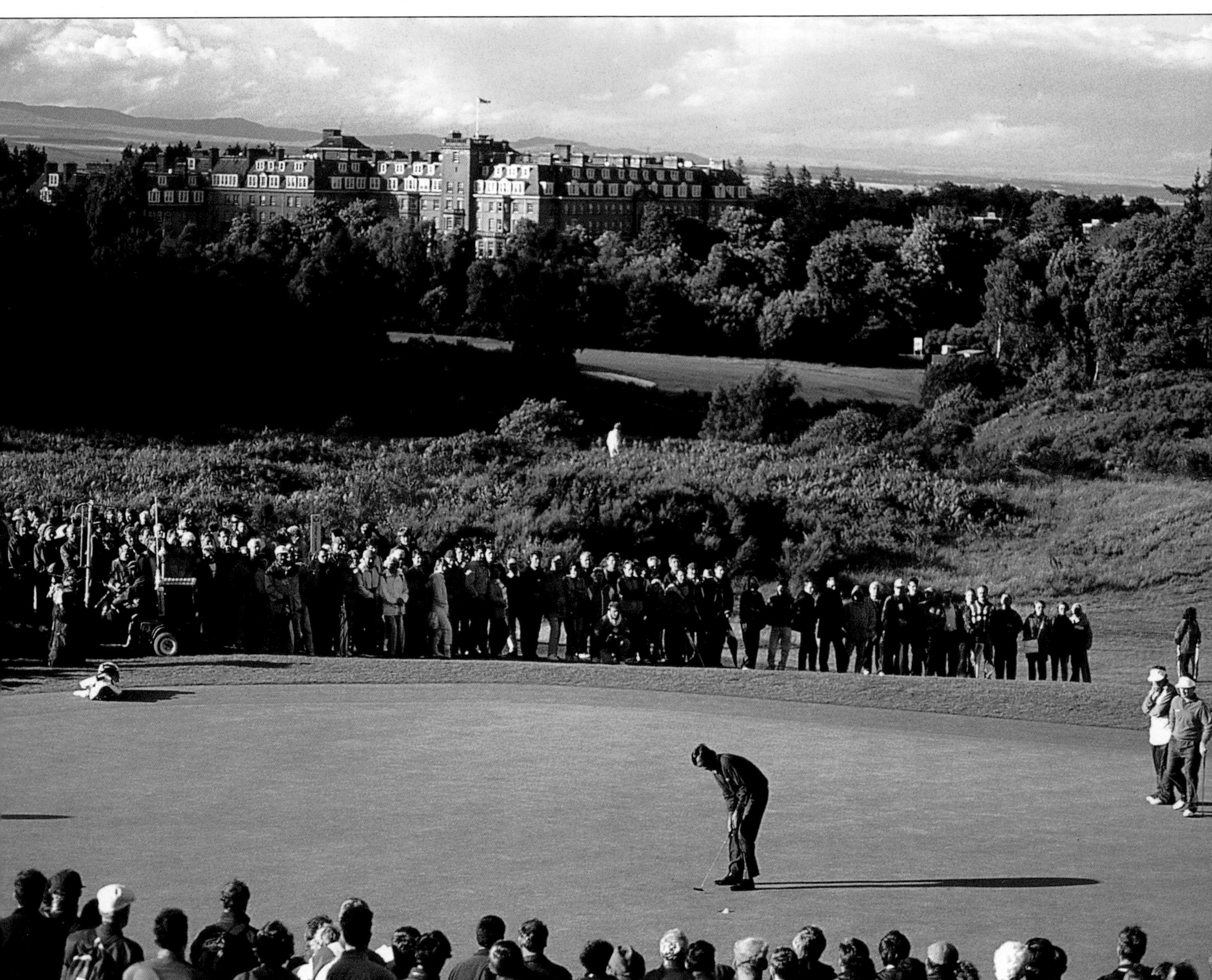

Gleneagles – set in the heart of some glorious Perthshire countryside

Fujioka 94

Fujioka may well be the best course to emerge from the feverish development that went on in Japan in the 1970s and 1980s. Situated on land to the north of Nagoya, the owner was a Mr Furukowa, who set the great Australian Peter Thomson the brief that the course should be strictly in the traditions set by Kasumigaseki.

Thomson has lived up to the request, converting the 180-acre site of moderately hilly land into a splendid test of golf that uses the natural habitat of tall pines and a large lake to great effect.

Almost 6,000 workers spent six months creating Fujioka, whose most distinctive feature is the expressive use of water. A number of holes call for accurate approach shots to avoid such hazards, something that was virtually unheard of in Japan when the course was built in 1971. Hitherto, water was used timidly, and rarely threatened the shot to the green.

One of the holes where it does at Fujioka is the 16th, which is a par five in every sense of the word. From the rarely used back tees this hole stretches for a monstrous 605 yards – and the drive is all uphill. Out of bounds threatens the draw and even from the top of the hill, which is where the good drive will finish, the green is still not visible. A good second down the V-shaped fairway will leave a mid-iron approach to a large green that curves along the side of a small lake.

Mauna Kea 93

In 1960 William F. Quinn, Hawaii's first state governor, asked Laurance Rockefeller if he would build a major resort that would attract tourists to the islands. During the feasibility studies that followed, Rockefeller was accompanied by the golf architect Robert Trent Jones, and they both plumped for a site on the Big Island.

In truth it was hardly perfect for golf, but Jones built the course to fit the land. The result is one of the most spectacular venues anywhere and certainly among the most unusual. Carved out of desolate volcanic lava beds beside the ocean and over the foothills of vast mountains, it has become recognized as one of the great golf resort destinations.

As ever, Jones is not sparing on those with lesser ability. The dramatic par-three 3rd calls for a tee shot over the Pacific with no dry land until the green. Unfortunately, the problems do not end there either; the green is full of sharp borrows and is impossibly quick.

Not all the holes, however, are quite so demanding. The 6th is a lovely short par four, while the 9th sweeps down to a well-protected green. The tumbling waves crash behind the tee at the par-three 11th, a downhill tee shot to a green that by Trent Jones's standards can be classed as positively generous.

Gleneagles 92

Few architects have ever been blessed with a more majestic site than that presented to James Braid to design the King's Course at Gleneagles. Situated on a sheltered moorland plateau in the heart of some glorious Perthshire countryside, the layout is characterized by the rolling hills and the splash of purple heather, golden gorse and tall stands of dark pine.

It has its share of memorable holes. Perhaps the pick of them is the one that carries the architect's name: Braid's Brawest, where the fairway rolls narrowly away from the tee, demanding a long, straight drive to avoid the heather and bracken. Then the ground rises for the approach, to an elevated green that is well protected by bunkers.

If par is an elusive reward on that hole, then any player who fails to secure a regulation figure at the next, an absurdly easy par four, ought really to head to the practice ground.

The sequence rather sums up the challenge of the King's Course, where precious little middle ground exists between holes sheathed either in an iron fist or a velvet glove.

Take the last two holes: the 17th, a winding par four where the fairway can be a slippery target; then the 18th, where the fairway is almost impossible to miss. And down the hole bounds, offering the satisfaction of a par five or better to finish, before coming to a halt in sight of the famous hotel where the privileged few who can afford the complete Gleneagles experience rest for the night.

Waterville 91

Few inward halves can compare with the glory of Waterville's back nine. Set amidst the dunes, the fairways tumble over spectacular rolling terrain, and three of the holes at least are exceptional.

The course was the brainchild of an American, John A. Mulcahey, who bought the land just knowing it would make an exceptional golf course. In the early 1970s he hired the noted Irish architect Eddie Hackett, and set about creating his own distinctive contribution to links play.

Upon its opening, Waterville received due praise. Mulcahey, a wealthy industrialist with good connections, brought over his pals like Sam Snead and Julius Boros, and they quickly spread the word.

For nine holes, however, the visitor could be forgiven for wondering if he has not made some terrible mistake, for the outward half is plain fare. The change from the 10th is quite dramatic. The 11th, meanwhile, is considered by many judges to be the finest par five in Ireland. Then to the 12th, a wonderful long par three where the tee shot must carry a dune.

The other great hole is another par three, the 196-yard 17th, played from "Mulcahey's Peak", the highest point on the course. Then to the long 18th, which runs its entire length along the Atlantic, leaving anyone brave enough to venture out a second time wondering if they could just play the back nine twice, please.

Prestwick 90

To play golf at Prestwick is to take a stroll around a live golf museum. All right, so the airport and several industrial establishments that disfigure the view along the 7th and 8th holes rather spoil the idea, but otherwise the golf engenders a feeling of being transported back to another age, when players did not look upon blind shots as being unfair but part of the capricious challenge that links golf presents.

Prestwick can be a forbidding place if the wind whips in from the Irish Sea, and its 6,544 yards can feel like 1,000 yards longer. All these years on from its inception it remains a demanding challenge, where sound technique and the rub of the green are prerequisites to a competent score.

The club was formed in 1851 and, nine years later, the members got together and decided to host an annual Open competition. Thus, the first Open was born, one so heavily imitated, but never surpassed; it remains the world's most prestigious golf championship. Prestwick fell from the Open roster when the plethora of blind shots began to endanger the health of spectators.

The 5th hole is perhaps Prestwick's most celebrated, the controversial par three being known as the Alps, owing to the hill that blocks the green from view. It is not a hole that has stood the test of time, however; far better the holes from the turn, the ferocious 10th leading to a stretch along the shore where the dunes offer merciful shelter on doleful days.

Formby – another of Lancashire's quality courses

Formby 89

Embedded within the sandhills that characterize much of the south-Lancashire coastline are at least five courses of championship quality. Formby is the third course to be included in this guide alone, and a splendid place it is, too, for intertwined with the holes that engender the spirit of a true links are several where pine trees induce a feeling of privacy so rarely found on a links, and where golf's reputation as a relaxing pursuit is amply fulfilled.

Some of the best holes, however, come at the start. The 1st is a wonderful opening hole, the drive menaced by the same railway line that causes palpitations over the initial tee shot at Hillside. This time, however, it is the player that slices the ball who has cause to fear. The 2nd and 3rd holes continue to journey straight out from the clubhouse, the latter a fabulously rugged par five which can be reached in two blows in the dry summer months. Now the course begins the first of no fewer than 11 switches of direction for the short par-four 4th, and then on to the pick of the short holes.

The middle part of the course was changed some 20 years ago due to coastal erosion, and the holes have sadly suffered as a result. But then the true character of the venue is once more apparent, as the player comes to Formby's distinguished quartet of closing holes.

Royal Rabat 88

In the last 20 years Morocco has tried hard to re-invent itself as a golfing destination for tourists. Under the watching eye of King Hassan II, over a dozen courses have been constructed to satiate the madding hordes, but the best of them lies in the royal grounds – the Red course at Royal Rabat.

Designed by Robert Trent Jones, it can be stretched to almost 7,500 yards if necessary, but generally plays around the 7,000 mark when the Moroccan Open, is staged there.

The course is cut from strands of cork oak trees, and any golfer having a bad day with the driver will soon take an instant dislike to them, such is their proliferation. Neither is there any alternative but to plough away with the driver if he wishes to reach the green in regulation, so demanding is the yardage.

For the straight hitter, however, a rosier picture awaits. Emerald-green fairways, which are invariably in pristine condition, assure the most perfect of lies to try to execute what is almost always a demanding approach stroke.

One hole where Jones allows the player a breather from the oak is the par-three 9th; here instead the trouble is all water. It is a lovely picturesque hole, the lake which surrounds the green dancing to the sounds of various geese, ducks and flamingoes.

Killarney 87

I suppose under the weight of all those tourists and the attractions laid on for them, a town called Killarney in the west of Ireland still exists, but it is not one that anyone looking for the true spirit of the country would choose to visit. Thankfully the golf courses that share its name have not given themselves over quite so readily to such rabid commercialism.

And so it is still possible to walk over its broad acres and appreciate the full majesty of the view, and stand on the 18th tee of the Mahoney's Point course and understand why Henry Longhurst once said: "What a lovely place to die."

Killarney was originally designed in the 1930s by Sir Guy Campbell, but little of his work remains. Instead the architecture owes much to the owner of the land, Lord Castlerosse, a scratch golfer who spent much of his time in the early 1940s pursuing his dream of the perfect golf course. He certainly had the setting: the imposing loom of Macgillicuddy's Reeks, and the tranquil beauty of Lough Leane have inspired many a songwriter. Sadly, he died in 1943, and his idea of decorating the course with extravagantly coloured shrubs such as he had seen at Augusta went with him.

Ironically, three of the holes that remain of Campbell's original design are some of the most dramatic: the long 16th unfolds gently downhill to a green set against the backdrop of the lake; the par-four 17th then runs along the lake shore, while the par-three 18th, where Longhurst lingered, requires a tee shot that must carry the corner of the lake's rugged shore to locate the narrow green.

Wild Dunes 86

The Links Course at Wild Dunes was once described by a writer as "a cross between Scotland and the Caribbean". Blatant hyperbole is the initial reaction, but personal inspection reveals the writer to be not that far out after all.

Wild Dunes lies on the eastern tip of the Isle of Palms along the golfing mecca that Myrtle Beach in South Carolina has become. It is an established residential community, complete with a variety of colourful abodes.

As for the Links Course, stretches of palm trees alongside manicured fairways give way to unkempt areas of sandy sea-grasses: hence the writer's comparison.

It is the ocean finish for which Wild Dunes has rightly become famous, the final two holes that run breathtakingly along the stunning beach. This is seaside golf at its finest, the 405-yard par-four 17th giving away to the 501-yard closer, which curves majestically over an area of the coastline steeped in history from the Civil War.

For it was these same wild dunes and tortured oaks that greeted the British troops more than 200 years ago when Lord Cornwallis put ashore with his army of Redcoats before being defeated by the Colonialists in the first victory of the war. May your shots be more successful.

Cruden Bay – Harry Vardon won the course's opening event in 1898

Royal Johannesburg 85

The Scots brought golf to South Africa, as they did everywhere else, in the final years of the last century, but it was not until this century was well into its stride that the game gained a foothold in Johannesburg. Then, as the city took shape, so did its courses. In 1906 money was advanced to allow the founder members of Royal Johannesburg to purchase a site. So the march of steady progress began. In 1933, as the membership increased, more land was bought to construct a second course on the high veldt.

The east was quickly considered the championship test. Built under the guiding hand of that master architect, Bob Grimsdell, it was refurbished in 1955 and now stands comparison with the best on the sub-continent. Certainly, none other judge than nine-time major winner Gary Player believes that to be the case.

The championship 18 wanders quietly over wooded parkland. The short holes in particular are memorable, from the monstrous beauty of the long 2nd to the subtle touch necessary to gauge the strength of shot required for the tender 5th.

The 11th, 511 yards long, may be the best hole of all. A gentle dog-leg to the right, the drive must be long and accurately placed to allow any prospect of making the green in two, since a stream runs across its front edge.

Cruden Bay 84

Cruden Bay earned a certain fame in Scotland within a month of its opening in May, 1898, when Harry Vardon, James Braid and Ben Sayers took part in a professional tournament in which the first prize was £30. Vardon, the reigning Open Champion, emerged as the winner.

The scene that greeted the trio is much the same as today. Blind shots, stunning views and classic par threes are the order of the day for this course, which is situated on the Buchan coast some 25 miles north of Aberdeen.

One of the best stretches of holes comes early, from the 4th to the 7th. The 193-yard 4th is a gem of its kind, the 5th, a long and winding par four where a good tee shot is crucial, the 6th a genuine par five with a short-iron approach over a burn, and the 7th a medium-length par four where a pulled drive needs to be avoided at all costs.

Thereafter, the golf struggles somewhat to live up to such quality, but it remains picturesque to the eye. The 9th tee offers wonderful views of Slains Castle, Cruden Bay itself, and the fishing village of Port Errol in the distance.

Bram Stoker, who spent some time in these parts, is reputed to have used the castle as the inspiration for his *Dracula* stories. At Cruden Bay, the welcome is somewhat more convivial, and never more so than in the magnificently appointed clubhouse.

Bali Handara 83

It is never a hindrance when a keen golfer is elected to office, and so it was with the election to power of President of General Suharto in 1965. Soon after he received the call, so word went out that Indonesia needed a golf course of the highest international standing. General Ibnu Sutowo oversaw the project, eventually selecting a site on Bali, that island of almost mythical beauty that lies at the eastern end of the Indonesian archipelago.

The former Ryder Cup player Guy Wolstenholme arrived in the autumn of 1973 to supervise the project, and discovered that the only earth-moving piece of machinery at his disposal was a converted bulldozer. No matter – he did have the enthusiastic co-operation of the whole island, and no fewer than 1,500 people set to work on the course.

It took six months to construct, and has matured well to retain its position among the leading courses in the Far East. One of the best holes is the 3rd, which was the hardest to build, but perhaps the most rewarding. From an elevated teeing area, all manner of wild shrubs and flowers must be carried to reach the fairway. For the long hitter the temptation is to aim down the right of the fairway, leaving a shorter shot to the green. But the penalty of failure is severe indeed, with water and trees awaiting the unwitting slice.

The stream carries all along this hole, presenting a very real hazard for the approach, which must cross both it and an imposing trap to find the safe haven of the green.

Falsterbo 82

Falsterbo is that rarity in mainland Europe: a true links. It lies on a tiny peninsula in the southernmost corner of Sweden, with Copenhagen just 30 miles distant, across the Øresund.

Strange as it seems now, with the European Tour filled with its professionals and tournaments there attracting over 25,000 spectators every day, the sport's beginnings in Sweden were at best hesitant. It was not until 1929 that the first 18-hole course was built.

Falsterbo, which opened for play in 1909, acquired its second nine in 1930. It incorporates all the true links qualities of turf, natural hazards, and changes of wind. It calls for unrelenting concentration and good technique.

The challenge begins from the 1st, a stiff dog-leg with the right side of the hole protected by out of bounds. The 4th and 5th are splendid holes, the water haunting all slicers.

The 14th is an enchanting par three, the old Falsterbo lighthouse standing proudly beyond the green. Then to the finish, the 15th and 18th two par fives, the 16th and 17th among the best of the par fours. The tee at the last is deep into the sand dunes, from which the hole dog-legs to the right with bunkers protecting the angle. Any shot to the green has to take on three treacherous bunkers.

Banff Springs 81

There are some courses where the majesty of the setting simply overrides any shortcomings regarding the course. One such venue is Crans-sur-Sierre, high up a Swiss mountain and the home each year of the European Masters. Another is Banff Springs, never tested in major competition, but boasting some of the most scenic views on any golf course, anywhere.

Situated in the Canadian Rockies, the course is a greenkeeper's nightmare. For months on end it lies unplayable and that is the good news: then comes spring, when the course thaws out during the warm and sunny days and then freezes again in the sub-zero evening temperatures.

The beauty of Banff Springs is obvious from the first tee. It lies directly below the clubhouse pavilion and right in front of the player is the steep precipice leading to the churning Spray river. The carry across is only 100 yards or so, but concentrating with so much going on is not easy.

The 7th is called Gibraltar, for reasons which are easily apparent. To the right of the tee are the rising cliffs of Mount Rundle, which also dominate the beautiful short 8th, Devil's Cauldron. This is universally recognized as one of the world's great par threes, the requirement being a precise mid-iron over a miniature glacial lake.

Banff Springs lies within a National Park, and deer and even the odd bear cub can be seen from time to time, making their contribution to the ethereal beauty.

Paraparaumu Beach Golf Club 80

Paraparaumu Beach is a wonderfully natural links situated some 35 miles north of Wellington on New Zealand's North Island. It takes up a parcel of land of only 130 acres, yet crammed within that space are a number of memorable holes – not least the short 5th, which that most famous of all golfing Kiwis, Bob Charles, maintains is equal to any short hole in the world.

It measures just 164 yards and offers comparisons with the Postage Stamp at Troon. A totally different ball game is the 13th, a long and uncompromising par four along a severely undulating fairway where even a long, straight drive will leave a similar shot with a long iron to find the plateau green.

Paraparaumu was designed in 1930 by Alex Russell, the co-architect with Alister Mackenzie of Royal Melbourne. What a wonderful job he did considering the flimsy acreage available, but then it did lead to him utilizing every natural undulation, and to place the tees with great care.

The course was built to accommodate a moderate breeze from the west, and on such days when the wind obliges it is an exhilarating experience. The finish is completely memorable: the 16th a gem of a par three, with the green cut into the side of a small hill; the 17th has a split fairway, offering an array of options; the 18th tumbles towards the clubhouse and offers the chance of a birdie four to finish.

Mid Ocean 79

Some courses have such evocative names that golfers are keen to visit without knowing much about them. One links course that fits this outline is The National on Long Island; The Country Club is another such venue; perhaps the best of the lot, however, is Mid Ocean, which is such a dreamy name one can almost envisage the Edenesque setting simply by closing one's eyes.

The reality does not disappoint. Many of the holes wind their way through pines that give it an almost cathedral-like feel; it is the Atlantic, though, that provides a glorious backdrop while playing little part in the overall design.

The signature hole is undoubtedly the 5th, one of the most photographed holes in the world. "A play upon courage, fear and greed," was how Herb Warren Wind once described it, a beautiful way of sketching a hole where the braver the tee shot over Mangrove Lake, the easier the approach.

Given that there is a terrible finality about finishing at the bottom of a water hazard, most players will err on the cautious side, and play it almost as a par four-and-a-half.

The 5th brings to a climax an unforgettable sequence of opening holes, where the majesty of the setting is matched by the quality of the golf. The finish is similarly memorable, the 17th, a long downhill par three, followed by the par-four 18th, which follows the line of the cliffs.

Olympic Golf Club 78

Only three courses in California have ever played host to the US Open, and none has held it as often as the Olympic Club, on the outskirts of San Francisco. Whether the Lakeside course has deserved the honour on four occasions is a different matter, for while there is undeniably a selection of great holes scattered throughout its acreage, there are also a number that leave the visitor wondering: "Have I not just seen this hole?"

The course traverses the San Andreas fault, which explains the savage tilt of many of the fairways. At US Open time, these fairways can be the very devil to hit, since they are usually only 30 yards wide and not as soft as they were intended to play.

At other times, the course's true nature reveals itself: on those occasions it remains extremely penal, but, crucially, never less than fair.

The great holes at Olympic begin from the off, and an opening par five which is reachable in two, albeit exceedingly accurate blows, then the arduous par-three 3rd, with the Golden Gate Bridge shimmering on clear days in the distance; the lovely, short par-four 8th, where strategy is everything, and the monstrously long par-four 17th, where it is as much as any player can do to make this green in two, let alone think about getting near the flag.

The 18th, meanwhile, makes up for its modest distance with a green that slopes wickedly from back to front.

Ganton 77

Several architects were responsible for creating Ganton, which lies on open heathland in the tranquil Vale of Pickering just a few miles from Scarborough. Given such information, one would not have been too surprised to find a course without a distinct character; in the event, such a synopsis could hardly be more misplaced.

In this instance, the committee of designers has made admirable play of the contours of the land. Ganton has been a leading light in the history of English golf since its then resident professional, Harry Vardon, won the first of his six Open Championships. Since then, it has been home to any number of prestigious tournaments, although these days it is more readily associated with the amateur, rather than the professional game.

A characteristic of the course is the cavernous bunkers, into which a player can easily disappear from view. It is a keen bunker exponent who gets down in two more often than three from these hazards.

Deep sand traps protect the fairway at the 15th, which heralds Ganton's stiff finish. The hole measures 437 yards, while the par-four 16th is even longer. Another monstrous blow is needed if the 251 yards of the 17th are to be covered in a single stroke, while the drive at the wonderful dog-leg 18th has to be precise to allow a clear view of the green through the stately pines that guard the outer limits of the fairway.

Olympic Golf Club – the San Andreas fault traversing the course has created its savagely tilting fairways

Durban Country Club 76

Durban Country Club was born of necessity. Royal Durban, the country's oldest club, proved a decidedly soggy venue for the 1919 South African Open and, with no guarantee that the low-lying course would not flood again, there was the real danger that Durban would lose its place on the national tournament roster.

The solution was a venue that, bar the resiting of several tees and renumbering of holes, has changed little since its inception in 1922.

The course is one of two halves: there are the holes on the dunes where either tee or green is elevated; and those on the flatland, which are slightly easier since they come without the fear of a hanging lie.

The signature hole on the course comes early. The 3rd, a short par five, is played from the highest point on the course into a valley. Then the ground rises again towards the green with trees protecting the rear.

The 18th is a tempting hole at 273 yards and, in favourable weather conditions, is certainly more than driveable. It is among the shortest finishing holes in championship golf, but Bob Grimsdell, who updated the course in 1959, described it thus: "A little longer and the hole would be mediocre – just another drive and pitch. But at this awkward and tempting distance it is just the finish needed for a course which rewards good golf, but ruthlessly exposes all our weaknesses." A fair testimony to the course.

Kennemer 75

Just a 30-minute car ride from the centre of Amsterdam, Kennemer is perhaps the finest links course on mainland Europe. Here, the land contradicts the widely held belief that Holland is completely flat, the wild, tumbling dunes seemingly made for golf.

Nine new holes were created in time for the 1989 Dutch Open, but it is the original 18, conceived by Harry Colt in the late 1920s, for which the venue is rightly feted. The course runs in two loops from the clubhouse, and both are instantly inviting. The first hole falls away to a widening fairway flanked on either side by the dunes. The drive to the 10th, meanwhile, is over an untamed valley to a distant, unseen fairway.

The outward half runs along the perimeter of the links in an anti-clockwise direction, and offers wonderfully varied and challenging golf. Then to the inner nine, designed in the space within, with several holes threaded pleasingly through the dunes.

Perhaps the most memorable tournament to be held at Kennemer was the 1976 Dutch Open, with a young Spaniard called Severiano Ballesteros making his first appearance since finishing runner-up in the Open. Ballesteros showed that performance was no fluke, winning what would prove to be the first of many professional victories.

Quaker Ridge 74

The affluent Manhattan suburb of Westchester has long been fertile ground for golf designers, the characteristic rolling terrain and spectacular woodland lending itself to some wonderful sites. Winged Foot and Westchester Country Club are both marvellous layouts and so, too, is Quaker Ridge, which is situated quite literally across the street from the former.

Both were designed by Albert Tillinghast, and both offer similar examinations. Like Winged Foot, Quaker Ridge requires no great carries to make the fairways, but the emphasis instead is placed upon the approach shot, where par quickly becomes a fanciful figure if the green is not found.

Not that the problems end there. In 1997, the course played host to the Walker Cup, and the visiting Great Britain and Ireland side simply could not come to terms with the slickly contoured greens.

The course is not overly long at 6,745 yards from the back tees, but it has its share of stern holes. The 13th, for example, is a par three measuring 234 yards, while the par-four 18th requires two mighty blows if it is to be reached in regulation.

The best hole may well be the 387-yard par-four 11th, where a stream that begins in front of the tee runs down the left-hand side of the fairway before snaking back again in front of the green.

Interlachen 73

Interlachen Country Club lies west of the city of Minnesota, and is rightly regarded as the state's premier course. For it is sacred ground, another course designed by the great Donald Ross and the place where Bobby Jones secured the third leg of his Grand Slam in 1930, collecting the US Open by two strokes from Macdonald Smith.

It was Jones's fourth US Open win, but the quality of the course was evident in his winning score; he was the only man under par. The par-three 17th had something to do with that, a hole that has now taken its place in US Open history. At the time it measured a monstrous 262 yards, making it the longest par-three ever. The best Jones could do in four rounds was a bogey four. Mind you, the entire field managed but two birdies between them. Thankfully, the hole has now been shortened to a more reasonable, but still daunting, 226 yards.

Interlachen lost some of its sheen until the mid-1980s, when Geoffrey Cornish was hired to refurbish it, while holding true to Ross's original concepts. He did an excellent job, one that was much appreciated by the competitors in the 1993 Walker Cup, although perhaps more by the Americans than the British and Irish, since the winning margin was 19–5 in the home side's favour. The visitors simply could not cope with the fast, undulating greens that have always been a Ross trademark.

Nevis 72

Nevis is another modern course that owes its construction to the wonders of technology. Set on a spectacular mountainous site that is decorated with a magnificent range of foliage, it boasts a series of dramatic holes that add up to a memorable holiday golf experience.

Most theatrical of all is the 663-yard par-five 15th, where the drive is from the highest point on the course and thus offers the most commanding views. They are stunning, too, portraying a delightful little island in all its glory.

From the back tee the first requirement is a drive that will carry 240 yards over a cavernous ravine to a plunging fairway. No wonder most people decide to give the championship tee a miss.

This, though, is a rare excursion into the macho; for the most part, Robert Trent Jones Jnr has designed a course that is playable for most levels of golfer, although accuracy from the tee will not go amiss. Be prepared for the hospitable welcome from the locals as well; several greens are gathering places for harmless monkeys.

Apart from the 15th, perhaps the most memorable hole is the 18th. Step 10 yards from the back of the green and you're on the beach; progress another five yards and you're in the water. Afternoon golfers have the best of worlds here, as the tourists gather behind the 18th – not to watch you play, it should be quickly added – to gaze at the setting sun.

Hillside 71

This is another course that is probably the victim of its location. Would Hillside's reputation have spread far and wide by now, were it not for the fact that it lies adjacent to Royal Birkdale? Whatever the case, it is a testament to its quality that many would prefer to play it instead of big brother next door.

Hillside has many of the virtues traditionally associated with great links courses. A railway line even runs alongside the 1st and 2nd holes, and is particularly in play off the opening drive. The 2nd is a fine par five, while the par-four 3rd comes back the other way. The 7th is a lovely short hole, played downhill towards a generous green; the short 10th may be even better, to a green shaped like an upturned saucer. Thus begins a wonderful inward half, the 11th and the 17th in particular being fabulous par fives that weave their way through the dunes.

Hillside has always had a jealously protected reputation for offering some of the best-conditioned greens in the country. Like Birkdale, it does not offer commanding views of the sea, nor do mountains gather imposingly in the distance. But again, like Birkdale, it is simply an aesthetically pleasing course in its own right, and rightly the venue for many prestigious championships, including the 1982 PGA Championship, where Tony Jacklin scored his last big win – over the up-and-coming Bernhard Langer.

Hillside – undermined by its proximity to Royal Birkdale

Kiawah Island – a course with a tigerish reputation

Kiawah Island 70

The ocean course at Kiawah Island is aptly named. Designed by Pete Dye with no concession to golfing weaknesses, it is a punishing layout set hard against the South Carolina shore of the Atlantic. From the very back tees it can be stretched to 7,700 yards. Don't try it. Not even in jest.

It was built to host the 1991 Ryder Cup, and suffered many a growing pain along the way. A hurricane swept through the area a year before the matches, and played havoc with the timetable. When it opened it was both raw and impossibly beautiful. "It does not look like a links course from Ireland or Scotland; it looks like something from Mars," David Feherty commented.

Almost a decade on, the Ocean course has matured, and deservedly hosted its second major international event in 1997 when the World Cup came to town. It measured a shade under 6,900 yards for that event, and Alex Cejka demonstrated that a venue regularly named "America's toughest resort course" could be tamed, with a new course-record 63.

The pivotal hole remains the long par-three 17th. Almost all carry over water, and invariably into the wind, it can play anything from a six iron to a driver depending on the velocity of the breeze. At the Ryder Cup it was blowing hard on the final day, and a stream of famous casualties resulted – which in turn did nothing, naturally, to harm the hole's tigerish reputation.

County Sligo 69

County Sligo, of course, is far too formal a name for an Irish golf course, so it is little wonder that it is known far and wide as "Rosses Point". It does not lack for supporters either – Tom Watson and Peter Alliss have both been particularly vociferous in that department – who believe that it deserves to be ranked right alongside the big four in the Emerald Isle: Portmarnock, Ballybunion, and the two Royals north of the border, County Down and Portrush.

Rosses Point has the two main prerequisites to be considered a truly great links: there is nothing contrived about the layout and the views are glorious. It is situated on the sweep of Sligo Bay, and is dominated by the extraordinary mountain, Benbullen.

The 14th is perhaps the choice hole, and a stringent par four into the wind. It forms part of a testing quartet to challenge any player's card: the 15th is played the same way, and the tee shot calls for a substantial carry over the dunes; the 16th is a 200-yard par three, while the 17th is a long, uphill par four. Finally, the 18th offers some respite, the calm following the storm. A slight dog-leg to the right, on a fine summer's day the sun drops gently away behind the green.

Chicago Golf Club 68

Chicago Golf Club is another that has fallen off the tournament roster in recent times, partly due to political correctness – it has no women members – but also due to its length. At 6,574 yards, it cannot meet today's demands. Once more it is the game's loss.

One of the original five clubs that formed the United States Golf Association, the club moved in 1894 to its present site at Wheaton. The original designer was Charles Blair Macdonald, who was responsible for the National, but much of his work disappeared when the course was rebuilt in 1921 with the assistance of Seth Raynor.

The 8th is one of the feature holes, a double dog-leg par four which is further protected by no fewer than eight bunkers, of which three surround the green. The 10th is a lovely short hole across a lake, while the 18th calls for a long, straight drive to escape a cluster of bunkers.

In the years before its exile Chicago staged many important championships, including the US Amateur on four occasions and the US Open three times. Two of the latter were memorable occasions: in 1900 Harry Vardon won his only US Open at Chicago, and in 1911 Johnny McDermott became the first native American to win his national championship.

Southern Hills 67

Southern Hills was one of the few courses built in America during the Depression. The citizenry of Tulsa who made their money from oil escaped its devastating effects and decided to build a golf course of which the state could be proud, providing some employment into the bargain.

Oklahoma remains proud, and rightly so, for the local architect Perry Maxwell constructed a layout that has confidently stood the test of time. Even in the clement weather that prevailed for the 1994 USPGA Championship, Southern Hills was far from overwhelmed as Nick Price came in with a winning score of 11 under par. The next best score was five under.

It was the sort of lead a player likes to have when tackling the awesome 18th, for no one wants to step on to that tee needing a par four to win. Contained within its 430 yards are all the hazards that make Southern Hills such a wonderful test: the trees, the curves, the bunkers and the impenetrable rough. There is also a narrow pond at the crook of the dog-leg, lending urgency to the quest for accuracy.

Straightness from the tee is generally a prerequisite at most championship venues, but at Southern Hills it is pivotal: quite simply, no man can hope to break par there unless he has with him his "A" game from the tee.

Sahalee 66

When the PGA of America made the brave decision to host the 1998 USPGA Championship in the Pacific north-west, it raised the stakes by choosing a course of which few people had heard.

The gamble, however, proved a spectacular success. Sahalee, a 40-minute ride from the beautiful city of Seattle, is a wondrous layout where each fairway is guarded by stately fir trees. Where the PGA of America did err was in allowing the rough to grow under the firs; how much more exciting the tournament would have been had the daring recovering shot from under the woodland been an option – although the eventual champion, Vijay Singh, wasn't complaining. Naturally, such rough was immediately cut back at the end of the tournament, allowing the members to play the course as it was meant to be played.

Sahalee gets quickly into its stride with the par-five 2nd, an exciting hole where the green is reachable in two but the water that protects the right side of the putting surface will capture the errant stroke. To follow is a lovely short par four, where accuracy with the approach is essential.

The finish is suitably stringent, the narrow par-four 18th, a hole where everyone in the PGA was thankful to make a regulation figure.

Sahalee's first professional was Paul Runyon, who won the PGA Championship twice in the 1930s. He has no doubts as to its quality: "It is a heavenly place, and unquestionably one of the 25 finest golf courses in the world," he said.

Royal Antwerp 65

Belgian golfers of note have been non-existent since the great Flory van Donck, which is surprising given a number of majestic courses. There is Waterloo, where Henry Cotton was professional between the wars; Royal Club de Belgique, where van Donck played; the Royal Zoute, a splendid links that is home to the Belgacom Open on the European Tour; and the Royal Club des Fagnes at Spa.

Best of all, perhaps, is Royal Antwerp, which like the others had the regal prefix bestowed by Belgian kings. It is also the oldest course in the country, and the current lay-out is partly the work of Willie Park and Tom Simpson, who was brought in after the First World War to create what became the middle ten holes.

Several holes are hauntingly beautiful. The 6th is a dog-leg around woodland, and narrows where the drive is meant to finish; the fairway of the 8th is almost an oasis of heather, where a mid-iron needs to carry to the middle of the green, behind which stands a wall of birch.

A conspicuous feature of the middle part of the course is the dog-leg holes: the 9th, 10th and the 14th. Simpson was one of the pioneers of such holes and here is a classic triumvirate, each presenting its own, beguilingly different problems.

Firestone 64

To anyone who has tried to play his way around the fearsome south course at Firestone, the idea of anyone shooting 61 is simply fantastical. For the first 15 holes, maybe? Yet Jose-Maria Olazabal managed it in the World Series of 1990. No wonder he went on to win the tournament by 12 shots.

Firestone ranks amongst the finest work of Robert Trent Jones. A man renowned for his tough layouts, this was one of the foundation posts upon which that reputation was made. From the back tees it measures almost 7,200 yards, and yet the par is just 70 strokes.

It was Harvey Firestone who instigated this country club. A millionaire industrialist, it was his gift to his workforce, and few employees have been the recipients of such a munificent gift.

Television has brought familiarity to the daunting last four holes, where birdies are desperately difficult to achieve. The 15th goes down on the card as a short hole, but at 230 yards long, most people will feel inclined to dispute the word "short".

No such ambiguity about the long 16th, which measures 625 yards, although it is not quite as monstrous as it sounds, since it is entirely downhill. The 17th is back up the hill and then to the 18th, one of those stringent par fours that have earned Firestone its rightful reputation as one of golf's most unforgiving of venues.

The European 63

The European lies on the shores of Brittas Bay in the county of Wicklow and, as is so often the case with great courses, is testament to the love and devotion of one man. The difference in this case is that this man is still very much among us, and his creation only opened for business in 1993.

It was in the late 1980s that Pat Ruddy took a helicopter round the shores of Ireland in search of a piece of suitable linksland. He bought the current site of the European for £330,000 and then sold off a chunk of it for almost as much. Naturally he kept the best bits for himself.

Built at a total cost of less than £1 million, the European opened in the same year as the K Club and Mount Juliet, both of which cost 25 times as much. When the annual survey of top Irish courses came out for that year, the European was perched in the top six – the other two were much lower down – a true reward for one man's labour.

For those who love true links golf, Ruddy's pride and joy is a wonderful thing. Most of the holes have been finely threaded through the dunes, with three that run directly along the shore. The one discordant note comes at the 18th; what should be one of the best holes on the course happens to be the worst. One day, I'm hoping to persuade Ruddy to change it, but so far he refuses to budge!

Medinah 62

Medinah number three is a haven for those who like their golf to be of the sado-masochistic variety. From the back tees, no fewer than six of the par fours measure over 440 yards, and none of the par fives measures under 520 yards. Even the par threes have a bit of length to them – the shortest, the 17th, coming in at a shade under 170 yards.

Harry Cooper is probably to blame for this penal state of affairs. In winning the 1930 Medinah Open, he shot a course record 63, which horrified the membership. This shall not happen again, was the collective view, and so the original design was changed out of all recognition. And it has not happened again – if anything it has reached the other extreme. When Lou Graham won the 1975 US Open, it was with a score of three over par.

Medinah will be in the news again in 1999, when it hosts the USPGA Championship. It will be interesting to see if the latest generation of professionals can fare any better.

No fewer than four of the holes swing back and forth across Lake Kadijah, which splits the course in two. These include the par-three 17th, where the lake sits in front of the green, and demands a perfectly judged shot. The full-blooded 18th is no less demanding, the requirement being two heavy hits to a gently undulating target.

The Red Course at The Berkshire 61

The Blue and Red courses at The Berkshire are almost equal in merit, but perhaps the Red deserves the nod if only for its unusual configuration of six par fours, six par threes, and six par fives. Certainly few inland courses can offer such an outstanding opening hole, played out against a wonderful backdrop of mature pine, silver birch and chestnut trees.

Given the abundance of par fives, it is hardly surprising that the Berkshire lends itself to spectacular scoring, although any player who thinks it a pushover is undoubtedly heading for a rude awakening.

In all prbability, the Berkshire may be the only course in the world where no par four is to be found amongst the last four holes. The 15th is a par five with the green within reach of two blows; the short 16th may well see any shot picked up at the 15th instantly dropped again, since a wood is often necessary to reach the plateau green. The 17th is a longer par five, again to an elevated green, before a gentle finishing hole, a short- to mid-iron the requirement to reach a target that is slightly deceptive, since the putting surface rises sharply from the front of the green.

As for the par fours, the 8th is a corker, where the approach must clear a shallow valley.

Medinah – host to the 1999 USPGA Championship

The Links at Spanish Bay 60

Perhaps only Kerry on Ireland's west coast, Ayrshire in Scotland, and the Southport area of Lancashire come close to the Monterey Peninsula in terms of the abundance of quantity links courses. None, however, comes really close.

Suffice to say that if the links at Spanish Bay were situated anywhere other than in close proximity to Pebble Beach and Cypress Point, players would travel continents to discover their special virtues.

Designed by Robert Trent Jones Jnr, with input from Tom Watson, the opening par five illustrates the beauty of the site, as it tumbles down towards the ocean, the green sitting prettily on a plateau. Thereafter the links unfolds in a tradition more in keeping with the old Scottish courses than any updated theories that were in fashion at the time of its construction in the 1980s.

Ten holes, for example, have but a single bunker around the green for protection; the greens are hard and invite the chip-and-run rather than any shot where the ball spends most of its time airborne. Most of the greens are also undulating, including the par-three 16th, which has a hog's back running through it.

For much of the time, the course runs pleasingly through the small sandy hummocks, but it is the ocean holes, naturally, that cause the most excitement. Another is the 14th – again a par five – where once more the hole falls down towards the sea.

Royal Dornoch 59

No great golf course is further from the madding crowds than Royal Dornoch, which lies beyond the Highlands of Scotland along the shores of Embo Bay at the mouth of Dornoch Firth. A testament to its virtues is the fact that few of the pilgrims who have made the long journey have come away feeling it was not worth their while.

The club was formed in 1877, although a decade would pass before Old Tom Morris was called upon to supplement the existing nine holes with a further nine. Morris was impressed by the place from the outset, the naturalness of the setting, and while alterations have been made since, the characteristics of the course – the dunes, the hummocks, the undulating fairways – continue to owe little to the existence of man.

The first two holes are gentle enough, but then the course falls away to a curving valley and reveals its qualities as it does so. From the 9th in particular, as the golfer turns for home to be greeted by the force of the prevailing wind, a player suddenly realizes that if he has not made his score by now, then he is not going to do so.

It is not easy to pick the finest of Dornoch's holes, but the glorious par-four 14th has to be close. Long known as "foxy", it measures the best part of 450 yards and requires two special shots to overcome it.

Hollinwell 58

On a sunlit day in either spring or autumn, few inland golf courses in Britain can compete for visual splendour with Nottingham golf club, or Hollinwell, as it is more popularly known. This truly is a hidden gem.

Designed around the turn of the century by Willie Park Jnr, with some additional touches by J.H. Taylor, the course initially came in for some heavy criticism from the membership, since they already had a course at Bulwell Forest and were reluctant to move. Once Messrs Park and Taylor had finished, however, any criticism was rendered mute.

The glory of Hollinwell lies in its boundless variety. The holes switch back and forth, with only the par-three 13th and the 14th running in the same direction. The former, incidentally, is a beauty, an inviting shot from an elevated tee to a green situated far below.

The finish sums up the differing challenges that Hollinwell presents. The 16th is all strategy, a short par four requiring a precise approach to a heavily protected green. The par-five 17th can be played strategically, too, although the bigger hitters will be unable to resist the temptation of trying for the green in two. Then the stiff par four to finish, where any second shot that finds the large putting surface is an excellent one. Behind stands the fine old clubhouse, a graceful landmark in the distance.

Lahinch 57

In the 108 years since it was first designed, Lahinch has been lauded in the highest quarter, right from its first architect, Old Tom Morris. Spying the land that lies on the spectacular coast of County Clare, just a couple of miles from the Cliffs of Moher, Morris declared that there was little for him to do except build tees and greens. "I consider the links is as fine a natural course as it has ever been my good fortune to play over," he said.

In 1928, Dr Alister Mackenzie was invited to make some adjustments, and went away saying that it was the "finest and most popular course that I, or I believe anyone else, ever constructed".

Even allowing for the fact that Mackenzie probably had these words in mind for Irish ears only, it is lavish praise indeed from the man who had already designed Royal Melbourne and Cypress Point, and would go on to design Augusta National.

Yet any visitor can easily understand the sentiments behind those laudatory statements. This is links golf in the raw, the holes tumbling around and over the dunes rather like they do down the coast at Ballybunion.

The most famous holes are two designed by Morris that Mackenzie was forbidden to touch. Both call for blind shots – the second to the par-five 5th is over a vast sandhill with the green remote in the distance. The 6th, more controversially, is a par three with the green nestling between two steep sand dunes.

Tournament Players' Club, Sawgrass – the home of the Players' Championship

Tournament Players' Club, Sawgrass 56

The TPC course in Jacksonville, North Florida, is the site every year of the Players' Championship, and was one of the first stadium courses to be built. It probably remains the best.

Certainly there is no shortage of room for spectators to watch in comfort; most of the holes are flanked by steep banks where golf fans can gather to watch their favourites.

The course was designed by Pete Dye and drew criticism early on for being too penal. Now it has been softened around the edges and, while it remains a stiff test, the player in form will gain his true reward.

Some of the best – and certainly the most dramatic – holes come at the finish. The 16th is a long par five where the green is reachable for the long hitter prepared to take on the water that protects both the right side of the fairway and the green. Then the player swings round the other way to confront the famous par-three 17th, complete with its island green, the first of its kind but now heavily imitated.

The shot required is only an eight iron or so in calm conditions, but the fun begins if the prevailing wind is blowing into the player's face or, better still, across the hole.

The 18th is protected by water all down its left-hand side, the hole curving gently to a two-tier green that has drawn many a three putt from players who thought their problems were over once they reached it with two exacting blows.

Westmoreland 55

Westmoreland is situated on a beautiful rolling 480-acre site in the parish of St James on Barbados's fabled Platinum Coast. Designed by Robert Trent Jones, it may be the only course in the world where the sea is visible on every hole, and yet it is not a links course.

It is, however, exceedingly playable – one of those courses that golfers of most standards can enjoy. From the back tees, with the omnipresent trade winds, it is a stern test. Yet off the blue tees, for the average golfer, it is an example of what holiday golf should be all about.

The par threes, in particular, are sublime examples of an architect's craft. There are also two wonderful short par fours.

Jones considers this among the best courses he has designed, in a full portfolio that reaches around the world. It is some tribute to the site he was presented with, and one round is sufficient to leave the visitor with the view that he has done justice to it.

The first sets out the challenge presented at Westmoreland. A good long drive will leave just an eight or nine iron to the green, but deviate from this plan and the problems begin.

A third nine has been lined by houses within the price range of only the exceedingly wealthy. Ian Woosnam has one, which indicates the sort of money we are talking about.

Tryall – a true Caribbean experience

Tryall 54

Tryall first came to public prominence in the early 1990s when it began hosting the Johnnie Walker World Championship. A more evocative venue would be hard to find. The event was always held the week before Christmas and, while half the world shivered beside the fireside, they tuned in to watch an event played in a Caribbean idyll, with a number of holes lapping up against sleepy Jamaican shores.

Fourteen new tees were built for that event, and 400 yards added to its length. In its tournament guise, especially with additional fortification from the trade winds, it became the stiffest challenge.

The original designer was Ralph Plummer, and a fine job he made of it, too. At first, most of the land appeared unsuitable for a golf course: much of it was on an upslope. In the hands of a less skilled architect, the result would have been a plethora of sidehill lies, plus the sort of exercise more suitable to triathlon training than a gentle holiday golfing workout.

In practice, there are few sidehill lies, indeed hardly any at all if the ball is struck where it is supposed to be. Given the setting, it was hardly surprising that Plummer should choose to place the 18th green practically on the beach, the second shot on a balmy evening played directly towards the setting sun.

Kasumigaseki 53

Kasumigaseki remains the most famous course in Japan. Situated within the sprawling metropolis of Tokyo, it was designed originally by a talented local player, and then improved upon by the English architect Charles Alison.

He was drawn particularly to the par-three 10th, which required a medium-length stroke to reach the green. Alison toughened the requirements, introducing several deep sandtraps into the side of a steep slope leading up to the green. Their depth was an innovation to the Japanese, who immediately christened them "Arisons". The name has stuck.

It was hardly Alison's only intervention, indeed the championship East Course is fundamentally his work. His simple guideline was that no shot struck straight and true should be punished, while any stroke that deviated from such a path would inevitably flirt with a hazard.

Another characteristic of the course is the concept of two greens, which lie side by side on many holes. One green of bent grass is used during the winter, giving way to the Korai grass green in the summer, as the latter can survive the oppressive heat and humidity.

One of the great holes at Kasumigaseki is the 18th, a par five within reach of the mighty hitters who are prepared to take on the challenge of a second shot that has to cross the deepest part of a valley to a green well protected by Arisons – sorry, deep bunkers.

Seminole 52

Seminole is one of the most attractive of America's courses, but also one of the most exclusive. It lies against the shore of North Palm Beach, and was the first great course to be built in Florida. For all the frantic building that has gone on in the state these past 30 years, it probably remains the number-one venue, but it is unfortunate that it has never been tested in tournament conditions.

Certainly Ben Hogan, who used to winter there, never had any doubts as to its quality. "If you can play well there, you can play well anywhere," he said. Having said that, Claude Harmon, for many years Seminole's professional in the winter months, once shot 60, and a card of his remarkable achievement hangs proudly in the clubhouse.

The course was laid out by the ubiquitous Donald Ross, the architect of so many outstanding venues in America. His creation is a true linksland course over the Florida sand ridges, and is influenced entirely by the winds that blow in from the Atlantic Ocean.

Its most conspicuous feature remains the large bunkers, housing gleaming white sand. Like many designers, Ross saved the land available by the sea for his closing holes. The short 17th, into the prevailing wind, requires a precise shot from an elevated tee to a plateau green; the 18th is a long par four requiring a fine drive simply to bring the green within reach of another wood or one or two iron.

The National 51

On the eastern seaboard of the United States, adjacent to the glory that is Shinneock Hills, stands another course that many believe to be its equal both in terms of standing and quality. Certainly The National is a joy to play, where the winds blowing either from the Atlantic or down Long Island Sound provide additional fortification to a layout that is a fearsome test of skill.

The designer was Charles Macdonald, who built The National after spending five consecutive summers trawling through England and Scotland, taking notes on the characteristics of all the great links courses.

Some of his designs are close imitations of celebrated holes in Britain: the third, for example, replicates some of the problems of the fifth at Prestwick, while the 7th and the 13th seek to recreate some of the drama to be had at St Andrews.

One of the further characteristics of the course are its sharply contoured bunkers, most notably at the stern 14th, where the green is protected by seven bunkers of varying size and shape.

For all its quality, its evocative title, just one event of international note has been held at the National – the 1922 Walker Cup. Among the players on that occasion was Bernard Darwin, the doyen of all golf writers, who had no hesitation in considering it "a truly great course".

Walton Heath 50

The Old Course at Walton Heath is a wonderful golfing experience from first to last, but it is the final three holes that elevate it above the fine cluster of courses to be found in this fertile region for golf just south of London.

The 16th, a par five measuring just over 500 yards, requires a long drive down a narrow heather-lined fairway to open up the possibility of a full-blooded shot to a green that slopes from left to right, and which is further fortified down the right side by bunkers.

The 17th is a lovely short hole, a precise iron the requirement to carry the enormous bunker that guards the front. And so to the 18th, a thunderous par four, where another long drive is necessary to eliminate any awkward decisions regarding a sand trap that cuts across the fairway some 40 yards short of the green.

Walton Heath was assured of a certain kind of fame from the moment James Braid agreed to become its first professional in 1904. Since then it has staged some of the great golfing occasions, including five European Open Championships and, in 1981, the Ryder Cup.

The event was a walkover for the Americans, but remains memorable for the quality of the visiting side; indeed, few doubt that it was the finest team that has ever played in the event, with no fewer than 11 members who had won, or would win, major championships.

Saunton 49

There is a possibility before the next century is too many years old that Saunton will realize its dream to host an Open Championship. Certainly the course is challenging enough, a wonderfully rugged links situated on the serene shoreline of North Devon.

Once considered too remote to host such an event, the argument simply does not hold water any more. It is certainly no less remote than Carnoustie.

Built among the sandhills, scrubland and rushes of Braunton Burrows, the course was closed for 11 years in 1939. It was C.K. Cotton who aided the reconstruction with three new holes, the 1st, 17th and the 18th. The start would test any professional, with the first three par fours all measuring over 400 yards; the first indeed, runs to 470, while there is only one par three in the first 12 holes. The toughest hole, however, is still to come: the 16th, a daunting par four of 430 yards that requires two all-but-perfect shots to find the putting surface.

The drive must carry a high sandhill and be played with a touch of draw to follow the dog-leg. This brings the elevated green within reach, but only with a long iron over the deep bunker that guards the front of the putting surface.

Baltusrol 48

"Forget Nicklaus," opined one newspaper man, when the US Open came to the Lower Course at Baltusrol in 1980. If ever a headline were designed to leave its inventor with egg on its face it was, of course, that one. Nicklaus enjoyed perhaps his finest moment, and Baltusrol was witness once more to a cherished piece of American golfing history.

The courses were built in the 1920s on land that was once owned by a wealthy Dutch farmer named Baltus Roll, who was murdered in 1831. These days, of course, the shots are of a more peaceful nature.

The designer was the great eccentric, Albert Tillinghast, although little of his work is recognizable, and certainly not the configuration adopted by the United States Golf Association for US Opens, whereby there are no par fives for 16 holes and then two come at once.

The 17th is a beauty, mind, all 630 yards of it, which remained out of reach to allcomers in two until John Daly managed the feat with a drive and one iron in the 1993 US Open.

One of the great golf stories concerns the par-three 4th. Redesigned by Robert Trent Jones, he came under flak from the members for making it too tough. So he played it with the club's professional and two committee men, and duly holed in one. "As you can see, gentlemen," Jones said, "the hole is not too tough."

Royal Aberdeen 47

There is no escaping "the gowf" on Scotland's east coast, and first-class golf at that. From North Berwick to Royal Dornoch, these courses lie as sacred ground for pilgrims to visit. Some are justly more famous than others; some, like Royal Aberdeen, are hidden gems, and perhaps slight victims of their location. Certainly, if this course were situated 200 miles down the coastline, the Royal and Ancient would be seeing what they could do to lengthen it for Open Championship consideration.

For the average player, no such thoughts are necessary. At 6,372 yards from the medal tees, it might not sound unduly taxing, but it is subject to every whim and mercy of the winds that are the east coast's almost constant companion.

The outward nine, in particular, are a wonderful stretch of holes. The noted Scottish writer Sam Mckinlay was moved to describe this nine as offering testing and picturesque golf to stand comparison with any other links in the British Isles. The holes run loosely in an anti-clockwise fashion, concluding with the forbidding par-four 18th.

Royal Aberdeen was founded in 1780, which makes it the sixth-oldest golf club in the world. The present course, however, was built in 1866, after two earlier moves. The Royal prefix was bestowed in 1903.

The Emirates Course, Dubai – a marvel of modern architecture

The Emirates Course, Dubai 46

The Emirates course in Dubai is a geological miracle; seen from the air, the full scope of man's ingenuity is apparent, the land outside the course's confines being the desert from which it emerged. Up to 750,000 gallons of water are desalinated daily and pumped via almost 19 miles of pipeline and 700 sprinklers on to the course. Without this watering, it would be desert once more within a month.

The layout is a fine example of modern architecture, the course eminently playable for most standards of golfer. There are five lakes, but they do not intrude excessively. Neither is there an injudicious use of bunkers, as there would be under a less stylish designer than Karl Litten.

To help aesthetically, thousands of trees were flown in: Royal palms from South America, date and coconut palms, Washingtonians and giant Arizona cactii line the fairways and greens.

The clubhouse is in keeping with the course it overlooks, an extravagant £10 million cluster of concrete buildings linked together and shaped like bedouin tents.

The best holes on the course may well be those that close the front and back nines, which are linked by a double green, and the lake that separates the fairways comes into play on both: the 9th is a fearsome par four, where the water is a factor both off the drive and the approach; the 18th, a fine par five, where a good drive shaped around the angle of the dog-leg fairway brings the green into view.

Royal Sydney 45

Royal Sydney plays a full role in the cultural life of this splendid city. It is situated just a 10-minute drive from its commerical heart, a thriving establishment that also offers tennis and social activities to fully engage its 5,000-strong membership.

Golf, however, came first and remains its primary function. The course is an elegant rolling layout, where the penalties for straying off line can be severe indeed.

Perhaps it is at its best in the autumn and winter months, but a sea breeze is a year-round hazard with which all golfers will invariably have to contend.

Perhaps the pick of the short holes is the 14th, where the green is protected by a veritable Sahara of bunkers. Its difficulty is indicated by the fact that a tournament once offered a $100,000 prize to anyone who made a hole-in-one. No one managed it, from a cumulative total of 440 attempts.

The course draws to a climax with one of the best finishing holes in Australia. Measuring a shade over 400 yards, it is a sharp dog-leg left, where the drive has to be shaped around a copse. Then comes the approach to an elevated green – a wonderful gathering spot at tournament time – that sits in front of the huge clubhouse.

Wentworth – worthy of any golfer's attention

Wentworth 44

The West and East courses at Wentworth are both worth any golfer's attention. The East is the easier upon which to score and, in many ways, the more enjoyable. The West is one to tackle when in form, otherwise the scorecard at the end can have a forlorn appearance.

This is the venue each spring and autumn for the Volvo PGA Championship and the World Matchplay events, respectively. These are the two seasons when the course is wearing its finest colours.

The first three holes set out the challenge ahead. The 1st and the 3rd are par fours that require heavy ammunition to reach in two; sandwiched in between is a strategic par three offering the sharpest contrast.

The finish is inspired. Not too many courses close with two par fives, but it works wonderfully: the 17th a sharp dog-leg left, the 18th going the other way. The first of the two long holes is out of reach for all but the longest; the green at the last is more inviting for two well-placed shots.

Wentworth has changed character over the last 20 years. It has become more corporate-friendly, with prices to match. On the positive side, the year-round condition of the two main courses compares favourably with any venue to be found in Britain.

Nairn 43

In 1899 Nairn became the first Scottish club to make an admission charge for a golf match. One hundred years later, it will host the Walker Cup. In the intervening century its reputation has not been enhanced quite as much as it deserves: thousands of pilgrims make the long march each year to Dornoch, but they would be fools not to play Nairn on the way back down. Situated some 12 miles from Inverness, it may not have quite the kudos of its more northerly neighbour, but it just happens to make up for that by being a better course.

The first seven holes, in particular, make for an entrancing opening stretch. Perched along the banks of the Moray Firth, the mountains of Caithness stand guard in the distance. This is links golf in its truest sense.

Yet some of the best holes fall when the course finally turns inward. The 13th is a marvellous par four up a steep hill, where the second shot appears much longer than the yardage marked on the card. Back down the hill, the par-three 14th makes for an inviting tee shot to a green protected heavily at the entrance by two deep bunkers.

The large undulating greens and cavernous sand traps are two of the characteristic features of a course laid out in 1887 by Archie Simpson, and modified two years later by Old Tom Morris and James Braid.

Peachtree 42

Bobby Jones will forever be associated with Augusta, of course, but it was not quite his only foray into golf-course architecture. At Peachtree, just outside Atlanta, Robert Trent Jones followed his ideas to the letter for a course that Bobby Jones considered his golfing home in later years.

The two men got along famously, and the fruit of their efforts solidified Trent Jones's burgeoning reputation.

Shades of Augusta abound. The terrain is rolling, the holes weaving their way amongst dogwoods and magnolia. A characteristic of the course is the greens, which were huge by the standards of the austere time – they were built in the 1940s. But it was in-keeping with the emphasis both men placed on the value of flexible hole locations, and set a trend.

The start is wonderful, away from the historic Cobb Caldwell mansion that serves as the clubhouse. The 1st is a dog-leg par four heavily protected by two fairway bunkers at the angle. The par-five 2nd, over 500 yards in length, can be reached with two monstrous blows, but the second shot has to take on both a lake and stream that makes it a three-shotter for all but the most cavalier.

In 1989 Peachtree played host to an historic Walker Cup, as a side representing Great Britain and Ireland won for the first time on American soil.

Loch Lomond 41

The best golf course built in Britain in the last 25 years sits snug to the ethereal shores of Loch Lomond, and was designed by that elegant-player-cum-architect, Tom Weiskopf. It was a troubled birth, and at one stage it looked as if it would lie in some half-completed state, an unfinished symphony. Lyle Anderson, a wealthy native of Arizona, rode to the rescue and all of golf has since rejoiced in his munificence.

The course is home each year to the Loch Lomond Invitational, which is played the week before the Open Championship. In those years when the Open is played in Scotland, it means a fortnight when all the best the game's home country has to offer is on show. One week there's the finest inland course it has to offer; the next a venerable links.

Like all the best courses, Loch Lomond works both the mind and the power cells. The 14th is a wonderfully treacherous short par four, with the green temptingly in reach from the tee for most of today's players. So, too, is the trouble. By contrast, the 6th runs along the loch for no less than 635 yards, making it the longest hole in Scotland.

A particularly fine stretch of golf follows the turn: the 10th is an imposing four, where the second shot has to avoid water that guards the green's left flank; the 11th is a daunting uphill par three that requires a perfectly-struck long iron; the 12th is Weiskopf's homage to Donald Ross, with a green that slopes sharply away at all angles.

Harbour Town 40

It is symptomatic of the allure of Harbour Town that few players in America feel like taking the week off after the Masters: they may be fatigued following their exertions in the first major championship of the year, but who wants to skip the Heritage Classic and its charming venue which sits towards the southern shores of Hilton Head Island in South Carolina?

The finest compliment that perhaps can be paid to the architects, Pete Dye and Jack Nicklaus, is that Harbour Town looks 100 years old even though it is only 30. The course was out of character for both men, and it becomes them. For once Dye forgot his trademark railroad tracks, and Nicklaus left behind his obsession with building courses that only men of his ability can play.

The result is a beguiling venue, with fairways flanked by a dazzling array of woodland and vegetation. And, appropriately, the best hole is saved until last, one of the best closing holes in America. At 478 yards and par four, few players want to stand on this tee in the Heritage Classic needing a regulation figure to ensure victory.

Played boldly, the hole calls for two absolutely straight shots, but the fairway and green are both cut into the tidal saltmarsh along Calibogue Sound, and it is a brave player who is not unduly influenced. Behind the green, the ceremonial lighthouse completes an enchanting backcloth.

Princeville 39

Princeville is situated beneath the Bali Hai mountains on the most westerly of the Hawaiian islands, Kauai. The sumptuousness of the surroundings is matched by the quality of the golf, although the Prince course is not one that a player who has a handicap of worse than 18 should attempt to play. Some of the carries invariably trouble a scratch player, let alone someone of a modest standard.

Trent Jones's brief was to build the best course in Hawaii and, despite competition from a number of quality venues, most objective judges believe he succeeded. *Golf Digest* usually rates it as such in its periodic guide to the best resort golf on the islands; one enthusiastic critic even called it "the Pine Valley of Hawaii".

The architect is the first to agree he had a wonderful site to begin with, and most of it remains intact as the holes wind their way through lush undergrowth with lots of wonderful views of the azure Pacific.

One of the best holes comes early, the menacing 2nd, where a good drive is required to enable a player to carry a ravine that is almost 100 yards long.

The winds are a constant factor on virtually all the Hawaiian courses, and Princeville is no exception. The 3rd, for example, measures 180 yards but can play as little as a wedge if the wind is helping.

Chantilly 38

To walk through the gates of Chantilly is to leave all trace of the outside world behind. Situated just 25 miles north of Paris, the first impression is also the one that lasts: this is a place of both peace and tranquillity.

For more than 90 years now the club has been the exclusive preserve of the Parisian bourgeoisie, who value its serene qualities. It was founded under the presidency of Prince Murat, and in 1920 the noted European architect Tom Simpson was commissioned to design another 18 holes. Much of his work was damaged during the course of the the Second World War, and nine of the new holes were abandoned, but there is little question that his work on the main course, which included reducing the number of bunkers, was the cornerstone to its greatness.

Two series of holes in particular stand out. The 9th to the 11th are daunting holes, calling for accurate placement from the tee to bring about the desired results. Similarly, the 13th to the 15th: the first of the three features a lovely second shot over a grassy chasm; then comes the longest of the short holes is followed by a tee shot that ranks among the most formidable on the course.

Chantilly has been host to the French Open on many occasions, and most recently for a trio of events from 1988. Two of them were won by that arch-strategist, Nick Faldo, who found a course well suited to his particular talent.

The Jockey Club 37

Golf in South America remains imperfectly formed. Even at places like the Jockey Club in Buenos Aires, where the game is played, the courses were built – as the title implies – as an adjunct to racing. In this particular instance, however, the two courses are no less impressive for that perceived indifference. They were designed by Dr Alister Mackenzie, and are more worthy examples of his unrivalled craft.

The Jockey Club is also home to Roberto de Vicenzo, the most famous golfer South America has ever produced, who remains strong and able well into his 70s. On home turf he is thought of as something of a demi-god; the pity is that few of his fellow countrymen took up his example and played the sport.

Given that it is both a playground for the rich and Buenos Aires has a temperate climate, it will come as no surprise to learn that the courses at the Jockey Club are always in impeccable condition. The Red was used for the 1970 World Cup, and while not long at 6,700 yards, it has plenty of variety. In common with most Mackenzie courses, mental acumen is a more telling virtue than brute strength.

Perhaps inevitably, the individual title at that World Cup was won by de Vicenzo himself, with Argentina finishing runner-up, 10 strokes behind the Australians.

Oakmont – Augusta's greens are considered by many to be slow in comparison

Oakmont 36

America contains many examples of penal golf architecture, but Oakmont scores highly not only in terms of toughness, but also quality. The former is perhaps not surprising, given that it was the stated aim of the designer to build such a course, but the latter is given that Oakmont is sliced almost in two by the Pennsylvania Turnpike. There is not another course in the world that wears such an aesthetic calamity so well.

Oakmont's most fabled feature is its greens, with contours designed to enhance their speed. Many players consider Augusta's to be slow by comparison. "I did well, I only had six three putts in nine holes," Tom Watson remarked, after practising one day for the 1994 US Open. "If this course were a woman it would never say 'I do'."

Yet it has been humbled, most memorably by Johnny Miller in the 1973 US Open. Granted, overnight rain had softened the greens so they uncharacteristically resembled dartboards, but still Miller's 63 to win was an astounding effort. It was the lowest score ever seen in a major championship, and a mark that has been equalled on many occasions since in grand-slam events, but still, at the time of writing, has never been beaten.

Oakmont will also be forever synonymous with the name of the Pennsylvania native Arnold Palmer, who played his first US Open there in 1953 and his last in 1994 – winning only once in 1960.

Royal Porthcawl 35

Royal Porthcawl is not Wales's most senior course in terms of age, but it is in terms of prestige. So much so indeed, that when the Walker Cup was held in the Principality for the first time in 1996 it would have been wrong for it to have been staged anywhere else.

It led to a rare home victory, as the Americans, including one Tiger Woods, struggled to cope with the trying conditions. Many an average mortal will have understood his sullen expression, for on such days when the elements are merciless, Porthcawl can be a doleful experience.

On warm spring days, however, it is a grand place to be. The members are among the most convivial, and the Bristol Channel is a polished diamond that never becomes hidden from view on any of the 18 holes. Yet Porthcawl is not a links in the traditional sense. From the 4th, the holes move inland and the terrain changes with them. Golf on the uplands in the middle of the course possesses more of a heathland character.

Yet it is the start and finish that most visitors will eagerly remember. The first three are all classic seaside holes, hugging the rock-fringed shore, while the last four are all wonderful, and particularly the 18th, played back towards the sea with the second shot from an elevated fairway to a green lying snug against the water's edge being one of the most evocative in golf.

Royal Adelaide 34

Royal Adelaide is as near to a links course as exists among the top Australian championship venues. For the 1998 Australian Open it measured a mammoth 7,200 yards and subtle changes, instigated by Peter Thomson, drew both praise and brickbats. The fact that the latter came mostly from players who struggled to locate the narrow fairways perhaps indicates they would have been better leaving their comments unsaid.

Those changes by Thomson formed a pattern of evolution that has been going on since the club acquired the Seaton site back in 1904. In 1926 Dr Alister Mackenzie arrived to make modifications, and the work he carried out forms the basis of the current championship route. The whole layout has the flat appearance of a links, save for a rise in the centre where the tees for the 8th and the 12th are situated. The best hole is probably the 11th, one that Thomson believes would be considered among the finest on the continent if it were somewhere pivotal on the card, such as the 17th.

No mention of Royal Adelaide is complete without the story of the stroke played by Kevin Simmonds at the 2nd in a national amateur event. A vicious hooked tee shot, it landed in the carriage of a passing train, whereupon the shocked passenger gathered his wits before throwing it back, the ball coming to rest a yard from the hole. Sadly, Simmonds missed what would have been the game's most astonishing albatross.

Portmarnock 33

In terms of hosting prestigious championships, no course in Ireland comes close in seniority to Portmarnock, that stately links close to the environs of Dublin. Accordingly it has become a professional's favourite. It boasts little of the scenic splendour of Royal County Down or Portrush but, as far as the pros are concerned, little of their capriciousness either.

Nothing is contrived at Portmarnock. The holes unfold on gently rolling land, with few tricks and still fewer blind shots. A feature is the trio of short holes, which display boundless variety. The 7th is into a small depression, the 12th high in the dunes, while the celebrated 15th has been described by no less a personage than Arnold Palmer as among the best par threes in golf. It is Portmarnock's signature hole, the sea finally visible behind the dunes. If the wind is blowing from this direction it can be a beast, the line towards the beach in the hope of watching the ball sail back on to the narrow table of green. The par fives are excellent examples of their genre as well.

The oft-heard cliché, to judge a course on the quality of its champions, leaves Portmarnock to puff out its chest with justifiable pride: the Irish Open winners there include Severiano Ballesteros, Bernhard Langer, Ian Woosnam and Jose-Maria Olazabal.

Merion 32

Few great golf courses are squeezed into such a small acreage as Merion. The venue is so landlocked that there is no way of extending its 6,482 yards from the back tees, which in turn is the reason why no United States Open has been staged there since 1981, when David Graham became the first Australian to win the tournament. It is an acute loss.

Merion was designed by an architectural amateur named Hugh Wilson, who spent six months in Britain on a post-graduate course in British linksland before returning home to design a venue that rightly remains the pride of all Philadelphia.

The course has been home to some of the great moments in golfing history: it was here in 1930 that Bobby Jones completed what then constituted the Grand Slam, winning the US Amateur to add to his earlier victories in the Open, the Amateur and the US Open. Twenty years later, a triumph every bit as remarkable was achieved by Ben Hogan as he won the US Open just 13 months after being told he would never walk again following a road accident.

The beauty of Merion is that because so much had to be crammed into just 110 acres – most country clubs take up a plot twice that size – there is no excess. Each of the 120 bunkers, for example, serves a purpose. Nicknamed the "white faces of Merion", by the 1916 US Amateur champion, Chick Evans, they remain one of the course's hallmarks.

Portmarnock – it has become a professional's favourite

County Louth 31

Baltray, as it is known by one and all, is undoubtedly one of the best-kept secrets in Irish golf. The course lies in the small fishing village from which it takes its less formal name, about an hour's drive north of Dublin.

Here we find a course of traditional links character. The opening nine are characterized by the tumbling land from which architect Tom Simpson has carved holes of rare variety. The back nine are still better in parts, and particularly the holes from the 12th to the 16th that run along the shore, and which are flanked by towering dunes. Three of the short holes are memorable, too: none calls for a long shot, but all are heavily fortified, leading to scorecards marked with double bogeys almost as often as they are with pars.

The first two holes go on the card as a four and a five, but each is as hard as the other: a par four-and-a-half for each would be about right, if such a scoring system were allowed.

If Baltray has one weakness then it is the last two holes. After 16 glorious holes, one looks for a fitting crescendo, but instead the opposite occurs. Given what has gone before, the plain and colourless par-three 17th comes as a complete shock. The 18th is not much better either, a par five with little to commend it.

Royal Montreal 30

Royal Montreal was the first properly constituted club in North America, pre-dating the first in the United States by 15 years. The club has moved twice since forming in 1873, however, due to urban sprawl, and now occupies a site on Ile Bizard in the Lake of Two Mountains.

The 45 holes there were designed by Dick Wilson, whose training as a civil engineer came in handy. Rocks, boulders and tree stumps had to be removed, a swamp to be drained and lakes created, and all in a climate in which snow and ice hampered the operation for months on end.

He completed the work in just over two years, and was rightly proud of his creations. "There is a sweep and dimension to this layout which can only be described as exciting," he wrote. "The vista of the Lake of Two Mountains is the perfect backdrop to these courses."

It is the Blue Course that has become the tournament venue, although both are exacting. After competing in the 1997 Canadian Open over the Blue, Davis Love said: "It is such a trying course, just like a major championship venue. The rough is very penalizing and the greens are fast." In particular, the 16th is one of the most intimidating par fours on the continent. Small wonder that it is accepted that a Royal member can play to his handicap anywhere.

Royal Troon 29

It is fashionable to consider Royal Troon as the least distinguished of the eight courses on the Open Championship rota; indeed, I have done as much with this list. Only a fool would belittle it on that score, however, for it remains to my mind one of the top-30 places in the world to play golf.

"As much by skill as by strength" is the club's motto, with the front nine justifying the first part of that clause, and the inward nine justifying the second. If the wind is blowing from the prevailing direction, the golfer may well find himself in fantasy land after the first six holes, where only the tee shot to the short 5th requires a precise stroke. Certainly Greg Norman did in the final round of the 1989 Open: he birdied all of them.

At the loop at the far end of the course, things get interesting. The 8th, the Postage Stamp, justifies everything written about it: it is one of the world's great short holes. The 9th is a fine hole, too, though disfigured somewhat by an unsightly caravan site nearby.

And so to the back nine, where the gains of the outward half can all so easily slip away. The 11th, a par five for mortals, is an awesomely difficult four for the Open protagonists. Four pars to finish, meanwhile, will invariably lead to progress against the vast majority of any field.

Valderrama 28

Jaime Patino made no secret of his ambition for Valderrama when he acquired the land in 1988. "I want to make it the Augusta of Europe," he boldly declared. In many ways he has succeeded. Valderrama is the most exclusive club in southern Spain, with few tee-times open to non-members. It is also the best-conditioned course on the continent, where the fairways are so pristine you almost feel like you should take off your shoes before you walk on them.

Valderrama is unusual among modern courses in that it does not seek to overpower a player with length. Even from the back tees it is well under 7,000 yards, and unless the breeze is fresh into the face at either the 7th or 9th holes, all the par fours are reachable.

The fairways are nowhere near as generous as they are at Augusta, however. Most are protected by the beautiful cork trees that characterize the plot. The greens and their environs are every bit as problematic. A tee shot that finishes above the 6th hole, just as at the Georgia original, will almost certainly result in a three putt.

The best hole on the course may well be the par-five 4th, where it is a brave man who tries for the green in two, since its right side is protected by a scenic waterfall. Even the third shot with a short iron is not easy.

Congressional 27

Just a short helicopter ride from the White House, Congressional has long been the favourite haunt of senators, congressmen and even First Golfers themselves. Their playground is a 36-hole country club with a composite course that stretches to 7,200 yards when the US Open comes to town.

It sounds monstrous, but the 1997 version was one of the best US Opens in recent years. This is because Congressional is a man-sized course in the best sense of the phrase. Because it is so long, the United States Golf Association strayed slightly from their usual policy of suffocatingly tight fairways, to the extent that all the players could relax a little and, instead of using irons off the tees, employ all the clubs in the bag. The result was a thrilling victory for Ernie Els, despite the close attentions of Colin Montgomerie and Tom Lehman.

One thing the USGA got wrong, however, was to change the composite layout in 1997 so that what had been the par-three 15th became the closing hole. Par threes as finishing holes are always a huge mistake: the requirement of any golfer must always be more than one good stroke to make a regulation figure at the last. Congressional would have been better served with the layout used for the 1964 US Open, when the wonderfully treacherous 17th proved a fitting finishing hole.

Oakland Hills 26

Few courses have metamorphosed as often as Oakland Hills. When it first began hosting major championships in the 1920s, it was thought of as an excellent layout, but one that fell some way short of greatness. Then it was redesigned by that lord of penal golf architecture, Robert Trent Jones, in time for the 1951 US Open. It was there that Ben Hogan came up with the soubriquet "the monster" – little could he have known that he was launching what would become one of the most overused clichés in the book, with seemingly half the courses in America being so described at one point or another.

Oakland Hills – the orginal monster – has, however, gone the other way. It has matured into a venue that remains punishingly stringent, but one that is never less than fair. When Nick Faldo first set eyes on it before the 1996 US Open, he instantly declared it to be one of the finest courses in America. Suffice to say that it now deserves to be called great.

Oakland Hills does have one unique and dubious distinction among such courses, however: it generally produces odd winners. This trend began in 1924 when a little-known golfer called Cyril Walker won the US Open. Then, in 1937, Ralph Guldahl prevailed over Sam Snead. Hogan himself did win in 1951, but since then the US Open has gone to Andy North in 1985 before going in 1996 – most bizarrely of all – to a qualifier, Steve Jones.

Valderrama – played host to the 1997 Ryder Cup

Royal West Norfolk 25

One look at the card at Brancaster would lead a player to conclude that a score must be made on the inward nine; after all, is it not over 300 yards shorter? This is true, but it invariably feels 300 yards longer, owing to the prevailing wind that sweeps across the course from the ancient, rambling clubhouse.

Royal West Norfolk is not a masterpiece of design, but it is a wonderful place to be if the elements are at all favourable. Much of the course is set in a sliver of land, with the Norfolk coast screened behind a dune. The inward holes are perilously close to this backdrop, so much so that coastal erosion has threatened the life of quite a few of them over the last 30 years. It would be a tragedy if any were lost.

Some of the most interesting holes are at the far end of the course. The par-five 8th is on islands in the marsh, while the 9th is a wonderful dog-leg par four, where the tee shot is again played over the marsh and the green is protected by a creek.

The course was designed in 1891 by Horace Hutchinson and Holcombe Ingleby, and although alterations were made by C.K. Hutchinson in 1928, the character of golf remains little changed more than a century on.

Woodhall Spa – a course in harmony with its surroundings

Royal Lytham and St Annes 24

Not the prettiest of links courses, it is true, but a wonderfully formidable test of golf for all that. Lytham shares with Southport and Ainsdale the unusual distinction of opening with a par three, and what a devil of a shot this can be, for the tee is sheltered from the elements and many a player has seen a stroke heading straight for the flag, only to be creased in sorrow as it has come up either a club short, or shot through the back.

Lytham has a proud history of hosting the important championships, its parade of winners standing comparison with any. It was here in 1926 that Bobby Jones won the first of his three Open titles; Gary Player triumphed with a remarkable shot from against the backdrop of the clubhouse wall in 1974, while Tony Jacklin raised a cheer for all Britain in 1969, when he became the first home player to lift the Claret Jug for 18 years. Then there were the two triumphs for Severiano Ballesteros...

Lytham is characterized by the five par fours to finish, a dramatic series of holes that stretch both mind and sinew. Only the 16th offers any sort of respite in terms of length, but neither the drive nor the approach shot are easy. The 18th, meanwhile, is one of the great finishing holes, the requirement from the tee a long straight drive to avoid a seemingly endless cluster of bunkers, and all the while the stately Victorian clubhouse stands imposingly in the distance.

Woodhall Spa 23

Woodhall Spa is one of those courses that gladdens the heart, as one makes the long drive to its remote Lincolnshire location. Since the English Golf Union bought it in 1994 it has become a thriving centre of excellence, with an academy added, and an excellent second course designed by Donald Steel.

It is the course that was completely redesigned in 1920 by the then owner, Colonel S.V. Hotchkin, that will continue to draw most of the plaudits. Built on sandy soil, the holes are beautifully constructed to complement the surrounding terrain, which abounds in heather, silver birch and pine trees.

The three shorts holes are particularly fine examples. Two of them are no more than a seven iron, and the third measures under 200 yards, but all require an exact stroke to secure a regulation figure; all are protected by particularly severe bunkers.

A player has to be quickly into his stride at Woodhall Spa. The first is benevolent enough, but the next three holes all demand precise shots to secure pars. The 9th, meanwhile, can be a brute of a par five if played into the wind; not only does it measure 560 yards, but the fairway is traversed at just over half-way by a series of bunkers, leaving a difficult decision for the player who has struck less than a fulsome drive.

Royal Liverpool 22

No course is more greatly missed from the Open Championship rota than Royal Liverpool, that fabled links that lies at the mouth of the broad Dee Estuary, on the Wirral peninsula. The last of the 10 Opens to be staged there was as long ago as 1967, which resulted in a popular and emotional victory for the Argentinian, Roberto de Vicenzo.

Hoylake, as it is more popularly known, became a victim of the event's popularity. It is landlocked, and accordingly there is no space for the paraphernalia that comes with the modern Open. The pity is that the golf course remains a singular challenge for all who tackle its prime acres.

Some of the vintage years for Hoylake fell at the end of the last century. Firstly, it was responsible for the founding of the Amateur Championship; then it had the particular pleasure of watching two of its members, John Ball and Harold Hilton, completely dominate the event for the next decade and more. Indeed, Ball's total of eight wins in the event has never been surpassed, nor will it be.

The feature holes are undoubtedly the quartet, starting at the 9th, that run along the coast. Here the golf is of traditional links character, the fairways dipping and twisting beneath the sandhills. Hilbre Island and its bird sanctuary are apparent in the distance, as are the Welsh hills. The purist, however, may well prefer the four holes to finish, a powerful foursome that make up in sheer quality what they may lack aesthetically.

Muirfield Village 21

Jack Nicklaus has built over a thousand golf courses since his first design in his native Ohio, but arguably none has improved on the original. This is not necessarily a criticism of his architectural skills, more a lasting tribute to the qualities of Muirfield Village, which is the only course in the top 25 of this list that was built after 1970.

The Golden Bear selected the land for the course and, together with Desmond Muirhead, designed each hole with pristine care. Muirfield Village is a glorious blend of the old and new, of what can be achieved with a nod both to the future but also to tradition.

It is the home every year to the Memorial tournament each May, but it is in the autumn that it is arguably seen at its best. The weather at that time is typically crisp and sunny – instead of cold and wet, as it usually is for the Memorial – and as the leaves turn colour so a pleasant legacy is left to recall before the onset of harsh winter.

In addition to the Memorial, the course has hosted both the Solheim Cup and the Ryder Cup, which were both held in the best month of September. The former in 1998 produced an easy victory for the Americans, but the latter, in 1987, was the scene of a historic first victory for Europe on US soil. Not a great weekend for the designer, though – he was the American captain.

The Country Club 20

The United States is positively cluttered with country clubs; there can hardly be a village, never mind a town or a state, that does not have one. When it comes to The Country Club, however, there is but one. It lies just outside the beautiful city of Boston, in the suburb of Brookline.

Given its use of the definite article, it is perhaps appropriate that this particular Country Club has more tradition and history than practically the rest put together. In 1999 another memorable chapter will be written, too, as the Ryder Cup comes to town.

The club was one of the original five to form the United States Golf Association, and its first US Open in 1913 was to prove a watershed for the game in America. A victory for a young unknown amateur from Brookline called Francis Ouimet, in a play-off against the great British professionals Harry Vardon and Ted Ray, set off an explosion of interest in the game. It was the first time that an American had shown he could compete against the best the home country had to offer, and it helped, too, that Ouimet was not from wealthy stock, as it demonstrated that the game was open not just to those with deep pockets.

The Country Club does not have a reputation as one of the more daunting tests to be found in American golf, but it can prove fearsome; when the US Open returned there in 1963, on the fiftieth anniversary of Ouimet's victory, Julius Boros's winning score was the highest for 18 years.

Any golfer hoping for a good score needs to make inroads over the first eight holes. In truth there is not much to distinguish them from a thousand other holes in America. From the 9th, the test begins in earnest, and the interest heightens. In quick succession are a quartet of par fours where the accumulation of regulation figures truly amounts to something.

On the card the 17th does not reek of menace – it is less than 400 yards – but in reality it has decided no fewer than three US Opens. In 1913 Ouimet birdied the hole in regulation play to force a tie with Vardon and Ray, and then birdied it again the following day in the play-off. Ouimet had stood on the tee with just a one-stroke advantage, but increased it to three shots as Vardon fell prey to the bunker that guards the dog-leg.

Fifty years later, Tony Lema bogeyed it to fall out of a tie for first, Arnold Palmer's bogey cost him outright victory, while Jacky Cupit, needing only a bogey and a par to win, took a double-bogey six. Boros, meanwhile, single-putted the hole to get into a play-off he would eventually win. Twenty-five years later it was Nick Faldo's turn to overshoot the green for a bogey to lose a play-off to Curtis Strange.

With its small, compact greens which can be frighteningly quick, The Country Club is a worthy venue for the Ryder Cup, a test not dissimilar to that which faced the players at Valderrama in 1997. Once more, the 17th will undoubtedly prove a focal point for the drama.

The Country Club – a worthy venue for the 1999 Ryder Cup

Oak Hill – has staged virtually all the great American championships

Oak Hill 19

Each autumn, when the leaves turn their varying colours and there is still a firmness to the turf, Oak Hill is a wonderful place to be. It was thus in 1995 when it played host to the Ryder Cup, when 24 players and two captains queued up regardless of whether they had won or lost, to pay homage to its virtues.

After Pinehurst and Royal Dornoch, this may be Donald Ross's third most famous work. Situated close to Rochester, high in New York State, it is a course with few weaknesses. Oak Hill was named by a club member called Dr John R. Williams, a physician by trade, but a botanist by calling. He developed 28 different types of oak and planted them throughout the property.

Now it is not just for varieties of oak that the course is renowned: today there are more than 30,000 trees that fit into a number of classifications. Accordingly, they give the layout its character, but never do they become overpowering – as they can at, say, Woburn.

But the fairways are narrow, and have got narrower still over the years as the United States Golf Association has followed Ben Hogan's lead of long ago and demanded that the test be stiffened to host the US Open. They certainly accorded with such a brief in the Ryder Cup. In a singles match Severiano Ballesteros, admittedly never the straightest of drivers, managed to play the first nine holes without ever finding a fairway.

The finish is particularly daunting, and many a player has seen a good score tarnished by recording three fives to close. The par-four 16th measures 441 yards and, after an accurate drive, requires a good long iron to escape the attentions of three mean bunkers. Similarly the 17th, which meanders gently to the right, and once more a long iron is necessary to set up a regulation par.

The best hole of all is the 18th, a sharp dog-leg to the right which caused havoc at the Ryder Cup. Only the straightest of drives will offer any chance of finding the plateau green. This is because the rough has been allowed to grow on the bank that guards the putting surface, and no one wants to finish there. The tee shot, however, has to be threaded to the angle of the dog-leg with trees and rough lying in wait on both sides to catch the stroke that strays. From the rough the only option is to play short of the green and hope for a chip and putt.

Even a straight drive will mean a long iron or a wood to a green that falls away at the back in characteristic Ross fashion. A small shelf in the putting surface makes this a treacherous stroke, too.

Oak Hill has deservedly played host to virtually all the great championships that America has to offer. It has been the venue for the US Open on three occasions, and has also hosted one USPGA. Cary Middlecoff won the first of the former in 1956, to be followed in turn by Lee Trevino and Curtis Strange. Jack Nicklaus won the latter.

The quality of champion in turn illustrates the quality of Oak Hill. No doubt the finest of players will continue to turn in low scores in ideal weather conditions in majors to come. But, far from being a sign of weakness, isn't this how it should be?

Winged Foot – one of the finest courses in America

Winged Foot 18

When Albert Tillinghast was commissioned to design a new layout in the Manhattan suburb of Westchester County, he was solemnly instructed: "Give us a man-sized course." The message was delivered by the gentlemen of the New York Athletic Club, from whose emblem the golf club takes its name, and the net result is not only a testament to penal golf architecture, but also to one of the finest courses in America.

To build his creation, Tillinghast had to move 7,200 tons of rock and cut down almost 8,000 trees. In the end he created enough room for two courses, but it is the longer and more treacherous West that is known and respected throughout the game.

The key to Winged Foot is its 12 gruelling par fours, 10 of which measure more than 400 yards. Tillinghast believed that a "controlled shot to a closely guarded green was the surest test of any man's golf". Winged Foot certainly meets such exacting requirements. Finding the fairways is stringent enough, but that is almost the easy bit: what must follow is a precise approach, where failure will invariably mean either a sand shot from a cavernous bunker, or a deft pitch from a thick collar of rough.

Winged Foot has produced a number of excellent golfers, all of whom were not surprisingly adept at the art of the sand shot. At one time in the early 1940s it boasted not just the US Open champion but the US Amateur title holder, too. Claude Harmon, who won the Masters in 1948, became professional six years later, while among his assistants were two major championship winners in Jack Burke and Dave Marr. Claude Harmon's son, Butch, is now coach to Tiger Woods.

The course comprises two nine-hole loops that head off in parallel directions from the clubhouse like two outstretched tentacles. Perhaps the two best holes are on the back nine. The 10th is a wonderful short hole, which stretches out in front of the player. At 190 yards it is not too long, and the green tilts invitingly towards the tee. The temptation to play long, however, has to be counterbalanced against the prospect of a downhill putt that will add new life to the word "slippery". But who would dabble with the two giant bunkers that guard the front of the green, both of which are taller than any man?

The 17th was said by Jack Nicklaus to be a "text book test of golf – a hole that really pits the player against the designer". It measures 444 yards, and a straight drive must reach the angle of the dog-leg to have any prospect of a long iron to a narrow green protected on either side by bunkers.

Did Tillinghast succeed in his "man-sized" brief? Few people have sought to quibble with his own assessment: "As the various holes came to life, they were of a sturdy breed. The contouring of the greens places a premium on the placement of the drives, but never is there the necessity of facing a prodigious carry of the sink-or-swim sort. It is only the knowledge that the next shot must be played with rifle accuracy that brings the realization that the drive must be placed. The holes are like men, all rather similar from foot to neck, but with the greens showing the same varying characters as human faces."

Royal St George's 17

A belief took hold among certain American professionals in the 1980s that Royal St George's was something less than a true venue for the Open Championship, that its sloping fairways containing devilish pin-pricks of land were somehow too capricious to host such a prestigious event. Quite who perpetuated this preposterous scenario is unknown: some have pointed the finger at Jack Nicklaus, but he firmly denies it.

And so he should, for St George's is unequivocally among the noblest of links courses, and a venue for the Open that has stood the test of time. Indeed, the setting has changed little since Dr Laidlaw Purves "spied the land with a golfer's eye" from the tower of a Sandwich church. The sight so stirred his imagination that a syndicate was formed and in 1887 the club was founded.

Sandwich was a stern test from the start. The first Open to be played there was the first outside Scotland, in 1894. It was won by J.H. Taylor with the fairly mind-boggling score of 326 strokes.

It was Pat Ward-Thomas who may have best described the golfing experience at St George's. "What a glorious place Sandwich is for golf," he wrote. "When sunlight is dancing on the waves of Pegwell Bay, the white cliffs of Ramsgate shining in the distance, the larks singing as they always seem to sing at Sandwich, and a sea wind stirring in the sand grasses, the golfer may share Bernard Darwin's view that it is as 'nearly my idea of heaven as is to be attained on any earthly links'." The opening hole is a formidable beast, and almost as difficult as the first at Muirfield or Birkdale. The fairway is narrow, and the second shot has to fly a cross bunker. The short 3rd is relatively new, having been redesigned by Frank Pennink a quarter of a century ago. The requirement is a long iron or more to a narrow shelf of green.

Quite quickly the golfer will be aware of the variety of stances needed to play approach shots. Rarely do the fairways fail to roll or rise at Sandwich; perhaps this is one of the factors that irked the Americans. If so, they know nothing of the true nature of links golf.

The start of the back nine is none too difficult, which is perhaps just as well given what lies ahead. The 13th begins a daunting trio of holes, calling for a long drive towards a green that lies next to the neighbouring Prince's course, remote and desolate in the distance.

The 14th is one of the hardest driving holes in golf, with dunes to be carried and out of bounds all down the right; a stream then cuts the fairway, calling for more debate. The 15th is a seriously long par four, with no fewer than seven bunkers to negotiate from the tee. A good, long drive brings the green into range, but now three more bunkers lie in wait, protecting a putting surface that on grey days can seem a league away. The 17th is another strong four, as is the 18th, where from a downhill fairway a precise stroke is needed to carry a green protected by sand on the right and which falls away nastily to the left.

It makes for a demanding conclusion to a course that requires more than its share of well-struck shots to prosper.

Royal St George's – a venue for the Open Championship that has stood the test of time

Sunningdale – a magnificent inland course

Sunningdale 16

The best inland course in Britain lies on heath ground ideal for golf on a stretch of country west of London. In the vicinity are such noble courses as Swinley Forest, the Berkshire and New Zealand, while the complex that constitutes the modern Wentworth lies but a few short miles away. No pleasures can match those to be found on Sunningdale's Old Course on a sunlit day in late spring, when nature displays her full bounty.

Sadly it is no longer part of the professional rota in Britain, and perhaps its 6,609 yards are not enough to stretch the very best of today's power hitters. But it is the game that is undoubtedly poorer for this development. When courses like Sunningdale can no longer be considered for the modern game, then the time has come to do something to rein in the ever-increasing lengths that people can strike the ball.

The Old Course begins with the gentlest of par fives, a long straight drive in mid-summer opening up the inviting possibility of reaching the green in two blows. Any shot gained at the 1st, however, is immediately under threat at the 2nd, a long four to a green that lies sheltered below a crest.

A feature of Sunningdale is a series of delightful short par fours that begin at the 3rd. The green can be driven, but even a short pitch is not an easy shot, for the sloping green falls subtly away and invariably takes a ball with it. The 9th is another where the green can be reached from the tee, but requires a shot of rare accuracy to do so. Then there is the 11th, the best of the lot, with a blind drive to a falling fairway with a delicate approach required from even a straight drive to finish close to a flag which is usually tucked away somewhere on the raised table of green.

Some of the tees at Sunningdale command glorious views of the course's trademark pines, birch and heather. The 5th is one such hole, containing as it does the course's one water hazard; the short 15th is another, from an elevated tee to kickstart a finish that is rather more difficult than the holes before might have led one to expect.

At the 16th the drive must be long enough to allow a comfortable approach over cross bunkers. At the 17th the fairway falls away to the left, and the second shot will often be played from a hanging lie. And so to the 18th, where a German bomber left its mark on golf-course architecture in the Second World War. The bomb that fell on this hole left an enormous crater to the right of the green, which prompted the idea of filling it in with bunkers. It has improved the hole immeasurably, the second shot one of the most imposing on the course, with a stern oak adding to the scene, standing guard behind the green.

Sunningdale is a course that lends itself to spectacular scoring. Ian Woosnam averaged 65 shots per round when winning the European Open there in 1988. But equally the shots can slip away if they are struck less than true. Few players can break 70 while playing average golf. For all the gentility of many of the holes, there lies plenty of menace, too.

Royal Portrush 15

No course in the British Isles can boast a more inviting path towards it than Royal Portrush. To take the Antrim coast road on a clear, sunny day is to luxuriate in a road trip with few parallels. Shortly after the road passes the ancient ruins of Dunluce Castle the course lies before the eye, while to the east and west lie the dark headlands of Benbane and Inishowen, rising from the sea.

The main course, named Dunluce after the ancestral home of the lords of Antrim, has changed much since the club was formed in 1888, with Harry Colt responsible for many of the improvements. The focal point is driving, for Portrush is particularly penal on anyone who consistently misses its fairways. What makes driving more difficult than on most courses is that few of the holes travel in a straight line. When the rough is allowed to grow for important championships the temptation to cut any of the dog-legs diminishes considerably.

The 1st is one of the few straight holes, while the 2nd winds down a long path through the dunes. The 4th is a wonderful par four, with out of bounds threatening on the right and the green nestling in the sandhills. The 5th is one of the most famous of Portrush's holes, as the fairway tumbles down to a green built just yards from the Antrim beach. The 6th, with its tee adjacent to the 5th green, is a lovely short hole. The middle holes wind their way this and that, a succession of dog-legs, but never monotonous. Only the 9th and 10th holes travel in the same direction, with the same shape.

The 14th may well be the most famous short hole in Ireland, which well deserves its wonderful name: Calamity Corner. Often played into the prevailing wind, from the back tee it calls for a full carry of 200 yards to make the green. In the Senior British Open, which was played for four successive years at Portrush from 1995, many of the competitors were often reduced to using a wood. It is not just the length that is the problem, however: a solid stroke that veers off to the right will also court disaster.

It is an immense pity that Portrush has hosted the Open on but one occasion. That was in 1951, when the flamboyant Englishman Max Faulkner registered his only success. In 1995 there was a delightful twist in the story when his son-in-law, Brian Barnes, prevailed over the old links in the Senior Open.

The reason the Open has not returned has nothing to do with the quality of the course, more simply the circus that the modern Championship has become. Could 40,000 people get easily and safely around the course? Could they find accommodation for the week? Then there were the years of the troubles, when the Americans would undoubtedly have stayed away.

It is unlikely that the Open will return anytime in the near future. But at least other visitors can, and they should leave plenty of time to do so, to sample the rare pleasures of the Antrim coast road, past the Giant's Causeway and Dunluce Castle, to a links course with a character all its own.

Royal Portrush – hosted the Open Championship the only time it was played outside England or Scotland in 1957

Carnoustie 14

For too long Carnoustie was hidden from view, like a masterpiece that had been taken down from the walls and discarded to a vault. No wonder its return to the Open rota in 1999 was greeted by general rejoicing. The grey and austere links situated on the northern shores of the Firth of Tay are a challenge for any man, even on a day of flat calm.

On a day when the wind is breezing in from the sea it can be a bear. "How can anyone be expected to play here on a day like this?" was Colin Montgomerie's general reaction following a storm-tossed day at the Scottish Open. And he is the course record-holder.

Carnoustie's contribution to golf lies not only through the splendour of its 18 holes. Many sons of the town left in the late years of the last century to help spread the gospel of the game in America. It is written that, at various times, every state title was held by one of them.

Since its formation in 1842, Carnoustie has proved a melting pot in which great champions have proved their worth. In 1867 it was Young Tom Morris, just 16, but already playing against and defeating all-comers. In 1953, Ben Hogan crossed the Atlantic for the first time and demonstrated his greatness by collecting the Open. In 1968 Gary Player embellished the belief that he is the finest golfer ever to emerge from outside America, and then, seven years later, Tom Watson collected the first of five Open titles, as if he had demonstrated to himself that if he could win at Carnoustie he could win anywhere.

Carnoustie is steeped in wonderful holes. From the short par-four 3rd, with its little pitch over Jockie's Burn, to the stern challenge presented by the long 6th, a hole to test the straightest of drivers. There are only three short holes, and none surrenders a par cheaply.

The most stringent is undoubtedly the 16th, which forms part of the most awesome finish in possibly all golf. Except in a helping wind, the 15th is a demanding par four, playing all of its 421 yards; then to a par three only in name, where even the best players invariably resort to a wood to reach a narrow shelf of green protected on either side by bunkers.

A fine drive at the 17th will carry the Barry Burn twice, but against a strong wind the tee shot must find what amounts to an island between its curves. Such a resort leaves a perilously difficult second shot. The final hole, protected again by the burn and out of bounds, is no less formidable.

Naturally such a finish has produced its share of heroics to procure victory – no wonder Carnoustie's roll of champions compares with any. In the 1968 Open Player was being chased hard by Jack Nicklaus, but a four-wood second shot over the Spectacle bunkers to two feet to set up an eagle three ended any argument. In 1975 the 18th was playing long, but in the play-off Watson had the clubs for the job, a drive and a wonderful two iron that enabled him to beat Jack Newton.

Now, after 24 long years, Carnoustie is back on the Open rota, a spanking new hotel and clubhouse ready to greet visitors into the new millennium. The links will offer no more luxury than before, however: only the very best will prosper.

Carnoustie – a melting pot in which great champions have proved their worth

Cypress Point – one of Dr Alister Mackenzie's masterpieces

Cypress Point 13

The Monterey Peninsula may well stand as the most fertile site for golf in the world. In addition to Pebble Beach, the links at Spanish Bay, Spyglass Hill and Poppy Hills are all worthy of any golfer's attention. And then there is Cypress Point, which many believe to be a better course than Pebble Beach itself. "Pebble has six great holes – all those that lie on the coastline," Julius Boros once proclaimed. "Cypress has 18 of them, whether they lie on the coast or not." As with Pebble, however – which lies barely a mile away – it is the ocean holes for which it has become famous, and in particular a wonderful trio beginning at the 15th. This is the first of successive par threes, just a nine iron or so, but what a nine iron, across a rocky inlet. Then the 16th, allegedly a short hole, but measuring 231 yards from the back tee. Few holes have been more photographed than this one: whether from above or from behind the tee, the scene is truly spectacular. Once more the carry is over water, but this time the ocean threatens; even those who are just relieved to make it across may be less so if their ball comes to rest in a rather harsh bunker. Naturally there have been few holes-in-one, but among those who did manage the singular feat was Bing Crosby, whose celebrated Pro-Am used to be held here (as well as at Pebble Beach and Spyglass Hill).

The 17th is perhaps even more admired among the professionals. It measures less than 400 yards, but the drive is from an elevated tee high above the steep cliffs behind the 16th green. The approach must then escape the attentions of a strategic pine front right of the green, and bunkers both to the rear and to the right.

Of the holy trinity at the forefront of Dr Alister Mackenzie's work, Cypress Point came first. He was given the job by the club's promoter, Marion Hollins, the 1921 Women's Amateur Champion.

A lovelier site would be hard to imagine. Cypress Point sits at the foothills of the Santa Lucia Mountains, and bordering many of the fairways are the picturesque Monterey cypress from which it takes its name. At dusk a fine mist invariably envelops many of the fairways and deer come out of the woods to roam freely.

On a windy day the noise from the surf can be truly dramatic; on calm days the Pacific merely gleams and dazzles. In either instance, to secure a passport to play is to feel privileged indeed.

For much of its length it winds its way through sandy dunes and sylvan glades, and while the holes at the finish grab all the attention, it would not be the special golf course it is if that were all there was to it. The 2nd, for example, is a magnificent par five.

Alas, Cypress Point has faded from public view since the club chose to back down from being one of the host courses for the Crosby Pro-Am, which is now run by AT&T. To get to play it requires friends in the highest of places.

Turnberry – the venue for one of the greatest Open Championships of all time in 1977

Turnberry 12

No greater pleasure exists in golf than to play the game in beautiful surroundings. The top ten in this list is littered with excellent golf courses, but what invariably makes them so special is the backdrop. And so it is with Turnberry, which sits snug against a wonderful stretch of Ayrshire coastline.

Only Royal County Down of the British links can truly compare with being at Turnberry on a golden summer day; to play the holes that run along the craggy shore as the evening sky dims and blazes is a special privilege.

Turnberry did not stage its first Open until 1977, but it was well worth the wait. Indeed it was probably the Open of the century, as Jack Nicklaus and Tom Watson played out their memorable duel over the final 36 holes.

That was Turnberry at its most generous. When the Open returned nine years later it was at its most malign, the sky an angry black and grey as the best players of the day struggled to keep their scores within respectable bounds.

The start is modest, the first three holes interesting enough, but mere appetizers for the feast to come. The 4th begins the trawl along the shore, a wonderful short hole with a heavily fortified green – rightly, it is named "Woe-be-tide". The 5th is a stringent par four, followed by a par three that never seems to end. The 7th is another long hole, the fairway narrow, the green just about within reach of a strong second blow. The 8th fairway leans from left to right, towards some bunkers that will catch a drive unless enough provision is made. The showboat tee at the 9th is Turnberry's signature, at the far end of the course above some craggy inlet, with the famous lighthouse to the left.

To stand on the 10th tee in the height of summer is to know the full beauty of Turnberry. Past the remains of a castle, the base for some stirring deeds of yore from Robert the Bruce, the hole plunges down beside the rocky shore. Small wonder that it is at this point that many golfers from America's West Coast find their thoughts turning to the equally dramatic settings that embrace the courses on the Monterey Peninsula.

After all this the par-three 11th is something of a disappointment; now the course has swung inland, and along the 12th there are traces of the airfield that Turnberry became on two occasions. The monument placed on the hill high above the green commemorates those who died in the First World War.

Of the closing holes, the 15th is a classic par three, and the 16th a fine par four, where the second shot has to carry a deceptive stream in front of the green. The 17th is a monstrous par five measuring a shade under 600 yards, and then to the finish, with the imposing Turnberry hotel on a hill in the distance.

There was a time not so long ago when Turnberry looked a sorry, neglected mess. No longer. Countless millions have been spent to make the hotel among the finest in Britain and a splendid clubhouse has been built next to the 18th green. Once more, one of Britain's best courses fully lives up to its status.

Pine Valley 11

The terrifying beauty of Pine Valley is perhaps best summed up in the story of a gifted local amateur named Woody Platt, who stood on the 5th tee, which comes back to the clubhouse, having gone birdie-eagle-eagle-birdie. Platt had been in his own fantasy world. He had struck a four-iron approach to the first and holed from 30 feet; a seven-iron second shot into the hole at the 2nd for an eagle; a five iron into the hole at the 3rd for a hole-in-one, before a driver and four wood to 30 feet for a birdie at the 4th. What to do for an encore? Platt decided to pop into the clubhouse for a stiff drink. And stayed there.

It was probably a wise choice. The clubs that a low-handicap amateur like Platt had to use give some idea of the penal nature of Pine Valley. No one could hope to maintain such a lucky streak.

For the course hardly gets any easier thereafter. One professional grumpily dismissed George Crump's most famous work as a "184-acre bunker". Perhaps it is just as well that there is no room for spectators, and no professional tournaments of note have been staged there. There are a number of pros who hardly need an excuse to gripe and moan: imagine what they would be like if confronted by a course that would strain every sinew?

Not that Pine Valley has ever sought professional golf. It is the most private of private clubs, an exclusive oasis in the most unpromising area of New Jersey. Open the gates, however, and a golfing paradise awaits.

To be fair to the professional who felt the place was one long bunker, to stand on the 7th tee is to know exactly what he means. This is a par five measuring 585 yards, and the hole truly does contain more sand than grass. The problem is an area of sand and scrub that begins some 285 yards from the tee and goes on for more than 100 yards. It is so punishing that it has become known as "hell's half-acre". The dilemma for the player, therefore, becomes obvious: a ball has to travel at least 385 yards, and the last 100 on the fly, to have any hope of reaching the green in two. For no one can hope to hit the green from hell's half-acre.

If that was one hole that old Woody Platt was thrilled to skip on his day of days, then another is the 13th, where a par four counts as a triumph. This was a hole that was finished off by Hugh and Allen Wilson after George Crump's untimely death. The great American writer, Herb Warren Wind, once opined: "It takes the true heart of a heavyweight to play the hole successfully." The hole dog-legs to the left, but so difficult is the second shot – even off a good drive – that the best strategic shot is to lay up 40 yards short and hope for a pitch and putt.

One of the great stories about Pine Valley concerns "Laddie" Lucas during the 1936 Walker Cup. The great British amateur struck a wild slice that was heading for the woods.

"Watch it! Watch it!" he yelled at his caddie.

"You don't have to watch 'em here," the caddie wearily replied. "Just listen for 'em."

Pine Valley – the most private of private clubs

Muirfield 10

A survey of the top professionals as to their favourite course on the Open Championship rota would undoubtedly lead to Muirfield finishing in pole position. It is not just the challenge of the links, but its unquestioned fairness that particularly appeals. At Muirfield there are no pimples of land on the fairways to send a straight drive tumbling unfairly towards the rough. Some of the more capricious aspects of links golf are therefore absent. Equally, it is almost impossible to get away with a poor stroke, for the likelihood of it missing any trouble is slim indeed.

The course as it now stands was largely the work of Harry Colt, who conceived the two loops of nine holes, both ending at the clubhouse. In this sense it is far from a traditional links; no hole is more than a few minutes' walk from the clubhouse, which makes it an ideal spectator venue. And it has hosted more than its share of prestigious championships, the Open returning once more in 2002.

Muirfield is also home to the Honourable Company of Edinburgh Golfers, which is generally recognized as the oldest club in the world. Continuous records date back to 1744, when "several Gentlemen of Honour skilful in the ancient and healthful exercise of Golf" petitioned the city of Edinburgh to provide a silver club for annual competition on the links at Leith.

There the club stayed for half a century, competing over just five holes. Encroachment led to them moving to Musselburgh before the same overcrowding problems caused them to move east, down the Firth of Forth, to Muirfield. It was not a popular move at first, not least because the Open moved with them from Musselburgh. Andrew Kirkaldy, one of the most famous professionals of the time, declared it a poor course by comparison, dismissing it as an old water meadow.

Muirfield – a true test of golf which punishes any poor stroke

The first Open to be played there was in 1892 and it has its place in history, not least for the fact it was the first over 72 holes rather than 36. Thereafter the reputation of Muirfield started to grow, the Open returning every few years and invariably producing a quality champion. Harry Vardon won the first of his six Open victories there; another member of the Great Triumvirate, James Braid, was also triumphant at Muirfield. Other winners include Walter Hagen, Henry Cotton, Gary Player, Tom Watson and Jack Nicklaus – while Nick Faldo, the greatest player of his generation, has the honour alongside Braid of being the only man to win the Open over the venerable links on two occasions.

Muirfield has also been witness to a Ryder Cup, Curtis Cup and, on many occasions, the Amateur Championship. The most recent of these was in 1998, the winner being the Spanish prodigy Sergio Garcia. Few would bet against his victory proving to be the launchpad for a highly successful career in the professional ranks.

Much of the greatness of Muirfield lies in its test of driving, and this is apparent from the opening hole, a daunting par four where the tee shot has to find a narrow waist of fairway between two bunkers. Even so, if the wind is against, another wood may be needed to locate the green, or at least a long iron.

At the 2nd, John Daly drove green high in the 1992 Open: the small matter of 351 yards. The third requires another well-placed drive before the first of the short holes, at once disturbing and beautiful. The plateau green is heavily protected on three sides, and the temptation is to take up the fourth option, and go long. But this will leave a long downhill putt.

At the 5th the temptation is to try to cut the corner, but any attempt to cheat the hole will almost certainly see the ball vanish into a nest of bunkers. Similarly, a pulled drive at the 6th will result in at least a bogey. Then, after the second of the par threes, there follow two holes to test the calibre of any player. The 8th is a wonderful long par four while the 9th is simply one of the best par fives in existence.

From the far south-eastern corner of the course, where Acherfield Wood comes to an end, the drive has to locate an ever-narrowing fairway with a large bunker defying those who try to play the hole absolutely straight. To have a simple pitch for the approach, the second shot must be played to a broad expanse of fairway, but this Elysian field ends abruptly against the wall that runs the length of the hole.

Now the clubhouse stands imposingly in view, guarding the 10th tee, and the narrow ribbon of fairway that stretches in the distance. The 10th completes an unremitting trio of holes.

The drive to the 11th is a blind one, but not worryingly so; the 12th, with its long falling fairway and narrow green, a hole full of character; the 13th a difficult three if a crosswind is blowing. The two par fours to follow both demand accurate tee shots before the last of the short holes, and surprisingly the longest at just 188 yards.

Then to the 17th, an obvious birdie hole since it is a par five that can be reached in two blows, but how often it trips up players. It did John Cook in 1992, Paul Azinger in 1987 and, most memorably, Tony Jacklin in 1972, and it cost all three their chance of Open glory. Jacklin's mistake was misjudging the length of the green with his third shot, and he followed that with three putts.

The 18th is one of the great finishing holes. It is a characteristic of many of the best links courses that they have closing holes to test a player to the full; perhaps only St Andrews truly fails in this respect. Muirfield's 18th rivals any, demanding a long, straight drive and a well-struck mid-to-long iron to set up an orthodox par. It was here that Nick Faldo's career really took off, a five-iron approach that never left the flag to lead to victory in the 1987 Open. It was confirmation of all the swing changes that he had worked upon, for Faldo knew that if he could find the 18th green at Muirfield, with all the attendant pressure of the Open, he could cope anywhere.

And so Muirfield had crowned another worthy winner. Kirkaldy's abuse has turned only to praise 100 years later.

Royal Melbourne 9

No architect has left a more bountiful legacy to golf than Dr Alister Mackenzie. Three of his creations adorn the top 13 of this guide, and all are a lasting tribute to the extraordinary breadth of his vision.

Of course, no architect can make a silk purse out of a sow's ear, and Mackenzie could hardly have asked for better sites on which to design his masterpieces than those that now house the courses of Cypress Point, Augusta and Royal Melbourne.

The latter is located in a 25-square-mile area known as the Sand Belt. Here, the rolling terrain containing fine grasses and indigenous trees, reeds, heather and bracken is absolutely ideal for golf. Sandy subsoils have always proved the perfect ingredients to support golf courses, as can be seen in the various courses along the stockbroker belt that straddles the Surrey/Berkshire border, and those on the Lancashire and Ayrshire coastlines.

The club was founded in 1891, making it the oldest in Australia, but it had two other locations before eventually moving to its present site and building its reputation as among the finest of courses. The prime land was acquired in 1924 and club officials, many of whom had links with St Andrews, were in no doubt that they wanted "the best expert advice", irrespective of cost. And so in 1926 Alister Mackenzie set to work with the 1924 Australian Open champion, Alex Russell, to create the West Course.

Although Mackenzie invariably gets the lion's share of the credit, Russell's part in the building of Royal Melbourne should not be understated. Indeed he created the East Course a short while later, a course that supplies six holes to the composite layout that is now used for championships such as the President's Cup, the biennial match between the United States and Australia that took place in December, 1998. The result is a layout of almost 7,000 yards, and a tough par of 71.

Aesthetically, Royal Melbourne leaves something to be desired

Royal Melbourne – the oldest club in Australia

because, over the years, the city's development has seen it surrounded by roads while houses back on to parts of the playing area. However, closer inspection reveals its true quality, notably in the thoughtful arrangements of humps and ridges, adding character, not to mention the odd hazard.

Apart from the overall design, another significant feature of Royal Melbourne is the large greens. These are usually extremely fast and among the truest to be found anywhere. Here the credit goes to the former head greenkeeper, Claude Crockford; indeed, such was his role in the rise to eminence of Royal Melbourne that it could almost be stated that three architects were at work.

As well as making the course justly famous for its greens Crockford, who was taken on to the staff in 1934, redesigned the par-three 7th after the original Mackenzie concoction was deemed unsatisfactory. Here Mackenzie envisaged an elevated green, which the members felt was a blind shot. Crockford's solution has resulted in a gem of planning and construction. Built on a sandy hill by horse and scoop, like the rest of the course, the green slopes from back to front, although there are one or two flat parts for pin positions. Several deep bunkers lie in wait for the stray shot. Sand traps, indeed, are one of the features of the course. In all there are 114 of various shapes, sizes and depths to be avoided or confronted before a good score can be contemplated.

Three holes in particular stand out at Royal Melbourne. The 6th is a wonderful place to watch golf during a championship. The temptation to bite off too much of the dog-leg from the tee has to be avoided at all costs, to leave a second shot to a green set in a natural amphitheatre.

The 8th is one of the great short par fours in golf. It is a stiff test of an architect's skill to ask him to make something out of a hole of only 300 yards, and Mackenzie succeeds wonderfully here. The length of the hole inevitably inspires visions of glory, of driving the green and holing the putt for an eagle. But the consequences of failure are dire indeed, and all but the most confident are likely to feel inhibited.

A dog-leg left, the hole crosses a pleasant valley from one crest to the next, but guarding the angle of the dog-leg, the line the bold player must take, is a cavernous bunker. Land in there and it is a bogey or worse that a player will be considering, not an eagle. Even the player who opts for the safe route has to box clever. Failure to reach the top of the crest will result in a blind second shot to a green that is invariably firm and fast.

The 14th is an altogether different kind of par four, indeed it is a par five for all but the most proficient of players. Measuring 433 yards, it twists and rolls dramatically for much of its length. It rises over a substantial hill before descending through a long valley and ending on roughly the same elevation at which it started.

The drive therefore is blind, and has to carry a complex of Mackenzie bunkers; the second shot sees the player aiming some 45 degrees to the right, with the sweep of the hole guarded by some beautiful tea trees. Even the green, with a number of subtle contours that are usually spotted too late, is of devilish construction.

The hole rather sums up the character of Royal Melbourne: it is a course that takes some time to get to know. Never was this more baldly summed up than in the President's Cup, where an International team, containing six Australasians who knew the course well, demolished the cream of American golf, many of whom were seeing the place for the first time. The American captain, Jack Nicklaus, said afterwards: "Royal Melbourne really showed herself this week. It was very difficult for our players to understand all the little nuances."It was, however, another memorable occasion for a course that has now hosted virtually all the great international tournaments available to it. Over the years Melbourne has witnessed a 65 in competition by Sam Snead and a 105 by Sam Surrudhin from Indonesia. It is that sort of place: one to inspire the mighty, but also one to cause terror among those with pretensions to greatness.

Ballybunion 8

Rather like its Scottish cousin, Royal Dornoch, Ballybunion has achieved a mystique and allure owing to the remoteness of its setting. Only in recent times have visitors come in any great numbers, when tourist operators began to appreciate that while one great course in itself may not attract significant golfers, packaging it alongside its Kerry brethren, Waterville and Killarney, would be a different matter.

The Old Course at Ballybunion is, in the judgement of this visitor at least, by some distance the pick of the bunch. The first surprise on seeing the land tumble out in front of you is to find that it was designed by man, not evolution. Tom Watson considers it a course that all architects should live and play before practising their art; certainly there are few finer examples of a course so perfectly in tune with its surroundings.

And so the word has spread. In 1998 Bill Clinton even stopped off for a visit. Come the early years of the millennium, Ballybunion will probably be behind only St Andrews among the favourite destinations of Americans. Quite how it will cope is a wholly different proposition.

Over the first few holes, a number of these transatlantic passengers no doubt wonder why on earth they bothered. The 1st is made interesting only by the fact that any hooked drive will end up in a portentous graveyard. The 2nd hole is good enough, a long par four where a steep saddle has to be overcome with the second shot. The 3rd, meanwhile, is a victim of its surroundings; it would be a lovely downhill par three, but for the fact that there is an unspeakable caravan site perched behind the green and dominating the eye line.

Then there are the 4th and 5th, both par fives and two more holes that one would not struggle across the road to play, let alone journey to such a remote location to tackle. To think these mundane long holes used to be the 17th and 18th. No wonder it was only when a new clubhouse was built and the configuration of the holes changed, tucking this pair into the obscurity of the front nine that they deserve, that Ballybunion became justly famous.

All starts to be forgiven at the 6th, a dog-leg par four where the ocean finally comes into view. At the 7th it is frighteningly close. Lose your balance on the tee and you could end up on the beach. This is a truly awesome par four, preceding a triangle of holes that loop inland. The pick of them is the 8th, a fabulous little short hole where the architect tries and usually succeeds in intimidating the life out of his poor opponent standing on the tee. The hole only measures 150 yards, but all the golfer can see is three huge bunkers, all of which are screaming: "Double bogey, double bogey!" Even Tom Watson said it was one of the most demanding tee shots he had faced.

At the 10th, a par four of no great length, the urge to look west is irresistible, but the pleasures are only starting to unfold. The 11th is quite simply one of the great par fours, and demands to be included in any card of the world's best 18 holes. This is another dramatic hole that runs along the clifftop, the ocean ever present, ever threatening. Dunes guard the left-hand side. The prospect of a par recedes into the distance with every stroke that is not struck absolutely flush.

The short 12th and the 13th offer a chance for a player to recover his breath before the tribulations to come. First, to complement the back-to-back par fives on the front nine are successive short holes on this half. The difference is that this pair are both wonderful, offering a sublime contrast in terms of what can be achieved in the name of a par three. The first is just 131 yards long and if the wind is blowing, as it nearly always is, it represents complete torment over club selection. The 15th offers a vivid contrast: here the task is to find a club long enough to locate the green – well, certainly if the wind is fresh into your face.

The 16th and 17th holes are dog-legs of quite breathtaking severity. The first swings sharply to the left, where the drive is away from the sea to a small target. Then the penultimate hole, back towards the Atlantic, where a good long drive will leave the green an inviting target, a rare treat over this forbidding stretch.

Now the 18th. Do we have to talk about this hole? One critic, when asked to summarize its virtues, drily concluded that its one quality was as a device to get from the 17th green to the 19th hole. Perhaps it is not quite as bad as that, but in truth it does have little to commend it. The cause of the vexation is a grotesque bunker named Sahara that sits in the middle of the fairway and allows no strategy. One plays before it, and then one guesses what to hit over it.

The hole is a relic of a bygone age, when earthmoving equipment was not available. At a younger links like Birkdale, the dunes are used to create amphitheatres. At Ballybunion they both straddle the links and dominate it; you play around them, over them, on top of them.

It works gloriously, at least for most of the way round. But could not something be done about the 18th, not to mention the 4th and 5th, to develop still further the world's greatest 15-hole golf course? No matter. Ballybunion remains one of those venues where each hole – yes, even the bad ones – can be recalled with little difficulty over the days that follow. As for how well a player scored, the elements will undoubtedly have had their say. On rare calm days, Ballybunion can seem simple enough. It possesses no great length, and a number of excellent birdie opportunities. A zephyr is enough to change matters, however, and on doleful days, when the Atlantic closes in and the surf fills the nostrils, there is not a hole that possesses any mercy.

Ballybunion is one of the most honest of courses: its virtues and its boils are all there in plain view. It is a rare man indeed who does not conclude that the former are so obvious and overwhelming as to render the latter a small blemish on a mightily impressive creation.

Ballybunion – Bill Clinton's visit in 1998 proved how the word on this great course has spread

Pinehurst 7

Thousands upon thousands of golf resorts have sprung up in the United States since Pinehurst first opened for business, but I have yet to come across any that I would choose to visit ahead of it. Situated in the sandhills of North Carolina, about a three-hour drive from Augusta, the place offers a unique blend of New England charm and Southern hospitality. There are also more golf courses contained within the resort's acreage than days in the week, but the one that all pilgrims descend upon to play is known modestly as number two.

Donald Ross was responsible for many of the world's great golf courses, including Oak Hill and Royal Dornoch, but Pinehurst number two is, unquestionably, his masterpiece. In a country with far too many courses that rely simply on water to intimidate the player, Pinehurst has but one such hazard, and that is hardly in play. It has fairways that every golfer ought to be able to locate, but what happens from there on in depends purely on the standard of shot played.

Pinehurst's greens are wonderful. They are chiefly upraised saucers, and the effect is that any iron shot that is not purely struck will be rejected, and run away to leave a difficult chip shot. They can be of Augusta speed as well, and certainly were when number two hosted its first US Open in the summer of 1999.

The North Carolina Sandhills assure a springiness to the turf that is similar to that to be found on heathland courses like Sunningdale and The Berkshire. Accordingly, when James W. Tufts, a pharmacist from Boston, conceived the idea of a golf course in 1896 to complement the resort he had built as a means of escaping the bitter New England winter, he found by a stroke of fortune – the perfect turf on which to build.

By 1900 the somewhat primitive Pinehurst number one had attracted the great Harry Vardon as a tourist. The visit generated an explosion of interest in the sport among the locals, and by

the end of the year Donald Ross had arrived to assume his duties as professional.

Ross had such a feel for the game that before the year was out he had laid nine holes of what would become known as number two. When the project was finished in 1907 it was immediately considered a triumph; so much so that Ross's fame spread far and wide, and he became the doyen of American golf-course architecture.

Its virtues stand to this day. In the years that have passed since Tufts first developed his resort, the trees have grown back to full maturity. The result is that each hole now stands virtually in its own glorious setting, is different from the one that came before it, and offers a peace and tranquillity that allows the player to be completely isolated from the rest of the world. There are plenty of bunkers, but not an abundance of them; the emphasis is more on strategy, challenging a golfer's mental prowess rather than his physical strength. Having said that, Pinehurst now measures over 7,000 yards from the back tees, thus calling for mastery of every club in the bag.

The 1st is an uncomplicated par four which looks further from the tee than it actually plays. The 2nd is a rather more difficult proposition and requires a strong shot with a long iron to locate the green. The 3rd, a shortish par four, is all about finesse, while at the 4th the accent is on power with the green at this par five reachable with two extremely long shots. The 5th is a majestic par four, a gentle dog-leg where the fairway falls away towards a heavily protected green. And so to the 6th, the first of a quartet of unusually long and demanding short holes.

The next three holes ought to pass without a proficient golfer experiencing any undue difficulty, and then to the 10th, the one par five on the course beyond the reach in two of all mortal golfers. It is followed by four par-fours, all of which present a considerable challenge in terms of both length and stringency.

The finish unusually contains two short holes, neither of which offers any respite. Positioned after each are the 16th, a long par five measuring 531 yards, and the 18th, a wonderful finishing hole requiring two exacting shots to set up a regulation figure.

It is both because of its remoteness and its relatively close proximity to Augusta – the site every year of the Masters – that Pinehurst has staged so few prestigious championships. The 1999 US Open is only its second major, the first being the 1936 USPGA, won by Denny Shute. The Ryder Cup brought international competition to Pinehurst in 1951, and in 1962 the US Amateur was held there for the first time.

The lack of tournaments has not stopped the top players showering number two with praise. Sam Snead declared: "You have got to hit every shot on old number two." While Tom Weiskopf, now a noted architect in his own right, declared it better than Augusta National. "Augusta is only a great golf course for one week of the year when they host the Masters, but Pinehurst number two is a great course for 52 weeks," he declared. "I have played Augusta three weeks before the Masters, and it is a piece of cake, a piece of cake. But number two is never a piece of cake." The advances made in the field of travel – both on land and in the air – have made the place an accessible site for tournaments in the 1990s. Pinehurst played host to the Tour Championship on two occasions, in 1991 and 1992, the respective winners being Craig Stadler and Paul Azinger, and also the 1994 US Senior Open, which was won by the South African Simon Hobday.

What now for Pinehurst? In 1996 the resort celebrated its centenary by building an eighth course. Improvements are going on all the time. In the autumn of 1999 number four is due to re-open having been completely refurbished from first tee to last. In short, the resort has become a mecca for golfers everywhere.

And the one above all they want to play is number two, offering lasting pleasure to those who appreciate that golf is a game played with the head as well as the hands.

Pinehurst – a mecca for golfer's everywhere

St Andrews 6

Quite what a golfer who strolled across the broad acres of St Andrews more than 150 years ago would make of the present customers who take on the links is hard to imagine. Clubs of metal and titanium, you say? Over 100 varieties of golf ball that can land hard or soft on the greens; can roll for ever or just a little on the fairways; can be white or pink, yellow or orange? We are talking about the same game, I take it?

Then he would walk the links and realize that while the language and equipment may have changed beyond all recognition, the course has remained essentially untouched.

This, then, is the appeal of St Andrews, and why it attracts more pilgrims from all over the globe than any other course: everything may have changed, but everything has stayed the same. The home of golf has lost none of its charm.

Yet there are legitimate concerns about what will happen in the next century, and how St Andrews will cope with the legions who lay siege to its portals every year. Quite simply, the demand for tee-times has exceeded those that are available, and so far the worrying response from those in charge of the links appears to be to price sufficient numbers out of the market to bring equilibrium.

The great joy of St Andrews always used to be that golf came at a price for all. I remember travelling with my father to play in the early 1970s; we took in St Andrews, Carnoustie and Gleneagles. Could we make the same trip now, on the equivalent salary to what my father earned and myself once more an eager boy on the verge of his teenage years? Sadly, no.

And so as the British have moved out of St Andrews, the Americans have moved in. In the summer, more than 70 percent of the green fees on offer are now taken up by golfers from the United States, for whom $150 a round is a bargain. It would be a tragedy for the sport if this trend were to continue, and the home of golf to be transported back a century, when the game in many parts of the world was a sport exclusively for the wealthy.

But so far the madness shows little signs of abating: the Open

St Andrews – attracts more pilgrims than any other course

returns to St Andrews in 2000, and a 12-room bed and breakfast around the corner from the links has already let out its rooms for the all-in price of £20,000. You could probably have bought the place for that a decade ago.

St Andrews, of course, is home not just to the oldest of Old Courses, but the Royal and Ancient Golf Club, whose forbidding clubhouse sits majestically behind the first tee.

More than one visitor has looked at the scene that surrounds him, at the sight of some of Scotland's finest architecture and the wonderful sweep of St Andrews Bay to the right, and done himself less than justice with his opening tee shot.

Without the setting, it would be the easiest shot in all golf; without the setting it would be the dullest, too. But it sets the scene for what follows, a course that came before all others, but one which was hardly a trendsetter. Nowhere else will you find so many holes fitted into such a small sliver of land, where 14 of them share seven greens.

More than any other great links course, St Andrews depends on the weather for protection. On placid days when the wind is absent, and particularly during the Alfred Dunhill Cup in October when the greens are full of autumn moisture, it can present little challenge to the great players of the day. In 1997 Joakim Haeggman played the front nine in level threes, while 10 years earlier Curtis Strange shot 62.

When the wind blows at a more characteristic speed, however, any player would be thrilled to break 70, while on the last day at the 1995 Open the par of 72 was such a good score that only eight of the top 20 managed to sneak below it.

The one area where St Andrews did set a trend was in the layout. The first seven holes all head out in the same direction, loosely along the curve of the bay; the next three then form a loop at the far end of the course, before the last seven complete the journey home. It became the standard pattern for links courses built before the turn of the last century.

As Haeggman proved in 1997, and as Tony Jacklin showed in the 1970 Open when he reached the turn in 29, it is the outward half where a player hopes to make his score before protecting it when homeward bound. On days when the wind is favouring the outward player, only the fourth is not a birdie chance. For the big hitter, the rest offer the minimum of resistance, with a plethora of wedge approach shots; in addition, the par-five 5th is reachable in two blows and the par-four 9th in one.

At which point, more than one golfer has found himself wondering what all the fuss is about. Surely there must be more to the Old Course than this? Not at the 10th, an orthodox par four. But the 11th is a wonderful par three, the green sloping sharply from back to front and protected by the evil Hill bunker. Woe betide the player who comes up short and finishes in this sandy grave.

The 12th is a lovely short par four with all manner of hazards contained within its 316 yards. The temptation to go for the green is impossible to resist for the long hitter on a good day, but a bogey rather than a birdie is more likely if the drive strays at all from the straight and narrow.

The 15th begins a formidable trinity of holes to test any golfer. Each is harder than the last, coming to a crescendo with the second shot to the 17th, perhaps the hardest single shot in golf. And so to the 18th, a gentle stroll after the terrors of what have preceded it. A par here is within the scope of just about every golfer, and the prospect of a satisfying finish, therefore, a real one.

The joy of St Andrews is obvious if one camps out during the evening in any of its splendid bars. Golfers will regale one another with their tales of derring-do. The scene is agreeably convivial. My sole complaint is that increasingly these days the occupants speak with one accent. I have nothing against Americans *per se*, but it is sad indeed to descend on St Andrews and hear tourists discussing not which country they come from, but which state.

Royal County Down 5

The Amateur Championship returned to Royal County Down for just the second time in 1999, thereby allowing a new generation of players the chance to savour the lasting glories of a links course that is among the most rewarding to play anywhere.

Put simply, the views are unrivalled in the British Isles: on gentle days in early summer, when the gorse is in full bloom, the sea sparkling like diamonds and above all the spectacular glory of the Mourne Mountains which really do sweep down to the sea, there is no better place to be.

Royal County Down lies on a curve of Dundrum Bay, and is an old-fashioned links in the sense that there is a proliferation of "blind" shots. Indeed there may be one or two too many for the taste of some golfers. Not, however, for this golfer. One would have to be blind oneself to the many compensations to worry unduly on that score.

The course came into being in 1889, following a meeting of the founder members who instructed Tom Morris to lay out 18 holes for a sum not exceeding £4. How far he managed to get with such a sum is not known, but within a decade Royal County Down was being written of as the finest links in all Ireland. In the intervening century it has been reconstructed, but the essence of the golf on offer has remained the same; and, in all that time, only Portmarnock to the south, Ballybunion to the west and Portrush to the north have come to be spoken of in the same breath. To my mind, it remains better than all of them.

Like many links courses the strictness of the examination depends largely upon the weather conditions at the time. Royal County Down depends on them less than most, however; even in a flat calm, it is no pushover. On less kind days it can be unplayable. One international meeting has entered golf folklore, a day when the cloud cover was so low that the Mourne Mountains were practically invisible, and eight of the par fours lay out of range with two wooden shots. One golfer, forgetting the sea was just over yonder, cried out: "How high are we here?" The opening holes run along the edge of the shore, which is screened from view by a bank of dunes. The first is an inviting drive for the straight hitter into a narrow valley, and at once the characteristic challenge of Royal County Down has presented itself. Miss the fairway either to the left or right and the green becomes a forbidding target in three, never mind two shots. The straight driver, however, can reach the putting surface if the wind is behind, or at least leave himself with an orthodox pitch.

The second is another hole where par is a reasonable target, which is more than can be said for the third, a glorious par four where the idea of reaching the green in two appears insurmountable from a tee perched high in the dune adjacent to the sea. Similarly, the par-three 4th, played into a stiff breeze on my last visit. From the back tee it measures 212 yards with little respite outside the sanctuary of the green. If the carpet of gorse does not gather the poorly struck tee shot, then one of no fewer than ten bunkers most assuredly will.

The 5th is a fine dog-leg par four, followed by two holes that offer some light relief: the 6th is a short par four, the second shot a short wedge from a basin fairway to a raised green; the 7th a par three that can be reached with a shortish iron, although the penalty for missing left or right is severe enough. Then the challenge rises once more; to the par-four 8th, where the second shot required is among the most taxing on the course; and then the 9th, one of the most photographed holes on earth. Even on doleful days, when the mountains are covered in mist and one can smell the rain approaching, it is a haunting sight.

Tom Watson called Royal County Down's outward half "as fine a nine holes of golf as I have ever played". Praise indeed, of course, but one that implies the second nine is something of a letdown. And perhaps it is, for no course could hope to maintain

Royal County Down – no better place to be

such quality. But for all that the inward half has more than its share of delights. The 10th is a short hole from a characteristically raised tee to a generous green. The 11th is one of five blind tee shots to an open fairway, the 12th a weakish long hole where no player of reasonable ability would hope to stray over five shots to complete.

The 13th is a wonderful hole, situated in a sweeping valley all its own. A good drive leaves a mid-iron over the corner of a mound to a green nestling in a natural amphitheatre. The 14th is a long par three to a well-bunkered green, but the target is large enough, as it generally is at Royal County Down. The challenge may be severe and test a player beyond his abilities, but only if the wind is a beast does it ever become unfair.

The 15th is another splendid two-shotter, the 16th a short par four that should be fun for every golfer. For the big hitter the green which sits on a shelf 276 yards away is inviting indeed. For players with more modest means at their disposal, the fairway is situated in a valley and the second shot is all about judgement of distance. The 17th is a more testing par four where an incongruous pond guards the middle of the fairway, before we finish as we began, with a long par five where accuracy from the tee is paramount.

The first Amateur Championship to have been played over the course was in 1970, and was won by the current Royal and Ancient secretary, Michael Bonallack. It was his third successive win, and fifth in all, a tally surpassed only by John Ball around the turn of the last century. Remarkably his opponent in the final was Bill Hyndman, as it had been the previous year at Royal Liverpool. In 1927 the petite Simone Thion de la Chaûme (later Madame René Lacoste) became the first Frenchwoman to win the British Championship.

The blind shots have been one reason for the absence of more prestigious championships from Royal County Down; while the troubles in Northern Ireland have been a far more threatening impediment in more recent times. Hopefully that will now all change with the concerted drive towards peace, and in the next century Royal County Down will be bathed in the glorious light it deserves.

Augusta 4

It has been open for business for just 65 years, but during that time Augusta has transcended golf to become a fabled, enchanting place for anyone interested in sport. Naturally, make anywhere difficult to get into and you create a situation where thousands will be hammering at the doors; nothing is more powerful than human curiosity, after all. But it is the glimpse of heaven that people witness every second weekend in April that adds to the intoxicating allure: the verdant green pastures, the gleaming sand, the brilliant whites and reds of the dogwoods, magnolias and azaleas.

Augusta, of course, will forever be associated with the genius of Bobby Jones and Alister Mackenzie. The former was the great golfer of the age, who had enough wisdom and modesty to employ the best architect of the day to oversee the building of his golf course on land of rolling hills positively teeming with fruit-bearing trees and flowers. Jones's reputation was such that he could have built the course himself and people would have flocked to applaud. Instead he chose to work hand in hand with a man who had already shown that he knew how to work in harmony with nature at the spectacular Cypress Point in California.

Together they proved an unbeatable combination. One knew all about shot values, while the other knew that a good hole that emphasized such things was worthless if it destroyed the surroundings. Both men wanted a course that would appeal to every man, or at least every golfer; one that would prove a challenge to the most able, but which was still playable by the humblest 18 handicapper.

Would that the architects who have followed in their wake had stuck to such a brief, instead of building their monstrosities with water everywhere and 180-yard carries simply to make the fairway.

At Augusta water is used sparingly, to protect the two par fives on the back nine that would all too easily be reached in two shots otherwise, plus the left side of the 11th green.

All these hazards will be familiar to the millions worldwide who tune in every year to the Masters. The front nine remains an enigma, for the authorities at Augusta have never allowed this half to be televised. "We like to retain a little air of mystery," explained Jack Stephens, who retired in 1998 as chairman.

The first is a fairly straightforward par four; there is a bunker to carry at 260 yards, but unless the wind is fresh into the players' faces, this presents no problems to today's power hitters. A straight drive leaves a wedge to a green that has seen more than its share of three-putts: everyone playing the course for the first time just cannot believe its speed.

Finding the fairways at Augusta is no problem at all; finding the right spots on the fairways to enable a player to attack the pins is a different matter. After the birdieable par-five 2nd comes the short par-four 3rd which emphasizes the point. Here, Tiger

Woods can almost drive the green, but whether he goes for it or not depends entirely on the pin position. If it is on a little shelf in the back right corner, there is no point: he needs to stop the ball quickly and he has more chance of doing that from 80 yards than 20. Augusta is full of such mental exercises.

The 4th is one of the hardest holes on the course, a brute of a par three to a severely sloping green where the margin of error is tiny. Similarly the 5th, a winding par four to a green that will reject any shot that does not land on the narrow shelf in the middle. The 6th is a gorgeous downhill par three to another treacherous putting surface. Such is the slope, it is often better to be 25 feet away putting uphill than four feet away downhill.

The 7th is another lovely short par four, the green heavily protected by a series of intimidating bunkers. The 8th is not the longest par five on the card, but plays that way owing to the fact it rises steeply uphill. Then the 9th plunges down into a valley, before rising again to an elevated green where the penalty for being short is severe indeed: in the final round in 1996 Greg Norman had a 70-yard pitch for his second shot, came up a yard

Augusta – a course with a magic all of its own

short – and found the ball almost back at his feet.

The first-time visitor to Augusta is always astonished by how much the land rises and falls. The 10th is a case in point, the drive finishing some 100ft below the point from where it was struck. Then we reach Amen Corner, the trinity of holes that do not need an introduction, so familiar have they become. On a good day any player would hope to play them in 11 shots, which is one under par. But the potential for calamity is so obvious that the nickname is well deserved; on balance any player is simply thankful to pass through without any damage to his scorecard.

The 14th is an orthodox hole rendered awkward by the shelf that runs through the green. Often the pin is perched nearby, to the effect that a shot that pitches three feet right of the flag can finish 70 feet away, as it is ushered from the target by the green's contours.

The 15th is one of two par fives – the other was the second, where the tee was moved back 30 yards – that were altered in 1999, to take into account the greater distances that players now strike the ball: the mounds on the right of the fairway have been lowered, to stop players landing on downslopes and finding their drives racing down the steep slope towards the green. The par-three 16th is another hole made difficult by the contours of the putting surface; the 17th, by contrast, may be the weakest hole on the course.

Then we come to the 18th, a glorious par four where the drive has to find a steeply rising fairway that is protected to the left by two bunkers and to the right by trees. Tucked some 70 yards behind the green lies the splendid clubhouse, and in front of it the lawn where members sip iced tea and sample food at prices that have hardly changed for 15 years.

During Masters week no advertising graffiti is allowed inside the Augusta gates: no billboards behind any tee, no deliberately placed signage to catch television's all-seeing eye. Even the sandwiches are served in green wrapping.

Augusta, therefore, remains unsullied, even when 25,000 patrons are allowed through the doors. Jones and Mackenzie would surely feel blessed at what has happened to the course that so proudly carries their legacy.

Shinnecock Hills 3

The two great links courses to be found on America's seaboards could hardly be more contrasting, and not just for the fact that Pebble Beach looks west and Shinnecock Hills east. The former is a public course and is open to all upon production of a handicap certificate and the appropriate green fee; the latter, meanwhile, probably needs an introductory letter from the First Golfer himself, Bill Clinton.

It was this obsession with privacy that meant 100 years passed without Shinnecock Hills hosting a US Open. When it returned to the rota in 1986, it was as if the gates to Eden had been opened. "How I wish all our courses were like this," Lee Trevino said.

Shinnecock, indeed, is the nearest America gets to the rumpled look of many of the best links courses to be found in Britain. It has the tradition as well; it has a claim to being the first "formalized" golf club in the United States and the first 18-hole course.

Situated towards the extreme tip of Long Island, NY, in the stylish summer resort of Southampton, the course's formation mirrors the almost casual way that golf came to lay down roots in America. Impressed by an exhibition of the game they had witnessed while on holiday in Biarritz, William K. Vanderbilt and his friends considered how "spiffing" it would be to have a golf course of their own in the Hamptons.

They set about their task wholeheartedly. Willie Dunn, the Scottish professional who had so impressed them in the south of France, was brought to New York and taken on a tour of the area in search of an appropriate location to build a course. Dunn settled upon an area of low-lying sandhills a couple of miles from the sea and a few minutes' drive from where Vanderbilt and Co. had their summer colony.

He set to work with the help of 150 Indians from the nearby Shinnecock Reservation. "Except for several horse-drawn road scrapers, all the work was done by hand," he wrote. "The fairways were cleaned off and the natural grass left in. The place was

dotted with Indian burial mounds, and we left some of these intact as bunkers in front of the greens. We scraped out some of the mounds and made sandtraps. It was here that the Indians buried their empty whisky bottles but we did not find this out until playing the course. One never knew when an explosion shot in a trap would bring out a couple of firewater flasks, or perhaps a bone or two." Within a year of its opening, Shinnecock had been enlarged from 12 to 18 holes and Stanford White, the most stylish architect of the age, commissioned to build a clubhouse. Golf had become the game for the fashionable and the wealthy, just as Vanderbilt had envisaged.

In 1894 Shinnecock became one of the five founding clubs that gave birth to the United States Golf Association. Two years later, it played host to the US Open.

The event was won by James Foulis, but as far as the members were concerned it was not a great success. The scoring was sufficiently low for them to believe that the course did not present much of a challenge, and so a series of alterations was undertaken, and it was not until after the innovative work of Dick Wilson in 1931 that the current beauty finally emerged.

At 6,950 yards and fortified by capricious winds it is a complete challenge, with few golfers managing its 18 holes without having used every club, and the long irons in particular being given a rigorous examination.

"Each hole is different and requires a great amount of skill to play properly," Ben Hogan remarked in 1962. "You know exactly where to shoot and the distance is easy to read. All in all, I think Shinnecock is one of the finest courses I have played." Above all, it is a shotmakers' course, as exemplified by the US Open victories for Raymond Floyd in 1986 and Corey Pavin in the centenary tournament nine years later. Neither player could be said to have the prettiest of swings; indeed, let us be honest here and say it would be hard to find two uglier.

But both players are mirror images when it comes to determination and their ability to shape the ball this way and that, qualities that were shown to ample effect by Pavin on the 72nd hole in 1995. This hole measures 425 yards, and the little American still had a four wood to go after his drive if he was to reach the green. That was not the only problem; there were mounds in front of him, mounds everywhere. Yet Pavin shaped his shot around them – so expertly, in fact, that the ball finished just five feet from the flag. That he was the only player to match par in that Championship speaks volumes.

Hitting the fairways is paramount and, rather like Augusta, the ability to carry crests invariably sets up an easier approach. A poor day with the driver will inevitably lead to an ugly scorecard.

Not that good driving alone will produce the opposite; the four short holes, for example, are nicely varied and extremely challenging. Perhaps the pick of them is the pivotal 17th, where Greg Norman saw another major championship pursuit come up heartbreakingly short in 1995 and Pavin holed what he would later describe as the best putt he ever made under pressure.

In Scotland the traditional links courses generally run away from the clubhouse for the front nine and back for the inward half, with perhaps a loop of holes through the turn.

Shinnecock Hills is completely different. Its immense variety of holes tumble this way and that, turning through every point on the compass. The winds from the Atlantic always blow, and so anyone who hopes to be successful has to cope not only with holes into the breeze or helping, but across from both directions as well. In short it is the course that has everything.

At the turn of the last century, it may not have been considered either tough enough or good enough to challenge the best; no one of sane mind would proffer the same judgement at the turn of this one.

Shinnecock Hills – the nearest America gets to a British links course

Royal Birkdale 2

For a tall, dark Australian named Ian Baker-Finch, the 1991 Open at Birkdale was the happiest of occasions. That his downfall over the coming years should be so complete as to render him incapable of playing in the same event over the same course just seven seasons later is as cruel a fate as the game can summon.

For many of those intervening years, the decline of Baker-Finch was mirrored by the decline of Birkdale itself. Its greens in 1991 had been exposed as riddled by disease. "If they want consistent greens they should dig them up and start again," was Payne Stewart's uncompromising verdict.

Which is exactly what the good members at Birkdale decided to do. But they did not just replace like with like: subtle borrows were added where before there were none; at the 17th a second tier was built.

The difference was dramatic, the response from the professionals who returned for the 1998 Open equally contrasting. It was not just the winner Mark O'Meara who left the arena believing that he had just completed the best course on the Championship rota. Even players like Phil Mickelson and the defending champion Justin Leonard, who had been blown away in the gales that afflicted the third round, could not find it in their hearts to say anything bad about the place. Three months later, *Golf World* pronounced it the best course in Britain, the first time it had enjoyed such lofty status in the magazine's comprehensive biennial survey. For those of us who had always thought of it in such terms, this restoration of Birkdale's reputation was gratifying indeed.

Situated on the coast road out of Liverpool about a mile or so from the tourist town of Southport, the journey to the course hardly gladdens the heart, such as the trip to St Andrews along the Anstruther road. But once row upon row of houses has finally given way to crumpled land that falls away from the road towards

Royal Birkdale – the area was made for golf

the sea, it is clear that a stretch of acreage has fallen into view upon which a golf course was just aching to be made. The fairways sit between dunes as if nature had always intended this to be the order of things; the greens are often tucked in sheltered coves no designer could have improved upon even if he had bulldozed them into view.

Alongside Muirfield, Birkdale is the fairest of all Open courses. A drive that finds the middle of its narrow fairways will invariably be rewarded with a flat stance and a perfect lie. Furthermore, the drive at the 9th is the only "blind" tee shot on the course. Elsewhere the targets lie in plain view of the player as, alas, do the dangers.

They begin at the 1st, which may be the hardest opening hole in British golf. A par four measuring 450 yards, it is essentially a double dog-leg, with the top players generally taking an iron to avoid the trouble presented by a bunker and a dune on the left, leaving them another long iron to locate the green.

The 2nd offers no respite, another long par four into the prevailing wind to a tight, well-protected green. Here a player must trust the yardage book or his caddy, for two bunkers short of the green have the effect of foreshortening the hole, offering encouragement to take less club than is really needed.

The 5th is a lovely short par four; the green has been reached from the tee, but really the risk in tournament play is too great, since the carry is over 260 yards of marshland to another heavily fortified green.

Another daunting par four is followed by a par three that was significantly improved by the construction of a new tee for the 1998 Open. It had the effect of changing the angle of attack, and strengthened the hole's line of defence.

The best short hole, however, is the 12th, and a firm contender for the title of best short hole in Britain. Constructed for the 1965 Open, it sits almost on its own in duneland at the far end of the course. When Tom Watson first set eyes on it, he could not believe it only measured 181 yards, such is the deceiving effect of a tee shot from a cloistered setting to a small green sheltered on three sides by the dunes; he thought it a par four. Watson grew to like it so much that a picture of the hole now has pride of place in his study at home.

Birkdale is a fairly new course in the sense that it was only in 1931 that Fred Hawtree and J.H. Taylor instigated the redesign that would render it suitable for major championships. Since then, there has been constant evolution. Not just the 7th and 12th, but the 13th and the 18th have been converted from par fives into par fours. The 15th, where Arnold Palmer played his shot of shots to secure the 1965 Open, is now the 16th.

Through the changes Birkdale has grown in eminence; not even St Andrews has played host to so many important tournaments over the last 30 years, and naturally they have produced an abundance of drama.

None was more memorable than the 1969 Ryder Cup, when Jack Nicklaus conceded a putt to Tony Jacklin to produce a tied match. The 18th was also witness to one of the great shots, too, when Watson rifled a three iron at the pin on the closing day in 1983 to set up his fifth Open victory in eight years.

In 1998 a little-known American called Brian Watts conjured up a shot from a terrible lie in a greenside bunker at the 18th to within inches of the hole to set up a play-off against Mark O'Meara. Had he won it there is no question that his bunker shot would have been recalled until the end of time. Sadly for Watts, every great shot needs a context, and with O'Meara's subsequent victory that context was heavily diminished.

But it was a great Open for all that, and undoubtedly the highlight of the golfing year. And in the rather odd-looking clubhouse that sits behind the 18th green, the members of Royal Birkdale were more than justified in allowing themselves a pat on the back. A brave decision had produced a windfall, and bathed the club in the greatness it truly deserves.

Pebble Beach 1

There is no finer place in the world to play golf than on the links at Pebble Beach, a wondrous stretch of real estate situated along the steep and rocky shore of Carmel Bay, some 120 miles south of San Francisco. Give most golfers a choice of one place they would dearly like to visit once, and the majority would plump for St Andrews, and so they should, for no place gives so much of itself to the grand old game; but equally, not one of its seven courses possesses a stretch of holes that remotely compares to those that run alongside the ocean at Pebble Beach, where a player comes close to an ethereal experience.

In 1999 they have even improved on perfection, too. The weakest hole on the course used to be the short 5th, a nothing hole that took the player back inland and whose only purpose appeared to be to place the holes that followed in a still more dazzling light. Now Jack Nicklaus has seen a lifetime's ambition realized. Pebble Beach always was his favourite course, and he always wanted to do something about the 5th; now he has, owing to the purchase of a copse that used to run along the ocean. The 5th has taken its place, adding still further to the glittering collection of shore holes so beautifully designed by Jack Neville in the years immediately following the First World War.

The United States Golf Association's reluctance to take its showpiece event, the US Open, to the West Coast meant that it was 1972 before Pebble Beach played host to the event. It has been held there on two subsequent occasions, and will be again in 2000.

It has become famous throughout the country, however, because it is beamed into American homes every January as one of the courses that played host to the AT&T Pro-Am.

How those television pictures must stir up dreams in the minds of golfers all over America! At $250 a round, the dream hardly comes cheap, but then the person who said that all the best things in life were free was wrong.

Pebble Beach begins some way away from the ocean with a couple of inland holes that give little hint of the pleasures to come. Only at the 3rd does the sea heave into view, courtesy of a fine par four that meanders down towards the shore.

The par-five 6th is reachable in two for the longer hitters, and from its upper shelf the dramatic scenery for which the course has become famous reveals itself. The 7th is just about as delightful a short hole as can be found in golf. It is downhill and measures less than 120 yards, but nobody ridicules it because of that. For behind and to the right of the player is the ocean, the surf often crashing against the rocks to provide the most theatrical of backdrops. Six bunkers provide further protection, and if the prevailing wind is blowing then club selection becomes a nightmare. On a good day it can be a soft wedge; in the final round of the 1992 US Open, Tom Kite hit a six iron.

As tough a test as the 7th can be, it is as nothing compared to the vicious triumvirate of par fours that follows. For the amateur golfer enjoying the Pebble Beach experience for the first time, the views are ample compensation for the damage being inflicted on your scorecard; for the professionals, however, these holes represent the ultimate golfing combination of beauty and danger.

The 8th measures 431 yards and commences with a blind drive from the side of a cliff that falls away severely to the sea below. The perfect drive still leaves a daunting 170-yard second shot, which is all carry across the elbow of the bay to a green protected on three sides by bunkers.

The 9th is simply a beast, and surely one of the toughest par fours in golf. In the 1992 US Open it is estimated that nearly half of the pars made here came courtesy of a single putt. It measures 462 yards, but since the fairway runs towards the sea, plays even longer unless a player is prepared to take on the boldest of drives. The 10th, though a little shorter, presents the same intimidating problems.

Pebble Beach then turns inland for a stretch of holes that

Pebble Beach – no finer place in the world to be. The ultimate golfing experience

appear tame to what has gone before; there again, who could hope to keep up such quality? It returns to the sea, however, for the 17th and the 18th, two of the most famous holes in golf.

The former is a daunting par three, straight towards the ocean and usually into the wind. Measuring 209 yards, it was the scene for a dramatic finale to the 1982 US Open when Tom Watson hooked his approach into thick rough. Needing to finish par, par to tie Nicklaus, his chance appeared to have gone. The chip he was left with emphasized that the tee shot is not the only forbidding one the hole can offer: the green ran away from him, and to have missed the pin would have presented him, at best, with a 20-foot uphill putt for par. Watson, though, did not miss the pin, the ball disappearing below ground for the most tumultuous of birdies.

Just for good measure, Watson birdied the wonderful 18th as well, a par five that hugs the shoreline for all of its 548 yards. As Jimmy Demaret once said: "Hook your ball here and you take a drop in Hawaii." One of golf's oldest and truest sayings is that you can tell the quality of a golf course by the champions it produces. After Watson's US Open victory in 1982 there was one for Tom Kite 10 years later; but the player who has enjoyed the most success at the greatest course is appropriately the greatest golfer, Nicklaus. In addition to his near miss in the 1982 US Open, he won that event in 1972 and also won the AT&T on three occasions.

Not that he ever completely mastered it. In 1976, when sharing the lead with nine holes to play, Nicklaus had two triple bogeys in a horrific back nine of 45 for an 82. It was a reminder that while the mighty may have the best chance of conquering Pebble Beach, even the mightiest of all can come unstuck when confronted by its stringent beauty.

Chapter 7

RECORDS

GOLF LENDS ITSELF TO THE STATISTICALLY INCLINED. COLIN MONTGOMERIE WILL NOT ONLY BE ABLE TO TELL YOU WHICH COUNTRY WON THE DUNHILL CUP IN WHATEVER YEAR YOU CARE TO MENTION, BUT WHO REPRESENTED THEM AND PROBABLY WHAT BREAKFAST THEY HAD AS WELL. THE FOLLOWING SECTION IS FOR ALL THE MONTYS OF THIS WORLD: THE MAD KEEN GOLFERS WHO WANT TO KNOW WHO DID WHAT, HOW AND WHERE.

RECORDS

The Major Championships

MOST WINS:

		BO	US	M	PGA	Total
18	Jack Nicklaus	3	4	6	5	18
11	Walter Hagen	4	2	-	5	11
9	Ben Hogan	1	4	2	2	9
	Gary Player	3	1	3	2	9
8	Tom Watson	5	1	2	-	8
7	Bobby Jones	3	4	-	-	7
	Arnold Palmer	2	1	4	-	7
	Gene Sarazen	1	2	1	3	7
	Sam Snead	1	-	3	3	7
	Harry Vardon	6	1	-	-	7
6	Nick Faldo	3	-	3	-	6
	Lee Trevino	2	2	-	2	6
5	Seve Ballesteros	3	-	2	-	5
	James Braid	5	-	-	-	5
	Byron Nelson	-	1	2	2	5
	J.H. Taylor	5	-	-	-	5
	Peter Thomson	5	-	-	-	5
4	Willie Anderson Jr	-	4	-	-	4
	Jim Barnes	1	1	-	2	4
	Ray Floyd	-	1	1	2	4
	Bobby Locke	4	-	-	-	4
	Tom Morris Jr	4	-	-	-	4
	Tom Morris Sr	4	-	-	-	4
	Willie Park Sr	4	-	-	-	4
3	Jamie Anderson	3	-	-	-	3
	Tommy Armour	1	1	-	1	3
	Julius Boros	2	-	-	1	3
	Billy Casper	-	2	1	-	3
	Henry Cotton	3	-	-	-	3
	Jimmy Demaret	-	-	3	-	3
	Bob Ferguson	3	-	-	-	3
	Ralph Guldahl	-	2	1	-	3
	Cary Middlecoff	-	2	1	-	3
	Hale Irwin	-	3	-	-	3
	Larry Nelson	1	-	-	2	3

		BO	US	M	PGA	Total
	Nick Price	1	-	-	2	3
	Denny Shute	1	-	-	2	3
2	Jack Burke Jr	-	-	1	1	2
	Ben Crenshaw	-	-	2	-	2
	John Daly	1	-	-	1	2
	Leo Diegel	-	-	-	2	2
	Olin Dutra	-	1	-	1	2
	Ernie Els	-	2	-	-	2
	Doug Ford	-	-	1	1	2
	David Graham	-	1	-	1	2
	Hubert Green	-	1	-	1	2
	Harold Hilton	2	-	-	-	2
	Jock Hutchinson	1	-	-	1	2
	Tony Jacklin	1	1	-	-	2
	Lee Janzen	-	2	-	-	2
	Bernhard Langer	-	-	2	-	2
	Sandy Lyle	1	-	1	-	2
	Bob Martin	2	-	-	-	2
	John McDermott	-	2	-	-	2
	Johnny Miller	1	1	-	-	2
	Greg Norman	2	-	-		2
	Andy North	-	2	-	-	2
	Mark O'Meara	1	-	1	-	2
	Jose-Maria Olazabal	-	-	2	-	2
	Willie Park Jr	2	-	-	-	2
	Henry Picard	-	-	1	1	2
	Paul Runyan	-	-	-	2	2
	Horton Smith	-	-	2	-	2
	Payne Stewart	-	1	-	1	2
	Dave Stockton	-	-	-	2	2
	Curtis Strange	-	2	-	-	2
	Ted Ray	1	1	-	-	2
	Craig Wood	-	1	1	-	2
	Fuzzy Zoeller	-	1	1	-	2
1	Tommy Aaron	-	-	1	-	1
	George Archer	-	-	1	-	1
	Laurie Auchterlonie	-	1	-	-	1
	Willie Auchterlonie	1	-	-	-	1
	Paul Azinger	-	-	-	1	1
	Ian Baker-Finch	1	-	-	-	1

	BO	*US*	*M*	*PGA*	*Total*
John Ball Jr	1	-	-	-	1
Jerry Barber	-	-	-	1	1
Tommy Bolt	-	1	-	-	1
Gay Brewer	-	-	1	-	1
Mark Brooks	-	-	-	1	1
David Brown	1	-	-	-	1
Billy Burke	-	1	-	-	1
Walter Burkemo	-	-	-	1	1
Jack Burns	1	-	-	-	1
Dick Burton	1	-	-	-	1
Mark Calcavecchia	1	-	-	-	1
Bob Charles	1	-	-	-	1
Charles Coody	-	-	1	-	1
Fred Couples	-	-	1	-	1
Tom Creavy	-	-	-	1	1
Fred Daly	1	-	-	-	1
Roberto de Vicenzo	1	-	-	-	1
George Duncan	1	-	-	-	1
Steve Elkington	-	-	-	1	1
Charles Evans Jr	-	1	-	-	1
Johnny Farrell	-	1	-	-	1
Max Faulkner	1	-	-	-	1
Willie Fernie	1	-	-	-	1
Jim Ferrier	-	-	-	1	1
Dow Finsterwald	-	-	-	1	1
Jack Fleck	-	1	-	-	1
James Foulis	-	1	-	-	1
Ed Furgol	-	1	-	-	1
Al Geiberger	-	-	-	1	1
Vic Ghezzi	-	-	-	1	1
Bob Goalby	-	-	1	-	1
Johnny Goodman	-	1	-	-	1
Wayne Grady	-	-	-	1	1
Lou Graham	-	1	-	-	1
Bob Hamilton	-	-	-	1	1
Chick Harbert	-	-	-	1	1
Claude Harmon	-	-	1	-	1
Chandler Harper	-	-	-	1	1
Arthur Havers	1	-	-	-	1
Jay Hebert	-	-	-	1	1
Lionel Hebert	-	-	-	1	1
Fred Herd	-	1	-	-	1
Sandy Herd	1	-	-	-	1
Don January	-	-	-	1	1
Steve Jones	-	1	-	-	1
Herman Keiser	-	-	1	-	1
Tom Kidd	1	-	-	-	1
Hugh Kirklaldy	1	-	-	-	1
Tom Kite	-	1	-	-	1
Tom Lehman	1	-	-	-	1
Tony Lema	1	-	-	-	1
Justin Leonard	1	-	-	-	1

	BO	*US*	*M*	*PGA*	*Total*
Lawson Little	-	1	-	-	1
Gene Littler	-	1	-	-	1
Joe Lloyd	-	1	-	-	1
Davis Love III	-	-	-	1	1
Willie MacFarlane	-	1	-	-	1
John Mahaffey	-	-	-	1	1
Tony Manero	-	1	-	-	1
Lloyd Mangrum	-	1	-	-	1
Dave Marr	-	-	-	1	1
Arnaud Massy	1	-	-	-	1
Dick Mayer	-	1	-	-	1
Fred McLeod	-	1	-	-	1
Larry Mize	-	-	1	-	1
Orville Moody	-	1	-	-	1
Kel Nagle	1	-	-	-	1
Bobby Nichols	-	-	-	1	1
Francis Ouimet	-	1	-	-	1
Alf Padgham	1	-	-	-	1
Mungo Park	1	-	-	-	1
Sam Parks Jr	-	1	-	-	1
Jerry Pate	-	1	-	-	1
Corey Pavin	-	1	-	-	1
Alf Perry	1	-	-	-	1
Horace Rawlins	-	1	-	-	1
Johnny Revolta	-	-	-	1	1
Bill Rogers	1	-	-	-	1
Bob Rosburg	-	-	-	1	1
Alex Ross	-	1	-	-	1
George Sargent	-	1	-	-	1
Jack Simpson	1	-	-	-	1
Scott Simpson	-	1	-	-	1
Vijay Singh	-	-	-	1	1
Jeff Sluman	-	-	-	1	1
Alex Smith	-	1	-	-	1
Willie Smith	-	1	-	-	1
Craig Stadler	-	-	1	-	1
Andrew Strath	1	-	-	-	1
Hal Sutton	-	-	-	1	1
Jerome Travers	-	1	-	-	1
Jim Turnesa	-	-	-	1	1
Bob Tway	-	-	-	1	1
Ken Venturi	-	1	-	-	1
Lanny Wadkins	-	-	-	1	1
Cyril Walker	-	1	-	-	1
Art Wall	-	-	1	-	1
Tom Weiskopf	1	-	-	-	1
Reg Whitcombe	1	-	-	-	1
Jack White	1	-	-	-	1
Tiger Woods	-	-	1	-	1
Ian Woosnam	-	-	1	-	1
Lew Worsham	-	1	-	-	1

MOST WINS IN INDIVIDUAL MAJORS:

The Open Championship:

6	Harry Vardon
5	James Braid
	J.H. Taylor
	Peter Thomson
	Tom Watson
4	Walter Hagen
	Tom Morris Jr
	Tom Morris Sr
	Willie Park Sr

The US Open:

4	Wille Anderson Jr
	Ben Hogan
	Bobby Jones
	Jack Nicklaus
3	Hale Irwin
2	Julius Boros
	Billy Casper
	Ernie Els
	Ralph Guldahl
	Walter Hagen
	John McDermott
	Cary Middlecoff
	Andy North
	Gene Sarazen
	Alex Smith
	Curtis Strange
	Lee Trevino

The US PGA Championship:

5	Walter Hagen
	Jack Nicklaus
3	Gene Sarazen
	Sam Snead
2	Jim Barnes
	Leo Diegel
	Ray Floyd
	Ben Hogan
	Byron Nelson
	Larry Nelson
	Gary Player
	Nick Price
	Paul Runyan
	Denny Shute
	Dave Stockton
	Lee Trevino

The Masters:

6	Jack Nicklaus
4	Arnold Palmer
3	Jimmy Demaret
	Nick Faldo
	Gary Player
	Sam Snead
2	Seve Ballesteros
	Ben Crenshaw
	Ben Hogan
	Bernhard Langer
	Byron Nelson
	Jose-Maria Olazabal
	Horton Smith
	Tom Watson

MULTIPLE WINS IN THE SAME YEAR:

Jack Nicklaus (5)	1963	M, PGA
	1966	M, BO
	1972	M, US
	1975	M, PGA
	1980	US, PGA
Ben Hogan (3)	1953	M, US, BO
	1948	US, PGA
	1951	M, US
Bobby Jones (2)	1926	US, BO
	1930	US, BO
Arnold Palmer (2)	1960	M, BO
	1962	M, BO
Gene Sarazen (2)	1922	US, PGA
	1932	US, BO
Tom Watson (2)	1977	M, BO
	1982	US, BO
Jack Burke Jr (1)	1956	M, PGA
Nick Faldo (1)	1990	M, BO
Walter Hagen (1)	1924	BO, PGA
Mark O'Meara (1)	1998	M, BO
Gary Player (1)	1974	M, BO
Nick Price (1)	1994	BOP, PGA

Sam Snead (1)	1949	M, PGA
Lee Trevino (1)	1971	US, BO
Craig Wood (1)	1941	M, US

YOUNGEST WINNERS:

Tom Morris Jr (BO, 1868), 17 years, 5 months, 8 days
Tom Morris Jr (BO, 1869), 18 years, 5 months, 1 day
Tom Morris Jr (BO, 1870), 19 years, 5 months
John McDermott (US, 1911), 19 years, 10 months, 12 days
Francis Ouimet (US, 1913), 20 years, 4 months, 11 days
Gene Sarazen (US, 1922), 20 years, 4 months, 16 days
Gene Sarazen (PGA, 1922), 20 years, 5 months, 20 days
Tom Creavy (PGA, 1931), 20 years, 7 months, 7 days
John McDermott (US, 1912), 20 years, 11 months, 21 days
Willie Auchterlonie (BO, 1893), 21 years, 24 days
Tiger Woods (M, 1997), 21 years, 3 months, 15 days

OLDEST WINNERS:

Julius Boros (PGA, 1968), 48 years, 4 months, 18 days
Tom Morris Sr (BO, 1867), 46 years, 3 months, 9 days
Jack Nicklaus (M, 1986), 46 years, 2 months, 23 days
Jerry Barber (PGA, 1961), 45 years, 3 months, 6 days
Hale Irwin (US, 1990), 45 years, 15 days
Lee Trevino (PGA, 1984), 44 years, 8 months, 18 days
Roberto de Vicenzo (BO, 1967), 44 years, 3 months, 3 days
Ray Floyd (US, 1986), 43 years, 9 months, 11 days
Ted Ray (US, 1920), 43 years, 4 months, 16 days
Ben Crenshaw (M, 1995), 43 years, 2 months, 29 days

LARGEST WINNING MARGINS

13	Tom Morris Sr	BO, 1862
12	Tom Morris Jr	BO, 1870
	Tiger Woods	M, 1997
11	Willie Smith	US, 1899
9	Jim Barnes	US, 1921
	Jack Nicklaus	M, 1965
8	James Braid	BO, 1908
	Ray Floyd	M, 1976
	J.H. Taylor	BO, 1900
	J.H. Taylor	BO, 1913
7	Fred Herd	US, 1898
	Tony Jacklin	US, 1970
	Cary Middlecoff	M, 1955
	Jack Nicklaus	PGA, 1980

MOST RUNNERS-UP

19	Jack Nicklaus	BO(7), US(4), PGA(4), M(4)
10	Arnold Palmer	BO(1), US(4), PGA(3), M(2)
8	Greg Norman	BO(1), US(2), PGA(2), M(3)
	Sam Snead	US(4), PGA(2), M(2)
7	J.H. Taylor	BO(6), US(1)
	Tom Watson	BO(1), US(2), PGA(1), M(3)
6	Ben Hogan	US(2), M(4)
	Byron Nelson	US(1), PGA(3), M(2)
	Gary Player	US(2), PGA(2), M(2)
	Harry Vardon	BO(4), US(2)
5	Ben Crenshaw	BO(2), PGA(1), M(2)
	Ray Floyd	BO(1), PGA(1), M(3)
	Tom Weiskopf	US(1), M(4)
	Craig Wood	BO(1), US(1), PGA(1), M(2)

MOST RUNNERS-UP POSITIONS WITHOUT EVER WINNING A MAJOR TITLE

4	Harry Cooper	US(2), M(2)
	Bruce Crampton	US(1), PGA(2), M(1)
	Doug Sanders	BO(2), US(1), PGA(1)
	Macdonald Smith	BO(2), US(2)
3	Andy Bean	BO(1), PGA(2)
	Chip Beck	US(2), M(1)
	Johnny Bulla	BO(2), M(1)
	Andrew Kirkaldy	BO(3)
	Tom McNamara	US(3)
	Colin Montgomerie	US(2), PGA(1)
	Ed Oliver	US(2), PGA(1)
	Dai Rees	BO(3)
	Frank Stranahan	BO(2), M(1)
	Davie Strath	BO(3)

LOWEST SCORES IN THE MAJORS

267	Steve Elkington	Riviera CC	PGA, 1995
	Colin Montgomerie	Riviera CC	PGA, 1995
	Greg Norman	Royal St George's	BO, 1993
268	Nick Price	Turnberry	BO, 1994
	Tom Watson	Turnberry	BO, 1977
269	Ernie Els	Riviera CC	PGA, 1995
	Nick Faldo	Royal St George's	BO, 1993
	Davis Love III	Winged Foot	PGA, 1977
	Jeff Maggert	Riviera CC	PGA, 1995

	Jack Nicklaus	Turnberry	BO, 1977
	Jesper Parnevik	Turnberry	BO, 1994
270	Nick Faldo	St Andrews	BO, 1990
	Bernhard Langer	Royal St George's	BO, 1993
	Tiger Woods	Augusta National	M, 1997
271	Brad Faxon	Riviera CC	PGA, 1995
	Ray Floyd	Augusta National	M, 1976
	Tom Lehman	Royal Lytham	BO, 1996
	Bobby Nichols	Columbus CC	PGA, 1964
	Jack Nicklaus	Augusta National	M, 1965
	Tom Watson	Muirfield	BO, 1980
	Fuzzy Zoeller	Turnberry	BO, 1994
272	Paul Azinger	Inverness	PGA, 1993
	Ian Baker-Finch	Royal Birkdale	BO, 1991
	Ben Crenshaw	Oakland Hills	PGA, 1979
	Nick Faldo	Muirfield	BO, 1992
	Ray Floyd	Southern Hills	PGA, 1982
	David Graham	Oakland Hills	PGA, 1979
	Lee Janzen	Baltusrol	US, 1993
	Jack Nicklaus	Baltusrol	US, 1980
	Greg Norman	Inverness	PGA, 1993
	Corey Pavin	Royal St George's	BO, 1993
	Peter Senior	Royal St George's	BO, 1993
	Jeff Sluman	Oak Tree GC	PGA, 1988

AFTER 18 HOLES

63	Michael Bradley	Riviera CC	PGA, 1995
	Ray Floyd	Southern Hills	PGA, 1982
	Jack Nicklaus	Baltusrol	US, 1980
	Greg Norman	Augusta National	M, 1996
	Tom Weiskopf	Baltusrol	BO, 1987
64	Rodger Davis	Muirfield	BO, 1987
	Mike Donald	Augusta National	M, 1990
	Ray Floyd	Muirfield	BO, 1992
	Jim Gallacher Jr	Riviera CC	PGA, 1995
	Lee Mackey Jr	Merion	US, 1950
	Lloyd Mangrum	Augusta National	M, 1940
	Bobby Nichols	Columbus CC	PGA, 1964
	Christy O'Connor Jr	Royal St George's	BO, 1985
	Mark O'Meara	Riviera CC	PGA, 1995
	Steve Pate	Muirfield	BO, 1982
	Scott Simpson	Inverness	PGA, 1993
	Craig Stadler	Royal Birkdale	BO, 1983
	Doug Tewell	Cherry Hills	PGA, 1985

AFTER 36 HOLES

130	Nick Faldo	Muirfield	BO, 1992
131	Ernie Els	Riviera CC	PGA, 1995
	Ray Floyd	Augusta National	M, 1976
	Mark O'Meara	Riviera CC	PGA, 1995
	Vijay Singh	Inverness	PGA, 1993
	Hal Sutton	Riviera CC	PGA, 1983
132	Nick Faldo	St Andrews	BO, 1990
	Nick Faldo	Royal St George's	BO, 1993
	Ray Floyd	Southern Hills	PGA, 1982
	Nick Price	Southern Hills	PGA, 1994

AFTER 54 HOLES

197	Ernie Els	Riviera CC	PGA, 1995
198	Tom Lehman	Royal Lytham	BO, 1996
199	Nick Faldo	St Andrews	BO, 1990
200	Ray Floyd	Southern Hills	PGA, 1982
	Jeff Maggert	Riviera CC	PGA, 1995
	Mark O'Meara	Riviera CC	PGA, 1995
201	Ray Floyd	Augusta National	M, 1976
	Tiger Woods	Augusta National	M, 1997

LOW ROUND: 2ND ROUND

63	Bruce Crampton	Firestone CC	PGA, 1975
	Nick Faldo	Royal St George's	BO, 1993
	Mark Hayes	Turnberry	BO, 1977
	Greg Norman	Turnberry	BO, 1993
	Gary Player	Shoal Creek	PGA, 1984
	Vijay Singh	Inverness	PGA, 1993

LOW ROUND: 3RD ROUND

63	Isao Aoki	Muirfield	BO, 1980
	Paul Broadhurst	St Andrews	BO, 1990
	Nick Price	Augusta National	M, 1986

LOW ROUND: 4TH ROUND

63	Brad Faxon	Riviera CC	PGA, 1995
	Johnny Miller	Oakmont	US, 1973
	Jodie Mudd	Royal Birkdale	BO, 1991
	Payne Stewart	Royal St George's	BO, 1993

RYDER CUP: Individual records

(from 1927–1971 matches were contested between Great Britain and the USA; as Great Britain and Ireland between 1973 and 1977 and as Europe from 1979)

Europe:

Name	*Year*	*P*	*W*	*L*	*H*
Jimmy Adams	1939/47/49/51/53	7	2	5	0
Percy Alliss	1929/33/35/37	6	3	2	1
Peter Alliss	1953/57/59/61/63/65/67/69	30	10	15	5
Laurie Ayton	1949	0	0	0	0
Peter Baker	1993	4	3	1	0
Severiano Ballesteros	1979/83/85/87/89/91/93/95/***97(c)***	37	20	12	5
Harry Bannerman	1971	5	2	2	1
Brian Barnes	1969/71/73/75/77/79	25	10	14	1
Maurice Bembridge	1969/71/73/75	16	5	8	3
Thomas Bjorn	1997	2	1	0	1
Aubrey Boomer	1927/29	4	2	2	0
Ken Bousfield	1949/51/55/57/59/61	10	5	5	0
Hugh Boyle	1967	3	0	3	0
Harry Bradshaw	1953/55/57	5	2	2	1
Gordon J Brand	1983	1	0	1	0
Gordon Brand Jr	1987/89	7	2	4	1
Paul Broadhurst	1991	2	2	0	0
Eric Brown	1953/55/57/59/***69(c)***/***71(c)***	8	4	4	0
Ken Brown	1977/79/83/85/87	13	4	9	0
Stewart Burns	1929	0	0	0	0
Dick Burton	1935/37/49	5	2	3	0
Jack Busson	1935	2	0	2	0
Peter Butler	1965/69/71/73	14	3	9	2
Jose Maria Canizares	1981/83/85/89	11	5	4	2
Alex Caygill	1969	1	0	0	1
Clive Clark	1973	1	0	1	0
Howard Clark	1977/81/85/87/89/95	15	7	7	1
Darren Clarke	1997	2	1	1	0
Neil Coles	1961/63/65/67/69/71/73/77	40	12	21	7
Archie Compston	1927/29/31	6	1	4	1
Henry Cotton	1929/37/**47(c)**/***53(c)***	6	2	4	0
Bill Cox	1935/37	3	0	2	1
Allan Dailey	1933	0	0	0	0
Fred Daly	1947/49/51/53	8	3	4	1
Eamonn Darcy	1975/77/81/87	11	1	8	2
William Davies	1931/33	4	2	2	0
Peter Dawson	1977	3	1	2	0
Norman Drew	1959	1	0	0	1
George Duncan	1927/**29(c)**/31	5	2	3	0
Syd Easterbrook	1931/33	3	2	1	0
Nick Faldo	1977/79/81/83/85/87/89/91/93/95/97	46	23	19	4
John Fallon	1955/***63(c)***	1	1	0	0
Max Faulkner	1947/49/51/53/57	8	1	7	0
David Feherty	1991	3	1	1	1
George Gadd	1927	0	0	0	0
Bernard Gallacher	1969/71/73/75/77/79/81/83/***91(c)***/***93(c)***	31	13	13	5
John Garner	1971/73	1	0	1	0

Name	*Year*	*P*	*W*	*L*	*H*
Antonio Garrido	1979	5	1	4	0
Ignacio Garrido	1997	4	0	1	3
David Gilford	1991/95	6	3	3	0
Malcolm Gregson	1967	4	0	4	0
Tom Haliburton	1961/63	6	0	6	0
Joachim Haeggman	1993	2	1	1	0
Jack Hargreaves	1951	0	0	0	0
Arthur Havers	1927/31/33	6	3	3	0
Jimmy Hitchcock	1965	3	0	3	0
Bert Hodson	1931	1	0	1	0
Tommy Horton	1975/77	8	1	6	1
Brian Huggett	1963/67/69/71/73/75/***77(c)***	25	9	10	6
Bernard Hunt	1953/57/59/61/63/65/67/69/***73(c)***/***75(c)***	28	6	16	6
Geoffrey Hunt	1963	3	0	3	0
Guy Hunt	1975	3	0	2	0
Tony Jacklin	1967/69/71/73/75/77/79/***83(c)*** ***/85(c)/87(c)/89(c)***	35	13	14	8
John Jacobs	1955/***79(c)***/***81(c)***	2	2	0	0
Mark James	1977/79/81/89/91/93/95	24	8	15	1
Edward Jarman	1935	1	0	1	0
Per/Ulrik Johannson	1995/97	5	3	2	0
Herbert Jolly	1927	2	0	2	0
Michael King	1979	1	0	1	0
Sam King	1937/47/49	5	1	3	1
Arthur Lacey	1933/37/***51(c)***	3	0	3	0
Barry Lane	1993	3	0	3	0
Bernhard Langer	1981/83/85/87/89/91/93/95/97	38	18	15	5
Arthur Lees	1947/49/51/55	8	4	4	0
Sandy Lyle	1979/81/83/85/87	18	7	9	2
Jimmy Martin	1965	1	0	1	0
Peter Mills	1957/59	1	1	0	0
Abe Mitchell	1929/31/33	6	4	2	0
Ralph Moffitt	1961	1	0	1	0
Colin Montgomerie	1991/93/95/97	18	9	6	3
Christy O'Connor Jr	1975/89	4	1	3	0
Christy O'Connor Sr	1955/57/59/61/63/65/67/69/71/73	36	11	21	4
Jose-Maria Olazabal	1987/89/91/93/97	25	14	8	3
John O'Leary	1975	4	0	4	0
Peter Oosterhuis	1971/73/75/77/79/81	28	14	11	3
Alf Padgham	1933/35/37	6	0	6	0
John Panton	1951/53/61	5	0	5	0
Jesper Parnevik	1997	4	1	1	2
Alf Perry	1933/35/37	4	0	3	1
Manuel Pinero	1981/85	9	6	3	0
Lionel Platts	1965	5	1	2	2
Eddie Polland	1973	2	0	2	0
Ronan Rafferty	1989	3	1	2	0
Ted Ray	**1927(c)**	2	0	2	0
Dai Rees	1937/47/49/51/53/**55(c)** **/57(c)/59(c)/61(c)/*67(c)***	18	7	10	1
Steven Richardson	1991	4	2	2	0
Jose Rivero	1985/87	5	2	3	0
Fred Robson	1927/29/31	6	2	4	0
Costantino Rocca	1993/95/97	11	6	5	0
Syd Scott	1955	2	0	2	0
Des Smyth	1979/81	7	2	5	0

Name	*Year*	*P*	*W*	*L*	*H*
Dave Thomas	1959/63/65/67	18	3	10	5
Sam Torrance	1981/83/85/87/89/91/93/95	28	7	15	6
Peter Townsend	1969/71	11	3	8	0
Brian Waites	1983	4	1	3	0
Philip Walton	1995	2	1	1	0
Charlie Ward	1947/49/51	6	1	5	0
Paul Way	1983/85	9	6	2	1
Harry Weetman	1951/53/55/57/59/61/63/***65(c)***	15	2	11	2
Lee Westwood	1997	5	2	3	0
Charles Whitcombe	1927/29/**31(c)**/33/**35(c)**/**37(c)**/***49(c)***	9	3	2	4
Ernest Whitcombe	1929/31/35	6	1	4	1
Reg Whitcombe	1935	1	0	1	0
George Will	1963/65/67	15	2	11	2
Norman Wood	1975	3	1	2	0
Ian Woosnam	1983/85/87/89/91/93/95/97	31	14	12	5

United States:

Name	Year	P	W	L	H
Tommy Aaron	1969/73	6	1	4	1
Skip Alexander	1949/51	2	1	1	0
Paul Azinger	1989/91/93	14	5	7	2
Jerry Barber	1955/**61(c)**	5	1	4	0
Miller Barber	1969/71	7	1	4	2
Herman Barron	1947	1	1	0	0
Andy Bean	1979/87	6	4	2	0
Frank Beard	1969/71	8	2	3	3
Chip Beck	1989/91/93	9	6	2	1
Homero Blancas	1973	4	2	1	1
Tommy Bolt	1955/57	4	3	1	0
Julius Boros	1959/63/65/67	16	9	3	4
Gay Brewer	1967/73	9	5	3	1
Billy Burke	1931/33	3	3	0	0
Jack Burke	1951/53/55/**57(c)**/59/***73(c)***	8	7	1	0
Walter Burkemo	1953	1	0	1	0
Mark Calcavecchia	1897/89/91	11	5	5	1
Billy Casper	1961/63/65/67/69/71/73/75/***79(c)***	37	20	10	7
Bill Collins	1961	3	1	2	0
Charles Coody	1971	3	0	2	1
John Cook	1993	2	1	1	0
Fred Couples	1989/91/93/95/97	20	7	9	4
Wilfred Cox	1931	2	2	0	0
Ben Crenshaw	1981/83/87/95	12	3	8	1
Jimmy Demaret	1947/49/51	6	6	0	0
Gardner Dickinson	1967/71	10	9	1	0
Leo Diegel	1927/29/31/33	6	3	3	0
Dale Douglass	1969	2	0	2	0
Dave Douglas	1953	2	1	0	1
Ed Dudley	1929/33/37	4	3	1	0
Olin Dutra	1933/35	4	1	3	0
Lee Elder	1979	4	1	3	0
Al Espinosa	1927/29/31	4	2	1	1
Johnny Farrell	1927/29/31	6	3	2	1
Brad Faxon	1995/97	6	2	4	0
Dow Finsterwald	1957/59/61/63/***77(c)***	13	9	3	1
Ray Floyd	1969/75/77/81/83/85/***89(c)***/91/93	31	12	16	3
Doug Ford	1955/57/59/61	9	4	4	1

Name	*Year*	*P*	*W*	*L*	*H*
Ed Furgol	1957	1	0	1	0
Marty Furgol	1955	1	0	1	0
Jim Furyk	1997	3	1	2	0
Jim Gallagher Jr	1993	3	2	1	0
Al Geiberger	1967/75	9	5	1	3
Bob Gilder	1983	4	2	2	0
Bob Goalby	1963	5	3	1	1
Johnny Golden	1927/29	3	3	0	0
Lou Graham	1973/75/77	9	5	3	1
Hubert Green	1977/79/85	7	4	3	0
Ken Green	1989	4	2	2	0
Ralph Guldahl	1937	2	2	0	0
Fred Haas Jr	1953	1	0	1	0
Jay Haas	1983/95	8	3	4	1
Walter Hagen	**1927(c)/29(c)/31(c)/35(c)/*37(c)***	9	7	1	1
Bob Hamilton	1949	2	0	2	0
Chick Harbert	1949/55	2	2	0	0
Chandler Harper	1955	1	0	1	0
Dutch (E.J.) Harrison	1947/49/51	3	2	1	0
Fred Hawkins	1957	2	1	1	0
Mark Hayes	1979	3	1	2	0
Chandler Haefner	1949/51	4	3	0	1
Jay Hebert	1959/61/***71(c)***	4	2	1	1
Lionel Hebert	1957	1	0	1	0
Dave Hill	1969/73/77	9	6	3	0
Scott Hoch	1997	3	2	0	1
Ben Hogan	**1947(c)**/***49(c)***/51/***67(c)***	3	3	0	0
Hale Irwin	1975/77/79/81/91	20	13	5	2
Tommy Jacobs	1965	4	3	1	0
Peter Jacobsen	1985/95	6	2	4	0
Don January	1965/77	7	2	3	2
Lee Janzen	1993/97	5	2	3	0
Herman Keiser	1947	1	0	1	0
Tom Kite	1979/81/83/85/87/89/93/***97(c)***	28	15	9	4
Ted Kroll	1953/55/57	4	3	1	0
Ky Laffoon	1935	1	0	1	0
Tom Lehman	1995/97	7	3	2	2
Tony Lema	1963/65	11	8	1	2
Justin Leonard	1997	4	0	2	2
Wayne Levi	1991	2	0	2	0
Bruce Lietzke	1981	3	0	2	1
Gene Littler	1961/63/65/67/69/71/75	27	14	5	8
Davis Love III	1993/95/97	13	5	8	0
John Mahaffey	1979	3	1	2	0
Mark McCumber	1989	3	2	1	0
Jerry McGee	1977	2	1	1	0
Jeff Maggert	1995/97	7	4	3	0
Tony Manero	1937	2	1	1	0
Lloyd Mangrum	1947/49/51/**53(c)**	8	6	2	0
Dave Marr	1965/***81(c)***	6	4	2	0
Billy Maxwell	1963	4	4	0	0
Dick Mayer	1957	2	1	0	1
Bill Mehlhorn	1927	2	1	1	0
Phil Mickelson	1995/97	7	4	1	2
Name	*Year*	*P*	*W*	*L*	*H*
Cary Middlecoff	1953/55/59	6	2	3	1

Johnny Miller	1975/81	6	2	2	2
Larry Mize	1987	4	1	1	2
Gil Morgan	1979/83	6	1	2	3
Bob Murphy	1975	4	2	1	1
Byron Nelson	1937/47/***65(c)***	4	3	1	0
Larry Nelson	1979/81/87	13	9	3	1
Bobby Nichols	1967	5	4	0	1
Jack Nicklaus	1969/71/73/75/77/81/***83(c)***/***87(c)***	28	17	8	3
Andy North	1985	3	0	3	0
Ed Oliver	1947/51/53	5	3	2	0
Mark O'Meara	1985/89/91/97	12	4	7	1
Arnold Palmer	1961/**63(c)**/65/67/71/73/***75(c)***	32	22	8	2
Johnny Palmer	1949	2	0	2	0
Sam Parks	1935	1	0	0	1
Jerry Pate	1981	4	2	2	0
Steve Pate	1991	1	0	1	0
Corey Pavin	1991/93/95	13	8	5	0
Calvin Peete	1983/85	7	4	2	1
Henry Picard	1935/37	4	3	1	0
Dan Pohl	1987	3	1	2	0
Johnny Pott	1963/65/67	7	5	2	0
Dave Ragan	1963	4	2	1	1
Henry Ransom	1951	1	0	1	0
Johnny Revolta	1935/37	3	2	1	0
Loren Roberts	1995	3	2	1	0
Chi Chi Rodriguez	1973	2	0	1	1
Bill Rogers	1981	4	1	2	1
Bob Rosburg	1959	2	2	0	0
Mason Rudolph	1971	3	1	1	1
Paul Runyan	1933/35	4	2	2	0
Doug Sanders	1967	5	2	3	0
Gene Sarazen	1927/29/31/33/35/37	12	7	2	3
Densmore Shute	1931/33/37	6	2	2	2
Dan Sikes	1969	3	2	1	0
Scott Simpson	1987	2	1	1	0
Horton Smith	1929/31/33/35/37	4	3	0	1
J.C. Snead	1971/73/75	11	9	2	0
Sam Snead	1937/47/49/**51(c)**/53/55/**59(c)**/***69(c)***	13	10	2	1
Ed Sneed	1977	2	1	0	1
Mike Souchak	1959/61	6	5	1	0
Craig Stadler	1983/85	8	4	2	2
Payne Stewart	1987/89/91/93	16	8	7	1
Ken Still	1969	3	1	2	0
Dave Stockton	1971/77/***91(c)***	5	3	1	1
Curtis Strange	1983/85/87/89/93	20	6	12	2
Hal Sutton	1985/87	9	3	3	3
Lee Trevino	1969/71/73/75/79/81/***85(c)***	30	17	7	6
Jim Turnesa	1953	1	1	0	0
Joe Turnesa	1927/29	4	1	2	1
Ken Venturi	1965	4	1	3	0
Lanny Wadkins	1977/79/83/85/87/89/91/93/***95(c)***	34	20	11	3
Art Wall Jr	1957/59/61	6	4	2	0
Al Watrous	1927/29	3	2	1	0
Tom Watson	1977/81/83/89/***93(c)***	15	10	4	1
Tom Weiskopf	1973/75	10	7	2	1
Name	*Year*	*P*	*W*	*L*	*H*
Craig Wood	1931/33/35	4	1	3	0

Tiger Woods	1997	5	1	3	1
Lew Worsham	1947	2	2	0	0
Fuzzy Zoeller	1979/83/85	10	1	8	1

NB: Bold type indicates a playing captain, bold type in italics indicates non-playing captain.

MOST APPEARANCES:

11 Nick Faldo
10 Christy O'Connor, Sr
9 Dai Rees
Ray Floyd
Billy Casper
Bernhard Langer
8 Peter Alliss
Neil Coles
Ray Floyd
Bernard Gallacher
Bernard Hunt
Sam Torrance
Lanny Wadkins
Ian Woosnam
Peter Oosterhuis
Sam Torrance

YOUNGEST PLAYER:

1929, Horton Smith, (21 years, 4 days)
1977, Nick Faldo, (21 years, 1 month, 28 days)

OLDEST PLAYER:

1993, Ray Floyd, (51 years, 20 days)
1927, Ted Ray, (50 years, 2 months, 5 days)

MOST MATCHES PLAYED:

46 Nick Faldo
40 Neil Coles
38 Bernhard Langer
37 Billy Casper
Seve Ballesteros
36 Christy O'Connor Sr
35 Tony Jacklin
34 Lanny Wadkins
32 Arnold Palmer
31 Ray Floyd
Bernard Gallacher
Ian Woosnam
30 Peter Alliss
Lee Trevino
28 Bernard Hunt
Tom Kite
Jack Nicklaus

MOST POINTS WON:

25.0 Nick Faldo
23.5 Billy Casper
23.0 Arnold Palmer
22.5 Seve Ballesteros
21.5 Lanny Wadkins
20.5 Bernhard Langer
20.0 Lee Trevino
18.5 Jack Nicklaus
17.0 Tony Jacklin
Tom Kite
16.5 Ian Woosnam
15.5 Bernard Gallacher
Jose-Maria Olazabal
Peter Oosterhuis

BEST POINT PERCENTAGE (MIN. 3 MATCHES):

100% Jimmy Demaret (6-0-0)
88% Jack Burke (7-1-0)
Horton Smith (3-0-1)
68% Jose-Maria Olazabal (14-8-3)
67% Abe Mitchell (4-2-0)
61% Seve Ballesteros (20-12-5)

MOST MATCHES WON:

23 Nick Faldo
22 Arnold Palmer
20 Lanny Wadkins
Seve Ballesteros
Billy Casper
18 Bernhard Langer

MOST MATCHES LOST:

21 Christy O'Connor, Sr
Neil Coles
16 Ray Floyd
Bernard Hunt
11 Lanny Wadkins

WALKER CUP: Individual Records

Great Britain and Ireland

Name	*Year*	*P*	*W*	*L*	*H*
M.F. Attenborough	1967	2	0	2	0
C.C. Aylmer	1922	2	1	1	0
P. Baker (R)	1985	3	2	1	0
J.B. Beck	1928/***38(c)***/***47(c)***	1	0	1	0
P.J. Benkra	1969	4	2	1	1
H.G. Bentley	1934/36/38	4	0	2	2
D.A. Blair	1955/61	4	1	3	0
C. Bloice	1985	3	0	2	1
M.F. Bonallack	1957/59/61/63/65/ 67/**69(c)**/**71(c)**/**73(c)**	25	8	14	3
G. Brand	1979	3	0	3	0
O.C. Bristowe	1923(c)/24	1	0	1	0
A. Brodie	1977/79	8	5	2	1
A. Brooks	1969	3	2	0	1
M. Brooks	1997	2	0	2	0
Hon W.G.E. Brownlow	1926	2	0	2	0
J. Bruen	1938/49/51	5	0	4	1
J.A. Buckley	1979	1	0	1	0
J. Burke	1932	2	0	1	1
R. Burns	1993	2	1	1	0
A.F. Bussell	1957	2	1	1	0
I. Caldwell	1951/55	4	1	2	1
S. Cage	1993	3	0	2	1
W. Campbell	1930	2	0	2	0
J.B. Carr	1947/49/51/53/55/57/ 59/61/63/***65(c)***/**67(c)**	20	5	14	1
R.J. Carr	1971	4	3	0	1
D.G. Carrick	1983/87	5	0	5	0
I.A. Carslaw	1979	3	1	1	1
C. Cassells	1989	3	2	1	0
J.R. Cater	1955	1	0	1	0
J. Caven	1922	2	0	2	0
B.H.G. Chapman	1961	1	0	1	0
R. Chapman	1981	4	3	1	0
M.J. Christmas	1961/63	3	1	2	0
C.A. Clark (R)	1965	4	2	0	2
G.J. Clark	1965	1	0	1	0
H.K. Clark (R)	1973	3	1	1	1
R. Claydon	1989	4	2	2	0
A. Coltart	1991	3	2	1	0
G.B. Cosh	1965	4	3	1	0
R. Coughlan	1997	4	0	3	1
T. Craddock	1967/69	6	2	3	1
L.G. Crawley	1932/34/38/47	6	3	3	0
B. Critchley	1969	4	1	1	2
D. Curry	1987	4	1	3	0
C.R. Dalgleish	1981	3	1	2	0
B. Darwin	1922	2	1	1	0
J.C. Davies	1973/75/77/79	13	3	8	3
P. Deeble	1977/81	5	1	4	0
F.W.G. Deighton	1957	2	0	2	0

Name	*Year*	*P*	*W*	*L*	*H*
S.C. Dodd	1989	4	1	1	2
B. Dredge	1993	3	0	3	0
N.V. Drew (R)	1953	1	0	1	0
J.M. Dykes	1936	2	0	1	1
R. Eggo	1987	2	0	2	0
D. Evans	1981	3	1	1	1
G. Evans	1991	4	2	2	0
R.C. Ewing	1936/38/47/49/51/55	10	1	7	2
G.R.D. Eyles	1975	4	2	2	0
J. Fanagan	1995	2	2	0	0
E.W. Fiddian	1932/34	4	0	4	0
J. de Forest	1932	1	0	1	0
M. Foster	1995	4	2	0	2
R. Foster	1965/67/69/71/73/ **79(c)**/**81(c)**	17	2	13	2
D.W. Frame	1961	1	0	1	0
S. Gallacher	1995	4	2	2	0
D. Gilford (R)	1985	1	0	1	0
P. Girvan	1987	3	0	3	0
G. Godwin	1979/81	7	2	4	1
C.W. Green	1963/69/71/73/ 75/**83(c)**/**85(c)**	17	4	10	3
R.H. Hardman	1928	1	0	1	0
A. Hare	1989	3	2	0	1
P. Harrington	1991/93/95	9	3	5	1
R. Harris	**1922(c)**/23(c)/26(c)	4	1	3	0
R.W. Hartley	1930/32	4	0	4	0
W.L. Hartley	1932	2	0	2	0
J. Hawksworth	1985	4	2	1	1
G. Hay	1991	3	1	2	0
P. Hedges	1973/75	5	0	2	3
C.O. Hezlet	1924/26/28	6	0	5	1
G.A. Hill	1936/**55(c)**	2	0	1	1
Sir E.W.E Holderness	1923/26/30	6	2	4	0
T.W.B. Homer	1973	3	0	3	0
C.V.L. Hooman	1922/23	3	1*	2	0*
W.L. Hope	1923/24/28	5	1	4	0
B. Howard	1995/97	7	0	5	2
D. Howell	1995	2	1	0	1
G. Huddy	1961	1	0	1	0
W. Humphreys	1971	3	2	1	0
I.C. Hutcheon	1975/77/79/81	15	5	8	2
R.R. Jack	1957/59	4	2	2	0
L. James	1995	2	1	1	0
M. James (R)	1975	4	3	1	0
A. Jamieson Jr	1926	2	1	1	0
M.J. Kelley	1977/79	7	3	3	1
S.D. Keppler	1983	4	0	3	1
M.G. King (R)	1969/73	7	1	5	1
A.T. Kyle	1938/47/51	5	2	3	0
D.K. Kyle	1924	1	0	1	0
J.D.A. Langley	1936/51/53	6	0	5	1
C.D. Lawrie	**1961(c)**/**63(c)**	0	0	0	0
M.E. Lewis	1983	1	0	1	0
P.B. Lucas	**1936(c)**/47/**49(c)**	2	1	1	0
M.S.R. Lunt	1959/61/63/65	11	2	8	1

Name	*Year*	*P*	*W*	*L*	*H*
A.W.B. Lyle (R)	1977	3	0	3	0
A.R. McCallum	1928	1	0	1	0
S.M. McCready	1949/51	3	0	3	0
J.S. Macdonald	1971	3	1	1	1
P. McEvoy	1977/79/81/85/89	18	5	11	2
G. McGimpsey	1985/89/91	11	4	5	2
P. McGinley	1991	3	1	2	0
G. MacGregor	1971/75/83/85/87	14	5	8	1
R.C. MacGregor	1953	2	0	2	0
J. McHenry	1987	4	2	2	0
P. McKellar	1977	1	0	1	0
W.W. Mackenzie	1922/23	3	1	2	0
S.L. McKinlay	1934	2	0	2	0
J. McLean	1934/36	4	1	3	0
E.A. McRuvie	1932/34	4	1	2	1
J.F.D. Madelay	1963	2	0	1	1
L.S. Mann	1983	4	2	1	1
B. Marchbank	1979	4	2	2	0
G.C. Marks	1969/71(c)/***87(c)/89(c)***	6	2	4	0
D.M. Marsh	***1959(c)/*****71(c)*****/73(c)/75(c)***	3	2	1	0
G.N.C. Martin	1928	1	0	1	0
S. Martin	1977	4	2	2	0
P. Mayo	1985/87	4	0	3	1
G.H. Micklem	1947/49/53/55/***57(c)/59(c)***	6	1	5	0
D.J. Millenstad	1967	2	1	1	0
J.W. Milligan	1989/91	7	3	3	1
E.B. Millward	1949(c)/55	2	0	2	0
W.T.G. Milne	1973	4	2	2	0
C.S. Montgomerie (R)	1985/87	8	2	5	1
J.L. Morgan	1951/53/55	6	2	4	0
P. Mulcare	1975	3	2	1	0
G.H. Murray	1977	2	1	1	0
S.W.T. Murray	1963	4	2	2	0
W.A. Murray	1923/24/26(c)	4	1	3	0
K. Nolan	1997	3	0	3	0
E. O'Connell	1989	4	2	0	2
A. Oldcorn	1983	4	4	0	0
P.A. Oosterhuis (R)	1967	4	1	2	1
R. Oppenheimer	***1951(c)***	0	0	0	0
P. Page	1993	2	0	2	0
D. Park	1997	3	0	3	0
R. Parkin	1983	3	2	1	0
J. Payne	1991	4	2	2	0
J.J.F. Pennick	1938	2	1	1	0
T.P Perkins	1928	2	0	2	0
A.H. Perowne	1949/53/59	4	0	4	0
G.B. Peters	1936/38	4	2	1	1
V. Phillips	1993	3	1	2	0
A.D. Pierse	1983	3	0	2	1
A.K. Pirie	1967	3	0	2	1
M.A. Poxon	1975	2	0	2	0
D. Prosser	1989	1	0	1	2
I. Pyman	1993	3	0	3	0
R. Rafferty (R)	1981	4	2	2	0
G. Rankin	1995/97	4	0	4	0
D. Robertson	1993	3	1	2	0

Name	*Year*	*P*	*W*	*L*	*H*
J. Robinson	1987	4	2	2	0
R.N. Roderick	1989	2	0	1	1
J. Rose	1997	4	2	2	0
R. Russell	1993	3	0	3	0
A.C. Saddler	1963/65/67/***77(c)***	10	3	5	2
Hon M. Scott	1924/**34(c)**	4	2	2	0
R. Scott Jr	1924	1	1	0	0
P.F. Scrutton	1955/57	3	0	3	0
D.N. Sewell	1957/59	4	1	3	0
R.D.B.M Shade	1961/63/65/67	14	6	6	2
G. Shaw	1987	4	1	2	1
D.B. Sheahan	1963	4	2	2	0
G. Sherry	1995	4	2	2	0
A.E. Shepperson	1957/59	3	1	1	1
A.F. Simpson	1926(c)	0	0	0	0
J.N. Smith	1930	2	0	2	0
W.D. Smith	1959	1	0	1	0
S. Stanford	1993	3	1	2	0
A.R. Stephen	1985	4	2	1	1
E.F. Storey	1924/26/28	6	1	5	0
J.A. Stout	1930/32	4	0	3	1
C. Stowe	1938/47	4	2	2	0
H.B. Stuart	1971/73/75	10	4	6	0
A. Thirlwell	1957	1	0	1	0
K.G. Thom	1949	2	0	2	0
M.S. Thompson	1983	3	1	2	0
H. Thomson	1936/38	4	2	2	0
C.J.H. Tolley	1922/23/**24(c)**/26/30/34	12	4	8	0
T.A. Torrance	1924/28/30/32(c)/34	9	3	5	1
W.B. Torrance	1922	2	0	2	0
P.M. Townsend (R)	1965	4	3	1	0
L.P. Tupling	1969	2	1	1	0
W. Tweddell	1928(c)/36(c)	2	0	2	0
J. Walker	1961	2	0	2	0
P. Walton (R)	1981/83	8	6	2	0
C. Watson	1997	3	1	1	1
P Way (R)	1981	4	2	2	0
R.H. Wethered	1922/23/26/**30(c)**/34	9	5	3	1
L. White	1991	2	1	1	0
R.J. White	1947/49/51/53/55	10	6	3	1
R. Willson	1991	4	1	3	0
J. Wilson	1923	2	2	0	0
J.C. Wilson	1947/53	4	0	4	0
G. Wolstenholme	1995/97	7	3	4	0
G.B. Wolstenholme	1957/59	4	1	2	1
S. Young	1997	4	2	2	0

UNITED STATES

Name	*Year*	*P*	*W*	*L*	*H*
T.D. Aaron (R)	1959	2	1	1	0
B. Alexander	1987	3	2	1	0
D.C. Allen	1965/67	6	0	4	2
B. Andrade	1987	4	2	2	0
E.S. Andrews	1961	1	1	0	0

Name	*Year*	*P*	*W*	*L*	*H*
D. Ballenger	1973	1	1	0	0
R. Baxter Jr	1957	2	2	0	0
N. Begay	1995	3	1	2	0
D.R. Beman	1959/61/63/65	11	7	2	2
D. Berganio	1993	3	1	2	0
R.E. Billows	1983/49	4	2	2	0
S.E. Bishop	1947/49	3	2	1	0
A.S. Blum	1957	1	0	1	0
J. Bohmann	1969	3	1	2	0
M. Brannan	1977	3	1	2	0
A. Bratton	1995	3	1	0	2
G.F. Burns	1975	3	2	1	0
C. Burroughs	1985	3	1	2	0
A.E. Campbell	1936	2	2	0	0
J.E. Campbell	1957	1	0	1	0
W.C. Campbell	1951/53/***55(c)***/57/65/67/71/75	18	11	4	3
R.J. Cerrudo	1967	4	1	1	2
R.D. Chapman	1947/51/53	5	3	2	0
D. Cherry	1953/55/61	5	5	0	0
D. Clarke	1979	3	2	0	1
R.E. Cochran	1961	1	1	0	0
C.R. Coe	1949/51/53/***57(c)***/**59(c)**/61/63	13	7	4	2
R. Commans	1981	3	1	1	1
J.W. Conrad	1955	2	1	1	0
T. Courville	1995/97	6	4	2	0
K. Cox	1995	3	1	2	0
N. Crosby	1983	2	1	1	0
B.H. Cudd	1955	2	2	0	0
R.D. Davies	1963	2	0	2	0
J.W. Dawson	1949	2	2	0	0
D. Delcher	1997	3	2	1	0
T. Demsey	1993	3	3	0	0
R.B. Dickson	1967	3	3	0	0
A. Doyle	1991/93	6	5	1	0
G.T. Dunlap Jr	1932/34/36	5	3	1	1
D. Duval	1991	3	2	1	0
D. Edwards	1973	4	4	0	0
H.C. Egan	1934	1	1	0	0
D. Eger	1991	3	2	1	0
H.C. Eger	1989	3	1	2	0
D. Eichelberger	1965	3	1	2	0
B. Elder	1997	4	4	0	0
J. Ellis	1973	3	2	1	0
W. Emery	1936	2	1	0	1
C. Evans Jr	1922/24/28	5	3	2	0
J. Farquar	1971	3	1	2	0
B. Faxon (R)	1983	4	3	1	0
R. Fehr	1983	4	2	1	1
J.W. Fischer	1934/36/38/***65(c)***	4	3	0	1
D. Fischesser	1979	3	1	2	0
M.A. Fleckman	1967	2	0	2	0
B. Fleisher	1969	4	0	2	2
J. Fought	1977	4	4	0	0
W.C. Fownes Jr	**1922(c)**/24	3	1	2	0
F. Fuhrer	1981	3	2	1	0
J.R. Gabrielsen	1977/81(c)/91(c)	3	1	2	0

Name	*Year*	*P*	*W*	*L*	*H*
R. Gamez	1989	4	3	0	1
R.A. Gardner	1922/***23(c)***/***24(c)***/***26(c)***	8	6	2	0
R.W. Gardner	1961/63	5	4	0	1
B. Gay	1993	2	0	1	1
M. Giles	1969/71/73/75	15	8	2	5
H.L. Givan	1936	1	0	0	1
J.G. Goodman	1934/36/38	6	4	2	0
J. Gore	1997	3	3	0	0
M. Gove	1979	3	2	1	0
J. Grace	1975	3	2	1	0
J.A. Grant	1967	2	2	0	0
A.D. Gray Jr	1963/65/67	12	5	6	1
J.P. Guilford	1926/28	4	4	0	0
F. Haas Jr (R)	1939	2	0	2	0
J. Haas (R)	1975	3	3	0	0
J Haas	1985	3	1	2	0
G. Hallberg	1977	3	1	2	0
G.S. Hamer Jr	***1947(c)***	0	0	0	0
J. Harris	1993/95/97	11	10	1	0
L.E. Harris Jr	1963	4	3	1	0
V. Haefner	1977	3	3	0	0
T. Herron	1993	3	3	0	0
S.D. Herron	1923	2	0	2	0
S. Hoch (R)	1979	4	4	0	0
W. Hoffer	1983	2	1	1	0
J. Holtgrieve	1979/81/83	10	6	4	0
J.M. Hopkins	1965	3	0	2	1
R. Howe	1989	1	0	1	0
W. Howell	1932	1	1	0	0
W. Hyndman	1957/59/61/69/71	9	6	1	2
J. Inman	1969	2	2	0	0
J.G. Jackson	1953/55	3	3	0	0
T. Jackson	1995	3	1	1	1
K. Johnson	1989	3	1	2	0
H.R. Johnston	1923/24/28/30	6	5	1	0
R.T. Jones Jr	1922/24/26/**28(c)**/**30(c)**	10	9	1	0
A.F. Kammer	1947	2	1	1	0
T. Keuhne	1995	3	0	3	0
M. Killian	1973	3	1	2	0
C. Kite	1987	3	2	1	0
T.O. Kite (R)	1971	4	2	1	1
R.E. Knepper	***1922(c)***	0	0	0	0
R.W. Knowles	1951	1	1	0	0
G. Koch	1973/75	7	4	1	2
C.R. Kocsis	1938/49/57	5	2	2	1
J. Kribel	1997	3	1	2	0
F. Langham	1991	3	1	2	0
R. Leen	1997	3	2	1	0
J. Leonard (R)	1993	3	3	0	0
G. Lesher	1989	4	1	3	0
B. Lewis Jr	1981/83/85/87	14	10	4	0
J.W. Lewis	1967	4	3	1	0
W.L. Little Jr	1934	2	2	0	0
G.A. Littler (R)	1953	2	2	0	0
B. Loeffler	1987	3	2	1	0
D. Love (R)	1985	3	2	0	1

Name	*Year*	*P*	*W*	*L*	*H*
M.J. McCarrthy Jr	1932	1	1	0	0
B.N. McCormick	1949	1	1	0	0
J.B. McHale	1949/51	3	2	0	1
R.R. Mackenzie	1926/28/30	6	5	1	0
M.R. Marston	1922/23/24/34	8	5	3	0
D. Martin	1989	4	1	1	2
B. Marucci	1995/97	6	4	1	1
L. Mattiace	1987	3	2	1	0
R. May	1991	4	3	1	0
B. Mayfair	1987	3	3	0	0
E. Meeks	1989	1	0	0	1
S.N. Melnyk	1969/71	7	3	3	1
P. Mickelson (R)	1989/91	8	4	2	2
A.L. Miller	1969/71	8	4	3	1
L. Miller	1977	4	4	0	0
K. Mitchum	1993	3	2	0	1
D.K. Moe	1930/32	3	3	0	0
B. Montgomery	1987	2	2	0	0
G. Moody	1979	3	1	2	0
G.T. Moreland	1932/34	4	4	0	0
D. Morey	1955/65	4	1	3	0
J. Mudd	1981	3	3	0	0
R.T. Murphy (R)	1967	4	1	2	1
J.F. Neville	1923	1	0	1	0
J.W. Nicklaus (R)	1959/61	4	4	0	0
L.W. Oehmig	***1977(c)***	0	0	0	0
F.D. Ouimet	1922/23/24/26/30/32(c)/**34(c)**/ **36(c)**/***38(c)***/***47(c)***/***49(c)***	16	9	5	2
H.D. Paddock Jr	1951	1	0	0	1
J. Pate (R)	1975	4	0	4	0
W.J. Patton	1955/57/59/63/65/***69(c)***	14	11	3	0
C. Pavin (R)	1981	3	2	0	1
M. Peck	1979	3	1	1	1
M. Pfeil	1973	4	2	1	1
M. Podolak	1985	2	1	0	1
S.L. Quick	1947	2	1	1	0
S. Randolph	1985	4	2	1	1
J. Rassett	1981	3	3	0	0
F. Ridley	1977/***87(c)***/***89(c)***	3	2	1	0
R.H. Riegel	1947/49	2	0	1	1
C. Riley	1995	3	1	1	1
H. Robbins Jr	1957	2	0	1	1
W. Rogers (R)	1973	2	1	1	0
G.V. Rotan	1923	2	1	1	0
E.M. Rudolph	1957	2	1	0	1
B. Sander	1977	3	0	3	0
T. Scherrer	1991	3	0	3	0
S. Scott	1997	3	2	1	0
C.H. Seaver	1932	2	2	0	0
R.L. Siderowf	1969/73/75/77/***79(c)***	14	4	8	2
J. Sigel	1977/79/81/**83(c)**/85/87/89/91/93	33	18	10	5
R.H. Sikes	1963	3	1	2	0
J.B. Simmons	1971	2	0	2	0
S. Simpson (R)	1977	3	3	0	0
C.B. Smith	1961/63	2	0	1	1
R. Smith	1936/38	4	2	2	0

Name	*Year*	*P*	*W*	*L*	*H*
R. Sonnier	1985	3	0	2	1
J. Sorensen	1987	3	1	1	1
M. Sposa	1991	3	2	1	0
C. Stadler (R)	1975	3	3	0	0
F.R. Stranahan	1947/49/51	6	3	2	1
C. Strange (R)	1975	4	3	0	1
H. Sutton (R)	1979/81	7	2	4	1
J.W. Sweetser	1922/23/24/26/28/32/***67(c)***	12	7	4*	1*
F.M. Taylor	1957/59/61	4	4	0	0
D. Tentis	1983	2	0	1	1
R.S. Tufts	***1963(c)***	0	0	0	0
W.P. Turnesa	1947/49/**51(c)**	6	3	3	0
B. Tuten	1983	2	1	1	0
E.M. Tutweiler	1965-67	6	5	1	0
E.R. Updegraff	1963/65/69/***75(c)***	7	3	3	1
S. Urzetta	1951/53	4	4	0	0
K. Venturi	1953	2	2	0	0
S. Verplank	1985	4	3	0	1
M. Voges	1991	3	2	1	0
G.J. Voigt	1930/32/36	5	2	2	1
G. Von Elm	1926/28/30	6	4	1	1
D von Tacky	1981	3	1	2	0
J.L. Wadkins (R)	1969/71	7	3	4	0
D. Waldorf	1985	3	1	2	0
E.H. Ward	1953/55/59	6	6	0	0
M.H. Ward	1938/47	4	2	2	0
M. West	1973/79	6	2	3	1
J. Westland	1932/34/53/***61(c)***	5	3	0	2
H.W. Wettlaufer	1959	2	2	0	0
E. White	1936	2	2	0	0
O.F. Willing	1923/24/30	4	4	0	0
J.M. Winters Jr	***1971(c)***	0	0	0	0
C. Wollmann	1997	3	1	1	1
W. Wood	1983	4	1	2	1
T. Woods (R)	1995	4	2	2	0
F.J. Wright	1923	1	1	0	0
C.R. Yates	1936/38/***53(c)***	4	3	0	1
D. Yates	1989/93	6	3	2	1
R.L. Yost	1955	2	2	0	0

Key: Bold type indicates playing captain. Bold italic type indicates a non-playing captain. (R) after a player's name, indicates that the player went on to play in the Ryder Cup. * C.V.L. Hooman and J. Sweetser were all square after their single's match in 1922, played on as no other instructions were readily available and Hooman went on to win at the 37th hole. On all other occasions halved matches have been recorded as thus.

US TOUR LEADING MONEY WINNERS

1934	Paul Runyan	$6,767
1935	Johnny Revolta	$9,543
1936	Horton Smith	$7,682
1937	Harry Cooper	$14,138
1938	Sam Snead	$19,534
1939	Henry Picard	$10,303
1940	Ben Hogan	$10,655
1941	Ben Hogan	$18,358
1942	Ben Hogan	$13,143
1943: *No statistics compiled*		
1944:	Byron Nelson	*37,967
1945	Byron Nelson	*63,335
1946	Ben Hogan	42,556
1947	Jimmy Demaret	27,936
1948	Ben Hogan	32,112
1949	Sam Snead	31,593
1950	Sam Snead	35,758
1951	Lloyd Mangrum	26,088
1952	Julius Boros	37,032
1953	Lew Worsham	34,002
1954	Bob Toski	65,819
1955	Julius Boros	63,121
1956	Ted Kroll	72,835
1957	Dick Mayer	65,835
1958	Arnold Palmer	42,607
1959	Art Wall	53,167
1960	Arnold Palmer	75,262
1961	Gary Player	64,540
1962	Arnold Palmer	81,448
1963	Arnold Palmer	128,230
1964	Jack Nicklaus	113,284
1965	Jack Nicklaus	140,752
1966	Billy Casper	121,944
1967	Jack Nicklaus	188,998
1968	Billy Casper	205,168
1969	Frank Beard	164,707
1970	Lee Trevino	157,037
1971	Jack Nicklaus	244,490
1972	Jack Nicklaus	320,542
1973	Jack Nicklaus	308,362
1974	Johnny Miller	353,021
1975	Jack Nicklaus	298,149
1976	Jack Nicklaus	266,438
1977	Tom Watson	310,653
1978	Tom Watson	362,428
1979	Tom Watson	462,636
1980	Tom Watson	530,808
1981	Tom Kite	375,698
1982	Craig Stadler	446,462
1983	Hal Sutton	426,668
1984	Tom Watson	476,260
1985	Curtis Strange	542,321
1986	Greg Norman	653,296
1987	Curtis Strange	925,941
1988	Curtis Strange	1,147,644
1989	Tom Kite	1,395,278
1990	Greg Norman	1,165,477
1991	Corey Pavin	979,430
1992	Fred Couples	1,344,188
1993	Nick Price	1,478,557
1994	Nick Price	1,499,927
1995	Greg Norman	1,654,959
1996	Tom Lehman	1,780,159
1997	Tiger Woods	2,066,833
1998	David Duval	2,591,031

(**Note:** all earnings in US dollars other than * which denote war bonds.)

PGA EUROPEAN TOUR MONEY WINNERS

1962	Peter Thomson	5,764
1963	Bernard Hunt	7,209
1964	Neil Coles	7,890
1965	Peter Thomson	7,011
1966	Bruce Devlin	13,205
1967	Gay Brewer	20,235
1968	Gay Brewer	23,107
1969	Billy Casper	23,483
1970	Christy O'Connor	31,532
1971	Gary Player	11,281
1972	Bob Charles	18,538
1973	Tony Jacklin	24,839
1974	Peter Oosterhuis	32,127
1975	Dale Hayes	20,507
1976	Seve Ballesteros	39,504
1977	Seve Ballesteros	46,436
1978	Seve Ballesteros	54,348
1979	Sandy Lyle	49,233
1980	Greg Norman	74,829
1981	Bernhard Langer	95,991
1982	Sandy Lyle	86,141
1983	Nick Faldo	140,761
1984	Bernhard Langer	160,883
1985	Sandy Lyle	254,711
1986	Seve Ballesteros	259,275
1987	Ian Woosnam	439,075
1988	Seve Ballesteros	502,000
1989	Ronan Rafferty	465,981
1990	Ian Woosnam	737,977
1991	Seve Ballesteros	790,811
1992	Nick Faldo	1,220,540
1993	Colin Montgomerie	798,145
1994	Colin Montgomerie	877,135
1995	Colin Montgomerie	1,038,718
1996	Colin Montgomerie	875,146
1997	Colin Montgomerie	798,947
1998	Colin Montgomerie	933,077

(**Note:** all earnings are in pounds sterling)

US TOUR ALL-TIME CAREER MONEY WINNERS (TOP 100)

1	Greg Norman	$12,292,543
2	Davis Love III	$11,335,561
3	Fred Couples	$11,062,520
4	Mark O'Meara	$10,935,168
5	Payne Stewart	$10,875,263
6	Nick Price	$10,572,795
7	Tom Kite	$10,462,511
8	Scott Hoch	$9,793,504
9	Tom Watson	$9,405,792
10	Mark Calcavecchia	$9,246,382
11	David Duval	$9,134,791
12	Corey Pavin	$8,568,870
13	Paul Azinger	$8,200,355
14	Hal Sutton	$7,836,523
15	Steve Elkington	$7,800,175
16	Craig Stadler	$7,653,781
17	John Cook	$7,612,495
18	Phil Mickelson	$7,484,903
19	Jeff Sluman	$7,313,585
20	Vijay Singh	$7,289,674
21	Curtis Strange	$7,280,566
22	Tom Lehman	$7,115,315
23	Jay Haas	$7,079,477
24	Ben Crenshaw	$7,075,996
25	Loren Roberts	$6,996,258
26	Lee Janzen	$6,967,295
27	Jeff Maggert	$6,931,885
28	John Huston	$6,641,455
29	David Frost	$6,629,043
30	Brad Faxon	$6,456,297
31	Bruce Lietzke	$6,316,759
32	Lanny Wadkins	$6,293,137
33	Bob Tway	$6,183,576
34	Tiger Woods	$6,138,742
35	Steve Pate	$6,050,572
36	Chip Beck	$6,022,579
37	Justin Leonard	$5,986,598
38	Hale Irwin	$5,907,550
39	Jim Furyk	$5,866,389
40	Larry Mize	$5,833,964
41	Scott Simpson	$5,828,343
42	Fuzzy Zoeller	$5,733,292
43	Jack Nicklaus	$5,691,673
44	Billy Mayfair	$5,687,481
45	Andrew Magee	$5,552,036
46	Peter Jacobsen	$5,461,948
47	Mark Brooks	$5,448,817
48	Jim Gallagher, Jr	$5,327,936
49	Ray Floyd	$5,323,075
50	Mark McCumber	$5,296,232
51	Ernie Els	$5,282,393
52	Gil Morgan	$5,259,164
53	Fred Funk	$5,120,727
54	Bill Glasson	$5,051,481
55	Steve Jones	$4,818,500
56	Joey Sindelar	$4,749,570
57	Kenny Perry	$4,722,473
58	Wayne Levi	$4,652,170
59	Nick Faldo	$4,559,670
60	Bob Estes	$4,432,487
61	D.A. Weibring	$4,377,040
62	Billy Andrade	$4,369,397
63	David Edwards	$4,237,596
64	Rocco Mediate	$4,218,441
65	Mike Reid	$4,122,869
66	Dan Forsman	$4,058,543
67	Steve Stricker	$4,028,676
68	Jesper Parnevik	$3,997,547
69	Tom Purtzer	$3,918,239
70	Russ Cochran	$3,896,716
71	John Mahaffey	$3,876,852
72	Mike Hulbert	$3,870,937
73	Larry Nelson	$3,827,401
74	Duffy Waldorf	$3,632,408
75	Jay Don Blake	$3,601,640
76	Ken Green	$3,585,926
77	Kirk Triplett	$3,557,312
78	Lee Trevino	$3,478,328
79	Rick Fehr	$3,452,293
80	Brad Bryant	$3,437,971
81	Andy Bean	$3,437,512
82	Nolan Henke	$3,433,927
83	Tim Simpson	$3,406,017
84	Blaine McCallister	$3,345,939
85	Mark Wiebe	$3,320,619
86	Gene Sauers	$3,290,841
87	Don Pooley	$3,285,743
88	Chris Perry	$3,259,838
89	Glen Day	$3,127,600
90	Donnie Hammond	$3,096,060
91	Dan Pohl	$3,033,203
92	Phil Blackmar	$3,029,592
93	Steve Lowery	$2,973,695
94	Bob Gilder	$2,951,820
95	Scott Verplank	$2,936,580
96	Bobby Wadkins	$2,810,972
97	Jodie Mudd	$2,806,955
98	Craig Parry	$2,782,411
99	Dudley Hart	$2,763,080
100	Johnny Miller	$2,747,484

(**Note:** all listings correct as of May 1, 1999)

PGA EUROPEAN TOUR ALL-TIME CAREER MONEY WINNERS (TOP 80)

1	Colin Montgomerie	8,639,534
2	Bernhard Langer	7,359,915
3	Ian Woosnam	6,296,756
4	Nick Faldo	5,527,625
5	Seve Ballesteros	5,244,450
6	Jose-Maria Olazabal	5,225,913
7	Sam Torrance	4,774,332
8	Mark James	3,855,852
9	Mark McNulty	3,798,559
10	Darren Clarke	3,795,493
11	Costantino Rocca	3,591,713
12	Miguel Angel Jimenez	3,235,785
13	Gordon Brand Jr	3,191,874
14	Eduardo Romero	3,046,245
15	Ronan Rafferty	3,039,719
16	Lee Westwood	3,002,071
17	Barry Lane	2,805,855
18	Sandy Lyle	2,771,366
19	Anders Forsbrand	2,642,103
20	David Gilford	2,589,111
21	Howard Clark	2,507,193
22	Ernie Els	2,478,643
23	José Rivero	2,475,028
24	Per-Ulrik Johansson	2,449,839
25	Peter Baker	2,427,082
26	Rodger Davis	2,410,896
27	Paul Broadhurst	2,362,655
28	Peter Mitchell	2,257,119
29	Tony Johnstone	2,123,989
30	Mark Roe	2,123,788
31	Jesper Parnevik	2,042,021
32	Eamonn Darcy	2,023,300
33	Greg Turner	2,014,410
34	Des Smyth	1,956,143
35	David Feherty	1,952,191
36	Roger Chapman	1,933,084
37	Robert Karlsson	1,928,341
38	Jamie Spence	1,921,481
39	Miguel Angel Martin	1,911,014
40	Russell Claydon	1,885,044
41	Philip Walton	1,874,439
42	Retief Goosen	1,825,711
43	Steven Richardson	1,821,512
44	Robert Allenby	1,813,207
45	Peter O'Malley	1,794,526
46	Jean van de Velde	1,785,302
47	Andrew Coltart	1,764,110
48	Paul McGinley	1,745,332
49	Joakim Haeggman	1,743,365
50	Carl Mason	1,717,708
51	Thomas Bjorn	1,517,935
52	Wayne Riley	1,510,309
53	Mats Lanner	1,506,479
54	Phil Price	1,491,497
55	Sven Struver	1,484,309
56	Santiago Luna	1,465,544
57	Ignacio Garrido	1,440,493
58	Mike Harwood	1,428,717
59	Padraig Harrington	1,417,595
60	José Coceres	1,370,651
61	Andrew Sherborne	1,364,259
62	Mark Mouland	1,355,442
63	Patrik Sjoland	1,351,372
64	Christy O'Connor Jr	1,342,666
65	Richard Boxall	1,327,957
66	Derrick Cooper	1,314,413
67	Wayne Westner	1,306,001
68	Gary Orr	1,300,265
69	Alex Cejka	1,263,941
70	Jarmo Sandelin	1,228,835
71	Paul Lawrie	1,214,423
72	Malcolm Mackenzie	1,202,446
73	Peter Fowler	1,200,749
74	Gordon J Brand	1,148,816
75	Jim Payne	1,101,943
76	Mark Davis	1,094,367
77	Mathias Gronberg	1,093,463
78	Mike McLean	1,076,316
79	John Bland	1,058,466
80	Manuel Pinero	1,056,359

(**Note:** all figures are in Euros and are correct as of May 17, 1999)

INDEX

Note: page numbers in italics refer to illustrations.

A

B

F

G

H

M

O

P

T

U

V

Z

PICTURE ACKNOWLEDGMENTS

Allsport UK Ltd./Jack Atley; Simon Bruty; David Cannon; Chris Cole; J.D. Cuban; Elsa Hasch; Historical Collection/Hulton Getty/MSI; Michael Hobbs; Hobbs Golf Collection; Harry How; Craig Jones; Ross Kinnaird; Clive Mason; Tim Matthews; Stephen Munday; Andrew Redington; Pascal Rondeau; Jamie Squire; Rick Stewart; Matthew Stockman; Peter Taylor;
Associated Press; Colorsport; Corbis/Bettmann; Tony Roberts; Peter Dazeley; Mary Evans Picture Library; Jon Ferrey; Hulton Getty; Mark Newcombe; /Visions In Golf; Popperfoto; Phil Sheldon; Sporting Pictures (UK) Ltd

420-099